PACIFIC
NORTHWEST

WELCOME TO THE PACIFIC NORTHWEST

With its rugged coast, commanding peaks, forested islands, and cool cities, the Pacific Northwest strikes an ideal balance between outdoorsy and cosmopolitan. In Seattle, Portland, and Vancouver, farm-to-table restaurants, sophisticated hotels, and cutting-edge galleries await. Beyond the cities, the wineries of Oregon's Willamette Valley, cute towns of Washington's San Juan Islands, and national parks from Crater Lake to Olympic beg to be explored. Whether your ideal trip involves hiking a trail or window shopping, the Pacific Northwest delivers.

TOP REASONS TO GO

★ **Hip Cities:** Quirky Portland, eclectic Seattle, and gorgeous Vancouver entice.

★ **Coastal Fun:** Beaches, whale sightings, tidal pools, headland walks.

★ **Mountains:** Mt. Rainier, Mt. Hood, Mt. Olympus, and Mt. St. Helens inspire awe.

★ **Craft Beverages:** Wineries, microbreweries, artisan coffee, and boutique distilleries.

★ **Seafood:** Fresh local crab, razor clams, sea scallops, oysters, and salmon.

★ **Scenic Drives:** On the Oregon coast, in the Cascade Range, through evergreen forests.

Fodor's PACIFIC NORTHWEST

Publisher: Amanda D'Acierno, *Senior Vice President*

Editorial: Arabella Bowen, *Executive Editorial Director*; Linda Cabasin, *Editorial Director*

Design: Fabrizio La Rocca, *Vice President, Creative Director*; Tina Malaney, *Associate Art Director*; Chie Ushio, *Senior Designer*; Ann McBride, *Production Designer*

Photography: Melanie Marin, *Associate Director of Photography*; Jessica Parkhill and Jennifer Romains, *Researchers*

Maps: Rebecca Baer, *Senior Map Editor*; Mark Stroud (Moon Street Cartography) and David Lindroth, *Cartographers*

Production: Linda Schmidt, *Managing Editor*; Evangelos Vasilakis, *Associate Managing Editor*; Angela L. McLean, *Senior Production Manager*

Sales: Jacqueline Lebow, *Sales Director*

Marketing & Publicity: Heather Dalton, *Marketing Director*; Katherine Fleming, *Senior Publicist*

Business & Operations: Susan Livingston, *Vice President, Strategic Business Planning*; Sue Daulton, *Vice President, Operations*

Fodors.com: Megan Bell, *Executive Director, Revenue & Business Development*; Yasmin Marinaro, *Senior Director, Marketing & Partnerships*

Copyright © 2014 by Fodor's Travel, a division of Random House LLC

Writers: Shelley Arenas, Kimberly Bowker, Cedar Burnett, Andrew Collins, Christina Cooke, Rebekah Denn, Paige Donner, Allison Ellis, Carolyn B. Heller, Adriana Janovich, Brian Kevin, Rob Phillips, Dave Sandage, AnnaMaria Stephens, Lee van der Voo, Christine Vovakes, Crystal Wood

Editors: Salwa Jabado (*lead project editor*), Jess Moss

Editorial Contributors: Caroline Trefler (*Seattle editor*), Mark Sullivan and Maria Hart (*Vancouver and Victoria editors*), Bethany Beckerlegge, Stephen Brewer, Penny Phenix

Production Editor: Carolyn Roth

19th Edition

ISBN 978-0-89141-957-0

ISSN 1098–6774

All details in this book are based on information supplied to us at press time. Always confirm information when it matters, especially if you're making a detour to visit a specific place. Fodor's expressly disclaims any liability, loss, or risk, personal or otherwise, that is incurred as a consequence of the use of any of the contents of this book.

SPECIAL SALES

This book is available at special discounts for bulk purchases for sales promotions or premiums. For more information, e-mail specialmarkets@randomhouse.com

PRINTED IN COLOMBIA

10 9 8 7 6 5 4 3 2 1

CONTENTS

Fodor's Features

MAPS

ABOUT
THIS GUIDE

Fodor's Recommendations

Everything in this guide is worth doing—we don't cover what isn't—but exceptional sights, hotels, and restaurants are recognized with additional accolades. **Fodor's Choice★** indicates our top recommendations; and **Best Bets** call attention to notable hotels and restaurants in various categories. Care to nominate a new place? Visit Fodors.com/contact-us.

Trip Costs

We list prices wherever possible to help you budget well. Hotel and restaurant price categories from **$** to **$$$$** are noted alongside each recommendation. For hotels, we include the lowest cost of a standard double room in high season. For restaurants, we cite the average price of a main course at dinner or, if dinner isn't served, at lunch. For attractions, we always list adult admission fees; discounts are usually available for children, students, and senior citizens.

Hotels

Our local writers vet every hotel to recommend the best overnights in each price category, from budget to expensive. Unless otherwise specified, you can expect private bath, phone, and TV in your room. For expanded hotel reviews, facilities, and deals visit Fodors.com.

Restaurants

Unless we state otherwise, restaurants are open for lunch and dinner daily. We mention dress code only when there's a specific requirement and reservations only when they're essential or not accepted. To make restaurant reservations, visit Fodors.com.

Credit Cards

The hotels and restaurants in this guide typically accept credit cards. If not, we'll say so.

Top Picks	Hotels & Restaurants
★ Fodor's Choice	⊞ Hotel
	↵ Number of rooms
Listings	⫯⊙⫯ Meal plans
⊠ Address	✗ Restaurant
✉ Branch address	⌖ Reservations
☎ Telephone	👔 Dress code
🖷 Fax	⊟ No credit cards
⊕ Website	$ Price
✑ E-mail	
✒ Admission fee	**Other**
☉ Open/closed times	⇨ See also
Ⓜ Subway	☞ Take note
⊹ Directions or Map coordinates	⅄ Golf facilities

EXPERIENCE THE PACIFIC NORTHWEST

WHAT'S WHERE

Numbers refer to chapters

2 Portland. With its pedestrian-friendly downtown and super public transit, Portland is easy to explore. The city has become a magnet for fans of artisanal food, beer, wine, and spirits, and its leafy parks and miles of bike lanes make it a prime spot for outdoors enthusiasts.

3 The Oregon Coast. Oregon's roughly 300 miles of rugged coast are every bit as scenic as the more crowded and famous California coast. Oregon Dunes National Recreation Area, the Oregon Coast Aquarium, and the Columbia River Maritime Museum are key highlights.

4 The Willamette Valley and Wine Country. Just beyond the Portland city limits and extending south for 120 miles to Eugene, the Willamette Valley is synonymous with exceptional wine-making.

5 The Columbia River Gorge and Mt. Hood. Less than an hour east of Portland, the Columbia Gorge extends for about 160 miles along the Oregon-Washington border. Wind sports and white-water rafting abound. Just 35 miles south of Hood River—a growing wine and culinary mecca—iconic Mt. Hood is renowned for hiking and skiing.

6 Central Oregon. The semi-arid and generally sunny swatch of Oregon immediately east of the Cascade Range takes in a varied landscape, with the outdoorsy city of Bend as the regional hub. Make time for the funky mountain town of Sisters and the world-famous rock climbing of Smith Rock State Park near Redmond.

7 Crater Lake National Park. The 21-square-mile sapphire-blue expanse is the nation's deepest lake and a scenic wonder. You can drive the loop road around the lake, hike, or take a guided boat tour.

8 Southern Oregon. The Klamath Falls region provides some of Oregon's best, under-visited scenery, while artsy Ashland and Old West–looking Jacksonville have sophisticated restaurants, shops, and wineries. Nearby, Oregon Caves National Monument is a fascinating natural attraction.

9 Seattle. This sprawling city is shaped by many beautiful bodies of water. On the west is Puget Sound; on the east is massive Lake Washington. The Emerald City sits in the middle, bisected by highway I-5 and further divvied up by more lakes and canals.

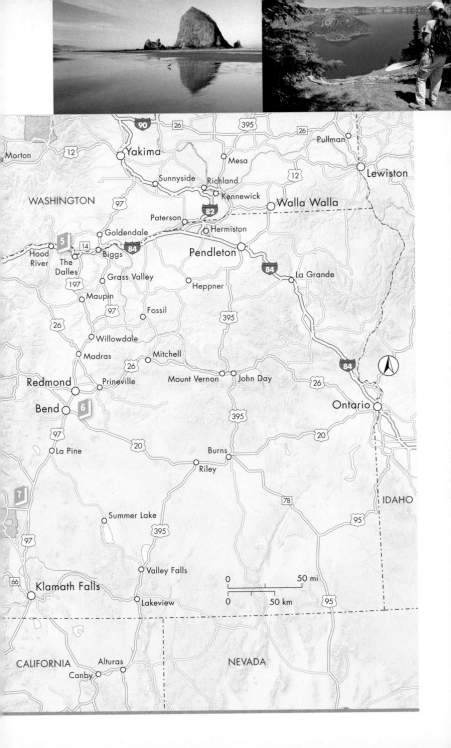

WASHINGTON

Morton

Yakima

Sunnyside

Richland

Kennewick

Walla Walla

Lewiston

Pullman

Mesa

Paterson

Hermiston

Pendleton

La Grande

Goldendale

Hood River

The Dalles

Biggs

Grass Valley

Heppner

Maupin

Fossil

Willowdale

Madras

Mitchell

Mount Vernon

John Day

Redmond

Prineville

Bend

La Pine

Burns

Riley

Summer Lake

IDAHO

Ontario

Valley Falls

Klamath Falls

Lakeview

0   50 mi

0   50 km

CALIFORNIA

Alturas

NEVADA

Canby

WHAT'S WHERE

10 Washington Cascade Mountains and Valleys. Right outside Seattle, you can tour the cities of Olympia and Tacoma, marvel at navy warships and vintage Boeing airplanes, or bike past tulip fields in the Skagit Valley. Olympia is also a good jumping off point for exploring the towns in the Cascade range and Mount St. Helens National Volcanic Monument.

11 The San Juan Islands. You haven't experienced a Washington summer if you haven't made a trip to the islands; this is prime whale-watching territory.

12 Olympic National Park. Centered on Mt. Olympus and framed on three sides by water, this 922,651-acre park covers much of Washington's forest-clad Olympic Peninsula.

13 Olympic Peninsula and Washington Coast. Wilderness envelops most of the Olympic Peninsula, with the Olympic Mountains at its core. Rugged terrain and few roads limit interior accessibility, but U.S. Highway 101 offers breathtaking forest, ocean, and mountain vistas.

14 North Cascades National Park. This 505,000-acre expanse of mountain wilderness is part of an area with more than half of the glaciers in America.

15 North Central Washington. Along the beautiful North Cascades Highway you'll encounter spectacular scenery and logging towns such as Sedro Wooley and Marblemount, as well as Winthrop.

16 Mount Rainier National Park. The fifth-highest mountain in the Lower 48, Mt. Rainier is massive and unforgettable.

17 Washington Wine Country. This fertile valley east of the Cascades has long been known for apple and cherry orchards, and in recent years as a highly prized wine-making area—including the vineyards around Zillah, Prosser, and Benton City.

18 Spokane and Eastern Washington. Characterized by rolling, dry, treeless hills and anchored by the state's second-largest city, Spokane, this area takes in the vast Columbia River valley and an eclectic mix of cities and towns, including wine-centric Walla Walla.

19 Vancouver and Victoria. Cosmopolitan Vancouver is a glorious city with tall fir trees, rock spires, the ocean at your doorstep, and a vibrant atmosphere. Victoria, with its stately Victorian structures, is a stunner.

THE PACIFIC NORTHWEST PLANNER

Fast Facts

Currency and Exchange. The units of currency in Canada are the Canadian dollar (C$) and the cent, in almost the same denominations as U.S. currency. A good way to be sure you're getting the best exchange rate is by using your credit card or ATM/debit card. The issuing bank will convert your bill at the current rate.

Packing. It's all about layers here. The weather can morph from cold and overcast to warm and sunny and back again in the course of a few hours, especially in spring and early fall.

Taxes. Oregon has no sales tax, although many cities and counties levy a tax on lodging and services. Room taxes, for example, vary from 6% to 9.5%. The state retail sales tax in Washington is 6.5%, but there are also local taxes that can raise the total tax to 11.5%, depending on the goods or service and the municipality; Seattle's retail sales tax is 8.9%. A Goods and Services Tax (GST) of 5% applies on virtually every transaction in Canada except for the purchase of basic groceries.

Border Crossing into Canada

Air and Ferry Travel. You are required to present a passport to enter or reenter the United States. To enter Canada (or more precisely, to reenter the U.S. from Canada) by air you must present a valid passport or an Air NEXUS card; by land or sea you need to present one of the following: 1) passport, 2) a trusted-traveler program card (i.e., Global Entry, NEXUS, SENTRI, or FAST card, 3) a U.S. Passport Card, or 4) an Enhanced Driver's License (issued only in the states of Michigan, New York, Vermont, and Washington).

Car Travel. You will need one of the aforementioned documents (see above) to cross the border by car. In addition, drivers must carry owner registration and proof of insurance coverage, which is compulsory in Canada. The Canadian Non-Resident Inter-Provincial Motor Vehicle Liability Insurance Card, available from any U.S. insurance company, is accepted as evidence of financial responsibility in Canada. If you are driving a car that is not registered in your name, carry a letter from the owner that authorizes your use of the vehicle.

The main entry point into British Columbia from the United States by car is on I–5 at Blaine, Washington, 48 km (30 miles) south of Vancouver. Three highways enter British Columbia from the east: Highway 1, or the Trans-Canada Highway; Highway 3, or the Crowsnest Highway, which crosses southern British Columbia; and Highway 16, the Yellowhead Highway, which runs through northern British Columbia from the Rocky Mountains to Prince Rupert.

Border-crossing procedures are usually quick and simple, although the wait can be trying on weekends and during busy holiday periods. Every British Columbia border crossing is open 24 hours (except the one at Aldergrove, which is open from 8 am to midnight). The I–5 border crossing at Blaine, Washington (also known as the Douglas, or Peace Arch, border crossing), is one of the busiest border crossings between the United States and Canada. Listen to local radio traffic reports for information about wait times.

U.S. Passport Information U.S. Department of State ☎ 877/487–2778 ⊕ www.travel.state.gov/passport.

Getting Around

Car Travel. You'll need a car to get around all but the major cities of the Pacific Northwest. Although a car will also grant you more freedom to explore the outer areas of Portland, Seattle, Vancouver, and Victoria, these four cities have adequate public transportation and taxi fleets. This is not the case in most other towns in the region, so even if bus or train service exists between two points, you'll likely need a car to get around once you arrive.

I–5 is the major north-south conduit of the U.S. part of the region, offering a straight shot at high speeds—when there aren't traffic snarls, of course—from Oregon's southern border all the way up to the Canadian border. Seattle and Portland are both along I–5, and Vancouver is about 30 miles across the border from where it ends. This makes driving between the major hubs an easy option, though it's also possible to travel between them by train or bus—except for the beautiful lower half of Oregon, below Eugene, I–5 is pleasant and green but not especially dramatic as far as the scenery goes, at least compared with the rest of the region as a whole.

U.S. 101, on the other hand, is one of the main attractions of the region. It starts in Washington west of Olympia, makes a very wide loop around Olympic National Park and then heads south through Oregon, hugging the coast almost the whole way down. Most of the road is incredibly scenic, but this is not a very quick way to traverse either state. Make sure you want to commit to the coastal drive, which can be windy and slow-going in some parts, before getting on the 101—it takes some time to work your way over from I–5, so jumping back and forth between the two isn't very practical.

The Cascade Range cuts through the middle of Washington and Oregon, which means that east–west journeys often meander over mountain passes and can be either beautiful and relaxing (summer) or beautiful and treacherous (winter). I–90 is the main east–west artery in Washington, connecting Seattle with Spokane, but Highway 20, which passes through the North Cascades National Park, is more scenic. I–84 is Oregon's major east–west artery; not far east of Portland it enters the stunningly picturesque Columbia River Gorge.

⇨ *See also Car Travel in Travel Smart for driving times to various regions from Seattle and Portland.*

When to Go

Hotels in the major tourist destinations often book up early in July and August, so it's important to make reservations well in advance. Spring and fall are also excellent times to visit, although rain is more prevalent then. Prices for accommodations, transportation, and tours can be lower and crowds smaller in the most popular destinations. In winter, snow is uncommon in the lowland areas but abundant in the nearby mountains, where ski resorts abound and chains and snow tires are often required for driving.

CLIMATE

Average daytime summer highs are in the 70s but occasional hot spells do produce temperatures as high as 100 degrees in Portland and Seattle; winter temperatures are generally in the 40s, but this depends heavily on elevation—in the mountains temperatures can drop much lower. Rainfall varies greatly from one locale to another. In the coastal mountains, for example, 160 inches of rain falls annually, creating temperate rain forests. In much of the eastern two-thirds of Oregon, Washington, and British Columbia, near-desert conditions prevail, with rainfall as low as 6 inches per year. Seattle and Portland average only around 36 inches of rainfall a year—less than New York, Chicago, or Miami—however, from October through March a light rain is present nearly every day.

OREGON
TOP ATTRACTIONS

Cannon Beach

(A) The nearest town on the dramatically rocky, windswept Oregon coast from Portland also happens to be one of the most idyllic communities in the coastal Northwest. This town anchored by 235-foot-tall Haystack Rock is rife with beach-side hiking trails, fine art galleries, and cafés specializing in organic coffee, Oregon wines, and fresh-caught seafood.

Columbia River Gorge

(B) The 75-mile section of the breathtaking Columbia River that extends just east of Portland to The Dalles provides some of the most stunning scenery in the Pacific Northwest. Towering cliffs on both the Washington and Oregon sides of the river form a dramatic backdrop, and meandering highways line both banks. Water and wind sports abound.

Columbia River Maritime Museum, Astoria

(C) At this dazzling, contemporary facility in the steadily gentrifying town of Astoria, where the northern Oregon coast meets the Columbia River, you can tour a fully operational U.S. Coast Guard lightship, and check out engaging exhibits on local shipwrecks, marine life, and how the mighty Columbia has driven the economic and cultural development of the Pacific Northwest.

Crater Lake National Park

(D) The deepest lake in the United States is also the clearest, a fact readily grasped as soon as you behold this searing-blue body of water. It formed from rain and snowmelt that filled an ancient volcanic caldera. It's closed much of the year due to snow, but in summer this 21-square-mile lake is southern Oregon's foremost attraction—the nearly century-old Crater Lake Lodge, perched on the southern

shore, makes a memorable overnight and dinner venue.

High Desert Museum, Bend

(E) Evocative and intricate walk-through dioramas and an indoor-outdoor zoo with creatures great and tiny convey the High Desert's past and present in a delightfully airy and family-friendly space just south of Bend.

Oregon Sand Dunes

(F) The 41 miles of rolling bluffs that make up Oregon Dunes National Recreation Area bring out the kid in visitors of all ages—there's something inherently happy about frolicking amid these massive mountains of sand, some of them climbing nearly 500 feet higher than the surf. Here you can hike, ride horseback, and race on a dune buggy, and there's great boating and fishing (plus several excellent seafood restaurants) in the nearby town of Florence.

Mount Hood

(G) Just 60 miles east of Portland, the state's highest mountain is the only place in the Lower 48 where you can ski year-round. There are five different facilities, Timberline Lodge Ski Area being the most scenic.

Powell's Bookstore, Portland

(H) The downtown Portland legend is the world's largest bookstore carrying both new and used titles, and with its coffee-house, late hours, and endless aisles of reading, it's also a prime spot for literary-minded people-watching.

Willamette Valley Wine Country

(I) Within easy day-tripping of Portland, this swath of fertile, hilly countryside is home to more than 200 wineries and has earned a reputation as one of the finest producers of Pinot Noir in the world—some say the best outside Burgundy. Winemakers in these parts also produce first-rate Pinot Gris and Chardonnay.

WASHINGTON TOP ATTRACTIONS

Hurricane Ridge, Olympic National Park

(A) Of the dozens of stunning panoramas within Olympic National Park, this 5,200-foot-high bluff offers the most memorable views—it takes in the vast Olympic mountain range as well as the Strait of Juan de Fuca and, beyond that, Vancouver Island. In summer, rangers lead tours through the wildflower- and wildlife-rich terrain.

Johnston Observatory, Mt. St. Helens

(B) Named for a brave volcanologist who perished in the terrifying 1980 eruption of Mt. St. Helens, this visitor center and observatory affords mind-blowing views of the hulking—often steaming—lava dome that lies deep within the mountain's crater. You reach this spot by driving the scenic Spirit Lake Highway.

Long Beach Peninsula

(C) Just two hours by car from Portland and three from Seattle, this 28-mile-long barrier peninsula rises from the mouth of the Columbia River north along the state's southwestern coast, providing visitors with rolling stretches of sand dunes, family-friendly amusements, and endless opportunities to view wildlife, from migrating birds to black bears.

Mount Rainier National Park

(D) Don't be intimidated by the formidable reputation of Mt. Rainier's 14,411-foot summit. It's true that only highly experienced hikers with guides should attempt this climb, but the national park that surrounds this snowcapped peak has plenty of terrain accessible to everyone, including 240 miles of well-maintained trails. The Skyline Trail makes for a moderately challenging 5-mile loop along alpine ridges and wildflower-strewn meadows—it's one of the best Mt. Rainier hikes if

1

you have only one day to explore the mountain.

Orcas Island, San Juan Islands

(E) Of the three main islands in this laid-back, friendly, and beautiful archipelago that sits snug between Bellingham and Vancouver Island, Orcas has the best balance of scenery, seclusion, and diversions. It's home to 2,409-foot Mt. Constitution and surrounding Moran State Park, several picturesque harbors popular for fishing and kayaking, and a sophisticated mix of country inns and farm-to-table restaurants.

Pike Place Market, Seattle

(F) The Pacific Northwest abounds with stellar farmers' markets, but downtown Seattle's creaky and colorful Pike Place is the mother of them all, established in 1907 and still thriving (despite a near brush with the wrecking ball during the 1960s).

SAM (Seattle Art Museum)

(G) Downtown's Seattle Art Museum is known for its collection of modern and Native American art. SAM'S Olympic Sculpture Park, in Belltown, overlooks Puget Sound and the Olympic Mountains and showcases works by Calder and Serra amidst lovely green spaces. On Capitol Hill, peruse the Seattle Asian Art Museum's fascinating collection of Chinese, Japanese, and Korean art before venturing into surrounding Volunteer Park.

Seattle Center and the Space Needle

(H) Almost every trip includes a stop at Seattle Center, which was built for the 1962 World's Fair and is home to the Space Needle, museums, and performance halls. Most of the city's major events are held here, but even on quiet weekends there's still something for everyone: Pacific Science Center and Children's Museum, Experience Music Project (EMP), and the Chihuly Garden and Glass exhibit.

VANCOUVER AND VICTORIA TOP ATTRACTIONS

The Bill Reid Gallery, Vancouver

(A) If First Nations heritage is your thing, be sure to visit this repository of regional art, one of the best of its kind in North America. It is as much a showcase for new artists as it is a showcase of Bill Reid's work, most famous of which is the statue The Spirit of Haida Gwaii, The Jade Canoe, on display at the Vancouver International Airport.

Capilano Suspension Bridge, Vancouver

(B) It's just a 20-minute drive across Burrard Inlet from downtown Vancouver to reach the surprisingly momentous North Shore mountains, home to Grouse Mountain and its aerial tramway, and the famed Capilano Suspension Bridge, a 450-foot cedar-plank swing bridge that crosses 230 feet above the frothy Capilano River.

Dr. Sun Yat-Sen Chinese Garden, Vancouver

(C) "Life is not measured by the number of breaths we take," according to the old saying, "but by the places and moments that take our breath away." That sentiment sums up this elegant downtown destination. It's the first authentic Ming Dynasty–style garden outside of China to incorporate symbolism and design elements from centuries-old Chinese gardens.

Granville Island, Vancouver

(D) Take the foot-passenger ferry across the inlet from downtown, and bring your appetite. This small island houses an extremely popular indoor market, a marina, theaters, restaurants, coffee shops, parks, and dozens of crafts shops and artist studios. Wander the stalls in the market, then grab a bench outside to get your fill of delicacies and the view.

Museum of Anthropology, Vancouver

(E) The city's most spectacular museum displays art from the Pacific Northwest and around the world—dramatic totem poles and canoes; exquisite carvings of gold, silver, and argillite; and masks, tools, and textiles from many cultures.

Stanley Park, Vancouver

(F) An afternoon in this gorgeous 1,000-acre wilderness, just blocks from downtown Vancouver, can include beaches, the ocean, the harbor, Douglas fir and cedar forests, First Nations sculptures, and a view of the North Shore Mountains. Walk, bike, picnic, or just take the trolley tour around the perimeter, but don't miss it.

Butchart Gardens, Victoria

(G) Just 20 minutes from downtown Victoria, the 55-acre Butchart Gardens was planted in a limestone quarry in 1904. Highlights include the Japanese and Italian gardens, as well as the proliferation of roses and 700 other varieties of flowers. On summer nights you can enjoy a fireworks display.

Inner Harbour, Victoria

(H) The lovely capital of British Columbia has a remarkably intimate and pedestrian-friendly downtown that wraps around the harbor. Street entertainers and crafts vendors—and lots of people—come out to stroll the waterfront walkway in summer.

Royal British Columbia Museum, Victoria

(I) At this superb museum, you can learn about the culture and human history of British Columbia, dating back several thousand years to the earliest First Peoples inhabitants. Other exhibits touch on natural history, European settlement, and maritime heritage.

TOP EXPERIENCES

Shopping at the Portland Saturday Market and Portland Farmers' Market, Portland, OR

The expansive outdoor Saturday market is actually open Saturday and Sunday (from March through Christmas). At the attractive market grounds you'll find every imaginable creation: offbeat patio sculptures, jewelry made from recycled wares, and stylish yet practical housewares to name a few. Several blocks away on Saturday mornings, the unrelated Portland Farmers' Market at PSU campus, on the verdant Park Blocks, is one of the nation's most acclaimed foodie gatherings—several vendors sell delish breakfast and lunch fare.

Skiing Mt. Hood, OR

Just 60 miles east of Portland, the state's highest mountain is the only place in the Lower 48 where you can ski year-round. There are actually three different facilities on this mammoth, snowcapped mountain. Timberline Lodge Ski Area is the one that remains open year-round, and its runs pass beside the venerable Timberline Lodge, a restaurant and hotel dating to the 1930s. Nearby Mt. Hood Ski Bowl has less interesting terrain but the most night-skiing acreage in the country. Around the north side of the mountain, you'll find the most challenging, extensive, and interesting terrain at Mt. Hood Meadows Ski Resort, which offers some 2,000 acres of winter snowboarding and ski fun.

White-water Rafting on the Rogue River, Grants Pass, OR

Of the many excellent places for white-water rafting in Oregon, the Rogue River offers some of the most thrilling rides. Several outfitters offer trips along this frothy, 215-mile river in the southwestern part of the state, from half-day adventures well suited to beginners to multiday trips that include camping or overnights in local lodges.

Picnicking at Silver Falls State Park, OR

The lush Silver Falls State Park, about 25 miles east of Salem, is so impressive that serious campaigns to admit it to the national park system have taken place recently. In the meantime, it's something of a secret treasure. The 8,700-acre swath of sky-scraping old-growth Douglas firs climbs into the foothills of the Cascade Range, where rain and melting snow supply the torrent that roars through 14 different waterfalls, several of them more than 100 feet tall.

Driving Through the Columbia Gorge, OR/WA

The roughly 75-mile section of the mighty Columbia River that extends from just east of Portland to The Dalles provides some of the most stunning scenery in the Pacific Northwest. Towering cliffs on both the Washington and Oregon sides of the river form a dramatic backdrop, and meandering highways line both banks (on the Washington side, Hwy. 14 is slower but offers better views). There's much to see and do in the Gorge: visit the 620-foot-high Multnomah Falls, stroll among the sophisticated restaurants, shops, and wineries in charming Hood River, or try your luck at sailboarding, a sport well suited to the river's high winds.

Attending the Oregon Shakespeare Festival in Ashland, OR

Sunny, hilly, and attractive Ashland is a charming, small city in its own right, with a bustling downtown popping with notable restaurants specializing in farm-to-table cuisine and wines from nearby

ineyards. But the Oregon Shakespeare 'estival, which presents world-class plays from Shakespeare to classics to contem->orary) on three different stages from 1id-February to early November, really >ut this town on the map. Try to see a >lay in the largest venue, the Elizabethan, vhich replicates London's famed Fortune ^heatre.

Coffeehouse-Crawling in Seattle, WA

>ure, for kicks, it's worth stopping by the >riginal branch of Starbucks, which is across the street from Pike Place Market. 3ut as arguably the nation's coffeehouse apital, Seattle has far more interesting ava joints to consider. Especially fertile coffee) grounds for coffeehouse-hopping nclude the Capitol Hill, Queen Anne, 3allard, and Fremont neighborhoods— ry Espresso Vivace, Caffe Vita, Fremont Coffee Company, or Caffe Fiore for stel-ar espresso.

Biking around Lopez Island, WA

Whether you're an ardent cyclist or an >ccasional weekender, Lopez Island >ffers some of the best biking terrain in he West. This laid-back, gently undu-ating island that's part of Washington's abled San Juan archipelago is ringed by a beautiful main road and dedicated bike >aths. As you cycle past lavender fields, >lackberry bushes, horse farms, and >ccasional patches of woodland, you'll ncounter little automobile traffic. There are several bike-rental shops, and the Lopez Island Soda Fountain is a fine spot for refreshments.

The Laser-Light Show at Grand Coulee Dam, WA

You truly get a sense of the awesome magnitude of the Columbia River when you view some of the enormous hydro-electric facilities set along this meandering Northwest river. The Grand Coulee Dam, built in 1932, ranks among the world's biggest concrete structures, and towers over the landscape. On summer evenings, grab a seat and watch the nightly laser-light show projected across the dam. This is a favorite family activity in this otherwise relatively remote part of northeastern Washington.

Wine-tasting in Walla Walla, WA

Although you'll find super wine-making in several parts of the region, including Oregon's Willamette Valley and Washington's nearby Yakima and Columbia valleys, the dapper college town of Walla Walla has evolved into the Northwest's best overall wine-country hub. The handsomely revived historic downtown abounds with smart boutiques, lively cafés and restaurants, and several prominent tasting rooms. And throughout the surrounding vineyard-studded hills you'll find elegant inns and some of the most critically acclaimed, if still somewhat underrated, wineries in the country.

Riding the Ferry to Victoria, BC

This is a perfectly simple way to admire the region's coastal scenery, from the mountains in Olympic National Park to the meandering shorelines of the San Juan Islands (if you're coming from Washington) and Gulf islands (if you're coming from mainland British Columbia). Numerous ferries of many sizes ply the waters around Victoria and Vancouver Island, and the trip is best enjoyed on an open deck, while devouring a cup of clam chowder.

FLAVORS OF THE PACIFIC NORTHWEST

Pacific Northwest cuisine highlights regional seafood, locally grown produce, and locally raised meats, often prepared in styles that borrow Pan-Asian, French, and Italian influences. All the region's major and even many smaller cities have top-rated, nationally renowned dining spots, as well as funky, inexpensive little eateries that also pride themselves on serving seasonal and often organic ingredients.

Seafood

The Northwest's dining scene is forever eclectic because of the combined abundance of fresh seafood and the imaginative ways it's cooked. Many restaurants, such as the Portland-based chain McCormick & Schmick's, print menus daily and feature a "fresh list" with more than 30 types of seafood represented, most of which are caught from local waters. And since Dungeness crab, salmon, tuna, sole, oysters, spotted prawns, scallops, and swordfish are all within pole's reach, chefs take serious and artful pleasure in discovering ways to fry, grill, bake, stir-fry, sear, poach, barbecue, and sauté the latest catch in new, inventive ways.

Jake's Famous Crawfish, Portland, OR. For more than 100 years Portlanders have come to Jake's. You should, too, especially during crawfish season (May–September).

Matt's in the Market, Seattle, WA. Right next to Seattle's prime source of fresh fish, Pike Place Market, Matt's serves a must-try oyster po'boy and Penn Cove mussels with chorizo or Dungeness crab bisque, and pan-roasted fillets of wild salmon and lingcod served with light vinaigrettes.

Blue Water Café, Vancouver, BC. Ask the staff to recommend wine-pairings from the BC-focused list, and enjoy exquisitely prepared seafood, which may include overlooked varieties such as mackerel, sardines, and herring.

Locavore Movement

Pacific Northwest chefs are fanatical, in a delicious way, about sustainability, presenting dishes with ingredients raised, grown, or foraged within about 100 miles. Northwest chefs are so determined to maintain an unwavering connection to the land that many hire professional foragers, or on occasion can be found tromping off into the woods themselves. Bounties of morels, chanterelles, and bolete mushrooms (fall), stinging nettles and fiddlehead ferns (spring), and huckleberries and blackberries (summer) now grace the menus of many restaurants. From both Portland and Seattle, farmland immediately surrounds urban boundaries; therefore, daily deliveries of asparagus, eggplant, pears, cherries, and other fruits and vegetables is achievable, along with locally raised game from area ranches and farms.

Higgins, Portland, OR. One of Portland's longtime culinary stars, chef Greg Higgins relies heavily on herbs and produce from nearby farms in such stand-out dishes as warm beets, asparagus, and artichokes; and venison terrine with dried sour cherries and roasted-garlic mustard.

Paley's Place, Portland, OR. Talented chef Vitaly Paley produces incomparably fresh and complex fare utilizing strictly seasonal and regional ingredients, from local rabbit and squab to razor clams and wild mushrooms.

Sitka & Spruce, Seattle, WA. Wild greens and edible flowers always show up in salads or as garnishes alongside fresh seafood or free-range chicken from Vashon Island farms at Chef Matt Dillon's tiny temple to the Northwest.

...ark, Seattle, WA. Naturally raised veal sweetbreads come with a sunchoke puree, and spring nettles are stuffed into spinach ravioli at Lark, where the small menu names every local farm that contributes to its dishes.

The Herbfarm, Woodinville, WA. Every year the Herbfarm honors mushroom season with the Mycologist's Dream menu, which sees the fungi go into everything from ravioli to flan. The rest of the year, blackberries may mingle with rose geranium in ice cream, or caviar may be accompanied by a jelly flavored with wild ginger and local rhizomes.

Wineries

Thanks to a mild climate with soil, air, water, and temperature conditions comparable to regions of France, the Northwest is recognized for producing prime varieties of wine. In charming, rural settings, some just outside the cities, petite to larger vineyards offer behind-the-scenes tours where sampling the merchandise is encouraged. The Northwest is also a notable region for its production of organic and biodynamic wines. In keeping with the sustainable food and farm movement, vineyards are developing fertilization, production, harvesting, and fermentation techniques that produce flavorful, eco-friendly varieties that set the standard in the wine world. A few of our favorites include:

Abacela Vineyards, Umpqua Valley, OR
Amity Vineyards, Willamette Valley, OR
Sokol Blosser, Willamette Valley, OR
Hedges Cellars, Yakima Valley, WA
L'Ecole No. 41, Walla Walla, WA

Artisanal Cocktails

Thanks to the growing number of craft distilleries that have sprung up in the Northwest, with the bulk of them in Portland (Clear Creek eau de vie, Aviation gin, New Deal vodka), bars and restaurants in Oregon and Washington have begun turning their attention to producing creative, artisanal cocktails, often using local and seasonal ingredients, including fresh juices and herbs garnered from farmers' markets. Bourbon and gin lovers never had it so good, as these drinks seem to be at the base of most creations; for the rest, there are plenty of obscure lavender-infused liqueurs to choose from. Classic drinks are also much appreciated. In Seattle, several bartenders are single-handedly restoring the dignity of the martini, the Manhattan, and the French 75.

Mint/820, Portland, OR. Bartender and owner Lucy Brennan wrote the book on creative cocktails—literally; she's the author of *Hip Sips*, which features more than 60 recipes.

Zig Zag, Seattle, WA. Zig Zag pours the best martinis in Seattle, along with more exotic fare like the Trident (cynar, aquavit, dry sherry, and peach bitters) and inventive, improvised cocktails.

Beaker & Flask, Portland, OR. This chic East Side restaurant and lounge has sophisticated elixirs utilizing everything from house-made bitter-orange liqueur to coconut-water ice cubes; the owners also operate liquor-oriented Rum Club, next door.

Spur Gastropub, Seattle, WA. This lively and trendy Belltown gastropub turns out artful, colorful cocktails, including the refreshing Empress, made with Jamaican rum, fresh grapefruit juice, and St. Germain liqueur.

PORTLAND WITH KIDS

Many of Oregon's best kids-oriented attractions and activities are in greater Portland. Just getting around the Rose City—via streetcars and light-rail trains on city streets and kayaks, excursion cruises, and jet boats on the Willamette River—is fun. For listings of family-oriented concerts, performances by the Oregon Children's Theatre, and the like, check the free *Willamette Weekly* newspaper.

Museums and Attractions

On the east bank of the Willamette River, the **Oregon Museum of Science and Industry** (OMSI) is a leading interactive museum, with touch-friendly exhibits, an Omnimax theater, the state's biggest planetarium, and a 240-foot submarine moored just outside in the river. Along Portland's leafy Park Blocks, both the **Oregon Historical Society** and the **Portland Art Museum** have exhibits and programming geared toward kids.

In Old Town, kids enjoy walking amid the ornate pagodas and dramatic foliage of the **Lan Su Chinese Garden.** This is a good spot for a weekend morning, followed by a visit to the **Portland Saturday Market,** where food stalls and musicians keep younger kids entertained, and the cool jewelry, toys, and gifts handcrafted by local artisans appeal to teens. Steps from the market is the **Oregon Maritime Museum,** set within a vintage stern-wheeler docked on the river. And just up Burnside Street from the market, **Powell's City of Books** contains enormous sections of kids' and young adults' literature.

Parks

Portland is dotted with densely wooded parks—many of the larger ones have ball fields, playgrounds, and picnic areas. The most famous urban oasis in the city, **Forest Park** (along with adjoining **Washington Park**) offers a wealth of engaging activities. You can ride the MAX light rail right to the park's main hub of culture, a complex comprising the **Oregon Zoo, Portland Children's Museum,** and **World Forestry Discovery Center Museum.** Ride the narrow-gauge railroad from the zoo for 2 miles to reach the **International Rose Test Garden** and **Japanese Garden.** From here it's an easy downhill stroll to **Northwest 23rd and 21st avenues'** pizza parlors, ice-cream shops, and bakeries.

Outdoor Adventures

Tour boats ply the **Willamette River,** and a couple of marinas near OMSI rent **kayaks** and conduct **drag-boat races** out on the water. There are also several shops in town that rent **bikes** for use on the city's many miles of dedicated bike lanes and trails. There's outstanding **white-water rafting** just southeast of Portland, along the Clackamas River. On your way toward the Clackamas, check out **North Clackamas Aquatic Park** and **Oaks Amusement Park,** which have rides and wave pools galore.

Nearby **Mt. Hood** has camping, hiking, and biking all summer, and three of the most family-friendly ski resorts in the Northwest—**Timberline** is especially popular for younger and less experienced boarders and skiers. From summer through fall, the pick-your-own berry farms and pumpkin patches on **Sauvie Island** make for an engaging afternoon getaway—for an all-day outing, continue up U.S. 30 all the way to **Astoria,** at the mouth of the Columbia River, to visit the **Columbia River Maritime Museum** and **Fort Stevens State Park,** where kids love to scamper about the remains of an early-20th-century shipwreck.

SEATTLE WITH KIDS

Seattle is great for kids. After all, a place where floatplanes take off a few feet from houseboats, and where harbor seals might be spotted on a routine ferry ride, doesn't have to try too hard to feel like a wonderland. And if the rain falls, there are plenty of great museums to keep the kids occupied. A lot of child-centric sights are easily reached via public transportation, and the piers and the Aquarium can be explored on foot from most Downtown hotels. A few spots (Woodland Park Zoo, the Ballard Locks, and the Discovery park) are easier to visit by car.

Museums

Several museums cater specifically to kids, and many are conveniently clustered at the Seattle Center. The Center's winning trio is the **Pacific Science Center**, which has interactive exhibits and IMAX theaters; the **Children's Museum**, which has exhibits on Washington State and foreign cultures plus plenty of interactive art spaces; and, of course, the **Space Needle**. For older, hipper siblings there's a skate park; the Vera Project, a teen music and art space; and the **Experience Music Project/Science Fiction Museum**.

Downtown there are miles of waterfront to explore along the piers. The **Seattle Aquarium** is here and has touch pools and otters—what more could a kid want?

Parks and Outdoor Attractions

Discovery Park has an interpretive center, a Native American cultural center, easy forest trails, and accessible beaches. **Alki Beach** in West Seattle is lively and fun; a wide paved path is the perfect surface for wheels of all kinds—you can rent bikes and scooters, or take to the water on rented paddleboats and kayaks. **Volunteer Park** has wide lawns and shallow pools made for splashing toddlers.

The **Woodland Park Zoo** has 300 different species of animals, from jaguars to mountain goats, cheap parking, and an adjacent playground; stroller rentals are available. Watching an astonishing variety of boats navigate the ship canal at the **Ballard Locks** will entertain visitors of any age.

Hotels

Downtown, the **Hotel Monaco** offers a happy medium between sophisticated and family-friendly. The colorful, eccentric decor will appeal to kids but remind adults that they're in a boutique property. Fun amenities abound, like optional goldfish in the rooms, and toys in the lobby. Surprisingly, one of the city's most high-end historic properties, the **Fairmont Olympic**, is also quite kid-friendly. The hotel's decor is a little fussy, but the grand staircases in the lobby will awe most little ones, and there's a great indoor pool area. In addition, the hotel offers babysitting, a kids' room-service menu, and toys and board games.

GREAT ITINERARIES

WASHINGTON AND OREGON

Northwest Coast and Cities, 10 days

The hip and urbane cities of Seattle and Portland bookend this itinerary, with the verdant Olympic Peninsula, rugged Oregon coast, and undulating Willamette Valley Wine Country at the heart, giving you the best of the city and the country in one trip.

Days 1 and 2: Seattle

Start in **Seattle,** where you can spend a couple of nights exploring this picturesque and dynamic city's highlights. Most of the must-see attractions—**Pike Place Market, Seattle Art Museum,** the **Seattle Aquarium**—are steps from downtown hotels, and it's only a short walk or monorail ride to reach the **Seattle Center,** with its iconic **Space Needle** and such family-friendly draws as the **Pacific Science Center, Children's Museum,** and **Experience Music Project/Science Fiction Museum.** You could cram several of these attractions into one busy day, but it's better to break them up over two days. Or spend your second day exploring some of the city's lively neighborhoods, including Capitol Hill, with its scenic **Volunteer Park,** and Ballard, where you can check out the **Lake Washington Ship Canal** and **Hiram M. Chittenden Locks** park.

Day 3: Bainbridge Island and Port Townsend

(2 hours by car ferry and car from Seattle)

Take the 35 minute car ferry from Seattle across Puget Sound to the laid-back and beautiful **Bainbridge Island,** stopping for lunch and browsing the shops in the village of Winslow and touring **Bloedel Reserve.** Continue on highways 305, 3, and 104, stopping in the cute Scandinavian town of **Poulsbo,** and continuing to the northeastern corner of the Olympic Peninsula, where the charming towns of **Port Townsend** and **Port Angeles** make good overnight bases and have several fine dinner options.

Days 4 and 5: Olympic National Park

(1 hour by car from Port Townsend, 15 minutes by car from Port Angeles)

The next morning, launch into a full day at **Olympic National Park.** Explore the **Hoh Rain Forest** and **Hurricane Ridge** (the nearest section to Port Angeles) before heading back to Port Angeles or Port Townsend for the evening. Start day 5 with a drive west on U.S. 101 to **Forks** and on to **La Push** via Highway 110, a total of about 45 miles. Here, an hour-long lunchtime stroll to **Second or Third Beach** will offer a taste of the wild Pacific coastline. Back on U.S. 101, head south to **Lake Quinault,** which is about 100 miles from Lake Crescent. Check into the **Lake Quinault Lodge,** then drive up the river 6 miles to one of the rain-forest trails through the lush Quinault Valley.

Days 6 and 7: The Oregon Coast

(3 hours from Lake Quinault to Astoria)

Leave Lake Quinault early on day 6 for the scenic drive south on U.S. 101. Here the road winds through coastal spruce forests, periodically rising on headlands to offer Pacific Ocean panoramas. Spend your first night in the up-and-coming town of **Astoria,** just across the Columbia River from Washington. The next day, after visiting Astoria's excellent **Columbia Maritime Museum,** continue south on U.S. 101, where small coastal resort towns like **Cannon Beach** and **Manzanita** beckon with cafés, shops, and spectacular beach parks. Be sure to walk out to the gorgeous beach at **Oswald West State Park** in Manzanita. Take a detour onto the **Three Capes Loop**, a stunning 35-mile byway off U.S. 101. Stop in **Newport** (on the loop), 130 miles south of Astoria, for your second night on the coast—this bustling town has several good restaurants and is home to the **Oregon Coast Aquarium.**

Day 8: Eugene and the Willamette Valley

(2½ hours by car from Newport to Eugene or 4 hours by car stopping at Oregon Dunes)

From Newport, continue south along the coast on U.S. 101 for 50 miles, stopping in the charming village of **Florence** for lunch. Then head south another 20 miles to briefly get a look at the soaring mountains of sand that make up **Oregon Dunes National Recreation Area,** before backtracking back to Florence and cutting inland on Highway 126 about 60 miles to the artsy, friendly college town of **Eugene,** which is at the southern end of the Willamette Valley wine region. Eugene has plenty of overnight options, or you could continue north 90 miles on Interstate 5 to spend the night in the heart of the wine country at **Newberg,** where you'll find dozens of wineries, several fine restaurants, and a few upscale inns and hotels.

Days 9 and 10: Portland

(1 hour 45 minutes by car from Eugene, 40 minutes by car from Newberg)

On day 9, visit some of the Willamette Valley's wineries and then from either Eugene or Newberg, continue into the hip, outdoorsy, and food-driven city of **Portland.** Be sure to visit the several attractions found at green and beautiful **Washington Park,** the chic shops and restaurants of the **Pearl District, Old Town** neighborhood, home to the excellent **Lan**

Su Chinese Garden, and the **Portland Art Museum,** situated along downtown's dapper Park Blocks. Like Seattle, the Rose City is renowned for its quirky, inviting neighborhoods, which abound with locavore-minded restaurants, artisan-coffee roasters, swanky cocktail lounges, and smart boutiques—**Hawthorne, Mississippi,** and **Alberta** are among the best areas for exploring. From Portland, it's a straight three-hour drive back up to Seattle; if you have an extra day, consider a detour east into the magnificent **Columbia River Gorge.** En route to Seattle, you could also easily detour to **Mt. St. Helens, Mt. Rainier,** and the cities of **Olympia** and **Tacoma.**

GREAT ITINERARIES

OREGON

Best of Oregon, 10 days

With 10 days, you can get a taste of Oregon's largest city, eco-conscious Portland, while also getting a nice sense of the state's geographical diversity—the mountainous and sweeping coast, gorgeous Crater Lake, the rugged Cascade Mountains, and the eastern high-desert regions.

Days 1 and 2: Portland

Start by spending a couple of days in Portland, where you can tour the museums and attractions that make up **Washington Park,** as well as the **Lan Su Chinese Garden** in Old Town, and the excellent museums and cultural institutions along downtown's leafy **Park Blocks.** This city of vibrant, distinctive neighborhoods offers plenty of great urban exploring, with Nob Hill, Hawthorne, and the Mississippi Avenue Arts District among the best areas for shopping, café hopping, and people-watching. If you have a little extra time, consider spending a couple of hours just south of the city in the **Willamette Valley Wine Country**—it's an easy jaunt from Portland.

Days 3 and 4: Oregon Coast
(1½ hours by car from Portland to Cannon Beach)

Leave Portland early on day 3 for the drive west about 100 miles on U.S. 30 to the small city of **Astoria,** which has several excellent spots for lunch and the **Columbia River Maritime Museum.** Pick the main scenic highway down the Oregon coast, U.S. 101, and continue south stopping at **Fort Stevens State Park** and the **Fort Clatsop National Memorial.** End the day in charming **Cannon Beach** (26 miles south of Astoria), which has a wealth of oceanfront hotels and inns, many with views of one of the region's seminal features, 235-foot-tall **Haystack Rock.**

The following morning, continue south down U.S. 101. In **Tillamook** (famous for its cheese), take a detour onto the **Three Capes Loop,** a stunning 35-mile byway. Stop in small and scenic **Pacific City** (at the south end of the loop) for lunch. Once you're back on U.S. 101, continue south to **Newport,** spending some time at the excellent **Oregon Coast Aquarium** as well as Oregon State University's fascinating **Hatfield Marine Science Center.** Your final stop is the charming village of **Florence,** 160 miles (four to six hours) from Cannon Beach.

Day 5: Eugene
(2½ hours by car from Florence to Eugene with detour at Oregon Dunes)

Spend the morning driving 20 miles south of Florence along U.S. 101 to scamper about the sandy bluffs at **Oregon Dunes National Recreation Area** near Reedsport. Then backtrack to Florence for lunch in Old Town before taking Highway 126 east for 60 miles to the attractive college city of **Eugene,** staying at one of the charming inns or bed-and-breakfasts near the leafy campus of the University of Oregon. Take a walk to the summit of **Skinner Butte,** which affords fine views of the city, and plan to have dinner at one of the top-notch restaurants at the **5th Street Public Market.** Budget some additional time in Eugene the following morning to visit two excellent University of Oregon museums, the **Jordan Schnitzer Museum of Art** and the **Oregon Museum of Natural History.**

Days 6 and 7: Crater Lake and Ashland
(3 hours by car from Eugene to Crater Lake National Park or Prospect)

From Eugene, take Interstate 5 south for 75 miles to Roseburg, and then head east along Highway 138 (the Umpqua River Scenic Byway), which twists and turns over the Cascade Range for 85 miles to the northern entrance of **Crater Lake National Park**. Once inside the park, you can continue along Rim Drive for another half hour for excellent views of the lake. Overnight in the park or in nearby **Prospect**.

The following morning, take the lake boat tour to **Wizard Island** and hike through the surrounding forest. In the afternoon, head southwest on Highway 62 to Interstate 5, and then on to **Ashland**, 95 miles (about two hours) from Crater Lake. Plan to stay the night in one of Ashland's many superb bed-and-breakfasts. Have dinner and attend one of the **Oregon Shakespeare Festival** productions (mid-February through early November).

Days 8 and 9: Bend
(3½ hours by car from Ashland)

Get an early start out of Ashland, driving east along scenic Highway 66 for 60 miles to **Klamath Falls**, where you can stop for lunch and to tour the excellent **Favell Museum of Western Art and Native American Artifacts** and the extensive **Klamath County Museum**. Then drive north on U.S. 97, stopping if you have time at **Collier Memorial State Park**, to reach the outdoorsy resort town of **Bend**, where you can spend two nights checking out the parks, mountain hikes, microbreweries, and restaurants of the state's largest city east of the Cascades. Be sure to visit the outstanding **High Desert Museum**, the **Old Mill District**, and **Mt. Bachelor Ski Area**.

Day 10: Hood River
(3 hours by car from Bend)

From Bend, continue north up U.S. 97, and then northwest up U.S. 26 to **Mt. Hood**, 105 miles total. Have lunch at the historic **Timberline Lodge**, admiring the

stunning views south down the Cascade Range. Pick up Highway 35 and drive around the east side of Mt. Hood and then north 40 miles up to the dapper town of **Hood River**, in the heart of the picturesque Columbia Gorge. Spend the night at one of the attractive inns, and try one of this town's stellar restaurants for dinner. From here it's just a 60-mile drive west along a scenic stretch of Interstate 84 to reach Portland.

GREAT ITINERARIES

WASHINGTON

Best of Washington, 10 days

It's hard to say which is more alluring for Washington visitors: the island and sculpted bays of Puget Sound, the volcanic peaks of the Cascade Range, or the lively neighborhoods and first-rate attractions, locavore-minded restaurants, and trendy music clubs of Seattle. Here's a tour that reveals all of the state's charms.

Days 1 and 2: Seattle

Begin with two days of touring this world-class hub of acclaimed arts, culture, and dining, visiting downtown's must-see sites, including **Pike Place Market**, the **Seattle Art Museum**, and—a bit north—the **Seattle Center** (and its iconic **Space Needle**). Set aside at least a half-day to investigate some of the city's liveliest neighborhoods, including **Capitol Hill**, with its indie shops, hipster bars, and diverting cafés, and similarly inviting **Ballard** and **Fremont**. If you have a little extra time, consider a quick day-trip to up-and-coming **Tacoma**, with its several fine attractions, and the wine-tasting hub of **Woodinville.**

Days 3 and 4: Olympic National Park
(3 hours by car ferry and car from Seattle, via Bainbridge Island)

Get an early start from Seattle on day 3, taking the ferry from downtown across Puget Sound to scenic **Bainbridge Island** for lunch and shopping in the village of **Winslow**, and perhaps a quick tour of **Bloedel Reserve**, before continuing the drive to historic **Port Angeles**, which you can use as an overnight base for exploring **Olympic National Park.**

Hurricane Ridge is the park's nearest section, but on day 4, depending on how ambitious you are, you could drive west to the **Hoh Rain Forest** section of the park, as well as the coastal areas out at **La Push**, and possibly all the way down to **Lake Quinault** (125 miles from Port Angeles). Try to visit at least one of the rain forests, where you can hike amid huge stands of Douglas firs and Sitka spruces.

Day 5: Whidbey Island
(1½ hours by car and car ferry from Port Angeles)

Drive from Port Angeles to the Victorian-era town of **Port Townsend**, a good stop for lunch and a look at the **Northwest Maritime Center**, and then catch the ferry to **Whidbey Island**, where there are plenty of sophisticated shops, galleries, restaurants, and inns in the laid-back, friendly hamlets of **Langley**, **Greenbank**, and **Coupeville** (where you disembark the ferry). Nature lovers shouldn't miss **Ebey's Landing National Historic Reserve**. To be closer to where you're headed on day 6, you might consider staying just north of Whidbey on **Fidalgo Island**, which is home to **Anacortes**, where ferries leave for the San Juan Islands.

Days 6 and 7: The Northern Cascades
(2½ hours by car from Whidbey Island to North Cascades National Park)

Leave the Puget Sound region, perhaps stopping in the picturesque Skagit Valley towns of **La Conner** and **Mount Vernon** for lunch, and head for Washington's stunning, sky-scraping Cascades range, passing through the old logging town of **Sedro-Woolley** and making your way up the dramatic **North Cascades Highway** (Highway 20) into **North Cascades National Park.** You could stay in the park at **Skagit River Resort** or a bit farther east in **Winthrop.**

On day 7, turn south and follow the upper Columbia River down into **Chelan** (2½ hours from North Cascades), the base

CANADA
U.S.

North Cascades National Park

San Juan Island
Anacortes
Sedro-Woolley 20
Mount Vernon
Winthrop
Port Angeles
Coupeville
Whidbey Island
Port Townsend
Olympic National Park
Lake Chelan
Chelan
Bainbridge Island
Leavenworth
Seattle
Lake Quinault
Mount Rainier Nat'l Park
12
Yakima
82
Zillah
Richland
Pasco
Walla Walla
Prosser
Kennewick
OREGON

area for exploring fjordlike, 55-mile-long **Lake Chelan,** the state's deepest lake, which you can explore by boat or even floatplane. Stay in Chelan, up at the north end of the lake at **Stehekin** (go by floatplane to save time), or a bit farther south and west in the endearingly cute, if kitschy, Bavarian-style town of **Leavenworth,** with its gingerbread architecture and cozy German restaurants.

Day 8: Walla Walla
(4 hours by car from Chelan)

From the Lake Chelan area, it's a long but pleasant 200-mile drive southeast, much of it along the mighty Columbia River, to reach what's developed into the most impressive of the Pacific Northwest's wine-producing areas, **Walla Walla.** This once-sleepy college and farming town has blossomed with stylish restaurants and shops in recent years, and you'll find dozens of tasting rooms, both in town and in the surrounding countryside.

Day 9: Yakima Valley
(2½ hours from Walla Walla)

The great wine-touring continues as you return west from Walla Walla through the **Tri-Cities** communities of Pasco, Kennewick, and Richland, following Interstate 82 to **Yakima.** Good stops for visiting wineries include **Richland, Benton City, Prosser,** and **Zillah.** Yakima itself is a good overnight stop.

Day 10: Mount Rainier National Park
(2½ hours from Yakima)

On the morning of day 10, take U.S. 12 west from Yakima 102 miles to Ohanapecosh, the southern entrance to **Mount Rainier National Park.** When you arrive, take the 31-mile two-hour drive on Sunrise Road, which reveals the "back" (northeast) side of Rainier. A room at the **Paradise Inn** is your base for the night. On the following day, energetic hikers could tackle one of the four- to six-hour trails that lead up among the park's many peaks. Or if it's your last day of traveling, try one of the shorter ranger-led walks through wildflower meadows. It's about a two-hour drive back to Seattle.

Alternatives

You really need a couple of days to enjoy one of Washington's loveliest areas, the **San Juan Islands,** ideally spending a night on two of the three main islands. If you're unable to add two days, you could easily make time by cutting out the Walla Walla/ Yakima portion.

GREAT ITINERARIES

VANCOUVER AND VICTORIA

British Columbia's Top Cities, 7 days

Easily reached from Washington via a combination of ferry and roads, Vancouver and Victoria are a pair of gems. The former is a fast-growing, contemporary city—Canada's third-largest—with a mix of enchanting outdoor activities and world-class cultural and culinary diversions. Much smaller, Victoria is surprisingly relaxed and compact for a provincial capital—it's renowned for its colorful gardens, well-groomed bike paths, and picturesque Inner Harbour.

Days 1 through 4: Vancouver

Start with two or three days in Vancouver itself. You'll want to dedicate a full day to touring 1,000-acre **Stanley Park**, with its 9-km (5½-mile) seawall for walking, cycling, and skating; and the **Vancouver Aquarium Marine Science Center**, a family favorite. From the park, you're at the edge of Vancouver's bustling **West End**, which is rife with interesting shopping and breezy cafés. Continue up the city's main retail drag, **Robson Street**, to reach some of Vancouver's top museums, including the **Vancouver Art Gallery** and the **Bill Reid Gallery of Northwest Coast Art**.

On additional days in Vancouver, explore the Victorian-era **Gaslamp Quarter** and adjacent **Chinatown**, home to the very interesting **Dr. Sun Yat-Sen Classical Chinese Garden**. Stroll over to hip and exciting **Yaletown**, a trendy warren of dining and shopping, and catch the Aquabus across False Creek to **Granville Island**, a former industrial wasteland that's become arguably—with Stanley Park—Vancouver's premier attraction. Here you can eat and shop your way through 50,000-square-foot **Granville Island Public Market**, taking a seat outside and admiring the yachts and sailboats plying False Creek. It's also well worth detouring from the downtown area to stroll through the charming **Kitsilano** neighborhood, near Granville Island, a gentrified patch of dining and shopping with a lovely beach park affording fine views of the city skyline. On this side of town, you're within easy driving or busing distance to a pair of top attractions, the **Museum of Anthropology** on the campus of University of British Columbia, and **Queen Elizabeth Park**, the highest point in the city.

On your final day in Vancouver, explore the mountains and parks of the **North Shore**, hiking across **Capilano Suspension Bridge** and through the adjoining rain forest, and taking the aerial tram to the top of **Grouse Mountain**. You could visit these attractions before catching the ferry from Horseshoe Bay across the Georgia Strait to Nanaimo, and then making the two-hour drive south to Victoria. Or if you're headed to Victoria directly from downtown Vancouver, you could instead drive south from Vancouver to Tsawwassen, and catch a ferry to Swartz Bay, from which it's a 30-minute drive south to Victoria.

Days 5 through 7: Victoria

(4 hours from Vancouver via Horseshoe Bay–Nanaimo ferry, 3 hours via Tsawwassen–Swartz Bay ferry)

British Columbia's compact, verdant, and welcoming capital city, Victoria, is compact enough to explore mostly on foot, although with a car you can more easily reach some of the city's interesting outlying attractions, as well as the wineries of the Saanich Peninsula. Give yourself a couple of days to see the top sites, including the artful architecture of Chinatown; the **Emily Carr House,** dedicated to one of the nation's most celebrated artists; and the fascinating **Royal British Columbia Museum,** where you could easily spend a few hours. Plan to have high tea at the regal **Fairmont Empress** hotel, which overlooks the city's picturesque **Inner Harbour.**

This is a great area for biking, with older residential areas like **Oak Bay, Rockland,** and **Fairfield** popular for touring on foot or on two wheels—highlights include Abkhazi Garden and **Craigdarroch Castle.**

Set aside a full day for a side trip outside of Victoria proper to the **Saanich Peninsula,** with its wineries, bike paths, and perhaps the most impressive attraction in the entire region, 55-acre **Butchart Gardens.**

Alternatives

En route from Vancouver to Victoria, many travelers tack on a couple of days in the nearby **Gulf Islands,** which are just off of Vancouver Island and bear a strong resemblance in scenery and personality to the **San Juan Islands.**

OUTDOOR ADVENTURES

HIKING

In the Pacific Northwest, hiking is potentially a year-round sport, though only experts should attempt hiking in the snowy higher elevations in winter. One of the greatest aspects of this region is the diverse terrain, from high alpine scrambles that require stamina to flowered meadows that invite a relaxed pace to stunning coastal areas that offer a mix of level and precipitous terrain.

Of course, many of the best trails in the region are in national parks (Crater Lake, Olympic, Mt. Rainier, and North Cascades among them). We've focused on trails elsewhere in the region, including some spectacular hidden gems.

Best Hikes

Forest Park, Portland, OR. You can easily walk to the network of more than 70 densely forested trails, many leading to spectacular vistas, from downtown hotels, making this 5,000-acre urban wilderness one of the most accessible in the country. A good place to start is Washington Park, with its Japanese Garden and International Rose Test Garden.

Oswald West State Park, Manzanita, OR. The trails at this state park just south of popular Cannon Beach lead to sweeping headlands, to a sheltered beach popular for surfing, and to the top of Neahkahnie Mountain, from which you have a view of more than 20 miles of coastline.

Smith Rock State Park, Redmond, OR. Although world-famous for rock-climbing, this maze of soaring rock formations has a number of trails well-suited to casual hikers; the 3-mile Smith Rocks Loop hike is a favorite.

Table Rock, Central Point, OR. Comprising a pair of monolithic rocky peaks outside Medford, Table Rock makes a great quick and relaxing scramble—from the top, you're treated to wonderful views of the Cascades.

Wallowa Mountains, Enterprise, OR. This range of granite peaks in eastern Washington, near Hells Canyon, is rife with crystalline alpine lakes and meadows, rushing rivers, and thickly forested valleys that fall between mountain ridges. Trails lead from both Enterprise and La Grande.

Beacon Rock State Park, North Bonneville, WA. Although Multnomah Falls, on the Oregon side of the Columbia Gorge, provides access to plenty of cool trails, the hiking at this park across the river provides bigger wows and fewer crowds. Scaling the 848-foot rock for which the park is named is fun and easy, but you can also access longer and more challenging day hikes to Hamilton Mountain and Table Mountain.

Cape Disappointment State Park, Ilwaco, WA. One of the top spots on the Washington coast for a beach hike, Cape Disappointment is at the mouth of the Columbia River and also contains exhibits documenting Lewis and Clark's journey, which ended here.

Moran State Park, Orcas Island, WA. Explore the 14 hiking trails at Moran State Park, which contains the largest mountain in the San Juan Islands, for exhilarating views of the islands, the Cascades, the Olympics, and Vancouver Island.

Snow Lake, Snoqualmie, WA. Relative proximity to Seattle makes this 8-mile trail into the dramatic Alpine Lakes Wilderness a bit crowded on weekends, but don't let that deter you—this hike is one of the state's true stunners.

BEACHES

Unless you're a truly hardy soul, or you've brought your wetsuit, taking a trip to the beach in the Pacific Northwest probably won't involve much swimming—water temperatures in these parts rarely exceed 55 degrees, even in late summer. However, the residents of this part of the world love going to the coast. The mountainous coastline in Oregon—which frequently inspires comparisons with everywhere from Big Sur to New Zealand—is home to rugged, curvy, smooth-as-glass beaches ideal for tide-pooling, strolling, and surfing. And you'll find similarly spectacular scenery as you continue into Washington, along the Long Beach Peninsula, up around the coast of Olympic National Park, and in the many islands of Puget Sound. Across the border, both Victoria and Vancouver have lovely, graceful beaches set against gorgeous mountain backdrops. Throughout the region, from spring through fall, there's a good chance of spotting whales swimming and diving just offshore (and plenty of tour boats offer cruises that afford better views).

Best Beaches

Cannon Beach, OR. The nearest coastal town to Portland also contains some of the state's most breathtaking beaches, including a stretch that fringes downtown. The 235-foot-tall Haystack Rock rises monumentally above the beach, and on the north side of town, Ecola State Park is a long stretch of rocky headlands punctuated by secluded, beaches.

Cape Kiwanda State Natural Area, Pacific City, OR. Yet another formation called Haystack Rock, this one soaring to 340 feet, defines the coast at this dramatic stretch of beach that's part of Oregon's famed Three Capes Loop scenic drive. Massive waves pound the wide beach here, which has dozens of tidal pools at low tide.

Cape Perpetua Scenic Area, Yachats, OR. This 2,700-acre oceanfront wilderness on the central coast of Oregon is home to an 800-foot-high coastal lookout point, steep and easy hiking trails (including one through a fern-filled rain forest), an educational nature center, and a rocky but beautiful beach.

Oregon Dunes National Recreation Area, Reedsport, OR. Smooth, wind-sculpted dunes—some rising as high as 500 feet—are the highlight of this recreation area near Florence, the largest expanse of coastal sand dunes on the continent.

Port Orford, OR. The westernmost town in the continental United States, this artsy small town along the southern coast is home to several great little beaches, including Battle Rock Wayside Park, which is just steps from downtown, and Garrison Beach State Wayside, a long stretch of sand extending north from Port Orford headland.

Alki Point and Beach, Seattle, WA. The quintessential sunning, beachcombing, and kite-flying stretch of sand, this West Seattle park encompasses 2½ miles of beachfront and is steps from several restaurants.

Second and Third Beaches, Olympic National Park, WA. These national park beaches are ideal for tide-pooling, kayaking, surfing, and watching gray whales frolic off-shore in spring and fall.

Kitsilano Beach, Vancouver, BC. A lovely urban beach in the quiet and charming Kitsilano neighborhood, the shore here has plenty of diversions (tennis, a huge pool) and gorgeous views of the city skyline and North Shore Mountains in the distance.

BICYCLING

From the cities to the coastal and mountain highways, the Pacific Northwest is ideal for—and hugely popular with—biking enthusiasts. You'll find rental shops as well as a handful of bike-tour operators in Portland, Seattle, Vancouver, and Victoria, and in all of these cities as well as a number of smaller towns, dedicated bike lanes and separate multiuse trails (for bikes, runners, and pedestrians) proliferate. And although bikes aren't permitted on many hiking trails, including many of those in national parks, roads in parks and many other scenic regions have wide shoulders and are well-suited to cycling adventures.

Best Bicycling Routes

Columbia Historic Highway, OR. Just 17 miles east of Portland, this narrow, rolling highway climbs through the spectacular Columbia Gorge, past Multnomah Falls and by the Vista House at Crown Point, a dramatic scenic overlook.

Portland and Sauvie Island, OR. Among America's most bike-crazy cities, Portland has miles of dedicated bike lanes and plenty of rental shops. In town, biking is a great way to explore leafy East Side neighborhoods like Hawthorne, Mississippi, and Alberta, which all abound with hip shops and cafés. Nearby are the rural and relatively flat roads of Sauvie Island, with its bounty of pick-your-own berry farms.

U.S. 97, near Bend, OR. The 40 miles or so north from Lava Butte through Bend and on up to Smith Rock State Park have awesome high-desert scenery and receive plenty of sunshine year-round.

Burke-Gilman Trail, Seattle, WA. Extending along an abandoned rail line through Seattle, including part of the lively Ballard community, this multiuse trail draws plenty of bikers year-round. The city itself has many miles of bike lanes and paths.

Hwy. 20, North Cascades National Park, WA. You'll want to be in pretty good shape before tackling the hilly and spectacular North Cascades Highway, but few roads in the state offer more mesmerizing scenery.

Lopez Island, San Juan Islands, WA. All of the islands in Puget Sound, including Whidbey and Bainbridge to the south, are massively popular with cyclists, but rural Lopez Island—with its gently rolling terrain and very little auto traffic—is especially well-suited to two-wheel traffic.

Mount Vernon and La Conner, WA. Bicycling around these two picturesque Skagit County communities is popular year-round, but this activity is especially fun in spring, when Tulip Country Bike Tours arranges trips through the region's glorious tulip fields.

Lochside Regional Trail, Victoria, BC. A fun way to get from the ferry terminal at Swartz Bay to downtown Victoria, and to access a number of wineries, this 29-km (18-mile) level route is along a former rail track.

Lower Seymour Valley Conservation Reserve, Vancouver, BC. Easily reached from downtown Vancouver, the reserve in the soaring North Shore Mountains comprises some 25 km (15.5 miles) of trails through leafy rain forests, plus an easier paved 10-km (6-mile) track.

Seaside Route, Vancouver, BC. The 32-km (20-mile) Seaside route, which curves around the seawall through False Creek and Stanley Park and then south into Kitsilano, is particularly dramatic.

WHALE-WATCHING
IN THE PACIFIC NORTHWEST

The thrill of seeing whales in the wild is, for many, one of the most enduring memories of a trip to the Pacific Northwest. In this part of the world, you'll generally spot two species—gray whales and killer "orca" whales.

About 20,000 grays migrate up the West Coast in spring and back down again in early winter (a smaller group of gray whales live off the Oregon coast all summer). From late spring through early autumn about 80 orcas inhabit Washington's Puget Sound and BC's Georgia Strait. Although far fewer in number, the orcas live in pods and travel in predictable patterns; therefore chances are high that you will see a pod on any given trip. Some operators claim sighting rates of 90 percent; others offer guaranteed sightings, meaning that you can repeat the tour free of charge until you spot a whale.

COMMON PACIFIC NORTHWEST SPECIES

| 0 | 20 | 40 | 60 | 80 | 100 (ft) |

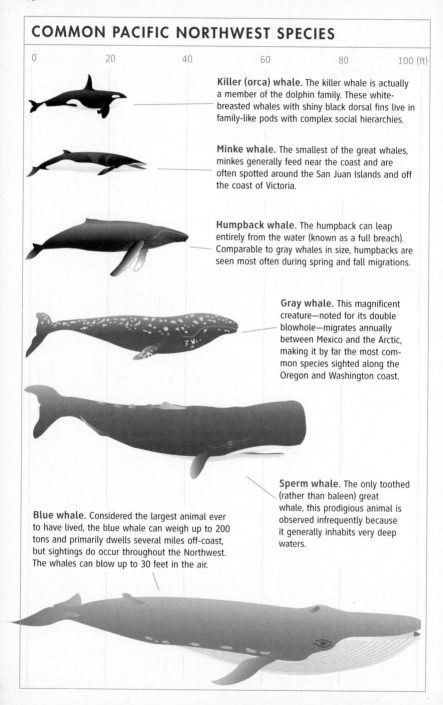

Killer (orca) whale. The killer whale is actually a member of the dolphin family. These white-breasted whales with shiny black dorsal fins live in family-like pods with complex social hierarchies.

Minke whale. The smallest of the great whales, minkes generally feed near the coast and are often spotted around the San Juan Islands and off the coast of Victoria.

Humpback whale. The humpback can leap entirely from the water (known as a full breach). Comparable to gray whales in size, humpbacks are seen most often during spring and fall migrations.

Gray whale. This magnificent creature—noted for its double blowhole—migrates annually between Mexico and the Arctic, making it by far the most common species sighted along the Oregon and Washington coast.

Sperm whale. The only toothed (rather than baleen) great whale, this prodigious animal is observed infrequently because it generally inhabits very deep waters.

Blue whale. Considered the largest animal ever to have lived, the blue whale can weigh up to 200 tons and primarily dwells several miles off-coast, but sightings do occur throughout the Northwest. The whales can blow up to 30 feet in the air.

TAKING A TOUR

Spotting an orca in the Haro Strait between British Columbia and Washington

CHOOSING YOUR BOAT

The type of boat you choose does not affect how close you can get to the whales. For the safety of whales and humans, government regulations require boats to stay at least 100 meters (328 feet) from the pods, though closer encounters are possible if whales approach a boat when its engine is off.

Motor Launches. These cruisers carry from 30 to more than 80 passengers. They are comfortable, with washrooms, protection from the elements, and even snack-and-drink concessions. They can be either glass-enclosed or open-air.

Zodiacs. Open inflatable boats, Zodiacs carry about 12 passengers. They are smaller and more agile than cruisers and offer both an exciting ride bouncing over the waves and an eye-level view of the whales. Passengers are supplied with warm, waterproof survival suits. Note: Zodiac tours are not recommended for people with back or neck problems, pregnant women, or small children.

Most companies have naturalists on board as guides, as well as hydrophones that, if you get close enough, allow you to listen to the whales singing and vocalizing. Although the focus is on whales, you also have a good chance of spotting marine birds, Dall's porpoises, dolphins, seals, and sea lions, as well as other marine life. And, naturally, there's the scenery of forested islands, distant mountains, and craggy coastline.

MOTION SICKNESS

Seasickness isn't usually a problem in the sheltered waters of Puget Sound and the Georgia Strait, but seas can get choppy off the Washington and Oregon coasts. If you're not a good sailor, it's wise to wear a seasickness band or take anti-nausea medication. Ginger candy often works, too.

THE OREGON AND WASHINGTON COAST

A full breach in open waters is a thrilling sight

WHEN TO GO

Mid-December through mid-January is the best time for viewing the southbound migration, with April through mid-June the peak period for the northbound return (when whales swim closer to shore). Throughout summer, several hundred gray whales remain in Oregon waters, often feeding within close view of land. Mornings are often the best time for viewing, as it's more commonly overcast at this time, which means less glare and calmer seas. Try to watch for vapor or water expelled from whales' spouts on the horizon.

WHAT IT COSTS

Trips are generally 2 hours and prices for adults range from $25 to $35.

RECOMMENDED OUTFITTERS

Depoe Bay, with its sheltered, deepwater harbor, is Oregon's whale-watching capital, and here you'll find several outfitters.

Dockside Charters (☎ 800/733–8915 ⊕ www. docksidedepoebay.com) and **Tradewind Charters** (☎ 800/445–8730 ⊕ www. tradewindscharters.com) have excellent reputations. Green-oriented **Eco Tours of Oregon** (☎ 888/868–7733, ⊕ www.ecotours-of-oregon. com) offers full day tours that depart from Portland hotels and include a stop along the coast at Siletz Bay, a 75-minute charter boat tour, lunch, and stops at state parks near Newport and Lincoln.

Along the Washington coast, several of the fishing-charter companies in Westport offer seasonal whale-watching cruises, including **Deep Sea Charters** (☎ 800/562–0151 ⊕ www.deepseacharters. net) and **Ocean Charters** (☎ 800/562–0105, ⊕ www. oceansportfishingcharters. net).

BEST VIEWING FROM SHORE

Washington: On Long Beach Peninsula, the North Head Lighthouse at the mouth of the Columbia River, makes an excellent perch for whale sightings. Westport, farther up the coast at the mouth of Grays Harbor, is another great spot.

Oregon Coast: You can spot gray whales all summer long and especially during the spring migration—excellent locales include Neahkanie Mountain Overlook near Manzanita, Cape Lookout State Park, the Whale Watching Center in Depoe Bay, Cape Perpetua Interpretive Center in Yachats, and Cape Blanco Lighthouse near Port Orford.

PUGET SOUND AND GEORGIA STRAIT

Killer whales in the Puget Sound

WHEN TO GO

Prime time for viewing the three pods of orcas that inhabit this region's waterways is April through September. Less commonly, you may see minke, gray, and humpback whales around the same time.

WHAT IT COSTS

Trips in the San Juan waters are from 3 to 6 hours and prices range from $59 to $99 per adult. Trips in Canada are generally 4 to 6 hours and prices range from $115 to $175 per adult.

RECOMMENDED OUTFITTERS

Many tours depart from Friday Harbor on San Juan Island, among them **Eclipse Charters** (☎ 360/376–6566 ⊕ www.orcasislandwhales. com), **San Juan Excursions** (☎ 800/809–4253 ⊕ www. watchwhales.com), and **Western Prince Cruises** (☎ 800/757–6722 ⊕ www.

orcawhalewatch.com). **San Juan Cruises** (☎ 800/443–4552 ⊕ www.whales.com) offers both day- and overnight whale-watching cruises between Bellingham and Victoria.

One rather fortuitous approach to whale-watching is simply to ride one of the **Washington State Ferries** (☎ 888/808–7977 ⊕ www. wsdot.wa.gov/ferries) out of Anacortes through the San Juans. During the summer killer-whale season, naturalists work on the ferries and talk about the whales and other wildlife.

In Canada, **Wild Whales Vancouver** (☎ 604/699–2011 ⊕ www.whalesvancouver.com) departs from Granville Island on both glass-domed and open-air vessels. **Vancouver Whale Watch** (☎ 604/274–9565 ⊕ www.vancouverwhale-

watch.com) is another first-rate company.

Victoria has an even greater number of whale-watching outfitters. **Great Pacific Adventures** (☎ 877/733–6722 ⊕ www.greatpacificadventures.com), **Ocean Explorations** (☎ 888/442–6722 ⊕ www.oceanexplorations. com), **Springtide Whale Tours** (☎ 800/470–3474 ⊕ www.springtidecharters. com) and **Prince of Whales** (☎ 888/383–4884 ⊕ www. princeofwhales.com) use boats equipped with hydrophones. The latter also offer trips on a 74-passenger cruiser.

BEST VIEWING FROM SHORE

A prime spot for viewing orcas is Lime Kiln State Park, on the west side of San Juan Island. On the Canadian side, you can sometimes see whales right off Oak Bay in Victoria.

CRUISES

Alaska Cruises

During the Alaska cruise season (May–Sept.), Seattle and Vancouver are among North America's busiest ports of embarkation. Ships debarking from these ports proceed directly to Alaska, with one exception: those leaving from Seattle usually make one stop in Victoria or, occasionally, Prince Rupert, BC. Additionally, many of the cruise lines that sail in Alaska (Carnival, Celebrity, Holland America, Norwegian, Princess, Regent Seven Seas, Royal Caribbean, Seabourn, and Silversea are the biggies) stop in Astoria, on the northern Oregon coast, during their seasonal repositioning cruises, when they move ships between Alaska and California, the Mexican Riviera, or even the Caribbean via the Panama Canal. These cruises typically take place in April or May and then again in October, usually starting or ending in Vancouver or Seattle, and sometimes calling in Victoria; additionally, Norwegian Cruise Line often calls on the BC port of Nanaimo during these repositioning cruises. **Cruise Lines International Association** (⊕ *www.cruising. org*) is a good starting point if you don't have a specific carrier in mind.

Pacific Northwest Cruises

From early April through early November, a few cruise lines with smaller ships offer excursions focused specifically on the Pacific Northwest, usually around the San Juan Islands and Puget Sound (leaving from Seattle), or along the Columbia and Snake rivers (leaving from Portland or Clarkston, WA). **Un-Cruise Adventures** (formerly America Safari Cruises) offers seven-day trips exploring Puget Sound, the San Juan Islands, the Gulf Islands, Victoria, and other parts of Vancouver Island; and seven-day excursions along the Columbia and Snake rivers, calling at Bonneville Dam, Richland, Clarkston/Hells Canyon, Walla Walla, The Dalles, and Astoria.

American Cruise Lines runs seven-day excursions along the Columbia and Snake rivers, departing either from Portland or Clarkston (WA), on a Victorian-style sternwheeler, the *Queen of the West*. The same company offers seven-day Puget Sound cruises that stop at Anacortes, Port Townsend, Poulsbo, Port Angeles, and the San Juan Islands. **Fantasy Cruises** is an intimate, high-end outfitter running eight-day cruises through the San Juan Islands. And **Bluewater Adventures** provides a number of tours along the coast of British Columbia, with a particular focus on the Gulf Islands and northern Vancouver Island.

Cruise Line Contacts

American Cruise Lines ☎ *800/460–4518* ⊕ *www.americancruiselines.com.*

Bluewater Adventures ☎ *888/877–1770* ⊕ *www.bluewateradventures.ca.*

Fantasy Cruises ☎ *800/234–3861* ⊕ *www. sanjuanislandcruises.com.*

Un-Cruise Adventures ☎ *888/862–8881* ⊕ *www.un-cruise.com.*

PORTLAND

WELCOME TO PORTLAND

TOP REASONS TO GO

★ **Unleash your inner foodie:** Don't miss an amazingly textured range of global delights, created with fresh, locally harvested ingredients.

★ **Beer "hop":** Over fifty local microbrews, producing offbeat varieties of beer with such names as Hallucinator, Doggie Claws, and Sock Knocker await.

★ **Experience McMenamins:** Visit one of the local chain's beautifully restored properties, such as a renovated elementary school turned hotel.

★ **Take a stroll through Washington Park:** The International Rose Test Garden, Japanese Garden, Oregon Zoo, and Children's Museum are all here.

★ **Peruse pages at Powell's City of Books:** The aisles of this city block–sized shop are filled with more than a million new and used books. Top off hours of literary wanderlust with a mocha or ginseng tea downstairs at World Cup Coffee and Tea House.

1 Downtown. At the center of it all, Portland's downtown boasts the Portland Art Museum, Pioneer Courthouse Square, and the Portland Farmers Market along with notable restaurants.

2 Old Town/Chinatown. This is the area for Asian-inspired public art and the LanSu Chinese Garden. It's also home to the Portland Saturday Market, North America's largest open-air handicraft market.

2

4 Nob Hill. From funky to fabulous, the exciting shopping, restaurants, and bars draw a younger but still sophisticated crowd.

5 Forest Park. Forest Park is the largest forested area within city limits in the nation. Trailheads are easily accessible from Nob Hill.

6 North. The "fifth quadrant," North Portland sits on the peninsula formed by the joining of the Willamette River and the Columbia River. North Mississippi Avenue and North Williams Street are hip dining and drinking destinations.

7 Northeast. Containing the Rose Garden basketball arena, the Lloyd Center Mall, the Alberta Arts District. Portland's Northeast quadrant is diverse to say the least.

8 Southeast. The vibrant pockets of foodie-approved restaurants make the Southeast a cultural must-see. It is also kid-friendly with the OMSI science museum and Mount Tabor Park.

9 Southwest. This neighborhood is home to Washington Park, which contains many must-sees, including the Hoyt Arboretum, International Rose Test Garden, Japanese Garden, and Portland Children's Museum.

EAST OF WILLAMETTE RIVER

3 Pearl District. Bordering Old Town to the northwest is Portland's trendy and posh neighborhood teaming with upscale restaurants, bars, and shopping. Don't leave Portland without visiting Powell's City of Books here.

GETTING ORIENTED

Geographically speaking, Portland is relatively easy to navigate. The city's 200-foot-long blocks are highly walkable, and mapped out into quadrants. The Willamette River divides east and west and Burnside Street separates north from south. "Northwest" refers to the area north of Burnside and west of the river; "Southwest" refers to the area south of Burnside and west of the river; "Northeast" refers to the area north of Burnside and east of the river; "Southeast" refers to the area south of Burnside and east of the river. As you travel around the Portland metropolitan area, keep in mind that named east and west streets intersect numbered avenues, run north to south, and begin at each side of the river. For instance, Southwest 12th Avenue is 12 blocks west of the Willamette. Most of downtown's streets are one-way.

Updated by
Crystal Wood

What distinguishes Portland, Oregon, from the rest of America's cityscapes? Or from the rest of the world's urban destinations for that matter? In a Northwest nutshell: everything. For some, it's the wealth of cultural offerings and never-ending culinary choices; for others, it's Portland's proximity to the ocean and mountains, or simply the beauty of having all these attributes in one place.

Strolling through downtown or within one of Portland's numerous neighborhoods, there's an unmistakable vibrancy to this city—one that is encouraged by clean air, infinite trees, and a blend of historic and modern architecture. Portland's various nicknames—Rose City, Bridgetown, Beervana, Brewtopia—tell its story.

Portland has a thriving cultural community, with ballet, opera, symphonies, theater, and art exhibitions both minor and major in scope. Portland also has long been considered a hub for indie music. Hundreds of bands flock to become part of the creative flow of alternative, jazz, blues, and rock that dominate the nightclub scene seven nights a week. Factor in an outrageous number of independent brewpubs and coffee shops—with snowboarding, windsurfing, or camping within an hour's drive—and it's easy to see why so many young people take advantage of Portland's eclectic indoor and outdoor offerings.

For people on a slower pace, there are strolls through never-ending parks, dimmed dining rooms for savoring innovative regional cuisine, and gorgeous cruises along the Willamette River aboard the *Portland Spirit*. Families can explore first-rate museums and parks, including the Children's Museum, the Oregon Museum of Science and Industry, and Oaks Park. At most libraries, parks, and recreational facilities, expect to find hands-on activities, music, story times, plays, and special performances for children. Many restaurants in and around Portland are family-friendly, and with immediate access to the MAX light rail and streetcars, toting kids around is easy.

PORTLAND PLANNER

WHEN TO GO

Portland's mild climate is best from June through September. Hotels are often filled in July and August, so it's important to book reservations in advance. Spring and fall are also excellent times to visit. The weather usually remains quite good, and the prices for accommodations, transportation, and tours can be lower (and the crowds much smaller) in the most popular destinations. In winter, snow is uncommon in the city but abundant in the nearby mountains, making the region a skier's dream.

Average daytime summer highs are in the 70s; winter temperatures are generally in the 40s. Rainfall varies greatly from one locale to another. In the coastal mountains, for example, 160 inches of rain fall annually, creating temperate rain forests. Portland has an average of only 36 inches of rainfall a year—less than New York, Chicago, or Miami. In winter, however, the rain may never seem to end. More than 75% of Portland's annual precipitation occurs from October through March.

FESTIVALS

SPRING Every May, McCall Waterfront Park fills with live entertainment, rides, and food for **Cinco de Mayo Fiesta**, one of the largest of its kind in America.

SUMMER ⇨ *There are a number of summer beer festivals; see Portland Beer Fests in Nightlife.* In early August, support the Special Olympics while stuffing your face with delectable foods at **Bite of Oregon.** From the pet parade to the Pride Parade, **Portland Pride Festival and Parade** in June is never dull. Now more than 100 years old, the **Portland Rose Festival** in June has two parades, a carnival, fireworks, and dragon boat races. Help stock the local food bank and listen to top headliners from around the nation each July at the **Waterfront Blues Festival,** the largest blues festival west of the Mississippi.

WINTER The holiday spirit is vibrant at **Festival of Lights,** with 500,000 lights and the Pacific Northwest's largest choral gathering. In the heart of downtown, **Holiday Ale Festival** helps chase away the chill of a long winter's night. The top short films, features, and documentaries from the Northwest are chosen by prominent filmmakers and critics each November at the **Northwest Film and Video Festival.** For more than 30 years film lovers have enjoyed the **Portland International Film Festival,** featuring works from throughout the world each February.

GETTING HERE AND AROUND

AIR TRAVEL

It takes about 5 hours to fly nonstop to Portland from New York, 4 hours from Chicago, and 2½ hours from Los Angeles. Flying from Seattle to Portland takes just under an hour; flying from Portland to Vancouver takes an hour and 15 minutes.

Portland International Airport (PDX) is a sleek, modern airport with service to many national and international destinations. It's easily accessible from downtown Portland.

Portland International Airport *(PDX).* Portland International Airport is the only nearby airport receiving commercial flights. The restaurants and shops within are mostly local brands. ☏ *877/739–4636* ⊕ *www. pdx.com.*

GROUND TRANSPORTATION

Taking the MAX, Portland's light-rail train, to and from Portland International Airport is relatively straightforward. The Red Line MAX stops at the east end of the airport, just steps from the door. The approximately 35-minute ride to downtown costs $2.50. Though the train operates seven days a week, it is not available 24 hours a day. Tickets are purchased before boarding at ticket machines located at the stop. MAX tickets are also good on TriMet buses and the Portland Streetcar.

A 5½-mile extension of the MAX light-rail system runs from the Gateway Transit Center (at the intersection of I–84 and I–205) directly to and from the airport. Trains arrive at and depart from inside the passenger terminal near the south baggage-claim area.

Contacts TriMet/MAX ☏ *503/238–7433* ⊕ *www.trimet.org.*

CAR TRAVEL

I–5 enters Portland from the north and south. I–84, the city's major eastern corridor, terminates in Portland. U.S. 26 and U.S. 30 are primary east–west thoroughfares. Bypass routes are I–205, which links I–5 and I–84 before crossing the Columbia River into Washington, and I–405, which arcs around western downtown. Most city-center streets are one-way only, and Southwest 5th and 6th avenues between Burnside and Southwest Madison streets are limited to bus traffic.

From the airport to downtown, take I–205 south to westbound I–84. Drive west over the Willamette River and take the City Center exit. If going to the airport, take I–84 east to I–205 north; follow I–205 to the airport exit.

Traffic on I–5 north and south of downtown and on I–84 and I–205 east of downtown is heavy between 6 am and 9 am and between 4 and 8 pm. Four-lane U.S. 26 west of downtown can be bumper-to-bumper any time of the day going to or from downtown.

PARKING   Though there are several options, parking in downtown Portland can be tricky and expensive. If you're parked for more than several hours, your most affordable and accessible option is to park in one of seven city-owned "Smart Park" lots. Rates start at $1.60 per hour (short-term parking, four hours or less) to $3–$5 per hour (long-term parking, weekdays 5 am–6 pm), with a $15 daily maximum; weekends and evenings have lower rates. The best part about Smart Park is that hundreds of participating merchants will validate tickets and cover the first two hours of parking when you spend at least $25 in their stores.

There are numerous privately owned lots around the city as well; fees for those vary and add up quickly.

Street parking is metered only and requires you to visibly display a sticker on the inside of your curbside window. The meters that dispense the stickers take coins or credit cards (though you'll be charged a bank fee for using a debit card). Metered spaces are mostly available for 90 minutes to three hours; parking tickets for exceeding the limit are regularly issued.

Once you get out of downtown and into residential areas, there's plenty of nonmetered street parking available.

TAXI TRAVEL

Taxi fare is $2.50 at flag drop plus $2.30 per mile. The first person pays by the meter, and each additional passenger pays $1. Cabs cruise the city streets, but it's better to phone for one. The major companies are Broadway Cab, New Rose City Cab, Portland Taxi Company, and Radio Cab. The trip between downtown Portland and the airport takes about 30 minutes by taxi. The fare is about $35.

Taxi Contacts Broadway Cab ☎ *503/227–1234, 503/333–3333* ⊕ *www. broadwaycab.com.* **New Rose City Cab** ✉ *1533 NE Alberta St., Vernon, Northeast* ☎ *503/282–7707* ⊕ *www.newrosecitycabco.biz.* **Portland Taxi Company** ☎ *503/256–5400* ⊕ *www.portlandtaxi.net.* **Radio Cab** ☎ *503/227–1212* ⊕ *www. radiocab.net.*

TRIMET/MAX TRAVEL

TriMet operates an extensive system of buses, streetcars, and light-rail trains. The Central City streetcar line runs between Legacy Good Samaritan hospital in Nob Hill, the Pearl District, downtown, Portland State University and South Waterfront. From the Pearl District, the Central Loop streetcar line crosses to the east side of the Willamette River taking riders to the Oregon Convention Center, then heads south ending at Oregon Museum of Science and Industry (OMSI). The many stops on the line make travel to the charismatic east side of Portland charming and simple. To Nob Hill it travels along 10th Avenue and then on Northwest Northrup; from Nob Hill it runs along Northwest Lovejoy and then on 11th Avenue. Trains stop every few blocks.

Metropolitan Area Express, or MAX, links the eastern and western Portland suburbs with downtown, Washington Park and the Oregon Zoo, the Lloyd Center district, the Convention Center, and the Rose Quarter. From downtown, trains operate daily 5:30 am–1 am, with a fare of $2.50 for 2 hours of travel, and $5 for an unlimited all-day ticket. A seven-day visitor pass is also available for $26. Trains run about every 10 minutes Monday through Saturday and every 15 minutes on Sunday and holidays.

Bus, MAX, and streetcar fare is $2.50 for two hours, which covers most places you'll have cause to go. If you've heard tales of the "fareless square," where travel from downtown to the Lloyd Center was fare-free, sadly it is no more. The ticket for riding without a fare is a stiff one and arrests can be made.

Day passes for unlimited system-wide travel cost $5. Seven- and fourteen-day and monthly passes are available. As you board the bus, the driver will hand you a transfer ticket that is good for one to two hours, depending on the time of day, on all buses and MAX trains. Be sure to hold on to it whether you're transferring or not; it also serves as proof that you have paid for your ride. MAX trains run every 10 minutes Monday to Saturday before 8 pm and every 15 minutes after 8 pm and all day Sunday and holidays. Buses can operate as frequently as every five minutes or once an hour. Bikes are allowed on designated areas of MAX trains, and there are bike racks on the front of all buses that everyone is free to use.

Contacts TriMet/MAX. ⊠ *Ticket Office at Pioneer Courthouse Square, 701 SW 6th Ave., Downtown* ☎ *503/238–7433* ⊕ *www.trimet.org.*

TOURS

BIKE TOURS

Pedal Bike Tours take riders into the heart of the city or out to the beauty that surrounds it. If one the many tours offered here doesn't meet your criteria, custom tours are available too. Bikes and helmets are included with each tour.

Trust your guide at Portland Bike Tours to know Portland's popular and lesser known spots, the places locals like to go, and to get you there in one piece. A well-stocked bike shop is located on-site and serves beer on tap. Bike and helmet are included with tours.

FAMILY   **Bike Tour Contacts Pedal Bike Tours** ⊠ *133 SW 2nd Ave., Downtown* ☎ *503/243–2453* ⊕ *www.pedalbiketours.com.* **Portland Bike Tours and Rentals** ⊠ *117 NW 2nd Ave., Pearl District* ☎ *503/902–5035* ⊕ *www. portlandbicycletours.com.*

BOAT TOURS

Two major rivers shored with pleasant scenery make Portland Spirit Cruises a good tour option. There are brunch, lunch, and dinner cruises, as well as those centered on themes like magic, holidays, tea parties, or live music. Some cruises have a sightseeing option that doesn't include the meal and are less expensive.

For adventurous types, Willamette Jetboat Excursions offers whirling, swirling one- and two-hour tours along the Willamette River that include an up-close visit with Willamette Falls.

Boat Tour Contacts Portland Spirit Cruises ⊠ *110 SE Caruthers St., Hosford-Abernethy, Southeast* ☎ *503/224–3900, 800/224–3901* ⊕ *www.portlandspirit. com.* **Willamette Jetboat Excursions** ⊠ *1945 SE Water Ave., Hosford-Abernethy, Southeast* ☎ *503/231–1532* ⊕ *www.willamettejet.com.*

BUS TOURS

Gray Line operates City of Portland and Pacific Northwest sightseeing tours, including service to Multnomah Falls and the Columbia Gorge. For getting around some of Portland's more major attractions, May through October they also operate Big Pink, a pink trolley that visits 11 stops in the downtown area or close by. One- and two-day passes are available. A one-hour 20-minute narrated tour is included and you can get off and on at designated stops as often as you wish. Call for departure times and tours.

Bus Tour Contacts Gray Line ☎ *503/241–7373* ⊕ *www.graylineofportland.net.*

WALKING TOURS

Walk the Portland beat with guides who share their personal Portland knowledge: its history, food, brews, arts, and sights. Travel Portland (⇨ *Visitor Information*), which is open weekdays 8:30–5:30 and Saturday 10–4, has brochures, maps, and guides to art galleries and select neighborhoods.

Take a tour with Food Carts Portland and Brett Burmeister, chief scribe of Portland's food cart scene since 2008. This 90-minute tour is not just to sample tastes from some favorite carts, but also an opportunity to learn more about the culture behind the carts. The tour starts at a predetermined downtown food cart.

Forktown Food Tours offers gastro-centered walking tours. Each of their three hour tours centers on a different epicurean area of Portland and includes a 1.5-mile walk to help burn off the calories. All tours meet up in the selected neighborhood at a specific location given at time of ticket purchase.

A slew of tours are offered by Portland Walking Tours but it's their Beyond Bizarre tour that garners lots of talk. Ghost hunter wannabes and paranormal junkies make this a popular tour that can sell out during the peak season. If it's unavailable, there's also the Underground Portland tour, which highlights the sinister history of Portland.

Walking Tour Contacts Food Carts Portland ☎ *503/896–2771* ⊕ *www. foodcartsportland.com/tours.* **Forktown Food Tours** ☎ *503/234–3663* ⊕ *www. forktown.com.* **Portland Walking Tours** ⊠ *115 SW Ash St., Suite 400F, Downtown* ☎ *503/774–4522* ⊕ *www.portlandwalkingtours.com.*

VISITOR INFORMATION

Travel Portland Information Center ⊠ *Pioneer Courthouse Square, 701 SW 6th Ave., Downtown* ☎ *503/275-8355, 877/678-5263* ⊕ *www.travelportland. com* ⊙ *May–Oct., weekdays 8:30–5:30, Sat. 10–4, Sun. 10–2; closed Nov.–Apr..*

EXPLORING

Updated by
Crystal Wood

One of the greatest things about Portland is that there's so much to explore. This city rightfully boasts that there's something for everyone. What makes discovering Portland's treasures even more enticing is that its attractions, transportation options, and events are all relatively accessible and affordable.

DOWNTOWN

Portland has one of the most attractive, inviting downtown centers in the United States. It's clean, compact, and filled with parks, plazas, and fountains. Architecture fans find plenty to admire in its mix of old and new. Hotels, shops, museums, restaurants, and entertainment can all be found here. Portland's superb public transportation system includes MAX light-rail, buses, and the streetcar, making it easy to get to all your interests downtown. A day pass is recommended.

TOP ATTRACTIONS

Central Library. The elegant, etched-graphite central staircase and elaborate ceiling ornamentation make this no ordinary library. With a gallery space on the second floor and famous literary names engraved on the walls, this building is well worth a walk around. ■ **TIP→ A 20-minute tour of the impressive eco-roof garden is given during the spring and summer seasons. Pre-registering is required.** ⊠ *801 SW 10th Ave.,*

GREAT ITINERARIES

IF YOU HAVE 1 DAY

Spend the morning exploring downtown. Visit the **Portland Art Museum** or the **Oregon History Center**, stop by the historic **First Congregational Church** and Pioneer Courthouse Square, and take a stroll along the **Park Blocks** or **Waterfront Park**. Eat lunch and do a little shopping along Northwest 23rd Avenue in the early afternoon, and be sure to get a look at the beautiful historic homes in Nob Hill. From there, drive up into the northwest hills to **Pittock Mansion**, and finish off the afternoon at the **Japanese Garden** and the **International Rose Test Garden** in Washington Park. If you still have energy, head across the river for dinner on Hawthorne Boulevard; then drive up to **Mt. Tabor Park** for Portland's best view of the sunset.

IF YOU HAVE 3 DAYS

On your first day, follow the itinerary above, but stay on the west side for dinner, and take your evening stroll in **Waterfront Park**. On your second morning, visit the **Lan Su Chinese Garden** in Old Town, and then head across the river to the Sellwood District for lunch and antiquing. Stop by the **Crystal Springs Rhododendron Garden**, then head to the Hawthorne District in the afternoon. Wander through the Hawthorne and Belmont neighborhoods for a couple hours, stop by **Laurelhurst Park**, and take a picnic dinner up to **Mt. Tabor Park** to watch the sun go down. In the evening, catch a movie at the **Bagdad Theatre and Pub**, or get a beer at one of the many east side brewpubs. On Day 3, take a morning hike in **Hoyt Arboretum** or **Forest Park**; then spend your afternoon exploring shops and galleries in the Pearl District and on northeast Alberta Street. Drive out to the Grotto, and then eat dinner at the **Kennedy School** or one of the other McMenamins brewpubs.

Downtown ☎ *503/988–5123* ⊕ *multcolib.org* ☉ *Thurs.–Sat. 10–6, Tues. and Wed. noon–8, Sun. 10–5, Mon. 10–8.*

Old Church. This building erected in 1882 is a prime example of Carpenter Gothic architecture. Tall spires and original stained-glass windows enhance its exterior of rough-cut lumber. The acoustically resonant church hosts free classical concerts at noon each Wednesday. If you're lucky, you'll get to hear one of the few operating Hook and Hastings tracker pipe organs. ■ TIP➔ Check the Old Church calendar for other special events such as the blues and jazz series. Tickets are reasonably priced, especially for the caliber of performance. ⊠ *1422 SW 11th Ave., Downtown* ☎ *503/222–2031* ⊕ *www.oldchurch.org* ☉ *Weekdays 11–3.*

Oregon Historical Society. Impressive eight-story-high trompe l'oeil murals of Lewis and Clark and the Oregon Trail cover two sides of this downtown museum, which follows the state's story from prehistoric times to the present. A pair of 9,000-year-old sagebrush sandals, a covered wagon, and an early chainsaw are displayed in "Oregon My Oregon," a permanent exhibit that provides a comprehensive overview of the state's past. Other spaces host large traveling exhibits and changing regional shows. The center's research library is open to the public Tuesday

WHAT'S FREE (OR CHEAPER) WHEN

Children's Museum: Free from 4–8 pm the first Friday of each month.

Crystal Springs Rhododendron Garden: Free the day after Labor Day through February.

Oregon Historical Society: Six free days each year. Call or check website for dates.

Oregon Museum of Science and Industry: $2 admission the first Sunday of each month.

Oregon Zoo: $4 admission the second Tuesday of each month.

Portland Art Museum: Free from 5–8 pm the fourth Friday of each month.

through Saturday; its bookstore is a good source for maps and publications on Pacific Northwest history. Every month the Oregon Historical Society has a day on which kids are admitted for free. Check the website for dates. ⊠ *1200 SW Park Ave., Downtown* ☎ *503/222–1741* ⊕ *www.ohs.org* ⊠ *$11* ⊙ *Mon.–Sat. 10–5, Sun. noon–5.*

Pioneer Courthouse Square. In many ways the living room, public heart, and commercial soul of downtown, Pioneer Square is not entirely square, rather an amphitheater-like brick piazza. Special seasonal, charitable, and festival-oriented events often take place in this premier people-watching venue. Directly across the street is one of downtown Portland's most familiar landmarks, the classically sedate **Pioneer Courthouse.** Built in 1869, it's the oldest public building in the Pacific Northwest. ⊠ *701 SW 6th Ave., Downtown* ⊕ *www.thesquarepdx.org.*

Vintage Trolley. On select Sundays May through December, vintage trolleys run between PSU and Union Station, with free service every half hour between 10:30 am and 5 pm. A round trip takes roughly 30 minutes with stops at each MAX station on the route. The ride is free but donations are accepted. ⊠ *Downtown* ☎ *503/323–7363* ⊕ *www.trimet.org/schedules/trolley.*

Portland/Oregon Information Center. You can pick up maps and literature about the city and the state here at the Portland/Oregon Information Center. Easy to miss, the center is located between the water features, through the glass doors, at Pioneer Courthouse Square. ⊠ *701 SW Sixth Ave., Downtown* ☎ *503/275–8355* ⊕ *www.travelportland. com* ⊙ *May–Oct. weekdays 8:30–5:30, Sat. 10–4, Sun. 10–2; Nov.–Apr. weekdays 8:30–5:30, Sat. 10–4.*

FAMILY **Portland Art Museum.** The treasures at the Pacific Northwest's oldest arts
Fodor's Choice facility span 35 centuries of Asian, European, and American art. A high
★ point is the Center for Native American Art, with regional and contemporary art from more than 200 tribes. The **Jubitz Center for Modern and Contemporary Art** contains six floors devoted entirely to modern art, with the changing selection chosen from more than 400 pieces in the museum's permanent collection. The film center presents the annual Portland International Film Festival in February and the Northwest

Downtown

← TO JELD-WEN FIELD

First Congregationalist Church

GOVERNOR TOM McCALL WATERFRONT PARK

S.W. Pine St.
S.W. Oak St.
S.W. Stark St.
S.W. Washington St.
S.W. Alder St.
MAX LIGHT RAIL
S.W. Morrison St.
S.W. Yamhill St.
S.W. Taylor St.
BUS
S.W. Salmon St.
S.W. Main St.
S.W. Madison St.
S.W. Jefferson St.
S.W. Columbia St.
S.W. Market St.
S.W. Clay St.
S.W. Mill St.
Harrison St.

S.W. 12th Ave.
S.W. 11th Ave.
S.W. 10th Ave.
S.W. 9th Ave.
S.W. Park Ave.
S.W. Broadway
S.W. 6th Ave.
S.W. 5th Ave.
S.W. 4th Ave.
S.W. 3rd Ave.
S.W. 2nd Ave.
S.W. 1st Ave.

6th Ave. Transit Mall
5th Ave. Transit Mall
S.W. 4th Ave.
S.W. 3rd Ave.
S.W. 2nd Ave.

CENTRAL CITY STREETCAR
South Park Blocks
S.W. Naito Pkwy./Front Ave.
Hawthorne Bridge

26
26

Willamette River

KEY

- ○ Max Light Rail
- ← Streetcar
- ... Bus
- 🚲 Bike only

0 .... 1/4 mile
0 .... 1/4 kilometer

Pioneer Square, Downtown

Film Festival in early November. Also, take a moment to linger in the peaceful outdoor sculpture garden. Kids under 17 are admitted free. ⊠ *1219 SW Park Ave., Downtown* ☎ *503/226–2811, 503/221–1156 film schedule* ⊕ *www.portlandartmuseum.org* ⊠ *$15* ⊗ *Tues., Wed., and Sat. 10–5, Thurs. and Fri. 10–8, Sun. noon–5.*

Portland Farmers Market. On Saturday from March through mid-December, local farmers, bakers, chefs, and entertainers converge at the South Park Blocks near the PSU campus for Oregon's largest open-air farmers' market. It's a great place to sample the regional bounty and to witness the local-food obsession that's revolutionized Portland's culinary scene. There's a Wednesday market, May through October, between Southwest Salmon and Southwest Main. And on Monday, June through September, the market can be found at Pioneer Courthouse Square. ⊠ *South Park Blocks at SW Park Ave. and Montgomery St., Downtown* ☎ *503/241–0032* ⊕ *www.portlandfarmersmarket.org* ⊗ *Mar.–mid-Dec., Sat. 8:30–2; May–Oct., Mon. and Wed. 10–2.*

WORTH NOTING

Chapman and Lownsdale squares. During the 1920s these parks were segregated by sex: Chapman, between Madison and Main streets, was reserved for women, and Lownsdale, between Main and Salmon streets, was for men. The elk statue on Main Street, which separates the parks, was given to the city by David Thompson, mayor from 1879 to 1882. It recalls the elk that grazed in the area in the 1850s. ⊠ *Between SW Salmon St. and SW Jefferson St. and SW 4th and 3rd Ave., Downtown.*

Director Park. Low on greenery but high on gathering space, this is the newest addition to the city's downtown park blocks. Opened in 2009, it was designed as a public piazza that hides the 700-space parking garage below. A glass canopy/light display provides cover and a fountain dedicated to teachers cools off summer visitors. Chess players will enjoy the giant (16-foot by 16-foot) board with 25-inch-high pieces, available on a first come, first served basis. ⊠ *815 SW Park Ave., Downtown* ⊕ *www.directorpark.org.*

Governor Tom McCall Waterfront Park. Named for a former governor revered for his statewide land-use planning initiatives, this park stretches north along the Willamette River for about a mile to Burnside Street. Broad and grassy, Waterfront Park's got a fine ground-level view of downtown Portland's bridges and skyline. Once an expressway, it's now the site for many events, among them the Rose Festival, classical and blues concerts, Cinco de Mayo, and the Oregon Brewers Festival. The arching jets of water at the **Salmon Street Fountain** change configuration every few hours, and are a favorite cooling-off spot during the dog days of summer. ⊠ *SW Naito Pkwy. (Front Ave.), from south of Steel Bridge to south of Hawthorne Bridge, Downtown.*

Ira Keller Fountain. This series of 18-foot-high stone waterfalls across from the front entrance of the Keller Auditorium is worth a look. Each minute, 13,000 gallons of water fall and churn through this beauty. ⊠ *SW 3rd Ave. and Clay St., Downtown* ☎ *503/274–6560.*

Portland Center for the Performing Arts. The "old building" and the hub of activity here is the **Arlene Schnitzer Concert Hall,** host to the Oregon Symphony, musical events of many genres, and lectures. Across Main Street, but still part of the center, is the 292-seat **Delores Winningstad Theatre,** used for plays and special performances. Its stage design and dimensions are based on those of an Elizabethan-era stage. The 916-seat **Newmark Theatre** is also part of the complex. ⊠ *SW Broadway and SW Main St., Downtown* ☎ *503/274–6560* ⊕ *www.pcpa.com* ☉ *Free tours Wed. at 11 am, Sat. every ½ hr 11–1.*

OLD TOWN/CHINATOWN

The Skidmore Old Town National Historic District, commonly called Old Town/Chinatown, is where Portland was born. The 20-square-block section, bounded by Oak Street to the south and Hoyt Street to the north, includes buildings of varying ages and architectural designs. Before it was renovated, this was skid row. Vestiges of it remain in parts of Chinatown; older buildings are slowly being remodeled and over the last several years the immediate area has experienced a surge in development. Lan Su Chinese Garden is also here. MAX serves the area with a stop at the Old Town/Chinatown station.

TOP ATTRACTIONS

Japanese-American Historical Plaza. Take a moment to study the evocative figures cast into the bronze columns at the plaza's entrance; they show Japanese and Japanese-Americans before, during, and after World War II—living daily life, fighting in battle for the United States, and marching off to internment camps. Simple blocks of granite carved with haiku poems describing the war experience powerfully evoke this dark episode

in American history. ⊠ *NW Naito Pkwy. and Davis St., in Waterfront Park, Old Town/Chinatown.*

Fodor's Choice ★ **Lan Su Chinese Garden.** In a twist on the Joni Mitchell song, the city of Portland and private donors took down a parking lot and unpaved paradise when they created this wonderland near the Pearl District and Old Town/Chinatown. It's the largest Suzhou-style garden outside China, with a large lake, bridged and covered walkways, koi- and water lily–filled ponds, rocks, bamboo, statues, waterfalls, and courtyards. A team of 60 artisans and designers from China literally left no stone unturned—500 tons of stone were brought here from Suzhou—in their efforts to give the windows, roof tiles, gateways, including a "moongate," and other architectural aspects of the garden some specific meaning or purpose. Also on the premises are a gift shop and a two-story teahouse overlooking the lake and garden. ⊠ *239 NW Everett, Old Town/Chinatown* ☎ *503/228–8131* ⊕ *www.lansugarden.org* ⊠ *$9.50* ☉ *Nov.–Mar., daily 10–5; Apr.–Oct., daily 10–6.*

FAMILY **Oregon Maritime Museum.** Local model makers created most of this museum's models of ships that once plied the Columbia River. Contained within the stern-wheeler steamship *Portland*, this small museum provides an excellent overview of Oregon's maritime history with artifacts and memorabilia. The Children's Room has nautical items that can

Lan Su Chinese Garden, Old Town/Chinatown

be touched and operated. The *Portland* was the last steam-powered stern-wheeler operating in the United States, and volunteer-guided tours include the pilothouse and engine room. ⊠ *Portland steamship, end of SW Pine St., in Waterfront Park, Old Town/Chinatown* ☏ *503/224–7724* ⊕ *www.oregonmaritimemuseum.org* ✉ *$7* ⊗ *Wed., Fri., and Sat. 11–4, Sun. 12:30–4:30.*

FAMILY

Fodor'sChoice

★

Portland Saturday Market. On weekends from March to Christmas, the west side of the Burnside Bridge and the Skidmore Fountain area has North America's largest open-air handicraft market. If you're looking for jewelry, yard art, housewares, and decorative goods made from every material under the sun, then there's an amazing collection of works by talented artisans on display here. Entertainers and food and produce booths add to the festive feel. If taking the MAX train to the market, get off at the Skidmore Fountain stop. ⊠ *2 SW Naito Pkwy. and SW Ankeny, Waterfront Park and Ankeny Plaza, Old Town/Chinatown* ☏ *503/222–6072* ⊕ *www.saturdaymarket.org* ⊗ *Mar.–Dec., Sat. 10–5, Sun. 11–4:30.*

WORTH NOTING

Chinatown Gate. Recognizable by its 5 roofs, 64 dragons, and 2 huge lions, the Chinatown Gate is the official entrance to the Chinatown District. During the 1890s Portland had the second-largest Chinese community in the United States. Today's Chinatown has shrunk to a handful of blocks with a few shops, grocery stores, and so-so restaurants (there are better places for Chinese food outside the district). ⊠ *NW 4th Ave. and Burnside St., Old Town/Chinatown.*

PEARL DISTRICT

Bordering Old Town to the northwest is the Pearl District. Formerly a warehouse area along the railroad yards, this is the fastest-growing part of Portland. Mid-rise residential lofts have sprouted on almost every block, and boutiques, outdoor retailers, galleries, and trendy restaurants line the streets. The Portland streetcar line passes through here on its way from Nob Hill to downtown and Portland State University, with stops at two new, ecologically themed city parks.

Fodor's Choice
★

Powell's City of Books. The largest independent bookstore in the world, with more than 1.5 million new and used books, this Portland landmark can easily consume several hours. It's so big it has its own map available at the info kiosks, and rooms are color-coded according to the types of books, so you can find your way out again. Be sure to look for the pillar bearing signatures of prominent sci-fi authors who have passed through the store—the scrawls are protected by a jagged length of Plexiglas. At the very least, stop into Powell's for a peek or grab a cup of coffee at the adjoining branch of World Cup Coffee and Tea. ⊠ *1005 W Burnside St., Pearl District* ☎ *503/228–4651* ⊕ *www.powells.com* ⊙ *Daily 9 am–11 pm.*

NOB HILL

The showiest example of Portland's urban chic is Northwest 23rd Avenue—sometimes referred to with varying degrees of affection as "trendy-third"—a 20-block thoroughfare that cuts north–south through the neighborhood known as Nob Hill. Fashionable since the 1880s and still filled with Victorian houses, the neighborhood is a mixed-use cornucopia of old Portland charm and new Portland hip. With its cafés, restaurants, galleries, and boutiques, it's a great place to stroll, shop, and people-watch. More restaurants, shops, and nightspots can be found on Northwest 21st Avenue, two blocks away. The Portland Streetcar runs from Legacy Good Samaritan Hospital in Nob Hill, through the Pearl District on 10th and 11th avenues, connects with MAX light-rail near Pioneer Courthouse Square downtown, and then continues on to Portland State University and ends at the South Waterfront District.

Clear Creek Distillery. The distillery keeps such a low profile that it's practically invisible. But ring the bell and someone will unlock the wrought-iron gate and let you into a dim, quiet tasting room where you can sample Clear Creek's world-famous Oregon apple and pear brandies, liqueurs, and grappas. ⊠ *2389 NW Wilson St., Nob Hill* ☎ *503/248–9470* ⊕ *www.clearcreekdistillery.com* ⊙ *Mon.–Sat. 9–5.*

NEED A BREAK?

Vivace Coffee. This creperie and coffeehouse is in Pettygrove House, a restored Victorian gingerbread house built in 1892. It was once the home of Francis Pettygrove, the man who named Portland after winning a coin toss. Today it's a good place to take a break, with colorful walls and comfortable chairs. ⊠ 1400 NW 23rd Ave., Nob Hill ☎ 503/228-3667.

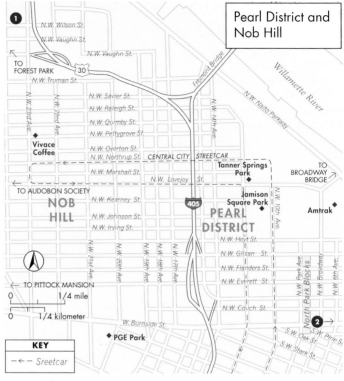

Pearl District and
Nob Hill

FOREST PARK

One of the largest city parks in the country, Forest Park stretches eight miles along the hills overlooking the Willamette River west of downtown. More than 70 miles of trails through forests of Douglas fir, hemlock, and cedar (including a few patches of old growth) offer numerous options for those looking to log some miles or spend some time outside. The Wildwood Trail serves as the backbone for many loop or spur trail routes. Trailheads easily accessible from Nob Hill begin at the west ends of NW Thurman and Upshur streets.

Forest Park. One of the nation's largest urban wildernesses (5,000 acres), this city-owned, car-free park, has more than 50 species of birds and mammals and more than 70 miles of trails. Running the length of the park is the 24½-mile Wildwood Trail, which extends into Washington Park. The 11-mile Leif Erikson Drive, which picks up from the end of Northwest Thurman Street, is a popular place to jog or ride a mountain bike. ■ TIP→ Trail information and maps can be found at the Forest Park Conservancy office. ⊠ *Forest Park Conservancy, 1505 NW 23rd Ave., Northwest* ☎ *503/223–5449* ⊕ *www.forestparkconservancy.org* ⊙ *Daily dawn–dusk.*

Portland Audubon Society. The 150-acre sanctuary has 4.5 miles of trails, including one known for ample woodpecker sightings. There's also a hospital for injured and orphaned birds here, as well as a gift shop stocked with books and feeders. The society supplies free maps and sponsors a flock of bird-related activities, including guided bird-watching events. ✉ *5151 NW Cornell Rd., Forest Park, Northwest* ☎ *503/292–6855* ⊕ *www.audubonportland.org* ☯ *Trails daily dawn–dusk; Nature Store Mon.–Sat 10–6, Sun. 10–5.*

NORTH

Long dismissed as the "fifth quadrant," North Portland has come into its own in recent years. Marked by a 31-foot-tall roadside statue of the strapping lumberman Paul Bunyan (on the National Register of Historic Places), North Portland sits on the peninsula formed by the joining of the Willamette River (to the west) and the Columbia River (to the north). In the working-class, port-side neighborhood of St. Johns, old-school barbershops and hardware stores sit alongside newer shops, restaurants, and cafés. Further south, North Mississippi Avenue and North Williams Street have become home to some of the most popular food, drink, and music destinations in the city.

North Mississippi Avenue. Four blocks of old storefronts reinvented as cafés, collectives, shops, and music venues along this north Portland street in the Boise neighborhood showcase the indie spirit of the city's do-it-yourselfers and creative types. Bioswale planter boxes, found-object fences, and café tables built from old doors are some of the innovations you'll see around this hip new district. At the hub of it all is the ReBuilding Center, an outlet for recycled building supplies that has cob (clay-and-straw) trees and benches built into the facade. Take MAX light-rail to the Albina/Mississippi station. ✉ *N Mississippi Ave. between N Fremont and N Shaver Sts., Boise, North.*

NORTHEAST

Containing the Rose Garden basketball arena, the Lloyd Center Mall, the Alberta Arts District, and some of the city's poorest and most affluent neighborhoods, Portland's Northeast quadrant is diverse to say the least. Once the epicenter of the city's African American community, the inner parts of Northeast have slowly gentrified over the last half century. In the Irvington, Laurelhurst, and Alameda neighborhoods, you'll find some of the largest, most historic homes in town. Lined with a number of high-quality restaurants, bars, galleries, and boutiques, Alberta Street hosts a bustling street art fair the last Thursday of every month during summer (primarily between 12th and 31st avenues), and the Hollywood District, built around the 1920s-era Hollywood Theater, offers a number of interesting shops as well.

EXPLORING

The Grotto. Owned by the Catholic Church, the National Sanctuary of Our Sorrowful Mother, as it's officially known, displays more than 100 statues and shrines in 62 acres of woods. The grotto was carved into the base of a 110-foot cliff, and has a replica of Michelangelo's *Pietà*. The real treat is found after ascending the cliff face via elevator, as you enter

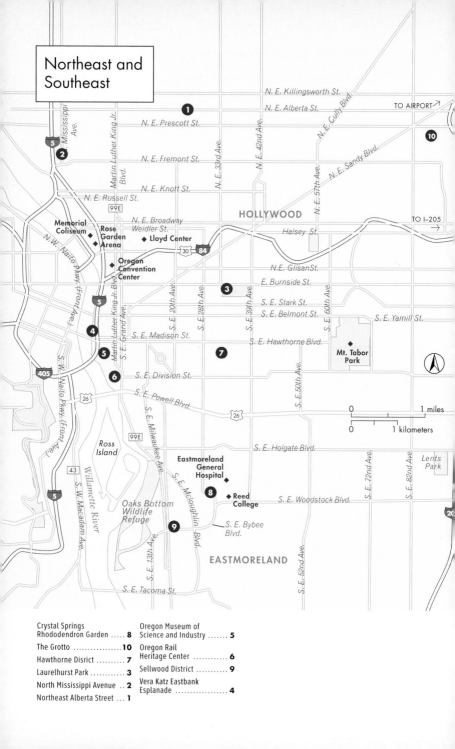

Northeast and Southeast

N. E. Killingsworth St.

N. E. Alberta St.

TO AIRPORT →

N. E. Prescott St.

N. E. Fremont St.

N. E. Knott St.

N. E. Russell St.

99E

Memorial
Coliseum

Rose
Garden
Arena

Lloyd Center

N. E. Broadway
Weidler St.

HOLLYWOOD

Halsey St.

TO I-205 →

Oregon
Convention
Center

30 84

N.E. Glisan St.

E. Burnside St.

S. E. Stark St.

S. E. Belmont St.

S. E. Yamill St.

S. E. Madison St.

S. E. Hawthorne Blvd.

Mt. Tabor
Park

S. E. Division St.

S. E. Powell Blvd.

405

26

26

99E

Ross
Island

Eastmoreland
General
Hospital

S. E. Holgate Blvd.

Lents
Park

Reed
College

S. E. Woodstock Blvd.

43

Oaks Bottom
Wildlife
Refuge

S. E. Bybee
Blvd.

EASTMORELAND

S. E. Tacoma St.

0   1 miles

0   1 kilometers

N. W. Naito Pkwy. (Front Ave.)

S. W. Naito Pkwy. (Front Ave.)

S. W. Macadam Ave.

Willamette River

Mississippi Ave.

Martin Luther King Jr. Blvd.

Martin Luther King Jr. Blvd.

S. E. Grand Ave.

N. E. 33rd Ave.

N. E. 42nd Ave.

N. E. Cully Blvd.

N. E. 57th Ave.

N. E. Sandy Blvd.

S. E. 20th Ave.

S. E. 28th Ave.

S. E. 39th Ave.

S. E. 60th Ave.

S. E. 50th Ave.

S. E. 72nd Ave.

S. E. 82nd Ave.

S. E. 52nd Ave.

S. E. Milwaukie Ave.

S. E. McLoughlin Blvd.

S. E. 13th Ave.

a wonderland of gardens, sculptures, and shrines, and a glass-walled cathedral with an awe-inspiring view of the Columbia River and the Cascades. There's a dazzling Festival of Lights at Christmastime (late November and December), with 250,000 lights and holiday concerts in the 600-seat chapel. Daily masses are held here, too. ⊠ *8840 N.E. Skidmore St. Main entrance: N.E. Sandy Blvd. at N.E. 85th Ave., Madison South, Northeast* ☎ *503/254–7371* ⊕ *www.thegrotto.org* 🖾 *Plaza level free; elevator to upper level $4* ⊗ *Mid-May–Labor Day, daily 9–8:30; day after Labor Day–late Nov. and Feb.–mid-May, daily 9–5:30; late Nov.–Jan., daily 9–4.*

Northeast Alberta Street. Quirky handicrafts by local artists are for sale inside the galleries, studios, coffeehouses, restaurants, and boutiques lining this street in the northeast Portland neighborhood. It's a fascinating place to witness the intersection of cultures and lifestyles in a growing city. Shops unveil new exhibits during an evening event called the Last Thursday Art Walk. The Alberta Street Fair in September showcases the area with arts-and-crafts displays and street performances. ⊠ *NE Albert St. between NE Martin Luther King Jr. Blvd. and NE 30th Ave., Alberta Arts District, Northeast.*

SOUTHEAST

Bounded on the west by the Willamette River and in the north by Burnside Avenue, the Southeast neighborhood is typical Portland: funky, creative, hip. Packed with shade trees, Craftsman-style houses, and backyard chicken coops, this neighborhood is industrial close in (the river to 7th) and middle-class residential further out (8th to 82nd). Its vibrant pockets of foodie-approved restaurants, as well as bars, coffee shops, and boutiques along east–west running Division, Hawthorne, Belmont, Stark, and Burnside streets, make the Southeast a Portland cultural must-see. Other features of this 'hood: the riverside, kid-focused science museum OMSI, and the sprawling park on the inactive volcano Mt. Tabor.

TOP ATTRACTIONS

Fodor'sChoice
★
Hawthorne District. Stretching from the foot of Mt. Tabor to Southeast 30th Avenue, this smaller neighborhood within the Buckman neighborhood in Southeast attracts a more college-age, bohemian crowd than Downtown or Nob Hill. With many bookstores, coffeehouses, taverns, restaurants, antiques stores, and boutiques filling the streets, it's easy to spend a few hours wandering here. Highlights include a smaller but still impressive branch of Powell's Books, Bagdad Theater & Pub, and the Goodwill Boutique. ⊠ *SE Hawthorne Blvd., between SE 30th and SE 42nd Aves., Buckman, Southeast.*

Laurelhurst Park. Manicured lawns, stately trees, and a wildfowl pond make this 25-acre southeast Portland park a favorite urban hangout since 1912. **Laurelhurst,** one of the city's most beautiful neighborhoods, surrounds the park. In 2001, it was the first city park to be named on the National Register of Historic Places. ⊠ *SE 39th Ave. between SE Ankeny and SE Oak Sts., Laurelhurst, Southeast* ⊕ *www. portlandparks.org* ⊗ *Daily dawn–dusk.*

NEED A
BREAK?

Bagdad Theatre and Pub. Here you can buy a pint of beer, a slice of pizza, and watch a movie in a large classic theater complete with dining tables. Built by Universal Pictures, the theater was state-of-the-art in 1927. In 1991 after being lovingly restored, it was reopened to feature films, live shows, and the occasional readings from authors invited by Powell's Books. ⊠ *3702 SE Hawthorne Blvd., Richmond, Southeast* ☎ *503/236–9234* ⊕ *www.mcmenamins.com/219-bagdad-theater-pub-home.*

Mt. Tabor Park. A playground on top of a volcano cinder cone? Yup, that's here. The cinders, or glassy rock fragments, unearthed in the park's construction, were used to surface the respite's roads; the ones leading to the top are closed to cars, but popular with cyclists. They're also popular with cruisers—each August there's an old-fashioned soapbox derby. Picnic tables and tennis, basketball, and volleyball courts make Mt. Tabor Park perfection. The whole park is closed to cars every Wednesday. ⊠ *SE 60th Ave. and SE Salmon St., Mt. Tabor, Southeast* ⊕ *www.portlandparks.org* ☉ *Daily dawn–dusk.*

FAMILY
Fodor's Choice
★

Oregon Museum of Science and Industry (*OMSI*). Hundreds of hands-on exhibits draw families to this interactive science museum, which also has an Omnimax theater and the Northwest's largest planetarium. The many permanent and touring exhibits are loaded with enough hands-on play for kids to fill a whole day exploring robotics, ecology, rockets, computers, animation, and outer space. Moored in the Willamette River as part of the museum is a 240-foot submarine, the USS *Blueback,* which can be toured for an extra charge. ⊠ *1945 SE Water Ave., Hosford-Abernathy, Southeast* ☎ *503/797–4000, 800/955–6674* ⊕ *www. omsi.edu* 🖃 *Museum $12, planetarium $5.75, Omnimax $8.50, submarine $5.75. Combined ticket $21* ☉ *Mid-June–Labor Day, daily 9:30–7; day after Labor Day–mid-June, daily 9:30–5:30.*

Sellwood District. The pleasant neighborhood that begins east of the Sellwood Bridge was once a separate town. Annexed by Portland in the 1890s, it retains a modest charm and on weekends the stores along 13th Avenue do a brisk business. Many storefronts are identified by a plaque giving the date of construction and the original purpose of the building. The eclectic shopping choices here include local designers, toy and games stores, art supplies, food carts, antiques, and locally crafted gifts, art and foods. ⊠ *SE 13th Ave. between SE Malden and SE Clatsop Sts., Sellwood, Southeast.*

Vera Katz Eastbank Esplanade. A stroll along this 1½-mile pedestrian and cycling path across from downtown is one of the best ways to experience the Willamette River and Portland's bridges close up. Built in 2001, the esplanade runs along the east bank of the Willamette River between the Hawthorne and Steele bridges, and features a 1,200-foot walkway that floats atop the river, a boat dock, and public art. Pedestrian crossings on both bridges link the esplanade to Waterfront Park, making a 3-mile loop. Take MAX light-rail to the Rose Quarter station. ⊠ *SE Water Ave. between Hawthorne Bridge and Steel Bridge, Southeast.*

2

WORTH NOTING

FAMILY **Crystal Springs Rhododendron Garden.** For much of the year, this 7-acre retreat near Reed College is frequented mainly by bird-watchers and those who want a restful stroll. But starting in April, thousands of rhododendron bushes and azaleas burst into flower, attracting visitors in larger numbers. The peak blooming season for these woody shrubs is May; by late June the show is over. ⊠ *SE 28th Ave., one block north of Woodstock Blvd., Eastmoreland, Southeast* ☎ *503/771–8386* ⊕ *www. portlandparks.org* ✉ *$4 Mar.–Labor Day, otherwise free* ☼ *Mar.–Labor Day, Thurs.–Mon. 10–6, Apr.–Sept. daily 6 am–10 pm, Oct.–Mar., daily 6–6.*

FAMILY **Oregon Rail Heritage Center.** Train history buffs aren't the only ones who'll appreciate the three steam-driven locomotives on display here. The center, which runs mostly on donations, also plays host to diesel locomotives, historic passenger cars, and other nuggets of train days gone by. Train rides are occasionally run. ⊠ *2250 SE Water Ave., Hosford-Abernathy, Southeast* ☎ *503/680–8895* ⊕ *www.orhf.org* ✉ *Free* ☼ *Thurs.–Sun. 1–5.*

SOUTHWEST

The most utilitarian of Portland's quadrants, the Southwest neighborhood, bounded by the West Hills to the west, the Willamette River to the east, and Burnside Avenue to the north, houses city government buildings, Portland State University, and the Oregon Health and Science University hospital. Though it offers fewer restaurants, bars and shops than other parts of town, the Southwest does have a few worthwhile attractions, including the Japanese Garden, Hoyt Arboretum, International Rose Test Garden, Portland Children's Museum, and Oregon Zoo, all within Washington Park.

The best way to get to Washington Park in Southwest is via MAX lightrail, which travels through a tunnel deep beneath the city's West Hills. Be sure to check out the Washington Park station, the deepest (260 feet) transit station in North America. Graphics on the walls depict life in the Portland area during the past 16.5 million years. There's also a core sample of the bedrock taken from the mountain displayed along the walls. Elevators to the surface put visitors in the parking lot for the Oregon Zoo and the Portland Children's Museum.

TOP ATTRACTIONS

Aerial Tram. On a clear day, the short ride on the aerial tram is worth the ticket for a view that includes Mt. Hood and perhaps Mt. St. Helens. The surrounding neighborhood at the base is posh and includes a park with splash pad. At the top are two hospitals but not much else, and it's best to just enjoy the view from the landing pad before heading back down. The tram departs every six minutes and can be more crowded during the morning and evening commute hours. ⊠ *3303 SW Bond Ave., South Waterfront, Southwest* ☎ *503/865–8726* ⊕ *www.gobytram. com* ✉ *$4* ☼ *Weekdays 5:30 am–9:30 pm; Sat. 9–5.*

Hoyt Arboretum. Twelve miles of trails wind through the arboretum, which has more than 1,000 species of plants and one of the nation's

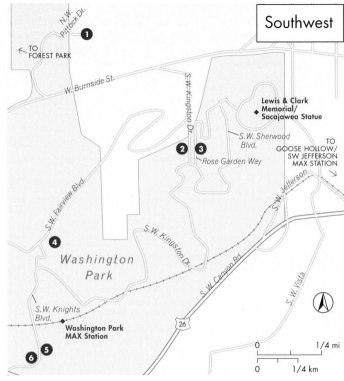

largest collections of coniferous trees; pick up trail maps at the visitor center. Also here are the Winter Garden and a memorial to veterans of the Vietnam War. The visitor center is a half-mile from the Washington Park MAX station. ⊠ *4000 SW Fairview Blvd., Arlington Heights, Southwest* ☎ *503/865–8733* ⊕ *www.hoytarboretum.org* ☞ *Free* ☉ *Arboretum daily, dawn–dusk; visitor center weekdays 9–4, Sat. 11–3.*

Fodor'sChoice ★ **International Rose Test Garden.** Despite the name, these grounds are not an experimental greenhouse laboratory, but rather three terraced gardens, set on 4 acres, where 10,000 bushes and 400 varieties of roses grow. The flowers, many of them new varieties, are at their peak in June, July, September, and October. From the gardens you can see highly photogenic views of the downtown skyline and, on fine days, the Fuji-shaped slopes of Mt. Hood, 50 miles to the east. Summer concerts take place in the garden's amphitheater. Take MAX light-rail to Washington Park station, and transfer to Bus No. 63 (no weekend service) or Washington Park Shuttle (May–August only). ⊠ *400 SW Kingston Ave., Arlington Heights, Southwest* ☎ *503/823–3636* ⊕ *www.rosegardenstore.org* ☞ *Free* ☉ *Daily dawn–dusk.*

Fodor'sChoice ★ **Japanese Garden.** The most authentic Japanese garden outside Japan takes up 5½ acres of Washington Park above the International Rose Test Garden. This serene spot, designed by a Japanese landscape master,

ortland Rose Festival parade

represents five separate garden styles: Strolling Pond Garden, Tea Garden, Natural Garden, Sand and Stone Garden, and Flat Garden. The Tea House was built in Japan and reconstructed here. The west side of the Pavilion has a majestic view of Portland and Mt. Hood. Take MAX light-rail to Washington Park station, and transfer to Bus No. 63 (no weekend service) or the Washington Park Shuttle (May–August only). ▥TIP→ **The public tours are given by knowledgeable volunteers. Check for tour times at the admission gate.** ⊠ *611 SW Kingston Ave., Arlington Heights, Southwest* ☎ *503/223–1321* ⊕ *www.japanesegarden.com* ✉ *$9.50* ⊘ *Oct.–Mar., Mon. noon–4, Tues.–Sun. 10–4; Apr.–Sept., Mon. noon–7, Tues.–Sun. 10–7.*

FAMILY **Portland Children's Museum.** Colorful sights and sounds offer a feast of sensations for kids of all ages where hands-on play is the order of the day. Visit nationally touring exhibits, catch a story time, a sing-along, or a puppet show in the Play It Again theater, create sculptures in the clay studio, splash hands in the waterworks display, or make a creation from junk in the Garage. To reach the museum's complex, take the Zoo exit off U.S. 26, or take MAX light-rail to Washington Park station. ⊠ *4015 SW Canyon Rd., Arlington Heights, Southwest* ☎ *503/223–6500* ⊕ *www.portlandcm.org* ✉ *$9* ⊘ *Mar.–Aug., daily 9–5; Sept.–Feb., Tues.–Sun. 9–5.*

WORTH NOTING

FAMILY **Oregon Zoo.** This beautiful animal park in the West Hills is famous for its Asian elephants. Major exhibits include an African section with rhinos, hippos, zebras, and giraffes. Steller Cove, a state-of-the-art aquatic exhibit, has two Steller sea lions and a family of sea otters. Other exhibits include polar bears, chimpanzees, an Alaska Tundra exhibit with wolves and grizzly bears, a penguin house, and habitats for beavers, otters, and reptiles native to the west side of the Cascade Range. In summer a 4-mile round-trip narrow-gauge train operates from the zoo, chugging through the woods to a station near the International Rose Test Garden and the Japanese Garden. Take the MAX light-rail to the Washington Park station. ⊠ *4001 SW Canyon Rd., Arlington Heights, Southwest* ☎ *503/226–1561* ⊕ *www.oregonzoo.org* ✉ *$11.50, $4 2nd Tues. of month* ⊗ *mid-May–Labor Day, daily 9–6; Mar.–mid-May and Sept.–Dec., daily 9–4; Jan.–Feb., daily 10–4.*

Pittock Mansion. Henry Pittock, the founder and publisher of the *Oregonian* newspaper, built this 22-room, castlelike mansion, which combines French Renaissance and Victorian styles. The opulent manor, built in 1914, is filled with art and antiques. The 46-acre grounds, north of Washington Park and 1,000 feet above the city, have superb views of the skyline, rivers, and the Cascade Range. There's a short hiking trail. If taking the bus, the mansion is a half-mile uphill hike. ⊠ *3229 NW Pittock Dr., Hillside, Northwest* ⊹ *from W Burnside St. heading west, turn right on NW Barnes Rd. and follow signs* ☎ *503/823–3623* ⊕ *www. pittockmansion.com* ✉ *$8.50* ⊗ *July and Aug., daily 10–5; Sept.–Dec. and Feb.–June, daily 11–4.*

WHERE TO EAT

Updated
by Christina
Cooke

These days, rising-star chefs are flocking to Portland. In this playground of sustainability and creativity, lots of the city's hottest restaurants change menus weekly—sometimes even daily—depending upon the ingredients they have delivered to their door that morning from local farms. A combination of fertile soils, temperate weather, nearby waters, and an urban growth boundary means that a bountiful harvest (be it lettuces or hazelnuts, mushrooms or salmon) is within any chef's reach.

While most of the city's reliable classics are concentrated in Nob Hill, the Pearl District, and Downtown, true food enthusiasts will be well rewarded by visiting eateries east of the Willamette River.

HOURS, PRICES, AND DRESS

Compared to other major cities, Portland restaurants aren't open quite as late, and it's unusual to see many diners after 11 pm even on weekends.

One aspect to Portland's dining scene that many locals and out-of-towners find appealing is how reasonably priced top-notch restaurants are. Particularly welcome in Portland is happy hour, when both inventive cocktails as well as small plates of food can be a good value. *Prices in the reviews are the average cost of a main course at dinner or, if dinner is not served, at lunch.*

In Portland, many diners dress casually for even higher-end establishments—a proclivity that's refreshing to some and annoying to others. In any case, jeans are acceptable almost everywhere.

In alphabetical order by neighborhood. Use the coordinate (⊹ B2) at the end of each listing to locate a site on the corresponding map.

DOWNTOWN

Finding a fabulous place to dine downtown is almost as easy as closing your eyes and pointing on the map. There are a plethora of food carts lining the streets and filling empty parking lots of downtown. As the noon hour approaches, smells of Greek, Russian, Japanese, Lebanese, and Mexican food permeate the air, and lines of workers hover around the makeshift kitchen trailers, waiting to get their fill of the inexpensive and authentic selection of food. For more info on where the various cart pods are located and what individual carts offer, check out the online guide at 🌐 *www.foodcartsportland.com*, and for daily specials, check out the Twitter thread at @pdxfoodcarts.

$ AMERICAN 🍴 **Bijou Cafe.** This spacious, sunny restaurant with high ceilings has excellent breakfasts, and they're served all day: French-style crepes and oyster hash are both popular, as are the buckwheat pancakes and French toast made with cinnamon bread. At lunchtime, salads, soups, and sandwiches, including burgers and panini, join the breakfast dishes on the menu. [$] *Average main: $10* ✉ *132 SW 3rd Ave., Downtown* ☎ *503/222–3187* 🌐 *www.bijoucafepdx.com* 🕒 *No dinner* ✣ *E4.*

$$$ PACIFIC NORTHWEST 🍴 **Clyde Common.** If you want to experience community Portland-style, then this hip, bustling spot adjacent to the Ace Hotel is for you. Visitors from all walks of life—politicians, rock stars, socialites, and hipsters—eat and drink at this European tavern-style restaurant. Long communal tables dominate the space, which means you never know who you'll end up sitting next to or where conversation may lead. With wood-and-canvas decor, expansive front windows, and an open kitchen, the restaurant has a warm, airy feel. Menu offerings include a number of delicious house-made pastas, fresh salads and fish. The specialty cocktail menu is one of the best in the neighborhood; try the barrel-aged Negroni made with Beefeater gin, Cinzano sweet vermouth, Campari, and orange peel, or the bartender's daily punch. [$] *Average main: $24* ✉ *Ace Hotel, 1014 SW Stark St., Downtown* ☎ *503/228–3333* 🌐 *www.clydecommon.com* ✣ *D4.*

$$$$ STEAKHOUSE 🍴 **El Gaucho.** The specialty at this upscale steak house in the elegant Benson Hotel is 28-day, dry-aged, certified Angus beef, but chops, ribs, and chicken entrées, also cooked over a bed of glowing coals in the open kitchen, are delicious as well. Attentive tuxedo-clad servers prepare the chateaubriand, from-scratch Caesar salad, and bananas Foster flambé tableside, and live Spanish guitar music serenades dinner guests every night. While the service is impeccable at this Seattle transplant restaurant, brace yourself for the hefty bill. Reservations are recommended. [$] *Average main: $65* ✉ *Benson Hotel, 319 SW Broadway, Downtown* ☎ *503/227–8794* 🌐 *www.elgaucho.com* 🕒 *No lunch* ✣ *D4.*

$$$ PACIFIC NORTHWEST Fodor's Choice ★ 🍴 **Higgins.** One of Portland's original farm-to-table restaurants, this classic eatery, opened in 1994, built its menu—and its reputation—on its use of local, seasonal, organic ingredients. Higgins' dishes display the diverse bounty of the Pacific Northwest, incorporating ingredients like heirloom tomatoes, forest mushrooms, mountain huckleberries, Pacific oysters, Oregon Dungeness crab, and locally raised pork. A bistro menu is available in the adjoining bar, where comfortable leather booths and tables provide an alternative to the formal, white-tableclothed main

BEST BETS FOR PORTLAND DINING

Fodor's writers and editors have selected their favorite restaurants by price, cuisine, and experience in the lists below. You can also search by neighborhood for excellent eats—just peruse our reviews on the following pages.

Fodor'sChoice ★

Andina, p. 76
Apizza Scholls, p. 85
Biwa, p. 86
Broder, p. 87
Bunk Sandwiches, p. 86
Higgins, p. 71
Laurelhurst Market, p. 89
Le Pigeon, p. 89
Lemongrass, p. 89
Natural Selection, p. 82
Ned Ludd, p. 82
Pok Pok & Whiskey Soda Lounge, p. 90
Russell St. Bar-B-Que, p. 84
Screen Door, p. 84
Tasty n Sons, p. 84

By Price

$

Broder, p. 87
Bunk Sandwiches, p. 86
Kenny and Zuke's Delicatessen, p. 74
Nicholas Restaurant, p. 89

Russell St. Bar-B-Que, p. 84
Pambiche, p. 83
Pok Pok & Whiskey Soda Lounge, p. 90
Savoy Tavern + Bistro, p. 90
Screen Door, p. 84
Tin Shed Garden Café, p. 85

$$

Accanto, p. 88
Bamboo Sushi, p. 86
Beaker and Flask, p. 86
Biwa, p. 86
Lemongrass, p. 89
Ned Ludd, p. 82
Nostrana, p. 90
Tasty n Alder, p. 75
Tasty n Sons, p. 84

$$$

Andina, p. 76
Apizza Scholls, p. 85
Aviary, p. 82
Clarklewis, p. 87
Clyde Common, p. 71
Higgins, p. 71
Laurelhurst Market, p. 89
Le Pigeon, p. 89

Meriwether's Restaurant, p. 80
St. Jack, p. 90
Wildwood Restaurant and Bar, p. 81

$$$$

Beast, p. 82
Castagna Restaurant, p. 87
Genoa, p. 88
Natural Selection, p. 82

By Cuisine

ASIAN

Aviary, p. 82
Lemongrass, p. 89
Pok Pok, p. 90

PACIFIC NORTHWEST

Clarklewis, p. 87
Clyde Common, p. 71
Higgins, p. 71
Laurelhurst Market, p. 89
Ned Ludd, p. 82

PIZZA

Apizza Scholls, p. 85
Hot Lips, p. 77

Ken's Artisan Pizza, p. 88
Nostrana, p. 90

By Experience

BRUNCH

Broder, p. 87
The Country Cat, p. 87
Meriwether's Restaurant, p. 80
Screen Door, p 84
Tasty n Alder, p. 75
Tasty n Sons, p. 84
Tin Shed Garden Café, p. 85

HOT SPOTS

Andina, p. 76
Clyde Common, p. 71

BEST HAPPY HOUR

23 Hoyt, p. 77
Beaker and Flask, p. 86
Clarklewis, p. 87
Clyde Common, p. 71
St. Jack, p. 90
Tasty n Sons, p. 84

ADVENTUROUS FOOD

Aviary, p. 82
Beast, p. 82
Le Pigeon, p. 89
Natural Selection, p. 82
Ned Ludd, p. 82
Pok Pok, p. 90

CLOSE UP

Portland's Food Carts

Throughout Portland at any given mealtime, around 500 food carts are dishing up steaming plates of everything from Korean tacos to shawarma to artisan cupcakes. While food carts have seen a rise in popularity throughout the country, the culture is especially strong in Portland.

Brightly colored and mostly stationary, the carts tend to cluster in former parking lots in pods ranging from 3 to 60 establishments, oftentimes ringing a cluster of picnic tables or a covered awning.

With plate prices averaging $6 to $7, cart fare provides a quick, inexpensive, and delicious alternative to traditional sit-down restaurants if you don't mind sitting outside. Cart dining is also an easy way to sample Portland's many ethnic food offerings.

For up-to-date information on hours and locations, check out the extensive local blog **Food Carts Portland** (⊕ *www.foodcartsportland.com*), the corresponding iPhone app Food-CartsPDX, and the Twitter thread @ pdxfoodcarts.com.

TOP FOOD CART PODS

Downtown, SW 9th (and 10th) and Alder: Covering more than an entire city block, this downtown pod, home to more than 50 carts, is the largest in the city. The spot is lively during the workweek but slower on the weekends. We recommend the signature Thai chicken dish at **Nong's Khao Man Gai**; battered fish-and-chips at **The Frying Scotsman**; kielbasa and other Polish classics at **EuroDish**; the porchetta and arugula sandwich at the **People's Pig Wood-Fired Grill**; and kalua pig at the Hawaiian cart **808 Grinds**.

Downtown, SW 3rd and Washington: This pod has an international bent, with some of the city's oldest Mexican carts on site, plus Egyptian, Greek, Indonesian, Lebanese, and Vietnamese establishments. We recommend the muffuletta at **Built to Grill**; falafel or chicken shawarma at **El Masry Egyptian** cart; and vegan cheesesteak at **DC Vegetarian**.

Northeast, Mississippi Marketplace (the corner of N. Mississippi and N. Skidmore): Situated beside the brick-and-mortar German bar Prost! (which allows cart diners to bring over food), this lot of about 15 carts surrounding a cluster of picnic tables is quite busy on weekends. We recommend the decadent breakfast at **The Big Egg**; bulgogi beef tacos or sliders at the **Koi Fusion Korean** cart; and Chinese flatbread sandwiches at **Prickly Ash**.

Southeast, Good Food Here (SE 43rd and Belmont): With covered seating and Rogue Brewing on site, this is a welcoming pod in quiet Southeast Portland. We recommend: the lamb gyro at the **Aybla Grill Mediterranean** cart; meatball- or smoked salmon-filled Norwegian lefse wraps at **Viking Soul Food**; chorizo and chips at **Euro Trash**.

Southeast, Cartopia (the corner of SE 12th and Hawthorne Blvd.): The go-to spot for late-night cravings, this pod of six carts stays open until 3 am most nights. We recommend: sweet or savory crepes at **Perierre Creperie**; fried hand pies at **Whiffies**; poutine at **Potato Champion**; and wood-fired margherita pizza at **Pyro Pizza**.

El Gaucho, Downtown

dining room. Don't miss the house-made charcuterie plate with Higgins pickles or the tender duck confit entrée. Vegetarian options are available. Reservations are recommended. [$] *Average main: $28* ⊠ *1239 SW Broadway, Downtown* ☎ *503/222–9070* ⊕ *higginsportland.com* ⊙ *No lunch weekends* ✛ *D5.*

$
DELI

✕ **Kenny & Zuke's Delicatessen.** The best word to describe this Jewish deli is simply, pastrami. Cured for seven days, then smoked for 10 hours and steamed for three, the rich and flavorful meat is best tasted on a rye bread sandwich or, if your appetite is heartier, the warm, sauerkraut-packed Reuben. Holding its own against East Coast delis, Kenny & Zuke's makes its own pickles and produces its own bagels, proofing the dough for 36 hours before hand-forming the circles then boiling and baking them in small batches. The open and airy downtown location serves omelets, Benedicts, biscuits, and breakfast sandwiches all day, along with a wide selection of soups, salads, and meaty sandwiches. The Thurman Street location, in a no-frills space furnished with picnic tables, specializes in the bagels, and the North Williams location, which bills itself as a deli-bar, stays open late serving hot food and cocktails. [$] *Average main: $14* ⊠ *1038 SW Stark St., Downtown* ☎ *503/222–3354* ⊕ *www.kennyandzukes.com* ✛ *D4.*

$$$$
AMERICAN

✕ **Portland City Grill.** On the 30th floor of the U.S. Bank Tower, the Portland City Grill offers one of the best views in town. Gaze over the city skyline and the distant Cascade Mountains from a window table while eating fine steak and seafood dishes with Asian and Island flair. The adjoining bar and lounge has comfortable armchairs along its windowed walls, which are the first to get snatched up during the extremely popular happy hour each day. [$] *Average main: $38* ⊠ *111*

SW 5th Ave., Downtown ☎ *503/450–0030* ⊕ *www.portlandcitygrill. com* ☽ *No lunch weekends* ✢ *E4.*

$$$ ✕ **Southpark Seafood Grill & Wine Bar.** This comfortable, art deco–tinged
SEAFOOD room with two bars specializes in wood-fired seafood. The Northwest-
influenced menu includes wild king salmon with bacon bread pudding,
squash, and pickled peppers, as well as prosciutto-wrapped trout with
root vegetables, hazelnuts, and lemon aioli. There's a wide selection
of fresh Pacific Northwest oysters, and fine regional wines are avail-
able by the glass. Some of the desserts are baked to order. $ *Average
main: $25* ✉ *901 SW Salmon St., Downtown* ☎ *503/326–1300* ⊕ *www.
southparkseafood.com* ✢ *D5.*

$$ ✕ **Tasty n Alder.** The latest venture of celebrated Portland chef John
ECLECTIC Gorham, this all-day brunch spot takes the success of the eastside estab-
lishment, Tasty n Sons, and moves it across the river to downtown.
Designed for sharing, the tapas-style menu draws on global influences
and delivers bold, delicious flavors. Try the potatoes bravas, served with
fried egg on top and aioli on the side, and the Korean fried chicken
(yes, for breakfast), served with rice, house kimchi, and eggs cooked
two ways (pickled and over-easy). At dinnertime, Tasty n Alder turns
up the class, offering a selection of top-notch steaks from family-run
ranches, along with a variety of original cocktails. The atmosphere is
modern, clean and inviting. $ *Average main: $20* ✉ *580 SW 12th Ave.,
Downtown* ☎ *503/621–9251* ⊕ *www.tastyntasty.com* ✢ *D4.*

$$$$ ✕ **Urban Farmer.** In the atrium of the upscale hotel the Nines, you'll
STEAKHOUSE discover why this restaurant calls itself a modern steak house. Making
much use of organic and sustainable ingredients, the dishes here are
presented with flair in glass canning jars and mini cast-iron skillets. The
focus is understandably on steaks (choose from corn-fed or grass-fed),
but there are also interesting alternatives, such as slow-braised lamb
flavored with apricot, and roasted Alaskan halibut served with chanterelles. Leave room for moonshine whiskey or the milk chocolate soufflé
served with huckleberry compote. $ *Average main: $42* ✉ *525 SW Morrison St., Downtown* ☎ *503/222–4900* ⊕ *www.urbanfarmerrestaurant.
com* ⌂ *Reservations essential* ✢ *D4.*

$$$ ✕ **Veritable Quandary.** There are so many delicious options at this long-
AMERICAN standing local favorite like the tantalizing French toast and revered
chocolate soufflé. The beautiful outdoor patio overlooking the Willa-
mette River is an oasis of roses, fuchsias, and hanging begonia baskets.
The menu emphasizes fresh, flavorful produce and seafood; prices are
reasonable for the quality, and the 200-plus wine list is one of the
best in town. $ *Average main: $27* ✉ *1220 SW 1st Ave., Downtown*
☎ *503/227–7342* ⊕ *www.veritablequandary.com* ✢ *E5.*

OLD TOWN/CHINATOWN

The original city center of Portland (located, incidentally, atop a net-
work of underground Shanghai Tunnels), the once-seedy Old Town
has a number of bistros, restaurants, pubs, and nightclubs (though it's
still not the best neighborhood to explore alone at night). Chinatown,
which makes up a large portion of the district, contains a few traditional
dim sum restaurants.

$ CAFÉ

🍴 **Backspace.** Taking "eclectic" to a new level, this hipster hangout is a coffee shop, art gallery, all-age concert and poetry slam venue, Internet café, LAN gaming center, and vegetarian nosh stop all rolled in one. While the art on the walls, the pool table and gaming room in the back, and the regular nighttime shows occupy and entertain, the tables, chairs, and couches up front invite rest and relaxation. The menu offers freshly brewed Stumptown coffee and a number of vegetarian and vegan soups, salads, and sandwiches as well. [$] *Average main: $8* ✉ *115 NW 5th Ave., Old Town/Chinatown* ☎ *503/248–2900* 🌐 *www.backspace.bz* ✥ *E3.*

$ CHINESE

🍴 **Fong Chong.** Some people believe that this rundown Chinatown restaurant serves the best dim sum in town, and that includes the dumplings filled with shrimp, pork, or vegetables, accompanied by plenty of different sauces. If you haven't eaten dim sum before, just take a seat: the food is brought to you on carts, and you pick what you want as it comes by; your ticket will be stamped based on the cost of the individual dish (ask if you aren't sure how this works). [$] *Average main: $10* ✉ *301 NW 4th Ave., Old Town/Chinatown* ☎ *503/228–6868* ✥ *E3.*

PEARL DISTRICT

The Pearl District, once full of worn, empty warehouses, and little more than a reminder of Portland's industrial past, is now one of the city's most bustling destinations for arts and dining. Many of the warehouses have been refurbished into hot spots to gather for drinks and food. Restaurants here tend to be slightly more upscale. Keep in mind that the city's gallery walk event, held the first Thursday of every month, keeps restaurants jammed on that night.

$$$ PERUVIAN Fodor's Choice ★

🍴 **Andina.** This popular upscale Pearl District restaurant offers an interesting and inventive menu—a combination of traditional Peruvian and contemporary "Novoandina" cuisines—served in a large but arch- and nook-filled space. The extensive seafood offerings include four kinds of ceviche, grilled octopus, and pan-seared scallops with white and black quinoa. There are also entrées with chicken, duck, beef, and lamb. A late-night bar offers sangria, small plates, and cocktails; downstairs, a shrinelike wine shop hosts private multicourse meals. Don't miss the traditional Peruvian pisco sour, a lemon and pisco liqueur cocktail topped with a froth of egg whites and bitters. Live music Sunday through Saturday. Reservations are recommended. [$] *Average main: $27* ✉ *1314 NW Glisan St., Pearl District* ☎ *503/228–9535* 🌐 *www.andinarestaurant.com* ✥ *C3.*

$$ GREEK

🍴 **Eleni's Philoxenia.** An unassuming gem in the Pearl District, this upscale version of its sister restaurant in Sellwood offers an extensive menu of Mediterranean specialties and a delicious commitment to first-press olive oil and fresh vegetables. The chef's favorite dish is the *kalatsounia* (spinach, fresh dill, and green onions rolled inside phyllo dough). Other surprising standouts are the *lahano salata* (thinly sliced cabbage and shaved fennel, toasted almonds, and lemon paprika dressing) and the *makaronia me kima* (ground beef simmered with peppers, onion, tomatoes, zucchini, and garlic served over spaghetti). In the Cretan tradition, the appetizer selection encourages sharing. $ *Average main: $18* ✉ *112 NW 9th Ave., Pearl District* ☎ *503/227–2158* ⊕ *www.elenisrestaurant. com* ⊙ *Closed Mon. No lunch* ✛ *D3.*

$$$

EUROPEAN

✕ **The Gilt Club.** Cascading gold curtains, ornate showpiece chandeliers, and high-back booths complement the sultry rich-red dining room. ■TIP➜ *Portlandia* **fans may recognize the restaurant from the episode about Colin, the free-range chicken.** The food is equally lush—like the charred New York steak with pumpkin purée, chanterelle marmalade, kale, and veal reduction, and the risotto-style farro with squash, tomatoes, pecorino, leeks, and gold beets. The drink menu is loaded with flavor-embellished drinks such as Tracy's First Love, with vodka, cucumber, basil, and lime. $ *Average main: $21* ✉ *306 NW Broadway, Pearl District* ☎ *503/222–4458* ⊕ *www.giltclub.com* ⊙ *Closed Sun.* ✛ *E3*

$$

PIZZA

✕ **Hot Lips Pizza.** A favorite of Portland's pizza lovers, Hot Lips bakes organic and regional ingredients into creative pizzas, available whole or by the slice. Seasonal variations might feature squash, wild mushrooms, pears, and Brie cheese. Soups, salads, and sandwiches are also available. Beverages include house-made berry sodas, a large rack of wines, and microbrew six-packs. Dine inside the Ecotrust building, outside on the "eco-roof," or take it all across the street for an impromptu picnic in Jamison Square. This is one of five different citywide locations. $ *Average main: $20* ✉ *721 NW 9th Ave., Pearl District* ☎ *503/595–2342* ⊕ *www.hotlipspizza.com* ✛ *D3.*

$

FRENCH

✕ **Le Happy.** This tiny creperie outside the hubbub of the Pearl District can serve as a romantic dinner-date spot or just a cozy place to enjoy a drink and a snack. You can get sweet crepes with fruit, cheese, chocolate, and cream or savory ones with meats and cheeses; in addition, the dinner menu is rounded out with steaks and salads. It's a classy joint, but not without a sense of humor: Le Trash Blanc is a bacon-and-cheddar crepe served with a can of Pabst. $ *Average main: $8* ✉ *1011 NW 16th Ave., Pearl District* ☎ *503/226–1258* ⊕ *www.lehappy.com* ⊙ *Closed Sun. No lunch* ✛ *C2.*

NOB HILL

Head northwest to sample the broadest scope of this city's food scene. From the finest of the fine (Paley's Place, Wildwood, Meriwether's) to the come-as-you-are casual (Pastini Pastaria, St. Honoré Boulangerie, MacTarnahan's Taproom), there's something for everyone within a handful of blocks. Most restaurants in the Nob Hill area are open for lunch and dinner and on the weekends; reservations are recommended for the higher-end establishments. This neighborhood draws an eclectic crowd: progressives and conservatives, lifetime residents and recent transplants, wealthy as well as struggling students. There are numerous retail shops and galleries in the neighborhood to help you work up an appetite before your meal.

$$$

ECLECTIC

✕ **23 Hoyt.** A chic, high-end tavern, 23 Hoyt takes happy hour to a new level, offering a wide selection of interesting small plates grouped by price, from $1 to $8. Snack plate choices, which change seasonally, may

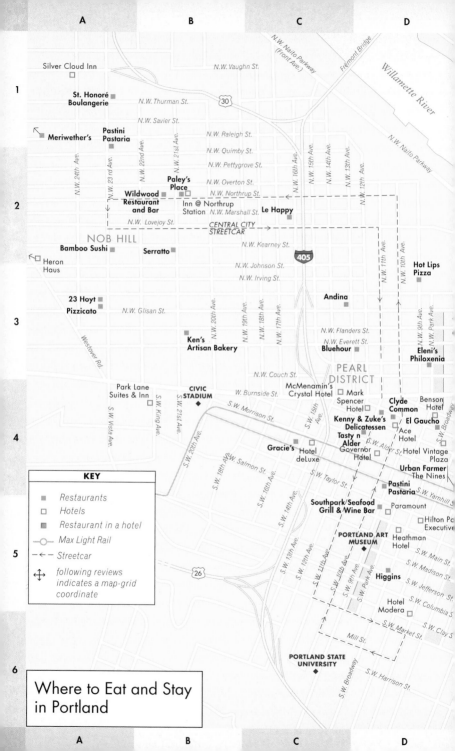

Where to Eat and Stay in Portland

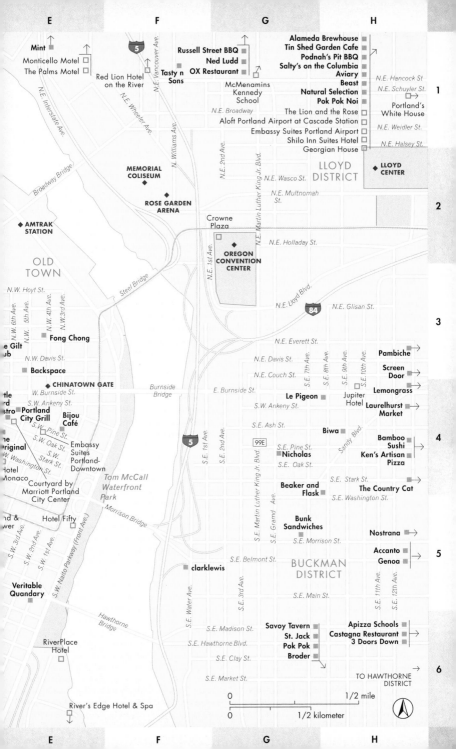

include roasted beets, chèvre, and walnuts; onion rings and harissa aioli; and seared steak bites. With a cool, clean ambience and the owner's private collection of contemporary art on the walls, this corner establishment makes an excellent place to partake in early-evening or late-night weekend noshing. The happy hour menu is available 4–6 pm daily and 9 pm to midnight on Friday and Saturday. There are also more substantial entrées such as buttermilk fried chicken and steak frites on the rotating dinner menu. [$] *Average main: $22* ✉ *529 NW 23rd Ave., Nob Hill* ☎ *503/445–7400* 🌐 *www.23hoyt.com* 🕓 *No lunch* ✥ *A3.*

$ CAFÉ 🍴 **Ken's Artisan Bakery.** Golden crusts are the trademark of Ken's rustic breads, croissants, tarts, and puff pastries, good for breakfast, lunch, and light evening meals. Sandwiches, barbecue pulled pork, and croque monsieur are served on thick slabs of freshly baked bread, and local berries fill the flaky pastries. If the dozen tables inside the vibrant blue bakery are crammed (they usually are), you can sit outside at one of the sidewalk tables on nice days. On Monday nights, Ken's serves pizza and stays open until 9:30 pm. [$] *Average main: $12* ✉ *338 NW 21st Ave., Nob Hill* ☎ *503/248–2202* 🌐 *www.kensartisan.com* 🕓 *No dinner Tues.–Sun.* ✥ *B3.*

$$$ EUROPEAN 🍴 **Meriwether's Restaurant.** The 5-acre Skyline Farm less than 20 minutes away grows all the produce for this high-end, yet quaint and unpretentious restaurant on the edge of the Northwest 23rd and 21st Avenue shopping districts. A lush covered and heated garden patio allow diners to eat alfresco even during cooler months. The farm-to-table offerings include the Skyline Farm beet salad with spiced coconut, feta, and almonds, and the Dungeness crab risotto. The dessert menu features tasty seasonal treats like pumpkin pots de crème. The weekend brunch, where the omelets, scrambles, and Benedicts are made with farm-fresh eggs, is wildly popular—and for good reason. [$] *Average main: $26* ✉ *2601 NW Vaughn St., Nob Hill* ☎ *503/228–1250* 🌐 *www.meriwethersnw.com* ✥ *A1.*

$$$$ FRENCH 🍴 **Paley's Place.** Open since 1995 in an old Victorian house, this acclaimed bistro serves French cuisine prepared with organic, Pacific Northwest ingredients. Among the entrées are seared steelhead with veggies and olive chili relish and a grilled pork loin chop with cauliflower grits, bacon, and brussels sprouts. The cheese selection, on display under a glass case just inside the front door, is extensive and exquisite. Two plainly decorated dining rooms and a bar area make up the interior; in warmer months, you can sit on the front porch or back patio. Reservations are recommended. [$] *Average main: $32* ✉ *1204 NW 21st Ave., Nob Hill* ☎ *503/243–2403* 🌐 *www.paleysplace.net* 🕓 *No lunch* ✥ *B2.*

$ ITALIAN FAMILY 🍴 **Pastini Pastaria.** With a wide selection of pasta dishes under $10, it's hard to go wrong with anything at this Italian bistro, which has four locations in Portland. Rigatoni *zuccati* comes in a light cream sauce with butternut squash, wild mushrooms, and spinach; *linguini misto mare* is a seafood linguine in white wine. There are also panini, antipasti, and dinner salads on the menu. There's often a crowd, but from this location you can browse the shops while waiting for a table. [$] *Average main: $10* ✉ *1506 NW 23rd Ave., Nob Hill* ☎ *503/595–1205* 🌐 *www.pastini.com* ✍ *Reservations not accepted* 🕓 *No lunch Sun.* ✥ *A2, D4.*

2

$$$ ✕ **Serratto Restaurant and Bar.** Good for a date night, business meeting,
ITALIAN   or even a casual outing with a friend, this open, elegant dining room
comes with warm service, a knowledgeable staff, and a solid Medi-
terranean-influenced menu. Made from scratch, the pasta is artfully
prepared. Good options include the ravioli filled with Dungeness crab,
ricotta, and caramelized fennel and the rigatoni with spicy sausage,
garlic, fresh mozzarella, and basil. The meat entrées, like the lamb osso
bucco with spaetzle, are equally tantalizing. Top off the meal with the
bittersweet chocolate cobbler, served warm with vanilla-bean gelato.
Ⓢ *Average main: $22* ✉ *2112 N.W. Kearney St., Nob Hill* ☎ *503/221–
1195* ⊕ *www.serratto.com* ✛ *B2.*

$ ✕ **St. Honoré Boulangerie.** Named for the patron saint of bakers, this
CAFÉ   French bakery on a quiet corner near Forest Park serves light meals and
pastries. Start the day off with a plain or chocolate croissant, or café
au lait. For lunch and dinner there's quiche, sandwiches, salads, savory
puff pastries, and tarts. Or simply unwind from shopping with a glass
of wine and a luscious dessert at one of the sidewalk café tables. Ⓢ *Av-
erage main: $9* ✉ *2335 NW Thurman St., Nob Hill* ☎ *503/445–4342*
⊕ *www.sainthonorebakery.com* ✛ *A1.*

$$$ ✕ **Wildwood Restaurant and Bar.** A devotion to fresh, sustainable, local
MODERN   ingredients means the menu changes weekly at this upscale restaurant.
AMERICAN   The chef works with lamb, pork loin, chicken, steak, and seafood, as
well as a wide array of vegetables, to create entrées as innovative as they
are delicious such as duck confit with kimchi mashed potatoes. You can
watch your meal being prepared in the open kitchen or sip a cocktail
at the busy center bar. At the casual, family-style supper on Sunday,
the restaurant waives the corkage fee on wines brought from home.
Ⓢ *Average main: $25* ✉ *1221 NW 21st Ave., Nob Hill* ☎ *503/248–9663*
⊕ *www.wildwoodrestaurant.com* ☾ *No lunch Sun.* ✛ *B2.*

NORTH

$$ ✕ **Mint.** The food offerings at this cool, romantic spot are as hard to
MODERN   categorize as the drinks offered at the boundary-pushing companion bar
AMERICAN   next door. Global flavors influence the changing dishes like the seafood
pot-au-feu made with the fish-of-the-day, scallops, mussels, and shrimp,
as well as the lamb burger with mint chimichurri and garlic aioli. Before
or after dinner, slip next door for a cocktail, where bar 820 is tended
by top-notch bartender Lucy Brennan. Ⓢ *Average main: $18* ✉ *816 N.
Russell St., Eliot, North* ☎ *503/284–5518* ⊕ *www.mintrestaurant.com*
☾ *Closed Sun. and Mon. No lunch* ✛ *E1.*

NORTHEAST

$ ✕ **Alameda Brewhouse.** With light wood, high ceilings, and stretches of
AMERICAN   stainless steel, this spacious neighborhood microbrewery feels chic while
managing to remain friendly and casual. Many people come for the
smooth microbrews produced on-site—including the award-winning
Black Bear XX Stout—but the food is worth a look, too. With creative
pasta dishes such as artichoke-mushroom linguine, salmon gyros, tuna
tacos, and delicious burgers, it seems this brewpub puts nearly as much

thought into its menu as its ales. $ *Average main: $9* ✉ *4765 NE Fremont St., Cully, Northeast* ☎ *503/460–9025* ⊕ *www.alamedabrewing. com* ⊘ *Closed Mon.* ✛ *H1.*

$$$
ASIAN FUSION

✕ **Aviary.** Disregarding culinary conventions, this visionary Alberta Street eatery serves up innovative dishes that will likely push your boundaries while also delighting your palate. Its simple menu of small plates (order 2-3 per person) influenced by Asian flavors and using European cooking techniques, combines unusual ingredients into dishes that work not in spite of, but because of their contrasts in flavor and texture. For example, the charred octopus, cooked to the perfect tenderness, is served with scallion pancakes and a salad of papaya, beans, and cashews. The signature dish, a mini wok containing crispy pig ears over mildly sweet coconut rice, is served with Chinese sausage, avocado, mint, and cilantro. Both dishes are well worth a try. The dining room is warm yet simple with white walls and concrete floors—a nice contrast to the boldness of the plates. The helpful waitstaff is available to guide and explain, easing adventurous eaters outside their comfort zones, where the payoff is big. $ *Average main: $27* ✉ *1733 NE Alberta St., Vernon, Northeast* ☎ *503/287–2400* ⊕ *aviarypdx.com* ⊘ *Closed Sun. No lunch* ✛ *H1.*

$$$$
PACIFIC
NORTHWEST

✕ **Beast.** This quintessential example of Portland's innovative cuisine is in a nondescript red building with subtle signage. Inside, the seating is communal, at two large tables that seat 8 and 16. The six-course prix-fixe dinner (and four-course brunch on Sunday) changes weekly, depending on the meat at the market. The dishes that come from the open kitchen live up to the restaurant's name: there might be chicken and duck-liver mousse, wine- and truffle-braised beef, foie-gras bon bons, or steak tartare with quail-egg toast. ■ TIP➔ **Vegetarians may find it a struggle to eat here.** There are two seatings per night at 6 and 8:45; view the week's menu online starting Tuesday afternoon. $ *Average main: $75* ✉ *5425 NE 30th Ave., Concordia, Northeast* ☎ *503/841–6968* ⊕ *www.beastpdx.com* ⌒ *Reservations essential* ⊘ *Closed Mon. and Tues. No dinner Sun.* ✛ *H1.*

$$$$
VEGETARIAN
Fodor's Choice
★

✕ **Natural Selection.** This rustic European-style café proves you don't need meat to create a meal you'll want to write home about. A small vegetarian restaurant with cocoa-colored walls and exposed-filament Edison bulbs over each table, Natural Selection serves a four-course, fixed-price menu whose brilliance rests in the pure and natural flavors of its ingredients. Assembled in new combinations—tomato almond soup with fennel, parsnip and watercress, for example, or chard gnocchi with winter squash, apple, basil and balsamic vinegar—the ingredients, which change by season, send your taste buds on lovely explorations with each bite. With a full two hours of table time from the start of your reservation, this restaurant encourages you to slow down and savor your meal. $ *Average main: $35* ✉ *3033 NE Alberta St., Concordia, Northeast* ☎ *503/288–5883* ⊕ *www.naturalselectionpdx.com* ⊘ *Closed Sun.–Wed.* ✛ *H1.*

$$
PACIFIC
NORTHWEST
Fodor's Choice
★

✕ **Ned Ludd.** Named for the founder of the Luddites, the group that resisted the technological advances of the Industrial Revolution, this Northwest-inspired craft kitchen prepares its food the most low-tech

2

way possible: in a wood-burning brick oven, over an open flame. Sourcing all its ingredients locally (or carefully, if they come from afar), Ned Ludd's menu varies completely depending on the season and weather. The whole roasted trout, a delicious constant on the menu, has a crisp, charred exterior and a moist, flavorful interior and comes with charred leeks and carrot and fennel salad. Consider the house-made pickle plate and any one of the salads or roasted vegetable dishes to accompany the meal. Fitting the simple, from-the-earth theme, the decor incorporates salvaged wood, dried flowers, and small succulent plants under glass domes. $ *Average main: $19* ⊠ *3925 NE Martin Luther King Blvd., King, Northeast* ⊕ *www.nedluddpdx.com* ⊙ *No lunch* ✛ *G1.*

$$$$
ARGENTINE

✕ **Ox Restaurant.** Specializing in "Argentine inspired Portland food," Ox is all about prime cuts of meat prepared well. In a dimly lit dining room with hardwood floors, exposed brick walls, and a bar against the front window, the flannel-shirt-and-white-apron-clad waitstaff serves beef, lamb, pork, and fish dishes cooked over flames in a large, hand-cranked grill. The asado Argentino, a platter of short ribs, chorizo, *morcilla* (blood sausage), and skirt steak with a few sides, is an ideal choice for two. Or try the grass-fed Uruguayan rib eye for one, which is a better choice than the skirt steak. The vegetable-based sides provide cool complements to the rich asados: try the chopped endive salad with pear, Gruyère, arugula, pecans, and Dijon vinaigrette, or the buttered beet salad with sweet onion, blue cheese, and walnuts. Save room for the chef's dessert specialty, a vanilla bean tres leches cake accompanied by banana pudding, dulce de leche, and a traditional *alfajor* cookie. $ *Average main: $34* ⊠ *2225 NE Martin Luther King Blvd., Eliot, Northeast* ☎ *503/284–3366* ⊕ *oxpdx.com* ⊙ *Closed Mon. No lunch* ✛ *G1.*

$
CUBAN

✕ **Pambiche.** Painted in bright purples, pinks, and greens, this hot spot offers traditional Cuban fare: slow-roasted meats, tropical root vegetables, hearty stews, rice, and beans. The meat plates—featuring slow-roasted pork, oxtail, shredded beef, rubbed chicken, or giant prawns—with various rich and saucy accompaniments, are all tasty. The empanadas make an excellent prelude and the fried plantains a sweet complement to any meal. Drinkwise, sangria and mojitos, garnished with fresh fruit and mint, respectively, are the way to go. Because this neighborhood joint is often packed, be prepared to wait for a table. $ *Average main: $15* ⊠ *2811 NE Glisan St., Kerns, Northeast* ☎ *503/233–0511* ⊕ *www. pambiche.com* ⚞ *Reservations not accepted* ✛ *H3.*

$
BARBECUE

✕ **Podnah's Pit BBQ.** Firing up the smoker at 5 every morning, the pit crew at Podnah's spends the day slow cooking some of the best Texas- and Carolina-style barbeque in Portland. Melt-in-your-mouth brisket, ribs, pulled pork, chicken, and lamb are all served up in a sassy vinegar-based sauce. Some sides, like the delicious green chili mac and cheese, rotate on and off the menu, but the collard greens, barbecue baked beans, and the iceberg wedge, topped with blue cheese and a punchy Thousand Island dressing, are excellent mainstays. $ *Average main: $15* ⊠ *1625 NE Killingsworth St., Vernon, Northeast* ☎ *503/281–3700* ⊕ *podnahspit.com* ✛ *H1.*

$
ASIAN

✕ **Pok Pok Noi.** An outpost of the Southeast Asian street fare legend Pok Pok, this restaurant (Little Pok Pok) offers a limited menu of its namesake's favorites. You can still get the legendary Vietnamese fish sauce wings, the green papaya salad, the rotisserie roasted game hen, and nine other dishes, along with yummy drinking vinegars and original cocktails. Originally a take-out only establishment, most of the seating is on stools at counters, though there are a few tables in front and in the enclosed tent out back. $ *Average main: $11* ⊠ *1469 NE Prescott St., Sabin, Northeast* ☎ *503/287–4149* ⊕ *www.pokpoknoi.com* ⊗ *No lunch weekdays* ✛ *H1.*

$ ✕ **Russell St. Bar-B-Que.** Pig-themed bric-a-brac indicates the specialty at this casual neighborhood joint, known for its fall-off-the-bone baby back ribs, but there's also beef, poultry, seafood, and smoked tofu dishes on the menu. Big eaters might consider the meatapalooza tray, with your choice of three meats. The candied yams, barbecue baked beans, hush puppies, mac and cheese, and braised mess o' collard greens make excellent accompaniments. $ *Average main: $13* ⊠ *325 NE Russell St., Eliot, Northeast* ☎ *503/528–8224* ⊕ *www.russellstreetbbq.com* ⌖ *Reservations not accepted* ⊗ *Closed Mon.* ✛ *G1.*

BARBECUE
FAMILY
Fodor's Choice
★

$$$$ ✕ **Salty's on the Columbia.** Pacific Northwest salmon (choose blackened or grilled, a half or full pound) is what this comfortable restaurant over-looking the Columbia River is known for. Loaded with prawns, oysters, crab, shrimp and scallops, the seafood platter offers plenty of variety. The menu also includes chicken and steak. Both a heated, covered deck and an open-air, uncovered deck offer views of the boats on the river. $ *Average main: $35* ⊠ *3839 NE Marine Dr., Portland International Airport, Northeast* ☎ *503/288–4444* ⊕ *www.saltys.com* ✛ *H1.*

SEAFOOD

$ ✕ **Screen Door.** The line that forms outside this Southern cooking res-taurant at brunch and dinner is as epic as the food itself. But think of the wait that precedes the meal—which you can spice up with cocktails from the bar—as a chance to ramp up your appetite and fully anticipate the experience to come. A large, packed dining room with canned pick-les and peppers along the walls, this Portland hot spot does justice to the Southern cooking tradition. Try the fried chicken plate—two moist pieces of meat in crisp and peppery buttermilk batter, accompanied by creamy mashed potatoes and collard greens cooked in bacon fat—or the Screen Door plate with your choice of four sides (we like the mac and cheese, creamy grits, and most any of the salads on the rotating seasonal menu). $ *Average main: $14* ⊠ *2337 E. Burnside St., Kerns, Northeast* ☎ *503/542–0880* ⊕ *www.screendoorrestaurant.com* ⊗ *No lunch weekdays* ✛ *H3.*

SOUTHERN
Fodor's Choice
★

$$ ✕ **Tasty n Sons.** Offering one of the best brunches in Portland, this North Williams Avenue eatery will motivate you to get up and go in the morning. With an open kitchen and happily munching diners pack-ing each table, the industrial, sky-lit dining room has a light and lively atmosphere. Pre-brunch appetizers like the bacon-wrapped date, along with a number of other small plates, serve as melt-in-your-mouth pre-cursors to larger dishes like French toast with pear-maple syrup and whipped cream, shakshuka red pepper and tomato stew topped with a baked egg and served with crusty bread, and a flaky biscuit filled with a fried egg, fried chicken, and cheddar cheese. The happy hour and dinner menus are also worth getting excited about. Designed to

AMERICAN
Fodor's Choice
★

be shared, both breakfast and dinner plates are served family-style. As you'll likely have to wait for a table, the other establishments on the block (Ristretto Roasters, Hopworks BikeBar, and various studios and boutiques) can keep you entertained. [$] *Average main: $16* ✉ *3808 N. Williams Ave., Ste. C, Boise, Northeast* ☎ *503/621–1400* 🌐 *www.tastynsons.com* ✥ *F1.*

$ CAFÉ FAMILY 🍴 **Tin Shed Garden Cafe.** Sided in metal, this busy restaurant on Alberta Street is known for its hearty breakfasts—namely, its biscuits and gravy, shredded-potato cakes, egg and tofu scrambles, and breakfast burritos—and the morning wait for a table can be long. The lunch and dinner menus have creative choices as well, like a creamy artichoke sandwich and a mac and cheese of the day. There's a kids' menu containing simple scrambles, sandwiches, and noodles (in the $2-$4 range). Dogs are allowed on the comfortable outdoor patio; there's even a dog menu with a variety of free-range meat dishes (in the $6-$7 range). With a large stone fireplace and chimney, the covered, comfortable outdoor area doubles as a beer garden on warm spring and summer evenings, and the adjacent garden rounds off the property with a peaceful sitting area. [$] *Average main: $11* ✉ *1438 N.E. Alberta St., King, Northeast* ☎ *503/288–6966* 🌐 *www.tinshedgardencafe.com* ✍ *Reservations not accepted* ✥ *H1.*

SOUTHEAST

A whole new food movement has sprouted up southeast of the Willamette River, just outside downtown Portland. As restaurants become more daring and inventive, they are also finding less predictable locations. One benefit of dining outside of downtown is that parking is less expensive and easier to find. Getting from place to place, though, takes more time as these establishments are not necessarily concentrated in any one area. But with some of Portland's most sought-after dining spots—such as Genoa, Pok Pok, Clarklewis—on the east side, a little research will go a long way toward uncovering amazing new flavors.

$$$ ITALIAN 🍴 **3 Doors Down Cafe and Lounge.** Three doors down a side street from the bustling Hawthorne Boulevard, this small restaurant is known for its high-quality Italian food. The intimate restaurant brings people back again and again for exquisite seafood dishes, skillful pasta concoctions, and rich desserts. [$] *Average main: $23* ✉ *1429 SE 37th Ave., Sunnyside, Southeast* ☎ *503/236–6886* 🌐 *www.3doorsdowncafe.com* ⏲ *Closed Mon. No lunch* ✥ *H6.*

$$$ PIZZA Fodor's Choice ★ 🍴 **Apizza Scholls.** The pizzas at Apizza Scholls, lauded by Anthony Bourdain, Rachel Ray, and most any pizza lover who visits, deserve the first-class reputation they enjoy. The greatness of the pies rests not in innovation or complexity, but in the simple quality of the ingredients. The dough is made by hand in small batches and baked to crispy-outside, tender-inside perfection. The toppings—including basil, pecorino Romano, and house-cured bacon—are fresh and delicious and served no more than three per pie. While the decor is rather plain and you'll likely have to wait for a table (reservations are recommended), you'll forget all that once you take your first bite and start basking in the

glory of some of the best pizza anywhere. [$] *Average main: $23* ✉ *4741 SE Hawthorne Blvd., Sunnyside, Southeast* ☎ *503/233–1286* 🌐 *www.apizzascholls.com* 🕒 *No lunch* ✣ *H6.*

$$ SUSHI 🍴 **Bamboo Sushi.** Conveniently, the best sushi spot in Portland is also the most environmentally sustainable, sourcing its fish conscientiously from fishing operations that follow guidelines set by the Monterey Bay Aquarium and Blue Ocean Institute. Try the black cod with smoked soy and roasted garlic glaze or the house-smoked wild ivory salmon nigiri. Or, opt for a couple of the signature rolls, like the Lucky 13, an albacore tuna, cucumber, and avocado roll topped with red crab, scallops, yuzu tobiko, and cilantro; or the vegetarian Green Machine, with tempura fried asparagus and green onion topped with avocado and cilantro sweet chili aioli. The sleek, modern interior gives the place a polished, classy feel. Seats around the sushi bar in the back set you front and center to the expert sushi-making operation, and on nice days, sidewalk tables allow you to bask in the sunshine while enjoying your meal. There's a second location on 23rd Avenue in Northwest. Expect a wait at this popular spot. [$] *Average main: $18* ✉ *310 SE 28th Ave., Kerns, Southeast* ☎ *503/232–5255* 🌐 *bamboosushi.com* 🕒 *No lunch* ✣ *H4, A2.*

$$ MODERN AMERICAN 🍴 **Beaker and Flask.** Known primarily for its innovative cocktails *(⇨ see review in Nightlife)*, the food offerings also unite ingredients in unconventional ways. Take the raw brussels sprout salad with golden raisins, angostura vinaigrette, and crispy pig ears, for example, or the grilled venison flank with caraway creamed cabbage and apple compote. A large, curved bar anchors the warm, industrial space with tall windows and welcoming, semicircular booths. [$] *Average main: $20* ✉ *727 SE Washington St., Buckman, Southeast* ☎ *503/235–8180* 🌐 *www.beakerandflask.com* 🕒 *Closed Sun.* ✣ *H4.*

$ AMERICAN Fodor's Choice ★ 🍴 **Bunk Sandwiches.** Watch out: you're about to have a new favorite sandwich shop. This trendy hole-in-the-wall establishment serves up inventive creations like the pork belly cubano with ham, Swiss, pickles, and mustard on a light poppy-seed bun that will put all other sandwiches to shame. Try the meatball parmigiana hero, the albacore tuna melt, or the roasted butternut squash with caramelized onions, Gruyère, and arugula. Long lines form at lunchtime in this narrow soda-shop style bar, but once you settle in at a table and experience the rich flavors and high-quality ingredients, you'll forget you had to wait. [$] *Average main: $9* ✉ *621 SE Morrison St., Buckman, Southeast* ☎ *503/477–9515* 🌐 *www.bunksandwiches.com* 🕒 *No dinner* ✣ *G5.*

$$ JAPANESE Fodor's Choice ★ 🍴 **Biwa.** A sleek, modern subterranean Japanese restaurant in industrial Southeast Portland, Biwa takes ramen and small plates to a delicious new level. Homemade noodles are the focal point of aromatic, flavorful soups you can enrich with add-ons such as smoked pork shoulder, crispy chicken thighs, kimchi greens, and seaweed. Other adventurous options include *yakimono* (skewered and grilled meats and vegetables, like trout, chicken livers, and button mushrooms), *sashimi* (fresh raw meats like scallops and tuna), and *agemono* (deep fried tofu, chicken, or kimchi). If you want to embark on a true epicurean adventure, consider the $35 per person Omakase, or chef's choice dinner. Sake choices

abound. $ *Average main: $17* ✉ *215 SE 9th Ave., Buckman, Southeast* ☎ *503/239–8830* ⊕ *www.biwarestaurant.com* ⊗ *No lunch* ✛ *H4.*

$ ✕ **Broder.** This delightful neighborhood café—one of the most unique brunch spots in town—serves up fresh and delicious Scandanavian food with fun-to-pronounce names like *friterade applen* (apple fritter) and *aebleskivers* (Danish pancakes). All of the food—the hashes, the baked egg scrambles, the Swedish breakfast bords—is exceedingly delicious and comes on tiny square plates and skillets, arranged simply and artfully on wooden boards with sauces and garnishes in separate bowls. On the lunch menu, the Stockholm hot dog, a beef frank wrapped in a potato pancake and flatbread, served with pickled onions and mustard, may change your life. Get the grilled shrimp add-on and the sautéed greens on the side. The Swedish meatballs and egg, shrimp, and chicken salads are also excellent midday choices. The light and narrow space, decorated with rustic modern furniture and accented with white tile and mirrors, has a laid-back and friendly vibe. Though you'll likely have to wait for a table at breakfast, the café serves complimentary coffee and borrows seating from neighboring Savoy, which opens later in the day. $ *Average main: $10* ✉ *2508 SE Clinton St., Hosford-Abernethy, Southeast* ☎ *503/736–3333* ⊕ *www.broderpdx.com* ⊗ *No dinner Sun.– Tues.* ✛ *H6.*

SWEDISH
Fodor's Choice
★

$$$$ ✕ **Castagna Restaurant.** Enjoy artful new Northwest cuisine—like sturgeon with brown butter, lemon, and parsley, or aged lamb with black carrots and lemon thyme—at this at this tranquil Hawthorne restaurant. Or, splurge for the fixed-price meal and revel in the array of 10 separate courses. Vegetarian options are available. Next door is the more casual Cafe Castagna, a bistro and bar open nightly, serving pizzas, hamburgers, meat, seafood, and other slightly less expensive, lighter fare. $ *Average main: $32* ✉ *1752 SE Hawthorne Blvd., Hosford-Abernethy, Southeast* ☎ *503/231–7373* ⊕ *www.castagnarestaurant. com* ⊗ *Restaurant: Closed Sun.–Tues. No lunch. Cafe: No lunch* ✛ *H6.*

PACIFIC
NORTHWEST

$$$ ✕ **Clarklewis.** Located in a former warehouse between the Willamette River and the train tracks in Industrial Southeast, this classy restaurant serves an excellent happy hour and inventive farm-fresh meals. The daily changing menu features sides, pastas, and entrées like tagliatelle topped with braised lamb ragù, pecorino, and rosemary or grilled pheasant with brussels sprouts, squash, and foraged mushroom sauce. If you're feeling indecisive, let the chef bring you a four-course fixed-price meal. The glass-paned garage doors that run along the front wall let in natural light and refreshing breezes when open during the summer. $ *Average main: $23* ✉ *1001 SE Water Ave., Buckman, Southeast* ☎ *503/235–2294* ⊕ *www.clarklewispdx.com* ⊗ *Closed Sun. No lunch weekends* ✛ *F5.*

PACIFIC
NORTHWEST

$$ ✕ **The Country Cat.** Pork lovers rejoice: you've found hog heaven. House-cured, slow-cooked country ham and bacon and samplers of pork shoulders, head, and belly await you at this craft eatery. Menu items include Southern dishes with a Northwest twist such as fish and shellfish chowder potpie, hickory-smoked duck leg, skillet fried chicken, and bacon-wrapped steelhead. There's also a bar here where the Bloody Mary comes garnished with beef jerky, pickled vegetables, and a giant

SOUTHERN

Laurelhurst Market, Southeast

olive. $ *Average main: $17* ✉ *7937 SE Stark St., Montavilla, Southeast* ☎ *503/408–1414* 🌐 *www.thecountrycat.net* ✣ *H4.*

$$$$ ITALIAN **Genoa.** Widely regarded as one of the finest restaurants in Portland, Genoa serves a five-course prix-fixe Italian menu that changes with the availability of ingredients and the season. In addition to appetizers, pastas, salads, and desserts, diners can chose from well-portioned, thoughtfully crafted entrées that might include seared duck breast with onions, apples, and arugula or steelhead trout with brioche, caramelized yogurt, and butternut squash. The dining room's dark antique furnishings, long curtains, and dangling light fixtures lend it an air of sophistication, and with seating limited to under a few dozen diners, service is excellent. For delicious, less expensive small plates as well as a full bar, head to sister property café Accanto next door. $ *Average main: $65* ✉ *2832 SE Belmont St., Sunnyside, Southeast* ☎ *503/238–1464* 🌐 *www.genoarestaurant.com* *Reservations essential* *Closed Mon. and Tues. No lunch* ✣ *H5.*

$ PIZZA **Ken's Artisan Pizza.** Doug fir beams, old wine barrels, and hungry crowds surround the glowing, igloo-shaped wood oven in the prep area of this thin-crust pizza joint. Ken, also of Ken's Artisan Bakery & Café, uses fresh, organic ingredients for the dough, sauces, and toppings of his pies. Fans rave about the margherita with arugula, the handpressed fennel sausage with onion, and the soppressata with basil. While the roasted vegetable plate and Caeser salad are delicious and the wine selection is solid, pizza is the real star. Be prepared for a wait. $ *Average main: $13* ✉ *304 SE 28th Ave., Kerns, Southeast* ☎ *503/517–9951* 🌐 *www.kensartisan.com* *Reservations not accepted* *No lunch* ✣ *H4.*

2

$$$ PACIFIC NORTHWEST Fodor's Choice ★

🍴 **Laurelhurst Market.** With an artisanal butcher shop anchoring the right side of the building, Laurelhurst Market offers some of the best meat in Portland. Case in point: the Wagyu brisket smoked for 12 hours and marinated in Ozark barbecue sauce, and the beef short ribs braised with red wine and prunes. Despite the meat-centric focus, Laurelhurst delivers when it comes to veggies too: the reasonably priced seasonal salads and sides can serve as interesting, flavorful complements to the meaty main courses or, mixed and matched, as meals themselves. The candlelit dining room is comfortable and sophisticated and the stainless steel kitchen along the back wall underneath the beef cuts diagram serves as a reminder of what the place is all about: the preparation and serving of outstanding meat. The butcher shop sells sandwiches at lunchtime; you can take your purchase to go or eat at one of the restaurant tables, though there's no waitstaff on duty. [$] *Average main: $23* ✉ *3155 East Burnside St., Laurelhurst, Southeast* ☎ *503/206–3097* 🌐 *www.laurelhurstmarket.com* ✥ *H4.*

$$ THAI Fodor's Choice ★

🍴 **Lemongrass.** Set in an old Victorian in a residential neighborhood, this lovely establishment serves consistently delicious Thai food—and isn't afraid to turn up the heat. In fact, during the spring and summer pepper growing season, the spice meter goes all the way up to 20 (the 2 is already hot). Cooked to order, the pad thai stands out among other pad thais in town, and the garlic basil chicken, peanut curry chicken, and various curry dishes are delectable as well. The small rooms, white-linen tablecloths, and fresh-cut flowers throughout the old house create an intimate dining atmosphere. [$] *Average main: $17* ✉ *1705 NE Couch St., Kerns, Northeast* ☎ *503/231–5780* 💳 *No credit cards* 🕒 *Closed Sun. and Mon. No lunch Sat.* ✥ *H4.*

$$$ FRENCH Fodor's Choice ★

🍴 **Le Pigeon.** Specializing in adventurous meat dishes of extraordinary quality, this cozy French restaurant is one of the best in Portland. Changing weekly, the menu features items like beef cheek bourguignon, grilled venison, rabbit, foie gras (especially exceptional), and, yes, pigeon too, all prepared with balance, nuance, and attention to detail. Less adventurous eaters can opt for the burger, delicious in its own right, and there's always a vegetarian option as well. With exposed brick, mismatched antique china, communal tables, and a counter overlooking the open kitchen that allows diners to interact with the chefs, the atmosphere at this 42-seat restaurant is trendy yet casual. Little Bird Bistro, Le Pigeon's sister restaurant, serves downtown diners French bistro fare for lunch and dinner. [$] *Average main: $26* ✉ *738 E. Burnside St., Buckman, Southeast* ☎ *503/546–8796* 🌐 *www.lepigeon.com* ✍ *Reservations essential* 🕒 *No lunch* ✥ *G4.*

$$$ BISTRO

🍴 **Little Bird Bistro.** ⇨ *See Le Pigeon review above.* [$] *Average main: $26* ✉ *219 SW 6th Ave., Downtown* ☎ *503/688–5952* 🌐 *littlebirdbistro.com* 🕒 *No lunch weekends* ✥ *E4.*

$ MIDDLE EASTERN

🍴 **Nicholas Restaurant.** In a small streetfront along an unimpressive stretch of Grand Avenue, this hidden gem serves some of the best Lebanese food in Portland, for prices that can't be beat. Everything from the fresh homemade pita to the hummus, falafel, tabbouleh, baba ghanoush, and kebabs is delicious, and comes in enormous portions. The meat, vegetable, or vegan mezza platters offer a smattering of the kitchen's best, and the lamb gyro is delish. No alcohol is offered at this location. [$] *Average main: $11* ✉ *318 SE Grand Ave., Buckman, Southeast* ☎ *503/235–5123* 🌐 *www.nicholasrestaurant.com* ✣ *G4.*

$$ PIZZA 🍴 **Nostrana.** This casual yet elegant restaurant delivers delicious, thin-crusted pizzas and wood-grilled specialties (even desserts) from their signature oven. Pies come topped with garnishings like shiitake mushrooms, housemade mozzarella, and arugula or Calabrese salami, pickled peppers, and honey. Pasta and meat entrées and salads round out the menu. Though large and windowed, the dining room still manages to feel warm and cozy. Reservations are recommended. [$] *Average main: $17* ✉ *1401 SE Morrison St., Buckman, Southeast* ☎ *503/234–2427* 🌐 *nostrana.com* ⏲ *No lunch weekends* ✣ *H5.*

$ ASIAN Fodor's Choice ★ 🍴 **Pok Pok & Whiskey Soda Lounge.** Serving thoroughly researched Southeast Asian street fare, Pok Pok takes taste buds on wild culinary adventures that leave them burning and craving more. The Vietnamese chicken wings, deep fried in caramelized fish sauce and garlic, are legendary in Portland and a must-try. Other favorites include the namesake green papaya salad with Thai chili, lime juice, fish sauce, tamarind, dried shrimp, and peanuts; and the curry coconut milk soup with pickled mustard greens, crispy yellow noodles, shallots, and roasted chili paste. Share plates for the liveliest culinary experience. Diners have the option of sitting outside under tents, or in the funky, cave-like interior. The affiliated Whiskey Soda Lounge (across the street at 3131 SE Division Street), is both a Pok Pok waiting area and restaurant in its own right and offers a full bar and a limited Pok Pok menu. Rest assured, you can get the wings there, too. Part of the Pok Pok mini-empire, Pok Pok Noi (Little Pok Pok) is an excellent alternative if you're Downtown. [$] *Average main: $14* ✉ *3226 S.E. Division St., Richmond, Southeast* ☎ *503/232–1387* 🌐 *www.pokpokpdx.com* ✣ *G6.*

$ AMERICAN 🍴 **Savoy Tavern + Bistro.** A hip restaurant specializing in Midwestern cuisine, Savoy offers diners the choice of sitting in either a dark and cozy tavern or a light, open bistro. The deep-fried cheese curds, beer bratwurst, and mac and cheese carry on the Midwestern tradition of comfort food, though you can also find fish and salads on the menu. The tavern board, a collection of meat cuts, cheeses, and house pickles, makes a nice appetizer or lighter meal. Try the Milwaukie mule, a mix of ginger vodka and ginger beer topped with a lime, and served in a traditional copper mug. A comfortable atmosphere and reasonably priced, seasonal menu make this a favorite for no-fuss drinking and dining. [$] *Average main: $14* ✉ *2500 SE Clinton St., Hosford-Abernethy, Southeast* ☎ *503/808–9999* 🌐 *www.savoypdx.com* ⏲ *No lunch* ✣ *H6.*

$$$ FRENCH 🍴 **St. Jack.** With sumptuous wax drip candles along the counters and French hip-hop playing softly in the background, this bistro on a busy street in Southeast has a certain *je ne sais quoi*. Serving hearty portions of rich and creamy food, the chic yet cozy restaurant takes its inspiration from the *bouchons*, or rustic cafés, of Lyon, the culinary capital of France. The pan-seared scallops, drenched in a cognac, leek, and Gruyère sauce, with a bread crumb crunch, make a delicious precursor to the main course. For dinner, try the moist and flavorful roasted trout, served whole with a warm lentil salad, or the perfectly tender

mussels, which arrive in a large white bowl with garlic, shallots, fennel, vermouth—and a crusty baguette for dunking. Regulars rave about the light and honeyed chicken liver mousse, and the house cocktails are killer too—particularly the Lost Weekend. During the day, the Patisserie St. Jack serves espresso along with croissants, *canelés* (a caramelized pastry with a custard center), macarons, and fresh-baked madeleines, as well as a variety of lunch plates. [$] *Average main: $24* ✉ *2039 SE Clinton St., Hosford-Abernethy, Southeast* 🌐 *stjackpdx.com* ✣ *G6.*

WHERE TO STAY

Updated by Christina Cooke

When it comes to lodging, Portland runs the gamut: modern to historical, fancy to basic, innovative to conventional. Reputable, large chains are here, and so are luxury boutique hotels that emphasize service and splendor. Convenient options abound for destinations like the convention center and airport; and sprinkled throughout the city are one-of-a-kind bed-and-breakfasts that offer travelers a glimpse of authentic Portland living.

Aside from price, the main thing to consider is where in the city you want to be. Many of the elegant hotels near the city center and on the riverfront also have appeal because of their proximity to Portland's attractions. MAX light-rail is within easy walking distance of most properties. The additional accommodations clustered near the Convention Center and the airport are almost all chain hotels that tend to be less expensive than those found downtown.

An alternative to the standard city hotel scene is to stay at one of the several beautiful B&Bs spread throughout residential neighborhoods in the northwest and northeast. These are usually lovely houses, with unique and luxurious guest rooms, deluxe home-cooked breakfasts, and friendly and knowledgeable innkeepers.

HOTEL PRICES

Portland's hotels will please visitors used to big-city lodging prices. Even most the more luxurious hotels can be booked for under $250 per night, and there are a lot of options for around $169 per night or less. If you are willing to stay outside of the downtown area (though this is the most convenient place to stay), you can easily find a room in a suburban chain hotel for well under $100 per night. Unlike in some cities, you will not see quite as many weekend discounts, although some of the top hotels for business travelers do offer these. *Prices in the reviews are the lowest cost of a standard double room in high season.*

Before booking your stay, visit 🌐 *www.travelportland.com* to check out "Portland Perks," packages that usually include double-occupancy accommodations, free nightly parking, a Continental breakfast for two, and visitor vouchers for savings on dining, tax-free shopping, and more.

In alphabetical order by neighborhood. Use the coordinate (✣ B2) at the end of each listing to locate a site on the corresponding map. For expanded hotel reviews, visit Fodors.com.

DOWNTOWN

Staying downtown ensures you'll have immediate access to just about everything Portland offers, including events, restaurants, cultural venues, shops, movie theaters, and more. Transportation options are abundant thanks to the MAX, bus lines, streetcar, and taxis; in addition, many hotels offer shuttle service. Portland has clean streets and, overall, is considered relatively safe.

$$
HOTEL
Fodor's Choice
★

Ace Hotel. The quintessential Portland hotel, Ace makes the "hipster" aesthetic available to anyone and, sandwiched between Stumptown Coffee and Clyde Common restaurant a block from Powell's Books, Ace positions you well to enjoy all downtown has to offer. **Pros:** "Portland" lodging experience; prime downtown location; unique touches, like original wall artwork in each room; free city bicycles available for guests. **Cons:** water pressure can be weak; some rooms can be noisy; Wi-Fi can be patchy; parking is $25 a day. $ *Rooms from: $130* ⊠ *1022 S.W. Stark St., Downtown* ☎ *503/228–2277* ⊕ *www.acehotel. com* ⋗ *78 rooms* ⫶⊙⫶ *No meals* ✛ *D4.*

$$$
HOTEL

Benson Hotel. Portland's grandest hotel has hosted most every president since it opened in 1913. **Pros:** historic building; beautiful lobby; excellent location. **Cons:** rooms and hallways could use updating. $ *Rooms from: $189* ⊠ *309 S.W. Broadway, Downtown* ☎ *503/228–2000, 800/663–1144* ⊕ *www.bensonhotel.com* ⋗ *230 rooms, 57 suites* ⫶⊙⫶ *No meals* ✛ *D4.*

$$$
HOTEL

Courtyard by Marriott–Portland City Center. Built in 2009, this LEED (Leadership in Energy and Design) gold certified hotel falls right in line with green Portland ideals. **Pros:** environmental consciousness; central location; comfy beds; good on-site restaurant. **Cons:** bathtubs available only in some rooms. $ *Rooms from: $179* ⊠ *550 SW Oak St., Downtown* ☎ *503/505–5000* ⊕ *www.marriott.com* ⋗ *253 rooms, 3 suites* ⫶⊙⫶ *No meals* ✛ *E4.*

$$$
HOTEL

Embassy Suites Portland–Downtown. In the former Multnomah Hotel, built in 1912, the grand lobby of this hotel offers an extravagant welcome to the spacious two-room suite accommodations. **Pros:** central location; the character of the beautiful old building; breakfast and evening drinks and snacks included in price. **Cons:** you have to pay for Internet in the rooms (though free in lobby); no in-and-out privileges in self-park garage across the street. $ *Rooms from: $229* ⊠ *319 S.W. Pine St., Downtown* ☎ *503/279–9000, 800/643–7892* ⊕ *www. embassyportland.com* ⋗ *276 suites* ⫶⊙⫶ *Breakfast* ✛ *E4.*

$$$$
HOTEL

The Governor Hotel. With mahogany walls and murals of Lewis and Clark's Pacific Northwest journey, the historic lobby of the distinctive Governor helps set the 1920s Arts and Crafts style that's followed throughout the hotel. **Pros:** central location; beautiful 1920s property; large rooms; well-lit and well-equipped gym. **Cons:** the valet parking is pricey. $ *Rooms from: $279* ⊠ *614 S.W. 10th Ave., Downtown* ☎ *503/224–3400, 888/246–5631* ⊕ *www.governorhotel.com* ⋗ *76 rooms, 24 suites* ⫶⊙⫶ *No meals* ✛ *D4.*

2

BEST BETS FOR PORTLAND LODGING

Fodor's offers a selective listing of quality lodging experiences in every price range, from the city's best budget beds to its most sophisticated luxury hotels. Here we've compiled our top recommendations by price and experience. The very best properties—in other words, those that provide a particularly remarkable experience in their price range—are designated in the listings with the Fodor's Choice logo.

$$$$ ⬚ **Heathman Hotel.** More than deserving of its reputation for quality,
HOTEL from the teak-paneled lobby to the marble fireplaces to the rosewood
Fodor'sChoice elevators with Warhol prints at each landing, this hotel exudes refine-
★ ment. **Pros:** superior service; central location adjoining the Performing
Arts Center; renowned on-site restaurant. **Cons:** small rooms; expensive parking. $ *Rooms from: $259* ✉ *1001 S.W. Broadway, Downtown* ☎ *503/241–4100, 800/551–0011* ⊕ *www.heathmanportland.com*
↪ *110 rooms, 40 suites* ❍ *No meals* ✛ *D5.*

$$$ ⬚ **Hilton Portland & Executive Tower.** Encompassing two buildings—a main
HOTEL building and a newer, more upscale tower—this gargantuan complex
offers luxurious bedrooms and a convenient location. **Pros:** nice work-
out facilities and indoor pools; prime downtown location near attrac-
tions and restaurants. **Cons:** not for visitors looking for homier lodging;
$32/night valet parking only. $ *Rooms from: $179* ✉ *921 S.W. 6th
Ave., Downtown* ☎ *503/226–1611, 800/445–8667* ⊕ *www.hilton.com*
↪ *773 rooms, 9 suites* ❍ *No meals* ✛ *D5.*

$$$ ⬚ **Hotel deLuxe.** If you want a taste of Hollywood's Golden Era, this
HOTEL one's for you: the original chandeliers and guilded ceilings of the historic
Fodor'sChoice building's golden lobby evoke the necessary glitz and glamour; 400-plus
★ black-and-white photographs on the hallway walls are arranged by
movie themes; and the for-loan collection of DVDs includes 50 classics
(*Casablanca*, anyone?). **Pros:** fun and artistic vibe; friendly and helpful
staff; pillow menu and other extra touches lend an air of luxury; cool
bar. **Cons:** rooms on the small side; can be noisy. $ *Rooms from: $179*
✉ *729 S.W. 15th Ave., Downtown* ☎ *503/219–2094, 866/986–8085*
⊕ *www.hoteldeluxeportland.com* ↪ *97 rooms, 33 suites* ❍ *No meals*
✛ *C4.*

$$$ ⬚ **Hotel Fifty.** This boutique property overlooking the Willamette River
HOTEL provides stellar views of the water and easy access to the waterfront
park and the events that take place there (Rose Festival, Blues Festival,
events featuring food and beer). **Pros:** central location on the river-
front; comfortable beds; easy access to the MAX. **Cons:** only east-facing
rooms have river views; no on-site fitness facility; expensive parking.
$ *Rooms from: $209* ✉ *50 S.W. Morrison St., Downtown* ☎ *503/221–
0711, 877/237–6775* ⊕ *www.hotelfifty.com* ↪ *140 rooms 1 suite* ❍ *No
meals* ✛ *E5.*

$$$ ⬚ **Hotel Modera.** Decorated with local artwork, sleek, contemporary
HOTEL furnishings, and wood and marble accents, this boutique property is at
once accessible and sophisticated. **Pros:** friendly staff; outdoor garden,
patio, and firepits; large massage showerheads; individually bagged ice
in hand-carved chests in every hall. **Cons:** rooms on the small side; in the
business district and far from restaurants and nightlife. $ *Rooms from:
$209* ✉ *515 S.W. Clay St., Downtown* ☎ *503/484–1084, 877/484–1084*
⊕ *www.hotelmodera.com* ↪ *167 rooms, 7 suites* ❍ *No meals* ✛ *D6.*

$$$ ⬚ **Hotel Monaco.** A departure from the safe earth tones of most hotels,
HOTEL this luxury boutique hotel is bright and bold, with a cacophony of col-
Fodor'sChoice ors and patterns that feels decadent rather than overwhelming—and is
★ a lot of fun. **Pros:** prime location; historic building; sumptuous interior;
impeccable service; well-equipped fitness center; free Starbucks coffee in
the morning. **Cons:** colors and patterns might not appeal to everyone;

business center is small. Ⓢ *Rooms from: $249 ✉ 506 S.W. Washington St., Downtown* ☎ *503/222–0001, 888/207–2201* ⊕ *www.portland-monaco.com* ↪ *86 rooms, 135 suites* ⦿| *No meals* ✛ *E4.*

$$$$
HOTEL
▦ **Hotel Vintage Plaza.** This historic landmark takes its theme from Oregon vineyards, with rooms named after local wineries, complimentary wine served every evening, and an extensive collection of Oregon vintages displayed in the tasting room. **Pros:** excellent complimentary wine selections; friendly staff; pet-friendly rooms; central location. **Cons:** pricey parking; those with allergies should request pet-free rooms; some street noise on the lower levels on the Washington Street side. Ⓢ *Rooms from: $289 ✉ 422 S.W. Broadway, Downtown* ☎ *503/228–1212, 800/263–2305* ⊕ *www.vintageplaza.com* ↪ *96 rooms, 21 suites* ⦿| *No meals* ✛ *D4.*

$$$
HOTEL
▦ **Mark Spencer Hotel.** This family-owned hotel, centrally located near Powell's Books, is one of the best values in town, and the rooms, which all have full kitchenettes, are clean and comfortable. **Pros:** commitment to the arts; afternoon tea and cookies and evening local wine tasting. **Cons:** some rooms are small and dark; the interior design is uninspiring (though renovations are scheduled); noise can be a problem; those with allergies should request a pet-free space. Ⓢ *Rooms from: $239 ✉ 409 S.W. 11th Ave., Downtown* ☎ *503/224–3293, 800/548–3934* ⊕ *www.markspencer.com* ↪ *36 rooms, 66 suites* ⦿| *Breakfast* ✛ *D4.*

$$
HOTEL
▦ **McMenamins Crystal Hotel.** Travelers who appreciate good music and good beer—especially in combination—will love this latest addition to the McMenamin brothers' unorthodox empire, which shares a building with three bars and is affiliated with the Crystal Ballroom concert venue a block up the road. **Pros:** historic building with lots of character; central location; guests-only soaking pool; three bars on site; affiliation with the Crystal Ballroom. **Cons:** few frills; shared bathrooms in some rooms; no televisions. Ⓢ *Rooms from: $105 ✉ 303 S.W. 12th Ave., Downtown* ☎ *503/972–2670, 855/205–3930* ⊕ *www.mcmenamins.com/crystalhotel* ↪ *51 rooms, 9 with bath* ⦿| *No meals* ✛ *C4.*

$$$$
HOTEL
Fodor'sChoice
★
▦ **The Nines.** If you're looking for the cosmopolitan flair of a larger city or want to spot visiting celebrities, this swanky hotel is the place for you. **Pros:** central location; stunning views; swanky vibe and cool design; spacious marble bathrooms; two restaurants; excellent gym. **Cons:** rooms facing the atrium and overlooking the bar and restaurant can be noisy. Ⓢ *Rooms from: $299 ✉ 525 S.W. Morrison St., Downtown* ☎ *503/222–9996, 877/229–9995* ⊕ *www.thenines.com* ↪ *318 rooms, 13 suites* ⦿| *No meals* ✛ *D4.*

$$$
HOTEL
▦ **The Paramount Hotel.** This pale-stone, 15-story hotel overlooking Director Park is a few blocks from Pioneer Square, the Arlene Schnitzer Concert Hall, the Portland Art Museum, the MAX, and the streetcar. **Pros:** central location; beautiful granite bathrooms; in-room honor bars. **Cons:** small fitness facility; parking is expensive. Ⓢ *Rooms from: $209 ✉ 808 S.W. Taylor St., Downtown* ☎ *503/223–9900* ⊕ *www.portlandparamount.com* ↪ *152 rooms, 2 suites* ⦿| *No meals* ✛ *D5.*

$$
HOTEL
▦ **Park Lane Suites & Inn.** A few blocks from Washington Park, the Nob Hill shopping district, and downtown, this hotel provides a comfortable alternative to fancier properties in the central area. **Pros:** proximity to

several of Portland's most prominent neighborhoods; expanded kitchen capacity in suites; complimentary coffee, tea, fruit, and cookies in the lobby. **Cons:** parking is free but limited; not enough soundproofing; not as luxurious as alternatives. $\boxed{\$}$ *Rooms from: $109* ✉ *809 S.W. King Ave., Downtown* ☎ *503/226–6288* ⊕ *www.parklanesuites.com* ⬅ *41 rooms, 45 suites* ◎ *No meals* ✛ *B4.*

$$$$
HOTEL

🏨 **RiverPlace Hotel.** With textured wall coverings, pillows made of Pendleton wool, and a color palette of slate blue, mustard yellow, and a variety of browns, this hotel on the banks of the Willamette River captures the look and feel of the Pacific Northwest. **Pros:** stellar views; riverfront location adjoining a city park; wide selection of room options; comfortable beds. **Cons:** some distance from the bars and restaurants in the city center. $\boxed{\$}$ *Rooms from: $299* ✉ *1510 S.W. Harbor Way, Downtown* ☎ *503/228–3233, 888/869–3108* ⊕ *www.riverplacehotel. com* ⬅ *39 rooms, 45 suites* ◎ *No meals* ✛ *E6.*

NOB HILL

$$$
B&B/INN

🏨 **Heron Haus.** In a stately, ivy-covered mansion built in 1904, this bright and lovely bed-and-breakfast sets you on a lush, fern-covered hillside bordering Forest Park and overlooking the Nob Hill shopping area. **Pros:** serene environment; modern amenities; discerning owners have good local knowledge to impart; off-street parking. **Cons:** in a residential neighborhood; no tubs in bathrooms. $\boxed{\$}$ *Rooms from: $225* ✉ *2545 N.W. Westover Rd., Nob Hill* ☎ *503/274–1846* ⊕ *www.heronhaus.com* ⬅ *6 rooms* ◎ *Breakfast* ✛ *A2.*

$$$
HOTEL
FAMILY

🏨 **Inn @ Northrup Station.** Bright colors, bold patterns, and retro designs characterize this Nob Hill hotel containing luxurious suites with full kitchens or kitchenettes. **Pros:** roomy suites have kitchens and feel like home; close to the shopping and dining on N.W. 21st Avenue; free parking; streetcar runs nearby. **Cons:** the bold colors might not appeal to everyone; some have commented on the lack of noise insulation. $\boxed{\$}$ *Rooms from: $184* ✉ *2025 N.W. Northrup St., Nob Hill* ☎ *503/224–0543, 800/224–1180* ⊕ *www.northrupstation.com* ⬅ *70 suites* ◎ *Breakfast* ✛ *B2.*

$$$
HOTEL
FAMILY

🏨 **Silver Cloud Inn–Portland.** Staying here, adjacent to lively N.W. 23rd Avenue, is a great alternative to being right downtown, and during the week a select local-area shuttle service is available, if you schedule in advance. **Pros:** spacious rooms; free parking; proximity to 23rd Avenue shopping district; easy access to bus and streetcar. **Cons:** gym but no pool; a trek to downtown area. $\boxed{\$}$ *Rooms from: $159* ✉ *2426 N.W. Vaughn St., Nob Hill* ☎ *503/242–2400, 800/205–6939* ⊕ *www. silvercloud.com* ⬅ *75 rooms, 6 suites* ◎ *Breakfast* ✛ *A1.*

NORTH

$
HOTEL

🏨 **Monticello Motel.** This is a smaller, family-owned property with several accommodation options, and is close to freeway access, the MAX line, and buses. **Pros:** kitchen suites are well equipped; free parking and Wi-Fi; affordable. **Cons:** not immediately near shops and restaurants; little character; no elevator. $\boxed{\$}$ *Rooms from: $76* ✉ *4801 N. Interstate*

McMenamins Kennedy School

Hotel deLuxe

Heathman Hotel

Ave., Overlook, North ☎ *503/285–6641* 🌐 *www.monticellomotel.com* 🛏 *5 rooms, 4 suites* 🍴 *No meals* ✥ *E1.*

$ HOTEL 🏨 **The Palms Motel.** Clean, simple, and accessible to downtown, this motel offers an affordable alternative to some of the larger chains. **Pros:** affordable; free parking; access to public transit; cool old neon sign out front. **Cons:** no frills; not immediately near shops and restaurants. [$] *Rooms from: $62* ✉ *3801 N. Interstate Ave., Overlook, North* ☎ *503/287–5788, 800/620–9652* 🌐 *www.palmsmotel.com* 🛏 *54 rooms, 1 suite* 🍴 *No meals* ✥ *E1.*

$$ HOTEL 🏨 **Red Lion Hotel on the River–Jantzen Beach.** The beige and red rooms in this four-story hotel on the Columbia River have balconies and excellent views of the river and Vancouver, Washington. **Pros:** river location; views from room balconies; close to the Jantzen Beach shopping center; complimentary airport transportation. **Cons:** pool is outdoors; far from downtown Portland. [$] *Rooms from: $135* ✉ *909 N. Hayden Island Dr., Hayden Island, North* ✥ *east of I–5's Jantzen Beach exit* ☎ *503/283–4466, 800/733–5466* 🌐 *www.redlion.com* 🛏 *296 rooms, 24 suites* 🍴 *No meals* ✥ *F1.*

NORTHEAST

The area east of the Willamette is not nearly as condensed as downtown Portland, which means fewer interesting buildings. It's also a little harder to get around, though because of the MAX and excellent bus service, it's still doable. Properties tend to be older, with lower prices than downtown, and with more rooms available. The majority of chain hotels are clustered around the convention center; nearby is Lloyd Center Mall. There are also a number of B&Bs on this side of town, tucked away in historical neighborhoods like Irvington.

$$ HOTEL 🏨 **Crowne Plaza Portland.** This sleek, modern hotel, with attractive rooms and ample facilities, is a reliable and convenient option for both business travelers and tourists. **Pros:** indoor pool; good selection of accommodations and room sizes; proximity to public transit; complimentary shuttle within 5 miles. **Cons:** location near the Rose Quarter means traffic congestion during basketball games and concerts. [$] *Rooms from: $149* ✉ *1441 N.E. 2nd Ave., Lloyd District, Northeast* ☎ *503/233–2401, 877/777–2704* 🌐 *www.cpportland.com* 🛏 *239 rooms, 2 suites* 🍴 *No meals* ✥ *G2.*

$$ B&B/INN 🏨 **Georgian House.** This red-brick Georgian colonial with neoclassical columns is on a quiet, tree-lined street in a historic neighborhood. **Pros:** warm hospitality; home-cooked breakfast; intimate environment; ample convenient parking. **Cons:** residential neighborhood; some rooms have shared bathrooms; no elevator; credit card accepted to hold room only. [$] *Rooms from: $132* ✉ *1828 N.E. Siskiyou St., Irvington, Northeast* ☎ *503/281–2250, 888/282–2250* 🌐 *www.thegeorgianhouse.com* 🛏 *2 rooms with shared bath, 2 suites* 🍴 *Breakfast* ✥ *H1.*

$$$ B&B/INN Fodor's Choice ★ 🏨 **Lion and the Rose Victorian Bed & Breakfast Inn.** Oak and mahogany floors, original light fixtures, and a coffered dining-room ceiling set a tone of formal elegance in this 1906 mansion, while the wonderfully friendly, accommodating, and knowledgeable innkeepers make sure

that you feel perfectly at home. **Pros:** gorgeous house; top-notch service; home-cooked meals. **Cons:** young children not allowed in main house; no elevator; not in an immediately exciting area. $ *Rooms from: $185* ⊠ *1810 N.E. 15th Ave., Irvington, Northeast* ☎ *503/287–9245, 800/955–1647* ⊕ *www.lionrose.com* ⤳ *8 rooms* ⦿ *Breakfast* ✛ *H1.*

$$ 🏨 **McMenamins Kennedy School.** In a renovated elementary school in HOTEL northeast Portland, this may well be one of the most unusual (and awesome) hotels you'll ever encounter. **Pros:** funky and authentic Portland experience; many opportunities for fun on site; room rates include movies and use of year-round soaking pool. **Cons:** no bathtubs, only shower stalls; no TVs in rooms; no elevator; food mediocre. $ *Rooms from: $145* ⊠ *5736 N.E. 33rd Ave., Concordia, Northeast* ☎ *503/249–3983* ⊕ *www.kennedyschool.com* ⤳ *57 rooms* ⦿ *No meals* ✛ *G1.*

Fodor'sChoice ★

$$$ 🏨 **Portland's White House Bed and Breakfast.** Hardwood floors with oriental rugs, chandeliers, antiques, and fountains create a warm and romantic mood at this elegant bed-and-breakfast in the historic Irvington District. **Pros:** romantic; authentic historic Portland experience; excellent service. **Cons:** in residential neighborhood; shops and restaurants several blocks away; no elevator; no pets. $ *Rooms from: $180* ⊠ *1914 N.E. 22nd Ave., Irvington, Northeast* ☎ *503/287–7131, 800/272–7131* ⊕ *www.portlandswhitehouse.com* ⤳ *8 suites* ⦿ *Breakfast* ✛ *H1.*

B&B/INN

AIRPORT

If you're flying in and out for a quick business trip, then staying by the airport may be a good idea. The lodging options here are only the larger chains. The airport is about a 20- to 25-minute drive away from downtown Portland.

$$$ 🏨 **Aloft Portland Airport at Cascade Station.** High-end vibrant design, HOTEL sophisticated amenities, and fresh new concepts in a hotel experience make the first Aloft in Oregon a standout amid airport hotel mediocrity. **Pros:** lots of high-tech amenities; welcoming social areas; unique, spacious rooms; near IKEA. **Cons:** airport location; no sit-down restaurant; no complimentary breakfast. $ *Rooms from: $169* ⊠ *9920 N.E. Cascades Pkwy., Airport, Northeast* ☎ *503/200–5678* ⊕ *www. aloftportlandairport.com* ⤳ *136 rooms* ⦿ *No meals* ✛ *H1.*

$$$ 🏨 **Embassy Suites Portland Airport.** Suites in this eight-story atrium hotel HOTEL come with separate bedrooms, living areas with sleeper sofas, and flat screen TVs. **Pros:** spacious suites; full breakfast included; free cocktails at happy hour. **Cons:** airport location. $ *Rooms from: $209* ⊠ *7900 N.E. 82nd Ave., Airport, Northeast* ☎ *503/460–3000* ⊕ *www. portlandairport.embassysuites.com* ⤳ *251 suites* ⦿ *Breakfast* ✛ *H1.*

$$ 🏨 **Shilo Inn Suites Hotel.** Each room in this large, four-level all-suites inn is HOTEL spacious (500 square feet) and bright, and has a fridge, microwave, wet FAMILY bar, and three TVs (including one in the bathroom!). **Pros:** large indoor pool, steam room, and sauna; large rooms; free local and domestic long distance calls; complimentary breakfast and airport shuttle. **Cons:** airport location. $ *Rooms from: $119* ⊠ *11707 N.E. Airport Way, Airport, Northeast* ☎ *503/252–7500, 800/222–2244* ⊕ *www.shiloinns. com* ⤳ *200 rooms* ⦿ *Breakfast* ✛ *H1.*

SOUTHEAST

$$ **The Jupiter Hotel.** The hip, creative, and adventurous flock to this
HOTEL   contemporary boutique hotel, formerly a motor inn, adjacent to a res-
taurant/bar and one of the city's most popular concert venues, the Doug
Fir Lounge. **Pros:** funky lodging; built-in nightlife; easy access to down-
town. **Cons:** not to everyone's taste; request a room on the "chill side"
if you want distance from the patio/bar scene. $ *Rooms from: $149*
⊠ *800 E. Burnside, Buckman, Southeast* ☎ *503/230–9200, 877/800–*
0004 ⊕ *www.jupiterhotel.com* ⤷ *80 rooms, 1 suite* ⊙ *No meals* ✛ *H4.*

SOUTHWEST

$$$ **River's Edge Hotel & Spa.** On the edge of Portland's progressive South
HOTEL   Waterfront District and just a few minutes from downtown, this tran-
quil boutique property is sheltered among trees along the meandering
Willamette River. **Pros:** great river views; trails nearby for walking and
jogging; complimentary Continental breakfast served on each hotel
floor; suites have gas fireplaces. **Cons:** not in the center of downtown;
steep overnight parking fee; Wi-Fi connection weak in some rooms.
$ *Rooms from: $189* ⊠ *455 S.W. Hamilton Ct., Southwest* ☎ *503/802–*
5800, 888/556–4402 ⊕ *www.riversedgehotel.com* ⤷ *81 rooms, 18*
suites ⊙ *Breakfast* ✛ *E6.*

NIGHTLIFE AND THE ARTS

Updated
by Christina
Cooke

Portland is quite the creative town. Every night performances from top-
ranked dance, theater, and musical talent take the stage somewhere in
the city. Expect to find never-ending choices for things to do, from taking in true independent films, performance art, and plays, to checking
out some of the Northwest's (and the country's) hottest musical groups
at one of the city's many nightclubs or concert venues.

As for the fine art scene, galleries abound in all four corners of Portland.
Painted, recycled, photographed, fired, fused, welded, or collaged—the
scope and selection of art is one of the most notable attributes of what
makes this city so metropolitan and alive.

EVENT LISTINGS

"A&E, The Arts and Entertainment Guide," published each Friday
in the *Oregonian* (⊕ *www.oregonlive.com*), contains listings of performers, productions, events, and club entertainment. *Willamette Week*
(⊕ *wweek.com*), published free each Wednesday and widely available
throughout the metropolitan area, contains similar, but hipper, listings.
The *Portland Mercury* (⊕ *www.portlandmercury.com*), also free, is an
even edgier entertainment publication distributed each Wednesday. The
glossy newsstand magazine *Portland Monthly* (⊕ *www.portlandmonth-*
lymag.com) covers Portland news, culture, and lifestyle and frequently
offers guides to the city. The free monthly publication *Portland Family*
Magazine (⊕ *www.portlandfamily.com*) has an excellent calendar of
events for recreational and educational opportunities for families. And

Just Out (⊕ www.justout.com), the city's gay and lesbian newspaper, is published monthly.

NIGHTLIFE

Portland has become something of a base for young rock bands, which perform in dance clubs and live music venues scattered throughout the metropolitan area. Good jazz groups perform nightly in clubs and bars as well. Top-name musicians and performers in every genre regularly appear at the city's larger venues.

From chic to cheap, cool to cultish, Portland's diverse bars and lounges blanket the town. Dozens of small breweries operate in the metropolitan area and produce pale ales, bitters, bocks, barley wines, and stouts. Some have attached pub operations, where you can sample a foaming pint of house ale. "Brew theaters," former neighborhood movie houses where patrons enjoy food, suds, and recent theatrical releases, are part of the microbrewery phenomenon here *(⇨ see Film in the Arts section)*. Many are branches of McMenamins, a locally owned chain of bars, restaurants, nightclubs, and hotels, and some of these pubs can be found in restored historic buildings.

Coffee is to Portland as tea is to England. For Portlanders, sipping a cup of coffee is a right, a ritual, and a pastime that occurs no matter the time of day or night. There's no shortage of cafés in which to park and read, reflect, or rejuvenate for the long day or night of exploration ahead.

Portland's gay community has a decent selection of places to mingle, dance, and drink; several of these night spots are open into the wee hours, until 4 am or so.

DOWNTOWN

BARS AND LOUNGES

Many of the best bars and lounges in Portland are found in its restaurants.

The Heathman Restaurant & Bar. At the elegant Heathman Hotel, you can sip tea in the eucalyptus-paneled Tea Court or beer, wine, and cocktails in the marble bar. ⊠ *1001 SW Broadway, Downtown* ☎ *503/790–7752* ⊕ *www.heathmanrestaurantandbar.com.*

Huber's Cafe. The city's oldest restaurant (est. 1879) is notable for its old-fashioned feel and Spanish coffee, which arrives on fire. The old bar in the back has great character. ⊠ *411 S.W. 3rd Ave., Downtown* ☎ *503/228–5686* ⊕ *www.hubers.com.*

Rialto Poolroom Bar & Cafe. The Rialto is a large bar with several pool tables and excellent Bloody Marys. The dark, divey, and slightly edgy Jack London Bar in the basement hosts regular literary events and history talks. ⊠ *529 S.W. 4th Ave., Downtown* ☎ *503/228–7605* ⊕ *www. rialtopoolroom.com.*

Saucebox. A sophisticated crowd flocks here to enjoy colorful cocktails and trendy DJ music many evenings a week. ⊠ *214 S.W. Broadway, Downtown* ☎ *503/241–3393* ⊕ *www.saucebox.com.*

Southpark. With its extensive wine list, the Southpark wine bar is a perfect spot for a postsymphony drink. ⊠ *901 SW Salmon St., Downtown* ☎ *503/326–1300* ⊕ *www.southparkseafood.com.*

Veritable Quandary. At this old riverside restaurant, you can eat and drink on the cozy, tree-filled patio or in the glass-walled dining room. ⊠ *1220 SW 1st Ave., Downtown* ☎ *503/227–7342* ⊕ *www. veritablequandary.com.*

BREWPUBS AND MICROBREWERIES

Ringlers Annex. Sip on beer, port, or single-malt scotch in the cozy, cellar-like basement of Ringlers Annex, a pie-shaped corner pub where Stark and Burnside streets meet. Ringlers is part of the local McMenamins chain. ⊠ *1223 S.W. Stark St., Downtown* ☎ *503/384–2700* ⊕ *www. mcmenamins.com/ringlersannex.*

COFFEEHOUSES

Stumptown Coffee Roasters. Serving a true Portland coffee experience, Stumptown Coffee Roasters has five local cafés, where hip baristas, well-versed in all things coffee, whip up delicious espresso drinks. There are two locations in Downtown; the Stark Street location is adjacent to the Ace Hotel lobby. ⊠ *128 S.W. 3rd Ave., Downtown* ☎ *503/295–6144* ⊕ *stumptowncoffee.com.*

DANCE CLUBS

Fez Ballroom. The funky, Moroccan-style Fez Ballroom draws a dancing crowd with its hip-hop, goth, dance, and '80s music. ⊠ *316 S.W. 11th St., Downtown* ☎ *503/221–7262* ⊕ *www.fezballroom.com.*

GAY AND LESBIAN

Scandals. At this low-key gay bar, there's a small dance floor, a pool table, and light food service noon to closing. The plate-glass windows offer a view of Stark Street and the city's streetcars. ⊠ *1125 S.W. Stark St., Downtown* ☎ *503/227–5887* ⊕ *www.scandalspdx.com.*

LIVE MUSIC

McMenamins Crystal Ballroom. With a 7,500-square-foot springy dance floor built on ball bearings to ramp up the energy, this historic former dance hall draws local, regional, and national acts every night but Monday. Past performers include Billy Idol, Jefferson Airplane, Emmylou Harris, Death Cab for Cutie, and the Shins. ⊠ *1332 W. Burnside St., Downtown* ☎ *503/225–0047* ⊕ *www.mcmenamins.com.*

MUSIC FESTIVALS

Bite of Oregon. This festival, held in early August as a benefit for Special Olympics Oregon, features the best in the local food and wine scene with eclectic choices in live entertainment. ⊠ *Tom McCall Waterfront Park, Downtown* ☎ *503/248–0600* ⊕ *www.biteoforegon.com.*

Waterfront Blues Festival. One of the nation's premier blues festivals, the four-day Waterfront Blues Festival, a benefit for the Oregon Food Bank, has been drawing big crowds and big names in blues over the July 4 weekend since 1987. Past performers have included Keb' Mo', Susan Tedeschi, Johnny Winter, and Sharon Jones & the Dap-Kings. ⊠ *Tom McCall Waterfront Park, Downtown* ☎ *503/973–3378* ⊕ *www. waterfrontbluesfest.com.*

Portland Beer Fests

Festivals that celebrate the city's most beloved beverage are quite common in Portland. The **North American Organic Brewers Festival** (⊕ *www. naobf.org*) kicks off summer in Portland the last weekend in June, pledging to "save the planet one beer at a time." This ode to sustainability spotlights beers and ciders made with organic ingredients from across the globe. July marks the start of **Oregon Craft Beer Month** (⊕ *www. oregoncraftbeer.com*) with more than 120 beer events throughout the state. The beertastic climax is the **Oregon Brewers Festival** (⊕ *www. oregonbrewfest.com*), one of the nation's longest-running craft-beer festivals, held the last full weekend in July on the banks of the Willamette River. This sun-soaked celebration features more than 80 craft breweries, live music, and Mt. Hood as the backdrop. Portland pays tribute to the world's most legendary brewing styles at the **Portland International Beer Festival** (⊕ *www.portland-beerfest. com*) in mid-July.

PEARL DISTRICT
BARS AND LOUNGES
Bluehour. The modern bar at Bluehour draws a chic crowd for specialty cocktails such as the Savannah Sunset (vodka, strawberries, lemon, and balsamic reduction swirl). ⊠ *250 N.W. 13th Ave., Pearl District* ☎ *503/226–3394* ⊕ *www.bluehouronline.com.*

Henry's 12th Street Tavern. In a building that was once the Blitz-Weinhard brewery, Henry's 12th Street Tavern has more than 100 local and regional beers on draft, plasma-screen TVs, and a billiards room. ⊠ *10 NW 12th Ave., Pearl District* ☎ *503/227–5320* ⊕ *www.henrystavern.com.*

Oba!. Plush tans and reds with lime-green backlit walls create a backdrop for Latin American cuisine and drinks here. ⊠ *555 NW 12th Ave., Pearl District* ☎ *503/228–6161* ⊕ *www.obarestaurant.com.*

BREW PUBS AND MICROBREWERIES
BridgePort BrewPub & Restaurant. Visit the oldest microbrewery in Portland, a beautiful brick-and-ivy building that is listed on the National Register of Historic Places. Brewery tours are free and take place on Saturday at 1, 3, and 5 pm. ⊠ *1313 N.W. Marshall St., Pearl District* ☎ *503/241–3612* ⊕ *www.bridgeportbrew.com.*

Deschutes Brewery. The Portland branch of the Bend-based Deschutes Brewery has 18 beers on tap, including mainstays Mirror Pond Pale Ale, Inversion IPA, and Black Butte Porter, plus seasonal and experimental brews as well. ⊠ *210 N.W. 11th Ave, Pearl District* ☎ *503/296–4906* ⊕ *www.deschutesbrewery.com.*

LIVE MUSIC
Jimmy Mak's. Dubbed one of the world's "top 100 places to hear jazz" by *DownBeat Magazine*, Jimmy Mak's also serves Greek and Middle Eastern dishes. ⊠ *221 N.W. 10th Ave., Pearl District* ☎ *503/295–6542* ⊕ *www.jimmymaks.com* ☉ *Closed Sun.*

OLD TOWN

GAY AND LESBIAN

C.C. Slaughters Nightclub & Lounge. Attracting mostly gay men, C.C. Slaughters has a restaurant, a martini-serving bar, and a crowded dance floor. ⊠ *219 N.W. Davis Ave., Old Town* ☎ *503/248–9135* ⊕ *www. ccslaughterspdx.com.*

Embers. Open late, Embers is a popular after-hours place to dance; the club hosts regular drag shows and theme nights. ⊠ *110 NW Broadway Ave., Old Town* ☎ *503/222–3082.*

The Fox and Hounds. Popular with the gay crowd, the friendly Fox and Hounds bar serves a full menu in the evenings and brunch on Sunday. ⊠ *217 N.W. 2nd Ave., Old Town* ☎ *503/243–5530.*

LIVE MUSIC

Kells Irish Restaurant & Pub. There's terrific Irish food here as well as Celtic music nightly. ⊠ *112 S.W. 2nd Ave., Old Town* ☎ *503/227–4057* ⊕ *www.kellsirish.com.*

Roseland Theater. The Roseland Theater, which holds 1,400 people (standing-room only except for the 21+ balcony seating area), primarily stages rock and blues shows. Past performers have included Miles Davis, Pearl Jam, Bonnie Raitt, and Prince. ⊠ *8 N.W. 6th Ave., Old Town* ☎ *503/230–0033* ⊕ *www.roselandpdx.com.*

NOB HILL

BARS AND LOUNGES

Muu-Muu's Restaurant & Bar. A young hip crowd packs the cool booths at Muu-Muu's for happy hour cocktails and Asian fusion comfort food. ⊠ *612 NW 21st Ave., Nob Hill* ☎ *503/223–8169* ⊕ *www.muumuus.net.*

COFFEEHOUSES

Coffeehouse Northwest. With hardwood floors, exposed brick walls, and friendly, knowledgeable baristas, Coffeehouse Northwest serves up some of the best coffee in Portland. It's daughter store, Sterling Coffee Roasters, serves a mean cup, too. ⊠ *1951 W. Burnside St., Nob Hill* ☎ *503/248–2133.* ⊠ *417 N.W. 21st Ave., Nob Hill* ⊕ *www. sterlingcoffeeroasters.com.*

World Cup Coffee and Tea. Excellent organic coffee and espresso are for sale at this location of World Cup as well as within Powell's City of Books on Burnside. ⊠ *1740 N.W. Glisan St., Nob Hill* ☎ *503/228–4152* ⊕ *www.worldcupcoffee.com.*

NORTH

BREWPUBS AND MICROBREWERIES

Widmer Brothers Brewing Gasthaus Pub. Founded in 1984, this brewery produces more beer than any other in Oregon, and their Hefeweizen is still the top-selling craft beer in the state. Free brewery tours take place Friday, Saturday, and Sunday afternoons (reservations required). There is also a full lunch and dinner menu. ⊠ *955 N. Russell St., Eliot, North* ☎ *503/281–3333* ⊕ *www.widmerbrothers.com.*

LIVE MUSIC

Fodor's Choice **Mississippi Studios.** An intimate neighborhood music venue, with a seated
★ balcony and old Oriental carpets covering the standing-room only floor,
Mississippi Studios offers high-quality live music performances every
night of the week in a wide range of genres. Between sets, you can jump
back and forth from the adjacent BarBar, a hip, comfortable bar with a
delicious hamburger and a covered back patio. ✉ *3939 N. Mississippi,
Boise, North* ☎ *503/288–3895* ⊕ *www.mississippistudios.com.*

Ponderosa Lounge at Jubitz Truck Stop. Not your ordinary truck stop, the
Ponderosa Lounge at Jubitz Truck Stop presents live country music and
line dancing on weekends. ✉ *10350 N. Vancouver Way, East Columbia, North* ☎ *503/345–0300* ⊕ *www.portlanderinn.com/entertainment.*

NORTHEAST

BARS AND LOUNGES

Bink's. This neighborhood spot on Northeast Alberta, which offers cozy
seats around a fireplace in cold weather and an open garage door in
warm, has a pool table, a jukebox, and a friendly vibe. ✉ *2715 N.E.
Alberta St., Alberta Arts District, Northeast* ☎ *503/493–4430* ⊕ *www.
binksbar.com.*

Mint/820. Green lanterns glow on the curvy bar of this hot spot where
hip patrons sip inventive cocktails, many incorporating fresh fruit. The
cocktails are the creations of an award-winning mixologist. ✉ *820 N.
Russell St., Eliot, Northeast* ☎ *503/284–5518* ⊕ *www.mintand820.com*
☽ *Closed Sun. and Mon.*

Noble Rot Wine Bar. Perched atop a hillside building on the east side,
Noble Rot offers expansive views of the river and downtown skyline
from its outdoor patio and large south- and west-facing windows. Sip
a glass of wine from its extensive wine list or try a wine flight. ✉ *1111
E. Burnside St., 4th fl., Kerns, Northeast* ☎ *503/233–1999* ⊕ *www.
noblerotpdx.com.*

Swift Lounge. The bird-themed Swift Lounge, a popular hipster hangout,
offers a menu of Mason-jar cocktails including the Guilty Sparrow
(citrus vodka, lemongrass, and house limoncello), the Stoned Finch
(cucumber infused vodka and house elderflower syrup), and the Top-
less Robin (ginger-lemongrass infused vodka and apricot brandy).
You can order the drinks in two sizes—the 32-ounce "Fatty" or the
16-ounce "Sissy." ✉ *1932 N.E. Broadway, Sullivan's Gulch, Northeast*
☎ *503/288–3333* ⊕ *www.swiftloungepdx.com.*

LIVE MUSIC

LaurelThirst Public House. Locals crowd the LaurelThirst Public House to
eat tasty food, sit in cozy red booths, and listen to folk, jazz, country,
or bluegrass music on its tiny stage. There are pool tables in an adjoining room. ✉ *2958 NE Glisan St., Kerns, Northeast* ☎ *503/232–1504*
⊕ *www.laurelthirst.com.*

SOUTHEAST

BARS AND LOUNGES

Aalto Lounge. Artsy, hip east-siders, not to be mistaken for the jet-setters downtown, hang and drink martinis and wine at the minimalist, bubble lamped Aalto Lounge. ⊠ *3356 SE Belmont St., Belmont District, Southeast* ☎ *503/235–6041* ⊕ *www.aaltolounge.com.*

Beaker & Flask. In an unmarked gray building, the mixologists at the swanky Beaker & Flask serve innovative twists on classic cocktails like the rum-based Sal's Minion, served over coconut-water ice cubes or the tart And & And, which combines blackberry liqueur and lemon. Drink choices—which tend toward absolutely delicious—change frequently based on seasons and available ingredients. ⊠ *727 S.E. Washington St., Buckman, Southeast* ☎ *503/235–8180* ⊕ *beakerandflask.com* ⊗ *Closed Sun. and Mon.*

Caldera Public House. Located in a cozy turn-of-the-century wooden building at the foot of Mount Tabor, the candlelit Caldera Public House serves beer, wine, and cocktails over a 100-year-old oak bar, as well as a menu of soups, salads, and sandwiches (and Cajun tater tots!). Its expansive patio out back, strung with glass lights and shaded by a full canopy of trees, is one of the best in the city. ⊠ *6031 S.E. Stark, Mount Tabor, Southeast* ☎ *503/233–8242* ⊕ *calderapublichouse.com.*

Fodor'sChoice
★
Horse Brass Pub. A laid-back beer-drinking crowd fills the dark-wood Horse Brass Pub, as good an English-style pub as you will find this side of the Atlantic, with more than 50 beers on tap (including some cask-conditioned too). ■ **TIP**➜ **Try the fish and chips.** ⊠ *4534 SE Belmont St., Belmont District, Southeast* ☎ *503/232–2202* ⊕ *www.horsebrass.com.*

Fodor'sChoice
★
Sapphire Hotel. In the lobby of a former brothel, the deep red, candlelit Sapphire Hotel serves cocktails, beer, and wine with an intimate, sultry atmosphere. ⊠ *5008 S.E. Hawthorne Blvd., Hawthorne District, Southeast* ☎ *503/232–6333* ⊕ *www.thesapphirehotel.com.*

BREWPUBS AND MICROBREWERIES

Hopworks Urban Brewery. A bicycle-themed microbrewery with tasty beer and pub fare, Hopworks Urban Brewery (H.U.B. for short) occupies an industrial ski lodge–type building that's 100% renewably powered and water neutral. Hopworks BikeBar, located on the bike highway of North Williams, offers similar fare with the same bikey, eco-friendly vibe. ⊠ *2944 S.E. Powell Blvd., Creston-Kenilworth, Southeast* ☎ *503/232–4677.* ⊠ *3947 N. Williams Ave., Boise, Northeast* ☎ *503/287–6258* ⊕ *www.hopworksbeer.com.*

Lucky Labrador Brew Pub. Inside an old warehouse with high ceilings and rustic wooden tables, the Lucky Lab Brew Pub serves handcrafted ales and pub food both in the brewery and on the patio, where four-legged friends are welcome to join. The Nob Hill location, which also offers ample outdoor seating, is large and casual as well. Frequented by families with kids, the newest location in North Portland often has mediocre service. ⊠ *915 S.E. Hawthorne Blvd., Hosford-Abernethy, Southeast* ☎ *503/236–3555.* ⊠ *1700 N. Killingsworth, Overlook, North* ☎ *503/505–9511.* ⊠ *1945 N.W. Quimby St, Nob Hill* ☎ *503/517–4352* ⊕ *www.luckylab.com.*

COFFEEHOUSES

Fodor's Choice ★ **Coava Coffee Roasters.** Located next door to the roastery, the light and open, bamboo wood-filled Coava Coffee Roasters offers some of the most delicious single-origin, pour-over coffees you'll ever taste. ⊠ *1300 SE Grand Ave., Buckman, Southeast* ☎ *503/894–8134* ⊕ *coavacoffee. com.*

Common Grounds Coffee House. This coffee shop is a nice place to take a break, with plush couches and serving sandwiches, soup, and desserts. ⊠ *4321 S.E. Hawthorne Blvd., Hawthorne District, Southeast* ☎ *503/236–4835.*

Palio Dessert & Espresso House. Located in the middle of peaceful, green Ladd's Addition neighborhood, Palio has delicious desserts and espresso, and is open later than many coffee shops in the area. ⊠ *1996 SE Ladd Ave., Ladd's Addition, Southeast* ☎ *503/232–9412* ⊕ *www. palio-in-ladds.com.*

Pied Cow Coffeehouse. In a creaky old Victorian with a large, nook-filled patio, the laid-back Pied Cow serves dessert, coffee, steamers, beer, wine, and hookahs (to people 21 and older, outside only). ⊠ *3244 S.E. Belmont St., Belmont District, Southeast* ☎ *503/230–4866.*

Rimsky Korsakoffee House. Located in an odd old Victorian with a few haunted tables (you have to see them to undestand), Rimsky Korsakoffee serves up coffee, tea, and desserts. ⊠ *707 S.E. 12th Ave., Buckman, Southeast* ☎ *503/232–2640.*

Stumptown Coffee Roasters. Stumptown Coffee Roasters has three cafés on the east side. At the original site (SE Division), which opened in 1999, organic beans are still roasted on a regular basis. At The Annex (now located at Stumptown's headquarters on S.E. Salmon), patrons can participate in "cuppings," or tastings, at 3 pm each day. ⊠ *4525 S.E. Division St., Richmond, Southeast* ☎ *503/230–7702* ⊕ *stumptowncoffee.com* ⊠ *3356 SE Belmont St., Belmont District, Southeast* ☎ *503/232–8889* ⊕ *stumptowncoffee.com.*

Stumptown Coffee Roasters Annex ⊠ *100 S.E. Salmon St, Buckman, Southeast* ☎ *503/467–4123* ⊕ *stumptowncoffee.com.*

Tao of Tea. With soft music and the sound of running water in the background, the Tao of Tea serves more than 80 loose-leaf teas as well as vegetarian snacks and sweets. ⊠ *3430 S.E. Belmont St., Belmont District, Southeast* ☎ *503/736–0119* ⊕ *www.taooftea.com.*

DANCE CLUBS

Holocene. Hosting deejayed dance nights that range from '90s to bollywood to booty music, the 5,000-square-foot former auto parts warehouse gets hip crowds moving Wednesday through Saturday nights. ⊠ *1001 SE Morrison St., Buckman, Southeast* ☎ *503/239-7639* ⊕ *www. holocene.org* ☾ *Closed Sun.–Tues.*

GAY AND LESBIAN

Crush. A gay-friendly bar in Southeast, Crush serves up tasty food, strong, delicious cocktails, and DJ-fueled dance parties. ⊠ *1400 S.E. Morrison St., Belmont District, Southeast* ☎ *503/235–8150* ⊕ *crushbar. squarespace.com* ☾ *Closed Mon.*

Last Thursday Art Walk on Alberta Street

LIVE MUSIC

Aladdin Theater. The Aladdin Theater music venue, located in an old movie theater in Southeast, offers microbrews and pizza along with quality musical performances many nights of the week. ✉ *3017 S.E. Milwaukie Ave., Brooklyn, Southeast* ☎ *503/234–9694* ⊕ *www. aladdin-theater.com.*

Doug Fir Lounge. Part 1950s diner and part log cabin, the Doug Fir serves food and booze and hosts DJs and live rock shows from up-and-coming bands seven nights a week. ✉ *830 E. Burnside St., Buckman, Southeast* ☎ *503/231–9663* ⊕ *www.dougfirlounge.com.*

THE ARTS

The conundrum of delving into Portland's art scene won't be *if* you can find something to do—it will be *what* to do when you discover there's almost too much to choose from. For a city of this size, there is truly an impressive—and accessible—scope of talent from visual artists, performance artists, and musicians. The arts are alive, with outdoor sculptural works strewn around the city, ongoing festivals, and premieres of traveling Broadway shows. Top-named international acts, such as David Byrne, St. Vincent, Joan Baez, and Mumford and Sons regularly include Portland in their worldwide stops.

PERFORMANCE VENUES

The Antoinette Hatfield Hall. Home to the Portland Center for Performing Arts, this hall contains Dolores Winningstad, Newmark, and Brunish theaters and is across the street from the Arlene Schnitzer Concert

Hall. ⊠ *1111 S.W. Broadway, Downtown* ☎ *503/248–4335* ⊕ *www.pcpa.com.*

Keller Auditorium. With 3,000 seats and outstanding acoustics, Keller Auditorium hosts performances by the Portland Opera and Oregon Ballet Theater, as well as country and rock concerts and touring Broadway shows. ⊠ *222 S.W. Clay St., Downtown* ☎ *503/248–4335* ⊕ *www.pcpa.com/keller.*

The Veterans Memorial Coliseum. This 12,000-seat venue on the MAX light-rail line serves as home to the WHL Winterhawks and books 150 events a year, including rock groups, touring shows, the Ringling Brothers circus, ice-skating extravaganzas, and sporting events. ⊠ *Rose Quarter, 1 Center Ct., Lloyd District, Northeast* ☎ *503/235–8771* ⊕ *www.rosequarter.com.*

Portland Center for the Performing Arts. Portland Center for the Performing Arts hosts opera, ballet, rock shows, symphony performances, lectures, and Broadway musicals in its three venues (⇨ *Downtown in Exploring Portland).* ⊠ *1111 SW Broadway, Downtown* ☎ *503/248–4335* ⊕ *www.pcpa.com.*

Rose Garden. The 21,000-seat Rose Garden is home to the Portland Trail Blazers basketball team and the site of other sporting events and rock concerts. The arena is on the MAX light-rail line. ⊠ *Rose Quarter, 1 Center Ct., Lloyd District, Northeast* ☎ *503/235–8771* ⊕ *www.rosequarter.com.*

CLASSICAL MUSIC

The Oregon Symphony, established in 1896, is Portland's largest classical group—and one of the largest orchestras in the country. Its season officially starts in September and ends in May, but throughout the summer the orchestra and its smaller ensembles can be seen at Waterfront Park and Washington Park for special outdoor summer performances.

CHAMBER MUSIC

Chamber Music Northwest. Some of the most sought-after soloists, chamber musicians, and recording artists from the Portland area and abroad perform here during the five-week summer concert series; performances take place at Reed College, Catlin Gabel School, and the Alberta Rose Theatre. ⊠ *522 S.W. 5th Ave., Suite 920, Downtown* ☎ *503/294–6400* ⊕ *www.cmnw.org.*

OPERA

Portland Opera. The opera, its orchestra, and chorus perform five productions a year at the Keller Auditorium. ⊠ *Keller Auditorium, 222 S.W. Clay St., Downtown* ☎ *503/241–1802, 866/739–6737* ⊕ *www.portlandopera.org.*

ORCHESTRAS

FAMILY **Oregon Symphony.** Established in 1896, the symphony is Portland's largest classical group—and one of the largest orchestras in the country. Its season officially starts in September and ends in May, but throughout the summer the orchestra and its smaller ensembles can be seen at Waterfront Park and Washington Park for special outdoor performances. It also presents about 40 classical, pop, children's, and family concerts each year at the Arlene Schnitzer Concert Hall. ⊠ *923 S.W. Washington, Downtown* ☎ *503/228–1353, 800/228–7343* ⊕ *www. orsymphony.org.*

DANCE

Portland has a wonderful variety of both progressive and traditional dance companies. As part of their productions, many of these companies bring in international talent for choreography and guest performances.

BodyVox. Led by Emmy Award-winning choreographers, Body Vox performs energetic contemporary dance–theater works internationally, as well as at several locations in Portland. ⊠ *1201 N.W. 17th Ave., Pearl District* ☎ *503/229–0627* ⊕ *www.bodyvox.com.*

Do Jump! Extremely Physical Theater. Check out the creative acrobatic work of Do Jump! at the Echo Theatre near Hawthorne. ⊠ *1515 S.E. 37th Ave., Richmond, Southeast* ☎ *503/231–1232* ⊕ *www.dojump.org.*

Oregon Ballet Theatre. Oregon Ballet Theatre produces several classical and contemporary works a year, including a much-loved holiday *Nutcracker.* Most performances are at Keller Auditorium. ⊠ *818 SE 6th Ave., Buckman, Southeast* ☎ *503/222–5538, 888/922–5538* ⊕ *www. obt.org.*

White Bird Dance. Since its founding in 1997, White Bird Dance has been dedicated to bringing exciting local, regional, national, and international dance performances to Portland stages including the Arlene Schnitzer Concert Hall, Lincoln Hall at Portland State University, and the Newmark Theater. ☎ *503/245–1600* ⊕ *www.whitebird.org.*

FILM

The McMenimans "brew theaters" are a great place to catch a flick while chowing down and sipping on local beer. They are not-to-be-missed Portland landmarks when it comes to movie viewing, and offer inexpensive tickets to second-run blockbusters in uniquely renovated buildings that avoid any hint of corporate streamlining.

If you're a film buff, be sure to check out the Northwest Film Center's calendar of events for special screenings and film festivals, with genres that include international, gay, and animation. These occur throughout the year.

Cinema 21. An old-school, one-screen movie theater in Nob Hill, Cinema 21 shows independent and foreign films and hosts the annual gay and lesbian film festival. ⊠ *616 N.W. 21st Ave., Nob Hill* ☎ *503/223–4515* ⊕ *www.cinema21.com.*

CineMagic Theater. Single-screen CineMagic shows everything from mainstream to progressive to foreign to cult films, both new and second-run. ⊠ *2021 S.E. Hawthorne Blvd., Hawthorne District, Southeast* ☎ *503/231–7919* ⊕ *www.thecinemagictheater.com.*

Hollywood Theatre. A landmark movie theater that showed silent films when it first opened in 1926, the not-for-profit Hollywood Theatre screens everything from obscure foreign art films to old American classics and second-run Hollywood hits, and hosts an annual Academy Awards viewing party. ⊠ *4122 N.E. Sandy Blvd., Hollywood District, Southeast* ☎ *503/281–4215* ⊕ *www.hollywoodtheatre.org.*

Laurelhurst Theater. With a classic neon sign out front, Laurelhurst Theater serves beer and pizza and shows excellent second-run features and cult classics for only $4. ⊠ *2735 E. Burnside, Buckman, Northeast* ☎ *503/232–5511* ⊕ *www.laurelhursttheater.com.*

Living Room Theater. The sleek, upscale Living Room Theater, which has a lobby café and full bar, shows 3-D blockbuster, foreign, and independent films in auditoriums furnished with spacious but fixed movie seats and moveable couches and tables. ⊠ *341 S.W. 10th Ave., Downtown* ⊕ *pdx.livingroomtheaters.com.*

Northwest Film Center. A branch of the Portland Art Museum, the Northwest Film Center screens art films, documentaries, and independent features and presents the three-week Portland International Film Festival every February. Films are shown at the Whitsell Auditorium, next to the museum. ⊠ *1219 S.W. Park Ave., Downtown* ☎ *503/221–1156* ⊕ *www.nwfilm.org.*

THEATER

From the largest of productions to the smallest of venues, theater comes to life in Portland year-round. Comedy, puppetry, tragedy, and artistry can be found at any of these theater company performances.

Artists Repertory Theatre. The theater company performs seven to nine productions a year including regional premieres, occasional commissioned works, and classics. ⊠ *1516 S.W. Alder St., Downtown* ☎ *503/241–1278* ⊕ *www.artistsrep.org.*

Imago Theatre. Considered by some to be Portland's most outstanding innovative theater company, the Imago specializes in movement-based work for both young and old. ⊠ *17 S.E. 8th Ave., Buckman, Southeast* ☎ *503/231–9581* ⊕ *www.imagotheatre.com.*

FAMILY **Oregon Children's Theatre.** The Oregon Children's Theatre puts on three to five shows a year for school groups and families in Hatfield Hall. ⊠ *1111 S.W. Broadway, Downtown* ☎ *503/228–9571* ⊕ *www.octc.org.*

Portland Center Stage. The largest producing theater in Portland, Portland Center Stage puts on contemporary and classical works in an historic armory building, built in 1891, between September and June. ⊠ *Gerding Theater at the Armory, 128 N.W. 11th Ave., Downtown* ☎ *503/445–3700* ⊕ *www.pcs.org.*

FAMILY **Tears of Joy Puppet Theatre.** Tears of Joy Puppet Theatre stages six children's productions a year at the Portland Center for Performing Arts' Winningstad Theatre. ⊠ *Winningstad Theatre, 1111 S.W. Broadway, Downtown* ☎ *503/248–0557* ⊕ *www.tojt.org.*

SPORTS AND THE OUTDOORS

Updated by
Crystal Wood

Portlanders gravitate to the outdoors and they're well acclimated to the elements year-round—including winter's wind, rain, and cold. Once the sun starts to shine in spring and into summer, the city fills with hikers, joggers, and mountain bikers, who flock to Portland's hundreds of miles of parks, paths, and trails. The Willamette and Columbia rivers are used for boating and water sports—though it's not easy to rent any kind of boat for casual use. Locals also have access to a playground for fishing, camping, skiing, and snowboarding all the way through June, thanks to the proximity of Mt. Hood.

As for competitive sports, Portland is home to the Winterhawks, a major junior league hockey team, and the Timbers, a major league soccer team with a devout local fan base. Big-sports fervor is reserved for Trail Blazers basketball games, held at the Rose Quarter arena on the east side of the river. Travel Portland provides information on sports events and outdoor activities in the city.

PARTICIPANT SPORTS

If there's something recreational to be done outdoors, Portlanders will find a way to do it. Because of the many parks, rivers, streams, mountains, and beaches within reach of the city, this region is a playground.

BICYCLING

Bicycling is a cultural phenomenon in Portland—possibly the most beloved mode of transportation in the city. Besides the sheer numbers of cyclists you see on roads and pathways, you'll find well-marked bike lanes and signs reminding motorists to yield to cyclists.

There are more than 300 miles of bicycle boulevards, lanes, and off-street paths in Portland. Accessible maps, specialized tours, parking capacity (including lockers and sheltered racks downtown), and bicycle-only traffic signals at confusing intersections make biking in the city easy. Cyclists can find the best routes by following green direction-and-distance signs that point the way around town, and the corresponding white dots on the street surface.

BIKE RENTALS

Fat Tire Farm. For treks in Forest Park, mountain bikes can be rented at Fat Tire Farm. Reservations are not taken though. The staff here really knows their stuff. If you brought your own bike to town and it is giving you trouble, they can likely help. ⊠ *2714 N.W. Thurman St., near Forest Park, Northwest* ☎ *503/222–3276* ⊕ *www.fattirefarm.com* ⊗ *Weekdays 11–7, Sat. 10–6, Sun. 12–5.*

Waterfront Bicycle Rentals. For jaunts along the Willamette River, try renting from Waterfront Bicycles. This bike shop has most everything a visiting bicyclist needs. They have multiple types and styles of bikes for the whole family, including balance bikes for the little rider. Reservations can be made online at least 48 hours ahead. Guided bike tours are offered as well. ⊠ *10 S.W. Ash St., Suite 100, Downtown* ☎ *503/227–1719* ⊕ *www.waterfrontbikes.com* ⊗ *Weekdays 11:30–6, weekends 10–4.*

BIKE ROUTES

Department of Transportation. For information on bike routes and resources in and around Portland, visit the Department of Transportation website. You can download maps, or order "Bike There," a glossy detailed bicycle map of the metropolitan area. ⊕ *www.portlandonline.com/transportation.*

Walkers crossing the Hawthorne Bridge

Bike paths on both sides of the **Willamette River** continue south of down-town, so you can easily make a mild, several-mile loop through Water-front Park by crossing the Steel, Hawthorne, or Sellwood bridges to get from one side to the other.

Leif Erikson Drive is an 11-mile off-road ride through Northwest Port-land's Forest Park, accessible from the serene west end of Northwest Thurman Street. Leif's wide, double-track trail is popular with runners and mountain bikers, winding through a 5,000-acre city park far from the noise and distraction of neighborhood traffic. Its dense canopy occasionally gives way to river views. To reach the trailhead, bike up steep Thurman Street or shuttle there via TriMet Bus 15.

Bicycling **Sauvie Island's** 12-mile loop is a rare treat. Situated near the mouth of the Willamette River and Columbia Slough, the island is entirely rural farmland. Besides the main loop, it also offers out-and-back jaunts to beaches and pristine wetlands. To get to Sauvie Island from Portland, you can brave the 10-mile ride in the wide bike lane of U.S. 30 or shuttle your bike there via TriMet Bus 17.

The **Springwater Corridor,** when combined with the Vera Katz Eastbank Esplanade ride on the east side of the Willamette, can take you all the way from downtown to the far reaches of southeast Portland along a former railroad line. The trail heads east beginning near Sellwood, close to Johnson Creek Boulevard.

FISHING

The Columbia and Willamette rivers are major sportfishing streams with opportunities for angling virtually year-round.

OUTFITTERS

Outfitters throughout Portland operate guide services. Few outfitters rent equipment, though, so bring your own or be prepared to buy.

Northwest Flyfishing Outfitters. For all things fly-fishing, including tackle, rentals, and guided outings, head here. Destinations for the guided trips include the Deschutes, Sandy, and Willamette rivers, as well as some rivers in southwest Washington. ☒ *10910 N.E. Halsey St., Hazelwood, Northeast* ☏ *503/252–1529, 888/292–1137* ⊕ *www.flyshopnw. com* ☉ *Weekdays 9–6, Sat. 9–5.*

GOLF

There are several public and top-class golf courses within Portland and just outside the city where you can practice your putt or test your swing. Even in the wet months, Portlanders still golf—and you can bet the first clear day after a wet spell will mean courses fill up with those who have so faithfully waited for the sun.

Eastmoreland Golf Course. This is a highly regarded 18-hole, 72-par course close to the Rhododendron Gardens, Crystal Springs Lake, shopping in the Sellwood neighborhood, and Reed College. The course opened in 1917 and has a driving range. ☒ *2425 S.E. Bybee Blvd., Eastmoreland, Southeast* ☏ *503/775–2900* ⊕ *www.eastmorelandgolfcourse.com.*

Heron Lakes Golf Course. Two 18-hole, par-72 courses are available to play: the Great Blue, generally acknowledged to be the most difficult links in the greater Portland area; and the Greenback. The greens fee at the Green, as it's locally known, is $26–$37, while the fee at the Blue runs $30–$42. An optional cart at either course costs $26. Rental clubs are available. ☒ *3500 N. Victory Blvd., Kenton, North* ⊕ *west of airport, off N. Marine Dr.* ☏ *503/289–1818* ⊕ *www.heronlakesgolf.com.*

Pumpkin Ridge Golf Club. The club has 36 holes, with the 18-hole Ghost Creek par-71 course open to the public. According to *Golf Digest,* Ghost Creek is one of the best public courses in the nation. Pumpkin Ridge hosted the U.S. Women's Open in 1997 and in 2003. The greens fee is $150; the cart fee is $16. ☒ *12930 NW Old Pumpkin Ridge Rd., North Plains* ☏ *503/647–4747, 888/594–4653* ⊕ *www. pumpkinridge.com.*

Rose City Golf Course. The second oldest course in the city has one 18-hole, par-72 course. Greens fees are $31–$36; carts are $26 for 18 holes. ☒ *2200 NE 71st Ave., Madison South, Northeast* ☏ *503/253–4744* ⊕ *www.rosecitygc.com.*

PARKS

The variety of Portland's parks ensures that there's something for just about everyone, from the world's smallest park (Mill Ends) to one of the largest urban natural areas in the country (Forest Park).

Cathedral Park. Whether it's the view of the imposing and stunning Gothic St. John's Bridge or the historic significance of Lewis and Clark having camped here in 1806, this park is divine. Though there's no church, the park gets its name from the picturesque arches supporting the bridge. It's rumored that the ghost of a young girl haunts the bridge, and that may be true, but if you're told that it was designed by the same man who envisioned the Golden Gate Bridge, that's just a popular misconception. Dog lovers, or those who aren't, should take note of the off-leash area. ⊠ *N. Edison St. and Pittsburg Ave., St. John's, North* ⊙ *Daily 5 am–midnight.*

Council Crest Park. The second-highest point in Portland, at 1,073 feet, is a superb spot to watch sunsets and sunrises. If you visit on a weekday, there are far fewer folks than on the busy weekends. Along with great views of the Portland metro area, a clear day also affords views of the surrounding peaks—Mt. Hood, Mt. St. Helens, Mt. Adams, Mt. Jefferson, and Mt. Rainier. A bronze fountain depicting a mother and child has been erected in the park twice; first in the 1950s and the second in the 1990s. The peaceful piece was stolen in the 1980s, uncovered in a narcotics bust ten years later, and then returned to the park. ⊠ *3400 Council Crest Dr., Southwest Hills, Southwest* ⊙ *Daily 5 am–midnight, closed to cars after 9 pm.*

Marquam Nature Park. Itching to get a hike in but no time to get out of Portland? Just minutes from downtown are 176 acres of greenery and 5 miles of trails to explore. No playgrounds or dog parks here, just peace and quiet. Maps of trails that range from 1 to 3.5 miles are available at the shelter at the base of the trails or on the Friends of Marquam Park website. ⊠ *SW Marquam St. and SW Sam Jackson Park Rd., Homestead, Southwest* ⊕ *www.fnmp.org* ⊙ *Daily 5 am–midnight.*

Oaks Bottom Wild Refuge. Bring your binoculars, because birds are plentiful here; more than 400 species have been spotted, including hawks, quail, pintails, mallards, coots, woodpeckers, kestrels, widgeons, hummingbirds, and the sedately beautiful blue heron. The 140-acre refuge is a flood-plain wetland—rare because it is in the heart of the city. The hiking isn't too strenuous, but wear sturdy shoes, as it can get muddy; part of the park is on top of a landfill layered with soil. ⊠ *SE 7th Ave. and SE Sellwood Ave., Sellwood, Southeast* ⊙ *Daily 5 am–midnight.*

Peninsula Park & Rose Garden. The "City of Roses" moniker started here, at this park that harks back to another time. The city's oldest (1909) public rose garden (and the only sunken one) houses almost nine thousand plantings and 65 varieties of roses. The daunting task of deadheading all these flowers is covered in classes taught to volunteers twice a season. The bandstand is a historic landmark, and the last of its kind in the city. There's also a 100-year-old fountain, playground, wading pool, tennis and volleyball courts, and picnic tables. ⊠ *700 N. Rosa Parks Way, Piedmont, North* ⊙ *Daily 5 am–midnight.*

Sellwood Park. Sixteen acres of tall old pines make a visit here purely relaxing. A paved path circles the park and most of the action—ballpark, pool, football field, playground, and tennis court. Sellwood also sports a terrific location; Oaks Bottom Refuge, Oaks Amusement Park, and the Willamette River are nearby, and the Sellwood neighborhood has charming shops and restaurants, convenient for a takeout picnic. ⊠ *SE 7th Ave. and SE Miller St., Sellwood, Southeast* ⊙ *Daily 5 am–midnight.*

Tryon Creek State Natural Area. Portland is chock-full of parks, but this is the only state park within city limits. And at 670 acres, there's plenty of room for all its admirers. The area was logged starting in the 1880s, and the natural regrowth has produced red alder, Douglas fir, big leaf maple, and western red cedar, giving home to more than 50 bird species. The eastern edge has a paved trail, in addition to 14 miles of trails for bikes, hikers, and horses. Before heading to the trails, stop by the nature center to check out the exhibits and topographical relief map. ⊠ *SW Boones Ferry Rd. and SW Terwilliger Blvd., Collins View, Southwest* ☎ *503/636–4398* ⊕ *www.tryonfriends.org* ⊘ *Daily 7 am–8 pm, Nature Center 9–4.*

SPECTATOR SPORTS

Since Portland isn't home to a large national football or baseball team, fans tend to show a lot of support for the NBA's Portland Trail Blazers and MLS's Portland Timbers.

BASKETBALL

Portland Trail Blazers. The National Basketball Association's Portland Trail Blazers play in the Rose Garden Arena, which can hold up to 20,000 spectators. Whether attending a game or concert, the MAX train pulls up just a couple blocks from the arena front door. ⊠ *Rose Garden, 1 N. Center Ct., Rose Quarter, North* ☎ *503/797–9617* ⊕ *www.trailblazers.com.*

ICE HOCKEY

Portland Winterhawks. Part of the Western Hockey League, the Portland Winterhawks play home games September to March at Memorial Coliseum or next door at the Rose Garden Arena. The MAX train stops just a couple of blocks away. Driving and parking to the venue can be a hassle and pricey. ⊠ *Memorial Coliseum, 300 N. Winning Way, Rose Quarter, North* ☎ *503/236–4295* ⊕ *www.winterhawks.com.*

SOCCER

Portland Timbers. Portland's major-league soccer team plays at the downtown Jeld-Wen Field from April through September. The city has many ardent soccer fans known as the Timbers Army. Sitting near this group means a raucous time with drumming, chanting, and cheers. The MAX stops in easy walking distance from the stadium. ⊠ *Jeld-Wen Field, 1844 S.W. Morrison St., Downtown* ☎ *503/553–5555 Portland Timbers ticket sales, 503/553–5400 Jeld-Wen Field* ⊕ *www.portlandtimbers.com.*

SHOPPING

Updated by
Crystal Wood

One of Portland's greatest attributes is its neighborhoods' dynamic spectrum of retail and specialty shops. The Pearl District is known for chic interior design and high-end clothing boutiques. Trek over to the Hawthorne area and you'll discover wonderful stores for handmade jewelry, clothing, and books. The Northwest has some funky shops for housewares, clothing, and jewelry, while in the Northeast there are fabulous galleries and crafts. Downtown has a blend of it all as well as

2

bigger options, including the Pioneer Place mall and department stores such as Nordstrom's and Macy's.

No Portland shopping experience would be complete without a visit to the nation's largest open-air market, Saturday Market, where an array of talented artists converge to peddle handcrafted wares beyond your wildest do-it-yourself dreams. It's also open Sunday.

DOWNTOWN

Shopping downtown is not only fun, it's also easy, thanks to easy transportation access and its proximity to many of Portland's hotels. Locally based favorites Nike and Columbia Sportswear both have major stores downtown; REI has one in the Pearl District.

CLOTHING

Magpie. For funky retro garb that dates from the '50s through the '80s look no further than Magpie. Lots of jewelry, shoes, dresses, coats, and even rhinestone tiaras can be found here. ⊠ *520 S.W. 9th Ave., Downtown* ☎ *503/220–0920* ⊘ *Weekdays 12–7.*

Mario's. Portland's best store for fine men's and women's clothing, Mario's carries designer lines by Prada, Dolce & Gabbana, Etro, and Loro Piana—among others. ⊠ *833 S.W. Broadway, Downtown* ☎ *503/227–3477* ⊕ *www.marios.com* ⊘ *Mon.–Sat. 10–6, Sun. 12–5.*

Nike Portland. Nike's flagship retail store has the latest and greatest in swoosh-adorned products. The high-tech setting has athlete profiles, photos, and interactive displays. ⊠ *638 S.W. 5th Ave., Downtown* ☎ *503/221–6453* ⊕ *www.nike.com* ⊘ *Mon.–Sat. 10–8, Sun. 11–6.*

Portland Outdoor Store. If you want authentic western gear—saddles, Stetsons, boots, or cowboy shirts—head to this store, which stubbornly resists all that is trendy, both in clothes and decor. ⊠ *304 S.W. 3rd Ave., Downtown* ☎ *503/222–1051* ⊘ *Weekdays 9:30–5:30, Sat. 11–4.*

Portland Pendleton Shop. This store stocks clothing by the famous local apparel maker. The store entrance is at S.W. Salmon Street and S.W. 4th Avenue. ⊠ *900 S.W. 5th Ave., Suite 96, Downtown* ☎ *503/242–0037* ⊕ *www.pendleton-usa.com* ⊘ *Weekdays 9:30–5:30, Sat. 10–5, Sun. 12–5.*

GIFTS

Made in Oregon. This store, which sells books, smoked salmon, local wines, Pendleton woolen goods, carvings made of myrtle wood, and other products made in the state, also has shops at Portland International Airport, the Lloyd Center, Washington Square, and Clackamas Town Center. ⊠ *Pioneer Place Mall, 340 S.W. Morrison St., Suite 1300, Downtown* ☎ *503/241–3630, 866/257–0938* ⊕ *www.madeinoregon. com* ⊘ *Mon.–Sat. 10–8, Sun. 11–6.*

JEWELRY

Maloy's Jewelry Workshop. This store specializes in fine antique pieces, including some from the 18th century. Rare and vintage designs fill the sparkling glass cases. ⊠ *717 SW 10th Ave., Downtown* ☎ *503/223–4720* ⊕ *www.maloys.com* ⊘ *Weekdays 10–5:30, Sat. 11–5.*

The Real Mother Goose. Selling mostly handcrafted, unique artistic pieces, current collections can include woodworking, furniture, blown glass and jewelry. Dangling earrings that incorporate copper wire wrapped around brilliant, colored glass are a customer favorite. The clothing store next door, Changes Designs to Wear, is part of The Real Mother Goose as well. ⊠ *901 S.W. Yamhill St., Downtown* ☎ *503/223–9510* ⊕ *www.therealmothergoose.com* ⊙ *Mon.–Thurs. 10–5:30, Fri.–Sat. 10–6.*

MALLS AND DEPARTMENT STORES

Nordstrom. Seattle-based Nordstrom sells fine-quality apparel and accessories and has a large footwear department. If you can get a table by the window, the café upstairs offers a nice view of Pioneer Square. ⊠ *701 S.W. Broadway, Downtown* ☎ *503/224–6666* ⊕ *shop.nordstrom.com.*

Nordstrom Rack. Bargain lovers should head for the Nordstrom Rack outlet across from Pioneer Place Mall. ⊠ *245 SW Morrison St., Downtown* ☎ *503/299–1815* ⊕ *shop.nordstrom.com.*

Pioneer Place Mall. This mall has more than 80 upscale specialty shops (including Coach, J. Crew, Louis Vuitton, Tiffany & Co., and Fossil) in a three-story, glass-roof atrium setting. You can find good, inexpensive ethnic foods from more than a dozen vendors in the Cascades Food Court in the basement. Paradise Bakery is known for fresh home-baked breads and delicious chocolate-chip cookies. Suki Hana has some yummy soups and noodle dishes. ⊠ *700 SW 5th Ave., Downtown* ☎ *503/228–5800* ⊕ *www.pioneerplace.com.*

OUTDOOR SUPPLIES

Columbia Sportswear. A local legend and global force in recreational outdoor wear, Columbia Sportswear is especially strong in fashionable jackets, pants, and durable shoes. A second smaller store can be found in the Sellwood neighborhood at 1323 S.E. Tacoma Street. ⊠ *911 S.W. Broadway, Downtown* ☎ *503/226–6800* ⊕ *www.columbia.com* ⊙ *Weekdays 9:30–7, Sat. 9:30–5, Sun. 11–6.*

SHOES

Clogs 'n' More. With locations on the west and east sides of the city, this shoe store carries quality clogs from brands such as Dansko, Troentorp, and Sanita, as well as other shoes. ⊠ *717 S.W. Alder St., Downtown* ☎ *503/279–9358* ⊕ *www.clogsnmore.com* ⊙ *Mon.–Sat. 10–6, Sun. 11–5.*

TOYS

Finnegan's Toys and Gifts. Downtown Portland's largest toy store, Finnegan's stocks artistic, creative, educational, and other types of toys. ⊠ *820 S.W. Washington St., Downtown* ☎ *503/221–0306* ⊕ *www. finneganstoys.com* ⊙ *Mon.–Sat. 10–6, Sun. 11–5.*

OLD TOWN/CHINATOWN

MARKETS

Fodor'sChoice
★

Portland Saturday Market. The open-air Portland Saturday Market, which runs from March to December on weekends (including Sunday, despite the name), is a favorite place to experience the people of Portland and

Portland Saturday Market

also find one-of-a-kind handcrafted home, garden, and gift items. ✉ *Waterfront Park and Ankeny Plaza, near Burnside Bridge, Old Town/Chinatown* ☎ *503/222–6072* ⊕ *www.saturdaymarket.org* ☽ *Mar. 2–Dec. 24, Sat. 10–5, Sun. 11–4:30.*

PEARL DISTRICT

What was once an industrial area is now a classy, hip, and dapper neighborhood to shop, dine and explore in. An entire day could be spent here sipping cocktails, checking out fashionable stores and galleries. The Pearl District is located north of Burnside Street, from NW Broadway to NW 15 Street.

BOOKS

Fodor's Choice **Powell's City of Books.** The largest retail store of used and new books in ★ the world (with more than 1.5 million volumes) covers an entire city block on the edge of the Pearl District. It also carries rare and collectible books. There are also three branches in the Portland International Airport. ✉ *1005 W. Burnside St., Pearl District* ☎ *503/228–4651* ⊕ *www. powells.com* ☽ *Daily 9 am–11 pm.*

GALLERIES

Butters Gallery, Ltd. Monthly exhibits of the works of nationally known and local artists are on view in this 5,000-square-foot Pearl District loft space. ✉ *520 N.W. Davis St., Pearl District* ☎ *503/248–9378* ⊕ *www. buttersgallery.com* ☽ *Tues.–Fri. 10–5:30, Sat. 11–5.*

First Thursday. This gallery walk the first Thursday of every month gives art appreciators a chance to check out new exhibits while enjoying music and wine. Typically the galleries, which are largely located in the Pearl District, are open in the evening from 6 to 9, but hours vary. Find out which galleries are participating on the website. Be prepared for a lively scene including throngs of people, street musicians, and local art vendors. ⊠ *Pearl District* ☎ *503/295–4979* ⊕ *www. firstthursdayportland.com.*

Quintana Galleries. The only Native American art gallery in Portland, Quintana focuses on Pacific Northwest Coast, Navajo, and Hopi art, pottery, and jewelry. ⊠ *124 N.W. 9th Ave., Pearl District* ☎ *503/223–1729, 800/321–1729* ⊕ *www.quintanagalleries.com* ☉ *Tues.–Sat. 10:30–5:30, First Thursday 10:30–8:30.*

OUTDOOR SUPPLIES

REI. You'll find clothes and accessories for hiking, biking, camping, fishing, bicycling, or just about any other outdoor activity you can possibly imagine here. REI has a great 100% satisfaction guarantee, which makes buying expensive gear less risky. Other locations include Clackamas, Hillsboro, and Tualatin. ⊠ *1405 N.W. Johnson St., Pearl District* ☎ *503/221–1938* ⊕ *www.rei.com* ☉ *Mon.–Sat. 10–9, Sun. 10–7.*

NOB HILL

ANTIQUES

Shogun's Gallery. The specialty here is Japanese and Chinese furniture, especially the lightweight wooden Japanese cabinets known as *tansu.* Also here are chairs, tea tables, altar tables, armoires, ikebana baskets (originally for flower arrangements), and Chinese wooden picnic boxes, most at least 100 years old and at reasonable prices. ⊠ *1111 N.W. 23rd Ave., Nob Hill* ☎ *503/224–0328* ⊕ *www.shogunsgallery.com* ☉ *Mon.– Sat. 11–6, Sun. 12–5.*

BOOKS

New Renaissance Bookshop. Between Overton and Pettygrove, this bookstore is dedicated to New Age and metaphysical books and tapes. ⊠ *1338 N.W. 23rd Ave., Nob Hill* ☎ *503/224–4929* ⊕ *www.newrenbooks.com* ☉ *Mon.–Thurs. and Sat. 10–9, Fri.10–9:30, Sun. 10–6.*

CLOTHING

Hanna Andersson. This retail store, which sells high-quality, comfortable clothing for children and families, is next to the company's corporate office. Clothing is also sold through their outlet store in Oswego Towne Square, south of Portland. ⊠ *327 N.W. 10th Ave., Nob Hill* ☎ *503/321–5275* ⊕ *www.hannaandersson.com* ☉ *Weekdays 10–6, Sat. 10–5, Sun. 11–5.*

GALLERIES

Laura Russo Gallery. A longtime staple of the Portland arts scene, the Laura Russo Gallery displays contemporary Northwest work of all styles, including landscapes and abstract expressionism. ⊠ *805 N.W. 21st Ave., Nob Hill* ☎ *503/226–2754* ⊕ *www.laurarusso.com* ☉ *Tues.– Fri. 11–5:30, Sat. 11–5.*

Twist. This huge space in Nob Hill is well stocked with contemporary American ceramics, glass, furniture, sculpture, and handcrafted jewelry often with a pop, whimsical touch. ⊠ *30 N.W. 23rd Pl., Nob Hill* ☎ *503/224–0334* ⊕ *www.twistonline.com* ⊙ *Mon.–Sat., 10–6, Sun. 11–6.*

GIFTS

Elephants Delicatessen. In addition to offering the best eat-in or take-out soups, salads, and desserts, Elephants Delicatessen has a vast gourmet food, cooking utensils, and household section. ⊠ *115 N.W. 22nd Ave., Nob Hill* ☎ *503/299–6304* ⊕ *www.elephantsdeli.com* ⊙ *Mon.–Sat. 7 am–7:30 pm, Sun. 9:30–6:30.*

La Vita Vera. Find Mamma Ro, La Gabbianella, and Ricardo Marzi Italian tabletop and home accessories here, including tablecloths and napkins. ⊠ *1801 N.W. Upshur St., Nob Hill* ☎ *503/274–0687* ⊕ *www.lavitavera.com* ⊙ *Tues.–Sat. 10–4.*

Moonstruck Chocolate Cafe. Even without getting a nod from Oprah in her magazine, Moonstruck would still be known as a chocolatier extraordinaire. There are five cafés in the Portland metro area, including Pioneer Place Mall. All offer made-to-order hot chocolate, cocoa, shakes, and mochas, as well as truffles, chocolate bars, and dynamic holiday treats. ⊠ *526 N.W. 23rd Ave., Nob Hill* ☎ *503/542–3400* ⊕ *www.moonstruckchocolate.com* ⊙ *Weekdays 8–6, Sat. 10–6, Sun. 10–5.*

Stella's on 21st. At Stella's there are eccentric, colorful, and artsy items for the home, including lamps, candles, and decorations, as well as jewelry. ⊠ *1108 NW 21st Ave., Nob Hill* ☎ *503/295–5930* ⊕ *www.stellason21st.com* ⊙ *Mon.–Sat. 10–6, Sun. 11–5.*

SHOES

Zelda's Shoe Bar. These two connected boutiques in Nob Hill carry a sophisticated, highly eclectic line of women's clothes, accessories, and shoes. ⊠ *633 N.W. 23rd Ave., Nob Hill* ☎ *503/226–0363* ⊕ *www.zeldaspdx.com* ⊙ *Mon.–Sat. 10–6, Sun. noon–5.*

NORTHEAST

BOOKS

Broadway Books. This fabulous independent bookstore has books on all subjects, including the Pacific Northwest. The staff is unpretentious and helpful. ⊠ *1714 N.E. Broadway, Sullivan's Gulch, Northeast* ☎ *503/284–1726* ⊕ *www.broadwaybooks.net* ⊙ *Mon.–Sat. 10–7, Sun. noon–5.*

In Other Words. A nonprofit bookstore, In Other Words carries feminist literature and hosts feminist events and readings. For *Portlandia* fans, the Women & Women First bookstore sketches were filmed here (though the staff is undoubtedly friendlier and more helpful than on the show). ⊠ *14 N.E. Killingsworth St., Humboldt, Northeast* ☎ *503/232–6003* ⊕ *www.inotherwords.org* ⊙ *Tues.–Sat., noon–7.*

CLOTHING

Tumbleweed. Carrying fun and stylish designer clothing, you might describe Tumbleweed as "country chic," for the woman who likes to wear flirty feminine dresses with cowboy boots. There's also unique baby and toddler clothing in their children's shop next door, called Grasshopper. ⊠ *1812 N.E. Alberta St., Alberta Arts District, Northeast* ☎ *503/335–3100* ⊕ *www.tumbleweedboutique.com* ☉ *Sun. and Mon. 11–5, Tues.–Fri. 11–6, Sat. 10–6.*

GALLERIES

Last Thursday Arts Walk. The Alberta Arts District hosts an arts walk on the last Thursday of each month. An answer to the ever-popular First Thursday, this one is a bit more Portland and little less posh. ⊠ *N.E. Alberta St., Alberta Arts District, Northeast* ☎ *503/972–2206* ⊕ *www. lastthursdayonalberta.com.*

Talisman Gallery. Formed in 1999, the cooperative Talisman Gallery showcases two artists each month—they may include local painters and sculptors. ⊠ *1476 NE Alberta St., Alberta Arts District, Northeast* ☎ *503/284–8800* ⊕ *talismangallery.com* ☉ *Fri.–Sun. 12–6; Last Thurs. 5:30–9.*

MALLS

Lloyd Center. On the MAX light-rail line, Lloyd Center has more than 170 shops (including Nordstrom, Sears, and Macy's), an international food court, a multiscreen cinema, and an ice-skating pavilion. The mall is within walking distance of Northeast Broadway, which has many specialty shops, boutiques, and restaurants. ⊠ *2201 Lloyd Center, Lloyd District, Northeast* ☎ *503/282–2511* ⊕ *www.lloydcenter.com.*

MUSIC

Music Millennium. The oldest record store in the Pacific Northwest, Music Millennium stocks a huge selection of new and used music in every possible category, including local punk groups. The store's offering of in-store performances is well worth checking out. ⊠ *3158 E. Burnside St., Kerns, Northeast* ☎ *503/231–8926* ⊕ *www.musicmillennium.com* ☉ *Mon.–Sat. 10–10, Sun. 11–9.*

SOUTHEAST

ANTIQUES

Stars Antique Mall. Portland's largest antiques mall, Stars has two stores across the street from each other in the Sellwood–Moreland neighborhood. Since it rents its space to about 75 antiques dealers, you might find anything from low-end 1950s kitsch to high-end treasures. The sister location across the street, Stars and Splendid, gives even more opportunities to find that special treasure. The surrounding neighborhood has restaurants, boutiques, and gift stores. ⊠ *7027 S.E. Milwaukie Ave., Sellwood, Southeast* ☎ *503/235–5990* ⊕ *starsantique.com* ☉ *Daily 11–6.*

BOOKS

ExLibris Anonymous. Journals and sketchbooks are the focus at ExLibris Anonymous, which is filled with thousands of recycled books with colorful, kitschy, or striking covers. Once you choose a book, it's transformed into a spiral journal for you using the original cover and some of the book's original pages interspersed within the blank journal pages. With so many books to choose from—science, art, classics, children's, travel, and many more—it's the perfect spot to pick up a unique and well-priced gift. ✉ *916 S.E. 29th Ave., Belmont, Southeast* ☎ *360/350–2927* ⊕ *www.bookjournals.com* ⊗ *Mon. and Fri. 10–5, Sat. 12–5; call for additional hrs.*

Powell's Books for Home and Garden. The inventory at this Powell's location focuses on cooking and gardening books, with a sizable selection of crafting books and unique gift items. There is also a small gourmet grocery adjoining the store. ✉ *3747 S.E. Hawthorne Blvd., Hawthorne District, Southeast* ☎ *503/235–3802* ⊕ *www.powells.com* ⊗ *Mon.–Sat. 9–9, Sun. 9–8.*

CLOTHING

Eight Women. This tiny boutique "for mother and child" has baby clothes, women's nightgowns, jewelry, and handbags. ✉ *3614 SE Hawthorne Blvd., Hawthorne District, Southeast* ☎ *503/236–8878.*

Union Rose. For unique women's fashion and accessories designed and made in Portland, check out Union Rose. Though there are scores of dresses for any season, there is also more everyday wear like hoodies and hats. ✉ *7909 S.E. Stark St., Montavilla, Southeast* ☎ *503/287–4242* ⊕ *www.unionrosepdx.com* ⊗ *Tues.–Sat. 10:30–6, Sun. 12–5.*

GIFTS

Pastaworks. Fancy deli foods, organic produce, beer, wine, cookware, and fresh pasta are all sold at Pastaworks. Sandwiches, salads, and small plates for dining-in are available in the afternoon and early evenings at this location. A second location can be found on N.W. 21st Avenue. ✉ *3735 S.E. Hawthorne Blvd., Richmond, Southeast* ☎ *503/232–1010* ⊕ *www.pastaworks.com* ⊗ *Mon.–Sat. 9:30–7, Sun. 10–7.*

Perfume House. Hundreds of brand-name fragrances for women and men, including hard-to-find scents, can be found at Perfume House. Perfume is taken very seriously here; this store is an olfactory experience and the place to go to find your signature scent, not just a trip to the perfume counter at a large department store. ✉ *3328 S.E. Hawthorne Blvd., Richmond, Southeast* ☎ *503/234–5375* ⊗ *Mon.–Sat. 10–5.*

OUTDOOR SUPPLIES

Next Adventure Sports. It all about the gear here. Next Adventure Sports carries new and used sporting goods, including camping gear, snowboards, kayaks, and mountaineering supplies. Kayak classes and Outdoor School provide plenty of opportunities to get out and enjoy Oregon like a local. Their Paddle Sports Center is just a few blocks southeast at 624 S.E. 7th Avenue. ✉ *426 S.E. Grand Ave., Buckman, Southeast* ☎ *503/233–0706* ⊕ *www.nextadventure.net* ⊗ *Weekdays 10–7, Sat. 10–6, Sun. 11–5.*

SHOES

Imelda's Designer Shoes. This upscale boutique has funky, fun shoes for women with flair. ✉ *3426 SE Hawthorne Blvd., Hawthorne District, Southeast* ☎ *503/233–7476* ⊕ *imeldas.com* ⊗ *Weekdays 10–7, Sat. 10–6, Sun. 11–6.*

TOYS

Kids at Heart. This small, colorful toy store sells models and stuffed animals as well as other toys. ⊠ *3445 S.E. Hawthorne Blvd., Sunnyside, Southeast* ☎ *503/231–2954* ⊕ *www.kidsathearttoys.com* ☉ *Mon.–Sat. 10–7, Sun. 10–6.*

Cloud Cap Games. There's more than just run-of-the-mill board games at Cloud Cap. For children and grown-ups alike, the games here challenge the mind and provide hours of entertainment. There's a room with tables to play or try out a game. The knowledgeable owners and staff may sit down and join in the fun and are always happy to answer questions and offer suggestions. ⊠ *1226 S.E. Lexington St., Sellwood, Southeast* ☎ *503/505–9344* ⊕ *www.cloudcapgames.com.*

THE OREGON COAST

WELCOME TO THE OREGON COAST

TOP REASONS TO GO

★ **A beach for everyone:** The Oregon Coast has breathtaking beaches, from romantic, bluffy stretches perfect for linking fingers with loved ones to creature-teeming tide pools great for exploring with kids.

★ **Blown glass:** Artisan glass shops dot the coastline, where you can craft your own colorful creations.

★ **Ride the dunes:** Whether you're a screaming dune-buggy passenger or an ATV daredevil, southern Oregon's mountainous sand dunes are thrilling.

★ **Par a hole:** Oregon's golf Shangri-La, Bandon Dunes, has four beach courses of pure bliss.

★ **Wine and dine:** You don't have to spend a lot to enjoy fresh seafood, rich microbrews, and local wines. There are delicious coastal eateries for every budget.

1 North Coast. The north coast is the primary getaway for Portland and Vancouver residents. Its lighthouse-dotted shoreline stretches from the mouth of the Columbia River at Oregon's far northwestern corner south to Pacific City. The 90-mile region includes the revitalized working community of Astoria, the art-fueled and refined Cannon Beach, the well-photographed Manzanita Beach, and Pacific City, where a colorful fleet of dories dots the wide, deep beach.

2 Central Coast. The 75-mile stretch from Lincoln City to Florence offers whale-watching, incomparable seafood, shell-covered beaches, candy confections, and close-up views of undersea life. At the north end, in Lincoln City, visitors can indulge in gaming, shopping, golfing, and beachcombing. The harbor town of Depoe Bay is a center for whale-watching, and nearby Newport offers a stellar aquarium and science center. It's also home to one of Oregon's largest fishing fleets. Yachats is a true vacation community, where the only demands are to relax and enjoy. Visitors will want to check in at the Sea Lion Caves in Florence, and enjoy crabbing, shopping, or riding the Oregon dunes.

3 South Coast. From the heart of Oregon dunes country in Reedsport to the southernmost Oregon town of Brookings, riding, hiking, and even surfing along the 134-mile south coast is a rollicking thrill. Coos Bay is a center for timber, commercial fishing, and commerce. There's also clamming, gaming, sport fishing, and plenty of shopping. Bandon offers a wealth of golfing, camping, lighthouse gazing, and cranberries. Port Orford has gorgeous beach landscapes and windsailing, while Gold Beach, farther south, bathes in sunshine, and gives its visitors a chance to rip up the Rogue River on a jet boat. At Oregon's farthest southwestern corner is Brookings—the "Banana Belt" of the Oregon Coast.

GETTING ORIENTED

3

Oregon's coastline begins in the north in the town of Astoria, which lies at the mouth of the Columbia River on the Washington state line. It is a 363-mile drive south along U.S. Highway 101 to reach the small town of Brookings at Oregon's southwestern corner, just 6 miles from the California border. The Oregon Coast is bordered by the Pacific Ocean on the east and by the Coast Range on the west. Farther east across the Coast Range is the Willamette Valley, which includes the larger Oregon communities of Portland, Salem, Corvallis, and Eugene.

EXPLORING OREGON'S BEST BEACHES

Oregon's 300 miles of public coastline is the backdrop for thrills, serenity, rejuvenation, and romance. From yawning expanses of sand dotted with beach chairs to tiny patches bounded by surf-shaped cliffs, they're yours to explore.

(above) Surfing the Oregon Coast (opposite page, top) Oregon Dunes National Recreation Area (opposite page, bottom) Cannon Beach Sandcastle Contest

Most awe-inspiring are the massive rock formations just offshore in the northern and southern sections of the coast, breaking up the Pacific horizon. Beaches along the north coast, from Astoria to Pacific City, are perfect for romantic strolls on the sands. The central-coast beaches, from Lincoln City to Florence, are long and wide, providing perfect conditions for sunbathers, children, clam diggers, horseback riders, and surfers. The southern-coast beaches from Reedsport to Brookings are less populated, ideal for getting away from it all.

In late July and August the climate is kind to sun worshipers. During the shoulder months, keep layers of clothing handy for the unpredictable temperature swings. Winter can be downright blustery, but plenty of beachfront hotels cater to visitors who enjoy bundling up to walk along the wet, wind-whipped surf.

GLASS FLOATS: FINDERS KEEPERS

Since 1997, between mid-October and Memorial Day, more than 2,000 hand-crafted glass floats made by local artists have been hidden along Lincoln City's 7½-mile public beach. If you happen to come upon one, call ☎ 800/452–2151 to register it, and find out which artist made it. While antique glass floats are extremely rare, these new versions make great souvenirs.

THE OREGON COAST'S BEST BEACHES

Cannon Beach. In the shadow of glorious **Haystack Rock,** this beach is wide, flat, and perfect for bird-watching, exploring tide pools, building sand castles, and romantic walks in the sea mist. Each June the city holds a **sand-castle contest,** drawing artists and thousands of visitors. The rest of the year the beach is far less populated. The beachfront town is a cultural destination featuring much of Oregon's finest dining, lodging, and boutique shopping.

Pacific City. This beach is postcard perfect, with its colorful fleet of dories sitting on the sand. Dozens of them lie tilted in between early-morning fishing excursions to catch lingcod, surf perch, and rockfish. Like Cannon Beach, this town also has a huge (less famous) Haystack Rock that provides the perfect scenic backdrop for horseback riders, beachcombers, and people with shovels chasing sand-covered clams. With safe beach breaks that are ideal for beginners and larger peaks a bit to the south, this is a great spot for surfers. Storm-watchers love Pacific City, where winds exceeding 75 miles per hour twist Sitka spruce, and tides deposit driftwood and logs on the beach. Most stay inside to watch, but there are plenty of bold (or crazy) folks who enjoy the blast in their faces.

Winchester Bay. One reason the Pacific Northwest isn't known for its amusement parks is because nature hurls more thrills than any rattling contraption could ever provide. This certainly is true at **Oregon Dunes National Recreation Area.** Here riders of all-terrain vehicles (ATVs) will encounter some of the most radical slips, dips, hills, and chills in the nation. It is the largest expanse of coastal sand dunes in North America, extending for 40 miles, from Florence to Coos Bay. More than 1.5 million people visit the dunes each year. For those who just want to swim, relax, and marvel at the amazing expanse of dunes against the ocean, there are spaces off-limits to motorized vehicles. Overlooking the beach is the gorgeous **Umpqua River Lighthouse.**

Samuel H. Boardman State Scenic Corridor. It doesn't get any wilder than this—or more spectacular. The 12-mile strip of forested, rugged coastline is dotted with smaller sand beaches, some more accessible than others. Here visitors will find the amazing **Arch Rock** and **Natural Bridges** and can hike 27 miles of the **Oregon Coast Trail.** Beach highlights include **Whaleshead Beach, Secret Beach,** and **Thunder Rock Cove,** where you might spot migrating gray whales. From the 345-foot-high **Thomas Creek Bridge** you can take a moderately difficult hike down to admire the gorgeous, jagged rocks off **China Beach.**

Updated by
Lee van der
Voo

The Oregon Coast truly epitomizes the finest in Pacific Northwest living. Thanks to its friendly seaside towns, outstanding fresh seafood, and cozy wine bars sprinkled among small hotels and resorts, visitors have the region's finest choices for sightseeing, dining, and lodging. But the true draw here is the beaches, where nature lovers will delight at their first site of a migrating whale or a baby harbor seal sitting on a rock.

Oregon's coastline is open to all; not a grain of its 300 miles of white-sand beaches is privately owned. The coast's large and small communities are linked by U.S. Highway 101, which runs the length of the state. It winds past sea-tortured rocks, brooding headlands, hidden beaches, historic lighthouses, and tiny ports. This is one of the most picturesque driving routes in the country, and should not be missed. Embracing it is the vast, gunmetal-gray Pacific Ocean, which presents a range of moods with the seasons. On summer evenings it might be glassy and reflective of a romantic sunset. In winter the ocean might throw a thrilling tantrum for storm-watchers sitting snug and safe in a beachfront cabin.

Active visitors can indulge in thrills from racing up a sand dune in a buggy to making par at Bandon Dunes, one of the nation's finest golf experiences. Bicyclists can pedal along misty coastline vistas, cruising past historic lighthouses. Boaters can explore southern-coast rivers on jet boats, or shoot a rapid on a raft. If the weather turns, indoor venues such as the Oregon Coast Aquarium capture the imagination.

Shoppers will be equally engaged perusing fine-art galleries in Toledo, Newport, or Cannon Beach; for more quirky shopping fun, giggle in the souvenir shops of Lincoln City while eating fistfuls of caramel corn or chewing saltwater taffy.

THE OREGON COAST PLANNER

WHEN TO GO

December through June are generally rainy months, but once the fair weather comes coastal Oregon is one of the most gorgeous, greenest places on earth. July through September offer wonderful, dry days for beachgoers. Autumn is also a great time to visit, as the warm-enough weather is perfect for crisp beachcombing walks followed by hearty harvest meals with local ales.

Even with the rain, coastal winter and spring do have quite a following. Many hotels are perfectly situated for storm-watching, and provide a romantic proposition. Think of a toasty fire, sweet music, a smooth Oregon Pinot, and your loved one, settled in to watch the waves dance upon a jagged rocky stage.

FESTIVALS

If you're looking for one time of year to experience what friendly frivolity can be found on the coast, check out the **Cannon Beach Sandcastle Contest** in May—if you can find a room or a parking spot. The **Newport Seafood and Wine Festival** occurs the last full weekend in February, and calls itself the premier seafood and wine event of the West Coast. Dozens of wineries are represented at this expansive celebration, which also features myriad crafts and eateries. In Bandon each October the **Cranberry Festival** comprises a fair and parade.

GETTING HERE AND AROUND

AIR TRAVEL

The north coast is accessible from **Astoria Regional Airport** (AST) (☎ 800/860–4093 or 503/741–3300), which has daily flights from Portland on SeaPort Airlines. The central coast has daily flights into **Newport Municipal Airport** (ONP) (☎ 541/867–3655) on SeaPort Airlines. The southern coast has flights from its new **Southwest Oregon Regional Airport** (OTH) (☎ 541/756–8531) in North Bend to Portland and San Francisco on United Express. Taxis are available at all airports; Hertz car rental is at the Astoria and Southwest airports.

Portland's airport is roughly 100 miles away from both Astoria and Lincoln City, and the drive takes about two hours; Newport is 150 miles and a three-hour drive away. **OmniShuttle** (☎ 800/741–5097) provides shuttle service from Eugene airport to the coast. The fare to Yachats is $140. It is more economical to rent a car.

BUS TRAVEL

Greyhound (☎ 800/231–2222 ⊕ www.greyhound.com) serves Coos Bay, Newport, Toledo, Florence, Astoria, and Cannon Beach, connecting them with Grants Pass, Eugene, Corvallis, Salem, and Portland. **Sunset Empire Transportation** (☎ 503/861–7433 ⊕ www.ridethebus.org) travels between Portland and Astoria seven days a week, and serves the north coast cities of Astoria, Warrenton, Hammond, Gearhart, and Cannon Beach. **Porter Stage Lines** (☎ 541/269–7183 ⊕ www.porterstageline.com) connects Florence, Coos Bay, and Reedsport with Eugene six days weekly. Closed Saturdays.

CAR TRAVEL

Driving the coast is one of the singular pleasures of visiting Oregon. Car-rental agencies are available in the coast's larger towns; a branch of Enterprise is in Newport, Hertz is at the airports. U.S. 101 runs the length of the coast, sometimes turning inland for a few miles. The highway enters coastal Oregon from Washington State at Astoria and from California near Brookings. U.S. 30 heads west from Portland to Astoria. U.S. 20 travels west from Corvallis to Newport. Highway 126 winds west to the coast from Eugene. Highway 42 leads west from Roseburg toward Coos Bay.

RESTAURANTS

Deciding which restaurant has the best clam chowder is just one of the culinary fact-finding expeditions you can embark upon along the Oregon Coast. Chefs here take full advantage of the wealth of sturgeon, chinook, steelhead, and trout found in coastal rivers. Fresh mussels, shrimp, and oyster shooters are also standard fare in many establishments. Newport's bounty is its Dungeness crab. When razor clams are in season, they appear as a succulent addition to restaurant menus throughout the state. Also popular are desserts made from Oregon's wealth of blueberries, marionberries, and huckleberries.

Away from the upscale resorts, most restaurants tend to be low-key and affordable. There are cozy pubs and bistros, and tasty fish-and-chips are easy to come by. In addition, Oregon Coast restaurants proudly serve reds and whites from Willamette Valley wineries and rich ales from local or on-site breweries. *Prices in the reviews are the average cost of a main course at dinner or, if dinner is not served, at lunch.*

HOTELS

The Oregon Coast offers a pleasant variety of properties for visitors who either wish to wallow in luxury, stay at a beachside golf course, watch storms through picture windows, or take river-running fishing trips. There are plenty of chains in the area, as well as an eclectic assortment of properties: fascinating bed-and-breakfasts hosted by friendly folks with stories to tell, properties perched on cliffs, and hotels set in the midst of wilderness and hiking trails.

Properties in much of the North and Central coast fill up fast in the summer, so book in advance. Between June and October hotel rates nudge up for many properties, but with some research you'll find plenty that keep their rates fairly steady throughout the year. Many will require a minimum two-night stay on a summer weekend. *Prices in the reviews are the lowest cost of a standard double room in high season.*

TOURS

Marine Discovery Tours. Sealife cruises, departing throughout the day, are conducted on a 65-foot excursion boat *Discovery*, with inside seating for 49 people and two viewing levels. Its public cruise season is March to October, while reserved group tours are welcome throughout the year. ✉ *345 SW Bay Blvd., Newport* ☎ *800/903–2628* ⊕ *www. marinediscovery.com.*

VISITOR INFORMATION

Central Oregon Coast Association ⊠ *137 NE 1st St., Newport* ☎ *503/265–2064, 800/767-2064* ⊕ *www.coastvisitor.com.* **Eugene, Cascades & Coast Adventure Center** ⊠ *754 Olive St., Eugene* ☎ *541/484-5307* ⊕ *www. eugenecascadescoast.org.* **Oregon Coast Visitors Association** ⊠ *137 NE 1st St., Newport* ☎ *541/574-2679, 888/628-2101* ⊕ *www.visittheoregoncoast.com.*

NORTH COAST

Every winter Astoria celebrates fisherman poets: hardworking men and women who bare their souls as to what makes their relationship to Oregon's north-coast waters so magical. It's easy to understand their inspiration, whether in the incredibly tempestuous ocean or the romantic beaches. Throw in Victorian homes, tony art galleries, and memorable wine bars and restaurants, and you have yourself one heck of a vacation.

This is the primary beach playground for residents of Portland. What distinguishes the region historically from other areas of the Oregon Coast are its forts, its graveyard of shipwrecks, Lewis and Clark's early visit, and a town—Astoria—that is closer in design and misty temperament to San Francisco than any other in the West. Just south, Cannon Beach has more amazing cheese, quality ales, and fine-dining venues than any other coastal town.

ASTORIA

96 miles northwest of Portland.

The mighty Columbia River meets the Pacific at Astoria, the oldest city west of the Rockies. It is named for John Jacob Astor, owner of the Pacific Fur Company, whose members arrived in 1811 and established Fort Astoria. In its early days Astoria was a placid amalgamation of small town and hard-working port city. With rivers rich with salmon, the city relied on its fishing and canning industries. Settlers built sprawling Victorian houses on the flanks of Coxcomb Hill; many of the homes have since been restored and are no less splendid as bed-and-breakfast inns or as stages and backdrops for a recent spate of movies. In recent years the city itself has awakened with a greater variety of trendy dining and lodging options, staking its claim as a destination resort town and cultivating its cinematic appeal. But it retains the soul of a fisherman's town, celebrated each February during its Fisher Poets Gathering. Astoria has wonderful views from most areas, and a richly treed backdrop to the east, yet it remains a working waterfront and there is little public beach access in the town proper—you have to cross the bridge and go from Fort Stevens in Warrenton.

GETTING HERE AND AROUND

Astoria is about a two-hour drive from Portland on U.S. Highway 30. It's also accessible from Washington on U.S. Highway 101. SeaPort Airlines offers an air shuttle between Portland and Seattle and Astoria's airport. The airport is 7 miles from downtown Astoria, with taxi

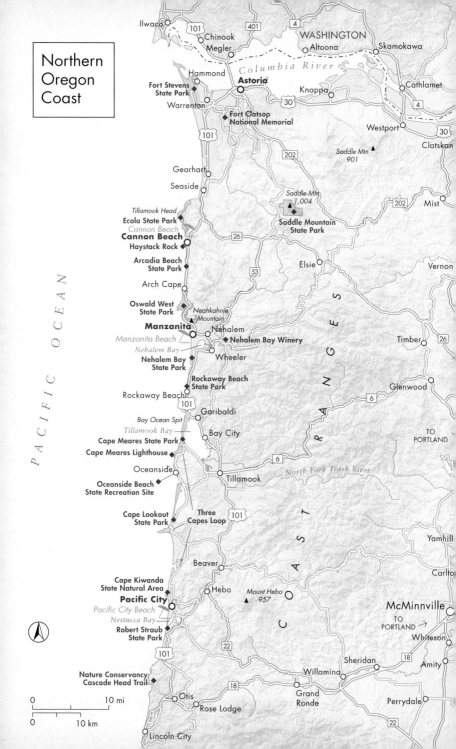

Northern Oregon Coast

Ilwaco
101
Chinook
Megler
401
4
WASHINGTON
Altoona
Skamokawa

Columbia River

Hammond
Astoria
Knappa
Cathlamet

Fort Stevens
State Park
Warrenton
30
4

Fort Clatsop
National Memorial
Westport
30

Clatskan

202
Saddle Mtn
901

Gearhart
Saddle Mtn
1,004
202
Mist

Seaside
Saddle Mountain
State Park

Tillamook Head
Ecola State Park
Cannon Beach
Cannon Beach
Haystack Rock
26
Elsie
Vernon

Arcadia Beach
State Park
53

Arch Cape

Oswald West
State Park
Neahkahnie
Mountain

R
A
N
G
E
S

Manzanita
Nehalem
Timber
26

Manzanita Beach
Nehalem Bay Winery

Nehalem Bay
Wheeler

Nehalem Bay
State Park

Rockaway Beach
State Park
Glenwood

Rockaway Beach
101
Garibaldi
6

Bay Ocean Spit
Tillamook Bay
Bay City
TO
PORTLAND

Cape Meares State Park
Cape Meares Lighthouse
6

Oceanside
Tillamook
North Fork Trask River

Oceanside Beach
State Recreation Site

C
O
A
S
T

Cape Lookout
State Park
Three
Capes Loop
101

Yamhill

Carlto

Beaver

Cape Kiwanda
State Natural Area
Hebo
Mount Hebo
957

Pacific City
McMinnville

Pacific City Beach
Nestucca Bay
TO
PORTLAND →

Robert Straub
State Park
Whiteson

R
A
N
G
E
S

22

Nature Conservancy
Cascade Head Trail
101
18
Amity

Sheridan
18

Willamina

Otis
Grand
Ronde
Perrydale

Rose Lodge
22

Lincoln City

PACIFIC OCEAN

0 ——— 10 mi
0 ——— 10 km

service and car rental available. **Sunset Empire** (☏ *503/861–7433* ⊕ *www. ridethebus.org*) buses connect Portland with the northern coastal cities of Astoria, Warrenton, Hammond, Gearhart, and Cannon Beach.

ESSENTIALS

Visitor Information Astoria–Warrenton Area Chamber of Commerce ⊠ *111 W. Marine Dr.* ☏ *503/325–6311, 800/875–6807* ⊕ *www.oldoregon.com.*

EXPLORING

Astoria Column. For the best view of the city, the Coast Range, volcanic Mt. St. Helens, and the Pacific Ocean, scamper up the 164 spiral stairs to the top of the Astoria Column. When you get to the top, you can throw a small wooden plane and watch it glide to earth; each year some 35,000 gliders are tossed. The 125-foot-high structure sits atop Coxcomb Hill, and was patterned after Trajan's Column in Rome. There are little platforms to rest on if you get winded, or, if you don't want to climb, the column's 500 feet of artwork, depicting important Pacific Northwest historical milestones, are well worth study. ⊠ *16th St. S, 1 mile south of downtown Astoria* ☏ *503/325–2963* ⊕ *www. astoriacolumn.org* 🎫 *$1 per car donation* ☾ *Daily dawn–dusk.*

Astoria Riverfront Trolley. Also known as "Old 300," this is a beautifully restored 1913 streetcar that travels for 4 miles along Astoria's historic riverfront. The hour-long ride gives you a close-up look at the waterfront from the Port of Astoria to the East Morring Basin; the Columbia River; and points of interest in between. ⊠ *1095 Dwayne St.* ☏ *503/325–6311* ⊕ *www.oldoregon.com/visitor-info/entry/Astoria-Riverfront-Trolley* 🎫 *$1 per boarding, $2 all-day pass* ☾ *Fri.–Sun. 10–5 (hours change seasonally; check website for details).*

FAMILY
Fodor's Choice
★

Columbia River Maritime Museum. One of Oregon's best coastal attractions illuminates the maritime history of the Pacific Northwest and provides visitors with a sense of the perils of guiding ships into the mouth of the Columbia River. Guests can experience what it was to pilot a tugboat and participate in a Coast Guard rescue on the Columbia River Bar. There's the actual bridge of a WWII-era U.S. Navy destroyer, the U.S. Coast Guard lightship *Columbia*, and a 44-foot Coast Guard motor lifeboat. A captivating exhibit displays the personal belongings of some of the ill-fated passengers of the 2,000 ships that have foundered here since 1811. ⊠ *1792 Marine Dr.* ☏ *503/325–2323* ⊕ *www.crmm.org* 🎫 *$12* ☾ *Daily 9:30–5.*

Flavel House. The Queen Anne-style mansion helps visitors imagine what life was like for the wealthy in late-19th-century Astoria. It rests on parklike grounds covering an entire city block, and is listed on the National Register of Historic Places. Completely restored, its three-story octagon tower is an area landmark. It was built for George Flavel, an influential Columbia River bar pilot and businessman who was one of the area's first millionaires. Visits start in the Carriage House interpretive center. ⊠ *441 8th St.* ☏ *503/325–2203* ⊕ *www.cumtux.org* 🎫 *$5* ☾ *May–Sept., daily 10–5; Oct.–Apr., daily 11–4.*

FAMILY Fodor's Choice ★ **Fort Clatsop National Memorial.** See where the 30-member Lewis and Clark Expedition endured a rain-soaked winter in 1805–06, hunting, gathering food, making salt, and trading with the local Clatsops, Chinooks, and Tillamooks. This memorial is a faithful replica of the log fort depicted in Clark's journal. The park has evolved into a 3,000-acre, forested wonderland, including an exhibit hall, gift shop, film, and trails. Park rangers dress in period garb during the summer and perform such early-19th-century tasks as making fire with flint and steel. Hikers will enjoy the 1.5-mile Netul Landing trail and the 6.5-mile Fort to Sea trail. ✉ *92343 Fort Clatsop Rd., 5 miles south of Astoria* ☎ *503/861–2471* 🌐 *www.nps.gov/lewi* 🎟 *$3* 🕓 *Daily 9–5 (summer 9–6).*

FAMILY **Fort Stevens State Park.** This earthen fort at Oregon's northwestern tip was built during the Civil War to guard the Columbia River against attack. None came until World War II, when a Japanese submarine fired upon it. The fort still has cannons and an underground gun battery. The park has year-round camping, with full hook-up sites and 15 yurts. There are also bike paths, boating, swimming, hiking trails, and a short walk to a gorgeous, wide beach where the corroded skeleton of the *Peter Iredale* pokes up through the sand. This century-old English four-master shipwreck is a reminder of the nearly 2,000 vessels claimed by these treacherous waters. ✉ *100 Peter Iredale Rd, 8½ miles west of Astoria via Hwy. 101 and Warrenton, Hammond* ☎ *503/861–1671, 800/457–5687, 503/861–1470* 🌐 *www.visitfortstevens.com* 🎟 *$5 per vehicle* 🕓 *Mid-May–Sept., daily 10–6; Oct.–mid-May, daily 10–4.*

Oregon Film Museum. Housed in the old Clatsop County Jail, this museum celebrates Oregon's long history of filmmaking and contains artifacts from and displays about prior productions. The location is apt because it was featured prominently in famous cult film *The Goonies*. The state's film productions date back to 1908 for *The Fisherman's Bride*. Oregon has helped give birth to such classics as *The General*, *The Great Race*, *One Flew Over the Cuckoo's Nest*, *Paint Your Wagon*, *Animal House*, and *Twilight*, leading some to call the state Hollywood North. *Kindergarten Cop*, *The Ring II*, *Free Willy I* and *II*, and *Short Circuit* are among those filmed in Astoria. The Astoria-Warrenton Chamber of Commerce sells a tour guide ($2) to filmed sites, a fun way to see the city's oft-unsung landmarks, especially during the annual Goonies festival, typically held in June. ✉ *732 Duane St.* ☎ *503/325–2203* 🌐 *www.oregonfilmmuseum.org* 🎟 *$4* 🕓 *May–Sept. daily 10–5; Oct.–Apr. daily 11–4.*

WHERE TO EAT

$ CAFÉ FAMILY 🍴 **Blue Scorcher Bakery Café.** "Joyful work, delicious food, and strong community," is this family-friendly café's rallying cry. It serves up everything from Huevos Scorcheros (poached eggs with rice, beans, cheese, and salsa) and organic, handcrafted breads to a variety of foods using local, fair trade, and organic ingredients. The offerings change with the seasons, but there's always a vegan or gluten-free option. This workers collective also has a Pie-of-the-Month Club. Big windows overlook the Columbia river, and there's a children's play area. [$] *Average main: $10* ✉ *1493 Duane St.* ☎ *503/338–7473* 🌐 *www.bluescorcher.com* 🕓 *No dinner.*

$$ SEAFOOD Fodor's Choice ★ 🍴 **Clemente's.** Serving possibly the best seafood on the Oregon Coast, chefs Gordon and Lisa Clemente are making a significant critical and popular splash in Astoria. Grounded in Mediterranean cuisine from Italy and the Adriatic Coast, Clemente's inventive specials feature the freshest catches of that day, from a succulent sea-bass salad to a hearty sturgeon sandwich—all dished up for reasonable prices. Dungeness crab cakes stuffed with crab rather than breading, and wild scallop fish-and-chips liven up a varied menu. Not interested in fish? Try the spaghetti with authentic meatballs. The Clementes have a strong commitment to locally sourced ingredients and environmentally friendly practices. [$] *Average main: $22* ✉ *1198 Commercial St.* ☎ *503/325–1067* 🌐 *www.clementesrestaurant.com* 🕒 *No lunch Mon.*

$$ ECLECTIC 🍴 **Columbian Cafe.** Locals love this unpretentious diner that defies categorization by offering inventive, fresh seafood and spicy vegetarian dishes, and meats cured and smoked on the premises. Open for breakfast, lunch, and dinner, it serves simple food, such as crepes with broccoli, cheese, and homemade salsa for lunch; grilled salmon and pasta with a lemon-cream sauce for dinner. The restaurant isn't shy about its culinary prowess, claiming that the experience "will change your life." Dishes are served by a staff that usually includes owner/chef Uriah Hulsey. Come early; this place always draws a crowd. [$] *Average main: $23* ✉ *1114 Marine Dr.* ☎ *503/325–2233* 🌐 *www.columbianvoodoo.com/cafe* 💳 *No credit cards* 🕒 *Closed Mon. and Tues.*

WHERE TO STAY

For expanded hotel reviews, visit Fodors.com.

$$$$ HOTEL Fodor's Choice ★ 🏨 **Cannery Pier Hotel.** From every room in this captivating property there's a gorgeous view of the mighty Columbia River flowing into the Pacific Ocean, and it's almost hypnotic to watch the tugboats shepherding barges to and fro. **Pros:** amazing river views; great in-room amenities; hotel hot tub and day spa; outstanding restaurants nearby. **Cons:** no on-site restaurant or room service. [$] *Rooms from: $299* ✉ *10 Basin St.* ☎ *503/325–4996, 888/325–4996* 🌐 *www.cannerypierhotel.com* 🛏 *46 rooms, 8 suites* 🍽 *Breakfast.*

$$ HOTEL 🏨 **Hotel Elliott.** This upscale, five-story hotel stands in the heart of Astoria's historic district and retains the elegance of yesteryear, updated with modern comforts like cozy underfloor heating in the bathrooms. **Pros:** captures the city's historic ambience beautifully; every effort made to infuse the rooms with upscale amenities; popular wine bar. **Cons:** some areas have a lingering smell of cigar smoke; no on-site dining. [$] *Rooms from: $179* ✉ *357 12th St.* ☎ *877/378–1924, 503/325–2222* 🌐 *www.hotelelliott.com* 🛏 *32 rooms* 🍽 *Breakfast.*

CANNON BEACH

25 miles south of Astoria.

Cannon Beach is a mellow, trendy place to enjoy art, wine, and fine dining, and to take in the sea air. Shops and galleries selling surfing gear, upscale clothing, local art, wine, coffee, and food line Hemlock Street, Cannon Beach's main thoroughfare. One of the most charming hamlets on the coast, the town has beachfront homes and hotels. On the downside, the Carmel of the Oregon coast can be more expensive and crowded than other towns along Highway 101.

Every May the town hosts the Cannon Beach Sandcastle Contest, for which thousands throng the beach to view imaginative and often startling works in this most transient of art forms.

GETTING HERE AND AROUND

Cannon Beach is about an hour and a half's drive from Portland on U.S. Highway 26, and 25 miles south of Astoria on U.S. Highway 101. **Sunset Empire** (☎ *503/861–7433 ⊕ www.ridethebus.org*) buses connect Portland with the northern coastal cities of Astoria, Warrenton, Hammond, Gearhart, and Cannon Beach.

ESSENTIALS

Visitor Information Cannon Beach Chamber of Commerce ⊠ *207 N. Spruce St., Cannon Beach* ☎ *503/436–2623* ⊕ *www.cannonbeach.org.*

EXPLORING

Haystack Rock. Towering over the broad, sandy beach is a gorgeous, 235-foot-high dome that is one of the most-photographed natural wonders on the Oregon Coast. ▪▪▪**TIP→** For safety, stay off the rock and enjoy the view from the beach. The rock is temptingly accessible during low tide, but the Coast Guard regularly airlifts stranded climbers from its precipitous sides, and falls have claimed numerous lives over the years.

EN ROUTE

A portion of the Oregon Trail crosses the summit of **Neahkahnie Mountain,** just south of Cannon Beach. Cryptic carvings on the beach rocks below and old Native American legends of shipwrecked Europeans have sustained the belief that survivors of a sunken Spanish galleon buried a fortune in doubloons somewhere on the side of the 1,661-foot-high mountain. U.S. 101 climbs 700 feet above the Pacific, providing dramatic views and often hair-raising curves as it winds along the flank of the mountain. There's a moderate but steep 3-mile climb to the summit, gaining 900 feet of elevation.

WHERE TO EAT

$$
IRISH
× **Irish Table.** This restaurant has made a favorable splash into Cannon Beach's dining scene. Built adjacent to the Sleepy Monk café, it serves seasonal food with an Irish twist, such as potato kale soup and its heralded Irish stew. Other offerings include a perfect steak or delicate fresh halibut. Start with chicken-bacon chowder or the curried mussels, and soak up the sauce with slices of piping-hot soda bread. Naturally, there are plenty of libations, including Irish whiskey. It's a terrific stop for people seeking something a little different at the coast. $ *Average main: $17* ⊠ *1235 S. Hemlock St., Cannon Beach* ☎ *503/436–0708* ☉ *Closed Wed. and Jan. No lunch.*

$
CAFÉ
× **Sleepy Monk.** In a region famous for its gourmet coffee, one small roaster brews a cup more memorable than any chain. Sleepy Monk attracts java aficionados on caffeine pilgrimages from near and far to sample it's specially roasted, certified organic, and fair trade beans. They are roasted without water, which adds unnecessary weight. Local, fresh pastries are stacked high and deep. If you're a coffee fan, this is your

Shangri-la. If you are a tea fan, there's a good selection, including herbal and green teas. The Irish Table restaurant next door is under the same management. $ *Average main: $5* ✉ *1235 S. Hemlock St., Cannon Beach* ☎ *503/436–2796* ⊕ *www.sleepymonkcoffee.com* ☽ *Mon.–Thurs.*

$$$$
EUROPEAN
Fodor'sChoice
★

✕ **Stephanie Inn Restaurant.** As diners enjoy a romantic view of Haystack Rock, this upscale hotel's four-star dining room prepares a new menu nightly, crafting exquisite, four-course, prix-fixe dinners using fresh, local ingredients. Diners can expect dishes such as butternut squash risotto, cedar plank–roasted salmon, savory duck confit, and a lemon-curd tart with wild berry sauce. Naturally, it has an extensive regional and international wine list. The view, cuisine, and attentive service combine to make it one of the finest dining experiences in the Pacific Northwest. $ *Average main: $59* ✉ *2740 S. Pacific St., Cannon Beach* ☎ *503/436–2221, 800/633–3466* ⊕ *www.stephanie-inn.com* ⚓ *Reservations essential.*

WHERE TO STAY

For expanded hotel reviews, visit Fodors.com.

$$$$
B&B/INN

⌂ **Arch Cape Inn & Retreat.** Between the artsy beach communities of Manzanita and Cannon Beach, this romantic getaway property—away from the summer hordes—lies along some of the most gorgeous stretch of coast in the region. **Pros:** elegant, distinctive rooms; fireplaces great in winter; most rooms have terrific ocean views; free Wi-Fi. **Cons:** 200 yards from the beach; not a family destination. $ *Rooms from: $268* ✉ *31970 E. Ocean La., Cannon Beach* ☎ *503/436–2800, 800/436–2848* ⊕ *www.archcapeinn.com* ⮐ *10 rooms* ⦿ *Breakfast.*

$$$$
RESORT

⌂ **Ocean Lodge.** Designed to capture the feel of a 1940s beach resort, this lodge is perfect for special occasions and romantic getaways. **Pros:** beachfront location; spacious rooms; turndown service; warm cookies delivered to rooms. **Cons:** one guest bemoaned the lack of privacy on the balcony. $ *Rooms from: $239* ✉ *2864 S. Pacific St., Cannon Beach* ☎ *503/436–2241, 888/777–4047* ⊕ *www.theoceanlodge.com* ⮐ *45 rooms* ⦿ *Breakfast.*

$$$$
RESORT
Fodor'sChoice
★

⌂ **Stephanie Inn.** One of the coastline's most beautiful views is paired with one of its most splendid hotels, where the focus is firmly on romance, superior service, and luxurious rooms. **Pros:** one of the finest romantic getaways in Oregon; lots of little extras included. **Cons:** expensive; not for families with younger children; some minimum stay requirements. $ *Rooms from: $419* ✉ *2740 S. Pacific St., Cannon Beach* ☎ *503/436–2221, 800/633–3466* ⊕ *www.stephanie-inn.com* ⮐ *27 rooms, 14 suites* ⦿ *Breakfast.*

SHOPPING

Cannon Beach Art Galleries. The numerous art galleries that line Cannon Beach's Hemlock Street are an essential part of the town's spirit and beauty. A group of 12 galleries featuring beautifully innovative works in ceramic, bronze, photography, painting, and other mediums have collaborated to form the Cannon Beach Gallery Group. Through its website, it helps to promote exhibitions and special events for all 10 venues. ✉ *Hemlock St., Cannon Beach* ⊕ *cbgallerygroup.com.*

Puffin Kite Festival, Cannon Beach

SPORTS AND THE OUTDOORS
BEACHES

FAMILY
Fodor'sChoice
★

Cannon Beach and Ecola State Park. Beachcombers love Cannon Beach for its often low foamy waves and the wide stretch of sand that wraps the quaint community, making it ideal for fair-weather play or for hunting down a cup of coffee and strolling in winter. This stretch can get feisty in storms, however, which also makes Cannon Beach a good place to curl up indoors and watch the show. Haystack Rock sits just to the south of town, one of 1,853 protected rocks that's part of the Oregon Ocean Island Wildlife Refuge, providing a nesting habitat for birds. Continue south past Tolovana Park—a playground located in the flood plain—to find the quiet side of Cannon Beach with a bevy of tide pools and few other souls. To the north of town, the beach gives way to Ecola State Park, a site where William Clark spotted a beached whale in 1806 and visitors still come to view them offshore during the twice-yearly migrations. From here, Sitka spruce and barbecues feature along the sands. A 6-mile trail first traced by Lewis and Clark runs from this spot all the way to Seaside. **Amenities:** parking; toilets. **Best for:** partiers; walking. ⊠ *Hwy. 101, Cannon Beach* ☎ *503/436–2844, 800/551–6949* ⊕ *www. cannon-beach.net.*

MANZANITA

20 miles south of Cannon Beach.

Manzanita is a secluded seaside community with only a few more than 500 full-time residents. It's on a sandy peninsula peppered with tufts of grass on the northwestern side of Nehalem Bay, a popular windsurfing destination. It is a tranquil small town, but its restaurants, galleries, and 18-hole golf course have increased its appeal to tourists.

GETTING HERE AND AROUND

Manzanita is in Tillamook County, a little under two hours from Portland on U.S. Highway 26. The town sits on Highway 101, about 40 miles south of Astoria and 27 miles north of Tillamook. The nearest airport is in Astoria. Tillamook County's bus, **The Wave** (☎ *503/815–8283* 🌐 *www.tillamookbus.com*), leaves from Portland's Union Station. The bus connects Manzanita, Tillamook, and Pacific City.

EXPLORING

Nehalem Bay Winery. Established in 1974, this winery is known for its Pinot Noir, Chardonnay, blackberry, and plum fruit wines. The winery also has a busy schedule of events, with concerts, barbecues, an occasional pig roast, children's activities, and a bluegrass festival the third week of August. ✉ *34965 Hwy. 53, Nehalem Bay, 3 miles south of Manzanita* ☎ *503/368–9463* 🌐 *www.nehalembaywinery.com* 🕒 *Daily 9–6.*

WHERE TO EAT AND STAY

For expanded hotel reviews, visit Fodors.com.

$ AMERICAN 🍴 **San Dune Pub.** Once just a tavern, the Sand Dune is now a local magnet for delicious seafood, bodacious burgers, sweet-potato fries, and, on Tuesdays, baby back ribs. On weekends they serve a cream-based seafood bisque, with lobster, crab, bay shrimp and other fish. There are 17 beers on tap, regular live music ($5 cover charge), and a 50-inch screen for sports, so it's a one-stop shop. Patio seating on nicer days is a bonus, particularly if you brought the dog along. [$] *Average main: $12* ✉ *127 Laneda Ave.* ☎ *503/368–5080* 🌐 *www.sandunepub.com* 🕒 *Closed Sun.*

QUICK BITE

Karla's Smokehouse. This weather-beaten yellow building along U.S. 101 is home to some of the best smoked fish on the Oregon Coast. Still produced on-site by Karla, the salmon, halibut, tuna, and oysters hold their moisture long after absorbing her long-nurtured house bastings and spices. There's no place to eat here, and Karla doesn't take credit cards, but a passerby with a pocket of cash and a good loaf of bread and cheese will quickly be in the way of a most rewarding picnic. Pre-orders are taken by phone, and be advised: when it's gone for the day, it's gone. ✉ ***2010 U.S. 101, just north of downtown, Rockaway Beach*** ☎ ***503/355-2362*** 🌐 ***www.karlassmokehouse.com*** 💳 ***No credit cards*** 🕒 ***Fri., Sat. and some weekdays; phone to check.***

$$ B&B/INN 🏨 **Inn at Manzanita.** Shore pines around this 1987 Scandinavian structure give upper-floor patios a tree house feel, and it's just half a block from the beach. **Pros:** wonderful ambience with a Japanese garden atmosphere; very light and clean; good for families. **Cons:** 20-day cancellation notice required; two-night minimum stay on weekends. [$] *Rooms from: $179* ✉ *67 Laneda Ave.* ☎ *503/368–6754* 🌐 *www.innatmanzanita.com* 🛏 *13 rooms, 1 penthouse* 🍽 *No meals.*

SPORTS AND THE OUTDOORS

BEACHES

Manzanita Beach and Nehalem Bay State Park. The long stretch of white sand that separates the Pacific Ocean from the town of Manzanita is as loved a stretch of coastline as the next, its north side sidled up to Neahkanie Mountain, right where the mountain puts its foot in the ocean. The beach is frequented by vacationers, day-trippers, kite flyers, and dogs on its north end, but it extends a breezy 7 miles to the tip of Nehalem Bay State Park, accessible on foot over sand or by car along the road. At the south end of the park's parking lot, a dirt horse trail leads all the way to a peninsula's tip, a flat walk behind grassy dunes. Cross to the right for a secluded patch of windy sand on the ocean, or to the left for a quiet, sunny place in the sun on Nehalem Bay, out of the wind. **Amenities:** toilets. **Best for:** sunset; walking. ⊠ *Manzanita.*

RECREATIONAL AREAS

Oswald West State Park. Adventurous travelers will enjoy a sojourn at one of the best-kept secrets on the Pacific coast, at the base of Neahkahnie Mountain. Park in one of the two lots on U.S. 101 and hike a half-mile trail. There are several trails to the beach that lead to the Cape Falcon overlook or to the Oregon Coast Trail. The spectacular beach has caves and tidal pools. The trail to the summit (about 2 miles south of the parking lots marked only by a "hikers" sign) provides rewarding views of the surf, sand, forest, and mountain. Come in December or March and you might spot pods of gray whales. ⊠ *U.S. 101 just north of Manzanita* ☎ *800/551–6949* ⊕ *www.oregonstateparks.org* 🖼 *Free* ⊙ *Daily dawn–dusk.*

GOLF

Manzanita Golf Course. This short, 9-hole course is a fun, coastal option for a quick, pleasant round. Designed by Ted Erickson, it offers tree-lined fairways, easy walking, and a 5th hole with a 60-foot drop to the fairway below. With only 280 yards from the back tees, it provides players with a great chance for an eagle. The course is open year-round, and has a full-service pro shop. The driving range is open May to September. Call for reservations, since many other vacationers have the same idea. ⊠ *908 Lakeview Dr.* ☎ *503/368–5744* ⊕ *www.oregongolf. com/courses/manzanita/manzanita-gc* 🖼 *$10–$20.*

NIGHTLIFE

Vino Manzanita Wine Bar. The best place in Manzanita for a glass of wine and live guitar background music, this tiny place is tucked away from the Manzanita nightlife, and perfect for a couple's night out or an evening with a good friend. The tapas menu is small but tasty. Enjoy outdoor seating in summer. ⊠ *387 Laneda Ave, Manzanita* ☎ *503/368–8466* ⊕ *www.facebook.com/vinomanzanita.*

PACIFIC CITY

24 miles south of Tillamook.

There's a lot to like about Pacific City, mostly that it's 3 miles off of Oregon's busy coastal Highway 101. That means fewer sputtering recreation vehicles or squeaking truck brakes breaking up the serenity

Three Capes Loop

Coastal views from the Three Capes Loop

The **Three Capes Loop,** a gorgeous 35-mile byway off U.S. 101, winds along the coast between Tillamook and Pacific City, passing three distinctive headlands—Cape Meares, Cape Lookout, and Cape Kiwanda. Bayocean Road heading west from Tillamook passes what was the thriving resort town of Bay Ocean, which washed into the sea more than 30 years ago. A road still crosses the levy to Bayocean, and along the beach on the other side you can find the remnants of an old hotel to the north. The panoramic views from the north end of the peninsula are worth the walk. A warm and windless road returns hikers on the bayside.

WHAT YOU'LL SEE

Cape Meares State Park. Cape Meares State Park is on the northern tip of the Three Capes Loop. The restored **Cape Meares Lighthouse,** built in 1890 and open to the public May to September, provides a sweeping view over the cliff to the caves and sea lion rookery on the rocks below. A many-trunked Sitka spruce known as the Octopus Tree grows near the lighthouse parking lot. ⊠ *Three Capes Loop, 10 miles west of Tillamook* ☎ *800/551–6949* ⊕ *www. oregonstateparks.org* ⌦ *Free* ⊙ *Park daily dawn–dusk. Lighthouse Apr.– Oct., daily 11–4.*

Cape Lookout State Park. Located south of the beach towns of Oceanside and Netarts, this park includes a fairly easy 2-mile trail—marked on the highway as "wildlife viewing area"— that leads through giant spruces, western red cedars, and hemlocks, and ends with views of Cascade Head to the south and Cape Meares to the north. Wildflowers, more than 150 species of birds, and migrating whales passing by in early April make this trail a favorite with nature lovers. The park has a picnic area overlooking the sea and a year-round campground. ⊠ *Three Capes Loop, 8 miles south of Cape Meares, Oceanside* ☎ *800/551– 6949* ⊕ *www.oregonstateparks.org* ⌦ *Day use $5* ⊙ *Daily dawn–dusk.*

Cape Kiwanda State Natural Area. Huge waves pound the jagged sandstone cliffs and caves here, and the much-photographed, 235-foot-high **Haystack Rock** juts out of the Pacific Ocean to the south. Surfers ride some of the longest waves on the coast, hang gliders soar above the shore, and beachcombers explore tidal pools and take in unparalleled ocean views. ⊠ *Three Capes Loop, 15 miles south of Cape Lookout* ☎ *800/551–6949* ⊕ *www.oregonstateparks.org* ⌦ *Free* ⊙ *Daily sunrise–sunset.*

of the sea. Also, there's no backup at the town's only traffic light—a blinking-red, four-way stop in the center of town. There's just the quiet, happy ambience of a town living the good life in the midst of extraordinary beauty. The dining venues and brewery are outstanding, and the lodging is stellar. Plus, the opportunities for recreation and tourism epitomize the best of the Oregon Coast. The beach at Pacific City is one of the few places in the state where fishing dories (flat-bottom boats with high, flaring sides) are launched directly into the surf instead of from harbors or docks. Pacific City's windy climes tend to keep even the summer months quieter than most.

GETTING HERE AND AROUND

Between Tillamook and Lincoln City, the unincorporated village of Pacific City is off U.S. Highway 101 on the south end of the beautiful Three Capes Loop. It is a two-hour drive from Portland on U.S. Highway 26 to Route 6. From Salem, Pacific City is a 90-minute drive on Route 22. Tillamook County's bus, **The Wave** (☎ *503/815–8283* 🌐 *www.tillamookbus.com*), leaves from Portland's Union Station. The bus connects Manzanita, Tillamook, and Pacific City. The nearest airport is in Newport, 47 miles south.

ESSENTIALS

Visitor Information **Pacific City-Nestucca Valley Chamber of Commerce** ☎ *503/392–4340, 888/549–2632* 🌐 *www.pacificcity.com.*

WHERE TO EAT AND STAY

For expanded hotel reviews, visit Fodors.com.

$ CAFÉ FAMILY 🍴 **Grateful Bread Bakery & Restaurant.** Open since 1991, this café uses the cod caught by the local dories for its fish-and-chips. Everything it makes is fresh and from scratch. Its breads, pastries, breakfasts, and pizzas are simply perfect. [$] *Average main: $9* ✉ *34805 Brooten Rd.* ☎ *503/965–7337* 🕒 *Closed Tues. and Wed. No dinner.*

$$ AMERICAN FAMILY 🍴 **Pelican Pub & Brewery.** This beer-lover's jewel stands on the oceanfront by Haystack Rock. While its microbrewery has garnered national and international acclaim for its beers, the Pelican Pub has elevated the art of beer cuisine by listing beer pairings on its menu. Many of its fine entrées are infused with its beers, such as the linguine with fresh clams flavored with Kiwanda Cream Ale, and the Tsunami Stout brownie sundae. The pub periodically hosts Brewers Dinners—splendid affairs that have explored beer pairings with Scottish, Greek, Italian, and Belgian cooking. Kids love the gourmet pizzas and children's menu. [$] *Average main: $17* ✉ *33180 Cape Kiwanda Dr.* ☎ *503/965–7007.*

$$$$ RESORT 🏨 **Cottages at Cape Kiwanda.** For a five-star resort experience with a glorious beach view, this complex has 18 units for rent that can sleep four or six people—perfect for families or that beach get-together with friends. **Pros:** upscale; comfortable; next to Pacific City eateries. **Cons:** there are ownership opportunities, so there might be a sales pitch; the beach is lively, and tail-gating cars can be a fixture. [$] *Rooms from: $299* ✉ *33000 Cape Kiwanda Dr.* ☎ *866/571–0605* 🌐 *www.kiwandacottages.com* 🛏 *18 rooms* 🍽 *No meals.*

$$ HOTEL FAMILY 🏨 **Inn at Cape Kiwanda.** You won't find a weather-beaten beach cottage here—each of the 35 deluxe, fireplace-warmed rooms has a gorgeous view of Haystack Rock. **Pros:** great views; some pets are welcome; terrific restaurants nearby. **Cons:** guests might get hit up with a sales pitch. [$] *Rooms from: $199* ✉ *33105 Cape Kiwanda Dr.* ☎ *888/965–7001, 503/965–7001* 🛏 *35 rooms* 🍴 *No meals.*

SPORTS AND THE OUTDOORS

BEACHES

Fodor's Choice ★ **Pacific City beach.** The town's public beach sits between Cape Kiwanda State Natural Area and Bob Straub State Park. Adjacent to Cape Kiwanda's massive dune, it's a favorite for kids who often climb its bulk (by some estimates 500 feet) just for the thrill of sliding back down again. Hikers also get a thrill from the top, where the view opens on a tiny cove and tide pools below, and the walk down is infinitely easier than the climb. The beach is also popular with tailgaters—it's one of the few places on the Oregon Coast where it's legal to park your vehicle on the sand. Other parking is available off Cape Kiwanda Drive. For quieter outings, try the Bob Straub. **Amenities:** none. **Best for:** partiers; walking. ✉ *Cape Kiwanda Drive, Pacific City* 🌐 *pacificcity.org.*

RECREATIONAL AREAS

Robert Straub State Park. An often sand-blasting walk along the flat white-sand beach leads down to the mouth of the Nestucca River, considered by many to be the best fishing river on the north coast. The beach along the Pacific is frequently windy, but it's separated from the stiller, warmer side of the peninsula by high dunes. Multiple trails cross the dunes into a forest that leads to small beaches on the Nestucca. Relax here with a book, and easily find stillness and sunshine. It's possible to skip the Pacific stroll all together, and find trails to the Nestucca straight from the parking lot, but it's hard to resist the views from the top of the dunes at the Bob Straub. If you choose the ocean side, pitch your beach-camp in the dunes, not the flat sand, and you'll find respite from the sometimes unrelenting wind. ✉ *West from main intersection in downtown Pacific City across Nestucca River* ☎ *800/551–6949* 🎟 *Free* 🕒 *Daily sunrise–sunset.*

OFF THE BEATEN PATH

Nature Conservancy Cascade Head Preserve and trail. This dense, green trail winds through a rain forest where 100-inch annual rainfalls nourish 250-year-old Sitka spruces, mosses, and ferns. Emerging from the forest, hikers come upon grassy and treeless Cascade Head, a rare maritime prairie. There are magnificent views down to the Salmon River and east to the Coast Range. Continuing along the headland, black-tailed deer often graze and turkey vultures soar in the strong winds. You need to be in fairly good shape for the first and steepest part of the hike, which can be done in about an hour. The 270-acre area has been named a United Nations Biosphere Reserve. Coastal bluffs also make this a popular hang-gliding and kite-flying area. The website has detailed driving directions to reach the preserve. ✉ *Savage Rd., 6 miles south of Neskowin off U.S. 101* ☎ *503/230–1221* 🌐 *www.nature.org* 🎟 *Free* 🕒 *Upper trail closed Jan.–mid-July.*

FISHING

FAMILY **Eagle Charters Fishing.** Within three minutes of launching from the beach, you can be fishing in a dory and catching rockfish right in front of Haystack Rock. Groups of up to five people can be accommodated, and families with children are welcome. Fishing and ecotourism trips last six hours, except for halibut and tuna fishing, which are 10 to 12 hours. ✉ *Cape Kiwanda Dr., launches from parking lot at the Pelican Pub (No. 33180)* ☎ *877/892–3679* ⊕ *www.eaglechartersfishing.com.*

Haystack Fishing Club, Inc. Offering ocean fishing for salmon, bottom fish, halibut, and crab, Haystack Fishing targets lingcod larger than 10 lbs. After a day of fishing, they'll fillet your catch. These guided dory trips last between four and six hours and accommodate up to six people. Fishing tours are held between June and September. ✉ *35170 Brooten Rd.* ☎ *503/965–7555, 866/965–7555* ⊕ *www.haystackfishing.com.*

HORSEBACK RIDING

FAMILY **Oregon Beach Rides.** Saddle up for horseback rides that journey along the beach, up coastal trails, to Robert Straub State Park and Nestucca River. Reserved rides can last from one hour to a full day. There's even a romantic sunset trot along the beach. Appropriate for ages six and up. ☎ *971/237–6653* ⊕ *www.oregonbeachrides.com* ⚞ *Reservations essential.*

CENTRAL COAST

This is Oregon's coastal playland, drawing shoppers, kite flyers, deep-sea fishing enthusiasts, surfers, and dune-shredding daredevils. Lincoln City offers a wealth of shops devoted to antiques and knickknacks, and visitors can even blow their own glass float. Depoe Bay has the world's smallest harbor, and Newport is designated the Dungeness crab capital of the world. The best barbecue is in Toledo, and Oregon Dunes National Recreation Area provides the best thrills. Even if you're not intent on making tracks in the sand, the dunes provide vast, unforgettable scenery.

LINCOLN CITY

16 miles south of Pacific City; 78 miles west of Portland.

Lincoln City is a captivating destination for families and lovers who want to share some time laughing on the beach, poking their fingers in tide pools, and trying to harness wind-bucking kites. Once a series of small villages, Lincoln City is a sprawling town without a center. But the endless tourist amenities make up for a lack of a small coastal-town ambience. Clustered like barnacles on the offshore reefs are fast-food restaurants, gift shops, supermarkets, candy stores, antiques markets, dozens of motels and hotels, a factory-outlet mall, and a busy casino. Lincoln City is the most popular destination city on the Oregon Coast, but its only real geographic claim to fame is the 445-foot-long D River, stretching from its source in Devil's Lake to the Pacific; *Guinness World Records* lists the D as the world's shortest river.

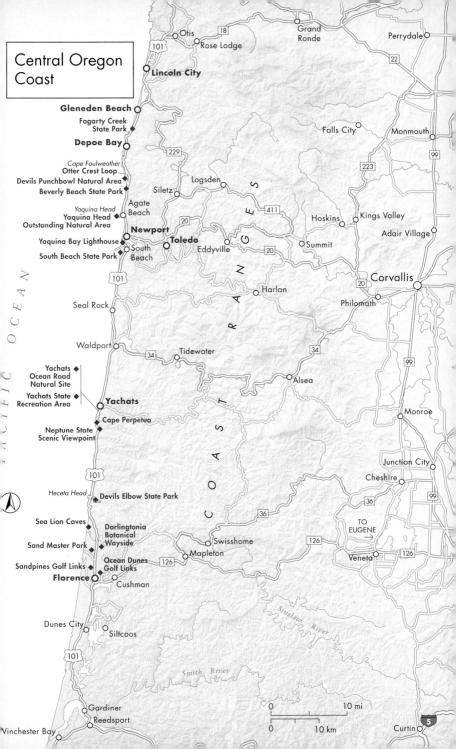

Central Oregon Coast

Lincoln City

Gleneden Beach
Fogarty Creek
State Park
Depoe Bay

Cape Foulweather
Otter Crest Loop
Devils Punchbowl Natural Area
Beverly Beach State Park

Yaquina Head
Yaquina Head
Outstanding Natural Area

Yaquina Bay Lighthouse
South Beach State Park

Seal Rock

Waldport

Yachats ◆
Ocean Road
Natural Site
Yachats State
Recreation Area

Yachats
Cape Perpetua
Neptune State
Scenic Viewpoint

Heceta Head
Devils Elbow State Park

Sea Lion Caves
Darlingtonia
Botanical
Wayside
Sand Master Park
Ocean Dunes
Golf Links
Sandpines Golf Links
Florence
Cushman

Dunes City
Siltcoos

Gardiner
Reedsport
Vinchester Bay

Otis
Rose Lodge
Grand
Ronde
Perrydale

18
101
22

Falls City
Monmouth

229
99
223

Logsden
411
Hoskins
Kings Valley

Siletz
Agate
Beach
20
Summit
Adair Village

Newport
Toledo
Eddyville
20
South
Beach

101
Harlan
Corvallis
20
Philomath

Tidewater
34
34
99

Alsea

Monroe

Junction City
Cheshire
99

36

TO
EUGENE
→
36
126
Veneta
126

Swisshome
Mapleton
126

Siuslaw River

Smith River

PACIFIC OCEAN

COAST RANGES

0   10 mi
0   10 km

Curtin

5

GETTING HERE AND AROUND

Lincoln City is a two-hour drive from Portland on Hwy. 99 W and Hwy. 18. From Astoria, it's a two-hour and 30 minute drive along U.S. 101. **Lincoln Transit** buses connect riders with Newport, Siletz, Lincoln City, and Yachats. Newport has the nearest airport, 31 miles away.

ESSENTIALS

Visitor Information **Lincoln City Visitors Center** ✉ *801 SW U.S. 101, 4th Floor* ☎ *541/996–1274, 800/452–2151* 🌐 *www.oregoncoast.org.*

WHERE TO EAT

$$$ PACIFIC NORTHWEST 🍴 **Bay House.** Inside a charming bungalow, this restaurant serves meals to linger over while you enjoy views across sunset-gilded Siletz Bay. The seasonal Pacific Northwest cuisine includes Dungeness crab cakes with roasted-chili chutney, fresh halibut Parmesan, and roast duckling with cranberry compote. Naturally, there's lamb, pork, and tasty fillets. A new wine bar/cocktail lounge has been added, and small-plate meals are available here from 5 pm. The wine list is extensive, and the service impeccable. [$] *Average main: $30* ✉ *5911 SW U.S. 101, about 5 miles south of Lincoln City* ☎ *541/996–3222* 🌐 *www.thebayhouse.org* ⏲ *Closed Mon. and Tues. No lunch.*

$ AMERICAN Fodor's Choice ★ 🍴 **Beach Dog Café.** Dang, these are good dogs, dressed in 16 different ways. You'll find everything from Coney, Philly, and Kosher to Hot Diggity. This family-owned joint has a galaxy of dog photos adorning its walls. But its breakfasts have the morning crowds gathering. Roger and Sonja Seals offer a menu full of hearty potato dishes, scrambles, stuffed French toast, and incredible breakfast sandwiches. The apple potato pancake with sour cream and a Polish sausage is the keystone to any nutritious breakfast. [$] *Average main: $9* ✉ *6042 SE Hwy. 101* ☎ *541/996–3647* 🌐 *www.thebeachdogcafe.com* 💳 *No credit cards* ⏲ *Closed Mon. and Tues. No dinner.*

$$ SEAFOOD Fodor's Choice ★ 🍴 **Blackfish Café.** Owner and chef Rob Pounding serves simple-but-succulent dishes that blend fresh ingredients from local fishermen and gardeners. Before starting his own restaurant in 1999, Pounding was the executive chef of acclaimed Salishan Lodge for 14 years, winning top national culinary awards. His skillet-roasted, "ocean trolled" chinook salmon, basted with fennel lime butter, and Oregon blue-cheese potatoes are flavorful and perfect. The Blackfish Ding Dong dessert, with mixed-berry sauce and whipped cream, is the best way to finish a meal. [$] *Average main: $18* ✉ *2733 U.S. 101* ☎ *541/996–1007* 🌐 *www.blackfishcafe.com* ⏲ *Closed Tues.*

$ BAKERY 🍴 **Rockfish Bakery.** The seed for this phenomenal bakery began when Rob Pounding, owner and chef for Blackfish Café, couldn't find any hamburger buns that met his standards. Now his bakery publishes a weekly bread schedule so customers will know when to buy the freshest sourdough, olive ciabatta, rye, or brioche with raisins. It makes the coast's best cinnamon rolls, cookies, excellent pizza, hearty sandwiches, and a soup du jour from the nearby Blackfish Café. The Rockfish is a must for anyone who loves an upper-crust bakery. [$] *Average main: $10* ✉ *3026 NE Hwy. 101* ☎ *541/996–1006* 🌐 *www.rockfishbakery.com* ⏲ *Closed Mon. and Tues. No dinner.*

WHERE TO STAY

For expanded hotel reviews, visit Fodors.com.

$ HOTEL FAMILY Fodor's Choice ★ **Coho Oceanfront Lodge.** Set on a romantic cliff, the renovated Coho is a perfect hybrid of family-friendly lodging and a quiet, intimate hideaway for couples. **Pros:** great value; family-friendly; concierge service; shuttle to nearby casino. **Cons:** no restaurant. [$] *Rooms from: $94* ✉ *1635 NW Harbor Ave.* ☎ *541/994–3684* 🌐 *www.thecoholodge.com* 🛏 *33 studios, 32 suites* 🍴 *Breakfast.*

$ B&B/INN **The Historic Anchor Inn.** This quirky bungalow might not be for everyone, but for those who appreciate a warm, spirited inn with a decidedly inventive and whimsical touch, this is a remarkable find. **Pros:** a memorable, truly unique property; everything you need to explore Lincoln City. **Cons:** not on the beach; very quirky and rustic, which could be a pro too. [$] *Rooms from: $79* ✉ *4417 SW U.S. 101* ☎ *541/996–3810* 🌐 *historicanchorinn.com* 🛏 *19 rooms* 🍴 *Breakfast.*

$$$ RESORT **Inn at Spanish Head.** Driving up to this luxury resort hotel, you'd think it might be small, but on further investigation you'll see that the property takes up the entire side of a bluff like a huge staircase. **Pros:** sweeping views of the ocean through floor-to-ceiling windows; restaurant on-site; easy beach access via elevator; great place to watch winter storms. **Cons:** pricey. [$] *Rooms from: $205* ✉ *4009 S. U.S. 101* ☎ *541/996–2161, 800/452–8127* 🌐 *www.spanishhead.com* 🛏 *78 rooms, 49 suites* 🍴 *Some meals.*

NIGHTLIFE AND THE ARTS

Chinook Winds Casino Resort. Oregon's only beachfront casino has a great variety of slot machines, blackjack, poker, keno, and off-track betting. The Rogue River Steakhouse serves a great fillet and terrific appetizers. There's also the Siletz Bay Buffet, the Chinook Seafood Grill, a snack bar, and a lounge. An arcade will keep the kids busy while you are on the gambling floor. Big-name entertainers perform in the showroom. Players can take a break from the tables and enjoy a round of golf at the Chinook Winds Golf Resort next door. ✉ *1777 NW 44th St.* ☎ *541/996–5825, 888/244–6665* 🌐 *www.chinookwindscasino.com* 🕓 *Daily 24 hrs.*

SHOPPING

Alderhouse Glassblowing. The imaginative crafts folk at this studio turn molten glass into vases and bowls, which are available for sale. It is the oldest glass-blowing studio in the state. ✉ *611 Immonen Rd.* ☎ *541/996–2483* 🌐 *www.alderhouse.com* 🎟 *Free* 🕓 *May–Nov., daily 10–5.*

Culinary Center. Whether she's conducting a small, hands-on class or orchestrating a full-blown cooking demonstration for dozens, executive chef Sharon Wiest loves sharing her passion for Pacific Northwest ingredients. Directly above the visitor bureau, the Culinary Center is a wonderful stop for newcomers to the area. Guests can sign up to get their hands onto some food and learn, or they can sit back, sip wine, and enjoy learning what makes Oregon such a special place to dine. The center's schedule includes classes in oysters, pizza, sushi, tapas, Mexican, seafood, and even bacon. Chocolate-chip bacon-pecan cookie, anyone?

✉ *801 SW Hwy. 101, Suite 401* ☎ *541/557–1125* ⊕ *www.oregoncoast. org/culinary* ⊗ *Closed Mon.*

Jennifer L. Sears Glass Art Studio. Blow a glass float or make a glorious glass starfish, heart, or fluted bowl of your own design (it costs $65 for a glass float). The studio's expert artisans will guide you every step of the way. It's a fun, memorable keepsake of the coast. ✉ *4821 SW Hwy. 101* ☎ *541/996–2569* ⊕ *www.jennifersearsglassart.com* ⊗ *Wed.–Sun. 10–6.*

Lincoln City Surf Shop. Darn right they surf on the Oregon Coast. Maybe the surfers are dressed from head to toe in wet suits, but they're riding some tasty waves just the same. At Lincoln City's oldest surf shop there's equipment and apparel for purchase or rent. Lessons provide a great family activity, and rates include board, wet suits, hood, and booties. The shop also has a collection of kiteboards, skimboards, and skateboards. ✉ *4792 SE Hwy. 101* ☎ *541/996–7433* ⊕ *www.lcsurfshop.com.*

SPORTS AND THE OUTDOORS

BOATING

Devil's Lake State Recreation Area. Canoeing and kayaking are popular on this small lake, also loved by coots, loons, ducks, cormorants, bald eagles, and grebes. Visitors can sign up in advance for popular kayaking tours in the summer, for which bird guides are provided. It has the only Oregon Coast campground within the environs of a city. Hookups, tent sites, and yurts are available. ✉ *1452 NE 6th St.* ☎ *541/994–2002, 800/551–6949* ⊕ *www.oregonstateparks.org* ⊗ *Daily.*

GLENEDEN BEACH

7 miles south of Lincoln City.

Gleneden Beach is primarily a resort town with Salishan, its most famous property, perching high above placid Siletz Bay. This expensive collection of guest rooms, vacation homes, condominiums, restaurants, golf fairways, tennis courts, and covered walkways blends into a forest preserve; if not for the signs, you'd scarcely be able to find it.

GETTING HERE AND AROUND

By road, take U.S. 101 from Lincoln City. The closest airport to Gleneden Beach is in Newport, 23 miles south. Bus service to Newport is provided by **Lincoln County Transit Bus/Dail-A-Ride** (☎ *541/265–4900*). **Caravan Airport Transportation** (☎ *541/994–9645*) provides shuttle service to Portland International Airport for Lincoln City, Depoe Bay, and Newport.

ESSENTIALS

Visitor Information **Central Oregon Coast Association** ✉ *137 NE 1st St., Newport* ☎ *503/265–2064, 800/767–2064* ⊕ *www.coastvisitor.com.*

WHERE TO EAT AND STAY

For expanded hotel reviews, visit Fodors.com.

$$$$
STEAKHOUSE
✕ **Dining Room at Salishan.** If you're not on a budget, pull up a chair and slurp a bowl of Dungeness crab bisque, relish some oysters Rockefeller, and slice into a 28-day-aged steak or a mouthwatering seared scallop. It also serves game, lamb, and elegant desserts. The white-linen dining

Salishan Golf Resort, Gleneden Beach

room has a gorgeous view of Siletz Bay and the private Salishan Spit, and there's a private dining room for those very special occasions. You could spend all evening perusing the wine list, as the resort's cellar has more than 17,000 bottles. [$] *Average main: $35* ✉ *7760 N. U.S. 101* ☎ *541/764–2371, 800/452–2300* ✍ *Reservations essential* ⊙ *No lunch.*

$$$ PACIFIC NORTHWEST 🍴 **Side Door Café.** This dining room, with a high ceiling, exposed beams, a fireplace, and many windows just under the eaves, shares a former tile factory with the Eden Hall performance space. The menu changes constantly—fresh preparations have included mushroom-crusted rack of lamb and broiled swordfish with citrus-raspberry vinaigrette over coconut-ginger basmati rice. [$] *Average main: $27* ✉ *6675 Gleneden Beach Loop Rd.* ☎ *541/764–3825* 🌐 *www.edenhall.com* ⊙ *Closed Tues.*

$ RENTAL 🏨 **Beachcombers Haven vacation rentals.** This cluster of properties is right off the beach, and features spacious one-, two-, and three-bedroom accommodations, some with a hot tub or in-room Jacuzzi. **Pros:** very friendly; comfortable; near the beach. **Cons:** expect a rustic beach property, not a resort. [$] *Rooms from: $149* ✉ *7045 NW Glen* ☎ *541/764–2252, 800/428–5533* 🌐 *www.beachcombershaven.com* 🛏 *14 homes* 🍽 *No meals.*

$$ RESORT 🏨 **Salishan Lodge and Golf Resort.** Secluded and refined, this upscale resort in a hillside forest preserve has long been revered as a luxury weekend getaway as well as a destination for tony corporate retreats, with plenty of reasons to stay on the property. **Pros:** very elegant; secluded resort with a terrific golf course; plenty of activities on the property. **Cons:** ocean views are few; some find service can be a bit lax. [$] *Rooms from: $189* ✉ *7760 N. U.S. 101* ☎ *541/764–3600, 800/452–2300* 🌐 *www.salishan.com* 🛏 *205 rooms* 🍽 *No meals.*

SPORTS AND THE OUTDOORS

GOLF

Salishan Golf Resort. Redesigned by Peter Jacobsen, this par-71 course is a year-round treat for hackers and aficionados alike. The front nine holes are surrounded by a forest of old-growth timber, while the back nine holes provide old-school, links-style play. It has an expansive pro shop with fine men's and women's sportswear, and a great bar and grill for relaxing after a "rough" day out on the links. It has rental clubs available, as well as lessons on its driving range and practice green. ⊠ 7760 N. U.S. 101 ☎ 541/764–3600, 800/452–2300 ⊕ www.salishan. com ⌨ Summer rates, 18 holes: $99 Mon.–Thurs., $118 Fri.–Sun.; after 2 pm, $79 weekdays, $89 weekends.

DEPOE BAY

5 miles south of Gleneden Beach.

Depoe Bay calls itself the whale-watching capital of the world. The small town was founded in the 1920s and named in honor of Charles DePoe of the Siletz tribe, who was named for his employment at a U.S. Army depot in the late 1800s. With a narrow channel and deep water, its tiny harbor is also one of the most protected on the coast. It supports a thriving fleet of commercial and charter fishing boats. The Spouting Horn, a natural cleft in the basalt cliffs on the waterfront, blasts seawater skyward during heavy weather.

GETTING HERE AND AROUND

Depoe Bay is a 12-mile drive north of Newport and its airport on Highway 101. **Lincoln Transit** provides bus service to Newport, Depoe Bay, Siletz, Lincoln City, and Yachats. Bus connections to Portland are accessible in Newport and are provided by **Greyhound** Newport and the **Valley Retriever** (☎ 541/265–2253 ⊕ www.kokkola-bus.com/ ValleyRetrieverBuslines.html). **Caravan Airport Transportation** (☎ 541/994–9645) provides shuttle service to Portland International Airport.

ESSENTIALS

Visitor Information **Depoe Bay Chamber of Commerce** ⊠ 223 SW Hwy. 101, Suite B ☎ 541/765–2889, 877/485–8348 ⊕ www.depoebaychamber.org.

EXPLORING

EN
ROUTE

Five miles south of Depoe Bay off U.S. 101 (watch for signs), the **Otter Crest Loop,** another scenic byway, winds along the cliff tops. Only parts of the loop are open to motor vehicles, but you can drive to points midway from either end and turn around. The full loop is open to bikes and hiking. British explorer Captain James Cook named the 500-foot-high **Cape Foulweather,** at the south end of the loop, on a blustery March day in 1778. Backward-leaning shore pines lend mute witness to the 100-mph winds that still strafe this exposed spot. At the viewing point at the **Devil's Punchbowl,** 1 mile south of Cape Foulweather, you can peer down into a collapsed sandstone sea cave carved out by the powerful waters of the Pacific. About 100 feet to the north in the rocky tidal pools of the beach known as **Marine Gardens,** purple sea urchins and orange starfish can be seen at low tide. The Otter Crest Loop rejoins U.S. 101 about 4 miles south of Cape Foulweather near **Yaquina Head,** which has been designated an Outstanding Natural Area. Harbor seals, sea lions, cormorants, murres, puffins, and guillemots frolic in the water and on the rocks below the gleaming, white tower of the **Yaquina Bay Lighthouse.**

WHERE TO EAT AND STAY

For expanded hotel reviews, visit Fodors.com.

$$ X **Gracie's Sea Hag.** In 1963, Gracie Strom founded Gracie's Sea Hag
SEAFOOD   Restaurant & Lounge, which specializes in fresh seafood, with an extensive buffet on Friday nights. On Saturday the focus is prime rib with Yorkshire pudding. Several booths at the front of the restaurant have views of the "spouting horns" across the highway. The restaurant is kid-friendly, and there's an adjoining grown-up-friendly bar that gets hopping with live entertainment at night. $ *Average main: $23* ⊠ *58 U.S. 101* ☎ *541/765–2734* ⊕ *www.theseahag.com.*

$ ⊞ **The Harbor Lights Inn.** This harbor-front bed-and-breakfast provides
B&B/INN   a dreamy setting for watching boats and relaxing in a quaint, quiet atmosphere. **Pros:** small, quiet, and pretty; great breakfasts. **Cons:** on the water of the bay but no beach. $ *Rooms from: $139* ⊠ *235 SE Bay View Ave.* ☎ *541/765–2322, 800/228–0448* ⊕ *www.theharborlightsinn. com* ⤳ *13 rooms* ⦿ *Breakfast.*

SPORTS AND THE OUTDOORS
RECREATIONAL AREAS
Fogarty Creek State Park. Bird-watching and viewing the tidal pools are the key draws here, but hiking and picnicking are also popular at this park 4 miles north of Depoe Bay on U.S. 101. Wooden footbridges arch through the forest. The beach is rimmed with cliffs. ⊠ *U.S. 101* ☎ *800/551–6949* ⊕ *www.oregonstateparks.org* ⤳ *Free* ۞ *Daily.*

NEWPORT

12 miles south of Depoe Bay.

Called the Dungeness crab capital of the world, Newport offers accessible beaches, a nationally renowned aquarium, a lively performing-arts center, and a local laid-back attitude. Newport exists on two levels: the highway above, threading its way through the community's main business district, and the old Bayfront along Yaquina Bay below (watch for signs on U.S. 101). With its high-masted fishing fleet, well-worn buildings, seafood markets, and art galleries and shops, Newport's Bayfront is an ideal place for an afternoon stroll. So many male sea lions in Yaquina Bay loiter near crab pots and bark from the waterfront piers that locals call the area the Bachelor Club. Visit the docks to buy fresh seafood or rent a kayak to explore the bay. In 2010 Newport was designated the National Oceanic and Atmospheric Administration's (NOAA) Pacific Marine Operations Center and a new, $38 million, 5-acre facility (and a port for four ships) opened in 2011.

Oregon Coast Aquarium, Newport

GETTING HERE AND AROUND

Newport is on U.S. 101. Daily flights on SeaPort Airlines land at Newport Municipal Airport (ONP), just 5 miles from town. The city is served by **Greyhound, Valley Retriever** (☎ *541/265–2253 ⊕ www.kokkolabus.com/ValleyRetrieverBuslines.html*), and **Lincoln Transit** buses, connecting to Siletz, Lincoln City, Yachats, and Portland.

ESSENTIALS

Visitor Information Greater Newport Chamber of Commerce ⊠ *555 SW Coast Hwy.* ☎ *503/262–8801, 800/262–7844 ⊕ www.newportchamber.org.*

EXPLORING

The Flying Dutchman Winery. Perched on a cliff, this small, family-owned winery enjoys one of the most spectacular locations on the Oregon Coast. It buys grapes from five Oregon vineyards, and brings them over the Coast Range to its salt-air environment for fermenting. Guests can enjoy its award-winning vintages in the cozy tasting room, or take a quick tour of the oak barrels next door with owner Dick Cutler. ⊠ *915 First St., Otter Rock* ☎ *541/765–2553 ⊕ www.dutchmanwinery.com ⊘ June–Sept., daily 11–6; Oct.–May, daily 11–5.*

FAMILY **Hatfield Marine Science Center.** Interactive and interpretive exhibits at Oregon State University appeal to the kid in everyone. The star of the show is a large octopus in a touch tank near the entrance. She seems as interested in human visitors as they are in her; guided by a staff volunteer, you can sometimes reach in to stroke her suction-tipped tentacles. But more than just showcasing sea life, the center holds programs and classes that teach the importance of scientific research in managing and sustaining coastal and marine resources. ⊠ *2030 S. Marine Science Dr.*

☎ *541/867–0100* 🌐 *hmsc.oregonstate.edu/visitor/exhibits-and-events* 🎟 *Donation $5* 🕓 *Memorial Day–Labor Day, daily 10–5; rest of year Thurs.–Mon. 10–4.*

FAMILY **Oregon Coast Aquarium.** This 4½-acre complex brings visitors face to face with the creatures living in offshore and near-shore Pacific marine habitats: Flirting, frolicking sea otters, colorful puffins, pulsating jellyfish, and even a 60-pound octopus. There's a hands-on interactive area for children, including tide pools perfect for "petting" sea anemones and urchins. The aquarium houses one of North America's largest seabird aviaries, including glowering turkey vultures. Permanent exhibits include Passages of the Deep, where visitors walk through a 200-foot underwater tunnel with 360-degree views of sharks, wolf eels, halibut, and a truly captivating array of sea life. Large coho salmon and sturgeon can be viewed in a naturalistic setting through a window wall 9-feet high and 20-feet wide. The sherbet-colored nettles are hypnotizing. ✉ *2820 SE Ferry Slip Rd.* ☎ *541/867–3474* 🌐 *www.aquarium.org* 🎟 *$18.95* 🕓 *Summer, daily 9–6; winter, daily 10–5.*

Yaquina Bay Lighthouse. The state's oldest wooden lighthouse was only in commission for three years (1871–1874), because it was determined that it was built in the wrong location. Today the well-restored lighthouse with a candy-apple top shines a steady white light from dusk to dawn. Open to the public, it is thought to be the oldest structure in Newport, and the only Oregon lighthouse with living quarters attached. ✉ *U.S. 101 S* ☎ *541/265–5679* 🌐 *www.yaquinalights.org* 🎟 *Free, donations suggested* 🕓 *Memorial Day–Sept., daily 11–5; Oct.–Memorial Day, daily noon–4.*

FAMILY **Yaquina Head Lighthouse.** The tallest lighthouse on the Oregon Coast has been blinking its beacon since its head keeper first walked up its 114 steps to light the wicks on the evening of August 20, 1873. Next to the 93-foot tower is an interpretive center. Bring your camera. ✉ *4 miles north of bridge in Newport* ☎ *541/574–3100* 🌐 *www.yaquinalights.org* 🎟 *Free. Donation suggested* 🕓 *Thurs.–Tues. noon–4.*

WHERE TO EAT

$$ SEAFOOD FAMILY Fodor's Choice ★ 🍴 **Georgie's Beachside Grill.** This stand-alone restaurant for the Hallmark Inns and Resorts serves up some surprisingly innovative dishes. From the sea scallops blackened in house-mixed herbs to coconut shrimp in pineapple salsa with chili slaw, the menu here lives up to the ocean view. Local ingredients are frequently mixed with tropical ones like the Dungeness crab cakes topped in mango salsa, and the plates are often layered—the bed of honey-mustard romaine is dressed apart from the blueberry barbecued salmon that lands on top. On the oceanside of Newport, Georgie's is one of few places in town with ocean views. Windows line a half-moon of table seating, and tiered booths mean even the back of the room has decent views. Popular with families and tourists alike, Georgie's is also extremely popular for its breakfasts. [$] *Average main: $20* ✉ *744 SW Elizabeth St, Newport* ☎ *503/265–9800, 888/448–4449.*

$$ SEAFOOD FAMILY Fodor's Choice ★ 🍴 **Local Ocean Seafoods.** This fish market and grill is truly one-of-a-kind. On picturesque Yaquina Bay, its operators purchase fish directly from more than 60 boats in the fishing fleet right outside and take the mission of locally sourced, sustainable seafood seriously. This is also one of few restaurants on the Oregon Coast that doesn't own a deep fryer—even its fish-and-chips are pan-fried. The menu includes such fish-lovers fare as tuna mignon, king salmon seared and served with local cheeses, and Fishwives Stew—a tomato broth stew loaded with both shell- and fin-fish, but come early because it closes at 8 pm (9 in summer). From the bustling interior, there are views through windowed garage doors that roll up in summer. Those tempted to take home more than a doggie bag can dive into the fish case, where house-smoked offerings include a rare smoked black cod and every fish comes with details about the boat that caught it. [$] *Average main: $20* ✉ *213 S.E. Bay Blvd., Newport* ☎ *514/574–7959* 🌐 *localocean.net.*

$ CAFÉ 🍴 **Panini Bakery.** The owner, who operates this local favorite bakery and espresso bar, prides himself on hearty and home-roasted meats, hand-cut breads, and friendly service. The coffee's organic, the eggs free range, the orange juice fresh-squeezed, and just about everything is made from scratch. Take a seat inside, or, in good weather, streetside tables are a great place to view the Nye Beach scene. The café closes at 7 pm. [$] *Average main: $10* ✉ *232 NW Coast Hwy.* ☎ *541/265–5033* 💳 *No credit cards.*

$$ SEAFOOD 🍴 **Tables of Content.** The well-plotted prix-fixe menu at the restaurant of the outstanding Sylvia Beach Hotel changes nightly. Chances are that the main dish will be fresh local seafood, perhaps a moist grilled salmon fillet in a sauce Dijonnaise, served with sautéed vegetables, fresh-baked breads, and rice pilaf; a decadent dessert is also included. The interior is functional and unadorned, with family-size tables, but be forewarned, dinners can be long, so young children may get restless. Dinner is at a fixed time—7 pm in summer, 6 pm most days in winter, but at 7 pm on Friday and Saturday. [$] *Average main: $23* ✉ *267 NW Cliff St., from U.S. 101 head west on 3rd St.* ☎ *541/265–5428, 888/795–8422* 🌐 *www.sylviabeachhotel.com* ✍ *Reservations essential.*

WHERE TO STAY

For expanded hotel reviews, visit Fodors.com.

$$ HOTEL 🏨 **Sylvia Beach Hotel.** Make reservations far in advance for this 1913-vintage beachfront hotel, where reading, writing, and conversation eclipse technological hotel-room isolation. **Pros:** unique; great place to disconnect. **Cons:** no TV, telephone, or Internet access; sharing tables with other guests at mealtimes doesn't suit everyone; not all rooms have an ocean view. [$] *Rooms from: $160* ✉ *267 NW Cliff St.* ☎ *541/265–5428, 888/795–8422* 🌐 *www.sylviabeachhotel.com* 🛏 *20 rooms* 🍽 *Breakfast.*

$ HOTEL 🏨 **The Whaler.** Across the roadway from the coast, guests here enjoy wide views of the Pacific Ocean—magnificent gray whales are often spotted offshore, and it's pleasant to watch the fishing boats leaving or returning to port. **Pros:** great location; ocean views from every room; roomy and clean; heated pool and hot tub. **Cons:** bland breakfast and rooms. [$] *Rooms from: $114* ✉ *155 SW Elizabeth St.* ☎ *541/265–9261, 800/433–9444* 🌐 *www.whalernewport.com* 🛏 *73 rooms* 🍽 *Breakfast.*

NIGHTLIFE AND THE ARTS

Newport Symphony Orchestra. The only year-round, professional symphony orchestra on the Oregon Coast plays at the 400-seat Newport Performing Arts Center, just a few steps away from the seashore in Nye Beach. Adam Flatt is the music director and conductor, and actor and narrator David Ogden Stiers serves as associate conductor. The orchestra performs a popular series of concerts in the Newport Performing Arts Center September through May, and special events in the summer, including its popular free community concert every July 4. ⊠ *777 W. Olive St.* ☎ *541/574–0614* ⊕ *newportsymphony.org.*

SPORTS AND THE OUTDOORS

RECREATIONAL AREAS

Beverly Beach State Park. Seven miles north of Newport, this beachfront park extends from Yaquina Head, where you can see the lighthouse, to the headlands of Otter Rock. It's a great place to fly a kite, surf the waves, or hunt for fossils. The campground is well equipped, with a wind-protected picnic area and a yurt meeting hall. It has 53 full hookups ($26), 75 electrical ($26), 128 tent sites ($21), a hiker/biker camp ($6), and 21 yurts ($40). ⊠ *U.S. 101* ☎ *541/265–9278, 800/551–6949* ⊕ *www.oregonstateparks.org* ☜ *Free* ⊙ *Daily.*

Devil's Punch Bowl State Natural Area. A rocky shoreline separates the day-use from the surf. It's a popular whale-watching site and has excellent tidal pools. ⊠ *U.S. 101, 9 miles north of Newport* ☎ *541/265–9278, 800/551–6949* ⊕ *www.oregonstateparks.org* ☜ *Free* ⊙ *Daily.*

South Beach State Park. Fishing, crabbing, boating, windsurfing, hiking, and beachcombing are popular activities at this park. Kayaking tours are available for a fee. Pets welcome through September. A campground with Wi-Fi access has 228 electrical hookups ($27), 27 yurts ($40), 59 tent sites ($21), three group tent sites ($77), and a hiker/biker camp ($6). ⊠ *U.S. 101 S* ☎ *541/867–4715, 800/551–6949* ⊕ *www. oregonstateparks.org* ⊙ *Daily.*

Yaquina Head Outstanding Natural Area. Thousands of birds—cormorants, gulls, common murres, pigeon guillemots—make their home just beyond shore on Pinnacle and Colony rocks, and nature trails wind through fields of sea grass and wildflowers, leading to spectacular views. There is also an interpretive center. ⊠ *750 NW Lighthouse Dr.* ☎ *541/574–3100* ⊕ *www.yaquinalights.org* ☜ *Free; donations suggested* ⊙ *Interpretive center, daily 10–4; Park daily 8–5.*

TOLEDO

7 miles east of Newport.

Once a rustic mill town, Toledo has reinvented itself as an enclave for painters, artisans, antiques, and the most amazing barbecue this side of Missouri. Landscape artists Ivan Kelly and Michael Gibbons reside here, as well as metal sculptor Sam Briseno, potter Jean Inglis, and contemporary artist Jon Zander. Just seven miles inland from the coast on the Yaquina River, it is the only inland coastal community with a deep-water channel. The Yaquina is fished for sturgeon, fall-run chinook, and steelhead.

GETTING HERE AND AROUND

Toledo is on U.S. 101 and is served by **Greyhound** to Corvallis and Newport. The Newport Municipal Airport is the closest airport, just 12 miles away.

ESSENTIALS

Visitor Information **Toledo Chamber of Commerce** ✉ *311 NE 1st St., Toledo* ☎ *541/336–3183* 🌐 *www.visittoledooregon.com.*

WHERE TO EAT

$ SOUTHERN Fodor's Choice ★ 🍴 **Pig Feathers.** "Everyone loves a great rack" is the rallying cry of the best barbecue restaurant in the Pacific Northwest. Owner and chef Stu Miller's sauces and rubs transform mere wings, pulled pork, and baby back ribs into tastes so rich and rare that they've brought grown men to tears. The OUCH, Slather, and Smokey Sweet sauces are available to purchase. [$] *Average main: $8* ✉ *300 S. Main St., Toledo* ☎ *541/336–1833* 🌐 *www.pigfeathers.com* 🕒 *Closed Sun.*

YACHATS

31 miles south of Toledo.

The small town of Yachats (pronounced "yah-*hots*") is at the mouth of the Yachats River, and from its rocky shoreline, which includes the highest point on the Oregon coast, trails lead to beaches and dozens of tidal pools. A relaxed alternative to the more touristy communities to the north, Yachats has all the coastal pleasures: B&Bs, good restaurants, deserted beaches, tidal pools, surf-pounded crags, fishing, and crabbing.

GETTING HERE AND AROUND

Yachats is on U.S. 101, 24 miles from Newport Municipal Airport, 84 miles from Eugene Airport, and 166 miles from Portland International Airport. **Lincoln Transit** provides bus service to Newport, Siletz, and Lincoln City. **Valley Retriever** (☎ *541/265–2253* 🌐 *www.kokkola-bus.com/ValleyRetrieverBuslines.html*) and **Greyhound** bus connections to Corvallis are in Newport. The **Omni Shuttle** runs to the Eugene airport, and **Caravan Airport Transportation** runs shuttles to the Portland airport.

ESSENTIALS

Visitor Information **Yachats Visitors Center** ✉ *241 U.S. 101* ☎ *800/929–0477* 🌐 *www.yachats.org.*

WHERE TO EAT

$$ SEAFOOD 🍴 **Adobe Restaurant.** The extraordinary ocean views sometimes upstage the meal, but if you stick to the seafood, and don't mind the aging interior, you'll be satisfied. The Baked Crab Pot is a rich, bubbling casserole filled with Dungeness crab and cheese in a shallot cream sauce. Its best dish is the Captain's Seafood Platter, heaped with prawns, scallops, grilled oysters, and razor clams. [$] *Average main: $22* ✉ *1555 U.S. 101* ☎ *541/547–3141, 800/522–3623* 🌐 *www.adoberesort.com/dining.*

$ BAKERY 🍴 **Bread and Roses Baking.** Artisan breads are handmade in small batches here, along with pastries, muffins, scones, cookies, cinnamon rolls, and desserts. In the bright, yellow-cottage bakery you can also nosh on the daily soup and sandwiches at lunchtime, or just while away the morning with pastries and good coffee. Off the beaten path, it's located en route to Yachats State Park and the community walkway, and is across the road from Yachats Commons Park. **TIP→ Let the kids out to play in the park, then settle in here for lunch.** [$] *Average main: $10* ✉ *238 4th Street, Yachats* ☎ *541/547–4454* ⊗ *No dinner.*

$$ SEAFOOD Fodor's Choice ★ 🍴 **The Drift Inn.** This restaurant is a terrific find, with the best fresh razor clams on the coast. Each night a musician plays to the crowd that sits below a ceiling full of umbrellas, with views of the Yachats River where it meets the ocean. Friday is open-mike night, and Saturday there's a dance rock band. Family-friendly and lively, the Drift Inn features fresh seafood, all-natural steaks, and other local meats and produce. The bar stools are usually crowded, and it has a great selection of Oregon craft brews and wines. [$] *Average main: $18* ✉ *124 U.S. 101 N* ☎ *541/547–4477* 🌐 *www.the-drift-inn.com.*

$ SEAFOOD 🍴 **Luna Sea Fish House.** The freshest Dungeness crab around is one of the seasonal attractions in this small weathered restaurant, coming straight from owner Robert Anthony's boat—he catches much of the fish served here using sustainable hook-and-line methods for salmon, cod, and albacore tuna. And in season, he pots the crab seen bubbling in outdoor kettles. Diners often eat family style here, bellied up to a few colorful tables. Fish-and-chips of all stripes, including clam and salmon, are served, but the fish tacos and a sinful dish called slumgullion—chowder baked with cheese and bay shrimp—are the most popular choices. The house special adds three cheeses to a bowl of thick, rich clam chowder, then tops it off with bay shrimp. You can also buy fresh fish here. [$] *Average main: $12* ✉ *153 N.W. Hwy. 101, Yachats* ☎ *541/547–4794, 888/547–4794* 🌐 *www.lunaseafishhouse.com.*

WHERE TO STAY

For expanded hotel reviews, visit Fodors.com.

$$ HOTEL Fodor's Choice ★ 🏨 **Overleaf Lodge.** On a rocky shoreline at the north end of Yachats, this is a romantic place to enjoy a spectacular sunset in splendid comfort. **Pros:** best hotel in one of the coast's best communities. **Cons:** no dining; exercise room is small; a bit of a walk from the action. [$] *Rooms from: $195* ✉ *280 Overleaf Lodge La.* ☎ *541/547–4885* 🌐 *www.overleaflodge.com* 🛏 *54 rooms and 4 suites* 🍽 *Breakfast.*

$$$ B&B/INN 🏨 **Sea Spirit House B&B.** Perched on the beach north of town, this property was built specifically as a bed-and-breakfast and each room offers privacy, a deck entrance to the beach, and its own Jacuzzi tub—and, of course, views of the ocean. Its white carpets and walls, and steeply pitched ceilings, make this more modern than most B&Bs. Combined with pastel paints, bright bedding, and wicker furniture, the architecture has a tropical feel. Communal space includes a loft observatory with a television, deep, comfortable seating, and a small movie collection. Breakfast—three thoughtful courses—is served in a room with two walls of windows overlooking the water and some much-frequented bird feeders. The owners have two small dogs, but they don't intrude on guests' quarters. **Pros:** right on the beach; delicious food. **Cons:** can be tough to locate; scented sheets: allergy-sufferers should request

the fragrance-free bedding. ⊠ *7304 U.S. 101, Yachats* ☏ *866/771–4888, 541/563–4888* ⊕ *seaspirithousebb.com.*

SPORTS AND THE OUTDOORS

RECREATIONAL AREAS

Cape Perpetua Scenic Area. The highest lookout point on the Oregon Coast, Cape Perpetua towers 800 feet above the rocky shoreline. Named by Captain Cook on St. Perpetua's Day in 1778, the cape is part of a 2,700-acre scenic area popular with hikers, campers, beachcombers, and naturalists. General information and a map of 10 trails are available at the **Cape Perpetua Visitors Center,** on the east side of the highway, 2 miles south of Devil's Churn. The easy 1-mile **Giant Spruce Trail** passes through a fern-filled rain forest to an enormous 500-year-old Sitka spruce. Easier still is the marked Auto Tour; it begins about 2 miles north of the visitor center and winds through Siuslaw National Forest to the ¼-mile **Whispering Spruce Trail.** Views from the rustic rock shelter here extend 150 miles north and south, and 37 miles out to sea. The **Cape Perpetua Interpretive Center,** in the visitor center, has educational movies and exhibits about the natural forces that shaped Cape Perpetua. ⊠ *2400 U.S. 101, 9 miles south of Yachats* ☏ *541/547–3289* ⊕ *www.fs.usda.gov/siuslaw* 🅿 *Parking fee $5* ☉ *Visitor's Center: Daily 10–5:30.*

Neptune State Park. Visitors will have fun searching for animals, watching the surf, or hunting for agates. The benches set above the beach on the cliff provide a great view of Cumming Creek. It's also a terrific spot for whale-watching. At low tide, beachcombers have access to a natural cave and tidal pools. ⊠ *U.S. 101 S, 3 miles south of Yachats* ☏ *800/551–6949* ⊕ *www.oregonstateparks.org* 🅿 *Free* ☉ *Daily.*

Yachats Ocean Road Natural Site. Drive this one-mile loop south of Yachats, and discover one of the most scenic viewpoints on the Oregon Coast. Park along the loop to see where the Yachats River meets the Pacific Ocean. There's fun to be had playing on the beach, poking around tide pools, and watching blowholes, summer sunsets, and whales spouting. ⊠ *Yachats Ocean Rd., off U.S. 101* ☏ *800/551–6949* ⊕ *www.oregonstateparks.org.*

Yachats State Recreation Area. The public beach in Yachats is more like the surface of the moon than most other places, and certainly most beaches. A wooden platform overlooks the coastline, where the waves roll in sideways and splash over the rocks at high tide. As is the case throughout most of the town, the beach itself is paralleled by an upland walking trail and dotted with picnic tables, benches, and interpretive signs. Visit to spot the sea lions that frequent this stretch of coast. Or join the intrepid beachcombers who climb the rocks for a closer look

TILLICUM BEACH CAMPGROUND

The Oceanside campsite 3½ miles north of Yachats is so popular there is a 14-day stay limit. Many of the campsites have beachfront views. Open July 1–Sept. 6, there are 59 sites, $30 for electric and water hookups. ⊠ *U.S. 101, 4 miles south of WaldportYachats, OR* ☏ *877/444–6777* ⊕ *www.fs.usda.gov.*

at tide pools populated by sea urchin, hermit crabs, barnacles, snails, and sea stars. **Amenities:** parking; toilets. **Best for:** walking; sunset. ✉ *In the heart of Yachats, turn west on 2nd St., Yachats* ☎ *800/551–6949* ⊕ *www.oregonstateparks.org.*

FLORENCE

25 miles south of Yachats; 64 miles west of Eugene.

Tourists and retirees have been flocking to Florence in ever-greater numbers in recent years. Its restored waterfront Old Town has restaurants, antiques stores, fish markets, and other diversions, but what really makes the town so appealing is its proximity to remarkable stretches of coastline. Seventy-five creeks and rivers empty into the Pacific Ocean in and around Florence, and the Siuslaw River flows right through town. When the numerous nearby lakes are added to the mix, it makes for one of the richest fishing areas in Oregon. Salmon, rainbow trout, bass, perch, crabs, and clams are among the water's treasures. Fishing boats and pleasure craft moor in Florence's harbor, forming a pleasant backdrop for the town's restored buildings. South of town, miles of white-sand dunes lend themselves to everything from solitary hikes to rides aboard all-terrain vehicles.

GETTING HERE AND AROUND
From Yachats, take U.S. 101, or travel Hwy. 126 from Eugene. The closest airport is in Newport. **Eugene Porter Stage Lines** provides bus transportation from Florence to Eugene and Coos Bay.

ESSENTIALS
Visitor Information Florence Area Chamber of Commerce ✉ *290 U.S. 101* ☎ *541/997–3128* ⊕ *www.florencechamber.com.*

EXPLORING
FAMILY **Sea Lion Caves.** In 1880 a sea captain named Cox rowed a small skiff into a fissure in a 300-foot-high sea cliff. Inside, he was startled to discover a vaulted chamber in the rock, 125 feet high and 2 acres in size. Hundreds of massive sea lions—the largest bulls weighing 2,000 pounds or more—covered every available surface. Cox's discovery would become one of the Oregon Coast's premier tourist attractions. An elevator near the cliff-top ticket office descends to the floor of the cavern, near sea level, where vast numbers of Steller's and California sea lions relax on rocks and swim about (their cute, fuzzy pups can be viewed from behind a wire fence). This is the only known hauling-out area and rookery for wild sea lions on the mainland in the Lower 48, and it's an awesome sight and sound. In spring and summer the mammals usually stay on the rocky ledges outside the cave; in fall and winter they move inside. You'll also see several species of seabirds here, including migratory pigeon guillemots, cormorants, and three varieties of gulls. Gray whales are visible during their northern and southern migrations, October through December and March through May. The gift shop has amazing fudge—try the jalapeño. ✉ *91560 U.S. 101, 10 miles north of downtown Florence* ☎ *541/547–3111* ⊕ *sealioncaves. com* ⬛ *$12* ☉ *Daily 9–5.*

NEED A BREAK?

Siuslaw River Coffee Roasters. This small, homey business serves cups of drip-on-demand coffee—you select the roast and they grind and brew it on the spot. Beans are roasted on-site, muffins and breads are freshly baked, and a view of the namesake river can be savored from the deck out back. It closes at 5 pm. ✉ *1240 Bay St.* ☎ *541/997–3443* 🌐 *www.coffeeoregon.com.*

WHERE TO EAT AND STAY

For expanded hotel reviews, visit Fodors.com.

$$ SEAFOOD 🍴 **Bridgewater Seafood Restaurant and Zebra Lounge.** Freshly caught seafood—20 to 25 choices nightly—is the mainstay of this creaky-floored, Victorian-era restaurant in Florence's Old Town. Whether you opt for patio dining during summer or lounge seating in winter, the varied menu of pastas, burgers, and soups offers something for everyone. A live jazz band provides some foot-tapping fun, and the sounds otherwise trend toward reggae and southern influence. For a light snack, try the peel-and-eat shrimp and a cup of chowder in the Zebra Lounge. [$] *Average main: $18* ✉ *1297 Bay St.* ☎ *541/997–1133.*

$ SEAFOOD 🍴 **Waterfront Depot Restaurant and Bar.** The detailed chalkboard menu says it all: from the fresh, crab-encrusted halibut to Bill's Flaming Spanish Coffee, this is a place serious about fresh food and fine flavors. Located in the old Mapleton train station, it has a great view of the Siuslaw River and the Siuslaw River Bridge. In the summer diners can enjoy patio seating right at the water's edge and chomp on the nice variety of tapas plates. [$] *Average main: $13* ✉ *1252 Bay St.* ☎ *541/902–9100* 🌐 *www.thewaterfrontdepot.com.*

$$$ B&B/INN Fodor's Choice ★ 🏨 **Heceta Head Lighthouse B&B.** On a windswept promontory, this unusual late-Victorian property is one of Oregon's most remarkable bed-and-breakfasts, owned by the U.S. Forest Service and managed by two certified executive chefs. **Pros:** unique property—as though you were living in a novel; exceptionally good food. **Cons:** not within walking distance of the town or other activities; some rooms share a bathroom. [$] *Rooms from: $209* ✉ *92072 U.S. 101* ☎ *541/547–3696, 866/547–3696* 🌐 *www.hecetalighthouse.com* 🛏 *6 rooms, 4 with bath* 🍽 *Breakfast.*

$ B&B/INN 🏨 **River House Inn.** On the beautiful Siuslaw River, this property has terrific accommodations and is near quaint shops and restaurants in Florence's Old Town. **Pros:** spacious; great views. **Cons:** not on the beach; interior style is a bit bland. [$] *Rooms from: $119* ✉ *1202 Bay St.* ☎ *541/997–3933, 888/824–2750* 🌐 *www.riverhouseflorence.com* 🛏 *40 rooms* 🍽 *Breakfast.*

NIGHTLIFE AND THE ARTS

Three Rivers Casino and Hotel. This casino has 700 of the newest slots and video games. It also has table games, including roulette, craps, blackjack, no-limit Texas hold 'em, as well as keno and bingo. Five dining venues—from the refined to the casual—suit every taste. Nearby are beaches, shopping, fishing, and two popular golf courses. ✉ *5647 Highway 126* ☎ *541/997–7529, 877/374–8378* 🌐 *www.threeriverscasino.com.*

Umpqua Sand Dunes in Oregon Dunes National Recreation Area

SPORTS AND THE OUTDOORS

RECREATIONAL AREAS

Devil's Elbow State Park. A ½-mile trail from the beachside parking lot leads to **Heceta Head Lighthouse,** whose beacon, visible for more than 21 miles, is the most powerful on the Oregon Coast. ⊠ *U.S. 101* ☎ *541/547–3696, 800/551–6949* ⊕ *www.oregonstateparks.org* ⊴ *Day use $5, lighthouse tours free.*

FAMILY

Fodor'sChoice

★

Oregon Dunes National Recreation Area. Open year-round, the Oregon Dunes National Recreation Area is the largest expanse of coastal sand dunes in North America, extending for 40 miles, from Florence to Coos Bay. The area contains some of the best ATV riding in the United States, with 5,930 acres of open sand and 6,140 acres with designated trails. More than 1.5 million people visit the dunes each year, and about 350,000 are ATV users, nearly half of them from outside Oregon. Honeyman Memorial State Park, 522 acres within the recreation area, is a base camp for dune-buggy enthusiasts, mountain bikers, hikers, boaters, horseback riders, and dogsledders (the sandy hills are an excellent training ground). It's campground has 41 full sites ($26); 121 electrical ($26); 187 tent sites ($21); hiker/biker sites ($5); and yurts ($39). The dunes are a vast playground for children, particularly the slopes surrounding cool **Cleawox Lake.** ⊠ *855 U.S. 101 (office), Reedsport* ☎ *541/271–6000* ⊴ *Day use $5* ☉ *Office hours weekdays 8–4:30 (also open Sat. in summer).*

FAMILY

Fodor'sChoice

★

Sandland Adventures. This has everything you need to get the whole family together for the ride of their lives. Start off with a heart-racing dune-buggy ride with a professional that will take you careening up, over, down, and around some of the steepest sand in the Oregon Dunes National Recreation Area. After you're done screaming and smiling, Sandland's park has bumper boats, a go-kart track, a miniature golf course, and a small railroad. ⊠ *85366 U.S. 101* ☏ *541/997–8087* ⊕ *www.sandland.com.*

GOLF

Ocean Dunes Golf Links. A favorite of locals year-round, Oregon Dunes Golf Links is a straightforward 18 holes that rewards great shots and penalizes the poor ones. You won't find many sand bunkers, because the narrow course is surrounded by sand dunes. Instead, you'll encounter fairways winding about dunes lined with ball-swallowing gorse, heather, shore pines, and native sea grasses. Pot bunkers guard small greens, and play can get pretty frisky if the frequent wind picks up. However, the course is well drained and playable—even under the wettest conditions. ⊠ *3345 Munsel Lake Rd.* ☏ *541/997–3232, 800/468–4833* ⊕ *threeriverscasino.com/golf* 🖫 *Summer rates: 18 holes $48, 9 holes $25.*

Sandpines Golf Links. This Scottish Links-style course is playable year-round. Designed by Rees Jones, the outward nine is cut out of pine forest and near blue lakes; and the inward nine provides some undulating fun, with the rolling dunes at the forefront from tee to green. While challenging, the course is generous enough to provide a great day on the links for beginners and more polished players. Sandpines has a fully equipped practice area with a driving range, bunkers, and putting greens. When it opened in 1993, *Golf Digest* named it the Best New Public Course in America. ⊠ *1201 35th St.* ☏ *800/917–4653, 541/997–1940* ⊕ *www.sandpines.com* 🖫 *Summer rates: 18 holes $79 or $35 after 2 pm.*

HIKING

Carl G. Washburne Memorial State Park. A trail from this park connects you to the Heceta Head Trail, which you can use to reach the Heceta Head Lighthouse. Its campground has 56 full hookups ($26), 7 tent sites ($21), hiker/biker sites ($5), and 2 yurts ($39). ⊠ *U.S. 101, 14 miles north of Florence* ☏ *541/547–3416, 800/551–6949* ⊕ *www. oregonstateparks.org.*

HORSEBACK RIDING

C & M Stables. Ride year-round along the Oregon Dunes National Recreation Area. The area is rich with marine life, including sea lions, whales, and coastal birds. Sharp-eyed riders also might spot bald eagles, red-tailed fox, and deer. Rides range from hour-long trots to half-day adventures. Children must be at least eight years old for the beach ride or six years old for the dune trail rides. There are also six overnight RV spaces. ⊠ *90241 U.S. 101 N* ☏ *541/997–7540* ⊕ *www.oregonhorsebackriding. com* 🖫 *$50–$175* ⊙ *Daily 10–5.*

SANDBOARDING

Sand Master Park. Everything you need to sandboard the park's private dunes is right here: Board rental, wax, eyewear, clothing, and instruction. The staff is exceptionally helpful, and will get beginners off on their sandboarding adventure with enthusiasm. However, what must be surfed, must first be hiked up, and so on. ⊠ *5351 U.S. 101* ☎ *541/997–6006* ⊕ *www.sandmasterpark.com* ⊗ *June–Sept. 10, daily 9–6:30; Sept. 11–May, Mon., Tues. and Thurs.–Sat. 10–5, Sun. 12–5.*

SOUTHERN COAST

Outdoors enthusiasts will find a natural amusement park along this gorgeous stretch of coast from Reedsport to Brookings. Its northern portion has a continuation of the Oregon Dunes National Recreation Area, and is the location for its visitor center. The Umpqua Discovery Center is a perfect trip with (or without) the kids, to learn about the region's history and animals. In Bandon golfers will find one of the most celebrated cluster of courses in the nation at Bandon Dunes, including its fourth course, Old Macdonald, which opened in 2010. Lovers of lighthouses, sailing, fishing, crabbing, elk-viewing, camping, and water sports will wonder why they didn't venture south sooner.

REEDSPORT

20 miles south of Florence; 90 miles southwest of Eugene.

The small town of Reedsport owes its existence to the Umpqua River, one of the state's great steelhead-fishing streams. Hikers will enjoy the picturesque, quiet hiking trails that wander through the forest, onto the dunes, and through the beach grass to the beaches. As in Florence to the north, there are plenty of ATV and dune-buggy riders on the dunes. The area is also a favorite of campers and nature lovers who watch herds of majestic elk in the Deer Creek Preserve.

GETTING HERE AND AROUND

From Florence, take U.S. 101 south; from Eugene travel via I-5 and Hwy. 38. From Reedsport, **Greyhound** bus lines provides limited service to Eugene. The nearest airport is 25 miles to the south in North Bend. Reedsport is 196 miles from Portland.

ESSENTIALS

Visitor Information Reedsport/Winchester Bay Chamber of Commerce ⊠ *855 U.S. 101* ☎ *541/271–3495, 800/247–2155* ⊕ *www.reedsportcc.org.*

EXPLORING

Oregon Dunes National Recreation Area Visitors Center. The natural forces that created the towering sand dunes along this section of the Oregon Coast (⇨ *see the listing in Florence*) are explained in interpretive exhibits. The center, which also sells maps, books, and gifts, is a good place to pick up free literature on the area. ⊠ *855 Highway Ave., south side of Umpqua River Bridge* ☎ *541/271–6000* ⊕ *www.fs.usda.gov* ⊠ *Free* ⊗ *July 13–Sept. 7, Mon.–Sat. 8–4:30; Sept. 8–July 12, weekdays 8–4:30.*

FAMILY **Umpqua Discovery Center.** Exhibits at this waterfront location provide a good introduction to the Lower Umpqua estuary and surrounding region. One of two state-of-the-art wings focuses on cultural history; the other, on natural history, has an indoor simulated walking trail, which whisks you through four seasons. ⊠ *409 Riverfront Way* ☎ *541/271–4816* ⊕ *www.umpquadiscoverycenter.com* ⊠ *$8.50*

⊙ *mid-Mar–mid-Oct., Mon.–Sat. 9:30–5; mid-Oct.–mid-Mar., daily 10–4.*

Umpqua Lighthouse Park. Some of the highest sand dunes in the country are found in this 50-acre park 6 miles south of Reedsport. The first **Umpqua River Lighthouse,** built on the dunes at the mouth of the Umpqua River in 1857, lasted only four years before it toppled over in a storm. It took local residents 33 years to build another one. The "new" lighthouse, built on a bluff overlooking the south side of Winchester Bay and operated by the U.S. Coast Guard, is still going strong, flashing a warning beacon out to sea every five seconds. The **Douglas County Coastal Visitors Center** adjacent to the lighthouse has a museum and can arrange lighthouse tours. ⊠ *Lighthouse Rd., Umpqua Hwy., west side of U.S. 101* ☎ *541/271–4118, 800/452–5687* ⊕ *www. oregonstateparks.org* ⊴ *Donations suggested* ⊙ *Lighthouse May–Sept., Wed.–Sat. 10–4, Sun. 1–4.*

EN ROUTE
A public pier at **Winchester Bay's Salmon Harbor,** 3¼ miles south of Reedsport, juts out over the bay and yields excellent results for crabbers and fishermen (especially those after rockfish). There's also a full-service marina with a fish market, **the Sportsmen's Cannery,** which serves a fresh seafood barbecue on weekends (from Memorial Day to Labor Day).

WHERE TO EAT

$

AMERICAN

✕ **Bedrocks on the Bay.** Outstanding pizza, sandwiches, and fresh fish-and-chips highlight this casual local restaurant on Winchester Bay's Salmon Harbor. Be sure and try the halibut fish-and-chips. It also serves breakfast. $ *Average main: $12* ⊠ *105 Coho Point Loop, Winchester Bay* ☎ *541/271–2431* ⊕ *bedrocksrestaurants.com.*

SPORTS AND THE OUTDOORS
RECREATIONAL AREAS

FAMILY **Dean Creek Elk Viewing Area.** A herd of wild Roosevelt elk, Oregon's largest land mammal, roams within sight. Abundant forage and a mild winter climate enable the elk to remain at Dean Creek year-round. The best viewing times are early morning and just before dusk. ⊠ *48819 Hwy. 38, 3 miles east of Reedsport* ☎ *541/756–0100* ⊕ *www.blm.gov (search: Dean Creek)* ⊴ *Free* ⊙ *Daily dawn–dusk.*

William M. Tugman State Park. On Eel Lake near the town of Lakeside, a dense forest of spruce, cedar, fir, and alder surrounds the little-known park. Recreational activities include fishing, swimming, canoeing, and sailing. ⊠ *U.S. 101, 8 miles south of Reedsport* ☎ *541/888–4902 info, 800/551–6949 info, 541/759–3604 camping reservations* ⊕ *www. oregonstateparks.org* ⊴ *$5 per vehicle day-use fee.*

BAY AREA: COOS BAY AND NORTH BEND

27 miles south of Reedsport on U.S. 101.

The Coos Bay–Charleston–North Bend metropolitan area, collectively known as the Bay Area (population 25,000), is the gateway to rewarding recreational experiences. The town of Coos Bay lies next to the largest natural harbor between San Francisco Bay and Seattle's Puget Sound. A century ago, vast quantities of lumber cut from the Coast

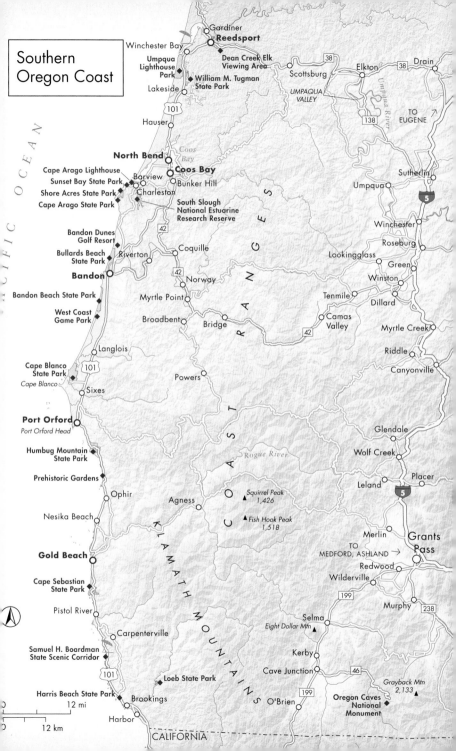

Southern Oregon Coast

PACIFIC OCEAN

Gardiner
Reedsport
Winchester Bay
Umpqua Lighthouse Park
Dean Creek Elk Viewing Area
Scottsburg
Elkton
Drain
William M. Tugman State Park
Lakeside
UMPQUA VALLEY
Umpqua River
TO EUGENE
101
Hauser
138
Coos Bay
North Bend
Sutherlin
Cape Arago Lighthouse
Coos Bay
Barview
Bunker Hill
Umpqua
Sunset Bay State Park
Charleston
Shore Acres State Park
Cape Arago State Park
South Slough National Estuarine Research Reserve
Winchester
42
Roseburg
Bandon Dunes Golf Resort
Coquille
Lookingglass
Green
Bullards Beach State Park
Riverton
42
Norway
Winston
Bandon
Tenmile
Dillard
Bandon Beach State Park
Myrtle Point
West Coast Game Park
Broadbent
Bridge
42
Camas Valley
Myrtle Creek
Langlois
Riddle
Cape Blanco State Park
Powers
Canyonville
Cape Blanco
101
Sixes
Port Orford
Port Orford Head
Glendale
Humbug Mountain State Park
Rogue River
Wolf Creek
Prehistoric Gardens
Placer
Ophir
Agness
Squirrel Peak 1,426
Leland
5
Nesika Beach
Fish Hook Peak 1,518
Merlin
Grants Pass
Gold Beach
TO MEDFORD, ASHLAND →
Redwood
Cape Sebastian State Park
Wilderville
Pistol River
KLAMATH MOUNTAINS
COAST RANGES
Murphy
238
Carpenterville
199
Selma
Eight Dollar Mtn
Samuel H. Boardman State Scenic Corridor
Kerby
101
Loeb State Park
Cave Junction
46
Grayback Mtn 2,133
Harris Beach State Park
Brookings
O'Brien
199
Oregon Caves National Monument
Harbor
12 mi
12 km
CALIFORNIA

Range were milled in Coos Bay and shipped around the world. Coos Bay still has a reputation as a rough-and-ready port city, but with mill closures and dwindling lumber reserves it is looking to tourism and other industries for economic growth.

To see the best of the Bay Area, head west from Coos Bay on Newmark Avenue for about 7 miles to **Charleston.** Though it's a Bay Area community, this quiet fishing village at the mouth of Coos Bay is a world unto itself. As it loops into town, the road becomes the Cape Arago Highway and leads to several oceanfront parks.

GETTING HERE AND AROUND

The area is on U.S. 101. Private and commercial jets use the Southwest Oregon Regional Airport in North Bend. Bus service to the airport and to south-coast communities is provided by **Curry Public Transit's Coastal Express** (☎ *800/921–2871* ⊕ *www.currypublictransit.org*).

ESSENTIALS

Visitor Information **Coos Bay—North Bend Visitors & Convention Bureau** ⊠ *50 Central Ave.* ☎ *541/269–0215, 800/824–8486* ⊕ *www. oregonsadventurecoast.com.*

EXPLORING

Cape Arago Lighthouse. On a rock island just 12 miles offshore south of Coos Bay, this lighthouse has had several iterations; the first lighthouse was built here in 1866, but it was destroyed by storms and erosion. A second, built in 1908, suffered the same fate. The current white tower, built in 1934, is 44 feet tall and towers 100 feet above the ocean. If you're here on a foggy day, listen for its unique foghorn. The lighthouse is connected to the mainland by a bridge. Neither is open to the public, but there's an excellent spot to view this lonely guardian and much of the coastline. From U.S. 101, take Cape Arago Highway to Gregory Point, where it ends at a turnaround, and follow the short trail. ⊠ *Cape Arago Highway, 2½ miles north of Cape Arago, Charleston* ☎ *800/551–6949* ⊕ *www.oregonstateparks.org.*

Coos County Historical Society Museum. The highlight here is a 1922 steam locomotive used in Coos County logging. On display are a formal 1900 parlor, a pioneer kitchen, and exhibits on Native American history, agriculture, and industry such as logging, shipping, and mining. ⊠ *1220 Sherman Ave., North Bend* ☎ *541/756–6320* ⊕ *www.cooshistory.org* 🖭 *$4* ⊙ *Tues.–Sat. 10–4.*

South Slough National Estuarine Research Reserve. The reserve's fragile ecosystem supports everything from algae to bald eagles and black bears. More than 300 species of birds have been sighted at the reserve, which has an interpretive center, guided walks (summer only), and nature trails that give you a chance to see things up close. ⊠ *61907 Seven Devils Rd., 4 miles south of Charleston* ☎ *541/888–5558* ⊕ *www.oregon.gov/ dsl/ssnerr* 🖭 *Free* ⊙ *Trails daily dawn–dusk; interpretive center daily 10–4:30.*

WHERE TO EAT AND STAY

For expanded hotel reviews, visit Fodors.com.

$ MODERN AMERICAN 🍴 **Blue Heron Bistro.** You'll find subtle preparations of local seafood, chicken, and homemade pasta at this busy bistro. There are no flat spots on the far-ranging menu; even the innovative soups and desserts are excellent. The skylit, tile-floor dining room seats about 70 amid natural wood and blue linen. The seating area outside has blue awnings and colorful Bavarian window boxes that add a festive touch. Eighteen microbrews are available. [$] *Average main: $12* ✉ *100 W. Commercial St.* ☎ *541/267–3933* 🌐 *www.blueheronbistro.com* 🕓 *Closed Sun. Oct.–May.*

$$$ SEAFOOD 🍴 **Portside Restaurant.** The fish served at this restaurant overlooking the Charleston boat basin come straight to the kitchen from the dock outside. Try the steamed Dungeness crab with drawn butter. The nautical furnishings—vintage bayside photos, boat lamps, navigational aids, coiled rope—reinforce the view of the harbor through the restaurant's picture windows. [$] *Average main: $25* ✉ *63383 Kingfisher Rd., Charleston* ☎ *541/888–5544* 🌐 *www.portsidebythebay.com.*

$ B&B/INN 🏨 **Coos Bay Manor.** Built in 1912 on a quiet residential street, this 15-room Colonial Revival manor is listed on the National Register of Historic Places. **Pros:** very nicely kept and decorated; family-friendly. **Cons:** not on the beach. [$] *Rooms from: $135* ✉ *955 S. 5th St.* ☎ *541/269–1224, 800/269–1224* 🌐 *www.coosbaymanor.com* 🛏 *5 rooms* 🍽 *Breakfast.*

NIGHTLIFE AND THE ARTS

The Mill Casino. Lively gaming, top-name touring entertainers, and a spacious hotel make up this complex. Gamblers will find more than 700 slots, craps, blackjack, poker, roulette, and bingo. Included in the property's five dining venues are a waterfront restaurant and a bakery. ✉ *3201 Tremont Ave., North Bend* ☎ *541/756–8800, 800/953–4800* 🌐 *www.themillcasino.com.*

SPORTS AND THE OUTDOORS

RECREATIONAL AREAS

Cape Arago State Park. The distant barking of sea lions echoes in the air at a trio of coves connected by short but steep trails. The park overlooks the **Oregon Islands National Wildlife Refuge,** where offshore rocks, beaches, islands, and reefs provide breeding grounds for seabirds and marine mammals. ✉ *End of Cape Arago Hwy., 1 mile south of Shore Acres State Park* ☎ *800/551–6949* 🌐 *www.oregonstateparks.org* 🎟 *Free* 🕓 *Daily dawn–dusk. Trail closed Mar.–June.*

Shore Acres State Park. An observation building on a grassy bluff overlooking the Pacific marks the site that held the mansion of lumber baron Louis J. Simpson. The view over the rugged wave-smashed cliffs is splendid, but the real glory of Shore Acres lies a few hundred yards to the south, where an entrance gate leads into what was Simpson's private garden. Beautifully landscaped and meticulously maintained, the gardens incorporate formal English and Japanese designs. From March to mid-October the grounds are ablaze with blossoming daffodils, rhododendrons, azaleas, roses, and dahlias. In December the garden is decked out with a dazzling display of holiday lights. ✉ *10965 Cape Arago Hwy., 1 mile south of Sunset Bay State Park* 🕾 *800/551–6949 park access, 541/888–2472 info center, 541/888–4902 park access* ⊕ *www. oregonstateparks.org* ✉ *$5 per vehicle day-use fee* ☉ *Daily 8–dusk.*

BANDON

25 miles south of Coos Bay.

Referred to by some who cherish its romantic lure as Bandon-by-the-Sea, Bandon is both a harbor town and a popular vacation spot, famous for its cranberry products, its cheese factory, and its artists' colony, complete with galleries and shops. Two national wildlife refuges, Oregon Islands and Bandon Marsh, are within the city limits. The Bandon Dunes links-style course is a worldwide attraction, often ranked in the top three golf courses in the U.S.

It may seem odd that tiny Bandon bills itself as Oregon's cranberry capital. But 10 miles north of town lie acres of bogs and irrigated fields where tons of the tart berries are harvested every year. Each October there's the Cranberry Festival, featuring a parade and a fair.

GETTING HERE AND AROUND

Bandon, on U.S. 101 is 29 miles from the North Bend airport. Bus service is provided by **Curry Public Transit's Coastal Express** (🕾 *800/921–2871* ⊕ *www.currypublictransit.org*), which travels the U.S. 101 corridor from Smith River, Calif., northward through Gold Beach, Port Orford, Bandon, and Coos Bay.

ESSENTIALS

Visitor Information Bandon Chamber of Commerce ✉ *300 Second St.* 🕾 *541/347–9616* ⊕ *www.bandon.com.*

EXPLORING

Bandon Historical Society Museum. In the old city hall building, this museum depicts the area's early history, including Native American artifacts, logging, fishing, cranberry farming, and the disastrous 1936 fire that destroyed the city. Its gift shop has books, knickknacks, jewelry, myrtlewood, and other little treasures. ✉ *270 Fillmore St.* 🕾 *541/347–2164* ⊕ *bandonhistoricalmuseum.org* ✉ *$2* ☉ *Mon.–Sat. 10–4.*

FAMILY **Oregon Islands National Wildlife Refuge.** Each of the colossal rocks jutting from the ocean between Bandon and Brookings is protected as part of this refuge, in total comprising a string of 1,853 rocks, reefs, islands, and two headland areas spanning 320 miles. Thirteen species of seabirds, totaling 1.2 million birds, nest here, and harbor seals, California sea lions, Steller sea lions, and Northern elephant seals also breed within the refuge. Coquille Point, a mainland unit of Oregon Islands Refuge, is one of many places to observe seabirds and harbor seals. The point overlooks a series of offshore rocks, and a paved trail that winds over the headland ends in stairways to the beach on both sides, allowing for a loop across the sand when tides permit. Visitors are encouraged to steer clear of harbor seals and avoid touching seal pups. A complete list of viewpoints and trails is available online. ✉ *11th Street W, drive west* *to road's end for Coquille Point and parking, Bandon* ☎ *541/347–1470* ⊕ *www.fws.gov/oregoncoast/oregonislands.*

West Coast Game Park. The "walk-through safari" on 21 acres has free-roaming wildlife (it's the visitors who are behind fences): 450 animals and 75 species, including lions, tigers, snow leopards, bears, chimps, cougars, and camels, make it one of the largest wild-animal petting parks in the United States. The big attractions here are the young animals: bear cubs, tiger cubs, whatever is suitable for actual handling. ✉ *46914 U.S. 101, 7 miles south of Bandon on U.S. 101* ☎ *541/347–3106* ⊕ *www.gameparksafari.com* 💲 *$16* ☉ *Mid-June–Labor Day, daily 9–5 (last admittance 4:30).*

WHERE TO EAT AND STAY

For expanded hotel reviews, visit Fodors.com.

$$$
MODERN FRENCH
Fodor's Choice
★

✕ **The Loft Restaurant & Bar.** The owners of this one-of-a-kind eatery in Bandon's Old Town like to call it "casual fine dining," a perfectly apt description of the chef's innovative, modern spin on French basics. On the second floor of an old Port of Bandon property, The Loft's vaulted wood-trimmed ceilings, three-sided view of the Coquille River, and classic wooden tables are all ingredients for a pleasant ambience. But it's the food that makes this restaurant truly memorable. There are no accidental sides dishes here, no multiple choice between potatoes and rice pilaf. Every dish on the menu is as intentional as the next, prepared with thoughtful sauces, delicate chopping, and artful presentation, often combining unexpected flavors into single servings with fantastic results. Most ingredients are organic and locally sourced. Daring diners will be mightily rewarded by the roasted butterfish served over spinach salad with porcini sauce and sesame scallion butter. 💲 *Average main: $25* ✉ *315 1st St., Bandon* ☎ *541/329–0535* ⊕ *www.theloftofbandon.com.*

$$$
STEAKHOUSE
Fodor's Choice
★

✕ **Lord Bennett's.** His lordship has a lot going for him: a cliff-top setting, a comfortable and spacious dining area, sunsets visible through picture windows overlooking Face Rock Beach, and occasional musical performers on weekends. The rich dishes include prawns sautéed with sherry and garlic and steaks topped with shiitake mushrooms. A Sunday brunch is served. 💲 *Average main: $25* ✉ *1695 Beach Loop Rd.* ☎ *541/347–3663* ⊕ *www.lordbennett.com* ☉ *No lunch Mon.–Thurs.*

$$
SEAFOOD

✕ **The Shanghai Lounge at Edgewaters Restaurant.** This second-story bar above Edgewaters Restaurant in Bandon has some of the best west-facing views of the ocean from Bandon, and is among few properties in Old Town that don't face north toward the Coquille River. Servers say you can often see whales from this spot during whale-watching season. It makes a great happy hour stop with its tall ceilings, warm fireplace, and many windows. 💲 *Average main: $18* ✉ *480 1st St., Bandon* ☎ *541/347–8500* ⊕ *www.edgewaters.net.*

$$$
RESORT
Fodor's Choice
★

▥ **Bandon Dunes Golf Resort.** This golfing lodge provides a luxurious place to relax after a day on the links, with accommodations ranging from single rooms to four-bedroom suites, many with beautiful views of the famous golf course. **Pros:** if you're a golfer, this adds to an incredible overall experience; if not, you'll have a wonderful stay anyway. **Cons:** the weather can be coarse in the shoulder-season months. 💲 *Rooms* *from: $210* ✉ *57744 Round Lake Dr.* ☎ *541/347–4380, 800/345–6008* ⊕ *www.bandondunesgolf.com* ⌁ *186 rooms* ⏐⊙⏐ *Some meals.*

SPORTS AND THE OUTDOORS

RECREATIONAL AREA

Bullards Beach State Park. The octagonal **Coquille Lighthouse,** built in 1896 and no longer in use, stands lonely sentinel at the mouth of the Coquille River. From the highway the 2-mile drive to reach it passes through the Bandon Marsh, a prime bird-watching and picnicking area. The beach beside the lighthouse is a good place to search for jasper, agate, and driftwood. The campground has 104 full hookups, 81 electrical ($24); 13 yurts ($36); horse camp: 8 sites (3 single corrals, 3 double corrals, 2 four-space corrals; $19); hiker/biker camp ($5). ✉ *52470 U.S. 101, 2 miles north of Bandon* ☎ *800/551–6949, 541/347–3501* ⊕ *www.oregonstateparks.org* ⌁ *Free* ⊙ *Lighthouse: May–mid-Oct., Mon.–Thurs. 2–5, Fri.–Sun. 11–5.*

GOLF

Fodor'sChoice
★
Bandon Dunes Golf Resort. This playland for the nation's golfing elite is no stranger to well-heeled athletes flying in to North Bend on private jets to play on the resort's four distinct courses, including the Old Macdonald course, which opened in 2010. The expectations at Bandon Dunes are that you will walk the course with a caddy—adding another refined, traditional touch. Greens fees range, according to season and other factors, $220 to $280 a round from May to October, $75 to $210 other months. Caddy fees are determined by the player. ✉ *57744 Round Lake Dr.* ☎ *541/347–4380, 800/345–6008* ⊕ *www.bandondunesgolf.com.*

PORT ORFORD

30 miles south of Bandon.

The westernmost incorporated city in the contiguous United States, Port Orford is surrounded by forests, rivers, lakes, and beaches. The jetty at Port Orford offers little protection from storms, so every night the fishing boats are lifted out and stored on the docks. Commercial fishing boats search for crab, tuna, snapper, and salmon in the waters out of Port Orford, and diving boats gather sea urchins for Japanese markets. Visitors can fish off the Port Orford Dock or the jetty for smelt, sardine, herring, lingcod, halibut, and perch. Dock Beach provides beach fishing. The area is a favorite spot for sport divers because of the near-shore, protected reef, and for whale-watchers in fall and early spring.

GETTING HERE AND AROUND

Port Orford is 56 miles from the North Bend airport. Bus service is provided by **Curry Public Transit's Coastal Express** (☎ *800/921–2871* ⊕ *www.currypublictransit.org*), which travels the U.S. 101 corridor from Smith River, California, northward through Gold Beach, Port Orford, Bandon, and Coos Bay.

ESSENTIALS

Visitor Information **Port Orford Visitor's Center Information** ✉ *520 Jefferson St.* ☎ *541/332–4106* ⊕ *www.discoverportorford.com.*

EXPLORING

OFF THE BEATEN PATH

Prehistoric Gardens. As you round a bend between Port Orford and Gold Beach, you'll see one of those sights that make grown-ups groan and kids squeal with delight: a huge, open-jawed Tyrannosaurus rex, with a green brontosaurus peering out from the forest beside it. Twenty-three life-size dinosaur replicas are on display. ✉ *36848 U.S. 101* ☎ *541/332–4463* 🌐 *prehistoricgardens.com* 🎟 *$10* 🕒 *Summer, daily 9–7; winter, daily 10–4.*

THE FAB 50

U.S. 101 between Port Orford and Brookings, often referred to as the "fabulous 50 miles," soars up green headlands, some of them hundreds of feet high, and past a seascape of cliffs and sea stacks. The ocean is bluer and clearer—though not appreciably warmer—than it is farther north, and the coastal countryside is dotted with farms, grazing cattle, and small rural communities.

WHERE TO EAT AND STAY

For expanded hotel reviews, visit Fodors.com.

$ SEAFOOD
🍴 **Crazy Norwegians Fish and Chips.** This small and casual eatery in Port Orford excels at what they do: good old-fashioned fish-and-chips. With everything from shrimp to cod to halibut paired with fries, the Crazy Norwegians serve it up with a side of pasta salad or coleslaw. Dine in at wooden tables with the mostly family crowd or take it to go to nearby Battle Rock Park. [$] *Average main: $12* ✉ *259 6th St., Port Orford* ☎ *541/332–8601.*

$ B&B/INN
🏨 **Floras Lake House by the Sea.** This comfortable cedar home rests beside spring-fed, freshwater Floras Lake, which is separated from the ocean by only a sand spit. **Pros:** perfect for windsurfing enthusiasts. **Cons:** a bit tricky to find. [$] *Rooms from: $150* ✉ *92870 Boice Cope Rd., Langlois* ☎ *541/348–2573* 🌐 *www.floraslake.com* 🛏 *4 rooms* 🕒 *Closed Nov.–mid-Feb.* 🍽 *Breakfast.*

$$$$ RESORT
Fodor's Choice ★
🏨 **WildSpring Guest Habitat.** This rustic outpost in the woods above Port Orford blends all the comforts and privacy of a vacation rental with the services of a resort. **Pros:** relaxing, secluded, and private. **Cons:** need to drive to the beach and stores. [$] *Rooms from: $278* ✉ *92978 Cemetery Loop Rd., Port Orford* ☎ *541/332–0977, 866/333–9453* 🌐 *www.wildspring.com* 🛏 *5 cabins* 🍽 *Breakfast.*

SPORTS AND THE OUTDOORS

RECREATIONAL AREAS

Cape Blanco State Park. The westernmost point in Oregon and perhaps the windiest—gusts clocked at speeds as high as 184 mph have twisted and battered the Sitka spruces along the 6-mile road from U.S. 101 to the **Cape Blanco Lighthouse.** The lighthouse, atop a 245-foot headland, has been in continuous use since 1870, longer than any other in Oregon. No one knows why the Spaniards sailing past these reddish bluffs in 1603 called them *blanco* (white). One theory is that the name refers to the fossilized shells that glint in the cliff face. Campsites at the 1,880-acre park are available on a first-come, first-served basis. Four cabins are available for reservation. ✉ *Cape Blanco Rd., follow signs from U.S. 101, Sixes* ☎ *541/332–6774* 🌐 *www.oregonstateparks.org*

🎟 *Day use and Hughes House tour free; Lighthouse tour $2* ⏲ *Park daily dawn–dawn; lighthouse Apr.–Oct., Tues.–Sun. 10–3:30.*

Humbug Mountain State Park. Six miles south of Port Orford, this park, especially popular with campers, usually has warm weather, thanks to the nearby mountains, which block the ocean breezes. Windsurfing and scuba diving are popular here. Hiking trails lead to the top of Humbug Mountain. The campground has 32 electrical ($20) and 62 tent sites ($17), and a hiker/biker camp ($5). Three electrical and four tent sites are accessible to the disabled. ✉ *U.S. 101* ☎ *541/332–6774, 800/551–6949* 🌐 *www.oregonstateparks.org.*

GOLD BEACH

28 miles south of Port Orford.

The fabled Rogue River is one of the few U.S. rivers to merit Wild and Scenic status from the federal government. From spring to late fall an estimated 50,000 visitors descend on the town to take one of the daily jet-boat excursions that roar upstream from Wedderburn, Gold Beach's sister city across the bay, into the Rogue River Wilderness Area. Black bears, otters, beavers, ospreys, egrets, and bald eagles are seen regularly on these trips.

Gold Beach is very much a seasonal town, thriving in summer and nearly deserted the rest of the year because of its remote location. It marks the entrance to Oregon's banana belt, where mild, California-like temperatures take the sting out of winter and encourage a blossoming trade in lilies and daffodils.

GETTING HERE AND AROUND

Gold Beach, on U.S. 101, is 84 miles south of the North Bend airport. Bus service is provided by **Curry Public Transit's Coastal Express** (☎ *800/921–2871* 🌐 *www.currypublictransit.org*), which travels the U.S. 101 corridor from Smith River, California, northward through Brookings, Gold Beach, Port Orford, Bandon, Coos Bay, and North Bend.

ESSENTIALS

Visitor Information **Gold Beach Visitors Center** ✉ *94080 Shirley La.* ☎ *541/247–7526, 800/525–2334* 🌐 *www.goldbeach.org.*

WHERE TO EAT

$$ MODERN AMERICAN

🍴 **Anna's by the Sea.** Dining at Anna's by the Sea is like stepping into one man's artisan universe: bowed and wood-trimmed ceilings, handmade cheeses, and blackberry honey lemonade, even a hydroponic herb garden, crafted by owner/head cook Peter Dower. The unique eatery seats only 18, six of those seats stools with a view into the kitchen. Diners get a dash of personality with their meal service, which offers such choices as wild shrimp in black truffle oil and seared albacore and chicken thighs in chanterelle gravy. A former wine retailer, Dower also stocks more than 80 Old World wines and an Oregon Spirits Collection that's a menu standout. Dower is as much entertainer as curator of the restaurant, so drop in ready for the performance and the bistro's buoyant atmosphere. [$] *Average main: $20* ✉ *29672 Stewart St., Gold Beach* ☎ *514/247–2100* 🌐 *www.annasbythesea.com* ⏲ *No lunch.*

$ MODERN AMERICAN 🍴 **The Chowder House.** At the Pacific Reef Resort, this stand-alone new restaurant is quickly becoming a Gold Beach hot spot, sharing a sous chef with Tu Tu Ton Lodge whose innovative, lively menu makes it also worth the stop. While the offerings include some standards, regular specials include dishes like shrimp and lobster-mousse-stuffed jalapeños and a chilled marinated prawn entrée that mingles with feta, mint, mixed greens and lime for a truly fantastic salad. In season, you'll find fresh whole Dungeness crab here, a coastal delicacy served with dipping butter. The building itself was recently remodeled. It's updated design—wood beams above a tiled wall and accent fireplace—add comfort to the menu's sophistication. An extremely well-priced experience. [$] *Average main: $15* ✉ *Pacific Reef Resort, 29374 Ellensburg Ave., Gold Beach* ☎ *541/425–5201.*

$ BAKERY Fodor's Choice ★ 🍴 **Rollin 'n Dough Bakery & Bistro.** Patti Joyce greets people like family in her kitchen. Not only does she create exquisite pastries, cheesecakes, and breads, but her Rollin 'n Dough Deli also carries imported cheeses, ethnic meats, and gourmet lunches. The bistro has table service for soups, salads, pasta dishes, specialty sandwiches, and desserts. It's a little tough to find, but worth seeking out: it's on the north bank of the Rogue River, across the street from Lex's Landing. [$] *Average main: $15* ✉ *94257 North Bank Rogue River Rd.* ☎ *541/247–4438* ⏲ *Closed Mon. No dinner. Sporadic hrs in winter.*

WHERE TO STAY

For expanded hotel reviews, visit Fodors.com.

$$$$ RESORT Fodor's Choice ★ 🏨 **Tu Tu' Tun Lodge.** Pronounced "too-*too*-tin," this renowned fishing resort is a slice of heaven on the Rogue River, and owner Kyle Ringer is intent on providing his guests with a singular Northwest experience. **Pros:** warm, beautiful, and luxurious; gourmet dining and wine tasting; activities to suit every taste. **Cons:** no TV; not well suited for young kids. [$] *Rooms from: $250* ✉ *96550 N. Bank Rogue River Rd., 7 miles upriver from Gold Beach* ☎ *541/247–6664* 🌐 *www.tututun.com* 🛏 *16 rooms, 2 suites* 🍴 *Breakfast.*

SPORTS AND THE OUTDOORS

RECREATIONAL AREAS

Cape Sebastian State Park. The parking lots at this park are more than 200 feet above sea level. At the south parking vista you can see up to 43 miles north to Humbug Mountain. Looking south, you can see nearly 50 miles toward Crescent City, California, and the Point Saint George Lighthouse. A deep forest of Sitka spruce covers most of the park. There's a 1½-mile walking trail. Be warned: there's no drinking water. ✉ *U.S. 101* ☎ *800/551–6949* 🌐 *www.oregonstateparks.org.*

EN ROUTE

Between Gold Beach and Brookings you'll cross Thomas Creek Bridge, the highest span in Oregon. Take advantage of the off-road coastal viewing points along the 10-mile-long **Samuel H. Boardman State Scenic Corridor**—especially in summer, when highway traffic becomes heavy and rubbernecking can be dangerous.

Samuel H. Boardman State Scenic Corridor. This forested, 12-mile corridor contains some of Oregon's most spectacular stretches of coastline, though seeing some of them up close requires effort. About 27 miles of the Oregon Coast Trail weaves its way through this area, a reach dominated by sitka spruce trees that stretch up to 300 feet and by rocky coast interspersed with sandy beaches. Starting from the north, walk a short path from the highway turnoff to view Arch Rock. The path travels a meadow that blooms in spring time. Down the road, find **Secret Beach**—hardly a secret—where trails run from two parking lots into three separate beaches below. Visit at low tide to make your way through all three, including through a cave that connects to the third beach close to Thunder Rock. At **Thunder Rock**, just north of milepost 345 on U.S. 101, walk west for a 1-mile loop that traces inlets and headlands, edging right up to steep drops. Find the highest bridge in Oregon just south—the **Thomas Creek Bridge**—from which a moderately difficult trail extends to wide, sandy **China Beach.** Find some sun on China Beach, or continue south to walk the unusual sculpted sandstone at **Indian Sands.** Easy beach access is had at Whaleshead Beach, where shaded picnic tables shelter the view. From farther south at **Lone Ranch,** climb the grassy hillside to the top of **Cape Ferrelo** for a sweeping view of the rugged coastline, also a great spot for whale-watching in fall and summer. ⊠ *U.S. 101 between Gold Beach and Brookings, Gold Beach* ☎ *800/551–6949* ⊕ *www.oregonstateparks.org.*

BOATING

Jerry's Rogue Jets. These jet boats operate in the most rugged section of the Wild and Scenic Rogue River, offering 64, 80, and 104-mile tours. Whether visitors choose a shorter, 6-hour lower Rogue scenic trip or an 8-hour white-water trip, folks will have a rollicking good time. Its largest vessels are 40-feet long and can hold 75 passengers. The smaller, white-water boats are 32-feet long and can hold 42 passengers. ⊠ *29985 Harbor Way* ☎ *541/247–4571, 800/451–3645* ⊕ *www. roguejets.com.*

FISHING

Five Star Charters. Fishing charter trips range from a four-hour bottom-fish outing to a full-day salmon, steelhead, or halibut charter. They offer all the tackle needed, and customers don't even need experience—they'll take beginners and experts. The outfit has four riverboats, including two drift boats and two powerboats, as well as two ocean boats. They operate year-round. ⊠ *29957 Harbor Way* ☎ *541/247–0217, 888/301–6480* ⊕ *www.goldbeachadventures.com.*

4

THE WILLAMETTE
VALLEY AND
WINE COUNTRY

WELCOME TO THE WILLAMETTE VALLEY AND WINE COUNTRY

TOP REASONS TO GO

★ **Swirl and sip.** Each region in the Willamette Valley offers some of the finest vintages and dining experiences found anywhere.

★ **Soar through the air.** Newberg's hot-air balloons will give you a bird's eye view of Yamhill's wine country.

★ **Run rapids.** Feel the bouncing exhilaration and the cold spray of white-water rafting on the wild, winding McKenzie River outside Eugene.

★ **Walk on the wild side.** Newberg's Jackson Bottom Nature Preserve gives walkers a chance to view otters, beavers, herons, and eagles.

★ **Back the Beavers or Ducks.** Nothing gets the blood pumping like an Oregon State Beaver or University of Oregon Ducks football game.

1 **North Willamette Valley.** Most visitors begin their journey into wine country here, an area rich with upscale dining, shopping, the arts, and wineries. Close to Portland, North Willamette's communities provide all the amenities of urban life with a whole lot less concrete. Wine enthusiasts will relish the excellent vineyards in Beaverton, Hillsboro, and Forest Grove.

2 **Yamhill County.** This part of the state has undergone a renaissance in the past 20 years, as the world has beaten a path to its door, seeking the perfect Pinot. Many of the Willamette's highest-rated wineries are here. There are gorgeous inns, wine bars, and unforgettable restaurants providing a complete vacation experience.

3 **Mid-Willamette Valley.** Agriculture is the mainstay of this region; roadsides are dotted with fruit and veggie stands, and towns boast farmers' markets. Its flat terrain is ideal for bicycle trips and hikes. The state capitol is Salem, and Oregon State University is in Corvallis.

4 **South Willamette Valley.** Here visitors soak in natural hot springs, hike in dense forest, run the rapids, or cheer on the Oregon Ducks. Eugene has a friendly, youthful vibe, which is enhanced by the natural splendor of the region.

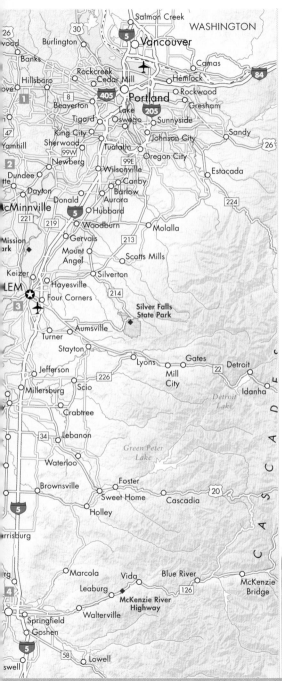

GETTING ORIENTED

The Willamette Valley is a fertile mix of urban, rural, and wild stretching from Portland at the north to Cottage Grove at the south. It is bordered by the Cascade Range to the east and the Coast Range to the west. The Calapooya Mountains border it to the south and the mighty Columbia River runs along the north. Running north and south, Interstate 5 connects communities throughout the valley. In the mid-1800s the Willamette Valley was the destination of emigrants on the Oregon Trail, and today is home to about two-thirds of the state's population. The Willamette Valley is 150 miles long and up to 60 miles wide, which makes it Oregon's largest wine-growing region.

Updated
by Dave
Sandage

The Willamette (pronounced "wil-*lam*-it") Valley has become a wine-lovers Shangri-La, particularly in the northern Yamhill and Washington counties. An entire tourism industry has sprung up between Interstate 5 and the Oregon Coast, encompassing small hotels and inns, cozy restaurants, and casual wine bars.

The valley divides two mountain ranges (the Cascade and Coast), and contains more than 200 wineries. The huge wine region is made up of six sub-appellations: Chehalem Mountains, Ribbon Ridge, Dundee Hills, Yamhill-Carlton, Eola-Amity Hills, and McMinnville. With its incredibly rich soil perfect for growing pinot noir, pinot gris, chardonnay, and Riesling, the valley has received worldwide acclaim for its vintages. The region's farms are famous for producing quality fruits, vegetables, and cheeses that are savored in area restaurants. During spring and summer there are many roadside stands dotting the country lanes, and farmers' markets appear in most of the valley's towns. Also delicious are the locally raised lamb, pork, chicken, and beef. The valley also is a huge exporter of plants and flowers for nurseries, with a large number of farms growing ornamental trees, bulbs, and plants.

The valley definitely has an artsy, expressive, and fun side, with its wine and beer festivals, theater, music, crafts, and even ballooning. Many residents and visitors are serious runners and bicyclists, particularly in Corvallis and Eugene, so pay attention while driving.

The entire state is riveted by the collegiate rivalry between the Willamette Valley–based Oregon State Beavers in Corvallis and University of Oregon Ducks in Eugene. In these towns businesses think nothing of closing for the home football games, and getting a ticket to the "Civil War" game between the two is a feat in itself.

THE WILLAMETTE VALLEY AND WINE COUNTRY PLANNER

WHEN TO GO

July to October are the best times to wander the country roads in the Willamette Valley, exploring the grounds of its many wineries. Fall is spectacular, with leaves at their colorful peak in late October. Winters are usually mild, but they can be relentlessly overcast and downright rainy. Visitors not disturbed by dampness or chill will find excellent deals on lodging. In the spring rains continue, but the wildflowers begin to bloom, which pays off at the many gardens and nature parks throughout the valley.

FESTIVALS

International Pinot Noir Celebration. Wine lovers flock to McMinnville to sample fine regional vintages in late July and early August during the International Pinot Noir Celebration.

Oregon Bach Festival. Eugene hosts the world-class Oregon Bach Festival, with 19 summer days of classical music performances.

Oregon State Fair. In late August and early September the Oregon State Fair in Salem has 8,000 things to do, see, and taste, ranging from carnival rides, top-name concert performances, animals, carnival-style games, and bodacious rides. ☎ *503/947–3247* ⊕ *www.oregonstateparks.org.*

Tigard Festival of Balloons. Look high in the sky for evidence of the colorful Tigard Festival of Balloons in June—hot-air balloons soar above the town throughout the weekend.

GETTING HERE AND AROUND

AIR TRAVEL

Portland's airport is an hour's drive east of the northern Willamette Valley. The **Aloha Express Airport Shuttle** and the **Beaverton Airporter** provide shuttle service. **Eugene Airport** is more convenient if you're exploring the region's southern end. It's served by Delta, Horizon, and United/United Express. The flight from Portland to Eugene is 40 minutes. Smaller airports for private aircraft are scattered throughout the valley.

Rental cars are available at the Eugene airport from Budget, Enterprise, and Hertz. Taxis and airport shuttles will transport you to downtown Eugene for about $22. **Omni Shuttle** will provide shuttle service to and from the Eugene airport from anywhere in Oregon.

Air Contacts **Aloha Express Airport Shuttle** ☎ *503/356–8848* ⊕ *www. alohaexpressshuttle.com.* **Beaverton Airporter** ☎ *503/760–6565* ⊕ *www. beavertonairporter.com.* **Omni Shuttle** ☎ *541/461–7959* ⊕ *www.omnishuttle.com.*

BUS TRAVEL

Buses operated by **TriMet** connect Forest Grove, Hillsboro, Beaverton, Tigard, Lake Oswego, and Oregon City with Portland and each other; light-rail trains operated by MAX run between Portland and Hillsboro. Many of the **Lane Transit District** buses will make a few stops to the outskirts of Lane County, such as McKenzie Bridge. All buses have bike racks.

Bus Contacts **TriMet** ☏ 503/238–7433 ⊕ www.trimet.org. **Lane Transit District** (*LTD*). ☏ 541/687–5555 ⊕ www.ltd.org.

CAR TRAVEL

I–5 runs north–south the length of the Willamette Valley. Many Willamette Valley attractions lie not too far east or west of I–5. Highway 22 travels west from the Willamette National Forest through Salem to the coast. Highway 99 travels parallel to I–5 through much of the Willamette Valley. Highway 34 leaves I–5 just south of Albany and heads west, past Corvallis and into the Coast Range, where it follows the Alsea River. Highway 126 heads east from Eugene toward the Willamette National Forest; it travels west from town to the coast. U.S. 20 travels west from Corvallis. Rental cars are available from Budget (Beaverton), Enterprise, and Hertz (both Beaverton, Salem).

RESTAURANTS

The buzzwords associated with fine dining in this region are "sustainable," "farm-to-table," and "local." Fresh salmon, Dungeness crab, mussels, shrimp, and oysters are harvested just a couple of hours away on the Oregon Coast. Lamb, pork, and beef are local and plentiful, and seasonal game appears on many menus. Desserts made with local blueberries, huckleberries, raspberries, and marionberries should not be missed. But what really sets the offerings apart are the splendid, local wines that receive worldwide acclaim.

Restaurants in the Willamette Valley are low-key and unpretentious. Expensive doesn't necessarily mean better, and locals have a pretty good nose for good value. Reasonably priced Mexican, Indian, Japanese, and Italian do very well. Food carts in the cities are a growing phenomenon. But there's still nothing like a great, sit-down meal at a cozy bistro for some fresh fish or lamb, washed down with a stellar Pinot Noir. *Prices in the reviews are the average cost of a main course at dinner or, if dinner is not served, at lunch.*

HOTELS

One of the great pleasures of touring the Willamette Valley is the incredible selection of small, ornate bed-and-breakfast hotels sprinkled throughout Oregon's wine country. In the summer and fall they can fill up quickly, as visitors come from around the world to enjoy wine tastings at the hundreds of large and small wineries. Many of these have exquisite restaurants right on the premises, with home-baked goods available day and night. There are plenty of larger properties located closer to urban areas and shopping centers, including upscale resorts with expansive spas, as well as national chains that are perfect for travelers who just need a place to lay their heads. *Prices in the reviews are the lowest cost of a standard double room in high season.*

TOURS

Oregon Wine Tours and **EcoTours of Oregon** provide informative, guided outings across the Willamette Valley wine country.

Contacts **EcoTours of Oregon** ☏ 503/245–1428, 888/868–7733 ⊕ www. ecotours-of-oregon.com. **Oregon Wine Tours** ☏ 503/681–9463 ⊕ www. orwinetours.com.

VISITOR INFORMATION

Contacts **Chehalem Valley Chamber of Commerce** ✉ *115 N. College St., Newberg* ☎ *503/538–2014* ⊕ *www.chehalemvalley.org.* **Oregon Wine Country/ Willamette Valley Visitors Association** ☎ *866/548–5018* ⊕ *www.oregonwinecountry.org.* **Travel Lane County** ✉ *754 Olive St., Eugene* ☎ *541/484–5307, 800/547–5445* ⊕ *www.eugenecascadescoast.org.* **Washington County Visitors Association** ✉ *11000 S.W. Stratus St., Suite 170, Beaverton* ☎ *503/644–5555, 800/537–3149* ⊕ *www.oregonswashingtoncounty.com.*

NORTH WILLAMETTE VALLEY

Just outside Portland the suburban areas of Tigard, Hillsboro, and Forest Grove have gorgeous wineries, wetlands, rivers, and nature preserves. The area has a wealth of golfing, bicycling, and trails for running and hiking, and, appropriately, is home to the headquarters of Nike. From wetlands to residential neighborhoods, it's not unusual to spot red-tail hawks, beavers, and ducks on your route. Shopping, fine dining, and proximity to Portland make this a great area in which to begin your exploration of the Willamette Valley and the wine country.

EN ROUTE

Vineyard and Valley Scenic Tour. A 60-mile driving route through the lush Tualatin Valley runs between the city of Sherwood in the southern part of the valley and Helvetia at the northern end. The rural drive showcases much of Washington County's agricultural bounty, including 17 of the county's 21 wineries and several farms (some with stands offering seasonal fresh produce and/or U-pick), along with pioneer and historic sites, wildlife refuges, and scenic viewpoints of the Cascade Mountains. For more information, contact the **Washington County Visitors Association** (⊕ *www.oregonswashingtoncounty.com*).

HILLSBORO

20 miles southwest of Portland.

Hillsboro offers a wealth of eclectic shops, preserves, restaurants, and proximity to the valley's fine wineries. In the past 20 years Hillsboro has experienced rapid growth associated with the Silicon Forest, where high-tech business found ample sprawling room. Several of Intel's industrial campuses are in Hillsboro, as are the facilities of other leading electronics manufacturers. Businesses related to the town's original agricultural roots remain a significant part of Hillsboro's culture and economy. Alpaca ranches, nurseries, berry farms, nut and fruit orchards, and numerous wineries are among the area's most active agricultural businesses.

GETTING HERE AND AROUND

Hillsboro is about a 45-minute drive west from Portland International Airport. The **Aloha Express Airport Shuttle** ☎ *503/356–8848* ⊕ *www.alohaexpressshuttle.com*) and the **Beaverton Airporter** ☎ *503/760–6565* ⊕ *www.beavertonairporter.com*) provide shuttle service.

From downtown Portland it's a short, 20-minute car ride, or visitors can ride the MAX light rail. The TriMet Bus Service connects to the

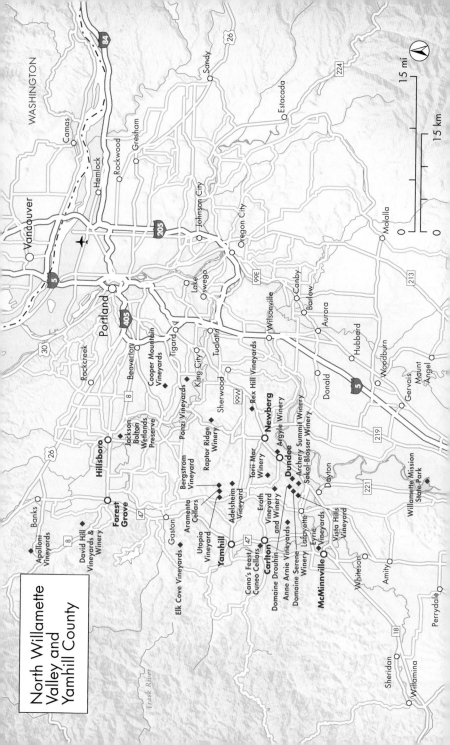

North Willamette Valley and Yamhill County

WASHINGTON

Camas

Vancouver

Hemlock

Rockwood

Gresham

Portland

Beaverton

Cooper Mountain Vineyards

Tigard

King City

Sherwood

Tualatin

Lake Oswego

Johnson City

Oregon City

Wilsonville

Canby

Barlow

Aurora

Donald

Hubbard

Woodburn

Gervais

Mount Angel

Molalla

Estacada

Sandy

Rockcreek

Banks

Hillsboro

Forest Grove

Gaston

Jackson Bolton Wetlands Preserve

Ponzi Vineyards

Raptor Ridge Winery

Rex Hill Vineyards

Newberg

Argyle Winery

Dundee

Archery Summit Winery

Sokol-Blosser Winery

Dayton

Apolloni Vineyards

David Hill Vineyards & Winery

Elk Cove Vineyards

Aramenta Cellars

Bergstrom Vineyard

Adelsheim Vineyard

Torii Mor Winery

Utopia Vineyard

Yamhill

Cana's Feast/ Cuneo Cellars

Carlton

Domaine Drouhin

Anne Amie Vineyards

Erath Vineyard and Winery

Domaine Serene

Lafayette

Eyrie Vineyards

Vista Hills Vineyard

McMinnville

Whiteson

Amity

Perrydale

Sheridan

Willamina

Willamette Mission State Park

Trask River

15 mi

15 km

MAX light rail in Hillsboro, with connections to Beaverton, Aloha, and other commercial areas.

EXPLORING

Hillsboro Saturday Market. Fresh local produce—some from booths, some from the backs of trucks—as well as local arts and crafts are on sale. Live music is played throughout the day. The market is just a block from the light-rail line. ⊠ *Main St. between 1st and 2nd Aves., and along 2nd Ave. between Main and Lincoln Sts.* ☎ *503/844–6685* ⊕ *www.hillsboromarkets.org* ⊗ *May–Oct., Sat. 8–1:30.*

Fodor'sChoice

★

Ponzi Vineyards. One of the founding families of Willamette Valley wine, Dick and Nancy Ponzi planted their original estate vineyard in 1970. The tasting room looks out over these old vines, and offers red and white flights of the current releases, as well as the occasional older vintage from the library. Pictures on the walls provide a wonderful visual history of this winery that is still family owned and operated. The Ponzi family also launched the BridgePort Brewing Company in 1984, and runs a wine bar and restaurant in Dundee (⇨ *Dundee Bistro in Dundee).* ⊠ *14665 S.W. Winery La., Beaverton* ☎ *503/628–1227* ⊕ *www.ponziwines.com* ⊗ *Daily 10–5.*

FAMILY **Rice Northwest Museum of Rocks and Minerals.** Richard and Helen Rice began collecting beach agates in 1938, and over the years they developed one of the largest private mineral collections in the United States. The most popular item here is the Alma Rose rhodochrosite, a 4-inch red crystal. The museum (in a ranch-style home) also displays petrified wood from all over the world and a gallery of Northwest minerals—including specimens of rare crystallized gold. Tours are offered Saturday at 2 pm. ⊠ *26385 N.W. Groveland Dr.* ☎ *503/647–2418* ⊕ *www.ricenorthwestmuseum.org* ▦ *$8* ⊗ *Wed.–Sun. 1–5.*

Washington County Museum and Historical Society. This impressive space on the second floor of the Hillsboro Civic Center houses a range of exhibits focusing on the history and culture of the area. Most of the exhibits include activities for children. ⊠ *210 E. Main St.* ☎ *503/645–5353* ⊕ *www.washingtoncountymuseum.org* ▦ *$6* ⊗ *Wed.–Fri. 10–5, Sat. 10–8, Sun. noon–5.*

WHERE TO EAT

$

MEXICAN

✕ **Mazatlan Mexican Restaurant.** Though this popular spot is hidden away in a small shopping mall, once you're inside and surrounded by stunning murals and ceramica you'll feel like you're in a charming village. Try the Mazatlan Dinner, a house specialty with sirloin, a chile relleno, and an enchilada; or *arroz con camarones,* prawns sautéed with vegetables. Save room for the flan or the *sopapillas* (fried dough). The kids' menu is a good value. ⑀ *Average main: $13* ⊠ *20413 S.W. TV Hwy., Aloha* ☎ *503/591–9536* ⊕ *www.mazatlanmexicanrestaurant.com.*

$

JAPANESE

✕ **Syun Izakaya.** A large assortment of sushi and sashimi, soups, and salads are served in quiet surroundings in the basement of the old Hillsboro Library. Wonderful grilled and fried meats and vegetables are also available, accompanied by a vast sake selection. A nice selection of small plates, only $3–$7, is served during happy hour, between 5 and 6 pm.

$ *Average main: $13* ⊠ *209 N.E. Lincoln St.* ☎ *503/640–3131* ⊕ *www. syun-izakaya.com* ⊘ *No lunch Sun.*

SPORTS AND THE OUTDOORS

RECREATIONAL AREAS

Jackson Bottom Wetlands Preserve. Several miles of trails in this 710-acre floodplain and woods are home to thousands of ducks and geese, deer, otters, beavers, herons, and eagles. Walking trails allow birders and other animal watchers to explore the wetlands for a chance to catch a glimpse of indigenous and migrating creatures in their own habitats. The **Education Center** has several hands-on exhibits, as well as a real bald eagle's nest that was rescued from the wild, and completely preserved (and sanitized) for public display. No dogs or bicycles are allowed. ⊠ *2600 S.W. Hillsboro Hwy.* ☎ *503/681–6206* ⊕ *www. jacksonbottom.org* ⊡ *$2 suggested donation* ⊘ *Trails daily dawn–dusk, Education Center weekdays 10–4.*

FAMILY **L.L. "Stub" Stewart State Park.** This 1,654-acre, full-service park has hiking, biking, and horseback riding trails for day use or overnight camping. There are full hookup sites, tent sites, small cabins, and even a horse camp. Lush rolling hills, forests, and deep canyons are terrific for bird-watching, wildflower walks, and other relaxing pursuits. An 18-hole disc golf course winds its way through a dense forest. In case you don't know, in disc golf players throw a disc at a target and attempt to complete the course with the fewest throws. ⊠ *30380 N.W. Hwy. 47, Buxton* ☎ *503/324–0606* ⊕ *www.oregonstateparks.org.* ⊡ *$5 for day use permit.*

FOREST GROVE

24 miles west of Portland on Hwy. 8.

This small town is surrounded by stands of Douglas firs and giant sequoia, including the largest giant sequoia in the state. There are nearby wetlands, birding, the Hagg Lake Recreation Area, a new outdoor adventure park, and numerous wineries and tasting rooms. To get to many of the wineries, head south from Forest Grove on Highway 47 and watch for the blue road signs between Forest Grove, Gaston, and Yamhill. To the west of town, you'll find some of the oldest Pinot Noir vines in the valley at David Hill Winery.

GETTING HERE AND AROUND

Forest Grove is about an hour's drive west from Portland International Airport. The **Aloha Express Airport Shuttle** ☎ *503/356–8848* ⊕ *www. alohaexpressshuttle.com*) and the **Beaverton Airporter** (☎ *503/760–6565* ⊕ *www.beavertonairporter.com*) provide shuttle service.

From downtown Portland it's a short 35-minute car ride with only one traffic light during the entire trip. TriMet Bus Service provides bus service to and from Forest Grove every 15 minutes, connecting to the MAX light rail 6 miles east in Hillsboro, which continues into Portland. Buses travel to Cornelius, Hillsboro, Aloha, and Beaverton.

ESSENTIALS

Visitor Information Forest Grove Chamber of Commerce ⊠ *2417 Pacific Ave., Forest Grove* ☎ *503/357–3006* ⊕ *www.visitforestgrove.com.*

EXPLORING

David Hill Vineyards and Winery. In 1965 Charles Coury came to Oregon from California and planted some of the Willamette Valley's first Pinot Noir vines on the site of what is now the David Hill Winery. The original farmhouse now serves as the tasting room and offers splendid views of the Tualatin Valley. They produce Pinot Noir, some of which comes from the original vines planted by Coury, along with Chardonnay, Gewürztraminer, Merlot, Tempranillo, Pinot Gris, and Riesling. The wines are well made and pleasant, especially the eclectic blends called Farmhouse Red and Farmhouse White and the estate Pinot Gris. ⊠ *46350 N.W. David Hill Rd.* ☎ *503/992–8545* ⊕ *www. davidhillwinery.com* ⊘ *Daily 11–5.*

Elk Cove Vineyard. Founded in 1974 by Pat and Joe Campbell, this well-established winery covers 600 acres on four separate vineyard sites. The focus is on Willamette Valley Pinot Noir, Pinot Gris, and Pinot Blanc. ⊠ *27751 N.W. Olson Rd., Gaston* ☎ *503/985–7760, 877/355–2683* ⊕ *www.elkcove.com* ⊠ *$5* ⊘ *Daily 10–5.*

Montinore Estate. Locals chuckle at visitors who try to show off their French savvy when they pronounce it "Mont-in-or-ay." The estate, originally a ranch, was established by a tycoon who'd made his money in the Montana mines before he retired to Oregon; he decided to call his estate "Montana in Oregon." Montinore has 232 acres of vineyards, and its wines reflect the high-quality soil and fruit. Highlights include a crisp Gewürztraminer, a light Müller-Thurgau, an off-dry Riesling, several lush Pinot Noirs, and a refreshing Pinot Gris that's a perfect partner for Northwest seafood. The winery also produces a Pinot Noir Port. The tasting-room staff is among the friendliest and most knowledgeable in Oregon wine country. ⊠ *3663 S.W. Dilley Rd.* ☎ *503/359–5012, 888/359–5012* ⊕ *www.montinore.com* ⊘ *Daily 11–5.*

Pacific University. Founded in 1849, this is one of the oldest educational institutions in the western United States. Concerts and special events are held on the shady campus in the Taylor-Meade Performing Arts Center. ⊠ *2043 College Way, Forest Grove* ☎ *503/352–6151, 877/722–8648* ⊕ *www.pacificu.edu.*

SakéOne. After SakéOne's founders realized that the country's best water supply for sake was in the Pacific Northwest, they built their brewery in Forest Grove in 1997. It's one of only six sake brewing facilities in America and produces award-winning sake under three labels. The tasting room offers three different flights ($3–$10), including one with food pairing. ⊠ *820 Elm St.* ☎ *503/357–7056, 800/550–7253* ⊕ *www. sakeone.com* ⊠ *Free* ⊘ *Daily 11–5.*

WHERE TO STAY

For expanded hotel reviews, visit Fodors.com.

$ **McMenamins Grand Lodge.** On 13 acres of pastoral countryside, this
HOTEL converted Masonic rest home has accommodations that run from

David Hill Vineyards and Winery, Forest Grove

bunk-bed rooms to a three-room fireplace suite, with some nice period antiques in all. **Pros:** relaxed, friendly brewpub atmosphere. **Cons:** not as refined as some tourists would like; most rooms have shared bathrooms. $ *Rooms from: $60* ✉ *3505 Pacific Ave.* ☎ *503/992–9533, 877/992–9533* ⊕ *www.mcmenamins.com/grandlodge* ⤳ *77 rooms* ✿ *No meals.*

SPORTS AND THE OUTDOORS

RECREATIONAL AREAS

Scoggin Valley Park and Henry Hagg Lake. This beautiful area in the Coast Range foothills has a 15-mile-long hiking trail that surrounds the lake. Bird-watching is best in spring. Recreational activities include fishing, boating, waterskiing, picnicking, and hiking, and a 10.5-mile, well-marked bicycle lane parallels the park's perimeter road. ✉ *50250 S.W. Scoggins Valley Rd., Gaston* ☎ *503/846–8715* 🖾 *$5* ⊙ *Mar.–Nov., daily sunrise–sunset.*

Tree to Tree Adventure Park. At the first public aerial adventure park in the Pacific Northwest—and only the second of its kind in the United States—the aerial adventure course features 19 zip lines and more than 60 treetop elements and obstacles. You can experience the thrills of moving from platform to platform (tree to tree) via wobbly bridges, tight ropes, Tarzan swings, and more. The courses range from beginner to extreme, with certified and trained instructors providing guidance to adventurers. "Woody's Ziptastic Voyage" zip-line tour features six extreme zip lines (including one that is 1,280 feet long), a bridge, and a 40-foot rappell. Harnesses and helmets are provided, and no open-toed shoes are allowed. ✉ *2975 S.W. Nelson Rd., Gaston* ☎ *503/357–0109*

⊕ *www.treetotreeadventurepark.com* ✉ *Aerial park $45, zip tour $75*
⊙ *Mar.–mid Nov., daily 9–3 hrs before sunset.*

YAMHILL COUNTY

Yamhill County, at the northern end of the Willamette Valley, has a fortunate confluence of perfect soils, a benign climate, and talented winemakers who craft world-class vintages. In recent years several new wineries have been built in Yamhill County's hills, as well as on its flatlands. While vineyards flourished in the northern Willamette Valley in the 19th century, viticulture didn't arrive in Yamhill County until the 1960s and 1970s, with such pioneers as Dick Erath (Erath Vineyards Winery), David and Ginny Adelsheim (Adelsheim Vineyard), and David and Diana Lett (The Eyrie Vineyards). The focus of much of the county's enthusiasm lies in the Red Hills of Dundee, where the farming towns of Newberg, Dundee, Yamhill, and Carlton have made room for upscale bed-and-breakfasts, spas, wine bars, and tourists seeking that perfect swirl and sip.

The Yamhill County wineries are only a short drive from Portland, and the roads, especially Route 99W and Route 18, can be crowded on weekends—that's because these roads link suburban Portland communities to the popular Oregon Coast.

NEWBERG

15 miles west of Tigard, 24 miles south of Portland on Hwy. 99 W.

Newberg sits in the Chehalem Valley, known as one of Oregon's most fertile wine-growing locations, and is called the Gateway to Oregon Wine Country. Many of Newberg's early settlers were Quakers from the Midwest, who founded the school that has become George Fox University, an accredited four-year institution. Newberg's most famous resident, likewise a Quaker, was Herbert Hoover, the 31st president of the United States. For about five years during his adolescence, he lived with an aunt and uncle at the Hoover-Minthorn House, now a museum listed on the National Register of Historic Places. Now the town is on the map for the nearby wineries, fine-dining establishments, and a spacious, spectacular resort, the Allison. St. Paul, a historic town with a population of about 325, is about 8 miles south of Newberg, and every July holds a professional rodeo.

GETTING HERE AND AROUND

Newberg is just under an hour's drive from Portland International Airport; **Caravan Airport Transportation** (☎ *541/994–9645* ⊕ *www. caravanairporttransportation.com*) provides shuttle service. The best way to visit Newberg and the Yamhill County vineyards is by car.

Situated on Highway 99W, Newberg is 15 miles outside of Tigard and 90 minutes from Lincoln City, on the Oregon Coast.

Yamhill County Transit Area (*YCTA* ☎ *503/472–0457 Ext. 122* ⊕ *www. yctransitarea.org*) provides bus service for Yamhill County, with links to Hillsboro/MAX, Sherwood/TriMet, and Salem/SAMT. Greyhound provides bus service to McMinnville.

VISITOR INFORMATION

See Chehalem Valley Chamber of Commerce in Planning, above.

EXPLORING

Fodor'sChoice **Adelsheim Vineyard.** David Adelsheim is the knight in shining armor of
★ the Oregon wine industry—tirelessly promoting Oregon wines abroad, and always willing to share the knowledge he has gained from his long viticultural experience. He and Ginny Adelsheim founded their pioneer winery in 1971. They make their wines from grapes picked on their 230 acres of estate vineyards, as well as from grapes they've purchased. Their Pinot Noir, Pinot Gris, Pinot Blanc, and Chardonnay all conform to the Adelsheim house style of rich, balanced fruit and long, clean finishes. They also make a spicy cool-climate Syrah from grapes grown just outside the beautiful tasting room. Tours are available by appointment. ⊠ *16800 N.E. Calkins La.* ☎ *503/538–3652* ⊕ *www.adelsheim. com* ➅ *$15* ⊘ *Daily 11–4.*

Aramenta Cellars. Owners Ed and Darlene Looney have been farming this land for more than 40 years. In 2000, they planted grape vines after keeping cattle on the property. The winery and tasting room are built on the foundation of the old barn, and Ed makes the wine while Darlene runs the tasting room. Of the 27 acres planted in vines, 20 acres are leased to Archrey Summit for their Looney Vineyard Pinot Noir, and the Looneys farm 7 acres for their own wines which have very limited distribution. If you're looking for a break from all the Pinot Noir, try the Tillie Claret—a smooth Bordeaux blend made with grapes from eastern Washington and southern Oregon. Aramenta offers a great opportunity to interact with farmers who have worked the land for several generations and to taste some great small production wine. ⊠ *17979 NE Lewis Rogers La., Newberg* ☎ *503/538–7230* ⊕ *www. aramentacellars.com* ⊘ *Daily 10:30–5.*

Bergstrom Winery. Focusing on classic Oregon Pinot Noir and Chardonnay, this family-owned winery produces elegant and refined wines that represent some of the best the Willamette Valley has to offer. The tasting room is surrounded by the de Lancellotti vineyard, and offers beautiful views of several neighboring vineyards. French-trained winemaker Josh Bergstrom sources fruit from his estate vineyard as well as several other local sites to produce a wide range of single-vineyard Pinots. Enjoy your tasting on the deck on a warm summer day. ⊠ *18215 N.E. Calkins La., Newberg* ☎ *503/554–0468* ⊕ *www.bergstromwines.com* ➅ *$15* ⊘ *Daily 10–4.*

Champoeg State Heritage Area. Pronounced "sham-*poo*-ee," this 615-acre state park on the south bank of the Willamette River is on the site of a Hudson's Bay Company trading post, granary, and warehouse that was built in 1813. This was the seat of the first provisional government in the Northwest. The settlement was abandoned after a catastrophic flood in 1861, then rebuilt and abandoned again after the flood of 1890. The park's wide-open spaces, groves of oak and fir, modern visitor center, museum, and historic buildings provide vivid insight into pioneer life. Tepees and wagons are displayed here, and there are 10 miles of hiking and cycle trails. ⊠ *8239 Champoeg Rd. N.E., St. Paul* ☎ *503/678–1251* ⊕ *www.oregonstateparks.org* ◱ *$5 per vehicle.*

Newell House Museum. Robert Newell was among the inaugural American settlers in the Willamette Valley and helped establish the town of Champoeg; a replica of his 1844 home, now the Newell House Museum, was built inside the park grounds in 1959 and paid for by the Oregon State Society Daughters of the American Revolution. The first floor is furnished with 1860s antiques. Pioneer quilts and a collection of gowns worn by the wives of Oregon governors at inaugurations are displayed on the second floor. There's also a pioneer jail and schoolhouse. ⊠ *8089 Champoeg Rd. N.E., St. Paul* ☎ *503/678–5537* ⊕ *www. newellhouse.com* ◱ *$4* ◷ *Mar.–Oct., Fri.–Sun. 1–5.*

Pioneer Mothers Memorial Log Cabin. This 1929 construction of a pioneer cabin on the grounds of Champoeg State Park showcases artifacts from the Oregon Trail era. The cabin is part of the Newell House museum, which exhibits many furnishings, textiles, hand crafts, and firearms from Oregon's pioneer days. ⊠ *8039 Champoeg Rd. N.E., St. Paul* ☎ *503/678–5537* ⊕ *newellhouse.com/PMMC.html* ◱ *$4* ◷ *Mar.– Oct., Fri.–Sun. 1–5.*

Fox Farm Vineyards. Fox Farm Vineyards produces small lots of Pinot Noir, Pinot Gris, Pinot Blanc, and Syrah made by local winemaker Joe Dobbes. In addition to showcasing their own small production wines, the Fox Farm Vineyards tasting room offers wines from seven other boutique wineries in the area. Conveniently located in downtown Newberg, the tasting room is a fun and easy stop if you're interested in trying fine wines from small producers that you won't likely find anywhere else. ⊠ *602 E. 1st St., Newberg* ☎ *503/538–8466* ⊕ *www. foxfarmvineyards.com* ◷ *Daily 12–8.*

Hoover-Minthorn House Museum. In 1885 Dr. Henry Minthorn invited his orphan nephew "Bertie" Hoover to come west and join the Minthorn family in Newberg. This boyhood home of President Herbert Hoover is the oldest and most significant of Newberg's original structures. Built in 1881, the restored frame house still has many of its original furnishings, including Hoover's bed and dresser. Hoover maintained his connection to Newberg, and visited several times after his presidency. ⊠ *115 S. River St., Newberg* ☎ *503/538–6629* ⊕ *www.thehooverminthornhousemuseum.org* ◱ *$3* ◷ *Mar.–Dec., Wed.–Sun. 1–4; Feb., weekends 1–4.*

Penner-Ash Wine Cellars. Lynn Penner-Ash brings years of experience working in Napa and as Rex Hill's winemaker to the eponymous winery that she and her husband Ron started in 1998. Although focused primarily on silky Pinot Noir, Penner-Ash also produces very good Syrah, Viognier, and Riesling. From its hilltop perch in the middle of the Dussin vineyard, this state of the art gravity-flow winery and tasting

Bountiful vineyards stretch along many of Willamette Valley's south-facing slopes.

room offers commanding views of the valley below. ✉ *15771 N.E. Ribbon Ridge Rd., Newberg* ☎ *503/554–6696* ⊕ *www.pennerash.com* ⏰ *Wed.–Sun. 11–5.*

Raptor Ridge Winery. The huge windows in the new tasting room look out over the vines of their estate vineyard on the northeast slope of the Chehalem Mountains. If you keep a sharp eye, you may even catch a glimpse of the many raptors (red-tail hawks, sharp-shinned hawks, and kestrels) that give this small winery its name. Raptor Ridge specializes in single vineyard Pinot Noirs that capture the sense of place of their estate vineyard as well as several other vineyards throughout the Willamette Valley. They also produce Chardonnay, Pinot Gris, and a very nice Tempranillo. During the summer, enjoy your tasting at a table on the outside deck that overlooks the vineyards. Tours of the wine-making facility are available by appointment. ✉ *18700 S.W. Hillsboro Hwy, Newberg* ☎ *503/628–8463* ⊕ *www.raptoridge.com* ⏰ *Mid-Jan.–mid Mar., weekends 11–4; mid-Mar.–mid-Dec., Thurs.–Mon. 11–4; mid-Dec.–mid Jan., by appt.*

Rex Hill Vineyards. A few hundred feet off the busy highway, surrounded by conifers and overlooked by vineyards, Rex Hill seems to exist in a world of its own. The winery opened in 1982, after owners Paul Hart and Jan Jacobsen converted a former nut-drying facility. It produces first-class Pinot Noir, Pinot Gris, Chardonnay, Sauvignon Blanc, and Riesling from both estate-grown and purchased grapes. The tasting room has a massive fireplace, elegant antiques, and an absorbing collection of modern art. Another highlight is the beautifully landscaped garden, perfect for picnicking. ✉ *30835 N. Hwy. 99W, Newberg*

☎ 503/538–0666, 800/739–4455 🌐 *www.rexhill.com* 🎫 *$10* 🕒 *Daily 10–5; closed major holidays.*

Utopia Vineyard. Take a trip back in time to when the Oregon wine industry was much smaller and more intimate. Utopia owner and winemaker Daniel Warnhius moved north from California looking for a vineyard site that would produce world-class Pinot Noir, and found this location with the right combination of location, climate, and soil structure. In the tasting room, you're likely to be served by Daniel himself. In addition to several great Pinot Noirs, they also produce a light, crisp Pinot Blanc, and a Pinot Noir Rosé. ✉ *17445 N.E. Ribbon Ridge Rd., Newberg* ☎ *503/687–1671* 🌐 *utopiawine.com* 🕒 *Daily 11–6.*

Vercingetorix. This small winery south of Newberg, which produces only Pinot Gris, Pinot Blanc, and Pinot Noir, is part of Willamette Farms, a grower of hazelnuts, trees, and wine grapes. The crisp, fruity Pinot Gris is especially worth seeking out. The winery has a half mile of Willamette River frontage, so you can claim a picnic table and keep your eyes peeled for wildlife (beavers, deer, ducks, geese, and raptors). ✉ *8000 N.E. Parrish Rd., Newberg* ☎ *503/538–9895* 🌐 *www.vxvineyardwine.com* 🕒 *May–Nov., weekends 11–5.*

WHERE TO EAT AND STAY

For expanded hotel reviews, visit Fodors.com.

$$$$ MODERN AMERICAN

🍴 **Jory.** This exquisite hotel dining room is named after one of the soils in the Oregon wine country. Here you can order grilled Muscovy duck over roasted grapes and watch it cook over a wood grill. Start off with butternut squash soup with shreds of fresh apple. Fish lovers will relish the saffron fettuccine in a tomato-fennel broth with bay scallops, prawns, and mussels. The dessert menu has orange-cardamom doughnuts accompanying a vanilla crème brûlée, and a brown-butter cake with hazelnut praline ice cream. Naturally, the restaurant has an expansive wine list focused on Oregon wines. [$] *Average main: $35* ✉ *The Allison Inn, 2525 Allison La., Newberg* ☎ *503/554–2525* 🌐 *www.theallison.com* 🕒 *No lunch Sun.*

$$$$ RESORT Fodor's Choice ★

🏨 **The Allison Inn & Spa.** At this luxurious, relaxing base for exploring the region's 200 wineries, each bright, comfortable room includes a gas fireplace, original works of art, a soaking tub, impressive furnishings, bay-window seats, and views of the vineyards from the terrace or balcony. **Pros:** outstanding on-site restaurant; excellent gym and spa facilities; located in the middle of wine country. **Cons:** not many nearby off-property activities other than wine tasting. [$] *Rooms from: $315* ✉ *2525 Allison La., Newberg* ☎ *503/554–2525* 🌐 *www.theallison.com* 🛏 *65 rooms, 20 suites.*

$$ B&B/INN

🏨 **Le Puy A Wine Valley Inn.** This beautiful wine country inn caters to wine enthusiasts with amenities that include wine bars in each individually decorated room, along with hot tubs and gas fireplaces in some. **Pros:** beautiful surroundings; lots of nice architectural and decorative touches. **Cons:** a distance from sights other than wineries. [$] *Rooms from: $195* ✉ *20300 N.E. Hwy. 240, Newberg* ☎ *503/554–9528* 🌐 *lepuy-inn.com* 🛏 *8 Rooms* 🍽 *Breakfast.*

Balloon festival in the Willamette Valley

NIGHTLIFE AND THE ARTS

99W Drive-in. Ted Francis built this drive-in in 1953, and operated it until his death at 98; the business is now run by his grandson. The first film begins at dusk. ✉ *3110 Portland Rd. (Hwy. 99W), Newberg* ☎ *503/538–2738* ⊕ *www.99w.com* 💲 *$8, vehicles with single occupant $12* 🕓 *Fri.–Sun.*

SPORTS AND THE OUTDOORS

BALLOONING

Hot-air balloon rides are nothing less than a spectacular, breathtaking thrill—particularly over Oregon's beautiful Yamhill County.

Vista Balloon Adventures. Several balloons are launched daily from Sportsman Airpark in Newberg. They rise about 1,500 feet, and the FAA-licensed pilots often can steer the craft down to skim the water, then up to view hawk's nests. A brunch is included afterwards. ✉ *Newberg* ☎ *503/625–7385, 800/622–2309* ⊕ *www.vistaballoon.com* 💲 *$189 per person* 🕓 *Apr.–Oct., Mon., Wed., Fri., weekends and holidays.*

DUNDEE

3 miles southwest of Newberg on Hwy. 99 W.

Dundee used to be known for growing the lion's share (more than 90%) of the U.S. hazelnut crop. Today, some of Oregon's top rated wineries are just outside of Dundee, and the area is now best-known for wine tourism and wine bars, bed-and-breakfast inns, and restaurants.

GETTING HERE AND AROUND

Dundee is just under an hour's drive from Portland International Airport; **Caravan Airport Transportation** (☎ *541/994–9645* ⊕ *www. caravanairporttransportation.com*) provides shuttle service.

What used to be a pleasant drive through quaint Dundee on Highway 99W now can be a traffic hassle, as it serves as the main artery from Lincoln City on the Oregon Coast to suburban Portland. Others will enjoy wandering along the 25 miles of Highway 18 between Dundee and Grande Ronde, in the Coast Range, which goes through the heart of the Yamhill Valley wine country.

Yamhill County Transit Area (*YCTA* ☎ *503/472–0457 Ext. 122* ⊕ *www. yctransitarea.org*) provides bus service for Yamhill County, with links to Hillsboro/MAX, Sherwood/TriMet, and Salem/SAMT.

VISITOR INFORMATION

⇨ *See Chehalem Valley Chamber of Commerce in Planning, above.*

EXPLORING

Fodor'sChoice ★ **Archery Summit Winery.** The winery that Gary and Nancy Andrus, owners of Pine Ridge winery in Napa Valley, founded in the 1990s has become synonomous with premium Oregon Pinot Noir. Because they believed that great wines are made in the vineyard, they adopted such innovative techniques as narrow spacing and vertical trellis systems, which give the fruit a great concentration of flavors. In addition to the standard flight of Pinot Noirs in the tasting room, you can call ahead and reserve a private seated tasting or a sensory tasting paired with small bites or a tour of the winery and, weather permitting, a walk out to the vineyard. You're welcome to bring a picnic, and as at many Oregon wineries, you can bring your dog too. ⊠ *18599 N.E. Archery Summit Rd., Dayton* ☎ *503/864–4300* ⊕ *www.archerysummit.com* ☜ *$15* ⊗ *Daily 10–4.*

Argyle Winery. A beautiful establishment, Argyle has its tasting room in a Victorian farmhouse set amid gorgeous gardens. The winery is tucked into a former hazelnut processing plant—which explains the Nuthouse label on its reserve wines. Since Argyle opened in 1987, it has consistently produced sparkling wines that are crisp on the palate, with an aromatic, lingering finish and bubbles that seem to last forever. And these sparklers cost about a third of their counterparts from California. The winery also produces Chardonnay, dry Riesling, Pinot Gris, and Pinot Noir. ⊠ *691 Hwy. 99 W* ☎ *503/538–8520, 888/427–4953* ⊕ *www. argylewinery.com* ⊗ *Daily 11–5.*

Dobbes Family Estate. Joe Dobbes makes a lot of wine, but he's definitely not a bulk winemaker. He provides custom wine-making services to many Oregon wineries that are too small to have their own winery or winemaker. But he also makes several lines of his own wine, ranging from his everyday "Wine By Joe" label to the premium Dobbes Family Estate label featuring great Pinot Noir, Syrah, Sauvignon Blanc, Viognier, and Grenache Blanc. In addition to a few single vineyard Pinot Noir bottlings, Dobbes focuses on blends from multiple vineyards to provide consistent, balanced, and interesting wines. Two different

Continued on page 206

The Willamette Valley is Oregon's premier wine region. With a milder climate than any growing area in California, cool-climate grapes like Pinot Noir and Pinot Gris thrive here, and are being transformed into world-class wines.

There may be fewer and smaller wineries than in Napa, but the experience is often more intimate. The winemaker himself may even pour you wine.

Touring is easy, as most wineries are well marked, and have tasting rooms with regular hours. Whether you're taking a day trip from Portland, or staying for a couple of days, here's how to get the most out of your sipping experience.

By Dave Sandage and John Doerper

Above and right, Willamette Valley

Wine Tasting
in the
Willamette Valley

OREGON'S WINES: THEN AND NOW

Rex Hill Vineyards

THE EARLY YEARS

The French made wine first—French Canadians, that is. In the 1830s, retired fur trappers from the Hudson's Bay Company started to colonize the Willamette Valley and planted grapes on the south-facing buttes. They were followed by American settlers who made wine.

Although wine-making in the region languished after these early efforts, it never quite vanished. A few wineries hung on, producing wines mainly for Oregonians of European descent.

It wasn't until the 1970s that the state's wine industry finally took off. Only after a group of young California winemakers started making vinifera wines in the Umpqua and Willamette Valleys and gained international acclaim for them, did Oregon's wines really take hold.

WINEMAKING TODAY

Today, Oregon's wine industry is racing ahead. Here the most prolific white and red grapes are Pinot Gris and Pinot Noir, respectively. Other prominent varietals include Riesling, Gewürztraminer, Viognier, Chardonnay, Carbernet Franc, and Syrah.

The wine industry in Oregon is still largely dominated by family and boutique wineries that pay close attention to quality and are often keen to experiment. That makes traveling and tasting at the source an always-interesting experience.

OREGON CERTIFIED SUSTAINABLE WINE

The latest trend in Oregon winemaking is a dedication to responsible grape growing and winemaking. When you see the Oregon Certified Sustainable Wine (OCSW) logo on the back of a wine bottle, it means the winery ensures accountable agricultural and winemaking practices (in conjunction with agencies such as USDA Organic, Demeter Biodynamic, the Food Alliance, Salmon-Safe, and Low Input Viticulture and Enology) through independent third-party certification. For more information on Oregon Certified Sustainable wines and participating wineries, check ⊕ www.ocsw.org.

WINE TASTING PRIMER

Ordering and tasting wine—whether at a winery, bar, or restaurant—is easy once you master a few simple steps.

LOOK AND NOTE

Hold your glass by the stem and look at the wine in the glass. Note its color, depth, and clarity.

For whites, is it greenish, yellow, or gold? For reds, is it purplish, ruby, or garnet? Is the wine's color pale or deep? Is the liquid clear or cloudy?

SWIRL AND SNIFF

Swirl the wine gently in the glass to intensify the scents, then sniff over the rim of the glass. What do you smell? Try to identify aromas like:

- **Fruits**—citrus, peaches, berries, figs, melon
- **Minerals**—earth, steely notes, wet stones
- **Flowers**—orange blossoms, honey, perfume
- **Dairy**—butter, cream, cheese, yogurt
- **Spices**—baking spices, pungent, herbal notes
- **Oak**—toast, vanilla, coconut, tobacco
- **Vegetables**—fresh or cooked, herbal notes
- **Animal**—leathery, meaty notes

Are there any unpleasant notes, like mildew or wet dog, that might indicate that the wine is "off?"

SIP AND SAVOR

Prime your palate with a sip, swishing the wine in your mouth. Then spit in a bucket or swallow.

Take another sip and think about the wine's attributes. Sweetness is detected on the tip of the tongue, acidity on the sides of the tongue, and tannins (a mouth-drying sensation) on the gums. Consider the body—does the wine feel light in the mouth, or is there a rich sensation? Are the flavors consistent with the aromas? If you like the wine, try to pinpoint what you like about it, and vice versa if you don't like it.

Take time to savor the wine as you're sipping it—the tasting experience may seem a bit scientific, but the end goal is your enjoyment.

WINE TOURING AND TASTING

Wine tasting at Argyle and Rex Hill

WHEN TO GO

In high season (June through October) and on weekends and holidays during much of the year, wine-country roads can be busy and tasting rooms are often crowded. If you prefer a more intimate tasting experience, plan your visit for a weekday.

To avoid the frustration of a fruitless drive, confirm in advance that wineries of interest will be open when you plan to visit.

Choose a designated driver for the day: Willamette wine-country roads are often narrow and curvy, and you may be sharing the road with bicyclists and wildlife as well as other wine tourists.

IN THE TASTING ROOM

Tasting rooms are designed to introduce newcomers to the pleasures of wine and to the wines made at the winery. At popular wineries you'll sometimes have to pay for your tasting, anything from a nominal $2 fee to $30 and up for a tasting that might include a glass you can take home. This fee is often deducted if you buy wine before leaving.

WHAT'S AN AVA?

AVAs (American Viticultural Areas) are geographic winegrowing regions that vaguely reflect the French concept of terroir, or "sense of place." The vineyards within a given AVA have similar characteristics such as climate, soil types, and/or elevation, which impart shared characteristics to the wines made from grapes grown in that area. AVAs are strictly geographic boundaries distinct from city or county designations. AVAs can also be subdivided into sub-AVAs; each of the AVAs mentioned here is actually part of the larger Willamette Valley AVA.

Each taste consists of an ounce or two. Feel free to pour whatever you don't finish into one of the dump buckets on the bar. If you like, rinse your glass between pours with a little water. Remember, those sips add up, so pace yourself. If you plan to visit several wineries, try just a few wines at each so you won't suffer from palate fatigue, when your mouth can no longer distinguish subtleties. It's also a good idea to bring a picnic lunch, which you can enjoy on the deck of a winery, taking in the surrounding wine country vistas.

FALL FOLIAGE

In autumn, Willamette Valley vineyards are particularly stunning as the leaves change color.

DAY TRIP FROM PORTLAND

With nearly 150 vineyards, the Chehalem Mountain and Ribbon Ridge AVAs offer widely varied soil types and diverse Pinot Noirs. The region is less than an hour away from Portland.

Ponzi Vineyards

CHEHALEM MOUNTAIN AND RIBBON RIDGE AVAS

❶ PONZI VINEYARDS

First planted in 1970, Ponzi has some of Oregon's oldest Pinot Noir vines. In addition to current releases, the tasting room sometimes offers older library wines. **Try:** *Arneis, a crisp Italian white varietal.*

✉ 14665 SW Winery La., Beaverton

☎ 503/628–1227

🌐 www.ponziwines.com

❷ REX HILL VINEYARDS

Before grapevines, the Willamette Valley was widely planted with fruits and nuts. Enjoy classic Oregon Pinot Noir in this tasting room built around an old fruit and nut drying facility. **Try:** *dark and spicy Dundee Hills Pinot Noir.*

✉ 30835 N. Hwy. 99W, Newberg

☎ 800/739–4455

🌐 www.rexhill.com

❸ VERCINGETORIX (VX) VINEYARD

This 10-acre vineyard sits in the middle of a 210-acre farm near the Willamette River. The tasting room is in one of the barns; a relaxed, friendly atmosphere for sampling. **Try:** *crisp and refreshing Pinot Blanc.*

✉ 8000 N.E. Parrish Rd., Newberg

☎ 503/538–9895

🌐 www.vxvineyard.com

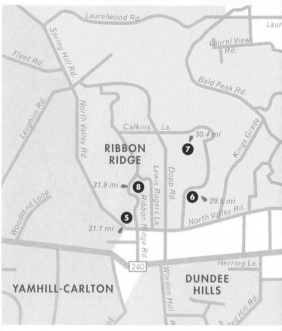

❹ FOX FARM VINEYARDS TASTING ROOM

In addition to offering their own wines, this multi-winery tasting room in downtown Newberg features samples from several small local producers. The menu changes periodically.

✉ 602 E. First St., Newberg

☎ 503/538–8466

🌐 www.foxfarmvineyards.com

❺ UTOPIA VINEYARD

The tasting room at this small Oregon winery is quite intimate—you'll likely be served by the winemaker himself. **Try:** *light and slightly sweet Rosé.*

✉ 17445 N.E. Ribbon Ridge Rd., Newberg

☎ 503/298–7841

🌐 www.utopiawine.com

Vercingetorix (VX) Vineyard

Adelsheim Vineyard

Rex Hill

Pinot Gris grapes

MAP

219 Scholls Ferry Rd.
Scholls
Winery La.
❶
15.7 mi

219
Scholls Sherwood Blvd.

TO PORTLAND ↗
Beef Bend Rd.

la Hill

LeBeau Rd.
99W

CHEHALEM MOUNTAINS

Edy Rd.

Bell Rd.
Sunset Blvd.
O Sherwood

I Rd.
23 mi
❾
Quarry Rd.

Pleasant Hill Rd.

Haugen Rd.
❷
21.1 mi
❿

Newberg
Ladd Hill

99W
❹
23.9 mi
Corral Cr.

219

Ladd Hill

Parrish Rd.
Wilsonville Rd.
❸
25.8 mi

5th St.

KEY
| Driving distance from Portland |
| 00 mi |

---

❻ ADELSHEIM VINEYARD

One of Oregon's older Pinot Noir producers, Adelsheim has just opened a new tasting room inside its modern winery, with friendly, knowledgeable employees. **Try:** *dark and smoky Elizabeth's Reserve Pinot Noir.*

✉ 16800 N.E. Calkins La., Newberg
☎ 503/538-3652
⊕ www.adelsheim.com

❼ BERGSTROM WINERY

A beautiful tasting room, but the real high point here is the classic Oregon Pinot Noir sourced from several of its estate vineyards as well as other local sites. **Try:** *earthy Bergstrom Pinot Noir.*

✉ 18215 N.E. Calkins La., Newberg
☎ 503/554-0468
⊕ www.bergstromwines.com

❽ ARAMENTA CELLARS

A small, family-run operation that offers tastings in its winery, built on the foundation of an old barn. The on-site vineyard grows primarily Pinot Noir and Chardonnay. **Try:** *smooth and structured Tillie Claret.*

✉ 17979 N.E. Lewis Rogers La., Newberg
☎ 503/538-7230
⊕ www.aramentacellars.com

STOP FOR A BITE

❾ JORY RESTAURANT

Located within the luxurious Allison Inn and Spa, Jory serves creative dishes that highlight the bounty of the Willamette Valley.

✉ 2525 Allison La., Newberg
☎ 503/554-2526
⊕ www.theallison.com

❿ SUBTERRA

Casual fine dining in a wine cellar atmosphere underneath the Dark Horse wine bar. The menu features global cuisine and a good selection of local wines.

✉ 1505 Portland Rd., Newberg
☎ 503/538-6060
⊕ www.subterrarestaurant.com

TWO DAYS IN WINE COUNTRY

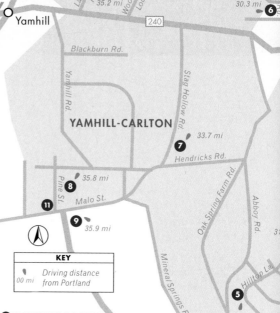

DAY 1

DUNDEE HILLS AVA

The Dundee Hills AVA is home to some of Oregon's best known Pinot Noir producers. Start your tour in the town of Dundee, about 30 miles southwest of Portland, then drive up into the red hills and enjoy the valley views from many wineries.

❶ ARGYLE WINERY

If you don't want to drive off the beaten path, this winery is right on Highway 99W in Dundee. They specialize in sparkling wines, but also make very nice still wines. **Try:** *crisp Brut Rosé.*

- ✉ 691 Hwy. 99 W, Dundee
- ☎ 503/538–8520
- ⊕ www.argylewinery.com

❷ PONZI WINE BAR

This tasting room close to Argyle has a huge selection of local wines. It's a good choice for those who want to sample a large selection side-by-side. **Try:** *bright and fruity Ponzi Pinot Gris.*

- ✉ 100 S.W. 7th St., Dundee
- ☎ 503/554–1500
- ⊕ www.ponziwinebar.com

❸ ARCHERY SUMMIT

An Oregon Pinot Noir pioneer, Archery Summit features memorable wines and equally pleasing views. Call in advance to schedule a tour of the winery and aging caves. **Try:** *dark and rich Premier Cuvée Pinot Noir.*

- ✉ 18599 NE Archery Summit Rd., Dayton
- ☎ 503/864–4300
- ⊕ www.archerysummit.com

❹ DOMAINE DROUHIN OREGON

Started in the late 1980s by the Drouhin family of Burgundy fame, this winery makes notable Oregon Pinot Noir, as well as Chardonnay. **Try:** *smooth and earthy Willamette Valley Pinot Noir.*

- ✉ 6750 Breyman Orchards Rd., Dayton
- ☎ 503/864–2700
- ⊕ www.domainedrouhin.com

❺ VISTA HILLS VINEYARD

The so-called Treehouse is arguably the most stunning tasting room in Oregon. Sample wine made from estate fruit on a deck that overlooks the vineyards of the Dundee Hills. **Try:** *fruity Treehouse Pinot Noir.*

- ✉ 6475 N.E. Hilltop La., Dayton
- ☎ 503/864–3200
- ⊕ www.vistahillsvineyard.com

DAY 2

YAMHILL-CARLTON AVA

To the west of the Dundee Hills AVA is the horseshoe-shaped Yamhill-Carlton AVA. Vineyards here are found on the slopes that surround the towns of Yamhill and Carlton. Carlton has become a center of wine tourism, and you could easily spend a day visiting tasting rooms in town.

❻ PENNER-ASH WINE CELLARS

This state-of-the-art winery and tasting room is atop a hill with an excellent view of the valley below. **Try:** *smooth and dark Shea Vineyard Pinot Noir.*

- ✉ 15771 N.E. Ribbon Ridge Rd., Newberg
- ☎ 503/554–5545
- ⊕ www.pennerash.com

nner-Ash Wine Cellars

Ponzi Wine Bar

STOP FOR A BITE

DUNDEE HILLS

TO ↗ NEWBERG, PORTLAND

99W

Red Hill Rd.

Fox Farm Rd.

Fairview

26.5 mi

7th St.

5th St.

9th St.

26.4 mi

Albert St.

29.4 mi

Archery Summit Rd.

Orchards Rd.

⑭

⑫

②

①

⑬

○ Dundee

③

⑦ LEMELSON VINEYARDS
Although it specializes in single-vineyard Pinot Noir, Lemelson also makes several crisp white wines. The deck overlooking the vineyards is perfect for picnics. **Try:** *crisp and fruity Riesling.*
- ✉ 12020 N.E. Stag Hollow Rd., Carlton
- ☎ 503/852-6619
- 🌐 www.lemelsonvineyards.com

⑧ TYRUS EVAN WINE
Well-known winemaker Ken Wright's second label features big reds. The tasting room is in the historic Carlton train station. **Try:** *bold and spicy Del Rio Claret.*
- ✉ 120 N. Pine St., Carlton
- ☎ 503/852-7070
- 🌐 www.tyrusevanwine.com

⑨ SCOTT PAUL WINES
In addition to making Oregon Pinot Noir, Scott Paul Wines also runs a Burgundy import company, allowing you to taste locally grown Pinot Noir alongside some of the best Burgundies. **Try:** *structured and elegant La Paulée Pinot Noir.*
- ✉ 128 S. Pine St., Carlton
- ☎ 503/852-7300
- 🌐 www.scottpaul.com

⑩ LENNÉ ESTATE
Lenné specializes in highly regarded Pinot Noir, although it's often pouring a couple of non-Pinot wines from other wineries as well. The tasting room in a small stone building overlooks the vineyards. **Try:** *complex and earthy Estate Pinot Noir.*
- ✉ 18760 Laughlin Rd., Yamhill
- ☎ 503/956-2256
- 🌐 www.lenneestate.com

⑪ THE HORSERADISH WINE AND CHEESE BAR
Located in downtown Carlton, The Horseradish offers a wide selection of local wines as well as cheese from around the world. The sandwiches and small plates make for a great quick lunch.
- ✉ 211 W. Main St., Carlton
- ☎ 503/852-6656
- 🌐 www.thehorseradish.com

⑫ DUNDEE BISTRO
A favorite of winemakers, Dundee Bistro serves seasonal local ingredients paired with Willamette Valley wines. Enjoy outdoor seating, or watch chefs work in the open kitchen inside.
- ✉ 100-A S.W. 7th St., Dundee
- ☎ 503/554-1650
- 🌐 www.dundeebistro.com

⑬ TINA'S
The warm and intimate Tina's features dishes made with seasonal ingredients, organic vegetables, and free-range meats. Stop by for lunch Tuesday–Friday, or nightly dinner.
- ✉ 760 Hwy. 99 W, Dundee
- ☎ 503/538-8880
- 🌐 www.tinasdundee.com

⑭ RED HILLS PROVINCIAL DINING
French and Italian fare made with fresh ingredients from the Willamette Valley. It has an extensive wine list with local and global selections.
- ✉ 276 N. Hwy. 99 W, Dundee
- ☎ 503/538-8224
- 🌐 www.redhills-dining.com

tasting flights are available in the tasting room, and seated tastings and tours can be arranged by appointment. ✉ *240 S.E. 5th St., Dundee* ☎ *503/538–1141* ⊕ *www.joedobbeswines.com* ☉ *Daily 11–6.*

Fodor's Choice
★

Domaine Drouhin Oregon. When the French winery magnate Robert Drouhin ("the Sebastiani of France") planted a vineyard and built a winery in the Red Hills of Dundee back in 1987, he set local oenophiles abuzz. His daughter Veronique is now the winemaker and produces silky and elegant Pinot Noir and Chardonnay. Ninety acres of the 225-acre estate have been planted. The hillside setting was selected to take advantage of the natural coolness of the earth and to establish a gravity-flow winery. No appointment is needed to taste the Oregon wines, but if you can plan ahead for the tour (reservations required), you can taste Oregon and Burgundy side-by-side. ✉ *6750 N.E. Breyman Orchards Rd., Dayton* ☎ *503/864–2700* ⊕ *www.domainedrouhin.com* ✑ *$10* ☉ *Wed.–Sun. 11–4. Tours by appointment only.*

Domaine Serene. This world-class winery in Dundee's Red Hills is a well-regarded producer of Oregon Pinot Noir and Chardonnay. Bring a picnic and enjoy the beautiful grounds of the estate. As an alternative to the standard drop-in tasting in the high ceiling tasting room, call ahead to reserve a tour or private seated tasting, which includes an extended flight of rare wines. ✉ *6555 N.E. Hilltop La., Dayton* ☎ *503/864–4600* ⊕ *www.domaineserene.com* ☉ *Wed.–Mon. 11–4.*

Erath Vineyards Winery. When Dick Erath opened one of Oregon's pioneer wineries more than a quarter century ago, he focused on producing distinctive Pinot Noir from grapes he'd been growing in the Red Hills since 1972—as well as full-flavored Pinot Gris, Pinot Blanc, Chardonnay, Riesling, and late-harvest Gewürztraminer. The wines are excellent and reasonably priced. In 2006 the winery was sold to Washington State's giant conglomerate Ste. Michelle Wine Estate. The tasting room is in the middle of the vineyards, high in the hills, with views in nearly every direction; the hazelnut trees that covered the slopes not so long ago have been replaced with vines. The tasting-room terrace, which overlooks the winery and the hills, is a choice spot for picnicking. Crabtree Park, next to the winery, is a good place to stretch your legs after a tasting. ✉ *9409 N.E. Worden Hill Rd.* ☎ *503/538–3318, 800/539–9463* ⊕ *www.erath.com* ✑ *$10* ☉ *Daily 11–5.*

Maresh Red Barn. When Jim and Loie Maresh planted two acres of vines in 1970, theirs became the fifth vineyard in Oregon and the first on Worden Hill Road. The quality of their grapes was so high that some of the Dundee Hills' best and most famous wineries soon sought them out. When the wine industry boomed in the 1980s, the Mareshes decided they might as well enjoy some wine from their renowned grapes, now planted on 45 acres of their land. They transformed their old barn into a tasting room, where you can taste and purchase exceptional Chardonnay, Pinot Noir, Pinot Gris, Riesling, and Sauvignon Blanc made by several acclaimed local winemakers from Maresh family grapes. ✉ *9325 N.W. Worden Hill Rd.* ☎ *503/537–1098* ⊕ *www.vineyardretreat.com* ✑ *$5* ☉ *Mar.–Dec., Wed.–Sun. 11–5 and by appointment.*

Ponzi Wine Bar. A huge array of local wines is available for tasting or purchase by the glass, bottle, or case. The tasting menu features current releases of Ponzi wines, as well as a rotating selection of other local wines. If you've had enough wine for a while, you can also get snacks, Italian coffee, or a craft beer as you browse the selection of wine country books, gifts, and gourmet food products. ✉ *100 S.W. 7th St., Dundee* ☎ *503/554–1500* ⊕ *ponziwinebar.com.*

Sokol Blosser. One of Yamhill County's oldest wineries (it was established in 1971) makes consistently excellent wines and sells them at reasonable prices. Set on a gently sloping south-facing hillside and surrounded by vineyards, lush lawns, and shade trees, it's a splendid place to learn about wine. A demonstration vineyard with several rows of vines contains the main grape varieties and shows what happens to them as the seasons unfold. Winery tours are available by reservation as well as vineyard hikes and ATV tours during the summer. ✉ *5000 Sokol Blosser La., 3 miles west of Dundee off Hwy. 99W* ☎ *503/864–2282, 800/582–6668* ⊕ *www.sokolblosser.com* ☉ *Daily 10–4.*

Torii Mor Winery. One of Yamhill County's oldest vineyards, established in 1993, makes small quantities of handcrafted Pinot Noir, Pinot Gris, and Chardonnay and is set amid Japanese gardens with breathtaking views of the Willamette Valley. The gardens were designed by Takuma Tono, the same architect who designed the renowned Portland Japanese Garden. The owners, who love things Japanese, named their winery after the distinctive Japanese gate of Shinto religious significance; they added a Scandinavian mor, signifying "earth," to create an east–west combo: "earth gate." Jacques Tardy, a native of Nuits Saint Georges, in Burgundy, France, is the current winemaker. Under his guidance Torii Mor wines have become more Burgundian in style. ✉ *18323 N.E. Fairview Dr.* ☎ *800/839–5004* ⊕ *www.toriimorwinery.com* 🍷 *$10* ☉ *Daily 11–5.*

Vista Hills Vineyard. The Treehouse tasting room is arguably the most beautiful in Oregon. Step out onto the deck and enjoy the view from underneath the towering trees. Vista Hills is a bit different in that they don't actually have a winery but partner with several well-known local winemakers to create wine from their grapes to sell under the Vista Hills label. The result is a range of distinctive wine styles, all made from the same vineyard. Also available are Hawaiian chocolate and coffee from their sister farm in Kona. ✉ *6475 Hilltop La., Dayton* ☎ *503/864–3200* ⊕ *www.vistahillsvineyard.com* ☉ *Daily noon–5.*

White Rose Estate. Like many of its better-known neighbors in the Dundee Hills, White Rose Estate produces elegant Pinot Noir that reflects the land where it is grown. In addition to their own estate vineyard, they purchase grapes from several highly regarded vineyards around the Willamette Valley. They describe their wines as "neo-classical," using traditional techniques in the vineyard, and state of the art equipment and handling in the winery. Somewhat unusual for Oregon, most of the wines have a fairly high percentage of whole clusters included during fermentation, giving the wines more complexity and a bit of spice. ⊠ *6250 N.E. Hilltop La., Dayton* ☎ *503/864–2328* ⊕ *www. whiteroseestate.com* ☉ *Daily 11–5.*

Winderlea. The tasting room looks over the acclaimed former Goldschmidt vineyard, first planted in 1974, and the view can be enjoyed on the outside deck on a warm summer day. Winemaker Robert Brittan crafts lush Pinot Noir and Chardonnay from several nearby vineyards in both single-vineyard offerings and blends from multiple vineyards. Proceeds from the tasting fee are donated to Salud, a partnership between Oregon winemakers and local medical professionals to provide healthcare services for Oregon's seasonal vineyard workers and their families. ⊠ *8905 N.E. Worden Hill Rd, Dundee* ☎ *503/554–5900* ⊕ *www. winderlea.com* ☉ *June–Sept., daily 11–4; Oct.–May, Thurs.–Mon.11–4.*

WHERE TO EAT AND STAY
For expanded hotel reviews, visit Fodors.com.

$$$
CONTEMPORARY

✕**Dundee Bistro.** The Ponzi wine family are capable restaurateurs as well and use Northwest organic foods such as Draper Valley chicken, Carlton Farms pork and locally produced wines, fruits, vegetables, nuts, mushrooms, fish, and meats. Vaulted ceilings provide an open feeling inside, warmed by abundant fresh flowers and the works of local Oregon artists. $ *Average main: $25* ⊠ *100-A S.W. 7th St.* ☎ *503/554–1650* ⊕ *www.dundeebistro.com.*

$$$
PACIFIC
NORTHWEST

✕**Paulée.** Fresh, local, seasonal, and sustainable are the hallmarks in this dining room that attracts winemakers, winery workers, locals, and visitors with a creative take on Northwest cuisine. The menu changes daily and is available à la carte or as tasting menus. The wine list is extensive and includes selections from around the world in addition to a good selection of local offerings. If you're not in the mood for more wine after a day of tasting, try one of the many local craft beers on tap. $ *Average main: $27* ⊠ *1410 N. Hwy. 99W, Dundee* ☎ *503/538–7970* ⊕ *pauleerestaurant.com.*

$$$
MODERN
AMERICAN

✕**Red Hills Provincial Dining.** A beautifully restored Craftsman home provides a warm and intimate atmosphere in which to enjoy dishes made with local season ingredients prepared using traditional European techniques. The braised lamb shank is perfect on a cool winter evening, and there's usually fresh local seafood on the menu. The wine list is extensive and features both local and global selections. You'll want to linger over one of their irresistible house-made desserts. $ *Average main: $28* ⊠ *276 N. Hwy. 99W, Dundee* ☎ *503/538–8244* ⊕ *redhillsdining.com* ☉ *Closed Mon.*

$$$
FRENCH
Fodor's Choice
★

✕**Tina's.** Chef–proprietors Tina and David Bergen bring a powerful one-two punch to this Dundee favorite that often lures Portlanders away from their own restaurant scene. The couple shares cooking duties—Tina does the baking and is often on hand to greet you, and David brings his experience as a former caterer and employee of nearby Sokol Blosser Winery to the table, ensuring that you have the right glass of wine to match your course. Fish and game vie for attention on the country-French menu: entrées might include grilled Oregon salmon or Alaskan halibut, or a braised rabbit, local lamb, or tenderloin. Avail yourself of any special soups, particularly if there's corn chowder in the house. The lunch menu includes soup, sandwiches, and creative salads with local, seasonal ingredients. Service is as intimate and laid-back as the interior. A double fireplace divides the dining room, with heavy glass brick shrouded by bushes on the highway side, so you're not bothered by the traffic on Highway 99. $ *Average main: $30* ⊠ *760 Hwy. 99 W* ☎ *503/538–8880* ⊕ *www.tinasdundee.com* ⊙ *No lunch Sat.–Mon.*

$$
B&B/INN
Fodor's Choice
★

🏠 **Dundee Manor Bed and Breakfast.** This 1908-built traditional home on expansive grounds is filled with treasures and collectibles that add intrigue to each themed room: African, Asian, European, and North American. **Pros:** terrific amenities; lots of activities; attentive staff. **Cons:** few rooms. $ *Rooms from: $175* ⊠ *8380 N.E. Worden Hill Rd.* ☎ *503/554–1945, 888/262–1133* ⊕ *www.dundeemanor.com* ⋌ *4 rooms* ⍾⊘ *Breakfast.*

$$
HOTEL

🏠 **The Inn at Red Hills.** These spacious and extremely comfortable rooms, each with its own layout, offer plenty of local flavor, from the materials in the building, the wines served, and the ingredients used in the kitchen. **Pros:** contemporary, stylish surroundings; close to many wineries. **Cons:** located on the main highway through town rather than the country. $ *Rooms from: $199* ⊠ *1410 N. Hwy. 99 W* ☎ *503/538–7666* ⊕ *www. innatredhills.com* ⋌ *18 rooms, 2 suites* ⍾⊘ *No meals.*

YAMHILL-CARLTON

14 miles west of Dundee.

Just outside the small towns of Carlton and Yamhill are neatly combed benchlands and hillsides, an American Viticultural Area (AVA) established in 2004, and home to some of the finest Pinot Noir vineyards in the world. Carlton has exploded with many small tasting rooms in the past few years, and you could easily spend an entire day tasting wine within three or four blocks. The area is a gorgeous quilt of nurseries, grain fields, and orchards. Come here for the wine tasting, but don't expect to find too much else to do.

GETTING HERE AND AROUND

Having your own car is the best way to explore this rural region of Yamhill County, located a little more than an hour's drive from Portland International Airport. The towns of Yamhill and Carlton are about an hour's drive from downtown Portland, traveling through Tigard, to Newberg and west on Highway 240.

Yamhill County Transit Area (*YCTA* ☎ *503/472–0457 Ext. 122* ⊕ *www. yctransitarea.org*) provides bus service for Yamhill County, with links to Hillsboro/MAX, Sherwood/TriMet, and Salem/SAMT.

EXPLORING

Anne Amie Vineyards. Early wine country adopters Fred and Mary Benoit established this hilltop winery as Chateau Benoit in 1979. When the winery changed hands in 1999, it was renamed Anne Amie and has been concentrating on Pinot Blanc, Pinot Gris, and Pinot Noir, but still makes a dry Riesling. In addition, they also make Syrah and a Bordeaux blend from eastern Washington grapes. Both the tasting room and the picnic area have spectacular views across the hills and valleys of Yamhill County. ⊠ *6580 N.E. Mineral Springs Rd., Carlton* ☎ *503/864–2991*

⊕ *www.anneamie.com* ☜ *$5–$10* ☉ *Open Mar.–Dec., daily 10–5; Jan.–Feb., Fri.–Sun. or by appointment.*

Carlton Winemakers Studio. Oregon's first cooperative winery was specifically designed to house multiple small premium wine producers. This gravity-flow winery has up-to-date winemaking equipment as well as multiple cellars for storing the different makers' wines. You can taste and purchase bottles from the different member wineries: Andrew Rich, Bachelder, Dukes Family Vineyeard, Hamacher Wines, Lazy River Vineyard, Merriman Wines, Montebruno Wines, Omero Cellars, Retour Wine Co., Trout Lily Ranch, Utopia Vineyard, and Wahle Vineyards and Cellars. The emphasis is on Pinot Noir, but more than a dozen other types of wines are poured, from Cabernet Franc to Gewürztraminer to Mourvèdre on a rotating basis. The selection of wines available to taste changes every few days. ⊠ *801 N. Scott St., Carlton* ☎ *503/852–6100* ⊕ *www.winemakersstudio.com* ☉ *Mar.–Oct., daily 11–5; Nov.–Feb., daily 11–4.*

The Horse Radish. The perfect stop in the middle of a day of wine tasting offers a wide selection of artisan cheese and meats, as well as a great lunch menu. Pick up some sandwiches and a soup or salad to go, and you're all set for a picnic at your favorite winery. The Horse Radish is also a wine bar with a wide selection of local wines, and features live music every Friday and Saturday night. ⊠ *211 W. Main St., Carlton* ☎ *503/852–6656* ⊕ *www.thehorseradish.com.*

Ken Wright Cellars Tasting Room. Carlton's former train depot is now the tasting room for Ken Wright and his warm-climate label, Tyrus Evan. The winery specializes in single-vineyard Pinot Noirs, each subtly different from the next depending on the soil types and grape clones. The wines are poured side by side, giving you an opportunity to go back and forth to compare them. The Tyrus Evan wines are quite different from the Ken Wright Pinots: they are warm-climate varieties like Cabernet Franc, Malbec, Syrah, and red Bordeaux blends, from grapes Wright buys from vineyards in eastern Washington and southern Oregon. You can also pick up cheeses and other picnic supplies, as well as wine country gifts and souvenirs. ⊠ *120 N. Pine St., Carlton* ☎ *503/852–7010* ⊕ *www.kenwrightcellars.com* ☉ *Fri.–Sat. 11–6, Sun.–Thurs. 11–5.*

Lemelson Vineyards. This winery was designed from the ground up to be a no-compromises Pinot Noir production facility with an eye to Willamette Valley aesthetics, and the highlight is a diverse range of single-vineyard Pinot Noirs. But don't neglect the bright Pinot Gris and Riesling, perfect with seafood or spicy fare. The spacious high-ceiling tasting room is a great place to relax and take in the view through the floor-to-ceiling windows, or bring a picnic and enjoy the deck on a warm summer day. ⊠ *12020 N.E. Stag Hollow Rd, Carlton* ☎ *503/852–6619* ⊕ *www.lemelsonvineyards.com* ☉ *Thurs.–Mon. 11–4.*

Lenné Estate. The small stone building that houses the tasting room is surrounded by the estate vineyard and looks like something right out of Burgundy. Steve Lutz was looking for the perfect site to grow Pinot Noir and bought the property in 2000. In addition to offering his own rich and elegant estate Pinot Noirs for tasting, he often pours other

Carlton Winemakers Studio

varietals from other wineries. ✉ *18760 N.E. Laughlin Rd., Yamhill* ☎ *503/956–2256* ⊕ *www.lenneestate.com* 🍷 *$10* ☻ *Weekends 12–5.*

Scott Paul Tasting Room and Winery. Pinot Noir fans, listen up: this small spot in the center of Carlton not only makes Pinot Noir from local grapes, but it also imports and sells Pinot Noirs from Burgundy. The three Pinot Noirs made from local grapes are Audrey, the finest wine of the vintage; La Paulée, a selection of the best lots of each vintage; and Cuvée Martha Pirrie, a fruit-forward, silky wine meant to be drunk young. All are splendid examples of the wines that can be made from this great, challenging grape. The tasting room, a quaint red-brick building, is across the street from the winery. Winery tours are by appointment only. Wine seminars are offered in the evenings, and private guided tastings are available by appointment. ✉ *128 S. Pine St., Carlton* ☎ *503/852–7300* ⊕ *www.scottpaul.com* ☻ *Sat. noon–5.*

MCMINNVILLE

11 miles south of Yamhill on Hwy. 99 W.

The Yamhill County seat, McMinnville lies in the center of Oregon's thriving wine industry. There is a larger concentration of wineries in Yamhill County than in any other area of the state. Among the varieties are Chardonnay, Pinot Noir, and Pinot Gris. Most of the wineries in the area offer tours and tastings. McMinnville's downtown area, with a pleasantly disproportionate number of bookstores and art galleries for its size, is well worth exploring; many of the historic district buildings, erected 1890–1915, are still standing, and are remarkably well maintained.

GETTING HERE AND AROUND

McMinnville is a little more than an hour's drive from downtown Portland; **Caravan Airport Transportation** (☎ 541/994–9645 ⊕ *www. caravanairporttransportation.com*) provides shuttle service to Portland International Airport. McMinnville is just 70 minutes from Lincoln City on the Oregon Coast, and 27 miles west of Salem.

Yamhill County Transit Area (*YCTA* ☎ 503/472–0457 *Ext. 122* ⊕ *www. yctransitarea.org*) provides bus service for Yamhill County, with links to Hillsboro/MAX, Sherwood/TriMet, and Salem/SAMT.

ESSENTIALS

Visitor Information McMinnville Chamber of Commerce ⊠ *417 N.W. Adams St.* ☎ *503/472–6196* ⊕ *www.mcminnville.org.*

EXPLORING

FAMILY

Fodor'sChoice

★

Evergreen Aviation and Space Museum. Howard Hughes' *Spruce Goose*, the largest plane ever built and constructed entirely of wood, is on permanent display, but if you can take your eyes off the giant you will also see more than 45 historic planes and replicas from the early years of flight and World War II, as well as the postwar and modern eras. Across the parking lot from the aviation museum is the space museum with artifacts that include a German V-2 rocket and a Titan missile, complete with silo and launch control room. A water park has 10 waterslides, including one that starts at a Boeing 747-100 that sits on *top* of the building. The IMAX theater is open daily and features several different films each day. There's a museum store and two cafés, as well as ongoing educational programs and special events. ⊠ *500 N.E. Michael King Smith Way* ☎ *503/434–4185* ⊕ *www.evergreenmuseum. org* ⊡ *$25, includes IMAX movie* ⊙ *Daily 9–5, closed holidays.*

The Eyrie Vineyards. When David Lett planted the first Pinot Noir vines in the Willamette Valley in 1965, he was setting in motion a series of events that has caused Willamette Valley Pinot Noir to be recognized as among the best in the world. Affectionately known as Papa Pinot, Lett, along with several other pioneering winemakers, nurtured the Oregon wine industry to what it is today. Today David's son Jason Lett is now the winemaker and vineyard manager, and continues to make Pinot Noir, Pinot Gris, and Chardonnay that reflect the gentle touch that has always characterized Eyrie wines. In recent years, many small wineries have sprung up in the neighborhood around this historic winery. ⊠ *935 N.E. 10th Ave., McMinnville* ☎ *503/472–6315, 888/440–4970* ⊕ *www. eyrievineyards.com* ⊙ *Wed.–Sun. noon–5.*

NEED A
BREAK?

Serendipity Ice Cream. Historic Cook's Hotel, built in 1886, is the setting for a true, old-fashioned ice-cream parlor experience. Try a sundae, and take home cookies made from scratch. If you don't feel like ice cream, the homemade soup is a great choice on a rainy day. ⊠ *502 N.E. 3rd St.* ☎ *503/474–9189* ⊕ *serendipityicecream.com.*

WHERE TO EAT AND STAY

For expanded hotel reviews, visit Fodors.com.

$$$$ CONTEMPORARY 🍴 **Joel Palmer House.** Joel Palmer was an Oregon pioneer, and his 1857 home in Dayton is now on the National Register of Historic Places. There are three small dining rooms, each seating about 15 people. The chef specializes in wild-mushroom dishes; a popular starter is Heidi's three-mushroom tart. The menu changes seasonally, but the mushroom tart, Joe's wild mushroom soup, and wild mushroom risotto with Oregon truffle oil are traditions that are always available. Or, if you really, really like mushrooms, have your entire table order Chef Christopher's Mushroom Madness Menu, a six-course extravaganza. [$] *Average main: $50* ✉ *600 Ferry St., Dayton* ☎ *503/864–2995* 🌐 *www.joelpalmerhouse.com* 🕒 *Closed Sun. and Mon. No Lunch.*

$$$$ ITALIAN 🍴 **Nick's Italian Cafe.** Famed for serving Oregon's wine country enthusiasts, this fine-dining venue is a destination for a special evening or lunch. Modestly furnished but with a voluminous wine cellar, Nick's serves spirited and simple food, reflecting the owner's northern Italian heritage. A five-course prix-fixe menu changes nightly. À la carte options are also available. [$] *Average main: $35* ✉ *521 N.E. 3rd St.* ☎ *503/434–4471* 🌐 *www.nicksitaliancafe.com* ✍ *Reservations essential* 🕒 *No lunch Mon.*

$ HOTEL 🏨 **Hotel Oregon.** Rooms in the former Elberton Hotel, built in 1905, have tall ceilings and high windows, are outfitted in late-Victorian furnishings, and filled with whimsical art—sometimes serene, often bizarre—as well as photos and sayings scribbled on the walls. **Pros:** inexpensive; casual and lively; plenty of food and drink on the premises. **Cons:** shared baths for most rooms; those seeking upscale ambience should look elsewhere. [$] *Rooms from: $60* ✉ *310 N.E. Evans St.* ☎ *503/472–8427, 888/472–8427* 🌐 *www.mcmenamins.com* 🛏 *42 rooms* 🍽 *No meals.*

$$ B&B/INN Fodor's Choice ★ 🏨 **Joseph Mattey House Bed & Breakfast.** The four upstairs rooms in this Queen Anne Victorian mansion are whimsically named after locally grown grape varieties and are decorated in keeping with the character of those wines: crisp white furnishings in the Chardonnay Room, dark-wood pieces and reddish wine accents in the Pinot Noir room. **Pros:** refined bed-and-breakfast atmosphere. **Cons:** not many modern amenities in the rooms. [$] *Rooms from: $160* ✉ *10221 N.E. Mattey La., off Hwy. 99 W, ¼ mile south of Lafayette* ☎ *503/434–5058* 🌐 *www.matteyhouse.com* 🛏 *4 rooms* 🍽 *Breakfast.*

NIGHTLIFE AND THE ARTS

Spirit Mountain Casino and Lodge. Located 24 miles southwest of McMinnville on Highway 18, this popular gambling getaway is owned and operated by the Confederated Tribes of the Grande Ronde Community of Oregon. The 90,000-square-foot casino has more than a thousand slots, as well as poker and blackjack tables, roulette, craps, Pai Gow poker, keno, bingo, and off-track betting. Big-name comedians and rock and country musicians perform in the 1,700-seat concert hall, and there's an arcade for the kids. There's complimentary shuttle service from Portland and Salem. Dining options include an all-you-can-eat buffet, a deli, and a café. ✉ *27100 S.W. Hwy. 18, Grand Ronde* ☎ *503/879–2350, 800/760–7977* ⊕ *spiritmountain.com.*

MID-WILLAMETTE VALLEY

While most of the wineries are concentrated in Washington and Yamhill counties, there are several finds in the Mid-Willamette Valley that warrant extending a wine enthusiast's journey. There are also flower, hops, berries, and seed gardens scattered throughout Salem, Albany, and Corvallis. The huge number of company stores concentrated on Interstate 5 will have you thinking about some new Nikes, and Oregon State University will have you wearing orange and black long after Halloween is over. Be aware that many communities in this region are little more than wide spots in the road. In these tiny towns you might find only a gas station, a grocery store, a church or two, and a school. Watch out for any "School Crossing" signs: Oregon strictly enforces its speed-limit laws.

SALEM

24 miles from McMinnville, south on Hwy. 99 W and east on Hwy. 22; 45 miles south of Portland on I–5.

Salem has a rich pioneer history, but before that it was the home of the Calapooia Indians, who called it Chemeketa, which means "place of rest." Salem is said to have been renamed by missionaries. Although trappers and farmers preceded them in the Willamette Valley, the Methodist missionaries had come in 1834 to minister to Native Americans, and they are credited with the founding of Salem. In 1842 they established the first academic institution west of the Rockies, which is now known as Willamette University. Salem became the capital when Oregon achieved statehood in 1859 (Oregon City was the capital of the Oregon Territory). Salem serves as the seat to Marion County as well as the home of the state fairgrounds. Government ranks as a major industry here, while the city's setting in the heart of the fertile Willamette Valley stimulates rich agricultural and food-processing industries. More than a dozen wineries are in or near Salem. The main attractions in Salem are west of I–5 in and around the Capitol Mall.

GETTING HERE AND AROUND

Salem is located on I–5 with easy access to Portland, Albany, and Eugene. **Hut Portland Airport Shuttle** (☎ *503/364–4444* ⊕ *www.portlandairportshuttle.com*) provides transportation to Portland International Airport, which is 1 hour and 15 minutes away. Salem's McNary Field no longer has commercial airline service, but serves general aviation aircraft.

Bus transportation throughout Salem is provided by **Cherriot's** (⊕ *www.cherriots.org*). Amtrak operates regularly, and its train station is located at 500 13th Street SE.

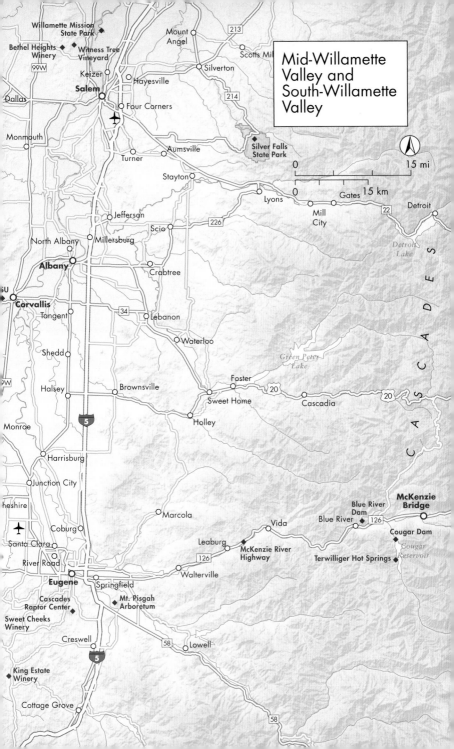

Mid-Willamette Valley and South-Willamette Valley

Willamette Mission State Park
Mount Angel
213
Scotts Mill
Bethel Heights Winery
Witness Tree Vineyard
Silverton
99W
Keizer
Hayesville
Salem
214
Dallas
Four Corners
Monmouth
Aumsville
Silver Falls State Park
Turner
Stayton
0   15 mi
0   15 km
Lyons
Gates
22
Detroit
Jefferson
Mill City
226
Detroit Lake
Scio
North Albany
Millersburg
Albany
Crabtree
OSU
Corvallis
Tangent
34
Lebanon
Shedd
Waterloo
Green Peter Lake
Halsey
Brownsville
Foster
20
Cascadia
20
C A S C A D E S
Sweet Home
Monroe
Holley
Harrisburg
Junction City
Cheshire
Marcola
Blue River Dam
McKenzie Bridge
Coburg
Vida
Blue River
126
Santa Clara
Leaburg
McKenzie River Highway
Cougar Dam
River Road
126
Terwilliger Hot Springs
Cougar Reservoir
Eugene
Walterville
Springfield
Cascades Raptor Center
Mt. Pisgah Arboretum
Sweet Cheeks Winery
Creswell
58
Lowell
5
King Estate Winery
Cottage Grove
58

Oregon Capitol building in Salem

ESSENTIALS

Visitor Information **Salem Convention & Visitors Center** ✉ *181 High St. N.E.*
☎ *503/581–4325, 800/874–7012* ⊕ *www.travelsalem.com.*

EXPLORING

Bethel Heights Vineyard. Founded in 1977, Bethel Heights was one of
the first vineyards planted in the Eola Hills region of the Willamette
Valley. It produces Pinot Noir, Chardonnay, Pinot Blanc, and Pinot
Gris. The tasting room has one of the most glorious panoramic views
of any winery in the state; its terrace and picnic area overlook the
surrounding vineyards, the valley below, and Mount Jefferson in the
distance. ✉ *6060 Bethel Heights Rd. N.W.* ☎ *503/581–2262* ⊕ *www.
bethelheights.com* ✉ *$5, refundable with purchase* ☉ *Feb.–Dec., Tues.–
Sun. 11–5; Jan., weekends 11–5.*

Bush's Pasture Park. These 105 acres of rolling lawn and formal English
gardens include the remarkably well-preserved Bush House, an 1878
Italianate mansion at the park's far-western boundary. It has 10 marble
fireplaces and virtually all of its original furnishings, and can be visited
only on informative tours. Bush Barn Art Center, behind the house,
exhibits the work of Northwest artists and has a sales gallery. ✉ *600
Mission St. S.E.* ☎ *503/363–4714* ⊕ *www.salemart.org* ✉ *House $4*
☉ *Gorunds: daily, dawn–midnight; house: Mar.–Dec. 23, Wed.–Sun.,
tours at 1, 2, 3, and 4.*

Elsinore Theatre. This flamboyant Tudor Gothic vaudeville house opened
on May 28, 1926, with Edgar Bergen in attendance. Clark Gable (who
lived in Silverton) and Gregory Peck performed on stage. The theater
was designed to look like a castle, with a false-stone front, chandeliers,

ironwork, and stained-glass windows. It's now a lively performing arts center with a busy schedule of bookings, and there are concerts on its Wurlitzer pipe organ. ⊠ *170 High St. S.E.* ☎ *503/375–3574* ⊕ *www. elsinoretheatre.com.*

Mount Angel Abbey. This Benedictine monastery on a 300-foot-high butte was founded in 1882 and is the site of one of two Modernist buildings designed by Finnish architect Alvar Aalto. A masterpiece of serene and thoughtful design, Aalto's library opened its doors in 1970, and has become a place of pilgrimage for students and aficionados of modern architecture. ⊠ *1 Abbey Dr., St. Benedict* ⊹ *18 miles from Salem; east on Hwy. 213 and north on Hwy. 214* ☎ *503/845–3030* ⊕ *www. mountangelabbey.org* ▨ *Free* ☉ *Daily 10–11:30 and 1–5.*

Oregon Capitol. A brightly gilded bronze statue of the *Oregon Pioneer* stands atop the 140-foot-high Capitol dome, looking north across the Capitol Mall. Built in 1939 with blocks of gray Vermont marble, Oregon's Capitol has an elegant yet austere neoclassical feel. East and west wings were added in 1978. Relief sculptures and deft historical murals soften the interior. Tours of the rotunda, the House and Senate chambers, and the governor's office leave from the information center under the dome. ⊠ *900 Court St. N.E.* ☎ *503/986–1388* ⊕ *www.leg. state.or.us* ▨ *Free* ☉ *Weekdays 7:30–5.*

Willamette Heritage Center at The Mill. Take a trip back in time to experience the story of Oregon's early pioneers and the industrial revolution. The **Thomas Kay Woolen Mill Museum** complex (circa 1889), complete with working waterwheels and millstream, looks as if the workers have just stepped away for a lunch break. Teasel gigging, napper flock bins, and the patented Furber double-acting napper are but a few of the machines and processes on display. The **Jason Lee House,** the **John D. Boon Home,** and the **Methodist Parsonage** are also part of the village. There is nothing grandiose about these early pioneer homes, the oldest frame structures in the Northwest, but they reveal a great deal about domestic life in the wilds of Oregon in the 1840s. ⊠ *1313 Mill St. S.E.* ☎ *503/585–7012* ⊕ *www.willametteheritage.org* ▨ *$6* ☉ *Mon.–Sat. 10–5.*

Willamette University. Behind the Capitol, across State Street but half a world away, are the brick buildings and grounds of Willamette University, the oldest college in the West. Founded in 1842, Willamette has long been a breeding ground for aspiring politicians. **Hatfield Library,** built in 1986 on the banks of Mill Stream, is a handsome brick-and-glass building with a striking campanile; tall, prim **Waller Hall,** built in 1867, is one of the oldest buildings in the Pacific Northwest. ⊠ *900 State St.* ☎ *503/370–6300* ⊕ *www.willamette.edu* ☉ *Weekdays 8–5.*

Witness Tree Vineyard. Named for the ancient oak that towers over the vineyard (it was used as a surveyor's landmark in the 1850s), this winery produces premium Pinot Noir made entirely from grapes grown on its 100-acre estate nestled in the Eola Hills northwest of Salem. The vineyard also produces limited quantities of estate Chardonnay, Viognier, Pinot Blanc, Dolcetto, and a sweet dessert wine called Sweet Signé. Tours are available by appointment. ⊠ *7111 Spring Valley Rd. N.W.*

☎ *503/585–7874* 🌐 *www.witnesstreevineyard.com* 🎟 *$5* ⏲ *May–Oct., Tues.–Sun. 11–5; Mar.–Apr. and Nov.–mid-Dec., Thurs.–Sun. 11–5.*

WHERE TO EAT AND STAY

For expanded hotel reviews, visit Fodors.com.

$$$ PACIFIC NORTHWEST 🍴 **Bentley's Grill.** This steak and seafood eatery strives to serve ingredients from the Northwest, whether it's Oregon bay shrimp, Rogue Valley bleu cheese, Oregon hazelnuts, or local beef. The menu occasionally also includes wild game entrées. Rounding out the menu are selections from its pizza oven. [$] *Average main: $25* ✉ *Grand Hotel, 291 Liberty St. S.E.* ☎ *503/779–1660* 🌐 *bentleysgrill.com.*

$$$ ITALIAN Fodor's Choice ★ 🍴 **DaVinci.** Salem politicos flock to this two-story downtown gathering spot for Italian-inspired dishes cooked in a wood-burning oven. No shortcuts are taken in the preparation, so don't come if you're in a rush. But if you're in the mood to linger over seafood and fresh pasta that's made on the premises, this may be your place. The wine list is one of the most extensive in the Northwest; the staff is courteous and extremely professional. There's live music most evenings. [$] *Average main: $25* ✉ *180 High St. S.E.* ☎ *503/399–1413* 🌐 *www.davincisofsalem.com* ⏲ *No lunch.*

$ HOTEL 🏨 **Grand Hotel in Salem.** Large rooms, with comfortable and luxurious furnishings, are the best in town, a good base for guests attending shows and meetings at Salem Conference Center or touring the region. **Pros:** spacious rooms; centrally located. **Cons:** some street noise; not a lot of character. [$] *Rooms from: $129* ✉ *201 Liberty St. S.E.* ☎ *503/540–7800, 877/540–7800* 🌐 *www.grandhotelsalem.com* 🛏 *143 rooms, 50 suites* 🍽 *Breakfast.*

$ RESORT 🏨 **Oregon Garden Resort.** Bright, roomy, and tastefully decorated rooms, each with a fireplace and a private, landscaped patio or balcony, neighbor the Oregon Garden (admission is included in the rates). **Pros:** gorgeous grounds; luxurious rooms; pool and plenty of other amenities. **Cons:** a distance from other activities. [$] *Rooms from: $110* ✉ *895 W. Main St., Silverton* ☎ *503/874–2500* 🌐 *www.oregongardenresort.com* 🛏 *103 rooms* 🍽 *Breakfast.*

SHOPPING

Reed Opera House. These days an 1869 opera house in downtown Salem contains a compelling collection of locally owned stores, shops, restaurants, bars, and bakeries. Its Trinity Ballroom hosts special events and celebrations. ✉ *189 Liberty St. N.E.* ☎ *503/391–4481* 🌐 *www.reedoperahouse.com.*

Woodburn Company Stores. Located 18 miles north of Salem on Interstate 5 are more than 100 brand-name outlet stores, including Nike, Calvin Klein, Bose, Gymboree, OshKosh B'Gosh, Ann Taylor, Levi's, Chico's, Fossil, Forever 21, Polo, and Columbia Sportswear, and plenty of places to eat. Chances are that someone in your traveling party would enjoy burning an hour or three perusing famous outlet stores. ✉ *1001 Arney Rd., Woodburn* ☎ *503/981–1900, 888/664–7467* 🌐 *www.woodburncompanystores.com* ⏲ *Mon.–Sat. 10–8, Sun. 10–7.*

SPORTS AND THE OUTDOORS
RECREATIONAL AREAS

Silver Falls State Park. Hidden amid old-growth Douglas firs in the foothills of the Cascades, Silver Falls is the largest state park in Oregon (8,700 acres). South Falls, roaring over the lip of a mossy basalt bowl into a deep pool 177 feet below, is the main attraction here, but 13 other waterfalls—half of them more than 100 feet high—are accessible to hikers. The best time to visit is in the fall, when vine maples blaze with brilliant color, or early spring, when the forest floor is carpeted with trilliums and yellow violets. There are picnic facilities and a day lodge; in winter you can cross-country ski. Camping facilities include tent and trailer sites, cabins, and a horse camp. ⊠ *20024 Silver Falls Hwy. S.E., Sublimity* ☎ *503/873–8681, 800/551–6949* ⊕ *www.oregonstateparks. org* ⊠ *$5 per vehicle* ⊙ *Daily dawn–dusk.*

Willamette Mission State Park. Along pastoral lowlands by the Willamette River, this serene park holds the largest black cottonwood tree in the United States. A thick-barked behemoth by a small pond, the 275-year-old tree has upraised arms that bring to mind J.R.R. Tolkien's fictional Ents. Site of Reverend Jason Lee's 1834 pioneer mission, the park also offers quiet strolling and picnicking in an old orchard and along the river. The Wheatland Ferry, at the north end of the park, began carrying covered wagons across the Willamette in 1844, using pulleys and is still in operation today. ⊠ *Wheatland Rd., 8 miles north of Salem, I–5 Exit 263* ☎ *503/393–1172, 800/551–6949* ⊕ *www.oregonstateparks. org* ⊠ *$5 per vehicle* ⊙ *Daily 7–5.*

ALBANY

20 miles from Salem, south on I–5 and west on U.S. 20.

Known as the grass-seed capital of the world, Albany has some of the most historic buildings in Oregon. Some 700 buildings, scattered over a 100-block area in three districts, include every major architectural style developed in the United States since 1850. The area is listed on the National Register of Historic Places. Eight covered bridges can also be seen on a half-hour drive from Albany.

GETTING HERE AND AROUND

Albany is located on I–5 with easy access to Portland, Salem, and Eugene. Portland International Airport is 1 hour, 40 minutes away, and the Eugene airport is 1 hour away to the south. Several shuttle services are available from both airports.

Albany Transit System provides two routes for intercity travel. The Linn-Benton loop system provides for transportation between Albany and Corvallis. Albany is served by Amtrak.

ESSENTIALS

Visitor Information Albany Visitors Association ⊠ *110 3rd Ave. S.E.* ☎ *541/928–0911, 800/526–2256* ⊕ *www.albanyvisitors.com.*

EXPLORING

Benton County Historical Society and Museum. The collection of 66,000 items features local themes ranging from logging and technology to the arts. Also on view are articles from Camp Adair, which was a World War II military cantonment, and Philomath College, a United Brethren college that now houses the museum. ✉ *1101 Main St., Philomath* ☎ *541/929–6230* 🌐 *www.bentoncountymuseum.org* 🕓 *Tues.–Sat. 10–4:30.*

Monteith House Museum. The first frame house in Albany, built in 1849, is now a museum, restored and filled with period furnishings and historic photos. It is widely thought to be the most authentic restoration of a Pacific Northwest pioneer-era home. ✉ *518 2nd Ave. S.W.* ☎ *800/526–2256, 541/928–0911* 🎟 *Donation* 🕓 *Mid-June–mid-Sept., Wed.–Sat. noon–4; mid-Sept.–mid-June, by appointment.*

WHERE TO EAT

$ HUNGARIAN

🍴 **Novak's Hungarian.** Since 1984, the Novak family has been a delightful fixture in Albany's dining scene. From Hungarian hash and eggs in the morning to chicken paprika served over homemade Hungarian pearl noodles, you can't go wrong in this establishment. There's a huge assortment of desserts as well. On Sunday they serve brunch. [$] *Average main: $14* ✉ *2306 Heritage Way S.E.* ☎ *541/967–9488* 🌐 *www.novakshungarian.com* 🕓 *No breakfast Mon.–Tues.*

$$ ECLECTIC Fodor's Choice ★

🍴 **Sybaris.** A rotating menu at this fine bistro in Albany's historic downtown changes monthly and features flavorful cuisine at reasonable prices. The restaurant strives to ensure that most of the ingredients, including the lamb, eggs, and vegetables, are raised within 10 miles. Even the huckleberries in the ice cream are gathered in secret locations by the restaurant's mushroom picker. [$] *Average main: $20* ✉ *442 1st Ave. W.* ☎ *541/928–8157* 🌐 *www.sybarisbistro.com* 🕓 *Closed Sun.–Mon. No lunch.*

CORVALLIS

10 miles southwest of Albany on U.S. 20.

To some, Corvallis is a brief stopping place along the way to Salem or Portland. To others, it's a small town that gives you a chance to escape the bigger cities. To still others, it's an academic and sports center, home to Oregon State University and its Beavers. Driving the area's economy are a growing engineering and high-tech industry, a burgeoning wine industry, and more traditional local agricultural crops, such as grass and legume seeds. The town and its environs offer plenty of outdoor activities as well as scenic attractions, from covered bridges to wineries and gardens.

GETTING HERE AND AROUND

Corvallis Transit System (CTS) operates eight bus routes throughout the city. **Hut Shuttle** (☎ *503/364–4444* 🌐 *www.portlandairportshuttle.com*) provides transportation between Corvallis and the Portland airport, located 1 hour, 53 minutes away. **OmniShuttle** (☎ *541/461–7959* 🌐 *www.omnishuttle.com*) provides transportation between Corvallis and the Eugene airport, 50 minutes away. Corvallis Municipal Airport is a public airport 4 miles south of the city.

ESSENTIALS

Visitor Information **Corvallis Tourism** ✉ *553 N.W. Harrison* ☎ *541/757–1544, 800/334–8118* 🌐 *www.visitcorvallis.com.*

EXPLORING

Oregon State University. It's a thrill to be on campus on game day, when students are a sea of orange and black cheering on their beloved Beavers. This 400-acre campus, west of the city center, was established as a land-grant institution in 1868. OSU has more than 26,000 students, many of them studying the university's nationally recognized programs in conservation biology, agricultural sciences, nuclear engineering, forestry, fisheries and wildlife management, community health, pharmacy, and zoology. ✉ *15th and Jefferson Sts.* ☎ *541/737–1000* 🌐 *oregonstate.edu.*

WHERE TO EAT AND STAY

For expanded hotel reviews, visit Fodors.com.

$$$ MODERN AMERICAN Fodor's Choice ★

🍴 **Gathering Together Farm.** When spring arrives, it means that the organic farmers outside of Philomath are serving their bounty. Fresh vegetables, pizzas, local lamb, pork, and halibut are frequent menu highlights. Local wines and tempting desserts make the evening perfect. If you don't see coppa (cured pork from the shoulder of the pig) on the menu, ask your server if the chef has any available. They can often add it to a dish, and it's fantastic. [$] *Average main: $25* ✉ *25159 Grange Hall Rd., Philomath* ☎ *541/929–4270* 🌐 *www.gatheringtogetherfarm.com* ✍ *Reservations essential* ⏲ *Closed Sun.–Wed. in winter, Sun.–Mon. in summer.*

$ HOTEL

🏨 **Comfort Suites Corvallis.** Spacious, clean rooms are equipped with comfortable and attractive furnishings, though the place doesn't shake the chain hotel feel. **Pros:** close to Corvallis sights; pleasant surroundings. **Cons:** suites seem a little cramped; bland and corporate. [$] *Rooms from: $120* ✉ *1730 N.W. 9th St.* ☎ *541/753–4320* 🌐 *www.comfortsuitescorvallis.com* 🛏 *95 rooms* 🍽 *Breakfast.*

SPORTS AND THE OUTDOORS

RECREATIONAL AREAS

Fodor's Choice ★

Siuslaw National Forest. The highest point in the Coast Range (4,097 feet), Mary's Peak offers panoramic views of the Cascades, the Willamette Valley, and the rest of the Coast Range. On a clear day you can see as far as the Pacific Ocean. There are several picnicking areas, more than 10 miles of hiking trails, and a small campground. There are stands of noble fir and alpine meadows. The forest, just 2 miles from Corvallis, includes the Oregon Dunes National Recreation Area and the Cape Perpetua Interpretive Center. People usually access the Forest using one of several major highways: highways 26, 6, and 18 all access the north central coast; highways 20 and 34 access Newport and the central coast; Highway 126 accesses Florence and the north part of the Oregon Dunes; and Highway 38 accesses Reedsport and the southern section of the Oregon Dunes. ✉ *Forest office, 3200 S.W.*

Jefferson Way ☎ *541/750–7000* ⊕ *www.fs.usda.gov/siuslaw* ✉ *Free* ⊙ *Daily dawn–dusk.*

SWIMMING

Osborn Aquatic Center. This is not your ordinary lap pool. There are waterslides, a water channel, water cannons, and floor geysers. The indoor pools are open all year. ⊠ *1940 N.W. Highland Dr.* ☎ *541/766–7946* ✉ *$4.75* ⊙ *Daily, hours vary.*

SOUTH WILLAMETTE VALLEY

Lane County rests at the southern end of the Willamette Valley. It encompasses Eugene, Springfield, Drain, McKenzie Bridge, and Cottage Grove to the south. There are plenty of wineries to enjoy, but visitors can also sprinkle their sipping fun with some white-water rafting, deep-woods hiking, and cheering on the Oregon Ducks. To the west lies the Oregon Dunes Recreation Area, and to the east are the beautiful central Oregon communities of Sisters, Bend, and Redmond.

EUGENE

63 miles south of Corvallis on I–5.

Eugene was founded in 1846, when Eugene Skinner staked the first federal land-grant claim for pioneers. Eugene is consistently given high marks for its "livability." As the home of the University of Oregon, a large student and former-student population lends Eugene a youthful vitality and countercultural edge. Full of parks and oriented to the outdoors, Eugene is a place where bike paths are used, pedestrians *always* have the right-of-way, and joggers are so plentiful that the city is known as the Running Capital of the World. Shopping and commercial streets surround the Eugene Hilton and the Hult Center for the Performing Arts, the two most prominent downtown buildings. During football season you can count on the U of O Ducks being the primary topic of most conversations.

GETTING HERE AND AROUND

Eugene's airport has rental cars, cabs, and shuttles that make the 15-minute trip to Eugene's city center. By train, Amtrak stops in the heart of downtown. Getting around Lane County's communities is easy with **Lane Transit District** (*LTD* ☎ *541/687–5555* ⊕ *www.ltd.org*) public transportation. Eugene is very bicycle-friendly.

ESSENTIALS

Visitor Information **Eugene, Cascades and Coast Adventure Center** ⊠ *3312 Gateway St., Springfield* ☎ *541/484–5307, 800/547–5445* ⊕ *www. eugenecascadescoast.org.*

EXPLORING

5th Street Public Market. A former chicken-processing plant is the site of this popular shopping mall, filled with small crafts, art, and gifts stores. Dining includes sit-down restaurants, decadent bakeries, and the international diversity of the second-floor food esplanade. ⊠ *296 E.*

5th Ave. ☎ *541/484–0383* ⊕ *www.5stmarket.com* ☉ *Shops Mon.–Sat. 10–7, Sun. 11–5.*

Alton Baker Park. This parcel of open land on the banks of the Willamette River is named after the late publisher of Eugene's newspaper, the *Register-Guard,* and is the site of many community events. Live music is performed in summer. There's fine hiking and biking on a footpath that runs along the river for the length of the park. Also worth seeing is the Whilamut Natural Area, an open space with 13 "talking stones," each with an inscription. ⊠ *200 Day Island Rd.* ☎ *541/682–4800.*

FAMILY **Cascades Raptor Center.** This birds-of-prey nature center and hospital hosts more than 30 species of birds. A visit is a great outing for kids, who can learn what owls eat, why and where birds migrate, and all sorts of other raptor facts. Some of the full-time residents include turkey vultures, bald eagles, owls, hawks, falcons, and kites. ⊠ *32275 Fox Hollow Rd.* ☎ *541/485–1320* ⊕ *www.eraptors.org* 🎫 *$7* ☉ *Apr.–Oct., Tues.–Sun. 10–6, Nov.–Mar., Tues.–Sun 10–4.*

King Estate Winery. This certified organic estate is committed to producing world-class Pinot Gris and Pinot Noir. The visitors center offers wine tasting and production tours, and the restaurant highlights organic produce grown in the estate gardens. ⊠ *80854 Territorial Rd.* ☎ *541/685–5189* ⊕ *www.kingestate.com* ☉ *Mon.–Tues. 11–5, Wed.–Sun. 11–8.*

FAMILY **Mount Pisgah Arboretum.** This beautiful nature preserve near southeast Eugene includes extensive all-weather trails, educational programs for all ages, and facilities for special events. Its visitor center holds workshops, and features native amphibian and reptile terraria; microscopes for exploring tiny seeds, bugs, feathers, and snakeskins; "touch me" exhibits; reference books; and a working viewable beehive. ⊠ *34901 Frank Parrish Rd.* ☎ *541/747–3817* ⊕ *www.mountpisgaharboretum. org* 🎫 *Parking $3* ☉ *Park, daily dawn–dusk; visitor center, hours vary.*

FAMILY **Science Factory.** Formerly the Willamette Science and Technology Center (WISTEC), and still known to locals by its former name, Eugene's imaginative, hands-on museum assembles rotating exhibits designed for curious young minds. The adjacent **planetarium,** one of the largest in the Pacific Northwest, presents star shows and entertainment events. ⊠ *2300 Leo Harris Pkwy.* ☎ *541/682–7888* ⊕ *www.sciencefactory.org* 🎫 *$7 for science hall and planetarium, $4 each* ☉ *Wed.–Sun. 10–4; closed Oregon Ducks home football games and major holidays.*

Sweet Cheeks Winery. This estate vineyard lies on a prime sloping hillside in the heart of the Willamette Valley appellation. It also supplies grapes to several award-winning wineries. Friday-night tastings are embellished with cheese pairings and live music. ⊠ *27007 Briggs Hill Rd.* ☎ *541/349–9463, 877/309–9463* ⊕ *www.sweetcheekswinery.com* ☉ *Sat.–Thurs. noon–6, Fri. noon–9.*

University of Oregon. The true heart of Eugene lies southeast of the city center at its university. Several fine old buildings can be seen on the 250-acre campus; **Deady Hall,** built in 1876, is the oldest. More than 400 varieties of trees grace the bucolic grounds, along with outdoor sculptures that include *The Pioneer* and *The Pioneer Mother.* The two

Fresh produce from Hey Bayles! Farm at the Lane County Farmer's Market in Eugene.

bronze figures by Alexander Phimster Proctor were dedicated to the men and women who settled the Oregon Territory and less than a generation later founded the university. ✉ *1585 E. 13th Ave.* ☎ *541/346–1000* ⊕ *www.uoregon.edu.*

Jordan Schnitzer Museum of Art. Works from the 20th and 21st centuries are a specialty in these handsome galleries, which feature works by many leading Pacific Northwest artists. European, Korean, Chinese, and Japanese works are also on view, as are 300 works commissioned by the Works Progress Administration in the 1930s and '40s. ✉ *1430 Johnson La.* ☎ *541/346–3027* ⊕ *jsma.uoregon.edu* ✉ *$5* ☼ *Tues. and Thurs.–Sun. 11–5, Wed. 11–8.*

University of Oregon Museum of Natural and Cultural History. Relics of a more local nature are on display at the University of Oregon Museum of Natural History, devoted to Pacific Northwest anthropology and the natural sciences. Its highlights include the fossil collection of Thomas Condon, Oregon's first geologist, and a pair of 9,000-year-old sandals made of sagebrush. ✉ *1680 E. 15th Ave.* ☎ *541/346–3024* ⊕ *www.natural-history.uoregon.edu* ✉ *$3, free on Wed.* ☼ *Wed.–Sun. 11–5.*

WHERE TO EAT

$$$ ✗ **Marché.** The name translates into "market," meaning that this
FRENCH renowned Eugene restaurant works with a dozen local farmers to bring the freshest, most organic local food to the table. Specialties include salmon, halibut, sturgeon, and beef tenderloin, braised pork shoulders, and outstanding local oysters. It has an extensive wine list with an emphasis on Oregon and France. There's also a Sunday brunch.

$ *Average main: $30* ✉ *296 E. 5th Ave.* ☎ *541/342–3612* ⊕ *www. marcherestaurant.com.*

$$$ ✕ **Ristorante Italiano.** The chef uses fresh local produce from the restau-
ITALIAN rant's own farm, but this bistro-style café across from the University of
Oregon is best known for its authentic Italian cuisine, such as a delec-
table osso bucco Milanese and house-made artisan pasta. The menu
changes according to the season, but staples include delicious salads
and soups, gnocchi, grilled chicken, broiled salmon, and sandwiches.
The dining room, shaded by blossoming cherry trees in the spring, has
a quiet, understated European feel, and there's outdoor seating on the
patio in good weather. Breakfast and Sunday brunch are served. $ *Av-
erage main: $26* ✉ *754 E. 13th Ave.* ☎ *541/342–6963, 800/321–6963*
⊘ *No lunch Sat.*

$$$ ✕ **Sweetwaters.** The dining room at the Valley River Inn, which over-
AMERICAN looks the Willamette at water level, specializes in Pacific Northwest
cuisine. Try the salmon with Szechuan peppercorn crust and cranberry
vinaigrette or the grilled beef fillet with Oregon blue-cheese crust.
There is a bar area outside, as well as a deck for open-air dining. Sunday brunch and a kids' menu are available, too. $ *Average main: $26*
✉ *1000 Valley River Way* ☎ *541/743–1000, 800/543–8266* ⊕ *www.
valleyriverinn.com.*

WHERE TO STAY
For expanded hotel reviews, visit Fodors.com.

$ 🛏 **Campbell House.** One of the oldest structures in Eugene, built in 1892,
B&B/INN combines architectural details and a mixture of century-old antiques
and reproductions to lend each of the rooms a distinctive personality. **Pros:** classic architecture; comfortable rooms; well-kept grounds.
Cons: rooms lack some of the amenities of nearby hotels. $ *Rooms
from: $129* ✉ *252 Pearl St.* ☎ *541/343–1119, 800/264–2519* ⊕ *www.
campbellhouse.com* ⤳ *12 rooms, 7 suites, 1 cottage* ⦿| *Breakfast.*

$ 🛏 **C'est la Vie Inn.** Listed on the National Register of Historic Places,
B&B/INN this 1891 Queen Anne Victorian bed-and-breakfast provides Old World
Fodor'sChoice comfort and modern-day amenities in its luxurious and romantic guest
★ rooms. **Pros:** outstanding service and value. **Cons:** few rooms. $ *Rooms
from: $150* ✉ *1006 Taylor St.* ☎ *866/302–3014, 541/302–3014* ⊕ *www.
cestlavieinn.com* ⤳ *3 rooms, 1 suite* ⦿| *Breakfast.*

$ 🛏 **Excelsior Inn.** Quiet sophistication, attention to architectural detail,
B&B/INN and rooms furnished in a refreshingly understated manner, each with
Fodor'sChoice a marble-and-tile bath and some with fireplaces, suggest a European
★ inn. **Pros:** romantic accommodations; excellent service and restaurant.
Cons: formal in a casual town. $ *Rooms from: $99* ✉ *754 E. 13th
Ave.* ☎ *541/342–6963, 800/321–6963* ⊕ *www.excelsiorinn.com* ⤳ *14
rooms* ⦿| *Breakfast.*

$$ 🛏 **Valley River Inn.** At this inn on the banks of the Willamette River, some
HOTEL rooms have an outdoor patio or balcony, some have river or pool views,
and concierge rooms have access to a private lounge. **Pros:** location on
the river; lots of amenities; great restaurant. **Cons:** basic and fairly banal
room decor. $ *Rooms from: $119* ✉ *1000 Valley River Way* ☎ *541/743–
1000, 800/543–8266* ⊕ *www.valleyriverinn.com* ⤳ *257 rooms.*

NIGHTLIFE AND THE ARTS

Hult Center for the Performing Arts. This is the locus of Eugene's cultural life. Renowned for the quality of its acoustics, the center has two theaters that are home to Eugene's symphony and opera. ⊠ *7th Ave. and Willamette St.* ☎ *541/682–5087 Administration, 541/682–5000 Tickets* ⊕ *www.hultcenter.org.*

Oregon Bach Festival. Conductor Helmuth Rilling leads the internationally known Oregon Bach Festival every summer. Concerts, chamber music, and social events—held mainly in Eugene at the Hult Center and the University of Oregon School of Music but also in Corvallis and Florence—are part of this three-week event. ⊠ *1787 Agate St.* ☎ *541/682–5000 for tickets, 800/457–1486 for information* ⊕ *oregonbachfestival.com.*

SPORTS AND THE OUTDOORS

RECREATIONAL AREAS

FAMILY **Skinner Butte Park.** Rising from the south bank of the Willamette River, this park provides the best views of any of the city's parks; it also has the greatest historic cachet, since it was here that Eugene Skinner staked the claim that put Eugene on the map. Children can scale a replica of Skinner Butte, uncover fossils, and cool off under a rain circle. Skinner Butte Loop leads to the top of Skinner Butte, traversing sometimes difficult terrain through a mixed-conifer forest. ⊠ *248 Cheshire Ave.* ☎ *541/682–4800* ⌧ *Free* ⊘ *Dawn–dusk.*

BIKING AND JOGGING

The **River Bank Bike Path,** originating in Alton Baker Park on the Willamette's north bank, is a level and leisurely introduction to Eugene's topography. It's one of 120 miles of trails in the area. **Prefontaine Trail,** used by area runners, travels through level fields and forests for 1½ miles.

SKIING

Willamette Pass. With a summit 6,683 feet high in the Cascade Range, this pass packs an annual average snowfall of 430 inches and has access to 29 ski runs with a vertical drop of 1,563 feet. Four triple chairs and one six-person detachable service the downhill ski areas, and 13 miles of Nordic trails lace the pass. Facilities include a ski shop; day care; a bar and restaurant; and Nordic and downhill rentals, repairs, and instruction. ⊠ *Hwy. 58, 69 miles southeast of Eugene* ☎ *541/345–7669* ⊕ *www.willamettepass.com* ⊘ *Wed.–Sun. 9–4 during ski season.*

SWIMMING

FAMILY **Splash! Lively Park Swim Center.** This indoor water park has wave surfing and a waterslide. There are family, lap, and kids' pools, as well as a spa, concessions, playground, park, and picnic shelters. ⊠ *6100 Thurston Rd., Springfield* ☎ *541/736–4244* ⊕ *www.willamalane.org* ⌧ *$6.50* ⊘ *Daily, hours vary.*

SHOPPING

Tourists coming to the Willamette Valley, especially to Eugene, can't escape without experiencing the **5th Street Public Market** in downtown Eugene. There are plenty of small crafts shops, and the food mall offers many cuisines, including vegetarian, pizza, and seafood.

Valley River Center. The largest shopping center between Portland and San Francisco has five department stores, including Macy's and JCPenney, plus 130 specialty shops and a food court. ✉ *293 Valley River Center* ☎ *541/683–5511* 🌐 *www.valleyrivercenter.com.*

MCKENZIE BRIDGE

58 miles east of Eugene on Hwy. 126.

On the beautiful McKenzie River, lakes, waterfalls, and covered bridges surround the town of McKenzie Bridge and wilderness trails in the Cascades. Fishing, skiing, backpacking, and rafting are among the most popular activities in the area.

4

GETTING HERE AND AROUND

McKenzie Bridge is about an hour from Eugene, on Highway 126. It is just 38 miles from Hoodoo Ski Area, but its proximity can be deceiving if the snow is heavy. Bend also is close at 64 miles to the east.

EXPLORING

McKenzie River Highway. Highway 126, as it heads east from Eugene, is known as the McKenzie River Highway. Following the curves of the river, it passes grazing lands, fruit and nut orchards, and the small riverside hamlets of the McKenzie Valley. From the highway you can glimpse the bouncing, bubbling, blue-green McKenzie River, one of Oregon's top fishing, boating, and white-water rafting spots, against a backdrop of densely forested mountains, splashing waterfalls, and jet-black lava beds. The small town of McKenzie Bridge marks the end of the McKenzie River Highway and the beginning of the 26-mile McKenzie River National Recreation Trail, which heads north through the Willamette National Forest along portions of the Old Santiam Wagon Road.

WHERE TO EAT AND STAY

For expanded hotel reviews, visit Fodors.com.

$ AMERICAN FAMILY 🍴 **Takoda's Restaurant.** A popular roadside café serves burgers, great soups, salads, pizza, and daily specials. A video game room keeps kids happy. [$] *Average main: $10* ✉ *91806 Mill Creek Rd., Milepost 47.5 McKenzie Hwy., Blue River* ☎ *541/822–1153.*

$ RESORT 🏨 **Belknap Hot Springs Resort.** A pleasant lodge, with comfortable though not luxurious rooms, and a campground with trailer sites, are nestled onto the banks of the beautiful McKenzie River. **Pros:** hot springs; wooded location. **Cons:** 14-day cancellation policy; two-night minimum on weekends; trailers and motor homes detract from the rustic atmosphere. [$] *Rooms from: $120* ✉ *59296 Belknap Springs Rd.* ☎ *541/822–3512* 🌐 *www.belknaphotsprings.com* 🛏 *19 rooms, 7 cabins* 🍽 *Breakfast.*

$ B&B/INN 🏨 **Eagle Rock Lodge.** These wood-paneled rooms filled with quilts and antiques are surprisingly luxurious and provide a romantic, relaxing retreat in the woods. **Pros:** great location on the McKenzie River; comfortable atmosphere. **Cons:** a distance from non-outdoor activities. [$] *Rooms from: $130* ✉ *49198 McKenzie Hwy., Vida* ☎ *541/822–3630, 888/773–4333* 🌐 *www.eaglerocklodge.com* 🛏 *7 rooms* 🍽 *Breakfast.*

$$ RENTAL **Holiday Farm Resort.** Originally built in 1910, this atmospheric little resort with 11 distinctive cottages on or near the McKenzie River banks served for many years as a stagecoach stop, and later a favorite stopover for President Herbert Hoover. **Pros:** great place for relaxation and outdoor activities. **Cons:** far from town. [$] *Rooms from: $175* ✉ *54455 McKenzie River Dr., Blue River* ☎ *541/822–3725* 🌐 *www.holidayfarmresort.com* 🛏 *11 cottages* 🍴 *No meals.*

SPORTS AND THE OUTDOORS

RECREATIONAL AREAS

Cougar Dam and Lake. Four miles outside of McKenzie Bridge is the highest embankment dam ever built by the Army Corps of Engineers—452 feet above the streambed. The resulting reservoir, on the South Fork McKenzie River, covers 1,280 acres. The public recreation areas are in the Willamette National Forest. You can visit the dam year-round, but the campgrounds are open only from May to September. ✉ *Forest Rd. 19, Willamette National Forest* ☎ *541/822–3381* 🎟 *Free* 🕒 *June–Sept., daily.*

Terwilliger Hot Springs (Cougar Hot Springs). An hour east of Eugene near Highway 126, take a short hike to a natural hot-springs area. Soaking aficionados will find Terwilliger to be rustic, which many regard as an advantage, though the popularity of this beautiful spot can be a drawback. The pools are in a forest of old-growth firs and cedars. Clothing is optional. ✉ *Off Forest Rd. 19, Blue River* ☎ *541/822–3381* 🎟 *$6* 🕒 *Dawn–dusk.*

Willamette National Forest. Stretching 110 miles along the western slopes of the Cascade Range, this forest boasts boundless recreation opportunities, including camping, hiking, boating, ATV riding, and winter sports. It extends from the Mt. Jefferson area east of Salem to the Calapooya Mountains northeast of Roseburg, encompassing 1,675,407 acres. ✉ *57600 McKenzie Hwy.* ☎ *541/225–6300* 🌐 *www.fs.usda.gov/willamette.*

GOLF

Tokatee Golf Club. Ranked one of the best golf courses in Oregon by *Golf Digest*, this 18-hole beauty is tucked away near the McKenzie River with views of the Three Sisters Mountains, native ponds, and streams. *Tokatee* is a Chinook word meaning "a place of restful beauty." The course offers a practice range, carts, lessons, rentals, a coffee shop and snack bar, and Wi-Fi. ✉ *54947 McKenzie Hwy.* ☎ *541/822–3220, 800/452–6376* 🌐 *www.tokatee.com* 🎟 *18 holes $45; 9 holes $26.*

WHITE-WATER RAFTING

FAMILY Fodor's Choice ★ **High Country Expeditions.** Raft the white waters of the McKenzie River on a guided full- or half-day tour. You'll bounce through rapids, admire old-growth forest, and watch osprey and blue herons fishing. The outfit provides life jackets, splash gear, wet suits, booties (if requested), boating equipment, paddling instructions, river safety talk, a three-course riverside meal, and shuttle service back to your vehicle. ✉ *Belknap Hot Springs Resort, 59296 Belknap Springs Rd.* ☎ *541/822–8288, 888/461–7238* 🌐 *www.highcountryexpeditions.com* 🎟 *Full day $90, half day $60.*

THE COLUMBIA RIVER GORGE AND MT. HOOD

WELCOME TO THE COLUMBIA RIVER GORGE AND MT. HOOD

TOP REASONS TO GO

★ **Waterfall walkabout:** Hikers will discover dozens of gorgeous cascades along the Historic Columbia River Highway and its adjoining trail network, including 620-foot Multnomah Falls.

★ **Outdoor rec mecca:** From kiteboarding the gorge to mountain biking the slopes of Mt. Hood, this is a region tailor-made for adventure junkies. Get the gear and the beta from outfitters in Hood River and Government Camp.

★ **Historico-luxe:** Grand and gaudy landmarks like McMenamins Edgefield, Timberline Lodge, and the Columbia Gorge Hotel are guest favorites and entries on the National Register of Historic Places.

★ **Suds-tacular:** Western Oregon is the national seat of craft brewing, and the Gorge/Hood area has its share of inviting taprooms, from Stevenson's tiny Walking Man Brewing to Full Sail's upbeat national headquarters in Hood River.

1 Columbia River Gorge. The dams of the early 20th century transformed the Columbia River from the raging torrent that vexed Lewis and Clark in 1805 to the breathtaking but comparatively docile waterway that hosts kiteboarders and windsurfers today. Auto visitors have been scoping out the gorge's picturesque bluffs and waterfalls for quite a while now—the road between Troutdale and the Dalles, on which construction began in 1913, was the country's first planned scenic highway.

2 Mt. Hood. Visible from 100 miles away, Mt. Hood (or "the Mountain," as Portlanders often call it) is the kind of rock that commands respect. It's holy ground for mountaineers, about 10,000 of whom make a summit bid each year. Sightseers are often shocked by the summer snows, but skiers rejoice, keeping the mountain's resorts busy year-round. Mingle with laid-back powderhounds and other outdoorsy types in the hospitality villas of Welches and Government Camp.

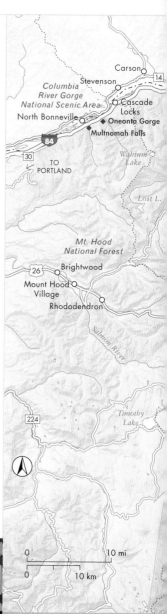

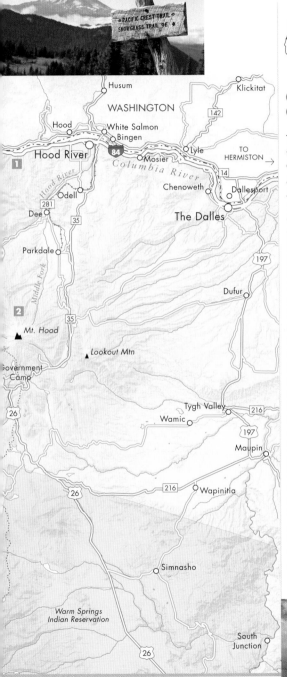

GETTING ORIENTED

The mighty Columbia River flows west through the Cascade Range, past the Mount Hood Wilderness Area, to Astoria. It's a natural border between Oregon and Washington to the north, and bridges link roads on both sides at Biggs Junction, the Dalles, Hood River, and Cascade Locks. The watery recreation corridor stretches from the Dalles in the east to the east Portland 'burbs. For most of that drive, snow-capped Mt. Hood looms to the southwest. Hood River drains the mountain's north side, emptying into the Columbia at its namesake town. Follow it upstream and you'll trade the warm, low-elevation climes of the gorge for the high country's tall pines and late-season snows. While it feels remote, the massive peak is just outside Portland. Look up from almost any neighborhood in town to see its white dome, just 60 miles east and accessible via U.S. 26 through Gresham.

Updated by
Brian Kevin

Volcanoes, lava flows, Ice Age floodwaters, and glaciers were Nature's tools of choice when carving a breathtaking 80-mile landscape now called the Columbia River Gorge. Proof of human civilization here reaches back 31,000 years, and excavations near the Dalles have uncovered evidence that salmon fishing is a 10,000-year-old tradition in these parts. In 1805 Lewis and Clark discovered the Columbia River to be the only waterway that led to the Pacific. Their first expedition was a treacherous route through wild, plunging rapids, but their successful navigation set a new exodus in motion.

Today the towns are laid-back recreation hamlets whose residents harbor a fierce pride in their shared natural resources. Sightseers, hikers, and skiers have long found contentment in this robust region, officially labeled a National Scenic Area in 1986. They're joined these days by epicures trolling the Columbia's banks in search of gourmet cuisine, artisan hop houses, and top-shelf vino. Highlights of the Columbia River Gorge include Multnomah Falls, Bonneville Dam, and the rich orchard land of Hood River. Sailboaters, windsurfers, and kiteboarders take advantage of the blustery gorge winds in the summer, their colorful sails decorating the waterway like windswept confetti.

To the south of Hood River are all the alpine attractions of the 11,245-foot-high Mt. Hood. With more than two million people living just up the road in Portland, you'd think this mountain playground would be overrun, but it's still easy to find solitude in the 67,000-acre wilderness surrounding the peak. Some of the world's best skiers take advantage of the powder on Hood, and they stick around in summertime for ski conditions that are as close to year-round as anyplace in the country.

THE COLUMBIA RIVER GORGE AND MT. HOOD PLANNER

WHEN TO GO

Winter weather in the Columbia Gorge and the Mt. Hood area is much more severe than in Portland and western Oregon. At times I–84 may be closed because of snow and ice. If you're planning a winter visit, be sure to carry plenty of warm clothes. High winds and single-digit temps are par for the course around 6,000 feet in January. Note that chains are a requirement for traveling over mountain passes.

Temperatures in the gorge are mild year-round, rarely dipping below 30 degrees in winter and hovering in the high 70s in mid-summer. As throughout Oregon, however, elevation is often a more significant factor than season, and an hour-long drive to Mt. Hood's Timberline Lodge can reduce those mid-summer temps by 20–30 degrees. Don't forget that the higher reaches of Mt. Hood retain snow as late as August.

In early fall, look for maple, tamarack, and aspen trees around the gorge, bursting with brilliant red and gold color. No matter the season, the basalt cliffs, the acres of lush forest, and that glorious expanse of water make the gorge worth visiting time and again.

FESTIVALS

Columbia Gorge Bluegrass Festival. One of the premier bluegrass fests in the West takes place in Stevenson, Washington every fourth weekend in July. ⊕ *www.columbiagorgebluegrass.net.*

RESTAURANTS

A prominent locavore mentality pervades western Oregon generally, and low elevations around the gorge mean long growing seasons for dozens of local producers. Fresh foods grown, caught, and harvested in the Northwest dominate menus in gourmet restaurants around the gorge and Mt. Hood. Columbia River salmon is big, fruit orchards proliferate around Hood River, and the gorge nurtures a glut of excellent vineyards. Of course, beer culture is king across Oregon, and even the smallest towns around the region have their own lively brewpubs with casual American pub fare and tap after tap of craft ales. In keeping with the region's green and laid-back vibe, outdoor dining is big, Hood River's superb Stonehedge Gardens being the quintessential example. *Prices in the reviews are the average cost of a main course at dinner or, if dinner is not served, at lunch.*

HOTELS

The hospitality industry is first-rate around the gorge and Mt. Hood, and the region's accommodations run the gamut from luxury hotels and sophisticated conference resorts to historic lodges, ski chalets, and cabin rentals. Cozy bed-and-breakfasts abound along the gorge, many of them historic structures overlooking the river. The slopes of Mt. Hood are spotted with smart ski resorts, and towns like Government Camp and Welches are long on rustic vacation rentals. The closer you are to Mt. Hood in any season, the earlier you'll want to reserve. With ski country working ever harder to attract summer patrons, Mt. Hood resorts like Timberline Lodge and Mt. Hood Skibowl offer some worthwhile seasonal specials. *Prices in the reviews are the lowest cost of a standard double room in high season.*

GETTING HERE AND AROUND

AIR TRAVEL

Air Contacts **Portland International Airport.** All major carriers serve PDX, the only nearby airport receiving commercial flights. Taxis out to Mt. Hood or the gorge are not particularly practical, but the airport has several door-to-door shuttle options. ⊠ *Portland* ☎ *877/739–4636* ⊕ *www.flypdx.com.*

Rates vary by destination, but a one-way trip to Hood River runs $90–$120. If you're heading to Hood, ski resorts like Timberline and Mt. Hood Meadows offer Portland shuttles in season.

Shuttles **Blue Star Transportation** ☎ *541/249–1837* ⊕ *www.bluestarbus.com.* **Green Shuttle** ☎ *541/252–4422* ⊕ *www.greentrans.com.*

BUS TRAVEL

Bus Contacts **Columbia Area Transit.** On Thursdays a fixed-route bus runs between the Dalles and Portland via Hood River. ☎ *541/386–4202* ⊕ *community.gorge.net/hrctd.*

CAR TRAVEL

I–84 is the main east–west route into the Columbia River Gorge. U.S. 26, heading east from Portland and northwest from Prineville, is the main route into the Mt. Hood area. Portions of I–84 and U.S. 26 that pass through the mountains pose winter-travel difficulties, though the state plows these roadways regularly. The gorge is closed frequently during harsh winters due to ice and mud slides. Extreme winds can also make driving hazardous, and potentially result in highway closures.

The Historic Columbia River Highway (U.S. 30) from Troutdale to just east of Oneonta Gorge passes Crown Point State Park and Multnomah Falls. I–84/U.S. 30 continues on to the Dalles. Highway 35 heads south from the Dalles to the Mt. Hood area, intersecting with U.S. 26 at Government Camp. From Portland, the Columbia Gorge–Mt. Hood Scenic Loop is the easiest way to see the gorge and the mountain. Take I–84 east to Troutdale and follow U.S. 26 to Bennett Pass (near Timberline), where Highway 35 heads north to Hood River; then follow I–84 back to Portland. Or make the loop in reverse.

Major rental-car agencies are available in Gresham (3 miles west of Troutdale); Enterprise is also in Hood River and the Dalles.

Local Agencies **Apple City Rental Cars** ⊠ *3250 Bonneville Rd., Hood River* ☎ *541/386–5504.*

TOURS

Americas Hub World Tours. Explore the gorge by bus or van on waterfall and wine tours. ☎ *800/673–3110* ⊕ *www.americashubworldtours.com.*

EcoTours of Oregon Day Tours. Day trips with an emphasis on natural history take in the waterfalls of the Historic Columbia River Highway and a scenic loop around Mt. Hood. ☎ *888/868–7733* ⊕ *www.ecotours-of-oregon.com.*

Explore the Gorge. Customizable tours of the gorge, Mt. Hood, and the Hood River Valley explore everything from the Lewis and Clark Trail to the region's microbreweries. ☎ 800/899–5676 ⊕ *www.explorethegorge. com.*

Martin's Gorge Tours. Wine tours, waterfall hikes, and spring wildflower tours are among the popular trips with this Portland-based guide. ☎ 888/290–8687 ⊕ *www.martinsgorgetours.com.*

VISITOR INFORMATION

Columbia River Gorge Visitors Association ☎ *800/984-6743* ⊕ *www.crgva.org.*

Oregon Tourism Commission ☎ *800/547-7842* ⊕ *www.traveloregon.com.*

COLUMBIA RIVER GORGE

When glacial floods carved out most of the Columbia River Gorge at the end of the last Ice Age, they left behind massive, looming cliffs where the river bisects the Cascade mountain range. The size of the canyon and the wildly varying elevations make this small stretch of Oregon as ecologically diverse as anyplace in the state. In a few days along the gorge you can mountain bike through dry canyons near the Dalles, hike through temperate rainforest in Oneonta Gorge, and take a woodland wildflower stroll just outside of Hood River. At night you'll be rewarded with historic lodging and good food in one of a half-dozen mellow river towns. The country's first National Scenic Area remains one of its most inviting ones.

TROUTDALE

16 miles east of Portland on I–84.

Troutdale is known for its great fishing spots, as well as antiques stores and the Columbia Gorge Premium Outlets. The city has a funky, walkable downtown, and it's the western terminus of the 22-mile-long **Historic Columbia River Highway,** U.S. 30 (also known as the Columbia River Scenic Highway and the Scenic Gorge Highway). In 1911, two years before work on the scenic road began, Troutdale became home to the Multnomah County Poor Farm, a massive Colonial Revival estate that housed Oregon's aged, indigent, and sick for most of the 20th century. After falling into disarray in the 1980s, the historic poor farm was reinvented in 1990 as the funky art resort McMenamins Edgefield, one of Troutdale's biggest draws today.

GETTING HERE AND AROUND

Troutdale is 16 miles east of downtown Portland on I–84, about a $40 cab ride from the airport. Reach Troutdale "the back way" by coming in from the east on U.S. 30, the Historic Columbia River Highway.

ESSENTIALS

Visitor Information **West Columbia Gorge Chamber of Commerce** ✉ *226 W. Historic Columbia River Hwy.* ☎ *503/669-7473* ⊕ *www. westcolumbiagorgechamber.com.*

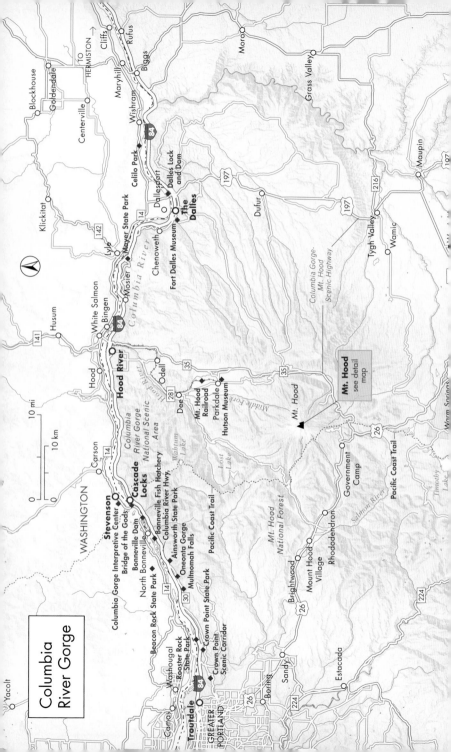

Columbia River Gorge

WASHINGTON

To HERMISTON →

Yacolt
Blockhouse
Goldendale
Centerville
Klickitat
142
141
Husum
Carson
Camas
Washougal
Stevenson

Cliffs
Rufus
Biggs
Maryhill
Wishram
Celilo Park
Dallesport
The Dalles
Dalles Lock and Dam
Chenoweth
Fort Dalles Museum
Moro
Grass Valley
Maupin
197

84

Lyle
Mosier
Mayer State Park
Bingen
White Salmon
Hood River
14

Columbia River

Dufur
216
Tygh Valley
Wamic

Columbia Gorge–Mt. Hood Scenic Highway

84

Columbia Gorge Interpretive Center
Bridge of the Gods
Cascade Locks
Bonneville Dam
North Bonneville
Bonneville Fish Hatchery
Columbia River Hwy.
Ainsworth State Park
Oneonta Gorge
Multnomah Falls
Beacon Rock State Park

14
30

Hood
Odell
35
281
Dee
Mt. Hood Railroad
Parkdale
Hutson Museum

Columbia River Gorge National Scenic Area

Wahtum Lake
Lost Lake
Middle Fork Hood River

Mt. Hood

Mt. Hood
see detail map

Warm Springs

Pacific Coast Trail
Crown Point State Park
Crown Point Scenic Corridor
Rooster Rock State Park

Troutdale

84

GREATER PORTLAND

Sandy
Boring
26
224
Estacada

Brightwood
Mount Hood Village
Rhododendron

Mt. Hood National Forest

Government Camp
Salmon River
Timothy Lake
Pacific Coast Trail

26
224

N

10 mi
10 km

WHERE TO EAT AND STAY

For expanded hotel reviews, visit Fodors.com.

$$$
MODERN
AMERICAN
✕ **Black Rabbit Restaurant & Bar.** Veteran Portland chef Kenny Giambalvo brought a new sizzle to Edgefield's flagship restaurant in 2013. Smart dishes like salmon tartare and wild mushroom crepes are served alongside fresh produce from the Edgefield garden. Vivid murals depicting the gorge's history enrich your view as you linger over dinner in a high-backed wooden booth. Enjoy an Edgefield wine or any one of a rotating cast of McMenamins brews (made on-site, approximately 50 yards away). Patio seating is available, with plenty of heaters to handle the unpredictable Oregon weather. Top off your meal with a homemade dessert and, wouldn't you know, a McMenamins home-roasted cup of coffee. $ *Average main: $26* ⊠ *2126 SW Halsey St.* ☎ *503/492–3086* ⊕ *www.mcmenamins.com.*

$
RESORT
Fodor's Choice
★
⊤ **McMenamins Edgefield.** Set in 74 acres of gardens, murals, orchards, and vineyards, this Georgian Revival manor is what the Four Seasons would be if it were operated by dreamers and Deadheads—which essentially describes Northwest brewers and hospitality innovators par excellence Mike and Brian McMenamin. **Pros:** plenty of eating and drinking choices; large variety of rooms and prices; great spa; on-site movie theater (only $3); live music events. **Cons:** crowds can get large at this busy place. $ *Rooms from: $100* ⊠ *2126 SW Halsey St.* ☎ *503/669–8610, 800/669–8610* ⊕ *www.mcmenamins.com* ⌁ *114 rooms, 20 with bath* ○| *No meals.*

SPORTS AND THE OUTDOORS

RECREATIONAL AREAS

Rooster Rock State Park. The most famous beach lining the Columbia River is here, right below Crown Point. Three miles of sandy beaches, panoramic cascades, and a large swimming area makes this a popular spot. True naturists appreciate that one of Oregon's two designated nude beaches is at the east end of Rooster Rock, and that it's not visible to conventional sunbathers. Rooster Rock is several miles east of Troutdale, and it's accessible only via the interstate. ⊠ *I–84, 7 miles east of Troutdale* ☎ *503/695–2261* ⊕ *www.oregonstateparks.org* ⌁ *Day use $5 per vehicle* ○ *Daily 7–dusk.*

FISHING

Just east of town, the Sandy River is fed by Mt. Hood snowmelt, and has a reputation as one of the state's best salmon and steelhead fisheries.

SHOPPING

Columbia Gorge Premium Outlets. Forty-five outlet stores, including Eddie Bauer and Coach, will keep you looking sharp for your trip through the gorge. Oregon's lack of a sales tax is a big draw for out-of-towners. ⊠ *450 NW 257th Way* ☎ *503/669–8060* ⊕ *www.premiumoutlets.com/ columbiagorge* ○ *Mon.–Sat. 10–8, Sun. 10–6.*

HISTORIC COLUMBIA RIVER HIGHWAY

U.S. 30, paralleling I–84 for 22 miles between Troutdale and interstate Exit 35.

The oldest scenic highway in the U.S. is a construction marvel that integrates asphalt path with cliff, river, and forest landscapes. Paralleling the interstate to the south, U.S. 30 climbs to forested riverside bluffs, passes half a dozen waterfalls, and provides access to hiking trails leading to still more falls and scenic overlooks. Completed in 1922, the serpentine highway was the first paved road in the gorge built expressly for automotive sightseers. The route is peppered with state parks. Eight of them are day-use only, with camping only available at Ainsworth State Park. Near the Dalles, an additional 15 miles of U.S. 30 are designated as part of the scenic byway, but the 22-mile western segment is the real draw.

GETTING HERE AND AROUND

U.S. 30 heads out of downtown Troutdale going east, and the route can be accessed from I–84 along the way, via Exit 22 near Corbett, Exit 28 near Bridal Veil Falls, Exit 31 at Multnomah Falls, and Exit 35, where it rejoins the interstate.

ESSENTIALS

Visitor Information **West Columbia Gorge Chamber of Commerce** ⊠ *226 W. Historic Columbia River Hwy., Troutdale* ☎ *503/669–7473* ⊕ *www. westcolumbiagorgechamber.com.* **Multnomah Falls Visitor Center** ⊠ *50000 Historic Columbia River Hwy., Exit 31 off I–84, Bridal Veil* ☎ *503/695–2372* ⊕ *www.multnomahfallslodge.com* ☉ *Daily 9–5.*

EXPLORING

Fodor's Choice ★ **Crown Point State Scenic Corridor.** This 730-foot-high bluff has an unparalleled 30-mile view down the Columbia River Gorge. Vista House, the two-tier octagonal structure on the side of the cliff, opened its doors to visitors in 1916; the rotunda has displays about the gorge and the highway. Vista House's architect Edgar Lazarus was the brother of Emma Lazarus, author of the poem displayed at the base of the Statue of Liberty. ⊠ *U.S. 30, 10 miles east of Troutdale* ☎ *503/695–2261, 800/551–6949* ⊕ *www.oregonstateparks.org* ☒ *Free* ☉ *Daily.*

Multnomah Falls. A 620-foot-high double-decker torrent, the second-highest year-round waterfall in the nation, Multnomah is by far the most spectacular of the cataracts east of Troutdale. The scenic highway leads down to a parking lot; from there a paved path winds to a bridge over the lower falls. A much steeper trail climbs to a viewing point overlooking the upper falls. It's quite a hike to the top, but worth it to avoid the crowds that swarm Multnomah in every season. ⊠ *Exit 31 off I–84, or 15 miles east of Troutdale on U.S. 30, Bridal Veil, Oregon* ☎ *503/695–2376* ⊕ *www.multnomahfallslodge.com.*

Oneonta Gorge. Following the old highway east from Multnomah Falls, you come to a narrow, mossy cleft with walls hundreds of feet high. Oneonta Gorge is most enjoyable in summer, when you can walk up the streambed through the cool green canyon, where hundreds of plant species—some found nowhere else—flourish under the perennially moist conditions. At other times of the year, take the trail along the west side of the canyon. The clearly marked trailhead is 100 yards west of the gorge, on the south side of the road. The trail takes you to Oneonta Falls, about ½ mile up the stream, where it links with an extensive regional trail system exploring the region's bluffs and waterfalls. Bring boots or submersible sneakers—plus a strong pair of ankles—because the rocks are slippery. ✉ *Exit 31 off I–84 ✢ 2 miles east of Multnomah Falls on U.S. 30, Oregon* ☎ *503/308–1700* 🌐 *www.fs.usda.gov/crgnsa.*

WHERE TO EAT

$$ AMERICAN 🍴 **Multnomah Falls Lodge.** Vaulted ceilings, stone fireplaces, and exquisite views of Multnomah Falls are complemented by wonderful service and an extensive menu at this restaurant, which is listed on the National Register of Historic Places. Consider the halibut fish-and-chips, the miso-and-seasame wild salmon, or the Oregon-beef sirloin with gnocchi. Breakfast favorites include blueberry, buttermilk, or huckleberry pancakes. A particular pleaser for out-of-town guests, the champagne Sunday brunch is held 8–2. Try the brown sugar–glazed Salmon Multnomah. For a treat during warmer months, sit on the patio and get close to the falls without feeling a drop. [$] *Average main: $20* ✉ *50000 Historic Columbia River Hwy., Exit 31 off I–84, Bridal Veil, Oregon* ☎ *503/695–2376* 🌐 *www.multnomahfallslodge.com.*

5

CASCADE LOCKS

7 miles east of Oneonta Gorge on Historic Columbia River Hwy. and I–84; 30 miles east of Troutdale on I–84.

In pioneer days, boats needing to pass the bedeviling rapids near the town of Whiskey Flats had to portage around them. The locks that gave the town its new name were completed in 1896, allowing waterborne passage for the first time. In 1938 they were submerged beneath the new Lake Bonneville when the Bonneville Lock and Dam became one of the most massive Corps of Engineers projects to come out of the New Deal. The town of Cascade Locks hung on to its name, though. A historic stern-wheeler still leads excursions from the town's port district, and the region's Native American tribes still practice traditional dip-net fishing near the current locks.

GETTING HERE AND AROUND

Reach Cascade Locks heading 45 miles east of Portland on I–84. If you're planning to come and go from Stevenson, Washington, carry cash for the $1 toll on the gorge-spanning Bridge of the Gods. The closest airport is Portland International, 40 miles west.

ESSENTIALS

Visitor Information **West Columbia Gorge Chamber of Commerce** ✉ *226 W. Historic Columbia River Hwy., Troutdale, Oregon* ☎ *503/669–7473* 🌐 *www.westcolumbiagorgechamber.com.*

EXPLORING

FAMILY **Bonneville Dam.** This is the first federal dam to span the Columbia, and was dedicated by President Franklin D. Roosevelt in 1937. Its generators (visible from a balcony on a self-guided tour or up close during thrice-daily guided tours in summer) have a capacity of more than

DID YOU KNOW?

The Columbia River Highway travels over graceful stone bridges built by Italian immigrant masons and winds through quiet forest glades. More than a dozen waterfalls pour over fern- and lichen-covered cliffs in a 10-mile stretch, including Multnomah Falls (pictured), the second-highest year-round waterfall in the nation.

a million kilowatts, enough to supply power to more than 200,000 single-family homes. There is a modern visitor center on Bradford Island, complete with underwater windows where gaggles of kids watch migrating salmon and steelhead as they struggle up fish ladders. The best viewing times are between April and October. In recent years the dwindling runs of wild Columbia salmon have made the dam a subject of much environmental controversy. ✉ *from I–84 take Exit 40, head northeast, and follow signs 1 mile to visitor center, Cascade Locks, Oregon* ☎ *541/374–8820* ⊕ *www.nwp.usace.army.mil/Locations/ColumbiaRiver/Bonneville* 💵 *Free* ☉ *Visitor center daily 9–5; tours mid-June–Aug., daily at 11, 1, and 3; Sept.–early June, weekends only.*

Cascade Locks. This is the home port of the 500-passenger stern-wheeler *Columbia Gorge*, which churns upriver, then back again, on two-hour excursions through some of the Columbia River Gorge's most impressive scenery, mid-May to early October. The ship's captain will talk about the gorge's fascinating 40-million-year geology and about pioneering spirits and legends, such as Lewis and Clark, who once triumphed over this very same river. Group bookings and private rentals are available. ✉ *Marine Park, 355 Wanapa St., Cascade Locks, Oregon* ☎ *541/224–3900, 800/224–3901* ⊕ *www.portlandspirit.com* 💵 *Prices vary* ⚓ *Reservations essential* ☉ *May–Oct.*

SPORTS AND THE OUTDOORS

HIKING

Pacific Crest Trail. Cascade Locks bustles with grubby thru-hikers refueling along the 2,650-mile Canada-to-Mexico Pacific Crest Trail. Check out a scenic and strenuous portion of it, heading south from the trailhead at Herman Creek Horse Camp, just east of town. The route heads up into the Cascades, showing off monster views of the gorge. Backpackers out for a longer trip will find idyllic campsites at Wahtum Lake, 14 miles south. ✉ *1 mile east of Cascade Locks off N.W. Forest Ln., Cascade Locks, Oregon* ☎ *541/308–1700* ⊕ *www.pcta.org.*

STEVENSON, WASHINGTON

Across the river from Cascade Locks via the Bridge of the Gods and 1 mile east on Hwy. 14.

With the Bridge of the Gods toll bridge spanning the Columbia River above the Bonneville Dam, Stevenson acts as a sort of "twin city" to Cascade Locks on the Oregon side. Tribal legends and the geologic record tell of the original Bridge of the Gods, a substantial landslide that occurred here sometime between AD 1000 and 1760, briefly linking the two sides of the gorge before the river swept away the debris. The landslide's steel namesake now leads to tiny Stevenson, where vacationers traverse the quiet Main Street, planning excursions to nearby Mt. Adams or Mt. St. Helens. Washington's Highway 14 runs through the middle of town, and since the cliffs on the Oregon side are more dramatic, driving this two-lane highway actually offers better views.

Dog Mountain Trail, Columbia River Gorge National Scenic Area

GETTING HERE AND AROUND

To get to Stevenson from the Oregon side of the gorge, cross the Columbia River at the Bridge of the Gods. Bring cash for the $1 toll. Stevenson proper is a mile east on Highway 14. The closest airport is Portland International, 43 miles west on the Oregon side of the river.

ESSENTIALS

Visitor Information **Skamania County Chamber of Commerce** ✉ *167 NW 2nd Ave.* ☎ *509/427–8911* ⊕ *www.skamania.org.*

EXPLORING

Bridge of the Gods. For a magnificent vista 135 feet above the Columbia, as well as a speedy route between Oregon and Washington, $1 will pay your way over the grandly named bridge. Here also, hikers cross from Oregon to reach the Washington segment of the **Pacific Crest Trail**, which picks up just west of the bridge. ⊕ *www.portofcascadelocks. org/bridge.htm.*

FAMILY **Columbia Gorge Interpretive Center Museum.** A petroglyph whose eyes seem to look straight at you, "She Who Watches" or "Tsagaglalal" is the logo for this museum. Sitting among the dramatic basaltic cliffs on the north bank of the Columbia River Gorge, the museum explores the life of the gorge: its history, culture, architecture, legends, and much more. The younger crowd may enjoy the reenactment of the gorge's formation in the Creation Theatre. Or a 37-foot high fishwheel from the 19th century. Historians will appreciate studying the water route of the Lewis & Clark Expedition. There's also an eye-opening exhibit that examines current environmental impacts on the area. ✉ *990 SW Rock Creek Dr.*

✛ *1 mile east of Bridge of the Gods on Hwy. 14* ☎ *509/427–8211, 800/991–2338* ⊕ *www.columbiagorge.org* 🎫 *$10* ☉ *Daily 10–5.*

WHERE TO EAT AND STAY

For expanded hotel reviews, visit Fodors.com.

$$$
MODERN
AMERICAN

✕ **The Cascade Room at Skamania Lodge.** Gaze at the perfect fusion of sky, river, and cliff scapes through the Cascade Room's expansive windows during an exquisite dining experience. Braised lamb with pasta and coastal cioppino are signature dishes; also try the potato gnocchi and stuffed mushroom strudel. Hearty organic carrot cake and fresh mixed-berry cobbler are grand finales. A champagne brunch buffet is offered on Sunday, and the seafood, salads, sushi, and pastas draw patrons from miles around. $ *Average main: $28* ⊠ *Skamania Lodge, 1131 SW Skamania Lodge Way* ☎ *509/427–7700* ⊕ *www.skamania.com.*

$$$
AMERICAN

✕ **Pacific Crest Dining Room.** After a rejuvenating spa treatment or hike, the fresh healthy cuisine here is a special treat. You can dine in the low light of the muted main room (metal pine-tree light fixtures are custom made) or in the adjoining lounge, its 12-foot-high glass wall overlooking the manicured courtyard and the forest beyond. The pastry chef works through the night, ensuring fresh-baked breads and pastries by sunrise. Healthy never tasted so good, with crisp salads, Pacific Northwest fish (amazing smoked salmon), Cascade-area beef, and gourmet vegetarian fare. Late afternoons, the lounge serves goodies such as house-baked pretzels and IPA-battered halibut and chips. $ *Average main: $26* ⊠ *Bonneville Hot Springs Resort, 1252 E. Cascade Dr.* ✛ *3 miles west of Bridge of the Gods on Hwy. 14, North Bonneville* ☎ *509/427–9711* ⊕ *www.bonnevilleresort.com.*

$$
RESORT

🏨 **Bonneville Hot Springs Resort and Spa.** Enter an architectural wonderland of wood, iron, rock, and water, water everywhere—owner Pete Cam and his sons built the resort to share their love of these historic mineral springs with the public, especially those seeking physical renewal. **Pros:** glorious grounds; impressive architectural detail; attentive and knowledgeable spa staff; the Pacific Crest Trail passes directly through the property. **Cons:** must reserve spa appointments separately from room reservations; the dull, boxy exterior belies what's inside. $ *Rooms from: $169* ⊠ *1252 E. Cascade Dr., North Bonneville* ☎ *509/427–7767, 866/459–1678* ⊕ *www.bonnevilleresort.com* ⌂ *78 rooms* ⦿| *No meals.*

$$
RESORT
FAMILY

🏨 **Skamania Lodge.** So big you need a map, this warm, woodsy lodge impresses with a multitude of windows overlooking in the surrounding forests and gorge and an outstanding array of recreational facilities. **Pros:** works for active guests as well as kids; U.S. Forest Service kiosk in the lobby. **Cons:** expensive for a large family; can get crowded—sometimes there's a wait for a table in the dining room. $ *Rooms from: $179* ⊠ *1131 S.W. Skamania Lodge Way, north of Hwy. 14, 1½ miles east of Bridge of the Gods* ☎ *509/427–7700, 800/221–7117* ⊕ *www.skamania.com* ⌂ *254 rooms* ⦿| *No meals.*

NIGHTLIFE AND THE ARTS

Walking Man Brewing. Locals and tourists alike crowd this cozy brewery's sunshiny patio for creative pizzas and a dozen craft ales. After a couple of pints of the strong Homo Erectus IPA and Knuckle Dragger Pale Ale, you may go a little ape. Live music on summer weekends skews twangy and upbeat. ⊠ *240 S.W. 1st St.* ☎ *509/427–5520* ⊘ *Closed Mon. and Tues.*

SPORTS AND THE OUTDOORS

RECREATIONAL AREA

Beacon Rock State Park. For several hundred years this 848-foot rock was a landmark for river travelers, including Native Americans, who recognized this point as the last rapids of the Columbia River. Lewis and Clark are thought to have been the first white men to see the volcanic remnant. Picnic atop old lava flows after hiking a 1-mile trail, steep but safe, which leads to tremendous views of the Columbia Gorge and the river. A round-trip hike takes 45–60 minutes. ⊠ *Off Hwy. 14, 7 miles west of Bridge of the Gods, North Bonneville* ☎ *509/427–8265, 360/902–8844* ⊕ *www.parks.wa.gov* ⊠ *Day use $10 per vehicle.*

HOOD RIVER

17 miles east of Cascade Locks on I–84.

For years, the incessant easterly winds blowing through the town of Hood River were nothing more than a nuisance. Then somebody bolted a sail to a surfboard, waded into the fat part of the gorge, and a new recreational craze was born. A fortuitous combination of factors—mainly the reliable gale-force winds blowing against the current—has made Hood River the self-proclaimed windsurfing capital of the world. Especially in summer, this once-somnolent town swarms with colorful "boardheads" from as far away as Europe and Australia.

Hood River's rich pioneer past is reflected in its downtown historic district. The City of Hood River publishes a free self-guided walking tour (available through the city government office or the Hood River Chamber of Commerce) that will take you on a tour of more than 40 civic and commercial buildings dating from 1893 to the 1930s, some of which are listed in the National Register of Historic Places.

GETTING HERE AND AROUND

Reach Hood River by driving 60 miles east of Portland on I-84, or if you're coming from Mt. Hood, by heading north on Highway 35. The closest airport is in Portland.

ESSENTIALS

Visitor Information Hood River County Chamber of Commerce ⊠ *720 E. Port Marina Dr.* ☎ *541/386–2000, 800/366–3530* ⊕ *www.hoodriver.org.*

EXPLORING

Cathedral Ridge Winery. Run by fourth-generation winemaker Michael Sebastiani, this vineyard has racked up countless ribbons and awards from wine festivals and publications, and *Wine Press Northwest* called it one of the region's best wine-country picnic spots. Popular varietals include Riesling, Pinot Gris, and Syrah. The tasting room is

Vineyards in the Hood River Valley

open 11 to 5 daily. ✉ *4200 Post Canyon Dr.* ☎ *800/516–8710* ⊕ *www.cathedralridgewinery.com* 🎫 *Free* ⏱ *Daily 11–5.*

Fruit Loop. Either by car or bicycle, tour the quiet country highways of Hood River Valley, whose vast orchards surround the river. You'll see apples, pears, cherries, and peaches fertilized by volcanic soil, pure glacier water, and a conducive harvesting climate. Along the 35 miles of farms are a host of outlets for delicious baked goods, wines, flowers, and nuts. Festive farm activities from April to November also give a taste of the agricultural life. While on the loop, consider stopping at the town of **Parkdale** to lunch, shop, and snap a photo of Mt. Hood's north face. ✉ *Rte. begins on Hwy. 35* ⊕ *www.hoodriverfruitloop.com.*

OFF THE BEATEN PATH **Lost Lake.** One of the most-photographed sights in the Pacific Northwest, this lake's waters reflect towering Mt. Hood and the thick forests that line its shore. Cabins and campsites are available for overnight stays, and because no motorboats are allowed on Lost Lake, the area is blissfully quiet. ✉ *Lost Lake Rd., take Hood River Hwy. south to town of Dee* ☎ *541/352–6002* 🎫 *Day use $7.*

Mt. Hood Railroad. An efficient and relaxing way to survey Mt. Hood and the Hood River, this passenger and freight line was established in 1906. Chug alongside the Hood River through vast fruit orchards before climbing up steep forested canyons, glimpsing Mt. Hood along the way. There are several trip options: a four-hour excursion (serves light concessions), dinner, brunch, and several themed trips, like murder-mysteries and Old West robberies. Exceptional service is as impressive as the scenery. ✉ *110 Railroad Ave.* ☎ *541/386–3556, 800/872–4661* ⊕ *www.mthoodrr.com* 🎫 *$30–$82* ⏱ *Mar.–Oct.*

NEED A BREAK?

Full Sail Tasting Room and Pub. A glass-walled microbrewery with a windswept deck overlooking the Columbia, the Full Sail Tasting Room and Pub is one of the great microbrew success stories in the West, having won major awards at the Great American Beer Festival and the World Beer Cup. Savory snack foods complement fresh ales. Free, on-site brewery tours last about 25 minutes. ✉ *506 Columbia St.* ☎ *541/386–2247* 🌐 *www.fullsailbrewing.com.*

Western Antique Aeroplane and Automobile Museum. Housed at Hood River's tiny airport (general aviation only), the museum's meticulously restored, propeller-driven planes are all still in flying condition. The antique steam cars, Model Ts, and sleek Depression-era sedans are road-worthy, too. Periodic car shows and an annual fly-in draw thousands of history nerds and spectators. ✉ *1600 Museum Rd., off Hwy. 281, 2½ miles south of town* ☎ *541/308–1600* 🌐 *www.waaamuseum.org* 🎟 *$12* 🕒 *Daily 9–5.*

WHERE TO EAT AND STAY

For expanded hotel reviews, visit Fodors.com.

$ MODERN AMERICAN

🍴 **Cornerstone Cuisine.** An emphasis on wild-caught seafood and local meat and produce makes the Hood River Hotel restaurant a popular lunch stop. Try the sea-salted grilled asparagus or the hearty chorizo paella. Chef Mark Whitehead impresses with simple dishes and fresh ingredients, and the covered sidewalk patio lets you keep an eye on comings and goings downtown. [$] *Average main: $14* ✉ *102 Oak St.* ☎ *541/386–1900* 🌐 *www.hoodriverhotel.com* 🕒 *No dinner.*

$$ MODERN AMERICAN Fodor's Choice ★

🍴 **Stonehedge Gardens.** It's not just the cuisine that's out of this world, Stonehedge is of another time and place, surrounded by 7 acres of lush English-style gardens that gracefully frame its multitude of stone terraces and trickling fountains. There's a *petanque* (lawn bowling) court for quick predinner activity, and music on Wednesday nights in summer draws a full house. Each of the four dining rooms in the restored 1898 home has a distinct personality, from cozy to verdant to elegant, but the tiered patio is where summer diners gather. Classics like steak Diane and filet mignon appeal to more traditional diners, while buffalo-style prawns and curry shiitake mushroom soup show off the kitchen's creative side. Just when you think your meal is complete, along comes the Flaming Bread Pudding. This restaurant is a Columbia Gorge institution. [$] *Average main: $23* ✉ *3405 Cascade Ave.* ☎ *541/386–3940* 🌐 *www.stonehedgeweddings.com* 🕒 *No lunch.*

$$$$ HOTEL

🏨 **Columbia Gorge Hotel.** One selling point of this grande dame of gorge hotels is the view of a 208-foot-high waterfall, while charming period-style rooms and a great restaurant add to the appeal. **Pros:** historic structure built by Columbia Gorge Highway visionary Simon Benson; unbeatable gorge views. **Cons:** smallish rooms reflect their historic character. [$] *Rooms from: $259* ✉ *4000 Westcliff Dr.* ☎ *541/386–5566, 800/345–1921* 🌐 *www.columbiagorgehotel.com* 🛏 *39 rooms* 🍽 *No meals.*

$ HOTEL

🏨 **Hood River Hotel.** Another Hood River gem found on the National Register of Historic Places, the restored building has a grand, Old West facade with antique-heavy interiors that feel more like a European inn.

Pros: excellent downtown location; several available adventure packages; historic vibe. **Cons:** smallish rooms; no king-size beds. $ *Rooms from: $129* ⊠ *102 Oak St.* ☎ *541/386–1900* ⊕ *www.hoodriverhotel. com* ⤳ *41 rooms* ⊚| *Breakfast.*

$$

B&B/INN

⊡ **Lakecliff Bed & Breakfast.** Perched on a cliff overlooking the Columbia Gorge, this beautiful 1908 summer home, designed by architect A.E. Doyle (who also created the Multnomah Falls Lodge), sits in a stunning 3-acre magical land of ferns, fir trees, and water. **Pros:** glorious views; friendly and accommodating hosts; convenient-to-town location with a remote feel. **Cons:** no king-size beds; Wi-Fi in living room only, and a bit spotty. $ *Rooms from: $175* ⊠ *3820 Westcliff Dr.* ☎ *541/386–7000* ⊕ *www.lakecliffbnb.com* ⤳ *4 rooms* ⊘ *Closed Nov.–Apr.* ⊚| *Breakfast.*

SPORTS AND THE OUTDOORS

KAYAKING

Columbia Gorge Kayak School. Whether you want to practice your Eskimo roll in the safety of a pool, run the Klickitat River in an inflatable kayak, or try out a stand-up paddleboard on the Columbia, the gorge's premier kayak guides can arrange the trip. Book online, by phone, or at the Kayak Shed downtown. ⊠ *6 Oak St.* ☎ *541/806–4190* ⊕ *www. gorgekayaker.com* ⊠ *Kayaking lessons $40, flatwater and whitewater trips $60–$220, two-hour paddleboard rentals $30.*

WINDSURFING

Big Winds. The retail hub for Hood River's windsurfing and kiteboarding culture also rents gear and provides windsurfing lessons for beginners. ⊠ *207 Front St.* ☎ *541/386–6086* ⊕ *www.bigwinds.com* ⊠ *Lessons and clinics $65–$250.*

THE DALLES

20 miles east of Hood River on I–84.

The Dalles lies on a crescent bend of the Columbia River where it narrows and once spilled over a series of rapids, creating a flagstone effect. French voyagers christened it *dalle,* or "flagstone." The Dalles is the seat of Wasco County and the trading hub of north–central Oregon. It gained fame early in the region's history as the town where the Oregon Trail branched, with some pioneers departing to travel over Mt. Hood on Barlow Road and the others continuing down the Columbia River. This may account for the small-town, Old West feeling that still permeates the area. Several historic Oregon moments as they relate to the Dalles' past are magnificently illustrated on eight murals painted by renowned Northwest artists, located downtown within short walking distance of one another.

GETTING HERE AND AROUND

The Dalles is best reached by car, 84 miles east of Portland or 126 miles west of Pendleton on I–84. The closest airport is Portland International.

ESSENTIALS

Visitor Information The Dalles Area Chamber of Commerce ⊠ *404 W. 2nd St.* ☎ *541/296–2231* ⊕ *www.thedalleschamber.com.*

EXPLORING

FAMILY **Columbia Gorge Discovery Center–Wasco County Historical Museum.** Exhibits highlight the geological history of the Columbia Gorge, back 40 million years when volcanoes, landslides, and floods carved out the area. The museum focuses on 10,000 years of Native American life and exploration of the region by white settlers. ✉ *5000 Discovery Dr.* ☎ *541/296–8600* 🌐 *www.gorgediscovery.org* 🎟 *$9* 🕑 *Daily 9–5.*

The Dalles Lock and Dam. At this hydroelectric dam east of the Bonneville Dam, you can tour a visitor center with a surprisingly even-handed exhibit on differing views of Colombia River dams, with input from farmers, utility companies, environmentalists, and indigenous tribes. There's also a surreal live feed of salmon and sturgeon scaling the fish ladder. Call ahead for tours offered most weekends, photo ID required. ✉ *2 miles east of the Dalles at Lake Celilo, off I-84, Exit 87 (in summer) or Exit 88 other times* ☎ *541/296–9778* 🌐 *www.nwp.usace.army.mil/Locations/ColumbiaRiver/TheDalles.aspx* 🎟 *Free* 🕑 *Hours vary throughout the year.*

Fort Dalles Museum. The 1856-vintage Fort Dalles Surgeon's Quarters is the site of the oldest history museum in Oregon. The museum's first visitors came through the doors in 1905. On display in authentic hand-hewn log buildings, originally part of a military base, are the personal effects of some of the region's settlers and a collection of early automobiles. The entrance fee gains you admission to the **Anderson Homestead** museum across the street, which also has pioneer artifacts. ✉ *500 W. 15th St., at Garrison* ☎ *541/296–4547* 🌐 *www.fortdallesmuseum.org* 🎟 *$5* 🕑 *Apr.–Oct., daily 10–4.*

WHERE TO EAT

$$ AMERICAN 🍴 **Baldwin Saloon.** The walls of this historic watering hole-turned-hip-restaurant are a weirdly authentic mix of landscape art and early American oil-painting erotica. The immense menu likewise runs the gamut from pastas to seafood to burgers. Stop in at lunch for a bowl of the popular bouillabaisse, and make weekend reservations for a dinner set to music from the saloon's 1894 mahogany Schubert piano. [$] *Average main: $22* ✉ *205 Court St.* ☎ *541/296–5666* 🌐 *www.baldwinsaloon.com* 🕑 *Closed Sun.*

$ CAFÉ 🍴 **Petite Provence.** This popular downtown bistro/bakery/dessertery serves eggs, crepes, and croissants for breakfast; hot and cold sandwiches and salads for lunch, and fresh-baked pastries and breads (you can take a loaf home). The sparkling display case tempts with a goodly selection of napoleons, éclairs, tarts, and mousses. [$] *Average main: $10* ✉ *408 E. 2nd St.* ☎ *541/506–0037* 🌐 *www.provencepdx.com* 🕑 *No dinner.*

$ HOTEL Fodor's Choice ★ 🏨 **Celilo Inn.** On a hill overlooking the Columbia, The Dalles Dam, and Mt. Hood, the Celilo benefits from a knockout concept: it's a prototypical motor lodge gone high-design, with exterior-entry rooms and a '50s light-up motel sign that disguise the hotel's slick, boutique feel. **Pros:** sexy design; specializes in wine tours (bottles available on-site); great views. **Cons:** not all rooms have views; those on the far end feel miles away from the front desk. [$] *Rooms from: $95* ✉ *3550 E. 2nd St.* ☎ *541/769–0001* 🌐 *www.celiloinn.com* 🛏 *46 rooms* 🍽 *No meals.*

NIGHTLIFE AND THE ARTS

Rivertap Pub. Regional beers and wines are showcased at this hipster hangout with a feel like a friend's cool garage lair. Cocktails are also available, including the rare tap margarita, and the small menu appeals to a drinking crowd with nachos, hot wings, and fish tacos. Live music on the weekends draws a crowd of slick young professionals. ⊠ *703 E. 2nd St.* ☎ *541/296–7870* ⊕ *www.rivertap.com* ⊗ *Mon.–Thurs. 4–10, Fri.–Sat. noon–midnight, Sun. noon–8.*

SPORTS AND THE OUTDOORS

RECREATIONAL AREAS

Celilo Park. Named for the falls that challenged spawning salmon here in the predam days, this favorite spot for windsurfers also has swimming, sailboarding, and fishing. ⊠ *7 miles east of the Dalles, off I–84 Exit 99* ☎ *541/296–1181* ⊠ *Free* ⊗ *Daily.*

Mayer State Park. Views from atop the park's Rowena Crest bluff are knockout, especially during the March and April wildflower season. Recreational activities include swimming, boating, fishing, and picnicking. ⊠ *Exit 77 off I–84* ☎ *800/551–6949* ⊕ *www.oregonstateparks.org* ⊠ *Day use $5 per vehicle* ⊗ *Daily.*

MT. HOOD

The Multnomah tribe call Mt. Hood "Wy'East," named, according to popular legend, for a jealous lover who once sparred over a woman with his rival, Klickitat. When their fighting caught the Great Spirit's attention, Wy'East and Klickitat were transformed into two angry, smoke-bellowing mountains—one became Washington's Mt. Adams, the other became Mt. Hood. Wy'East has mellowed out a bit since then, but the mountain is still technically an active volcano, and it's had very minor, lava-free eruptive events as recently as the mid-1800s. Today Mt. Hood is better known for the challenge it poses to climbers, its deep winter snows, and a dozen glaciers and snowfields that make skiing possible almost year-round. Resort towns and colorful hospitality villages are arranged in a semicircle around the mountain, full of ski bars and rental cabins that host hordes of fun-loving Portlanders each weekend. In every direction from the postcard-perfect peak the million-acre Mount Hood National Forest spreads out like a big green blanket, and upwards of 300,000 acres of that are designated wilderness. Mule deer, black bears, elk, and the occasional cougar share the space with humans who come to hike, camp, and fish in the Pacific Northwest's quintessential wild ecosystem.

AROUND THE MOUNTAIN

About 60 miles east of Portland on I–84 and U.S. 26; 65 miles from the Dalles, west on I–84 and south on Hwy. 35 and U.S. 26.

Majestically towering 11,245 feet above sea level, Mt. Hood is what remains of the original north wall and rim of a volatile crater. Although the peak no longer spews ash or fire, active steam vents can be spotted high on the mountain. The mountain took its modern moniker in 1792,

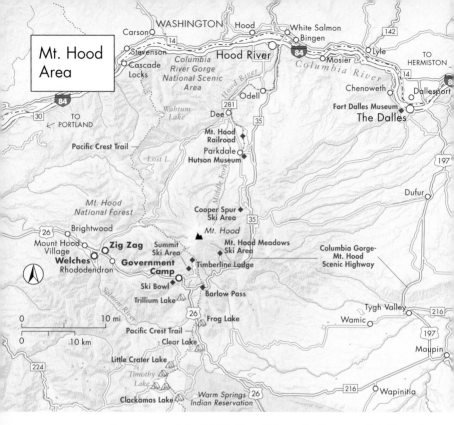

when a crew of the British Royal Navy, the first recorded Caucasians sailing up the Columbia River, spotted it and named it after a famed British naval officer by the name of—you guessed it—Hood.

Mt. Hood offers the only year-round skiing in the Lower 48 states, with three major ski areas and some 30 lifts, as well as extensive areas for cross-country skiing and snowboarding. Many of the ski runs turn into mountain-bike trails in summer. The mountain is also popular with climbers and hikers. In fact, some hikes follow parts of the Oregon Trail, and signs of the pioneers' passing are still evident.

GETTING HERE AND AROUND

From Portland, U.S. 26 heads east into the heart of Mount Hood National Forest, while Highway 35 runs south from Hood River along the mountain's east face. The roads meet 60 miles east of Portland, near Government Camp, forming an oblong loop with I–84 and the Historic Columbia Gorge Highway. The closest airport is Portland International, 53 miles northwest of Government Camp. Ski resorts like Timberline Lodge and Mt. Hood Meadows offer Portland shuttles in season—call for timetables and pick-up and drop-off sites.

A snowboarder catches some air on Mt. Hood.

ESSENTIALS

Visitor Information **Mt. Hood Area Chamber of Commerce** ✉ *24403 E. Welches Rd., Welches* ☎ *503/622–3017* 🌐 *www.mthood.org.* **Mt. Hood National Forest Headquarters** ✉ *16400 Champion Way, Sandy* ☎ *503/668–1700* 🌐 *www.fs.usda.gov/mthood.*

WHERE TO EAT AND STAY

For expanded hotel reviews, visit Fodors.com.

$$$$ | MODERN AMERICAN

🍴 **Cascade Dining Room.** If the wall of windows isn't coated with snow, you may get a good look at some of the neighboring peaks. Vaulted wooden beams and a wood-plank floor, handcrafted furniture, handwoven drapes, and a lion-size stone fireplace set the scene. The atmosphere is historic, but executive chef Jason Stoller Smith is a former wine-country *wunderkind* whose résumé includes orchestrating a salmon bake at the White House. The dinner menu's local/organic emphasis embraces, for example, Oregon lamb with goat-cheese-stuffed pear and poached duck eggs in red wine. The daily Farmers Market Brunch is itself worth the drive up to Timberline, highlighting different seasonal ingredients and purveyors each week, from Dungeness crab to local hazelnuts to Oregon cherries. Pick up a few culinary tips from the chef demonstrations. [$] *Average main: $34* ✉ *Timberline Rd., Timberline* ☎ *503/272–3104* 🌐 *www.timberlinelodge.com* ✍ *Reservations essential.*

$$$ | RESORT | FAMILY | Fodor's Choice ★

🏨 **Timberline Lodge.** The approach builds excitement, an unforgettable 6-mile ascent that circles Mt. Hood, then the Lodge materializes out of the mist and you momentarily forget about the snow-capped peak; no wonder Stanley Kubrick used shots of the exterior for *The*

Mt. Hood

Shining. **Pros:** a thrill to stay on the mountain itself; great proximity to all snow activity; plush featherbeds; amazing architecture; fun dining places. **Cons:** rooms are small; no air-conditioning; carloads of tourists. [$] *Rooms from: $250* ✉ *27500 E. Timberline Rd.* ☎ *503/272–3311, 800/547–1406* 🌐 *www.timberlinelodge.com* 🛏 *70 rooms, 60 with bath* 🍴 *Some meals.*

SPORTS AND THE OUTDOORS

Fodor's Choice ★ **Mount Hood National Forest.** The highest mountain in Oregon and the fourth-highest peak in the Cascades, "the Mountain" is a focal point of the 1.1-million-acre forest, an all-season playground attracting almost 3 million visitors annually. Twenty miles southeast of Portland, it extends south from the Columbia River Gorge for more than 60 miles and includes more than 311,000 acres of designated wilderness. These woods are perfect for hikers, horseback riders, mountain climbers, and cyclists. Within the forest are more than 80 campgrounds and 50 lakes stocked with brown, rainbow, cutthroat, brook, and steelhead trout. The Sandy, Salmon, and other rivers are known for their fishing, rafting, canoeing, and swimming. Both forest and mountain are crossed by an extensive trail system for hikers, cyclists, and horseback riders. The **Pacific Crest Trail,** which begins in British Columbia and ends in Mexico, crosses at the 4,157-foot-high Barlow Pass. As with most other mountain destinations within Oregon, weather can be temperamental, and snow and ice may affect driving conditions as early as October and as late as June. Bring tire chains and warm clothes as a precaution.

Since this forest is close to the Portland metro area, campgrounds and trails are potentially crowded over the summer months, especially on weekends. If you're planning to camp, get info and permits from the Mt. Hood National Forest Headquarters. Campgrounds are managed by the National Forest and a few private concessionaires, and standouts include a string of neighboring campgrounds on the south side of Mt. Hood: Trillium Lake, Still Creek, Timothy Lake, Little Crater Lake, Clackamas Lake, Summit Lake, Clear Lake, and Frog Lake. Each varies in what it offers and in price. The mountain is overflowing with day-use areas. There are also Mount Hood National Forest maps with details about well-marked trails. From mid-November through April, all designated Winter Recreation Areas require a Sno-Park permit, available from the Forest Service and many local resorts and sporting goods stores. ✉ *Single day $5–$7, annual Northwest Forest Pass $30 (not accepted in all day-use areas).*

SPORTS AND THE OUTDOORS

DOWNHILL SKIING

FAMILY **Cooper Spur Mountain Resort.** On the eastern slope of Mt. Hood, Cooper Spur caters to families and has one double chair and a towrope. The longest run is 2/3 miles, with a 350-foot vertical drop. Facilities and services include rentals, instruction, repairs, and a ski shop, day lodge, snack bar, and restaurant. Call for hours. ✉ *10755 Cooper Spur Rd., follow signs from Hwy. 35 for 2½ miles to ski area, Pinedale* ☎ *541/352–6692* ⊕ *www.cooperspur.com.*

Timberline Lodge Ski Area. The longest ski season in North America unfolds at this full-service ski area, where the U.S. ski team conducts summer training. Thanks to the omnipresent Palmer snowfield, it's the closest thing to a year-round ski area in the Lower 48 (closed only for a few weeks in September). Timberline is famous for its Palmer chairlift, which takes skiers and snowboarders to the high glacier for summer skiing. There are five high-speed quad chairs, one triple chair, and one double. The top elevation is 8,500 feet, with a 3,700-foot vertical drop, and the longest run is 3 miles. Facilities include a day lodge with fast food and a ski shop; lessons and equipment rental and repair are available. Parking requires a Sno-Park permit. The Palmer and Magic Mile lifts are popular with both skiers and sightseers. Construction on Timberline's long-awaited mountain-biking park began in 2013. ✉ *Off U.S. 26* ☎ *503/272–3311* ⊕ *www.timberlinelodge.com.* ✉ *Lift tickets $60–$66 per day* ⊘ *Sun.–Thurs. 9–4, Fri. and Sat. 9 am–10 pm; Palmer and Magic Mile lifts June–Aug., daily 7 am–2 pm.*

GOVERNMENT CAMP

45 miles from the Dalles, south on Hwy. 35 and west on U.S. 26; 54 miles east of Portland on I–84 and U.S. 26.

Government Camp is an alpine resort village with a bohemian vibe and a fair number of hotels and restaurants. A bonanza of ski and mountain-biking trails converge at "Govy," and it's a convenient drive to Welches, which also has restaurants and lodging. Several of Mt. Hood's five ski resorts are just outside of town, and the rest are a convenient drive away.

WHERE TO EAT AND STAY

For expanded hotel reviews, visit Fodors.com.

$ AMERICAN 🍴 **Charlie's Mountain View.** Old and new ski swag plasters the walls, lift chairs function as furniture, and photos of famous (and locally famous) skiers and other memorabilia are as abundant as the menu selections. Open flame–grilled steaks and hamburgers are worthy here, and the happy hour crowd shares plates piled high with waffle fries. When they're in season, try the apple dumplings. Charlie's is a local institution for powder hounds, and the fun, divey bar in back stays busy with ski bums and other lively degenerates. Live music packs them in on Friday and Saturday nights. [$] *Average main: $9* ✉ *88462 E. Government Camp Loop* ☎ *503/272–3333* 🌐 *www.charliesmountainview.com.*

$ AMERICAN 🍴 **Huckleberry Inn.** Whether it's 2 am or 2 pm, Huckleberry Inn welcomes you 24 hours a day with soups, milk shakes, burgers, sandwiches, and omelets. Well-known treats are made with huckleberries, and include pie, pancakes, tea, jelly, and vinaigrette salad dressing. Alongside the diner, a (very slightly) more upscale steak house opens on weekends during ski season. [$] *Average main: $7* ✉ *88611 E. Government Camp Loop* ☎ *503/272–3325* 🌐 *www.huckleberry-inn.com.*

$$$ RENTAL 🏨 **Thunderhead Lodge.** Within walking distance of the Mt. Hood Ski Bowl (its night lights visible from your cabin), the condo units at the lodge are great jumping-off sites for the many activities in the area. **Pros:** walking distance to activities and amenities; wonderful views. **Cons:** no-frills accommodations. [$] *Rooms from: $245* ✉ *87577 E. Government Camp Loop* ☎ *503/622–1142* 🌐 *www.mthoodrent.com* 🛏 *8 units* 🍽 *No meals.*

SPORTS AND THE OUTDOORS

DOWNHILL SKIING

Mt. Hood Meadows Ski Resort. The mountain's largest resort has more than 2,000 skiable acres, 85 runs, five double chairs, six high-speed quads, a top elevation of 9,000 feet, a vertical drop of 2,777 feet, and a longest run of 3 miles. Facilities include a day lodge, nine restaurants, two lounges, a ski school, and a ski shop. Equipment rental and repair are also available. ✉ *10 miles east of Government Camp off Hwy. 35* ☎ *503/337–2222, 800/754–4663* 🌐 *www.skihood.com.*

FAMILY **Mt. Hood Skibowl.** The ski area closest to Portland is also known as "America's largest night ski area." It has 960 skiable acres serviced by four double chairs and five surface tows, a top elevation of 5,027 feet, a vertical drop of 1,500 feet, and a longest run of 3½ miles. You can take advantage of two-day lodges, a midmountain warming hut, three restaurants, and two lounges. Sleigh rides are conducted, weather permitting. In summer the resort morphs into the Adventure Park at Skibowl, with mountain biking, disc golf, and kid-friendly tubing and alpine slides. ✉ *53 miles east of Portland, across U.S. 26 from Government Camp* ☎ *503/272–3206, 800/754–2695* 🌐 *www.skibowl.com.*

FAMILY **Summit Ski Area.** The longest run at this tiny hill is ½ mile, with a 300-foot vertical drop; there's one chairlift, some sledding hills, and a mess of Nordic trails passing through. Facilities include instruction, a ski shop, a cafeteria, and a day lodge. Summit's parking lot is also a highway rest stop, and the small cafeteria stays open in summer for travelers. ✉ *Government Camp Loop Hwy., east end* ☎ *503/272–0256* 🌐 *www.summitskiarea.com.*

SHOPPING

Govy General Store. Good thing this is a really nice grocery store, because it's the only one for miles around. Govy General stocks all the staples, plus a nice selection of gourmet treats like cheeses and chocolates. It's also a full-service liquor store and your one-stop shop for Mt. Hood sweatshirts, postcards, and other keepsake tchotchkes. Grab your Sno-Park permit here in winter. ✉ *30521 E. Meldrum St.* ☎ *541/272–3107* 🌐 *www.govygeneralstore.com* 🕒 *Daily 7 am–8 pm.*

WELCHES AND ZIGZAG

14 miles west of Government Camp on U.S. 26; 40 miles east of Portland, I–84 to U.S. 26.

One of a string of small communities known as the Villages at Mt. Hood, Welches' claim to fame is that it was the site of Oregon's first golf course, built at the base of Mt. Hood in 1928. Another golf course is still going strong today, and summer vacationers hover around both towns for access to basic services like gas, groceries, and dining. Others come to pull a few trout out of the scenic Zigzag River or to access trails and streams in the adjacent Salmon-Huckleberry Wilderness.

GETTING HERE AND AROUND

Most of Welches is found just off U.S. 26, often called the Mt. Hood Corridor here, about 45 miles east of Portland. On weekdays the **Mountain Express** (☎ *503/668–3466* 🌐 *www. villagesmthood.us/bus.htm*) bus line links the villages along the corridor, connecting in Sandy with a commuter line to Portland.

ESSENTIALS

Visitor Information **Mt. Hood Area Chamber of Commerce** ✉ *24403 E. Welches Rd., Welches* ☎ *503/622–3017* 🌐 *www.mthood.org.*

WHERE TO EAT AND STAY

For expanded hotel reviews, visit Fodors.com.

$$$ MODERN AMERICAN 🍴 **Altitude.** The flagship restaurant at the Resort at the Mountain is a little schizophrenic, aiming for a sleek, modernist concept in a dining room that's filled with booths and bad hotel art. Don't let that stop you, though, as the kitchen ably handles standards like short ribs and New York strip steak, along with a few adventurous dishes like foie gras custard. The adjacent lounge has fun, lighter fare (try the poutine), along with a few good specialty cocktails. [$] *Average main: $24* ✉ *68010 E. Fairway Ave., Welches* ☎ *503/622–2214* 🌐 *www. altituderestaurant.com.*

$$ AMERICAN 🍴 **The Rendezvous Grill & Tap Room.** "Serious food in a not-so-serious place" is the slogan of this upscale roadhouse, a locals' favorite for the last 20 years. For a landlocked joint, the 'Vous sure does a nice job with seafood, turning out appetizing plates of sautéed shrimp, Willapa Bay oysters, Dungeness crab, and more. In the adjacent taproom, ask about the seasonal, house-infused vodkas. The bar's strong rhubarb liqueur

is good enough to drink by the glass. $ *Average main: $20* ✉ *67149 E. Hwy. 26., Welches* ☎ *503/622–6837* ⊕ *www.rendezvousgrill.net.*

$
RENTAL

☐ **The Cabins Creekside at Welches.** Affordability, accessibility to recreational activities, and wonderful hosts make this a great lodging choice in the Mt. Hood area. **Pros:** family-run; quiet, off-highway location; anglers will benefit from the Thurmans' fly-fishing savvy. **Cons:** no dining within walking distance; no cabin-side parking. $ *Rooms from: $115* ✉ *25086 E. Welches Rd.* ☎ *503/622–4275* ⊕ *www.mthoodcabins. com* ↪ *10 cabins* ☉ *No meals.*

$$$
RENTAL

☐ **Mt. Hood Vacation Rentals.** Doggedly determined to ensure a great time for the two- and four-pawed vacationer alike, this company welcomes the family pet into the majority of its homes/cabins/condos, yet the properties are still on the upscale side. **Pros:** knowledgeable, hospitable staff; gorgeous homes nestled throughout the Mt. Hood area; many secluded sites; family- and pet-friendly. **Cons:** bring your own shampoo and hair dryer; two-night minimum. $ *Rooms from: $225* ✉ *67898 E. Hwy. 26* ☎ *800/424–9168* ⊕ *www.mthoodrentals.com* ↪ *13 units* ☉ *No meals.*

$$
RESORT

☐ **The Resort at the Mountains.** In the highlands of Mt. Hood, the Cascades are seemingly close enough for golfers to hit with a long drive. **Pros:** every sport available; plenty of choices in room size. **Cons:** there will be crowds; may not appeal to those who are not fans of golf; grounds seem more designed for golf carts than pedestrians. $ *Rooms from: $179* ✉ *68010 E. Fairway Ave.* ☎ *503/622–3101, 877/439–6774* ⊕ *www.theresort.com* ↪ *157 rooms* ☉ *No meals.*

SPORTS AND THE OUTDOORS

RECREATIONAL AREAS

Salmon–Huckleberry Wilderness. Named for the two main food groups of both black bears and frequent Mt. Hood restaurant diners, this sizeable wilderness area just south of Welches occupies the eroded foothills of the "Old Cascades," ancient mountains made mellow by time, water, and wind. Not surprisingly, trailside huckleberry picking is big here in late August and September. Inquire at the Zigzag Ranger Station for regulations and recommended trails. ✉ *Mt. Hood National Forest Zigzag Ranger Station, 70220 E. Hwy. 26., Welches* ☎ *503/622–3191* ☉ *Weekdays 7:45–4:30.*

GOLF

The Courses. The three nine-hole tracks at the Resort at the Mountain include the Pine Cone Nine, Oregon's oldest golf course, built on a rented hayfield in 1928. For families or more relaxed golfers, there's also an 18-hole putting course. Check the website to review the club's dress code, or cover that tee with a collared shirt from the pro shop. ✉ *68010 E. Fairway Ave., follow signs south from U.S. 26 in Welches, Welches* ☎ *503/622–3151, 877/439–6674* ⊕ *www.theresortcourses. com* 🗎 *Summer greens fees: 18 holes $57 weekdays, $60 weekends; off-season rates vary month to month. Putting course $8.*

CENTRAL
OREGON

WELCOME TO CENTRAL OREGON

TOP REASONS TO GO

★ **Become one with nature:** Central Oregonians live on the flanks of the Cascade Range and are bracketed by rock formations, rivers, lakes, forests, ancient lava flows, and desert badlands. Bring your golf clubs, carabiners, snowboard, or camera, and explore deeper.

★ **Visit Bend:** Downtown Bend is lively and walkable, with a variety of appealing restaurants, galleries, and stores.

★ **Kick back at Sunriver:** This family-oriented resort has bike paths, river trails, an airstrip, horse stables, tennis courts, a golf course, and several restaurants.

★ **Check out the craft brewing scene:** With more than a dozen breweries—and counting—you can find nearly any type of beer that fits your tastes.

★ **Discover the Old West:** Cowboy towns, such as Sisters and Prineville, offer a glimpse into what life was like when the West was wild.

1 West Central Oregon. The western portion of Central Oregon ranges from lush and green in the Cascades to dry and full of conifers down to the Deschutes River. It's the side with the ski areas, the high mountain lakes, most of the resorts, and the rushing waters. Conveniently, the region's largest town is Bend, and it straddles the forested west and the harshly beautiful east.

2 East Central Oregon. East of the Deschutes River this land is marked by rugged buttes, tough junipers, and bristly sagebrush. It's a place that still hugs the edge of the wilderness, with weathered barns, painted desert hills, a caldera holding two popular lakes, and some world-class rock climbing.

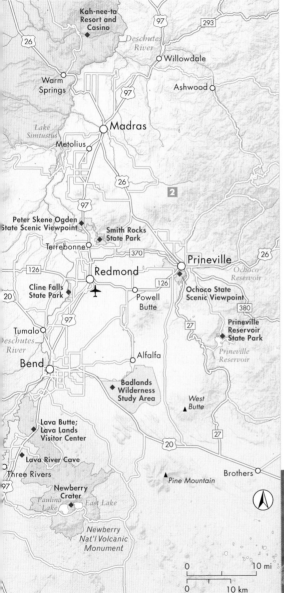

GETTING ORIENTED

Central Oregon provides a natural meeting place between the urban west side and the rural east side. It nestles neatly below the Columbia River basin and is drained by the Deschutes River, which flows from south to north. Skiers and snowboarders flock to winter sports areas on the western edge, anglers head to the Deschutes, the Metolius, and the Cascade Lakes, and climbers, campers, rockhounds, and wanderers explore the arid landscapes on the east side. Bend, the largest town for more than 120 miles in any direction, sits roughly in the center of this region.

6

Updated
by Kimberly
Bowker

After a day on the Sunriver bike paths, a first-time visitor from Germany shook her head. "This place is paradise," she declared. It's easy to see why she thought so. Central Oregon has snowfields so white they sharpen the edges of the mountains; canyons so deep and sudden as to induce vertigo; air so crisp that it fills the senses; water that ripples in mountain lakes so clear that boaters can see to the bottom, or rushes through turbulent rapids favored by rafters.

A region born of volcanic tumult is now a powerful lure for the adventurous, the beauty-seeking, and even the urbane—which, in Central Oregon, can all be found in the same person.

Bend has grown into a sophisticated city of 80,000-plus, a magnet for people retreating from larger, noisier city centers. For most visitors it is the sunny face of central Oregon, a haven for hikers, athletes, and aesthetes, but with the charm and elegance of much larger cities.

From Bend it's easy to launch to the attractions that surround it. To the northwest, Camp Sherman is a stunning place to fish for rainbow trout or kokanee. The Smith Rocks formation to the north draws climbers and boulderers, and, to the south, Lava Lands and the Lava River Caves fascinate visitors more than 6,000 years after they were chiseled out of the earth. The Oregon Badlands Wilderness to the east draws hikers and horseback riders wanting to connect with the untamed landscape. Lake Billy Chinook to the north is a startling oasis, where summer visitors drift in houseboats beneath the high walls of the Deschutes River canyon. The Deschutes River itself carries rafters of all descriptions, from young families to solo adventurers.

The area's natural beauty has brought it a diverse cluster of resorts, whether situated on the shores of high mountain lakes or cradling golf courses of startling green. They dot the landscape from the dry terrain around Warm Springs to the high road to Mount Bachelor.

CENTRAL OREGON PLANNER

WHEN TO GO

Central Oregon is a popular destination year-round. Skiers and snowboarders come from mid-December through March, when the powder is deepest and driest. During this time, guests flock to the hotels and resorts along Century Drive, which leads from Bend to Mount Bachelor. In summer, when temperatures reach the upper 80s, travelers are more likely to spread throughout the region. But temperatures fall as the elevation rises, so take a jacket if you're heading out for an evening at the high lakes or Newberry Crater.

You'll pay a premium at the mountain resorts during ski season, and Sunriver and other family and golf resorts are busiest in summer. It's best to make reservations as far in advance as possible; six months in advance is not too early.

FESTIVALS

The **Sisters Rodeo** takes place in June, the **Sisters Outdoor Quilt Show** in July, and Bend's **Pole, Pedal, Paddle**—a popular ski, bike, run, and kayak/canoe race—is in May. The **Sisters Folk Festival,** a celebration of American roots music, is in September. Bend celebrates the seasons with a **Fall Festival** in mid-September, **Summer Festival** in July and **WinterFest** in February, featuring outdoor sports, ice carving, live music, beer, and wine.

GETTING HERE AND AROUND

AIR TRAVEL

Visitors fly into **Redmond Municipal Airport–Roberts Field** (RDM), about 17 miles north of downtown Bend. Rental cars are available for pickup at the airport from several national agencies. The **Redmond Airport Shuttle** provides transportation throughout the region (reservations requested); a ride from the airport to downtown Bend costs about $35. Taxis are available at curbside, or can be summoned from the call board inside the airport; a cab ride to Bend from the airport is about $35. Portland's airport is 160 miles northwest of Bend.

Air Contacts **Redmond Airport Shuttle** ☎ 541/382–1687, 888/664–8449 ⊕ www.redmondairportshuttle.net. **Redmond Municipal Airport–Roberts Field** (RDM). ☎ 541/548–0646 ⊕ www.flyrdm.com.

BUS TRAVEL

The **Central Oregon Breeze,** a regional carrier, runs one bus a day each way between Portland and Bend, with stops in Redmond and Madras. **Cascades East Transit** is Bend's intercity bus service, and connects Redmond, La Pine, Madras, Prineville, Bend, and Sisters. Trips from the airport require reservations.

Bus Contacts **Cascades East Transit** ☎ 541/385–8680, 866/385–8680 ⊕ www.cascadeseasttransit.com. **Central Oregon Breeze** ☎ 541/389–7469, 800/847–0157 ⊕ www.cobreeze.com.

CAR TRAVEL

U.S. 20 heads west from Idaho and east from the coastal town of Newport into central Oregon. U.S. 26 goes southeast from Portland to Prineville, where it heads northeast into the Ochoco National Forest. U.S.

97 heads north from California and south from Washington to Bend. Highway 126 travels east from Eugene to Prineville; it connects with U.S. 20 heading south (to Bend) at Sisters. Major roads throughout central Oregon are well maintained and open throughout the winter season, although it's always advisable to have tire chains in the car. Some roads are closed by snow during winter, including Oregon 242. Check the **Oregon Department of Transportation's TripCheck** (⊕ *www.tripcheck. com*) or call **ODOT** (☏ *800/977–ODOT*).

RESTAURANTS

The center of culinary ambition is in downtown Bend, where the industry remains strong after a brutal recession, but good-to-excellent restaurants also serve diners in Sisters, Redmond, Tumalo, Prineville, and the major resorts. Styles vary, but many hew to the Northwest preference for fresh foods grown, caught, and harvested in the region.

Central Oregon also has many down-home places and family-friendly brewpubs, and authentic Mexican restaurants have emerged to win faithful followings in Prineville, Redmond, Madras, and Bend. *Prices in the reviews are the average cost of a main course at dinner or, if dinner is not served, at lunch.*

HOTELS

Central Oregon has lodging for every taste, from upscale resort lodges to an in-town brewpub village, eclectic bed-and-breakfasts, rustic Western inns, and a range of independent and chain hotels and motels. If you're drawn to the rivers, stay in a pastoral fishing cabin along the Metolius near Camp Sherman. If you came for the powder, you'll want a ski/snowboard condo at Mount Bachelor Village. For soaking up the atmosphere, you might favor downtown Bend's newest option, a sophisticated boutique inn called The Oxford Hotel, or Old St. Francis, the Catholic school–turned-brewpub village. *Prices in the reviews are the lowest cost of a standard double room in high season.*

TOURS

Cog Wild. Bicycle tours are offered for people of all skill levels and interests. ☏ *541/385–7002, 866/610–4822* ⊕ *www.cogwild.com.*

Cycle Pub. Friends bike for beer, or families bond over pedaling, as this multi-pedal-power vehicle, complete with stools and counters, carries groups around Bend on pub crawls and other themed tours. ✉ *Bend* ☏ *541/678–5051* ⊕ *www.cyclepub.com.*

Sun Country Tours. A longtime provider of raft and tube trips on central Oregon rivers, Sun Country's rafting excursions range from two hours to full days May through September. ☏ *541/382–6277, 800/537–8092* ⊕ *www.suncountrytours.com.*

Wanderlust Tours. Popular and family-friendly half-day excursions are offered in Bend, Sisters, and Sunriver. Options include kayaking, canoeing, snowshoeing, caving, and volcano exploring. ☏ *541/389–8359, 800/962–2862* ⊕ *www.wanderlusttours.com.*

VISITOR INFORMATION

Central Oregon Visitors Association ✉ *705 S.W. Bonnett Way, Suite 1000, Bend* ☏ *541/389–8799, 800/800–8334* ⊕ *www.visitcentraloregon.com.*

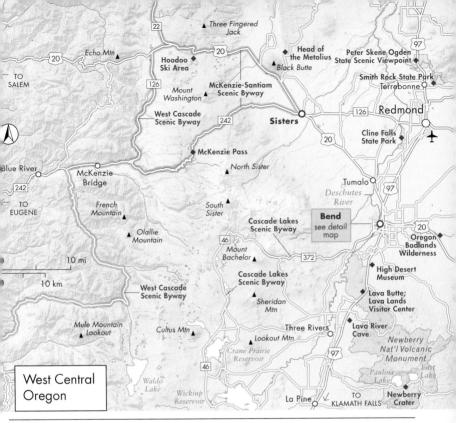

West Central Oregon

WEST CENTRAL OREGON

Sunshine, crisp pines, pure air, rushing waters, world-class skiing and snowboarding at Mt. Bachelor, destination golf resorts, a touch of the frontier West at Sisters, an air of sophistication in Bend—the forested side of Central Oregon serves up many recreational flavors. The area draws young couples, seniors, families, athletes, and adventurers, all of whom arrive with a certain sense of purpose, but also with an appreciation for the natural world. Travelers will have no problem filling a week in central Oregon's western half with memorable activities, from rafting to enjoying a sensational meal.

BEND

160 miles southeast of Portland.

Bend, Oregon's largest city east of the Cascades, is emerging from a boom-and-bust cycle, one that caused it to go from being the state's fastest-growing city to the city with the nation's steepest fall in housing prices. As banks have worked through their inventories of foreclosed properties, the people of Bend have continued to enjoy the elements that attracted all the attention in the first place: an enviable climate, proximity to skiing, and a reputation as a playground and recreational escape.

At times it seems that everybody in Bend is an athlete or a brewer, but it remains a tolerant, welcoming town, conscious of making a good first impression. Downtown Bend remains compact, vibrant, and walkable, and the Old Mill District draws shoppers from throughout the region. Chain stores and franchise restaurants have filled in along the approaches to town, especially along U.S. 20 and U.S. 97.

Neighboring Mt. Bachelor, though hardly a giant among the Cascades at 9,065 feet, is blessed by an advantage over its taller siblings—by virtue of its location, it's the first to get snowfall, and the last to see it go. Inland air collides with the Pacific's damp influence, creating skiing conditions immortalized in songs by local rock bands and raves from the ski press.

GETTING HERE AND AROUND

Portlanders arrive via car on U.S. 20 or U.S. 26, and folks from the mid-Willamette Valley cross the mountains on Oregon 126. Redmond Municipal Airport, 17 miles to the north, is an efficient hub for air travelers, who can rent a car or take a shuttle or cab into town. **Greyhound** also serves the area with a shuttle from Salem. The **Central Oregon Breeze,** a privately operated regional carrier, runs daily between Portland and Bend, with stops in Redmond and Madras. Bend is served by a citywide bus system called **Cascades East Transit,** which also connects to Redmond, La Pine, Sisters, Prineville, and Madras. To take a Cascades East bus between cities in Central Oregon, reservations are not required but recommended.

If you're trying to head out of or into Bend on a major highway during the morning or 5 pm rush, especially on U.S. 97, you may hit congestion. Parking in downtown Bend is free for the first two hours (three hours at the centrally located parking garage), or park for free in the residential neighborhoods just west of downtown. In addition to the car-rental counters at the airport, Avis, Budget, Enterprise, and Hertz also have rental locations in Bend.

Contacts Cascades East Transit ☎ 541/385–8680, 866/385–8680 ⊕ www.cascadeseasttransit.com. **Central Oregon Breeze** ☎ 541/389–7469, 800/847–0157 ⊕ www.cobreeze.com. **Greyhound Bend** ✉ 334 N.E. Hawthorne Ave. ☎ 541/923–1732, 800/231–2222 ⊕ www.greyhound.com.

ESSENTIALS

Visitor Information Bend Chamber of Commerce ✉ 777 N.W. Wall St., Ste. 200 ☎ 541/382–3221 ⊕ www.bendchamber.org. **Central Oregon Visitors Association** ✉ 705 S.W. Bonnett Way, Ste. 1000 ☎ 541/389–8799, 800/800–8334 ⊕ www.visitcentraloregon.com.

EXPLORING

FAMILY   **Des Chutes Historical Museum.** Originally built as a schoolhouse in 1914 from locally quarried volcanic tuff, the museum is operated by the Deschutes County Historical Society. Exhibits depict historical life in the area, including a pioneer schoolroom complete with studious children, native artifacts, and relics from the logging, ranching, homesteading, and railroading eras. Outdoor heritage walks are conducted

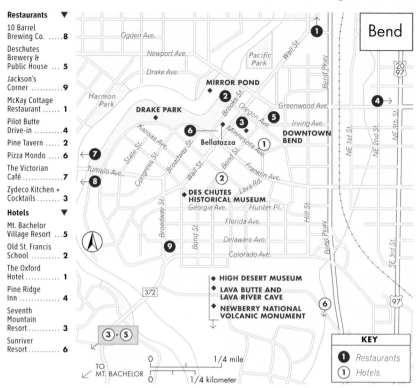

in the summer. ✉ *129 N.W. Idaho Ave.* ☎ *541/389–1813* ⊕ *www. deschuteshistory.org* ⊑ *$5* ⊙ *Tues.–Sat. 10–4:30.*

Fodor'sChoice ★ **Downtown Bend.** Bend's heart is an area of about four square blocks, centered on Wall and Bond streets. Here you'll find boutique stores, galleries, independent coffee shops, brewpubs, fine restaurants, lively nightlife establishments, and historic landmarks such as the Tower Theatre, built in 1940. A few traditional barbershops and taverns are also dispersed around, keeping it real.

Drake Park and Mirror Pond. At its western edge, downtown Bend slopes down to Drake Park and Mirror Pond. Thirteen acres of manicured greensward and trees line the edge of the Deschutes, attracting flocks of Canada geese as well as strollers from downtown. Various events, such as music festivals, occur in the park during the summer months. Note the 11-foot-high wheel log skidder in Drake Park, harkening back to Bend's logging industry in the early 20th century, when four draft horses pulled the wheel to move heavy logs. ✉ *Bounded on the west by N.W. Brooks St. and Drake Park; N.W. Lava Rd on the east; N.W. Franklin Ave. to the south; and N.W. Greenwood Ave. to the north* ⊕ *www.downtownbend.org.*

NEED A BREAK?

Bellatazza. A sleekly designed coffee shop with indoor and outdoor seating, Bellatazza starts with morning jolts and pastries in the heart of downtown Bend. Free Wi-Fi allows patrons to work on laptops while observing the world saunter by until early evening. ✉ ***869 N.W. Wall St., #100*** ☎ ***541/318–0606*** 🌐 ***www.bellatazza.com.***

FAMILY Fodor's Choice ★

High Desert Museum. The West was actually wild, and this combo museum/zoo proves it. Kids will love the up-close-and-personal encounters with gila monsters, snakes, porcupines, Vivi the bobcat, and Snowshoe the lynx. Actors in costume take part in the Living History series, where you can chat with stagecoach drivers, boomtown widows, pioneers, and homesteaders. Peruse the 110,000-square-feet of indoor and outdoor exhibits, or wander along a quarter-mile nature exhibit trail, to experience how the past can truly come alive. ✉ *59800 S. Hwy. 97, 7 miles south of downtown Bend* ☎ *541/382–4754* 🌐 *www.highdesertmuseum.org* 🎟 *$15 May–Oct., $12 Nov.–Apr.* 🕒 *May–Oct., daily 9–5; Nov.–Apr., daily 10–4.*

EN ROUTE

Cascade Lakes Scenic Byway. For about 90 miles, this forest-highway loop beginning and ending in Bend meanders past a series of high mountain lakes and is good for fishing, hiking, and camping in the summer months. (Much of the road is closed by snow during the colder months.) To find it, take Century Drive/Oregon 372 out of Bend, and then take U.S. 97 at La Pine to return.

Newberry National Volcanic Monument and Lava Lands. The last time Newberry Volcano blew its top was about 13 centuries ago. The north end of the monument has several large basalt flows, as well as the 500-foot **Lava Butte** cinder cone—a coal-black, symmetrical mound thrust from the depths 7,000 years ago. The cone is now home to the **Lava Lands Visitor Center,** which features interpretive exhibits covering the volcanic and early human history of the area. **Lava River Cave,** a 1-mile-long lava tube, takes about 90 minutes to explore on your own with a lantern (available for rent, $5). On the south end of the monument, **Paulina Peak,** on an unpaved road, has the best view into the caldera. Along the shores of **Paulina Lake** and **East Lake,** you can hike, fish, camp, or stay at the rustic resorts. ✉ *58201 S. Hwy. 97* ☎ *541/383–5700, 541/593–2421* 🌐 *www.fs.usda.gov/centraloregon* 🎟 *$5 per vehicle* 🕒 *May–Sept.*

WHERE TO EAT

$ AMERICAN

🍴 **10 Barrel Brewing Co.** Attracting locals and travelers of all ages, this trendy brewpub supplies good beer and compatible food. Pizzas are hand tossed daily, salads are fresh, and sandwiches—such as portobello mushroom—are served with shoestring fries. It's a popular place, so expect to wait during busy meal hours. Grab a table or stool in the bar for a cozier setting, and enjoy the windowed-garage doors that open to the central Oregon sun on summer days, and to the patio fires on crisp winter nights. [$] *Average main: $11* ✉ *1135 N.W. Galveston Ave.* ☎ *541/678–5228* 🌐 *www.10barrel.com.*

$ AMERICAN

🍴 **Deschutes Brewery & Public House.** Bendites are fiercely loyal to their city's original brewpub, established in 1988. Not only does the Brewery bake its own bread and pizza dough (adding in its own spent grain),

Paulina and East lakes in Newberry National Volcanic Monument

it makes its sausages, sauces, mustards, dressings, soups, etc. House favorites include sweet-and-spicy mac and cheese and fish-and-chips. Though the always-popular Black Butte Porter is a Public House classic, Deschutes brews a diverse lineup of craft beers, including such seasonals as Jubelale (winter holidays) and Twilight Ale (summer). It is almost always hopping, and you may find yourself waiting to be seated, as there are no reservations. However, time flies as you sip one of 19 Deschutes beers on tap and people-watch the boisterous crowd while you wait. [$] *Average main: $12* ✉ *1044 N.W. Bond St.* ☎ *541/382–9242* 🌐 *www.deschutesbrewery.com.*

$ AMERICAN FAMILY 🍴 **Jackson's Corner.** This family-friendly community restaurant is housed in an unassuming vintage building tucked into a neighborhood near downtown. The open, inviting space is a great place for casual gatherings, with frequent live music. The eclectic menu leans heavily on locally grown and organic dishes. Order seasonal market salads, house-made pasta dishes, or brick-oven pizza and sandwiches at the counter to be served at your table. [$] *Average main: $13* ✉ *845 N.W. Delaware Ave.* ☎ *541/647–2198* 🌐 *www.jacksonscornerbendor.com.*

$ AMERICAN 🍴 **McKay Cottage Restaurant.** This breakfast and lunch spot is housed in a 1916 pioneer cottage that was home to a former state senator. Locals relax throughout its cozy rooms and spill over onto the porch and patio below. The menu is long on comfort food, including fresh scones and sticky buns, and servers are friendly and attentive. On your way out, you can pick up baked goods and coffee drinks at the to-go bakery. [$] *Average main: $12* ✉ *62910 O.B. Riley Rd.* ☎ *541/383–2697* 🌐 *www.themckaycottage.com* ⏲ *No dinner.*

$ DINER

🍴 **Pilot Butte Drive-In.** If you are craving a lusty hamburger or a hearty chicken-fried steak, you can't go wrong with this local burger institution. With two locations in Bend, on both the east and west sides, be prepared to rub elbows with locals on lunch break and enjoy the casual flash-to-the-past atmosphere. Don't be afraid to open your mouth wide for the stacked sandwiches and steak dogs or, if you are feeling particularly courageous, for the infamous 18-ounce burger. [$] *Average main: $10* ✉ *917 N.E. Greenwood Ave.* ☎ *541/382–2972* 🌐 *www.pilotbutte.com.*

$$$ AMERICAN

🍴 **Pine Tavern.** Named for the Ponderosa pine tree growing through the back dining room, this locally loved restaurant has been dishing up high-end meals in the heart of downtown Bend since 1936. Specialties include steaks, prime rib, pot pie, and other traditional American cuisine. Longtime regulars share the dining room with out-of-towners. In summertime, seek a spot on the patio—named Best Patio in Bend for multiple years—overlooking Mirror Pond and Drake Park. [$] *Average main: $24* ✉ *967 N.W. Brooks St.* ☎ *541/382–5581* 🌐 *www.pinetavern.com* 🕒 *No lunch winter weekends.*

$$ PIZZA

🍴 **Pizza Mondo.** The Maui Wowie and Run Little Piggy are just a few topping combinations at this New York–style pizza restaurant in downtown Bend. Visit the cozy digs for the lunch special—pizza slice, salad, and soda for $5.75—or order an "after mountain special" (two slices and a beer for $7) in the late afternoon. Consider the garlic dough knots as an appetizer, or the melt-in-your-mouth brownies for dessert. Sandwiches, calzones, and two sizes of pies are made to order throughout the day, and gluten-free dough is available on certain nights. [$] *Average main: $20* ✉ *811 N.W. Wall St.* ☎ *541/330–9093* 🌐 *www.pizzamondobend.com.*

$ AMERICAN

🍴 **The Victorian Café.** In a renovated house on the west side of Bend, this breakfast and lunch restaurant offers a wide selection of surprising combinations of eggs Benedict, such as the Caribbean Benedict with Cuban seasoned ham, mango and black beans. Weekly mouthwatering specials may include deep-fried graham cracker–crusted Texas toast filled with mascarpone. With local accolades for Best Breakfast in Bend for many years, the restaurant is also known for its homemade applesauce and scones. There's often a long wait on weekends, so order a Bloody Mary or a "Man-mosa" (a mimosa in a pint glass) to enjoy around the outdoor fireplace. [$] *Average main: $12* ✉ *1404 N.W. Galveston Ave.* ☎ *541/382–6411* 🌐 *www.victoriancafebend.com* ✍ *Reservations not accepted* 🕒 *No dinner.*

$$ AMERICAN
Fodor's Choice ★

🍴 **Zydeco Kitchen & Cocktails.** The blended menu of Northwest specialties and Cajun influences has made this restaurant a popular spot. On the menu, fillet medallions, chicken, and pasta sit alongside jambalaya and redfish dishes, as you'd expect. The owners emphasize the preparation of fresh, organic foods and provide a gluten-free selection. The bar is trendy, but welcoming. In warm weather, ask to sit on the patio. Bonus: Kids eat free on Sunday. Reservations recommended. [$] *Average main: $22* ✉ *919 N.W. Bond St.* ☎ *541/312–2899* 🌐 *www.zydecokitchen.com* 🕒 *No lunch weekends.*

OFF THE BEATEN PATH

Cowboy Dinner Tree. Seventy miles south of Sunriver you'll find an authentic BBQ cook firing up a genuine taste of the Old West. Oregonians will tell you that the "true cowboy cut" 30-ounce steak or whole chicken over an open flame, plus all the fixings, is more than worth the trip. Don't expect to plug in your laptop: there's no electricity, nor is alcohol served, nor credit cards accepted. If you are making a day out of it, detour to Fort Rock State Natural Area to hike around a prehistoric volcanic tuff emerging from the flat horizon, and explore a nearby cave home to the oldest sandals ever discovered. If you journey from afar, lodging is available in rustic buckaroo bunkhouses. Plates are $25.00 per adult, $10.25 for kids 7–13; kids 6 and under free. ✉ *County Rd. 4-12/Forest Service Rd. 28, Silver Lake* ☎ *541/576–2426* 🌐 *www.cowboydinnertree.net* ✍ *Reservations required* 🕒 *June–Oct., Thurs.–Sun. 4 pm–8:30 pm; Nov.–May, Fri.–Sun. 4 pm–8:30 pm.*

WHERE TO STAY

For expanded hotel reviews, visit Fodors.com.

$ RENTAL **Mount Bachelor Village Resort.** Lodging units, from a single room to three-bedroom condos, accommodate small and large groups at this ski-themed resort within 2 miles of downtown and the Old Mill District. **Pros:** rich forest and river views promote feelings of retreat; ski racks adhered to walls outside each unit. **Cons:** no on-site restaurant or spa, but there are nearby options; out-of-date showers. $ *Rooms from: $139* ✉ *19717 Mount Bachelor Dr.* ☎ *888/272–5321* 🌐 *www.mtbachelorvillage.com* *45 rooms, 44 suites, 45 condos* *No meals.*

$ RESORT **Old St. Francis School.** This charming outpost is a restored 1936 Catholic schoolhouse converted to a destination village, with classrooms turned lodging quarters, restaurant and bars, brewery, stage, soaking pool, and movie theater with couches and food and beer service. **Pros:** a self-contained destination village, yet only footsteps from downtown Bend and Drake Park; kids and pets welcome. **Cons:** few modern appliances. $ *Rooms from: $135* ✉ *700 N.W. Bond St.* ☎ *541/382–5174, 877/661–4228* 🌐 *www.mcmenamins.com* *19 rooms* *No meals.*

$$$$ HOTEL Fodor's Choice ★ **The Oxford Hotel.** Stepping into the sleek, high-ceilinged lobby tells you you've found a new kind of accommodation in central Oregon—an attractive boutique hotel with stylish Northwest interiors and elegantly spacious rooms with a menu of five pillow choices. **Pros:** generous and environmentally sustainable amenities; luxurious spa and fitness room; loaner bikes, iPods, and Breedlove guitars; exceptional service. **Cons:** on the exterior, property appears inconspicuously wedged into a half block on the edge of downtown. $ *Rooms from: $289* ✉ *10 N.W. Minnesota Ave.* ☎ *877/440–8436* 🌐 *www.oxfordhotelbend.com* *59 rooms* *No meals.*

$$ HOTEL **Pine Ridge Inn.** Each room in this immaculate two-story hotel, surrounded by ponderosa pines and junipers, has a fireplace and either a deck or a patio. **Pros:** secluded feel although close to Bend happenings; four-poster beds reminiscent of a ranch atmosphere. **Cons:** the river view is also the bridge view with cars; rooms clean but slightly dated. $ *Rooms from: $189* ✉ *1200 S.W. Century Dr.* ☎ *541/389–6137, 800/600–4095* 🌐 *www.pineridgeinn.com* *20 rooms* *Breakfast.*

6

$ 🏨 **Seventh Mountain Resort.** "The closest accommodation to Mt.
RENTAL   Bachelor" (approximately 14 miles away), this resort encompasses
FAMILY   20 three-story buildings on the banks of the Deschutes River, with
white-water rafting and fishing right outside. **Pros:** kid-friendly; varied
accommodations, some moderately priced; setting is terrific. **Cons:**
golf course is not on-site, but ½ mile away; some guests have com-
plained that service is uneven. $ *Rooms from: $139* ⊠ *18575 S.W.*
Century Dr., 6½ miles southwest of Bend in Deschutes National For-
est 🕾 *541/382–8711, 877/765–1501* ⊕ *www.seventhmountain.com*
↝ *150 rooms* ⊘ *No meals.*

$$$ 🏨 **Sunriver Resort.** Central Oregon's premier family playground and lux-
RESORT   urious destination resort encapsulates so many things that are distinc-
FAMILY   tive about central Oregon, from the mountain views and winding river,
Fodor's Choice   to the biking, rafting, golfing, and skiing. **Pros:** many activities for kids
★   and adults; much pampering in elegant lodge facilities; close to The Vil-
lage at Sunriver. **Cons:** when visitors throng the shops, restaurants, and
bike paths, it can feel as if an entire city has relocated here. $ *Rooms*
from: $239 ⊠ *17600 Center Dr., 15 miles south of Bend on Hwy 97,*
Sunriver 🕾 *800/801–8765, 800/547–3922* ⊕ *www.sunriver-resort.com*
↝ *224 rooms, 300 houses* ⊘ *No meals.*

NIGHTLIFE AND THE ARTS

900 Wall Restaurant and Bar. In a historic corner brick building on a
downtown Bend crossroads, this sophisticated restaurant and bar serves
hundreds of bottles and about 60 different wines by the glass, earning
it the Wine Spectator Award of Excellence in 2012. ⊠ *900 N.W. Wall*
St. 🕾 *541/323–6295* ⊕ *www.900wall.com.*

Level 2. After a day of shopping, or before concert-going at the amphi-
theater, sip on a perfectly mixed cocktail at this trendy Old Mill Dis-
trict urban-esque lounge. The rich chai martini is a delectable winter
treat. ⊠ *360 S.W. Powerhouse Dr., #210* 🕾 *541/323–5382* ⊕ *www.*
bendlevel2.com.

SPORTS AND THE OUTDOORS

RECREATIONAL AREAS

Deschutes National Forest. This 1.6-million-acre forest has 20 peaks higher
than 7,000 feet, including three of Oregon's five highest mountains,
more than 150 lakes, and 500 miles of streams. If you want to park your
car at a trailhead, some of the sites require a Northwest Forest Pass;
day-use passes are also needed May through September at many loca-
tions for boating and picnicking. Campgrounds (fees payable) are oper-
ated by a camp host. ⊠ *63095 Deschutes Market Rd.* 🕾 *541/383–5300*
⊕ *www.fs.usda.gov/centraloregon* 🎟 *Park pass $5* ⊘ *Daily.*

BICYCLING

U.S. 97 north to the Crooked River Gorge and Smith Rock, or the
route along the **Cascade Lakes Highway** out of Bend, provides bikers
with memorable scenery and a good workout. **Sunriver** has more than
30 miles of paved bike paths.

Hutch's Bicycles. Road, mountain, and kids' bikes can be rented at
two locations in Bend. ⊠ *820 N.E. 3rd St.* 🕾 *541/382–6248* ⊕ *www.*
hutchsbicycles.com ⊠ *725 N.W. Columbia St.* 🕾 *541/382–9253.*

Sunriver Resort

BOATING

Deschutes River Float. A popular summer activity is floating the river at your own pace. Rent an inner tube at Riverbend Park (*799 S.W. Columbia St.*) from a kiosk run by **Sun Country Tours** (*541/382–6277*), and float two hours downriver to Drake Park, where you can catch a shuttle back for a minimal cash fee. Another option is to rent a kayak or Stand Up Paddleboard at **Tumalo Creek Kayak & Canoe** (*805 S.W. Industrial Way, Suite 6; 541/317–9407*) where you can enter the river from the store's backyard, but be prepared to paddle upriver before a leisurely float downstream. ⊕ *www.bendparksandrec.org* ✆ *Kiosk open Memorial Day–Labor Day, daily 10:30–5:50.*

SKIING

Deschutes National Forest. Many Nordic trails—more than 165 miles of them—wind through the Deschutes National Forest. ☎ *541/383–5300 for trail condition information.*

FAMILY **Mt. Bachelor.** This is one of the best alpine resort areas in the United States—60 percent of the downhill runs are rated advanced or expert, the rest geared for beginner and intermediate skiers and snowboarders. One of ten lifts takes skiers all the way to the mountain's 9,065-foot summit. The vertical drop is 3,265 feet; the longest of the 70 runs is 4 miles. Facilities and services include equipment rental and repair, a ski school, and ski shop, Nordic skiing, weekly races, and day care; you can enjoy restaurants, bars, and six lodges. Other activities include cross-country skiing, a tubing park, sled-dog rides, snowshoeing, and in summer, hiking and chairlift rides. The 36 miles of trails at the **Mt.**

Bachelor Nordic Center, most of them near the base of the mountain, are intermediate.

During the offseason, the lift to the **Pine Marten Lodge** provides sightseeing, stunning views, and fine sunset dining. Visitors can play disc golf on a downhill course that starts near the lodge. At the base of the mountain, take dry-land dog sled rides with four-time Iditarod musher Rachael Scdoris. ⊠ *Cascade Lakes Hwy.* ☎ *541/382–7888, 800/829–2442* ⊕ *www.mtbachelor.com* ▰ *Lift tickets $59–$69 per day* ⊙ *Nov.–May, daily 8–4, or as weather allows.*

SHOPPING

Cowgirl Cash. A funky western outfitter also buys vintage boots and western apparel. You never know exactly what you'll find, but you can expect a fair share of leather, turquoise, silver, and, always, boots. It's a quirky and welcome feature of the downtown scene. It's closed Thursday through Sunday in January and February. ⊠ *924 N.W. Brooks St.* ☎ *541/678–5162* ⊕ *www.cowgirlcashbend.com.*

Dudley's BookShop Café. This independent bookseller offers Wi-Fi, a small café, and seating areas that attract interesting people who meet amidst new and used books to participate in all kinds of activities, from knitting circles to philosophical debates. ⊠ *135 N.W. Minnesota Ave.* ☎ *541/749–2010.*

Goody's. If the aroma of fresh waffle cones causes a pause on your downtown stroll, you've probably hit one of central Oregon's favorite soda fountain and candy shops. Try the Oreo cookie ice cream, a local favorite, or the homemade chocolate. If you purchase a stuffed toy animal that calls the store home, expect for it to smell sweet for weeks to come. ⊠ *957 N.W. Wall St.* ☎ *541/389–5185* ⊕ *www.goodyschocolates.com.*

Local Joe. Selling clothing and accessories for men and women, this long-established boutique carries lines such as Lucky Brand, Seven For All Mankind, and Silver. ⊠ *929 N.W. Wall St.* ☎ *541/385–7137* ⊕ *www.localjoejeans.com.*

Newport Avenue Market. In business for more than 20 years, this culinary market not only offers a large selection of organic and gourmet foods, but also sells items such as high-end kitchen supplies and humorous gifts. Pick up a pair of squirrel underwear—it's as small as you might expect. ⊠ *1121 N.W. Newport Ave.* ☎ *541/382–3940* ⊕ *www.newportavemarket.com.*

Old Mill District. Bend was once the site of one of the world's largest sawmill operations, a sprawling industrial complex along the banks of the Deschutes. In recent years the abandoned shells of the old factory buildings have been transformed into an attractive shopping center, a project honored with national environmental awards. National chain retailers can be found here, along with restaurants, boutiques, the Central Oregon Visitors Association, a 16-screen multiplex and IMAX movie theater, and the Les Schwab Amphitheater that attracts nationally renowned artists, local bands, and summer festivals. ⊠ *520 S.W. Powerhouse Dr.* ☎ *541/312–0131* ⊕ *www.theoldmill.com.*

Patagonia@Bend. A friendly staff sells stylishly comfortable outdoor clothing, equipment, and footwear at a Patagonia concept store that's still independently owned. ✉ *1000 N.W. Wall St., Suite 140* ☎ *541/382–6694* ⊕ *www.patagoniabend.com.*

Pine Mountain Sports. Part of Bend's fleet of outdoors stores, this shop sells high-quality clothing, golf discs, and the locally famous Hydro Flask water bottles. It also rents and sells recreation equipment such as mountain bikes, skis, and snowshoes. ✉ *255 S.W. Century Dr.* ☎ *541/385–8080* ⊕ *www.pinemountainsports.com.*

SISTERS

21 miles northwest of Bend.

If Sisters looks as if you've stumbled into the Old West, that's entirely by design. The town fathers—or perhaps we should say "sisters"—strictly enforce an 1800s-style architecture. Rustic cabins border a llama ranch on the edge of town, and you won't find a stoplight on any street. Western storefronts give way to galleries, the century-old hotel now houses a restaurant and bar, and a bakery occupies the former general store. Although its population is just a little more than 2,000, Sisters increasingly attracts visitors as well as urban runaways who appreciate its tranquility and charm. If you're driving over from the Willamette Valley, note how the weather seems to change to sunshine when you cross the Cascades at the Santiam Pass and begin descending toward the town.

Black Butte, a perfectly conical cinder cone, rises to the northwest. The Metolius River/Camp Sherman area to the west is a special find for fly-fishermen and abounds with springtime wildflowers.

GETTING HERE AND AROUND

Travelers from Portland and the west come to Sisters over the Santiam Pass on Oregon Highway 126. This is also the route for visitors who fly into Redmond Municipal Airport, rent a car, and drive 20 miles west. Those coming from Bend drive 21 miles northwest on U.S. 20. **Cascades East,** a regional bus carrier, runs routes between Sisters and the Redmond airport by reservation.

Contacts Cascades East Transit ☎ *541/385–8680, 866/385–8680* ⊕ *www.cascadeseasttransit.com.*

ESSENTIALS

Visitor Information Sisters Chamber of Commerce ✉ *291 E. Main Ave.* ☎ *541/549–0251* ⊕ *www.sisterscountry.com.*

EXPLORING

Camp Sherman. Surrounded by groves of whispering yellow-bellied ponderosa pines, larch, fir, and cedars and miles of streamside forest trails, this small, peaceful resort community of 250 full-time residents (plus a few stray cats and dogs) is part of a designated conservation area. The area's beauty and natural resources are the big draw: the spring-fed Metolius River prominently glides through the community. In the early 1900s Sherman County wheat farmers escaped the dry summer heat by migrating here to fish and rest in the cool river environment, making Camp Sherman one of the first destination resorts in central Oregon. As legend has it, to help guide fellow farmers to the spot, devotees nailed a shoebox top with the name "camp sherman" to a tree at a fork in the road. Several original buildings still stand from the early days, including some cabins, a schoolhouse, and a tiny railroad chapel. The "action" is at the Camp Sherman Store & Fly Shop, built in 1918, adjacent to the post office. ✉ *25451 S.W. Forest Service Rd., #1419* ⊕ *10 miles northwest of Sisters on U.S. 20, 5 miles north on Hwy. 14* ☎ *541/595–6711* 🌐 *www.campshermanstore.com* 🕒 *June–Sept., Mon.–Thurs. 8–7, Fri. and Sat. 8–8, Sun. 8–6; Oct.–May, Fri. and Sat. 9–5, Sun. 9–4.*

WHERE TO EAT

$ AMERICAN
🍴 **The Boathouse.** From a simple marina tackle shop comes a woodsy boathouse, replete with pine, Mexican tiling, Native American art, and water as far as the eye can see. Sophisticated home-style dishes are zesty variations on such core elements as New York steak, salmon, pork, and duck. Many fine Northwest and California wines are available by the bottle or glass. Lovely food and the management's genuine joie de vivre give the Boathouse its unique flavor. Reservations are not required, but best to make them for dinner if you are driving from Sisters. [$] *Average main: $16* ✉ *The Lodge at Suttle Lake, 13300 U.S. Hwy. 20, 14 miles northeast of Sisters* ☎ *541/595–2628* 🌐 *www.thelodgeatsuttlelake.com.*

$ AMERICAN
🍴 **The Depot Café.** A railroad theme prevails at this main-street rustic café. A miniature train circles above as the kitchen dishes out sandwiches, salads, and dinner specials. Sit inside next to the rough-wood walls or out back on the deck. [$] *Average main: $10* ✉ *250 W. Cascade St.* ☎ *541/549–2572* 🌐 *www.sistersdepot.com* 🕒 *Closed Mon.–Tues. in winter; no breakfast weekdays.*

$$$ FRENCH Fodor's Choice ★
🍴 **Jen's Garden.** This "garden" has grown to become a top-class restaurant, and offers a three-course prix-fixe option as well as its traditional five-course meal. In keeping with the European custom of small servings, the courses are deliberately integrated so that the flavors complement each other. The menu changes often to incorporate seasonal specialties and fresh products, with choices for each course: smoked trout with Gruyère dip, pork chop with chanterelle risotto and roasted beets, olive oil cake with mascarpone icing. If one particular dish tantalizes the senses, ordering à la carte is also an option. [$] *Average main: $26* ✉ *403 E. Hood Ave.* ☎ *541/549–2699* 🌐 *www.intimatecottagecuisine.com* ✍ *Reservations essential* 🕒 *No lunch* 🕒 *Closed Mon. and Tues. in fall and spring and for a few weeks around Thanksgiving and after Valentine's Day.*

$$$ AMERICAN Fodor's Choice ★
🍴 **Kokanee Café.** The remarkable restaurant draws diners from across the mountains to sample artful Northwest dishes at this homey hideaway on the banks of the Metolius. Wild boar, fresh fish, and vegetarian options are presented with creative elegance. As if brilliant appetizers, entrées and full bar weren't enough, sample the house made desserts. Located 15 miles northwest of Sisters, reservations are highly recommended. [$] *Average main: $25* ✉ *25545 S.W. Forest Service Rd., #1419,*

The Lodge at Suttle Lake

Camp Sherman ☎ *541/595–6420* 🌐 *www.kokaneecafe.com* ⏲ *Closed Nov.–Apr. No lunch.*

$ ITALIAN 🍴 **The Open Door.** Serving simple and light Italian fare, such as panini and flatbread pizzas, this new quaint and cozy restaurant offers a different homemade pasta dish every night for dinner. The interior is an eclectic mix of mismatched tables and chairs, the restaurant and wine bar opens into Clearwater Gallery & Framing, which displays Northwest artwork. An outdoor patio is open in the summer, but since the indoor eating space is small and fills quickly, come early for lunch or try to make reservations for dinner. If it's busy on a winter's eve, you may find yourself eating in the gallery among paintings and pottery. [$] *Average main: $10* ✉ *303 W. Hood Ave.* ☎ *541/549–4994* 🌐 *www.theclearwatergallery.com* ⏲ *Closed Tues. in winter.*

WHERE TO STAY

For expanded hotel reviews, visit Fodors.com.

$$ RESORT Fodor's Choice ★ 🏨 **Five Pine Lodge.** Resembling a forest lodge, this luxury western-style resort features high-end furnishings built by Amish craftsmen and is a great spot for a romantic retreat or a family (and pet) getaway, with miles of trails on the doorstep. **Pros:** top-quality craftsmanship and fixtures, like the Kohler waterfall tubs; peaceful atmosphere but conveniently located on the fringes of downtown Sisters. **Cons:** only slightly set back from U.S. Highway 20, where traffic is sometimes heavy. [$] *Rooms from: $189* ✉ *1021 Desperado Trail* ☎ *541/549–5900, 866/974–5900* 🌐 *www.fivepinelodge.com* 🛏 *8 rooms, 24 cabins* 🍽 *Breakfast.*

$$ RESORT 🏨 **The Lodge at Suttle Lake.** Built in the Grand Cascadian style, this 10,000 square-foot lodge presides over the eastern side of Suttle Lake, with

supersized wooden architecture and whimsical charm. **Pros:** peaceful setting in luxurious accommodations; some waterfront cabins; accessibility to varied sports in all seasons; various rooms and prices. **Cons:** no air-conditioning in summer. $ *Rooms from: $199* ⊠ *13300 U.S. Hwy. 20, 13 miles northwest of Sisters* ☎ *541/595–2628* ⊕ *www. thelodgeatsuttlelake.com* ↝ *10 rooms, 14 cabins* ⦿ *No meals.*

$

RENTAL

⊡ **Metolius River Lodges.** Homespun cottages give you cozy river views, fireplaces, and woodsy interiors complemented by top-notch hospitality. **Pros:** cabins with decks on the river; within walking distance from the Camp Sherman store. **Cons:** few amenities, so bring supplies on winter weekdays; no pets. $ *Rooms from: $126* ⊠ *12390 S.W. Forest Service Rd., #1419* ✛ *15 miles northeast of Sisters, Camp Sherman* ☎ *800/595–6290, 541/595–6290* ⊕ *www.metoliusriverlodges.com* ↝ *13 cabins* ⦿ *No meals.*

$$$

RENTAL

Fodor's Choice

★

⊡ **Metolius River Resort.** Each of the immaculate, individually owned cabins that nestle amid the pines and aspen at this peaceful resort has splendid views of the sparkling Metolius River, decks furnished with Adirondack chairs, a full kitchen, and a fireplace. **Pros:** privacy; cabins feel like home—a very luxurious home; fall asleep and wake up to the sound of the river. **Cons:** no additional people (even visitors) allowed; no cell-phone service, and not all cabins have Wi-Fi and DVD; bring supplies on winter weekdays when Camp Sherman closes down. $ *Rooms from: $225* ⊠ *25551 S.W. Forest Service Rd., #1419, Camp Sherman* ✛ *Off U.S. 20, northeast 10 miles from Sisters, turn north on Camp Sherman Rd., stay to left at fork (1419), and then turn right at the only stop sign* ☎ *800/818–7688, 541/595–6281* ⊕ *www. metoliusriverresort.com* ↝ *11 cabins* ⦿ *No meals.*

NIGHTLIFE AND THE ARTS

Bronco Billy's Ranch Grill and Saloon. Pass through the swinging saloon doors into this Old West watering hole, originally built more than a century ago as the Hotel Sisters. Head to the bar, which is decorated with a mural of cancan dancers, weathered saddles hanging on the wall, and a mounted stuffed buffalo head. The saloon beckons to both residents and travelers alike, often staying open until 1 am on busy summer weekends. ⊠ *190 E. Cascade Ave.* ☎ *541/549–7427* ⊕ *www. broncobillysranchgrill.com.*

Three Creeks Brewing Co. The brewpub, with 10 of its beers on tap, also serves a wide range of food. Order a frothing pint of the popular Knotty Blonde, or the clever Stonefly Rye, and perhaps even sign-up for an in-house class to learn more about beers. ⊠ *721 Desperado Ct.* ☎ *541/549–1963* ⊕ *www.threecreeksbrewing.com.*

SHOPPING

Don Terra Artworks. This gallery represents local artists and craftspeople. You'll find stone sculptures, pottery, jewelry, glass, paintings, and photography. ⊠ *222 W. Hood Ave.* ☎ *541/549–1299* ⊕ *www.donterra.com* ☾ *Closed Tues.–Thurs. Jan.–Mar.*

Stitchin' Post. Owned by a mother and daughter team, the famous knitting, sewing, and quilting store opened its doors in 1975. The spacious store not only inspires the senses with colorful fabric patterns, but also conducts classes throughout the year. The Sisters Outdoor Quilt Show, annually held the second Saturday of July, is the largest in the world and intertwines its origins with the store's early years. ⊠ *311 W. Cascade St.* ☎ *541/549–6061* ⊕ *www.stitchinpost.com.*

SPORTS AND THE OUTDOORS

RECREATIONAL AREAS

Metolius Recreation Area. On the eastern slope of the Cascades and within the 1.6-million-acre Deschutes National Forest, this bounty of recreational wilderness is drier and sunnier than the western side of the mountains, giving way to bountiful natural history, outdoor activities, and wildlife. There are spectacular views of jagged, 10,000-foot snow-capped Cascade peaks, looming high above the basin of an expansive evergreen valley clothed in pine.

Five miles south of **Camp Sherman** (⇨ *See Exploring listings*), the dark and perfectly shaped cinder cone of **Black Butte** rises 6,400 feet. At its base the **Metolius River** springs forth. Witness the birth of this "instant" river by walking a short paved path embedded in ponderosa forest, eventually reaching a viewpoint with the dramatic snow-covered peak of **Mt. Jefferson** on the horizon. At this point, water gurgles to the ground's surface and pours into a wide trickling creek cascading over moss-covered rocks. Within feet it funnels outward, expanding its northerly flow; becomes a full-size river; and meanders east alongside grassy banks and a dense pine forest to join the Deschutes River downstream. In 1988 the 4,600-acre corridor of the Metolius was designated a National Wild and Scenic River, and in 2009 the state legislature designated the entire Metolius Basin Oregon's first "Area of Critical State Concern." Within the area and along the river, there are ample resources for camping, hiking, biking, and floating. Enjoy fly-fishing for rainbow, brown, and bull trout in perhaps the best spot within the Cascades. ⊠ *9 miles northwest of Sisters, off Hwy. 20* ⊕ *www.metoliusriver.org.*

FISHING

Fly-fishing the Metolius River attracts anglers who seek a challenge. A great fishing resource is the **Camp Sherman Store & Fly Shop** (☎ *541/595–6711* ⊕ *www.campshermanstore.com*), which sells gear and provides information about where and how best to fish. For fishing guides, try **Fly and Field Outfitters** (☎ *541/318–1616* ⊕ *www.flyandfield.com*) out of Bend.

GOLF

Aspen Lakes. Golfers give high marks to this 18-hole bentgrass course designed by William Overdorf, which takes full advantage of the Sisters area's stunning vistas. ⊠ *16900 Aspen Lakes Dr.* ☎ *541/549–4653* ⊕ *www.aspenlakes.com.*

Big Meadow and Glaze Meadow at Black Butte Ranch. The resort, which also offers accommodations, has two 18-hole golf courses praised for striking views and stately stands of fir and pine trees that girdle the fairways. ⊠ *13020 Hawks Beard* ☎ *541/595–1500, 866/901–2961* ⊕ *www.blackbutteranch.com.*

6

SKIING

Hoodoo Ski Area. On a 5,703-foot summit, this winter sports area has more than 800 acres of skiable terrain. With 32 runs and five lifts, skiers of all levels will find suitable thrills. Upper and lower Nordic trails are surrounded by silence, and an inner tube run and night skiing round out the range of activities. At a 60,000-square-foot lodge at the mountain's base you can take in the view, grab a bite, shop, or rest your weary feet. The ski area has kids' activities and child-care services available. Lift tickets range from $20 to $51 for adults, depending on time of day. ⊠ *U.S. 20, 20 miles northwest of Sisters* ☏ *541/822–3799* ⊕ *www.hoodoo.com.*

EAST CENTRAL OREGON

East of the Cascades, central Oregon changes to desert. The land is austere, covered mostly in sage and juniper, with a few hardy rivers and great extrusions of lava, which flowed or was blasted across the prehistoric landscape. In recent years resorts have emerged to draw west-side residents weary of the rain. They come over to bask in the sun and to soak up the feeling of the frontier, reinforced by ranches and resilient towns like Redmond and Prineville. They also come to fish and boat on the high lakes inside Newberry Crater and the man-made lakes near Culver and Prineville.

REDMOND

20 miles east of Sisters, 17 miles northeast of Bend.

Redmond sits at the western end of Oregon's high desert, a handful of miles from the Deschutes River and within minutes of several lakes. It is a place where desert ranches meet runways, as it serves as the regional hub for air travel. It is the town nearest to Eagle Crest Resort and Smith Rock, a magnet for rock climbers. As with Deschutes County, Redmond has experienced some of the most rapid growth in the state during the past 10 years, largely owing to a dry and mild climate and year-round downhill and cross-country skiing, fishing, hiking, mountain biking, and rock hounding. Still, this is no gentrified resort town à la Bend, as a stroll through the compact and historic downtown will attest. A few blocks of vintage buildings remain, but north–south traffic hustles through the city core, with most residents in neighborhoods strung out to the west. Centennial Park, a small but attractive open space with fountains and an expansive lawn, opened downtown in 2010.

GETTING HERE AND AROUND

A couple of highways—U.S. 97 and Oregon 126—cross in Redmond. Highway 97 carries travelers north and south to Washington and California, and Highway 126 runs between Sisters in the west to Prineville in the east. If driving on U.S. 26 from Portland, stop at **The Museum at Warm Springs** (☏ *541/553–3331* ⊕ *www.museumatwarmsprings.org*) at the Confederated Tribes of Warm Springs Reservation for a look at Native American artifacts and history. Taxis and the **Redmond Airport Shuttle** ferry travelers to the Redmond Municipal Airport. Two bus lines,

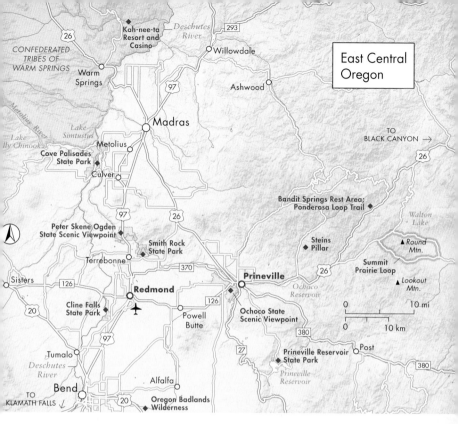

the **Central Oregon Breeze** and **Cascades East Transit,** serve Redmond. The Central Oregon Breeze links Bend, Redmond, Madras, and Portland, and Cascades East runs buses to and from Redmond and Madras, Prineville, and Bend. Passengers should call to ensure a ride.

Contacts **Central Oregon Breeze** ☎ 541/389-7469, 800/847-0157 ⊕ www. cobreeze.com. **Cascades East Transit** ☎ 541/385-8680, 866/385-8680 ⊕ www.cascadeseasttransit.com. **Redmond Airport Shuttle** ☎ 541/382-1687, 888/664-8449 ⊕ www.redmondairportshuttle.net.

ESSENTIALS

Visitor Information **Redmond Chamber of Commerce and Convention Visitor's Bureau** ⊠ 446 S.W. 7th St. ☎ 541/923-5191 ⊕ www. visitredmondoregon.com.

EXPLORING

Peter Skene Ogden Scenic Viewpoint. Even the most seasoned traveler may develop vertigo peering from the cliff top into a deep river canyon. It is a view that gives insight into why Oregon's high desert looks the way it does, with sheer drops and austere landscapes. You'll want to take pictures, but hang on to your camera. ⊠ U.S. 97 N, 9 miles north of Redmond ☎ 800/551-6949 ⊕ www.oregonstateparks.org.

Rock climbing in Smith Rock State Park

Petersen's Rock Gardens. Rasmus Petersen, a Danish immigrant who died in 1952, created this rock garden about halfway between Redmond and Bend. Petrified wood, thunder eggs, agate, jasper, lava, and obsidian were used to architecturally construct miniature buildings and bridges, terraces and towers. Among the structures are a micro–Statue of Liberty and five miniature castles. The attraction includes a small museum, gift shop, and picnic area. ✉ *7930 S.W. 77th St.* ☎ *541/382–5574, 541/408–8563* 🎟 *$5* 🕒 *Summer weekdays 10–7, weekends 9–8; spring and fall Tues.–Fri. 10–3, weekends 10–5; winter weekends by appointment.*

WHERE TO EAT AND STAY

For expanded hotel reviews, visit Fodors.com.

$$$ STEAKHOUSE 🍴 **Brickhouse.** An elegant dining experience in Redmond can be found at this white-tablecloth and brick-wall restaurant, which specializes in steaks and chops but also offers attractive plates of seafood, especially shellfish. The lighting is muted, but bright enough to let you see what you're eating. You can get lost in the list of cocktails and wines from Oregon and around the world. [$] *Average main: $25* ✉ *412 S.W. 6th St.* ☎ *541/526–1782* 🌐 *www.brickhousesteakhouse.com* 🕒 *Closed Sun. and Mon. No lunch.*

$ ITALIAN 🍴 **Sully's Italian Restaurant.** This home-style Italian restaurant is a Redmond favorite. With a redbrick interior and candles on every table, Sully's is proud to serve its take on the always-classic spaghetti and meatballs, pizza, manicotti, and eggplant Parmesan. [$] *Average main: $13* ✉ *314 S.W. 5th St.* ☎ *541/548–5483* 🌐 *www.sullysitalianrestaurant.com* 🕒 *No lunch.*

$$
AMERICAN

✕**Terrebonne Depot.** Within an old train depot, this Smith Rock restaurant matches the view. Offering an array of reasonably priced, tasty dishes, the kitchen plays it straight down the middle with nicely seasoned salmon, chicken, and pasta. You can also get lunch baskets to take with you on the climb. Service is friendly, and the menu is a cut above what you'd expect in this off-the-beaten-track location. The view allows you to reflect on the climb you've just made—or will inspire you to embark on one. $ *Average main: $18* ⊠ *400 N.W. Smith Rock Way* ☎ *541/548–5030* ⊕ *www.terrebonnedepot.com* ☽ *Closed Tues. year-round and Mon. Labor Day–Memorial Day.*

$
RESORT
FAMILY

⌂**Eagle Crest Resort.** On high-desert grounds covered with juniper and sagebrush, this luxurious resort offers vacation rental houses as well as lodgings, and is a good base for golfing, hiking, biking, and fishing. **Pros:** a full-service resort with a spa and three 18-hole golf courses; great for kids; pet-friendly. **Cons:** there can be crowds, kids, and pets. $ *Rooms from: $149* ⊠ *1522 Cline Falls Hwy., 5 miles west of Redmond* ☎ *541/923–2453, 888/306–9643* ⊕ *www.eagle-crest.com* ⊃ *100 rooms, 70 town houses* ⃝ *No meals.*

SPORTS AND THE OUTDOORS

RECREATIONAL AREAS

Cline Falls State Park. Picnicking and fishing are popular at this nine-acre rest area commanding scenic views on the Deschutes River. You'll feel free from civilization here. ⊠ *Hwy. 126, 4 miles west of Redmond* ☎ *800/551–6949* ⊕ *www.oregonstateparks.org.*

ROCK CLIMBING

Fodor'sChoice
★

Smith Rock State Park. Eight miles north of Redmond, this park is world famous for rock climbing, with hundreds of routes of all levels of difficulty. A network of trails serves both climbers and families dropping in for the scenery. In addition to the stunning rock formations, the Crooked River, which helped shape these features, loops through the park. You might spot golden eagles, prairie falcons, mule deer, river otters, and beavers. Due to the environmental sensitivity of the region, the animal leash law is strongly enforced. It can get quite hot in midsummer, so most prefer to climb in the spring and fall. The stunning scenery—specifically, a view of the river curving through the high rocks—was adopted by Deschutes Brewery for its Twilight Summer Ale label. ⊠ *Off U.S. 97, 9241 N.E. Crooked River Dr.* ☎ *541/548–7501, 800/551–6949* ⊕ *www. oregonstateparks.org* ⊃ *Day use $5 per vehicle.*

Smith Rock Climbing Guides. Professionals with emergency medical training take visitors to the Smith Rock formation for climbs of all levels of difficulty; they also supply equipment. Guided climbs—you meet at the rock—can run a half day or full day, and are priced according to the number of people. ☎ *541/788–6225* ⊕ *www.smithrockclimbingguides.com.*

PRINEVILLE

18 miles east of Redmond.

Prineville is the oldest town in central Oregon, and the only incorporated city in Crook County. Tire entrepreneur Les Schwab founded his regional empire here, and it remains a key hub for the company. Recently, Facebook and Apple chose Prineville as the location for its new data centers. Surrounded by verdant ranch lands and the purplish hills of the Ochoco National Forest, Prineville will likely interest you chiefly as a jumping-off point for some of the region's more secluded outdoor adventures. The area attracts thousands of anglers, boaters, sightseers, and rock hounds to its nearby streams, reservoirs, and mountains. Rimrocks nearly encircle Prineville, and geology nuts dig for free agates, limb casts, jasper, and thunder eggs. Downtown Prineville consists of a handful of small buildings along a quiet strip of Highway 26, dominated by the Crook County Courthouse, built in 1909. Shopping and dining opportunities are mostly on the basic side.

GETTING HERE AND AROUND

Travelers approaching Prineville from the west on Oregon 126 descend like a marble circling a funnel, dropping into a tidy grid of a town from a high desert plain. It's an unfailingly dramatic way to enter the seat of Crook County, dominated by the courthouse on Northeast Third Street, aka Highway 26, the main drag. Prineville is 19 miles east of Redmond Municipal Airport. If you're coming to Prineville from the airport, it's easiest to rent a car and drive. However, two bus lines, **Central Oregon Breeze** and **Cascades East Transit** run routes.

Contacts **Central Oregon Breeze** ☎ 541/389-7469, 800/847-0157 ⊕ www.cobreeze.com. **Cascades East Transit** ☎ 541/385-8680, 866/385-8680 ⊕ www.cascadeseasttransit.com.

ESSENTIALS

Visitor Information **Ochoco National Forest Headquarters** ✉ 3160 N.E. 3rd St. ☎ 541/416-6500 ⊕ www.fs.usda.gov/centraloregon. **Prineville-Crook County Chamber of Commerce and Visitor Center** ✉ 785 N.W. 3rd St. ☎ 541/447-6304 ⊕ www.visitprineville.org.

EXPLORING

A.R. Bowman Memorial Museum. A tough little stone building (it was once a bank, and banks out here needed to be tough) is the site of the museum of the Crook County Historical Society. The 1910 edifice is on the National Register of Historic Places, with the inside vault and teller cages seemingly untouched. Prominent in the museum are artifacts that define early Prineville, and recent expansion houses a research library and life-size representations of an Old West street. ✉ *246 N. Main St.* ☎ *541/447–3715* ⊕ *www.bowmanmuseum.org* 🎫 *Free* 🕙 *Memorial Day–Labor Day, weekdays 10–5, weekends 11–4; Labor Day–Dec. and Feb.–Memorial Day, Tues.–Fri. 10–5, Sat. 11–4. Closed Jan.*

Ochoco Viewpoint. This is a truly fantastic scenic overlook that commands a sweeping view of the city, including the prominent Crook County Courthouse built in 1909, and the hills, ridges, and buttes beyond. ✉ *U.S. Hwy. 126, ½ mile west of Prineville.*

WHERE TO EAT AND STAY

For expanded hotel reviews, visit Fodors.com.

$$ ✕ **Barney Prine's Steakhouse & Saloon.** Prineville is home to a startlingly
STEAKHOUSE appealing restaurant and saloon named after one of the town's founders.

It's a good place to get filet mignon, pepper steak, slow-smoked prime rib, 1-pound ribeye steak, or other cuts. Chicken, lamb, fish, and sometimes elk and veal, are also on the menu. The waitstaff is cheerful and attentive, and the ambience is part frontier western, part contemporary. [$] *Average main: $20* ✉ *380 N.E. Main St.* ☎ *541/362–1272* 🌐 *www.barneyprinessteakhouse.com* 🕒 *No lunch.*

$ DINER 🍴 **Tastee Treet.** Open since 1957, this local establishment is renowned for its traditional burgers, hand-cut french fries, and milk shakes. Saunter up to the horseshoe-shaped counter to sit on swiveling stools and chat with locals, or talk with out-of-towners, some of whom never miss a chance to drop by once a year while passing through. Claim a red-and-white leather booth for the family, a table on the patio, or pick up an order from the drive-through. Hearty breakfast plates, such as hamburger steak and eggs, are available until 11 am, when the menu switches to sandwiches, burgers, chili cheese fries, and other "Tastee Eats." [$] *Average main: $8* ✉ *493 N.E. 3rd St.* ☎ *541/447–4165.*

$$$$ RESORT Fodor's Choice ★ 🏨 **Brasada Ranch.** Dotty, the friendly ranch dog, is first to greet guests checking in at this luxurious guest ranch resort that offers authentic Western experiences with pristine modern amenities in the midst of exquisite mountain views, sagebrush, and juniper trees. **Pros:** extremely helpful staff; superb range of on-site facilities and activities; Wi-Fi. **Cons:** minimum two-night stay most summer weekends; not all units have hot tubs. [$] *Rooms from: $309* ✉ *16986 S.W. Brasada Ranch Rd.* ☎ *866/373–4822* 🌐 *www.brasada.com* 🛏 *8 suites, 51 cabins* 🍽 *No meals.*

SPORTS AND THE OUTDOORS

RECREATIONAL AREAS

Ochoco National Forest. Twenty-five miles east of the flat, juniper-dotted countryside around Prineville, the landscape changes to forested ridges covered with tall ponderosa pines and Douglas firs. Sheltered by the diminutive Ochoco Mountains and with only about a foot of rain each year, the national forest, established in 1906 by President Theodore Roosevelt, manages to lay a blanket of green across the dry, high desert of central Oregon. This arid landscape—marked by deep canyons, towering volcanic plugs, and sharp ridges—goes largely unnoticed except for the annual influx of hunters during the fall. The Ochoco, part of the old Blue Mountain Forest Reserve, is a great place for camping, hiking, biking, and fishing in relative solitude. In its three wilderness areas—Mill Creek, Bridge Creek, and Black Canyon—it's possible to see elk, wild horses, eagles, and even cougars. ✉ *Ranger Station, 3160 N.E. 3rd St. (U.S. 26)* ☎ *541/416–6500* 🌐 *www.fs.usda.gov/centraloregon* 🕒 *Daily; ranger station weekdays 8–4:30.*

Oregon Badlands Wilderness. This 29,000-acre swath of Oregon's high desert was designated a national wilderness in 2009, following the longtime advocacy of Oregonians enamored by its harshly beautiful landscape riven by ancient lava flows and home to sage grouse, pronghorn antelope, and elk. Motorized vehicles are prohibited, but visitors can ride horses on designated trails and low-impact hikers are welcome. Bring a camera to capture the lava flows, jagged rock formations, birds, and wildflowers. ✉ *3050 N.E. 3rd St. (U.S. 26)* ☎ *541/416–6700* 🌐 *www.blm.gov/or/resources/recreation/badlands.*

6

Prineville Reservoir State Park. Mountain streams flow out of the Ochoco Mountains and join together to create the Crooked River, which is dammed near Prineville. Bowman Dam on the river forms this park, where recreational activities include boating, swimming, fishing, hiking, and camping. ⊠ *19020 S.E. Parkland Dr.* ☎ *541/447–4363, 800/452–5687* ⊕ *www.oregonstateparks.org* ⌂ *Campsites $22–$26.*

FISHING

It's a good idea to check the **Oregon Department of Fish and Wildlife**'s (⊕ *www.dfw.state.or.us/rr/index.asp*) weekly recreation report before you head out.

Ochoco Reservoir. Annually stocked with fingerling trout, you might also find a rainbow, bass, or brown bullhead tugging on your line. ⊠ *6 miles east of Prineville on Highway 26* ☎ *541/447–1209* ⊕ *www.fs.usda.gov/centraloregon.*

Prineville Reservoir. Some anglers return here year after year, although temperatures can get uncomfortably hot and water levels relatively low by late summer. The reservoir is known for its bass, trout and crappie, with fly-fishing available on the Crooked River below Bowman Dam. ⊠ *19020 S.E. Parkland Dr.* ☎ *541/447–4363, 800/452–5687* ⊕ *www. oregonstateparks.org.*

HIKING

Pick up maps at the Ochoco/Prineville Ranger Station for trails through the nearly 5,400-acre **Bridge Creek Wilderness** and the demanding Black Canyon Trail (11½ miles one-way with a hazardous river crossing in spring) in the **Black Canyon Wilderness.** The 1½-miles **Ponderosa Loop Trail** follows an old logging road through ponderosa pines growing on hills. In early summer wildflowers take over the open meadows. The trailhead begins at Bandit Springs Rest Area, 29 miles east of Prineville on U.S. 26. A 2-mile, one-way trail winds through old-growth forest and mountain meadows to **Steins Pillar,** a giant lava column with panoramic views; be prepared for a workout on the trail's poorly maintained second half, and allow at least three hours for the hike. To get to the trailhead, drive east 9 miles from Prineville on U.S. 26, head north (to the left) for 6½ miles on Mill Creek Road (also signed as Forest Service Road 33), and head east (to the right) on Forest Service Road 500.

SKIING

Bandit Springs Rest Area. A network of cross-country trails starts at Bandit Springs Rest Area. Designed for all levels of skiers, the trails traverse areas near the Ochoco Divide and have great views. ⊠ *U.S. 26, 29 miles east of Prineville.*

Department of Motor Vehicles. Ochoco National Forest headquarters has a handout on skiing trails, and can provide the required Sno-Park permits, which are also available from the Department of Motor Vehicles. ⊠ *Ochoco Plaza, 1595 E. 3rd St., Suite A-3* ☎ *541/447–7855* ⊕ *www. oregondmv.com.*

CRATER LAKE
NATIONAL PARK

WELCOME TO CRATER LAKE NATIONAL PARK

TOP REASONS TO GO

★ **The lake:** Cruise inside the caldera basin and gaze into the extraordinary sapphire-blue water of the country's deepest lake.

★ **Native land:** Enjoy the rare luxury of interacting with totally unspoiled terrain.

★ **The night sky:** Billions of stars glisten in the pitch-black darkness of an unpolluted sky.

★ **Splendid hikes:** Accessible trails spool off the main roads and wind past colorful bursts of wildflowers and cascading waterfalls.

★ **Camping at its best:** Pitch a tent or pull up a motor home at Mazama Campground, a beautifully situated, guest-friendly, and well-maintained campground.

1 Crater Lake. The focal point of the park, this non-recreational, scenic destination is known for its deep blue hue.

2 Wizard Island. Visitors can take boat rides to this protruding landmass rising from the western section of Crater Lake; it's a great place for a hike or a picnic.

3 Mazama Village. This is your best bet for stocking up on snacks, beverages, and fuel in the park; it's about 5 miles from Rim Drive.

4 Cleetwood Cove Trail. The only safe, designated trail to hike down the caldera and reach the lake's edge is on the rim's north side off Rim Drive.

GETTING ORIENTED

Crater Lake National Park covers 183,224 acres. Located in southern Oregon less than 100 miles from the California border, it's surrounded by several Cascade Range forests, including the Winema and Rogue River national forests. Of the nearby towns, Medford is closest at 59 miles southwest of the park; Ashland, to the southwest, and Klamath Falls, to the south, are each approximately 90 miles from the lake, with Roseburg the farthest away at 119 miles northwest of the park.

KEY	
🚹	Ranger Station
▲	Campground
🌲	Picnic Area
🍴	Restaurant
🏨	Lodge
🥾	Trailhead
🚻	Restrooms
⇗	Scenic Viewpoint
-----	Walking/Hiking Trails

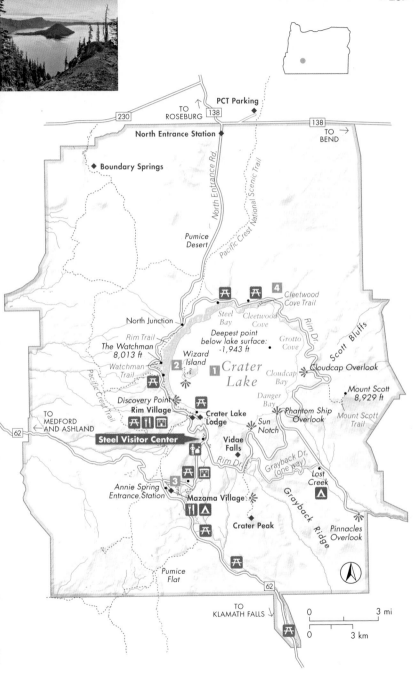

TO ROSEBURG

PCT Parking

230 138

North Entrance Station

138

TO BEND

Boundary Springs

North Entrance Rd.

Pacific Crest National Scenic Trail

Pumice Desert

Steel Bay

Cleetwood Cove Trail

4

Cleetwood Cove

North Junction

Rim Trail

The Watchman 8,013 ft

Watchman Trail

Deepest point below lake surface: -1,943 ft

Grotto Cove

Rim Dr.

Scott Bluffs

7

2

Wizard Island

1 *Crater Lake*

Cloudcap Bay

Cloudcap Overlook

Discovery Point

Pacific Crest Trail

Rim Village

Danger Bay

Phantom Ship Overlook

Mount Scott 8,929 ft

Mount Scott Trail

Crater Lake Lodge

Sun Notch

TO MEDFORD AND ASHLAND

62

Steel Visitor Center

Vidae Falls

Rim Dr.

Grayback Dr. (one way)

Annie Spring Entrance Station

3

Lost Creek

Mazama Village

Crater Peak

Grayback Ridge

Pinnacles Overlook

Pumice Flat

62

TO KLAMATH FALLS

0   3 mi

0   3 km

Updated by Christine Vovakes

The pure, crystalline blue of Crater Lake astounds visitors at first sight. More than 5 miles wide and ringed by cliffs almost 2,000 feet high, the lake was created approximately 7,700 years ago, following Mt. Mazama's fiery explosion. Days after the eruption, the mountain collapsed on an underground chamber emptied of lava. Rain and snowmelt filled the caldera, creating a sapphire-blue lake so clear that sunlight penetrates to a depth of 400 feet (the lake's depth is 1,943 feet). Today it's both the clearest and deepest lake in the United States—and the ninth deepest in the world.

CRATER LAKE NATIONAL PARK PLANNER

WHEN TO GO
The park's high season is July and August. September and early October tend to draw smaller crowds. From October through June, the entire park virtually closes due to heavy snowfall. The road is kept open just to the rim in winter, except during severe weather.

AVG. HIGH/LOW TEMPS.

JAN.	FEB.	MAR.	APR.	MAY	JUNE
34/18	35/18	37/19	43/23	50/29	58/34

JULY	AUG.	SEPT.	OCT.	NOV.	DEC.
69/41	69/41	63/37	52/31	40/24	35/20

FESTIVALS AND EVENTS
More than 400,000 Bard-loving buffs descend on Ashland (90 miles from Crater Lake) for the annual **Oregon Shakespeare Festival.** Plays run from February to November in three theaters; peak season is July, August, and September. ☎ *541/482–4331.*

PLANNING YOUR TIME
CRATER LAKE IN ONE DAY

Begin at **Steel Visitor Center,** where interpretive displays and a short video introduce you to the story of the lake's formation and its unique characteristics. Then begin your circumnavigation of the crater's rim by heading northeast on **Rim Drive,** allowing an hour to stop at overlooks—check out the Phantom Ship rock formation in the lake—before you reach **Cleetwood Cove Trail** trailhead, the only safe and legal access to the lake. Hike down the strenuous trail to reach the dock, and hop aboard one of the **tour boats** for a two-hour tour around the lake. If you have time, add on a trip to **Wizard Island** for a picnic lunch.

Back on Rim Drive, continue around the lake and stop at the **Watchman Trail.** A short but steep hike to this peak above the rim rewards you with a stunning view of the lake and the surrounding southern Cascades. Wind up your visit at **Crater Lake Lodge**—allow time to wander the lobby of the 1915 structure perched on the rim. Dinner at the lodge restaurant, overlooking the lake and the Cascade sunset, caps the day.

GETTING HERE AND AROUND

Most of the park is accessible only in late June–early July through mid-October. The rest of the year, snow blocks all park roadways and entrances except Highway 62 and the access road to Rim Village from Mazama Village. Rim Drive is typically closed because of heavy snowfall from mid-October to mid-July, and you could encounter icy conditions any month of the year, particularly in early morning.

PARK ESSENTIALS
PARK FEES AND PERMITS

Admission to the park is $10 per vehicle, good for seven days. Backcountry campers and hikers must obtain a free wilderness permit at Rim Visitor Center or Steel Visitor Center for all overnight trips.

PARK HOURS

Crater Lake National Park is open 24 hours a day year-round; however, snow closes most park roadways October through June. Lodging and dining facilities usually are open from late May to mid-October. The park is located in the Pacific time zone.

CELL PHONE RECEPTION

Cell phone reception in the park is unreliable. You'll find public telephones at Crater Lake Lodge and outside the Mazama Village store.

RESTAURANTS

There are a few casual eateries and convenience stores within the park. For fantastic upscale dining on the caldera's rim, head to the Crater Lake Lodge. *Prices in the reviews are the average cost of a main course at dinner or, if dinner is not served, at lunch.*

HOTELS

Crater Lake's summer season is relatively brief, and the park's main lodge is generally booked with guest reservations a year in advance. If you don't snag one, check availability as your trip approaches—cancellations are always possible. Outside the park are options in Prospect, Klamath Falls, Roseburg, Medford, and Ashland. *Prices in the reviews are the lowest cost of a standard double room in high season.*

VISITOR INFORMATION

PARK CONTACT INFORMATION

Crater Lake National Park ☎ *541/594–3000* ⊕ *www.nps.gov/crla.*

VISITOR CENTERS

Rim Visitor Center. In summer you can obtain park information here, take a ranger-led tour, or stop into the nearby Sinnott Memorial, with a small museum and a 900-foot view down to the lake's surface. In winter, snowshoe walks are offered on weekends and holidays. The Rim Village Gift Store and cafeteria are the only services open in winter. ⊠ *Rim Dr. on the south side of the lake, 7 miles north of Annie Spring entrance station* ☎ *541/594–3090* ⊕ *www.nps.gov/crla* ☉ *Late May–late Sept., daily 9:30–5.*

Steel Visitor Center. Open year-round, the information center is part of the park's headquarters; you'll find restrooms and a first-aid station here. There's also a small post office and a shop that sells books, maps, and postcards. In the auditorium, an 18-minute film, *The Mirror of Heaven,* describes Crater Lake's formation. ⊠ *Rim Dr., 4 miles north of Annie Spring entrance station* ☎ *541/594–3100* ⊕ *www.nps.gov/crla* ☉ *Early Apr.–early Nov., daily 9–5; mid-Nov.–early Apr., daily 10–4.*

EXPLORING

For most visitors, the star attractions of Crater Lake are the lake itself and the breathtakingly situated Crater Lake Lodge. Other park highlights include the natural, unspoiled beauty of the forest and the geological marvels that you can access along the 33-mile Rim Drive.

SCENIC DRIVES

Rim Drive. Take this 33-miles scenic loop for views of the lake and its cliffs from every conceivable angle. The drive alone is at least two hours long; frequent stops at overlooks and short hikes can easily stretch this to a half day. Be aware that Rim Drive is typically closed due to heavy snowfall from mid-October to mid-June, and icy conditions can be encountered any month of the year, particularly in early morning. ⊠ *Rim Dr. leads from Annie Spring entrance station to Rim Village where the drive circles around the rim; it's about 7 miles from the entrance station to Rim Village.* ✛ *To get to Rim Dr. from the park's north entrance, access the north entrance road via either Rte. 230 or Hwy. 138, and follow it for about 10 miles.*

HISTORIC SITES

Fodor'sChoice **Crater Lake Lodge.** First built in 1915, this classic log-and-stone struc-
★ ture still boasts the original lodgepole-pine pillars, beams, and stone
fireplaces. The lobby, fondly referred to as the Great Hall, serves as a
warm, welcoming gathering place where you can play games, socialize
with a cocktail, or gaze out of the many windows to view spectacular
sunrises and sunsets by a crackling fire. ⊠ *Rim Village, just east of Rim
Visitor Center.*

SCENIC STOPS

Cloudcap Overlook. The highest road-access overlook on the Crater Lake
rim, Cloudcap has a westward view across the lake to Wizard Island
and an eastward view of Mt. Scott, the volcanic cone that is the park's
highest point, just 2 miles away. ⊠ *2 mi off Rim Dr., 13 miles northeast
of Steel Visitor Center.*

Discovery Point. This overlook marks the spot at which prospectors first
spied the lake in 1853. Wizard Island is just northeast, close to shore.
⊠ *Rim Dr., 1½ miles north of Rim Village.*

Mazama Village. In summer a campground, motor inn, amphitheater,
gas station, post office, and small store are open here. No gasoline is
available in the park from mid-October to mid-May. ⊠ *Mazama Village
Rd., off Hwy. 62, near Annie Spring entrance station* ☎ *541/594–2255,
888/774–2728* ⊕ *www.nps.gov/crla* ☉ *Mid-to-late May, daily 10–5;
June–Aug., daily 7–9; Sept.–mid-Oct., daily 8–8.*

Phantom Ship Overlook. From this point you can get a close look at
Phantom Ship, a rock formation that resembles a schooner with furled
masts, and looks ghostly in fog. ⊠ *Rim Dr., 7 miles northeast of Steel
Information Center.*

Pinnacles Overlook. Ascending from the banks of Sand and Wheeler
creeks, unearthly spires of eroded ash resemble the peaks of fairy-tale
castles. Once upon a time, the road continued east to a former entrance.
A path now replaces the old road and follows the rim of Sand Creek
(affording more views of pinnacles) to where the entrance arch still
stands. ⊠ *5 miles northeast of Steel Visitor Center, then 2 miles east
on Pinnacles Spur Rd.*

Sun Notch. It's a moderate ¼-mile hike through wildflowers and dry
meadow to this overlook, which has views of Crater Lake and Phantom
Ship. Mind the cliff edges. ⊠ *Rim Dr., 4.4 miles east of Steel Visitor
Center, east side of the lake.*

Wizard Island. To get here, hike down the steep Cleetwood Cove Trail
(and back up upon your return) and board the tour boat (⇨ *Educational
Offerings)* for a 2-hour ride. Bring a picnic. If you're in top shape take
the very strenuous 2-mile hike to Wizard Summit that leads to a path
around the 90-foot deep crater at the top. A more moderate hike is the
1.8-mile trek on a rocky trail along the shore of the island. ⊠ *Via Cleetwood Cove Trail to the Wizard Island dock* ☎ *541/594–2255, 888/774–
2728* ⊕ *www.craterlakelodges.com* ☉ *Late June–mid-Sept., daily.*

CLOSE UP

Wildlife in Crater Lake

Two primary types of fish swim beneath the surface of Crater Lake: kokanee salmon and rainbow trout. It's estimated that hundreds of thousands of kokanee inhabit the lake, but since boating and recreational access is so limited they elude many would-be sportsmen. Kokanees average about 8 inches in length, but they can grow to nearly 18 inches. Rainbow trout are larger than the kokanee but are less abundant in Crater Lake. Trout—including bull, Eastern brook, rainbow, and German brown—swim in the park's many streams and rivers; they usually remain elusive because these waterways flow near inaccessibly steep canyons.

Remote canyons shelter the park's elk and deer populations, which can sometimes be seen at dusk and dawn feeding at the forest's edge. Black bears and pine martens—cousins of the short-tailed weasel—also call Crater Lake home. Birds such as hairy woodpeckers, California gulls, red-tailed hawks, and great horned owls are more commonly seen in summer in forests below the lake. Clark's nut-cracker, a big raucous bird, is essential to seeding new whitebark pine trees around the lake rim.

EDUCATIONAL OFFERINGS

RANGER PROGRAMS

FAMILY **Boat Tours.** The most extensively used guided tours in Crater Lake are on the water, aboard launches that carry 48 passengers on a two-hour tour accompanied by a ranger. The boats circle the lake; two of the eight daily boats stop at Wizard Island, where you can get off and reboard a minimum of three hours later, or six hours later if you catch the morning boat. The first tour leaves the dock at 9:30 am; the last departs at 3:30 pm. To get to the dock you must hike down Cleetwood Cove Trail, a strenuous 1.1-mile walk that drops 700 feet; only those in excellent physical shape should attempt the hike. Bring adequate water with you. Purchase boat-tour tickets at the top of the trail or through advance reservations. Restrooms are available at the top and bottom of the trail. ⊠ *Cleetwood Cove Trail, off Rim Dr., 11 miles north of Rim Village on the north side of the lake* ☎ *541/594–2255, 888/774–2728* ⊕ *www.craterlakelodges.com* ✉ *$32; $42 with island drop-off* ☉ *Late June–mid-Sept., daily.*

FAMILY **Junior Ranger Program.** Kids ages 6–12 learn about Crater Lake while earning either a Junior Ranger patch or badge in daily sessions during summer months at the Rim Visitor Center, and year-round at the Steel Visitor Center. Pick up free activity booklets at either visitor center. ☎ *541/594–3100.*

SPORTS AND THE OUTDOORS

FISHING

Fishing is allowed in the lake, but you may find the experience frustrating—in such a massive body of water, the problem is finding the fish. Try your luck near the Cleetwood Cove boat dock, or take poles on the boat tour and fish off Wizard Island. Rainbow trout and kokanee salmon lurk in Crater Lake's aquamarine depths, and some grow to enormous sizes. You don't need a state fishing license, but to protect the lake's pristine waters, use only artificial bait as opposed to live worms. Private boats are prohibited on the lake.

> **BEST BETS FOR FAMILIES**
>
> ■ **Boat Tour.** Climb aboard for a close-up view of Crater Lake.
>
> ■ **Annie Creek Restaurant.** Chow down on a picnic feast at this eatery's outdoor seating area.
>
> ■ **Crater Lake Lodge.** Tour this historic inn.

HIKING

EASY

Castle Crest Wildflower Trail. This 1-mile loop that passes through a spring-fed meadow is one of the park's flatter hikes. Wildflowers burst into full bloom here in July. *Easy.* ✉ *Across the street from Steel Visitor Center parking lot, Rim Dr.*

Godfrey Glen Trail. This 1-mile loop trail is an easy stroll through an old-growth forest with canyon views. Its dirt path is accessible to wheelchairs with assistance. *Easy.* ✉ *2.4 miles south of Steel Visitor Center.*

MODERATE

Annie Creek Canyon Trail. This somewhat strenuous 1.7-mile hike loops through a deep stream-cut canyon, providing views of the narrow cleft scarred by volcanic activity. This is a good area to look for flowers and deer. *Moderate.* ✉ *Mazama Campground, Mazama Village Rd., near Annie Spring entrance station.*

Boundary Springs Trail. If you feel like sleuthing, take this moderate 5-mile round-trip hike to the headwaters of the Rogue River. The trail isn't always well marked, so a detailed trail guide is necessary. You'll see streams, forests, and wildflowers along the way before discovering Boundary Springs pouring out of the side of a low ridge. *Moderate.* ✉ *Pullout on Hwy. 230, near milepost 19, about 5 miles west of the junction with Hwy. 138.*

The Watchman Trail. This is one of the best hikes in the park. Though it's less than a mile each way, the trail climbs more than 400 feet—not counting the steps up to the actual lookout, which has great views of Wizard Island and the lake. *Moderate.* ✉ *Watchman Overlook, 3.8 miles northwest of Rim Village on Rim Dr., west side of the lake.*

7

DIFFICULT

Cleetwood Cove Trail. This strenuous 2.2-mile round-trip hike descends 700 feet down nearly vertical cliffs along the lake to the boat dock. Be in top shape before you take this one. *Difficult.* ⊠ *Cleetwood Cove trailhead, Rim Dr., 11 miles north of Rim Village, north side of the lake.*

Fodor's Choice ★ **Mt. Scott Trail.** This strenuous 5-mile round-trip trail takes you to the park's highest point—the top of Mt. Scott, the oldest volcanic cone of Mt. Mazama, at 8,929 feet. The average hiker needs 90 minutes to make the steep uphill trek—and nearly 60 minutes to get down. The trail starts at an elevation of about 7,450 feet, so the climb is not extreme but does get steep in spots. Views of the lake and the broad Klamath Basin are spectacular. *Difficult.* ⊠ *14 miles east of Steel Visitor Center on Rim Dr., east side of the lake, across from the road to Cloudcap Overlook.*

Pacific Crest Trail. You can hike a portion of the Pacific Crest Trail, which extends from Mexico to Canada and winds through the park for 33 miles. For this prime backcountry experience, catch the trail off Highway 138 about a mile east of the north entrance, where it heads south and then toward the west rim of the lake and circles it for about 6 miles, then descends down Dutton Creek to the Mazama Village area. You'll need a detailed map for this hike; check online or with the PCT association. *Difficult.* ⊠ *Pacific Crest Trail parking lot, north access road off Hwy. 138, 2 miles east of the Hwy. 138–north entrance road junction* ⊕ *www.pcta.org.*

> ### SERIOUS SAFETY
>
> There is only one safe way to reach Crater Lake's edge: the Cleetwood Cove Trail from the north rim. The rest of the inner caldera is steep and composed of loose gravel, basalt, and pumice—extremely dangerous, in other words. That's why all hiking and climbing are strictly prohibited inside the rim, and rangers will issue citations for violations.

SKIING

There are no maintained ski trails in the park, although some backcountry trails are marked with blue diamonds or snow poles. Most cross-country skiers park at Rim Village and follow a portion of West Rim Drive toward Wizard Island Overlook (4 miles). The road is plowed to Rim Village, but it may be closed temporarily due to severe storms. Snow tires and chains are essential. The park's online brochure (available at ⊕ *www.nps.gov/crla*) lists additional trails and their length and difficulty.

SWIMMING

Swimming is allowed in the lake, but it's not advised. Made up entirely of snowmelt, Crater Lake is very cold—about 45°F to 59°F during summer. The lagoons on Wizard Island and at Cleetwood Cove are your best choices—but only when the air temperature rises above 80°F, which is rare. If you're able to brave the cold, though, you can say that you've taken a dip in the deepest lake in the United States.

WHERE TO EAT

$$
ECLECTIC
FAMILY

✕ **Annie Creek Restaurant.** It's family-style buffet dining here for lunch and dinner; pizza and pasta, along with ham and roast beef, are the main features. Less expensive sandwich selections are available. The outdoor seating area is surrounded by towering pine trees. $ *Average main: $14* ⊠ *Mazama Village Rd., near Annie Spring entrance station* ☎ *541/594–2255* ⊘ *Closed mid-Oct.–late May.*

$$$
AMERICAN
Fodor's Choice
★

✕ **Dining Room at Crater Lake Lodge.** Virtually the only place where you can dine well once you're in the park, the lodge's culinary emphasis is on fresh, regional Northwest cuisine. The dining room is magnificent, with a large stone fireplace and views of Crater Lake's clear-blue waters. Breakfast and lunch are enjoyable here, but the evening menu is the main attraction, with tempting delights such as wild Alaskan salmon, pork loin with apple-pear chutney, steak, and vegetarian offerings. An extensive wine list tops off the gourmet experience. No reservations accepted for breakfast and lunch; they're essential for dinner. $ *Average main: $29* ⊠ *Crater Lake Lodge, 1 Lodge Loop Rd., Rim Village* ☎ *541/594–2255* ⊕ *www.craterlakelodges.com* ⌂ *Reservations essential* ⊘ *Closed mid-Oct.–late May.*

PICNIC AREAS

Rim Drive. About a half-dozen picnic-area turnouts encircle the lake; all have good views, but they can get very windy. Most have pit toilets, and a few have fire grills, but none have running water. ⊠ *Rim Dr.* ▭ *No credit cards.*

Rim Village. This is the only park picnic area with running water. The tables are set behind the visitor center, and most have a view of the lake below. There are flush toilets inside the visitor center. ⊠ *Rim Dr. on the south side of the lake, 7 miles north of Annie Spring entrance station* ▭ *No credit cards.*

Wizard Island. The park's best picnic venue is on Wizard Island; pack a picnic lunch and book yourself on one of the early morning boat tour departures, reserving space on an afternoon return. There are no formal picnic areas and just pit toilets, but you'll discover plenty of sunny, protected spots where you can have a quiet meal and appreciate the astounding scene that surrounds you. The island is accessible by boat tour only (⇨ *Educational Offerings).* ▭ *No credit cards.*

7

CLOSE UP

Best Campgrounds in Crater Lake

Both tent campers and RV enthusiasts will enjoy the heavily wooded and well-equipped setting of Mazama Campground. Drinking water, showers, and laundry facilities help ensure that you don't have to rough it too much. Lost Creek Campground is much smaller, with minimal amenities and a more "rustic" Crater Lake experience.

Lost Creek Campground. The small, remote tent sites here are usually available on a daily basis; in July and August arrive early to secure a spot. ✉ *3 miles south of Rim Rd. on Pinnacles Spur Rd. at Grayback Dr.* ☎ *541/594–3100.*

Mazama Campground. This campground is set well below the lake caldera in the pine and fir forest of the Cascades not far from the main access road (Highway 62). About half the spaces are pull-throughs, some with electricity; no hookups are available. The best tent spots are on some of the outer loops above Annie Creek Canyon. ✉ *Mazama Village, near Annie Spring entrance station* ☎ *541/594–2255 or 888/774–2728* 🌐 *www.craterlakelodges.com.*

WHERE TO STAY

For expanded hotel reviews, visit Fodors.com.

$$ HOTEL 🏨 **The Cabins at Mazama Village.** In a wooded area 7 miles south of the lake, this complex is made up of several A-frame buildings. **Pros:** clean and well-kept facility. **Cons:** lots of traffic into adjacent campground. [$] *Rooms from: $138* ✉ *Mazama Village, near Annie Spring entrance station* ☎ *541/594–2255, 888/774–2728* 🌐 *www.craterlakelodges.com* 🛏 *40 rooms* 🕓 *Closed mid-Oct.–late May* 🍴 *No meals.*

$$$ HOTEL 🏨 **Crater Lake Lodge.** The period feel of this 1915 lodge on the caldera's rim is reflected in its lodgepole-pine columns, gleaming wood floors, and stone fireplaces in the common areas. **Pros:** ideal location for watching sunrise and sunset reflected on the lake. **Cons:** very difficult to reserve rooms; some rooms have tubs only, no shower. [$] *Rooms from: $164* ✉ *Rim Village, east of Rim Visitor Center, 1 Lodge Loop Rd., Crater Lake* ☎ *541/594–2255, 888/774–2728* 🌐 *www.craterlakelodges.com* 🛏 *71 rooms* 🕓 *Closed mid-Oct.–late May* 🍴 *No meals.*

8

SOUTHERN OREGON

WELCOME TO SOUTHERN OREGON

TOP REASONS TO GO

★ **The other wine regions:** The underrated and fast-growing Umpqua and Rogue River wine regions offer picturesque pastoral views and numerous tasting rooms.

★ **Oregon Caves National Monument:** Explore deep into mysterious underground chambers and marble caves at this off-the-beaten-path natural wonder.

★ **Oregon Shakespeare Festival:** This acclaimed festival draws drama lovers to Ashland nine months a year, presenting a wide variety of both classic and contemporary theater.

★ **Quaint towns:** Southern Oregon's own throwback to the Old West, Jacksonville abounds with well-preserved buildings. Ashland claims one of the prettiest downtowns in Oregon, with its hip cafés and urbane boutiques.

★ **Wild wonders:** Each fall more than 1 million waterfowl descend upon Klamath Basin National Wildlife Refuge Complex. The Rogue River is Oregon's white-water rafting capital.

1 Umpqua Valley. Known increasingly for its up-and-coming wineries, including award-winning Abacela, this valley is home to historic Oakland, Roseburg and its family-friendly Wildlife Safari park, and the Umpqua River Scenic Byway, a particularly scenic route to Crater Lake.

2 Rogue Valley. This fertile, mild-temperature region that extends from Grants Pass southeast through Medford and down to Ashland takes in the most populous communities in the area—it's also the gateway for reaching Klamath Falls, to the east, and the remote but fascinating Oregon Caves National Monument to the southwest. The Oregon Shakespeare Festival and an abundance of historic buildings have turned Ashland into a hub of arts, culture, and fine bed-and-breakfasts. Grants Pass is the launch point for some of the best white-water rafting around, while Medford and historic Jacksonville are surrounded by vineyards and farms that produce some of the state's tastiest local edibles, from pears to Pinot Gris.

GETTING ORIENTED

To locals, southern Oregon really refers to the southwestern corner of the state, encompassing the Rogue and several other river valleys that lie between the Coast and Cascade mountain ranges, from a little north of Roseburg down to the California border. The area is due south of Eugene and the Willamette Valley, and has a similarly lush, hilly, and fertile terrain that lends itself perfectly to agriculture and winemaking. Towns in the valleys, such as Ashland and Roseburg, have elevations ranging from about 500 to 2000 feet, while peaks to the east, in the Cascade Range, rise as high as 9,000 feet. This area is also the gateway to Crater Lake National Park—many visitors to that park overnight in Medford or Ashland, which is about 85 miles away.

8

Updated
by Andrew
Collins

Southern Oregon begins where the verdant lowlands of the Willamette Valley give way to a complex collision of mountains, rivers, and ravines. The intricate geography of the "Land of Umpqua," as the area around Roseburg is somewhat romantically known, signals that this is territory distinct from neighboring regions to the north, east, and west.

Wild rivers—the Rogue and the Umpqua are legendary for fishing and boating—and twisting mountain roads venture through the landscape that saw Oregon's most violent Indian wars and became the territory of a self-reliant breed. "Don't-Tread-on-Me" southern Oregonians see themselves as markedly different from fellow citizens of the Pacific Wonderland. In fact, several early-20th-century attempts to secede from Oregon (in combination with northern California) and proclaim a "state of Jefferson" survive in local folklore and culture. That being said, Ashland and parts of the surrounding area have gradually become more progressive and urbane in recent decades, as wineries, art galleries, and hip restaurants continue to proliferate. The mix of folks from all different political, social, and stylistic bents is a big part of what makes southern Oregon so interesting—and appealing.

Some locals refer to this sun-kissed, sometimes surprisingly hot landscape as the Mediterranean; others call it Oregon's banana belt. It's a climate built for slow-paced pursuits and a leisurely outlook on life, not to mention agriculture—the region's orchards, farms, and increasingly acclaimed vineyards have lately helped give southern Oregon cachet among food and wine aficionados. The restaurant scene has grown partly thanks to a pair of big cultural draws, Ashland's Oregon Shakespeare Festival and Jacksonville's open-air, picnic-friendly Britt Festivals concert series.

Roseburg, Medford, and Klamath Falls are also all popular bases for visiting iconic Crater Lake National Park (⇨ *see Chapter 7*), which lies at the region's eastern edge, about two hours away by car. Formed nearly 8,000 years ago by the cataclysmic eruption of Mt. Mazama, this stunningly clear-blue lake is North America's deepest.

SOUTHERN OREGON PLANNER

WHEN TO GO

Southern Oregon's population centers, which all lie chiefly in the valleys, tend to be warmer and quite a bit sunnier than Eugene and Portland to the north, receiving almost no snow in winter and only 2 to 3 inches of rain per month. In summer, temperatures regularly climb into the 90s, but the low humidity makes for a generally comfortable climate. This makes most of the region quite pleasant to visit year-round, with spring and fall generally offering the best balance of sunny and mild weather.

The exception, during the colder months, are southern Oregon's mountainous areas to the east and west, which are covered with snow from fall through spring. Some of the roads leading from the Umpqua and Rogue valleys up to Crater Lake are closed because of snow from mid-October through June, making summer the prime time to visit.

Jacksonville hosts the world-class summer music **Britt Festivals,** and the **Oregon Shakespeare Festival** in Ashland lasts from February to early November. Each February nature enthusiasts flock to the Klamath Basin for the **Winter Wings Festival,** the nation's oldest birding festival.

GETTING HERE AND AROUND

AIR TRAVEL

Medford's **Rogue Valley International Airport (MFR)** (☎ *541/772–8068* ⊕ *www.co.jackson.or.us*) is the state's third-largest facility, with direct flights to Denver, Las Vegas, Los Angeles, Phoenix, Portland, Salt Lake City, San Francisco, and Seattle, and service by Allegiant, Air, Horizon Air (part of Alaska Airlines), Delta Connection, and United Express. Most national car-rental branches are at the airport, with rates starting around $25 a day. A few taxi and shuttle companies provide transportation from the airport to other towns in the area; these are used mostly by locals, as a car is the only practical way to explore this relatively rural part of Oregon. The one exception is Ashland, where many attractions, restaurants, and accommodations are within walking distance. **Cascade Airport Shuttle** (☎ *541/488–1998* ⊕ *www.cascadeshuttle.com*) offers door-to-door service from the airport to Ashland for about $30. Among taxi companies, **Valley Cab** (☎ *541/772–1818* ⊕ *www.myvalleycab.com*) serves the Rogue Valley region, with fares costing $3 base per trip, plus $2.50 per mile thereafter.

Roseburg is a 75-mile drive from Oregon's second-largest airport, in Eugene (EUG). Ashland is about 300 miles south of the state's largest airport, in Portland, and 350 miles north of San Francisco. Although it's often cheaper to fly into these larger airports than it is to Medford, what you lose in gas costs, time, and inconvenience will likely outweigh any savings.

CAR TRAVEL

Unquestionably, your best way to explore the region is by car, although most of Ashland's key attractions, hotels, and dining are downtown and within walking distance of one another. Interstate 5 runs north–south the length of the Umpqua and Rogue River valleys, linking Roseburg,

8

Grants Pass, Medford, and Ashland. Many regional attractions lie not too far east or west of Interstate 5. Jacksonville is a short drive due west from Medford. Highway 138 winds scenically along the Umpqua River east of Roseburg to the less-visited northern end of Crater Lake National Park. Highway 140 leads from Medford east to Klamath Falls, which you can reach from Bend via U.S. 97.

RESTAURANTS

Southern Oregon's dining scene varies greatly from region to region, with the more tourism-driven and upscale communities of Ashland and Jacksonville leading the way in terms of sophisticated farm-to-table restaurants, hip coffeehouses, and noteworthy bakeries and wine bars. Other larger towns in the valleys, including Roseburg, Grants Pass, and Medford, have grown in culinary stature and variety of late, while Klamath Falls and Cave Junction have few dining options of note. In the former communities you'll find chefs emphasizing Oregon-produced foods; Oregon wines, including many from the Rogue and Umqua valleys, also find their way onto many menus. *Prices in the reviews are the average cost of a main course at dinner or, if dinner is not served, at lunch.*

HOTELS

Ashland has the region's greatest variety of distinctive lodgings, from the usual low- to mid-priced chain properties to plush B&Bs set in restored Arts and Crafts and Victorian houses. Nearby Jacksonville also has several fine, upscale inns. Beyond that, in nearly every town in southern Oregon you'll find two or three interesting B&Bs or small hotels, and in any of the communities along Interstate 5—including Roseburg, Grants Pass, and Medford—a wide variety of chain motels and hotels. Rooms in this part of the state book up earliest in summer, especially on weekends. If you're coming to Ashland or Jacksonville, try to book at least a week or two ahead. Elsewhere, you can usually find a room in a suitable chain property on less than a day's notice. *Prices in the reviews are the lowest cost of a standard double room in high season.*

TOURS

You'll see some of Oregon's most magnificent scenery with **Hellgate Jetboat Excursions** (☎ *541/479–7204 or 800/648–4874 ⊕ www.hellgate. com*), which depart from the Riverside Inn in Grants Pass. The 36-mile round-trip runs through Hellgate Canyon and takes two hours. There is also a five-hour, 75-mile round-trip from Grants Pass to Grave Creek, with a stop for a meal on an open-air deck (cost of meal not included). Trips are available May through August, and sometimes into September, if conditions permit.

Main Street Adventure Tours (☎ *541/482–9852 ⊕ www.southernoregon winetours.com*), based in Ashland, offers custom limo tours through the region's key wine regions, the Rogue, Applegate, Illinois, and Umpqua valleys. The company can also customize tours to Crater Lake, fly-fishing and skiing trips, and other activities and explorations throughout the region.

VISITOR INFORMATION
Southern Oregon Visitors Association ⊠ *332 W. 6th St., Medford* ☎ *541/779–4691* ⊕ *www.southernoregon.org.*

UMPQUA VALLEY

The northernmost part of southern Oregon, beginning about 40 miles south of Eugene and the Willamette Valley, the rural and sparsely populated Umpqua Valley is the gateway to this part of the state's sunny and relatively dry climate. As you drive down Interstate 5 you'll descend through twisting valleys and climb up over scenic highlands. In summer you can follow the dramatic Umpqua River Scenic Byway (Hwy. 138) east over the Cascades to access Crater Lake from the north—it's the prettiest route to the lake. Within the Umpqua Valley, attractions are relatively few, but this area has several excellent wineries, some of the best river fishing in the Northwest, and one of the region's top draws for animal lovers, the Wildlife Safari park.

ROSEBURG

73 miles south of Eugene on Interstate 5.

Fishermen the world over hold the name Roseburg sacred. The timber town on the Umpqua River attracts anglers in search of a dozen popular fish species, including bass, brown and brook trout, and chinook, coho, and sockeye salmon. The native steelhead, which makes its run to the sea in the summer, is king of them all.

The north and south branches of the Umpqua River meet up just north of Roseburg. The roads that run parallel to this river provide spectacular views of the falls, and the North Umpqua route also provides access to trails, hot springs, and the Winchester fish ladder. White-water rafting is also popular here, although not to the degree that it is farther south in the Rogue Valley.

About 80 miles west of the northern gateway to Crater Lake National Park and in the Hundred Valleys of the Umpqua, Roseburg produces innovative, well-regarded wines. Wineries are sprouting up throughout the mild, gorgeous farm country around town, mostly within easy reach of Interstate 5.

GETTING HERE AND AROUND

Roseburg is the first large town you'll reach driving south from Eugene on Interstate 5. It's also a main access point into southern Oregon via Highway 138 if you're approaching from the east, either by way of Crater Lake or U.S. 97, which leads down from Bend. And from the Bandon–Coos Bay region of the Oregon Coast, windy but picturesque Highway 42 leads to just south of Roseburg. It's a 75-mile drive north to Eugene's airport, and a 95-mile drive south to Rogue Valley Airport in Medford. Attractions in the region are spread over a large area—a car is a must.

8

ESSENTIALS

Visitor Information **Roseburg Visitors & Convention Bureau** ✉ *410 S.E. Spruce St., Roseburg* ☎ *541/672–9731, 800/444–9584* 🌐 *www.visitroseburg.com.*

EXPLORING

Fodor's Choice ★ **Abacela Vineyards and Winery.** The name derives from an archaic Spanish word meaning "to plant grapevines," and that's exactly what this winery's husband-wife team did not so very long ago. Abacela released its first wine in 1999 and has steadily established itself as one of the state's most acclaimed producers—one of the best outside the Willamette Valley. Hot-blooded Spanish Tempranillo is Abacela's pride and joy, though inky Malbec and torrid Sangiovese also highlight a repertoire heavy on Mediterranean varietals. The winery unveiled a sleek, airy new tasting room in 2012. ✉ *12500 Lookingglass Rd.* ☎ *541/679–6642* 🌐 *www.abacela.com* 🕒 *June–Oct., daily 11–6; Nov.–May, daily 11–5.*

Douglas County Museum. One of the best county museums in the state surveys 8,000 years of human activity in the region. The fossil collection is worth a stop, as is the state's second-largest photo collection, numbering more than 24,000 images, some dating to the 1840s. ✉ *123 Museum Dr.* ☎ *541/957–7007* 🌐 *www.co.douglas.or.us/museum* 🎟 *$5* 🕒 *Tues.–Sat. 10–5.*

FAMILY Fodor's Choice ★ **Wildlife Safari.** Come face-to-face with some 500 free-roaming animals at the 600-acre drive-through wildlife park. Inhabitants include alligators, bobcats, cougars, gibbons, lions, giraffes, grizzly bears, Tibetan yaks, cheetahs, Siberian tigers, and more than 100 additional species. There's also a petting zoo, a miniature train, and elephant rides. The admission price includes two same-day drive-throughs. This nonprofit zoological park is a respected research facility with full accreditation from the American Zoo and Aquarium Assocation, with a mission to conserve and protect endangered species through education and breeding programs. ✉ *1790 Safari Rd., Winston* ☎ *541/679–6761* 🌐 *www.wildlifesafari.net* 🎟 *$18* 🕒 *Mid-Mar.–Oct., daily 9–5; Nov.–mid-Mar., daily 10–4.*

WHERE TO EAT AND STAY

For expanded hotel reviews, visit Fodors.com.

$$ AMERICAN 🍴 **The Mark V.** This cheery corner bar and grill in downtown Roseburg lends a bit of much-needed urbanity to this workaday downtown. Tall windows look onto the street from the plant-filled, warmly lighted dining room, where a friendly and easygoing staff serves both tapas-size and more substantial fare three meals a day. Try the sashimi-style blackened ahi tuna, crab cakes, and hefty New York strip steak. [$] *Average main: $18* ✉ *563 S.E. Main St.* ☎ *541/229–6275* 🌐 *www.themark5.com.*

$$ B&B/INN Fodor's Choice ★ 🏨 **The Steamboat Inn.** Every fall a who's who of the world's top fly-fishermen converges at this secluded forest inn, high in the Cascades above the emerald North Umpqua River, in search of the 20-pound steelhead that haunt these waters; guide services are available, as are equipment rentals and sales. **Pros:** good option if en route to Crater Lake; access to some of the best fishing in the West; great escape. **Cons:** extremely far from civilization. [$] *Rooms from: $185* ✉ *42705 N. Umpqua Hwy., 38 miles east of Roseburg on Hwy. 138, near Steamboat Creek, Idleyld*

Wine production in southern Oregon

Park ☎ *541/498–2230, 800/840–8825* ⊕ *www.thesteamboatinn.com*
⤵ *8 cabins, 5 cottages, 2 suites, 5 houses* ⦿ *Multiple meal plans.*

SPORTS AND THE OUTDOORS

FISHING

You'll find some of the best river fishing in Oregon along the Umpqua, with smallmouth bass, shad, steelhead, salmon (coho, chinook, and sockeye), and sturgeon—the biggest reaching 10 feet in length—among the most prized catches. In addition to the Steamboat Inn, several outfitters in the region provide full guide services, which typically include all gear, boats, and expert leaders. There's good fishing in this region year-round, with sturgeon and steelhead at their best during the colder months, chinook and coho salmon thriving in the fall, and most other species prolific in spring and summer.

Oregon Angler. The Oregon Angler, run by one of the state's most respected and knowledgeable guides, Todd Hannah, specializes in jet-boat and drift-boat fishing excursions along the famed "Umpqua Loop," an 18-mile span of river that's long been lauded for exceptional fishing. Full-day trips start at $175 per person. ☎ *800/428–8585* ⊕ *www.theoregonangler.com.*

Big K Guest Ranch. Set along a 10-mile span of the upper Umpqua River near Elkton (about 35 miles north of Roseburg), Big K is a pastoral 2,500-acre guest ranch. The accommodations are geared primarily to groups and corporate retreats, but the ranch offers individual fishing packages starting at $400 per person, per day (meals and lodging included), with three- and four-night deals available at a better rate. Adventures include fly-fishing for smallmouth bass and summer steelhead, as well as spin-casting and drift-boat fishing. ☎ 541/584–2295 ⊕ www.big-k.com.

RAFTING

There's thrilling Class III and higher white-water rafting along the North Umpqua River, with several outfitters providing trips ranging from a few hours to a few days throughout the year.

North Umpqua Outfitters. Since 1987, this trusted provider has offered both half- and full-day rafting and kayaking trips along the frothy North Umpqua. ⊠ Idleyld Park ☎ 888/454–9696 ⊕ www.nuorafting.com.

Oregon Ridge & River Excursions. This popular company offers white-water rafting and kayaking throughout the Umpqua Basin, along with milder canoeing adventures on nearby lakes. ⊠ Idleyld Park ☎ 541/496–3333 ⊕ www.umpquarivers.com.

ROGUE VALLEY

Encompassing the broad, curving, southeasterly swath of towns from Grants Pass through Medford down to Ashland, the mild and sun-kissed Rogue Valley is southern Oregon's main population center, and also where you'll find the bulk of the region's lodging, dining, shopping, and recreation.

Interstate 5 cuts through the valley en route to northern California, but venture away from the main thoroughfare to see what makes this part of Oregon so special, including the superb—if underrated—wineries. With warmer temperatures, this area is conducive to many more varietals than the Willamette Valley—from reds like Syrah, Tempranillo, and Cabernet Sauvignon to increasingly well-known old-world whites like Viognier and Pinot Gris. Foodies are drawn to the region's abundance of local food producers, from nationally acclaimed cheese makers and chocolatiers to farms growing juicy pears, blackberries, and cherries. Access to excellent food has helped turn the small but artsy city of Ashland into one of Oregon's top restaurant destinations, with nearby communities also growing in culinary cachet. Additionally, the area's reputation for performing arts, which manifests itself in the famed Oregon Shakespeare Festival in Ashland and Britt Music Festival in historic Jacksonville, continues to grow.

Flanked by 1.8-million-acre Rogue-Siskiyou National Forest, which has rangers' offices near Grants Pass and Medford, the Rogue Valley is a hub of outdoor recreation, from fishing and white-water rafting along its clear rivers to mountain-biking, hiking, and even skiing in the higher elevations—peaks in the Cascade Range, to the east, rise to nearly 10,000 feet. Klamath Falls lies technically a bit east of the Rogue Valley but shares the region's abundance of unspoiled wilderness and opportunities for getting in touch with nature.

Kayaking Rainey Falls on the Rogue River

GRANTS PASS

70 miles south of Roseburg on I–5.

"It's the Climate!" So says a confident 1950s vintage neon sign presiding over Josephine County's downtown. Grants Pass bills itself as Oregon's white-water capital: the Rogue River, preserved by Congress in 1968 as a National Wild and Scenic River, runs right through town. Downtown Grants Pass is a National Historic District, a stately little enclave of 19th-century brick storefronts housing folksy businesses harking back to the 1950s. It's all that white water, however, that compels most visitors—and not a few moviemakers (*The River Wild* and *Rooster Cogburn* were both filmed here). If the river alone doesn't serve up enough natural drama, the sheer rock walls of nearby Hellgate Canyon rise 250 feet.

GETTING HERE AND AROUND

Grants Pass is easily reached from elsewhere in the region via Interstate 5, and it's also where U.S. 199 cuts southwest toward Oregon Caves National Monument and, eventually, the northernmost section of California's coast (as well as the northern sections of Redwood National Park). Many visitors to the southern Oregon coastline backtrack inland up U.S. 199 to create a scenic loop drive, ultimately intersecting with Interstate 5 at Grants Pass. Medford's airport is a 30-mile drive away.

ESSENTIALS

Visitor Information Grants Pass Tourism ⌧ *198 S.W. G St.* ☎ *800/547–5927* ⊕ *www.visitgrantspass.org.*

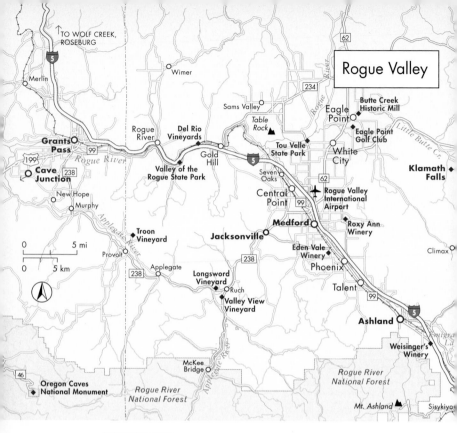

Rogue Valley

EXPLORING

★

Troon Vineyards. Few winemakers in southern Oregon have generated more buzz than Troon, whose swank tasting room and winery is patterned after a French country villa. Troon produces relatively small yields of exceptional wines more typical of Sonoma than Oregon (Cabernet Sauvignon, Zinfandel, and Syrah are the heavy hitters), but they also plant less typical U.S. varietals, such as Viognier and Cabernet Franc. The winery is 14 miles southeast of downtown Grants Pass, in the northern edge of the Applegate Valley. ⊠ *1475 Kubli Rd.* ☎ *541/846–9900* ⊕ *www.troonvineyard.com* ⊘ *Daily 11–5.*

WHERE TO EAT AND STAY
For expanded hotel reviews, visit Fodors.com.

$$
ECLECTIC

✕ **Blondies' Bistro.** Sophisticated but affordable Blondies' serves globally inspired food and cocktails in a dapper downtown space with high ceilings and hardwood floors—the lone aesthetic drawback is the sometimes boisterous acoustics. The kitchen, however, prepares first-rate food, including an especially good list of starters, from Portuguese-style steamed clams with herbed sausage to a substantial Mediterranean antipasto platter. Cedar plank–grilled wild coho salmon and the innovative Kung Pao chicken spaghetti rank among the better main courses. Live bands perform some nights. $ *Average main: $20* ✉ *226 S.W. G St.* ☎ *541/479–0420* ⊕ *www.facebook.com/blondiesbistro.*

$ ✕**Taprock Northwest Grill.** This cavernous family-friendly restaurant
AMERICAN   designed to resemble a Cascade mountain lodge lies on the southern edge of downtown, its dining room lined with tall windows overlooking the Rogue River. Expect hearty, reasonably priced fare that uses primarily regional ingredients, including such popular starters as pan-fried oysters and smoked chicken salad with candied Oregon hazelnuts. Burgers, sandwiches, and heftier main dishes like meatloaf and chicken potpie round out the menu. $ *Average main: $13* ✉ *971 S.E. 6th St.* ☎ *541/955–5998* ⊕ *www.taprock.com.*

$ ✕**Twisted Cork Wine Bar.** Opened in 2012 with a mission to show-
WINE BAR   case southern Oregon's fast-growing reputation for acclaimed vino, this dapper, art-filled space has lent a bit of urbane sophistication to downtown Grants Pass. In addition to pouring varietals from throughout the Umpqua and Rogue valleys, Twisted Cork carries wines from more than 100 wineries throughout the Northwest, along with a few from California. The menu focuses on small plates ideal for sharing—fruit-and-cheese plates, cured meats—as well as creative and quite affordable larger plates, including pomegranate-cinnamon flank steak, ginger-glazed salmon, and wild-mushroom flatbread with butternut-mint hummus. There's a nice list of local ports, too. $ *Average main: $15* ✉ *210 S.W. 6th St., Grants Pass* ☎ *541/295–3094* ⊕ *www.thetwistedcorkgrantspass.com* ☾ *Closed Sun.–Mon.*

$ ⊤ **Lodge at Riverside.** The pool and many of the rooms of this airy,
HOTEL   contemporary downtown hotel overlook the Rogue River as it passes through the southern end of downtown Grants Pass. **Pros:** central location; beautiful modern furnishings; attractively landscaped pool overlooks Rogue River. **Cons:** among the highest rates in town; no restaurant on-site. $ *Rooms from: $139* ✉ *955 S.E. 7th St.* ☎ *541/955–0600, 877/955–0600* ⊕ *www.thelodgeatriverside.com* ⤳ *29 rooms, 4 suites* ❏ *Breakfast.*

$$ ⊤ **Weasku Inn.** Although posh in a country-chic sort of way, the rambling
B&B/INN   Weasku Inn fits in perfectly with its piney surroundings—the rambling
Fodor'sChoice   timber-frame home overlooking the Rogue River was built as a vacation
★   retreat in 1924, and has hosted the likes of Walt Disney, Clark Gable, and Carol Lombard. **Pros:** set directly on the Rogue River; impeccably decorated; fireplaces in many rooms. **Cons:** it's a 10-minute drive east of downtown; among the highest rates in the region. $ *Rooms from: $200* ✉ *5560 Rogue River Hwy.* ☎ *541/471–8000, 800/493–2758* ⊕ *www.weaskuinn.com* ⤳ *5 rooms, 12 cabins* ❏ *Breakfast.*

SPORTS AND THE OUTDOORS

RECREATIONAL AREAS

Rogue River and Siskiyou National Forests–Grants Pass. In the Klamath Mountains and the Coast Range of southwestern Oregon, the 1.8-million-acre forest contains the 35-mile-long Wild and Scenic section of the Rogue River, which races through the Wild Rogue Wilderness Area, and the Illinois and Chetco Wild and Scenic rivers, which run through the 180,000-acre Kalmiopsis Wilderness Area. Activities include white-water rafting, camping, and hiking, but many hiking areas require trail-park passes—check the website for details. ⊠ *Off U.S. 199* ☎ *541/618–2200* ⊕ *www.fs.usda.gov/rogue-siskiyou.*

Valley of the Rogue State Park. A 1¼-mile hiking trail follows the bank of the Rogue, the river made famous by novelist and fisherman Zane Grey. A campground along 3 miles of shoreline has 88 full hookups ($24), 59 electrical ($24), 21 tent sites ($19), and 6 yurts ($36). There are picnic tables, walking trails, playgrounds, and restrooms. The park is 12 miles east of downtown Grants Pass. ⊠ *3792 N. River Rd., Gold Hill* ☎ *541/582–1118, 800/551–6949* ⊕ *www.oregonstateparks.org* ⊙ *Daily.*

RAFTING

Fodor'sChoice More than a dozen outfitters guide white-water rafting trips along the
★ Rogue River in and around Grants Pass. In fact, this stretch of Class III rapids ranks among the best in the West. The rafting season lasts from about July through August and often into September, and the stretch of river running south from Grants Pass, with some 80 frothy rapids, is exciting but not treacherous, making it ideal for novices, families, and others looking simply to give this enthralling activity a try.

Orange Torpedo Trips. One of the most reliable operators on the Rogue River, this outfitter offers half-day to several-day trips, as well as relaxed dinner-and-wine float trips along a calmer stretch of river. ⊠ *Merlin* ☎ *541/479–5061, 866/479–5061* ⊕ *www.orangetorpedo.com.*

Rogue River Raft Trips. If you're up for an adventure that combines rafting with overnight accommodations, consider booking a trip with Rogue River Raft Trips, whose exciting excursions run along a 44-mile stretch of the Rogue River and last for four days and three nights, with options for both lodge and camping stays along the way. ⊠ *Merlin* ☎ *800/826–1963* ⊕ *www.rogueriverraft.com.*

MEDFORD

30 miles southeast of Grants Pass on I–5.

Medford is the professional, retail, trade, and service center for eight counties in southern Oregon and northern California. As such, it offers more professional and cultural venues than might be expected for a city of its size. The workaday downtown has shown signs of gentrification and rejuvenation in recent years, and in the outskirts you'll find several major shopping centers and the famed fruit and gourmet-food mail-order company Harry & David.

Lodging tends to be cheaper in Medford than in nearby (and easily accessible) Ashland or Jacksonville, although cookie-cutter chain properties dominate the hotel landscape. But it's 71 miles southwest of Crater Lake and 80 miles northeast of the Oregon Caves, making it an affordable and convenient base for visiting either.

GETTING HERE AND AROUND

Medford is in the heart of the Rogue Valley on I–5, and is home to the state's third-largest airport, Rogue Valley International. **Valley Cab** (☎ *541/772–1818* ⊕ *www.myvalleycab.com*) serves the Rogue Valley region, with fares costing $3 base per trip, plus $2.50 per mile thereafter. Most attractions in Medford lie outside the downtown area, however, so a cab isn't an especially practical or cost-effective way to explore. Your best option is renting a car.

ESSENTIALS

Visitor Information **Medford Visitors & Convention Bureau** ✉ *1314 Center Dr.* ☎ *541/779–4847, 800/469–6307* 🌐 *www.visitmedford.org.*

EXPLORING

Butte Creek Mill. This 1872 water-powered gristmill, which is 12 miles north of Medford, is listed in the National Historic Register and still produces whole-grain food products, which you can buy at the country store here. There's also a modest display of antiques. ✉ *402 Royal Ave. N, Central Point* ☎ *541/826–3531* 🌐 *www.buttecreekmill.com* 🎟 *Free* 🕒 *Mon.–Sat. 9–5, Sun. 11–5.*

Crater Rock Museum. Jackson County's natural history and collections of the Roxy Ann Gem and Mineral Society are on display at this quirky museum in Central Point (6 miles northwest of Medford). Fossils, petrified wood, fluorescent rocks, and precious minerals from throughout Oregon and elsewhere in the West are included, plus works of glass by renowned artist Dale Chihuly. ✉ *2002 Scenic Ave., Central Point* ☎ *541/664–6081* 🌐 *www.craterrock.com* 🎟 *$4* 🕒 *Tues.–Sat. 10–4.*

EdenVale Winery. Four miles southwest of downtown Medford amid a bucolic patch of fruit orchards, this winery and tasting room, called the Rogue Valley Wine Center, adjoins a rather grand 19th-century white-clapboard farmhouse surrounded by flower beds and vegetable gardens. Inside the tasting room you can sample and buy not only EdenVale's noted reds and late-harvest whites but also other respected labels from vineyards throughout the region. ✉ *2310 Voorhies Rd.* ☎ *541/512–2955* 🌐 *www.edenvalewines.com* 🕒 *Mar.–Oct., Mon.–Sat. 11–6, Sun. noon–4; Nov.–Feb., Mon.–Thurs. 11–5, Fri.–Sat. 11–6, Sun. noon–4.*

WHERE TO EAT AND STAY

For expanded hotel reviews, visit Fodors.com.

$$ ECLECTIC Fodor's Choice ★

🍴 **38 Central.** Set inside a handsomely restored 1910 downtown building, this casual yet smartly furnished bistro specializes in comfort-driven fare with notably urbane flourishes. The classic fish-and-chips, for instance, is prepared with fresh local lingcod and battered in a champagne sauce, while "grown up" mac and cheese comes with Rogue Creamery cheddar, aged Parmesan, and hardwood-smoked bacon. An oft-changing roster of starters, soups, salads, and sides (try haricots verts with shallots) are ideal for sharing. [$] *Average main: $19* ✉ *38 N. Central Ave.* ☎ *541/776–0038* 🌐 *www.38oncentral.com* 🕒 *No lunch Sat. No dinner Sun.*

$$ AMERICAN

🍴 **Porters Dining at the Depot.** Set in an opulent 1910 train station, Porters is a favorite spot for special-occasion meals or even just relaxed dinners on a wisteria-shaded patio. The menu features aged-beef steaks, pork tenderloin, seafood fettuccine, lamb burgers, panfried oysters, and similarly straightforward American classics. Leave room for the decadent desserts, including a rich bread pudding drizzled with Jack Daniels crème anglaise. The bar is a popular spot for drinks or, during the early- and late-evening happy hours, less expensive fare, such as prime-rib sandwiches and chicken satay with Asian barbecue sauce. Ⓢ *Average main: $22* ✉ *147 N. Front St.* ☎ *541/857–1910* ⊕ *www. porterstrainstation.com* ☉ *No lunch.*

Ⓢ

B&B/INN

⬚ **Under the Greenwood Tree.** Regulars at this bed-and-breakfast between Medford and Jacksonville find themselves hard-pressed to decide what they like most: the luxurious and romantic rooms, the stunning 10-acre farm, or the hearty three-course country-style breakfasts. **Pros:** stunning setting amid farm fields and overlooking the Cascades; breakfast will fill you up well into the late afternoon. **Cons:** a few miles southwest of downtown (but en route to Jacksonville); old-fashioned rooms won't appeal to modernists or minimalists. Ⓢ *Rooms from: $140* ✉ *3045 Bellinger La.* ☎ *541/776–0000* ⊕ *www.greenwoodtree.com* ⟿ *4 rooms* ⫰⊙⫱ *Breakfast.*

SPORTS AND THE OUTDOORS

RECREATIONAL AREAS

Rogue River–Siskiyou National Forest, Medford. Covering 1.8 million acres, this immense tract of wilderness woodland has fishing, swimming, hiking, and skiing. Motorized vehicles and equipment—even bicycles—are prohibited in the 113,000-acre Sky Lakes Wilderness, south of Crater Lake National Park. Its highest point is the 9,495-foot Mt. McLoughlin. Access to most of the forest is free, but there are fees at some trailheads—check the website for details. ✉ *I–5 to Exit 39, Hwy. 62 to Hwy. 140* ☎ *541/618–2200* ⊕ *www.fs.usda.gov/rogue-siskiyou.*

OFF THE
BEATEN
PATH

Rogue River Views. Nature lovers who want to see the Rogue River at its loveliest can take a side trip to the Avenue of the Boulders, Mill Creek Falls, and Barr Creek Falls, off Highway 62, near Prospect, which is about 45 miles northeast of Medford—it's a scenic one-hour drive, and it's on the way to Crater Lake. Here the wild waters of the upper Rogue foam past volcanic boulders and the dense greenery of the Rogue River National Forest. ✉ *Hwy. 62, Prospect.*

FAMILY

Rogue Valley Fun Center. You'll find an impressive array of kids' games and recreation at Rogue Valley Fun Center, just off Exit 33 of Interstate 5 (about 5 miles north of Medford). Miniature golf, batting cages, a golf driving range, bumper boats, and go-karts are among the offerings, and there's also a video arcade and game room. ✉ *1A Peninger Rd., Central Point* ☎ *541/664–4263* ⊕ *www.rvfamilyfuncenter.com.*

FISHING

With close access to some of the best freshwater fishing venues in the Northwest, Medford has several companies that lead tours and provide gear.

Carson's Guide Service. Based 22 miles north of Medford along Hwy. 62 (going toward Crater Lake), Carson's provides expert instruction and knowledge of many of the area's rivers, including the Rogue, Umpqua, Coquille, and Chetco, as well as several lakes. Steelhead, salmon, shad, and smallmouth bass are the most common catches. ✉ *Trail* ☎ *541/261–3279* ⊕ *www.fishwithcarson.com.*

GOLF

Eagle Point Golf Club. By far the most challenging and best-designed in the area, this course is 10 miles northeast of Medford and was designed by legendary architect Robert Trent Jones Jr. Greens fees are $30 at this par 72, 6,576-yard course. ✉ *100 Eagle Point Dr., Central Point* ☎ *541/826–8225* ⊕ *eaglepointgolf.com.*

HIKING

Fodor'sChoice ★ **Table Rock.** One of the best venues for hiking in the Rogue Valley, Table Rock comprises a pair of monolithic rock formations that rise some 700 to 800 feet above the valley floor about 10 miles north of Medford and just a couple of miles north of TouVelle State Park. Operated by a partnership between the Bureau of Land Management and the Nature Conservancy, the Table Rock formations afford panoramic valley views from their summits. You reach Lower Table Rock by way of a moderately challenging 1.75-mile trail, and Upper Table Rock via a shorter (1.25-mile) and less steep route. The trailheads to these formations are a couple of miles apart—just follow the road signs from Table Rock Road, north of TouVelle State Park (reached from Exit 33 of Interstate 5). ✉ *Off Table Rock Rd., Central Point* ☎ *541/618–2200* ⊕ *www. blm.gov.*

RAFTING

Medford is close to a number of the region's great white-water rafting rivers, including the famed Rogue River. Both overnight and day trips are offered by several outfitters.

Rogue Klamath River Adventures. This popular outfitter for guided white-water rafting trips as well as fishing adventures (for salmon and steelhead) throughout the area also offers boating excursions on inflatable kayaks. The company visits a great variety of waterways, from gentle but scenic Class I rivers to wild and exciting Class V rapids. ☎ *541/779– 3708, 800/231–0769* ⊕ *www.rogueklamath.com.*

SHOPPING

Harry & David. Famous for their holiday gift baskets, Harry & David is based in Medford and offers hour-long tours of its huge facility on weekdays at 9:15, 10:30, 12:30, and 1:45. The tours cost $5 per person, but the fee is refunded if you spend a minimum of $40 in the mammoth Harry & David store, great for snagging picnic supplies to carry with you on any winery tour. ✉ *1314 Center Dr.* ☎ *541/864–2278, 877/322–8000* ⊕ *www.harryanddavid.com.*

Fodor'sChoice ★ **Lillie Belle Farms.** Next door to Rogue River Creamery, this artisan chocolatier handcrafts outstanding chocolates using local, often organic ingredients. A favorite treat is the Smokey Blue Cheese ganache made with Rogue River blue, but don't overlook the dark-chocolate–marionberry bonbons (made with organic marionberries grown on-site) or the delectable hazelnut chews. Most unusual, however, is the chocolate-covered bacon. Yes, you read that correctly—the bacon is coated in chipotle and brown sugar, hand-dipped in chocolate, and sprinkled with sea salt. ✉ *211 N. Front St., Central Point* ☎ *541/664–2815* ⊕ *www. lilliebellefarms.com.*

8

Fodor's Choice
★

Rogue River Creamery. Just a few miles up the road from Medford in the small and otherwise drab little town of Central Point, you'll find one of the nation's most respected cheese makers, Rogue River Creamery, which was started in 1935 by Italian immigrants. Current owners Cary Bryant and David Gremmels bought the company in 2002, and promptly won one of the highest honors for cheese making, the London World Cheese Award. You can purchase any of the company's stellar cheeses here, from Smokey Blue to a lavender-infused cheddar, and you can watch the production through a window on most days. There's a wine-tasting room that carries vintages by a few local vineyards; the best nearby place to enjoy a picnic is the small neighborhood park a few blocks north at Laurel and North 6th streets. ⊠ *311 N. Front St., Central Point* ☎ *541/664–1537, 866/396–4704* ⊕ *www.roguecreamery. com.*

JACKSONVILLE

5 miles west of Medford on Hwy. 238.

This perfectly preserved town founded in the frenzy of the 1851 gold rush has served as the backdrop for several Western flicks. It's easy to see why. Jacksonville is one of only eight towns corralled into the National Register of Historic Places lock, stock, and barrel. These days, living-history exhibits offering a glimpse of pioneer life and the world-renowned Britt Festivals of classical, jazz, and pop music are the draw, rather than gold. Trails winding up from the town's center lead to the festival amphitheater, mid-19th-century gardens, exotic madrona groves, and an intriguing pioneer cemetery.

GETTING HERE AND AROUND

Most visitors to Jacksonville come by way of Medford, 5 miles east, on Highway 238—it's a scenic drive over hilly farmland and past vineyards. Alternatively, you can reach the town coming the other way on Highway 238, driving southeast from Grants Pass. This similarly beautiful drive through the Applegate Valley takes about 45 minutes. **Valley Cab** (⊕ *541/772–1818* ⊕ *www.myvalleycab.com*) serves the Rogue Valley region, with fares costing $3 base per trip, plus $2.50 per mile thereafter. A cab ride from Medford's airport to Jacksonville costs about $20, and downtown Jacksonville can easily be explored on foot. However, if you plan on visiting any of the region's wineries and parks, you're better off renting a car.

ESSENTIALS

Visitor Information **Jacksonville Chamber of Commerce & Visitor Center** ⊠ *185 N. Oregon St.* ☎ *541/899–8118* ⊕ *www.jacksonvilleoregon.org.*

EXPLORING

FAMILY
Fodor's Choice
★

Jacksonville Cemetery. A trip up the winding road—or, better yet, a hike via the old cart track marked Catholic access—leads to the resting place of the clans (the Britts, the Beekmans, and the Orths) that built Jacksonville. You'll also get a fascinating, if sometimes unattractive, view of the social dynamics of the Old West: older graves (the cemetery is still in use) are strictly segregated, Irish Catholics from Jews from

Protestants. A somber granite plinth marks the pauper's field, where those who found themselves on the losing end of gold-rush economics entered eternity anonymously. The cemetery closes at sundown. ✉ *Oregon St., follow signs from downtown* ☎ *541/826–9939* 🌐 *www.friendsjvillecemetery.org.*

Valley View Vineyard. Perched on a bench in the scenic Applegate Valley, you can sample acclaimed Chardonnay, Viognier, Pinot Gris, Merlot, and Cabernet Sauvignon while soaking up some of the best views in southern Oregon. The valley's especially sunny, warm climate produces highly acclaimed vintages. Founded in the 1850s by pioneer Peter Britt, the vineyard was reestablished in 1972. A restored pole barn houses the winery and tasting room. ✉ *1000 Upper Applegate Rd., 10 miles southwest of downtown* ☎ *541/899–8468, 800/781–9463* 🌐 *www.valleyviewwinery.com* 🕒 *Daily 11–5.*

WHERE TO EAT AND STAY

For expanded hotel reviews, visit Fodors.com.

$$ SOUTHERN

🍴 **Back Porch BBQ.** For an excellent, midpriced alternative to Jacksonville's more upscale eateries, head to this roadhouse-style clapboard building six blocks northeast of the town's historic main drag. Authentic central Texas–style barbecue is served here: char-grilled red-hot sausage, slow-cooked pork ribs, chicken-fried steak, and ½-pound burgers, plus a few dishes to remind you that you're in Oregon, including wild local salmon baked with Cajun spices. [$] *Average main: $18* ✉ *605 N. 5th St.* ☎ *541/899–8821* 🌐 *www.backporchbbqinc.com.*

$$$ ECLECTIC Fodor's Choice ★

🍴 **Gogi's.** Many visitors overlook this small, low-key restaurant just down the hill from Britt Gardens—it's a favorite of foodies and locals, and word is out about the artful presentation and innovative style of chef-owner Gabriel Murphy's sophisticated international cuisine. The menu changes regularly, but has featured a tower of roasted beets and chèvre topped with toasted walnuts and a balsamic-truffle reduction, followed by grilled pan-smoked pork chop atop a sweet-potato pancake with haricots verts and caramelized-onion marmalade. The wine list is small but discerning. If you're in town on a Sunday, do not miss the super brunch. [$] *Average main: $26* ✉ *235 W. Main St.* ☎ *541/899–8699* 🌐 *www.gogis.net* 🕒 *Closed Mon.–Tues. No lunch Wed.–Sat.*

$$ B&B/INN

🏨 **Jacksonville Inn.** The spotless period antiques and the host of well-chosen amenities at this 1861-vintage inn evoke what the Wild West might have been had Martha Stewart been in charge. **Pros:** in heart of downtown historic district; one of the town's most historically significant buildings; very good restaurant on-site. **Cons:** rather old-fashioned decor for some tastes. [$] *Rooms from: $159* ✉ *175 E. California St.* ☎ *541/899–1900, 800/321–9344* 🌐 *www.jacksonvilleinn.com* 🛏 *8 rooms, 4 cottages* 🍽 *Breakfast.*

$ B&B/INN Fodor's Choice ★

🏨 **TouVelle House B&B.** This six-room inn set inside a grand 1916 Craftsman-style home a few blocks north of Jacksonville's tiny commercial strip manages that tricky balance between exquisite and comfy. **Pros:** situated on a gentle bluff surrounded by beautiful gardens; downtown dining is a 5-minute walk away; knowledgeable and friendly hosts. **Cons:** no TVs or phones in rooms. [$] *Rooms from: $135* ✉ *435*

8

N. Oregon St. ☎ 541/899–8938, 800/846–8422 ⊕ www.touvellehouse. com ⇌ 6 rooms ⎢○⎢ Breakfast.

SHOPPING

Jacksonville's historic downtown has several engaging galleries, boutiques, and gift shops. It's best just to stroll along California Street and its cross streets to get a sense of the retail scene.

Jacksonville Barn Co. This colorful shop specializes in both antiques and contemporary home decor, from Victorian pieces that have come from many nearby estates to modern garden accessories and country-house furnishings. ✉ *150 S. Oregon St.* ☎ *541/702–0307* ⊕ *www. jacksonvillebarnco.com.*

Jacksonville Company. Drop by to browse the stylish selection of handbags, footwear, and women's apparel. MOTO Denim, Nicole Shoes, and Bernardo Footwear are among the top brands carried here. ✉ *115 W. California St.* ☎ *541/899–8912, 888/271–1047* ⊕ *www. jacksonvillecompany.com.*

Jacksonville Mercantile. The racks of this gourmet-food store abound with sauces, oils, vinegars, jams, and tapenades. Watch for Lillie Belle Farms lavender–sea salt caramels, and the shop's own private-label Merlot-wine jelly. ✉ *120 E. California St.* ☎ *541/899–1047* ⊕ *www. jacksonvillemercantile.com.*

ASHLAND

20 miles southeast of Jacksonville and 14 miles southeast of Medford on I–5.

As you walk Ashland's twisting hillside streets, it seems like every house is a restored Victorian operating as an upscale B&B, though that's not quite all there is to this town: the Oregon Shakespeare Festival attracts thousands of theater lovers to the Rogue Valley every year, from mid-February to early November (though tourists don't start showing up en masse until June). That influx means that Ashland is more geared toward the arts, more eccentric, and more expensive than its size might suggest. The mix of well-heeled theater tourists, bohemian students from Southern Oregon University, and dramatic show folk imbues the town with some one-of-a-kind cultural frissons. The stage isn't the only show in town—skiing at Mt. Ashland and the town's reputation as a secluded getaway and growing culinary destination keep things hopping year-round.

GETTING HERE AND AROUND

Ashland is the first town you'll reach on Interstate 5 if driving north from California, and it's the southernmost community in this region. You can also get here from Klamath Falls by driving west on winding but dramatic Highway 66. **Cascade Airport Shuttle** (☎ *541/488–1998* ⊕ *www.cascadeshuttle.com*) offers door-to-door service from the airport to Ashland for about $30. A car isn't necessary to explore downtown and to get among many of the inns and restaurants, but it is helpful if you're planning to venture farther afield or visit more than one town, which most visitors do.

Ashland's Main Street

ESSENTIALS

Visitor Information Ashland Chamber of Commerce and Visitors Information Center ✉ *110 E. Main St.* ☎ *541/482–3486* ⊕ *www.ashlandchamber.com.*

EXPLORING

Fodor'sChoice ★ **Lithia Park.** The Elizabethan Theatre overlooks this park, a 93-acre jewel that is Ashland's physical and psychological anchor. The park is named for the town's mineral springs, which supply a water fountain by the band shell as well as a fountain on the town plaza—be warned that the slightly bubbly water has a strong and rather disagreeable taste. Whether thronged with colorful hippie folk and picnickers on a summer evening or buzzing with joggers and dog walkers in the morning, Lithia is a well-used, well-loved, and well-tended spot. On summer weekend mornings the park plays host to a '60s-ish artisans' market. Each June the Oregon Shakespeare Festival opens its outdoor season by hosting the Feast of Will in the park, with music, dancing, bagpipes, and food. Tickets ($15) are available through the festival box office (*541/482–4331*). ✉ *W. Fork and S. Pioneer Sts.*

Schneider Museum of Art. At the edge of the Southern Oregon University campus, this museum includes a light-filled gallery devoted to special exhibits by Oregon, West Coast, and international artists. The permanent collection has grown considerably over the years, and includes pre-Columbian ceramics and works by such notables as Alexander Calder, George Inness, and David Alfaro Siqueiros. Hallways and galleries throughout the rest of the 66,000-square-foot complex display many works by students and faculty. ✉ *1250 Siskiyou Blvd.* ☎ *541/552–6245* ⊕ *www.sou.edu/sma* ✉ *$5* ⏰ *Mon.–Sat. 10–4.*

Weisinger's Winery. Although downtown Ashland has wine bars and tasting rooms, the only major winery of note here is Weisinger's, which set up shop in 1988 and is set a few miles south of town on a hilltop with broad views of the surrounding mountains. Specialties here include a Chardonnay, a well-respected Viognier, and a nicely balanced Tempranillo. ✉ *3150 Siskiyou Blvd.* ☎ *541/488–5989, 800/551–9463* 🌐 *www.weisingers.com* 🕒 *May–Sept., daily 11–5; Oct.–Apr., Wed.–Sun. 11–5.*

WORD OF MOUTH

"In Ashland, there are a number of good restaurants including a microbrewery and wine bars, and some nice shops as well as a pleasant walk along the stream that runs through the town center. Weekends include an outdoor market of high quality arts and crafts within a few steps of the theater area." —saige

NEED A BREAK?

Noble Coffee Roasting. The fair-trade, organic beans used in the espresso drinks at Noble Coffee Roasting are among the best in town. ✉ ***281 4th St., Ashland*** ☎ ***541/488–3288*** 🌐 ***www.noblecoffeeroasting.com.***

Zoey's Cafe. Zoey's Cafe scores high marks for its creative, house-made ice cream in such enticing flavors as mountain blackberry and Rogue Valley pear. ✉ ***199 E. Main St., Ashland*** ☎ ***541/482–4794.***

WHERE TO EAT

$$$ ECLECTIC Fodor's Choice ★

🍴 **Amuse.** This locally celebrated restaurant features Northwest-driven French cuisine, infused with seasonal, organic meat and produce. Chef-owners Erik Brown and Jamie North prepare a daily-changing menu. You might sample wood-grilled beef tenderloin with sweet-potato-purée, cipollini onions, pickled turnip, and a mustard demi-glace, or truffle-roasted game hen with kale and tarragon jus. Try your best to save room for the warm hazelnut crepes filled with banana ganache and topped with brandy whipped cream. [$] *Average main: $28* ✉ *15 N. 1st St.* ☎ *541/488–9000* 🌐 *www.amuserestaurant.com* 🕒 *Closed Mon. and Tues. No lunch.*

$$$ AMERICAN

🍴 **Larks.** In this restaurant off the lobby of the historic Ashland Springs Hotel, owners Doug and Becky Neuman practice dedication to the farm-to-table movement. Larks pairs the freshest foods from local farms with great wines, artisan chocolate desserts, and drinks in a swanky yet soothing dining room. Modern interpretations of comfort food are the order of the day, with servings such as homemade meat loaf with mushroom gravy, Anniebelle's fried chicken, and maple-glazed pork chops with organic-apple compote and rosemary-roasted sweet potatoes. Dessert offerings include Dagoba chocolate sundaes, s'mores, and cheesecake of the day. The Sunday brunch is one of the best in town. [$] *Average main: $26* ✉ *212 E. Main St.* ☎ *541/488–5558* 🌐 *www.larksrestaurant.com.*

$ AMERICAN Fodor's Choice ★

🍴 **Morning Glory.** Breakfast reaches new heights at this distinctive café across the street from Southern Oregon University. In a blue Craftsman-style bungalow, the café has eclectic furnishings and an attractive patio space bounded by arbors. The extraordinarily good food emphasizes breakfast fare—omelets filled with crab, artichokes, Parmesan, and smoked-garlic cream; tandoori tofu scrambles with cherry-cranberry chutney; lemon-poppy waffles with seasonal berries; and cranberry-hazelnut French toast with lemon butter. Expect a wait on weekend mornings; it's first-come, first-served. $ *Average main: $11* ⊠ *1149 Siskiyou Blvd.* ☎ *541/488–8636* ⊕ *morninggloryrestaurant.com* ⚑ *Reservations not accepted* ⊘ *No dinner.*

$$
MODERN
AMERICAN
⨯**Peerless Restaurant & Bar.** This cosmopolitan, neighborhood bistro and wine bar anchors the up-and-coming Railroad District, on the north side of downtown, just a few blocks from Main Street and the Shakespeare theaters. It's adjacent to the Peerless Hotel, a stylish little boutique property with the same creative spirit and hipster vibe of the restaurant. Regulars here come as much for the well-crafted cocktails and thoughtful wine list as for the consistently tasty locally sourced American food. Start with the Manila clams in a broth of pernod, garlic confit, and smoked bacon, before tucking into a plate of sage-rubbed roast chicken, or baked ziti with sweet corn, chunks of lobster, and three cheeses. Desserts ($8–$11) are the one spendy item on the menu, but they're delicious, too. $ *Average main: $18* ⊠ *265 4th St., Ashland* ☎ *541/488–6067* ⊕ *www.peerlessrestaurant.com* ⊘ *Closed Sun.–Mon.*

WHERE TO STAY

For expanded hotel reviews, visit Fodors.com.

The Oregon Shakespeare Festival has stimulated one of the most extensive networks of B&Bs in the Northwest—more than 25 in all. High season for Ashland-area bed-and-breakfasts is between June and October.

Ashland B&B Network. The Ashland B&B Network provides referrals to roughly 22 of the town's top inns. ☎ *800/944–0329* ⊕ *www.abbnet. com.*

$$$
B&B/INN
⊡**Ashland Creek Inn.** Every one of the ten plush suites in this converted mill has a geographic theme—the Normandy is outfitted with rustic country French prints and furniture, while Moroccan, Danish, and New Mexican motifs are among the designs in other units. **Pros:** exceptionally good breakfasts; peaceful but central location; enormous suites. **Cons:** spendy for this part of the state; limited common areas. $ *Rooms from: $245* ⊠ *70 Water St.* ☎ *541/482–3315* ⊕ *www.ashlandcreekinn. com* ⇲ *10 suites* ⊙❘*Breakfast.*

$$
HOTEL
⊡**Ashland Springs Hotel.** Ashland's stately landmark hotel is a totally restored version of an original 1925 landmark building that towers seven stories over the center of downtown. **Pros:** rich with history; upper floors have dazzling mountain views; the excellent Larks restaurant *(*⇨ *see above)* is on-site. **Cons:** central location translates to some street noise and bustle; some rooms are on the small side. $ *Rooms from: $170* ⊠ *212 E. Main St.* ☎ *541/488–1700, 888/795–4545* ⊕ *www.ashlandspringshotel.com* ⇲ *70 rooms* ⊙❘*Breakfast.*

$$
B&B/INN
Fodor'sChoice
★
⊡**Chanticleer Inn.** This courtly, 1920 Craftsman-style bed-and-breakfast is one of the most picturesque structures in this hilly and historic residential neighborhood just a few blocks south of the Shakespeare theaters and Main Street restaurants. **Pros:** rooms all have expansive views

8

of the Cascade Mountains; only eco-friendly products are used. **Cons:** it's intimate and homey, so fans of larger and more anonymous lodgings may prefer a bigger inn or hotel. [$] *Rooms from: $170* ✉ *120 Gresham St.* ☎ *541/482–1919, 800/898–1950* 🌐 *www.ashland-bed-breakfast.com* 🛏 *6 rooms* 🍴 *Breakfast.*

$$ B&B/INN FAMILY **The Winchester Inn.** This posh yet unpretentious inn is often booked well in advance, so plan ahead. **Pros:** the adjacent wine bar and restaurant serve very good international fare; one of the more child-friendly B&Bs in town; surrounded by lush gardens. **Cons:** among the more expensive lodgings in town. [$] *Rooms from: $195* ✉ *35 S. 2nd St.* ☎ *541/488–1113, 800/972–4991* 🌐 *www.winchesterinn.com* 🛏 *11 rooms, 8 suites* 🍴 *Breakfast.*

NIGHTLIFE AND THE ARTS

With its presence of college students, theater types, and increasing numbers of tourists (many of them fans of local wine), Ashland has developed quite a festive nightlife scene. Much of the activity takes place at bars inside some of downtown's more reputable restaurants, such as Black Sheep and Creekside Pizza, which you'll have no trouble finding, as they're right in the center of town.

Standing Stone Brewing Company. A good bet for rich and flavorful craft beers, this centrally located brewpub has live jazz on the patio, pours some excellent microbrews—including Milk & Honey Ale and Oatmeal Stout—and serves reliably good food, too. ✉ *101 Oak St.* ☎ *541/482–2448* 🌐 *www.standingstonebrewing.com.*

Tabu. The Nuevo Latino restaurant Tabu keeps busy with revelers into the later hours. Live comedy, reggae, salsa, and other entertainment takes place most Thursday through Saturday nights. ✉ *76 N. Pioneer St.* ☎ *541/482–3900* 🌐 *www.tabuashland.com.*

Fodor's Choice ★ **Oregon Shakespeare Festival.** From mid-February to early November, more than 100,000 Bard-loving fans descend on Ashland for the Oregon Shakespeare Festival, presented in three theaters. Its accomplished repertory company mounts some of the finest Shakespearean productions you're likely to see outside of Stratford-upon-Avon—plus works by Ibsen, Williams, and contemporary playwrights. Between June and October plays are staged in the 1,200-seat Elizabethan Theatre, an atmospheric re-creation of the Fortune Theatre in London; the 600-seat Angus Bowmer Theatre, a state-of-the-art facility typically used for five different productions in a single season; and the 350-seat New Theater, which mostly hosts productions of new or experimental work. The festival generally operates close to capacity, so it's important to book ahead. ✉ *15 S. Pioneer St.* ☎ *541/482–4331* 🌐 *www.osfashland.org.*

SPORTS AND THE OUTDOORS

MULTISPORT OUTFITTERS

Adventure Center. This respected Ashland company offers "mild to wild" outdoor expeditions, including white-water rafting, fishing, and bike excursions. ✉ *40 N. Main St.* ☎ *541/488–2819, 800/444–2819* 🌐 *www.raftingtours.com.*

RAFTING

Noah's River Adventures. This long-running outfitter provides white-water rafting and wilderness fishing trips throughout the region—the company can lead single- or multiple-day adventures along the mighty Rogue River as well as just across the border, in northern California, on the Salmon and Scott rivers. ⊠ *53 N. Main St.* ☎ *800/858–2811* ⊕ *www.noahsrafting.com.*

SKIING

Mt. Ashland Ski Area. This winter-sports playground in the Siskiyou Mountains is halfway between San Francisco and Portland. The ski runs get more than 280 inches of snow each year. There are 23 trails, virtually all of them intermediate and advanced, in addition to chute skiing in a glacial cirque called the bowl. Two triple and two double chairlifts accommodate a vertical drop of 1,150 feet; the longest of the runs is 1 mile. Facilities include rentals, repairs, instruction, a ski shop, a restaurant, and a bar. A couple of days a week, usually Thursday and Friday, there's also lighted twilight skiing until 9 pm. Anytime of year the drive up the twisting road to the ski area is incredibly scenic, affording views of 14,162-foot Mt. Shasta, some 90 miles south in California. ⊠ *Mt. Ashland Access Rd., off Exit 6 from I–5, 18 miles southwest of downtown* ☎ *541/482–2897* ⊕ *www.mtashland.com* ✉ *Lift ticket $43* ☯ *Nov.–Apr., daily 9–4; twilight skiing 3 pm–9 pm most Thurs. and Fri.*

SHOPPING

Dagoba Organic Chocolate. A few miles' drive south of town you'll find Dagoba Organic Chocolate, the retail outlet of the company that produces those small, handsomely packed, superfine chocolate bars sold in fancy-food shops and groceries throughout the country. Although Hershey Company now owns the company, Dagoba was founded in Ashland, and its operation remains here, where a small retail shop sells its goods. ⊠ *1105 Benson St.* ☎ *866/608–6944* ⊕ *www.dagobachocolate.com.*

8

KLAMATH FALLS

65 miles east of Ashland via Hwy. 66; 75 miles east of Medford via Hwy. 140.

Often overlooked by visitors traveling the I–5 corridor, the greater Klamath Falls area is one of the most beautiful parts of Oregon. The small if not especially engaging city of Klamath Falls stands at an elevation of 4,100 feet, on the southern shore of Upper Klamath Lake. The highest elevation in Klamath County is the peak of Mt. Scott, at 8,926 feet. There are more than 82 lakes and streams in Klamath County, including Upper Klamath Lake, which covers 133 square miles.

The Klamath Basin, with its six national wildlife refuges, hosts the largest wintering concentration of bald eagles in the contiguous United States and the largest concentration of migratory waterfowl on the continent. Each February nature enthusiasts from around the world flock here for the Winter Wings Festival, the nation's oldest birding festival.

The Nature Conservancy has called the basin a western Everglades, because it is the largest wetland area west of the Mississippi. But humans have significantly damaged the ecosystem through farming and development. More than 25% of vertebrate species in the area are now endangered or threatened. As recently as the 1980s, about 6 million birds used the area every year; today that number is down to 2 to 3 million. Environmental organizations are working to reverse some of the damage.

GETTING HERE AND AROUND

Klamath Falls lies along U.S. 97, one of the Northwest's main north–south routes—it's a prime stop between Bend, 140 miles north, and Weed, California, about 70 miles south. You can also get here from the Rogue Valley, either by way of Highway 66 from Ashland or Highway 140 from Medford, which is home to the nearest airport (about a 90-minute drive).

ESSENTIALS

Visitor Information **Discover Klamath** ✉ *205 Riverside Dr., Suite B, Klamath Falls* ☎ *541/882–1501, 800/445–6728* 🌐 *www.discoverklamath.com.*

EXPLORING

Klamath County Museum. The anthropology, history, geology, and wildlife of the Klamath Basin are explained at this extensive museum set inside the city's historic armory building, with special attention given to the hardships faced by early white settlers. ✉ *1451 Main St.* ☎ *541/883–4208* 🌐 *www.co.klamath.or.us/museum/index.htm* 🎟 *$5* 🕒 *Tues.–Sat. 9–5.*

Fodor's Choice ★ **Klamath Basin National Wildlife Refuge Complex.** As many as 1,000 bald eagles make Klamath Basin their rest stop, amounting to the largest wintering concentration of these birds in the contiguous United States. Located along the Pacific Flyway bird migration route, the vast acres of freshwater wetlands in the refuge complex serve as a stopover for nearly 1 million waterfowl in the fall. Any time of year is bird-watching season; more than 400 species of birds have been spotted in the Klamath Basin. For a leisurely ramble by car take the tour routes in the Lower Klamath and Tule Lake Refuges. There's a superb bookstore at the visitor center. ✉ *4009 Hill Rd., 20 miles south of Klamath Falls via U.S. 97 or Hwy. 39, Tulelake, California* ☎ *530/667–2231* 🌐 *www.fws.gov/klamathbasinrefuges* 🎟 *Free* 🕒 *Visitor center: weekdays 8–4:30, weekends 9–4.*

WHERE TO EAT AND STAY

For expanded hotel reviews, visit Fodors.com.

$$ AMERICAN 🍴 **Basin Martini Bar.** Although the name of this swell-elegant storefront spot in the heart of the downtown historic district suggests an option for evening cocktails, Basin Martini Bar is just as well regarded for its reliably tasty dinner fare—New York strip steaks, burgers topped with Crater Lake blue cheese, and bacon-wrapped scallops are among the highlights. There's seating in a handful of comfy booths or at stools along the modern bar. The creative drinks are notable, too—consider the lemon-basil martini. [$] *Average main: $17* ✉ *632 Main St.* ☎ *541/884–6264* 🕒 *No lunch.*

Klamath Basin National Wildlife Refuge

$$$
FRENCH
✕ **Mr. B.'s Steakhouse.** The dark-wood dining room in this 1920s house suggests more formal pleasures but maintains a relaxed mood. A talented French chef prepares tried-and-true classics like chicken Cordon Bleu, filet mignon, shrimp scampi, veal dishes, and the house specialty, rack of lamb with rosemary and Dijon mustard. Fresh strawberry-blueberry shortcake often appears on the menu, and there's a good wine list. It's in the unappealing but convenient strip of motels and fast-food restaurants about 2 miles southeast of downtown. $ *Average main: $26* ✉ *3927 S. 6th St.* ☎ *541/883–8719* ⊕ *www.mrbssteaks.com* ⊘ *Closed Sun.–Mon. No lunch.*

$
RESORT
FAMILY
⌂ **Running Y Ranch Resort.** Golfers rave about the Arnold Palmer–designed course at this 3,600-acre Holiday Inn resort situated in a juniper-and-ponderosa–shaded canyon overlooking Upper Klamath Lake. **Pros:** kids enjoy their own playground; walkers and joggers have 8 miles of paved trails; property received an ambitious makeover in 2011. **Cons:** may be a bit too far off the beaten path for some. $ *Rooms from: $135* ✉ *5500 Running Y Rd., 8 miles north of Klamath Falls, Klamath Falls* ☎ *541/850–5500, 800/851–6013* ⊕ *www.runningy.com* ⌿ *82 rooms, 43 houses* ⦶ *No meals.*

SPORTS AND THE OUTDOORS

MULTISPORT OUTFITTERS

The Ledge Outdoor Store. For advice, gear, clothing, books, and maps for hiking, birding, mountaineering, canoeing, camping, and fishing throughout the area, visit this extensively stocked shop in downtown Klamath Falls, which carries all kinds of equipment, and also offers guided fly-fishing trips. ⊠ *369 S. 6th St.* ☎ *541/882–5586* ⊕ *www. theledgeoutdoorstore.com.*

RECREATIONAL AREAS

Fremont–Winema National Forest. With the nearest access to Klamath Falls about 12 miles north of downtown, this forest bordering Crater Lake National Park covers 2.3 million acres on the eastern slopes of the Cascades. Hiking, camping, fishing, and boating are popular. In winter snowmobiling and cross-country skiing are available. ⊠ *U.S. 97* ☎ *541/883–6714* ⊕ *www.fs.usda.gov/fremont-winema* ☉ *Daily; campgrounds and picnic areas Memorial Day–Labor Day.*

BOATING

Birding & Boating. For a chance to enjoy the beauty of Klamath Lake while also observing the region's abundant birdlife, rent a sailboat, canoe, or kayak from Birding & Boating, which has a prime spot on the lake and a staff that can offer expert advice on wildlife-viewing. You can also fish from a dock on the lake. ⊠ *658 Front St.* ☎ *541/885–5450* ⊕ *www.birdingandboating.com.*

FISHING

Roe Outfitters & Flyway Shop. This well-established outfitter leads fishing and hunting trips on nearby lakes and rivers, as well as guided canoe and white-water rafting excursions. ⊠ *9349 U.S. 97 S* ☎ *541/884–3825* ⊕ *www.roeoutfitters.com.*

GOLF

Running Y Ranch. The outstanding Arnold Palmer-designed 18-hole course at Running Y Ranch delights golfers of all abilities. Ponderosa pines line the relatively short, undulating course, which is heavy on doglegs and has a number of holes in which water comes into play. There's also an 18-hole putting course that's ideal for honing your short game, and fun for families. ⊠ *5115 Running Y Rd., 8 miles north of Klamath Falls* ☎ *541/850–5580, 877/866–1266* ⊕ *www.runningy.com* 🏌 *6,581 yards. Par 72. Green Fee: $99–$119 (discount for hotel guests).*

CAVE JUNCTION

30 miles southwest of Grants Pass via U.S. 199, 60 miles west of Jacksonville via Hwy. 238 and U.S. 199.

One of the least populated and most pristine parts of southern Oregon, the town of Cave Junction and the surrounding Illinois Valley attract outdoors enthusiasts of all kinds for hiking, backpacking, camping, fishing, and hunting. Expect rugged terrain and the chance to view some of the tallest Douglas fir trees in the state. Other than those passing through en route from Grants Pass to the northern California coast via U.S. 199, most visitors come here to visit the Oregon Caves National Monument, one of the world's only marble caves (formed by erosion from acidic rainwater). Sleepy Cave Junction makes an engaging little base camp, its main drag lined with a handful of quirky shops, short-order restaurants, and gas stations.

GETTING HERE AND AROUND

Cave Junction lies along U.S. 199, the main road leading from Grants Pass. You can also reach Cave Junction by heading west from Jacksonville on Highway 238 to U.S. 199. From Cave Junction, head east on Highway 46 to reach Oregon Caves National Monument. Cave Junction is a about a 75-minute drive southwest of Medford's regional airport. Alternatively, the small airport (served by United Airlines, with service from San Francisco) in Crescent City, California, is the same distance.

ESSENTIALS

Visitor Information **Illinois Valley Chamber of Commerce** ✉ *201 Caves Hwy. (Hwy. 46), just off U.S. 199, Cave Junction* ☎ *541/592–3326, 541/592–4076* 🌐 *www.cavejunction.com.*

EXPLORING

Bridgeview Vineyard and Winery. The producers of the well-distributed and reasonably priced Blue Moon wines (known especially for Riesling, Chardonnay, Pinot Gris, and Merlot), as well as more premium vintages such as Black Beauty Syrah and a very nice reserve Pinot Noir, established the winery in 1986, and—despite considerable skepticism from observers—have gone on to tremendous success. There's a second tasting room, open summer only, in Grants Pass. ✉ *4210 Holland Loop Rd., Cave Junction* ☎ *541/592–4688, 877/273–4843* 🌐 *www.bridgeviewwine.com* 🕒 *Daily 11–4.*

Fodor's Choice ★ **Oregon Caves National Monument.** Marble caves, large calcite formations, and huge underground rooms shape this rare adventure in geology. Above ground, the surrounding valley holds an old-growth forest with some of the state's largest trees. Guided cave tours take place on the hour in late spring and fall, and every half hour in July and August. The 90-minute 0.6-mile tour is moderately strenuous with low passageways, twisting turns, and more than 500 stairs; children must be at least 42 inches tall to go on the tour. Cave tours aren't given in winter; however, unless the road is closed temporarily due to snow, the monument itself is open year-round. ✉ *19000 Caves Hwy.(Hwy. 46) 20 miles east of U.S. 199, Cave Junction* ☎ *541/592–2100* 🌐 *www.nps.gov/orca* 🎟 *$8.50* 🕒 *Late Mar.–late May, and mid-Oct.–early Nov., daily 10–4; late May–early Sept., daily 9–6; early Sept.–mid-Oct., daily 9–5.*

WHERE TO STAY

For expanded hotel reviews, visit Fodors.com.

$ HOTEL FAMILY 🏨 **Oregon Caves Chateau.** If you're looking for a quiet retreat in an unusual place, consider this six-story wood-frame lodge on the grounds of the national monument. **Pros:** steps from national monument; historic and funky personality; wonderfully tranquil setting. **Cons:** no-frills rooms; no Internet or phones (and very limited cell reception); location well out of the way if you aren't visiting the caves. [$] *Rooms from: $109* ✉ *20000 Caves Hwy.* ☎ *541/592–3400, 877/245–9022* 🌐 *www.oregoncaveschateau.com* 🛏 *23 rooms* 🕒 *Closed Oct.–mid May* 🍴 *No meals.*

$ B&B/INN FAMILY

Out 'n' About. You sleep among the leaves in the tree houses of this extraordinary resort—the highest is 37 feet from the ground. **Pros:** kids love the Swiss Family Robinson atmosphere; it truly feels at one with the surrounding old-growth forest; amazingly quiet and peaceful. **Cons:** accommodations are extremely rustic; some units don't have bathrooms; two-night minimum during week and three-night minimum weekends during spring to fall. [$] *Rooms from: $120* ✉ *300 Page Creek Rd.* ☎ *541/592–2208* 🌐 *www.treehouses.com* 🛏 *15 tree houses, 1 cabin* 🍴 *Breakfast.*

SEATTLE

9

WELCOME TO SEATTLE

TOP REASONS TO GO

★ **Examine Seattle's architecture:** Chihuly Garden and Glass is conveniently located at the base of the Space Needle, which you can visit or just admire from below.

★ **Appreciate art:** Visit the Seattle Art Museum and make time for a stroll in SAM's Olympic Sculpture Park satellite location, right on Lake Washington.

★ **Drink coffee:** Seattle may be the birthplace of Starbucks, but there is also a variety of other excellent local chains.

★ **Indulge in fresh seafood:** First gawk at all the fabulous local produce and seafood at the Pike Place Market, and then visit some of Seattle's renowned restaurants to eat it.

★ **Stroll the "Republic of Fremont":** This pretty neighborhood is where you'll find boutiques, restaurants, a scenic canal-side path, the Theo Chocolate Factory, and the Fremont Troll.

1 Downtown and Belltown. Skyscrapers are here, along with most of the city's hotels and many popular spots, including the waterfront, Pike Place Market, and Seattle Art Museum. Just north of Downtown, Belltown is home to the Olympic Sculpture Park.

2 Seattle Center, South Lake Union, and Queen Anne. Queen Anne rises up from Denny Way to the Lake Washington Ship Canal. At the bottom are the Space Needle, the Seattle Center, and the Experience Music Project museum. South Lake Union has the REI superstore and lakefront.

3 Pioneer Square. Seattle's oldest neighborhood has lovely redbrick and sandstone buildings, galleries and antiques shops.

4 International District. This is a fun place to shop and eat. The stunning Wing Luke Museum and Uwajimaya shopping center anchor the neighborhood.

5 First Hill. There is one must-see here: the Frye Art Museum.

6 Capitol Hill. The Hill has two faces: young and sassy and elegant and upscale. It has fantastic restaurants and nightlife.

7 Fremont. There is a mix of pricey boutiques and yummy restaurants here; up the hill, residential Phinney Ridge includes the Woodland Park Zoo.

8 Ballard. Ballard's main attraction is the Hiram M. Chittenden Locks. This historically Scandinavian neighborhood is beloved for its eateries, trendy shops, and farmers' market.

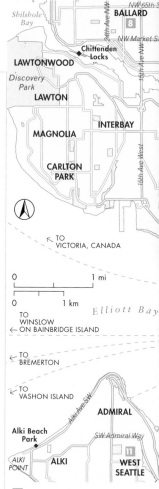

GETTING ORIENTED

Hemmed in by mountains, hills, and multiple bodies of water, Seattle is anything but a linear, grid-lined city. Twisty, turny, and very long, the city can be baffling to navigate, especially if you delve into its residential neighborhoods—and you should. Water makes the best landmark. Both Elliott Bay and Lake Union are pretty hard to miss. When you are trying to get your bearings Downtown, Elliott Bay is a much more reliable landmark than the Space Needle. Remember that I–5 bisects the city (north–south). The major routes connecting the southern part of the city to the northern part are I–5, Aurora Avenue/ Hwy. 99, 15th Avenue NW (Ballard Bridge), and Westlake (Fremont Bridge) and Eastlake avenues. Streets in the Seattle area generally travel east to west, whereas avenues travel north to south.

9 Wallingford. At the ship canal is the wonderful waterfront Gas Works Park. Its booming commercial strip along N. 45th Street has a few excellent restaurants.

10 The "U District." The university's vast campus is truly lovely, and the surrounding neighborhood has ethnic restaurants.

11 West Seattle. West Seattle's California Avenue has some lovely shops and restaurants. Gorgeous Alki Beach offers views of the Seattle skyline.

12 Eastside. The Eastside suburbs are home to Microsoft. Bellevue is the most citylike, with its own skyline, an art museum, and high-end shops and restaurants.

Updated by
Cedar Burnett

Seattle is a city of many neighborhoods: Eclectic, urban, outdoorsy, artsy, gritty, down-to-earth, or posh—it's all here, from the quirky character of the Seattle Waterfront and the eccentric "Republic of Fremont," to hipsters walking baby carriages past aging mansions on Capitol Hill. There's something for just about everyone within this vibrant Emerald City.

Indeed, part of Seattle's diversity lies in the topography: The city is a feat of environmental engineering. When the Denny party arrived on its shores, "Seattle" was a series of densely forested valleys covered by Douglas fir, Western hemlock, and red cedar. Where SoDo (the stadium district south of Downtown) currently is was nothing but mudflats. Pioneer Square was actually an island of sorts where Duwamish tribespeople crossed to the mainland over sandbars.

Once Seattle started to grow, its residents literally changed the landscape. Massive Denny Hill once occupied the Belltown neighborhood, but it simply had to go. The multi-stage "regrade" started in 1899 and was completed 32 years later. The Denny Hill Regrade was just one of dozens of projects; another equally ambitious earth-moving mission was the construction of the canal that links Lake Washington to Puget Sound. Today, the city is once again moving a lot of earth around with the construction of a light rail line across the city; it's changing the look, feel, and energy of neighborhoods as a result.

It's hard to think of Seattle as anything but natural, though. After all, the city owes much of its appeal to its natural features—the myriad hills that did survive settlement offer views of mountain ranges and water, water, water. Outside of Downtown and other smaller commercial cores, Seattle's neighborhoods fan out in tangles of tree-lined streets. Massive parks like Discovery, Magnuson, and Washington Park Arboretum make Seattle one of the greenest and most livable cities in the nation. From the peaks of the Olympics or Cascades to an artistically

A steel sculpture by Richard Serra at the Olympic Sculpture Park

landscaped garden in front of a classic Northwest bungalow, nature is in full effect every time you turn your head.

SEATTLE PLANNER

WHEN TO GO

Unless you're planning an all-indoor museum trip, Seattle is most enjoyable May through October. June can be surprisingly rainy, but July through September is almost always dry, with warm days reaching into the mid-70s and 80s; nights are cooler, though it doesn't get dark until 9 or 10 pm. Although the weather can be dodgy, spring (particularly April) and fall are also excellent times to visit, as lodging and tour costs are usually much lower (and the crowds much smaller). In winter, the days are short, dark, and wet, but temperatures rarely dip below the low 40s and winter events—especially around the holidays—are plentiful.

FESTIVALS

▓TIP→ The Seattle Convention and Visitors Bureau has a full calendar of events at ⊕ *www.visitseattle.org/cultural*. Foodies will want to hit up **Taste Washington** (spring ⊕ *www.tastewashington.org*) for the best of food and wine, as well as **Bite of Seattle** (July ⊕ *www.biteofseattle.com*), the Northwest Chocolate Festival (September ⊕ *www.nwchocolate. com*) and Seattle International Beer Fest (July ⊕ *www.seattlebeerfest. com*). The **Seattle International Film Festival** presents more than 200 features (May–June ⊕ *www.siff.net*).

Music lovers have three major events to keep them happy: **Bumbershoot** (September ⊕ *www.bumbershoot.org*) is Seattle's premier music festival, packed with major acts, as well as dance and theater, while Northwest Folklife Festival (May ⊕ *www.nwfolklife.org*) is a free, family-friendly event featuring folk music and dance from around the globe. Hipsters will want to check out Capitol Hill Block Party (July ⊕ *www.capitolhillblockparty.com*) for the best indie pop, rock, hip-hop, and alt-country.

The **Seattle Pride Festival** (June ⊕ *www.seattlepride.org*) has the Northwest's biggest gay, lesbian, and transgender pride parade. A local favorite, the quirky Fremont Fair Summer Solstice Parade (June ⊕ *www.fremontfair.org*) provides a glimpse into the true character of the city. **Seafair** (July–August ⊕ *www.seafair.com*) is the biggest summer festival; hydroplane races are just one major event.

GETTING HERE AND AROUND

AIR TRAVEL

The major gateway is Seattle–Tacoma International Airport (SEA), known locally as Sea-Tac. The airport is south of the city and reasonably close to it—non-rush-hours trips to Downtown sometimes take less than a half hour. Sea-Tac is a midsize, modern airport that is usually pleasant to navigate. Charter flights and small carriers, such as Kenmore Air, that operate shuttle flights between the cities of the Pacific Northwest land at Boeing Field, which is between Sea-Tac and Seattle.

AIRPORT TRANSFER You can take Sound Transit's **Link Light Rail** (⊕ *www.soundtransit.org*), which will take you right to Downtown in 36 minutes for just $2.75. Trains depart every 7½ or 15 minutes, depending on the time of day and run from 5 am to 1 am Monday through Saturday and 6 am to midnight on Sundays.

BIKING AND WALKING

Bicycling is popular but still somewhat of a cult endeavor, thanks to a shortage of safe bike routes and some daunting hills. Check out ⊕ *www.ridethecity.com/seattle*. Walking is fun, though distances and rain can sometimes get in the way. Several neighborhoods—from Pioneer Square to Downtown, or from Belltown to Queen Anne, for example—are close enough to each other that even hills and moisture can't stop walkers.

BUS TRAVEL

The bus system will get you anywhere you need to go, although some routes require a time commitment and several transfers. Within the downtown core, however, the bus is efficient and affordable, with off-peak fares starting at $2.25. The $4.50 weekend and holiday pass is a bargain if you're doing a lot of touring. The Trip Planner (⊕ *tripplanner.kingcounty.gov*) is a useful resource.

CAR TRAVEL

Access to a car is *almost* a necessity if you want to explore the residential neighborhoods beyond their commercial centers. Before you book a car for city-only driving, keep in mind that many high-end hotels offer complimentary town-car service around Downtown and the immediate areas.

The best advice about driving in Seattle is to avoid driving during rush hour whenever possible.

FERRY TRAVEL

Ferries are a major part of Seattle's transportation network, and they're the only way to reach such points as Vashon Island and the San Juans. You'll get outstanding views of the skyline and the elusive Mt. Rainier from the ferry to Bainbridge. Whale-watching/ferry ride vacation packages like those offered by the *Victoria Clipper* can be booked in advance. The Washington State Ferries to Puget Sound and San Juan Islands rarely accept reservations (only on international sailings to Sidney, B.C., for example), so be sure to plan island travel thoughtfully: leave enough time in your schedule to arrive at the piers early—and to wait for the next ferry if you're last in line.

LIGHT-RAIL TRAVEL

Sound Transit's Central Link Light Rail (⊕ *www.soundtransit.org*)—the first link of which was completed in 2009—will eventually accomplish what the buses can't: an efficient way to go north–south in this vertically oriented city. (Fare: $2.50)

MONORAIL TRAVEL

Built for the 1962 World's Fair, the monorail (⊕ *www.seattlemonorail. com*) is the shortest transportation system in the city. It runs from Westlake Center (on 5th and Pike) to Seattle Center. But this is great for visitors who plan to spend a day at the Space Needle and the Seattle Center's museums. (Fare: $4.50 round-trip)

SEATTLE STREETCAR TRAVEL

The second-shortest system in the city (⊕ *www.seattlestreetcar.org*) was built to connect Downtown to South Lake Union (directly east of Seattle Center). It runs from Westlake and Olive to the southern shore of Lake Union. (Fare: $2.50)

TAXI TRAVEL

Seattle has a smaller taxi fleet than most major cities do. Taking a cab is not a major form of transportation in the city, and you'll find that rates run higher here. Most people take cabs only to and from the airport and when they go out partying on weekends. You'll often be able to hail cabs on the street in Downtown, but anywhere else, you'll have to call. Expect long waits on Friday and Saturday nights. Two major cab companies are **Yellow Cab** (☎ *206/622–6500*) and **Farwest** (☎ *206/622–1717*).

TRAIN TRAVEL

Amtrak tickets to Portland and Vancouver, B.C., sell out on summer weekends, and last-minute fares can be quite expensive.

VISITOR INFORMATION

Contact the **Seattle Visitors Bureau and Convention Center** (⊕ *www. visitseattle.org* ☎ *206/461–5800*) for help with everything from sightseeing to booking spa services. You can also follow their Twitter feed (⊕ *twitter.com/seattlemaven*). The main visitor information center is Downtown, at the Washington State Convention and Trade Center on 8th Avenue and Pike Street; it has a full-service concierge desk open daily 9 to 5 (in summer; weekdays only in winter). There's also an info booth at Pike Place Market.

EXPLORING

Updated by
Allison Ellis

Each of Seattle's neighborhoods is distinctive in personality, and taking a stroll, browsing a bookstore, or enjoying a cup of coffee can feel different in every one. It's the adventure of exploring that will really introduce you to the character of Seattle.

DOWNTOWN AND BELLTOWN

Except for the busy areas around the Market and the piers, and the always-frenetic shopping district, a lot of Downtown can often seem deserted, especially at night. Still, while it may not be the soul of the city, it's definitely the heart, and there's plenty to do—nearly all of it easily reachable by foot. There's the city's premier art museum, the eye-popping Rem Koolhaus–designed Central Library, lively Pike Place Market, and a major shopping corridor along 5th Avenue and down Pine Street. And, of course, there's the water: Elliott Bay beckons from every crested hill.

Belltown is Downtown's younger sibling, just north of Virginia Street (up to Denny Way) and stretching from Elliott Bay to 6th Avenue. Not so long ago, Belltown was home to some of the most unwanted real estate in the city. Today, Belltown is increasingly hip, with luxury condos, trendy restaurants, swanky bars, and a number of boutiques. (Most of the action happens between 1st and 4th avenues and between Bell and Virginia streets.) You can still find plenty of evidence of its edgy past—including a gallery exhibiting urban street art, a punk-rock vinyl shop, and a major indie rock music venue that was a cornerstone of the grunge scene—but today Belltown is almost unrecognizable to long-term residents.

Fodor's Choice
★

Olympic Sculpture Park. This 9-acre open-air park is the spectacular outdoor branch of the Seattle Art Museum. The Sculpture Park is a favorite destination for picnics, strolls, and quiet contemplation. Nestled at the edge of Belltown with views of Elliott Bay, this gently sloping green space is planted with native plants and is crisscrossed with walking paths. On sunny days, the park flaunts an astounding panorama of the Olympic Mountain Range, but even the grayest afternoon casts a favorable light on the site's sculptures. The grounds are home to works by such artists as Richard Serra, Roy McMakin, Louise Bourgeois, Mark di Suvero, and Alexander Calder, whose bright-red steel "Eagle" sculpture is a local favorite—indeed, you may even see a real bald eagle passing by overhead. The PACCAR Pavilion has a gift shop, café, and more information about the park. ⊠ *2901 Western Ave., between Broad and Bay Sts., Belltown* ☎ *206/654–3100* ⊕ *www.seattleartmuseum.org/ visit/osp* ⌧ *Free* ⊙ *Park open daily sunrise–sunset. PACCAR Pavilion open May–Labor Day, Tues.–Sun. 10–5; Sept.–Apr., Tues.–Sun. 10–4.*

FAMILY

Fodor's Choice
★

Pike Place Market. ⇨ *For an in-depth description of the market, see the highlighted feature in this chapter.* One of the nation's largest and oldest public markets, Pike Place Market dates from 1907, when the city issued permits allowing farmers to sell produce from wagons parked at Pike Place. At one time the market was a madhouse of vendors hawking their produce and haggling with customers over prices; now you might find fishmongers engaging in frenzied banter and hilarious antics, but chances are you won't get them to waver on prices. There are many restaurants, bakeries, coffee shops (including the flagship Starbucks), lunch counters, and ethnic eateries. Go to the Market hungry and you won't be disappointed. The flower market is also a must-see—gigantic fresh arrangements can be had for as little as $5. Strap on some walking shoes and enjoy the Market's many corridors: Specialty-food items, quirky gift shops, tea, honey, jams, comic books, beads, eclectic crafts and cookware—you'll find it all here. ⊠ *Pike Pl. at Pike St., west of 1st Ave., Downtown* ☎ *206/682–7453* ⊕ *www.pikeplacemarket.org* ⊗ *Market opens daily for breakfast at 6 am; fresh produce and fish open 7 am–6 pm; Merchants open 10 am–6 pm; restaurants and bars last call, 1:30 am.*

A GOOD COMBO

If you plan to spend the morning exploring Pike Place Market or the Seattle Art Museum, but still have energy for a walk, head north into the Belltown neighborhood, grab lunch to go at Macrina Bakery, and stroll down to the Olympic Sculpture Park: Views, works of art, and chairs aplenty await.

FAMILY
Fodor's Choice
★

Seattle Aquarium. Located right at the water's edge, the Seattle Aquarium is one of the nation's premier aquariums. Among its most engaging residents are the sea otters—kids, especially, seem able to spend hours watching the delightful antics of these creatures and their river cousins. In the Puget Sound Great Hall, "Window on Washington Waters," a slice of Neah Bay life, is presented in a 20-foot-tall tank holding 120,000 gallons of water. The aquarium's darkened rooms and large, lighted tanks brilliantly display Pacific Northwest marine life. The "Life on the Edge" tide pools re-create Washington's rocky coast and sandy beaches. Huge glass windows provide underwater views of the renovated harbor seal exhibit; go up top to watch them play in their pools. Kids love the Discovery Lab, where they can touch starfish, sea urchins, and sponges. ■ TIP→ If you're visiting in fall or winter, dress warmly—the Marine Mammal area is outside on the waterfront and catches all of those chilly Puget Sound breezes. The café serves Ivar's chowder and kid-friendly food like burgers and chicken fingers; the balcony has views of Elliott Bay. ⊠ *1483 Alaskan Way, Pier 59, Downtown* ☎ *206/386–4300* ⊕ *www.seattleaquarium.org* ⊠ *$19.95; children 4–12, $13.95* ⊗ *Daily 9:30–6 (last entry at 5 pm).*

Seattle Art Museum. Long the pride of the city's art scene, SAM is better than ever after a massive expansion connected the iconic old building on University Street (where sculptor Jonathan Borofsky's several-stories-high *Hammering Man* still pounds away) to a sleek, light-filled high-rise adjacent space, on 1st Avenue and Union Street. Wander two floors of free public space. The first floor includes the museum's fantastic shop, a café that focuses on local ingredients, and drop-in workshops where the whole family can get creative. The second floor features free exhibitions, including awesome large-scale installations. ⊠ *1300 1st Ave., Downtown* ☎ *206/654–3100* ⊕ *www.seattleartmuseum.org* ⊠ *$17* ⊗ *Wed. and weekends 10–5, Thurs. and Fri. 10–9; closed Mon. and Tues. Free on First Thursdays.*

9

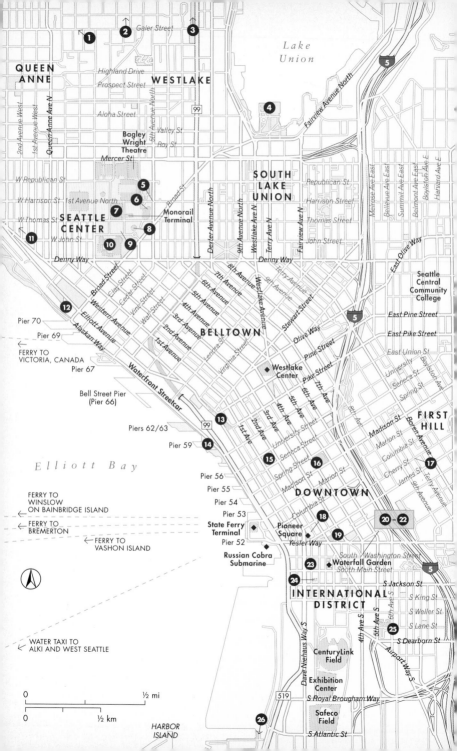

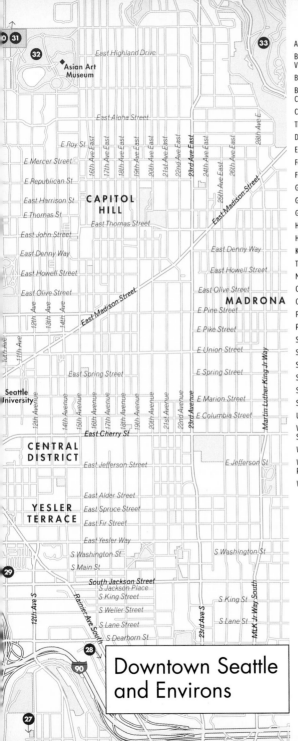

Downtown Seattle and Environs

Fodor's Choice   **The Seattle Public Library.** The hub of Seattle's 25-branch library system,
★   the Central Library is a stunning jewel of a building that stands out
against the concrete jungle of Downtown. Designed by renowned Dutch
architect Rem Koolhaas and Joshua Ramus, this 11-story structure
houses more than 1 million books, a language center, terrific areas for
kids and teens—plus hundreds of computers with Internet access, an
auditorium, a "mixing chamber" floor of information desks, and a café.
The building's floor plan is anything but simple; stand outside the bev-
eled glass-and-metal facade of the building and you can see the library's
floors zigzagging upward. Tours are self-guided via a laminated sheet
you can pick up at the information desk; there's also a number you can
call on your cell phone for an audio tour. The reading room on the 10th
floor has unbeatable views of the city and the water, and the building
has Wi-Fi throughout. Readings and free film screenings happen on a
regular basis; check the website for more information. ⊠ *1000 4th Ave.,
Downtown* ☏ *206/386–4636* ⊕ *www.spl.org* ☉ *Mon.–Thurs. 10–8, Fri.
and Sat. 10–6, Sun. noon–6.*

SEATTLE CENTER, SOUTH LAKE UNION, AND QUEEN ANNE

Almost all visitors make their way to Seattle Center at some point, to
visit the Space Needle or other key Seattle sites like the EMP building,
the Pacific Science Center, or the stunning new Chihuly Garden and
Glass. The neighborhoods that bookend Seattle Center couldn't be more
different: Queen Anne is all residential elegance (especially on top of
the hill), while South Lake Union, once completely industrial, is quickly
becoming Seattle's next hot neighborhood.

FAMILY   **Bill & Melinda Gates Foundation Visitor Center.** The Bill and Melinda Gates
Foundation has some lofty goals, and it's here at the Visitor Center,
conveniently located across the street from Seattle Center, where you
get to witness their plans in action. Exhibits are thought-provoking
and interactive, inviting you to offer up your own solutions to complex global problems like poverty and climate change. The "Innovation
and Inspiration" gallery is the most fun, providing dozens of creative
activities for visitors of all ages. ⊠ *440 5th Ave N, South Lake Union*
☏ *206/709–3100* ⊕ *www.visitorcenter.gatesfoundation.org* ▱ *Free*
☉ *Tues.–Sat. 10–5.*

Fodor's Choice   **Chihuly Garden and Glass.** Just steps from the base of the Space Needle,
★   Chihuly Garden and Glass is a magnificent addition to Seattle Center.
Fans of Dale Chihuly's glass works will be delighted to trace his early
influences—neon art, Native American Northwest Coast trade baskets,
and Pendleton blankets, to name a few—to the vibrant chandelier towers and architectural glass installations he is most known for today.
There are eight galleries total, plus a 40-foot-tall Glasshouse and an
outdoor Garden, which serves as a backdrop for colorful installations
that integrate with a dynamic Northwest landscape, including native
plants and a 500-year-old Western Cedar that washed up on the shores
of Neah Bay. Chihuly, who was born and raised in Tacoma, was actively
involved in the design of the exhibition as well as the whimsical Collections Cafe, where you'll find Chihuly's quirky personal collections on

The stunning Seattle Central Library

display—everything from tin toys to vintage cameras to antique shaving brushes. Indeed, so many of his personal touches are part of the exhibition space, you can almost feel his presence in every room (look for the guy with the unruly hair and the black eye patch).

For an extra few dollars, you can also get a combined Chihuly/Space Needle ticket, a great value. Other things to keep in mind are the two-entry admission ticket, which allows you two visit twice in one 24-hour period, so you can see the Glasshouse and Garden both during the day and night. Chihuly Garden and Glass is great for older kids, and their thoughtful Kid's Guide provides activities for further exploration.

If you're staying Downtown, skip the exorbitant parking prices around Seattle Center and ride the Monorail from Westlake Center ($2.25 each way, with departures every 10 minutes). There's plenty to do around Seattle Center and lower Queen Anne, so make a day of it here. ✉ *305 Harrison St., under the Space Needle, Seattle Center* ☎ *206/753–4940* ⊕ *www.chihulygardenandglass.com* ✉ *$19 one-time visit or $26 for a two-time pass* ⊙ *Daily 11–7; extended hours in summer.*

FAMILY **The Children's Museum, Seattle.** If you're traveling with kids, you already know that a good children's museum is like gold at the end of a rainbow. This colorful, spacious museum, located on the lower level of The Armory in the heart of Seattle Center, provides hours of exploration and fun. Enter through a Northwest wilderness setting, with winding trails, hollow logs, and a waterfall. From there, you can explore the Global Village where rooms with kid-friendly props show everyday life in Ghana, the Philippines, and Japan. Cog City is a giant game of pipes, pulleys, and balls; kids can also test their talent in a mock

Continued on page 346

9

PIKE PLACE MARKET
Nine Acres of History & Quirky Charm

With more than a century of history tucked into every corner and plenty of local personality, the Market is one spot you can't miss. Office workers hustle past cruise-ship crowds to take a seat at lunch counters that serve anything from pizza to piroshkies to German sausage. Local chefs plan the evening's menu over stacks of fresh, colorful produce. At night, couples stroll in to canoodle by candlelight in tucked-away bars and restaurants. Sure, some residents may bemoan the hordes of visitors, and many Seattleites spend their dollars at a growing number of neighborhood farmers' markets. But the Market is still one of Seattle's best-loved attractions.

The Pike Place Market dates from 1907. In response to anger over rising food prices, the city issued permits for farmers to sell produce from wagons parked at Pike Place. The impromptu public market grew steadily, and in 1921 Frank Goodwin, a hotel owner who had been quietly buying up real estate around Pike Place for a decade, proposed to build a permanent space.

More than 250 businesses, including 70 eateries. Breathtaking views of Elliott Bay. A pedestrian-friendly central shopping arcade that buzzes to life each day beginning at 6:30 AM. Strumming street musicians. Cobblestones, flying fish, and the very first Starbucks. Pike Place Market—the oldest continuously operated public market in the United States and a beloved Seattle icon—covers all the bases.

The Market's vitality ebbed after World War II, with the exodus to the suburbs and the rise of large supermarkets. Both it and the surrounding neighborhoods began to deteriorate. But a group of dedicated residents, led by the late architect Victor Steinbrueck, rallied and voted the Market a Historical Asset in the early 1970s. Years of subsequent restoration turned the Market into what you see today.

Pike Place Market is many buildings built around a central arcade (which is distinguished by its huge red neon sign).

Shops and restaurants fill buildings on Pike Place and Western Avenue. In the main arcade, dozens of booths sell fresh produce, cheese, spices, coffee, crafts, and seafood—which can be packed in dry ice for flights home. Farmers sell high-quality produce that helps to set Seattle's rigorous dining standards. The shopkeepers who rent store spaces sell art, curios, clothing, beads, and more. Most shops cater to tourists, but there are gems to be found.

EXPLORING THE MARKET

TOP EATS

❶ THE PINK DOOR. This adored (and adorable) Italian eatery is tucked into Post Alley. Whimsical decor, very good Italian food (such as the scrumptious *linguine alla vongole*), and weekend cabaret and burlesque make this gem a must-visit.

❷ LE PANIER. It's a self-proclaimed "Very French Bakery" and another Seattle favorite. The pastries are the main draw, but sandwiches on fresh baguettes and stuffed croissants offer more substantial snacks.

❸ PIROSHKY PIROSHKY. Authentic piroshky come in both standard varieties (beef and cheese) and Seattle-influenced ones (smoked salmon with cream cheese). There are plenty of sweet piroshky, too, if you need a sugar fix.

❹ CAMPAGNE. This French favorite and its charming attached café have you covered, whether you want a quick Croque Madame for lunch, a leisurely and delicious weekend brunch, or a white-tablecloth dinner.

❺ BEECHER'S. Artisanal cheeses—and mac-n-cheese to go—make this a spot Seattle-ites will brave the crowds for.

❻ THREE GIRLS BAKERY. This tiny bakery turns out piles of pastries and sandwiches on their fresh-baked bread (the baked salmon is a favorite).

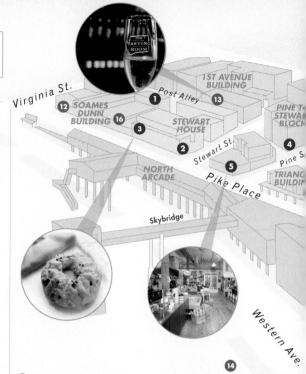

❼ MATT'S IN THE MARKET. Matt's is the best restaurant in the Market, and one of the best in the city. Lunch is casual (try the catfish po'boy), and dinner is elegant, with fresh fish and local produce showcased on the small menu. Reservations are essential.

❽ DAILY DOZEN DONUTS. Mini-donuts are made fresh before your eyes and are a great snack to pick up before you venture into the labyrinth.

❾ MARKET GRILL. This no-frills counter serves up the market's best fish sandwiches and a great clam chowder.

❿ CHUKAR CHERRIES. Look for handmade confections featuring—but not restricted to—local cherries dipped in all sorts of sweet, rich coatings.

TOP SHOPS

⓫ MARKET SPICE TEA. For a tin of the Market's signature tea, Market Spice Blend, which is infused with cinnamon and clove oils, seek out Market Spice shop on the south side of the main arcade.

⓬ PIKE & WESTERN WINE SHOP. The Tasting Room in Post Alley may be a lovely place to sample Washington wines, but Pike and Western is the place where serious oenophiles flock.

⓭ THE TASTING ROOM. With one of the top wine selections in town, the Tasting Room offers Washington wines for the casual collector and the experienced connoisseur. Stop by the bar for

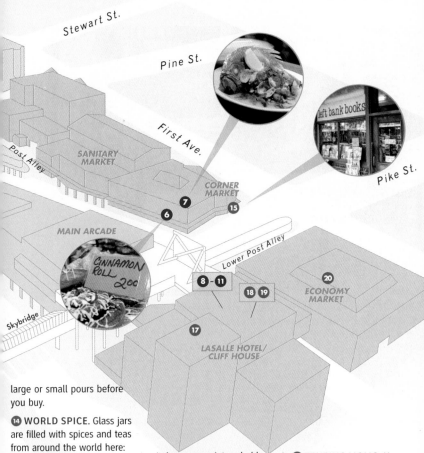

large or small pours before you buy.

⑭ WORLD SPICE. Glass jars are filled with spices and teas from around the world here: Buy by the ounce or grab a pre-packaged gift set as a souvenir.

⑮ LEFT BANK BOOKS. A collective in operation since 1973, this tiny bookshop specializes in political and history titles and alternative literature.

⑯ THE ORIGINAL STAR-BUCKS. At 1912 Pike Place, you'll find the tiny store that opened in 1971 and started an empire. The shop is defi-

nitely more quaint and old-timey than its sleek younger siblings, and it features the original, uncensored (read: bare-breasted) version of the mermaid logo.

⑰ THE SPANISH TABLE. Though not technically in the Market, this amazing specialty store is nearby. It's the Spanish equivalent of DeLaurenti's, and carries hard-to-find cured meats and cheeses plus a nice stock of sweets and clay cookware like cazuelas.

⑱ TENZING MOMO. Your obligatory New Age stop, Tenzing sells high-quality essential oils, natural herbs, teas, tarot cards, incense, soaps, and much more.

⑲ PAPPARDELLE'S PASTA. There's no type of pasta you could dream up that isn't already in a bin at Pappardelle's.

⑳ DELAURENTI'S. This amazing Italian grocery has everything from fancy olive oil to digestifs and wine to meats and fine cheeses.

TOP EXPERIENCES

Pike Place Flowers

Pike Place Fish Co.

Market buskers

FISHMONGERS. There are four spots to visit if you want to see some serious fish: Pike Place Fish Co. (where the fish-throwers are—look for the awestruck crowds); City Fish (the place for fresh crab); Pure Food Fish Market (selling since 1911); and Jack's Fish Spot.

FLOWER STALLS. Flower growers, many of them Hmong immigrants, dot the main arcade. The gorgeous, seasonal bouquets are among the market's biggest draws.

PILES OF PRODUCE. The bounty of the agricultural valleys just outside Seattle is endless. In summer, seek out sweet peaches and Rainier cherries. In fall, look for cider made from Yakima Valley apples. There are dozens of produce vendors, but Sosio's and Manzo Brothers have been around the longest.

BUSKERS. The market has more than 240 street entertainers in any given year; the parade of Pacific Northwest hippie quirkitude is entertainment in itself.

POST ALLEY. There are some great finds in the alley that runs the length of the Market, paralleling First Avenue, from the highbrow (The Tasting Room) to the very lowbrow (the Gum Wall, a wall speckled with discarded gum supposedly left by people waiting in line at the Market Theater).

GHOSTS. If you listen to local lore, Pike Place Market may be the most haunted spot in Seattle. The epicenter seems to be 1921 First Avenue, where Butterworths & Sons Undertakers handled most of Seattle's dead in the early 1900s. You might see visitors sliding flowers into the building's old mail slot.

***SLEEPLESS IN SEATTLE* STOP.** Though it's been more than a decade since Rob Reiner and Tom Hanks discussed dating mores at the bar of The Athenian Inn, tourists still snap pictures of the corner they occupied. Look for the bright red plaque declaring: TOM HANKS SAT HERE.

A DAY AT THE MARKET

6:30 AM Delivery vans and trucks start to fill the narrow streets surrounding Pike Place Market. Vendors with permanent stalls arrive to stack produce, arrange flowers, and shovel ice into bins for displaying salmon, crab, octopus, and other delicacies.

7:30 AM Breakfast is served! **TIP→ For freshly made pastries head to Three Girls and Le Panier.**

9 AM Craftspeople vying for day stalls sign in and are assigned spots based on seniority.

10 AM Craftspeople set up Down Under —the levels below the main arcade—as the main arcade officially opens. The Heritage Center on Western Avenue opens. Market tours ($10) start at the information booth. **TIP→ Make reservations for market tours at least a day in advance; call ☎ 206/774–5249.**

11 AM The Market madness begins. In summer, midday crowds make it nearly impossible to walk through the street-level arcades. **TIP→ Head Down Under where things are often a bit quieter.**

12 PM–2 PM Lunch counters at places like the Athenian Inn and the Market Grill fill up.

Pike Place Market

5 PM Down Under shops close and the cobblestones are hosed down. (The Market closes at 6 PM Mon.–Sat. and 5 PM on Sun.)

7 PM–2 AM Patrons fill the tables at the Alibi Room, Zig Zag Café, the Pink Door, Matt's at the Market, and Maximilien's.

9

RACHEL THE PIG

Rachel, the 550-lb bronze pig that greets marketgoers at the main entrance on Pike and 1st Avenue, is a popular photo stop. But she's also a giant piggy bank that contributes up to $9,000 per year to the Market Foundation. Rachel was sculpted by Georgia Gerber, of Whidbey Island, and was named for the 750-pound pig that won the 1985 Island County Fair.

PARKING

There are numerous garages in the area, including one affiliated with the market itself (the Public Market Parking Garage at 1531 Western Ave.), at which you can get validated parking from many merchants; some restaurants offer free parking at this garage after 5 PM. You'll also find several pay lots farther south on Western Ave. and north on 1st Ave. Street parking is next to impossible to find midday. From Downtown hotels, the Market is easy to reach on foot or on city buses in the "Ride Free Zone."

recording studio. There's a small play area for toddlers and plenty of crafts to keep everyone engaged. ✉ *305 Harrison St., Seattle Center* ☎ *206/441–1768* ⊕ *www.thechildrensmuseum.org* 🖾 *$7.50* ◷ *Weekdays 10–5, weekends 10–6.*

FAMILY

Fodor's Choice

★

EMP Museum. Seattle's most controversial architectural statement is the 140,000-square-foot complex designed by architect Frank Gehry, who drew inspiration from electric guitars to achieve the building's curvy metallic design. It's a fitting backdrop for rock memorabilia from the likes of Bob Dylan and the grunge-scene heavies. ✉ *325 5th Ave. N, between Broad and Thomas Sts., Seattle Center* ☎ *206/770–2700* ⊕ *www.empsfm.org* 🖾 *$20* ◷ *Daily 10–5.*

FAMILY

Museum of History & Industry. In its new location in the converted Naval Reserve Building in Lake Union Park, MOHAI offers visitors an in-depth slice of regional history. With 20,000 square feet devoted to the Seattle experience, recent exhibits include "Celluloid Seattle: A City at the Movies," examining Seattle's relationship with film, and "Still Afloat: A Contemporary History of Seattle's Floating Homes." MOHAI's Center for Innovation is a permanent exhibit that showcases Seattle's role as a place where innovation and entrepreneurship flourish; the exhibit is supported by a $10 million gift from Jeff Bezos, founder and CEO of Seattle-based Amazon.com (which has its corporate head-quarters a few blocks away). ✉ *860 Terry Avenue N., at Lake Union Park, South Lake Union* ☎ *206/324–1126* ⊕ *www.seattlehistory.org* 🖾 *$14, free 1st Thurs. of month* ◷ *Daily 10–5, 1st Thurs. of month 10–8.*

FAMILY

Fodor's Choice

★

Pacific Science Center. If you have kids, the Pacific Science Center is a must-visit. Located in the heart of Seattle Center, this nonprofit science center is home to more than 200 indoor and outdoor hands-on exhibits, two IMAX theaters, a Laser Dome, a butterfly house, and a state-of-the-art Planetarium. The dinosaur exhibit—complete with moving robotic reproductions—is a favorite, and tots can experiment with water at the ever-popular stream table. Machines analyze human physiology in the *Body Works* exhibit. When you need to warm up, The Tropical Butterfly House is 80 degrees and home to colorful butterflies from South and Central America, Africa, and Asia; other creatures live in the Insect Village and saltwater tide-pool areas. IMAX movies, Planetarium shows, Live Science Shows, and Laser Dome rock shows run daily. Look for the giant white arches near the Space Needle and make a day of the surrounding sights. ■TIP→ **Pacific Science Center offers a number of lectures, forums, and "Science Cafes" for adults, plus a variety of educational programs for kids, including camp-ins, monthly parents' nights out, workshops, and more. See website for schedule informa-tion.** ✉ *200 2nd Ave. N, Seattle Center* ☎ *206/443–2001* ⊕ *www.pacsci. org* 🖾 *Center $16, regular IMAX $9, laser shows $5–$9.25, combined museum/IMAX $20* ◷ *Weekdays 10–5, weekends 10–6.*

FAMILY

Space Needle. Over 50 years old, Seattle's most iconic building is as quirky and beloved as ever. The distinctive, towering structure of the 605-foot-high Space Needle is visible throughout much of Seattle—but the view from the inside out is even better. A less-than-one-minute ride

The Pioneer Square skyline is dominated by historic Smith Tower.

up to the observation deck yields 360-degree vistas of Downtown Seattle, the Olympic Mountains, Elliott Bay, Queen Anne Hill, Lake Union, and the Cascade Range. Built for the 1962 World's Fair, the Needle has educational kiosks, interactive trivia game stations for kids, and the glass-enclosed SpaceBase store and Pavilion spiraling around the base of the tower. The top-floor SkyCity restaurant is "revolutionary" (literally—watch the skyline evolve as you dine) and the elevator trip and observation deck are complimentary with your reservation. ■TIP→ If the forecast says you may have a sunny day during your visit, schedule the Needle for that day! If you can't decide whether you want the daytime or nighttime view, for $26 you can buy a ticket that allows you to visit twice in one day. ⊠ *400 Broad St., Seattle Center* ☎ *206/905–2100* ⊕ *www.spaceneedle.com* 🎟 *$19* ⊙ *Daily 9 am–midnight.*

Discovery Park. You won't find more spectacular views of Puget Sound, the Cascades, and the Olympics. Discovery Park, located on Magnolia Bluff, northwest of Downtown, is Seattle's largest park at 534 acres, and it has an amazing variety of terrain: shaded, secluded forest trails lead to meadows, saltwater beaches, sand dunes, a lighthouse, and 2 miles of protected beaches. The North Beach Trail, which takes you along the shore to the lighthouse, is a must-see. Head to the South Bluff Trail to get a view of Mt. Rainier. The park has several entrances—if you want to stop at the visitor center to pick up a trail map before exploring, use the main entrance at Government Way. The North Parking Lot is much closer to the North Beach Trail and to Ballard and Fremont, if you're coming from that direction. ■TIP→ Note that the park is easily reached from Ballard and Fremont. It's easier to combine a park day with an exploration of those neighborhoods than with a busy Downtown itinerary. ✉ *3801 W. Government Way, Magnolia* ✛ *From Downtown, take Elliot Ave. W (which turns into 15th Ave. W), and get off at the Emerson St. exit and turn left onto W. Emerson. Make a right onto Gilman Ave. W (which eventually becomes W. Government Way). As you enter the park, the road becomes Washington Ave.; turn left on Utah Ave.* ☎ *206/386–4236* ⊕ *seattle.gov/ parks/environment/discovery.htm* ✉ *Free* ☉ *Park open daily 6 am–11 pm, visitor center Tues.–Sun. 8:30–5.*

GALLERY WALKS

It's fun to simply walk around Pioneer Square and pop into galleries. South Jackson Street to Yesler between Western and 4th Avenue South is a good area. The first Thursday of every month, galleries stay open late for First Thursday Art Walk, a neighborhood highlight. Visit ⊕ *www. firstthursdayseattle.com.*

PIONEER SQUARE

The Pioneer Square district, directly south of Downtown, is Seattle's oldest neighborhood. It attracts visitors for elegantly renovated (or in some cases replica) turn-of-the-20th-century redbrick buildings and art galleries. It's the center of Seattle's arts scene and the galleries in this small neighborhood make up the majority of its sights.

Bill Speidel's Underground Tour. Present-day Pioneer Square is actually one story higher than it used to be. After the Great Seattle Fire of 1889, Seattle's planners regraded the neighborhood's streets one level higher. The result: there is now an intricate and expansive array of subterranean passageways and basements beneath Pioneer Square, and Bill Speidel's Underground Tour is the only way to explore them. Speidel was an irreverent historian, PR man, and former *Seattle Times* reporter who took it upon himself to preserve historic Seattle, and this tour is packed with his sardonic wit and playful humor. It's very informative, too—if you're interested in the general history of the city or anecdotes about the city's early politicians and residents, you'll appreciate it that much more. Younger kids will probably be bored, as there's not much to see at the specific sites, which are more used as launching points for the stories. ■TIP→ **Comfortable shoes, a love for quirky historical anecdotes, and an appreciation of bad puns are musts.** Several tours are offered daily, and schedules change month to month: call or visit the website for a full list of tour times. ✉ *608 1st Ave., Pioneer Square* ☎ *206/682–4646* ⊕ *www.undergroundtour.com* ✉ *$16* ☉ *May–Sept., 10–7; Oct.–Apr., 11–6.*

Smith Tower. The iconic Smith Tower opened on July 4, 1914, and was the tallest office building outside New York City and the fourth tallest building in the world. (It remained the tallest building west of the Mississippi for nearly 50 years.) The Smith Tower Observation Deck on the 35th floor is an open-air wrap-around deck providing panoramic views of the surrounding historic neighborhood, ball fields, the city skyline, and the mountains on clear days. The ride to the Observation

Deck is via a manually operated elevator (the last on the west coast) and the ground floor was recently restored and returned to its original 1914 footprint as part of a $28 million restoration. ✉ *506 2nd Ave. S, Pioneer Square* ☎ *206/622–4004* ⊕ *www.smithtower.com* 💲*$7.50* ⊗ *May–July, daily 10 am–8:30 pm; Apr. and Oct., daily 10–5; Sept., daily 10–7:30; Nov.–Mar., weekends only 10–4. Hours may vary based on the private events schedule; check online before you go.*

Occidental Park. This shady, picturesque cobblestone park is the geographical heart of the historic neighborhood—on first Thursdays it's home to a variety of local artisans setting up makeshift booths. Grab a sandwich or pastry at the Grand Central Bakery (arguably the city's finest artisan bakery) and get in some good people-watching at the outdoor patio. Note that this square is a spot where homeless people congregate; you're likely to encounter more than a few oddballs. The square is best avoided at night. ✉ *Occidental Ave. S and S. Main St., Pioneer Square.*

GALLERIES

Foster/White Gallery. One of the Seattle art scene's heaviest hitters, Foster/White has digs as impressive as the works it shows: a century-old building with high ceilings and 7,000 square feet of exhibition space. Works by internationally acclaimed Northwest masters Kenneth Callahan, Mark Tobey, Alden Mason, and George Tsutakawa are on permanent display. ✉ *220 3rd Ave. S, Pioneer Square* ☎ *206/622–2833* ⊕ *www.fosterwhite.com* 💲*Free* ⊗ *Tues.–Sat. 10–6.*

Fodor's Choice ★ **G. Gibson Gallery.** Vintage and contemporary photography is on exhibit in this elegant corner space, including work by the likes of Michael Kenna, Walker Evans, Jule Blackman, Lori Nix, and JoAnn Verburg. The gallery also shows contemporary paintings, sculpture, and mixed-media pieces. The gallery's taste is always impeccable and shows rotate every six weeks. ✉ *300 S. Washington St., Pioneer Square* ☎ *206/587–4033* ⊕ *www.ggibsongallery.com* 💲*Free* ⊗ *Wed.–Sat. 11–5 and Tues. by appointment.*

Fodor's Choice ★ **Greg Kucera Gallery.** One of the most important destinations on the First Thursday gallery walk, this gorgeous space is a top venue for national and regional artists. Be sure to check out the outdoor sculpture deck on the second level. If you have time for only one gallery visit, this is the place to go. You'll see big names that you might recognize—along with newer artists—and the thematic group shows are always thoughtful and well presented. ✉ *212 3rd Ave. S, Pioneer Square* ☎ *206/624–0770* ⊕ *www.gregkucera.com* 💲*Free* ⊗ *Tues.–Sat. 10:30–5:30.*

Stonington Gallery. You'll see plenty of cheesy tribal art knockoffs in tourist-trap shops, but this elegant gallery will give you a real look at the best contemporary work of Northwest Coast and Alaska tribal members (and artists from these regions working in the native style). Three floors exhibit wood carvings, paintings, sculpture, and mixed-media pieces from the likes of Robert Davidson, Joe David, Preston Singeltary, Dwane Pasco, Marvin Oliver, Susan Point, and Rick Barto. ✉ *119 S. Jackson St., Pioneer Square* ☎ *206/405–4040* ⊕ *www.stoningtongallery. com* 💲*Free* ⊗ *Weekdays 10–6, Sat. 10–5:30, Sun. noon–5.*

A striking show at Greg Kucera Gallery

INTERNATIONAL DISTRICT

Bright welcome banners, 12-foot fiberglass dragons clinging to lamp-posts, and a traditional Chinese gate confirm you're in the International District. The I.D., as it's locally known, is synonymous with delectable dining—it has many inexpensive Chinese restaurants (this is the neighborhood for barbecued duck and all manner of dumplings), but the best eateries reflect its Pan-Asian spirit: Vietnamese, Japanese, Malay, Filipino, Cambodian. With the endlessly fun Uwajimaya shopping center, the gorgeously redesigned Wing Luke Museum, and several walking tours to choose from, you now have something to do in between bites.

A GOOD COMBO

For a great day of walking and exploring, start your day with breakfast at Pike Place Market, then bus, cab, or stroll down 1st Avenue to Pioneer Square (you'll pass SAM en route—another option!). After visiting some art galleries (which generally open between 10:30 and noon) and stopping at any of the neighborhood's coffee shops (such as Zeitgeist or Grand Central Bakery), walk southeast to the International District for some retail therapy at Uwajimaya and a visit to the Wing Luke Museum. Then cab it back to your hotel.

Kubota Garden. A serene 20 acres of streams, waterfalls, ponds, and rock outcroppings, Kubota Garden, a designated historical landmark of the city of Seattle, was created by Fujitaro Kubota, a 1907 emigrant from Japan. The gardens on the Seattle University campus and the Japanese Garden at the Bloedel Reserve on Bainbridge Island are other examples of his work. The garden is free to visitors and tours are self-guided, though you can go on a docent-led tour on the fourth Saturday of every month, April through October, at 10 am. ✉ *9817 55th Ave. S., Mt. Baker ✛ From I–5, take Exit 158 and turn left toward Martin Luther King, Jr. Way; continue up the hill on Ryan Way. Turn left on 51st Ave. S., then right on Renton Ave. S. and right on 55th Ave. S. to the parking lot.* ☎ *206/684–4584* ⊕ *www.kubota.org* ☉ *Open daily during daylight hours.*

FAMILY

Fodor's Choice

★

Uwajimaya. This huge, fascinating Japanese supermarket is a feast for the senses. A 30-foot-long red Chinese dragon stretches above colorful mounds of fresh produce and aisles of delicious packaged goods—including spicy peas, sweet crackers, gummy candies, nut mixes, rice snacks, and colorful sweets from countries throughout Asia. A busy food court serves sushi, Japanese bento-box meals, Chinese stir-fry combos, Korean barbecue, Hawaiian dishes, Vietnamese spring rolls, and an assortment of teas and tapioca drinks. This is the best place to pick up all sorts of snacks; dessert lovers won't know which way to turn first. The housewares section is well stocked with dishes, cookware, appliances, textiles, and gifts. There's also a card section, a Hello Kitty corner, and Yuriko's cosmetics, where you can find Shiseido products that are usually available only in Japan. Last but not least, there's a delightful branch of the famous Kinokuniya bookstore chain, selling paper goods, pens, stickers, gift items, and many Asian-language books. The large parking lot is free for one hour with a minimum $7.50 purchase or two hours with a minimum $15 purchase—don't forget to have your ticket validated by the cashiers. ✉ *600 5th Ave. S, International District* ☎ *206/624–6248* ⊕ *www.uwajimaya.com* ☉ *Mon.–Sat. 8 am–10 pm, Sun. 9–9.*

FAMILY

Fodor's Choice

★

Wing Luke Museum of the Asian Pacific American Experience. The only museum in the U.S. devoted to the Asian Pacific American experience, this gorgeous museum provides a sophisticated and often somber look at how immigrants and their descendants have transformed (and been transformed by) American culture. The evolution of the museum has been driven by community participation—the museum's library has an oral history lab, and many of the rotating exhibits are focused around stories from longtime residents and their descendants. Museum admission includes a guided walk and talk tour through the East Kong Yick building, where scores of immigrant workers from China, Japan, and the Philippines first found refuge in Seattle. ✉ *719 S. King St., International District* ☎ *206/623–5124* ⊕ *www.wingluke.org* ✑ *$12.95, free 1st Thurs. and 3rd Sat. of month* ☉ *Tues.–Sun. 10–5.*

9

FIRST HILL

Smack between Downtown and Capitol Hill, First Hill is an odd mix of sterile-looking medical facility buildings (earning it the nickname "Pill Hill"), old brick buildings that look like they belong on a college campus, and newer residential towers. The main draws of the neighborhood are the Frye Art Museum, which is well worth a detour, and the fantastic historic Sorrento Hotel.

Frye Art Museum. The Frye was a forgotten museum for a while, frequented only by Seattleites who would come visit their favorite paintings from the permanent collection (mostly 19th- and 20th-century pastoral scenes). But a new curator shook the Frye out of its torpor, and now, in addition to its beloved permanent collection, this elegant building hosts eclectic and often avant-garde exhibits, putting this museum on par with The Henry in the U-District. Thanks to the legacy of Charles and Emma Frye, the museum is always free, and parking is free as well. Past shows have included "Susie J. Lee: Of Breath and Rain" a new-media sensualist who filters and distills technological noise in her work, and "Ties that Bind: American Artists in Europe." No matter what's going on in the stark, brightly lighted back galleries, it always seems to blend well with the permanent collection, which is rotated regularly. ✉ *704 Terry Ave., First Hill* ☎ *206/622–9250* ⊕ *www.fryemuseum.org* ✉ *Free* ⊗ *Tues.–Sat. 11–5 (Thurs. until 8), Sun. noon–5.*

WORD OF MOUTH

"Right in the city, Volunteer Park on Capitol Hill is nice, even in winter. There's a plant conservatory, the [Seattle Asian Art Museum], plus a great view out over the city. [There are] great shops and restaurants nearby, along 15th Avenue East or on Broadway." —suze

CAPITOL HILL

The Hill has two faces: On one side, it's young and edgy, full of artists, musicians, and students. Tattoo parlors and coffeehouses abound, as well as thumping music venues and bars. On the other side, it's elegant and upscale, with tree-lined streets, 19th-century mansions, and John Charles Olmsted's Volunteer Park and the Seattle Asian Art Museum. Converted warehouses, modern high-rises, colorfully painted two-story homes, and brick mansions all occupy the same neighborhood. There are parks aplenty and cute, quirky shops to browse, including one of the best bookstores in the city.

Volunteer Park and the Seattle Asian Art Museum. Nestled amongst the grand homes of North Capitol Hill sits 45-acre Volunteer Park, a grassy expanse perfect for picnicking, sunbathing (or stomping in rain puddles), and strolling. You can tell this is one of the city's older parks by the size of the trees and the rhododendrons, many of which were planted more than a hundred years ago. The Olmsted Brothers, the premier landscape architects of the day, helped with the final design in 1904; the park has changed surprisingly little since then. In the center of the park is the **Seattle Asian Art Museum (SAAM, a branch of the Seattle Art Museum)**, housed in a 1933 art moderne–style edifice. It fits surprisingly well with the stark plaza stretching from the front door to the edge of a bluff, and with the lush plants of Volunteer Park. The museum's collections include thousands of paintings, sculptures, pottery, and textiles from China, Japan, India, Korea, and several Southeast Asian countries. ✉ *Park entrance, 1400 East Prospect St., Capitol Hill* ☎ *206/654–3100 Museum, 206/684–4743 Conservatory* ✉ *Park* *free; museum $7, free 1st Thurs. (all day), 2nd Thurs. (5–9), and 1st Sat. (families)* ☉ *Park daily sunrise–sunset; museum Wed.–Sun. 10–5, Thurs. until 9; Conservatory Tues.–Sun. 10–4.*

Washington Park Arboretum. As far as Seattle's green spaces go, this 230-acre arboretum is arguably the most beautiful. On calm weekdays, the place feels really secluded; though there are trails, you feel like you're freer to roam here than at Discovery Park. The seasons are always on full display: in warm winters, flowering cherries and plums bloom in its protected valleys as early as late February, while the flowering shrubs in Rhododendron Glen and Azalea Way bloom March through June. In autumn, trees and shrubs glow in hues of crimson, pumpkin, and lemon; in winter, plantings chosen specially for their stark and colorful branches dominate the landscape. March through October, visit the peaceful **Japanese Garden,** a compressed world of mountains, forests, rivers, lakes, and tablelands. The pond, lined with blooming water irises in spring, has turtles and brightly colored koi. An authentic Japanese teahouse is reserved for tea ceremonies and instruction on the art of serving tea (visitors who would like to enjoy a bowl of tea and sweets can purchase a $5 tea ticket at the Garden ticket booth; see website for times and schedules). The Graham Visitors Center at the park's north end has descriptions of the arboretum's flora and fauna (which include 130 endangered plants), as well as brochures, a garden gift shop, and walking-tour maps. Free tours are offered most of the year; see website for schedule. ✉ *2300 Arboretum Dr. E, Capitol Hill* ☎ *206/543–8800 arboretum, 206/684–4725 Japanese garden* ⊕ *www.depts.washington. edu/uwbg/gardens/wpa.shtml* ☑ *Free, Japanese garden $6* ☉ *Park open daily 7 am–sunset; visitor center daily 10–4. Japanese garden May–Aug., daily 10–8, hrs vary seasonally, call to confirm.*

FREMONT AND PHINNEY RIDGE

For many years, Fremont enjoyed its reputation as Seattle's weirdest neighborhood, home to hippies, artists, bikers, and rat-race dropouts. But Fremont has lost most of its artist cachet as the stores along its main strip turned more upscale, luxury condos and town houses appeared above the neighborhood's warren of small houses, and rising rents sent many longtime residents reluctantly packing (many to nearby Ballard). On weekend nights, the Downtown strip sometimes looks like one big party, as a bunch of bars draw in a young crowd from Downtown, the University District, and the city's suburbs. Phinney Ridge, above Fremont, is almost entirely residential, though it shares the booming commercial street of Greenwood Avenue North with its neighbor to the north, Greenwood. Although not as strollable as similar districts in Fremont or Ballard, Greenwood Avenue has a lot of boutiques, coffee shops, and restaurants that range from go-to diner food to pricey Pacific Northwest.

FAMILY **Theo Chocolate factory tour.** If it weren't for a small sign on the sidewalk pointing the way, you'd never know that Fremont has its own chocolate factory. Theo has helped to boost the Northwest's growing artisan chocolate scene and has taken the city by storm, thanks to high-quality chocolate creations. Theo uses only organic, fair trade cocoa beans, usually in high percentages—yielding darker, less-sweet, and more complex flavors than some of their competitors. You'll see Theo chocolate bars for sale in many local businesses, from coffee shops to grocery stores. Stop by the factory to buy exquisite "confection" truffles—made daily in small batches—with unusual flavors like basil-ganache, lemon, fig-fennel, and burnt sugar. The super-friendly staff is known to be generous with samples. You can go behind the scenes as well: informative, yummy tours are offered daily; reservations aren't always necessary, but it's a good idea to reserve ahead, particularly on weekends. ✉ *3400 Phinney Ave. N, Fremont* ☎ *206/632–5100* ⊕ *www.theochocolate.com* ☑ *Tour $6* ☉ *Store daily 10–6. Daily tours at 10:30, 11, 12, 12:30, 1, 2 and 4.*

★ **Woodland Park Zoo.** Ninety-two acres are divided into bioclimatic zones
℃ here, allowing many animals to roam freely in habitat areas. A jaguar exhibit is the center of the Tropical Rain Forest area, where rare cats, frogs, and birds evoke South American jungles. The Humboldt penguin exhibit is environmentally sound—it uses geothermal heating and cooling to mimic the climes of the penguins' native home, the coastal areas of Peru. With authentic thatch-roof buildings, the African Village has a replica schoolroom overlooking animals roaming the savanna; the Asian Elephant Forest Trail takes you through a Thai village; and the Northern Trail winds past rocky habitats where brown bears, wolves, mountain goats, and otters scramble and play. Zoomazium is a nature-themed indoor play space for toddlers and young kids, and the Woodland Park Rose Garden (free; located near the zoo's south entrance) is always a hit. ✉ *5500 Phinney Ave. N, Phinney Ridge* ☎ *206/548–2604* ⊕ *www.zoo.org* ☑ *Oct.–Apr. $11.75, May–Sept. $17.75* ☉ *Oct.–Apr., daily 9:30–4; May–Sept., daily 9:30–6.*

BALLARD

Ballard is Seattle's sweetheart. This historically Scandinavian neighborhood doesn't have many sights outside of the Hiram M. Chittenden Locks; you'll spend more time strolling, shopping, and hanging out than crossing attractions off your list. It's got a great little nightlife, shopping, and restaurant scene on Ballard Avenue, and an outstanding farmers' market every Sunday.

FAMILY **Hiram M. Chittenden Locks.** There's no doubt—there's something intrigu-
Fodor's Choice ing and eerie about seeing two bodies of water, right next to each, at
★ different levels. The Hiram M. Chittenden Locks (also known as "Ballard Locks") are an important passage in the 8-mile Lake Washington Ship Canal that connects Puget Sound to freshwater Lake Washington and Lake Union. In addition to boat traffic, the Locks see an estimated half-million salmon and trout make the journey from saltwater to fresh each summer, with the help of a fish ladder.

Families picnic beneath oak trees in the adjacent 7-acre Carl S. English Botanical Gardens; various musical performances (from jazz bands to chamber music) serenade visitors on summer weekends; and steel-tinted salmon awe spectators as they climb a 21-step fish ladder en route to their freshwater spawning grounds—a heroic journey from the Pacific to the base of the Cascade Mountains.

In the 1850s, when Seattle was founded, Lake Washington and Lake Union were inaccessible from the tantalizingly close Puget Sound. The city's founding fathers—most notably, Thomas Mercer in 1854—began dreaming of a canal that would connect the freshwater lakes and the Sound. The lure of freshwater moorage and easier transport of timber and coal proved powerful, but it wasn't until 1917 that General Hiram M. Chittenden and the Army Corps of Engineers completed the Lake Washington Ship Canal and the locks that officially bear his name. More than 90 years later, the Locks are still going strong. Tens of thousands of boaters pass through the Locks each year, carrying over a million tons of commercial products—including seafood, fuel, and building materials.

Guided tours of the Locks are available departing from the visitor's center; however, plaques by the Locks will give you plenty of information if you don't have time for a tour. ⊠ *3015 NW 54th St., Ballard* ✢ *From Fremont, head north on Leary Way NW, west on NW Market St., and south on 54th St.* ☎ *206/783–7059* ⊕ *www.seattle.gov/tour/locks.htm* ☑ *Free* ☉ *Locks daily 7 am–9 pm; visitor center Thurs.–Mon. 10–4. Tours are offered May–Sept. at 1 and 3 daily and 11, 1 and 3 weekends. Call for winter tour information.*

WALLINGFORD

The laid-back neighborhood of Wallingford is directly east of Fremont—the boundaries actually blur quite a bit. There are several lovely parks and residential streets brimming with colorful Craftsman houses. The main drag, 45th Street NW, has an eclectic group of shops, from a gourmet beer store to an erotic bakery to a Hawaiian merchant, along with a few great coffeehouses, and several notable restaurants.

Fodor'sChoice
★
ⓒ
Gas Works Park. The park gets its name from the hulking remains of an old 1907 gas plant, which, far from being an eyesore, actually lends quirky character to the otherwise open, hilly, 20-acre park. Get a great view of Downtown Seattle while seaplanes rise up from the south shore of Lae Union; the best vantage point is from the zodiac sculpture at the top of a very steep hill, so be sure to wear appropriate walking shoes. This is a great spot for couples and families alike; the sand-bottom playground has monkey bars, wooden platforms, and a spinning metal merry-go-round. Crowds throng to picnic and enjoy outdoor summer concerts, movies, and the July 4th fireworks display over Lake Union. ▥ TIP➔ **Gas Works can easily be reached from Fremont Center, via the waterfront Burke-Gilman Trail—remember to stay in the clearly designated pedestrian lane, as you'll be sharing the trail with many other walkers, joggers, and speed-demon bicyclists.** ⊠ *2101 N. Northlake Way, at Meridian Ave. N (the north end of Lake Union), Wallingford* ⊕ *www.seattle.gov/parks/park_detail.asp?id=293* ☉ *Daily 6 am–10 pm.*

9

UNIVERSITY DISTRICT

The U-District, as everyone calls it, is the neighborhood surrounding the University of Washington (UW or "U-Dub" to locals). The campus is extraordinarily beautiful (especially in springtime, when the cherry blossoms are flowering), and the Henry Art Gallery, on its western edge, is one of the city's best small museums. Beyond that, the appeal of the neighborhood lies in its variety of cheap, delicious ethnic eateries, its proximity to the waters of Portage and Union Bays and Lake Washington, and its youthful energy.

FAMILY   **Burke Museum of Natural History and Culture.** Founded in 1899, the Burke is the state's oldest museum, featuring exhibits that survey the natural history of the Pacific Northwest. Highlights include artifacts from Washington's 35 Native American tribes, dinosaur skeletons, and dioramas depicting the traditions of Pacific Rim cultures. An adjacent ethnobotanical garden is planted with species that were important to the region's Native American communities. Check out the schedule for family events and adult classes. ⊠ *University of Washington campus, 17th Ave. NE and NE 45th St., University District* ☎ *206/543–5590* ⊕ *www.burkemuseum.org* ☜ *$10, free 1st Thurs. of month* ☉ *Daily 10–5, 1st Thurs. of each month 10–8.*

Fodor's Choice   **Henry Art Gallery.** The Henry is perhaps the best reason to take a side trip ★   to the U-District. The large gallery consistently presents sophisticated and thought-provoking contemporary work. Exhibits pull from many different genres and include mixed media, photography, and paintings. Richard C. Elliott used more than 21,500 bicycle and truck reflectors of different colors and sizes in his paintings that fit into the sculpture alcoves on the exterior walls of the museum; in another permanent installation, *Light Reign,* a "Skyspace" from artist James Turrell, an elliptical chamber allows visitors to view the sky. More than a few people have used this as a meditation spot; at night the chamber is illuminated by thousands of LED lights. ⊠ *University of Washington campus, 15th Ave. NE and NE 41st St., University District* ☎ *206/543–2280* ⊕ *www.henryart.org* ☜ *$10* ☉ *Thurs. and Fri. 11–9, Wed. and weekends 11–4.*

WEST SEATTLE

Cross the bridge to West Seattle and it's another world altogether. Jutting out into Elliott Bay and Puget Sound, separated from the city by the Duwamish waterway, this out-of-the-way neighborhood covers most of the city's western peninsula—and, indeed, it has an identity of its own. In summer, throngs of people hang out at Alki Beach—Seattle's taste of California—while others head for the trails and playgrounds of Lincoln Park to the west.

FAMILY   **Alki Point and Beach.** In summer, West Seattle's Alki Beach is as close
Fodor's Choice   to California as Seattle gets—and some hardy residents even swim in
★   the cold, salty waters of Puget Sound here (water temperature ranges from 46 to 56 degrees F). This 2½-mile stretch of sand has views of the Seattle skyline and the Olympic Mountains, and the beachfront

promenade is especially popular with skaters, joggers, strollers, and cyclists. Year-round, Seattleites come to build sand castles, beachcomb, and fly kites; in winter, storm-watchers come to see the crashing waves. Facilities include drinking water, grills, picnic tables, phones, and restrooms; restaurants line the street across from the beach. ■ TIP→ **To get here from Downtown, take either I–5 south or Highway 99 south to the West Seattle Bridge (keep an eye out, as this exit is easy to miss) and exit onto Harbor Avenue SW, turning right at the stoplight.** Alki Point is the place where David Denny, John Low, and Lee Terry arrived in September 1851, ready to found a city. The Alki Point Lighthouse dates from 1913. One of 195 Lady Liberty replicas found around the country lives near the 2700 block of Alki Avenue SW. Miss Liberty (or Little Liberty) is a popular meeting point for beachfront picnics and dates. ✉ *1702 Alki Ave SW, West Seattle* ⊕ *www.seattle.gov/parks/park_detail.asp?ID=445.*

OFF THE BEATEN PATH

The Museum of Flight. Boeing, the world's largest builder of aircraft, was founded in Seattle in 1916. This facility at Boeing Field houses one of the city's best museums, and it's especially fun for kids, who can climb in many of the aircraft and pretend to fly, make flight-related crafts, or attend special programs. The Red Barn, Boeing's original airplane factory, houses an exhibit on the history of flight. The Great Gallery, a dramatic structure designed by Ibsen Nelson, contains more than three-dozen vintage airplanes. The Personal Courage Wing showcases World War I and World War II fighter planes, and the Charles Simonyi Space Gallery is home to the NASA Full Fuselage Space Shuttle Trainer. ■ TIP→ **West Seattle is a good jumping-off point for a side trip to the Museum of Flight, which is farther south, close to Sea-Tac airport.** Take the West Seattle Bridge back toward I–5, and then head south on I–5. At Exit 158, merge right onto S. Boeing Access Road. Turn right at the first stoplight (E. Marginal Way S); the museum is on the right after ½ mile. ✉ *9404 E. Marginal Way S, Tukwila* ✛ *Take I–5 south to Exit 158, turn right on Marginal Way S* ☎ *206/764–5720* ⊕ *www.museumofflight.org* 🎫 *$18* ☉ *Daily 10–5; 1st Thurs. of every month, free from 5–9 pm.*

THE EASTSIDE

The suburbs east of Lake Washington can easily supplement any Seattle itinerary. The center of East King County is Bellevue, a fast-growing city with its own downtown core, high-end shopping, and a notable dining scene. Kirkland, north of Bellevue, has a few shops and restaurants (including fabulous Café Juanita) plus lakefront promenades. Redmond and Issaquah, to the northeast and southeast respectively, are gateways to greenery. Woodinville, north of Redmond, is the ambassador for Washington State's wine industry, with many wineries and tasting rooms. Redmond itself is home to Microsoft's gigantic campus.

WHERE TO EAT

Updated by
Rebekah Denn

Use the coordinate (✛ B2) at the end of each listing to locate a site on the corresponding map.

Thanks to inventive chefs, first-rate local produce, adventurous diners, and a bold entrepreneurial spirit, Seattle has become one of the culinary capitals of the nation. Fearless young chefs have stepped in and raised the bar. Nowadays, fresh and often foraged produce, local seafood, and imaginative techniques make the quality of local cuisine even higher.

Seattle's dining scene has been stoked like a wildfire by culinary rock stars who compete on shows like *Iron Chef, Top Chef,* and regularly dominate "best of" lists. Seattle chefs have won big in the prestigious James Beard competition, with Matt Dillon of Sitka & Spruce taking the "Best Chef Northwest" title in 2012 and empire-builder Tom Douglas named the national "Best Restaurateur." And the Fare Start culinary training program, which runs a restaurant and a popular "guest chef" series, was honored as the foundation's 2011 "Humanitarian of the Year." The city is particularly strong on New American, French, and Asian cuisines. Chefs continuously fine-tune what can best be called Pacific Northwest cuisine, which features fresh, local ingredients: nettles and mushrooms foraged in nearby forests; colorful berries, apples, and cherries grown by Washington State farmers; and outstanding seafood from the cold northern waters of the Pacific Ocean, like wild salmon, halibut, oysters, Dungeness crab, and geoduck. Seattle boasts quite a few outstanding bakeries, too, whose breads and desserts you'll see touted on many menus. *Prices in the reviews are the average cost of a main course at dinner or, if dinner is not served, at lunch.*

DOWNTOWN AND BELLTOWN

$
MODERN
AMERICAN
Fodor's Choice
★

✕ **Boat Street Café & Kitchen.** Tables at this French bistro–meets–Nantucket bistro often fill up with couples at night, but the lunchtime scene runs the gamut from Downtown office workers to tourists. Food is understated, fresh, and simply divine: start with raw oysters and a crisp glass of white wine. Next up, sautéed Medjool dates sprinkled with *fleur de sel* and olive oil, a radish salad with pine nuts, or a plate of the famous housemade pickles. Entrées, too, take advantage of whatever is in season, so expect anything from Oregon hanger steak with olive tapenade to Alaskan halibut with cauliflower. Though it's on the ground floor of an odd office building (just north of the Olympic Sculpture Park), Boat Street positively blooms in the quirky space. Monday through Sunday, brunch and lunch are served 10:30–2:30. Ⓢ *Average main: $16* ✉ *3131 Western Ave., Belltown* ☎ *206/632–4602* ⊕ *www.boatstreetcafe.com* ☽ *No dinner Sun.–Mon.* ✛ *C3.*

$
MEXICAN

✕ **El Puerco Lloron.** This funky, cafeteria-style diner perched on the Pike Place Market "Hillclimb" (a flight of stairs between Pike Place Market and the piers along Elliott Bay) has delightful open-air terrace seating perfect for sunny days. It's also got some of Seattle's best and most authentic Mexican cooking—simple, tasty, and inexpensive. Try fresh tacos filled with pork, chicken, or beef and spiked with cilantro and

BEST BETS FOR SEATTLE DINING

With so many restaurants to choose from, how to decide where to eat? Fodor's writers and editors have selected their favorite restaurants by price, cuisine, and experience in the Best Bets lists *below*. In the first column, Fodor's Choice properties represent the "best of the best" in every price category. Other favorites are listed by price category, cuisine, and experience.

Fodor's Choice ★

Anchovies & Olives, $$, p. 366

Boat Street Café & Kitchen, $, p. 358

Café Juanita, $$$$, p. 372

Cascina Spinasse, $$$, p. 366

La Carta de Oaxaca, $, p. 371

Lark, $$$, p. 367

Lola, $$$, p. 360

Ma'ono, $$, p. 372

Matt's in the Market, $$$, p. 360

Monsoon, $$$, p. 368

Poppy, $$$, p. 368

Quinn's, $$, p. 368

Salumi, $, p. 365

Shiro's Sushi, $$$, p. 361

Sitka & Spruce, $$$, p. 368

By Price

$

Boat Street Café & Kitchen, p. 358

Café Presse, p. 366

Delancey, p. 370

Green Leaf, p. 365

How to Cook a Wolf, p. 364

La Carta de Oaxaca, p. 371

Macrina Bakery, p. 360

Salumi, p. 365

$$

Anchovies & Olives, p. 366

Joule, p. 369

Ma'ono, p. 372

Quinn's, p. 368

Tamarind Tree, p. 365

$$$

Cascina Spinasse, p. 366

Lark, p. 367

Lola, p. 360

Monsoon, p. 368

Poppy, p. 368

Shiro's Sushi, p. 361

Sitka & Spruce, p. 368

$$$$

Café Juanita, p. 372

Canlis, p. 364

Crush, p. 367

Matt's in the Market, p. 360

By Cuisine

ASIAN

Joule, $$, p. 369

Monsoon, $$$, p. 368

Tamarind Tree, $$, p. 365

ITALIAN

Café Juanita, $$$$, p. 372

Cascina Spinasse, $$$, p. 366

LATIN

La Carta de Oaxaca, $, p. 371

Paseo, $, p. 370

MEDITERRANEAN

Lola, $$$, p. 360

PACIFIC NORTHWEST

Matt's in the Market, $$$, p. 360

Palace Kitchen, $$, p. 361

Canlis, $$$$, p. 364

SEAFOOD

Anchovies & Olives, $$, p. 366

Best by Experience

BRUNCH

Café Presse, $, p. 366

Lola, $$$, p. 360

Monsoon, $$$, p. 368

LATE-NIGHT DINING

Café Presse, $, p. 366

MOST ROMANTIC

Boat Street Café & Kitchen, $, p. 358

Canlis, $$$$, p. 364

Lark, $$$, p. 367

9

salsa. More ambitious highlights include perfect *chiles rellenos* (mild green peppers that are breaded, stuffed with cheese, and fried) and a flavorful guacamole. **TIP→ This is a fantastic spot for a casual lunch after a morning stroll at Pike Place Market.** [$] *Average main: $9* ✉ *1501 Western Ave., Downtown* ☎ *206/624–0541* 🌐 *www.elpuercolloron.com* ✥ *D4.*

$ ITALIAN

🍴 **Il Corvo.** Some of the city's best pasta is served at an incongruous counter sharing space with Procopio Gelateria on the Pike Place Market "Hillclimb" (a flight of stairs between the market and the piers along Elliott Bay). Experienced chef Mike Easton left the cooking line at higher-end restaurants to found this lunch-only (11 am to 3 pm), cash-only collection of tables where he prepares a few inexpensive hand-made dishes each day using antique pasta-makers and artisanal, seasonal ingredients—perhaps tender agnolotti stuffed with pecorino cheese and green peppercorns, or capellini with cured tuna heart, Calabrian chilis, bread crumbs, and parsley. A few antipasti round out the menu each day. [$] *Average main: $8* ✉ *217 James St., Downtown* ☎ *206/538–0999* 🌐 *www.ilcorvopasta.com* ✍ *Reservations not accepted* 💳 *No credit cards* ⏰ *Closed weekends, no dinner* ✥ *E5.*

$$$ MEDITERRANEAN Fodor's Choice ★

🍴 **Lola.** Tom Douglas dishes out his signature Northwest style, spiked with Greek and Mediterranean touches here—another huge success for the local celebrity chef. Try a glorious tagine of goat meat with mustard and rosemary; grape leaf–wrapped trout; lamb burgers with chickpea fries; and scrumptious spreads including hummus, tzatziki, and *harissa* (a red-pepper concoction). Booths are usually full at this bustling, dimly lighted restaurant, which anchors the Hotel Ändra. The fabulous weekend brunches are inventive: try Tom's Big Breakfast—octopus, mustard greens, cumin-spiced yogurt, bacon, and an egg. If you still have room, there are made-to-order doughnuts, too. [$] *Average main: $25* ✉ *2000 4th Ave., Belltown* ☎ *206/441–1430* 🌐 *www.tomdouglas.com* ✥ *E4.*

$ BAKERY

🍴 **Macrina Bakery.** One of Seattle's favorite bakeries is also popular for breakfast and brunch. With its perfectly executed breads and pastries—from Nutella brioche and ginger cookies to almond croissants and dark-chocolate, sugar-dusted brownies—it's become a true Belltown institution. The small spot is usually too frenzied to invite the hours of idleness that other coffee shops may inspire, but a recent remodel helped ease the crunch with additional seating. **TIP→ Macrina is an excellent place to take a delicious break on your way to or from the Olympic Sculpture Park.** You can also wait for a table and have a larger breakfast or lunch—sandwiches, quiches, and salads are all yummy and fresh. There's also a location in SODO and one in Queen Anne. [$] *Average main: $3* ✉ *2408 1st Ave., Belltown* ☎ *206/448–4032* 🌐 *www.macrinabakery.com* ✥ *D4.*

$$$ PACIFIC NORTHWEST Fodor's Choice ★

🍴 **Matt's in the Market.** Your first dinner at Matt's is like a first date you hope will never end. One of the most beloved of Pike Place Market's restaurants, Matt's is now owned by Dan Bugge, who continues to value intimate dining, fresh ingredients, and superb service. An expansion nearly doubled the number of seats, and some tables are now held for walk-ins. You can perch at the bar for pints and a delicious pulled pork or hot grilled-tuna sandwich or a cup of gumbo, or be

Matt's in the Market

seated at a table—complete with vases filled with flowers from the market—for a seasonal menu that synthesizes the best picks from the restaurant's produce vendors and an excellent wine list. Dinner entrées always include at least one catch of the day—perhaps a whole fish in saffron broth or Alaskan halibut with pea vines. ■ **TIP→ Looking for the original Matt, former owner Matt Janke? He's pleasing diners at his new joint, Lecosho, a few blocks down at 89 University St.** [$] *Average main: $32* ✉ *94 Pike St., Suite 32, Downtown* ☎ *206/467–7909* 🌐 *www.mattsinthemarket.com* 🕒 *Closed Sun.* ✥ *D4.*

$$ PACIFIC NORTHWEST

🍴 **Palace Kitchen.** The star of this chic yet convivial Tom Douglas eatery may be the 45-foot bar, but the real show takes place in the giant open kitchen at the back. Wood-grilled chicken wings, olive poppers, Penn Cove mussels, roast-pork ravioli, and a nightly selection of cheeses vie for your attention on the ever-changing menu of small plates. The half-pound Palace Burger is one of the city's best, and there are always a few entrées, mouthwatering desserts, and a rotisserie special from the apple-wood grill. ■ **TIP→ "Late night breakfast" is available in the wee hours—you can ask for it even if it's not on the menu.** [$] *Average main: $22* ✉ *2030 5th Ave., Belltown* ☎ *206/448–2001* 🌐 *www.tomdouglas.com* 🕒 *No lunch* ✥ *D4.*

$$$ JAPANESE Fodor's Choice ★

🍴 **Shiro's Sushi Restaurant.** Shiro Kashiba is the most famous sushi chef in Seattle; he's been in town for more than 40 years, and he still occasionally takes the time to helm the sushi bar at his popular restaurant. ■ **TIP→ If you get a seat at the sushi bar in front of Shiro, don't be shy—this is one place where ordering omakase (chef's choice) is a must.** Willfully unconcerned with atmosphere, this simple spot is a real curiosity amid Belltown's chic establishments, though it does seem to be charging

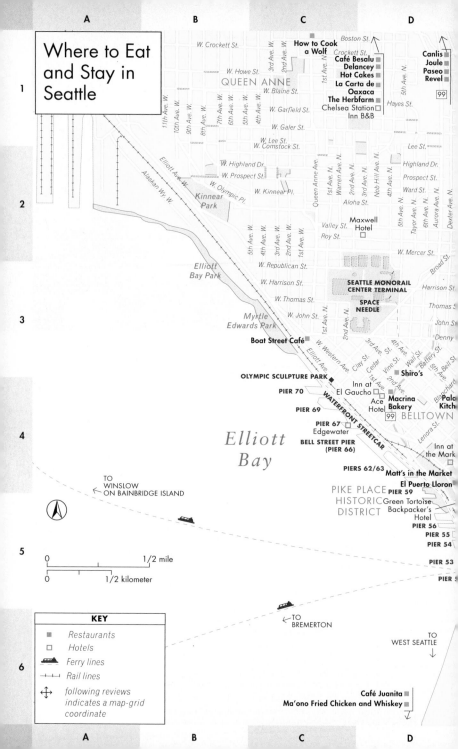

Where to Eat and Stay in Seattle

A

B

C

W. Crockett St.

Boston St.

How to Cook a Wolf

Crockett St.

Canlis
Joule
Paseo
Revel

D

W. Howe St.

Café Besalu
Delancey
Hot Cakes
La Carta de Oaxaca
The Herbfarm

QUEEN ANNE

W. Blaine St.

Hayes St.

Chelsea Station Inn B&B

W. Garfield St.

W. Galer St.

W. Lee St.
W. Comstock St.

Lee St.

W. Highland Dr.
W. Prospect St.

Highland Dr.

Prospect St.

W. Olympic Pl.
W. Kinnear Pl.

Kinnear
Park

Ward St.

Aloha St.

Maxwell Hotel

Valley St.

Roy St.

W. Mercer St.

Broad St.

Elliott
Bay Park

W. Republican St.

W. Harrison St.

SEATTLE MONORAIL CENTER TERMINAL

Harrison St.

Thomas S

SPACE NEEDLE

Myrtle
Edwards Park

W. Thomas St.

W. John St.

John St

Denny

Boat Street Café

Shiro's

OLYMPIC SCULPTURE PARK

Palo Kitch

PIER 70

Inn at El Gaucho

Macrina Bakery

Ace Hotel

PIER 69

BELLTOWN

PIER 67
Edgewater

Lenora St.

BELL STREET PIER (PIER 66)

*Elliott
Bay*

Inn at the Mark

PIERS 62/63

Matt's in the Market
El Puerto Lloron

TO
WINSLOW
ON BAINBRIDGE ISLAND

PIKE PLACE
HISTORIC
DISTRICT

PIER 59

Green Tortoise
Backpacker's
Hotel

PIER 56

PIER 55

PIER 54

0   1/2 mile

PIER 53

0   1/2 kilometer

PIER 5

TO
BREMERTON

TO
WEST SEATTLE

KEY

■	*Restaurants*
□	*Hotels*
⛴	*Ferry lines*
+++	*Rail lines*
⬌	*following reviews indicates a map-grid coordinate*

Café Juanita
Ma'ono Fried Chicken and Whiskey

A

B

C

D

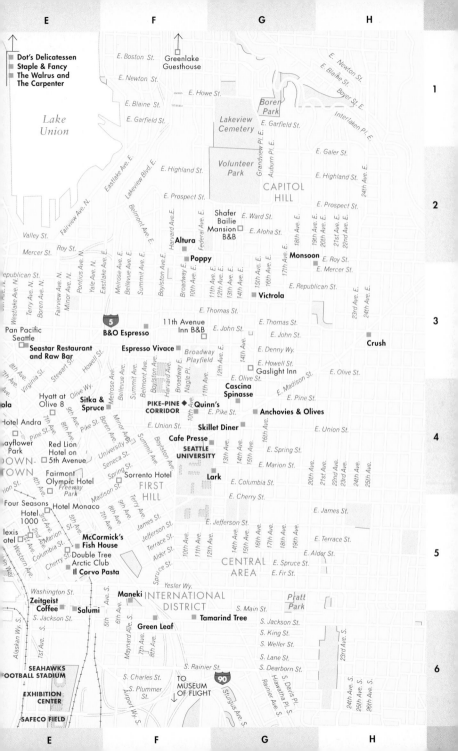

Belltown prices for simpler pleasures like teriyaki and tempura dinners. New fans have been drawn in by the documentary film *Jiro Dreams of Sushi*, which features Shiro's Tokyo mentor, Jiro Ono; one of Jiro's other protégés, Daisuke Nakazawa, now works at Shiro's. $ *Average main: $28* ⊠ *2401 2nd Ave., Belltown* ☎ *206/443–9844* ⊕ *www.shiros. com* ⊗ *No lunch* ✣ *D4.*

SOUTH LAKE UNION AND QUEEN ANNE

$$$$ ╳ **Canlis Restaurant.** Canlis has been setting the standard for opulent din-
PACIFIC ing in Seattle since the 1950s and although there are no longer kimono-
NORTHWEST clad waitresses, the food, the wine, the practically clairvoyant service, and the views overlooking Lake Union are still remarkable. Executive chef Jason Franey (formerly of Manhattan's acclaimed Eleven Madison Park) maintains the restaurant's signature insistence on the finest meat and the freshest produce but he has also refreshed the menu. The famous Canlis Salad of romaine, bacon, Romano cheese, and mint is always a crowd-pleaser, but the entrées are the stars here: 14-day dry-aged roasted duck breast accompanied by orange chutney, fennel, and caramelized cipollini onion, or perhaps an arresting smoked black cod with peaches, porcini, and pickled mustard seeds. ▓TIP➔ **If the dining room seems too formal, the bar menu is more wallet-friendly and you don't need a reservation.** $ *Average main: $48* ⊠ *2576 Aurora Ave. N, Queen Anne* ☎ *206/283–3313* ⊕ *www.canlis.com* ⇲ *Reservations essential* ⌂ *Jacket required* ⊗ *Closed Sun., no lunch* ✣ *D1.*

$ ╳ **Espresso Vivace.** A cozy and large outpost of the famed Capitol Hill
CAFÉ roaster, the Vivace coffee shrine in South Lake Union is right across from the REI megastore and amid a growing number of hip boutiques and design shops. Grab a seat, order an expertly prepared espresso beverage, and munch on a small variety of snacks—this is a perfect stop after an exhausting jaunt through REI and before you head out to the next adventure. $ *Average main: $3* ⊠ *227 Yale Ave. N, South Lake Union* ☎ *206/388–5164* ⊕ *www.espressovivace.com* ✣ *F3.*

$ ╳ **How to Cook a Wolf.** This sleek eatery—complete with loads of trendy
ITALIAN young couples perched at its tables—"pays homage to MFK Fisher and her philosophy of taking simple ingredients and transforming them into culinary splendor." As you would expect then, fresh, artisanal ingredients are the focus. Starters run the gamut from cured-meat platters, to roasted almonds, pork terrine, chicken-liver mousse, and arugula salad, while tasty mains focus on handmade pastas—the *casarecce* features bacon, onion, and black pepper. Fresh skate with brown butter and capers or quail with saffron aioli are examples of the rustic-chic Italian-inspired dishes chef Ethan Stowell has perfected in his various eateries around town. This restaurant is worth the trip even if you're far from Queen Anne. $ *Average main: $16* ⊠ *2208 Queen Anne Ave. N., Queen Anne* ☎ *206/838–8090* ⊕ *www.ethanstowellrestaurants.com* ⊗ *No lunch* ✣ *C1.*

$$$$ ╳ **Seastar Restaurant and Raw Bar.** Nestled in the Pan Pacific Hotel com-
SEAFOOD plex on the southern edge of South Lake Union, this sleek and spacious restaurant is known for its extensive happy hour. The raw bar features sushi and such delicacies as Thai seafood salad, giant black tiger

prawns, ceviche, and a Northwest oyster sampler. Delicious tempura rolls, hamburger sliders, and cedar-plank salmon are all popular. Order a chilled white wine and get comfortable in one of the spacious booths. $ *Average main: $33* ✉ *2121 Terry Ave., Pan Pacific Hotel, South Lake Union* ☎ *206/462–4364* ⊕ *www.seastarrestaurant.com* ✷ *No lunch Sat. or Sun.* ✥ *E3.*

PIONEER SQUARE

$

ITALIAN

Fodor's Choice

★

✗ **Salumi Cured Meats.** The lines are long for hearty, unforgettable sandwiches filled with superior house-cured meats and all other sorts of goodies at this shoebox shop owned by Gina Batali—sister of famed New York chef Mario Batali—and founded by their dad Armandino. The oxtail sandwich special is unbeatable, but if it's unavailable or sold out (as specials often are by the lunchtime peak) order a salami, bresaola, porchetta, meatball, sausage, or lamb prosciutto sandwich with onions, peppers, cheese, and olive oil. Most people opt for takeout, though there is limited indoor seating. ■ TIP➜ Note that Salumi is only open from 11 am to 4 pm. $ *Average main: $9* ✉ *309 3rd Ave. S, Pioneer Square* ☎ *206/621–8772* ⊕ *www.salumicuredmeats.com* ✷ *Closed Sat.–Mon.* ✥ *E5.*

INTERNATIONAL DISTRICT

$

VIETNAMESE

✗ **Green Leaf Vietnamese Restaurant.** Locals pack this friendly café for the expansive menu of fresh, well-prepared Vietnamese staples. The quality of the food—the spring rolls, *bánh xèo* (the Vietnamese version of an omelet), and lemongrass chicken are just a few standouts—and reasonable prices would be enough to make it an instant I.D. favorite. But Green Leaf also proves you don't have to sacrifice ambience to get cheap, authentic Asian food in Seattle: you'll find bamboo embellishments on lighting fixtures, tables, and chairs; and instead of glaring fluorescents, there is dim mood lighting in the evening. The staff greets everyone as though they're regulars—and there are plenty of regulars, enough to fill the small space. ■ TIP➜ If it's packed, try consider the newer Belltown branch, a large space with a full bar and late-night hours, at 2800 First Ave. $ *Average main: $11* ✉ *418 8th Ave. S, International District* ☎ *206/340–1388* ⊕ *www.greenleaftaste.com* ✥ *F5.*

$$

VIETNAMESE

✗ **Tamarind Tree.** Wildly popular with savvy diners from all across the city, this Vietnamese haunt on the eastern side of the I.D. *really* doesn't look like much from the outside, especially because the entrance is through a grungy parking lot (which it shares with Sichuanese Cuisine restaurant). Once you're inside, though, the elegantly simple, large, and warm space is extremely welcoming. The food is the main draw—try the spring rolls, which are stuffed with fresh herbs, fried tofu, peanuts, coconut, jicama, and carrots; authentic *bánh xèo*; spicy, authentic pho; the signature "seven courses of beef"; and, to finish, grilled banana cake with warm coconut milk. Service is attentive, but the waits can be long, even with reservations. $ *Average main: $21* ✉ *1036 S. Jackson St., Suite A, International District* ☎ *206/860–1404* ⊕ *www. tamarindtreerestaurant.com* ✥ *F6.*

9

CAPITOL HILL

$$$ ITALIAN

🍴 **Altura.** A hand-carved cedar angel statue watches over diners at this lively spot, where chef-owner Nathan Lockwood lends a Northwest focus to Italian cuisine. The weekly seasonal menu is presented as prix-fixe, but technically dishes are available à la carte as well. It's hard to go wrong with any of the starters or pastas: you might begin with a crudo misto of geoduck (a variety of clam) and scallops with dollops of urchin roe, then move on to pappardelle with braised tripe and oxtail ragu. Mains may include black cod with fragrant shavings of foraged matsutake mushrooms. Service is hyper-solicitous but the atmosphere is more casual and loud than you might expect given the price tag. **TIP→ When making your reservation, let them know if you prefer a table or a seat at the bar overlooking the open kitchen.** [$] *Average main: $32* ✉ *617 Broadway E., Capitol Hill* ☎ *206/402–6749* 🌐 *www.alturarestaurant.com* ✍ *Reservations essential* ⏲ *Closed Sun. and Mon., no lunch* ✥ *F2.*

$$ SEAFOOD Fodor's Choice ★

🍴 **Anchovies & Olives.** Artful lighting, an exposed kitchen, a well-edited Italian and Northwest wine list, and a lively small bar are the backdrop for some of the best, and most elegant, seafood dishes in the city at this sophisticated Ethan Stowell restaurant in the ground floor of a residential high-rise at the eastern end of the Pike–Pine Corridor. Appetizer plates are small and easily shared, while mains from the changing menu might include mackerel with cauliflower and radicchio; skate wing with asparagus and saffron leeks; clams with pine nuts and hot pepper; and octopus with corona beans and fennel. The "oyster power hour," from 5–6 pm, Sunday–Thursday, is popular for $1 oysters and drink specials. Dinner reservations are highly recommended. [$] *Average main: $24* ✉ *1550 15th Ave., at Pine St., Capitol Hill* ☎ *206/838–8080* 🌐 *ethanstowellrestaurants.com/anchoviesandolives* ✥ *G4.*

$ FRENCH

🍴 **Café Presse.** Two distinct rooms create plenty of space at this French bistro just off the Pike–Pine Corridor, where you can get such Parisian fare as pressed chicken with greens; a *croque madame*; mussels with french fries; pan-roasted quail with sautéed potatoes and apples; and simple cheese platters with slices of baguette. This is the spot to order some red table wine and people-watch. A quirky, low-key vibe pervades this beloved Capitol Hill haunt, thanks in part to Seattle University, which is just steps away. It's equally good for early birds and night owls, open from the 7 am *petit dejeuner* until 2 am. Reservations are only accepted for dinner. [$] *Average main: $16* ✉ *1117 12th Ave., Capitol Hill* ☎ *206/709–7674* 🌐 *www.cafepresseseattle.com* ✥ *F4.*

$$$ ITALIAN Fodor's Choice ★

🍴 **Cascina Spinasse.** Squeeze into this postage stamp–size eatery with its cream-colored lace curtains and true Italian soul—and come hungry, because chef Jason Stratton knows how to make pasta. It's made fresh daily and comes with such sauces and fillings as lamb or rabbit ragu, roasted carrot and goat cheese, or duck confit. *Secondi* options can range from braised pork belly with cabbage to stewed venison served over polenta. The dessert selections are lovely; a favorite is *panna cotta* with cardoon flower honey. With the friendly service and dynamite grappa, amaro, and an Italian-focused wine selection, you likely won't mind paying the price, even if the restaurant is loud and

Anchovies & Olives

small. ■ TIP→ For a well-crafted aperitif, start out next door at Stratton's companion bar-eatery, Artusi (1535 14th. Ave.). ⓢ *Average main: $26 ⊠ 1531 14th Ave., Capitol Hill* ☎ *206/251–7673* ⊕ *www.spinasse. com* ⊙ *Closed Tues., no lunch* ✛ *G4.*

$$$$
MODERN
AMERICAN
✕ **Crush.** Occupying a converted two-story house (with dining rooms on both levels), this sleek restaurant helmed by James Beard Award–winning chef Jason Wilson may have you thinking that you're Downtown, not on the southeastern edge of Capitol Hill. The food is always tasty, and often rises to sublime: braised short ribs are Crush's signature dish, and they're so good that the menu could begin and end right there. However, seafood dishes are also superbly executed, such as crusted Neah Bay black cod with Wagyu beef broth and salsify. The place doesn't attract a specific demographic—you'll see gourmands, couples, local families, and more. Despite the clamor for a table on the weekend, servers remain serene and you'll never be rushed out the door. For a budget-minded taste of Wilson's wizardry, go for happy hour. ⓢ *Average main: $34 ⊠ 2319 E. Madison St., Madison Park* ☎ *206/302–7874* ⊕ *www.chefjasonwilson.com* ⌒ *Reservations essential* ⊙ *Closed Mon., no lunch* ✛ *H3.*

$$$
MODERN
AMERICAN
Fodor's Choice
★
✕ **Lark.** Just off the Pike–Pine Corridor in a converted garage with exposed beams and gauzy curtain dividers, Lark was one of the restaurants that kick-started the small-plate trend in Seattle. The idea is to order several of the mouthwateringly delicious options per person. The expert servers can help you choose from an impressive wine list, and will happily offer their opinions of the long menu, which is divided into cheese; vegetables and grains; charcuterie; fish; meat; and, of course, dessert. Seasonally inspired dishes may include chicken-liver parfait

with grilled ramps; carpaccio of yellowtail with preserved lemons; veal sweetbreads with black truffle; and poached organic egg with chorizo. For dessert try the Theo-chocolate madeleines, which come wrapped in a white napkin with a small pot of dipping chocolate. Reservations are recommended. [$] *Average main: $28* ✉ *926 12th Ave., Capitol Hill* ☎ *206/323–5275* 🌐 *www.larkseattle.com* 🕓 *Closed Mon.* ✥ *G4.*

$$$ VIETNAMESE Fodor's Choice ★ 🍴 **Monsoon.** A small, serene space decorated with simple woven hats hanging on a bright wall, Monsoon serves delicious, upscale Vietnamese food to happy locals on this tree-lined residential stretch of Capitol Hill. Favorites, blending Vietnamese and Pacific Northwest elements, include wild gulf prawns with lemongrass, catfish clay pot with fresh coconut juice and green onion, and lamb with fermented soybeans and sweet onions. Homemade ice creams include lychee and mango, but the restaurant's most famous dessert is the coconut crème caramel. The wine cellar has nearly 250 varieties, including many French selections. **TIP→ The weekend brunch—which serves traditional Vietnamese offerings, dim sum, and "colonial" favorites like French toast and eggs en cocotte—is divine.** [$] *Average main: $25* ✉ *615 19th Ave. E, Capitol Hill* ☎ *206/325–2111* 🌐 *www.monsoonrestaurants.com* ✥ *G3.*

$$$ MODERN AMERICAN Fodor's Choice ★ 🍴 **Poppy.** Jerry Traunfeld's bright, airy restaurant on the northern end of Broadway is a feast for the senses, with funky design details, friendly staff, and a happening bar area. Start with one of the many interesting cocktails and an order of eggplant fries with sea salt and honey; then peruse the menu, which offers standard and vegetarian thali of various sizes—the idea is inspired by the Indian thali meal, in which a selection of different dishes is served in small compartments on a large platter but here the food is mainly seasonal New American cuisine. Dinner might include items like braised Wagyu beef cheek with ginger, rhubarb pickles, onion-poppy naan, and roasted halibut with saffron leeks. The concept may be gimmicky but somehow each small-portioned delight seems better than the last. [$] *Average main: $28* ✉ *622 Broadway E, Capitol Hill* ☎ *206/324–1108* 🌐 *www.poppyseattle.com* 🕓 *No lunch* ✥ *F2.*

$$ BRITISH Fodor's Choice ★ 🍴 **Quinn's.** Capitol Hill's coolest gastropub has friendly bartenders, an *amazing* selection of beers on tap (with the West Coast and Belgium heavily represented), an extensive list of whiskey, and an edgy menu of good food, which you can enjoy at the long bar or at a table on either of the two floors of the industrial-chic space. Spicy fried peanuts and country-style rabbit pâté are good ways to start—then you can choose from Painted Hills beef tartare with pumpernickel crisps, perfect marrow bones with baguette and citrus jam, or a cheese plate. The folks here take their libations seriously, so feel free to chat up the bartenders about their favorites. [$] *Average main: $17* ✉ *1001 E. Pike St., Capitol Hill* ☎ *206/325–7711* 🌐 *www.quinnspubseattle.com* ✍ *Reservations not accepted* 🕓 *No lunch* ✥ *F4.*

$$$ MODERN AMERICAN Fodor's Choice ★ 🍴 **Sitka & Spruce.** Anchoring the hot Melrose Market (between Pike and Pine), which houses a hip bar, a cheesemonger, and a butcher, Sitka & Spruce is the Capitol Hill eatery of James Beard Award–winner Matthew Dillon. Romantic, chic, friendly, and cutting edge all at once, S&S is a heaven for foodies—try to snag a table at the large butcher block

that extends from the chef's kitchen for a view of the cooks at work. Choose from seasonally rotating offerings such as king bolete mushrooms with blistered fava beans, whole baby turnips in tarragon with house-made yogurt with za'atar spice, and deliciously tender charcoal-grilled chicken served with rye berries grown in nearby Winthrop. The sourdough bread baked at Dillon's Georgetown project, The Corson Building, is a bargain even at $4 (fancy butters and spreads included). Mondays the menu is given over to authentic, inexpensive (and no-reservation) Mexican taco nights. $ *Average main: $29* ⊠ *1531 Melrose Ave., Capitol Hill* ☎ *206/324–0662* ⊕ *www.sitkaandspruce.com* ✛ *E4.*

$ ✕ **Skillet Diner.** Diner fare takes a modern turn on Capitol Hill at this AMERICAN stylishly retro, brick-and-mortar version of one of the city's preeminent food trucks. Skillet's hot, strong coffee is made with beans from the local Fonté micro-roastery, while their burgers are ridiculously savory, topped with signature "bacon jam" and blue cheese (max out the decadence with a side of cheesy poutine). A kale Caesar salad and a fried chicken "sammy" sporting a fennel seed crust are other signs you're not in the '50s anymore. Sit on counter stools or in comfy avocado-green booths, but allow plenty of time—while service is cheerful and prompt, lunch-hour waits are lengthy. $ *Average main: $14* ⊠ *1400 E. Union, Capitol Hill* ☎ *206/512–2000* ⊕ *www.skilletstreetfood.com* 🗎 *Reservations not accepted* ✛ *G4.*

$ ✕ **Victrola Coffee Roasters.** Victrola is probably the most loved of Capitol CAFÉ Hill's many coffeehouses, and it's easy to see why: the sizable space is lovely—the walls are hung with artwork by local painters and photographers—the coffee and pastries are fantastic, the baristas are skillful, and everyone, from soccer moms to indie rockers, is made to feel like this neighborhood spot exists just for them. If 15th Avenue E is too far off the beaten path for you, there are also branches at 310 East Pike Street (206/462–6259), between Melrose and Bellevue, as well as in Beacon Hill and South Lake Union. $ *Average main: $3* ⊠ *411 15th Ave. E, Capitol Hill* ☎ *206/462–6259* ⊕ *www.victrolacoffee.com* ✛ *G3.*

FREEMONT

$ ✕ **Dot's Delicatessan.** Go early for the Reuben at Dot's: it takes owner DELI Miles James roughly a week to brine and smoke his pastrami, and it sells out fast. If it's gone, though, there are always house-made hot dogs and sausages, fries, and the pâtés and charcuterie that James perfected in previous stints at high-end restaurants (as well as manning his own hot dog cart). There are only a handful of tables facing the glass display case and open kitchen at this casual combination of restaurant, deli, and butcher shop, but you'll find top chefs as well as locals stopping by for a bite. Note that it's a walk or short ride to get here from Fremont's main retail zone. $ *Average main: $9* ⊠ *4262 Fremont Ave. N., Fremont* ☎ *206/687–7446* ⊕ *www.dotsdelicatessen.com* 🗎 *Reservations not accepted* ☉ *Closed Sun. and Mon.* ✛ *E1.*

$$ ✕ **Joule.** This nouvelle take on a Korean steak house serves meat options KOREAN like brisket steak with sweet chili rub and pickled pearl onions, and short rib with Kalbi and grilled kimchi. The new Joule, in the modern-funky new Fremont Collective building, replaced the original, less

focused Wallingford restaurant of Rachel Yang and Seif Chirchi, who have generally wowed Seattle diners with their French-fusion spins on Asian cuisine (at Joule and at Fremont's Revel). Non-meat menu items include smoked tofu with *honshimejo* (mushroom) confit and soy truffle vinaigrette and mackerel with green curry cilantro crust and black currant, while a weekend brunch buffet goes slightly more mainstream with a fruit and pastry buffet, as well as entrées like oatmeal-stuffed porchetta. [$] *Average main: $19* ✉ *3506 Stone Way N., Fremont* ☎ *206/632–1913* 🌐 *www.joulerestaurant.com* 🕒 *No lunch* ✥ *D1.*

$ CUBAN 🍴 **Paseo.** The centerpiece of Lorenzo Lorenzo's slim, Cuban-influenced menu is the mouthwatering Caribbean Roast sandwich: marinated pork, topped with sautéed onions and served on a chewy baguette, is doused with an amazing sauce (the ingredients of which are known only by Lorenzo) that keeps folks coming back for more. The entrées are also delicious, from fresh fish in garlic tapenade to prawns in a spicy red sauce. There are a few tables, but Paseo gets so busy the line usually snakes way out the door, and most people opt for takeout. **TIP→ It's cash-only, so come prepared.** [$] *Average main: $13* ✉ *4225 Fremont Ave. N, Fremont* ☎ *206/545–7440* 🌐 *www.paseoseattle.com* 💳 *No credit cards* 🕒 *Closed Sun. and Mon.* ✥ *D1.*

$$ ASIAN FUSION 🍴 **Revel.** Adventurous enough for the most committed gourmands but accessible enough to be a neighborhood lunchtime favorite, Revel starts with Korean street food and shakes it up with a variety of influences, from French to Americana. Noodle dishes at this popular, sleek spot (try for a counter seat overlooking the open kitchen) might feature smoked tea noodles with roast duck or seaweed noodles with Dungeness crab, while irresistibly spicy dumplings might be stuffed with bites of short ribs, shallots, and scallions, or perhaps chickpeas, roasted cauliflower, and mustard yogurt. Plates are small enough so that you can save room for one of the playful desserts riffing off Junior Mints or butterscotch pudding. [$] *Average main: $22* ✉ *403 N. 36th St., Fremont* ☎ *206/547–2040* 🌐 *www.revelseattle.com* ✥ *D1.*

BALLARD

$ BAKERY 🍴 **Café Besalu.** A slice of France here in Ballard, this small, casual bakery gets patrons from across the entire city, thanks to its *I-swear-I'm-in-Paris* croissants—they are buttery, flaky perfection. Weekend lines are long, but if you score a table, you'll be in heaven. You can also, of course, take pastries to go, which is perfect if you're en route to Golden Gardens. Apple turnovers, *pain au chocolat,* decent espresso drinks, quiches, and sandwiches round out the offerings. Note that Besalu is a bit north of downtown Ballard on 24th Avenue, but the walk is worth it. **TIP→ Besalu has twice-yearly weekly closures, usually after Christmas and around July 4, so call ahead.** [$] *Average main: $3* ✉ *5909 24th Ave. NW, Ballard* ☎ *206/789–1463* 🌐 *www.cafebesalu.com* 🕒 *Closed Mon. and Tues.* ✥ *D1.*

$ PIZZA 🍴 **Delancey.** Brandon Pettit spent years developing his thin-but-chewy pizza crust, and the final product has made him a contender for the city's best pies from the day Delancey opened. Pettit himself is usually manning the wood-fired oven at this sweetly sophisticated little spot north of downtown Ballard that he owns with wife Molly Wizenberg (author of the "Orangette" food blog). Neighborhood families and far-flung travelers alike line up before opening time for seasonal pizzas topped with anything from fresh cheeses, local clams, pork fennel sausage, blistered padron peppers, nettles, and crimini mushrooms. The small wine list is well edited and elegant; desserts are simple but inspired— the homemade chocolate chip cookie with sea salt is delish. Charming service and quirky mismatched tables and lighting make this a Ballard experience to remember. $ *Average main: $14* ✉ *1415 N.W. 70th St., Ballard* ☎ *206/838–1960* ⊕ *www.delanceyseattle.com* ⊙ *Closed Mon. and Tues., no lunch* ✛ *D1.*

$

CAFÉ

× **Hot Cakes.** A few savory dishes are available at this Ballard "cak-ery," but consider passing on the chicken potpie in favor of the grilled chocolate sandwich. Autumn Martin, formerly head chocolatier at Theo Chocolate, specializes in creative, high-quality desserts such as a "s'mores" molten chocolate cake with house-made marshmallows and caramel, and cookies with house-smoked chocolate chips. Thick, rich milk shakes come in gourmet seasonal flavors like Meyer lemon with lavender, or grownup "boozy" shakes like smoked chocolate and scotch. Hot Cakes is open late night, too (till 10 pm Sunday through Thursday, and till 11 pm Friday and Saturday). A few long communal tables make for casual dining. ▮TIP➔ **There are a surprisingly large number of vegan options, too.** $ *Average main: $9* ✉ *5427 Ballard Ave. NW, Ballard* ☎ *206/420–3431* ⊕ *www.getyourhotcakes.com* ⌫ *Reservations not accepted* ✛ *D1.*

$

MEXICAN

Fodor's Choice

★

× **La Carta de Oaxaca.** True to its name, this low-key, bustling Ballard favorite serves traditional Mexican cooking with Oaxacan accents. The *mole negro* is a must, served with chicken or pork; another standout is the *albondigas* (a spicy vegetable soup with meatballs). The menu is mostly small plates, which works to your advantage because you won't have to choose just one savory dish. The small, casual space has an open kitchen enclosed by a stainless-steel bar, the walls are covered in gorgeous black-and-white photos. It gets very crowded on weekends and stays busy until late, though if you have a small party you usually don't have to wait too long for a table. $ *Average main: $16* ✉ *5431 Ballard Ave. NW, Ballard* ☎ *206/782–8722* ⊕ *www.lacartadeoaxaca. com* ⊙ *Closed Sun., no lunch Mon.* ✛ *D1.*

$$$

MODERN ITALIAN

× **Staple & Fancy.** The "Staple" side of this Ethan Stowell restaurant at the south end of Ballard Avenue might mean ethereal gnocchi served with corn and chanterelles, or a whole grilled branzino. But visitors to the glam remodeled historic brick building are best served by going "Fancy," meaning the $45 chef's choice dinner where diners are asked about allergies and food preferences, then presented with several courses (technically four, but the appetizer usually consists of a few different plates) of whatever the cooks (often including Stowell him-self) are playing with on the line that night—cured meats, salads made with exotic greens, handmade pastas, seasonal desserts. You won't know what's coming next, but it's usually remarkably good. $ *Average main: $27* ✉ *4739 Ballard Ave. NW, Ballard* ☎ *206/789–1200* ⊕ *www. ethanstowellrestaurants.com* ⊙ *No lunch* ✛ *E1.*

$$
SEAFOOD

✕ **The Walrus and the Carpenter.** Chef-owner Renee Erickson was inspired by the casual oyster bars of Paris to open this bustling shoebox of a restaurant on the south end of Ballard Avenue (in the rear of a historic brick building, behind Staple+Fancy). Seats fill fast at the zinc bar and the scattered tall tables where seafood fans slurp on fresh-shucked kusshis and shigokus and other local oysters, but the menu also offers refined small plates like grilled sardines with shallots and walnuts or roasted greengage plums in cream. ■ TIP→ Arriving soon after the 4 pm opening usually guarantees a seat, but not on Sundays, when the lineup starts early because of the popular Ballard Farmers Market. $ *Average main: $24* ⊠ *4743 Ballard Ave. NW, Ballard* ☎ *206/395–9227* ⊕ *www. thewalrusbar.com* ◱ *Reservations not accepted* ✛ *E1.*

WEST SEATTLE

$$
PACIFIC
NORTHWEST
Fodor'sChoice
★

✕ **Ma'ono Fried Chicken & Whiskey.** A quietly hip vibe pervades this culinary beacon in West Seattle, where the vast bar surrounds an open kitchen. Diners of all stripes relish the Hawaiian spin on fresh and high-quality Pacific Northwest bounty. Chef Mark Fuller's famous fried chicken dinners are offered nightly ($38 for a whole chicken, served with kimchi and rice), while his saiman soup with smoked ham broth, house-made noodles, mustard cabbage, and fish cake could cure any hangover. Spam musubi, Portuguese sweet bread, and other sides showcase expertly made but down-to-earth foods. There are some two-dozen whiskeys and a short cocktail list. $ *Average main: $18* ⊠ *4437 California Ave. SW, West Seattle* ☎ *206/935–1075* ⊕ *www.maono. springhillnorthwest.com* ⊗ *No lunch weekdays* ✛ *D6.*

THE EASTSIDE

$$$$
ITALIAN
Fodor'sChoice
★

✕ **Café Juanita.** There are so many ways for a pricey "destination restaurant" to go overboard, making itself nothing more than a special-occasion spectacle, but Café Juanita manages to get everything just right. This Kirkland space is refined without being overly posh, and the food—much of which has a northern Italian influence—is also perfectly balanced. One bite of lauded chef Holly Smith's tender saddle of Oregon lamb with baby artichokes, fava beans, and lemon emulsion and you'll be sold. The daily fish specials are almost always worth the plunge, and the restaurant is extremely accommodating for gluten-free guests. With advance notice, she'll craft individualized tasting menus at "Table 2" with its view of the kitchen. To top it all off, the restaurant has an excellent wine list. $ *Average main: $35* ⊠ *9702 NE 120th Pl., Eastside, Kirkland* ☎ *425/823–1505* ⊕ *www.cafejuanita.com* ◱ *Reservations essential* ⊗ *Closed Mon., no lunch* ✛ *D6.*

$$$$
PACIFIC
NORTHWEST

✕ **The Herbfarm.** You might consider fasting before dining at the Herbfarm. It's prix-fixe only and you'll get nine courses—dinner takes at least four hours and includes six fine wines (you might also want to arrange for transportation there and back). The dining room itself is reminiscent of a country estate, but before you tuck in, you'll be treated to a delightful tour of the herb garden. The set menus change roughly every other week, with clever themes like the 100-mile dinner where even the salt is harvested from local waters (if you have dietary restrictions, it's essential to call ahead). With all products coming from the restaurant's farm (including heritage pigs), or from other regional growers and suppliers, you can expect über-fresh ingredients, including rarities like Ozette potatoes and Roy's Calais flint corn. Book a room at elegant Willows Lodge to make a true getaway of it. [$] *Average main: $80* ✉ *14590 N.E. 145th St., Eastside, Woodinville* ☎ *425/485–5300* ⊕ *www.theherbfarm. com* ⌖ *Reservations essential* ⊗ *Closed Mon.–Wed., no lunch* ✛ *D1.*

WHERE TO STAY

Updated by Cedar Burnett

Use the coordinate (✛ B2) at the end of each listing to locate a site on the corresponding map. Prices in the reviews are the lowest cost of a standard double room in high season.

For expanded hotel reviews, visit Fodors.com.

Much like the eclectic city itself, Seattle's lodging offers something for everyone. There are grand, ornate vintage hotels; sleek and elegant, modern properties; green hotels with yoga studios and enough bamboo for an army of pandas; and cozy bed-and-breakfasts with sweet bedspreads and home-cooked breakfasts. Travelers who appreciate the anonymity of high-rise chains can comfortably stay here, while guests who want to feel like family can find the perfect boutique inn to lay their heads.

DOWNTOWN AND BELLTOWN

$
HOTEL
Fodor's Choice
★

Ace Hotel. The Ace is a dream come true for both penny-pinching hipsters and folks who appreciate unique minimalist decor. **Pros:** ultra-trendy but with some of the most affordable rates in town; good place to meet other travelers; free Wi-Fi. **Cons:** most rooms have shared bathrooms; not for people who want pampering; neighborhood rife with panhandlers; lots of stairs to get to lobby. [$] *Rooms from: $99* ✉ *2423 1st Ave., Belltown* ☎ *206/448–4721* ⊕ *www.acehotel.com* ⬎ *14 standard rooms, 14 deluxe rooms* ⊙ *No meals* ✛ *D4.*

$$
HOTEL

Alexis Hotel. Aesthetes and modern romantics will adore the Alexis Hotel, which occupies two historic buildings near the waterfront. **Pros:** great service; close to waterfront; unique, beautiful rooms; suites aren't prohibitively expensive. **Cons:** small lobby; not entirely soundproofed; some rooms can be a bit dark. [$] *Rooms from: $245* ✉ *1007 1st Ave., Downtown* ☎ *206/624–4844, 888/850–1155* ⊕ *www.alexishotel.com* ⬎ *88 rooms, 33 suites* ⊙ *No meals* ✛ *E5.*

$$$
HOTEL
Fodor's Choice
★

The Arctic Club Seattle – a DoubleTree by Hilton Hotel. From the Alaskan-marble-sheathed foyer and the antique walrus heads on the third floor, to the Northern Lights Dome room with its leaded glass ceiling and rococo touches, the Arctic Club pays homage to an era of Gold Rush opulence. **Pros:** cool, unique property; great staff; light-rail and bus lines just outside the door. **Cons:** not in the heart of Downtown; rooms are a bit dark; style may be off-putting for travelers who like modern hotels; charge for Wi-Fi. [$] *Rooms from: $289* ✉ *700 3rd Ave., Downtown*

9

WHERE SHOULD I STAY?

	Neighborhood Vibe	Pros	Cons
Downtown and Belltown	Downtown is central, with the hottest hotels with water views. If you're a fan of galleries and bars, stay in Belltown.	A day in Downtown and Belltown can take you from the Seattle Art Museum to Pike Place Market.	Parking can be pricey and hard to come by. This is not your spot if you want quiet, relaxing respite.
Seattle Center, South Lake Union, and Queen Anne	Queen Anne boasts great water views and easy access to Downtown. South Lake Union can feel industrial.	Seattle Center's many festivals (such as Bumbershoot) means you'll have a ringside seat.	If you're mostly focused on seeing the key Downtown sights or have limited mobility, parking can be difficult.
Capitol Hill	One of Seattle's oldest and quirkiest neighborhoods, Capitol Hill has cozy accommodations.	A great place to stay if you want to mingle with creative locals in great bookstores and cafés.	If you're uncomfortable with the pierced, tattooed, or GLBT set, look elsewhere.
Fremont	From the Woodland Park Zoo to the Locks, funky Fremont is an excellent jumping-off point.	This quintessential Seattle 'hood is a short trek from Downtown and has restaurants and shops.	The only lodgings to be found here are B&Bs—book ahead.
Green Lake	Laid-back and wonderfully situated near the Woodland Park Zoo and Gas Works Park.	Outdoorsy types will love the proximity to Green Lake, a great place to stroll or jog.	You won't find anything trendy here, and, after a few days, you'll have seen everything.
University District	It offers everything you'd expect from a college area—from bookstores to ethnic food.	If you're renting a car, this area offers centrality with a lower price tag.	Homeless and college kids populate University Avenue ("The Ave."). Not much in the way of sightseeing.
West Seattle	In summer, West Seattle can feel a lot like Southern California: It's a fun place to stay.	Alki Beach and Lincoln Park are fun, plus great restaurants and shopping on California Avenue.	You'll need a car to stay in this very removed 'hood. The only way in or out is over a bridge.
The Eastside	Proximity to high-end malls, Woodinville wineries, and Microsoft.	Woodinville is wine HQ; Kirkland offers cute boutiques; and Bellevue is a shopping mecca.	If you're here to experience Seattle, stick to the city. Traffic is a total nightmare.

☎ *206/340–0340, 800/445–8667* ⊕ *www.thearcticclubseattle.com* ⌂ *118 rooms, 2 suites* ⦿ *No meals* ✢ *E5.*

$$

B&B/INN

Fodor's Choice
★

🏠 **El Gaucho.** Hollywood Rat Pack enthusiasts will want to move right in to this dark, swank, and luxurious, retro-style inn, upstairs from Belltown's beloved El Gaucho steak house and the Big Picture—a fabulous movie theater with a full bar. **Pros:** unique aesthetic; some rooms have great views; location; warm, helpful staff. **Cons:** steep stairs with no elevator; some rooms only have showers; no outdoor spaces; rooms are (purposely) dark; no on-site fitness center. $ *Rooms from: $249* ⊠ *2505 1st Ave., Belltown* ☎ *206/728–1133, 866/354–2824* ⊕ *www.elgaucho. com* ⌂ *17 suites* ⦿ *No meals* ✢ *D4.*

BEST BETS FOR SEATTLE LODGING

Fodor's offers a selective listing of lodging experiences at every price range. Here, we've compiled our top recommendations by price and experience. The very best properties are designated in the listings with the Fodor's Choice logo.

9

$$$$ ⊡ **The Fairmont Olympic Hotel.** Grand and stately, the Fairmont Olympic

HOTEL   transports travelers to another time: with marble floors, brocade chairs,

FAMILY   massive chandeliers, and sweeping staircases, this old-world hotel per-

Fodor's Choice   sonifies class and elegance. **Pros:** great location; excellent service; fabu-

★   lous on-site dining and amenities. **Cons:** not much in the way of views;
may be a little too old-school for trendy travelers; remodel in 2013
means some rooms may be unavailable. $ *Rooms from: $409* ✉ *411
University St., Downtown* ☎ *206/621–1700, 888/363–5022* ⊕ *www.
fairmont.com/seattle* ⤳ *232 rooms, 218 suites* ⁙◎⁙ *No meals* ✛ *E4.*

$$$$ ⊡ **Four Seasons Hotel Seattle.** Just south of the Pike Place Market and

HOTEL   steps from the Seattle Art Museum, this Downtown gem is polished

FAMILY   and elegant, with Eastern accents and plush furnishings set against a

Fodor's Choice   modern-Northwest backdrop in which materials, such as stone and

★   fine hardwoods, take center stage. **Pros:** fantastic location with amazing views of Elliott Bay; large rooms with luxurious bathrooms; lovely
spa. **Cons:** Four Seasons regulars might not click with this modern take
on the brand; street-side rooms not entirely sound-proofed; some room
views are partially obscured by industrial sites. $ *Rooms from: $405*
✉ *99 Union St., Downtown* ☎ *206/749–7000, 800/332–3442* ⊕ *www.
fourseasons.com/seattle* ⤳ *134 rooms,13 suites* ⁙◎⁙ *No meals* ✛ *E5.*

$ ⊡ **Green Tortoise Backpacker's Hotel.** A Seattle institution, the Green Tor-

HOTEL   toise is still considered by many to be the best deal in town—and even
if you don't own a backpack and the word "hostel" gives you the
heebie-jeebies, the impressive cleanliness makes the Tortoise an option
for anyone on a budget who doesn't mind sacrificing a little privacy.
Pros: cheapest lodging in town; great place to make instant friends
from around the globe; across the street from Pike Place Market; great
bike rental program; free day storage. **Cons:** street noise; thin walls; if
you don't like the communal experience this isn't for you. $ *Rooms
from: $29* ✉ *105½ Pike St., Downtown* ☎ *206/340–1222* ⊕ *www.
greentortoise.net* ⤳ *30 rooms without en suite bath* ⁙◎⁙ *Breakfast* ✛ *D4.*

$$ ⊡ **Hotel 1000.** Chic and modern yet warm and inviting, the Hotel 1000

HOTEL   is luxe, with a distinctly Pacific Northwest feel, without being campy.

FAMILY   **Pros:** useful high-tech gadgets; guests feel pampered; hotel is hip without

Fodor's Choice   being alienating. **Cons:** rooms can be dark; rooms without views look

★   out on a cement wall; small gym. $ *Rooms from: $239* ✉ *1000 1st Ave.,
Downtown* ☎ *206/957–1000, 877/315–1088* ⊕ *www.hotel1000seattle.
com* ⤳ *101 rooms, 19 suites* ⁙◎⁙ *No meals* ✛ *E5.*

$$ ⊡ **Hotel Ändra.** Scandinavian sensibility and clean, modern lines define

HOTEL   this sophisticated hotel on the edge of Belltown. **Pros:** great lobby

Fodor's Choice   lounge; hip vibe; excellent service; spacious rooms. **Cons:** pricey

★   valet parking; street noise; not family-friendly. $ *Rooms from: $229*
✉ *2000 4th Ave., Belltown* ☎ *206/448–8600, 877/448–8600* ⊕ *www.
hotelandra.com* ⤳ *93 rooms, 4 studios, 22 suites* ⁙◎⁙ *No meals* ✛ *E4.*

$$ ⊡ **Hotel Monaco.** Thanks to a massive $5.2-million renovation completed

HOTEL   in 2012, the once slightly dated 189-room hotel has sprung back to

FAMILY   life with a modern-meets-global look. **Pros:** near Pike Place Market

Fodor's Choice   and the Space Needle; newly renovated; one of the best happy hours in

★   town. **Cons:** some street-facing rooms can be a little noisy; small gym.
$ *Rooms from: $239* ✉ *1101 4th Ave., Downtown* ☎ *206/621–1770,*

800/715–6513 ⊕ *www.monaco-seattle.com* ⇥ *152 rooms, 37 suites* |○| *No meals* ✛ *E5.*

$$ ⛭ **Hyatt at Olive 8.** In a city known for environmental responsibil-
HOTEL ity, being the greenest hotel in Seattle is no small feat—and green is
Fodor's Choice rarely this chic. **Pros:** central location; superb amenities; environmental
★ responsibility; wonderful spa. **Cons:** standard rooms have showers only;
guests complain of hallway and traffic noise; translucent glass bathroom
doors offer little privacy; fee for Wi-Fi. $ *Rooms from: $219* ⊠ *1635*
8th Ave., Downtown ☎ *206/695–1234, 800/233–1234* ⊕ *www.olive8.*
hyatt.com ⇥ *331 rooms, 15 suites* |○| *No meals* ✛ *E4.*

$$ ⛭ **Inn at the Market.** From its heart-stopping views and comfortable
B&B/INN rooms to the fabulous location and amazing fifth-floor deck perched
Fodor's Choice above Puget Sound, this is a place you'll want to visit again and again.
★ **Pros:** outstanding views from most rooms; steps from Pike Place Market; fantastic service; complimentary town-car service for Downtown
locations. **Cons:** little common space; a full renovation should take
place in early 2013 so some rooms may be unavailable; being in the
heart of the action means some street noise. $ *Rooms from: $265*
⊠ *86 Pine St., Downtown* ☎ *206/443–3600, 800/446–4484* ⊕ *www.*
innatthemarket.com ⇥ *63 rooms, 7 suites* |○| *No meals* ✛ *D4.*

$$ ⛭ **Mayflower Park Hotel.** Classic and comfortable, the Mayflower Park
HOTEL offers old-world charm in the center of the action. **Pros:** central Down-
Fodor's Choice town location; good value; direct connection to the airport via Light
★ Rail and Seattle Center via the Monorail; great service. **Cons:** rooms
are small; no pool. $ *Rooms from: $229* ⊠ *405 Olive Way, Downtown*
☎ *206/623–8700, 800/426–5100* ⊕ *www.mayflowerpark.com* ⇥ *160*
rooms, 29 suites |○| *No meals* ✛ *E4.*

$$$ ⛭ **Sorrento Hotel.** If you're the type who owns a smoking jacket, names
HOTEL aged Scotch as your poison, or wants to pretend you're on the set of
Fodor's Choice a period piece, look no further than this italianate hotel built in 1909.
★ **Pros:** serene and classy; fantastic service; great restaurant; fabulous
beds; free Downtown car service. **Cons:** not central; rooms are a bit
small. $ *Rooms from: $285* ⊠ *900 Madison St., First Hill* ☎ *206/622–*
6400, 800/426–1265 ⊕ *www.hotelsorrento.com* ⇥ *34 rooms, 42 suites*
|○| *No meals* ✛ *F4.*

SOUTH LAKE UNION AND QUEEN ANNE

$$ ⛭ **Pan Pacific Hotel Seattle.** Views of the Space Needle and Lake Union
HOTEL are one of the many perks at this stunning hotel, where the decor makes
FAMILY it feel full of light even during the gray Seattle winter. **Pros:** helpful
Fodor's Choice staff; feels more luxurious than it costs; away from the tourist throngs.
★ **Cons:** long walk to Downtown sights (though the streetcar stops right
out front); shoji doors are pretty but cut down on bathroom privacy in
standard rooms. $ *Rooms from: $225* ⊠ *2125 Terry Ave., South Lake*
Union ☎ *206/264–8111* ⊕ *www.panpacific.com/seattle* ⇥ *130 rooms,*
23 suites |○| *No meals* ✛ *E3.*

$$ ⛭ **The Maxwell Hotel.** This is *the* hotel for visitors frequenting the Seattle
HOTEL Center for opera or the ballet, or going to Teatro Zinzanni, whose huge,
colorful tent is just steps from the hotel. **Pros:** free parking and shuttle;
complimentary bikes; some rooms have great views of the Space Needle.

9

Fairmont Olympic Hotel

Four Seasons Hotel

Cons: hotel is on a busy street; pool and gym are tiny; guests complain of low water pressure. [$] *Rooms from: $219* ✉ *300 Roy St., Queen Anne* ☎ *206/286–0629, 866/866–7977* 🌐 *www.themaxwellhotel.com* 🛏 *139 rooms* 🍴 *No meals* ✛ *D2.*

CAPITOL HILL

$ B&B/INN Fodor's Choice ★ 🏨 **11th Avenue Inn Bed & Breakfast.** The closest B&B to Downtown, the 11th Avenue Inn offers all the charm of a classic bed-and-breakfast with the convenience of being near the action. **Pros:** unpretentious take on classic B&B; free on-site parking; wonderful owner and staff. **Cons:** no a/c; although most guests are courteous, sound does carry in old houses; no kids under 12. [$] *Rooms from: $129* ✉ *121 11th Ave. E, Capitol Hill* ☎ *206/720–7161, 800/720–7161* 🌐 *www.11thavenueinn.com* 🛏 *8 rooms* 🍴 *Breakfast* ✛ *F3.*

$ B&B/INN 🏨 **Gaslight Inn.** The Gaslight retains much of the charm of its single-family past, while offering contemporary and artistic touches not typically seen in a B&B. **Pros:** great art collection; house and rooms are quite spacious; pool; Wi-Fi. **Cons:** breakfast is unimpressive; street parking not always easy to find. [$] *Rooms from: $98* ✉ *1727 15th Ave., Capitol Hill* ☎ *206/325–3654* 🌐 *www.gaslight-inn.com* 🛏 *6 rooms with private bath; 2 rooms with shared bath* 🍴 *Breakfast* ✛ *G3.*

$ B&B/INN Fodor's Choice ★ 🏨 **Shafer Baillie Mansion Bed & Breakfast.** Guests have plenty of room to lounge and enjoy round-the-clock snacks, coffee, and tea in the library and salon of this gorgeous Grand Tudor Revival mansion, steps from Capitol Hill's Volunteer Park. **Pros:** wonderful staff; great interior and exterior common spaces; free Wi-Fi; location. **Cons:** no elevator and the walk to the third floor might be hard for some guests; while children are allowed, some guests say the mansion isn't kid-*friendly.* [$] *Rooms from: $149* ✉ *907 14th Ave. E, Capitol Hill, Sea-Tac* ☎ *800/985–4654* 🌐 *www.sbmansion.com* 🛏 *6 rooms; 2 suites* 🍴 *Breakfast* ✛ *G2.*

9

FREMONT

$$ B&B/INN Fodor's Choice ★ 🏨 **Chelsea Station Inn Bed & Breakfast.** On the edge of Fremont and Phinney Ridge, this 1920s brick colonial B&B is a convenient and luxurious jumping-off point for all the north end has to offer. **Pros:** great, unobtrusive host; huge rooms and 1½ bathrooms per suite; fabulous breakfasts and complimentary snacks. **Cons:** far from Downtown; no TVs; no elevator. [$] *Rooms from: $219* ✉ *4915 Linden Ave. N, Fremont* ☎ *206/547–6077* 🌐 *www.chelseastationinn.com* 🛏 *4 suites* 🍴 *Breakfast* ✛ *D1.*

GREEN LAKE

$ B&B/INN Fodor's Choice ★ 🏨 **Greenlake Guest House.** Outdoorsy types, visitors who want to stay in a low-key residential area, and anyone who wants to feel pampered and refreshed will enjoy this charming B&B, across the street from the eastern shore of beautiful Green Lake and a short walk from several restaurants. **Pros:** views of and quick access to Green Lake; thoughtful amenities and wonderful hosts; can accommodate kids over four years

Inn at the Market

Pan Pacific Hotel Seattle

Hotel 1000

old. **Cons:** five miles from Downtown; on a busy street. $\boxed{\$}$ *Rooms from: $164 ⊠ 7630 E. Green Lake Dr. N, Green Lake ☎ 206/729–8700, 866/355–8700 ⊕ www.greenlakeguesthouse.com ⥹ 4 rooms ⫛ Breakfast ⬩ F1.*

NIGHTLIFE

Updated by
Anna Maria
Stephens

Seattle's amazing musical legacy is well known, but there's more to the arts and nightlife scenes than live music. In fact, these days, there are far more swanky bars and inventive pubs than music venues in the city. To put it bluntly, Seattle's a dynamite place to drink. You can sip overly ambitious and ridiculously named specialty cocktails in trendy lounges, get a lesson from an enthusiastic sommelier in a wine bar or restaurant, or swill cheap beer on the patio of a dive bar. Though some places have very specific demographics, most Seattle bars are egalitarian, drawing loyal regulars of all ages.

The music scene is still kicking—there's something going on every night of the week in nearly every genre of music.

In addition to its bars, Downtown and Belltown in particular have notable restaurants with separate bar areas. ▮▮**TIP**➜ **Nearly all of Tom Douglas's restaurants have busy after-work and weekend bar scenes, as do trendy hotel restaurants.** Most restaurants have impressive bar menus, and food is often served until 11 pm, midnight, or even 1 am in some spots.

DOWNTOWN AND BELLTOWN

BARS AND LOUNGES

Alibi Room. Well-dressed locals head to this hard-to-find wood-paneled bar to sip double martinis while taking in views of Elliott Bay or studying the scripts, handbills, and movie posters that line the walls. The lower level is more crowded and casual. It's an ever-cool yet low-key, intimate place. Stop by for a drink or a meal, or stay to listen and dance to live music. Happy hour—weekdays from 3 to 6 and weekends from noon to 6—is quiet and a good respite from the Market. ⊠ *85 Pike St., in Post Alley, at Pike Place Market, Downtown ☎ 206/623–3180 ⊕ www.seattlealibi.com.*

Black Bottle. Sleek and sexy, Black Bottle makes the northern reaches of Belltown look good. The interior of this gastro-tavern is simple but stylish, with black chairs and tables and shiny wood floors. It gets crowded on nights and weekends with a laid-back but often dressed-up clientele. A small selection of beers on tap and a solid wine list (with Washington, Oregon, California, and beyond well represented) will help you wash down the sustainably sourced pub snacks, including house-smoked wild boar ribs, pork belly with kimchi, and oysters on the half shell. ⊠ *2600 1st Ave., Belltown ☎ 206/441–1500 ⊕ www.blackbottleseattle.com.*

Oliver's Twist. The most important question here: Shaken or stirred? Oliver's Twist, in the Mayflower Park Hotel, is famous for its martinis. In fact, having a cocktail here is like having afternoon tea in some other parts of the world. Wing chairs, low tables, and lots of natural light make it easy to relax after a hectic day. The likes of Frank Sinatra or Billie Holiday may be playing in the background; expect an unfussy crowd of regulars, hotel guests, and older Manhattan-sippers who appreciate old-school elegance. ⊠ *405 Olive Way, Downtown* ☎ *206/706–6673* ⊕ *oliverstwistseattle.com.*

Purple Café and Wine Bar. Wine-lovers come for the massive selection—the menu boasts 80 wines by the glass and some 600 bottles—but Purple Café and Wine Bar deserves props for its design, too. Despite the cavernous quality of the space and floor-to-ceiling windows, all eyes are immediately drawn to the 20-foot tower ringed by a spiral staircase that showcases thousands of bottles. There are full lunch and dinner menus (American and Pacific Northwest fare), as well as tasting menus. Try the popular lobster mac and cheese or a tasty baked Brie. Though Purple is surprisingly unpretentious for a place in the financial district of Downtown, it's sophisticated enough that you'll want to dress up a bit. ⊠ *1225 4th Ave., Downtown* ☎ *206/829–2280* ⊕ *www. thepurplecafe.com.*

Spur. The inventive small plates and carefully planned drink menu make this a very popular nightspot and a favorite with foodies. The decor, which pays subtle photographic homage to the pioneers, fishermen, and outlaws of Seattle's past, is also a draw. Sip a bourbon-infused cocktail and munch on stellar crostini with salmon or veal sweetbreads. Spur can be a bit spendy, so it may make sense to save your visit for happy hour (Sunday to Thursday 5 to 7) or for a late-night snack (it serves a special pairing menu from 11 to 1:30). ⊠ *113 Blanchard St., Belltown* ☎ *206/728–6706* ⊕ *www.spurseattle.com.*

Vessel. After being shuttered for nearly two years, one of Seattle's legendary cocktail bars is back on the scene. You'll find some of Seattle's expert mixologists at Vessel, where the artisanal drinks are stellar and the atmosphere of these sleek new digs is always buzzing. Accents of leather, steel and red resin lend a masculine vibe to the space, and the custom bar, made from a 24-foot slab of madrona wood, gives bartenders plenty of room to showcase their talent. Even the ice is custom made—out of view, alas—with a giant tray and a chainsaw. Vessel also serves a full lunch and dinner menu. ⊠ *624 Olive Way, Downtown* ⊕ *www.vesselseattle.com.*

Fodor's Choice
★
Zig Zag Café. When it comes to pouring perfect martinis, Zig Zag Café gives Oliver's a run for its money—and it's much more eclectic and relaxed here. A mixed crowd of mostly locals hunts out this unique spot at Pike Place Market's Street Hill Climb (a nearly hidden stairwell leading down to the piers). Several memorable cocktails include the Don't Give Up the Ship (gin, Dubonnet, Grand Marnier, and Fernet Branca), the One-Legged Duck (rye whiskey, Dubonnet, Mandarine Napoleon, and Fernet Branca), and Satan's Soulpatch (bourbon, sweet and dry vermouth, Grand Marnier, orange, and orange bitters). A very simple, ho-hum food menu includes cheese and meat plates, bruschetta, soup, salad, olives, and nuts. A small patio is the place to be on a summery happy-hour evening. Zig Zag is friendly—retro without being

obnoxiously ironic—and very Seattle, with the occasional live music show to boot. ⊠ *1501 Western Ave., Downtown* ☎ *206/625–1146* ⊕ *zigzagseattle.com.*

LIVE MUSIC

Fodor's Choice ★ **The Crocodile.** The heart and soul of Seattle's music scene since 1991, the Crocodile has hosted the likes of Nirvana, Pearl Jam, and Mudhoney, along with countless other bands. Seattleites mourned when it closed in 2007, and rejoiced even harder when it reopened, with much improved sightlines, in 2009. Nightly shows are complemented by cheap beer on tap and pizza right next door at Via Tribunali. All hail the Croc! ⊠ *2200 2nd Ave., Belltown* ☎ *206/441–7416* ⊕ *www.thecrocodile.com.*

Dimitriou's Jazz Alley. Seattleites dress up to see nationally known jazz artists at Dimitriou's. The cabaret-style theater, where intimate tables for two surround the stage, runs shows nightly. Those with reservations for cocktails or dinner, served during the first set, receive priority seating. ⊠ *2033 6th Ave., Downtown* ☎ *206/441–9729* ⊕ *www.jazzalley.com.*

Showbox. Just across from Pike Place Market, Showbox is a great place to see some pretty big-name acts. The acoustics are decent, the venue's small enough that you don't feel like you're miles away from the performers, and the bar areas flanking the main floor provide some relief if you don't want to join the crush in front of the stage. Another branch, **Showbox SoDo** (*1700 1st Ave. S, SoDo*), is named for its location south of Downtown. The converted warehouse, larger than the original, features big national acts. ⊠ *1426 1st Ave., Downtown* ☎ *206/628–3151* ⊕ *www.showboxonline.com.*

THEATER

Paramount Theatre. Built in 1928 as a venue for early talkies and vaudeville acts, this lovely beaux arts movie palace—which features an original Wurlitzer theatre pipe organ—now mostly hosts concerts, as well as the occasional comedy, dance, or Broadway event. ⊠ *907 Pine St., Downtown* ☎ *206/682–1414* ⊕ *www.stgpresents.org.*

9

QUEEN ANNE

MUSIC CLUB

Teatro ZinZanni. There's dinner theater, and then there's Seattle's famous Teatro ZinZanni, an over-the-top—and totally entertaining—five-course feast with a circus on the side. Featuring vaudeville, comedy, music and dance, the themed shows change every few months, but ZinZanni, in the heart of Seattle Center, remains a reliable favorite for locals and tourists alike. ⊠ *222 Mercer St., Queen Anne* ☎ *206/802–0015* ⊕ *dreams.zinzanni.org.*

PIONEER SQUARE

BARS AND LOUNGES

Collins Pub. The best beer bar in Pioneer Square, Collins Pub features 22 rotating taps of Northwest (including Boundary Bay, Chuckanut, and Anacortes) and California beers and a long list of bottles from the region. Its upscale pub menu features local and seasonal ingredients—try the grilled lamb chops or the Parmesan risotto cakes with your pint. ✉ *526 2nd Ave., Pioneer Square* ☎ *206/623–1016* ⊕ *www.thecollinspub.com.*

Saké Nomi. Whether you're a novice or expert, you'll appreciate the authentic offerings at Saké Nomi. The shop and tasting bar is open until 10 pm Tuesday through Saturday and from noon to 6 on Sunday. Don't be shy—have a seat, try a few of the rotating samples, and ask a lot of questions. Sake can be served up in a variety of temperatures and styles. ✉ *76 S. Washington St., Pioneer Square* ☎ *206/467–7253* ⊕ *www.sakenomi.us.*

CAPITOL HILL

BARS AND LOUNGES

Capitol Club. At this sumptuous Moroccan-themed escape, you can sprawl on tasseled floor cushions and dine on Mediterranean treats. Despite this being one of the neighborhood's see-and-be-seen spots, good attitudes prevail, and the waitresses are always affable and efficient, even during busy weekend nights. ✉ *414 E. Pine St., Capitol Hill* ☎ *206/325–2149.*

Linda's Tavern. Welcome to one of the Hill's iconic dives—and not just because it was allegedly the last place Kurt Cobain was seen alive. The interior has a vaguely Western theme, but the patrons are pure Capitol Hill indie-rockers and hipsters. The bartenders are friendly, the burgers are good (brunch is even better), and the always-packed patio is one of the liveliest places to grab a happy-hour drink. ✉ *707 E. Pine St., Capitol Hill* ☎ *206/325–1220* ⊕ *www.lindastavern.com.*

Fodor'sChoice ★ **Quinn's.** Laid-back but very cool, this is one of our go-to places for great beer. A friendly, knowledgeable staff tends the bar and the tables at the pub area, serving delicious food (especially the burgers)—and even better beers. It can get very busy on weekends, but if you arrive in early evening on a weekday, you can sidle up to the bar, order some nibbles, and chat up the bartender about the numerous (rotating) brews on tap, including Belgian favorites, local IPAs, Russian River winners, and more. ✉ *1001 E. Pike St., Capitol Hill* ☎ *206/325–7711* ⊕ *www.quinnspubseattle.com.*

The Pine Box. The clever name is just one reason to visit The Pine Box, a beer hall housed in a former funeral home on the corner of Pine Street. The churchlike interior is stately, with soaring ceilings, dark woodwork, and custom furniture made from huge Douglas fir timbers found in the basement—they were supposedly used to shelve coffins many years ago. The place is rumored to be haunted, but that doesn't stop a trendy crowd from congregating to sample from 30-plus taps of craft beer and a menu of wood-fired pizza and entrées like herbed lamb loin and pancetta scallops. ✉ *1600 Melrose Ave., Capitol Hill* ☎ *206/588–0375* ⊕ *www.pineboxbar.com.*

BREWPUBS

Elysian Brewing Company. Worn booths and tables are scattered across the bi-level warehouse space of this Capitol Hill mainstay. Its beers are a good representation of the thriving brewing scene in the Northwest.

The Crocodile

Always on tap are the hop-heavy Immortal IPA, the rich Perseus Porter, and the crisp Elysian Fields Pale Ale. The food (burgers, fish tacos, sandwiches, salads) is decent too. This is a favorite of Seattleites and Capitol Hill residents and a good alternative to the more trendy haunts and lounges in the area. There's another branch in Wallingford near Green Lake on North 55th and Meridien, but it's a bit off the beaten path unless you're staying in that area. ⊠ *1221 E. Pike St., Capitol Hill* ☎ *206/860–1920* ⊕ *www.elysianbrewing.com.*

LIVE MUSIC

Neumo's. Once one of the grunge era's iconic clubs (when it was Moe's), Neumo's has managed to reclaim its status as a staple of the Seattle rock scene, despite being closed for a six-year stretch. And it is a great rock venue: acoustics are excellent, and the roster of cutting-edge indie rock bands is the best in the city. That said, it's one of the most uncomfortable places in town to see a show (sight lines throughout the club can be terrible). It's also stuffy and hot during sold-out shows. ⊠ *925 E. Pike St., Capitol Hill* ☎ *206/709–9467* ⊕ *www.neumos.com.*

FREMONT, PHINNEY RIDGE, AND GREEN LAKE

BARS AND LOUNGES

Brouwer's. It may look like a trendy Gothic castle, but in fact this is heaven for Belgian-beer lovers. A converted warehouse provides an ample venue for a top selection of suds, which are provided by the owners of Seattle's best specialty-beer shop, Bottleworks. Brouwer's serves plenty of German and American beers, too, as well as English, Czech, and Polish selections. A menu of surprisingly good sandwiches, frites, and Belgian specialties help to lay a pre-imbibing foundation (remember that most Belgian beers have a higher alcohol content). Before settling on a seat downstairs, check out the balcony and the cozy parlor room. ✉ *400 N. 35th St., Fremont* ☎ *206/267–2437* ⊕ *www.brouwerscafe. com.*

Quoin. Even if you're not staying for dinner at the neighboring Revel— a Korean fusion restaurant that's won raves for its dumplings, rice, and noodle dishes—Quoin is worth a visit. The sliver of a bar makes a fantastic cocktail, and offers a much more intimate and stylish experience than most Fremont bars. There's also an outdoor deck with bench seating around a fire pit. ✉ *403 N 36th St., Fremont* ☎ *206/547–2040.*

Über Tavern. At what many serious aficionados claim may be one of the best beer bars on the planet, there's a constantly changing lineup of drafts—everything from Belgian imports to hop-heavy California DIPAs (double IPAs)—as well as a big list of bottles from around the globe. A digital menu shows what's on tap (and what's almost out) and there are Scrabble and checkers boards built into the bar tables—perfect for lazy afternoons. Über doesn't offer food, but you're free to order from a stack of takeout menus. ✉ *7517 Aurora Ave. N, Green Lake* ☎ *206/782–2337* ⊕ *www.uberbier.com.*

BREWPUBS

Hale's Ales. Opened in 1983, Hale's is one of the city's oldest craft breweries. It produces unique English-style ales, cask-conditioned ales and nitrogen-conditioned cream ales, plus a popular Mongoose IPA. The pub serves a full menu and has a great view of the fermenting room. Order a taster's flight if you want to try everything. ✉ *4301 Leary Way NW, Fremont* ☎ *206/706–1544* ⊕ *www.halesbrewery.com.*

BALLARD

BARS AND LOUNGES

The BalMar. One of Ballard's largest and most attractive bars, this former department store has exposed-brick walls, hardwood floors, comfy cocoa-color couches, and ottomans. The two stories include areas to dine (serving a small-plates menu), drink, and shoot pool. It can be a bit of a fratty meat market on Saturday, but other than that it's usually pretty mellow, and there's room enough to accommodate all the groups of friends and coworkers who enjoy this slightly more upscale alternative to Ballard's neighborhood joints. ✉ *5449 Ballard Ave. NW, Ballard* ☎ *703/289–9000* ⊕ *www.thebalmar.com.*

Moshi Moshi Sushi. Inventive cocktails are expertly poured beneath a tree with lighted faux-cherry blossoms at this Japanese restaurant's bar. Refreshingly, the cocktail menu steers clear of sake-tinis—there are one or two sake concoctions, but you're more likely to find whiskey, gin, brandy, or tequila put to good use, as in the Bella Donna (gin, black muscat, vermouth blanc, and lavender bitters) or the Sweet Savage (whiskey, Aperol, maple syrup, and grapefruit). There always seems to be a happy hour or nightly special at the bar, including the evening-long

Elysian Brewing Company

happy hour on Sunday. ✉ *5324 Ballard Ave., Ballard* ☎ *206/971–7424* ⊕ *www.moshiseattle.com.*

The Peoples Pub. Head to this Ballard institution to see what locals love about this unpretentious neighborhood. The pub (a dining room and a separate bar in the back) isn't much to look at—a lot of wood paneling, simple wood tables and chairs, and some unfortunate floral upholstery—but it has a "*Prost*"-worthy selection of German beers and one delicious fried pickle. True to its name, Peoples draws an interesting cross section of the neighborhood, from the young and trendy to old-school fishermen. ✉ *5429 Ballard Ave. NW, Ballard* ☎ *206/783–6521* ⊕ *www.peoplespub.com.*

Portalis. Serious oenophiles gather around communal tables and at the long bar to sample wines from around the world in this cozy, brick-lined bar. It's a full-service retail shop as well, so you can pick up a few bottles to take home. Though it's a bit stuffy for the neighborhood, it's a nice alternative to the frenetic scene on the upper part of Ballard Avenue. ✉ *5205 Ballard Ave. NW, Ballard* ☎ *206/783–2007* ⊕ *www. portaliswines.com.*

The Noble Fir. A rotating selection of great beer, cider, and wine and a truly varied crowd are just part of the appeal of this popular bar. Like many (most?) Seattleites, the husband-and-wife owners are outdoorsy—and it shows in the rustic-modern interior, which includes a library-like seating area stocked with large trail maps, as well as hundreds of travel books. The Noble Fir serves a few simple snacks, like cheese and charcuterie, in case you feel like settling in and planning your next big adventure. ⊠ *5316 Ballard Ave., Ballard* ☎ *206/420-7425* ⊕ *www. thenoblefir.com.*

Ocho. Blink and you'll miss it, and that would be a shame, because this tiny corner hot spot crafts some of the finest cocktails in town. Try the Donkey Tongue, made with chili-infused tequila, cucumber, pomegranate liqueur and lemon, or the San Miguel, a refreshing concoction of gin, St. Germain, lemon and rhubarb bitters. Dimly lit and loud, Ocho only has a few tables and bar seats, and it fills up fast with an attractive crowd that flocks here for the drinks and top-notch Spanish tapas. It's usually possible to snag a table without a wait during the weekend happy hour from noon to 6. Come summer, the slender sidewalk patio is an ideal spot for soaking up the sun and people-watching. ⊠ *2325 NW Market St., Ballard* ☎ *206/784–0699* ⊕ *www.ochoballard.com.*

LIVE MUSIC

Tractor Tavern. Seattle's top spot for roots music and alt-country has a large, dimly lighted hall with all the right touches—wagon-wheel fixtures, exposed-brick walls, and a cheery staff. The sound system is outstanding. ⊠ *5213 Ballard Ave. NW, Ballard* ☎ *206/789–3599* ⊕ *www. tractortavern.com.*

SPORTS AND THE OUTDOORS

Updated by
Anna Maria
Stephens

The question in Seattle isn't "Do you exercise?" Rather, it's "How do you exercise?" Athleticism is a regular part of most people's lives here, whether it's an afternoon jog, a sunrise rowing session, a lunch-hour bike ride, or an evening game of Frisbee.

The Cascade Mountains, a 60-minute drive east, have trails and peaks for alpinists of all skill levels. Snoqualmie Pass attracts downhill skiers and snowboarders, and cross-country skiing and snowshoeing are excellent throughout the Cascades. To the west of the city is Puget Sound, where sailors, kayakers, and anglers practice their sports. Lake Union and Lake Washington also provide residents with plenty of boating, kayaking, fishing, and swimming opportunities. Farther west, the Olympic Mountains beckon adventure-seeking souls to their unspoiled wilderness.

Spectator sports are also appreciated here, from the UW Huskies (Go Dawgs!) to the Sonics, Seattle's beloved pro soccer team.

PARKS INFORMATION

King County Parks and Recreation. This agency manages many of the parks outside city limits. ☎ *206/296–4232 information and reservations* ⊕ *www.kingcounty.gov/recreation/parks.aspx.*

Seattle Parks and Recreation Department. To find out whether an in-town park baseball diamond or tennis court is available, contact the Seattle Parks and Recreation Department, which is responsible for most of the parks, piers, beaches, playgrounds, and courts within city limits. The department issues permits for events, arranges reservations for facilities, and staffs visitor centers and naturalist programs. ☎ *206/684–4075* ⊕ *www.seattle.gov/parks.*

Bicyclists ride along Lake Washington in the Seattle-to-Portland (STP) event.

Washington State Parks. The state manages several parks and campgrounds in greater Seattle. ✉ *1111 Israel Rd. S.W.* ☎ *360/902–8844 for general information, 888/226–7688 for campsite reservations* ⊕ *www. parks.wa.gov.*

BASEBALL

Seattle Mariners. The Seattle Mariners play at **Safeco Field,** a retractable-roof stadium where there really isn't a bad seat in the house. One local sports columnist referred to the $656 million venue—which finished $100 million over budget—as "the guilty pleasure." You can purchase tickets through Ticketmaster or StubHub; online or by phone from Safeco Field (to be picked up at the Will Call); in person at Safeco's box office (no surcharges), which is open daily 10–6; or from the Mariners team store at 4th Avenue and Stewart Street in Downtown. The cheap seats cost $9; better seats cost $38–$98, and the best seats go for up to $300. ✉ *1st Ave. S and Atlantic St., Sodo* ☎ *206/346–4000* ⊕ *seattle. mariners.mlb.com.*

BICYCLING

Biking is probably Seattle's most popular sport. Thousands of Seattleites bike to work, and even more ride recreationally, especially on weekends. In the past, Seattle hasn't been a particularly bike-friendly city. But in 2007, city government adopted a sweeping Bicycle Master Plan, calling for 118 new miles of bike lanes, 19 miles of bike paths, and countless route signs and lane markings throughout the city by 2017. The plan can't erase the hills, though—only masochists should attempt Queen Anne Hill and Phinney Ridge. Fortunately, all city buses have easy-to-use bike racks (on the front of the buses, below the windshield) and drivers are used to waiting for cyclists to load and unload their bikes. If you're not comfortable biking in urban traffic—and there is a lot of urban traffic to contend with here—you can do a combination bus-and-bike tour of the city or stick to the car-free Burke-Gilman Trail.

Seattle drivers are fairly used to sharing the road with cyclists. With the exception of the occasional road-rager or clueless cell-phone talker, drivers usually leave a generous amount of room when passing; however, there are biking fatalities every year, so be alert and cautious, especially when approaching blind intersections, of which Seattle has many. You must wear a helmet at all times (it's the law) and be sure to lock up your bike—bikes do get stolen, even in quiet residential neighborhoods.

The Seattle Parks Department sponsors Bicycle Sundays on various weekends from May through September. On these Sundays, a 4-mile stretch of Lake Washington Boulevard—from Mt. Baker Beach to Seward Park—is closed to motor vehicles. Many riders continue around the 2-mile loop at Seward Park and back to Mt. Baker Beach to complete a 10-mile, car-free ride. Check with the **Seattle Parks and Recreation Department** (☎ 206/684–4075 ⊕ www.seattle.gov/parks/bicyclesunday) for a complete schedule.

The trail that circles **Green Lake** is popular with cyclists, though runners and walkers can impede fast travel. The city-maintained **Burke-Gilman Trail,** a slightly less congested path, follows an abandoned railroad line 14 miles roughly following Seattle's waterfront from Ballard to Kenmore, at the north end of Lake Washington. (From there, serious cyclists can continue on the Sammamish River Trail to Marymoor Park in Redmond; in all, the trail spans 42 miles between Seattle and Issaquah.) **Discovery Park** is a very tranquil place to tool around in. **Myrtle Edwards Park,** north of Pier 70, has a two-lane waterfront path for bicycling and running. The **islands of the Puget Sound** are also easily explored by bike (there are rental places by the ferry terminals), though keep in mind that Bainbridge, Whidbey, and the San Juans all have some tough hills.

King County has more than 100 miles of paved and nearly 70 miles of unpaved routes, including the Sammamish River, Interurban, Green River, Cedar River, Snoqualmie Valley, and Soos Creek trails. For more information contact the **King County Parks and Recreation** office (☎ 206/296–8687).

RENTALS

Montlake Bicycle Shop. Montlake, a mile south of the University of Washington and within easy riding distance of the Burke-Gilman Trail, rents mountain bikes, road bikes, basic cruisers, and tandems. Prices range from $35 to $90 for the day, with discounts for longer rentals. If you find yourself on the Eastside, you can rent a bike from its Kirkland branch. ✉ 2223 24th Ave. E, Montlake ☎ 206/329–7333 ⊕ www.montlakebike.com.

Agua Verde Paddle Club and Café

BOATING AND KAYAKING

Fodor's Choice
★ **Agua Verde Cafe & Paddle Club.** Start out by renting a kayak and paddling along either the Lake Union shoreline, with its hodgepodge of funky-to-fabulous houseboats and dramatic Downtown vistas, or Union Bay on Lake Washington, with its marshes and cattails. Afterward, take in the lakefront as you wash down some Mexican food (halibut tacos, anyone?) with a margarita. Kayaks and stand up paddleboards are available March through October and are rented by the hour—$15 for singles, $20 for doubles. It pays to paddle midweek: the third hour is free on weekdays. ⊠ *1303 NE Boat St., University District* ☎ *206/545–8570* ⊕ *www.aguaverde.com.*

Alki Kayak Tours & Adventure Center. For a variety of day-long guided kayak outings—from a Seattle Sunset Sea Kayak Tour to an Alki Point Lighthouse Tour—led by experienced, fun staff, try this great outfitter in West Seattle. In addition to kayaks, you can also rent skates, fishing boats, and longboards here. Custom sea-kayaking adventures can be set up, too. To rent a kayak without a guide, you must be an experienced kayaker; otherwise, sign up for one of the fascinating guided tours. ⊠ *1660 Harbor Ave. SW, West Seattle* ☎ *206/953–0237* ⊕ *kayakalki.com.*

The Center for Wooden Boats. Located on the southern shore of Lake Union, Seattle's free maritime heritage museum is a bustling community hub. Thousands of Seattleites rent rowboats and small wooden sailboats here every year; the Center also offers workshops, demonstrations, and classes. Rentals for nonmembers range from $25 to $30. There's also a $10 skills-check fee. Free half-hour guided sails and steamboat rides are offered on Sunday from 2 to 4 (arrive an hour early to reserve a spot). ✉ *1010 Valley St., Lake Union* ☎ *206/382–2628* ⊕ *www.cwb.org.*

Green Lake Boat Rental. This shop is the source for canoes, paddleboats, sailboats, kayaks, sailboards, and rowboats to take out on Green Lake's calm waters. On beautiful summer afternoons, however, be prepared to spend most of your time dealing with traffic, both in the parking lot and on the water. Fees are $17 an hour for paddleboats, single kayaks, rowboats, and sailboards, $20 an hour for sailboats. Don't confuse this place with the Green Lake Small Craft Center, which offers sailing programs but no rentals. ✉ *7351 E. Green Lake Dr. N, Green Lake* ☎ *206/527–0171* ⊕ *www.greenlakeboatrentals.net.*

Northwest Outdoor Center. This center on Lake Union's west side rents one- or two-person kayaks (it also has a few triples) by the hour or day, including equipment and basic or advanced instruction. The hourly rate is $13 for a single and $19 for a double (costs are figured in 10-minute increments after the first hour). If you want to find your own water, NWOC offers "to-go" kayaks. In summer, reserve at least three days ahead. NWOC also runs guided trips to the Nisqually Delta and Chuckanut Bay, as well as sunset tours near Golden Gardens Park and moonlight tours of Portage Bay. ✉ *2100 Westlake Ave. N, Lake Union* ☎ *206/281–9694* ⊕ *www.nwoc.com.*

Wind Works Sailing & Powerboating. Although members are given first pick at this club on Shilshole Bay, nonmembers can also arrange rentals. Experienced sailors are allowed to skipper their own boats after a brief qualifying process. Daily charter rental rates range from $150 to $350 during peak season. ✉ *7001 Seaview Ave. NW, Suite 110, Ballard* ☎ *206/784–9386* ⊕ *www.windworkssailing.com.*

FOOTBALL

Seattle Seahawks. The Seattle Seahawks play in the $430-million, state-of-the-art Qwest Field. Single-game football tickets go on sale in late July or early August, and all home games sell out quickly. Tickets are expensive, with the cheapest seats, in the 300 section (where you actually get a really good view of the field), starting at $42. Note that traffic and parking are both nightmares on game days; try to take public transportation—or walk the mile from Downtown. ✉ *800 Occidental Ave. S, Sodo* ☎ *425/203–8000* ⊕ *www.seahawks.com.*

GOLF

Gold Mountain Golf Complex. Most people make the trek to Bremerton to play the Olympic Course, a beautiful and challenging par 72 that is widely considered the best public course in Washington. The older, less-sculpted Cascade Course is also popular; it's better suited to those new to the game. There are four putting greens, a driving range, and a striking clubhouse with views of the Belfair Valley. Prime-time greens fees are $33–$40 for the Cascade and $45–$65 for the Olympic. Carts are $32. You can drive all the way to Bremerton via I–5, or you can take the car ferry to Bremerton from Pier 52. The trip will take roughly an hour and a half no matter which way you do it, but the ferry ride (60 minutes) might be a more pleasant way to spend a large part of the journey. Note, however, that the earliest departure time for the ferry is 6 am, so this option won't work for very early tee times. ☒ *7263 W. Belfair Valley Rd., Bremerton* ☎ *206/464–1175* ⊕ *www.goldmt.com.*

Jefferson Park. This golf complex has views of the city skyline *and* Mt. Rainier. The par-27, 9-hole course has a lighted driving range with heated stalls that's open from dusk until midnight. And the 18-hole, par-72 main course is one of the city's best. Greens fees are $38 on weekends and $33 on weekdays for the 18-hole course; you can play the 9-hole course for $8.50 daily. Carts are $26 and $17, and $2 buys you a bucket of 30 balls at the driving range. You can book tee times online up to 10 days in advance or by phone up to 7 days in advance. ☒ *4101 Beacon Ave. S, Beacon Hill* ☎ *206/762–4513* ⊕ *www.seattlegolf.com.*

Willows Run. Willows has it all: two 18-hole, links-style courses; a 9-hole, par-27 course; and a lighted, 18-hole putting course that's open until 11 pm. It also plays reasonably dry even in typically moist Seattle-area weather. Greens fees for 9 holes are $22 Monday through Thursday, $26 Friday through Sunday and on holidays; fees for 18 holes are $42 or $56. Carts cost $14 per rider. There are also two pro shops and a driving range (75 balls cost $7; 35 balls cost $4). ☒ *10402 Willows Rd. NE, Redmond* ☎ *425/883–1200* ⊕ *www.willowsrun.com.*

HIKING

■TIP➜ Within Seattle city limits, the best nature trails can be found in Discovery Park, Lincoln Park, Seward Park, and at the Washington Park Arboretum.

Cougar Mountain Regional Wildland Park. This spectacular park in the "Issaquah Alps" has more than 36 miles of hiking trails and 12 miles of bridle trails within its 3,000-plus acres. The Indian Trail, believed to date back 8,000 years, was part of a trade route that Native Americans used to reach North Bend and the Cascades. Thick pine forests rise to spectacular mountaintop views; there are waterfalls, deep caves, and the remnants of a former mining town. Local residents include deer, black bears, bobcats, bald eagles, and pileated woodpeckers, among many other woodland creatures. ☒ *18201 SE Cougar Mountain Dr., Issaquah* ✛ *From Downtown Seattle take I–90 East; follow signs to park beyond Issaquah* ☉ *Daily 8 am–dusk.*

Mt. Si. A good place to cut your teeth before setting out on more-ambitious hikes—or a good place to just witness the local hikers and trail-runners in all their weird and wonderful splendor. Mt. Si offers a challenging hike with views of a valley (slightly marred by the suburbs) and the Olympic Mountains in the distance. The main trail to Haystack Basin, 8 miles round-trip, climbs some 4,000 vertical feet, but there are several obvious places to rest or turn around if you'd like to keep the hike to 3 or 4 miles. Note that solitude is in short supply here—this is an extremely popular trail thanks to its proximity to Seattle. ✛ *Take I–90 East to Exit 31 (towards North Bend). Turn onto North Bend*

Way and then make a left onto Mt. Si Rd. and follow that road to the trailhead parking lot. ⊕ www.mountsi.com.

Snow Lake. Washington State's most popular wilderness trail may be crowded at times, but the scenery and convenience of this hike make it a classic. The 8-mile roundtrip sports a relatively modest 1,300-foot elevation gain; the views of the Alpine Lakes Wilderness are well worth the sweat. The glimmering waters of Snow Lake await hikers at the trail's end; summer visitors will find abundant wildflowers, huckleberries, and wild birds. ⊹ *Take I–90 East to Exit 52 (toward Snoqualmie Pass West). Turn left (north), cross under the freeway, and continue on to the trailhead, located in parking lot at the Alpental Ski Area. ⊕ www. wta.org-go-hiking/hikes/snow-lake.*

WALKING TOURS

Taking a tour is a great way to see the city if you specific interests, or if you have limited time.

Bill Speidel's Underground Tour. The guides of Bill Speidel's Underground Tour tell tales of Seattle's sometimes scandalous pioneering past as they lead guests through subterranean passageways that once were the main roads of old Seattle. A staple for visitors to Pioneer Square. ⊠ *608 1st Ave., Pioneer Square* ☎ *206/682–4646* ⊕ *www.undergroundtour.com* ▱ *$16.*

Market Ghost Tours. These weekend tours around the Pike Place Market weave in local ghost stories, eerie history, and fun facts about the market and its haunted places. ⊠ *1410 Post Alley, Downtown* ☎ *206/805–0195* ⊕ *www.seattleghost.com.*

Savor Seattle Food Tours. Serving up two- to three-hour culinary walking tours around town, Savor Seattle features a Chocolate Indulgence tour, a Gourmet Seattle tour (with stops at fine restaurants to meet chefs, and tasty meals with wine and beer pairings); and a Pike Place Market walking tour led by a local guide. ⊠ *1st Ave. and Pike St., Downtown* ☎ *888/987–2867* ⊕ *www.savorseattletours.com.*

SHOPPING

Updated by
Anna Maris
Stephens
Shopping in Seattle is something best done gradually. Don't expect to find it all in one or two days' worth of blitz shopping tours. Downtown is the only area that allows for easy daylong shopping excursions. Within a few blocks along 4th and 5th avenues, you'll find the standard chains (The Gap, Urban Outfitters, H&M, Anthropologie, Sephora, Old Navy), along with Nike's flagship store, and a few more glamorous high-end stores, some featuring well-known designers like Betsey Johnson. Downtown is also where you'll find department stores like Nordstrom, Macy's and Barneys New York. Belltown and Pioneer Square are also easy areas to patrol—most stores of note are within a few blocks.

To find many of the stores that are truly special to Seattle—such as boutiques featuring handmade frocks from local designers, independent record stores run by encyclopedic-minded music geeks, cozy used-book shops that smell of paper and worn wood shelves—you'll have to branch out to Capitol Hill, Queen Anne, and northern neighborhoods like Ballard. Shopping these areas will give you a better feel for the character of the city and its quirky inhabitants, all while you score that new dress or nab gifts for your friends.

DOWNTOWN

Best shopping: 4th, 5th, and 6th avenues between Pine and Spring streets, and 1st Avenue between Virginia and Madison streets.

BOOKS AND PRINTED MATERIAL

Fodor's Choice ★ **Peter Miller Architectural & Design Books and Supplies.** Aesthetes and architects haunt this shop, which is stocked floor to ceiling with all things design. Rare, international architecture, art, and design books mingle with high-end products from Alessi and Iittala; sleek notebooks, bags, portfolios, and drawing tools round out the collection. This is a great shop for quirky, unforgettable gifts, like a Black Dot sketchbook, an Arne Jacobsen wall clock, or an aerodynamic umbrella. ⊠ *1930 1st Ave., Downtown* ☎ *206/441–4114* ⊕ *www.petermiller.com.*

CHOCOLATE

Fodor's Choice ★ **Fran's Chocolates.** A Seattle institution, Fran's Chocolates (helmed by Fran Bigelow) has been making quality chocolates for decades. Its world-famous salted caramels are transcendent, as are delectable truffles, which are spiked with oolong tea, single malt whiskey, or raspberry, among other flavors. This shop is housed in the Four Seasons on 1st Avenue—how very elegant, indeed! ⊠ *1325 1st Ave., Downtown* ☎ *206/682–0168* ⊕ *www.franschocolates.com.*

CLOTHING

Alhambra. Sophisticated, casual, and devastatingly feminine, this pricey boutique delivers quality, European-style looks for women of all ages. Pop into the Moorish-inspired shop for a party dress, elegant jewelry, or separates, and be sure to check out the house line, designed by the owners. ⊠ *101 Pine St., Downtown* ☎ *206/621–9571* ⊕ *www.alhambrastyle.com.*

Mario's. Known for fabulous service and designer labels, this high-end boutique treats every client like a superstar. Men shop the ground floor for Armani, Etro, and Zegna; women ascend the ornate staircase for Prada, Emilio Pucci, and Lanvin. A freestanding Hugo Boss boutique sells the sharpest tuxedos in town. ⊠ *1513 6th Ave., Downtown* ☎ *206/223–1461* ⊕ *www.marios.com.*

DEPARTMENT STORES

Fodor's Choice ★ **Nordstrom.** Seattle's own retail giant sells quality clothing, accessories, cosmetics, jewelry, and lots of shoes—in keeping with its roots in footwear—including many hard-to-find sizes. Peruse the various floors for anything from trendy jeans to lingerie to goods for the home. A sky bridge on the store's fourth floor will take you to Pacific Place Shopping Center. Deservedly renowned for its impeccable customer service, the busy Downtown flagship has a concierge desk and valet parking.

TOP SPOTS TO SHOP

Shopping becomes decidedly less fun when it involves driving around and circling for parking. You're better off limiting your all-day shopping tours to one of several key areas than planning to do a citywide search for a particular item. The following areas have the greatest concentration of shops and the greatest variety.

5th and 6th Avenues, Downtown. Depending on where you're staying, you may not need to drive to this area, but if you do, the parking garage at Pacific Place mall (at 600 Pine Street) always seems to have a space somewhere (it also has valet parking). Tackling either Pacific Place or the four blocks of 5th and 6th avenues between Olive Way and University Street will keep you very busy for a day.

1st Avenue, Belltown. From Wall Street to Pine Street, you'll find clothing boutiques, shoe stores, and some sleek home and architectural design stores. 1st Avenue and Pike Street brings you to the Pike Place Market. There are numerous pay parking lots on both 1st and 2nd avenues.

Pioneer Square. Walk or bus here if you can. Art galleries are the main draw, along with some home decor and rug shops. If you do drive, many pay lots in the neighborhood participate in the "Parking Around the Square" program, which works with local businesses to offer shoppers validated parking; the website (⊕ www.pioneersquare.org) lists the lots and stores that offer it.

International District. Parking in the I.D. can be hit or miss depending on the time of day. It's best if you can walk here from Downtown or take a quick bus ride over. If you do drive, go directly to the Uwajimaya parking lot. They validate for purchases, and it's a safe bet you'll be buying something there. It's too fun to resist.

Pike–Pine Corridor, Capitol Hill. The best shopping in the Hill is on Pike and Pine streets between Melrose Avenue and 10th Avenue E. Most of the stores are on Pike Street; Pine's best offerings are clustered on the western end of the avenue between Melrose and Summit. There are pay lots on Pike Street (near Broadway) and one on Summit by E. Olive Way (next to the Starbucks).

Fremont and Ballard. Start in Fremont's small retail center, which is mostly along 36th Street. You may be able to snag street parking. After you've exhausted Fremont's shops, it's an easy drive over to Ballard. Ballard Avenue and NW Market Street are chockablock with great boutiques. Finding parking in Ballard can be tricky on weekends, but it's usually possible.

◼ TIP→ The Nordstrom Rack store at 1st Avenue and Spring Street, close to Pike Place Market, has great deals on marked-down items. ✉ *500 Pine St., Downtown* ☎ *206/628–2111* ⊕ *shop.nordstrom.com.*

GIFTS AND HOME DECOR

FAMILY
Fodor'sChoice
★
Schmancy. Weird and wonderful, this toy store is more surreal art funhouse than FAO Schwarz. Pick up a crocheted zombie (with a cute little bow), a felted Ishmael's whale, your very own Hugh Hefner figurine—or how about a pork-chop pillow? With collectibles from cult

favorites Plush You!, Kidrobot, and Lovemongers, this quirky shop is full of surprises. Warning: Sense of humor required. ⊠ *1932 2nd Ave., Downtown* ☎ *206/728–8008* ⊕ *www.schmancytoys.com.*

Sur La Table. Need a brass-plated medieval French duck press? You've come to the right place. Culinary artists and foodies have flocked to this popular Pike Place Market destination since 1972. Sur La Table's flagship shop is packed to the rafters with many thousands of kitchen items, including an exclusive line of copper cookware, endless shelves of baking equipment, tabletop accessories, cookbooks, and a formidable display of knives. ⊠ *84 Pine St., Downtown* ☎ *206/448–2244* ⊕ *www. surlatable.com.*

MALL

Pacific Place Shopping Center. Stores, restaurants, and an excellent movie multiplex are wrapped around a four-story, light-filled atrium, making this a cheerful destination even on a stormy day. The mostly high-end shops include Tiffany & Co., MaxMara, Coach, and True Religion, and there's also L'Occitane, Brookstone, Victoria's Secret, Ann Taylor, and J.Crew. A third-floor sky bridge provides a rainproof route to the neighboring Nordstrom. One of the best things about the mall is its parking garage, which is surprisingly affordable, given its location: valet parking is just a few bucks more. ⊠ *600 Pine St., Downtown* ☎ *206/652–1300* ⊕ *www.pacificplaceseattle.com.*

OUTDOOR CLOTHING AND EQUIPMENT

The North Face. This is one of the original stores by the California outfitter, and it doesn't take a rocket scientist to figure out why: You've probably heard about Seattle's often-dreary weather. If you showed up with an optimistic suitcase full of shorts and shirts, stop here for your requisite raincoat—an authentic souvenir if ever there was one. ⊠ *1023 1st Ave., Downtown* ☎ *206/622–4111* ⊕ *www.thenorthface.com.*

WINE AND SPECIALTY FOODS

Fodor's Choice ★ **DeLaurenti Specialty Food and Wine.** Attention foodies: clear out your hotel mini-bars and make room for delectable treats from DeLaurenti. And, if you're planning any picnics, swing by here first. Imported meats and cheeses crowd the deli cases, and packaged delicacies pack the aisles. Stock up on hard-to-find items like truffle-infused olive oil or excellent Italian vintages from the wine shop upstairs. Spring travelers will also want to stop by DeLaurenti's nosh nirvana, called Cheesefest, in May. ⊠ *Pike Place Market, 1435 1st Ave., Downtown* ☎ *206/622–0141* ⊕ *www.delaurenti.com.*

Pike and Western Wine Shop. The folks at Pike and Western have spent nearly four decades carving out a reputation as one of the best wine markets in the city. With more than 1,000 wines personally selected from the Pacific Northwest and around the world, this shop offers expert advice from friendly salespeople. ⊠ *1934 Pike Pl., Downtown* ☎ *206/441–1307* ⊕ *www.pikeandwestern.com.*

BELLTOWN

Best shopping: Along 1st Avenue between Cedar and Virginia streets.

CLOTHING

Karan Dannenberg Clothier. A favorite of Seattle executives and sophisticates, this boutique stocks classy, modern clothing for women, and doesn't bow to useless trends. The staff is very knowledgeable, and offers wardrobe consulting for their customers—they'll even make house calls to critique your closets in a What Not to Wear–style evaluation. Shop here for perfect jeans, business attire, or glamorous formal wear. ⊠ *2232 1st Ave., Belltown* ☎ *206/441–3442* ⊕ *karandannenberg.com.*

MUSIC

Singles Going Steady. If punk rock is more to you than anarchy symbols sewn on Target sweatshirts, then stop at Singles Going Steady. Punk and its myriad subgenres on CD and vinyl are specialties, though they also stock rockabilly, indie rock, and hip-hop. It's a nice foil to the city's indie-rock-dominated record shops, and a good reminder that Belltown is still more eclectic than its rising rents may indicate. ⊠ *2219 2nd Ave., Belltown* ☎ *206/441–7396.*

OUTDOOR CLOTHING

Patagonia. If the person next to you on the bus isn't wearing North Face, he or she is probably clad in Patagonia. This popular and durable brand excels at functional outdoor wear—made with earth-friendly materials such as hemp and organic cotton—as well as technical clothing hip enough for mountaineers or urban hikers. The line of whimsically patterned fleece wear for children is particularly charming. ⊠ *2100 1st Ave., Belltown* ☎ *206/622–9700* ⊕ *www.patagonia.com.*

WALLINGFORD

OUTDOOR CLOTHING

evo. For outdoor gear with an edgy vibe, locals head to evo, which specializes in snow sports and also carries a solid selection of urban street clothes. You'll find everything you need for shredding Washington's big mountains in style, including fat powder skis and snowboards with wild graphics to flashy ski jackets and thick woolen beanies. Evo also has a gallery space that hosts cool art shows. ⊠ *3500 Stone Way N, Wallingford* ☎ *206/973–4470* ⊕ *www.evo.com.*

SOUTH LAKE UNION

OUTDOOR CLOTHING AND EQUIPMENT

Fodor'sChoice
★

REI. The enormous flagship for Recreational Equipment, Inc. (REI) has an incredible selection of outdoor gear—polar-fleece jackets, wool socks, down vests, hiking boots, raingear, and much more—as well as its own 65-foot climbing wall. The staff is extremely knowledgeable; there always seems to be enough help on hand, even when the store is busy. You can test things out on the mountain-bike test trail or in the simulated rain booth. REI also rents gear such as tents, sleeping bags, skis, snowshoes, and backpacks. ✉ *222 Yale Ave. N, South Lake Union* ☎ *206/223–1944* ⊕ *www.rei.com.*

QUEEN ANNE

Best shopping: Along Queen Anne Avenue N between W. Harrison and Roy streets, and between W. Galer and McGraw streets.

BOOKS AND MUSIC

FAMILY **Queen Anne Books.** One of the most beloved neighborhood bookstores in Seattle, Queen Anne Books is well known for its friendly, knowledgeable staff and extensive book selection. Pop in for children's storytelling sessions on the third Sunday of every month, or browse at night and catch one of the many author events. After you grab your new books, slip into El Diablo, the cute coffee shop adjacent to the bookstore. ✉ *1811 Queen Anne Ave. N, Queen Anne* ☎ *206/283–5624* ⊕ *www. queenannebooks.com.*

CLOTHING

Peridot Boutique. Strapless animal-print pocket dresses, retro gingham tops, and ruffly skirts abound in this contemporary women's boutique in lower Queen Anne. The prices are reasonable, the accessories are abundant, and local designers are represented as well. ✉ *532 Queen Anne Ave. N, Queen Anne* ☎ *206/687–7130* ⊕ *www.peridotboutique. wordpress.com.*

WINE AND SPECIALTY FOODS

McCarthy & Schiering Wine Merchants. One of the best wine shops in the city, this attitude-free store offers an amazing selection of wines from around the world. Check out the selection of local wines to experience the true flavor of the Northwest. ✉ *2401B Queen Anne Ave. N, Queen Anne* ☎ *206/282–8500* ⊕ *www.mccarthyandschiering.com.*

PIONEER SQUARE

Best shopping: 1st Avenue S between Yesler Way and S. Jackson Street, and Occidental Avenue S between S. Main and Jackson streets.

ANTIQUES AND COLLECTIBLES

Cuttysark Nautical Antiques. Named for the famous Scottish tea clipper, Cuttysark is filled to the brim with nautical memorabilia: antique navigational instruments, signal flags, clocks, lanterns, ships' wheels, telegraphs, binnacles and other decorative items, along with books and ship models. It's worth wandering through even if you don't know your bow from your stern. ✉ *320 First Ave., Pioneer Square* ☎ *206/262–1265* ⊕ *www.cuttyantiques.com.*

ART AND GIFTS

Agate Designs. Amateur geologists, curious kids, and anyone fascinated by fossils and gems should make a trip to Agate Designs, where there's no shortage of eye-popping items on display. Between the 500 million-year-old fossils and the 250-pound amethyst geodes, this store is almost like a museum (but a lot more fun). ✉ *120 1st Ave. S, Pioneer Square* ☎ *206/621–3063* ⊕ *www.agatedesigns.com.*

The REI superstore in South Lake Union

Glass House Studio. Seattle's oldest glassblowing studio and gallery lets you watch fearless artisans at work in the "hot shop." Some of the best glass artists in the country work out of this shop, and many of their impressive studio pieces are for sale, along with around 40 other Northwest artists represented by the shop. ⊠ *311 Occidental Ave. S, Pioneer Square* ☎ *206/682–9939* ⊕ *www.glasshouse-studio.com.*

BOOKS AND TOYS

FAMILY **Magic Mouse Toys.** Since 1977, Magic Mouse has been supplying families with games, toys, puzzles, tricks, candy, figurines from a two-story, 7,000-square-foot shop in the heart of Pioneer Square. They claim a professional child runs this friendly store—and it shows. ⊠ *603 1st Ave., Pioneer Square* ☎ *206/682–8097* ⊕ *www.magicmousetoys.com.*

CLOTHING

Filson. Seattle's flagship Filson store is a shrine to meticulously well-made outdoor wear for men and women. The hunting lodge–like decor of the space, paired with interesting memorabilia and pricey, made-on-site clothing, makes the drive south of Pioneer Square worth it (we recommend catching a cab, not hoofing it). The attention to detail paid to the plaid vests, oil-treated rain slickers, and fishing outfits borders on the fetishistic. ⊠ *1555 4th Ave. S, Pioneer Square* ☎ *206/622–3147* ⊕ *www.filson.com.*

CAPITOL HILL

Best shopping: E. Pike and E. Pine streets between Bellevue Avenue and Madison Avenue E, E. Olive Way between Bellevue Avenue E and Broadway E, and Broadway E between E. Denny Way and E. Roy Street.

BOOKS AND MUSIC

Fodor's Choice ★ **Elliott Bay Book Company.** A major reason to visit this landmark bookstore is the great selection of Pacific Northwest history books and fiction titles by local authors, complete with handwritten recommendation cards from the knowledgeable staff. A big selection of bargain books, underground parking, lovely skylights, and an appealing café all sweeten the deal—and the hundreds of author events held every year mean that nearly every day is an exciting one for dropping by. ⊠ *1521 10th Ave., Capitol Hill* ☎ *206/624–6600* ⊕ *www.elliottbaybook.com.*

Wall of Sound. If you're on the hunt for Japanese avant-rock on LP, antiwar spoken word, spiritual reggae with Afro-jazz undertones, or old screen-printed show posters, you've found the place. Obscure, experimental, adventurous, and good? Wall of Sound probably has it. ⊠ *315 E. Pine St., Capitol Hill* ☎ *206/441–9880* ⊕ *www.wosound.com.*

CLOTHING

Le Frock. It may look like just another overcrowded consignment shop, but Le Frock is Seattle's classiest vintage and consignment store. Among the racks, you'll find classic steals for men and women from Burberry, Fendi, Dior, Missoni, and the like, while contemporary looks from Prada, Gucci, and Chanel round out the collection. ⊠ *317 E. Pine St., Capitol Hill* ☎ *206/623–5339* ⊕ *www.lefrockonline.com.*

The Red Light Clothing Exchange. Nostalgia rules in this cavernous space filled with well-organized, good-quality vintage clothing. Fantasy outfits from decades past are arranged by era or by genre. There's plenty of denim, leather, and disco threads alongside cowboy boots and eveningwear. There's a smaller branch in the University District. ⊠ *312 Broadway E, Capitol Hill* ☎ *503/963–8888* ⊕ *redlightclothingexchange.com.*

FOOTWEAR

Edie's Shoes. Super-comfy, effortlessly cool shoes can be found at this small, carefully planned shop. Plop down on the big purple couch and try on trendy but sensible footwear by Camper, Onitsuka Tiger, Biviel, Tretorn, and Tsubo. You won't find any outrageous designs or one-of-a-kind items here, but it does have a great selection of favored brands in perhaps a few more styles than you'd find at Nordstrom. ⊠ *319 E. Pine St., Capitol Hill* ☎ *206/839–1111* ⊕ *www.ediesshoes.com.*

GIFTS AND HOME DECOR

Area 51. Anything might materialize in this 10,000-square-foot industrial space, from Eames replicas to clever coffee mugs, but the mix of retro-inspired new items and vintage finds all looks like it's straight out of a handbook of the design trends from the middle of the last century. ⊠ *401 E. Pine St., Capitol Hill* ☎ *206/568–4782* ⊕ *www. area51seattle.com.*

NuBe Green. An emphasis on recycled goods and sustainability is the mission of this well-presented store anchoring a corner of the Oddfellows Building. All items are sourced and made in the United States, including linens, candles, glass art, and even dog beds made from old jeans. Our favorite items are by local **Alchemy Goods** (⊕ *www.alchemygoods. com*), which recycles bicycle tubes, reclaimed vinyl mesh, and seatbelts into distinctively cool wallets and messenger bags. ⊠ *921 East Pine St., Capitol Hill* ☎ *206/402–4515* ⊕ *www.nubegreen.com.*

SPECIALTY FOODS

Melrose Market. Seattle is famously foodie-friendly, and this historic triangular building packs several of the city's best culinary shops under one roof. Browse and sample artisanal meats, cheeses, shellfish, and liquor, all with locavore leanings. Unlike Pike Place, the relatively pint-size Melrose is more a hipster haunt than a tourist trap: Anthony Bourdain and the Seattle *Top Chef* contestants have been spotted here. ⊠ *1501–1535 Melrose Ave., Capitol Hill* ⊕ *melrosemarketseattle.com.*

FREMONT

Best shopping: Blocks bound by Fremont Place N and Evanston Avenue N to N. 34th Street and Aurora Avenue N.

CHOCOLATE

Fodor's Choice ★ **Theo Chocolate.** Seattleites love their chocolate nearly as much as their coffee (and preferably at the same time, thank you). This Fremont factory/storefront is one-stop fun, with factory tours on offer every day. Learn about the history of cacao, then stock up on free-trade organic tasty chocolate nibbles, such as spicy chili, cherry and almond, or coconut curry chocolate bars. ⊠ *3400 Phinney Ave. N, Fremont* ☎ *206/632–5100* ⊕ *www.theochocolate.com.*

CLOTHING

Les Amis. Women whose sartorial leanings go beyond low-rise jeans will adore the sophisticated dresses, gorgeous handknits, and the makings of great work outfits here, much of it from Europe and Japan. Younger fashionistas come here, too, for unique summer skirts and ultrasoft T-shirts. Everyone seems to love the whimsical lingerie collection. Les Amis carries some top designers, such as Dosa, Isabel Marant, and Nanette Lepore. ⊠ *3420 Evanston Ave. N, Fremont* ☎ *206/632–2877* ⊕ *www.lesamis-inc.com.*

BALLARD

Best shopping: Ballard Avenue between 22nd Avenue NW and 20th Avenue NW; Northwest Market Street between 20th and 24th avenues.

BOOKS AND MUSIC

FAMILY **Secret Garden Bookshop.** Named after the Francis Hodgson Burnett classic, this cozy shop has been delighting readers for 34 years. A favorite of teachers, librarians, and parents, the store stocks a wide array of imaginative literature and thoughtful nonfiction for all ages; their children's section is particularly notable. ⊠ *2214 NW Market St., Ballard* ☎ *206/789–5006* ⊕ *www.secretgardenbooks.com.*

CLOTHING AND ACCESSORIES

FAMILY **Clover.** Easily the cutest children's store in town, Clover carries wonderful handcrafted wooden toys, European figurines, works by local artists, and a variety of swoon-worthy, perfectly crafted little clothes. Even shoppers without children will be smitten—it's hard to resist the vintage French Tintin posters, knit-wool cow dolls, and classic Smurf figurines. ⊠ *5333 Ballard Ave. NW, Ballard* ☎ *206/782–0715* ⊕ *www. clovertoys.com.*

Velouria. The ultimate antidote to the mass-produced, unimaginative women's clothes choking much of the chains these days can be found at Velouria, where independent West Coast designers rule. Much on offer is one-of-a-kind: step in to this exquisitely feminine shop to find handmade, '70s-inspired jumpsuits; romantic, demure eyelet dresses; and clever screen-printed tees. Superb bags, delicate jewelry, and fun cards and gifts are also on display. It's worth a look just to check out all the wearable art. ⊠ *2205 NW Market St., Ballard* ☎ *206/788–0330* ⊕ *shopvelouria.com.*

GIFTS AND HOME ACCESSORIES

Fodor'sChoice **La Tienda.** Every item in this showroom of handmade art was lovingly
★ selected by the owners, who pride themselves on procuring art directly from craftspeople for a fair price. You'll find delicate Chinese puppets, figurines from Peru, and Indonesian Buddha sculptures, but many American-made items are also among the collection. This store has been a favorite shopping destination since 1962. ⊠ *2050 NW Market St., Ballard* ☎ *206/297–3605* ⊕ *www.latienda-folkart.com.*

THE EASTSIDE

Best shopping: Bellevue Square and The Shops at the Bravern.

CENTERS AND MALLS

FAMILY **The Bellevue Collection.** In this impressive trifecta of shopping centers, you'll find just about any chain store you've heard of (and some that you haven't). Bellevue Square alone has more than 200 stores, including Nordstrom, Macy's, Pottery Barn, Crate & Barrel, Aveda, Banana Republic, Coach, 7 For All Mankind, Build-a-Bear, and Helly Hansen. The Square's wide walkways and benches, its many children's clothing stores, the first-floor play area, and a children's museum on the third floor make this a great place for kids, too. You can park for free in the attached garage. Take the sky bridge to Lincoln Center, to catch a flick at their 16-screen cinema, organize your life at The Container Store, or sample an assortment of other retail and several popular chain restaurants. Bellevue Place, across from Lincoln Center, hosts a variety of retail along with the ever-popular Daniel's Broiler. ⊠ *Bellevue Way, 575 Bellevue Sq., Bellevue* ☎ *425/454–8096* ⊕ *www.bellevuesquare.com.*

The Shops at the Bravern. If you have some serious cash to burn, the sleek, upscale Bravern might be the Eastside spot for you. With high-end shops like Neiman Marcus, Hermès, Brooks Brothers, Jimmy Choo, Salvatore Ferragamo, and Louis Vuitton, it's tempting to empty your wallet—but save room for a spa treatment at the Elizabeth Arden Red Door Spa or

9

a meal at Northwest favorite Wild Ginger. Valet and complimentary parking (with validation) are available. ✉ *11111 NE 8th St., Bellevue* ☎ *425/456–8780* ⊕ *www.thebravern.com.*

SIDE TRIPS FROM SEATTLE: THE PUGET SOUND ISLANDS

Updated by
Allison Ellis

The islands of Puget Sound—particularly Bainbridge, Vashon, and Whidbey—are easy and popular day trips for Seattle visitors, and riding the Washington State ferries is half of the fun. There are a few classic inns and B&Bs in the historic towns of Langley and Coupeville if you want to spend the night. It's definitely worth planning your trip around mealtimes because the islands of Puget Sound have top-notch restaurants serving local foods—including locally grown produce, seafood, and even island-raised beef. On Vashon Island, Sea Breeze farm's restaurant La Boucherie is at the top of the locavore pack; Bainbridge, Whidbey, and the San Juans also have a myriad of small farms and charming restaurants worth a visit. Seafood of course, is a big draw. Local crab, salmon, and shellfish should be on your not-to-miss list, including the word renowned Penn Cove Mussels from Whidbey Island.

Whidbey Island has the most spectacular natural attractions, but it requires the biggest time commitment to get to (it's 30 miles northwest of Seattle). Bainbridge is the most developed island—it's something of a moneyed bedroom community—with higher end restaurants and shops supplementing its natural attractions. It's also the easiest to get to—just hop on a ferry from Pier 52 on the Downtown Seattle waterfront. Vashon is the most pastoral of the islands—if you don't like leisurely strolls, beachcombing, or bike rides, you might get bored there quickly. Bainbridge and Whidbey get tons of visitors in summer. Though you'll be able to snag a walk-on spot on the ferry, spaces for cars can fill up, so arrive early. Whidbey is big, so you'll most likely want to tour by car (you can actually drive there, too, as the north end of the island is accessible via Deception Pass), and a car is handy on Bainbridge as well, especially if you want to tour the entire island or visit spectacular Bloedel Reserve. Otherwise, Bainbridge is your best bet if you want to walk on the ferry and tour by foot.

BAINBRIDGE ISLAND

35 mins west of Seattle by ferry.

Of the three main islands in Puget Sound, Bainbridge has by far the largest population of Seattle commuters. Certain parts of the island are dense enough to have rush-hour traffic problems, while other areas retain a semi-rural, small-town vibe. Longtime residents work hard to keep parks and protected areas out of the hands of condominium builders, and despite the increasing number of stressed-out commuters, the island still has resident artists, craftspeople, and old-timers who can't be bothered to venture into the big city. Though not as dramatic as Whidbey or as idyllic as Vashon, Bainbridge always makes for a pleasant day trip.

The ferry, which departs from the Downtown terminal at Pier 52, drops you off in the charming village of Winslow. Along its compact main street, Winslow Way, it's easy to while away an afternoon among the antiques shops, art galleries, bookstores, and cafés. There are two bike-rental shops in Winslow, too, if you plan on touring the island on two wheels. Getting out of town on a bike can be a bit nerve-racking, as the traffic to and from the ferry terminal is thick, and there aren't a lot of dedicated bike lanes, but you'll soon be on quieter country roads. Be sure to ask for maps at the rental shop, and if you want to avoid the worst of the island's hills, ask the staff to go over your options with you before you set out.

Many of the island's most reliable dining options are in Winslow—or close to it. You'll also find the delightful Town & Country supermarket on the main stretch if you want to pick up some provisions for a picnic, though you can also easily do that in Seattle at the Pike Place Market before you get on the ferry.

GETTING HERE AND AROUND

Unless you're coming from Tacoma or points farther south, or from the Olympic Peninsula, the only way to get to Bainbridge is via the ferry from Pier 52 Downtown. Round-trip fares start at $7.70 per person; round-trip fare for a car and driver is $32.80. Crossing time is 35 minutes. If you confine your visit to the village of Winslow, as many visitors do, then you won't need anything other than a pair of walking shoes. Out on the island, besides driving or biking, the only way to get around is on buses provided by Kitsap Transit. Fares are only $2 one-way, but note that since routed buses are for commuters, they may not drop you off quite at the doorstep of the park or attraction you're headed to. Be sure to study the route map carefully or call Kitsap at least a day in advance of your trip to inquire about their Dial-A-Ride services.

Contacts Kitsap Transit ☎ *800/501–7433* ⊕ *www.kitsaptransit.com.*

ESSENTIALS

Visitor Information Chamber of Commerce. The Chamber of Commerce operates a visitor's kiosk just outside the ferry terminal near the taxi area, as well as a visitor center at 395 Winslow Way E. ☎ *206/842–3700* ⊕ *www. bainbridgechamber.com.*

EXPLORING

Bainbridge Island Studio Tour. Twice a year (the second weekend in August and the first weekend in December), the island's artists and craftspeople are in the spotlight with the Bainbridge Island Studio Tour. Participants put their best pieces on display for these three-day events, and you can buy anything from watercolors to furniture directly from the artists. Even if you can't make the official studio tours, check out the website, which has maps and information on studios and shops throughout the island, as well as links to artists' websites. Many of the shops have regular hours, and you can easily put together your own tour. ⊕ *www. bistudiotour.com.*

Bloedel Reserve, Bainbridge Island

Fodor's Choice **Bloedel Reserve.** The 150-acre internationally recognized Bloedel Reserve ★ is a stunning mix of natural woodlands and beautifully landscaped gardens—including a moss garden, Japanese garden, a reflection pool, and the impressive former Bloedel estate home. Dazzling rhododendrons and azaleas bloom in spring, and Japanese maples colorfully signal autumn's arrival. Picnicking is not permitted, and you'll want to leave the pooch behind—pets are not allowed on the property, even if they stay in the car. Check the website's events page for special events, lectures and exhibits. ✉ *7571 N.E. Dolphin Dr., 6 miles west of Winslow, via Hwy. 305* ☎ *206/842–7631* ⊕ *www.bloedelreserve.org* 🎫 *$13* ⊙ *Sept.–May, Tues.–Sun. 10–4; Jun.–Aug., Tues. –Sat. 10–7, Sun. 10–4.*

Fort Ward Park. On the southwest side of the island is the lovely and tranquil 137-acre Fort Ward Park. There are 2 miles of hiking trails through forest, a long stretch of (sometimes) sun-drenched rocky beach, several picnic tables, and even a spot for scuba diving. Along with views of the water and the Olympic Mountains, you might be lucky and get a peek of Mt. Rainier—or of the massive sea lions that frequent the near-shore waters. A loop trail through the park is suitable for all ability levels, and will take you past vestiges of the park's previous life as a military installation. ⊹ *Take Hwy. 305 out of Winslow; turn west on High School Rd. and follow signs to park* ☎ *206/842–3931* ⊕ *www.biparks.org/parksandfacilities/pkftward.html* ⊙ *Daily 8–dusk.*

WHERE TO EAT

$ ✕ **Blackbird Bakery.** A great place to grab a cup of coffee and a snack

BAKERY before exploring the island, Blackbird serves up rich pastries and cakes along with quiche, soups, and a good selection of teas and espresso drinks. Though there is some nice window seating that allows you to watch the human parade on Winslow Way, the place gets very crowded, especially when the ferries come in, so you might want to take your order to go. $ *Average main: $4* ⊠ *210 Winslow Way E, Winslow* ☎ *206/780–1322* ⊕ *www.blackbirdbakery.com* ▭ No credit cards ⊗ *No dinner.*

$$
BISTRO
✕ **Café Nola.** Café Nola is the best option for something a little fancier than pub grub or picnic fare. The bistro setting is pleasant, with pale yellow walls, white tablecloths, and jazz music, and there's a small patio area for alfresco dining. The food is basically American and European comfort cooking with a few modern twists. The lunch menu offers salads, burgers, and sandwiches, such as an open-faced Dungeness crab melt on foccacia or a fresh King Salmon sandwich with red pepper aioli. At dinner, classics like pan-seared scallops and roasted pork shoulder steal the show. The restaurant is within walking distance of the main ferry terminal. $ *Average main: $22* ⊠ *101 Winslow Way E, Winslow* ☎ *206/842–3822* ⊕ *www.cafenola.com.*

$
SEAFOOD
✕ **Harbor Public House.** An 1881 estate home overlooking Eagle Harbor was renovated to create this casual pub and restaurant at Winslow's Harbor Marina, where a complimentary boat tie-up is available for pub patrons. Local seafood—including steamed mussels, clams, and oyster sliders—plus burgers, fish-and-chips, and poutine are typical fare, and there are 12 beers on tap. This is where the kayaking and pleasure-boating crowds come to dine in a relaxed, waterfront setting. When the sun shines, the harbor-front deck is the place to be, and things get raucous during the first Tuesday night open-mike sessions. $ *Average main: $15* ⊠ *231 Parfitt Way SW, Winslow* ☎ *206/842–0969* ⊕ *www. harbourpub.com.*

VASHON ISLAND

20 mins by ferry from West Seattle.

Vashon is the most peaceful and rural of the islands easily reached from the city, home to fruit growers, commune-dwelling hippies, rat-race dropouts, and Seattle commuters.

Biking, beachcombing, picnicking, and kayaking are the main activities here. A tour of the 13-mile-long island will take you down country lanes and past orchards and lavender farms. There are several artists' studios and galleries on the island, as well as a small commercial district in the center of the island, where a farmers' market is a highlight every Saturday from May to October. The popular Strawberry Festival takes place every July.

GETTING HERE AND AROUND

Washington State Ferries leave from Fauntleroy in West Seattle (about 9 miles southwest of Downtown) for the 20-minute ride to Vashon Island. The ferry docks at the northern tip of the island. Round-trip fares are $5.00 per person or $20.90 for a car and driver. A water taxi also goes to Vashon from Pier 50 on the Seattle waterfront, but it's primarily for commuters, operating only on weekdays during commuter hours. One-way fares are $5. There's limited bus service on the island; the best way to get around is by car or by bicycle (bring your own or rent in Seattle. Note that there's the huge hill as you immediately disembark the ferry dock and head up to town). The site ⊕ *www.vashonchamber.com* is also a good source of information.

ESSENTIALS

Visitor Information **Vashon-Maury Island Chamber of Commerce.** Vashon-Maury Island Chamber of Commerce is open Monday–Saturday 10–3. ✉ *17141 Vashon Highway SW, Across from Ober Park* ☎ *206/463–6217* ⊕ *www. vashonchamber.com.*

EXPLORING

Jensen Point and Burton Acres Park. Vashon has many parks and protected areas. Located on the lush Burton Peninsula overlooking Quartermaster Harbor, Burton Acres Park is home to 64 acres of secluded hiking and horseback riding trails. The adjacent Jensen Point, a 4-acre shoreline park, has picnic tables, a swimming beach, and kayak and paddleboard rentals (May through September). ✉ *8900 SW Harbor Drive* ✛ *From the ferry terminal, take Vashon Highway SW to S.W. Burton Drive and turn left. Turn left on 97 Avenue SW and follow it around as it becomes S.W. Harbor Drive.* ⊕ *www.vashonparks.org/section_facilities/parks/m_burtonacres-jensenpt.htm.*

Point Robinson Park. You can stroll along the beach at Point Robinson Park, which is very picturesque thanks to **Point Robinson Lighthouse.** Free tours of the lighthouse are given from noon to 4 on Saturdays and Sundays from mid-May through the summer; call to arrange tours at other times. ✉ *3705 SW Pt. Robinson Rd* ☎ *206/463–9602* ⊕ *www. vashonparks.org.*

Vashon Allied Arts. Vashon Allied Arts at the Blue Heron Art Center is the best representative of the island's diverse arts community, presenting monthly exhibits and events that span all mediums, including dance, chamber music, and art lectures. The gallery's exhibits rotate monthly, featuring local and Northwest artists, and Heron's Nest *(17600 Vashon Hwy SW, 206/463–5252)*, the affiliated gift shop in town, is where you'll find fine art and handcrafted items by local artists. ✉ *19704 Vashon Hwy.* ☎ *206/463–5131* ⊕ *www.vashonalliedarts.org* ☉ *Weekdays 10–5, Sat. noon–5.*

WHERE TO EAT

$ ✕ **Hardware Store.** The restaurant's unusual name comes from its former

AMERICAN   life as a mom-and-pop hardware shop—it occupies the oldest commercial building on Vashon, and certainly looks like a relic from the outside. Inside, you'll find a charming restaurant that's a cross between a bistro and an upscale diner. The cuisine is "Northwest Americana," with breakfast highlights like rustic French toast and smoked salmon Benedict; sandwiches, salads, and burgers for lunch, and for dinner, hearty old standbys like buttermilk fried chicken, pasta, meat loaf, and grilled salmon. Almost everything on the menu can be made gluten-free. A decent wine list focuses on Northwest and Californian wines. $ *Average main: $16* ✉ *17601 Vashon Hwy. SW* ☎ *206/463–1800* ⊕ *www. thsrestaurant.com.*

$$$$ **✕ La Boucherie.** As the retail and restaurant side of the "beyond organic"
FRENCH Sea Breeze Farm, this much-discussed outpost of ultralocal cuisine
serves meats, poultry, and produce grown on or very close to the property. As a result, the menu is highly seasonal (changing twice weekly),
but it always highlights Vashon's growers and farmers. The charcuterie
plate is one of their most popular starters; it features all the pâtés they
make in-house. Foodies who flock here swear by the pork chops, too.
You can order off the à la carte menu (most items are $11) but the six-
course prix-fixe is the way to go. It's a tiny spot; reservations are essential. $ *Average main: $33* ⊠ *17635 100th Ave. SW* ☎ *206/567–4628*
⊕ *www.seabreezefarm.net* ⟋ *Reservations essential* ⊙ *Weds.–Sat. lunch
and dinner; Sun. lunch.*

$$ **✕ May Kitchen + Bar.** With the opening of May Kitchen + Bar, there's
THAI reason beyond La Boucherie for city dwellers to hop a ferry to come
Fodor's Choice to Vashon for dinner. Foodies swoon over the delectable Thai dishes
★ cooked to perfection, and the ambience is scene-y (atypical for Vashon):
dark with fully paneled walls in mahogany and teak—wood that owner
May Chaleoy had shipped from Thailand, where it previously lived
in the interior of a 150-year-old home. Reservations highly recom-
mended. $ *Average main: $18* ⊠ *17614 Vashon Hwy SW, Vashon
Island* ☎ *206/408–7196* ⊕ *www.maykitchen.com* ⊙ *Wed.–Sun, 4–9
pm. No lunch.*

WHIDBEY ISLAND

*20 mins by ferry from Mukilteo (20 miles north of Seattle) to Clinton, at
the southern end of Whidbey Island, or drive north 87 miles to Decep-
tion Pass at the north end of the island.*

Whidbey is a blend of low pastoral hills, evergreen and oak forests,
meadows of wildflowers (including some endemic species), sandy
beaches, and dramatic bluffs with a few pockets of unfortunate sub-
urban sprawl. It's a great place for a scenic drive, viewing sunsets over
the water, taking ridge hikes that give you uninterrupted views of the
Strait of Juan de Fuca, walking along miles of rugged seaweed-strewn
beaches, and for boating or kayaking along the protected shorelines of
Saratoga Passage, Holmes Harbor, Penn Cove, and Skagit Bay.

The best beaches are on the west side, where wooded and wildflower-
bedecked bluffs drop steeply to sand or surf—which can cover the
beaches at high tide and can be unexpectedly rough on this exposed
shore. Both beaches and bluffs have great views of the shipping lanes
and the Olympic Mountains. Maxwelton Beach, with its sand, drift-
wood, and amazing sunsets, is popular with the locals. Possession Point
includes a park and a beach, but it's best known for its popular boat
launch. West of Coupeville, Ft. Ebey State Park has a sandy spread and
an incredible bluff trail; West Beach is a stormy patch north of the fort
with mounds of driftwood. At 35 miles long, Whidbey's island vibe is
split between north and south; the historic southern and central towns
of Langley and Coupeville are quaint and offer the most to do; Clinton
(near the ferry terminal) isn't much of a destination, nor is the sprawl-
ing Navy town of Oak Harbor farther north. Yet Deception Pass at the

island's northern tip offers the most jaw-dropping splendor, so plan enough time to visit both ends of the island. One fun way to see it all is to arrive via the Clinton ferry and drive back to Seattle via Deception Pass, or vice versa.

GETTING HERE AND AROUND

You can reach Whidbey Island by heading north from Seattle on I–5, west on Route 20 onto Fidalgo Island, and south across Deception Pass Bridge. The Deception Pass Bridge links Whidbey to Fidalgo Island. From the bridge it's just a short drive to Anacortes, Fidalgo's main town and the terminus for ferries to the San Juan Islands. It's easier—and more pleasant—to take the 20-minute ferry trip from Mukilteo (30 miles northwest of Seattle) to Clinton, on Whidbey's south end, as long as you don't time your trip on a Friday evening, which could leave you waiting in the car line for hours. Fares are $4.65 per person for walk-ons (round trip) and $9.75 per car and driver (one way). Be sure to look at a map before choosing your point of entry; the ferry ride may not make sense if your main destination is Deception Pass State Park. Buses on Whidbey Island, provided by Island Transit, are free. Routes are fairly comprehensive, but keep in mind that Whidbey is big—it takes at least 35 minutes just to drive from the southern ferry terminal to the midway point at Coupeville—and if your itinerary is far-reaching, a car is your best bet.

Contact **Island Transit** ☎ *800/240–8747* ⊕ *www.islandtransit.org.*

ESSENTIALS

Visitor Information Central Whidbey Chamber of Commerce. Central Whidbey Chamber of Commerce's website has a great list of resources, from lodging to shopping, restaurants and local events. ⊠ *107 S. Main St., Coupeville* ☎ *360/678–5434* ⊕ *www.centralwhidbeychamber.com.*

Langley/South Whidbey Chamber of Commerce. Start off the "Langley Loop"—an 8.5-mile scenic driving or biking tour, at the Langley/South Whidbey Chamber of Commerce, which will point you in the right direction for South Whidbey's eclectic mix of restaurants, galleries, wineries, and markets. ⊠ *208 Anthes Ave., Langley* ☎ *360/221–6765* ⊕ *www.southwhidbeychamber.com.*

LANGLEY

The historic village of Langley, 7 miles north of Clinton on Whidbey Island, is above a 50-foot-high bluff overlooking Saratoga Passage, which separates Whidbey from Camano Island. A grassy terrace just above the beach is a great place for viewing birds on the water or in the air. On a clear day you can see Mt. Baker in the distance. Upscale boutiques selling art, glass, jewelry, books, and clothing line 1st and 2nd streets in the heart of town.

WHERE TO EAT AND STAY

For expanded hotel reviews, visit Fodors.com.

$ ✕ **Prima Bistro.** Langley's most popular gathering spot occupies a
BISTRO second-story space on First Street, right above the Star Store Grocery. Northwest-inspired French cuisine is the headliner here; classic bistro dishes like steak frites, salade niçoise, and confit of duck leg are favorites. Penn Cove mussels and oysters are always popular. The wine list

is by far the best in town. The bistro's outdoor deck offers views of Saratoga Passage, Camano Island, and beyond, and ample heat lamps ensure that guests enjoy the beauty of Whidbey summer's night. Live music every Thursday night and a daily happy hour from 3 to 6 pm keeps locals and tourists coming back for more. [$] *Average main: $17* ✉ *201½ 1st St.* ☎ *360/221–4060* 🌐 *www.primabistro.com.*

$$$$ B&B/INN Fodor's Choice ★ 🏨 **Inn at Langley.** Langley's most elegant inn, the concrete-and-wood Frank Lloyd Wright–inspired structure perches on a bluff above the beach, just steps from the center of town. **Pros:** island luxury; lovely views; amazing restaurant. **Cons:** some rooms can be on the small side; decor is starting to feel slightly dated. [$] *Rooms from: $390* ✉ *400 1st St.* ☎ *360/221–3033* 🌐 *www.innatlangley.com* 🛏 *28 rooms* 🍴 *Breakfast.*

$$ B&B/INN 🏨 **Saratoga Inn.** At the edge of Langley, this cedar-shake, Nantucket-style inn is a short walk from the town's shops and restaurants, and it overlooks the waters of Saratoga Passage and the stunning North Cascades. **Pros:** breathtaking views; cozy interiors. **Cons:** a bit rustic; some small bathrooms. [$] *Rooms from: $205* ✉ *201 Cascade Ave.* ☎ *360/221–5801, 800/698–2910* 🌐 *www.saratogainnwhidbeyisland.com* 🛏 *15 rooms, 1 carriage house* 🍴 *Breakfast.*

SHOPPING

Brackenwood Gallery. Brackenwood is known for its fine art and well-known Pacific Northwest artists. You can see pieces by Georgia Gerber, a famed island sculptor whose bronze pieces are regionally famous; Western-themed paintings and prints by Bruce Morrow; exquisite stone sculpture by Sharon Spencer; and Northwest landscape paintings by Pete Jordan. ✉ *302 1st St.* ☎ *360/221–2978* 🌐 *www.brackenwoodgallery.com* 🕒 *Wed.–Fri. 11–5, weekends 10–5. Closed Tue. and Wed. Jan.–Apr.*

Moonraker Books. Moonraker Books has been Langley's independent bookshop since 1972, and it stocks a wonderful and eclectic array of fiction, nonfiction, cookbooks—and, according to the owners, "books you didn't even know you wanted until you stepped inside." ✉ *209 1st St.* ☎ *360/221–6962.*

Museo. A contemporary fine art gallery focused on Northwest and regional artists, Museo is known for its glass art, sculpture, and handcrafted jewelry. Artist receptions are held on the first Saturday of each month from 5 to 7 pm. ✉ *215 1st St.* ☎ *360/221–7737* 🌐 *www.museo.cc* 🕒 *Wed.–Mon. 11–5; Tues. by appointment.*

The Wayward Son. Featuring both estate jewelry and custom creations by local jeweler Sandy Wainwright, The Wayward Son has antique-inspired rings, bracelets, and pendants incorporating gemstones of all styles. The gift shop also sells fine chocolates and candies. ✉ *107-B 1st St.* ☎ *360/221–3911* 🕒 *Wed.–Mon. 11–5.*

GREENBANK

About halfway up Whidbey Island, 14 miles northwest of Langley, is the hamlet of Greenbank, home to a loganberry farm encircled by views of the Olympic and Cascade ranges.

EXPLORING

FAMILY **Greenbank Farm.** You can't miss the huge, chestnut-color, two-story barn with the wine vat out front—the centerpiece to this picturesque, 125-acre property. Greenbank's loganberry wines and dessert wines (for which they are famous) can be sampled daily in the tasting room for $1 per taste. The adjacent Whidbey Pies Café creates gourmet sandwiches, soups, and pies, all of which disappear quickly as visitors head for the scattered picnic tables. Bring your dog (or horse!) and walk the scenic meadow trails. Besides wildlife, be on the lookout for the herd of fluffy alpacas raised onsite by the Whidbey Island Alpacas company. The 1904 barn, which once housed a winery, is now a community center for farmers' markets, concerts, flea markets, and other events, including the famous Loganberry Festival each July. ✉ *765 Wonn Rd.* ☎ *360/678–7700* 🌐 *www.greenbankfarm.com* 🎟 *Free* 🕒 *The property is open daily until dusk. Businesses are open daily 12–5.*

Meerkerk Rhododendron Gardens. The 53-acre Meerkerk Rhododendron Gardens contain 1,500 native and hybrid species of rhododendrons and more than 100,000 spring bulbs on 10 acres of display gardens with more than 4 miles of nature trails. The flowers are in full bloom in April and May; summer flowers and fall color provide interest later in the year. The 43 remaining acres are kept wild as a nature preserve. ✉ *Hwy. 525 and Resort Rd.* ☎ *360/678–1912* 🌐 *www.meerkerkgardens.org* 🎟 *$5* 🕒 *Mar. 15–Sept. 15, daily 9–4; Sept. 16–Mar. 14, Wed.–Sun. 9–dusk.*

WHERE TO STAY

For expanded hotel reviews, visit Fodors.com.

$$ B&B/INN 🏨 **Guest House Cottages.** Surrounded by 25 secluded wooded acres, each of these six private cabins, resembling cedar-sided barns with towering stone chimneys, comes with a feather bed, a Jacuzzi, country antiques, a kitchen, and a fireplace. **Pros:** lots of privacy and amenities; good location between Langley and Coupeville. **Cons:** strict cancellation policy of 21 days; basic breakfast foods are provided but you have to make your own. [$] *Rooms from: $235* ✉ *24371 State Route 525 E, Christianson Rd.* ☎ *360/678–3115, 800/997–3115* 🌐 *www.guesthouselogcottages.com* 🛏 *6 cabins.*

9

COUPEVILLE

Restored Victorian houses grace many of the streets in quiet Coupeville, Washington's second-oldest city, on the south shore of Penn Cove, 12 miles north of Greenbank. It also has one of the largest national historic districts in the state, and has been used for filming movies depicting 19th-century New England villages. Stores above the waterfront have maintained their old-fashioned character. Captain Thomas Coupe founded the town in 1852. His house was built the following year, and other houses and commercial buildings were built in the late 1800s. Even though Coupeville is the Island County seat, the town has a laid-back, almost 19th-century air.

EXPLORING

FAMILY Fodor's Choice ★ **Ebey's Landing National Historic Reserve.** Ebey's Landing National Historic Reserve encompasses a sand-and-cobble beach, bluffs with dramatic views down the Strait of Juan de Fuca, two state parks *(Ft. Casey and Ft. Ebey; see separate listings)*, and several privately held pioneer farms homesteaded in the early 1850s. The reserve, the first and largest of its kind, holds nearly 400 nationally registered historic structures (including those located within the town of Coupeville), most of them from the 19th century. Miles of trails lead along the beach and through the woods. Cedar Gulch, south of the main entrance to Ft. Ebey, has a lovely picnic area in a wooded ravine above the beach. ✥ *From state Highway 20, turn south on Main Street in Coupeville. This road turns into Engles road as you head out of town. Turn right on Hill road and follow it to the reserve.* 🌐 *www.nps.gov/ebla/index.htm.*

FAMILY **Island County Historical Museum.** The Island County Historical Museum's collections include Ice Age relics, mammoth remains, and a strong Native American collection, including cedar dugout canoes. The square-timber **Alexander Blockhouse** outside dates from 1855. Note the squared logs and dovetail joints of the corners—no overlapping log ends. This construction technique was favored by many Western Washington pioneers. ✉ *908 N.W. Alexander St.* ☎ *360/678–3310* 🎟 *$3* ⏲ *May–Sept., Mon.–Sat. 10–5, Sun. 11–5; Oct.–Apr., Mon.–Sat. 10–4, Sun. 11–4.*

WHERE TO EAT AND STAY

For expanded hotel reviews, visit Fodors.com.

$$ PACIFIC NORTHWEST 🍴 **Christopher's on Whidbey.** A warm and casual place, Christopher's is in a house one block from the waterfront. The menu features many Whidbey favorites, including local mussels and clams, and such flavorful fare as raspberry barbecued salmon, bacon-wrapped pork tenderloin with mushrooms, Penn Cove seafood stew, and linguine with a smoked-salmon cream sauce. The wine list is extensive. [$] *Average main: $21* ✉ *103 N.W. Coveland* ☎ *360/678–5480* 🌐 *www.christophersonwhidbey.com* ⏲ *Closed Mon.*

$$ SEAFOOD Fodor's Choice ★ 🍴 **The Oystercatcher.** A dining destination for foodies from across the Northwest, the Oystercatcher is renowned for its local-inspired cuisine. The simple menu is heavily influenced by fresh, in-season ingredients. Owners Joe and Jamie Martin have crafted an intimate, romantic dining space in the heart of town, and the restaurant's wine list is stellar. [$] *Average main: $22* ✉ *901 Grace St. NW* ☎ *360/678–0683* 🌐 *www.oystercatcherwhidbey.com* ⏲ *Thurs.–Sun. 5–8.*

$$ B&B/INN 🏨 **Captain Whidbey Inn.** Over a century old, this venerable historic lodge on a wooded promontory offers a special kind of old-world romance and charm now rarely found. **Pros:** private cabins with hot tubs; rustic yet comfortable. **Cons:** poor soundproofing in the main motel; shared bathrooms. [$] *Rooms from: $170* ✉ *2072 Captain Whidbey Inn Rd., off Madrona Way* ☎ *360/678–4097, 800/366–4097* 🌐 *www.captainwhidbey.com* 🛏 *23 rooms, 2 suites, 4 cabins.*

$ B&B/INN 🏨 **Compass Rose Bed and Breakfast.** Inside this stately 1890 Queen Anne Victorian on the National Register of Historic Places, a veritable museum of art, artifacts, and antiques awaits you. **Pros:** wonderful hosts; great

This Historic Ferry House is part of Ebey's Landing National Historic Reserve on Whidbey Island.

breakfast; full of interesting antiques and collectibles. **Cons:** only two rooms, so it gets booked up fast. $ *Rooms from: $115* ✉ *508 S. Main St.* ☎ *360/678–5318, 800/237–3881* 🌐 *www.compassrosebandb.com* 🛏 *2 rooms* 💳 *No credit cards* 🍴 *Breakfast.*

OAK HARBOR

Oak Harbor, about 10 miles north of Coupeville, is the least attractive and least interesting part of Whidbey—it mainly exists to serve the Whidbey Island Naval Air Station, and has none of the historic or pastoral charm of the rest of the island. It is, however, the largest town on the island and the one closest to Deception Pass State Park. If you need to stock up on provisions, you'll find all the big box stores here, in addition to major supermarkets. In town, the marina, at the east side of the bay, has a picnic area with views of Saratoga Passage and the entrance of Penn Cove.

FAMILY **Deception Pass State Park.** The biggest draw of the park is the historic two-lane Deception Pass Bridge connecting Whidbey Island to Fidalgo Island, about 9 miles north of Oak Harbor. Park the car and walk across in order to get the best views of the dramatic saltwater gorges and churning whirlpools below. Then, spend a few hours walking the 19 miles of rocky shore and beaches, exploring three freshwater lakes, or walking along the many forest and meadow trails. A Washington State Discovery Pass is required ($10/day or $30/yr). ✉ *Rte. 20, 9 miles north of Oak Harbor* ☎ *360/675–2417* 🌐 *www.parks.wa.gov* 🎟 *Discovery Pass required ($30/yr or $10/day), campsite fees vary* 🕒 *Apr.–Sept., daily 6:30 am–dusk; Oct.–Mar., daily 8 am–dusk.*

CLOSE UP

Woodinville Wineries

Walla Walla wine country is too far to go from Seattle if you've only got a few days; instead, check out Woodinville's excellent wineries. It's only about 22 miles from Seattle's city center. You'll need a car unless you sign up for a guided tour. Check out ⊕ www.woodinvillewinecountry. com for a full list of wineries and touring maps.

Wineries

There are more than 50 wineries in Woodinville, though most of them don't have tasting rooms. This list provides a good survey, from the big guys to the smallest boutique producers:

Chateau Ste. Michelle (✉ 14111 NE 145th St. ⊕ www.ste-michelle.com) is the grande dame of the Woodinville wine scene, and perhaps the most recognizable name nationwide. Guided tours of the winery and grounds (which do include a château) are available daily 10:30–4:30. The tasting room is open daily 10–5. Check the website for special events like dinners and concerts.

Columbia Winery (✉ 14030 N.E. 145th St ⊕ www.columbiawinery. com) is another major player with a grand house anchoring its winery. Columbia's tasting room is open Sunday–Tuesday 11–6 and Wednesday–Saturday 11–7. Regular tastings are $10 and private tastings are available for $25 per person.

Novelty Hill-Januik (✉ 14710 Woodinville-Redmond Rd. NE ⊕ www. noveltyhilljanuik.com) is often described as the most Napa-esque experience in Woodinville. The tasting room (open daily 11–5) for these sister wineries is sleek and modern. Themed tastings are $7–$10 per person. Brick-oven pizza is available on weekends.

DeLille Cellars (✉ 14221 Woodinville-Redmond Rd. NE ⊕ www. delillecellars.com) is on the list of nearly every fancy restaurant in Seattle. Most recently it's garnered national acclaim for the predominantly Cab-Sauv blend Chaleur Estate. The Carriage House tasting room, slightly north of the winery, is open Sunday–Thursday noon–4:30, Friday noon–7 and Saturday 11–4:30.

Mark Ryan (✉ 14810 NE 145th St., #A-1 ⊕ www.markryanwinery.com) is an indie winery that has earned praise nationwide for its use of mostly Red Mountain AVA grapes—especially for the Dead Horse reds. The winery has a small tasting room open daily 12–5.

Ross Andrew (✉ 14810 NE 145th St, #A-2 ⊕ www.rossandrewwinery. com) is a newcomer that is already at the top of many enthusiasts' lists for Cabs and Syrah from Columbia Valley grapes and Pinot Blanc and Pinot Gris from Oregon grapes. The tasting room (next door to Mark Ryan) is open Thursday–Monday 12–5 (Saturday until 6).

Woodinville Warehouse Wineries (⊕ www.woodwarewine.com) is a collective of all the wineries, breweries and distilleries in and around Woodinville. "Wine Walk" tastings are held on first and third Thursdays for $20 (BYOG, or bring your own glass). Producers and themed tastings vary; check the website for details.

—Updated by Allison Ellis

WASHINGTON CASCADE MOUNTAINS AND VALLEYS

With Tacoma, Olympia, and Mt. St. Helens

WELCOME TO WASHINGTON CASCADE MOUNTAINS AND VALLEYS

TOP REASONS TO GO

★ **Take flight:** See a Boeing in mid-construction or see a World War II chopper up close at Everett's Paine Field.

★ **Tiptoe through the tulips:** Bike past undulating fields of tulips and other spring blooms in La Conner and Mt. Vernon.

★ **Hang in glass houses:** Check out Dale Chihuly's biomorphic sculptures at Tacoma's Museum of Glass.

★ **View a volcano:** Visit Johnston Ridge Observatory, for a scarily close view of Mt. St. Helens.

★ **Paddle around Puget Sound:** Rent a kayak to explore the charming seaside communities of Poulsbo or Gig Harbor.

1 Cascade Foothills and Snohomish County. Short jaunts off the I–5 highway include attending a county fair in Puyallup and winding down a day of hiking or biking near Snoqualmie Pass with a snack in the cute town of Snoqualmie. North of Seattle are two important port towns, Edmonds and Everett. Edmonds has more of a seaside vibe, with waterfront parks and promenades, and a ferry terminal serving the islands of Puget Sound. Everett, on the other hand, is devoted to flight, with a Boeing factory tour and a collection of vintage airplanes being the main attractions.

2 Bellingham and Skagit Valley. The laid-back, outdoorsy college town of Bellingham is about as close as this area comes to bustle. Although not as tranquil as the central part of the state, the area is about roads less traveled: the farm roads that connect La Conner and Mt. Vernon and the bike and hiking paths that wind through state parks.

3 Kitsap Peninsula. Crawling around Bremerton's collection of naval vessels is a favorite family activity. The smaller, less industrial port towns provide beach parks plus glimpses of the region's Scandinavian

and logging pasts—a nice snapshot of coastal Washington life should you not be able to make it out to the Olympic Peninsula.

4 Tacoma and Olympia. Immortalized in song by Neko Case as the "dusty old jewel in the South Puget Sound," Tacoma is shining a bit more brightly these days with a walkable waterfront that includes several impressive museums. Farther south is the capital city Olympia, which is the perfect mix of quirky and stately.

5 Mt. Rainier Environs. Washington's rugged southern Cascades region is famous for two massive volcanic peaks, Mt. Rainier and Mt. St. Helens. Small, remote towns are strung along highways that meander through this dramatic area within day-tripping distance of Olympia and Tacoma. To really get to know this part of the state, however, spend a night in Ashford, Mossyrock, or Packwood.

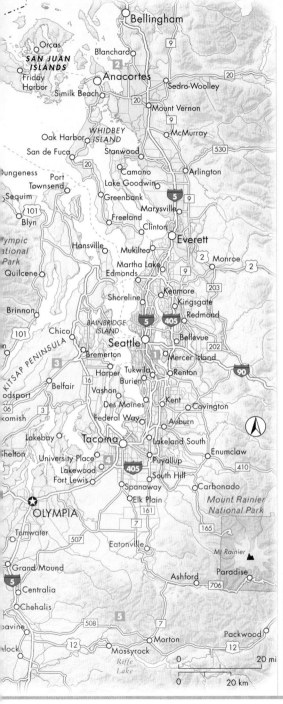

GETTING ORIENTED

Most of the major towns are along—or not far from—the I–5 corridor, stretching from the capital city of Olympia, 60 miles south of Seattle, and on north to Bellingham, 90 miles north of Seattle and the last city of size before the Canadian border. Many of the cities along the route are ports on Puget Sound. There's even more waterfront out on the Kitsap Peninsula, which is sandwiched between this corridor and the Olympic Peninsula. Three other outlying areas include the western edge of the Skagit Valley, an important agricultural area; Snoqualmie, in the foothills of the Cascades east of Seattle via I–90; and the towns around Mt. Rainier and Mt. St. Helens, which are south of Seattle and just east of the I–5 corridor.

10

Updated
by Andrew
Collins

Day trips—or long-weekend escapes—fan out from Seattle in every direction. The San Juan Islands, the Olympic Peninsula, and the great swaths of mid-state wilderness get the most photo ops, but there are plenty of adventures that don't require traveling on ferries or bumping along Forest Service roads.

Up and down I–5 you'll find most of the state's major cities: the ports of Tacoma, Olympia, and Bellingham may feel more like overgrown towns, but each has enough cultural and outdoorsy attractions to warrant an overnight.

Slightly farther afield you'll find smaller towns with some very specific draws: Poulsbo's proud Norwegian heritage, Puyallup's traditional state fair, Port Gamble's painstakingly preserved mill-town vibe, Everett's enthusiasm for all things flight-related, whether crafted by Boeing or not, and North Bend and Snoqualmie's breathtaking alpine scenery and friendly feel. And south of Mt. Rainier, towns like Packwood and Ashford in the Cascades offer rugged scenery and jumping-off points for visiting both Rainier and Mt. St. Helens.

Encompassing so many distinct geographical areas like the Kitsap Peninsula and the western fringe of the Skagit Valley, exploring this part of the state can bring you from industrial areas to tulip fields in one day. From naval warships to thundering falls, there's a lot to see within two hours of Seattle.

WASHINGTON CASCADE MOUNTAINS AND VALLEYS PLANNER

WHEN TO GO
The climate throughout the I–5 corridor, from the Skagit Valley down through Tacoma and Olympia, largely matches that of Seattle, with cool and damp winters (with low temperatures in the upper 30s) and largely dry and sunny summers, with temperatures in the 70s and low

80s. The more favorable weather of late spring through mid-October brings the largest crowds to the region, but rainy winter brings lower hotels rates and can be charmingly stormy—ideal for cozying up by the fireplace in a toasty room—on the Kitsap Peninsula or up in Bellingham and the Skagit Valley. In the Snoqualmie area, skiing and other winter sports are popular from December through April, when heavy snows come, although the towns in the foothills receive more rain than snow. In the towns up around Mt. Rainier and Mt. St. Helens, winter snow often brings temporary road closures, and many restaurants, lodges, and attractions are closed or have limited hours from mid-fall through mid-spring; it's definitely wise to check forecasts and call ahead if venturing into the Cascades at this time.

FESTIVALS AND EVENTS

Skagit Valley Tulip Festival. The Skagit Valley Tulip Festival in June is a monthlong celebration of these iconic flowers that bloom in the millions throughout Mt. Vernon and La Conner. ☎ *360/428–5959* ⊕ *www. tulipfestival.org.*

Washington State Fair. This fair in September brings thousands of visitors daily over two weeks to Puyallup, and features concerts, a rodeo, art and cultural exhibits, agricultural shows, and amusement rides. ☎ *253/845–1771* ⊕ *www.thefair.com.*

GETTING HERE AND AROUND

AIR TRAVEL

Seattle-Tacoma International Airport (Sea-Tac), 15 miles south of Seattle, is the hub for the Seattle environs. There are several regional airports, but the only one that sees much action is Bellingham's International Airport (which has direct flights to Seattle, Portland, Las Vegas, Denver, Phoenix, Oakland, and several other cities), because Bellingham is a hub between northwestern Washington and Canada and has a ferry terminal for cruises to British Columbia and beyond.

Contacts Bellingham International ✉ *1801 Roeder Ave., Bellingham* ☎ *360/676–2500* ⊕ *www.portofbellingham.com.* **Sea-Tac Airport** ✉ *17801 International Blvd., [Hwy. 99], Seattle* ☎ *206/787–5388, 800/544–1965* ⊕ *www. portseattle.org/sea-tac.*

AIRPORT TRANSFERS

Shuttle Express provides scheduled ride-share service hourly from Sea-Tac Airport to all of the cities and larger towns in this chapter. Bremerton–Kitsap Airporter shuttles passengers from Sea-Tac to points in Tacoma, Bremerton, Port Orchard, and Gig Harbor ($13–$21 one-way). The Capital Aeroporter connects Sea-Tac with Olympia ($30–$40 one-way). The Airporter Shuttle/Bellair Charters makes numerous trips daily between Sea-Tac and Bellingham ($34 one-way), with a few stops in between; and between Sea-Tac and North Bend ($21 one-way), continuing on to Yakima

Contacts Airporter Shuttle/Bellair Charters ☎ *866/235–5247* ⊕ *www.airporter. com.* **Bremerton–Kitsap Airporter** ☎ *360/876–1737* ⊕ *www.kitsapairporter.com.* **Capital Aeroporter** ☎ *360/754–7113, 800/962–3579* ⊕ *www.capair.com.* **Shuttle Express** ☎ *425/981–7000* ⊕ *www.shuttleexpress.com.*

10

BOAT AND FERRY TRAVEL

Washington State Ferries ply Puget Sound, including from Seattle to Bremerton and between Edmonds and Kingston on the Key Peninsula.

Contact **Washington State Ferries** ☎ *206/464-6400, 888/808-7977* ⊕ *www.wsdot.wa.gov/ferries.*

BUS TRAVEL

Greyhound Lines and Northwestern Trailways cover Washington and the Pacific Northwest. From Seattle, Greyhound connects to Tacoma, Olympia, Bellingham, and several other cities in the region. Pierce County Transit provides bus service around Tacoma

Greyhound Lines ☎ *800/231-2222* ⊕ *www.greyhound.com.*

Northwestern Trailways ☎ *800/366-3830* ⊕ *www.northwesterntrailways.com.*

Pierce County Transit ☎ *253/581-8000* ⊕ *www.piercetransit.org.*

CAR TRAVEL

Interstate 5 runs south from the Canadian border through Seattle, Tacoma, and Olympia to Oregon and California. Interstate 90 begins in Seattle and runs east through North Bend all the way to Idaho. U.S. 2 meanders east, parallel to I–90, from Everett to Spokane. Highways 7 and 167 connect the Tacoma area with the Puyallup suburbs and towns around Mt. Rainier. U.S. 101 begins northwest of Olympia and traces the coast of the Olympic Peninsula.

TRAIN TRAVEL

Amtrak's Cascades line serves Centralia, Tacoma, Olympia, Seattle, Edmonds, Everett, Mt. Vernon, and Bellingham. Sound Transit's Sounder trains (commuter rail, weekdays only) connect Seattle with Edmonds, Mukilteo, and Everett; and Seattle with Tacoma and Puyallup as well as a few other suburbs.

Amtrak ☎ *800/872-7245* ⊕ *www.amtrak.com.*

Sound Transit ☎ *206/398-5000, 888/889-6368* ⊕ *www.soundtransit.org.*

TRAVELING FROM SEATTLE

Tacoma, Bremerton, and Everett are good choices for day trips. Tacoma is only 30–40 minutes by car or train from Seattle; Bremerton and Everett are also easy to reach in under an hour, plus their major attractions (exhibits on naval and flight history, respectively) are of the type that don't require overnights. Just don't get stuck driving the I-5 corridor during weekday rush hours or on Sunday night in summer—the chaotic and heavy traffic will sour any outing.

Snoqualmie is also easily visited in a day, as it's close to Seattle, but because it's a popular base for outdoor recreation, many visitors overnight here.

Olympia is far enough from Seattle—technically it's only about 60 miles, but you almost always hit traffic, so expect a solid 1½ hours in the car—that it's often better for an overnight visit or as a stop on the way to the southern part of the Olympic Peninsula (Ocean Shores or Moclips, for example). You can pick up U.S. 101 on the outskirts of the city. Olympia is also a good leg-stretch between Seattle and Portland

and can be part of an itinerary to Mount Rainier National Park or Mount St. Helens National Monument—it's a good idea to spend the night near these parks if planning a visit, as they're a good drive from Seattle, and you'll want to get an early start if planning a hike or driving along these winding, narrow forest roads.

RESTAURANTS

Tacoma and Olympia both have increasingly hip and sophisticated dining scenes, with everything from laid-back cafés to seasonally driven restaurants with water views. After those cities, Gig Harbor has the best food scene—not terribly big, but with an across-the-board quality not quite found in Bellingham, which is, however, steadily developing a fine little crop of notable restaurants. You'll also find good brewpubs and indie coffeehouses in most of the larger towns in the area.

On the road, refueling takes place at country-style cafés, farm stands, and kitschy or specialty shops like the '50s-style sweets shops of Port Gamble and Snoqualmie or the Norwegian bakeries of Poulsbo. None of these is in short supply, and many eateries, however small, pride themselves on using local ingredients. *Prices in the reviews are the average cost of a main course at dinner or, if dinner is not served, at lunch.*

HOTELS

Many of the towns listed are easy day trips from Seattle, so staying there is always an option. On the other hand, hotel rates are nearly always lower outside Seattle, and overnight parking at smaller-town hotels is often very cheap or free. Tacoma, Olympia, and Bellingham have the widest variety of accommodations, with pricey hotels, midrange chains, and bed-and-breakfasts. Almost all but the smallest rural towns have mid-range chain motels; towns lacking those, like Port Gamble, have at least one B&B. The only truly great luxury resort in the region is the Salish Lodge in Snoqualmie. There are a few other noteworthy hotels in these parts—the Murano in Tacoma, the Chrysalis Inn in Bellingham, and some fine B&Bs elsewhere—but relatively prosaic chains dominate the lodging landscape. *Prices in the reviews are the lowest cost of a standard double room in high season.*

10

CASCADE FOOTHILLS AND SNOHOMISH COUNTY

Flanking the I–5 corridor are gateway towns to the scenically beautiful areas north and east of Seattle: Snoqualmie and North Bend are tried-and-true pit stops for hikers, bikers, and skiers heading over Snoqualmie Pass. The town of Snoqualmie is itself day-trip-worthy, with its stuck-in-time downtown full of vintage railroad cars, and beautiful, easily accessed falls.

The towns north of Seattle are a mixed bag. Edmonds and Everett, both close to Seattle, are important commuter hubs. Edmonds has a major ferry terminal and the more sophisticated dining and shopping scenes. Everett has slightly more tourist appeal because of its connection to Boeing and the great airplane-related attractions its Paine Field supports.

SNOQUALMIE

3 miles northwest of North Bend.

Spring and summer snowmelt turn the Snoqualmie (sno-*qual*-mie) River into a thundering torrent at **Snoqualmie Falls,** the sweeping cascades that provided the backdrop for the *Twin Peaks* opening montage. The water pours over a 268-foot rock ledge (100 feet higher than Niagara Falls) to a 65-foot-deep pool. These cascades, considered sacred by the Native Americans, are Snoqualmie's biggest attraction. A 2-acre park and observation platform afford views of the falls and the surrounding area. The 3-mile round-trip River Trail winds through trees and over open slopes to the base of the cascades.

GETTING HERE AND AROUND

To reach Snoqualmie from Seattle, take I–90 east to Exit 27. The old town area of Snoqualmie is very compact and walkable; the falls and Salish Lodge are a mile north of Old Town.

EXPLORING

FAMILY **Northwest Railway Museum.** Vintage cars line a paved path along Railroad Avenue, with signs explaining the origin of each engine, car, and caboose on display, and more history and memorabilia are on display inside the former waiting room of the stunning restored Snoqualmie depot. Several times a day, on weekends only, a train made of cars built in the mid-1910s for the Spokane, Portland, and Seattle Railroad, travels between Snoqualmie Depot and North Bend. The 70-minute (round-trip) excursion passes through woods, past waterfalls, and around patchwork farmland. Crowds of families pack the winter Santa Train journeys and the midsummer Railroad Days rides, when a helicopter drops balloons and prizes over the annual parade. ✉ *Snoqualmie Depot, 38625 S.E. King St.* ☎ *425/888–3030* 🌐 *www.trainmuseum.org* 🎟 *Depot free; rides $15* 🕒 *Depot daily 10–5; rides weekends only.*

WHERE TO EAT AND STAY

For expanded hotel reviews, visit Fodors.com.

$ AMERICAN 🍴 **Snoqualmie Taproom & Brewery.** This bustling, spacious Old Town brewpub and casual restaurant is renowned for its craft beers, including a much-acclaimed Steam Train Porter, named for the town's historic rail line. Food-wise, expect a nice range of hearty hot and cold sandwiches (the smoked turkey, provolone, jalapeño, and chipotle mayo on rosemary bread has plenty of kick), plus a nice variety of 12-inch pizzas. The Greek pie, with feta, kalamatas, artichokes, roasted red peppers, and pesto is a favorite. [$] *Average main: $9* ✉ *8032 Falls Ave. SE, Snoqualmie* ☎ *425/831–2357* 🌐 *www.fallsbrew.com.*

$$$ RESORT Fodor's Choice ★ 🏨 **Salish Lodge.** The stunning, chalet-style lodge sits right over Snoqualmie Falls and eight rooms have gorgeous views of the cascades, while others have a river panorama. **Pros:** right on the falls; most sophisticated dining in region; great spa. **Cons:** resort fee; not within easy walking

distance of Old Town. $ *Rooms from: $209* ✉ *6501 Railroad Ave. SE* ☎ *206/888–2556* ⊕ *www.salishlodge.com* ⌖ *80 rooms, 4 suites* ❖ *Some meals.*

SPORTS AND THE OUTDOORS

FAMILY
Fodor'sChoice
★

The Summit at Snoqualmie. This winter sports destination, 53 miles east of Seattle and about 25 miles east of North Bend, combines the Alpental, Summit West, Summit East, and Summit Central ski areas along Snoqualmie Pass. Spread over nearly 2,000 acres at elevations of up to 5,400 feet, the facilities include 65 ski trails (85% of them intermediate and advanced), 25 chairlifts, and two terrain parks. Those seeking tamer pursuits can head to the Summit Nordic Center, with groomed trails and a tubing area. Shops, restaurants, lodges (none of which are slope-side), and ski schools are connected by shuttle vans; there's even child care. For a different take on the mountains, head up to the pass after dinner; this is one of the nation's largest night-skiing areas. Full-day lift tickets, good for any of the four mountains, start at $60. ✉ *1001 Hwy. 906, exit 52 off I–90, Snoqualmie Pass* ☎ *425/434–7669, 206/236–1600 snow conditions* ⊕ *www.summitatsnoqualmie.com* ☉ *Oct.–Apr.*

WORD OF MOUTH

"In Snoqualmie, the Salish Lodge overlooking the falls has a superb restaurant. It's very fine for breakfast, and upscale for lunch, but a bargain compared to evening prices. Take your hiking shoes to walk the trail to the base of the falls. It's less than a mile, but steep with a boulder-to-boulder hop up the stream."

—stumpworks73

NORTH BEND

3 miles southeast of Snoqualmie.

This small town gets its name from a bend in the Snoqualmie River, which here turns toward Canada. The gorgeous surrounding scenery is dominated by 4,420-foot Mt. Washington, 4,788-foot Mt. Tenerife, and 4,167-foot Mt. Si. Named for early settler Josiah "Si" Merrit, Mt. Si can be climbed via a steep, four-hour trail that in summer provides views of the Cascade and Olympic peaks down to Puget Sound and Seattle. In winter, however, these mountains corner the rains: North Bend is one of the wettest places in western Washington, with an annual precipitation typically exceeding 65 inches (about double that of Seattle).

Scenes from the TV show *Twin Peaks*—notably the stunning opening waterfall sequence—were shot in North Bend, though most of the work was done in studios in Seattle. This is the last town on I–90 for gassing up before Snoqualmie Pass.

GETTING HERE AND AROUND

To reach North Bend from Seattle, take I–90 east to Exit 31. There's not much Old Town left in North Bend; navigating it requires a car.

10

The Summit at Snoqualmie

EXPLORING

Snoqualmie Valley Historical Museum. This local repository of history focuses on life centuries ago, with Native American tools, crafts, and attire as well as pioneer artifacts. The timber industry is another focus. ✉ *320 Bendego Blvd. S* ☎ *425/888–3200* 🌐 *www.snoqualmievalleymuseum.org* 🎟 *Donation suggested* 🕒 *Apr.–Oct., Sat.–Tues. 1–5; Nov.–Mar., Mon. noon–4.*

WHERE TO EAT AND STAY

For expanded hotel reviews, visit Fodors.com.

$ BAKERY 🍴 **George's Bakery.** A reliable fueling stop on the way to Snoqualmie Pass, George's has shelves of fresh-made doughnuts, pastries, and breads; decent coffee; and a full deli menu of sandwiches, soups, quiches, and calzones. [$] *Average main: $7* ✉ *127 W. North Bend Way* ☎ *425/888–0632* 🕒 *Closed Mon. No dinner.*

$$ B&B/INN 🏨 **Roaring River Bed & Breakfast.** On 2½ acres above the Snoqualmie River, this secluded B&B has unbeatable mountain and wilderness views, and rooms, with wainscoting and fireplaces, have private entrances and decks. **Pros:** pretty location; rustic-chic Herb's Place hunting cabin is spacious and reasonably priced. **Cons:** rooms are a little cluttered and overdone. [$] *Rooms from: $119* ✉ *46715 S.E. 129th St.* ☎ *425/888–4834, 877/627–4647* 🌐 *www.theroaringriver.com* 🛏 *4 rooms, 1 cabin* 🍽 *Breakfast.*

EDMONDS

45 miles northwest of Snoqualmie, 15 miles north of Seattle.

This charming, somewhat suburban small city just north of Seattle has a waterfront lined by more than a mile of boutiques and restaurants, seaside parks and attractions, and a string of broad, windswept beaches. Just beyond is the small but lively downtown area, where you can wander into hip cafés and wine shops, peruse attractive antiques stores and chic galleries, and browse the colorful Summer Market, which runs Saturday 9 to 3 from late June to early October. The Third Thursday Art Walk—one of the state's largest such events—shows off the work of local artists, and a host of events and festivals takes place year-round. On the east side of Puget Sound, Edmonds is also a gateway to the Kitsap Peninsula, as ferries from here connect to Kingston.

GETTING HERE AND AROUND

From Seattle, take I–5 north to Hwy. 104 west, which leads downtown and to the ferry terminal.

ESSENTIALS

Visitor Information Edmonds Chamber of Commerce ⊠ *120 5th Ave. N* ☎ *425/776–6711* ⊕ *edmondswa.com.*

EXPLORING

Edmonds Historical Museum. The lower level of the Edmonds Historical Museum is the place to find out about local legends and traditions; temporary exhibits upstairs often have a patriotic theme. The museum's Summer Garden Market sells handmade and hand-grown items on Saturday from 9 to 3 from late June through early October. ⊠ *118 5th Ave. N* ☎ *425/774–0900* ⊕ *www.historicedmonds.org* 🖃 *$5* 🕙 *Wed.–Sun. 1–4.*

Edmonds Underwater Park. Perhaps the best-known dive site in Puget Sound besides the Narrows Bridge area, the underwater park has 27 acres of sunken structures and developed dive trails. It's immediately north of the ferry landing at the foot of Main Street. Underwater Sports (*264 Railroad Ave., 425/771–6322, www.underwatersports.com*) in town offers tuition, equipment rentals, and underwater tours of the park. The adjacent Brackett's Landing Park—where there's parking—has trails, picnic areas, and restrooms. ⊠ *Brackett's Landing Park, Main St. and Railroad Ave., next to ferry terminal* ☎ *425/771–0230.*

FAMILY **Olympic Beach.** Get your dinner to go and watch the sun go down behind Whidbey Island and the Olympic Mountains at this lovely waterfront park. The Olympic Beach fishing pier attracts anglers all year and public art dots the landscape. In summer, a visitor station (open weekends noon–5) is a great place to pick up local info; kids like exploring the marine touch tank. ⊠ *200 Admiral Way* ☎ *425/775–1344.*

WHERE TO EAT

$$ ✕ **Arnie's in Edmonds.** Directly across from the sound, this classic, reasonably priced seafood restaurant (with another branch in Mukilteo) has expansive views of the water. You can count on fresh, seasonal fish and shellfish, with the menu varying depending on the day's catch.

SEAFOOD

One noted dish, Prawns Undecided, consists of prawns prepared in three different ways—stuffed with crab, roasted with garlic, and coated in a beer batter and fried. Pan-seared oysters, seared ahi tacos, and chopped seafood salad are other standouts. Sunday brunches, which last until 2, are a local tradition. $ *Average main: $23* ✉ *300 Admiral Way* ☎ *425/771–5688* ⊕ *www.arniesrestaurant.com.*

$$
ASIAN FUSION

✕ **Bar Dojo.** Although it's a couple of miles east of downtown in a strip mall, this newcomer has quickly established itself as a hot spot for creative, often complex modern Asian fare, with an emphasis on local ingredients. The early-evening and late-night happy hours are hugely popular, with great bargains on food and drinks. Pork belly ramen and wild salmon laksa with coconut shrimp broth are stars among the noodle bowls, but also look to honey-lemon pork belly and green-curry clams. Save room for the banana tarte tatin. $ *Average main: $18* ✉ *8404 Bowdoin Way, Edmonds* ☎ *425/967–7267* ⊕ *www.bardojo.com* ☾ *Closed Mon. No lunch.*

$$
MEDITERRANEAN
Fodor'sChoice
★

✕ **Epulo Bistro.** Darkly lighted, smartly furnished, and urbane, this hip bistro in the heart of downtown serves seasonally driven Mediterranean food with plenty of Northwestern influences. It's very easy to make a meal here of several tantalizing small plates, like sautéed brussels sprouts with bacon, chili, and garlic; and Penn Cove mussels with saffron, orange, and leeks. But there are plenty of tasty main dishes to consider, too, including braised-beef short rib with garlic-mashed potatoes. Wood-fired pizzas are another stellar option. $ *Average main: $21* ✉ *526 Main St., Edmonds* ☎ *425/678–8680* ⊕ *epulobistro.com* ☾ *Closed Mon. No lunch.*

$$
ITALIAN

✕ **Girardi's Osteria Italiana.** Coming here is like walking into an elegant yet comfortable Italian kitchen, where every space beneath the high, peaked ceiling glows with warm country colors and muted light. Small tables, with gleaming glass and white linens, are set on polished-wood floors and tucked in near exposed-brick walls. The menu is an induction into the Italian dining experience, with such entrées as *anitra della casa* (pan-seared duck breast on herb polenta) and *vitello del capitano* (veal medallions in a Madeira wine sauce). Come Monday and Tuesday for half-price bottled wines, and look for seasonal wine-tasting dinners focused on specific regions of Italy. $ *Average main: $19* ✉ *504 5th Ave. S* ☎ *425/673–5278* ⊕ *girardis-osteria.com.*

WHERE TO STAY
For expanded hotel reviews, visit Fodors.com.

$$
HOTEL

⌂ **Best Western Plus Edmonds Harbor Inn.** In downtown Edmonds, this inn has as much country style as you're likely to find in a chain property. **Pros:** proximity to the waterfront, and only 1½ blocks from the Kingston ferry terminal. **Cons:** no beach views. $ *Rooms from: $110* ✉ *130 W. Dayton St.* ☎ *425/771–5021, 800/441–8033* ⊕ *www.bestwesternwashington.com* ⤳ *91 rooms* ⏀| *Breakfast.*

EVERETT

19 miles north of Edmonds.

Much of this industrial town, the county seat of suburban Snohomish County, sits high on a bluff above Port Gardner Bay and the Snohomish River. The waterfront was once lined by so many lumber, pulp, and shingle mills that Everett proudly called itself "the city of smokestacks." Downtown Everett has many elegant old commercial buildings dating from the period when John D. Rockefeller heavily invested in the fledging town, hoping to profit from the nearby Monte Cristo mines—which turned out to be a flop. Another scheme failed when James J. Hill made Everett the western terminus of the Great Northern Railroad, hoping to turn it into Puget Sound's most important port. Everett is best known for the Boeing Aircraft plant and for having the second-largest Puget Sound port (after Seattle). The naval station here is home to the U.S.S. *Nimitz* aircraft carrier and a support flotilla of destroyers and frigates.

The pleasant waterfront suburb of Mukilteo, about 5 miles southeast of Everett, is the main departure point for ferries to Clinton, on Whidbey Island. The old lighthouse and waterfront park are fun to explore. An important Native American treaty was signed in 1855 at nearby Point Elliott.

Marysville, 6 miles north of Everett, was set up as a trading post in 1877. Pioneers exchanged goods with the Snohomish people, who once occupied southeastern Whidbey Island and the lower Snohomish Valley. Settlers drained and diked the lowlands, raised dairy cows, planted strawberry fields, cleared the forests, and in no time a thriving community was established. Marysville kept to itself for a century, until the I–5 freeway was built; today it's a thriving community and the home of the popular Tulalip (Too-*lay*-lip) Casino.

GETTING HERE AND AROUND

Everett is best explored by car; take I–5 north to exit 192.

ESSENTIALS

Visitor Information **Everett Visitor Information** ☎ 425/257–8700 ⊕ www.everettwa.org.

EXPLORING

The Flying Heritage Collection. Housed within a 51,000-square-foot airport hangar, this spectacular gathering of unique vintage aircraft belongs to local tycoon Paul Allen, who began collecting and restoring rare planes in 1988. The selections run the full length of 20th-century military history, including pieces from the two world wars and other international battles. A favorite plane is the P-51D Mustang from World War II. Tours are self-guided; exhibits help to explain the collection. In summer, try to time your visit for one of the Free Fly Days, when pilots are on-site to fly some of the craft as part of monthly maintenance. ⊠ *Paine Field, 3407 109th St. SW* ☎ *206/342–3404* ⊕ *www.flyingheritage.com* ☞ *$1* ☉ *Memorial Day–Labor Day, daily 10–5; day after Labor Day–day before Memorial Day, Tues.–Sun. 10–5.*

10

Boeing Everett Facility

Future of Flight Aviation Center & Boeing Tour. This facility showcases the Boeing Everett line (747, 767, 777, and 787), and the 98-acre site holds the world's largest building—so big that it often creates its own weather system inside. You can see planes in various stages of production on a 90-minute tour. Note that there are no bathroom breaks on the tour, and no purses, cameras, videos, or children under 48 inches tall are permitted. The tour includes a lot of walking and some stair-climbing, but the facility can accommodate people with mobility issues with advance arrangements. Reserving tour tickets a day in advance is recommended if you need a specific tour time, but same-day tickets are always available. The Future of Flight gallery includes cutaways of airplane fuselages, exhibits on the inner workings of navigation and hydraulic systems, and interactive exhibits that let you design your own commercial airliner. It also has a café. ⊠ *8415 Paine Field Blvd., Mukilteo* ☎ *425/438–8100, 800/464–1476 reservations* ⊕ *www.futureofflight. org* ⊠ *$18* ☉ *Facility daily 8:30–5:30, tours hourly 9–3.*

FAMILY **Imagine Children's Museum.** This engaging spot for kids is on a pioneer homestead built in the 1800s. Interactive exhibits and crafts are part of the fun; wee ones love the magic school bus as well. ⊠ *1502 Wall St.* ☎ *425/258–1006* ⊕ *www.imaginecm.org* ⊠ *$9 ($4.50 Thurs.)* ☉ *Tues.– Wed. 9–5, Thurs.–Sat. 10–5, Sun. 11–5.*

FAMILY **Jetty Island.** Open in summer only, this is a 2-mile-long, sand-fringed offshore haven full of wildlife and outdoor opportunities. Seasonal programs include guided walks, bonfires, and midsummer Jetty Island Days festivities. A free ferry (reservation recommended to avoid lines) provides round-trip transportation; group tours (book first) run daily at 10:45 and 3:30. ✉ *W. Marine View Dr.* ☎ *425/257–8304* 🌐 *www.ci.everett.wa.us* 🎟 *Free* 🕒 *Early July–early Sept., ferries depart on the half-hr, Mon.–Sat. 10–5:25, Sun. 11–5:25.*

Museum of Flight Restoration Center. At this branch of Seattle's Museum of Flight, vintage planes are restored by a volunteer staff who simply love bringing vintage aircraft back to life. You can wander among the mix of delicate and behemoth planes on a leisurely, self-guided tour at Paine Field. ✉ *2909 100th St. SW, Bldg. C-72* ☎ *425/745–5150* 🌐 *www.museumofflight.org/restoration-center* 🎟 *$5* 🕒 *June–Aug., Tues.–Sat. 9–5; Sept.–May, Tues.–Thurs. and Sat. 9–4.*

WHERE TO EAT AND STAY

For expanded hotel reviews, visit Fodors.com.

$$ SEAFOOD 🍴 **Anthony's Homeport.** Tucked into chic Marina Village, this elegant waterfront restaurant—part of a popular Washington-based seafood chain—has large windows opening to a panorama of Port Gardner Bay. In summer, sunsets appear to ooze into the water. The specials, which change daily, might include meaty Dungeness crab, wild chinook salmon, and other sea creatures caught just offshore. Desserts are fabulous, especially those crafted from the state's succulent berries and fruits. [$] *Average main: $18* ✉ *1726 W. Marine View Dr.* ☎ *425/252–3333* 🌐 *www.anthonys.com.*

$ AMERICAN 🍴 **The Sisters.** This funky breakfast and lunch café in Everett Public Market is as popular now as when it opened in 1983. Perhaps that's because the blueberry or pecan hotcakes, rich soups, and overflowing sandwiches are as good as ever. Eye-opening espresso drinks start the morning (from 7 am); homemade ice cream is a perfect end to the afternoon. Note that the café closes at 4 pm, but they shut down the grill at 3 pm. [$] *Average main: $7* ✉ *2804 Grand St.* ☎ *425/252–0480* 🌐 *www.thesistersrestaurant.com* 🕒 *Closed weekends. No dinner.*

$$ HOTEL 🏨 **Inn at Port Gardner.** Stroll along the marina and you'll encounter this gray, warehouse-style structure, which wraps around a cozy, modern hotel. **Pros:** right on the waterfront; close to area restaurants; nice patio and lobby. **Cons:** no pool; rooms are lovely but of the standard chain-hotel variety. [$] *Rooms from: $110* ✉ *1700 W. Marine Dr.* ☎ *425/252–6779, 888/252–6779* 🌐 *www.innatportgardner.com* 🛏 *27 rooms, 6 suites* 🍽 *Breakfast.*

10

PUYALLUP

35 miles south of Seattle, 10 miles southeast of Tacoma.

Set before the towering forests and snowfields of Mt. Rainier is Puyallup (pyoo-*al*-lup), one of western Washington's oldest towns. The Puyallup Fair attracts all of western Washington to its carnival rides, performers, produce, and animals. The annual event is held at the fairgrounds on the northwest end of town each September. The Spring Fair and Daffodil Festival (known as "The Little Puyallup") is another beloved event that takes place each April. These special events are really the only reason to make a detour to Puyallup unless you need a leg-stretch or a bite to eat on your way elsewhere. The downtown area is pleasant enough and has a few boutiques and restaurants, but doesn't have enough charm to warrant a special visit.

GETTING HERE AND AROUND

To reach Puyallup, take I–5 south to 405 north and then 167 south.

EXPLORING

Antique Shopping District. The city's developing Antique Shopping District has about a half-dozen cozy little stores clustered downtown. There are more vendors in the neighboring town of Sumner. Events and openings are guided by the Puyallup Antique District Association. ⊠ *Meridian and Main Sts.* ⊕ *www.antiquedistrict.net.*

FAMILY **Northwest Trek Wildlife Park.** This spectacular, 435-acre wildlife park 35 miles south of Puyallup is devoted to native creatures of the Pacific Northwest. Walking paths wind through natural surroundings—so natural that in 1998 a cougar entered the park and started snacking on the deer (it was finally trapped and relocated to the North Cascades). See beavers, otters, and wolverines; get close to wolves, foxes, coyotes; and observe several species of big cats and bears in wild environments. Admission includes a 50-minute tram ride through fields of wandering moose, bighorn sheep, elk, bison, and mountain goats. ⊠ *11610 Trek Dr. E, Eatonville* ☎ *360/832–6117* ⊕ *www.nwtrek.org* ✉ *$18.25* ⊗ *Hrs vary seasonally; call ahead.*

FAMILY **Pioneer Farm Museum and Ohop Indian Village.** This living history museum, 23 miles south of Puyallup, provides a look at pioneer and Native American life. Kids can learn how to hunt and fish in a realistic tribal village, grind grain, milk a cow, churn butter, and do other old-fashioned chores. A trading post shows the commodities of earlier eras. One-hour tours are available through both the farm and village. ⊠ *7716 Ohop Valley Rd. E, Eatonville* ☎ *360/832–6300* ⊕ *www.pioneerfarmmuseum. org* ✉ *Farm $9, village $9* ⊗ *Mid-June–early Sept., daily 11:15–4; mid-Mar.–mid-June and early Sept.–late Nov., weekends 11:15–4.*

Ezra Meeker Mansion. This grand, beige-colored italianate palace, built in 1891, was a fitting place for the richest man in the Northwest. Meeker, known locally as the "Hop King" for his beer empire, sank much of his profits into such elegant touches as inlaid fireplaces, ceiling murals, and stained-glass windows. The home is completely furnished in the style of its heyday. Seasonal events include the historic Meeker Days in June, the autumn Cider Squeeze, and Christmas at the Mansion each December. ⊠ *312 Spring St.* ☎ *253/848–1770* ⊕ *www.meekermansion. org* ✉ *$4* ⊗ *Mar.–mid-Dec., Wed.–Sun. noon–4.*

WHERE TO EAT

$ ✗ **Powerhouse Brewery and Restaurant.** The interior of what was once a AMERICAN   railroad powerhouse is adorned with glass insulators and high-voltage signs. About a dozen brews are served—some brewed on the premises and others from a sister brewery. The pub fare includes salads, pizzas, burgers, sandwiches, and pastas. $ *Average main: $13* ⊠ *454 E. Main Ave.* ☎ *253/845–1370* ⊕ *www.powerhousebrewpub.com.*

BELLINGHAM AND SKAGIT VALLEY

Most people blow through places like La Conner, Mt. Vernon, or Bellingham on their way west to the San Juans, east to the Cascades, or north to the Canadian border. But between Everett and Canada are some lovely miles of coastline, some impressive parkland, and charming farm towns—all of which are fairly easy to access from I–5. Collectively, the towns that anchor the northwestern edge of the state are seriously underappreciated: La Conner is a pleasantly laid-back farming community, and Mt. Vernon is a riverfront town with some great festivals. Between the two towns are the best of the Skagit Valley flower farms, which do draw big crowds in spring when the tulips bloom. Bellingham is a college town that's a fun and quirky mix of hippie and yuppie, and nearby Ferndale has some interesting historic sights to supplement the natural wonders. Any one of these towns makes a good stopover on other itineraries.

LA CONNER

14 miles southeast of Anacortes, 68 miles north of Seattle.

Morris Graves, Kenneth Callahan, Guy Anderson, Mark Tobey, and other painters set up shop in La Conner in the 1940s, and the village on the Swinomish Channel (Slough) has been a haven for artists ever since. In recent years the community has become increasingly popular as a weekend escape for Seattle residents, because it can be reached after a short drive but seems far away.

La Conner has several historic buildings near the waterfront or a short walk up the hill—use the stairs leading up the bluff, or go around and walk up one of the sloping streets—as well as several good shops and restaurants. In summer the village becomes congested with people and cars, and parking can be hard to find. The flat land around La Conner makes for easy bicycling along levees and through the tulip fields. You'll see plenty of fields and farms, and a major attraction in fall and summer are farm stands selling local produce.

GETTING HERE AND AROUND

The center of La Conner is roughly 12 miles off of I–5 (from Seattle, take Exit 221 for Hwy. 534). The town is very close to both Anacortes and the northern tip of Whidbey Island, and therefore it makes sense to pass through here on the way to one or the other. A car is by far the best way to reach and explore the area. In summer bike rentals ($30 for a half-day; $40 per day) are available at the Port of Skagit Marina in La Conner from Tulip Country Bike Tours.

Contact **Tulip Country Bike Tours** ☎ *360/424–7461* ⊕ *www.countrycycling. com.*

EXPLORING

Museum of Northwest Art. Here you can view some 2,500 works of regional creative minds past and present. Soaring spaces, circular exhibit rooms, a glass gallery, and a broad spiral staircase add to the free-form feeling of the displays. The small shop sells examples of what you see in

10

the exhibits. ⊠ *121 S. 1st St.* ☎ *360/466–4446* ⊕ *www.museumofnwart. org* ⊠ *$8* ⊗ *Sun. and Mon. noon–5, Tues.–Sat. 10–5.*

Skagit County Historical Museum. This hilltop museum surveys domestic life in early Skagit County and Northwest Coastal Native American history. ⊠ *501 4th St.* ☎ *360/466–3365* ⊕ *www.skagitcounty.net/museum* ⊠ *$5* ⊗ *Tues.–Sun. 11–5.*

WHERE TO EAT

$ ✕ **Calico Cupboard.** A local favorite, this chain of storefront bakeries
CAFÉ turns out some of the best pastries in Skagit County (there are branches
Fodor'sChoice in Anacortes and Mt. Vernon, too). Lunches focus on fresh and creative
★ salads, soups, and burgers; while huge and hearty breakfasts may leave you with little need for lunch—the roasted butternut-squash hash and migas are a couple of favorites. Buy goodies at the take-out counter for a picnic adventure. Ⓢ *Average main: $9* ⊠ *720 S. 1st St.* ☎ *360/466–4451* ⊕ *www.calicocupboardcafe.com* ⊗ *No dinner.*

$$ ✕ **La Conner Channel Grill.** A hot spot in downtown since it opened in
AMERICAN 2011, this casual but dapper spot with a pubby vibe, varnished-wood tables, and a lively bar scene has earned a popular following for fresh, deftly prepared seafood and steaks. Pecan-baked local wild salmon, panko-crusted panfried oysters, and filet mignon are favorites, and the burgers are a nice option for a lighter, less-spendy meal. Ⓢ *Average main: $22* ⊠ *110 N. 1st St., La Conner* ☎ *360/466–3800* ⊕ *www. laconnerrestaurant.com* ⊗ *Closed Tues. No lunch.*

WHERE TO STAY

For expanded hotel reviews, visit Fodors.com.

$$ ⊡ **Hotel Planter.** This smartly renovated hotel, the oldest in La Conner,
B&B/INN is on the National Register of Historic Places and its homey rooms have fine views of the hill or the waterfront. **Pros:** good value; central location; historic charm. **Cons:** old-fashioned decorative scheme isn't for everybody; some age restrictions. Ⓢ *Rooms from: $119* ⊠ *715 1st St.* ☎ *360/466–4710, 800/488–5409* ⊕ *www.hotelplanter.com* ⤹ *12 rooms* ⅠⓄⅠ *No meals.*

$$ ⊡ **La Conner Country Inn and Channel Lodge.** The stylish property com-
HOTEL prises two sections (a couple of blocks from one another): a rambling country inn and an understated lodge (*205 N. 1st St.*) overlooking the narrow Swinomish Channel. **Pros:** big stone fireplace; rustic charm wrapped around sleek modern amenities; two family suites. **Cons:** rooms are an odd mix of country coziness and chain hotel. Ⓢ *Rooms from: $139* ⊠ *107 S. 2nd St.* ☎ *360/466–1500, 888/466–4113* ⊕ *www. laconnerlodging.com* ⤹ *28 rooms, 17 suites* ⅠⓄⅠ *Breakfast.*

$ ⊡ **Queen of the Valley.** A white picket fence surrounds this stately, three-
B&B/INN story, early-20th-century country house about a mile east of downtown. **Pros:** great value; lovely views of the countryside; friendly staff. **Cons:** downtown shops and restaurants a bit of a walk. Ⓢ *Rooms from: $99* ⊠ *1075 Chilberg Rd.* ☎ *360/466–4578* ⊕ *www.queenofthevalleyinn. com* ⤹ *4 rooms, 1 cottage* ⅠⓄⅠ *Breakfast.*

Tulip fields, Mt. Vernon

$$ B&B/INN Fodor's Choice ★ 🏨 **Wild Iris.** The garden-laced exterior is a sprawling model of a Victorian-style inn, and the elegantly decorated interior begins with a river-rock fireplace. **Pros:** beautiful and tastefully decorated rooms; great amenities (good linens, DVD library, CD players) considering the decent rates. **Cons:** the least expensive rooms are quite small; layouts are a little odd, with whirlpool tubs very close to the beds and fireplaces. [$] *Rooms from: $119* ✉ *121 Maple Ave.* ☎ *360/466–1400, 800/477–1400* 🌐 *www.wildiris.com* 🛏 *4 rooms, 12 suites* 🍴 *Breakfast.*

MOUNT VERNON

11 miles northeast of La Conner.

This attractive riverfront town is the county seat of Skagit County and was founded in 1871. After a giant logjam on the lower Skagit was cleared, steamers began churning up the river, and Mount Vernon soon became the major commercial center of the Skagit Valley, a position it has never relinquished. The city is surrounded by dairy pastures, vegetable fields, and bulb farms, and is famous for its annual Tulip Festival in April, when thousands of people visit to admire the floral exuberance. Rising above downtown and the river, 972-foot-high Little Mountain is a city park with a view. It used to be an island until the mudflats were filled in by Skagit River silt. Glacial striations in rocks near the top of the mountain, dating from the last continental glaciation (10,000–20,000 years ago), were made when the mountain (and all of the Puget Sound region) was covered by some 3,500 feet of ice.

GETTING HERE AND AROUND

The best way to reach Mt. Vernon is by car, taking I–5 north to any of several exits right in town. In Mt. Vernon I–5 connects with Highway 536, which then merges with Highway 20 toward Anacortes.

Tulip Country Bike Tours arranges spring trips through the tulip fields, starting at $60 per person. In summer, tours take in other Skagit Valley sights like berry farms and Padilla Bay. You can also rent bikes for $40 per day.

Contacts Tulip Country Bike Tours ☎ 360/424–7461 ⊕ www.countrycycling. com.

EXPLORING

Bay View State Park. Adjoining the small waterfront community of the same name, this scenic 25-acre park has a campground in the woods and picnic tables on the low grassy bluff above the bay. Canoers and kayakers take note: Padilla Bay runs almost dry at low tide, when water is restricted to a few creek-like tidal channels. ⊠ *10905 Bay View–Edison Rd.* ☎ *360/757–0227* ⊕ *www.parks.wa.gov* ⊠ *$10 day pass, $30 annual Discover Pass (valid at all state parks)* ☉ *Daily 8 am–dusk.*

Little Mountain Park. Atop the eponymous mountain at the southeastern edge of town, this 480-acre park has great views of the Skagit Valley (especially in March and April, when the daffodils and tulips are in full bloom), the San Juan Islands, and the distant Olympic Mountains. ⊠ *Little Mountain Rd., off E. Blackburn Rd., 4 miles southeast of downtown* ☎ *360/336–6213* ⊠ *Free* ☉ *Daily dawn–dusk.*

Padilla Bay National Estuarine Reserve. At this serene wildlife preserve, the Breazeale Interpretive Center has great birding: there are black Brant (or Brent) geese, raptors, peregrine falcons, and bald eagles. Trails lead into the woods and to a rocky beach, with more good bird-watching opportunities. The 2¼-mile Padilla Bay Trail starts at the south end of Bayview; look for signs directing you to the parking area, which is away from the water off the east side of the road. ⊠ *10441 Bayview–Edison Rd.* ☎ *360/428–1558* ⊕ *www.padillabay.gov* ⊠ *Free* ☉ *Wed.–Sun. 10–5.*

Roozengaarde. This 1,200-acre estate was established by the Roozen family and Washington Bulb Company in 1985—it's the world's largest family-owned tulip-, daffodil-, and iris-growing business. Fifteen acres of greenhouses are filled with multicolored blossoms, and more than 200,000 bulbs are planted in the show gardens each fall. The Skagit Valley Tulip Festival, held in April, is the main event, when the flowers pop up in neat, brilliant rows across the flat land, attracting thousands of sightseers. The garden and store are open year-round, and the staff and website are full of helpful advice for both novice and experienced gardeners. ⊠ *15867 Beaver Marsh Rd., Mt. Vernon* ☎ *360/424–8531, 866/488–5477* ⊕ *www.tulips.com* ⊠ *Free* ☉ *Mon.–Sat. 9–6, Sun. 11–4.*

WHERE TO EAT

$$$ ✕ **Il Grainaio.** Tucked deep into the town's historic Old Granery, amid
ITALIAN displays of century-old farming equipment, is this cozy and rustic Italian restaurant. Dark-wood floors, small tables, and lanternlike lighting

give it the authentic ambience of a local trattoria. The waitstaff is quick and knowledgeable, turning out enormous pasta bowls, seafood salads, and pan-fried eggplant or salmon with flair. Excellent wines garnish the tables, and desserts are simple and rich. Slip in early on weekends, when dinners bustle with groups. $ *Average main: $27* ⊠ *100 E. Montgomery St.* ☎ *360/419–0674* ⊕ *www.granaio.com* ⊗ *No lunch weekends.*

$
CAFÉ
✕ **Rexville Grocery.** From Ben & Jerry's to Pocky sticks to local microbrews, Rexville is one well-stocked country store, with a great mix of everyday and gourmet snacks and drinks. There's a small café with a patio encircled by trees, vines, and blooming thistle. On weekends, you can sit down for a breakfast (served until noon) of scrambles or pancakes; the rest of the week, stop in for a sandwich or salad. You could put together quite a good picnic basket here. The store closes at 7 pm. $ *Average main: $10* ⊠ *19271 Best Rd.* ☎ *360/466–5522* ⊕ *www. rexvillegrocery.com* ⊗ *No dinner.*

BELLINGHAM

29 miles northeast of Mount Vernon.

The fishing port and college community of Bellingham is transforming itself from a grungy blue-collar area to the arts, retirement, and pleasure-boating capital of Washington's northwest corner. Downtown has cafés, specialty shops, and galleries, and the waterfront, once dominated by lumber mills and shipyards, is slowly being converted into a string of parks with connecting trails. College students and professors from Western Washington University make up a sizable part of the town's population and contribute to its laid-back intellectual climate. The lushly green bay-front, creeks meandering through town, and Lakes Whatcom and Padden attract wildlife like deer, raccoons, river otters, beavers, ducks, geese, herons, bald eagles, and the occasional cougar.

GETTING HERE AND AROUND

From Seattle, Bellingham is nearly a straight shot on I–5 north (Exit 254 will get you into the center of town).

Amtrak's Cascades train stops in Bellingham on its way to Vancouver, B.C. Greyhound buses also serve Bellingham from Seattle, as does the Airporter Shuttle from Sea-Tac and downtown Seattle.

Biking is popular in and around Bellingham, which has a series of designated bike paths and park trails. The city of Bellingham has a good high-res bike-route map that can be downloaded from its website.

The Coast Millennium Trail will eventually connect Skagit and Whatcom counties to British Columbia. So far, about 15 miles of the 50-mile trail are open to bikes and walkers. Fairhaven Bike & Ski rents road bikes, full-suspension bikes, and standard mountain bikes starting at $55 per day.

Contacts Amtrak ☎ *800/872–7245* ⊕ *www.amtrak.com.* **City of Bellingham Bike Routes** ⊕ *www.cob.org/services/transportation.* **Fairhaven Bike & Ski** ☎ *360/733–4433* ⊕ *www.fairhavenbike.com.*

10

EXPLORING

Bellingham Cruise Terminal. This massive brick building surrounded by gardens dispatches daily ferries to the San Juan Islands, Victoria, and Alaska. There's terrific wildlife-watching right off the docks and adjacent shoreline, where sea lions, otters, and gray whales frolic out in the water as great blue herons, cormorants, and harlequin ducks bob on the surface. **Fairhaven Marine Park,** a long, sandy beach at the foot of Harris Avenue a few blocks south, is the place to launch sea kayaks. A rough trail runs south from the park along the railroad tracks to shingle beaches and rocky headlands, where you'll find clams, summer blackberries, and splendid views of Lummi Island. ⊠ *355 Harris Ave.* ☎ *360/676–2500* ⊕ *www.portofbellingham.com.*

Bloedel Donovan Park. The only public access in Bellingham to 14-mile-long Lake Whatcom is at its north end, in Bloedel Donovan Park. Locals swim in the sheltered waters of a cove, but you might find the water too cold. If so, spend some time trying to spot beavers, river otters, ducks, great blue herons, and yellow pond lilies at Scudder Pond, which is another 100 feet west (reached by trail from a parking area at Northshore and Alabama). ⊠ *2214 Electric Ave.* ☎ *360/778–7000* ⊕ *www.cob.org/services/recreation* ☉ *Daily dawn–dusk.*

Fodor'sChoice **Chuckanut Drive.** Highway 11, also known as Chuckanut Drive, was once
★ the only highway heading south from Bellingham. The drive begins in Fairhaven, reaches the flat farmlands of the Samish Valley near the village of Bow, and joins up with I–5 at Burlington, in Skagit County; the full loop can be made in a couple of hours. For a dozen miles this 23-mile road winds along the cliffs above beautiful Chuckanut and Samish bays. It twists its way past the sheer sandstone face of Chuckanut Mountain and crosses creeks with waterfalls. Turnouts are framed by gnarled madrona trees and pines and offer great views of the San Juan Islands. Bald eagles cruise along the cliffs or hang out on top of tall firs. Drive carefully: the cliffs are so steep in places that rock slides are common; closures occasionally happen in winter. ⊠ *Hwy. 11, starting in Fairhaven at 12th St. and Old Fairhaven Pkwy.*

Fairhaven. Just shy of 3 miles south of Bellingham and at the beginning of Chuckanut Drive (Highway 11), this historic district was an independent city until 1903, and still retains its distinct identity as an intellectual and artistic center. The beautifully restored 1890s redbrick buildings of the Old Fairhaven District, especially on Harris Avenue between 10th and 12th streets, house restaurants, galleries, and specialty boutiques. ⊕ *www.fairhaven.com.*

Larrabee State Park. South of Chuckanut Bay along the Whatcom–Skagit county line, this rugged 2,683-acre tract is one of the state's most scenic and popular parks. It straddles a rocky shore that has quiet, sandy coves and runs high up along the slopes of Chuckanut Mountain. Even though the mountain has been logged repeatedly, some of it is still wilderness. Miles of trails lead through ferny fir and maple forests to hidden lakes, caves, and cliff-top lookouts from which you can see all the way to the San Juan Islands. At the shore there's a sheltered boat launch; you can go crabbing here or watch the birds—and the occasional harbor seal—that perch on the offshore rocks. The area west of Chuckanut Drive has picnic tables as well as tent and RV sites with hookups, which are open all year. ✉ *245 Chuckanut Dr.* ☎ *360/676–2093* 🌐 *www.parks.wa.gov* 🎟 *$10 day pass, $30 annual Discover Pass (valid at all state parks)* 🕒 *Daily dawn–dusk.*

FAMILY **Maritime Heritage Park.** Down a flight of steps behind the Whatcom Museum, this park pays tribute to Bellingham's fishing industry. Self-guided Marine Heritage Center tours take you through a salmon's life cycle, winding past hatcheries, aquarium tanks, and fish ladders. A boardwalk route from Holly Street leads to the ponds and a waterfall, where Bellingham was founded in 1852. Note that salmon runs occur annually around September and October. ✉ *500 W. Holly St.* ☎ *360/778–7000* 🌐 *www.cob.org/services/recreation* 🎟 *Free* 🕒 *Daily 6 am–10 pm.*

FAMILY **Squalicum Harbor Marina.** A good place to fish, lounge, picnic, or walk, the marina holds more than 1,900 commercial and pleasure boats. Zuanich Point Park, at the end of the spit, has a telescope for close-up views of the water and a marine-life center with touch tanks. ✉ *722 Coho Way* ☎ *360/676–2542* 🌐 *www.portofbellingham.com.*

FAMILY
Fodor's Choice ★
Whatcom Museum. Bellingham's art and history museum comprises three buildings near one another downtown. At its center is the Lightcatcher, a LEED-certified (Leadership in Energy and Environmental Design) building with an 180-foot-long translucent wall. Rotating shows are presented here, as are permanent collections of contemporary Northwest artists. The second building, Bellingham's 1892 former city hall, is a redbrick structure that was converted into a museum in 1941—it completed a dramatic renovation in 2010 and contains historic exhibits. The third building, the Syre Education Center, contains a photographic archive. ✉ *250 Flora St.* ☎ *360/778–8930* 🌐 *www.whatcommuseum.org* 🎟 *$10* 🕒 *Lightcatcher Building: Wed.–Sat. noon–5 (open to 8 pm Thurs.), Sun. 10–5. Old City Hall: Thurs.–Sun. noon–5. Syre Education Center: Wed.–Fri. afternoons; call for hours.*

WHERE TO EAT

$$
SEAFOOD
🍴 **Big Fat Fish Company.** Head to this spacious, brewpub-style restaurant for first-rate seafood—everything from panfried trout to cedar-planked salmon and sea bass Wellington. A lot of other fishy items round out the menu: king crab legs, scallops in truffle butter, and rich seafood cioppino. The sushi is spot-on, too; there's a nice sampler platter if you're seeking variety. Good non-aquatic options include the rib eye with wild mushrooms. Service is casual and fun, although weekends often bring long waits. [$] *Average main: $22* ✉ *1304 12th St.* ☎ *360/733–2284* 🌐 *www.bigfatfishco.com* 🕒 *No lunch Mon.*

$
AMERICAN
Fodor's Choice ★
🍴 **Boundary Bay Brewery & Bistro.** Long a top venue in downtown Bellingham, both for sampling distinctive, well-crafted microbrews and enjoying big portions of delicious pub fare, this convivial spot occupies a vintage former garage—the huge central door is rolled open in warm weather. Boundary garners high marks among beer lovers for its ruby-red Scottish ale, smooth oatmeal stout, and rotating seasonal ales. From the food menu, you won't go wrong with the Bavarian-style

pretzels (served with spicy brown mustard), smoked-clam chowder, beer-barbecue-sauce pizzas, and char-grilled lamb burger. $ *Average main: $12* ⊠ *1107 Railroad Ave., Bellingham* ☎ *360/647–5593* ⊕ *www. bbaybrewery.com.*

$$$
AMERICAN

× **Chuckanut Manor.** The old-fashioned, glassed-in dining room and bar overlook the mouth of the Samish River, Samish Bay, and the mudflats, where great blue herons hang out. It's a popular spot for sunset- and bird-watching: bird feeders outside the bar's picture windows attract finches, chickadees, red-winged blackbirds, and other songbirds. Occasionally bald eagles can be seen gliding past. Besides the view, folks come here for classic American fare with an emphasis on steak and fresh seafood—the mac-and-Jack-battered halibut is a novel take on fish-and-chips. There's also a very popular Sunday champagne brunch. $ *Average main: $28* ⊠ *3056 Chuckanut Dr., Bow* ☎ *360/766–6191* ⊕ *www.chuckanutmanor.com* ⊘ *Closed Mon.*

$
CAFÉ

× **Harris Avenue Café.** Occupying a light-filled, cheerfully painted late-Victorian building a few blocks from the port and train station in Fairhaven, this hugely popular breakfast and lunch spot adjoins an inviting little coffeehouse (Tony's), which is a nice option for lighter snacking and fueling up on espresso. In the main café, which has patio dining in summer, you can kick off a day of exploring with a filling Sitka omelet (smoked salmon, feta, roasted garlic, tomatoes, and pesto). Lunch options include the Matterhorn Burger, topped with mushrooms and Swiss cheese, and a poached pear salad with candied pecans and fresh wild salmon. The café closes at 2, but Tony's remains open till 6 pm. $ *Average main: $10* ⊠ *1101 Harris Ave., Bellingham* ☎ *360/738–0802* ⊕ *www.harrisavecafe.com* ⊘ *No dinner.*

$$$$
SEAFOOD
Fodor'sChoice
★

× **Oyster Bar.** Above the shore on a steep, wooded bluff, this intimate restaurant in the village of Bow is regionally famous for what may be the best marine view from any Washington restaurant. People come here to dine and watch the sun set over the islands to the west or to watch the full moon reflect off the waters of Samish Bay. The menu changes regularly, so it's hard to predict what you might find, but the oyster bar, along with the refined seafood dishes, wild game, and pastas never disappoint—and there are well-chosen wines to complement every dish. $ *Average main: $35* ⊠ *2578 Chuckanut Dr., 21.6 miles south of Bellingham, Bow* ☎ *360/766–6185* ⊕ *www.theoysterbar.net.*

WHERE TO STAY

For expanded hotel reviews, visit Fodors.com.

$$$
HOTEL
Fodor'sChoice
★

▦ **Chrysalis Inn and Spa at the Pier.** The facade of this elegant downtown boutique hotel, which rises above the waterfront, is gray and stark, but in the lobby warm wood predominates and rooms are comfortable and contemporary. **Pros:** utterly relaxing; great water views from most rooms. **Cons:** some noise from adjacent rail track. $ *Rooms from: $205* ⊠ *804 10th St.* ☎ *360/756–1005, 888/808–0005* ⊕ *www. thechrysalisinn.com* ⇆ *34 rooms, 9 suites* ❡❍ *Breakfast.*

$$$
HOTEL

▦ **Hotel Bellwether.** Bellingham's original waterfront hotel overlooks the entrance to bustling Squalicum Harbor, and its luxurious rooms are augmented by a lighthouse suite ensconced in its own tower. **Pros:** beautiful bay views; large private dock; wide variety of room configurations.

Cons: a hub for groups; one of the more expensive options in town. [$] *Rooms from: $215* ✉ *1 Bellwether Way, Squalicum Harbor Marina* ☎ *360/392–3100, 877/411–1200* 🌐 *www.hotelbellwether.com* 🛏 *50 rooms, 16 suites* 🍴 *Breakfast.*

$$$ B&B/INN 🏠 **Fairhaven Village Inn.** High on a bluff between the Fairhaven Village Green and the Port of Bellingham's south terminal, this charming, historic inn overlooks Bellingham Bay; on a clear day the eye ranges all the way to the San Juans. **Pros:** interesting part of town with good shops, galleries, and restaurants; convenient for Chuckanut Scenic Drive and the university; staff is helpful and knowledgeable. **Cons:** two-night minimum stay at certain times. [$] *Rooms from: $179* ✉ *1200 10th St.* ☎ *360/733–1311, 877/733–1100* 🌐 *www.fairhavenvillageinn.com* 🛏 *21 rooms, 1 suite* 🍴 *Breakfast.*

NIGHTLIFE AND THE ARTS

Mt. Baker Theatre. This restored vaudeville-era theater has a 110-foot-tall Moorish tower and a lobby fashioned after a Spanish galleon. The state's largest performing arts center north of Seattle, it's home to the Whatcom Symphony Orchestra. It's also a venue for movies, musicals, and headline performers. ✉ *104 N. Commercial St.* ☎ *360/734–6080* 🌐 *www.mountbakertheatre.com.*

Up and Up Tavern. This is a relaxed, endearingly dive-y spot for a beer, drawing a mix of locals, college students, and folks passing through town. ✉ *1234 N. State St.* ☎ *360/733–9739.*

SPORTS AND THE OUTDOORS

WHALE-WATCHING

Island Mariner Cruises. This long-respected tour company conducts whale-watching, nature, and sunset cruises around Bellingham Bay and on out to the San Juans. ☎ *360/734–8866, 877/734–8866* 🌐 *www.orcawatch.com.*

San Juan Cruises. This popular whale-watching excursion company sails around Bellingham Bay and out to the San Juan Islands, where there's a stop for lunch and exploring in Friday Harbor on San Juan Island. Under the right conditions, the views of whales and sunsets cannot be beat. ☎ *360/738–8099, 800/443–4552* 🌐 *www.whales.com.*

KITSAP PENINSULA

Branching off the southeastern edge of the Olympic Peninsula, the Kitsap Peninsula has Puget Sound on one side and the Hood Canal on the other. Though it doesn't possess the great wild beauty of the Olympic Peninsula, it does have several charming waterfront towns with beach parks, kayaking, and sailing opportunities, as well as a serene setting. Bremerton is the most developed (and least attractive) city on the peninsula, but it's home to a navy base, and its waterfront has many naval museums and retired ships to crawl around on. Gig Harbor's marinas, on the other hand, are full of pretty sailboats—it's the town that has the most to offer in terms of tourist amenities. Outside of these main cities, Poulsbo and Port Gamble get the most attention. The former is a pilgrimage point for anyone interested in tracing the Norwegian influence in the Pacific Northwest, and the latter is a twee little town made up mostly of historic buildings.

GIG HARBOR

23 miles south of Bremerton, 10 miles northwest of Tacoma.

One of the most picturesque and accessible waterfront cities on Puget Sound, Gig Harbor has a neat, circular bay dotted with sailboats and fronted by hills of evergreens and million-dollar homes. Expect spectacular views all along the town's winding 2-mile bayside walkway, which is intermittently lined by boat docks, quirky shops, cozy cafés, and broad expanses of open water.

The bay was a storm refuge for the 1841 survey team of Captain Charles Wilkes, who named the area after his small gig (boat). A decade later Croatian and Scandinavian immigrants put their fishing, lumber, and boat-building skills to profitable use, and the town still has strong seafaring traditions. By the 1880s, steamboats carried passengers and goods between the harbor and Tacoma, and auto ferries plied the narrows between the cities by 1917.

The town winds around the waterfront, centering at the intersection of Harborview Drive and Pioneer Way, where shops, art galleries, and restaurants often attract more foot traffic than vehicles. From here, Harborview makes a long, gentle curve around the bay toward the renovated Finholm Market building, which has shops, docks, a restaurant, kayak rentals, and more views. A Gig Harbor Historical Society self-guided walk brochure covers 49 sights (see if you can spot the 16 metal salmon sculptures, designed by local artists, placed in front of sights around town).

GETTING HERE AND AROUND

From Seattle, the fastest way (if there's no traffic) to Gig Harbor is to take I–5 south through Tacoma and take Exit 132 to Highway 16 toward Bremerton. A slightly longer approach—in minutes, not miles— is to take the ferry from the West Seattle terminal to the Southworth landing on the Kitsap Peninsula and take Highway 160 west and then Highway 16 south. Taking the ferry from Seattle to Bremerton also works—you'd take Highway 3 south to 16.

Contact Washington State Ferries ☎ *888/808–7977, 206/464–6400* ⊕ *www. wsdot.wa.gov/ferries.*

ESSENTIALS

Visitor Information Gig Harbor Chamber of Commerce ✉ *3125 Judson St.* ☎ *253/851–6865* ⊕ *www.gigharborchamber.com.*

EXPLORING

Fox Island. Surrounding Gig Harbor, pine forests and open woods alternate with rolling pastures; it's enjoyable scenery (even on rainy days) during the 10-minute drive to Fox Island. Crossing the Fox Island Bridge over Echo Bay, you'll see stunning views of the Olympic Mountains to the right and the Tanglewood Lighthouse against a backdrop of Mt. Rainier to the left. **Tanglewood Island,** the small drop of forest

Gig Harbor

on which the Tanglewood lighthouse sits, was once a Native American burial ground known as Grav Island. At low tide the boat ramp and boulder-strewn beach next to the bridge are scattered with stranded saltwater creatures.

Fox Island Historical Museum. This museum displays island pioneer memorabilia in an authentic log cabin. Pioneer-days children's activities, such as Maypole dances, memory boxes, and old-fashioned Valentine crafts, are scheduled the first Saturday of every month, and the local farmers' market runs summer Wednesdays. ⊠ *1017 9th Ave.* ☎ *253/549–2461* ⊕ *www.foxislandmuseum.org* ⊠ *$1* ⊗ *Wed. and weekends 1–4.*

10

Gig Harbor Museum. An excellent collection of exhibits here describes the city's maritime history, and there are photo archives, video programs, and a research library focusing on the area's pioneer and Native American ancestors. The facilities include a one-room, early-20th-century schoolhouse and a 65-foot, 1950s purse seiner, a type of fishing vessel from the community's famous seafaring fleets. News clippings and videos about "Galloping Gertie," the original bridge, are particularly eerie. ⊠ *4121 Harborview Dr.* ☎ *253/858–6722* ⊕ *www. harborhistorymuseum.org* ⊠ *$7* ⊗ *Mid-Apr.–Dec., Tues.–Sun. 10–5; Jan.–mid-Apr., Wed.–Sat. 10–4, Sun. noon–4.*

Kopachuck State Park. A 10-minute drive from Gig Harbor, this is a wonderful beachcombing area at low tide. Native American tribes once fished and clammed here, and you can still see people trolling the shallow waters or digging deep for razor clams in season. Children and dogs alike delight in discovering huge Dungeness crabs, sea stars, and sand dollars. Picnic tables and walking trails are interspersed throughout the steep, forested hills, and the campground is always full in summer. ✉ *11101 56th St. NW* ☎ *253/265–3606* 🌐 *www.parks.wa.gov* 🎟 *$10; $30 annual Discover Pass (valid at all state parks)* 🕓 *Daily 8–dusk.*

WHERE TO EAT

$$ MODERN AMERICAN Fodor's Choice ★ 🍴 **Brix 25.** Simple seafood dishes and classic European fare are beautifully presented in this cozy, glass-fronted setting at the base of Harborview Drive and the Gig Harbor bay. Dinners are elaborate affairs that feature seafood—perhaps Thai curry and coconut steamed mussels—and dishes such as the Brix signature boeuf bourguignonne or osso buco-style lamb shank. Tempting desserts include an array of sugary cakes, sorbets, and cobblers, and there's a fine wine to match every course. Seasonal events include chef-hosted, multicourse dinners. [$] *Average main: $22* ✉ *7707 Pioneer Way* ☎ *253/858–6626* 🌐 *www.harborbrix.com* 🕓 *No lunch.*

$ MEXICAN 🍴 **El Pueblito.** The mariachi music, cilantro and chili pepper scents from the kitchen, and a waitstaff that chats in Spanish are reminiscent of a compact cantina south of the border. Huge portions of better-than-average Mexican dishes and frothy margaritas are served amid much gaiety. The adjacent bar is a lively late-night hangout on weekends. There's a second branch in Port Gamble. [$] *Average main: $13* ✉ *3226 Harborview Dr.* ☎ *253/858–9077* 🌐 *www.elpueblitorestaurant.com.*

$$ PACIFIC NORTHWEST 🍴 **JW.** This elegant yet unfussy downtown bistro is one of Gig Harbor's top picks for memorable dinners. The kitchen turns out creative, seasonally driven fare—starters of honey-almond prawns, and duck-confit sliders, followed by seared sea scallops with candied bacon, and wild boar bourguignonne with sweet onions, carrots, fennel, and peppercorn sauce. The flourless dark-chocolate torte with white-chocolate ganache is worth preserving your appetite for, and the terrific wine list focuses on Washington and Oregon. JW doesn't cater to diners under the age of 21. [$] *Average main: $19* ✉ *4107 Harborview Dr., Gig Harbor* ☎ *253/858–3529* 🌐 *www.jwgigharbor.com* 🕓 *Closed Mon. No lunch.*

WHERE TO STAY

For expanded hotel reviews, visit Fodors.com.

$$$ HOTEL 🏨 **Inn at Gig Harbor.** The city's largest hotel has a multicolor exterior that makes it seem more like a mansion than a member of the Heritage chain. **Pros:** lodge-style ambience; professional staff. **Cons:** no pool; pricey for dated, unimpressive rooms. [$] *Rooms from: $154* ✉ *3211 56th St. NW* ☎ *253/858–1111, 800/795–9980* 🌐 *www.innatgigharbor.com* 🛏 *52 rooms, 12 suites* 🍽 *Breakfast.*

$$ HOTEL 🏨 **Maritime Inn.** On a hill across from Jersich Park and the docks, this dapper boutique hotel combines class and comfort with water views and highly personal service. **Pros:** right on the waterfront; friendly staff. **Cons:** front rooms absorb traffic noise. [$] *Rooms from: $145* ✉ *3112 Harborview Dr.* ☎ *253/858–1818* 🌐 *www.maritimeinn.com* 🛏 *15 rooms* 🍽 *Breakfast.*

SPORTS AND THE OUTDOORS
SAILING AND BOATING
Gig Harbor Rent-a-Boat. Look here to rent powerboats, kayaks, pedal boats, and stand-up paddleboards. ✉ *8829 N. Harborview Dr.* ☎ *253/ 858–7341* ⊕ *www.gigharborrentaboat.com.*

BREMERTON

18 miles west of Seattle by ferry, 68 miles southwest of Seattle by road, 25 miles north of Gig Harbor by road.

Nearly surrounded by water, and with one of the largest navy bases on the West Coast, Bremerton is a workaday city of about 30,000 with several attractions that center on the waterfront and its gardens, fountains, and ferry docks dwarfed by massive warships. Away from the waterfront, and especially around the ferry terminal, Bremerton looks a bit depressed in some parts. The western Charleston neighborhood, which had been run-down for years until some recent revitalization efforts, has the most going on, with a few art galleries and restaurants. Bremerton appeals primarily to fans of naval history and machinery.

GETTING HERE AND AROUND
From Seattle, Washington State Ferries provides regular hour-long service to Bremerton. The many navy sights are close to the ferry terminal, but Bremerton is best explored by car. You can also drive here via Gig Harbor—from Seattle, it takes a little over 90 minutes.

Bremerton Area Chamber of Commerce ✉ *286 4th St.* ☎ *360/479–3579* ⊕ *www.bremertonchamber.org.*

EXPLORING
Bremerton Marina. The waterfront expanse of the Bremerton Marina, lining the glistening blue bay between the warships and ferry docks, is the place to walk, bicycle, picnic, run through fountains in summer, and watch a mass of sailboats and military craft pass through the calm waters. It's an especially good place for spotting the host of birds and marine life around the docks. ✉ *off Washington Ave.* ⊕ *www. portofbremerton.org.*

Kitsap County Historical Society Museum. Pioneer artifacts, nautical items, and a collection of old photographs are on show at this small local history museum. The staff plans such special children's events as costume dress-up sessions and treasure hunts for the first Friday of the month, when the museum is open late in conjunction with the town's monthly Art Walk. ✉ *280 4th St.* ☎ *360/479–6226* ⊕ *www.kitsaphistory.org* 🏷 *$4* ⊙ *May–Sept., Tues.–Sat. 10–4, Sun. noon–4; Oct.–Apr. Tues.– Sat. 10–4.*

FAMILY **Naval Undersea Museum.** A 15-minute drive north of Bremerton (not far from Poulsbo), the museum is fronted by a can't-miss sight: the 88-ton *Trieste II* submarine, which dove to the deepest spot in the ocean (the Marianas Trench) in 1960. In the main building are exhibits on torpedoes, diving equipment, model submarines, and mines. ✉ *1 Garnett Way, Keyport* ☎ *360/396–4148* ⊕ *www.navalunderseamuseum.org* 🏷 *Free* ⊙ *May–Sept., daily 10–4; Oct.–Apr., Wed.–Mon. 10–4.*

10

FAMILY **Puget Sound Navy Museum.** One of Bremerton's several maritime-related attractions, this museum is right on the waterfront near the ferry terminal, bringing American naval history to life through war photos, ship models, historic displays, and American and Japanese war artifacts. *✉ 251 1st St. ☎ 360/479–7447 🌐 www.pugetsoundnavymuseum.org 🎟 Free ⏲ May–Sept., Mon.–Sat. 10–4, Sun. 1–4; Oct.–Apr. closed Tues.*

FAMILY **USS *Turner Joy*.** This vintage Navy destroyer, along the marina near the ferry docks, is open for self-guided tours. Allow about 90 minutes to walk through the narrow passages to view the cafeteria, medical office, barbershop, prison cell, cramped bunk rooms, and captain's quarters. *✉ 300 Washington Beach Ave. ☎ 360/792–2457 🌐 ussturnerjoy.org 🎟 $12 ⏲ Mar.–Oct., daily 10–5; Nov.–Feb., Fri–Sun. 10–4.*

WHERE TO EAT AND STAY

For expanded hotel reviews, visit Fodors.com.

$$ SEAFOOD 🍴 **Boat Shed.** At this deliberately rustic waterfront restaurant diners share a casual, seaside camaraderie as they slurp up clam chowder, steamed clams, and mussels, plus larger plates of creatively prepared seafood grills and pastas—cioppino, wasabi-spiced fresh halibut, and smoked-salmon linguine are some of the best bets. Sailors, who enjoy free boat moorage, arrive early for the famed Sunday brunch. *[$] Average main: $21 ✉ 101 Shore Dr. ☎ 360/377–2600 🌐 www.theboatshedrestaurant.com.*

$ HOTEL 🏨 **Flagship Inn.** Although it's a budget spot, rooms here have private balconies overlooking Oyster Bay and the Olympic Mountains. **Pros:** the price is right; nice views. **Cons:** place could use an update—some furnishings are worn. *[$] Rooms from: $75 ✉ 4320 Kitsap Way ☎ 360/479–6566, 800/447–9396 🌐 www.flagship-inn.com 🛏 29 rooms 🍽 Breakfast.*

$$ HOTEL 🏨 **Hampton Inn & Suites Bremerton.** Its splashy waterfront location—right in the center of the city marina, adjacent to the Bremerton Harborside Conference Center and just a block from the ferry terminal—makes this large, modern hotel a bit more interesting than your usual mid-range chain property. **Pros:** reliable chain hotel; good location. **Cons:** not much personality *[$] Rooms from: $139 ✉ 150 Washington Ave. ☎ 360/405–0200, 800/426–7866 🌐 hamptoninn3.hilton.com 🛏 105 rooms, 21 suites 🍽 Breakfast.*

POULSBO

19 miles north of Bremerton, 12 miles northwest of Bainbridge Island.

Velkommen til Poulsbo (*pauls*-bo), a charming village on lovely Liberty Bay. Soon after it was settled by Norwegians in the 1880s, shops and bakeries sprang up along Front Street, as did a cod-drying facility to produce the Norwegian delicacy called lutefisk. Although it's no longer produced here commercially, lutefisk is still served at holiday feasts. Front Street is crammed with authentic Norwegian bakeries, eclectic Scandinavian craft shops, small boutiques and bookstores, and art galleries. Norwegian flags flutter from the eaves of the town's chalet-style buildings. Grassy Liberty Bay Park is fronted by a network of slender docks where seals and otters pop in and out of the waves. One of the town's biggest events is the annual May Viking Festival (🌐 *www.vikingfest.org*), complete with Viking tents and weapons, costumed locals, and a lively parade.

GETTING HERE AND AROUND

To reach Poulsbo from Seattle, it's easiest to take Washington State ferry to Bainbridge Island and drive 12 miles from there via Highway 305 north across the Agate Pass Bridge. If driving up the Kitsap Peninsula, head north from Bremerton about 19 miles up Highway 3.

ESSENTIALS

Visitor Information **Greater Poulsbo Chamber of Commerce** ✉ *19351 8th Ave., Suite 108* ☎ *360/779–4848, 877/768–5726* 🌐 *www.poulsbochamber.com.*

EXPLORING

FAMILY **Poulsbo Marine Science Center.** Right along the shoreline and the edge of Liberty Bay Park, the center is raised above the water and jam-packed with exhibits of local sea creatures. An intertidal touch tank lets kids feel sea anemones, sea urchins, and starfish, while other displays house crabs, jellyfish, and plants. Puppets, puzzles, murals, and videos help youngsters learn more about what they see. Don't miss the giant Pacific octopus in a 2,000-gallon tank beneath the center. A small gift shop fronts the building, and the center organizes special activities during Poulsbo festivals. ✉ *18743 Front St. NE* ☎ *360/598–4460* 🌐 *www.poulsbomsc.org* 🎟 *Free* 🕒 *Thurs.–Sun. 11–4.*

WHERE TO EAT AND STAY

For expanded hotel reviews, visit Fodors.com.

$$ PACIFIC NORTHWEST Fodor's Choice ★ 🍴 **Mor Mor Bistro & Bar.** This lively, stylish restaurant in Poulsbo's historic district is something of a tribute to the grandmothers of chef-owners John and Laura Nesby—*mormor* is a Norwegian word for grandma. The talented pair perfected their cooking skills at some of the West Coast's finest restaurants before opening this venue for fresh and accessible Pacific Northwest (with Scandinavian accents) fare in 2004. You could easily make a meal of small plates like garlic-Parmesan fries with garlic aioli and Norwegian meatballs in lingonberry sauce; cedar-plank salmon with *guanciale*-spiked lentils and grilled asparagus is a noteworthy entrée. Sunday brunch is highly popular. Part of the fun here is the drinks menu, from complex craft cocktails to a nicely curated selection of craft beers and regional wines. [$] *Average main: $21* ✉ *18820 Front St., Poulsbo* ☎ *360/697–3449* 🌐 *www.mormorbistro.com* 🕒 *Closed Mon. No dinner Sun.*

$ BAKERY 🍴 **Sluys Bakery.** Rhyme it with "pies" and you'll sound like a local when you enter the town's most famous bakery. Gorgeous Norwegian pastries, braided bread, and *lefse* (traditional Norwegian round, flat bread) line the shelves. Kids often beg for one of the decorated cookies or frosted doughnuts displayed at eye level. There's only strong coffee and milk to drink, and there are no seats, but you can grab a bench along busy Front Street or take your goodies to the waterfront at Liberty Bay Park. [$] *Average main: $6* ✉ *18924 Front St.* ☎ *360/779–2798* 🕒 *No lunch or dinner.*

$$ B&B/INN 🏨 **Green Cat Guest House.** A few miles north of downtown Poulsbo on the way to Port Gamble, this dashing B&B with steep gabled roof has

10

a funky vibe, whimsical artwork, and a striking design, both inside and out. **Pros:** completely peaceful and enchanting setting; distinctive furnishings; good proximity both to Poulsbo and Port Gamble. **Cons:** not within walking distance of downtown; a bit remote. [$] *Rooms from: $120* ✉ *25819 Tytler Rd. NE, Poulsbo* ☎ *360/779–7569* 🌐 *www.greencatbb.com* 🛏 *3 rooms, 1 suite* 🍴 *Breakfast.*

PORT GAMBLE

6 miles northeast of Poulsbo.

Residents from the opposite side of America founded Port Gamble around a sawmill in 1853; hence its New England–style architecture mimicking founder Capt. William Talbot's hometown of East Machias, Maine. Its setting amid the Kitsap Peninsula's tall stands of timber brought in great profits, but the mill was later destroyed by fire, and much of the forest has disappeared. A walk through town takes you past the 1870 St. Paul's Episcopal Church as well as the Thompson House, thought to be the state's oldest continuously lived-in home, and a handful of shops and restaurants. The town also stages a popular medieval-inspired June Faire each summer. This is also an excellent hiking area, with numerous backcountry trails throughout the area.

GETTING HERE AND AROUND

Port Gamble is just 6 miles from Poulsbo via Hwy. 3 and Hwy. 104.

EXPLORING

FAMILY Fodor's Choice ★ **Port Gamble Historic Museum.** Beneath the town's quaint General Store, the Smithsonian-designed Port Gamble Historic Museum takes you through the region's timber heyday. Highlights include artifacts from the Pope and Talbot Timber Company, which built the town, and realistic ship's quarters. Above the General Store, the **Of Sea and Shore Museum** is open daily and houses more than 25,000 shells as well as displays on natural history. Kids love the weird bug exhibit. Stop at the General Store for souvenirs or a huge ice-cream cone or hand-dipped milkshake, or stay for lunch or dinner in the acclaimed restaurant in the back of the building. ✉ *32400 Rainier Ave. NE* ☎ *360/297–8078* 🌐 *www.portgamblegeneralstore.com* 🎟 *Historic Museum $4, Shell Museum free* ⏲ *May–Sept., daily 9:30–5; Oct.–Apr., Fri.–Sun. 11–4.*

WHERE TO EAT

$ PACIFIC NORTHWEST 🍴 **Taste Port Gamble.** The sunny yellow exterior of this colonial home provides a lovely front for this elegant spot that's a tearoom by day and bistro on weekend evenings. Enjoy specials like cream tea (with scones and cream), or take chocolate high tea with finger sandwiches and chocolate fondue during the day. It's also a popular stop for lunch or Sunday brunch, and on weekends it's a romantic dinner option for dining on eclectic Pacific Northwest food with an emphasis on seasonal ingredients—lamb chops with mission figs and a port wine reduction, or wild Alaskan ling cod piccata. The adjacent artisan chocolate shop whips up homemade dark- and white-chocolate truffles, as well as a variety of molded chocolate candies. [$] *Average main: $12* ✉ *32279*

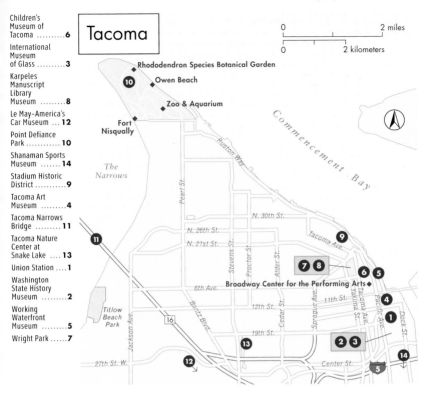

N.E. Rainier Ave. ☎360/297–4225 ⊕ *www.tasteportgamble.com* ☯ *Closed Mon.–Tues. No dinner Sun.–Thurs.*

TACOMA AND OLYMPIA

A trip south down I–5 quickly yields two important port cities: Tacoma, and Olympia, the state capital. Although Olympia is more practiced in winning over visitors with its tidy legislative campus and laid-back charms, Tacoma is determined to follow suit with an ambitious if somewhat stalled revitalization plan. Both have the same good foundation to work with: beautiful waterfront locations with historic cores and lots of adjacent parkland.

TACOMA

25 miles southeast of Gig Harbor, 34 miles southwest of Seattle.

After decades of decline, Tacoma has been steadily undergoing a renaissance in recent years, with development around the waterfront and in other parts of downtown showing the greatest progress—a number of urbane galleries, bars, and restaurants have popped up around Union Station and nearby blocks. Still, quite a few beautiful old buildings downtown remain vacant, and even on the busiest nights, Tacoma can seem a little quiet considering its population of 200,000. In this sense, proximity to Seattle is both a blessing and a curse, as locals still tend to drive there for a big night on the town.

Tacoma's got character, however, and it does have plenty to fill a day or two. The museums, the waterfront promenade, and the attractive old neighborhoods and suburbs make for a very pleasant side trip or overnight adventure. The waterfront stretches west from the busy port, past the city and Puget Sound islands to the cliff-lined Tacoma Narrows. Renovated 19th-century homes, pretty beaches, and parks pocket the outskirts, and a young, diverse population gives the city a spirited character. The Tacoma Dome—that wooden, blue-and-gray half-sphere stadium visible along I–5—hosts international expos, sporting events, and famous entertainers in its 28,000-seat arena. The city's convenient setting provides easy access to Seattle to the north; Mt. Rainier to the southeast; Olympia to the south; and the Kitsap and Olympic peninsulas to the west.

Tacoma was the first Puget Sound port connected by train to the East, and its economy was once based on the railroad. Old photos show tall-masted windjammers loading at the City Waterway, whose storage sheds were promoted by local boosters as the "longest warehouse under one continuous roof in the world." The city's shipping industry certainly weathered the tests of time, as Tacoma is the largest container port in the Northwest, slightly edging out Seattle.

GETTING HERE AND AROUND

Tacoma is close enough to Seattle that many people commute in both directions. It's a straight 30-mile shot down I–5 to Exit 133 toward the city center. Tacoma is served by Greyhound and Amtrak, with connections north to Seattle and beyond, as well as south to Olympia. Tacoma is also served by Sound Transit's commuter rail, though trains are limited to rush hours.

If you're not planning to go too far out of the downtown core—just seeing the museums and the waterfront—you won't need a car to get around, as Amtrak and Greyhound let you off at Union Station, which is within walking distance of the city's main museums and a handful of restaurants.

Contact Sound Transit ☎ 206/398–5000, 888/889–6368 ⊕ www. soundtransit.org.

ESSENTIALS

Visitor Information Tacoma Regional Convention & Visitors Bureau ✉ Courtyard by Marriott Hotel, 1516 Pacific Ave. ☎ 253/627–2836, 800/272–2662 ⊕ www.traveltacoma.com.

EXPLORING

TOP ATTRACTIONS

Fodor'sChoice
★

International Museum of Glass. The showpiece of this spectacular, 2-acre combination of delicate and creative exhibits is the 500-foot-long Chihuly Bridge of Glass, a tunnel of glorious color and light that stretches above I–705. Cross it to reach the building grounds, which sit above the

Chihuly Bridge of Glass, Tacoma

bay and next to a shallow reflecting pool dotted with large modern-art sculptures. Inside, you can wander with the crowds through the quiet, light-filled galleries, take a seat in the theater-like Hot Shop to watch glass-blowing artists, or try your own hand at arts and crafts in the studio. You'll also find a souvenir shop and café. ✉ *1801 E. Dock St.* ☎ *253/284–4750, 866/468–7386* ⊕ *www.museumofglass.org* 💲*$12* ☉ *Late May–early Sept., Mon.–Sat. 10–5, Sun. noon–5; early Sept.– mid-May, Wed.–Sat. 10–5, Sun. noon–5.*

LeMay—America's Car Museum. Harold LeMay was the ultimate collector of vintage cars; his collection of some 4,000 autos is in the *Guinness Book of World Records* as the largest privately owned collection in the world. Highlights include a 1906 Cadillac Model M, a 1926 Rolls-Royce Silver Ghost, a 1930 Lincoln L Brougham, a 1953 Citroen 2CV, a 1960 Corvette, and a 1963 Studebaker Avanti, along with fire engines, antique buses, and old-fashioned trucks. About 350 of the top models are on display is this sleek, striking new museum that opened on the south side of downtown in 2012. The café serves diner classics. ✉ *2702 E. D St.* ☎ *253/779–8490, 877/902–8490* ⊕ *www.lemaymuseum.org* 💲*$14* ☉ *Daily 10–5.*

FAMILY
Fodor's Choice
★

Point Defiance Park. Jutting into Commencement Bay, this hilly, 702-acre park surrounds Five Mile Drive with lush picnicking fields and patches of forest. Hiking trails, bike paths, and numerous gardens draw crowds year-round, particularly during summer festivals such as the Taste of Tacoma, in June. The park begins at the north end of Pearl Street as you drive toward the Point Defiance Ferry Terminal, where vehicles depart for Vashon Island just across the Sound. A one-way road branches off the ferry lane, past a lake and picnic area, a rose garden, and a Japanese garden, finally winding down to the beach.

A half-mile past the gardens is **Owen Beach,** a driftwood-strewn stretch of pebbly sand near the ferry dock and a wonderful place for beach-combing and sailboat-watching. Kayak rentals and concessions are available in summer. Continue around the looping drive, which offers occasional views of the narrows. Cruise slowly to take in the scenes—and watch out for joggers and bikers. ⊠ *5400 N. Pearl St.* ⊕ *www.metroparkstacoma.org/point-defiance-park.*

Point Defiance Zoo & Aquarium. One of the Northwest's finest collections of regional and international species, this winding and hilly site includes tigers, elephants, tapirs, and gibbons in the Asian Forest Sanctuary, where paw-print trails lead between lookouts so even the smallest tots can spot animals. The aquariums are also fun to explore, including a glass-walled, floor-to-ceiling shark tank; seahorse room; touch-tank marine area; and open-topped, two-level Pacific Northwest reef display. Other areas house such cold-weather creatures as beluga whales, wolves, polar bears, and penguins. Thirty-minute animal shows, run two to four times daily, let different creatures show off their skills. The fantastic playground area has friendly farm animals running between the slides, and seasonal special events include a Halloween trick-or-treat night and the famous nightly Zoolights holiday displays around Christmas. ⊠ *Point Defiance Park, 5400 N. Pearl St.* ☎ *253/305–1000* ⊕ *www.pdza.org* 🎫 *$15* ☉ *Daily, but hours vary from month to month, so call ahead.*

Rhododendron Species Botanical Garden. On Five Mile Drive, this is a 22-acre expanse of more than 10,000 plants—some 700 species—which bloom in succession. It's one of the finest rhododendron collections in the world. ⊠ *2525 S. 336th St.* ☎ *253/927–6960, 877/242–2528* ⊕ *www.rhodygarden.org* 🎫 *$8* ☉ *Tues.–Sun. 10–4.*

Ft. Nisqually. This restored Hudson's Bay Trading Post—a British outpost on the Nisqually Delta in the 1830s—was moved to Point Defiance in 1935. The compound houses a trading post, granary, blacksmith's shop, bakery, and officers' quarters. Docents dress in 1850s attire and demonstrate pioneer skills like weaving and loading a rifle. Queen Victoria's birthday in August is a big event, and eerie candlelight tours run throughout October. ⊠ *5400 N. Pearl St.* ☎ *253/591–5339* ⊕ *www.fortnisqually.org* 🎫 *$6.50* ☉ *Mid-May–early Sept., daily 11–5; May 1–mid-May and early Sept.–Sept. 30, Wed.–Sun 11–5; Oct.–Apr. Wed.–Sun. 11–4.*

WORTH NOTING

FAMILY **Children's Museum of Tacoma.** Fun activities for little ones take place at this hands-on, state-of-the-art museum that moved into an impressive new space in 2012. Areas for exploration are broken down into a variety of "playscapes"—woods, water, voyager, Becka's Studio, invention, and reflection. Admission is a "pay as you will" donation, and snacks are served in Café Play. ⊠ *1501 Pacific Ave.* ☎ *253/627–6031* ⊕ *www.playtacoma.org* 🎫 *Donation suggested* ☉ *Wed.–Sat. 10–5, Sun. 10–5.*

Karpeles Manuscript Library Museum. Housed in the former American Legion hall and across from Wright Park, the museum showcases rare and unpublished letters and documents by notables who have shaped history. Themes of the rotating exhibits have included the correspondence from the family of Presidents John and John Quincy Adams and Einstein's theory of relativity. ⊠ *407 S. G St.* ☎ *253/383–2575* ⊕ *www. rain.org/~karpeles* ✆ *Free* ☉ *Tues.–Fri. 10–4.*

Shanaman Sports Museum. Housed on the lower level of the atmospheric wooden Tacoma Dome, the museum highlights the accomplishments of local athletes. All sports are represented, from baseball, basketball, football, soccer, and tennis to gymnastics and volleyball. You must either hold a Tacoma Dome event ticket or make an appointment for a tour. ⊠ *2727 E. D St.* ☎ *253/627–5857* ⊕ *www.tacomasportsmuseum. com* ✆ *Free* ☉ *Open during events or by appointment.*

Stadium Historic District. Several of the Victorian homes in this charming neighborhood, high on a hill overlooking Commencement Bay, have been converted to bed-and-breakfast inns. Stadium High School at 111 North E Street is in an elaborate château-style structure built in 1891 as a luxury hotel for the Northern Pacific Railroad. The building was converted into a school after a 1906 fire.

Tacoma Art Museum. Adorned in glass and steel, this Antoine Predock masterpiece wraps around a beautiful garden. Inside, you'll find paintings, ceramics, sculptures, and other creations dating from the 18th century to the present. Look for the many glass sculptures by Dale Chihuly—especially the magnificent, flame-color *Mille Fiori* (Thousand Flowers) glass garden. ⊠ *1701 Pacific Ave.* ☎ *253/272–4258* ⊕ *www. tacomaartmuseum.org* ✆ *$10; free on 3rd Thurs. of month* ☉ *Wed.– Sun. 10–5 (until 8 pm every 3rd Thurs. of month).*

The Tacoma-Narrows Bridge. A mile-wide waterway is the boundary between the Tacoma hills and the rugged bluffs of the Kitsap Peninsula. From the twin bridges that span it, the view plunges hundreds of feet down to roiling green waters, which are often busy with barge traffic or obscured by fog. The original bridge, "Galloping Gertie," famously twisted itself to death and broke in half during a storm in 1940. Today its mint-green replacement and a sister bridge opened in 2007 form the world's largest man-made reef, and is a popular dive site. Note: The $5 toll is for eastbound cars only; westbound it's free from Tacoma into Gig Harbor. ⊠ *Hwy. 16 at N. Jackson Ave.*

10

FAMILY **Tacoma Nature Center at Snake Lake.** Comprising 71 acres of marshland, evergreen forest, and shallow lake that break up the urban sprawl of west Tacoma, the center shelters 20 species of mammals and more than 100 species of birds. The lake has nesting pairs of wood ducks, rare elsewhere in western Washington, and the interpretive center is a fun place for kids to look at small creatures, take walks and nature quizzes, and dress up in animal costumes. ⊠ *1919 S. Tyler St.* ☎ *253/591–6439* ⊕ *www.metroparkstacoma.org* ✆ *Free* ☉ *Center Mon.–Sat. 9–4; trails daily dawn–dusk.*

Union Station. This heirloom dates from 1911, when Tacoma was the western terminus of the Northern Pacific Railroad. Built by Reed and

Stem, architects of New York City's Grand Central Terminal, the copper-domed, beaux arts–style depot shows the influence of the Roman Pantheon and Italian baroque style. The station houses federal district courts, but its rotunda contains a gorgeous exhibit of glass sculptures by Dale Chihuly. Since it's a highly guarded government facility, be prepared to walk through a metal detector and show photo ID. ⊠ *1717 Pacific Ave.* ☏ *253/882–3900* ⊕ *www.wawb.uscourts.gov* ⌦ *Free* ☉ *Weekdays 8:30–4:30.*

Washington State History Museum. Adjacent to Union Station, and with the same opulent architecture, Washington's official history museum presents interactive exhibits and multimedia installations about the exploration and settlement of the state. Some rooms are filled with Native American, Inuit, and pioneer artifacts, while others display logging and railroad relics. The upstairs gallery has rotating exhibits, and summer programs are staged in the outdoor amphitheater. ⊠ *1911 Pacific Ave.* ☏ *253/272–3500* ⊕ *www.washingtonhistory.org* ⌦ *$9.50* ☉ *Tues.–Sun. 10–5 (to 8 pm every 3rd Thurs. of the month).*

Working Waterfront Maritime Museum. With its beautiful setting right along the Thea Foss waterfront, the turn-of-the-20th-century, wharf-style structure—which underwent a major renovation and the installation of a dashing new glass facade early in 2013—is easily reached along a walk by the bay. Inside the enormous timber building, displays trace the history of Tacoma's brisk shipping business. Extensive exhibits cover boat-making, importing and exporting, and the development of the waterfront. Photos and relics round out the exhibits, and children's activities are staged monthly. ⊠ *705 Dock St.* ☏ *253/272–2750* ⊕ *www. fosswaterwayseaport.org* ⌦ *$7* ☉ *Wed.–Fri. 10–5, weekends noon–5.*

Wright Park ⊠ *Yakima and Tacoma Aves., between 6th and Division Sts.* ☏ *253/591–5331* ⊕ *www.metroparkstacoma.org/wright-park* ⌦ *Park free, conservatory $3* ☉ *Park daily dawn–dusk, conservatory Tues.– Sun. 10–4:30.*

W.W. Seymour Botanical Conservatory. The chief attraction in the historic 28-acre Wright Park is the 1908 glass-dome W.W. Seymour Botanical Conservatory, a Victorian-style greenhouse (one of only three such structures on the West Coast) filled with exotic flora. Events include music, storytelling, food tastings, and cocktails. ⊠ *316 S. G St.* ☏ *253/591–5330* ⊕ *www.metroparkstacoma.org/conservatory.*

WHERE TO EAT

$$$

SEAFOOD

✕ **The Cliff House Restaurant.** For an unforgettable scene, witness the ocean panorama from the Rainier Room when there's a full moon. On any clear day, you'll probably get a view of Mt. Rainier across the bay. Clubby, curved banquettes provide the best positioning, but the cozier tables tucked in between offer more intimacy. When the succulent steaks, seafood, and wild game are served, your attention is turned away from the views. Entrées include Northwest seafood stew in a tomato-garlic broth, and boneless rib-eye steak with a green-peppercorn demi-glaze. Ⓢ *Average main: $26* ⊠ *6300 Marine View Dr.* ☏ *253/927–0400* ⊕ *cliffhousetacoma.com* ☉ *No lunch Sun., no brunch Mon.–Sat.*

$$$$
STEAKHOUSE

✕ **El Gaucho.** This Argentine-inspired steak house with a few branches around the Northwest serves prodigious, well-prepared dry-age steaks, plus a good mix of seafood and other grills. Service is straightforward, and there's an impressive wine list. This favorite of corporate honchos and tight-knit couples also has a cigar lounge and a piano bar that's open nightly. $ *Average main: $38* ✉ *2119 Pacific Ave.* ☎ *253/272– 1510* ⊕ *www.elgaucho.com* ☾ *No lunch.*

$$
ASIAN
Fodor's Choice
★

✕ **Indochine.** The elegant, pan-Asian conglomeration of sounds, scents, and sights takes place in a sleekly modern, yet darkly cozy space. Black-leather seats, curving banquettes, and steely metal accents set off plush red curtains and pavilion tables. The taste-dazzling array of Thai, Chinese, Indian, and Japanese cuisines includes curries, stir-fries, soups, and seafood. Standouts include coconut and galangal chicken soup, and the Oceans Five seafood and cilantro, served over vegetables. $ *Average main: $21* ✉ *1924 Pacific Ave.* ☎ *253/272–8200* ⊕ *indochinedowntown.com* ☾ *Closed Sun.*

$$$
SEAFOOD

✕ **Lobster Shop.** Built on stilts above the Dash Point tide flats, this former grocery store and beachside soda fountain is now an upscale, two-story seafood spot with panoramic bay views. Start with a house martini (always a double) or a taste of Washington wine, and perhaps Manila clams in white wine, or charbroiled artichoke with lemon-caper aioli. Move on to jumbo prawn étouffée with Southern grits, potato-crusted lingcod, or pearl couscous with mixed seafood. Finish with flourless chocolate cake with brown-sugar ice cream and house-made caramel. Twilight meals, served before 5:30, provide a mix of courses at a reduced price. $ *Average main: $30* ✉ *6912 Soundview Dr. NE* ☎ *253/927–1513* ⊕ *dash.lobstershop.com* ☾ *No lunch Mon.–Sat.* $ *Average main: $30* ✉ *4013 Ruston Way* ☎ *253/759–2165* ⊕ *wp.lobstershop.com*

$$
PACIFIC
NORTHWEST

✕ **Over The Moon Cafe.** Tucked down an alley near Wright Park and the Stadium Historic District, this quirky and cozy neighborhood bistro serves first-rate Northwest-influenced Italian fare, including bounteous salads and creative grills. It's worth seeking out this art-filled space with exposed-brick walls for such delectable fare as slow-cooked chicken ragu over rigatoni, and pan-seared, bourbon-glazed salmon fillet. Desserts, including banana pie with chocolate-fudge sauce, are a major draw. $ *Average main: $20* ✉ *709 Opera Alley* ☎ *253/284–3722* ⊕ *www.overthemooncafe.net* ☾ *Closed Sun. and Mon.*

$$$
MODERN
AMERICAN

✕ **Pacific Grill.** With its clubby interior, huge wine list, and proximity to downtown hotels and attractions, it's easy to see how this flashy restaurant is a favorite for special occasions and high-end business meals. Here you can expect a menu of contemporary variations on seafood and steak, including Columbia River steelhead with a maple-balsamic glaze, and New York steak with red flannel hash and a red wine sauce; vegetarians shouldn't pass up the unusual roasted cauliflower "steak" served with olive gremolata, tomatoes, orange, and capers. The ahi tartare with ginger-lime vinaigrette makes a fine starter. $ *Average main: $29* ✉ *1502 Pacific Ave.* ☎ *253/627–3535* ⊕ *www.pacificgrilltacoma. com* ☾ *No lunch weekends.*

10

$ SOUTHERN Fodor's Choice ★ 🍴 **Southern Kitchen.** Sure, it's awfully far north to be specializing in down-home Southern cooking, but this bustling, casual spot on Tacoma's north side, a little west of Wright Park, serves remarkably authentic and absolutely delicious soul food. In the morning, regulars swing by for heaping plates of chicken-fried steak with grits and eggs, or home-made biscuits and gravy. Later on, move on to fried catfish strips with a side of hush puppies, Texas-style hand-trimmed brisket, and hot-links sandwiches. Dinners come with corn cakes and lots of tasty sides—and do save room for the sweet potato pie. Note that the restaurant closes on the early side most evenings, usually around 8 pm. [$] *Average main: $12* ✉ *1716 6th Ave.* ☎ *253/627–4282* 🌐 *www.southernkitchen-tacoma.com.*

WHERE TO STAY

For expanded hotel reviews, visit Fodors.com.

$$$ B&B/INN 🏨 **Chinaberry Hill.** Original fixtures and stained-glass windows are among the grace notes in this 1889 Queen Anne–style B&B in the Stadium Historic District. **Pros:** wraparound porch with vast bay views; the suites are spacious and romantic. **Cons:** creaks and quirks of a century-old mansion. [$] *Rooms from: $169* ✉ *302 Tacoma Ave. N* ☎ *253/272–1282* 🌐 *www.chinaberryhill.com* 🛏 *1 room, 4 suites, 1 cottage* 🍽 *Breakfast.*

$$$ HOTEL 🏨 **Courtyard Marriott Tacoma Downtown.** Although set in the late-19th-century Waddell Building, this Marriott has spacious, modern rooms outfitted in bright Northwest colors with lots of 21st-century touches, and you'll find an upscale restaurant and bar. **Pros:** reliable chain hotel in historic building; close to convention center and museums; full-service spa. **Cons:** rooms get street noise; a little pricey for a mid-range chain hotel. [$] *Rooms from: $189* ✉ *1515 Commerce St.* ☎ *253/591–9100* 🌐 *www.marriott.com* 🛏 *156 rooms, 6 suites* 🍽 *Breakfast.*

$$ B&B/INN 🏨 **Green Cape Cod Bed & Breakfast.** Built in 1929, this house stands in a residential neighborhood only blocks from the historic Proctor shopping district. **Pros:** cozy, frilly rooms. **Cons:** need a car to explore the rest of the city. [$] *Rooms from: $140* ✉ *2711 N. Warner St.* ☎ *253/752–1977, 888/752–1977* 🌐 *www.greencapecod.com* 🛏 *3 rooms* 🍽 *Breakfast.*

$$$ HOTEL Fodor's Choice ★ 🏨 **Hotel Murano.** Named for the Italian island where some of the world's best glass is created, this big hotel with an intimate ambience centers around exhibits by world-famous glass artists. **Pros:** stylish rooms with beautiful art; luxury amenities; top-flight service. **Cons:** no pool. [$] *Rooms from: $179* ✉ *1320 Broadway Plaza* ☎ *253/238–8000, 888/862–3255* 🌐 *www.hotelmuranotacoma.com* 🛏 *319 rooms, 10 suites* 🍽 *Breakfast.*

$$$ HOTEL 🏨 **Silver Cloud Inn.** Tacoma's only waterfront hotel juts right out into the bay along picturesque Ruston Way and the historic Old Town area. **Pros:** waterside locale; Ruston Way walking paths and restaurants; free parking. **Cons:** summer traffic; compact rooms. [$] *Rooms from: $190* ✉ *2317 N. Ruston Way* ☎ *253/272–1300, 866/820–8448* 🌐 *www.silvercloud.com* 🛏 *90 rooms* 🍽 *Breakfast.*

$$$$ B&B/INN 🏨 **Thornewood Castle Inn and Gardens.** Spread over four lush acres along beautiful American Lake, this 27,000-square-foot, Gothic Tudor–style mansion built in 1908 has hosted two American presidents: William

Howard Taft and Theodore Roosevelt. **Pros:** castlelike ambience; lively events. **Cons:** one of the more expensive properties in the area; in a sort of no-man's-land between Tacoma and Fort Lewis. $ *Rooms from: $350* ✉ *8601 N. Thorne La. SW, 12 miles south of Tacoma, Lakewood* ☎ *253/589–9052* ⊕ *www.thornewoodcastle.com* ⏎ *2 rooms, 7 suites, 3 apartments* ⊠ *Breakfast.*

NIGHTLIFE AND THE ARTS

THE ARTS

Broadway Center for the Performing Arts. Cultural activity in Tacoma centers on this complex of performance spaces. ✉ *901 Broadway* ☎ *253/591–5894, 800/291–7593* ⊕ *www.broadwaycenter.org.*

Pantages. The famous theater architect B. Marcus Pritica designed this Greco-Roman–influenced music hall, decked out with classical figures, ornate columns, arches, and reliefs, in 1918. W.C. Fields, Mae West, Charlie Chaplin, Bob Hope, and Stan Laurel all performed here. The Tacoma Symphony Orchestra, Tacoma Concert Band, and Tacoma City Ballet perform at the Pantages, which also presents touring shows. ✉ *901 Broadway.*

Rialto Theater. In its early days, the Rialto Theater presented vaudeville performances and silent films. The Tacoma Youth Symphony now performs in the 1918 structure, which also hosts concerts and other shows. ✉ *301 S. 9th St.* ☎ *253/591–5894.*

Theatre on the Square. Adjacent to the Pantages, the contemporary Theatre on the Square presents performances by the Tacoma Opera as well as professional plays and musicals. ✉ *Broadway, between 10th and 11th Sts.* ☎ *253/591–5894.*

NIGHTLIFE

Jazzbones. This classy no-cover, no-fuss, just-great-music joint is on the Sixth Avenue strip, with live jazz on stage every night. ✉ *2803 6th Ave.* ☎ *253/396–9169* ⊕ *www.jazzbones.com.*

Swiss Pub. This lively pub inside a historic building has microbrews on tap, pool tables, and bands on stage Thursday through Saturday. Monday brings free admission for live blues night, and there's karaoke on Wednesday. The place is best early in the evening before the bands start playing—not only is the music not usually that good, but the pub morphs from a laid-back gem of a place to loud and obnoxious pretty quickly. ✉ *1904 S. Jefferson Ave.* ☎ *253/572–2821* ⊕ *www. theswisspub.com.*

SHOPPING

Antique Row. In this district, you'll find upscale antiques stores and boutiques selling collectibles and 1950s paraphernalia. The Broadway farmers' market is held here every Thursday in summer. ✉ *Broadway Ave. at St. Helen's St., between 7th and 9th Sts.*

Proctor District. This lively neighborhood contains a mix of upscale boutiques, restaurants, and specialty shops. ☎ *253/370–1748* ⊕ *www. proctordistrict.com.*

SCUBA DIVING
Tacoma Lighthouse Diving Center. This is a full-service dive operation with lessons, equipment, and regional trips. ⊠ *2502 Pacific Ave.* ☎ *253/627–7617* ⊕ *www.lighthousediving.com.*

Tacoma Underwater Sports. The area's largest scuba center sells and rents gear, plans trips, and has branches and repair facilities throughout Puget Sound. ⊠ *9608 40th Ave. SW, Lakewood* ☎ *253/588–6634* ⊕ *www. underwatersports.com.*

OLYMPIA

30 miles southwest of Tacoma.

Olympia has been the capital of Washington since 1853, the beginning of city and state. It is small for the capital city of a major state, but that makes it all the more pleasant to visit. The old and charming downtown area is compact and easy on the feet, stretching between Capitol Lake and the gathering of austere government buildings to the south, the shipping and yacht docks around glistening Budd Inlet to the west, the colorful market area capping the north end of town, and I–5 running along the eastern edge. There are little unexpected surprises all through town, from pretty little half-block parks and blossoming miniature gardens to clutches of Thai and Vietnamese restaurants and antiques shops. The imposing state capitol, finished in 1928, is set above the south end of town like a fortress, framed by a skirt of granite steps. The monumental 287-foot-high dome is the fourth-largest masonry dome in the world (only St. Peter's in Rome, St. Paul's in London, and the national Capitol in the other Washington are larger).

GETTING HERE AND AROUND
To reach Olympia from Seattle, take I–5 south to Exit 105—this is an easy city to drive and park in, and a car is your best way around. Both Greyhound and Amtrak serve Olympia, but the Amtrak station is 8 miles away, so from Seattle, if not driving, taking the bus is actually more convenient, as the bus station is centrally located and the sights clustered around downtown and the Capitol Campus are easily reached by foot.

EXPLORING
Capitol Campus. These attractive grounds, sprawling around the buildings perched above the Capitol Lake bluffs, contain memorials, monuments, rose gardens, and Japanese cherry trees. The 1939 conservatory is open year-round on weekdays from 8 to 3 and also on weekends in summer. Directly behind the legislative building, the modern state library has exhibits devoted to Washington's history. Free 45-minute tours from the visitor center take you around the area. If you want to see state government in action, the legislature is in session for 30 or 60 days from the second Monday in January, depending on whether it's an even- or odd-numbered year. ⊠ *Capitol Way, between 10th and 14th Aves.* ☎ *360/902–8880 tour information* ⊕ *www.des.wa.gov* ✆ *Free* ⊙ *Campus tours daily on the hr, 10–3 weekdays and 11–3 weekends.*

Hands On Children's Museum. This fun spot in a handsome new building just off Marine Drive overlooking East Bay is where children can touch, build, and play with all sorts of crafts and exhibits. Dozens of interactive, cleverly designed stations include an art studio and a special gallery for kids four and under. During the city's First Friday art walks the museum is open late and stages special programs and events. ⊠ *414 Jefferson St. NW* ☎ *360/956–0818* ⊕ *www.hocm.org* ☞ *$9.95 (free 5–9 on 1st Fri. of month)* ☉ *Mon.–Sat. 10–5, Sun. 11–5.*

Olympia Farmers' Market. Neat, clean, and well-run, this expanse of covered fruit, vegetable, pastry, and craft stalls at the north end of town includes organic produce. You'll also find all sorts of oddities such as ostrich eggs, button magnets, and glass sculptures. With a dozen tiny ethnic eateries tucked in between the vendors, it's also a terrific place to grab a bite and then walk over to the waterfront area. ⊠ *700 N. Capitol Way* ☎ *360/352–9096* ⊕ *www.olympiafarmersmarket.com* ☞ *Free* ☉ *Apr.–Oct., Thurs.–Sun. 10–3; Nov. and Dec., weekends 10–3.*

The Olympic Flight Museum. Housed in a hangar at the Olympic Regional Airport south of town, this museum brings to life an ever-changing collection of vintage aircraft. Important pieces include a colorful P-51D Mustang, a sleek BAC-167 Strikemaster, and a serious-looking AH-1S Cobra helicopter. On the annual schedule are winter lectures, weekly tours, monthly flights, and the Gathering of Warbirds event each June. The shop sells a model of just about everything you see on-site. ⊠ *7637 A Old Hwy. 99 SE* ☎ *360/705–3925* ⊕ *www.olympicflightmuseum.com* ☞ *$7* ☉ *Hours vary; call ahead.*

Percival Landing Waterfront Park. Framing nearly an acre of landscaped desert gardens and bird-watching areas, this lovely waterfront spot stretches along a 1-mile boardwalk through a beachy section of the Ellis Cove coastline. To the south are yachts bobbing in the water at the wooden docks and the waterfront Anthony's restaurant; to the north are the shipyards and cargo cranes; and to the east is the market. In the center is an open space with an outdoor stage for summer shows, music, and festivals. You can see it all from three stories up by climbing the winding steps of the timber viewing tower, where open benches invite visitors to relax and enjoy the city views. ⊠ *4th Ave. to Thurston Ave.* ☎ *360/753–8380* ⊕ *olympiawa.gov/community/parks/percival-landing* ☞ *Free* ☉ *Daily dawn–dusk.*

Priest Point Park. This leafy tract is a beautiful section of protected shoreline and wetlands. Thick swaths of forest and glistening bay views are the main attractions, with picnic areas and playgrounds filling in the open spaces. The 3-mile **Ellis Cove Trail,** with interpretive stations, bridges, and nature settings, runs right through the Priest Point Park area and around the Olympia coast. ⊠ *East Bay Dr.* ☎ *360/753–8380* ⊕ *olympiawa.gov/community/parks/parks-and-trails/priest-point-park.*

FAMILY **Wolf Haven International.** Guided tours of this 80-acre wolf sanctuary are given every hour on the hour and run about 50 minutes, during which docents explain the recovery programs and visitors can view the wolves. You must join a tour. In summer the facility hosts a so-called Howl-In (reservations essential), with tours, storytelling, arts and crafts, and howling contests. Note that it's worth taking a look at the website before visiting—the sanctuary has a few rules regarding conduct and photography (certain zoom lenses can only be used on special photography tours). Most importantly, parents should know that although the sanctuary can be a wonderful place for kids, it does not provide as much stimulation as a typical zoo and may bore kids with short attention spans. ✉ *3111 Offut Lake Rd. SE* ✛ *From Olympia, take I–5 south to Exit 99 and follow signs east for 7 miles* ☎ *800/448–9653* ⊕ *www. wolfhaven.org* ✉ *$12, Howl-In $17* ☉ *Apr.–Sept., Mon. and Wed.– Sat. 10–3, Sun. noon–3; Oct.–Jan. and Mar. Sat. 10–3, Sun. noon–3. Closed Feb.*

Yashiro Japanese Garden. A symbol of the sister-city relationship of Olympia and Yashiro, Japan, the garden opened in 1989. Within it are a waterfall, a bamboo grove, a koi pond, and stone lanterns. ✉ *1010 Plum St.* ⊕ *olympiawa.gov/city-services/parks/parks-and-trails/yashiro-japanese-garden* ✉ *Free* ☉ *Daily dawn–dusk.*

WHERE TO EAT

$

CAFÉ

Fodor's Choice ★

× **Batdorf & Bronson Dancing Goats Coffee Bar.** Here is a local roaster (also with branches in metro Atlanta, Georgia) that can stand up to the best of Seattle's coffeehouses. Several spacious and sleek shops, one across from the Farmers' Market and one in the heart of downtown, pair the best beans with just-baked pastries and tasty sandwiches. The tasting room at 200 Market Street is in the roastery. You can sample about a half-dozen of Batdorf's favorite blends in the tasting room Wednesday through Sunday from 9 to 4. $ *Average main: $6* ✉ *111 Market St. NE* ☎ *360/528–5555* ⊕ *www.dancinggoats.com* ☉ *No dinner* $ *Average main: $6* ✉ *513 S. Capitol Way* ☎ *360/786–6717* ⊕ *www. batdorfcoffee.com* ☉ *No dinner* $ *Average main: $6* ✉ *200 Market St.* ☎ *360/753–4057* ☉ *Closed Mon. and Tues. No dinner.*

$$$

PACIFIC
NORTHWEST

× **Dockside Bistro & Wine Bar.** The marina views are just part of the appeal of this bright, modern bistro overlooking West Bay. It's the innovative, beautifully presented Asia-meets-Northwest cuisine of chef Laurie Nguyen that has foodies buzzing, not to mention friendly and efficient service and a stellar wine list. The food here focuses strongly on what's local and organic, with Totten Inlet steamer clams in white wine, and local elk rib-eye carpaccio with juniper berries and green papaya salad starring among the starters. Worthy picks among the main dishes include pear-Gorgonzola ravioli with wild prawns, and seared sea scallops with a light watercress-saffron cream. $ *Average main: $24* ✉ *501 Columbia St. NW* ☎ *360/956–1928* ⊕ *www.docksidebistro.com* ☉ *Closed Mon. No lunch Sun.*

$$

MEDITERRANEAN

× **Mercato.** Tucked into a glitzy, glass-front office building on a sunny corner across from the Farmers' Market, the aptly named restaurant brings an Italian countryside ambience to this relaxed neighborhood. Tables line up against sponge-painted gold walls decorated with a series of Patés Baroni posters, with tiny stained-glass lamps lighting the scene. Specialties include the *piadina* sandwiches, slices of warmed flatbread slathered with such cold fillings as smoked duck on spinach vinaigrette, along with thin-crust pizzas, creative pastas, and hearty grills. $ *Average main: $18* ✉ *111 Market St. NE* ☎ *360/528–3663* ⊕ *www.ramblinrestaurants.com.*

$
AMERICAN
✕ **Sage's Brunchhouse.** This cute and homey West Bay neighborhood spot, a favorite for its namesake meal, sources much of its ingredients from Olympia Food Cooperative next door. The cozy, art-filled dining room, which does sometimes fill up quickly for weekend brunch, is an enchanting spot for feasting on huevos rancheros, eggs Benedict topped with salmon and dill sauce, fluffy biscuits and gravy, and other staples of the morning meal. $ *Average main: $9* ✉ *903 Rogers St. NW, Olympia* ☎ *360/352–1103* ⊕ *www.sagesbrunchhouse.com* ⊙ *Closed Mon. and Tues. No dinner.*

WHERE TO STAY
For expanded hotel reviews, visit Fodors.com.

$$
HOTEL
🛏 **Phoenix Inn Suites.** This polished inn is nestled right up to Budd Inlet and just a couple of blocks from the Farmers' Market. **Pros:** great rates considering size and look of rooms; lots of amenities; indoor pool open 24 hours. **Cons:** pedestrian hotel appearance. $ *Rooms from: $135* ✉ *415 Capitol Way N* ☎ *360/570–0555, 877/570–0555* ⊕ *www.phoenixinnsuites.com* ⤴ *102 suites* 🍽 *Breakfast.*

$$
B&B/INN
🛏 **Swantown Inn.** Antiques and lace ornament every room of this stylish, peak-roofed Victorian inn, built as a mansion in 1893 and then used for many years as a boardinghouse. **Pros:** 19th-century feel, but modern and business-friendly. **Cons:** A 20- to 30-minute walk to downtown. $ *Rooms from: $129* ✉ *1431 11th Ave. SE* ☎ *360/753–9123, 877/753–9123* ⊕ *www.swantowninn.com* ⤴ *3 rooms, 1 suite* 🍽 *Breakfast.*

MT. RAINIER ENVIRONS

The Cascade Mountains south of Snoqualmie Pass are more heavily eroded than those to the north and generally not as high. But a few peaks do top 7,000 feet, and two volcanic peaks are taller than any of the state's northern mountains. Mt. Adams is more than 12,000 feet high, and Mt. Rainier rises to more than 14,000 feet. The third of the southern peaks, Mt. St. Helens, blew its top in 1980, and is now little more than 8,000 feet high.

Ashford sits astride an ancient trail across the Cascades used by the Yakama Native Americans to trade with the coastal tribes of western Washington. The town began as a logging railway terminal; today, it's the main gateway to Mt. Rainier—and the only year-round access point to the park—with lodges, restaurants, grocery stores, and gift shops. Surrounded by Cascade peaks, Packwood is a pretty mountain village on U.S. 12, below White Pass. Between Mt. Rainier and Mt. St. Helens, it's a perfect jumping-off point for exploring local wilderness areas. The small town of Mossyrock is located between the large lakes of Riffe and Mayfield, which are popular for fishing, camping, and boating.

10

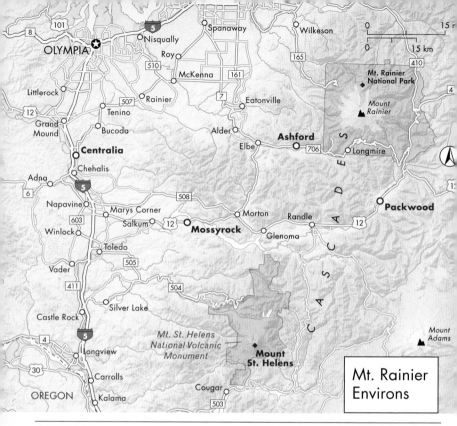

Mt. Rainier Environs

ASHFORD

85 miles from Seattle, 130 miles from Portland.

Adjacent to the Nisqually (Longmire) entrance to Mount Rainier National Park, it's hardly surprising that Ashford draws around 2 million visitors every year. Long a transit route for local aboriginal tribes, its more recent history began when it became a logging terminal on the rail line and developed into a tourism hot spot with lodges, restaurants, groceries, and gift shops along Highway 706.

GETTING HERE AND AROUND

Ashford is about 85 miles from Seattle via I–5 southbound to Highway 7, then southeast to Highway 706. An alternate route is via I–5 southbound to Highway 167, then continuing south to Highway 161 through Eatonville to Highway 7, then east to Highway 706. From the Portland area, it's about 130 miles via I–5 northbound, then east on Highway 12 to Morton and north via Highway 7 to Highway 706.

EXPLORING

FAMILY **Mount Rainier Scenic Railroad.** This train takes you through lush forests and across scenic bridges, covering 14 miles of incomparable beauty. Seasonal theme trips, such as the Great Pumpkin Express and the Snowball Express, are also available. The trains depart from Elbe, 11 miles west of Ashford, then bring passengers to a lovely picnic area near Mineral Lake before returning. ✉ *349 Mineral Creek Rd., Mineral* ☎ *360/569–2588, 888/783–2611* 🌐 *www.mrsr.com* 🎟 *$26–$29* ⏲ *Mid-May–Oct., weekends (also Thurs.–Fri. in summer); some seasonal trips in Dec. and Mar.*

WHERE TO EAT

$$ AMERICAN Fodor's Choice ★ 🍴 **Alexander's Country Inn Restaurant.** Without a doubt, this woodsy country inn near Mount Rainier National Park's Nisqually Entrance serves the best food in the area. Ceiling fans and wooden booths lining the walls add a touch of whimsy to the 1912 building. Try the steak, or trout that's freshly caught from the pond on the grounds. The homemade bread is fantastic, and the blackberry pie is a must for dessert. Dine inside or outside on a patio overlooking a waterfall. Box lunches for adventurers are available. [$] *Average main: $19* ✉ *37515 Hwy. 706 E, 4 miles east of Ashford* ☎ *360/569–2300* 🌐 *www.alexanderscountryinn.com* ⏲ *No lunch Mon.–Thurs.; no dinner Sun.–Thurs. Nov.–Mar.*

$ AMERICAN FAMILY 🍴 **Scaleburgers.** Once a 1939 logging-truck weigh station, the building is now a popular restaurant serving homemade hamburgers, fries, and shakes. Eat outside on tables overlooking the hills and scenic railroad. [$] *Average main: $6* ✉ *54109 Mountain Hwy. E, 11 miles west of Ashford, Elbe* ☎ *360/569–2247* 💳 *No credit cards* ⏲ *Limited hours in winter; call ahead.*

WHERE TO STAY

For expanded hotel reviews, visit Fodors.com.

$$ B&B/INN 🏨 **Alexander's Country Inn.** Serving guests since 1912, this top-notch lodging sits just a mile from Mt. Rainier's Nisqually Entrance. **Pros:** luxurious amenities, especially considering moderate rates; on-site day spa; home to the best restaurant in the region *(⇨ See Where to Eat)*. **Cons:** lots of breakables means it's not great for children. [$] *Rooms from: $130* ✉ *37515 Hwy. 706 E, 4 miles east of Ashford* ☎ *360/569–2323, 800/654–7615* 🌐 *www.alexanderscountryinn.com* 🛏 *12 rooms, 2 3-bedroom houses* 🍽 *Breakfast.*

$ HOTEL 🏨 **Nisqually Lodge.** Crackling flames from the massive stone fireplace lend warmth and cheer to the great room of this hotel, a few miles west of Mount Rainier National Park. **Pros:** spacious rooms; central to mountain activities and just a few miles from park; the price is right. **Cons:** no frills. [$] *Rooms from: $95* ✉ *31609 Hwy. 706 E* ☎ *360/569–8804, 888/674–3554* 🌐 *www.nisqually.whitepasstravel.com* 🛏 *24 rooms* 🍽 *Breakfast.*

$ B&B/INN 🏨 **Wellspring.** In the woods outside Ashford, the accommodations here include tastefully designed log cabins, tent cabins, a tree house, and a room in a greenhouse. **Pros:** unique lodging with a wide range of prices, depending on the room; some options good for groups; relaxing spa and hot soaking tubs. **Cons:** limited amenities. [$] *Rooms from: $100* ✉ *54922 Kernehan Rd.* ☎ *360/569–2514* 🌐 *wellspringspa.com* 🛏 *2 rooms, 6 cabins, 3 tent cabins, 5 cottages* 🍽 *Breakfast.*

$ HOTEL 🏨 **Whittaker's Bunkhouse Motel.** With inexpensive bunk spaces (available May–September) as well as large private rooms and a cottage, this comfortable 1912 motel once housed loggers and mill workers. **Pros:**

Mt. Rainier was named after British admiral Peter Rainier in the late 18th century.

inexpensive; convenient; historical draw for mountain buffs. **Cons:** no frills in most rooms; bunk room shares bathrooms. Ⓢ *Rooms from: $90* ✉ *30205 Hwy. 706 E* ☎ *360/569–2439* ⊕ *www.whittakersbunkhouse. com* ↪ *20 rooms, 1 12-bed bunk room, 1 cottage* ⦿ *No meals.*

PACKWOOD

25 miles southeast of Ashford via Skate Creek Rd. (closed in winter).

Its location, between Mt. Rainier and Mt. St. Helens, makes this delightful mountain village on U.S. 12 an attractive destination for those who plan to explore the nearby wilderness areas.

GETTING HERE AND AROUND
Packwood is about 140 miles from Portland via I–5 northbound to Exit 68, then 64 miles east via U.S. 12 (also called the White Pass Scenic Byway). From Seattle (about 120 miles away), take I–5 south to Highway 167 near Renton, then south via Highway 161 through Eatonville and southeast on Highway 7 through Morton, then east on U.S. 12.

ESSENTIALS
Visitor Information Destination Packwood Association ✉ *103 Main St. E* ☎ *360/494–2223* ⊕ *www.destinationpackwood.com.*

EXPLORING
Goat Rocks Wilderness. The crags in Gifford Pinchot National Forest, south of Mt. Rainier, are aptly named. You often see mountain goats here, especially when you hike into the backcountry. Goat Lake is a particularly good spot for viewing these elusive creatures. See the goats without backpacking by taking Forest Road 2140 south from U.S. 12.

The goats will be on Stonewall Ridge looming up ahead of you. ✉ *Gifford Pinchot National Forest Headquarters, 10600 N.E. 51st St. Circle, Vancouver* ☎ *360/891–5000* 🌐 *www.fs.usda.gov/giffordpinchot.*

WHERE TO STAY

For expanded hotel reviews, visit Fodors.com.

$ HOTEL 🏨 **Cowlitz River Lodge.** You can't beat the location of this comfortable two-story family motel: it's just off the highway in Packwood, the gateway to Mount Rainier National Park *and* the Mount St. Helens National Volcanic Monument. **Pros:** convenient location; knowledgeable staff. **Cons:** no pool; no restaurant; rooms are basic motel-style. [$] *Rooms from: $90* ✉ *13069 U.S. 12* ☎ *360/494–4444, 888/305–2185* 🌐 *www.escapetothemountains.com* 🛏 *31 rooms* 🍴 *Breakfast.*

$ HOTEL FAMILY 🏨 **Mountain View Lodge.** Just east of the town of Packwood, this convenient, quiet motel is 40 miles from both Mt. Rainier and Mt. St. Helens, and 17 miles from White Pass Ski Resort. **Pros:** roomy accommodations (some with kitchens); close to ski resort; friendly and helpful owners. **Cons:** no restaurant on-site. [$] *Rooms from: $80* ✉ *13163 U.S. Hwy. 12* ☎ *360/494–5555, 877/277–7192* 🌐 *www.mtvlodge.com* 🛏 *22 rooms* 🍴 *No meals.*

MOSSYROCK

45 miles west of Packwood.

Another great "outdoors" destination, with opportunities for camping, fishing and boating in abundance, Mossyrock is a charming small town with two lakefront parks. The large lakes—Riffe and Mayfield—were created in the 1960s when dams were constructed for generating electricity, and Tacoma Power (which generates the power) stocks the lakes with fish. At Mayfield Lake there are also a state park and a privately owned marina and resort.

GETTING HERE AND AROUND

Mossyrock is reached from Portland or Seattle via I–5, Exit 68, then 21 miles east via U.S. 12 (also called the White Pass Scenic Byway). A more scenic alternate route from Seattle that travels closer to Mt. Rainier is Highway 167 and Highway 161 through Eatonville, then Highway 7 to Morton and west on U.S. 12. Coming from the southwest (Nisqually) entrance to Mt. Rainier, take Highway 706 West to Highway 7 South, then follow the same route via Morton to Mossyrock.

EXPLORING

DeGoede Bulb Farm. Just outside of town, fields of tulips and other flowers grown at the DeGoede Bulb Farm provide a colorful backdrop along U.S. 12. Stroll through the manicured show gardens year-round. ✉ *409 Mossyrock Rd. W* ☎ *360/983–9000* 🌐 *www.degoedebulb.com* 🎟 *Free* 🕒 *Mar.–Aug., Mon.–Sat. 9–6; Sept.–Feb., Mon.–Sat. 9–5.*

Ike Kinswa State Park. This serene 454-acre preserve on the north side of Mayfield Lake is about 4 miles from Mossyrock. Many of the forested campsites provide a nice sense of seclusion, and some lake-view spots are situated for prime sunset views. Five cabins have electricity and bunk beds, but no bathrooms. There's year-round camping, two boat

MT. ST. HELENS

One of the most prominent peaks in the Northwest's rugged Cascade Range, Mount St. Helens National Volcanic Monument affords visitors an up-close look at the site of the most destructive volcanic blast in U.S. history.

Just 55 miles northeast of Portland, and 155 miles southeast of Seattle, this once soaring, conical summit stood at 9,665 feet above sea level. Then, on May 18, 1980, a massive eruption launched a 36,000-foot plume of steam and ash into the air and sent nearly 4 million cubic yards of debris through the Toutle and Cowlitz river valleys. The devastating eruption leveled a 230-square-mile area, claiming 57 lives and more than 250 homes. The mountain now stands at 8,365 feet, and a horseshoe-shape crater—most visible from the north—now forms the scarred summit. A modern highway carries travelers to within about 5 miles of the summit, and the surrounding region offers thrilling opportunities for climbing, hiking, and learning about volcanology.

BEST TIME TO GO

It's best to visit from mid-May through late October, as the last section of Spirit Lake Highway, Johnston Ridge Observatory, and many of the park's forest roads are closed the rest of the year. The other visitor centers along the lower sections of the highway are open year-round, but overcast skies typically obscure the mountain's summit in winter.

WORD OF MOUTH

"The visitor centers were excellent—far from the usual NPS centers that make one feel like they are on a 5th-grade field trip. I remember standing outside in awe at the power of the volcano."
—gail

PARK HIGHLIGHTS

Ape Cave. The longest continuous lava tube in the continental U.S., Ape Cave is one of the park's outstanding attractions. Two routes traverse the tube. The lower route is an easy hour-long hike; the upper route is challenging (expect uneven ground and some scrambles) and takes about three hours. Be sure to bring your own light source and warm clothing—temperatures in the cave don't rise above the mid-40s. In high season ranger-led walks are sometimes available; inquire at the **Apes' Headquarters** (☎ 360/449-7800), which is off Forest Service road 8303, 3 miles north of the junction of Forest Roads 83 and 90. ⊕ *www.fs.usda.gov/recarea/mountsthelens.*

Johnston Ridge Observatory. The visitor center closest to the summit, Johnston Ridge is named for scientist David Johnston, who was killed by the mountain's immense lateral blast. Open only from mid-May through early November, **Johnston Ridge Observatory Visitor Center** (✉ *end of Hwy. 504* ☎ *360/274-2140* ⊕ *www.fs.usda.gov/recarea/mountsthelens*) stands at the end of the park's Spirit Lake Highway, and contains fascinating exhibits on the mountain's geology and instruments measuring volcanic activity and seismic activity. Several short trails afford spectacular views of the summit.

Spirit Lake Highway. Officially known as Highway 504, this twisting, turning paved road rises some 4,000 feet from the town of Castle Rock (just off I-5, Exit 49) to within about 5 miles of the Mt. St. Helens summit. Along this road are several visitor centers that interpret the region's geology and geography, and several turnouts afford views of the destruction wrought upon the Toutle and Cowlitz river valleys. Don't miss the **Mount St. Helens Visitor Center at Silver Lake** (✉ *Hwy. 504, 5 miles east of I-5* ☎ *360/274-0962* ⊕ *www.parks. wa.gov/stewardship/mountsthelens*) in Seaquest State Park, which shows chilling video footage of the eruption, contains superb exhibits, and houses a scale model of the mountain that you can actually climb through.

STAY THE NIGHT

Mt. St. Helens is in a remote area. You'll find a handful of chain motels in Kelso and Longview, about 10 to 15 miles south. **Lewis River B&B.** In Woodland, 30 miles south of Castle Rock but right on Highway 503, the gateway for approaching great Mt. St. Helens hiking from the south, the charming Lewis River B&B is a terrific lodging option. The five rooms have upscale, contemporary furnishings, and most overlook the scenic Lewis River. ✉ *2339 Lewis River Rd., Woodland* ☎ *360/225-8630* ⊕ *www. lewisriverbedandbreakfast. com.*

Patty's Place at 19 Mile House. For a memorable meal midway up Spirit Lake Highway, drop by this rustic roadhouse with a veranda overlooking the North Fork Toutle River—burgers are a specialty, and be sure to save room for the fresh-fruit cobblers. ✉ *9440 Spirit Lake Hwy., Kid Valley* ☎ *360/274-8779, 888/342-1420* ⊕ *www. pattysplace-19milehouse. com* ☉ *Limited hrs in winter; call ahead.*

10

ramps, hiking trails, and fishing (including the challenging tiger muskie, stocked from a nearby hatchery). The park is named after a Cowlitz tribe that lived in this area; their burial grounds are nearby. ⊠ *873 Harmony Rd., Silver Creek* ☎ *360/983–3332* ⊕ *www.parks.wa.gov* ⌕ *$10 day pass; $30 for annual Discover Pass (valid in all state parks)* ⊙ *Summer, daily 6:30–dusk; winter, daily 8:30–dusk.*

Mayfield Lake Park. At this park right off U.S. 12, 4 miles west of Mossyrock, you'll find a handy boat launch. Camping spots are especially scenic, with lake views, forest settings, and even lakefront spots. Fish for trout, bass, and coho salmon. ⊠ *180 Beach Rd.* ☎ *360/985–2364, 888/502–8690* ⌕ *Parking $5* ⊙ *Daily; camping mid-Apr.–mid-Oct.*

Mossyrock Park. Fish, camp, and boat at this park on Riffe Lake, just a few miles east of town. The lake is stocked with cutthroat, rainbow and brown trout, coho salmon, steelhead, and bass. ⊠ *202 Ajlune Rd.* ☎ *360/983–3900, 888/502–8690* ⌕ *Parking $5.*

WHERE TO STAY

For expanded hotel reviews, visit Fodors.com.

$$$
B&B/INN
Fodor's Choice
★

☵ **Adytum Retreat.** This bed-and-breakfast is all about luxury in nature— set on a hill on nearly 16 acres of forested grounds, the castle-like home, with its stone front, towers, and 75 windows, faces Mayfield Lake and the valleys below. **Pros:** amazing views; beautiful grounds; unique amenities. **Cons:** a bit of a drive to restaurants and shopping. $ *Rooms from: $180* ⊠ *186 Skyview Drive* ☎ *360/983–8008* ⊕ *www. adytumsanctuary.com* ⇝ *2 suites* ⦿ *Breakfast.*

THE SAN JUAN
ISLANDS

WELCOME TO
THE SAN JUAN ISLANDS

TOP REASONS
TO GO

★ **Whale watch:** Spot whales and other marine life from a tour boat or sea kayak.

★ **Taste local flavors:** Talented chefs have turned Orcas and San Juan Islands into hot spots for sophisticated, locavore-driven cuisine.

★ **Gallery hop:** Dozens of acclaimed artists live year-round or seasonally in the San Juans, and you can find their work in studio galleries and group cooperatives throughout the islands.

★ **Indulge in a spa day:** Work out the kayaking or hiking kinks with a massage at the lovely seaside Rosario Resort and Spa on Orcas Island.

★ **Bike beautiful terrain:** Rent a bike and cycle the scenic, sloping country roads—Lopez Island has the gentlest terrain for this activity, but biking is popular on all of the islands.

1 Lopez Island. The smallest, least-populated, and most tranquil of the main islands, Lopez is a largely rural and wonderfully restive place with a handful of charming cafés, a few inns, and traffic-free roads ideal for biking.

2 Orcas Island. The rugged and hilly terrain contains the highest point in the San Juans and is the largest in the archipelago, although the pace is easygoing and relaxed. The main village of Eastsound, however, contains a number of sophisticated restaurants and galleries, and you'll find several fine eateries, inns, and boutique resorts elsewhere on this verdant island.

3 San Juan Island. The political seat and commercial center of the archipelago, and the only one of the islands with direct ferry service to British Columbia, San Juan is home to the bustling town of Friday Harbor, which abounds with good shopping and cheery cafés. There is a national historic park, and you can explore fine beaches, great roads for biking, and marinas that rent kayaks and boats.

GETTING ORIENTED

Spending time on the San Juans is all about connecting with the sea. A trip here requires a bit more travel, planning, and expense, but visitors nevertheless flock here to spot migrating whales, go kayaking, chill out in endearingly informal inns, and dine on creative, surprisingly urbane cuisine. The most popular boating activities include whale-watching, but each island has its share of parks, bluffs, and coastline to explore. The San Juan Islands are part of the same archipelago as the Gulf Islands of British Columbia—they're actually closer to Victoria, BC, than they are to Seattle. The closest Washington cities to them are Anacortes and Bellingham, about 90 minutes north of Seattle.

Updated
by Andrew
Collins

The coastal waters of the Pacific Northwest, between mainland Washington and Vancouver Island, contain hundreds of islands, some little more than sandbars, others rising 3,000 feet. Among these, the San Juans are considered by many to be the loveliest.

About 100 miles northwest of Seattle, these romantic islands abound with breathtaking rolling pastures, rocky shorelines, and thickly forested ridges, and their quaint villages draw art lovers, foodies, and city folk seeking serenity. Inns are easygoing and well-appointed, and many restaurants are helmed by highly talented chefs emphasizing local ingredients.

Each of the San Juans maintains a distinct character, though all share in the archipelago's blessings of serene farmlands, unspoiled coves, blue-green or gray tidal waters, and radiant light. Offshore, seals haul out on sandbanks and orcas patrol the deep channels. Since the late 1990s, gray whales have begun to summer here, instead of heading north to their arctic breeding grounds; you may see the occasional minke or humpback whale frolicking in the kelp.

Seattleites often escape to the San Juans in the course of a soggy, gray Northwest winter. There are 176 named islands in the archipelago. Sixty are populated (though most have only a house or two), and 10 are state marine parks, some of which are accessible only to kayakers navigating the Cascadia Marine Trail.

The San Juan Islands have valleys and mountains where eagles soar, and forests and leafy glens where the tiny island deer browse. Even a species of prickly pear cactus (*Opuntia fragilis*) grows here. Beaches can be of sand or shingle (covered in small pebbles), but all are scenic and invite beachcombers and kayakers to explore them. The islands are visited by ducks and swans, herons and hawks, otters and whales. The main draw is the great outdoors, but there's plenty to do once you've seen the whales or hiked. Each island, even tiny Lopez, has at least one commercial center, where you'll find shops, restaurants, and history museums. Not surprisingly, many artists take inspiration from the dramatic surroundings, and each island has a collection of galleries; Friday Harbor

11

even has an impressive sculpture park and art museum. Lavender and alpaca farms, spas and yoga studios, whale museums and lighthouse tours—the San Juans have a little bit of everything.

THE SAN JUAN ISLANDS PLANNER

WHEN TO GO

This part of Washington has a mild, maritime climate. Winter temperatures average in the low 40s, while summer temps hover in the mid 70s. July and August are by far the most popular months to visit these tourism-dependent islands—they can get busy during this time, with resorts, boating tours, and ferries often at capacity. To beat the crowds and avoid the worst of the wet weather, visit in late spring or early fall—September and early October can be fair and stunningly gorgeous, as can May and early June. Hotel rates are generally lower everywhere during these shoulder seasons—and even lower once the winter drizzle starts.

■TIP➔ Orcas, Lopez, and San Juan islands are extremely popular in high season; securing hotel reservations in advance is essential. Car lines for the ferries during this time can be very long. If you're traveling light, consider walking or biking on. Lot parking at Anacortes is $10 per day and $40 per week in summer and half that October–April.

FESTIVALS

August: The Orcas Island Chamber Music Festival (☎ *866/492–0003* ⊕ *www.oicmf.org*) comprises more than two weeks of "classical music with a view." These concerts are immensely popular with chamber-music fans around the Pacific Northwest.

October: Artstock (☎ *360/378–6550* ⊕ *www.artstocksanjuanisland.com*) is a weekend-long festival of open-studio and gallery art tours and receptions taking place in Friday Harbor during the first weekend of the month.

GETTING HERE AND AROUND

AIR TRAVEL

Port of Friday Harbor is the main San Juan Islands airport, but there are also small airports on Lopez, Shaw, and Orcas islands. Seaplanes land on the waterfront at Friday Harbor and Roche Harbor on San Juan Island; Rosario Resort, Deer Harbor, and West Sound on Orcas Island; and Fisherman Bay on Lopez Island. Daily scheduled flights link the San Juan Islands with mainland airports at Anacortes, Bellingham, and Seattle-Tacoma International Airport. Most of these airlines also offer charter services, and Island Air has sightseeing flights.

If traffic and ferry lines really aren't your thing, consider hopping aboard a seaplane for the quick flight from Seattle. **Kenmore Air** offers several daily departures from Seattle. Flying isn't cheap—around $120–$160 each way—but the scenic, hour-long flight is an experience in itself.

Air Contacts Kenmore Air. This is a major provider of regular flights from Seattle to Orcas, San Juan, and Lopez islands. ⊠ *Kenmore Air Harbor, 6321 N.E. 175th St., Kenmore* ☎ *425/486–1257, 866/435–9524* ⊕ *www.kenmoreair.com.*

San Juan Islands

Northwest Sky Ferry. This small airline has daily flights from Bellingham to all of the San Juan Islands. ✉ *4167 Mitchell Way, Bellingham* ☎ *360/676–9999* 🌐 *www.nwskyferry.com.* **San Juan Airlines.** This is a reliable option for daily flights to the islands from Bellingham and Anacortes. ☎ *800/874–4434* 🌐 *www.sanjuanairlines.com.*

CAR TRAVEL

Most visitors arrive by car, which is the best way to explore these mostly rural islands comprehensively, especially if you plan on visiting for more than a couple of days. You can also park your car at the Anacortes ferry terminal ($10/day or $40/week high season, and half that fall through spring), as fares are cheaper and lines much shorter for passengers without cars. B&B owners can usually pick guests up at the ferry terminal by prior arrangement, and you can rely on bikes and occasional taxis or on-island car rentals (on San Juan and Orcas) for getting around. From Seattle, it's a 90-minute drive via Interstate 5 north and Highway 20 west to reach Anacortes.

Island roads are narrow and often windy, with one or two lanes. Slow down and hug the shoulder when passing another car on a one-lane road. Expect rough patches, potholes, deer and rabbits, bicyclists, and other hazards—plus the distractions of sweeping water views. There are a few car-rental agencies on San Juan and Orcas, with daily rates running about $60 to $100 in summer, and as much as 25% less off-season. You'll likely save money renting a car on the mainland, even factoring in the cost of ferry transport (which is about $20 to $30 for a standard vehicle, plus driver and passengers, depending on which island you're headed to).

Rental Car Contacts M and W Rental Cars. This agency has an office on San Juan Island and also rents cars by arrangement on Orcas Island. ✉ *725 Spring St., Friday Harbor* ☎ *360/376–5266 Orcas, 360/378–2794 San Juan* ⊕ *www.sanjuanauto.com.* **Orcas Island Rental Cars.** This agency on Orcas Island rents both cars and vans; staff will meet you with a car at the ferry or deliver it to a location of your choice. ✉ *Orcas Island* ☎ *360/376–7433* ⊕ *www. orcasislandshuttle.com.* **Susie's Mopeds.** This company on San Juan rents cars and mopeds. ✉ *125 Nichols St., Friday Harbor* ☎ *360/378–5244, 800/532–0087* ⊕ *www.susiesmopeds.com.*

FERRY TRAVEL

The Washington State Ferries system can become overloaded during peak travel times, leading to lengthy waits at the Anacortes terminal for passengers bringing their vehicles aboard. Always arrive at least 45 minutes ahead of your departure, and as much as 90 minutes ahead on summer weekends or holidays, when you can also expect heavier road traffic reaching Anacortes. It's rarely a problem to get a walk-on spot, although arriving a bit early to ensure you get a ticket is wise. ⇨ *For more information, see Getting Here and Around in individual islands below.*

Ferry Contacts Washington State Ferries. These state-operated ferries depart from Anacortes, about 75 miles north of Seattle, for the San Juan Islands. That same ferry service also connects the San Juans to one another, and San Juan Island with Sidney, BC, near Victoria. ✉ *2100 Ferry Terminal Rd., Anacortes* ☎ *206/464–6400, 888/808–7977* ⊕ *www.wsdot.wa.gov/ferries.*

RESTAURANTS

The San Juans have myriad small farms and restaurants serving local foods and fresh-harvested seafood, and culinary agritourism—the recreational act of visiting local farmers, growers, and chefs at their places of business—is on the rise. *Prices in the reviews are the average cost of a main course at dinner or, if dinner is not served, at lunch.*

HOTELS

With the exception of Lopez Island, which has just a handful of lovely but rather homey inns, accommodations in the San Juans can be quite plush. Rosario Resort & Spa on Orcas Island is a favorite spot for special-occasion splurges, and both Orcas and San Juan have some very upscale inns. These often have perks like ornate breakfast and on-site outfitters and tour operators. *Prices in the reviews are the lowest cost of a standard double room in high season.*

LOPEZ ISLAND

45 mins by ferry from Anacortes.

Known affectionately as "Slow-pez," the closest significantly populated island to the mainland is a broad, bay-encircled bit of terrain amid sparkling blue seas, a place where cabinlike homes are tucked into the woods, and boats are moored in lonely coves. Of the three San Juan islands with facilities to accommodate overnight visitors, Lopez has the smallest population (approximately 2,400), and with its old orchards, weathered barns, and rolling green pastures, it's the most rustic and least crowded in the archipelago. Gently sloping roads cut wide curves through golden farmlands and trace the edges of pebbly beaches, while peaceful trails wind through thick patches of forest. Sweeping country views make Lopez a favorite year-round biking locale, and except for the long hill up from the ferry docks, most roads and designated bike paths are easy for novices to negotiate.

The only settlement is Lopez Village, really just a cluster of cafés and boutiques, as well as a summer market and outdoor theater, visitor information center, and grocery store. Other attractions—such as seasonal berry-picking farms, small wineries, kitschy galleries, intimate restaurants, and secluded bed-and-breakfasts—are scattered around the island.

GETTING HERE AND AROUND

The Washington State Ferries crossing from Anacortes take about 45 minutes; round-trip fares are about $13 per person, $40 for a car and driver. One-hour flights from Seattle cost about $120 to $160 each way. You can get around the island by car (bring your own—there are no rentals) or bike; there are bike-rental facilities by the ferry terminal.

ESSENTIALS

Visitor Information Lopez Island Chamber of Commerce ⊠ *6 Old Post Rd., Lopez Island* ☎ *360/468–4664, 877/433–2789* ⊕ *www.lopezisland.com.*

EXPLORING

Lopez Island Historical Museum. Artifacts from the region's Native American tribes and early settlers include some impressive ship and small-boat models and maps of local landmarks. You can also listen to fascinating digital recordings of early settlers discussing life on Lopez Island. ⊠ *Weeks Rd. and Washburn Pl.* ☎ *360/468–2049* ⊕ *www. lopezmuseum.org* ☉ *May–Sept., Wed.–Sun. noon–4, Oct.–Apr., by appointment.*

Lopez Island Vineyard. This popular winery is spread over 6 acres on Fisherman Bay Road and has a tasting room right in the heart of Lopez Village. The vineyards and orchards yield estate-grown white wines, including Madeleine Angevine and Siegerrebe; sweet wines using raspberries, blackberries, and other local fruits; and a number of reds sourced from eastern Washington's Yakima Valley, including Malbec, Cabernet Sauvignon, and Sangiovese. ⊠ *724 Fisherman Bay Rd., Lopez Island* ☎ *360/468–3644* ⊕ *www.lopezislandvineyards.com*

Free ⓢ July–Sept., Wed.–Sat. noon–5; Mar.–June and Oct.–mid-Dec., Fri.–Sat. noon–5.

Fodor's Choice
★
Shark Reef Sanctuary. A quiet forest trail along beautiful Shark Reef leads to an isolated headland jutting out above the bay. The sounds of raucous barks and squeals mean you're nearly there, and eventually you may see throngs of seals and seagulls on the rocky islets across from the point. Bring binoculars to spot bald eagles in the trees as you walk, and to view sea otters frolicking in the waves near the shore. The trail starts at the Shark Reef Road parking lot south of Lopez Village, and it's a 15-minute walk to the headland. ⊠ *Shark Reef Rd.* ✛ *2 miles south of Lopez Island Airport* *Free ⓢ Daily dawn–dusk.*

Spencer Spit State Park. Set on a spit along the Cascadia Marine Trail for kayakers, this popular spot for summer camping is on former Native American clamming, crabbing, and fishing grounds. A variety of campsites are available, from primitive tent sites to full hookups. This is one of the few Washington beaches where cars are permitted. ⊠ *521 A. Bakerview Rd., Lopez Island* ☎ *360/468–2251* ⊕ *www.parks.wa.gov/parks* *Free; Discover Pass ($10 one-day, $30 annual) required for parking ⓢ Mar.–Oct., daily 8–dusk.*

WHERE TO EAT AND STAY

For expanded hotel reviews, visit Fodors.com.

$$$
AMERICAN
Fodor's Choice
★
✕ **Bay Café.** Boats dock right outside this pretty waterside house at the entrance to Fisherman Bay. In winter, sunlight streams into the window-framed dining room; in summer you can relax on the wraparound porch before a gorgeous sunset panorama. The menu is highlighted by regionally sourced meats and seafood, including sea scallop risotto with porcini, leeks, and crème fraîche, and grilled rib eye with a green-peppercorn demi-glace, which is best enjoyed with a side of bacon-studded roasted brussels sprouts. Homemade sorbet and a fine crème caramel are among the desserts. Weekend breakfasts draw huge crowds. Ⓢ *Average main: $28* ⊠ *9 Old Post Rd.* ☎ *360/468–3700* ⊕ *www. bay-cafe.com ⓢ Closed Mon.–Tues. No lunch weekdays Oct.–May.*

$
BAKERY
✕ **Holly B's Bakery.** Tucked into a small, cabinlike strip of businesses set back from the water, this cozy, wood-paneled dining room is the highlight of daytime dining in the village. Fresh pastries and big homemade breakfasts are the draws. Sunny summer mornings bring diners out onto the patio, where kids play and parents relax. Ⓢ *Average main: $6* ⊠ *Lopez Plaza* ☎ *360/468–2133* ⊕ *www.hollybsbakery.com* ▭ *No credit cards ⓢ Closed Dec.–Mar. No dinner.*

$$
B&B/INN
🏠 **Edenwild.** In this large Victorian-style farmhouse, surrounded by gardens and framed by Fisherman Bay, large rooms are each painted or papered in different pastel shades and furnished with simple antiques; some have claw-foot tubs and brick fireplaces. **Pros:** bicycles provided; nice breakfast buffet using local produce; handy location. **Cons:** few in-room amenities (no TVs); some guests have reported uneven service. Ⓢ *Rooms from: $170* ⊠ *132 Lopez Rd.* ☎ *360/468–3238, 800/606–0662* ⊕ *www.edenwildinn.com* ⇲ *6 rooms, 2 suites* ⦿ *Breakfast.*

$$ **Mackaye Harbor Inn.** This former sea captain's house, built in 1904,
B&B/INN rises two stories above the beach at the southern end of the island and
Fodor'sChoice accommodates guests in cheerfully furnished rooms with golden-oak
★ and brass details and wicker furniture; three have views of MacKaye
Harbor. **Pros:** fantastic water views; mountain bikes (free) and kayaks
(reasonable daily fee) available; friendly and attentive hosts. **Cons:** on
far end of the island; several miles from the ferry terminal and airport;
some bathrooms are across the hall from rooms. $ *Rooms from: $175*
⌂ *949 MacKaye Harbor Rd., Lopez Island* ☎ *360/468–2253, 888/314–
6140* ⊕ *www.mackayeharborinn.com* ⤳ *4 rooms, 1 suite* ⎮⊙⎮ *Breakfast.*

SPORTS AND THE OUTDOORS

BICYCLING

Mountain-bike rental rates start at around $7 an hour and $30 a day.
Reservations are recommended, particularly in summer.

Lopez Bicycle Works. At the marina 4 miles from the ferry, this full-
service operation can bring bicycles to your door or the ferry. In addi-
tion to cruisers and mountain bikes, the shop also rents tandem and
recumbent bikes. ⌂ *2847 Fisherman Bay Rd.* ☎ *360/468–2847* ⊕ *www.
lopezbicycleworks.com.*

SEA KAYAKING

Cascadia Kayaks. Here you can rent kayaks for half days or full days.
The shop also organizes half-day, full-day, and two- to three-day guided
tours. Hour-long private lessons are available, too, if you need a little
coaching before going out on your own. ⌂ *135 Lopez Rd., Lopez Island*
☎ *360/468–3008* ⊕ *www.cascadiakayaks.com.*

Lopez Island Sea Kayak. Open May–September at Fisherman Bay, this
outfitter has a huge selection of kayaks, both plastic and fiberglass tour-
ing models. Rentals are by the hour or day, and the company can deliver
kayaks to any point on the island for an additional fee. ⌂ *Marinas on
Fisherman Bay, Lopez Island* ☎ *360/468–2847* ⊕ *www.lopezkayaks.
com.*

SHOPPING

Chimera Gallery. This local artists' cooperative exhibits and sells
crafts, jewelry, and fine art. ⌂ *Village Rd.* ☎ *360/468–3265* ⊕ *www.
chimeragallery.com.*

Islehaven Books. This longtime bookseller is stocked with publications on
San Juan Islands history and activities, as well as tomes about the Pacific
Northwest. There's also a good selection of mysteries, literary novels,
children's books, and craft kits, plus greeting cards, art prints, and
maps. Many of the items sold here are the works of local writers, artists,
and photographers. ⌂ *211 Lopez Rd., Plaza Building* ☎ *360/468–2132*
⊕ *www.islehavenbooks.com.*

ORCAS ISLAND

75 mins by ferry from Anacortes.

Orcas Island, the largest of the San Juans, is blessed with wide, pastoral valleys and scenic ridges that rise high above the neighboring waters. (At 2,409 feet, Orcas's Mt. Constitution is the highest peak in the San Juans.) Spanish explorers set foot here in 1791, and the island is actually named for their ship—not for the black-and-white whales that frolic in the surrounding waters. The island was also the home of Native American tribes, whose history is reflected in such places as Pole Pass, where the Lummi people used kelp and cedar-bark nets to catch ducks, and Massacre Bay, where in 1858 a tribe from southeast Alaska attacked a Lummi fishing village.

Today farmers, fishermen, artists, retirees, and summer-home owners make up the population of about 4,500. Houses are spaced far apart, and the island's few towns typically have just one major road running through them. Low-keyed resorts dotting the island's edges are evidence of the thriving local tourism industry. The beauty of this island is beyond compare; Orcas is a favorite place for weekend getaways from the Seattle area any time of the year, as well as one of the state's top settings for summer weddings.

GETTING HERE AND AROUND

The Washington State Ferries crossing from Anacortes to Orcas Village, in the island's Westsound area, takes about 75 minutes; round-trip fares are about $13 per person, $50 for a car and driver. One-hour flights from Seattle cost about $120 to $160 each way. Planes land at Deer Harbor, Eastsound, Westsound, and at the Rosario Resort and Spa.

The best way to get around the island is either by car or by bicycle. Most resorts and inns offer transfers from the ferry terminal.

ESSENTIALS

Visitor Information Orcas Island Chamber of Commerce ✉ *65 N. Beach Rd., Eastsound* ☎ *360/376–2273* ⊕ *www.orcasislandchamber.com.*

EXPLORING

Eastsound. The main town on Orcas Island lies at the head of the East Sound channel, which nearly divides the island in two. Small shops here sell jewelry, pottery, and crafts by local artisans. Several stores and restaurants stretch along Prune Alley.

FAMILY **Funhouse.** This big, nonprofit activity center and museum is especially popular with families. Interactive exhibits on age, hearing, kinetics, and video production, among other subjects, are all educational. Kids can explore an arts-and-crafts yurt, an audio production room, kinetic sculptures, a library, Internet stations, and more. Sports activities include indoor pitching cages and games, as well as an outdoor playground. Kids and adults can also take classes on music, theater, digital film, and poetry. There are free programs for preteens and teenagers on Friday nights from 6 to 11 (hint to Mom and Dad, who might want to enjoy dinner alone on this romantic island). ✉ *30 Pea Patch*

La., Eastsound ☎ 360/376–7177 🌐 www.funhousecommons.org 🎟 $5 ⏲ Sept.–June, weekdays 3–5:30; July and Aug., weekdays 1–5.

Fodor's Choice ★ **Moran State Park.** This pristine patch of wilderness comprises 5,200 acres of hilly, old-growth forests dotted with sparkling lakes, in the middle of which rises the island's highest point, 2,409-foot Mt. Constitution. A drive to the summit affords exhilarating views of the islands, the Cascades, the Olympics, and Vancouver Island. The observation tower up here was built by the Civilian Conservation Corps in the 1930s. You can explore the terrain along 30 miles of hiking trails and choose from among 151 campsites if you'd like to stay longer (reservations are available May–September, or first-come, first-served at other times). ✉ *Mt. Constitution Rd., Olga ☎ 360/376–2326, 888/226–7688 for reservations 🌐 www.parks.wa.gov/parks 🎟 Parking requires Discovery Pass ($10 one day, $30 annual) ⏲ Daily dawn–dusk.*

WHERE TO EAT

$$$ MODERN AMERICAN 🍴 **Allium.** Talented chef Lisa Nakamura has studied botany, worked as a flight attendant, and trained under French Laundry's Thomas Keller—all experiences that have helped inform her spirited, innovative, and global-meets-local approach to cuisine at this dapper but informal restaurant in the center of Eastsound, with an expansive deck overlooking the water. Flavorful fare like cider-glazed bone-in Lopez Island pork chop and a daily fish of the day with house-made red curry and a five-spice rice cake reveal Nakamura's bold but simple approach to cuisine. There's a fantastic Northwest-intensive wine list. Reservations are a good idea on summer weekends. [$] *Average main: $27* ✉ *310 Main St., Eastsound ☎ 360/376–4904 🌐 www.alliumonorcas.com ⏲ Closed Mon.–Wed. in winter. No lunch.*

$$ MODERN AMERICAN Fodor's Choice ★ 🍴 **Doe Bay Cafe.** Most of the tables in this warmly rustic dining room at Doe Bay Resort overlook the tranquil body of water for which the café is named. This is a popular stop for breakfast, lunch, or dinner before or after hiking or biking in nearby Moran State Park—starting your day off with an olive oil–poached local duck egg with spicy slow-cooked greens, smoked mushrooms, and grits will provide you with plenty of fuel for recreation. The kitchen uses ingredients foraged from the lush resort garden (tours are available) in such artful, healthy dinner creations as crisp-skinned wild salmon with roe, fennel confit, braised cabbage, and pickled apples; and crushed potatoes served with leek ash, allium aioli, braised sauerkraut, and smoked kale. [$] *Average main: $22* ✉ *107 Doe Bay Rd., Olga ☎ 360/376–8059 🌐 www.doebay.com/cafe.html ⏲ Closed Tues.–Thurs. No lunch Mon. and Fri. Oct.–May.*

$$$ PACIFIC NORTHWEST 🍴 **Inn at Ship Bay.** This restaurant at this stylish inn just a mile from Eastsound offers among the most memorable dining experiences on the island. Tucked into a renovated 1869 farmhouse, the dining room and bar serve food that's heavy on local, seasonal ingredients. Island greens, fruits, and seafood are served alongside a regionally focused wine list, and the results are spectacular. In early summer, for example, local veal is accompanied by a wild leek–potato puree and black currant–red wine sauce. Even the bread is memorable; the restaurant serves housemade

Rosario Point at Rosario Resort, on Orcas Island in the San Juans

sourdough from a starter that's more than 100 years old. $ *Average main: $28* ✉ *326 Olga Rd.* ☎ *360/376–5886* ⊕ *www.innatshipbay.com* ⊗ *Closed Sun. and Mon. and mid-Dec.–mid-Mar. No lunch.*

WHERE TO STAY

For expanded hotel reviews, visit Fodors.com.

$$　⬚ **All Dream Cottages and Kingfish Inn.** Spacious units in this atmospheric
B&B/INN　1902 house are equipped with a king or queen bed, private bath, and
all the serenity a guest could ever want, while four lovely cottages
come with plenty of privacy and beautiful views. **Pros:** decor is taste-
ful and contemporary; good café; water views. **Cons:** somewhat small
bathrooms in some rooms; although on the lesser-visited shore of West
Sound, the rooms do get some noise from road and busy marina; two-
night minimum. $ *Rooms from: $197* ✉ *Crow Valley Rd., at Deer
Harbor Rd.* ☎ *360/376–2500* ⊕ *www.kingfishinn.com* ⇨ *3 rooms, 1
suite, 4 cottages* ⊗ *Closed early Jan.–mid-Feb.* ⦿ *No meals.*

$　⬚ **Deer Harbor Inn.** Eight wood-paneled rooms have balconies and
B&B/INN　peeled-log furniture, while four cottages and the Harborview Suite
have whirlpool tubs and propane fireplaces; two houses have kitchens
and laundry facilities. **Pros:** cute spa cabin for solo or couples' mas-
sage; cottages are good for longer stays. **Cons:** decor is a bit outdated;
cottages are the best but also the most expensive accommodations.
$ *Rooms from: $149* ✉ *33 Inn La., Deer Harbor* ☎ *360/376–4110*
⊕ *www.deerharborinn.com* ⇨ *8 rooms, 1 suite, 4 cottages, 2 houses*
⦿ *Breakfast.*

$ RESORT 🏨 **Rosario Resort and Spa.** Shipbuilding magnate Robert Moran built this Arts and Crafts–style mansion on Cascade Bay in 1906, and it is now the centerpiece of a resort where 20 rooms and suites are in a nearby waterfront building and have sweeping views. **Pros:** gorgeous location; new management has immensely improved service and refurbished rooms; great spa. **Cons:** often busy with weddings and special events. [$] *Rooms from: $149* ✉ *1400 Rosario Rd., Eastsound* ☎ *360/376–2222, 800/562–8820* 🌐 *www.rosarioresort.com* 🛏 *16 rooms, 4 suites* 🍴 *No meals.*

$$ B&B/INN 🏨 **Turtleback Farm Inn.** Eighty acres of meadow, forest, and farmland in the shadow of Turtleback Mountain surround these pleasant and homey rooms in the carefully restored late-19th-century green-clapboard farmhouse and the newer cedar Orchard House. **Pros:** lovely grounds to stroll through; good location reasonably close to marina, ferries, and village of Eastsound. **Cons:** Orchard House gets some traffic noise; two-night minimum in high season. [$] *Rooms from: $165* ✉ *1981 Crow Valley Rd.* ☎ *360/376–3914, 800/376–4914* 🌐 *www.turtlebackinn.com* 🛏 *11 rooms* 🍴 *Breakfast.*

SPORTS AND THE OUTDOORS

BICYCLES AND MOPEDS

Mountain bikes rent for about $30 per day or $100 per week. Tandem, recumbent, and electric bikes rent for about $50 per day. Mopeds rent for $20 to $30 per hour or $60 to $70 per day. Three-wheel, two-passenger electric Scootcars rent for about $50 per hour or $140 per day.

Dolphin Bay Bicycles. This shop at the ferry landing rents road, mountain, and BMX bikes for children and adults. ✉ *Orcas Ferry Landing* ☎ *360/376–4157, 360/376–6734* 🌐 *www.rockisland.com/~dolphin.*

Orcas Moped Rentals. You can rent mopeds, three-wheel Scootcars, and bicycles at this agency by the ferry landing. ✉ *65 Orcas Hill Rd., Eastsound* ☎ *360/376–5266* 🌐 *www.orcasmopeds.com.*

Wildlife Cycles. This trusty shop rents bikes and can recommend great routes all over the island. ✉ *350 N. Beach Rd., Eastsound* ☎ *360/376–4708* 🌐 *www.wildlifecycles.com.*

BOATING AND SAILING

Orcas Boat Rentals. You can rent a variety of sailboats, outboards, and skiffs for full- and half-day trips, as well as book custom charter cruises, with this company. ✉ *5164 Deer Harbor Rd., Deer Harbor* ☎ *360/376–7616* 🌐 *www.orcasboats.com.*

West Beach Resort. This is a good option for renting motorized boats, kayaks and canoes, and fishing gear on the island's northwest shore. The resort is also a popular spot for divers, who can fill their tanks here. ✉ *190 Waterfront Way, Eastsound* ☎ *360/376–2240, 877/937–8224* 🌐 *www.westbeachresort.com.*

SEA KAYAKING

All equipment is usually included in a rental package or tour. One-hour trips cost around $30; three-hour tours, about $70; and day tours, $95–$120.

11

Orcas Outdoors Sea Kayak Tours. This outfitter offers one-, two-, and three-hour journeys, as well as day trips, overnight tours, and rentals. ⊠ *Orcas Ferry Landing, Eastsound* ☎ *360/376–4611* ⊕ *www. orcasoutdoors.com.*

Shearwater Adventures. This established company holds kayaking classes and runs three-hour, day, and overnight tours from Rosario, Deer Harbor, West Beach, and Doe Bay resorts. ⊠ *138 N. Beach Rd., Eastsound* ☎ *360/376–4699* ⊕ *www.shearwaterkayaks.com.*

WHALE-WATCHING

Cruises, which run about four hours, are scheduled daily in summer and once or twice weekly at other times. The cost is around $75 per person, and boats hold 20 to 40 people. Wear warm clothing and bring a snack.

Deer Harbor Charters. This eco-friendly tour company (the first in the San Juans to use biodiesel) offers whale-watching cruises around the island straits, with departures from both Deer Harbor Marina and Rosario Resort. Outboards and skiffs are also available, as is fishing gear. ⊠ *Deer Harbor Rd., Deer Harbor* ☎ *360/376–5989, 800/544–5758* ⊕ *www.deerharborcharters.com.*

Eclipse Charters. In addition to tours that search around Orcas Island for whale pods and other sea life, this charter company offers lighthouse tours. ⊠ *Orcas Island Ferry Landing, Eastsound* ☎ *360/376–6566* ⊕ *www.orcasislandwhales.com.*

SHOPPING

FodorsChoice
★
Crow Valley Pottery. Since 1959 this gallery with a lovely wooded setting has exhibited beautiful and distinctive ceramics, metalworks, blown glass, and sculptures; there's also a second branch in Eastsound's village center at 269 Eastman Road. ⊠ *2274 Orcas Rd., Eastsound* ☎ *360/376–4260, 877/512–8184* ⊕ *www.crowvalley.com.*

Darvill's Bookstore. This island favorite specializes in literary fiction, nautical literature, local guidebooks, and more. ⊠ *1 Main St., Eastsound* ☎ *360/376–2135* ⊕ *www.darvillsbookstore.com.*

Orcas Island Artworks. Stop by this cooperative gallery to see the impressive displays pottery, sculpture, jewelry, art glass, paintings, and quilts by resident artists. ⊠ *11 Point Lawrence Rd., Olga* ☎ *360/376–4408* ⊕ *www.orcasartworks.com.*

SAN JUAN ISLAND

45 mins by ferry from Orcas Island, 75–90 mins by ferry from Anacortes or Sidney, BC (near Victoria).

San Juan is the cultural and commercial hub of the archipelago that shares its name. Friday Harbor, the county seat, is larger and more vibrant than any of the towns on Orcas or Lopez, yet San Juan still has miles of rural roads, uncrowded beaches, and rolling woodlands. It's easy to get here, too, making San Juan the preferred destination for travelers who have time to visit only one island.

Lummi Indians were the first settlers on San Juan, with encampments along the north end of the island. North-end beaches were especially busy during the annual salmon migration, when hundreds of tribal members would gather along the shoreline to fish, cook, and exchange news. Many of the Lummi tribe were killed by smallpox and other imported diseases in the 18th and 19th centuries. Smallpox Bay was where tribal members plunged into the icy water to cool the fevers that came with the disease.

The 18th century brought explorers from England and Spain, but the island remained sparsely populated until the mid-1800s. From the 1880s Friday Harbor and its newspaper were controlled by lime-company owner and Republican bigwig John S. McMillin, who virtually ran San Juan Island as a personal fiefdom from 1886 until his death in 1936. The town's main street, rising from the harbor and ferry landing up the slopes of a modest hill, hasn't changed much in the past few decades, though the cafés and shops have become increasingly urbane.

GETTING HERE AND AROUND

With ferry connections from both Anacortes and Sidney, BC (on Vancouver Island, near Victoria), San Juan is the most convenient of the islands to reach, and the island is easily explore by car, public transportation, and bicycle.

AIR TRAVEL One-hour flights from Seattle to San Juan Airport, Friday Harbor, or Roche Harbor cost about $120 to $160 each way.

BUS TRAVEL San Juan Transit & Tours operates shuttle buses from mid-May to mid-September. Hop on at Friday Harbor, the main town, to get to all the island's significant points and parks, including the San Juan Vineyards, Krystal Acres Alpaca Ranch, Lime Kiln Point State Park, and Snug Harbor and Roche Harbor resorts. Different buses call on different stops, so be sure to check the schedule before you plan your day. Tickets are $5 one-way, or $15 for a day pass.

Contact **San Juan Transit & Tours** ☎ *360/378–8887* ⊕ *sanjuantransit.com.*

BOAT AND FERRY TRAVEL The Washington State Ferries crossings from Anacortes to Friday Harbor takes about 75 to 90 minutes; round-trip fares are about $13 per person, $60 for a car and driver. It's about the same distance from Sidney, BC, on Vancouver Island—this service is available twice daily in summer and one daily spring and fall (there's no BC service in winter). Round-trip fares are about $25 per person, $90 for car and driver. Clipper Navigation operates the passenger-only *Victoria Clipper* jet catamaran service between Pier 69 in Seattle and Friday Harbor. Boats leave daily mid-May–early September (and also on weekends through the end of September) at 7:45 am; reservations are strongly recommended. The journey costs $70 to $90 round-trip, depending on the day.

Contacts **Clipper Navigation** ☎ 250/382–8100 in Victoria, 206/448–5000 in Seattle, 800/888–2535 in the U.S. ⊕ www.clippervacations.com/ferry.

ESSENTIALS

Look to the San Juan Islands Visitors Bureau for general information on all of the islands—the website is very useful. The San Juan Island Chamber of Commerce has a visitor center (open daily 10–4) in Friday Harbor where you can grab brochures and ask for advice.

Visitor Information **San Juan Island Chamber of Commerce** ⊠ 135 Spring St., Friday Harbor ☎ 360/378–5240 ⊕ www.sanjuanisland.org. **San Juan Islands Visitors Bureau** ⊠ The Technology Center, 640 Mullis St., Suites 210–211, Friday Harbor ☎ 360/378–3277, 888/468–3701 ⊕ www.visitsanjuans.com.

EXPLORING

TOP ATTRACTIONS

FAMILY

Fodor's Choice

★

Lime Kiln Point State Park. To watch whales cavorting in Haro Strait, head to these 36 acres on San Juan's western side just 6 miles from Friday Harbor. A rocky coastal trail leads to lookout points and a little white 1919 lighthouse. The best period for sighting whales is from the end of April through August, but a resident pod of orcas regularly cruises past the point. This park is also a beautiful spot to soak in a summer sunset, with expansive views of Vancouver Island and beyond. ⊠ 1567 Westside Rd., San Juan Island ☎ 360/378–2044 ⊕ www.parks.wa.gov/parks ☞ Free; Discovery Pass required for parking, $10 single-day or $30 annual ☉ Daily 8 am–dusk; lighthouse tours May–Sept. at 3 and 5.

Pelindaba Lavender Farm. Wander a spectacular 20-acre valley smothered with endless rows of fragrant purple-and-gold lavender blossoms. The oils are distilled for use in therapeutic, botanical, and household products, all created on-site. The farm hosts the very popular San Juan Island Lavender Festival in late July. If you can't make it to the farm, stop at the outlet in the Friday Harbor Center on First Street, where you can buy their products and sample delicious lavender-infused baked goods and beverages. ⊠ 45 Hawthorn La., Friday Harbor ☎ 360/378–4248, 866/819–1911 ⊕ www.pelindabalavender.com ☞ Free ☉ May–Oct., Wed.–Sun. 9:30–5:30.

FAMILY

Fodor's Choice

★

San Juan Island National Historic Park. Fortifications and other 19th-century military installments commemorate the Pig War, in which the United States and Great Britain nearly went to war over their respective claims on the San Juan Islands. The dispute began in 1859 when an American settler killed a British soldier's pig, and escalated until roughly 500 American soldiers and 2,200 British soldiers with five warships were poised for battle. Fortunately, no blood was spilled, and the disagreement was finally settled in 1872 in the Americans' favor, with Kaiser Wilhelm I of Germany as arbitrator.

The park comprises two separate areas on opposite sides of the island. English Camp, in a sheltered cove of Garrison Bay on the northern end, includes a blockhouse, a commissary, and barracks. A popular (though steep) hike is to the top of Young Hill, from which you can get a great view of the northwest side of the island. American Camp, on the southern end, has a visitor center and the remains of fortifications; it stretches along driftwood-strewn beaches. Many of the American Camp's walking trails are through prairie; in the evening, dozens of rabbits emerge from their warrens to nibble in the fields. Great views greet you from the top of the Mt. Finlayson Trail—if you're lucky, you might be able to see Mt. Baker and Mt. Rainier along with the Olympics. From June to August you can take guided hikes and see reenactments of 1860s-era military life. ⊠ *park headquarters, 125 Spring St., American Camp, 6 miles southeast of Friday Harbor; English Camp, 9 miles northwest of Friday Harbor, Friday Harbor* ☎ *360/378–2240* ⊕ *www.nps.gov/sajh* ☎ *Free* ☉ *American Camp visitor center, June–Aug., daily 8:30–5; Sept.–mid-Oct., daily 8:30–4:30; mid-Oct.–May, Wed.–Sun. 8:30–4:30. English Camp visitor center, June–early Sept., daily 9–5; grounds open daily dawn–11 pm.*

WORTH NOTING

FAMILY **Krystal Acres Alpaca Farm.** On this enormous swath of farmland on the west side of the island, keep an eye out for the dozens of alpacas from South America. In the big barn, the shop displays beautiful, high-quality clothing and crafts, all handmade from alpaca hair. ⊠ *152 Blazing Tree Rd., Friday Harbor* ☎ *360/378–6125* ⊕ *www.krystalacres.com* ☎ *Free* ☉ *Apr.–Dec., daily 10–5; Jan.–Mar., daily 11–4.*

Roche Harbor. It's hard to believe that fashionable Roche Harbor at the northern end of San Juan Island was once the most important producer of builder's lime on the West Coast. In 1882 John S. McMillin gained control of the lime company and expanded production. But even in its heyday as a limestone quarrying village, Roche Harbor was known for abundant flowers and welcoming accommodations. McMillin transformed a bunkhouse into private lodgings for his invited guests, who included such notables as Teddy Roosevelt. The guesthouse is now the Hotel de Haro (part of the ⇨ *Roche Harbor Resort*), which displays period photographs and artifacts in its lobby. The staff has maps of the old quarry, kilns, and the Mausoleum, an eerie Greek-inspired memorial to McMillin.

McMillin's heirs operated the quarries and plant until 1956, when they sold the company to the Tarte family. Although the old lime kilns still stand below the bluff, the company town has become a posh resort. Locals say it took two years for the limestone dust to wash off the trees around the harbor. McMillin's former home is now a restaurant, and workers' cottages have been transformed into comfortable visitors' lodgings. With its rose gardens, cobblestone waterfront, and well-manicured lawns, Roche Harbor retains the flavor of its days as a hangout for McMillin's powerful friends—especially since the sheltered harbor is very popular with well-to-do pleasure boaters. ⊠ *End of Roche Harbor Road.*

San Juan Islands Museum of Art. Established in 2001 (and previously known as the Visual Arts Museum), this facility currently presents rotating art shows and exhibits out of a temporary space in Friday Harbor, a short walk from the ferry dock. The emphasis is on island and Northwest artists. Plans are afoot to create a permanent home for the

A solitary boat in San Juan Island's Friday Harbor

museum. ⊠ *232 A St., Friday Harbor* ☎ *360/370–5050* ⊕ *www.sjima. org* 🎫 *Free* 🕙 *Thurs.–Sun. 11–5.*

FAMILY **Westcott Bay Nature Preserve and Sculpture Park.** At this serene park overlooking beautiful Westcott Bay, you can stroll along winding trails to view more than 100 sculptures spread amid freshwater and saltwater wetlands, open woods, blossoming fields, and rugged terrain. The park is also a haven for birds; more than 120 species nest and breed here. ⊠ *Westcott Dr., off Roche Harbor Rd., Roche Harbor* 🎫 *Free* 🕙 *Daily dawn–dusk.*

FAMILY **Whale Museum.** A stairwell painted with a life-size underwater mural leads you into a world filled with models of whales and whale skeletons, recordings of whale sounds, and videos of whales. Head around to the back of the first-floor shop to view maps of the latest orca pod trackings in the area. ⊠ *62 1st St. N, Friday Harbor* ☎ *360/378–4710* ⊕ *www. whale-museum.org* 🎫 *$6* 🕙 *Daily 9–5.*

WHERE TO EAT AND STAY

For expanded hotel reviews, visit Fodors.com.

$$
ECLECTIC
Fodor's Choice
★
✕ **Backdoor Kitchen.** This local favorite has become well-known beyond the San Juans, thanks to the stellar service and inventive, globally inspired cuisine. As the name might indicate, it's a bit hard to find, tucked in an elegant courtyard a few blocks uphill from the water. Star dishes include pan-seared scallops with ginger-sake beurre blanc, and pork chops topped with a poblano–goat cheese sauce and served with caramelized onions and smoked bacon. Local greens and produce are

used often, and the Northwest-heavy wine list cements the Backdoor's status as a regional gem. [$] *Average main: $21* ✉ *400B A St., Friday Harbor* ☎ *360/378–9540* 🌐 *www.backdoorkitchen.com* 🕒 *Closed Tues. and additional days in winter; call off-season. No lunch.*

$$$$ PACIFIC NORTHWEST 🍴 **Duck Soup Inn.** Blossoming vines thread over the cedar-shingled walls and inside, island-inspired paintings and a flagstone fireplace are the background for creative meals served at comfortable booths. Everything is made from scratch daily, from the sourdough bread to the ice cream. You might start with crispy five-spice duck confit with hoisin-plum sauce; or perhaps Jones Family Farm manila clams from Lopez Island steamed with pancetta and sherry. For a second course, consider the pork meatballs with linguine, hazelnut-basil pesto, fresh figs, and Parmesan; or roasted-eggplant croquettes with garlic hummus, cucumber-mint yogurt, and toasted walnuts. An excellent selection of Northwest, Californian, and European wines is also on hand. [$] *Average main: $34* ✉ *50 Duck Soup La., off Roche Harbor Rd., Friday Harbor* ☎ *360/378–4878* 🌐 *www.ducksoupinn.com* 🕒 *Closed Mon. and Nov.–Mar.; also some other weekdays spring and fall; call ahead. No lunch.*

$ CAFÉ 🍴 **The Market Chef.** Only 50 yards from the ferry holding area, this café makes some unbelievable sandwiches (try the roast-beef-and-rocket version, which is served on a house-baked roll with spicy chili aioli). The soups and deli items—including a decadent macaroni and cheese—are also top-notch. Beer, wine, juices, and espresso are served as well. There may be no better place in town to wait for your ferry to depart. [$] *Average main: $9* ✉ *225 A St., Friday Harbor* ☎ *360/378–4546* 🕒 *No dinner.*

$ B&B/INN 🏨 **Kirk House Bed and Breakfast.** Rooms are all differently decorated in this 1907 Craftsman bungalow, the summer home of steel magnate Peter Kirk: the Garden Room has a botanical motif, the sunny Trellis Room is done in soft shades of yellow and green, and the Arbor Room has French doors leading out to the garden. **Pros:** gorgeous house full of stained glass and other lovely details; within walking distance of town. **Cons:** some noise from nearby airport; a couple of the rooms are on the small side. [$] *Rooms from: $140* ✉ *595 Park St., Friday Harbor* ☎ *360/378–3757, 800/639–2762* 🌐 *www.kirkhouse.net* 🛏 *4 rooms* 🍽 *Breakfast.*

$$ RESORT 🏨 **Roche Harbor Resort.** This sprawling resort, with accommodations ranging from historic hotel rooms to contemporary condos, occupies the site of the lime deposits that made John S. McMillin his fortune in the late 19th century. **Pros:** lots of different options for families and groups; very convenient for boaters; beautiful grounds. **Cons:** condos have less character and are far from the resort; a bit isolated from the rest of the island if you don't have a car; standard rooms in Hotel de Haro have private baths down the hall. [$] *Rooms from: $175* ✉ *248 Reuben Memorial Dr., Roche Harbor* ☎ *360/378–2155, 800/451–8910* 🌐 *www.rocheharbor.com* 🛏 *16 rooms, 18 suites, 9 cottages, 20 condos* 🍽 *No meals.*

SPORTS AND THE OUTDOORS

BEACHES

South Beach at American Camp. This 6-mile public beach on the southern end of the island is part of San Juan Island National Historical Park. ⊠ *off Cattle Point Road* ⊹ *6 miles southeast of Friday Harbor.*

San Juan County Park. You'll find a wide gravel beachfront at this park 10 miles west of Friday Harbor, overlooking waters where orcas often frolic in summer, plus grassy lawns with picnic tables and a small campground. ⊠ *380 Westside Rd., Friday Harbor* ☎ *360/378–8420* ⊕ *www. co.san-juan.wa.us.*

BICYCLES

You can rent standard, mountain, and BMX bikes for $40 to $50 per day or $175 to $225 per week. Tandem, recumbent, and electric bikes rent for about $70 to $80 per day.

Island Bicycles. This full-service shop rents bikes. ⊠ *380 Argyle Ave., Friday Harbor, Friday Harbor* ☎ *360/378–4941* ⊕ *www.islandbicycles.com.*

BOATING AND SAILING

At public docks, high-season moorage rates are $1–$2 per foot (of vessel) per night.

Port of Friday Harbor. The marina at the island's main port offers guest moorage, vessel assistance and repair, bareboat and skippered charters, overnight accommodations, and wildlife and whale-watching cruises. ⊠ *204 Front St., Friday Harbor* ☎ *360/378–2688* ⊕ *www. portfridayharbor.org.*

Snug Harbor Resort Marina. This well-located marina adjoins a popular small resort. It provides van service to and from Friday Harbor and rents small powerboats. ⊠ *1997 Mitchell Bay Rd., Friday Harbor* ☎ *360/378–4762* ⊕ *www.snugresort.com.*

SEA KAYAKING

You'll find many places to rent kayaks in Friday Harbor, as well as outfitters providing classes and tours. Be sure to make reservations in summer. Three-hour tours run about $65–$85, day tours cost around $90–$100, and overnight tours start around $125 per day. Equipment is always included in the cost.

Crystal Seas Kayaking. Sunset trips and multisport tours that might include biking, kayaking, yoga, and camping are among the options with this respected guide company. ⊠ *40 Spring St., Friday Harbor* ☎ *360/378–4223, 877/732–7877* ⊕ *www.crystalseas.com.*

Discovery Sea Kayaks. This outfitter offers both sea-kayaking adventures, including sunset trips and multiday excursions, and whale-watching tours. ⊠ *185 1st St. S, Friday Harbor* ☎ *360/378–2559, 866/461–2559* ⊕ *www.discoveryseakayak.com.*

San Juan Kayak Expeditions. This reputable company has been running kayaking and camping tours in two-person kayaks since 1980. ⊠ *16 Apple Tree La., Friday Harbor* ☎ *360/378–4436* ⊕ *www. sanjuankayak.com.*

Sea Quest Expeditions. Kayak eco-tours with guides who are trained naturalists, biologists, and environmental scientists are available through this popular outfitter. ✉ *Friday Harbor* ☎ *360/378–5767, 888/589–4253* ⊕ *www.sea-quest-kayak.com.*

WHALE-WATCHING

Whale-watching expeditions typically run three to four hours and cost around $50 per person. ■TIP→ For the best experience, look for tour companies with small boats that carry under 30 people. Bring warm clothing even if it's a warm day.

Island Adventures. Two San Juan tours operate out of Anacortes per day from June through August—you'll get right up next to the orcas. ✉ *1801 Commercial Ave., Anacortes* ☎ *360/293–2428, 800/465–4604* ⊕ *www.island-adventures.com.*

San Juan Cruises. Full-day whale-watching adventure cruises out of Bellingham include lunch and a two-hour stop at Friday Harbor and are offered on May weekends and daily from June through September. These trips depart Bellingham at 9:30 am and return at 5:30 pm. Two-night overnight trips to the islands are also sometimes available. ✉ *Fairhaven Terminal, 355 Harris Ave., Bellingham* ☎ *360/738–8099, 800/443–4552* ⊕ *www.whales.com.*

San Juan Excursions. Whale-watching cruises are offered aboard a converted 1940s U.S. Navy research vessel. ✉ *2 Spring St., Friday Harbor* ☎ *360/378–6636, 800/809–4253* ⊕ *www.watchwhales.com.*

Western Prince Cruises. Narrated whale-watching tours last three to four hours. ✉ *1 Spring St., Friday Harbor* ☎ *360/378–5315, 800/757–6722* ⊕ *www.orcawhalewatch.com.*

SHOPPING

Friday Harbor is the main shopping area, with dozens of shops selling a variety of art, crafts, and clothing created by residents, as well as a bounty of island-grown produce.

San Juan Island Farmers Market. From mid-April through late October, this open-air market with more than 30 vendors selling local produce and crafts takes place at Friday Harbor Brickworks on Saturdays from 10 to 1. The market is also open once or twice a month on Saturdays in winter; check the website for the schedule. ✉ *150 Nichols St., Friday Harbor* ⊕ *www.sjifarmersmarket.com.*

San Juan Vineyards. This winery 3 miles north of Friday Harbor has a tasting room and gift shop, and organizes such special events as a harvest festival in October and November barrel tastings. Noteworthy varietals here include Pinot Gris, Riesling Sangiovese, and Cabernet Franc. ✉ *3136 Roche Harbor Rd., Friday Harbor* ☎ *360/378–9463* ⊕ *www.sanjuanvineyards.com.*

Waterworks Gallery. This respected gallery represents about 30 eclectic, contemporary artists, from painters to jewelers. ✉ *315 Argyle St., Friday Harbor* ☎ *360/378–3060* ⊕ *www.waterworksgallery.com.*

OLYMPIC
NATIONAL PARK

WELCOME TO OLYMPIC NATIONAL PARK

TOP REASONS TO GO

★ **Exotic rain forest:** A rain forest in the Pacific Northwest? Indeed, Olympic National Park is one of a few places in the world with this unique temperate landscape.

★ **Beachcombing:** Miles of rugged, spectacular coastline hemmed with sea stacks and tidal pools edge the driftwood-strewn shores of the Olympic Peninsula.

★ **Nature's hot tubs:** A dip in Sol Duc's natural geothermal mineral pools offers a secluded spa experience in the wooded heart of the park.

★ **Lofty vistas:** The hardy can hike up meadowed foothill trails or climb the frosty peaks throughout the Olympics—or just drive up to Hurricane Ridge for endless views.

★ **A sense of history:** American Indian history is key to this region, where eight tribes have traditional ties to the park lands—there's 12,000 years of human history to explore.

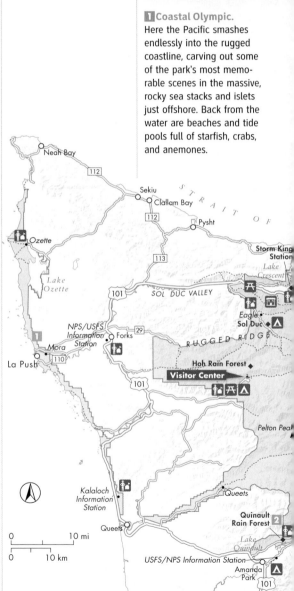

1 Coastal Olympic.
Here the Pacific smashes endlessly into the rugged coastline, carving out some of the park's most memorable scenes in the massive, rocky sea stacks and islets just offshore. Back from the water are beaches and tide pools full of starfish, crabs, and anemones.

Neah Bay
112
Sekiu
Clallam Bay
112
Pysht
STRAIT OF
Ozette
Storm King Station
Lake Crescent
113
Lake Ozette
SOL DUC VALLEY
101
Eagle
Sol Duc
NPS/USFS Information Station
Forks
29
RUGGED RIDGE
Mora
110
La Push
Hoh Rain Forest
Visitor Center
101
Pelton Peak
Kalaloch Information Station
Queets
Quinault Rain Forest
2
Lake Quinault
0   10 mi
0   10 km
Queets
USFS/NPS Information Station
Amanda Park
101

2 The Rain Forest. Centered on the Hoh, Queets, and Quinault river valleys, this is the region's most unique landscape. Fog-shrouded Douglas firs and Sitka spruces, some at more than 300 feet tall, huddle in this moist, pine-carpeted area, shading fern- and moss-draped cedars, maples, and alders.

3 The Mountains. Craggy gray peaks and snow-covered summits dominate the skyline. Low-level foliage and wildflower meadows make for excellent hiking in the plateaus. Even on the sunniest days, temperatures are brisk. Some roads are closed in winter months.

4 Alpine Meadows. In midsummer, the swath of colors is like a Monet canvas spread over the landscape, and wildlife teems among the honeyed flowers. Trails are never prettier, and views are crisp and vast.

12

GETTING ORIENTED

The Olympic peninsula's elegant snowcapped and forested landscape is edged on all sides by water: to the north the Strait of Juan de Fuca separates the United States from Canada, a network of Puget Sound bays laces the east, the Chehalis River meanders along the southern end, and the massive gray Pacific Ocean guards the west side.

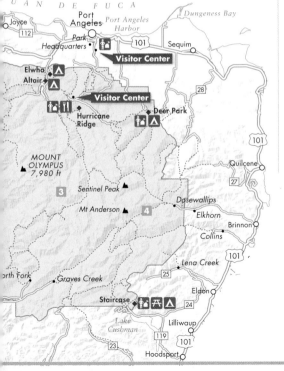

KEY	
🏠	Ranger Station
⛺	Campground
🏕	Picnic Area
🍴	Restaurant
🏨	Lodge
🚶	Trailhead
🚻	Restrooms
⇗	Scenic Viewpoint
-----	Walking/Hiking Trails

Updated by
Shelley Arenas

A spellbinding setting is tucked into the country's far-northwestern corner, within the heart-shaped Olympic Peninsula. Edged on all sides by water, the forested landscape is remote and pristine, and works its way around the sharpened ridges of the snowcapped Olympic Mountains. Big lakes cut pockets of blue in the rugged blanket of pine forests, and hot springs gurgle up from the foothills. Along the coast the sights are even more enchanting: wave-sculpted boulders, tidal pools teeming with sea life, and tree-topped sea stacks.

OLYMPIC NATIONAL PARK PLANNER

WHEN TO GO

Summer, with its long stretches of sun-filled days, is prime touring time for Olympic National Park. June through September are the peak months; Hurricane Ridge, the Hoh Rain Forest, Lake Crescent, and Ruby Beach are bustling by 10 am.

Late spring and early autumn are also good bets for clear weather; anytime between April and October, and you'll have a good chance of fair skies. Between Thanksgiving and Easter, it's a toss-up as to which days will turn out fair; prepare for heavy clouds, rain showers, and chilly temperatures, then hope for the best.

Winter is a great time to visit if you enjoy isolation. Locals are usually the only hardy souls during this time, except for weekend skiers heading to the snowfields around Hurricane Ridge. Many visitor facilities have limited hours or are closed from October to April.

AVG. HIGH/LOW TEMPS.

JAN.	FEB.	MAR.	APR.	MAY	JUNE
45/33	48/35	51/36	55/39	60/44	65/48

JULY	AUG.	SEPT.	OCT.	NOV.	DEC.
68/50	69/51	66/48	58/42	50/37	45/34

12

FESTIVALS AND EVENTS

MAY **Irrigation Festival.** Highlights of this Sequim festival include a beauty pageant, logging demonstrations, arts and crafts, classic car show, strongman competition, parades, and a picnic. ⊕ *www.irrigationfestival.com.*

JUNE–AUGUST **Centrum Summer Arts Festival.** Fort Worden State Park, a 19th-century army base near Port Townsend, hosts a summer-long line-up of concerts and workshops. ☎ *360/385–3102* ⊕ *www.centrum.org.*

JUNE–
SEPTEMBER **Olympic Music Festival.** A variety of classical concerts are performed in a renovated barn; picnic on the farm while you listen. ☎ *360/732–4800* ⊕ *www.olympicmusicfestival.org.*

JULY **Forks Old-Fashioned Fourth of July.** A salmon bake, parade, demolition derby, arts and crafts exhibits, kids activities, and plenty of fireworks mark Forks' weekend-long celebration. ☎ *360/374–2531, 800/443–6757* ⊕ *www.forkswa.com.*

Sequim Lavender Festival. Mid-month, a street fair and free self-guided farm tours celebrate Sequim's many fragrant lavender fields. ⊕ *www.lavenderfestival.com.*

SEPTEMBER **Wooden Boat Festival.** Hundreds of antique boats sail into Port Townsend. ☎ *360/385–3628* ⊕ *www.woodenboat.org.*

PLANNING YOUR TIME

OLYMPIC IN ONE DAY

Start at the **Lake Quinault Lodge,** in the park's southwest corner. From here, drive a half hour into the Quinault Valley via **South Shore Road.** Tackle the forested **Graves Creek Trail,** then head up **North Shore Road** to the Quinault Rain Forest Interpretive Trail. Next, head back to Highway 101 and drive to **Ruby Beach,** where a shoreline walk presents a breathtaking scene of sea stacks and sparkling, pink-hued sands.

Forks, and its **Timber Museum,** are your next stop; have lunch here, then drive 20 minutes to the beach at **La Push.** Next, head to **Lake Crescent,** around the corner to the northeast, where you can rent a boat, take a swim, or enjoy a picnic next to the sparkling teal waters. Drive through **Port Angeles** to **Hurricane Ridge;** count on an hour's drive from bottom to top if there aren't too many visitors. At the ridge, explore the visitor center or hike the 3-mile loop to **Hurricane Hill,** where you can see over the entire park north to Vancouver Island and south past Mt. Olympus.

GETTING HERE AND AROUND

You can enter the park at a number of points, but since the park is 95% wilderness, access roads do not penetrate far. The best way to get around and to see many of the park's top sites is on foot.

BOAT TRAVEL

Ferries provide another unique link to the Olympic area from Seattle; contact **Washington State Ferries** (☎ *800/843–3779 or 206/464–6400* ⊕ *www.wsdot.wa.gov/ferries*) for information.

BUS TRAVEL

Grays Harbor Transit runs daily buses from Aberdeen, Hoquiam, and Forks to Amanda Park, on the west end of Lake Quinault. Jefferson Transit operates a Forks–Amanda Park route Monday through Saturday.

Bus Contacts **Grays Harbor Transit** ☎ *360/532–2770, 800/562–9730* ⊕ *www. ghtransit.com.* **Jefferson Transit** ☎ *800/371–0497, 360/385-4777* ⊕ *www. jeffersontransit.com.*

CAR TRAVEL

U.S. 101 essentially encircles the main section of Olympic National Park, and a number of roads lead from the highway into the park's mountains and toward its beaches. You can reach U.S. 101 via Interstate 5 at Olympia, via Route 12 at Aberdeen, or via Route 104 from the Washington state ferry terminals at Bainbridge or Kingston.

PARK ESSENTIALS

ADMISSION FEES AND PERMITS

Seven-day vehicle admission fee is $15; an annual family pass is $30. Individuals arriving on foot, bike, or motorcycle pay $5 (ages 15 and under are admitted free).

An overnight wilderness permit, available at visitor centers and ranger stations, is $5 (covers registration of your party for up to 14 days), plus $2 per person per night. A frequent-hiker pass, which covers all wilderness-use fees, is $30 per year. Fishing in freshwater streams and lakes within Olympic National Park does not require a Washington state fishing license; however, anglers must acquire a salmon-steelhead punch card when fishing for those species. Ocean fishing and harvesting shellfish and seaweed require licenses, which are available at sporting goods and outdoor supply stores.

ADMISSION HOURS

Six park entrances are open 24/7; gate kiosk hours (for buying passes) vary according to season and location, but most are staffed during daylight hours. Olympic National Park is in the Pacific time zone.

CELL PHONE RECEPTION

Note that cell reception is sketchy in wilderness areas. There are public telephones at the Olympic National Park Visitor Center, Hoh River Rain Forest Visitor Center, and lodging properties within the park— Lake Crescent, Kalaloch, and Sol Duc Hot Springs. Fairholm General Store also has a phone.

RESTAURANTS

The major resorts are your best bets for eating out in the park. Each has a main restaurant, café, and/or kiosk, as well as casually upscale dinner service, with regional seafood, meat, and produce complemented by a range of microbrews and good Washington and international wines. Reservations are either recommended or required.

Outside the park, Port Angeles is the place to go for a truly spectacular meal; several restaurants are internationally renowned by diners and chefs alike, and most are run by famous former chefs. Dozens of small, easygoing eateries offering hearty American-style fare line the main thoroughfares in Forks and Sequim. *Prices in the reviews are the average cost of a main course at dinner or, if dinner is not served, at lunch.*

HOTELS

Major park resorts run from good to terrific, with generally comfortable rooms, excellent facilities, and easy access to trails, beaches, and activity centers. Midsize accommodations, like Sol Duc Hot Springs Resort, are often shockingly rustic—but remember, you're here for the park, not for the rooms.

The towns around the park have motels, hotels, and resorts for every budget. For high-priced stays with lots of perks, base yourself in Port Angeles. Sequim has many attractive, friendly B&Bs, plus lots of inexpensive chain hotels and motels. Forks is basically a motel town, with a few guesthouses around its fringes. *Prices in the reviews are the lowest cost of a standard double room in high season.*

VISITOR INFORMATION

PARK CONTACT INFORMATION

Olympic National Park ⊠ *600 E. Park Ave., Port Angeles* ☎ *360/565–3130* ⊕ *www.nps.gov/olym.*

VISITOR CENTERS

Forks NPS/USFS Recreation Information Center. The information center has park maps, brochures, and exhibits; they also provide permits and rent bear-proof containers. ⊠ *551 S. Forks Ave. (Hwy. 101), Forks* ☎ *360/374–5877* ⊕ *www.nps.gov/olym/planyourvisit/visitorcenters. htm* ☉ *Mid-June–Sept. 9–4; spring and fall Fri–Sun; closed in winter.*

Hoh Rain Forest Visitor Center. Pick up park maps and pamphlets, permits, and activities lists in this busy, woodsy chalet; there's also a shop and exhibits on natural history. Several short interpretive trails and longer wilderness treks start from here. ⊠ *Hoh Valley Road, West End* ☎ *360/374–6925* ⊕ *www.nps.gov/olym/planyourvisit/visitorcenters. htm* ☉ *Daily in summer; Fri.–Tues. rest of year.*

Hurricane Ridge Visitor Center. The upper level of this visitor center has exhibits and nice views; the lower level has a gift shop and snack bar. Guided walks and programs start in late June. In winter, find details on the surrounding ski and sledding slopes and take guided snowshoe walks. ⊠ *Hurricane Ridge Rd.* ☎ *360/565–3131* ⊕ *www.nps.gov/olym/ planyourvisit/visitorcenters.htm* ☉ *Memorial Day–Labor Day, daily 9–7; late Dec.–Apr., Fri.–Sun. 10–4.*

Olympic National Park Visitor Center. This modern, well-organized facility, staffed by park rangers, provides everything: maps, trail brochures, campground advice, listings of wildlife sightings, educational programs and exhibits, information on road and trail closures, and weather forecasts. ⊠ *3002 Mount Angeles Rd., Port Angeles* ☎ *360/565–3130* ⊕ *www.nps.gov/olym* ☉ *May–Sept., daily 9–4; Oct.–Apr., daily 10–4.*

South Shore Quinault Ranger Station. The National Forest Service's ranger station near the Lake Quinault Lodge has maps, campground information, and program listings. ✉ *353 S. Shore Road, Quinault* ☎ *360/288–2525* ⊕ *www.fs.usda.gov/recarea/olympic* ⊘ *Year-round, weekdays 8–4:30; Memorial Day–Labor Day, also open weekends 9–4.*

Wilderness Information Center (WIC). Located behind Olympic National Park Visitor Center, this facility provides all the information you'll need for a trip in the park, including trail conditions, safety tips, and weather bulletins. The office also issues camping permits, takes campground reservations, and rents bear-proof food canisters. ✉ *3002 Mount Angeles Rd., Port Angeles* ☎ *360/565–3100* ⊕ *www.nps.gov/olym* ⊘ *Daily except Thanksgiving and Christmas; hours vary.*

EXPLORING

Most of the park's attractions are found either off Highway 101 or down trails that require hikes of 15 minutes or longer. The west coast beaches are linked to the highway by downhill tracks; the number of cars parked alongside the road at the start of the paths indicates how crowded the beach will be.

SCENIC DRIVES

Port Angeles Visitor Center to Hurricane Ridge. The premier scenic drive in Olympic National Park is a steep ribbon of curves, which climbs from thickly forested foothills and subalpine meadows into the upper stretches of pine-swathed peaks. At the top, the visitor center at Hurricane Ridge has some truly spectacular views over the heart of the peninsula and across the Strait of Juan de Fuca. (Backpackers note wryly that you have to hike a long way in other parts of the park to get the kinds of views you can drive to here.) Hurricane Ridge also has an uncommonly fine display of wildflowers in spring and summer. In winter, vehicles must carry chains and the road is usually open Friday through Sunday only (call first to check conditions). ⊕ *www.nps.gov/olym.*

HISTORIC SITES

La Push. At the mouth of Quileute River, La Push is the tribal center of the Quileute Indians. In fact, the town's name is a variation on the French *la bouche,* which means "the mouth." Offshore rock spires known as sea stacks dot the coast here, and you may catch a glimpse of bald eagles nesting in the nearby cliffs. ✉ *Rte. 110, 14 miles west of Forks, La Push* ⊕ *www.forkswa.com/places-to-visit-near-forks.*

Lake Ozette. The third-largest glacial impoundment in Washington anchors the coastal strip of Olympic National Park at its north end. The small town of Ozette, home to a coastal tribe, is the trailhead for two of the park's better one-day hikes. Both 3-mile trails lead over boardwalks through swampy wetland and coastal old-growth forest to the ocean shore and uncrowded beaches. ✉ *At the end of Hoko-Ozette Rd., 26 miles southwest of Hwy. 112 near Sekiu, Ozette* ☎ *360/963–2725*

CLOSE UP

Plants and Wildlife in Olympic

Along the high mountain slopes hardy cedar, fir, and hemlock trees stand tough on the rugged land; the lower montane forests are filled with thickets of silver firs; and valleys stream with Douglas firs and western hemlock. The park's famous temperate rain forests are on the peninsula's western side, marked by broad western red cedars, towering red spruces, and ferns festooned with strands of mosses and patchwork lichens. This lower landscape is also home to some of the Northwest's largest trees: massive cedar and Sitka spruce near Lake Quinault can measure more than 700 inches around, and Douglas firs near the Queets and Hoh rivers are nearly as wide.

These landscapes are home to a variety of wildlife, including many large mammals and 15 creatures found nowhere else in the world. Hikers often come across Roosevelt's elk, black-tailed deer, mountain goats, beavers, raccoons, skunks, opossums, and foxes; Douglas squirrels and flying squirrels populate the heights of the forest. Less common are black bears (most prevalent from May through August); wolves, bobcats, and cougar

are rarely seen. Birdlife includes bald eagles, red-tailed hawks, osprey, and great horned owls. Rivers and lakes are filled with freshwater fish, while beaches hold crabs, starfish, anemones, and other shelled creatures. Get out in a boat on the Pacific to spot seals, sea lions, and sea otters—and perhaps a pod of porpoises, orcas, or gray whales.

Beware of jellyfish around the shores—beached jellyfish can still sting. In the woods, check for ticks after every hike and after each shower. Biting nasties include black flies, horseflies, sand fleas, and the ever-present mosquitoes. Yellowjacket nests populate tree hollows along many trails; signs throughout the Hoh Rain Forest warn hikers to move quickly through these sections. If one or two chase you, remain calm and keep walking; these are just "guards" making sure you're keeping away from the hive. Poison oak is common, so familiarize yourself with its appearance. Bug repellent, sunscreen, and long pants and sleeves will go a long way toward making your experience more comfortable.

12

Ozette Ranger Station ⊕ *www.nps.gov/olym/planyourvisit/visiting-ozette.htm.*

SCENIC STOPS

Fodor'sChoice **Hoh River Rain Forest.** South of Forks, an 18-mile spur road links High-★ way 101 with this unique temperate rain forest, where spruce and hemlock trees soar to heights of more than 200 feet. Alders and big-leaf maples are so densely covered with mosses they look more like shaggy prehistoric animals than trees, and elk browse in shaded glens. Be prepared for precipitation: the region receives 140 inches or more each year. The visitor center is open daily July through September from 9 to 6, and Friday through Tuesday from 10 to 4 in other months. ⊠ *From Hwy. 101, at about 20 miles north of Kalaloch, turn onto Upper Hoh*

Rd. 18 miles east to Hoh Rain Forest Visitor Center ☎ *360/374–6925* ⊕ *www.nps.gov/olym.*

Hurricane Ridge. The panoramic view from this 5,200-foot-high ridge encompasses the Olympic range, the Strait of Juan de Fuca, and Vancouver Island. Guided tours are given in summer along the many paved and unpaved trails, where wildflowers and wildlife such as deer and marmots flourish. ⊠ *Hurricane Ridge Rd., 17 miles south of Port Angeles* ☎ *360/565–3130 visitor center* ⊕ *www.nps.gov/olym* ⊙ *Visitor center open daily in summer; open rest of year on days road is open.*

Kalaloch. With a lodge, a huge campground, miles of coastline, and easy access from the highway, this is another popular spot. Keen-eyed beachcombers may spot sea otters just offshore; they were reintroduced here in 1970. ⊠ *Hwy. 101, 32 miles northwest of Lake Quinault* ☎ *360/565–3130 Olympic National Park visitor info* ⊕ *www.nps.gov/olym/planyourvisit/visiting-kalaloch-and-ruby-beach.htm.*

Lake Crescent. Visitors see Lake Crescent as Highway 101 winds along its southern shore, giving way to gorgeous views of teal waters rippling in a basin formed by Tuscan-like hills. In the evening, low bands of clouds caught between the surrounding mountains often linger over its reflective surface. ⊠ *Hwy. 101, 16 miles west of Port Angeles and 28 miles east of Forks* ☎ *360/565–3130 ONP Visitor Info* ⊕ *www.nps.gov/olym/planyourvisit/visiting-lake-crescent.htm.*

Lake Quinault. This glimmering lake, 4½ miles long and 300 feet deep, is the first landmark you'll reach when driving the west-side loop of U.S. 101. The rain forest is thickest here, with moss-draped maples and alders, and towering spruce, fir, and hemlock. Enchanted Valley, high up near the Quinault River's source, is a deeply glaciated valley that's closer to the Hood Canal than to the Pacific Ocean. A scenic loop drive circles the lake and travels around a section of the Quinault River. ⊠ *Hwy. 101, 38 miles north of Hoquiam* ☎ *360/288–2444 for Quinault Rain Forest ranger station* ⊕ *www.nps.gov/olym/planyourvisit/visiting-quinault.htm* ⊙ *Ranger station open part-time in summer.*

Second and Third Beaches. During low tide these flat, driftwood-strewn expanses are perfect for long afternoon strolls. Second Beach, accessed via an easy forest trail through Quileute lands, opens to a vista of Pacific Ocean and sea stacks; Third Beach offers a 1.3-mile forest hike for a warm-up before reaching the sands. ⊠ *Hwy. 101, 32 miles north of Lake Quinault* ☎ *360/565–3130 ONP Visitor Info.*

Sol Duc. Sol Duc Valley is one of those magical places where all the Northwest's virtues seem at hand: lush lowland forests, sparkling river scenes, salmon runs, and serene hiking trails. Here, the popular Sol Duc Hot Springs area includes three attractive sulfuric pools ranging in temperature from 98°F to 104°F. ⊠ *Sol Duc Rd., south of U.S. 101, 1 mile past the west end of Lake Crescent* ☎ *360/565–3130 ONP Visitor Info* ⊕ *www.nps.gov/olym/planyourvisit/visiting-the-sol-duc-valley.htm.*

Staircase. Unlike the forests of the park's south and west sides, Douglas fir is the dominant tree on the east slope of the Olympic Mountains. Fire has played an important role in creating the majestic forest here, as the Staircase Ranger Station explains in interpretive exhibits. ⊠ *At*

DID YOU KNOW?

Encompassing more than 70 miles of beachfront, Olympic is one of the few national parks of the West with an ocean beach (Redwood, Channel Islands, and some of the Alaskan parks are the others). The park is therefore home to many marine animals, including sea otters, whales, sea lions, and seals.

end of Rte. 119, 15 miles from U.S. 101 at Hoodsport ☎ 360/877–5569 Staircase Ranger Station.

EDUCATIONAL OFFERINGS

CLASSES AND SEMINARS

NatureBridge. This rustic educational facility offers talks and excursions focusing on park ecology and history. Trips range from canoe trips to camping excursions, with a strong emphasis on family programs. ✉ *111 Barnes Point Rd., Port Angeles* ☎ *360/928–3720, 800/775–3720* ⊕ *www.naturebridge.org/olympic-national-park.*

SPORTS AND THE OUTDOORS

BEACHCOMBING

★ The wild, shell-strewn Pacific coast teems with tide pools and crustaceans. Crabs, sand dollars, anemones, starfish, and all sorts of shellfish are exposed at low tide, when flat beaches can stretch out for hundreds of yards. The most easily accessible sand-strolling spots are Rialto, Ruby, First, and Second beaches, near Mora and La Push, and Kalaloch Beach and Fourth Beach in the Kalaloch stretch.

The Wilderness Act and the park's code of ethics instruct visitors to leave all nonliving materials where they are for others to enjoy.

BICYCLING

The rough gravel car tracks to some of the park's remote sites were meant for four-wheel-drive vehicles, but can double as mountain-bike routes. The Quinault Valley, Queets River, Hoh River, and Sol Duc River roads have bike paths through old-growth forest. Graves Creek Road, in the southwest, is a mountain-bike path; Lake Crescent's north side is also edged by the bike-friendly Spruce Railroad Trail. More bike tracks run through the adjacent Olympic National Forest. Note that Highway 101 has heavy traffic and isn't recommended for cycling, although the western side has broad roads with beautiful scenery and can be biked off-season. Bikes are not permitted on foot trails.

TOURS AND OUTFITTERS

Mike's Bikes. A bike, gear, and repair shop, Mike's is a great resource for advice on routes around the Olympic Peninsula. ✉ *150 W. Sequim Bay Rd., Sequim* ☎ *360/681–3868* ⊕ *www.mikes-bikes.net.*

Peak 6. This adventure store on the way to the Hoh Rain Forest Visitor Center rents mountain bikes. ✉ *4883 Upper Hoh Rd., Forks* ☎ *360/374–5254.*

Sound Bike & Kayak. This sports outfitter rents and sells bikes, kayaks, and related equipment. ✉ *120 E. Front St., Port Angeles* ☎ *360/457–1240* ⊕ *www.soundbikeskayaks.com.*

CLIMBING

At 7,980 feet, Mt. Olympus is the highest peak in the park and the most popular climb in the region. To attempt the summit, participants must register at the Glacier Meadows Ranger Station. Mt. Constance, the third-highest Olympic peak at 7,743 feet, has a well-traversed climbing route that requires technical experience; reservations are recommended for the Lake Constance stop, which is limited to 20 campers. Mt. Deception is another possibility, though tricky snows have caused fatalities and injuries in the last decade. Climbing season runs from late June through September. Note that crevasse skills and self-rescue experience are highly recommended. Climbers must register with park officials and purchase wilderness permits before setting out. The best resource for climbing advice is the Wilderness Information Center in Port Angeles.

TOURS AND OUTFITTERS

Alpine Ascents. This company offers a backpacking and wilderness navigation course in the Olympic ranges. ⊠ *121 Mercer St., Seattle* ☎ *206/378–1927* ⊕ *www.alpineascents.com.*

Mountain Madness. Choose from several adventure trips to summits around the Olympic Peninsula. ⊠ *3018 SW Charlestown St., Seattle* ☎ *800/328–5925* ⊕ *www.mountainmadness.com.*

The Olympia Mountaineers. A branch of the Seattle Mountaineers, this group schedules climbing-oriented activities throughout the park. ⊠ *Friends Meeting House at Priest Point, 3201 Boston Harbor Rd., Olympia* ☎ *360/570–0296* ⊕ *www.olympiamountaineers.org.*

FISHING

There are numerous fishing possibilities throughout the park. Lake Crescent is home to cutthroat and rainbow trout, as well as petite kokanee salmon; Lake Cushman, Lake Quinault, and Ozette Lake have trout, salmon, and steelhead; and Lake Mills has three trout varieties. As for rivers, the Bogachiel and Queets have steelhead salmon in season. The glacier-fed Hoh River is home to chinook salmon April to November, and coho salmon from August through November; the Sol Duc River offers all five species of salmon, plus cutthroat and steelhead trout. Rainbow trout are also found in the Dosewallips, Elwha, and Skykomish rivers. Other places to go after salmon and trout include the Duckabush, Quillayute, Quinault, and Salmon rivers. A Washington state punch card is required during salmon-spawning months; fishing regulations vary throughout the park. Licenses are available from sporting goods and outdoor supply stores.

TOURS AND OUTFITTERS

Bob's Piscatorial Pursuits. This company, based in Forks, offers salmon and steelhead fishing trips around the Olympic Peninsula from October through mid-May. ☎ *866/347–4232* ⊕ *www.piscatorialpursuits.com.*

Kalaloch Lodge. Lodge staff customize guided fishing expeditions around the Olympic Peninsula for guests. ⊠ *157151 U.S. 101, Forks* ☎ *360/962–2271, 866/525–2562* ⊕ *www.thekalalochlodge.com.*

BEST BETS FOR FAMILIES

■ **Head for the beach:** Dungeness Spit is one of the nation's finest, and you can't beat the stunning sea stacks along the western coast of the Olympic Peninsula.

■ **Learn from a ranger:** Take an informative guided walk, or attend a nature talk at a campground or visitor center.

■ **Stay up late:** Join park staff and fellow travelers around the campfire for stories, songs, and nature tales.

■ **Cast off for adventure:** Try your hand at paddling on a kayaking, canoeing, or white-water excursion.

■ **Look for Native American art:** Be on the lookout for characters and symbols from tribal legends on buildings and totem poles as you pass through small towns.

HIKING

Know your tides, or you might be trapped by high water. Tide tables are available at all visitor centers and ranger stations. Remember that a wilderness permit is required for all overnight backcountry visits.

EASY

FAMILY

Fodor's Choice

★

Hoh River Trail. From the Hoh Visitor Center, this rain-forest jaunt takes you into the Hoh Valley, wending its way for 17.4 miles alongside the river, through moss-draped maple and alder trees and past open meadows where elk roam in winter. *Easy.* ⊠ *Hoh Visitor Center, 18 miles east of U.S. 101* ⊕ *www.nps.gov/olym/planyourvisit/hoh-river-trail.htm.*

Hurricane Ridge Trail. A ¼-mile alpine loop, most of it wheelchair-accessible, leads through wildflower meadows overlooking numerous vistas of the interior Olympic peaks to the south and a panorama of the Strait of Juan de Fuca to the north. *Easy.* ⊠ *Hurricane Ridge Rd., 17 miles south of Port Angeles* ⊕ *www.nps.gov/olym/planyourvisit/visiting-hurricane-ridge.htm.*

MODERATE

Boulder Creek Trail. The 5-mile round-trip walk up Boulder Creek leads to a half-dozen hot spring pools of varying temperatures; some are clothing-optional. *Moderate.* ⊠ *End of the Elwha River Rd., 4 miles south of Altair Campground* ⊕ *www.nps.gov/olym/planyourvisit/boulder-creek-trail.htm.*

FAMILY **Cape Alava Trail.** Beginning at Ozette, this 3-mile boardwalk trail leads from the forest to wave-tossed headlands. *Moderate.* ⊠ *End of the Hoko-Ozette Rd., 26 miles south of Hwy. 112, west of Sekiu* ⊕ *ww. nps.gov/olym/planyourvisit/visiting-ozette.htm.*

Graves Creek Trail. This 6-mile-long moderately strenuous trail climbs from lowland rain forest to alpine territory at Sundown Pass. Due to spring floods, a fjord halfway up is often impassable in May and June. *Moderate.* ⊠ *End of S. Quinault Valley Rd., 23 miles east of U.S. 101* ⊕ *www.nps.gov/olym.*

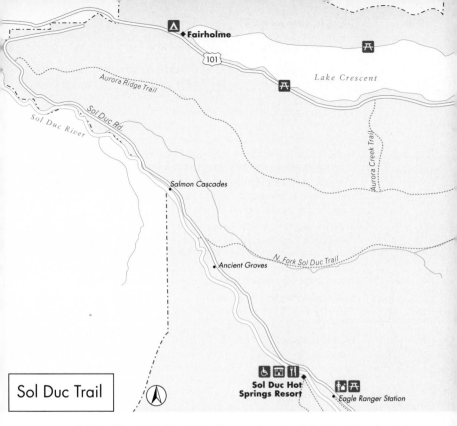

Sol Duc Trail

FAMILY
Fodor's Choice
★

Sol Duc River Trail. The 1.5-mile gravel path off Sol Duc Road winds through thick Douglas fir forests toward the thundering, three-chute Sol Duc Falls. Just 0.1 mile from the road, below a wooden platform over the Sol Duc River, you'll come across the 70-foot Salmon Cascades. In late summer and autumn, thousands of salmon negotiate 50 miles or more of treacherous waters to reach the cascades and the tamer pools near Sol Duc Hot Springs. The popular 6-mile **Lovers Lane Loop Trail** links the Sol Duc falls with the hot springs. You can continue up from the falls 5 miles to the **Appleton Pass Trail,** at 3,100 feet. From there you can hike on to the 8.5-mile mark, where views at the High Divide are from 5,050 feet. *Moderate.* ⊠ *Sol Duc Rd., 11 miles south of U.S. 101* ⊕ *www.nps.gov/olym/planyourvisit/sol-duc-river-trail.htm.*

DIFFICULT

High Divide Trail. A 9-mile hike in the park's high country defines this trail, which includes some strenuous climbing on its last 4 miles before topping out at a small alpine lake. A return loop along High Divide wends its way an extra mile through alpine territory, with sensational views of Olympic peaks. This trail is only for dedicated, properly equipped hikers who are in good shape. *Difficult.* ⊠ *End of Sol Duc River Rd., 13 miles south of U.S. 101* ⊕ *www.nps.gov/olym/planyourvisit/high-divide-loop.htm.*

KAYAKING AND CANOEING

Lake Crescent, a serene expanse of teal-colored waters surrounded by deep-green pine forests, is one of the park's best boating areas. Note that the west end is for swimming only; no speedboats are allowed here.

Lake Quinault has boating access from a gravel ramp on the north shore. From U.S. 101, take a right on North Shore Road, another right on Hemlock Way, and a left on Lakeview Drive. There are plank ramps at Falls Creek and Willoughby campgrounds on South Shore Drive, 0.1 mile and 0.2 mile past the Quinault Ranger Station, respectively.

Lake Ozette, with just one access road, is a good place for overnight trips. Only experienced canoe and kayak handlers should travel far from the put-in, since fierce storms occasionally strike—even in summer.

TOURS AND OUTFITTERS

Fairholm General Store. Rowboats and canoes on Lake Crescent are available to rent for $10 to $45. The store is at the lake's west end, 27 miles west of Port Angeles. ⊠ *U.S. 101, Fairholm* ☎ *360/928–3020* ⏾ *Closed after Labor Day until Memorial Day weekend.*

Lake Crescent Lodge. You can rent rowboats here for $9 per hour and $40 per day. ⊠ *416 Lake Crescent Rd.* ☎ *360/928–3211* ⊕ *www.olympicnationalparks.com.*

Log Cabin Resort. This resort, 17 miles west of Port Angeles, has boat rentals for $10 to $30. The dock provides easy access to Lake Crescent's northeast section. ⊠ *3183 East Beach Road, Port Angeles* ☎ *360/928–3325* ⊕ *www.olympicnationalparks.com.*

Rain Forest Paddlers. This company takes kayakers down the Lizard Rock and Oxbow sections of the Hoh River. ⊠ *4882 Upper Hoh Rd., Forks* ☎ *360/374–5254, 866/457–8398* ⊕ *www.rainforestpaddlers.com.*

RAFTING

Olympic has excellent rafting rivers, with Class II to Class V rapids. The Elwha River is a popular place to paddle, with some exciting turns. The Hoh is better for those who like a smooth, easy float.

TOURS AND OUTFITTERS

Olympic Raft and Kayak. Based in Port Angeles, this is the only rafting outfit allowed to venture into Olympic National Park. ⊠ *123 Lake Aldwell Rd.* ☎ *360/452–5268, 888/452–1443* ⊕ *www.raftandkayak.com.*

WINTER SPORTS

Hurricane Ridge is the central spot for winter sports. Miles of downhill and Nordic ski tracks are open late December through March, and a ski lift, towropes, and ski school are open 10 to 4 weekends and holidays. A snow-play area for children ages eight and younger is located near the Hurricane Ridge Visitors Center. Hurricane Ridge Road is open Friday through Sunday in the winter season and all vehicles are required to carry chains.

TOURS AND OUTFITTERS

Hurricane Ridge Visitor Center. Hurricane Ridge Visitor Center rents snowshoes and ski equipment December through March; prices are $17 to $42. Free 90-minute snowshoe tours also depart from here weekends from mid-December through March. Groups of 7 to 30 people can register in advance by phone for the 10:30 tour. The 2 pm tour is first-come, first-served, with sign-ups beginning at 1:30. A $5 per person donation is requested to cover trail and equipment maintenance. ✉ *Hurricane Ridge Rd., Port Angeles* ☎ *360/565–3131 information, 360/565–3136 tour reservations* 🌐 *www.nps.gov/olym.*

WHERE TO EAT

$$$ AMERICAN 🍴 **Creekside Restaurant.** A tranquil country setting and ocean views at Kalaloch Lodge's restaurant create the perfect backdrop for savoring local dinner specialties like cedar-planked salmon, fresh shellfish, wild mushrooms, and well-aged beef. Note that seating is every half hour after 5, and reservations are recommended. Hearty breakfasts and sandwich-style lunches are more casual. [$] *Average main: $25* ✉ *157151 Hwy. 101, Kalaloch* ☎ *866/525–2562, 360/962–2271* 🌐 *www.thekalalochlodge.com/Dine.aspx* 🕑 *Closed 3:30–5 (and hours vary seasonally).*

$$$ AMERICAN 🍴 **Lake Crescent Lodge.** Part of the original 1916 lodge, the fir-paneled dining room overlooks the lake; you also won't find a better spot for sunset views. Entrées include crab cakes, grilled salmon, halibut fish-and-chips, classic American steaks, and elk ribs. A good Northwest wine list complements the menu. Note that meals are only offered during set hours, but appetizers are served in the lounge or out on the Sun Porch. [$] *Average main: $24* ✉ *416 Lake Crescent Rd., Port Angeles* ☎ *360/928–3211* ✍ *Reservations essential* 🕑 *Closed mid-Oct.–May.*

$$$ AMERICAN 🍴 **The Springs Restaurant.** The main Sol Duc Hot Springs Resort restaurant is a rustic, fir-and-cedar paneled dining room surrounded by trees. Big breakfasts are turned out daily 7:30 to 10; dinner is served daily between 5:30 and 9 (lunch and snacks are available 11 to 4 at the Poolside Deli or Espresso Hut). Evening choices include Northwest seafood and game highlighted by fresh-picked fruits and vegetables. [$] *Average main: $22* ✉ *12076 Sol Duc Rd., at U.S. 101, Port Angeles* ☎ *360/327–3583* 🌐 *www.olympicnationalparks.com/activities/dining.aspx* 🕑 *Closed mid-Oct.–mid-May.*

PICNIC AREAS

All Olympic National Park campgrounds have adjacent picnic areas with tables, some shelters, and restrooms, but no cooking facilities. The same is true for major visitor centers, such as Hoh Rain Forest. Drinking water is available at ranger stations, interpretive centers, and inside campgrounds.

East Beach Picnic Area. Set on a grassy meadow overlooking Lake Crescent, this popular swimming spot has six picnic tables and vault toilets. ✉ *At the far east end of Lake Crescent, off Hwy. 101, 17 miles west of Port Angeles* 🌐 *www.nps.gov/olym.*

Rialto Beach Picnic Area. Relatively secluded at the end of the road from Forks, this is one of the premier day-use areas in the park's Pacific coast segment. This site has 12 picnic tables, fire grills, and vault toilets. ✉ *Rte. 110, 14 miles west of Forks* 🌐 *www.nps.gov/olym* 💳 *No credit cards.*

WHERE TO STAY

For expanded hotel reviews, visit Fodors.com.

$$$$ HOTEL **Kalaloch Lodge.** Overlooking the Pacific, Kalaloch has cozy rooms with sea views in the lodge and separate cabins along the bluff. **Pros:** ranger tours; clam digging; supreme storm watching in winter. **Cons:** some units are two blocks from main lodge; cabins can smell like pets. [$] *Rooms from: $202* ✉ *157151 U.S. 101, Forks* ☎ *360/962–2271, 866/662–9928* 🌐 *www.thekalalochlodge.com* 🛏 *10 lodge rooms, 7 motel rooms, 3 motel suites, 42 cabins* 🍴 *No meals.*

$$$ HOTEL **Lake Crescent Lodge.** Deep in the forest at the foot of Mt. Storm King, this 1916 lodge has a variety of comfortable accommodations, from basic rooms with shared baths to spacious two-bedroom fireplace cottages (the latter available even on winter weekends when the rest of the lodge is closed). **Pros:** gorgeous setting; free wireless access in the wilderness. **Cons:** no laundry; Roosevelt Cottages must be booked a year in advance for summer stays. [$] *Rooms from: $184* ✉ *416 Lake Crescent Rd., Port Angeles* ☎ *360/928–3211* 🌐 *www.lakecrescentlodge.com* 🛏 *30 motel rooms, 17 cabins, 5 lodge rooms with shared bath* ⏲ *Closed Nov.–Apr.* 🍴 *No meals.*

$$$ HOTEL **Lake Quinault Lodge.** On a lovely glacial lake in Olympic National Forest, this beautiful early-20th-century lodge complex is within walking distance of the lakeshore and hiking trails in the spectacular old-growth forest. **Pros:** hosts summer campfires with s'mores; family-friendly ambience. **Cons:** kayaks and canoes rent out quickly in the summer. [$] *Rooms from: $193* ✉ *P.O. Box 7, 345 South Shore Rd., Quinault* ☎ *360/288–2900, 800/562-6672* 🌐 *www.olympicnationalparks.com/accommodations/lake-quinault-lodge.aspx* 🛏 *92 rooms* 🍴 *No meals.*

$ **Log Cabin Resort.** This rustic hotel has an idyllic setting at the northeast end of Lake Crescent. **Pros:** bikes and boats available on-site; weekly ranger talks. **Cons:** cabins are very rustic. [$] *Rooms from: $68* ✉ *3183 E. Beach Rd., Port Angeles* ☎ *888/896-3818* 🌐 *www.olympicnationalparks.com/stay/lodging/log-cabin-resort.aspx* 🛏 *4 rooms, 24 cabins, 22 RV sites, 4 tent sites* ⏲ *Closed mid-Sept.–mid-May* 🍴 *No meals.*

$$$ HOTEL **Sol Duc Hot Springs Resort.** Deep in the brooding forest along the Sol Duc River, this remote 1910 resort is surrounded by 5,000-foot-tall mountains. **Pros:** nearby trails; peaceful setting. **Cons:** steep pool rates. [$] *Rooms from: $171* ✉ *12076 Sol Duc Hot Springs Rd.* ☎ *360/327–3583, 866/476–5382* 🌐 *www.olympicnationalparks.com/accommodations/sol-duc-hot-springs-resort.aspx* 🛏 *32 rooms, 6 cabins* ⏲ *Closed mid-Oct.–mid-Apr.* 🍴 *No meals.*

Best Campgrounds in Olympic

Note that only a few places take reservations; if you can't book in advance, you'll have to arrive early to get a place. Each site usually has a picnic table and grill or fire pit, and most campgrounds have water, toilets, and garbage containers; for hookups, showers, and laundry facilities, you'll have to head into the towns. Firewood is available from camp concessions, but if there's no store you can collect dead wood within 1 mile of your campsite. Dogs are allowed in campgrounds, but not on most trails or in the backcountry. Trailers should be 21 feet long or less (15 feet or less at Queets Campground) though a few campgrounds can accommodate up to 35 feet. There's a camping limit of two weeks. Nightly rates run $12–$18 per site.

Elwha Campground. The larger of the Elwha Valley's two campgrounds, this is one of Olympic's year-round facilities. ⊠ *Elwha River Rd., 7 miles south of U.S. 101, Olympic National Park* ☎ *No phone.*

Fairholme Campground. One of just three lakeside campgrounds in the park, Fairholm is near the Lake Crescent Resort. ⊠ *U.S. 101, 28 miles west of Port Angeles, on the west end of Lake Crescent, Olympic National Park* ☎ *No phone.*

Kalaloch Campground. Kalaloch is the biggest and most popular Olympic campground, and it's open all year. Its vantage of the Pacific is unmatched on the park's coastal stretch. ⊠ *U.S. 101, ½ mile north of the Kalaloch Information Station, Olympic National Park* ☎ *360/962–2271 group bookings.*

Lake Quinault Rain Forest Resort Village Campground. Stretching along the south shore of Lake Quinault, this RV campground has many recreation facilities, including beaches, canoes, ball fields, and horseshoe pits. The 31 RV sites, which rent for $30 per night, are open year-round but bathrooms are closed in winter. ⊠ *3½ miles east of U.S. 101, South Shore Rd., Lake Quinault* ☎ *360/288–2535 or 800/255–6936* ⊕ *www.rainforestresort.com.*

Mora Campground. Along the Quillayute estuary, this campground doubles as a popular staging point for hikes northward along the coast's wilderness stretch. ⊠ *Rte. 110, 13 miles west of Forks, Olympic National Park* ☎ *No phone.*

Ozette Campground. Hikers heading to Cape Alava, a scenic promontory that is the westernmost point in the Lower 48 states, use this lakeshore campground as a jumping-off point. ⊠ *Hoko-Ozette Rd., 26 miles south of Hwy. 112, Olympic National Park* ☎ *No phone.*

Sol Duc Campground. Sol Duc resembles virtually all Olympic campgrounds save one distinguishing feature—the famed hot springs are a short walk away. ⊠ *Sol Duc Rd., 11 miles south of U.S. 101, Olympic National Park* ☎ *360/327–3534.*

Staircase Campground. In deep woods away from the river, this campground is a popular jumping-off point for hikes into the Skokomish River Valley and the Olympic high country. ⊠ *Rte. 119, 16 miles northwest of U.S. 101, Olympic National Park* ☎ *No phone.*

OLYMPIC PENINSULA AND WASHINGTON COAST

WELCOME TO OLYMPIC PENINSULA AND WASHINGTON COAST

TOP REASONS TO GO

★ **Soak up the scene in Port Townsend.** Washington's Victorian seaport is home to artists, boat lovers, and foodies as well as festivals celebrating everything from American fiddle tunes and films to wooden boats.

★ **Explore the past at Fort Worden State Park.** Strategically situated on the northernmost point of the Quimper Peninsula, this old military fort features a marine science center, historic lighthouse, artillery museum, abandoned bunkers, and beaches.

★ **Inhale the aroma of lavender.** Pick your own in the fields surrounding Sequim, which grow an abundance of this fragrant herb.

★ **Meet the Makah.** Exhibits at the impressive Makah Cultural Center complex display authentic scenes of early life in the Northwest.

★ **Enjoy the great outdoors at Hurricane Ridge.** Drive to the top of this spectacular ridge for splendid summer hikes and winter snow sports.

1 **Northeastern Olympic Peninsula.** Anchored on the northeastern tip by the restored Victorian seaport of Port Townsend, this part of the peninsula is less remote than its northwestern counterpart. Here, the protected waters of Hood Canal meet the Strait of Juan de Fuca, providing a backdrop for boat-building, bird-watching, sailing and—at the turn of the 19th century—shanghai-ing. Farther west, bucolic farmland abounds in the rain shadow surrounding Sequim. Port Angeles provides a launch pad for skiing, snowboarding, hiking and biking at Hurricane Ridge, one of the most easily accessible parts of Olympic National Park.

2 **Northwestern Olympic Peninsula.** Driftwood-strewn secluded beaches and dense old-growth forests, featuring enormous ferns and moss-dripping evergreens, govern the rain-soaked west end. Marked by waterfalls, rivers, mountain lakes, and lodges, it's home to Cape Flattery, the most northwesterly edge of the contiguous United States, and the old logging town of Forks, the setting for the fictional *Twilight* series.

3 **Washington Coast.** The communities along this stretch of Pacific coastline range from new Cape Cod–style homes in the master-planned development of Seabrook, where bikes and flip-flops provide the preferred means of transportation, to Ocean Shores and Westport, guarding the entry to Grays Harbor. Tucked inside are the historic lumber and fishing towns of Hoquiam and Aberdeen, hometown of Nirvana front man Kurt Cobain and home port of the *Lady Washington*. The state's official ship offers dockside tours as well as sail training.

4 **Long Beach Peninsula.** Bookended by two state parks, this narrow stretch of land offers a series of ocean-side retreats, oyster farms, cranberry bogs, and beach after beach to comb. Kite-flying, kayaking, horse-back-riding, clam-digging and winter storm-watching are also popular pastimes. At the southern tip, Cape Disappointment is home to two lighthouses and the Lewis and Clark Interpretative Center.

Neah Bay

Stra

Ozette Lake

La Push

Olympic National Park

Kalaloc

Ta

PACIFIC OCEAN

0		20 mi
0		20 km

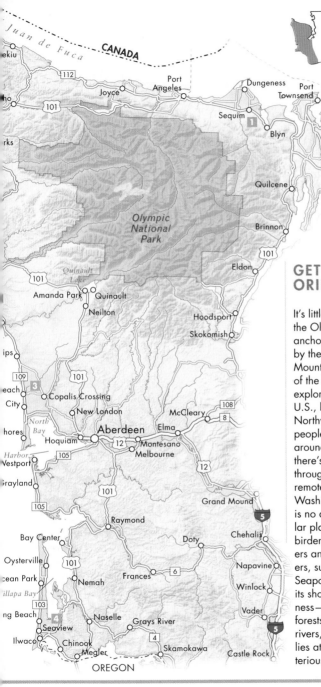

13

GETTING ORIENTED

It's little wonder that the Olympic Peninsula, anchored in the middle by the majestic Olympic Mountains, contains many of the last places to be explored in the contiguous U.S., let alone the Pacific Northwest. Even today, people must drive or sail around this mass of land—there's no direct route through the rugged and remote northwestern arm of Washington state. But this is no deterrent. It's a popular playground for anglers, birders, hikers, snowboarders and snowshoers, skiers, surfers, and sailors. Seaports and beaches hug its shores, but the wilderness—waterfalls, rain forests, hot springs, lakes, rivers, ridges, and peaks—lies at the heart of this mysteriously beautiful place.

Updated
by Adriana
Janovich

Wilderness envelops most of the Olympic Peninsula, an unrefined and enchanting place that promises craggy, snow-capped peaks, pristine evergreen forests, and driftwood-covered coastlines. This is a wonderland where the scent of saltwater and pine hang in the air and the horizon sometimes seems to make the entire world appear to be shades of blue and green. Historic lighthouses, seaports, and tidal pools trim its shores and a majestic mountain range rises up from its heart.

The Olympic Mountains form the core of the peninsula, skirted by saltwater on three sides. The area's highest point, Mount Olympus, stands nearly 8,000 feet above sea level. It's safeguarded in the 922,000-acre Olympic National Park (⇨ *see Chapter 12*), along with much of the extraordinary interior landscape. Several thousand acres more are protected in the Olympic National Forest. The peninsula also encompasses seven Native American reservations, five wilderness areas, five national wildlife refuges, the world's largest unmanaged herd of Roosevelt elk, and some of the wettest and driest areas in the coastal Pacific Northwest. The mountains catch penetrating Pacific storms, bringing an average annual rainfall of about 140 inches to the lush western river valleys and rain forests. The drier northeastern slopes of the peninsula's rain shadow see about 16 inches of precipitation per year, creating an ideal climate for the lavender that's grown commercially here.

Most residents live on the edges of the peninsula, anchored at its southwestern corner by Grays Harbor, named for Captain Robert Gray. He became the first European-American to enter the harbor in 1792. From there, the coast extends north along the Washington Coast to Cape Flattery and Neah Bay on the Makah Indian Reservation, then stretches to the Victorian seaport of Port Townsend, on the tip of the Quimper Peninsula, a narrow, crooked elbow of land at the northeastern end of the larger land mass. Rugged terrain and few roads limit interior accessibility to backpackers and climbers. But the 330-mile outer loop of U.S. Highway 101 offers breath-taking forest, ocean, and mountain vistas as well as rest stops at a variety of colorful outposts along the way.

OLYMPIC PENINSULA AND WASHINGTON COAST PLANNER

13

WHEN TO GO

Visitors trek to the Olympic Peninsula year-round, but summer is prime touring time for this outdoor-lovers' paradise. June through September, when it's least likely to rain, is busiest. Beaches, campgrounds, and downtown areas bustle during the sun-filled summer months, and festivals attract additional crowds. This is also the time of peak lodging rates.

Early and late spring and fall are likely to be less crowded, and in many cases the shoulder season also promises less expensive hotel rates. Anytime between April and October, there's a good chance of clear skies, even if temperatures dip. The rest of the year, prepare for heavy clouds, rain showers, and chilly temperatures.

Accommodations tend to fill up year-round on festival and holiday weekends. Some museums and other tourist attractions close or operate on a limited schedule in winter, when unrelenting storms pound Washington's Pacific coast. Mid-October through mid-March, pummeling waves crash into sea stacks and outcroppings, and wind speeds of up to 60 mph send rain spitting sideways. Winter storm watchers, weekend skiers and snowboarders heading to Hurricane Ridge, and locals are usually the only hardy souls around this time of the year. For some, that—coupled with off-season lodging rates—is a draw.

FESTIVALS AND EVENTS

The region has a number of festivals and events that are worth planning for.

Great Port Townsend Bay Kinetic Sculpture Race. Since 1983, contestants have been racing human-powered contraptions through sand, mud, neighborhoods, and saltwater in the hope of winning the most coveted prize: the Mediocrity Award for the sculpture that finishes in the middle of the pack. The race takes place in early October. ⊠ *Port Townsend* ☎ *360/379–4972* ⊕ *ptkineticrace.org.*

Irrigation Festival. Sequim has been celebrating the introduction of irrigation water to its once-parched prairie since 1896. Recent fests, held in May, feature an antique-car show, street fair, pageant, parade, dance, and logging demonstrations. ⊠ *Sequim* ☎ *360/683–6197* ⊕ *irrigationfestival.com.*

Olympic Music Festival. From June through September, concert-goers can picnic on the lawn while enjoying chamber music in a bucolic setting, complete with a renovated barn. ⊠ *Quilcene* ☎ *360/385–4800* ⊕ *www.olympicmusicfestival.org.*

Port Townsend Film Festival. Founded in 1999 by Rocky Friedman, owner and operator of the town's 1907 Rose Theatre, this mid-September fest features onstage discussions with Hollywood stars, a variety of documentary and narrative films, and outdoor screenings on Taylor Street. ⊠ *Port Townsend* ☎ *360/379–1333* ⊕ *www.ptfilmfest.com.*

Sequim Lavender Festival. A street fair and free self-guided farm tours celebrate Sequim's many fragrant lavender fields in July. ⊠ *Sequim* ☎ *360/681–3035* ⊕ *www.lavenderfestival.com.*

Wooden Boat Festival. Hundreds of wooden boats sail into Port Townsend in September for a weekend of demonstrations, presentations, tours, and sea shanties. The Wooden Boat Foundation, the festival's sponsor, offers seminars, sailing, rowing, regattas, and youth programming year-round. ⊠ *Port Townsend* ☎ *360/385–3628* ⊕ *woodenboat.org.*

GETTING HERE AND AROUND

AIR TRAVEL

Port Angeles is the major northern gateway to the Olympic Peninsula, while Olympia is the major entry point in the south. Kenmore Air connects Port Angeles with Boeing Field, near Seattle, where passengers make the 15-minute trip to Sea-Tac Airport via a free shuttle bus. Fairchild International Airport, the largest on the Olympic Peninsula, is 6 miles southwest of Port Angeles off U.S. 101 (take Airport Rd. north from U.S. 101). Jefferson County Airport, a small charter-flight base, is 4 miles southwest of Port Townsend off Hwy. 19.

Contacts **Fairchild International Airport** ⊠ *1402 Fairchild International Airport Rd., Port Angeles* ☎ *360/457–1138, 360/417–3433* ⊕ *www.portofpa.com.* **Jefferson County International Airport** ⊠ *310 Airport Rd., Port Townsend* ☎ *360/385–0656* ⊕ *www.portofpt.com/airport.htm.* **Kenmore Air** ☎ *866/435–9524* ⊕ *www.kenmoreair.com.* **San Juan Airlines** ☎ *360/293–4691, 800/874–4434* ⊕ *www.sanjuanairlines.com.*

AIRPORTS AND TRANSFERS

Olympic Bus Lines, a Greyhound affiliate, transports passengers twice daily from Port Angeles, Discovery Bay, and Port Townsend to Sea-Tac Airport ($49) and downtown Seattle ($39).

Contacts **Olympic Bus Lines** ☎ *360/417–0700, 800/457–4492* ⊕ *www.olympicbuslines.com.*

BOAT AND FERRY TRAVEL

Washington State Ferries offers the most direct route from Seattle to the Olympic Peninsula. Fares vary seasonally. Walk-ons pay less than vehicles with a driver and other passengers. A ferry from Whidbey Island takes travelers to downtown Port Townsend.

Nearby ferry terminals in Edmonds, Kingston and Bremerton also provide access to the Olympic Peninsula. From Port Angeles, travelers can reach Victoria, British Columbia, on the M.V. *Coho,* which makes 1½-hour Port Angeles–Victoria crossings four times daily from mid-May through mid-October and twice daily the rest of the year (except when it's docked for maintenance, from mid-January through mid-March). Rates are $58.50 per car and driver, $16 per passenger, and $6.50 per bike; travelers can reserve ahead online or by telephone for an additional fee. *Coho,* operated by Black Ball Transport, departs from the ferry terminal at the foot of Laurel Street.

Contacts **Black Ball Ferry Line** ☎ *360/457–4491 in Port Angeles, 250/386–2202 in Victoria* ⊕ *www.ferrytovictoria.com.* **Washington State Ferries** ✉ *Colman Dock, Pier 52, Downtown, Seattle* ☎ *206/464–6400, 888/808–7977, 800/843–3779 automated line in WA and BC* ⊕ *www.wsdot.wa.gov/ferries.*

CAR TRAVEL

U.S. 101, the main thoroughfare around the Olympic Peninsula, is a two-lane, well-paved highway. Rural back roads are blacktop or gravel, and tend to have potholes and get washed out during rains. In winter, landslides and wet weather frequently close roads. Highway 112 heads west from U.S. 101 at Port Angeles to Neah Bay. Highway 113 winds north from U.S. 101 at Sappho to Highway 112. Highway 110 travels west from U.S. 101 at Forks to La Push. Highway 109 leads west from U.S. 101 at Hoquiam to Copalis Beach, Moclips, and Taholah. Highway 8 heads west from Olympia and connects with U.S. 12, which travels west to Aberdeen. From the Hood Canal Bridge, State Routes 19 and 20 branch off State Route 104 to Port Townsend, Discovery Bay, and Sequim.

RESTAURANTS

Port Townsend reigns as the foodie capital of the Olympic Peninsula, where Pacific Northwest coastal cuisine prevails. For a small town, it features an impressive collection of casual yet upscale dining options, some with sweeping bay views. Influences include Italian, French, Spanish, and Southern American cooking. Many restaurants and pubs offer straight-from-the-farm organic herbs and vegetables as well as locally crafted artisanal breads and cheeses and, of course, shellfish and salmon from local waters.

The entire Olympic Culinary Loop—from Port Townsend, Sequim, Port Angeles, and Forks to the Long Beach Peninsula—is best known for its seafood, fresh from local bays and inlets or wild-caught in the Pacific Ocean by local fishermen. Many restaurants along the route feature fish-and-chips, chowders, oyster or salmon burgers, crab cakes, cioppino, clams, and mussels. The peninsula also offers many family-friendly and down-home eateries, from hearty burger and breakfast joints to authentic Thai, Japanese, and Mexican restaurants. *Prices in the reviews are the average cost of a main course at dinner or, if dinner is not served, at lunch.*

HOTELS

The Olympic Peninsula offers an array of lodging options, from Cape Cod-style cottages and rustic cabins to mid-range motels, timber-lined lodges, and Victorian-mansions-turned-bed-and-breakfasts, complete with claw-foot tubs, multicourse morning meals, and innkeepers dressed in turn-of-the-twentieth-century garb. Many offer beach access or views of the water or mountains. Holidays and during festivals are when it's most difficult to find rooms. Winter and shoulder seasons typically offer the most economical price points. Skiers, snowboarders, and day-hikers headed to Hurricane Ridge might opt to use Port Angeles as their home base. For foodies, history buffs, and maritime enthusiasts, Port Townsend offers numerous Victorian-themed B&Bs and hotels as well as inns and motels with bay views. Those seeking peace and quiet might consider accommodations in Sequim. The Washington Coast and Long Beach Peninsula are the best destinations for winter storm watchers and beachcombers. *Prices in the reviews are the lowest cost of a standard double room in high season.*

VISITOR INFORMATION

Contacts North Olympic Peninsula Visitor and Convention Bureau ⊠ *Port of Port Angeles, 338 W. 1st St., Suite 104, Port Angeles* ☎ *360/452–8552, 800/942–4042* ⊕ *www.olympicpeninsula.org.* **Northwest Interpretive Association** ⊠ *3002 Mt. Angeles Rd., Port Angeles* ☎ *360/565–3195* ⊕ *www. discovernw.org.* **Olympic National Forest** ⊠ *1835 Blacklake Blvd. SW, Olympia* ☎ *360/956–2400 Olympia Office, 360/765–2200 Hood Canal Ranger District, Quilcene, 360/374–6522 Pacific Ranger District North, Forks, 360/288–2525 Pacific Ranger District South, Quinault* ⊕ *www.fs.usda.gov/olympic.* **Olympic National Park** ⊠ *3002 Mt. Angeles Rd. (visitor center), Port Angeles* ☎ *360/565–3130 visitor information, 360/565–3131 road and weather hotline* ⊕ *www.nps.gov/olym.*

NORTHEASTERN OLYMPIC PENINSULA

The northeastern portion of the Olympic Peninsula is easily accessible, making it a favorite getaway for Seattleites and other Washingtonians who live along the urban corridor that follows the north-south ribbon of Interstate 5. The restored Victorian seaport of Port Townsend at the peninsula's northeastern tip is a mere hour-and-45-minute drive from Seattle, including a scenic half-hour ferry ride across Puget Sound. The town is small—some 9,000 people live here—but it's teeming with activity. With its thriving arts scene, main street lined with galleries and boutiques, rich maritime heritage, upscale eateries, and variety of festivals, PT—as locals call it—offers plenty to do. Travelers could easily spend an entire weekend in this town alone. But, farther west, past Discovery Bay, bucolic farmland abounds in the rain shadow surrounding Sequim, home of the Olympic Game Farm and Dungeness Spit, a 5-mile sandy finger of shoreline topped with a wide wishbone-shaped beach that juts into the Strait of Juan de Fuca. An 1857 lighthouse, which allows families to serve as lighthouse keepers for a week at a time, stands guard at the north end of the wishbone. At the western edge of this corner of the peninsula, Port Angeles provides a launchpad for skiing, snowboarding, hiking, and biking at Hurricane Ridge, one of the most easily accessible parts of Olympic National Park. It also offers ferry service to Victoria, British Columbia, sweeping views of the Strait of Juan de Fuca, and a chance for *Twilight* fans to relive some of their favorite scenes, including dinner at La Bella Italia, the restaurant that served as the backdrop for Bella and Edward's first date.

PORT TOWNSEND

99 miles north from Olympia.

Ship captains from around the world once sailed into this port, known for its parlors of ill repute, saloons, shanghaiing, and other mid-19th century waterfront shenanigans. In fact, it was developed into two separate urban centers: the waterfront, which catered to hard-drinking sailors and other adventurers, and uptown, on the cliff above the bay, where merchants and permanent residents lived and raised their families away from the riff-raff. The refined Victorian-era women who once shunned Water Street, the main drag through downtown, would likely want to be seen there now. The once rough-and tumble thoroughfare has given way to art galleries and antiques stores, trendy boutiques, coffeehouses, pubs, upscale eateries, and public docks.

Officially settled in 1851, Port Townsend was dubbed the "City of Dreams" because of the early idea that it would become the largest harbor on the West Coast with help from the impending railroad. Instead, the railroad opted for the east side of Puget Sound and the former boomtown experienced a bit of a bust. But the spirit of the town's maritime community and idea that open water lies just off the horizon continues to tinge this place with a certain romance. On a peninsula— the small, crooked arm of the Quimper on the northeastern tip of the larger, torch-shaped Olympic—Port Townsend is a place where the modern meets the Victorian, maritime trades meet the arts, and the sun sets over the water. Its inhabitants are a collection of artists, writers, musicians, mariners, and "shed boys," a term coined in the early 2000s for the mostly single men who live here off the grid. For all of them Port Townsend remains a city of dreams. These knit-cap and Carhartt-wearing residents are well-traveled and highly educated. It's not unusual to find waitresses, bartenders, and students at the boat school who have willingly given up more lucrative positions in larger cities to live here, in the most picturesque gateway to the Olympic Peninsula.

GETTING HERE AND AROUND

From downtown Seattle, Port Townsend is reached via the Washington State Ferries to Bainbridge Island, then north on State Route 305, north on State Route 3, west on State Route 104, and north on State Route 19, which connects to State Route 20 and takes travelers into town. From Edmonds (north of Seattle via I–5), take the Washington State Ferries to Kingston, then travel west via Hwy. 104 and north via State Route 19. Both routes run roughly an hour and 45 minutes, not including ferry waits. From Olympia and points south, there are two routes northbound: U.S. 101 and Hwy. 14. Both take about two hours.

Contact **Washington State Ferries** ☎ *888/808–7977, 800/843–3779, 206/464–6400* ⊕ *www.wsdot.wa.gov/ferries.*

GUIDED TOURS

Walking Tours. The Jefferson County Historical Society conducts hour-long walking tours of Port Townsend on weekends from June through September for $10. ⊠ *540 Water St.* ☎ *360/385–1003* ⊕ *www.jchsmuseum.org.*

ESSENTIALS

Visitor Information **Jefferson County Chamber of Commerce and Visitor Information Center** ⊠ *440 12th St.* ☎ *360/385–7869, 888/365–6978* ⊕ *jeffcountychamber.org.*

EXPLORING

Fire Bell Tower. Set high along the bayside bluffs, the tower is recognizable by its pyramid shape and red paint job. Built in 1890 to hold a 1,500-pound brass alarm bell, the 75-foot wooden structure was once the key alert center for local volunteer firemen. A century later it's considered one of the state's most valuable historic buildings. Inside are firefighting equipment and regional artifacts from pioneer days, including a 19th-century horse-drawn hearse. Reach the tower by climbing the stairs at Tyler Street. The tenth-of-an-acre plot also holds a park bench and five parking spots. ⊠ *Jefferson St. and Tyler St., Uptown* ☎ *360/385–1003* ⊕ *www.jchsmuseum.org* ☜ *$4* ⊙ *By appointment with Jefferson Co. Historical Society.*

FAMILY **Fort Worden State Park.** The manicured grounds of 434-acre Fort Worden State Park include a row of restored Victorian officers' houses, a World War II balloon hangar, and a sandy beach that leads to the 1913 Point Wilson Lighthouse. Built on Point Wilson in 1896, the fort hosts art events, music festivals, kayaking tours, camping, and outdoor activities. ⊠ *200 Battery Way* ☎ *360/385–4730, 360/344–4400* ⊕ *www.parks. wa.gov/fortworden* ☜ *Day pass: $10 per vehicle; Discovery Pass $30 (valid at all state parks)* ⊙ *Daily dawn–dusk.*

Northwest Maritime Center. The myriad traditions and trades of the Pacific Northwest's seafaring history are explained here, specifically citing the importance of Port Townsend as one of only three Victorian-era seaports on the country's register of National Historic Sites. It's the core of the Point Hudson district and the center of operations for the Wooden Boat Foundation, which stages the annual Wooden Boat Festival early each September. The center has interactive exhibits, hands-on sailing training, boatbuilding workshops, a wood shop, and a pilot house where you can test navigational tools. The boardwalk, pier, and sandy beach that front the buildings are laced with marine life, and are the perfect points to launch a kayak or watch sloops and schooners gliding along the coast. The chandlery features a variety of nautical gifts and gear, from brass fittings and rigging supplies to galley wares, illustrated knot books, and boats-in-a-bottle. In a well-lighted back corner overlooking the bay, Velocity Coffee Bar sells espresso and baked goods from 6:30 am to 5 pm Monday through Saturday. ⊠ *431 Water St.* ☎ *360/385–3628, 360/379–5383* ⊕ *www.nwmaritime.org* ☜ *Free* ⊙ *Weekdays 9–5.*

NEED A BREAK?

Elevated Ice Cream Company. Stop here for coffee, pastries, handmade truffles and chocolates, candy, or scoops of ice cream, sherbet and Italian ices, crafted on-site. Proprietors Julie and David McCulloch first served their homemade ice cream from an antique Victorian elevator cage in 1977 (the shop motto is "Lift Your Spirits"). It's open daily 10–9 (to 10 pm Friday and Saturday). ⊠ *627 and 631 Water St.* ☎ *360/385–1156* ⊕ *www. elevatedicecream.com.*

Port Townsend Marine Science Center. Along the waterfront at Fort Worden State Park, the center is divided into two sections. The marine lab and aquarium building, in a former World War II military storage facility at

Victorian building, Port Townsend

the end of a pier, houses numerous aquarium displays, as well as touch tanks with sea stars, crabs, and anemones. The separate, on-shore Natural History Exhibit Center is filled with displays detailing the region's geography and marine ecology. Beach walks, nature camps, cruises, and day camps run throughout the summer, and there's a Low Tide Festival each July. ✉ *520 Battery Way* ☎ *360/385–5582, 800/566–3932* 🌐 *www.ptmsc.org* 🎟 *$5* 🕒 *mid-June–early Sept., Wed.–Mon. 11–5; early Sept.–early June, Fri.–Sun. noon–4 (marine lab and aquarium building by appointment only Nov.–Mar.).*

WHERE TO EAT

$$ INTERNATIONAL 🍴 **Alchemy Bistro & Wine Bar.** This upscale eatery overlooking Haller Fountain offers a blend of Italian, Spanish, and French favorites alongside Pacific Northwest fare, including succulent salmon, oysters, and mussels. Start with rich, creamy stuffed poblano peppers, or oyster stew with leeks, ginger, garlic and fresh tarragon. Entrées include a selection of salads, seafood, and pastas as well as the often-requested Drunken Rabbit, slow-cooked in red wine with garlic, carrots, and onions. Other mainstays include duck breast with myrtle berry butter, cassoulet with rabbit, chicken garlic sausage, and braised lamb chops. Sunday brunch features wild salmon Benedict, crepes with fresh berry compote and mascarpone, crème brûlée French toast, and endless mimosas, and there's an evening "small bites" menu in the dimly lighted, intimate bar. [$] *Average main: $22* ✉ *842 Washington St.* ☎ *360/385–5225* 🌐 *alchemybistroandwinebar.com.*

$$ ✕ **The Belmont.** The town's only remaining 1880s saloon is tucked into
PACIFIC the line of brick-front buildings along the seaport's main street. Tall,
NORTHWEST waterfront windows let in light and afford broad bay views, which
make a perfect backdrop to the innovative seafood dishes and Pacific
Northwest fare. Dig into a pound of mussels or clams or a combination
poached in a pesto cream sauce, a char-grilled salmon filet topped with
Dungeness crab and béarnaise sauce, or the "three-masted" filet mignon
topped with Dungeness crab, three prawns and béarnaise sauce. A bar
on the mezzanine overlooks Water Street for people-watching. The sec-
ond floor is a hotel with Victorian furnishings to match the history and
architecture. $ *Average main: $18* ⊠ *925 Water St.* ☎ *360/385–3007*
⊕ *www.thebelmontpt.com.*

$ ✕ **Cellar Door.** The undertown entrance to this eclectic subterranean
CONTEMPORARY space, which opened in 2013, can be difficult to spot—at the bottom of
a Tyler Street staircase. There you'll find a sophisticated yet casual wine
and cocktail bar that melds vintage Victorian with a rustic industrial
feel and sense of whimsy (concrete floors, reclaimed wood, antiques).
Catering to the after-hours crew, it offers contemporary bites, hand-
crafted cocktails, and a distinctly steampunk vibe. Specials like bread
crumb–encrusted mac-n-cheese in tarragon béchamel sauce or pork ten-
derloin with roasted parsnips can be eaten at the force-rusted steel bar
or in any of the intimate nooks. Most of the sodas, syrups, bitters, and
infusions are made in-house. Quick bites include antipasto and hum-
mus plates and pulled pork or lamb sliders. $ *Average main: $8* ⊠ *940
Water St., Entrance on Tyler St.* ☎ *360/385–6959* ⊕ *www.cellardoorpt.
com* ⊘ *Closed Tues. and Wed. No lunch.*

$ ✕ **Courtyard Café.** This homey mom-and-pop coffee and baked goods
AMERICAN shop sells thick-crusted, overstuffed housemade berry and fruit pies,
cinnamon rolls, muffins, and other assorted pastries and breads. Order
at the deli-style counter and take treats to go, or seat yourself and enjoy
the family-friendly, cozy café, which also serves hearty breakfasts and
lunches like a skillet scramble; corned beef and hash; spinach, mush-
room, and cheese quiche; soups; salads; and a wide selection of amply
filled sandwiches. In warm weather, sit outside on the back deck or in
the fenced front patio, a few yards off the town's main street. $ *Average
main: $8* ⊠ *230 Quincy St.* ☎ *360/379–3355* ⊕ *www.courtyardcafept.
com* ⊘ *Closed Tues. No dinner.*

$$$ ✕ **Fins Coastal Cuisine.** This spacious, second-floor Pacific Northwest-
SEAFOOD style dining room, set above the main street and picturesque bay,
provides a perfect setting to sample fresh catch, from appetizers like
Dungeness crab cakes and calamari to full dinners of succulent, beautifully presented shellfish and salmon. Look for mains like creamy but not
too thick clam chowder with a hint of white wine and thyme, Dungeness
crab rigatoni with sweet corn sauce, macadamia crusted halibut, and
traditional cioppppino. The menu also features locally harvested oysters,
mussels, and clams, and desserts like pot de crème and crème brûlée.
Housemade pickles garnish dishes and housemade simple syrups and
infused vodkas add something special to a wide selection of spirits. In
warm weather, dine on the terrace, which overlooks the incoming and

outgoing ferries and sailboats. $ *Average main: $24* ✉ *1019 Water St.* ☎ *360/379–3474* ⊕ *www.finscoastal.com.*

$$ ✕ **Fountain Café.** Tucked inside a historic clapboard building a block off

ECLECTIC the main drag, this intimate and eclectic eatery is a local favorite. Artwork lines the walls of the small, funky café where seafood and pasta dishes carry Mediterranean, Moroccan, Indian, and Thai influences, and often include rich cream sauces as well as plenty of garlic. Chicken marsala and paella are mainstays. Full-bodied Pacific Northwest and Italian wines as well as simple sweets like tiramisu and gingerbread round out the menu. Most of the art on the walls is for sale, and the café forms part of the town's monthly gallery walks. $ *Average main: $17* ✉ *920 Washington St.* ☎ *360/385–1364* ⊜ *Reservations not accepted.*

$ ✕ **Hanazono Asian Noodle.** The regular menu at this small, long, thin,

JAPANESE authentic Japanese noodle house includes three types of egg noodles— ramen, *yakisoba*, and *champon*—as well as rice, soba and udon noodles in a variety of soups, stir-fries, and salads. The restaurant also serves a variety of sushi rolls, *donburi* (rice bowl dish), bento, and daily specials. Start with tofu fries, miso soup, seaweed salad, spring rolls, or *gyoza* (handmade potstickers stuffed with cabbage, pork, and green onion). Finish with green tea or ginger ice cream, green tea tiramisu, or cheesecake. The restaurant also serves, beer, wine, and sake. Don't be surprised if it's crowded; the place gets packed. $ *Average main: $9* ✉ *225 Taylor St.* ☎ *360/385–7622* ⊕ *hanazonoasiannoodle.com* ⊘ *Closed Mon.*

$ ✕ **Khu Larb Thai.** Some of the state's best Thai food is prepared at this

THAI unassuming restaurant, a few steps off the main street. Family-run for more than 20 years, its recipes reflect Chinese, Indian, and Malaysian influences on traditional Thai fare, including savory soups, curries, and fried rice and noodle dishes, many with fresh basil, sliced lime leaves, and hints of lemongrass. There's a wide array of meat and vegetarian dishes as well as seafood like tender scallops in red curry or local Marrowstone Island clams in ginger curry. The signature black rice pudding dessert far exceeds the usual coconut ice cream on Thai menus. $ *Average main: $13* ✉ *225 Adams St.* ☎ *360/385–5023* ⊕ *www.khularbthai.com* ⊘ *Closed Tues.*

$ ✕ **Lanza's Ristorante.** Intimate and romantic, this small Uptown eatery

ITALIAN exudes the warmth of Italy with welcoming and gracious staff, generous portions, and authentic, old-country recipes. Sit in the booth in the front window, and share the ample antipasto platter while waiting for pizza or pasta, from classic spaghetti and meatballs to ravioli Florentine, penne with sausage, mushrooms and spinach, and a rich, creamy linguine luna. Specialty dishes include rack of lamb, chicken marsala, and chicken piccata. A Port Townsend institution for nearly 30 years, Lanza's is popular with locals and there's usually a crowd, especially on weekends, when live music adds to the ambiance. Reservations are recommended. Save room for tiramisu. $ *Average main: $16* ✉ *1020 Lawrence St., Uptown* ☎ *360/379–1900* ⊕ *www.lanzaspt.com* ⊘ *Closed Sun. and Mon. No lunch.*

$$ ✕ **Silverwater Cafe.** On the first floor of the 1889 Elks' Lodge building,

PACIFIC
NORTHWEST this restaurant pairs elegant surroundings with a sophisticated menu. Start with sesame ahi, Grand Marnier prawns, or a plate of artisanal

cheeses from the local Mount Townsend Creamery, then opt for pan-seared halibut in a slightly sweet hazelnut cream sauce, cilantro ginger lime jumbo prawns, or lavender pepper ahi. Dessert offers such delicacies as Northwest blackberry pie, raspberry white chocolate cheesecake, and the signature coconut flan—caramel-topped custard with a wisp of coconut flavoring. Mezzaluna, the mezzanine-level lounge, serves dessert as well as salads, samplers, and sandwiches. $ *Average main: $22* ⊠ *237 Taylor St.* ☎ *360/385–6448* ⊕ *www.silverwatercafe.com* ☾ *No lunch Sun.*

$$$ ✕ **Sweet Laurette Café and Bistro.** Paris meets the Pacific Northwest in
BISTRO   this Uptown bistro. Starting out as a patisserie in 2001, it still serves espresso and baked treats in its cozy, French-inspired coffee shop, but don't forego a full meal in the lavender-lined courtyard or casually elegant, intimate dining room, with chocolate-colored wainscoting and pistachio-tinted walls. The menu is classic French bistro with a fresh, contemporary, farm-to-table flair—chef/owner Laurette Feit sources her ingredients, including grass-fed beef, organic eggs, and wild king salmon, from local farmers and fishermen. Exquisitely presented entrées—think lamb shanks with creamy polenta; steak au poivre; king salmon topped with black olive and sun-dried tomato butter—feature beautifully balanced flavors, colors, and textures. Profiteroles, flourless chocolate torte, and crème brûlée are signature desserts. Breakfast and lunch selections are equally accomplished. $ *Average main: $24* ⊠ *1029 Lawrence St., Uptown* ☎ *360/385–4886* ⊕ *www.sweetlaurette. com* ☾ *Closed Mon. and Tues.*

WHERE TO STAY
For expanded hotel reviews, visit Fodors.com.

$ ▨ **Ann Starrett Mansion.** Gables, turrets, and gingerbread trim deco-
B&B/INN   rate this glorious 1889 mansion, built for love—a gift from a wealthy
Fodor'sChoice   contractor to his young bride, the inn features well-appointed, unique
★   rooms, all beautifully decorated and furnished with antiques. **Pros:** sweeping views; a short walk to downtown and uptown restaurants and shops; a chance to experience Victorian elegance. **Cons:** no breakfast; no elevator. $ *Rooms from: $115* ⊠ *744 Clay St., Uptown* ☎ *360/385–3205, 800/321–0644* ⊕ *www.starrettmansion.com* ⇆ *8 rooms, 2 cottages* ⦿ *No meals.*

$$ ▨ **Bishop Victorian Hotel.** This brick inn abounds with 19th-century ele-
B&B/INN   gance and thoughtful service, and most of the one- and two-bedroom suites have garden, mountain, or water views. **Pros:** Victorian flair with contemporary conveniences; a stone's throw from the waterfront, restaurants, boutiques, and coffee shops; congenial staff. **Cons:** no elevator. $ *Rooms from: $155* ⊠ *714 Washington St.* ☎ *360/385–6122, 800/824–4738* ⊕ *www.bishopvictorian.com* ⇆ *16 suites* ⦿ *Breakfast.*

$ ▨ **Manresa Castle.** This expansive, imposing, hillside mansion, built in
HOTEL   1892 for Port Townsend's first mayor, has a fascinating history, lots of Victorian character, and some sweeping views of the bay. **Pros:** staying in a real slice of history. **Cons:** somewhat of a spooky vibe (ask the staff about reported ghost sightings). $ *Rooms from: $109* ⊠ *651 Cleveland St.* ☎ *360/385–5750, 800/732–1281* 🖷 *360/385–5883* ⊕ *www. manresacastle.com* ⇆ *30 rooms, 9 suites* ⦿ *Breakfast.*

$ 🛏 **Old Consulate Inn.** Perched on a bluff above the bay, this elegant red,
B&B/INN   turreted Victorian mansion with a sweeping veranda takes its name
Fodor's Choice   from the acting German consul, one of the inn's early boarders. **Pros:**
★   gourmet breakfast; gorgeous grounds and views; quiet; a real step-
ping-back-in-time experience. **Cons:** no children under 14; no elevator.
$ *Rooms from: $110* ⊠ *313 Walker St.* ☎ *360/385–6753, 800/300–
6753* ⊕ *www.oldconsulate.com* ⟿ *5 rooms, 3 suites* ❍| *Breakfast.*

$ 🛏 **Palace Hotel.** Built in 1889, the historic, three-story Captain Tibbals
B&B/INN   building is one of the most famous in town—a former bordello that
retains its 19th-century grandeur. **Pros:** a feeling of participating in a bit
of Port Townsend's history; a stone's throw from restaurants, boutiques,
and bars. **Cons:** might not suit travelers who don't appreciate Victorian charm. $ *Rooms from: $99* ⊠ *1004 Water St.* ☎ *360/385–0773,
800/962–0741* ⊕ *www.palacehotelpt.com* ⟿ *19 rooms, 17 with bath*
❍| *No meals.*

$ 🛏 **The Swan Hotel.** Tucked at the end of the downtown thoroughfare,
B&B/INN   this balcony-encased, four-story boutique hotel features well-lighted,
airy rooms with gorgeous sea views or, on the north side, overlooking
the Point Hudson Marina. **Pros:** central location; majestic views; comfortable and cozy; suite is good for small groups. **Cons:** no breakfast;
small, often crowded parking lot, with alternative lot a few blocks away.
$ *Rooms from: $130* ⊠ *216 Monroe St.* ☎ *360/379–1840, 800/824–
4738* ⊕ *www.theswanhotel.com* ⟿ *8 rooms, 1 suite, four cottages*
❍| *No meals.*

$ 🛏 **Tides Inn.** The multistory, peak-roofed inn resembles an expansive
HOTEL   beach house, and its setting on the water near to the ferry dock—as
well as its variety of rooms—makes it one of the town's most popular
accommodations. **Pros:** beach locale, with beautiful bay views; reasonable price; one of the few hotels in town with an elevator. **Cons:**
need to book far in advance for festivals and summer weekends; three
rooms don't have a sea view. $ *Rooms from: $89* ⊠ *1807 Water St.*
☎ *360/385–0595, 800/822–8696* ⊕ *www.tides-inn.com* ⟿ *23 rooms,
21 suites* ❍| *Breakfast.*

$ 🛏 **Washington Hotel.** With its keyless entry, Wi-Fi, and modern interi-
HOTEL   ors, this small boutique hotel on the second floor of a historic building in the heart of downtown caters to the independent traveler. **Pros:**
stylish city feel in a small-town environment; central location. **Cons:**
not the best choice for travelers who require 24-hour concierge services. $ *Rooms from: $109* ⊠ *825 Washington St.* ☎ *360/774–0213*
⊕ *washingtonhotelporttownsend.com* ⟿ *4 rooms* ❍| *No meals.*

NIGHTLIFE

Port Townsend Brewing Company. Boatyard workers and beer enthusiasts congregate at this casual and cozy Boat Haven brewery to enjoy
a pint and bowl of peanuts (and not worry about dropping the spent
shells on the floor). There's an outdoor beer garden during warmer
months. Proprietors Kim and Guy Sands opened the brewery in 1997
with only two beers. About 10 are on now the menu, including the
award-winning Boatyard Bitter, Port Townsend Pale Ale, and Hop Dig-
gidy, a classic Northwest-style IPA. The brewery closes early evening,
so nightlife-seekers might want to make this one of their first stops.

✉ *330 10th St., Port Townsend Boat Haven* ☎ *360/385–9967* ⊕ *www. porttownsendbrewing.com* ☯ *Daily noon–7 (open until 9 on Fri.).*

Pourhouse. Opened in 2012, this craft beer taproom and bottle shop has quickly become a gathering place for local and out-of-town beer enthusiasts. It features a dozen rotating taps, 200 bottles and cans of beer and hard cider, and wines by the glass. During warmer months, the bayside beer garden has sweeping views of the Cascade and Olympic mountains and nearby boat haven. There are picnic tables, a pétanque court, and a concrete table for table tennis. Some snacks are served, you can bring your own take-out, or order from one of the many in-town eateries that will deliver full meals; menus are available in the taproom. ✉ *2231 Washington St.* ☎ *360/379–5586* ⊕ *www.ptpourhouse.com.*

Sirens. Tucked away on the upper floor of a historic sandstone building on Port Townsend's main street, Sirens provides breathtaking bay views and regularly books West Coast rockabilly, alternative country, blues, jazz, and rock bands on weekends. Fiddlers jam here Tuesday nights, and Wednesday open mic nights are a local tradition. Microbrews, handcrafted martinis, and margaritas quench the thirst and there's a menu of hearty Pacific Northwest-inspired pub food. ✉ *832 Water St.* ☎ *360/379–1100* ⊕ *www.sirenspub.com.*

The Upstage. With its exposed brick walls and two open floors surrounding a grand piano and otherwise intimate performance space, there's a backstage feel here. It's difficult to find an empty night on the performance calendar. Live music ranges from blues and jazz to salsa, tango, swing, and folk, and there are comedians, open mic nights, dancing, and ukulele jam sessions. The entrance is across the parking lot at the end of Tyler Street. There's a cover charge ($5 to $30) most nights. Reservations are recommended; some premium acts require a seven-day cancellation notice. The dinner menu features Pacific Northwest cuisine with Mediterranean, Cajun, Indian, Russian and Balkan influences. ✉ *923 Washington St.* ☎ *360/385–2216* ⊕ *www.upstagerestaurant.com.*

SHOPPING

Port Townsend brims with antiques stores, art galleries, clothing boutiques, consignment shops, vintage and New Age-y bookstores, and upscale maritime, kitchen, home design, and gift shops. Water and Washington streets, which run parallel to the bay, are lined with storefronts. So are their block-long offshoots, cut off by the cliff that separates downtown from uptown. More stores are located uptown on Lawrence Street near an enclave of Victorian houses. To reach them, walk up the Terrace Steps behind Haller Fountain at Washington and Taylor streets. Along the way, plenty of pubs, coffeehouses, and eateries provide tired shoppers a place to revive and rest their feet.

Conservatory Coastal Home. With its high ceilings, exposed brick walls, array of upscale seaside luxe living essentials, and soy candles handpoured on-site in small batches in scents like sailcloth, fog, moss, and water, this home design and gift boutique smells as good and it looks. A variety of air plants in recycled glass terrariums are always in stock. Look for furniture fashioned from reclaimed wood, nautical-themed throw pillows, jewelry, and seashells. ✉ *639 Water St.* ☎ *360/385–3857* ⊕ *www.conservatorycoastalhome.com.*

Green Eyeshade. This well-stocked kitchen and gift shop features a wide array of linens, glassware, dishes, jewelry, wine accessories, candles, knickknacks, and gourmet gadgets. ✉ *720 Water St.* ☎ *360/385–3838.*

get-a-bles. An eclectic range of supplies makes this little shop as interesting and fun as the name suggests. There are eat-a-bles and drink-a-bles—sandwiches, cheese, pickles, pretzels, nuts, hard cider, soda, and beer—and gift-a-bles such as locally roasted coffee, gourmet salts, handmade sugar scrubs and soaps, toys, and flasks. ✉ *810 Water St.* ☎ *360/385–5560* ⊕ *www.getablespt.com.*

Maestrale. East meets West in this specialty shop, which imports fabrics, furniture, jewelry, and other handicrafts from India, Indonesia, Thailand, Nepal, and China. ✉ *821 Water St.* ☎ *360/385–5565* ⊕ *maestraleimports.com.*

Perfect Season. You'll find a little bit of everything here, including things for the home, pottery, planters, bath and baby items, books, birdhouses, and antiques. ✉ *1042 Lawrence St., Uptown* ☎ *360/385–9265* ⊕ *www.theperfectseason.com.*

Port Townsend Antique Mall. Three-dozen dealers at the two-story Port Townsend Antique Mall sell merchandise ranging from pricey Victorian collectors' items to cheap flea-market kitsch. ✉ *802 Washington St.* ☎ *360/379–8069.*

Port Townsend Farmers' Market. Port Townsend is proud of its farm-to-table food movement and visitors can witness and share in the region's bounty at the farmers' market. Approximately 70 vendors, including some 40 farmers, showcase their fare—fresh produce, artisan foods, crafts, and handmade soaps and salves. The market is open Saturday 9–2 April–December and also on Wednesday 3–6 late June–late September. ✉ *Tyler St.* ☎ *360/379–9098* ⊕ *jeffersoncountyfarmersmarket.org.*

Sport Townsend. This store has been stocking high-quality outdoor gear, including backpacks, hiking boots, camping supplies, and boating and fishing equipment, for more than 20 years. Winter sports gear is also available, including downhill and cross-country ski accessories, cold-weather clothing, and snowshoes. ✉ *1044 Water St.* ☎ *360/379–9711* ⊕ *www.sporttownsend.com.*

William James Bookseller. Used and out-of-print books covering all fields—with an emphasis on nautical, regional history, and theology titles—are arrayed from floor to ceiling of this jam-packed gem of a bookstore. ✉ *829 Water St.* ☎ *360/385–7313* ⊕ *williamjamesbookseller.com.*

SPORTS AND THE OUTDOORS
BICYCLING
The nearest place to go biking is Fort Worden State Park, but you can range as far afield as Fort Flagler, the lower Dungeness trails (no bikes are allowed on the spit itself), or across the water to Whidbey Island.

The Broken Spoke. This bike retail, repair, and rental shop in the heart of downtown promotes cycling at all levels. ✉ *835 Water St.* ☎ *360/379–1295* ⊕ *www.thebrokenspokept.blogspot.com.*

P. T. Cyclery. Mountain bikes are available for rent here, and they repair flats and can advise you on where to start your journey. ⊠ *252 Tyler St.* ☎ *360/385–6470* ⊕ *www.ptcyclery.com.*

BOAT CRUISE

P. S. Express. This company has run summer speedboat connections between Port Townsend and Friday Harbor for nearly 30 years. The round-trips cost $85 to $95 May through September; boats depart from Port Townsend at 9, arriving in Friday Harbor at noon; the return trip departs from Friday Harbor at 2:30 and arrives back in Port Townsend at 5. Four-hour guaranteed-sighting whale-watching trips ($95) depart from Friday Harbor at 10 and 2:30 May–late September to view orcas (killer whales) and at 10 from mid-March–end April to see migrating gray whales ($85). Whale-watching trips are subject to a minimum number of passengers. ⊠ *227 Jackson St., at the Point Hudson Marina* ☎ *360/385–5288* ⊕ *www.pugetsoundexpress.com.*

KAYAKING

PT Outdoors. Located at Fort Worden State Park and open seasonally, this company offers kayaking classes and guided trips. Waterfront tours are $60; three-hour tours to Bird Island are $80; specialty tours can also be arranged with at least a week's advance notice. All tours require reservations. Single kayaks rent for $25 per hour; double kayaks rent for $40 per hour. ⊠ *Fort Worden State Park, 200 Battery Way* ☎ *360/379–3608* ⊕ *www.ptoutdoors.com.*

SEQUIM

31 miles west of Port Townsend.

Sequim (pronounced *skwim*), incorporated in 1913, is a pleasant old mill town and farming center between the northern foothills of the Olympic Mountains and the southeastern stretch of the Strait of Juan de Fuca. With lots of sunshine, lovely views, and neat, quiet blocks, it's also a popular place to retire. Sequim's walkable downtown, marked by a historic grain elevator, features a variety of gift and other shops. A few miles to the north is the shallow and fertile Dungeness Valley, which enjoys some of the lowest rainfall in western Washington. Fragrant purple lavender flourishes in local fields. East of town, scenic Sequim Bay is home to the John Wayne Marina. The actor, who navigated local waters aboard his yacht, Wild Goose, donated land for the marina in 1975, four years before his death.

GETTING HERE AND AROUND

Sequim is about 2 hours from Seattle, via the Seattle-Bainbridge Island or Edmonds–Kingston ferries and U.S. 101. It's served by Clallam Transit to local Olympic Peninsula towns, and Olympic Bus Lines to Silverdale, Seattle, and Sea-Tac International Airport.

Contacts Clallam Transit ☎ *360/452–4511, 800/858–3747* ⊕ *www. clallamtransit.com.* **Olympic Bus Lines** ☎ *360/417–0700, 800/457–4492* ⊕ *www.olympicbuslines.com.*

13

ESSENTIALS

Visitor Information Sequim Chamber of Commerce ✉ *1192 E. Washington St.* ☎ *360/683–6197, 800/737–8462* ⊕ *www.sequimchamber.com.*

EXPLORING

Fodor'sChoice
★

Dungeness Spit. Curving 5½ miles into the Strait of Juan de Fuca, the longest natural sand spit in the United States is a wild, beautiful section of shoreline. More than 30,000 migratory waterfowl stop here each spring and fall, but you'll see plenty of birdlife any time of year. The entire spit is part of the **Dungeness National Wildlife Refuge.** ✉ *end of Voice of America Rd., 3 miles north from U.S. 101, 4 miles west of Sequim, Sequim* ☎ *360/457–8451 wildlife refuge* ⊕ *www.clallam.net/ Parks/Dungeness.html* ⊠ *$3 per family* ⊙ *Daily dawn–dusk.*

Dungeness Lighthouse. At the end of the Dungeness Spit is the towering white 1857 Dungeness Lighthouse; tours are available, though access is limited to those who can hike or kayak out 5 miles to the end of the spit. Guests also have the opportunity to serve as lighthouse keepers for a week at a time. An adjacent, 64-site camping area, on the bluff above the Strait of Juan de Fuca, is open February through September. ✉ *Sequim* ☎ *360/683–6638* ⊕ *www.newdungenesslighthouse.com.*

FAMILY

Olympic Game Farm. The 200-acre property—part zoo, part safari—is Sequim's biggest attraction after the Dungeness Spit. For years, the farm's exclusive client was Walt Disney Studios, and many of the bears here are the offspring of former movie stars. On the hour-long, drive-through tour, which covers some 84 acres of the picturesque property, be prepared to see large animals like buffalo surround your car and lick your windows. You'll also see zebras, llamas, lynx, lions, elk, Tibetan yak, emu, bobcat, Siberian and Bengal tigers, and Kodiak and black bears, among other animals. Facilities also include an aquarium, a studio barn with movie sets, a snack kiosk, and a gift shop. Guests are allowed to feed the uncaged animals (with wheat bread only), except for the buffalo and elk at the entrance gates, but must stay in their vehicles at all times. Even sunroofs must remain locked. ✉ *1423 Ward Rd.* ☎ *360/683–4295, 800/778–4295* ⊕ *www.olygamefarm.com* ⊠ *Drive-through tour $12; mini guided walking tour $5* ⊙ *Summer, daily 9–5 (open until 6 Sat.); winter daily 9–3; spring and fall daily 9–4.*

Open Aire Market. You'll find lavender and other local produce in abundance at this Saturday market, a tented affair with lots of color and live music, open from 9 to 3 between early May and late October. ✉ *Cedar St., between Seal St. and 2nd Ave.* ☎ *360/460–2668* ⊕ *www. sequimmarket.com.*

Railroad Bridge Park. Set along a beautifully serene, 25-acre stretch of the Dungeness River, the park is centered on a lacy ironwork bridge that was once part of the coastal line between Port Angeles and Port Townsend. Today the park shelters a pristine river environment. The River Walk hike-and-bike path leads from the River Center educational facility, on the banks of the Dungeness, into the woods, and a horseback track links Runnion Road with the waterway. In summer, families picnic at the River Shed pavilion, students participate in science programs at the Dungeness River Audubon Society office, and locals

The Dungeness National Wildlife Refuge

come to watch performances at the River Stage amphitheater. There are free guided bird walks every Wednesday morning from 8:30 to 10:15. You'll find the park 2 miles west of town, and a five-minute drive from the coast. ✉ *2151 Hendrickson Rd.* ☎ *360/681–4076* 🌐 *www.dungenessrivercenter.org* 🎟 *Free* 🕒 *Park, daily dawn–dusk. Audubon office Tues.–Sat. 10–4, Sun. noon–4.*

WHERE TO EAT

$$ ECLECTIC 🍴 **Alder Wood Bistro.** An inventive menu of local and organic dishes makes this one of the most popular restaurants in Sequim. Pizzas from the wood-fired oven include unique creations, like the chicken bianca with organic chicken, prosciutto, blue cheese, rosemary crème fraîche, caramelized leeks, arugula, and quattro formaggi. Some feature Mt. Townsend Creamery cheeses. The menu's sustainably harvested seafood selections highlight whatever is in season, from black cod and mussels to oysters and salmon; they also get the wood-fire treatment. Even the bacon-wrapped meat loaf features local beef, along with buttermilk mashed potatoes and greens. For dessert, try the housemade apple pie or organic carrot cake. On warmer days, enjoy alfresco dining in the pretty garden courtyard. [$] *Average main: $18* ✉ *139 W. Alder St.* ☎ *360/683–4321* 🌐 *www.alderwoodbistro.com* 🕒 *Closed Sun. and Mon. No lunch.*

$$ PACIFIC NORTHWEST 🍴 **Dockside Grill.** With tremendous views of John Wayne Marina and Sequim Bay, this family restaurant is a fun place to watch ships placidly sail by. The casual menu includes Dungeness crab fritters, steamed clams, cedar-plank salmon, bouillabaisse, cioppino, pasta, and grilled chicken. The kitchen also serves up excellent steak, surf-n-turf poutine,

and a duck confit burger. [$] *Average main: $18* ✉ *2577 W. Sequim Bay Rd., Sequim* ☎ *360/683–7510* 🌐 *www.docksidegrill-sequim.com* 🕒 *Closed Mon. and Tues.*

$ AMERICAN 🍴 **Oak Table Café.** Carefully crafted breakfasts and lunches, made with high-grade, fresh ingredients, are the focus of this well-run, family-friendly eatery, a Sequim institution since 1981. Breakfast is served throughout the 7 am–3 pm open hours; on Sunday, when the large, well-lighted dining room is especially bustling, it's the only meal, and the selection is extensive. Thickly sliced bacon and eggs are a top-seller, but the restaurant is best known for its creamy blintzes, golden-brown waffles, crepes, and variety of pancakes, particularly the cinnamony sweet soufflé-style apple pancake. Egg dishes include eggs Nicole—a medley of sautéed mushrooms, onions, spinach, and scrambled eggs served over an open-face croissant and covered with hollandaise sauce. Lunches include burgers, salads, teriyaki plates, and sandwiches. [$] *Average main: $12* ✉ *292 W. Bell St., Sequim* ☎ *360/683–2179* 🌐 *www.oaktablecafe.com* 🕒 *No dinner. No lunch Sun.*

WHERE TO STAY

For expanded hotel reviews, visit Fodors.com.

$ B&B/INN 🏨 **Greywolf Inn.** On a 5-acre hilltop overlooking town, this pastoral retreat among the trees is right on the Olympic Discovery Trail and a gazebo, Japanese-style hot tub, and warm front room encourage convivial gatherings. **Pros:** quiet garden setting; inexpensive. **Cons:** interior styling too frilly for some. [$] *Rooms from: $85* ✉ *395 Keeler Rd.* ☎ *360/683–5889, 800/914–9653* 🌐 *www.greywolfinn.com* 🛏 *5 rooms* 🍽 *Breakfast.*

$$ B&B/INN Fodor's Choice ★ 🏨 **Red Caboose Getaway.** Vintage metal railcars form the centerpiece of this bed-and-breakfast, where guests can experience the romance of the rails and sleep in luxury cabooses, each with a different theme. **Pros:** unique style; great breakfast. **Cons:** no children under 12. [$] *Rooms from: $175* ✉ *24 Old Coyote Way* ☎ *360/683–7350* 🌐 *www.redcaboosegetaway.com* 🛏 *6 suites* 🍽 *Breakfast.*

$ HOTEL 🏨 **Sequim Bay Lodge.** This sprawling, modern hotel on 17 acres is as resort-style as you'll get for the area. **Pros:** good value; suites are convenient for families; varied room styles; helpful staff. **Cons:** not too fancy; interior design is somewhat dated. [$] *Rooms from: $79* ✉ *268522 U.S. 101* ☎ *360/683–0691, 800/622–0691* 🌐 *www.sequimbaylodge.com* 🛏 *54 rooms* 🍽 *Breakfast.*

NIGHTLIFE

7 Cedars Casino. The Jamestown S'Klallam tribe's enormous casino has blackjack, roulette, and slots. One end of the casino is devoted to bingo. There are several restaurants as well as deli-style dining and music and other entertainment. The tribe also runs an excellent art gallery and gift shop across the highway near the information kiosk, which is accessed via an underpass footpath. ✉ *270756 U.S. 101* ☎ *360/683–7777* 🌐 *www.7cedarsresort.com.*

13

PORT ANGELES

17 miles west of Sequim.

Sprawling along the hills above the deep-blue Strait of San Juan de Fuca, Port Angeles is the crux of the Olympic Peninsula's air, sea, and land links. The town is capped off at the water's edge by a gathering of glittering hotels, restaurants, shops, and attractions, all set around the modern marina and the bone-white swath of Hollywood Beach. With a population of about 19,000, the town is the largest on the Olympic Peninsula and a major gateway to Olympic National Park. Summer foot traffic is shoulder-to-shoulder downtown with hopefuls rushing to ferries, vacationers strolling the waterfront, and locals relaxing at outdoor cafés.

It didn't start out this way, though, as the seasonal crowds have only been a phenomenon since the 1950s. The area was first settled by the Hoh, Makah, Quileute, Quinault, and S'Klallam tribes, and others had little reason to visit until a Greek pilot named Apostolos Valerianus—aka Juan de Fuca—sailed into the strait in 1610. In 1791 Spanish explorer Juan Francisco de Eliza followed him and named it Puerto de Nuestra Señora de Los Angeles, or Port of Our Lady of the Angels. George Vancouver shortened the name to Port Angeles in 1792, and the site was settled by pioneers in 1856. In the century that followed, Port Angeles became a timber-mill town, a military base, and a key regional fishing port.

GETTING HERE AND AROUND

Port Angeles is about 2 hours from Seattle via the Seattle–Bainbridge Island and Edmonds–Kingston ferries and Hwy. 104; it's about 17 miles west of Sequim on U.S. 101. It's served by Clallam Transit to local Olympic Peninsula towns, and Olympic Bus Lines to Silverdale, Seattle, and Sea-Tac airport. Kenmore Air runs flights between Port Angeles and Boeing Field, near Seattle.

Contacts Clallam Transit ☎ *360/452–4511, 800/858–3747* ⊕ *www. clallamtransit.com.* **Olympic Bus Lines** ☎ *360/417–0700, 800/457–4492* ⊕ *www.olympicbuslines.com.* **Kenmore Air** ☎ *866/435–9524* ⊕ *www. kenmoreair.com.*

TOURS

Olympic Raft & Kayak. White-water and scenic float trips are conducted on the Hoh and Elwha rivers, and the Sound Dive Center has scuba certification classes, dive equipment, and tours around the region, including Lake Crescent. ⊠ *123 Lake Aldwell Rd.* ☎ *360/452–1443* ⊕ *www. raftandkayak.com, www.sounddivecenter.com.*

ESSENTIALS

Visitor Information Port Angeles Regional Chamber of Commerce ⊠ *121 E. Railroad Ave.* ☎ *360/452–2363* ⊕ *www.portangeles.org.*

WHERE TO EAT

$$

PACIFIC
NORTHWEST

✕ **The Bushwhacker.** More than three decades of excellent surf-and-turf keep the locals coming back to this Northwest-style restaurant just east of the city. It's a big, friendly place where families gather to dig into huge cuts of meat or seafood dishes. Other tasty fare includes jam-packed

Colette's Bed & Breakfast

seafood fettuccine, sandwiches, wraps, and build-your-own, half-pound "Whacker" burgers. A salad and soup bar comes with every meal—but save room for decadent desserts like triple berry cobbler with ice cream. [$] *Average main: $18* ✉ *1527 E. 1st St.* ☎ *360/457–4113* 🌐 *www.bushwhackerpa.com* 🕒 *No lunch Sat.*

$$$$ FRENCH 🍴 **C'est Si Bon.** Far more Euro-savvy than is typical on the Olympic Peninsula, this longtime, first-rate restaurant stands out for its interior design as well as for its food. The fanciful dining room is done up in bold red hues, with crisp white linens, huge oil paintings, and glittering chandeliers; the spacious solarium takes an equally formal approach. The changing menu highlights homemade French onion soup, escargots, magret de canard with berry sauce, Dungeness crab soufflé, filet mignon, and rack of lamb. The wine list is superb, with French, Australian, and Northwest choices to pair with everything. [$] *Average main: $32* ✉ *23 Cedar Park Rd., Port Angeles* ☎ *360/452–8888* 🌐 *www.cestsibon-frenchcuisine.com* ✍ *Reservations essential* 🕒 *Closed Mon. No lunch.*

WHERE TO STAY

For expanded hotel reviews, visit Fodors.com.

$$ B&B/INN Fodor's Choice ★ 🏨 **Colette's Bed & Breakfast.** A contemporary mansion within 10 acres of gorgeous waterfront property, this appealing place offers more space, service, and luxury than any other property in the area. **Pros:** water views extend to Victoria, BC; discreet personal service. **Cons:** does not cater to families. [$] *Rooms from: $195* ✉ *339 Finn Hall Rd., 10 miles east of town, Port Angeles* ☎ *360/457–9197, 888/457–9777* 🌐 *www.colettes.com* 🛏 *5 suites* 🍽 *Breakfast.*

$$ B&B/INN 🏨 **Domaine Madeleine.** The owners of this luxury B&B, perched on five acres on a bluff above the Strait of Juan de Fuca, love to pamper their guests. **Pros:** the mosaic of colorful waterfront blossoms; abundant wildlife; well-appointed rooms; beautifully presented gourmet breakfast. **Cons:** no children under 12. [$] *Rooms from: $195* ✉ *146 Wildflower La., 8 miles east of town, Port Angeles* ☎ *360/457–4174, 888/811–8376* 🌐 *www.domainemadeleine.com* 🛏 *4 rooms, 1 cottage* 🍴 *Breakfast.*

$ B&B/INN 🏨 **Five Sea Suns Bed & Breakfast.** Just steps from town, within gardens that have won awards, this cozy 1926 inn overlooks the mountains and the bay. **Pros:** lovely garden setting close to town; home-baked chocolate-chip cookies; top-notch hospitality. **Cons:** on a busy street; no children under 12; strict 14-day cancellation policy. [$] *Rooms from: $135* ✉ *1006 S. Lincoln St.* ☎ *360/452–8248, 800/708–0777* 🌐 *www.seasuns.com* 🛏 *5 rooms* 🍴 *Breakfast.*

$$ HOTEL 🏨 **Quality Inn Uptown.** South of town, at the green edge of the Olympic Mountain foothills, this inn offers a stunning panorama of mountain and harbor views. **Pros:** central location; great views. **Cons:** always busy; basic interior design and amenities. [$] *Rooms from: $175* ✉ *101 E. 2nd St., Port Angeles* ☎ *360/457–9434, 800/858–3812* 🌐 *www.qualityinnportangeles.com* 🛏 *51 rooms* 🍴 *Breakfast.*

$$ B&B/INN Fodor's Choice ★ 🏨 **Sea Cliff Gardens Bed & Breakfast.** A gingerbread-style porch fronts this antiques-furnished waterfront Victorian home on three acres of landscaped grounds. **Pros:** sumptuous accommodations with stunning views; hot tubs; gorgeous flower gardens have been featured in national commercials; very romantic setting. **Cons:** a bit off the beaten path. [$] *Rooms from: $175* ✉ *397 Monterra Dr.* ☎ *360/452–2322, 800/880–1332* 🌐 *www.seacliffgardens.com* 🛏 *5 suites* 🍴 *Breakfast.*

SPORTS AND THE OUTDOORS

FAMILY **Ediz Hook.** At the western end of Port Angeles, this long natural sand spit protects the harbor from big waves and storms. The Hook is a fine place to take a walk along the water and watch shore- and seabirds, and to spot the occasional seal, orca, or gray whale. It's also a popular dive spot. From downtown, take Front Street west and follow it as it meanders past the shuttered lumber mill. **Amenities:** toilets. **Best for:** walking; sunset. ✉ *Ediz Hook Rd., off west end of Marine Dr.*

NORTHWESTERN OLYMPIC PENINSULA

The remote, rugged, and rain-soaked west end takes travelers more time to reach, but its unspoiled beaches, old-growth forests, and mountain lakes make for a spectacular geographic pilgrimage. This is where the forest meets the ocean and the wilderness runs into the water. It's lush, green, and wet, a land of fallen trees, ferns, moss-covered rocks, sea stacks, saltwater spray, and smoked salmon. Surfers seek out the coastline near Neah Bay, immortalized in Robert Sullivan's 2000 book *A Whale Hunt*, documenting the Makah Nation's quest to reclaim its cultural heritage. Artifacts from an ancient fishing village at the tribe's museum and cultural center offer an opportunity to learn about the people whose ancestors lived for thousands of years off the land and sea.

Nearby, in the old logging town of Forks, fans can celebrate the setting of the fictional *Twilight* series, and Cape Flattery offers views from the most northwesterly edge of the contiguous United States.

SEKIU

13

100 miles west of Port Townsend, 134 miles northwest of Seattle

The village of Sekiu (pronounced *see*-kyu) rests on the peninsula's northern shore, a rocky and roiling stretch of coastline inhabited for centuries by the Makah (ma-*kah*), Ozette, and S'Klallam tribes. White settlers moved to Sekiu after a salmon cannery opened near the fishing grounds in 1870. Logging became the mainstay of the local economy in the early 1900s. Both industries shut down when resources became overexploited, and now Sekiu is a scenic vacation town known for excellent fishing and scuba diving. As the twisted two-lane road rises and dips along the rugged edge of the land, the forest often yields to a panorama of surf-thrashing, boulder-strewn beaches, with distant views of mountainous Vancouver Island. Autumn attracts fishing pros to the Sekiu River for cutthroat trout and steelhead, and the town jetty is a base for sport divers.

GETTING HERE AND AROUND

Seiku is about an hour and 15 minutes from Port Angeles, via U.S. 101 west to Hwy. 113, then north.

GUIDED TOURS

Curley's Resort & Dive Center. This regional scuba shop has an air-fill station, launch ramps, moorage, a large supply of diving equipment, and beach dive sites. ✉ *291 Front St.* ☎ *360/963–2281, 800/542–9680* ⊕ *www.curleysresort.com.*

ESSENTIALS

Visitor Information Clallam Bay/Sekiu Chamber of Commerce ✉ *16795 Hwy. 112, Clallam Bay* ☎ *360/963-2339* ⊕ *www.sekiu.com.*

WHERE TO EAT AND STAY

For expanded hotel reviews, visit Fodors.com.

$
AMERICAN
✕ **Breakwater Restaurant.** This restaurant above the Strait of San Juan de Fuca claims to be the most northwesterly dining establishment in the continental United States. Look for seafood, of course, served by a friendly and accommodating staff. Chicken dishes, burgers, steaks, and generous breakfasts fill out the menu. There's a salad bar, selection of microbrews, and spectacular views. While you wait for your fish-and-chips, chicken-fried steak, or homemade pie, enjoy the collection of locally painted works hung along the walls. $ *Average main: $15* ✉ *15582 Hwy. 112, Clallam Bay* ☎ *360/963-2428.*

$
B&B/INN
⬚ **Winter Summer Inn.** From all around this pleasant, welcoming B&B there are panoramic views of the Clallam River and Strait of Juan de Fuca, and the spacious master suite has a full kitchen and private deck. **Pros:** central to upper Olympic Peninsula sights; stunning water views; hospitable innkeeper. **Cons:** two rooms have private half-bath but share the shower room; previous guests have complained about hot water shortages. $ *Rooms from: $85* ✉ *16651 Hwy. 112, Clallam Bay*

☎ *360/963–2264* ⊕ *www.wintersummerinn.com* ⟿ *3 rooms, 1 suite* ⧖ *Breakfast.*

SPORTS AND THE OUTDOORS

Clallam Bay Spit. On the former site of a Native American fishing village, the 33-acre Clallam Bay Spit, where eagles and osprey can be found feeding on the sand, attracts beachcombers, fishers, and divers. The 4-acre Pillar Point Fishing Camp to the east has campsites and a boat ramp. Dress warmly: Pysht Bay takes its name from a S'Klallam term meaning "where the wind blows from all directions." **Amenities:** toilets. **Best for:** walking; solitude; sunset. ⊠ *Off Hwy. 112 at Clallam Bay and Pysht Bay* ⊕ *www.clallam.net/Parks/clallambayspit.html.*

NEAH BAY

15 miles northwest of Sekiu.

One of the oldest villages in Washington, Neah (pronounced *nee*-ah) Bay is surrounded by the Makah Reservation at the northwestern tip of the Olympic Peninsula. Today it's still a quiet, seldom-visited seaside settlement of one-story homes, espresso stands, and bait shops stretched along about a mile of gravelly coastal road, which parallels the glistening, boat-filled bay. Stroll along the docks to watch boot-clad fishermen and shaggy canines motoring out on warped and barnacled vessels, and peer into the oil-stained water for views of anemones, shellfish, and sea lions. The rocky bulkhead rises behind the marina; look beyond that to view sunsets and Cape Flattery, the northwesternmost point in the contiguous United States.

Explorer James Cook named the cape in 1778 when his ship missed the fog-smothered Strait of Juan de Fuca and landed here instead. In 1792 Spanish mariners established a short-lived fort here, which was the first European settlement in what is now Washington State. The local Makah tribe is more closely related to the Nootka of Vancouver Island, just across the water, than to any Washington tribe. Like their ancestors, they embark on whale hunts by canoe, a right guaranteed by treaty, although fleets of kayaks skimming through the calm bay are all you're likely to see during your visit.

GETTING HERE AND AROUND

Neah Bay is quite remote, accessed only by Hwy. 112 west of Sekiu (about a half-hour drive).

EXPLORING

FAMILY

Fodor's Choice

★

Makah Cultural and Research Center. The outstanding Makah Cultural and Research Center displays thousands of Makah art pieces and artifacts, many eons old. Done in low lights and rich timbers, the space is divided into an easy route of intriguing exhibits. The centerpiece is a full-size cedar longhouse, complete with hand-woven baskets, fur skins, cattail wool, grass mats on the bed planks, and a background of tribal music. Another section houses full-size whaling and seal-hunting canoes and weapons. Other areas show games, clothing, crafts, and relics from the ancient Ozette Village mudslide. The small shop stocks a collection of locally made art pieces, books, and crafts; plan to spend some time looking around. This is· an impressive a museum as you'd find in any major city, and should be a stop on any itinerary in the region. ✉ *1880 Bayview Ave.* ☎ *360/645–2711* ⊕ *www.makah.com* ⊡ *$5* ⊗ *Daily 10–5 (unless harsh weather forces closure).*

Makah National Fish Hatchery. Here visitors can view chinook salmon as they make their way over fish ladders to the hatchery's spawning area. Spawning months are October through December, and the salmon are released in late April. Smaller numbers of coho and chum salmon as well as steelhead trout also populate the hatchery. Call to find out the best times to see hatchery activity. From Neah Bay, follow signs south for 7 miles. ✉ *897 Hatchery Rd.* ☎ *360/645–2521* ⊕ *www.fws.gov/ makahnfh* ⊡ *Free* ⊗ *Daily 7:30–4.*

13

FORKS

49 miles south of Neah Bay.

The former logging town of Forks is named for two nearby river junctions: the Bogachiel and Calawah rivers merge west of town, and a few miles farther they are joined by the Soleduck to form the Quileute River, which empties into the Pacific at the Native American village of La Push. Forks is a small, quiet gateway town for Olympic National Park's Hoh River valley unit. The surrounding countryside is exceptionally green, with an annual precipitation of more than 100 inches. As the setting for the popular *Twilight* movie series, the town has become a popular destination for fans in recent years, and Bella's Birthday Weekend, in October, has plenty of *Twilight*-related events.

GETTING HERE AND AROUND

From the Seattle area, Forks is about 3½ hours via the Seattle–Bainbridge Island and Edmonds–Kingston ferries and U.S. 101 west; it's about an hour past Port Angeles. Coming from the south, U.S. 101 north from Aberdeen to Forks takes about 2 hours. Clallam Transit runs from Forks to Port Angeles and other north peninsula towns. West Jefferson Transit provides service between Forks and Lake Quinault, including a stop at Kalaloch.

GUIDED TOURS

Peak 6 Tours and Gift Shop. Here you'll find gear and information for hiking, biking, camping, climbing, and sightseeing on the Olympic Peninsula. Guided hikes cost about $50 per day. ✉ *4883 Upper Hoh Rd.* ☎ *360/374–5254.*

ESSENTIALS

Visitor Information Forks Chamber of Commerce ✉ *1411 S. Forks Ave.* ☎ *360/374–2531, 800/443–6757* ⊕ *www.forkswa.com.*

EXPLORING

Big Cedar. Thought to be the world's largest, this monumental cedar tree stands 178 feet tall and is 19 feet 5 inches in diameter. Area loggers left it standing when they realized just how enormous it really was. The tree is off Nolan Creek Road. From U.S. 101, turn right onto Highway N1000 for 1.3 miles, then turn right onto N1100 for 2.4 miles. Turn right again onto N1112 for 0.4 miles, and then turn right once more for 0.1 miles.

Makah Indian Art

WHERE TO EAT

$ ✕ **Forks Coffee Shop.** This modest restaurant on the highway in down-
DINER town Forks serves home-style, classic American fare. From 5 am to 8 pm
you can dig into giant pancakes and Sol Duc scrambles (eggs, sausage,
hash browns, and veggies tumbled together). At lunch there's a choice
of soups, salads, and hot and cold sandwiches, which the waitstaff will
bag for pickup if you're on the run. Dinner specials come with free trips
to the salad bar and include entrées like baby back ribs and grilled Hood
Canal oysters. Top off the meal with a home-baked treat, like a slice
of flaky-crust pie made with locally grown marionberries, blueberries,
strawberries, cherries, or apples. $ *Average main: $8* ✉ *241 Forks Ave.*
☎ *360/374–6769* ⊕ *www.forkscoffeeshop.com.*

$ ✕ **Plaza Jalisco.** On the outside you can tell it was once a gas station, but
MEXICAN head past the painted Mexican bandit statue and suddenly you're in a
colorful world south of the border. Desert colors, ceramic bells, hand-
painted masks, and hand-knit blankets decorate the small, airy dining
room, where locals gather to down heaping plates of rice, beans, and
meat-filled burritos. Frothy and potent margaritas are the big draw on
weekends. This is a prime budget stop, where the home-cooked flavors
and low prices keep both your stomach and your wallet full. $ *Average
main: $9* ✉ *90 N. Forks Ave., Forks* ☎ *360/374–3108.*

$ ✕ **Smoke House Restaurant.** Rough-panel walls give a rustic appeal to
STEAKHOUSE the dining room of this two-story Forks favorite. Successful surf-and-
turf specials remain unchanged since the place opened as a smokehouse in 1975. Smoked salmon is a top-seller, but the steaks, other
seafood, and prime rib are also delicious. Burgers, fries, pies, and milk

shakes will please the kids. [$] *Average main: $10* ✉ *193161 U.S. 101* ☎ *360/374–6258.*

WHERE TO STAY

For expanded hotel reviews, visit Fodors.com.

$ B&B/INN 🏨 **Manitou Lodge.** If seclusion, quiet, and relaxation is what you seek, visit this cedar lodge in the rain forest, which bills itself as the westernmost B&B in the continental United States. **Pros:** guests are welcomed with cookies in their rooms; some lodgings are family-friendly. **Cons:** no TV, phones, or cell phone service, though there is Wi-Fi. [$] *Rooms from: $139* ✉ *813 Kilmer Rd.* ☎ *360/374–6295* 🌐 *www.manitoulodge.com* 🛏 *5 rooms, 2 suites, 2 cabins, 2 tents* 🍴 *Breakfast.*

13

WASHINGTON COAST

The communities along this stretch of Pacific coastline range from quiet and secluded getaways to busy beach towns, especially during the summer months when highways in and out of towns can become congested with vacationers. Pacific Beach and Moclips to the north are a little more remote and less crowded than their southern counterparts. Ocean Shores is one of the busier beaches, with horseback riders, kite-flyers, go-carts, dune buggies, and beachcombers all competing for space. While the sun shines here in summer, it gets gusty on the beach at any time of year so don't forget your windbreaker and polar fleece.

COPALIS BEACH

74 miles west of Olympia.

A Native American village for several thousand years, this small coastal town at the mouth of the Copalis (pronounced coh-*pah*-liss) River was settled by European-Americans in the 1890s. The beach here is known locally for its innumerable razor clams, which can be gathered by the thousands each summer, and for its watchtowers, built between 1870 and 1903 to spot and stalk sea otters—the animals are now protected by Washington state law. The first oil well in the state was dug here in 1901, but it proved to be unproductive. However, some geologists still claim that the continental shelf off the Olympic Peninsula holds major oil reserves.

GETTING HERE AND AROUND

Copalis Beach is about 30 miles from Aberdeen, via Hwy. 109. Bus service is provided by Grays Harbor Transit.

Contact **Grays Harbor Transit** ☎ *360/532–2770, 800/562–9730* 🌐 *www.ghtransit.com.*

EXPLORING

Griffiths-Priday Ocean State Park. You can hike or ride horses in this 364-acre marine park stretching more than a mile along both the Pacific Ocean and the Copalis River. A boardwalk crosses low dunes to the broad, flat beach. The Copalis Spit section of the park is a designated wildlife refuge for thousands of snowy plover and other bird life.

There is no camping at this park, but there's plenty of picnicking, bird-watching, mountain biking, fishing, clamming, kite-flying, and beachcombing. ✉ *3119 Hwy. 109* ☎ *360/902–8844* 🌐 *www.parks.wa.gov/parks* 🎟 *Day pass $10 per vehicle; annual Discovery Pass $30 (valid at all state parks)* ⏲ *Daily dawn–dusk.*

Pacific Beach State Park. Between Copalis Beach and the town of Moclips, this is a lovely spot for walking, surf-perch fishing, and razor-clam digging. There's also excellent fishing for sea-run cutthroat trout in the Moclips River—but be careful not to trespass onto Native American land, as the Quinault Reservation starts north of the river. The 10-acre park has developed tent and RV sites, as well as a few primitive beachfront campsites. ✉ *49 2nd St., Hwy. 109 S, 5 miles north of Copalis Beach* ☎ *360/276–4297* 🌐 *www.parks.wa.gov* 🎟 *Day pass $10 per vehicle; annual Discovery Pass $30 (valid t all state parks); camping $12–$37* ⏲ *Daily dawn–dusk.*

WORD OF MOUTH

"The coast and rain forest will be drippy and lovely . . . the elk have eaten all the low stuff over the winter . . . leaving a canopy of mossy trees vanishing into the mist, and spongy moss underfoot, with surprisingly long views available between. And of course there will be beach walks, booming surf, and all the drama you could want at the beaches: try Rialto and Ruby Beaches for starts."

—Gardyloo

WHERE TO EAT AND STAY

For expanded hotel reviews, visit Fodors.com.

$ RESORT 🏨 **Sandpiper Beach Resort.** This pet-friendly resort, on a secluded beach 3 miles south of Moclips, is a great place for getting away from it all and immersing yourself in nature. **Pros:** spacious lodgings; right on the beach; nearby restaurants. **Cons:** not for technology-dependent folks; no on-site restaurant. [$] *Rooms from: $79* ✉ *4159 Hwy. 109, Pacific Beach* ☎ *360/276–4580, 800/567–4737* 🌐 *www.sandpiper-resort.com* 🛏 *24 suites, 4 cabins* 🍴 *No meals.*

$ RENTAL FAMILY Fodor's Choice ★ 🏨 **Seabrook Cottage Rentals.** A range of individually owned rental properties is available in a charming new beach town that is still being developed. **Pros:** recreational amenities and beach within walking distance; homes are all new with full amenities. **Cons:** there is ongoing construction. [$] *Rooms from: $109* ✉ *4275 State Rte. 109, Pacific Beach* ☎ *360/276–0265, 877/779–9990* 🌐 *www.seabrookcottagerentals.com* 🛏 *76 cottages* 🍴 *No meals.*

SPORTS AND THE OUTDOORS

Ruby Beach. Named for the rosy fragments of garnet that color its sands, this is one of the peninsula's most beautiful stretches of coastline. A short trail leads to the wave-beaten sands, where sea stacks, caves, tidal pools, and bony driftwood make it a favorite place for beachcombers, artists, and photographers. It's 28 miles south of Forks, off U.S. 101. **Amenities:** none. **Best for:** walking; sunset. ✉ *Kalaloch.*

OCEAN SHORES

10 miles south of Copalis Beach.

Ocean Shores, a long stretch of resorts, restaurants, shops, and attractions, sits on the northern spit that encloses Grays Harbor. The whole area was planned by housing developers in the 1960s, and with its broad, flat white beach, shallow surf, and sunset panoramas, it's been a favorite seaside getaway since. Come summer, dune buggies and go-carts buzz up and down the sand road, weaving around clusters of horses trotting tourists over the dunes. Colorful kites flap overhead, dogs romp in the waves, and tide pools are filled with huge orange Dungeness crabs, live sand dollars, and delicate snails, to the delight of small children. It's no tropical haven, however, as summer can bring chilly breezes, and the water never warms up much for swimming—hence jackets are mandatory even in July. A fog of sea mist often blows in during the late afternoon, and in winter massive thunderstorms billow onto land directly before the line of coastal hotels. An indoor pool and in-room fireplace are coveted amenities year-round in this cool climate, and well worth the added expense.

GETTING HERE AND AROUND

Ocean Shores is the closest developed ocean-beach town to Seattle; it's about a 2½-hour drive via I–5 south to Olympia then west via U.S. 101 and north via Hwy. 109. The traffic through Aberdeen and Hoquiam can slow to a crawl on busy summer weekends; try especially to avoid heading back east on Sunday or holiday afternoons. Grays Harbor Transit serves the community locally.

Contact Grays Harbor Transit ☎ *360/532–2770, 800/562–9730* ⊕ *www. ghtransit.com.*

ESSENTIALS

Visitor Information Ocean Shores/North Beach Chamber of Commerce ✉ *873 Point Brown Ave. NW, Suite 1, Oak Harbor* ☎ *360/289-2451* ⊕ *www. oceanshores.org.*

EXPLORING

Coastal Interpretive Center. A great stormy-day educational spot for families, the center highlights the seaside environment, local history, and Native American traditions. Displays include tsunami debris, artifacts from the founding of the city, and Native American basketry. Reproduction seabirds, whale bones, and a vast shell collection let you examine the shoreline wildlife up close. ✉ *1033 Catala Ave. SE* ☎ *360/289–4617* ⊕ *interpretivecenter.org* ✍ *Free* ☉ *Apr.–Sept., daily 11–4; Oct.–Mar., weekends 11–4.*

WHERE TO EAT AND STAY

For expanded hotel reviews, visit Fodors.com.

$ ✕ **Alec's by the Sea.** One of the best restaurants in the region, conveniently set between the town and beach, this family-run place has been serving seafood for two decades. The best dishes are made with the ocean's bounty that's caught locally, such as steelhead, razor clams, and Grays Harbor oysters. Steaks, sandwiches, salads, burgers, and prime

AMERICAN

Seabrook Cottage Rentals

rib—one of its signature dishes—are also on the menu. $ *Average main: $16* ✉ *131 E. Chance a la Mer Blvd.* ☎ *360/289–4026.*

$$ SEAFOOD 🍴 **Mike's Steak and Seafood Restaurant.** Wander through the small, roadside seafood shop to see what's cooking before you sit down in the adjacent restaurant. Everything served is fresh-caught, and salmon is smoked on the premises. Italian specialties like puttanesca round out the menu, which includes burgers and fish-and-chips for lunch. Dinner specialties include whole Dungeness crab that diners pick out from the live-crab tank, crab-stuffed prawns, pepper pear prawns, and smoked salmon linguine. One of the best ways to sample it all is in the tomato-based cioppino. $ *Average main: $18* ✉ *830 Point Brown Ave. NE* ☎ *360/289–0532.*

$$$$ RESORT 🏨 **Quinault Beach Resort & Casino.** A half-mile of dunes and wild beach grasses separates this enormous resort from the crowds. **Pros:** grand rooms; upscale setting; on-site spa and dining. **Cons:** gambling crowds can be rowdy. $ *Rooms from: $349* ✉ *78 Hwy. 115* ☎ *360/289–5001, 888/461–2214* 🌐 *www.quinaultbeachresort.com* 🛏 *150 rooms, 9 suites* 🍽 *Some meals.*

$$ HOTEL 🏨 **Shilo Inn.** Framed by a Pacific Ocean seascape to the west and a dune-covered state park to the south, this all-suites hotel welcomes guests resort-style. **Pros:** great location; attractive lobby; lots of amenities. **Cons:** lots of tourists, families, and groups make hallways noisy late and early; rates spike during summer and special events. $ *Rooms from: $189* ✉ *707 Ocean Shores Blvd.* ☎ *360/289–4600, 800/222–2244* 🌐 *www.shiloinns.com* 🛏 *113 suites* 🍽 *No meals.*

SPORTS AND THE OUTDOORS

Ocean Shores Beaches. Six miles of wide, public, sandy beaches line a peninsula trimmed by the Pacific Ocean on the west and Grays Harbor on the east. With five access roads, it's possible to find secluded sections along the state's most visited beach destination. Highest tides occur in July and December, the latter when winter storm-watching is at its peak. Motor vehicles are allowed on **City Beach,** a popular place for clam-digging and kite-flying. **Ocean City State Park,** a 170-acre ocean-front park 2 miles north in Hoquiam, has year-round camping. Several hotels and resorts line the beach, including the **Quinault Beach Resort & Casino** and the **Shilo Inn** (⇨ *See Where to Stay*); trails provide access. **Amenities:** food and drink; parking; showers; toilets. **Best for:** solitude; sunrise; sunset; walking. ⊠ *Sand Dune Ave. SW and off Duck Lake Dr. SE, Ocean Shores* ☎ *360/289–2451* ⊕ *oceanshores.org.*

13

HOQUIAM

21½ miles east of Ocean Shores.

Hoquiam (pronounced *hoh*-quee-ahm) is a historic lumber town near Aberdeen and the mouth of the Hoquiam River. Both river and town were named with the Chehalis word meaning "hungry for wood." The town was settled in the mid-19th century, around the same time as Aberdeen, and is now a major Grays Harbor port for cargo and fishing vessels. Its industries include canneries and manufacturers of wood products and machine tools.

GETTING HERE AND AROUND

Hoquiam is about an hour from Olympia via U.S. 101. Grays Harbor Transit serves Hoquiam and neighboring towns.

Contact Grays Harbor Transit ☎ *360/532–2770, 800/562–9730* ⊕ *www. ghtransit.com.*

ESSENTIALS

Visitor Information Grays Harbor Chamber of Commerce ⊠ *506 Duffy St., Aberdeen* ☎ *800/321–1924, 360/532–1924* ⊕ *www.graysharbor.org.*

EXPLORING

Grays Harbor National Wildlife Refuge. In fall and spring, this refuge, established in 1990, is a perfect place to observe the multitude of migrating shorebirds that visit the area. Keep your binoculars handy as you stroll along the 1,800-foot-long boardwalk, and make sure to stop at the visitor center's shop and bookstore. ⊠ *Airport Way, west of Hoquiam via Hwy. 109 and Paulson Rd.* ☎ *360/753–9467* ⊕ *www.fws.gov/refuge/ grays_harbor* ☑ *$3 per family* ⊙ *Park: daily dawn–dusk; visitor center: Wed.–Sun. 9–4.*

The Polson Museum. In a 26-room mansion built in 1924, this museum is filled with artifacts and mementos relating to Grays Harbor's past. You can walk through the remodeled dining room, kitchen, and living room, where an exhibit traces the history of tall ships in the Pacific Northwest. Upstairs is the logging exhibit, with a replica Little Hoquiam Railroad; a period-costume room; and the Polson children's room and dollhouse. Outside you can wander the riverside grounds, which have exotic trees and a rose garden. ✉ *1611 Riverside Ave.* ☎ *360/533–5862* ⊕ *www. polsonmuseum.org* 🏷 *$4* ⊗ *Jan.–Aug., Wed.–Sat. 11–4, Sun. noon–4.*

ABERDEEN

4 miles east of Hoquiam.

The pretty town of Aberdeen, on Grays Harbor at the mouth of the Chehalis River, was settled in 1867 by farmers. Some of the earliest residents were Scottish immigrants who named it after their own city set along a harbor at the mouth of a river. Growth and prosperity came to the town after Scotsman George R. Hume started a salmon cannery here in 1878 and the town's first sawmill was built in 1884. Soon tall ships crowded the narrow harbor to load lumber, and waterfront bars were busy with sailors and lumberjacks.

Early homesteaders found the cleared forest land too soggy to support anything except cranberries, which still thrive in the bogs. Other farmers turned to cultivating oysters in the shallow harbor bays. In 1903 most of Aberdeen's buildings, made of wood and surrounded by streets of sawdust, burned down during a dry spell. These were replaced with stone and brick buildings, many of which still stand in the downtown area.

Aberdeen is known for its lovely harbor, spread glittering and gray along the west edge of town, where the bay bobs with sailboats and speed cruisers. Vast swaths of lumberyards are broken up by towering cranes, which transport the massive timbers onto immense metal barges. Forested hills serve as a backdrop to town, promising a picturesque entry into the Olympic Peninsula to the north. The town is also dotted with the classic, century-old mansions built by shipping and timber barons of the 20th century. Walking tours provide looks at some of the largest and most beautiful homes as well as local highlights from some of the town's best-known former residents, including Bill Boeing and Kurt Cobain.

GETTING HERE AND AROUND

Aberdeen is 4 miles east of Hoquiam and is served by Grays Harbor Transit.

Contact Grays Harbor Transit ☎ *360/532–2770, 800/562–9730* ⊕ *www. ghtransit.com.*

EXPLORING

Morrison Riverfront Park Walk. For a general look at the lay of Aberdeen, take the 1½-mile-long, paved Morrison Riverfront Park Walk to the 40-foot-wide Compass Rose mosaic, inlaid at the confluence of the Wishkah and Chehalis rivers. ✉ *1404 Sargent Blvd.*

Lady Washington. Tall, billowing white sails in the harbor mark the presence of the *Lady Washington*, a replica of the 1750s coastal freighter from Boston, which, in 1792, under the command of famous explorer Captain Robert Gray, was the first American vessel to reach the northwest American coast. The replica was famously converted into the multi-timasted HMS *Interceptor* sloop for the 2002 Disney movie *Pirates of the Caribbean.* Its main base is the Grays Harbor Historic Seaport, but you'll find the vessel at local coastal towns throughout the region, where it's open for self-guided tours.Three-hour cruises include the hands-on "Adventure Sail" and a mock "Battle Sail" war between two vessels, and if you're at least 18 you can volunteer as a deckhand for multiday trips. The free **Seaport Learning Center,** a 214-acre site spread across the harbor and surrounding wetlands, runs tours on two historic longboats, and schedules monthly boatbuilding, rope-climbing, and marine-trade programs for families and students. ✉ *712 Hagara St.* ☎ *360/532–8611, 800/200–5239* 🌐 *historicalseaport.org* 🎟 *Tours by donation; sailings $40–$60.*

WHERE TO EAT AND STAY

For expanded hotel reviews, visit Fodors.com.

$ AMERICAN 🍴 **Billy's.** This bar and grill used to be the most popular saloon and brothel in town, and the restaurant has a collection of prints recalling those bawdy days. Even the establishment's name was taken from the saloon's notorious original owner, Billy Ghol. It's said his ghost haunts the premises. Standard fare includes burgers and salads, but you can go exotic with grilled yak, and food is served until 11 pm. [$] *Average main: $10* ✉ *322 E. Heron St.* ☎ *360/533–7144.*

$ B&B/INN 🏨 **A Harbor View Inn.** You can see the harbor from every room in this 1905 Colonial Revivial-style mansion, furnished with Victorian-era antiques. **Pros:** special packages available; gourmet breakfast served in the sunroom overlooking the harbor; feeling of stepping back in time. **Cons:** not for those who don't enjoy an abundance of Victoriana. [$] *Rooms from: $129* ✉ *111 W. 11th St.* ☎ *360/533–7996, 877/533–7996* 🌐 *www.aharborview.com* 🛏 *4 rooms, 1 suite* 🍽 *Breakfast.*

WESTPORT

21 miles southwest of Aberdeen.

Westport is a bay-front fishing village on the southern spit that helps protect the entrance to Grays Harbor from the fury of the Pacific Ocean. Numerous charter companies based here offer salmon, lingcod, rockfish, and albacore fishing trips, as well as whale-watching tours. If you're not taking a cruise, you can stand on Westport's beach to look for gray whales migrating southward in November and December, toward their breeding grounds in Baja California, and northward in April and May, toward their feeding grounds in the Bering Sea. The serene beach is perfect for walking, surfing, or kite-flying—although it's too dangerous for swimming and too cold for sunbathing. In winter it's one of the best spots on the coast to watch oncoming storms.

GETTING HERE AND AROUND

Westport is about a half-hour southwest of Aberdeen via Hwy. 105. Grays Harbor Transit serves the town.

Contact **Grays Harbor Transit** ☎ *360/532–2770, 800/562–9730* 🌐 *www.ghtransit.com.*

ESSENTIALS

Visitor Information **Westport-Grayland Chamber of Commerce** ✉ *2985 S. Montesano* ☎ *360/268–9422, 800/345–6223* 🌐 *www.westportgrayland-chamber.org.*

EXPLORING

Harbor Walkway. A 2-mile-long paved promenade winds along the sandy beach between Grays Harbor Lighthouse and West Haven State Park. ✉ *Ocean Ave.*

FAMILY **Westport Aquarium.** Exhibits of local marine life include a wolf eel, an octopus, and a dog shark. Touch tanks let you feel shells, starfish, anemones, and other sea creatures. You can even hand-feed two seals. ✉ *321 Harbor St.* ☎ *360/268–7070* 🌐 *westportaquarium.weebly.com* 🎟 *$5* ⏲ *Thurs.–Mon. 10–4, and by appointment.*

Westport Maritime Museum. In a former Coast Guard station, the museum displays historic photos, equipment, clothing, and other relics from the life-saving service and such local industries as fishing, logging, and cranberry farming. Among the exhibits is a collection of sea-mammal bones, and the 17-foot-tall Destruction Island Lens, a lighthouse beacon that was built in 1888 and weighs almost 6 tons. The octagonal **Grays Harbor Lighthouse,** a 107-foot structure built in 1898, is the tallest on the Washington coast. It stands near the museum and adjacent to Westport Light State Park, a day-use area with picnic tables and a beach. A tour of the lighthouse base is included with museum admission; it costs extra to climb to the top. ✉ *2201 Westhaven Dr.* ☎ *360/268–0078* 🌐 *www.westportmaritimemuseum.com* 🎟 *$5, includes lighthouse base (extra $5 to climb to the top)* ⏲ *Apr.–Sept., daily 10–4; Oct.–Mar., Fri.–Mon. noon–4; lighthouse closed Dec. and Jan.*

WHERE TO STAY

For expanded hotel reviews, visit Fodors.com.

$ HOTEL 🏨 **Chateau Westport Motel.** This big motel sits near the dunes and is perfect for families who want a base near the beach. **Pros:** guests 21 and older receive a voucher for free wine and cheese tasting at local winery. **Cons:** parking lot can be noisy; two-night minimum stay some holiday weekends. [$] *Rooms from: $129* ✉ *710 Hancock Ave.* ☎ *360/268–9101, 800/255–9101* 🌐 *www.chateauwestport.com* 🛏 *104 rooms* 🍴 *Breakfast.*

SPORT AND THE OUTDOORS

Westport Beaches. At the southern mouth of Grays Harbor, **Westhaven State Park** encompasses some 80 acres, including oceanfront and easy pedestrian access to the beach. A 1.3-mile concrete boardwalk crosses the dunes, connecting Westhaven with the 212-acre **Westport Light State Park,** adjacent to the historic Westport Lighthouse, built in 1898. Farther south, the 172-acre **Twin Harbors State Park** provides another stretch of Pacific coastline, popular for clamming, bird-watching, and beachcombing. **Amenities:** parking (fee); showers; toilets. **Best for:** solitude; sunrise; sunset; walking. ✉ *St. Park Access Rd., off N. Montesano St.* ☎ *360/268–9422* 🌐 *www.westportwa.com.*

LONG BEACH PENINSULA

The seas are so turbulent beneath the cliffs of Cape Disappointment, where the mighty Columbia River meets the stormy waters of the Pacific Ocean, that several explorers, from James Cook to George Vancouver, mistook the river's mouth for surf breaking on a wild shore. Many ships have crossed (and many have come to grief) here since American sea captain Robert Gray sailed into the river on May 11, 1792, and named it after his ship.

Long Beach Peninsula stretches north from Cape Disappointment, protecting Willapa Bay from the ocean. The peninsula has vast stretches of sand dunes, friendly beach towns, dank cranberry bogs, and forests and meadows. Willapa Bay was once known as Shoalwater Bay because it runs almost dry at low tide. It's a prime oyster habitat, producing more of the creatures than any other estuary in the country.

The 28-mile-long, uninterrupted stretch of sand that runs along the peninsula's ocean shore is a great place to beachcomb. Don't even think about swimming here, however. Though surfers in wet suits brave the waves in some areas, the water is too cold and the surf too rough for most people; hypothermia, shifting sands underfoot, and tremendous undertows account for several drownings each year.

The peninsula is a great place to hike, bike, and bird-watch. Lakes and marshes attract migrating birds, among them trumpeter swans. Long Island, in southeastern Willapa Bay, has a stand of old-growth red cedar trees, home to spotted owls, marbled murrelets (a western seabird), elks, and black bears. The island is accessible only by private boat (the boat ramp is on the bay's eastern shore).

GETTING HERE AND AROUND

The Long Beach peninsula is a little more than 3 hours from Seattle via I–5 south to Olympia and then southwest via U.S. 101. From Portland, the drive takes about 2¼ hours via I–5 north to Kelso then west via Hwy. 30. Pacific Transit buses serve the towns of Aberdeen, Bay Center, Chinook, Ilwaco, Long Beach, Nahcotta, Naselle, Ocean Park, Oysterville, South Bend, Surfside, Raymond, and Astoria, Oregon.

Contact **Pacific Transit** ☎ *360/642–9418* ⊕ *www.pacifictransit.org.*

ILWACO

13 miles west of Chinook.

Ilwaco (ill-*wah*-co) has been a fishing port for thousands of years, first as a Native American village and later as an American settlement. A 3-mile scenic loop winds past Ft. Canby State Park to North Head Lighthouse and through the town. The colorful harbor is a great place for watching gulls and boats. Lewis and Clark camped here before moving their winter base to the Oregon coast at Ft. Clatsop.

EXPLORING

Columbia Pacific Heritage Museum. Dioramas and miniatures of Long Beach towns illustrate the history of southwestern Washington, and other displays cover Native Americans; the influx of traders, missionaries, and pioneers; and the contemporary workers of the fishing, agriculture, and forest industries. The original Ilwaco Freight Depot and a Pullman car from the Clamshell Railroad highlight rail history. ☒ *115 S.E. Lake St., off U.S. 101* ☎ *360/642–3446* ⊕ *columbiapacificheritagemuseum.org* ☜ *$5; free on Thurs.* ⊗ *Tues.–Sat. 10–4, Sun. noon–4.*

Cape Disappointment. The cape was named in 1788 by Captain John Meares, an English fur trader who had been unable to find the Northwest Passage. This rocky cape and treacherous sandbar—the so-called graveyard of the Pacific—has been the scourge of sailors since the 1800s. More than 250 ships have sunk after running aground on its ever-shifting sands. A ½-mile-long path from the Lewis & Clark Interpretive Center in Cape Disappointment State Park leads to the Cape Disappointment Lighthouse. Built in 1856, it's the oldest lighthouse on the West Coast that's still in use.

U.S. Coast Guard Station Cape Disappointment. This is the northwest coast's largest search-and-rescue station and the rough conditions of the Columbia River provide plenty of lessons for the students at the on-site National Motor Life Boat School. The only institution of its kind, the school teaches advanced skills in navigation, mechanics, firefighting, and lifesaving to elite rescue crews from around the world. The observation platform on the north jetty in Cape Disappointment State Park is a good place to watch the motor lifeboats. ☒ *322 Coast Guard Rd.* ☎ *360/642–2382* ⊕ *www.uscg.mil.*

FAMILY

Fodor's Choice

★

Cape Disappointment State Park. This 1,882-acre park (formerly Ft. Canby) was an active military installation until 1957. Emplacements for the guns that once guarded the Columbia's mouth remain, some of them hidden by dense vegetation. Trails lead to stunning beaches and eagles can sometimes be seen on the cliffs. All of the park's 240 campsites have stoves and tables; some have water, sewer, and electric hookups. The park also has three lightkeepers' residences (houses) available for rent, as well as 14 yurts and three cabins. Exhibits at the park's **Lewis & Clark Interpretive Center** tell the tale of the duo's 8,000-mile round-trip expedition. Displays include artwork, journal entries, and other items that elaborate on the Corps of Discovery, which left Wood River, Illinois, in 1804; arrived at Cape Disappointment in 1805; and got back to Illinois in 1806. ☒ *Robert Gray Dr., 2½ miles southwest of Ilwaco off U.S. 101* ☎ *360/642–3029, 360/642–3078* ⊕ *www.parks.wa.gov* ☜ *Day pass $10 per vehicle; annual Discovery Pass $30 (valid at all state parks); Interpretive center $5, campsites $21–$28* ⊗ *Daily dawn–dusk; Interpretive center: daily 10–5.*

North Head Lighthouse. Built in 1898, this lighthouse was needed to help skippers sailing from the north, who couldn't see the Cape Disappointment Lighthouse. Stand high on a bluff above the pounding surf here, amid the windswept trees, for superb views of the Long Beach Peninsula. Lodging is available in the Lighthouse Keepers' Residence. ☒ *North Head Lighthouse Rd., 2 miles from Cape Disappointment via Spur 100 Rd.* ☎ *360/642–3029* ⊕ *www.parks.wa.gov, northheadlighthouse.com* ☜ *$2.50* ⊗ *Hrs vary; call for info.*

Cape Disappointment State Park

WHERE TO EAT AND STAY

For expanded hotel reviews, visit Fodors.com.

$
DINER
✕ **Don's Portside Café and Pizzeria.** This local favorite, two blocks from the dock and boat launch, is known for its breakfasts and its lunches of biscuits and gravy, soups, and pies—all of them homemade. Pizza is also on the menu, along with burgers and platter cakes, pancakes the size of a platter. Ⓢ *Average main: $10* ⊠ *303 Main St. SE* ☎ *360/642–3477* 🕙 *No dinner.*

$
SEAFOOD
✕ **Imperial Schooner.** This is the place to go for fish-and-chips, fried shrimp, clam chowder, and grilled oysters. Overlooking the Port of Ilwaco marina, it serves six varieties of local Willapa Bay oysters, including chicken-fried and Angels and Devils on Horseback (wrapped in bacon). Thursday is oyster day, with varying specials. Ⓢ *Average main: $10* ⊠ *133 Howerton Way SE* ☎ *360/642–8667.*

$$
B&B/INN
🏨 **China Beach Retreat.** Between the port of Ilwaco and Cape Disappointment State Park, this secluded, elegant, and comfortable B&B is surrounded by serene wetlands and has wonderful views of Baker's Bay and the mouth of the Columbia River. **Pros:** secluded, back-to-nature setting; tideflat views will keep bird-watchers enthralled. **Cons:** sumptuous, complimentary breakfast served at sister property, Shelburne Inn, 5 miles away. Ⓢ *Rooms from: $199* ⊠ *222 Robert Gray Dr.* ☎ *360/642–2442* ⊕ *www.chinabeachretreat.com* ⤴ *3 rooms, 1 cottage* 🍽 *Breakfast.*

SPORTS AND THE OUTDOORS

FISHING AND WHALE-WATCHING

Gray whales pass the Long Beach Peninsula twice a year: December to February, on their migration from the Arctic to their winter breeding grounds in Californian and Mexican waters, and March to May, on the return trip north. The view from the **North Head Lighthouse** is spectacular. ■TIP➔ The best time for sightings is in the morning, when the water is calm and overcast conditions reduce the glare. Look on the horizon for a whale blow—the vapor, water, or condensation that spouts into the air when the whale exhales. If you spot one blow, you're likely to see others: whales often make several shorter, shallow dives before a longer dive that can last as long as 10 minutes.

The fish that swim in the waters near Ilwaco include salmon, rock cod, lingcod, flounder, perch, sea bass, and sturgeon. Charters generally cost from $100 to $200 per person.

Port of Ilwaco. Free tide charts are available from the port; check the website for information about fishing season and clam-digging dates. ☎ 360/642–3143 ⊕ www.portofilwaco.com.

SEAVIEW

3 miles north of Ilwaco.

Seaview, an unincorporated town, has 750 year-round residents and several homes that date from the 1800s. The Shelburne Inn, built in 1896, is on the National Register of Historic Places. In 1892 U.S. Senator Henry Winslow Corbett built what's now the Sou'wester Lodge.

WHERE TO EAT AND STAY

For expanded hotel reviews, visit Fodors.com.

$$
PACIFIC NORTHWEST
Fodor's Choice
★
✕ **42nd Street Cafe and Bistro.** Inspired and creative yet unpretentious, this cozy, cheerful place serves gourmet comfort food at its best. Make a meal of small plates like fried green tomatoes, Dungeness crab beignets, or Willapa Bay clams steamed in Heffewizen with lemon, garlic, chili flakes, and parsley. Dinner entrées—such as ravioli stuffed with butternut squash and Gorgonzola, eight-hour pot roast, and lemon crab and shrimp fettuccine—come with house-baked bread, marionberry conserve, corn relish, and seasonal local vegetables. Razor clams and panfried oysters are available for breakfast, lunch and dinner. Rich chocolate rum truffle cheesecake and a lighter mini mint chocolate sorbet are popular desserts. The excellent wine list has Pacific Northwest labels. $ *Average main: $20* ⊠ *4201 Pacific Hwy.* ☎ *360/642–2323* ⊕ *www.42ndstreetcafe.com.*

$
B&B/INN
Fodor's Choice
★
⌂ **Shelburne Inn.** A white picket fence and lovely gardens surround a Victorian hotel that's been continuously operating since it was built in 1896. **Pros:** excellent breakfast; historic appeal; attentive service. **Cons:** like many B&Bs, there are no in-room phones or TVs; some rooms are rather small. $ *Rooms from: $139* ⊠ *4415 Pacific Way* ☎ *360/642–2442, 800/466–1896* ⊕ *www.theshelburneinn.com* ⇱ *14* ⦶ *Breakfast.*

LONG BEACH

½-mile north of Seaview.

Long Beach bears a striking resemblance to Brooklyn's Coney Island in the 1950s. Along its main drag, which stretches southwest from 10th Street to Bolstadt Street, you'll find everything from cotton candy and hot dogs to go-carts and bumper cars.

EXPLORING

Cranberry Museum. Here, visitors can learn about more than a century of cranberry cultivation in this area, take a self-guided walking tour through the bogs, try some cranberry tea, and buy cranberry products to take home. ✉ *2907 Pioneer Rd.* ☎ *360/642-5553* ⊕ *www.cranberrymuseum.com* 🔄 *Free* ☉ *Apr.–mid-Dec., daily 10–5.*

FAMILY **Discovery Trail.** Created to memorialize Lewis and Clark's explorations here in 1805–06, the 8-mile Discovery Trail traces the explorers' moccasin steps from Ilwaco to north Long Beach. ☎ *800/451–2542* ⊕ *www.funbeach.com.*

FAMILY **Long Beach Boardwalk.** The ½-mile-long boardwalk runs through the dunes parallel to the beach, and is a great place for strolling, birdwatching, or just sitting and listening to the wind and the roar of the surf. It's ¼ mile west of downtown. ⊕ *funbeach.com.*

FAMILY **Marsh's Free Museum.** If you've got kids in your group, or simply an appreciation of oddities, be sure to visit this quirky museum. Best known for "Jake the Alligator Man," Marsh's is filled with plenty of other curiosities, like real shrunken heads, skeletons, and an eight-legged lamb. ✉ *400 S. Pacific Ave.* ☎ *360/642–2188* ⊕ *www.marshsfreemuseum.com* 🔄 *Free* ☉ *Daily 9–6, later in summer.*

World Kite Museum and Hall of Fame. Each August Long Beach hosts the Washington State International Kite Festival; the community is also home to the Northwest Stunt Kite Championships, a competition held each June. At the World Kite Museum and Hall of Fame, the only U.S. museum focused solely on kites and kiting, you can view an array of kites and learn about kite making and history. ✉ *303 Sid Snyder Dr. SW* ☎ *360/642–4020* ⊕ *www.worldkitemuseum.com* 🔄 *$5* ☉ *May–Sept., daily 11–5; Oct.–Apr., Fri.–Tues. 11–5.*

WHERE TO EAT AND STAY

For expanded hotel reviews, visit Fodors.com.

$$
SEAFOOD
✕ **Dooger's Seafood and Grill.** Locals will urge you to eat here—listen to them. The place serves seafood from 11 am to 9 pm in winter, and until 10 on summer weekends. The ample portions come with potatoes, shrimp-topped salad, and garlic toast. Clam chowder and fish-and-chips are popular lunch choices. Dinner entrées, served all day, include crab legs, razor clams, lobster tail, halibut, and salmon: panfried, poached, grilled, or Cajun-style. $ *Average main: $17* ✉ *900 Pacific Hwy. S* ☎ *360/642–4224* ⊕ *doogersseafood.com.*

$
RENTAL
FAMILY
🏠 **Anchorage Cottages.** Along a western ridge of the Long Beach Peninsula, these cozy cottages have been accommodating beach getaways since the early 1950s. **Pros:** pretty gardens and courtyard; affordable; near the beach. **Cons:** not very private; town is a mile away. $ *Rooms*

from: $90 ✉ *2209 Boulevard Ave. N* ☎ *800/646–2351, 360/642–2351* ⊕ *www.theanchoragecottages.com* ⌁ *10 cottages* ⏀ *No meals.*

$$
Boreas Bed and Breakfast. A private path leads from this vintage 1920s
B&B/INN beach house, on the Lewis and Clark Trail, through the dunes to the shore. **Pros:** great breakfast; helpful innkeepers. **Cons:** no bathtubs in two rooms; not for families. $ *Rooms from: $179* ✉ *607 N. Ocean Beach Blvd.* ☎ *360/642–8069, 888/642–8069* ⊕ *www.boreasinn.com* ⌁ *5 suites, 3 with shower only* ⏀ *Breakfast.*

$ **Breakers Motel and Condominiums.** Each of the contemporary one-
RESORT and two-bedroom condominiums here has a private balcony or patio,
FAMILY and many also have fireplaces and exceptional views of the dunes and the surf. **Pros:** very family-friendly, with lots of activities. **Cons:** units are individually owned, so style and quality differs. $ *Rooms from: $129* ✉ *210 26th St. NW* ☎ *360/642–4414, 800/219–9833* ⊕ *www. breakerslongbeach.com* ⌁ *144 rooms* ⏀ *No meals.*

$ **Our Place at the Beach.** Just a couple blocks from the main highway,
HOTEL and a five-minute walk from the beach, restaurants, and shops, this older, pet-friendly motel is both quiet and convenient. **Pros:** cheerful, accommodating staff; reasonably priced; convenient location. **Cons:** past guests have complained about thin walls and somewhat dated interiors. $ *Rooms from: $99* ✉ *1309 S. Ocean Beach Blvd.* ☎ *360/642–3793, 800/538–5107* ⊕ *www.ourplacelongbeach.weebly.com* ⌁ *26 rooms* ⏀ *Breakfast.*

SPORTS AND THE OUTDOORS

Back Country Wilderness Outfitters. One- and two-hour horseback rides are offered here for $25 per hour. The Ribeye Ride, which lasts nearly four hours, with a steak dinner on the beach costs $85. ✉ *409 S.W. Sid Snyder Dr.* ☎ *360/642–2576.*

Long Beach. The Long Beach Peninsula consists of 28 continuous miles of broad sandy beach, which fills with kite-flyers, sand-castle builders, sunbathers, bicyclists, horseback riders, and drivers during summer months. Watch out for horses, cars, and other motor vehicles—some sections are open for driving year-round, while other parts don't allow it in summer; the speed limit on the sand is 25 mph. Bonfires are also allowed. Bring a windbreaker—strong gusts are common near the water, which remains consistently frigid throughout the year. **Amenities:** toilets. **Best for:** solitude; sunrise; sunset; walking. ✉ *West off State Rte. 103* ☎ *360/642–2400* ⊕ *funbeach.com.*

Peninsula Golf Course. There are two 9-hole, par-33 courses here, on Long Beach's northern edge. Greens fees are $16 for 9 holes and $23 for 18 holes. After 2 pm, it's all-you-can-play for $15. ✉ *9604 Pacific Hwy.* ☎ *360/642–2828* ⊕ *peninsulagolfcourse.com.*

NORTH CASCADES
NATIONAL PARK

WELCOME TO NORTH CASCADES NATIONAL PARK

TOP REASONS TO GO

★ **Pure wilderness:** Nearly 400 miles of mountain and meadow trails immerse hikers in pristine natural panoramas, with sure sightings of bald eagles, deer, elk, and other wildlife.

★ **Majestic glaciers:** The North Cascades are home to 318 moving ice masses, more than half of the glaciers in the United States.

★ **Splendid flora:** A bright palette of flowers blankets the hillsides in midsummer, while October's colors paint the landscape in vibrant autumn hues.

★ **Thrilling boat rides:** Lake Chelan, Lake Ross, and the Stehekin River are the starting points for kayaking, white-water rafting, and ferry trips.

★ **19th-century history:** Delve into the state's farming, lumber, and logging pasts in clapboard towns and homesteads around the park.

1 North Unit. The park's creek-cut northern wilderness, centered on snowy Mount Challenger, stretches north from Highway 20 over the Picket Range toward the Canadian border. It's an endless landscape of pine-topped peaks and ridges.

2 South Unit. Hike lake-filled mountain foothills in summer to take in vistas of blue skies and flower-filled meadows. Waterfalls and wildlife are abundant here.

3 Ross Lake National Recreation Area. Drawing a thick line from British Columbia all the way down to the North Cascades Scenic Highway, placid Ross Lake is edged with pretty bays that draw swimmers and boaters.

4 Lake Chelan National Recreation Area. Ferries steam between small waterfront towns along this pristine waterway, while kayakers and hikers follow quiet trails along its edges. This is one of the Northwest's most popular summer escapes, with nature-bound activities and rustic accommodations.

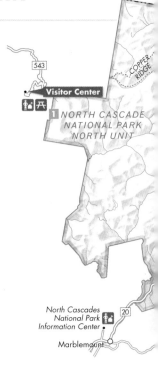

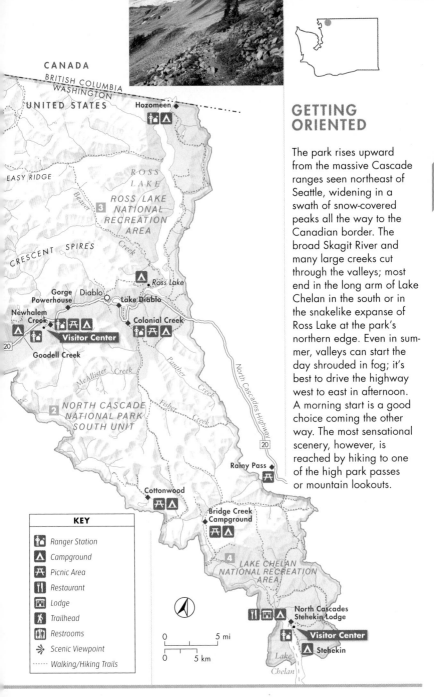

CANADA
BRITISH COLUMBIA
WASHINGTON
UNITED STATES

Hozomeen

EASY RIDGE

ROSS LAKE

ROSS LAKE NATIONAL RECREATION AREA

3

CRESCENT SPIRES

Beaver Creek

Ross Lake

Gorge / Diablo
Powerhouse
Newhalem Creek
Lake Diablo
Visitor Center
Colonial Creek
Goodell Creek
20

McAllister Creek

Panther Creek

Fisher Creek

North Cascades Highway

2 NORTH CASCADE NATIONAL PARK SOUTH UNIT

20

Rainy Pass

Cottonwood

Bridge Creek Campground

GETTING ORIENTED

The park rises upward from the massive Cascade ranges seen northeast of Seattle, widening in a swath of snow-covered peaks all the way to the Canadian border. The broad Skagit River and many large creeks cut through the valleys; most end in the long arm of Lake Chelan in the south or in the snakelike expanse of Ross Lake at the park's northern edge. Even in summer, valleys can start the day shrouded in fog; it's best to drive the highway west to east in afternoon. A morning start is a good choice coming the other way. The most sensational scenery, however, is reached by hiking to one of the high park passes or mountain lookouts.

14

KEY

👫	Ranger Station
⛺	Campground
🛆	Picnic Area
🍴	Restaurant
🏨	Lodge
🚶	Trailhead
🚻	Restrooms
☀	Scenic Viewpoint
⋯	Walking/Hiking Trails

4 LAKE CHELAN NATIONAL RECREATION AREA

North Cascades Stehekin Lodge
Visitor Center
Stehekin

0   5 mi
0   5 km

Lake Chelan

Updated by
Shelley Arenas

Countless snow-clad mountain spires dwarf narrow glacial valleys in this 505,000-acre expanse of the North Cascades, which encompasses three diverse natural areas. North Cascades National Park is the core of the region, flanked by Lake Chelan National Recreation Area to the south and Ross Lake National Recreation Area to the north; all are part of the Stephen T. Mather Wilderness Area. It's a spectacular gathering of snowy peaks, glacial meadows, plunging canyons, and cold, deep-blue lakes. Traditionally the lands of several American Indian tribes, it's fitting that it's still completely wild—and wildlife-filled.

NORTH CASCADES NATIONAL PARK PLANNER

WHEN TO GO

The spectacular, craggy peaks of the North Cascades—often likened to the Alps—are breathtaking anytime. Summer is peak season, especially along the alpine stretches of Route 20; weekends and holidays can be crowded. Summer is short and glorious in the high country, extending from snowmelt (late May to July, depending on the elevation and the amount of snow) to early September.

The North Cascades Highway is a popular autumn drive in September and October, when the changing leaves put on a colorful show. The lowland forest areas, such as the complex around Newhalem, can be visited almost any time of year. These are wonderfully quiet in early spring or late autumn on mild, rainy days. Snow closes the North Cascades Highway from November through mid-April.

AVG. HIGH/LOW TEMPS.

JAN.	FEB.	MAR.	APR.	MAY	JUNE
39/30	43/32	49/34	56/38	64/43	70/49

JULY	AUG.	SEPT.	OCT.	NOV.	DEC.
76/52	76/53	69/49	57/42	45/36	39/31

PLANNING YOUR TIME

NORTH CASCADES IN ONE DAY

The **North Cascades Highway,** with its breathtaking mountain and meadow scenery, is one of the most memorable drives in the United States. Although many travelers first head northeast from Seattle into the park and make this their grand finale, if you start from Winthrop, at the south end of the route, traffic is lighter and there's less morning fog. Either way, the main highlight is **Washington Pass,** the road's highest point, where an overlook affords a sensational panorama of snow-covered peaks.

Rainy Pass, where the road heading north drops into the west slope valleys, is another good vantage point. Old-growth forest begins to appear, and after about an hour you reach **Gorge Creek Falls overlook** with its 242-foot cascade. Continue west to Newhalem and stop for lunch, then take a half-hour stroll along the **Trail of the Cedars.** Later, stop at the **North Cascades Visitor Center** and take another short hike. It's an hour drive down the Skagit Valley to Sedro-Woolley, where bald eagles are often seen along the river in winter.

GETTING HERE AND AROUND

CAR TRAVEL

Highway 20, the North Cascades Highway, splits the park's north and south sections. The gravel Cascade River Road, which runs southeast from Marblemount, peels off Highway 20; Sibley Creek/Hidden Lake Road (USFS 1540) turns off Cascade River Road to the Cascade Pass trailhead. Thornton Creek Road is another rough four-wheel-drive track. For the Ross Lake area in the north, the unpaved Hozomeen Road (Silver–Skagit Road) provides access between Hope, British Columbia; Silver Lake; and Skagit Valley provincial parks. From Stehekin, the Stehekin Valley Road continues to High Bridge, Car Wash Falls, Bridge Creek, and Cottonwood campgrounds—although seasonal floods may cause washouts. Note that roads are narrow and closed from October to June, many sights are off the beaten path, and the scenery is so spectacular that, once you're in it, you'll want to make more than a day trip.

PARK ESSENTIALS

PARK FEES AND PERMITS

There are no entrance fees to the National Park and no parking fees at trailheads on park land. A Northwest Forest Pass, required for parking only at Forest Service trailheads, is $5 per vehicle for one calendar day or $30 for one year. A free wilderness permit is required for all overnight stays in the backcountry; these are available in person only. Dock permits for boat-in campgrounds are also $5 per day. Passes and permits are sold at visitor centers and ranger stations around the park area.

PARK HOURS

The park never closes, but access is limited by snow in winter. Route 20 (North Cascades Highway), the major access to the park, is partially closed from mid-November to mid-April.

CELL PHONE RECEPTION

Cell phone reception in the park is unreliable. Public telephones are found at the North Cascades Visitor Center and Skagit Information Center in Newhalem, and the Golden West Visitor Center and North Cascades Stehekin Lodge in Stehekin.

RESTAURANTS

There are no formal restaurants in North Cascades National Park, just a lakeside café at the North Cascades Environmental Learning Center. The only other place to eat out is in Stehekin, at the Stehekin Valley Ranch dining room, North Cascade Lodge, or the Stehekin Pastry Company; all serve simple, hearty, country-style meals and sweets. Towns within a few hours of the park on either side all have a few small eateries, and some lodgings have small dining rooms. Don't expect fancy decor or gourmet frills—just friendly service and generally delicious homemade stews, roasts, grilled fare, soups, salads, and baked goods. *Prices in the reviews are the average cost of a main course at dinner or, if dinner is not served, at lunch.*

HOTELS

Accommodations in North Cascades National Park are rustic, cozy, and comfortable. Options range from plush Stehekin lodges and homey cabin rentals to spartan Learning Center bunks and campgrounds. Expect to pay roughly $50 to $200 per night, depending on the rental size and the season. Book at least three months in advance, or even a year for popular accommodations in summer. Outside the park are numerous resorts, motels, bed-and-breakfasts, and even overnight boat rentals in Chelan, Concrete, Glacier, Marblemount, Sedro-Woolley, Twisp, and Winthrop. *Prices in the reviews are the lowest cost of a standard double room in high season.*

TOURS

North Cascades Institute (NCI). Come here for information on park hiking, wildlife watching, horseback riding, climbing, boat rentals, and fishing, as well as classroom education and hands-on nature experiences. Guided tours staged from the center include mountain climbs, pack-train excursions, and float trips on the Skagit and Stehekin rivers. Choices range from forest ecology and backpacking trips to explorations of the Cascades hot springs. There's even a research library, a dock on Lake Diablo, an amphitheater, and overnight lodging. ⊠ *810 Rte. 20, near Diablo Dam, Sedro-Woolley* ☎ *360/854-2599* ⊕ *www. ncascades.org.*

VISITOR INFORMATION

PARK CONTACT INFORMATION

North Cascades National Park ⊠ *810 Rte. 20, Sedro-Woolley* ☎ *360/856-5700, 360/854-7200* ⊕ *www.nps.gov/noca.*

VISITOR CENTERS

Chelan Ranger Station. The base for the Chelan National Recreation Area and Wenatchee National Forest has an information desk and a shop selling regional maps and books. ⊠ *Edge of Lake Chelan, 428 W. Woodin, Chelan* ☎ *509/682–4900* ⊕ *www.nps.gov/noca/planyourvisit/ visitorcenters.htm* ☾ *Weekdays 7:45–4:30 except federal holidays.*

Glacier Public Service Center. This office doubles as a headquarters for the Mt. Baker–Snoqualmie National Forest; it has maps, a book and souvenir shop, and a permits desk. The center is also right on the way to some of the park's main trailheads. ⊠ *Mt. Baker Hwy., east of Glacier, 10091 Mt Baker Hwy., Glacier* ☎ *360/599–2714* ⊕ *www.nps.gov/ noca/planyourvisit/visitorcenters.htm* ☾ *Mar.–mid-Oct., daily 8–4:30; mid-Oct.–Mar., weekends 9–3.*

Golden West Visitor Center. Rangers here offer guidance on hiking, camping, and other activities, as well as audiovisual and children's programs and bike tours. There's also an arts-and-crafts gallery. Maps and concise displays explain the layered ecology of the valley, which encompasses in its length virtually every ecosystem in the Northwest. Note that access is by floatplane, ferry, or trail only. ⊠ *Stehekin Valley Rd., ¼ mile north of Stehekin Landing, Stehekin* ☎ *360/854–7365* ⊕ *www.nps.gov/noca/ planyourvisit/visitorcenters.htm* ☾ *Mid-Oct.–March, Mon., Wed., Fri. 12:30–1:30; Apr., daily 12:30–1:30; May, weekdays 12:30–2, weekends 10–2; Memorial Day–Sept., daily 8:30–5; early Oct. –mid-Oct. daily 10–2.*

North Cascades National Park Headquarters Information Station. This is the park's major administrative center and the place to pick up passes, permits, and information about current conditions. ⊠ *810 Rte. 20, Sedro-Woolley* ☎ *360/856–7200* ⊕ *www.nps.gov/noca/planyourvisit/ visitorcenters.htm* ☾ *Mid-Oct.–late May, weekdays 8–4:30; late May– mid-Oct., daily 8–4:30.*

North Cascades Visitor Center. The main visitor facility for the park complex has extensive displays on surrounding landscape. Learn about the history and value of old-growth trees, the many creatures that depend on the rain-forest ecology, and the effects of human activity on the ecosystem. Park rangers frequently conduct programs; check bulletin boards for schedules. ⊠ *Milepost 20, N. Cascades Hwy., Newhalem* ☎ *206/386–4495* ⊕ *www.nps.gov/noca/planyourvisit/visitorcenters. htm* ☾ *May–June, daily 9–5; July–Aug., daily 9–6; Sept.–Oct., daily 9–5. Closed Nov.–Apr.*

Wilderness Information Center. The main stop to secure backcountry and climbing permits for North Cascades National Park and the Lake Chelan and Ross Lake recreational areas, this office has maps, a bookshop, and nature exhibits. If you arrive after hours, there's a self-register permit stop outside. ⊠ *Off milepost 105.9, N. Cascades Hwy., 7280 Ranger Station Rd., Marblemount* ☎ *360/854-7245* ⊕ *www.nps.gov/ noca/planyourvisit/visitorcenters.htm* ☾ *May–June and Sept.–mid-Oct., Sun.–Thurs. 8–4:30, Fri. and Sat. 7–6; July–Aug., Sun.–Thurs. 7–6, Fri. and Sat. 7–8. Closed mid-Oct.–Apr.*

14

EXPLORING

SCENIC DRIVES

North Cascades Highway. Also known as Highway 20, this classic scenic route first winds through the green pastures and woods of the upper Skagit Valley, the mountains looming in the distance. Beyond Concrete, a former cement-manufacturing town, the highway climbs into the mountains, passes the Ross and Diablo dams, and traverses Ross Lake National Recreation Area. Here several pullouts offer great views of the lake and the surrounding snowcapped peaks. From June to September, the meadows are covered with wildflowers, and from late September through October, the mountain slopes flame with fall foliage. The pinnacle point of this stretch is 5,477-foot-high Washington Pass: look east, to where the road descends quickly into a series of hairpin curves between Early Winters Creek and the Methow Valley. Remember, this section of the highway is closed from roughly November to April, depending on snowfall. From the Methow Valley, Highway 153 takes the scenic route along the Methow River's apple, nectarine, and peach orchards to Pateros, on the Columbia River; from here, you can continue east to Grand Coulee or south to Lake Chelan. ⊕ *www.cascadeloop.com/index.php?page_id=218.*

> ### PLANTS AND WILDLIFE IN NORTH CASCADES
>
> Bald eagles are present year-round along the Skagit River and the lakes—in December, hundreds flock to the Skagit to feed on a rare winter salmon run, and remain through January. Spring and early summer bring black bears to the roadsides in the high country. Deer and elk can often be seen in early morning and late evening, grazing and browsing at the forest's edge. Other mountain residents include beaver, marmots, pika, otters, skunks, opossums, and smaller mammals, as well as forest and field birds.

HISTORIC SITES

Buckner Homestead. Dating from 1889, this restored pioneer farm includes an apple orchard, farmhouse, barn, and many ranch buildings. One-hour ranger-guided tours of the property are offered Thursday through Sunday from late June through mid-September; otherwise, you can pick up a self-guided tour booklet from the drop box. ⊠ *Stehekin Valley Rd., 3½ miles from Stehekin Landing, Stehekin* ☎ *360/854–7365 option 14* ⊕ *www.bucknerhomestead.org* ☉ *June–Sept., daily 9–5.*

SCENIC STOPS

Gorge Powerhouse/Ladder Creek Falls and Rock Gardens. A powerhouse is a powerhouse, but the rock gardens overlooking Ladder Creek Falls, 7 miles west of Diablo, are beautiful and inspiring. ⊠ *Rte. 20, 2 miles east of North Cascades Visitor Center, Newhalem* ☎ *360/854-2589* ⊕ *www.seattle.gov/light/tours/skagit/* 💷 *Free* ☉ *May–Sept., daily, dawn to dusk.*

FodorśChoice **Stehekin.** One of the most beautiful and secluded valleys in the Pacific
★ Northwest, Stehekin was homesteaded by hardy souls in the late 19th
century. It's actually not a town, but rather a small community set at
the northwest end of Lake Chelan, and it's accessible only by boat,
floatplane, or trail. Year-round residents—who have intermittent outside communications, boat-delivered supplies, and just two-dozen cars
between them—enjoy a wilderness lifestyle. Even on a peak summer
season day, only around 200 visitors make the trek here.

EDUCATIONAL OFFERINGS

RANGER PROGRAMS

In the summer, rangers conduct programs at the visitor centers, where
you also can find exhibits and other park information. At the North
Cascades Visitor Center (in Newhalem) you can learn about rain-forest
ecology, while at the Golden West Visitor Center (in Stehekin) there's an
arts and crafts gallery as well as audiovisual and children's programs.
Check center bulletin boards for schedules.

14

SPORTS AND THE OUTDOORS

BICYCLING

Mountain bikes are permitted on highways, unpaved back roads, and
a few designated tracks around the park; however, there is no biking
on footpaths. Ranger stations have details on the best places to ride in
each season, as well as notes on spots that are closed due to weather,
mud, or other environmental factors. It's $24 round-trip to bring a bike
on the Lake Chelan ferry to Stehekin.

OUTFITTERS

Discovery Bikes. You can rent mountain bikes at a self-serve rack in
front of the Courtney Log Office in Stehekin for $3.50 per hour, $25 a
day through Discovery Bikes. Helmets are included. ☎ *509/682–3014*
⊕ *www.stehekindiscoverybikes.com.*

BOATING

The boundaries of North Cascades National Park touch two long and
sinewy expanses: Lake Chelan in the far south, and Ross Lake, which
runs toward the Canadian border. Boat ramps, some with speed- and
sailboat, paddleboat, kayak, and canoe rentals, are situated all around
Lake Chelan, and passenger ferries cross between towns and campgrounds. Hozomeen, accessible via a 39-mile dirt road from Canada,
is the boating base for Ross Lake; the site has a large boat ramp, and a
boat taxi makes drops at campgrounds all around the shoreline. Diablo Lake, in the center of the park, also has a ramp at Colonial Creek.
Gorge Lake has a public ramp near the town of Diablo.

Hiking in North Cascades National Park

HIKING

⚠ **Black bears are often sighted along trails in the summer; do not approach them.** Back away carefully, and report sightings to the Golden West Visitor Center. Cougars, which are shy of humans and well aware of their presence, are rarely sighted in this region. Still, keep kids close and don't let them run too far ahead or lag behind on a trail. If you do spot a cougar, pick up children, have the whole group stand close together, and make yourself look as large as possible.

EASY

FAMILY **Happy Creek Forest Walk.** Old-growth forests are the focus of this kid-friendly boardwalk route, which loops just 0.3 mile through the trees right off the North Cascades Highway. Interpretive signs provide details about flora along the way. *Easy.* ✉ *Trailhead at milepost 135, Hwy. 20* ⊕ *www.nps.gov/noca.*

Rainy Pass. An easy and accessible 1-mile paved trail leads to Rainy Lake, a waterfall, and a glacier-view platform. *Easy.* ✉ *Trailhead off Hwy. 20, 38 miles east of visitor center at Newhalem* ⊕ *www.nps.gov/noca.*

River Loop Trail. Take this flat and easy, 1.8-mile, wheelchair-accessible trail down through stands of huge, old-growth firs and cedars toward the Skagit River. *Easy.* ✉ *Trailhead near North Cascades Visitor Center* ⊕ *www.nps.gov/noca/planyourvisit/newhalem-area-trails.htm.*

Sterling Munro Trail. Starting from the North Cascades Visitor Center, this popular introductory stroll follows a boardwalk path to a lookout above the forested Picket Range peaks. *Easy.* ✉ *milepost 120, near Newhalem Creek Campground, Hwy. 20.*

Trail of the Cedars. Only 0.3-mile long, this trail winds its way through one of the finest surviving stands of old-growth western red cedar in Washington. Some of the trees on the path are more than 1,000 years old. *Easy.* ⊠ *Trailhead near North Cascades Visitor Center* ⊕ *www.nps. gov/noca/planyourvisit/newhalem-area-trails.htm.*

MODERATE

Fodor's Choice ★ **Cascade Pass.** The draws of this extremely popular 3.7-mile, four-hour trail are stunning panoramas from the great mountain divide. Dozens of peaks line the horizon as you make your way up the fairly flat, hairpin-turn track, the scene fronted by a blanket of alpine wildflowers from July to mid-August. Arrive before noon if you want a parking spot at the trailhead. *Moderate.* ⊠ *Trailhead at end of Cascade River Rd., 14 miles from Marblemount* ⊕ *www.nps.gov/noca/planyourvisit/ cascade-pass-trail.htm.*

Diablo Lake Trail. Explore nearly 4 miles of waterside terrain on this moderate route, which is accessed from the Sourdough Creek parking lot. An excellent alternative for parties with small hikers is to take the Seattle City Light Ferry one way. *Moderate.* ⊠ *Trailhead at milepost 135, Hwy. 20* ⊕ *www.nps.gov/noca.*

DIFFICULT

Thornton Lakes Trail. A 5-mile climb into an alpine basin with three pretty lakes, this steep and strenuous hike takes about five to six hours round-trip. *Difficult* ⊠ *Trailhead off Hwy. 20, 3 miles west of Newhalem, Thornton Lake Rd. and Hwy. 20* ⊕ *www.nps.gov/noca/planyourvisit/ thornton-lake-trail.htm.*

HORSEBACK RIDING

Many hiking trails and backwoods paths are also popular horseback-riding routes, particularly around the park's southern fringes.

TOURS AND OUTFITTERS

Cascade Corrals. This subsidiary of Stehekin Outfitters organizes 2½-hour horseback trips to Coon Lake and full-day rides (lunch included) to Moore Point and Bridge Creek. English- and western-style riding lessons are also available. Reservations are taken at the Courtney Log Office at Stehekin Landing. ⊕ *www.cascadecorrals.com* 🖃 *$55–$150* ☉ *June–mid-Sept., half-day rides daily at 8:15 and 2:15.*

KAYAKING

The park's tangles of waterways offer access to remote areas inaccessible by road or trail; here are some of the most pristine and secluded mountain scenes on the continent. Bring your own kayak and you can launch from any boat ramp or beach; otherwise, companies in several nearby towns and Seattle suburbs offer kayak and canoe rentals, portage, and tours. The upper basin of Lake Chelan (at the park's southern end) and Ross Lake (at the top edge of the park) are two well-known kayaking expanses, but there are dozens of smaller lakes and creeks between. The Stehekin River also provides many kayaking possibilities.

14

TOURS AND OUTFITTERS

Outward Bound. Based in the mountain-sports center of Mazama, Outward Bound stages backpacking and mountaineering expeditions for older teens and adults on peaks throughout the park, and offers a variety of special programs for youth and veterans, including sea kayaking, canoeing, and rock climbing. ⊠ *226 Lost River Rd.* ☎ *866/467–7651, 828/239–2359* ⊕ *www.outwardbound.com.*

Ross Lake Resort. The resort rents kayaks and offers portage service for exploring Ross Lake. A water-taxi service is also available; the resort is not accessible by road. ⊠ *503 Diablo St., Rockport* ☎ *206/386–4437, 206/708–3980* ⊕ *www.rosslakeresort.com.*

Stehekin Adventure Company. Book a two-hour trip along the lake's upper estuary and western shoreline with Stehekin Adventure Company, or just hire a kayak and set out on your own. ⊠ *Stehekin Landing, Stehekin* ☎ *509/682–4677, 800/536–0745* ⊕ *www.stehekinoutfitters.com* ⬗ *Tour $35* ⊙ *Tours June–Sept., daily at 10. Rentals June–Sept., daily 10–4.*

RAFTING

June through August is the park's white-water season, and rafting trips run through the lower section of the Stehekin River. Along the way take in views of cottonwood and pine forests, glimpses of Yawning Glacier on Magic Mountain, and placid vistas of Lake Chelan.

TOURS AND OUTFITTERS

Downstream River Runners. Downstream River Runners covers rafting throughout the Northwest. ⊠ *3924 SW 106th St., Seattle* ☎ *206/910–7102* ⊕ *www.riverpeople.com.*

North Cascades River Expeditions. June through October, North Cascades River Expeditions focuses on regional rivers; trips are offered on the Upper Skagit year-round. ☎ *800/634–8433, 360/435–9548* ⊕ *www.riverexpeditions.com.*

Orion River Expeditions. White-water tours are available on the Skykomish and other area rivers April through September with Orion River Expeditions. ☎ *509/548–1401, 800/553–7466* ⊕ *www.orionexp.com.*

Stehekin Valley Ranch. Guided trips on the class III Stehekin River leave from Stehekin Valley Ranch. ⊠ *Stehekin Valley Rd., 3½ miles from Stehekin Landing, Stehekin* ☎ *509/682–4677, 800/536–0745* ⊕ *www.stehekinvalleyranch.com* ⬗ *$55* ⊙ *June–Sept.*

Wildwater River Guides. Exciting half- and full-day rafting excursions with Wildwater River Guides include transportation and a picnic. ☎ *509/470–8558, 800/522–9453* ⊕ *www.wildwater-river.com.*

WINTER SPORTS

Mt. Baker, just off the park's far northwest corner, is one of the Northwest's premier skiing, snowboarding, and snowshoeing regions—the area set a world record for most snow in a single season during the winter of 1998–99 (1,140 inches). The Mt. Baker Highway (Route 542) cuts through the slopes toward several state snow parks; Salmon

Ridge Sno-Park, 46 miles east of Bellingham at exit 255, has groomed trails and parking. Mt. Baker Ski Area, 17 miles east of the town of Glacier, has eight chairlifts and access to backcountry skiing; its season runs roughly from November to April. Stehekin is another base for winter sports. The Stehekin Valley alone has 20 miles of trails; some of the most popular are around Buckner Orchard, Coon Lake, and the Courtney Ranch (Cascade Corrals).

Mt. Baker. Off the park's northwest corner, this is the closest winter-sports area, with facilities for downhill and Nordic skiing, snowboarding, and other recreational ventures. The main base is the town of Glacier, 17 miles west of the slopes, where lodging is available. Equipment rental and food service are on-site. ✉ *52 miles east of Bellingham, Mt. Baker Hwy. 542, Glacier* ☎ *360/734–6771, 360/671–0211 for snow reports* 🌐 *www.mtbaker.us* 🎟 *All-day lift ticket weekends and holidays $54, weekdays $49* 🕒 *Nov.–Apr.*

WHERE TO EAT

$ CAFÉ 🍴 **Stehekin Pastry Company.** As you enter this lawn-framed timber chalet, you're immersed in the tantalizing aromas of a European bakery. Glassed-in display cases are filled with trays of homemade baked goods, and the pungent espresso is eye-opening. Sit down at a window-side table and dig into an over-filled sandwich or rich bowl of soup—and don't forget dessert: we're guessing you'll never taste a better slice of pie, made with fruit fresh-picked from local orchards. Although it's outside of town, the shop is conveniently en route to Rainbow Falls. [$] *Average main: $5* ✉ *Stehekin Valley Rd., about 2 miles from Stehekin Landing, Stehekin* ☎ *509/682–7742* 🌐 *www.stehekinpastry.com* 💳 *No credit cards* 🕒 *Closed mid-Oct.–mid-June.*

$$ AMERICAN 🍴 **Stehekin Valley Ranch.** Meals in the rustic log ranch house, served at polished wood tables, include buffet dinners of steak, ribs, hamburgers, salad, beans, and dessert. Note that breakfast is served 7 to 9, lunch is noon to 1, and dinner is 5:30 to 7. Show up later than that and you'll find the kitchen's closed. Transportation from Stehekin Landing is included for day visitors. [$] *Average main: $15* ✉ *Stehekin Valley Rd., 9 miles north of Stehekin Landing, Stehekin* ☎ *509/682–4677, 800/536–0745* 🌐 *www.stehekinvalleyranch.com* 💳 *No credit cards* 🕒 *Closed Oct.–mid-June.*

PICNIC AREAS

Developed picnic areas at both Rainy Pass (Route 20, 38 miles east of the park visitor center) and Washington Pass (Route 20, 42 miles east of the visitor center) have a half-dozen picnic tables, drinking water, and pit toilets. The vistas of surrounding peaks are sensational at these two overlooks. More picnic facilities are located near the visitor center in Newhalem and at Colonial Creek Campground, 10 miles east of the visitor center on Highway 20.

CLOSE UP

Best Campgrounds in North Cascades

Tent campers can choose between forest sites, riverside spots, lake grounds, or meadow spreads encircled by mountains. Here camping is as easy or challenging as you want to make it; some campgrounds are a short walk from ranger stations, while others are miles from the highway. Note that many campsites, particularly those around Stehekin, are completely remote and without road access anywhere, so you have to walk, boat, ride a horse, or take a floatplane to reach them. Most don't accept reservations, and spots fill up quickly May through September. If there's no ranger on-site, you can often sign yourself in—and always check in at a ranger station before you set out overnight. Note that some areas are occasionally closed due to flooding, forest fires, or other factors.

Lake Chelan National Recreation Area. Many backcountry camping areas are accessible via park shuttles or boat. All require a free backcountry permit. Purple Point, the most popular campground due to its quick access to Stehekin Landing, has seven tent sites, bear boxes, and nearby road access. ✉ *Stehekin Landing, Stehekin* ☎ *360/856–5700.*

WHERE TO STAY

For expanded hotel reviews, visit Fodors.com.

$$ HOTEL
🏨 **North Cascades Lodge at Stehekin.** Large lodge-style buildings welcome you with crackling fires and Lake Chelan views. **Pros:** on the water; recreation center with pool table; tent-to-tent hiking excursions. **Cons:** no air-conditioning. [$] *Rooms from: $118* ✉ *About 5 miles south of Stehekin Landing on Lake Chelan* ☎ *509/682–4494* 🌐 *www.lodgeatstehekin.com* 🛏 *28 rooms, 1 house* 🍴 *No meals.*

$$$ B&B/INN
🏨 **Silver Bay Inn.** Perched on a slip of land at the head of Lake Chelan, Silver Bay's accommodations feature water and mountain views; all have their own kitchens. **Pros:** hot tub vistas; free use of boats and bikes. **Cons:** summertime mosquitoes; not for families with kids under 12. [$] *Rooms from: $195* ✉ *Silver Bay Rd., P.O. Box 85, Stehekin* ☎ *509/699–2023, 800/555–7781* 🌐 *www.silverbayinn.com* 🛏 *1 room, 2 cabins, 1 house* 🕒 *Closed Nov.–Apr.*

$$$$ B&B/INN
🏨 **Stehekin Valley Ranch.** Alongside pretty meadows at the edge of pine forest, this classic ranch is a center for hikers and horseback riders. **Pros:** many activities; free vehicle use with kitchen cabins. **Cons:** no bathrooms in tent cabins. [$] *Rooms from: $240* ✉ *Stehekin Valley Rd., 9 miles north of Stehekin Landing, Stehekin* ☎ *509/682–4677, 800/536–0745* 🌐 *www.stehekinvalleyranch.com* 🛏 *34 cabins* 🕒 *Closed Oct.–mid-June* 🍴 *All meals.*

NORTH CENTRAL
WASHINGTON

WELCOME TO NORTH CENTRAL WASHINGTON

TOP REASONS TO GO

★ **Winter sports:** The nonprofit Methow Valley Sport Trails Association maintains 120 miles of groomed trails in the North Cascades during winter, when the region is also busy with snowmobiling, heli-skiing, snowshoeing and other winter sports.

★ **Summer sports:** The groomed trails of winter are used for mountain biking, trail running, and hiking when the snow melts. Mountain lakes, ridges and rivers also provide a perfect playground.

★ **Cascade Loop:** Visitors to the North Cascades don't *have* to be athletic. This scenic byway circles through the mountains, offering some 400 miles of stunning sights.

★ **Winthrop:** With its wagon wheels, wooden sidewalks, false fronts, and hitching posts, this riverside town gives a glimpse into the Old West.

★ **Leavenworth:** This Bavarian-style mountain town lights up for the holidays, Oktoberfest, and its annual accordion festival.

1 North Cascades. West of Washington Pass, Highway 20 winds around the northern shore of Diablo Lake and southern tip of Ross Lake, continuing through the former cement-manufacturing town of Concrete and fertile Skagit Valley pastures. The route offers breathtaking views of snowcapped peaks, summer wildflowers, and fall foliage. Snowfall closes the pass from November to April, cutting the valley off from Okanogan County, which includes Old West–style Winthrop and the riverfront town of Twisp in the Methow Valley.

2 Central Cascades. This picturesque region encompasses not only the resort town and fjord-like lake Chelan, but also the Bavarian-style village of Leavenworth and Wenatchee, self-proclaimed "Apple Capital of Washington," surrounded by orchards. Bordered by the Columbia River to the east, this stretch offers the ultimate in outdoor experiences, from boating and mountain biking to hiking and fishing, as well as plenty of outposts at which to relax and recoup.

CANADA

Mt.
Challenger

Ross
Lake

Cascades
onal Park

Ross Lake
Nat'l Rec Area

20

Mount
Logan

Washington Pass

20

Marblemount

Buckner
Mountain

Winthrop

North Cascades
National Park

Twisp

20

Lake Chelan
Nat'l Rec Area

153

Glacier
Peak

C
A
S
C
A
D
E
S

Lake
Chelan

Chelan

Stevens Pass

2

97W

97

Entiat

2

nish

Leavenworth

Cashmere

2

Sunnyslope

Snoqualmie
Pass

97

Wenatchee

Rock
Island

Kachess
Lake

2

Cle Elum
Lake

0   20 mi

Easton

0   20 km

Cle Elum

Columbia River

Thorp

90

GETTING
ORIENTED

Former logging towns,
nestled in the shadow of
Mount Baker to the north,
line the upper ring of the
Cascade Loop, encircling a
vast series of national forests fanning north and east
from Seattle. The ridges
and valleys of the Cascade
Range form the heart of this
region, a mecca for skiers,
snowshoers, white-water
river rafters, campers, hikers, mountain bikers, and
other adventurers drawn to
its natural beauty. Fjord-like
Lake Chelan reaches into
the wilderness from the
eastern edge of the loop,
providing one of three
ways to get to the secluded
outpost of Stehekin, accessible only by boat or plane
or on foot. The alpine
area is anchored by the
orchards surrounding
Wenatchee to the south-
east, where the Columbia
River forms a natural border between North Central
and Eastern Washington.

15

Updated
by Adriana
Janovich

Wilderness embraces much of North Central Washington, replete with old timber towns, cascading creeks, glacial peaks, and low-hanging valleys dusted with wildflowers. The region's natural beauty creates a feeling of journeying to an out-of-the-way, rural retreat. This is the quintessential outdoors, a place of snowcapped summits, sparkling lakes, evergreen forests and—despite the remote outpost of Stehekin and a road closure that walls off the east and west in winter—surprising accessibility.

Because of the depth of their glaciated valleys, the North Cascades are uncommonly reachable. One of the most popular drives in the state encircles the region, from the old lumber towns of Sedro-Woolley and Marblemount to the northwest, over Washington Pass to Mazama, where the family-run country store is a must-stop for a bowl of soup and baked goods, through the riverside stops of Twisp and Winthrop to the northeast. Both boast riverfront brewpubs with live music on summer weekends as well as good selections of craft beer. Farther south, the resort community of Chelan chalks up some 300 days of sunshine per year on the southern tip of a pristine, 50-mile glacier-fed lake of the same name. It stretches 1½ miles at its widest and descends 1,486 feet at its deepest. Bavarian-style Leavenworth, 23 miles northwest of Wenatchee, bustles with shopping and a variety of festivals, including an annual Oktoberfest celebration.

Most permanent residents live along the loop, on ranches and orchards and in pocket-sized towns, all gateways to the northern ridges of the Cascade Range. In winter, these peaks, which climb 4,000 to 9,000 feet and higher, have the greatest measured snowfall in North America—more than 80 feet in high places of the western slopes. Washington Pass closes in November, cutting off the Cascade Loop until April, but the region remains accessible via Interstate 90. Still, when Highway 20 reopens in spring, travelers on both sides line up, waiting to be among the first to travel back over the byway.

NORTH CENTRAL WASHINGTON PLANNER

WHEN TO GO

With its evergreen foothills, impressive peaks, and general accessibility, the North Cascades—often likened to the Alps—is a popular destination year-round. Skiers, snowboarders, and snowshoers come here from December through March, relaxing après-ski in the area's lodges, boutique hotels, and bed-and-breakfasts. With Washington Pass closed, however, winter visitors have to take alternative routes, making some otherwise easily accessible destinations and accommodations seem out-of-the-way. Still, almost all lowland forest areas and valleys can be visited any time of year. Summer peak season extends from snowmelt (late May through July, depending on elevation) to early September. Many annual visitors to Lake Chelan book lodging for the following summer before leaving. Weekends and holidays can get crowded with hikers, backpackers, boaters, anglers, white-water rafters, and other outdoors enthusiasts.

In the fall, when the North Cascades glow with crimson, saffron, and rust-colored foliage against a backdrop of its evergreen trees, the Cascade Loop is a popular route. Leaf-peepers who don't mind the rainy days of late autumn can enjoy otherwise mild temperatures and a quieter drive. Early spring also offers peace and quiet as well as the promise of alpine air. Many hotels and other lodging options offer economical shoulder season pricing.

FESTIVALS AND EVENTS

If you want to match your visit up with a local event, there are highlights in each season.

Christkindlmarkt and Christmas Lighting Festival. Old World holiday traditions blend with modern rituals to turn downtown Leavenworth into a glittering holiday wonderland, complete with carriage rides, carols, sledding, tree-lighting, children's activities, and other festivities. ⊠ *Leavenworth* ☎ *509/548–6605* ⊕ *www.christkindlmarktleavenworth.com.*

Lake Chelan Winterfest Fire and Ice. Held during the long Martin Luther King Jr. Day weekend in January, this festival features a chili cook-off, music, winter ale tasting, a fun run, ice slide, wine walk, children's activities, and ice sculpture. ⊠ *Chelan* ☎ *509/682–3503* ⊕ *www. lakechelanwinterfest.com.*

Leavenworth International Accordion Celebration. Sponsored by the Northwest Accordion Society, this June fest features jam sessions, competitions, concerts, workshops, vendors, and free accordion lessons. ⊠ *Leavenworth* ⊕ *www.accordioncelebration.org.*

Maifest. Enjoy traditional German dancing, including an intricate Old World maypole dance, as well as a lederhosen contest and parade flower-decked Bavarian-style village of Leavenworth. As the name suggests, it takes place in May. ⊠ *Leavenworth* ☎ *509/548–5807* ⊕ *www. leavenworth.org.*

Oktoberfest. Show off your "chicken dance" and other oom-pah moves in Leavenworth at one of the most exuberant stateside celebrations of this German beer festival, complete with German food, German music, German dancing and, of course, beer. Needless to say, it's in October. ⊠ *Leavenworth* ☎ *509/548–7021* ⊕ *www.leavenworthoktoberfest.com.*

Winthrop Rhythm and Blues Fest. The Blues Ranch, 1 mile west of Winthrop, is the venue for this nonprofit, volunteer-run July music festival— an outdoor Methow Valley tradition. ⊠ *Winthrop* ☎ *509/997–3837* ⊕ *www.winthropbluesfestival.com.*

GETTING HERE AND AROUND

AIR TRAVEL

Commercial flights from Sea-Tac International Airport to Wenatchee's Pangborn Memorial Airport (☎ *509/884–2494* ⊕ *www.pangbornairport.com*) are available through Horizon Air, a regional carrier and subsidiary of Alaska Airlines.

Twisp-based Catlin Flying Service (☎ *509/997–4602 or 866/445–2359* ⊕ *www.catlinflyingservice.com*) offers direct flights to some 500 destinations, including Chelan, Winthrop, Stehekin, and Seattle's Boeing Field. Private flights, including scenic mountain flights, are available for up to five passengers.

CAR TRAVEL

From the Skagit Valley towns of Mt. Vernon and Burlington, about 65 miles north of Seattle on I–5, take Hwy. 20, the North Cascades Highway, east through Sedro-Woolley, Concrete, and Marblemount. From April to November, when Washington Pass is open, continue to Winthrop and Twisp, then use State Rte. 153 to get to Chelan, and U.S. Rte. 97—with a short jaunt on U.S. Rte. 2 heading west—to get to Leavenworth and Wenatchee. An hour and a half to the south, U.S. Rte. 97 connects with I–90 at Ellensburg, about an hour and 45 minutes from Seattle.

From Seattle, take I–90 to U.S. Rte. 97 to Wenatchee and Leavenworth— with a short jaunt on U.S. Rte. 2 heading east—to Chelan. From there, State Rte. 153 takes travelers north to Hwy. 20 through Twisp and Winthrop, and—from April to November—west over Washington Pass, through Marblemount, Concrete, Sedro-Woolley, and Burlington, where it connects with I–5, Washington's main north-south artery.

From Everett, about 28 miles north of Seattle on I–5, take U.S. Hwy. 2 east through Gold Bar, Index, Stevens Pass, and the Alpine Lakes Wilderness to Leavenworth and Wenatchee.

RESTAURANTS

This region has a good range of dining options, from American pub fare to fine dining, and many incorporate locally grown and produced ingredients, including organic produce, beef, chicken, eggs, and artisanal breads and cheeses. Around the region, there are low-key, affordable, and unpretentious eateries—coffee shops, bakeries, brewpubs, diners, and restaurants.

Wenatchee is the largest city in the North Cascades and features the most variety when it comes to dining. It's home to the most ethnically diverse cuisine in the region, including several Mexican restaurants as well as Italian, Thai, Japanese, Chinese, and others. The self-proclaimed "Apple Capital of Washington," this is the place to try to the fruit in a variety of forms, sweet and savory.

Bavarian-themed Leavenworth offers a number of restaurants specializing in traditional German fare as well as southern barbecue and American pub fare. Wine enthusiasts might want to make a stop in the Lake Chelan region, home to some two-dozen wineries. *Prices in the reviews are the average cost of a main course at dinner or, if dinner is not served, at lunch.*

HOTELS

Accommodations in the North Cascades range from rustic cabins and basic motels to charming bed-and-breakfasts, riverside inns, boutique hotels, and upscale mountain resorts, most featuring first-rate hospitality. Many also have picturesque mountain, lake, or river views. Splurge at the pricey but spectacular Sun Mountain Lodge, which offers spacious suites, abundant amenities and activities, and seemingly endless panoramic alpine vistas. Book well in advance for holiday and summer weekends, particularly during festivals and events. Winter and shoulder seasons tend to feature lower price points. Look for package deals online at many establishments. *Prices in the reviews are the lowest cost of a standard double room in high season.*

15

NORTH CASCADES

This is a backpacker's paradise, the perfect place to take a hike, enjoy winter snow sports, and go white-water rafting or fishing. In fall, the changing leaves provide a colorful backdrop along the Cascade Loop, one of the state's most popular scenic byways. In summer, the valleys and slopes are blanketed with wildflowers. The towns of Twisp and Winthrop—the latter with an appealing Old West feel—provide launchpads to the great outdoors, easily accessible from every corner of this gorgeous region, marked by snowcapped peaks and low-hanging valleys.

GLACIER

113 miles north of Seattle.

The canyon village of Glacier, just outside the Mt. Baker–Snoqualmie National Forest boundary, has a few shops, cafés, and lodgings. Highway 542 winds east from Glacier into the forest through an increasingly steep-walled canyon. It passes 170-foot-high Nooksack Falls, about 5 miles east of Glacier, and travels up the north fork of the Nooksack River and the slopes of Mt. Baker to a ski area, which is bright with huckleberry patches and wildflowers in summer.

GETTING HERE AND AROUND

Glacier is about 2 hours and 15 minutes from Seattle. Take I–5 north to Exit 230 at Burlington; go east 6 miles on Hwy. 20 then north via Hwy. 9, then northeast via Hwy. 542.

EXPLORING

Mt. Baker–Snoqualmie National Forest. A vast area, including much of the mountain and forest land around North Cascades National Park, the forest has many trails, but because the snowline is quite low in Washington State, the upper ridges and mountains are covered by snow much of the year. This makes for a short hiking, climbing, and mountain-biking season, usually from mid-July to mid-September or October—but winter brings skiing and snowmobiling. The wildflower season is also short, but it's spectacular; expect fall color by late August or early September. The 10,778-foot-high, snow-covered volcanic dome of **Mt. Baker** is visible from much of Whatcom County and from as far north as Vancouver and as far south as Seattle. ✉ *Ranger Station: 1405 Emens Ave. N, Darrington* ☎ *360/783–6000 Everett office, 800/627–0062 toll free, 360/436–1155 Darrington Ranger District office, 206/470–4060 Outdoor Recreation Information* 🌐 *www.fs.fed.us/r6/mbs* 🎟 *$5* 🕒 *Daily 24 hrs.*

WHERE TO STAY

For expanded hotel reviews, visit Fodors.com.

$$ B&B/INN 🏨 **The Inn at Mt. Baker.** Nestled into the upper Cascades, this stately country home offers airy spaces with vaulted ceilings—and sweeping mountain panoramas from every angle. **Pros:** easy to find; European-style luxuries; recreation packages can be arranged. **Cons:** simple room style can seem sparse; no children under 16. [$] *Rooms from: $165* ✉ *8174 Mt. Baker Hwy., at milepost 28* ☎ *360/599–1776, 877/567–5526* 🌐 *www.theinnatmtbaker.com* 🛏 *5 rooms* 🍴 *Breakfast.*

$ B&B/INN 🏨 **Kale House Bed & Breakfast.** The charming home gleams with polished wood and large windows, which look out to knobby apple trees and a weeping willow. **Pros:** small and inviting; lovely gardens; lots of art. **Cons:** no children or pets. [$] *Rooms from: $125* ✉ *201 Kale St., Everson* ☎ *360/966–7027* 🌐 *www.kalehouse.net* 🛏 *2 rooms* 🍴 *Breakfast.*

$ RENTAL 🏨 **The Logs at Canyon Creek.** This comfortable back-country destination, set on a creek and surrounded by forest, is a haven for deer, eagles, and other wildlife. **Pros:** your home in the woods; great ski access. **Cons:** a long drive from civilization; three-night minimum stay in summer. [$] *Rooms from: $135* ✉ *7577 Canyon View Dr., 3½ miles northwest of Glacier off Mt. Baker Hwy., Deming* ☎ *360/599–2711* 🌐 *www.thelogs.com* 🛏 *5 cabins, 3 chalets* 💳 *No credit cards* 🍴 *No meals.*

SPORTS AND THE OUTDOORS

Mt. Baker Ski Area. Here you can snowboard and ski downhill or cross-country from roughly November to the end of April. The area set a world snowfall record in winter 1998–99. Ski and snowboard equipment is available to rent. ✉ *17 miles east of Glacier at end of Hwy. 542* ☎ *360/734–6771, 360/671–0211 snow reports* 🌐 *www.mtbakerskiarea.com* 🎟 *Lift ticket $49 weekdays, $54 weekends and holidays.*

SEDRO-WOOLLEY

42 miles southwest of Glacier.

On its way east from I–5, Highway 20 skirts Burlington and Sedro-Woolley, the latter a former mill and logging town now considered "The

Gateway to the Cascades." Fronted by a huge black steam engine, the settlement has a bit of an old downtown and a smattering of Tar Heel culture, as it was settled by pioneer loggers and farmers from North Carolina. It also has an institute that arranges trips into the North Cascades National Park and a nearby park headquarters.

GETTING HERE AND AROUND

Sedro-Woolley is about 1 hour, 20 minutes from Seattle via I–5 north to Burlington (Exit 230), then 5 miles east via Hwy. 20.

ESSENTIALS

Visitor Information **Sedro-Woolley Chamber of Commerce** ⊠ *714-B Metcalf St.* ☎ *360/855–1841, 888/225–8365* ⊕ *www.sedro-woolley.com.*

EXPLORING

Lake Whatcom Railway. The steam-powered train makes short jaunts through the woods 11 miles north of Sedro-Woolley. Excursions run all summer and during special events, such as the Christmas train rides with Santa in December. During peak weekends, tours depart around 10, 12:30, and 3, and children pay half-price. Note that the schedule changes seasonally. ⊠ *Hwy. 9, Wickersham* ☎ *360/595–2218* ⊕ *www.lakewhatcomrailway.com* 🎫 *$20* ⏰ *Call for hrs.*

WHERE TO STAY

For expanded hotel reviews, visit Fodors.com.

$

HOTEL

🛏 **Three Rivers Inn.** This pleasant two-story motel is a handy place to stay on the way to or from North Cascades National Park. **Pros:** rooms are equipped with microwaves and refrigerators; seasonally open swimming pool; pet-friendly. **Cons:** no elevator; basic interior design. $ *Rooms from: $120* ⊠ *210 Ball St.* ☎ *360/855–2626, 800/221–5122* ⊕ *www.thethreeriversinn.com* 🛏 *40 rooms* 🍴 *Breakfast.*

MARBLEMOUNT

40 miles east of Sedro-Woolley.

Like Sedro-Woolley, Marblemount is a former logging town now depending on outdoor recreation for its fortunes. Anglers, campers, hikers, bird-watchers, and hunters come and go from the town's collection of motels, cafés, and stores, while day-trippers head in for sips at the area's small wineries. It's also a good base for exploring North Cascades National Park.

GETTING HERE AND AROUND

Marblemount is about 2 hours northeast of Seattle. It can be reached via I–5 north to Burlington then east past Sedro-Woolley on Highway 20. An alternate route is to take the exit from I–5 to Arlington/Darrington and proceed on Hwy. 530 until it reaches Hwy. 20, then continue east.

WHERE TO EAT

$

AMERICAN

✕ **Buffalo Run.** Buffalo, venison, elk, and ostrich are the specialties at this little place next to the Marblemount Post Office, but vegetarians will find a few nonmeat options on the menu too. The atmosphere is completely casual, with buffalo heads and Old West memorabilia lining the dining room walls. Outside, the patio adds warm-weather seating and garden views; it's a good spot to kick back with a glass of wine. The adjacent inn, under the same management, is an inexpensive overnight option. $ *Average main: $15* ✉ *60084 Hwy. 20, Marblemount* 📞 *360/873–2461* ⊕ *www.buffaloruninn.com* ⊙ *Closed Wed. and Nov.–Dec.*

WINTHROP

87 miles east of Marblemount, 128 miles east of Sedro-Woolley.

Before the cowboys came, the Methow Valley was a favorite gathering place for Native American tribes, who dug the plentiful and nutritious bulbs and hunted deer while their horses fattened on the tall native grasses. For wayward pioneers who came later, the cool, glacier-fed streams provided welcome relief on hot summer days, and the rich fields were a starting point for vast crops and orchards. The 1800s saw the burgeoning riverside settlement of Winthrop grow into a cattle-ranching town, whose residents inspired some of Owen Wister's colorful characters in his novel *The Virginian*. In 1972, inspired by Leavenworth's Bavarian theme, Winthrop business owners enacted a plan to restore its Old West feel, and many of the original, turn-of-the-20th-century buildings still stand.

Getting to town through the Washington countryside is a picturesque drive, with endless vistas of golden meadows, neatly sown crop fields, and rustic old barn frames. In winter the land is a crisp blanket of glittering frost; in summer little fruit-and-vegetable stands pop up along the back roads. Massive tangles of blackberry bushes produce kumquat-size fruit you can eat right off the vines, and the pungent aroma of apples pervades the breezes in autumn. Flat roads, small towns, incredible views, and plenty of camp spots make this the perfect weekend wandering territory by bike, car, or motorcycle.

GETTING HERE AND AROUND

When the North Cascades Highway is open, Winthrop can be reached via that scenic route; it takes about 3 hours, 45 minutes from Seattle. The rest of the year, it will take about an extra hour via Stevens Pass (Hwy. 2) or Snoqualmie Pass (I–90 then Hwy. 970 to Hwy. 2) to Wenatchee then north via Hwys. 97, 153, and 20. From Spokane, Winthrop is about 3½ hours west via Hwy. 2, then Hwys. 174, 17, 97, 153, and 20.

ESSENTIALS

Visitor Information Winthrop Chamber of Commerce ✉ *202 Hwy. 20* 📞 *509/996–2125, 888/463–8469* ⊕ *www.winthropwashington.com.*

WHERE TO EAT

$$$

PACIFIC NORTHWEST

✕ **Dining Room at Sun Mountain Lodge.** In a sylvan hilltop setting overlooking the Methow Valley, intimate tables and a woodsy interior design set the scene for an extraordinary dining experience. The upscale Pacific Northwest cuisine is based around often-organic, locally grown, raised, caught and crafted ingredients, providing for exquisite flavors to match the artful presentation and elegant yet unpretentious atmosphere. Delicacies include mushroom bisque, melt-in-your-mouth pork chops, spinach and goat cheese tortellini, and New York steak au poivre with truffled mashed potatoes. The dessert menu has many tempting choices, including a trio of vanilla, mocha, and lemon brûlée, rich passion fruit cheesecake, and "Chocolate Fantasy"—a quintet of chocolate delights. The 5,000-bottle wine cellar is one of the best and most extensive in the region. [$] *Average main: $25* ✉ *604 Patterson Lake Rd., Winthrop* ☎ *509/996–2211* 🌐 *www.sunmountainlodge.com/dining* 🕒 *Closed Sun.–Thurs. in winter.*

$ AMERICAN 🍴 **Old Schoolhouse Brewery.** Located in a red-painted building designed to resemble an old, one-room schoolhouse, this family-run craft brewpub sits between the town's main drag and the river. Live music plays on the outdoor stage in the beer garden on the banks of the Chewuch River on summer weekend nights. Seating is also available on the back deck, affectionately dubbed "The Hangover," as well as indoors in the long, one-room pub. While waiting for big burgers, fish-and-chips, baked mac-n-cheese, or a succulent pork sandwich, sip an Epiphany Pale, Hooligan Stout, or Ruud Awakening IPA, the latter named for the family that owns the place. [$] *Average main: $12* ✉ *155 Riverside Ave.* ☎ *509/996–3183* 🌐 *www.oldschoolhousebrewery.com* 🕒 *Closed Tues. and Wed. in winter.*

$ AMERICAN 🍴 **Twisp River Pub.** This popular brewpub produces a range of house beers, including IPA (the most popular), ESB, and porter, hard pear and apple ciders, and seasonal ales. Regional wines are also available. Within the industrial Craftsman-style interior, choose from burgers fashioned from local beef, fish-and-chips, and meaty sandwiches at lunch. Dinners include steak, salmon, coconut curry, and Thai peanut noodles—one of the most frequently requested dishes. Or you can snack on buffalo wings, nachos, and an array of homemade soups. Brunch is served on Sunday. There's live music every weekend and jazz in the riverside beer garden on summer Wednesday evenings. [$] *Average main: $15* ✉ *201 Hwy. 20, 9 miles south of Winthrop, Twisp* ☎ *509/997–6822, 888/220–3360* 🌐 *www.methowbrewing.com* 🕒 *Closed Mon.–Wed. mid-Oct.–mid-May (except Christmas–New Year period). No brunch Mon.–Sat.*

WHERE TO STAY

For expanded hotel reviews, visit Fodors.com.

$$$ RESORT Fodor's Choice ★ 🏨 **Freestone Inn.** At the heart of the 120-acre, historic Wilson Ranch, amid more than 2 million acres of forest, this upscale mountain retreat embraces luxury along with the pioneer spirit. **Pros:** gorgeous scenery; myriad activities. **Cons:** limited cell phone service; Wi-Fi signal isn't strong in guest rooms; breakfast only included for guests in main inn building. [$] *Rooms from: $225* ✉ *31 Early Winters Dr., about 14 miles northwest of Winthop, Mazama* ☎ *509/996–3906, 800/639–3809* 🌐 *www.freestoneinn.com* 🛏 *10 rooms, 7 suites, 15 cabins, 4 lodges* 🍽 *Breakfast.*

$ B&B/INN 🏨 **Methow Valley Inn.** Run with family-style friendliness, this historic country inn with lovely gardens has guest rooms furnished with antiques and decorated with a Scandinavian influence. **Pros:** gorgeous gardens in summer; lovely holiday decorations in winter; superb cleanliness. **Cons:** showers only, no bath tubs; no in-room TVs; some shared bathrooms;

no children under 12 unless you rent the entire inn. [$] *Rooms from: $89* ✉ *234 E. 2nd Ave., about 9 miles north Winthrop, Twisp* ☎ *509/997–2253* 🌐 *www.methowvalleyinn.com* 🛏 *7 rooms, 5 with private bath, 1 suite* 🍴 *Breakfast.*

$ RENTAL 🏨 **Rolling Huts.** There's camping, and then there are the Rolling Huts—this is roughing it with style and sophistication, in an alpine river valley meadow with mountain views. **Pros:** gorgeous views; serene setting; interesting architecture. **Cons:** limited cell phone service; portable toilets and water faucets outside each hut. [$] *Rooms from: $135* ✉ *18381 Hwy. 20, about 14 miles northwest of Winthrop on State Rte. 20, Mazama* ☎ *509/996–4442* 🌐 *www.rollinghuts.com* 🛏 *6 huts* 🍴 *No meals.*

$$$ RESORT Fodor's Choice ★ 🏨 **Sun Mountain Lodge.** This hilltop resort provides alpine elegance, spectacular mountain views, and a range of activities that make it a year-round destination. **Pros:** year-round outdoor activities; panoramic views. **Cons:** limited cell service; roundabout route from Seattle in winter. [$] *Rooms from: $235* ✉ *604 Patterson Lake Rd., Winthrop* ☎ *509/996–2211, 800/572–0493* 🌐 *www.sunmountainlodge.com* 🛏 *86 rooms, 10 suites, 16 cabins* 🍴 *Breakfast.*

$ HOTEL 🏨 **Twisp River Suites.** Opened in 2012 to rave reviews, this boutique hotel offers contemporary rooms and condominium-style suites on the banks of the Twisp River, lined by ponderosa pine and frequented by bald eagles. **Pros:** modern; congenial staff; riverfront views. **Cons:** not too much to do in Twisp. [$] *Rooms from: $99* ✉ *140 W. Twisp Ave., Twisp* ☎ *509/997–0100, 855/784–8328* 🌐 *www.twispriversuites.com* 🛏 *5 rooms, 8 suites* 🍴 *Breakfast.*

CENTRAL CASCADES

Lake Chelan, with its sparkling glacier-fed waters, is one of Washington's longtime destinations. Temperatures soar at this mountain lake in the summer, when vacationers flock to its shores. The remote outpost of Stehekin, not accessible by any road, hugs its northern end. To the south, the Bavarian-style town of Leavenworth hosts numerous festivals, along with outdoor fun and plenty of bratwurst. Wenatchee, known for the apples plucked from its local orchards, and Cashmere, with its candied aplets and cotlets, anchor the region's southeast corner. Like its North Cascades neighbor, this area is also good for hiking, backpacking, fishing, rafting, skiing, and other winter snow sports.

CHELAN

181 miles east of Seattle.

Long before the first American settlers arrived at the long, narrow lake, Chelan (sha-*lan*) was the site of a Chelan tribal winter village. The Native Americans would range far and wide on their horses in spring and summer, following the newly sprouting grass from the river bottoms into the mountains; in winter they converged in permanent villages to feast, perform sacred rituals, and wait out the cold weather and snow. During the winter of 1879–80, Chelan served briefly as

Sun Mountain Lodge

an army post, but the troops were soon transferred to Fort Spokane. European-American settlers arrived in the 1880s.

Today Chelan serves as the favorite beach resort of western Washingtonians. In summer Lake Chelan is one of the hottest places in Washington, with temperatures often soaring above 100°F. The mountains surrounding the 50½-mile-long fjord-like lake rise from a height of about 4,000 feet near Chelan to 8,000 and 9,000 feet near the town of Stehekin, at the head of the lake. There is no road circling the lake, so the only way to see the whole thing is by boat or floatplane or on foot. Several resorts line the lake's eastern (and warmer) shore. Its northwestern end, at Stehekin, just penetrates North Cascades National Park. South of the lake, 9,511-foot Bonanza Peak is the tallest nonvolcanic peak in Washington.

GETTING HERE AND AROUND

From Seattle it takes about 3 hours, 15 minutes to reach Chelan by either Hwy. 2 (Stevens Pass) or I–90 (Snoqualmie Pass) then north via Hwy. 97. From Spokane it's about 3 hours via Hwys. 2 and 17.

ESSENTIALS

Visitor Information **Lake Chelan Chamber of Commerce** ✉ *102 E. Johnson Ave.* ☎ *509/682–3503, 800/424–3536* ⊕ *www.lakechelan.com.*

Purple Point Information Center. Rangers here offer guidance on hiking and camping and information about the national parks and recreation areas. This is a good place to pick up permits and passes. Maps and concise displays explain the complicated ecology of the valley, which encompasses in its length virtually every ecosystem in the Northwest.

Stehekin River Valley

Hours vary in spring and fall. ⊠ *Stehekin Valley Rd., ¼ mile north of Stehekin Landing, Stehekin* ☎ *360/856–5700* ⊘ *Mid-Mar.–mid-Oct., daily 8:30–5.*

EXPLORING

Lake Chelan. This sinewy, 50.5-mile-long fjord—Washington's deepest lake—works its way from the town of Chelan, at its south end, to Stehekin, at the far northwest edge. The scenery is unparalleled, the flat blue water encircled by plunging gorges, with a vista of snow-slathered mountains beyond. No roads access the lake except for Chelan, so a floatplane or boat is needed to see the whole thing. Resorts dot the warmer eastern shores. ⊠ *U.S. 97A, Chelan* ☎ *360/856–5700 option 14* ⊕ *www.nps.gov/lach.*

Stehekin Boat Co. The *Lady of the Lake II* makes journeys from May to October, departing Chelan at 8:30 and returning at 6. Tickets are $40.50 round-trip, half price for ages 2 to 11. The *Lady Express*, a speedy catamaran, runs between Stehekin, Holden Village, the national park, and Lake Chelan year-round; schedules vary with the seasons. Tickets are $61 round-trip. The vessels also can drop off and pick up at lakeshore trailheads. ⊠ *1418 Woodin Ave., Chelan* ☎ *509/682–4584, 888/682–4584* ⊕ *www.ladyofthelake.com.*

Lake Chelan State Park. Right on the lake and 9 miles west of Chelan on the opposite (less crowded) shore, this 127-acre park with 6,000 feet of shoreline is a favorite hangout for folks from the cool west side of the Cascades who want to soak up some sun. There are docks, a boat ramp, RV sites with full hookups, and lots of campsites for those who prefer a less "citified" approach to camping. ⊠ *7544 S. Lakeshore*

Rd., U.S. 97A, west to South Shore Dr. or Navarre Coulee Rd. ☎ *360/902–8844, 509/687–3710, 88/226–7688* 🌐 *www.parks.wa.gov* 🎟 *Day pass $10 per vehicle, annual Discovery Pass $30 (valid at all state parks), camping $23–$37* ⏲ *Memorial Day–Labor Day, daily 6:30 am–10 pm.*

Fodor's Choice ★ **Stehekin.** One of the most beautiful and secluded valleys in the Pacific Northwest, Stehekin was homesteaded by hardy souls in the late 19th century. It's actually not a town, but rather a small community set at the northwest end of Lake Chelan, and it's accessible only by boat, floatplane, or trail. Year-round residents—who have intermittent outside communications, boat-delivered supplies, and just two-dozen cars between them—enjoy a wilderness lifestyle. Even on a peak summer season day, only around 200 visitors make the trek here.

WORD OF MOUTH

"Chelan is at the south end of Lake Chelan, which is a very narrow, very long fjord-like lake that extends from the sagebrush country around Chelan deep into the North Cascades. Partway up the lake is the little village of Stehekin, accessed by a passenger ferry from Chelan. . . . There's a variety of lodging in Stehekin, all of it quite rustic, but the lake itself and the surrounding mountains and waterfalls are quite something."

—Gardyloo

Twenty-Five Mile Creek State Park. Directly north of Lake Chelan State Park, this park also abuts the lake's eastern shore. It has many of the same facilities as the Chelan park, as well as a swimming pool, and because it's the more remote of the two, it's often less crowded. ✉ *20530 South Lakeshore Rd.* ☎ *509/687–3610, 800/452–5687* 🌐 *www.parks.wa.gov* ⏲ *Apr.–Sept., daily dawn–dusk.*

Buckner Homestead. Dating from 1889, this restored pioneer farm includes an apple orchard, farmhouse, barn, and many ranch buildings. One-hour ranger-guided tours of the property are offered Thursday to Sunday from late June through mid-September; otherwise, you can pick up a self-guided tour booklet from the drop box. ✉ *Stehekin Valley Rd., 3½ miles from Stehekin Landing, Stehekin* ☎ *360/854–7365 option 14* 🌐 *www.bucknerhomestead.org* ⏲ *June–Sept., daily 9–5.*

WHERE TO EAT

$ CAFÉ 🍴 **Stehekin Pastry Company.** As you enter this lawn-framed timber chalet, you're immersed in the tantalizing aromas of a European bakery. Glassed-in display cases are filled with trays of homemade baked goods, and the pungent espresso is eye-opening. Sit down at a window-side table and dig into an over-filled sandwich or rich bowl of soup—and don't forget dessert: we're guessing you'll never taste a better slice of pie, made with fruit fresh-picked from local orchards. Although it's outside of town, the shop is conveniently en route to Rainbow Falls. [$] *Average main: $5* ✉ *Stehekin Valley Rd., about 2 miles from Stehekin Landing, Stehekin* ☎ *509/682–7742* 🌐 *www.stehekinpastry.com* 💳 *No credit cards* ⏲ *Closed mid-Oct.–mid-June.*

15

$ AMERICAN
🍴 **Stehekin Valley Ranch.** Meals in the rustic log ranch house, served at polished wood tables, include buffet dinners of steak, ribs, hamburgers, salad, beans, and dessert. Note that breakfast is served 7 to 9, lunch is noon to 1, and dinner is 5:30 to 7. Show up later than that and you'll find the kitchen's closed. Transportation from Stehekin Landing is included for day visitors. [$] *Average main: $15* ✉ *Stehekin Valley Rd., 9 miles north of Stehekin Landing, Stehekin* ☎ *509/682–4677, 800/536–0745* 🌐 *www.stehekinvalleyranch.com* 💳 *No credit cards* 🕒 *Closed Oct.–mid-June.*

WHERE TO STAY

For expanded hotel reviews, visit Fodors.com.

$$$$ RESORT
🏨 **Campbell's Resort.** A long-established lakeshore landmark, this sand-color apartment-style resort sits on 8 acres of landscaped grounds, with 1,200 feet of pristine sandy beachfront on Lake Chelan and lots of activities for all ages. **Pros:** lots of activities as well as tranquil spaces; private beach; lake and mountain views; low off-season rates. **Cons:** very busy high season. [$] *Rooms from: $275* ✉ *104 W. Woodin Ave.* ☎ *509/682–2561, 800/553–8225* 📠 *509/682–2177* 🌐 *www.campbellsresort.com* 🛏 *170 rooms* 🍽 *No meals.*

$$$$ RENTAL
🏨 **The Lake House at Chelan.** Just across the street from lakeshore Don Morse Park you'll find these sophisticated and impeccable condominium-style rental units with one or three bedrooms and full modern kitchens with granite countertops. **Pros:** modern and immaculate; family-friendly; year-round pool; reasonable shoulder and off-season rates; secured underground parking. **Cons:** some traffic noise from State Route 150, which fronts the property; no restaurant or bar on-site. [$] *Rooms from: $299* ✉ *402 W. Manson Highway* ☎ *509/293–5982, 877/293–5982* 🌐 *www.lakehousechelan.com* 🛏 *40 condominiums* 🍽 *No meals.*

$$$ HOTEL
Fodor's Choice ★
🏨 **Lake View Hotel.** In the heart of Chelan's historic downtown, this exceptionally elegant boutique hotel, opened in 2010, tops a brick heritage building overlooking a riverfront park. **Pros:** sophisticated feel; prime location. **Cons:** not suitable for families; no on-site parking; $50 cancellation fee, or 50% of first night if canceled within two weeks. [$] *Rooms from: $225* ✉ *104 E. Woodin Ave.* ☎ *509/682–1334* 🌐 *chelanhotel.com* 🛏 *12 rooms* 🍽 *No meals.*

$ HOTEL
🏨 **North Cascades Lodge at Stehekin.** Large lodge-style buildings welcome you with crackling fires and Lake Chelan views. **Pros:** on the water; recreation center with pool table; tent-to-tent hiking excursions. **Cons:** no air-conditioning. [$] *Rooms from: $118* ✉ *About 5 miles south of Stehekin Landing on Lake Chelan* ☎ *509/682–4494* 🌐 *www.lodgeatstehekin.com* 🛏 *28 rooms, 1 house* 🍽 *No meals.*

$$$ B&B/INN
🏨 **Stehekin Valley Ranch.** Alongside pretty meadows at the edge of pine forest, this classic ranch is a center for hikers and horseback riders. **Pros:** many activities; free vehicle use with kitchen cabins. **Cons:** no bathrooms in tent cabins. [$] *Rooms from: $240* ✉ *Stehekin Valley Rd., 9 miles north of Stehekin Landing, Stehekin* ☎ *509/682–4677, 800/536–0745* 🌐 *www.stehekinvalleyranch.com* 🛏 *34 cabins* 🕒 *Closed Oct.–mid-June* 🍽 *All meals.*

SPORTS AND THE OUTDOORS

On a scenic half-day raft trip you can traverse the lower section of the Stehekin River, which winds through cottonwood and pine forest, from Yawning Glacier on the slopes of Magic Mountain southeast to Lake Chelan.

Stehekin Valley Ranch. From June through September, $55 guided trips on Class III waters leave from the Stehekin Valley Ranch, 9 miles from Stehekin Landing (there's a free shuttle). In addition to the whitewater rafting, they offer kayaking and horseback riding. The ranch is also a good launch pad for mountain biking and day hiking. ⊠ *Stehekin Valley Rd., Stehekin* ☎ *509/682–4677, 800/536–0745* ⊕ *stehekinvalleyranch.com.*

Mountain bikers also make their way into this rugged terrain.

Stehekin Discovery Bikes. Bikes can be rented for $4 per hour or $25 for 24 hours. The $35 Ranch Breakfast Ride is a popular package; riders are transported to Stehekin Valley Ranch for custom breakfasts, then explore the valley at their own pace. ⊠ *Stehekin Valley Rd., 5-minute walk from the boat landing, Stehekin* ☎ *509/682–2519* ⊕ *stehekindiscoverybikes.com.*

15

WENATCHEE

39 miles southwest of Chelan.

Wenatchee (we-*nat*-chee), the county seat of Chelan County, is an attractive city in a shallow valley at the confluence of the Wenatchee and Columbia rivers. Surrounded by orchards, Wenatchee is known as the "Apple Capital of Washington." Downtown has many old commercial buildings as well as apple-packing houses where visitors can buy locally grown apples by the case (at about half the price charged in supermarkets). The paved Apple Valley Recreation Loop Trail runs on both sides of the Columbia River. It crosses the river on bridges at the northern and southern ends of town and connects several riverfront parks. The Wenatchee section is lighted until midnight.

The town was built on an ancient Wenatchi tribal village, which may have been occupied as long as 11,000 years ago, as recent archaeological finds of Clovis hunter artifacts suggest. (The Clovis hunters, also known as Paleo-Indians, were members of the oldest tribes known to have inhabited North America.)

GETTING HERE AND AROUND

Horizon Air serves Wenatchee's Pangborn Memorial Airport. Amtrak's *Empire Builder,* which runs from Chicago to Seattle, stops in Wenatchee; Greyhound Bus Lines serves the town, too. From Seattle it's about a 2½ hour drive to Wenatchee via Hwy. 2 or I–90 and Hwy. 97; from Spokane it takes about 3 hours via Hwy. 2 or I–90.

Contacts Amtrak ☎ *800/872-7245* ⊕ *www.amtrak.com.* **Greyhound Bus Lines** ☎ *509/662-2183* ⊕ *www.greyhound.com.* **Pangborn Memorial Airport** ☎ *509/884-2494* ⊕ *www.pangbornairport.com.*

ESSENTIALS

Visitor Information Wenatchee Chamber of Commerce ✉ *300 S. Columbia St.* ☎ *509/662–2116, 800/572–7753* 🌐 *www.wenatcheevalley.org.* **Wenatchee Valley Convention and Visitor Bureau** ✉ *5 S. Wenatchee Ave., Ste. 100* ☎ *800/572–7753* 🌐 *www.wenatcheevalley.org.*

EXPLORING

Ohme Gardens. This is a lush green oasis, high atop bluffs near the confluence of the Columbia and Wenatchee rivers, where you can commune with a blend of native rocks, ferns, mosses, waterfalls, rock gardens, and conifers. ✉ *3327 Ohme Rd., north of Wenatchee near U.S. 2 at U.S. 97A* ☎ *509/662–5785* 🌐 *www.ohmegardens.com* 🎟 *$7* 🕒 *Mid-Apr.–mid-Oct, daily 9–6 (to 7 pm Memorial Day–Labor Day),.*

Okanogan-Wenatchee National Forest. More than 4 million acres of pines extend from the eastern slopes of the Cascades to the crest of the Wenatchee Mountains and north to Lake Chelan. Camping, hiking, boating, fishing, hunting, and picnicking are popular activities. ✉ *215 Melody La.* ☎ *509/664–9200* 🌐 *www.fs.usda.gov/okawen* 🎟 *$5 daily parking pass, or $30 Northwest Forest Pass* 🕒 *Daily 24 hrs.*

Rocky Reach Dam. There's a museum and visitor center here, as well as picnic tables and elaborately landscaped grounds. The Gallery of the Columbia has the pilothouse of the late-19th-century Columbia River steamer *Bridgeport,* Native American tools and replica dwellings, and loggers' and railroad workers' tools. The Gallery of Electricity has exhibits explaining why dams are good for you. ✉ *U.S. 97A N, about 10 miles north of Wenatchee* ☎ *509/663–7522, 509/663–8121* 🎟 *Free* 🕒 *Park, daily dawn–dusk. Museum, daily 8:30–5. Visitor center, daily 8:30–5:30.*

Wenatchee Valley Museum & Cultural Center. Displays include local Native American and pioneer artifacts, the story of the Washington apple industry, and the 1931 landing of the first-ever flight across the Pacific. Children enjoy the hands-on area and the model railway. There are also Northwest artist exhibits. ✉ *127 S. Mission St.* ☎ *509/888–6240* 🌐 *www.wvmcc.org* 🎟 *$5, free on first Fri. of month* 🕒 *Tues.–Sat. 10–4 (open until 7 on first Fri. of month).*

WHERE TO EAT AND STAY

For expanded hotel reviews, visit Fodors.com.

$$ ECLECTIC
🍴 **Shakti's.** Fine dining in a classy yet comfortable atmosphere is the vibe here, making it popular for dates and special occasions. Entrée prices are very reasonable considering the large serving sizes. The eclectic menu has several pasta dishes, including a spicy-hot chicken puttanesca and a seafood linguine; steaks, fish, crab, and lamb also are featured. The small, two-level restaurant and bar has twinkling white lights that add to the romantic ambience. There's also patio dining in the charming garden, open during the warmer months. [$] *Average main: $20* ✉ *218 N. Mission St.* ☎ *509/662–3321* 🌐 *www.shaktisfinedining.com* 🕒 *Closed Sun.*

$$$ AMERICAN
🍴 **The Windmill.** The comfortable old roadhouse, gamely topped by a windmill, was built in 1931. Here it's all about home-style food, particularly steak: famous entrées include whiskey pepper steak (pepper-coated

New York strip sautéed, flamed with whiskey, and finished with mush-rooms in a rich demi-glace) and the marinated tenderloin chunks. Sea-food isn't overlooked, though; try the charbroiled salmon coated with apple brandy barbecue sauce. Desserts include fresh-baked pies and regional wines are on offer. $ *Average main: $30* ⊠ *1501 N. Wenatchee Ave.* ☎ *509/665–9529* ⊕ *www.thewindmillrestaurant.com* ⊗ *No lunch*.

$ 🔄 **Coast Wenatchee Center Hotel.** A skywalk links this hotel to a conven-
HOTEL   tion center, but although it tends to attract business travelers, there are enough facilities and amenities to appeal to vacationing families too. **Pros:** convenient access to local sights and activities. **Cons:** stan-dard hotel atmosphere. $ *Rooms from: $118* ⊠ *201 N. Wenatchee Ave.* ☎ *509/662–1234, 800/716–6199* ⊕ *www.wenatcheecenter.com* 🔄 *147 rooms, 5 suites* ⦾ *Breakfast.*

SPORTS AND THE OUTDOORS
SKIING
Mission Ridge Ski Area. Four lifts, 33 downhill runs, powder snow, and some 30 miles of marked cross-country trails make Mission Ridge one of Washington's most popular ski areas. There's a 2,100-foot vertical drop, and the snowmaker scatters whiteness from the top to bottom slopes during the season. Snowboarding is allowed. Lift tickets cost $53 per day. ⊠ *7500 Mission Ridge Rd.* ☎ *509/663–6543, 800/374–1693 snow conditions* ⊕ *www.missionridge.com* ⊗ *mid-Nov.–Apr., Thurs.–Mon. 9–4 (daily during school breaks).*

EN
ROUTE   **Aplets and Cotlets/Liberty Orchards Co., Inc.** Surrounded by snow-capped mountain peaks, Cashmere is one of Washington's oldest towns, founded by Oblate missionaries back in 1853, when the Wenatchi and their vast herds of horses still roamed free over the bunch grasslands of the region. Some of the great Wenatchi leaders are buried in the mis-sion cemetery. Today Cashmere is the apple, apricot, and pear capital of the Wenatchee Valley. Aplets and Cotlets/Liberty Orchards Co., Inc. was founded by two Armenian brothers who escaped the massacres of Armenians by Turks early in the 20th century, settled in this peaceful valley, and became orchardists. When a marketing crisis hit the orchards in the 1920s, the brothers remembered dried-fruit confections from their homeland, re-created them, and named them aplets (made from apples) and cotlets (made from apricots). Sales took off almost imme-diately, and today aplets and cotlets are known as the combination that made Cashmere famous. Free samples are offered during the 15-minute tour of the plant. ⊠ *117 Mission Ave., Cashmere* ☎ *509/782–2191* ⊕ *www.libertyorchards.com* 🎫 *Free* ⊗ *Daily 8:30–5:30, tours every 20 min. with some exceptions for breaks.*

LEAVENWORTH

22 miles northwest of Wenatchee, 118 miles northeast of Seattle.

Leavenworth is a favorite weekend getaway for Seattle folks, and it's easy to see why: the charming (if occasionally *too* cute) Bavarian-style village, home to good restaurants and attractive lodgings, is a hub for some of the Northwest's best skiing, hiking, rock climbing, rafting, canoeing, and snowshoeing.

A railroad and mining center for many years, Leavenworth fell on hard times around the 1960s, and civic leaders, looking for ways to capitalize on the town's setting in the heart of the Central Cascade Range, convinced shopkeepers and other businesspeople to maintain a gingerbread-Bavarian architectural style in their buildings. Today, even the Safeway supermarket and the Chevron gas station adhere to the theme. Restaurants prepare Bavarian-influenced dishes, candy shops sell Swiss-style chocolates, and stores and boutiques stock music boxes, dollhouses, and other Bavarian items.

GETTING HERE AND AROUND

From Seattle, Leavenworth can be reached by either of Washington's most-developed mountain passes—Stevens (Hwy. 2) or Snoqualmie (I–90, then a short jog up Hwy. 97/Blewett Pass); either takes about 2½ hours. From Spokane, traveling west via Hwy. 2 takes about 3½ hours. Amtrak's *Empire Builder* now makes daily trips from Spokane and Seattle to Leavenworth, and Greyhound Bus Lines also serves the town.

Contacts **Amtrak** ☏ *800/872–7245* 🌐 *www.amtrak.com.* **Greyhound Bus Lines** ☏ *509/548–9601* 🌐 *www.greyhound.com.*

ESSENTIALS

Visitor Information **Leavenworth Chamber of Commerce** ☏ *509/548–5807* 🌐 *www.leavenworth.org.*

EXPLORING

Icicle Junction. Part of Icicle Village Resort, this is an amusement arcade in the wilderness replete with miniature golf, a rock wall, a movie theater, and other activities. ✉ *565 Hwy. 2, at Icicle Rd.* ☏ *509/548–2400, 800/558–2438* 🌐 *www.iciclejunction.com* ⏲ *School year, Mon.–Thurs. 3–8, Fri. 3–10, Sat. 10–10, Sun. 10–8; summer, daily 10–10.*

Leavenworth Upper Valley Museum. Settled into the 19th-century, barn-style Big Haus, this museum evokes pioneer days in the Cascades. The riverside grounds, where Arabian stallion were once put to graze, now host Audubon programs that take advantage of plentiful bird sightings. Exhibits highlight the lives and times of the Field family, local Native American tribes, and other prominent residents of Leavenworth and the Upper Wenatchee Valley. ✉ *347 Division St.* ☏ *509/548–0728* 🌐 *www.uppervalleymuseum.org* 🎫 *Donations* ⏲ *Apr.–Oct., Wed.–Sun. 10–5; Nov.–Mar., Thurs.–Sun. 10–4.*

Nutcracker Museum. More than 5,000 antique and modern nutcrackers are housed in the Nussknacker House, a shop selling nutcrackers and other knickknacks. ✉ *735 Front St.* ☏ *509/548–4573, 800/892–3989* 🌐 *www.nutcrackermuseum.com* 🎫 *$2.50* ⏲ *Museum May–Oct. daily 2–5; Nov.–Apr. weekends 2–5. Store daily 10–6.*

WHERE TO EAT

$ GERMAN ✕ **Andreas Keller German Restaurant.** Merry "oompah" music bubbles out from marching accordion players at this fun-focused dining hub, where the theme is "Germany without the Passport." Laughing crowds lap up strong, cold brews and feast on a selection of brat-, knack-, weiss-, and mettwursts, Polish sausage, and Wiener schnitzel, all nestled into heaping sides of sauerkraut, tangy German potato salad, and thick,

Holiday season in Leavenworth

dark rye bread. Get a taste of it all with the sampler plate—and save room for the knockout apple strudel. Note that service can be slow at times, so just sit back and enjoy the ambience. $ *Average main: $16* ✉ *829 Front St.* ☎ *509/548–6000* ⊕ *www.andreaskellerrestaurant.com.*

$$
GERMAN

✕ **Bären Haus.** The cuisine at this spacious, noisy, and often crowded beer hall–style room may not be haute, or even particularly interesting, but the generous servings and low prices will appeal to those traveling on a budget. Fill up on generous servings of basic American fare, like burgers and fries, sandwiches, salads, pizza, and pasta, as well as bratwurst, schnitzel, German sausage, and potato pancakes. For dessert, try German apple or German chocolate cake. $ *Average main: $17* ✉ *208 9th St.* ☎ *509/548–4535* ⊕ *www.barenhaus.com* ☾ *No breakfast weekdays (except most holidays).*

$$
ECLECTIC

✕ **Cafe Mozart.** This elegant café resembles a central European town house, capturing the essence of Gemütlichkeit (coziness) in the way the small dining rooms are decorated and the drapes are cut. Authentic aromas drift from the kitchen, too, promising superb, well-constructed dishes that will not disappoint. Start, perhaps, with cold-smoked Norwegian salmon on a potato pancake, followed by a "symphony of schnitzels" (veal or pork topped with a choice of sauces), duck breast in a ruby port reduction with sautéed bing cherries, or rainbow trout filet with toasted almond butter. Almond cream-filled marzipan torte, apple strudel, or a "chorus of crêpes" might conclude the meal. A pianist plays during weekend dinners. $ *Average main: $19* ✉ *829 Front St., upstairs* ☎ *509/548–0600* ⊕ *www.cafemozartrestaurant.com.*

$
BAKERY

✕ **Homefires Bakery.** Inside Dan's Food Market, this homey bakery turns out delicious breads, muffins, cinnamon rolls, almond cookies, and other baked goods. Try the "egg blossoms," a mini-omelette in puff pastry, for breakfast, or take berry pie to go. Open daily 6 am to 10 pm. $ *Average main: $4* ⊠ *1329 U.S. Hwy. 2* ☎ *509/548–7362* ⊕ *www. homefiresbakery.com.*

$

LATIN AMERICAN

✕ **South.** A nice change from all the Bavarian food in town, South features an innovative menu of Latin-inspired dishes, including sweet-potato and roasted poblano chili enchiladas, Yucatan chicken rojo, and Oaxacan black mole with chicken or pork. It's not all Latin, though. Although there's no Wiener schnitzel on the menu, they do have German sausage, burgers, steaks, and a popular pulled pork sandwich at lunch. The children's menu includes tacos, quesadillas, and even prawns, and oranges can be substituted for chips. More than two-dozen kinds of tequila and a margarita infused with basil are among the drink choices. $ *Average main: $12* ⊠ *913 Front St.* ☎ *509/888–4328* ⊕ *www.southleavenworth.com.*

WHERE TO STAY
For expanded hotel reviews, visit Fodors.com.

$

B&B/INN

Abendblume Pension. Wonderful views of the mountains and Leavenworth Valley are afforded from each room's private balcony, and the carved-wood walls and ceilings of this Bavarian-style country chalet give it an authentic alpine appearance. **Pros:** very romantic; Bavarian breakfast is authentic and ample; exceptional hospitality. **Cons:** fills up quickly during festivals; strict cancellation policy. $ *Rooms from: $145* ⊠ *12570 Ranger Rd., ¾ mile from downtown* ☎ *509/548–4059, 800/669–7634* ⊕ *www.abendblume.com* ⟳ *7 rooms* ⦿ *Breakfast.*

$$

RESORT
FAMILY

Icicle Village Resort. This nearly five-acre property has an array of unique amenities, including its own movie theater, soda fountain, minigolf, two outdoor pools (one covered and open year-round), hot tubs, a day spa, sport court, and game arcade. **Pros:** Lots of on-site activities, very kid-friendly; free shuttle into Leavenworth (except Sunday); full hot breakfast buffet included, even for condominium guests. **Cons:** 10-minute walk to town. $ *Rooms from: $199* ⊠ *505 Hwy. 2* ☎ *800/961–0162, 509/888–2776* ⊕ *www.iciclevillage.com* ⟳ *92 rooms, 27 condominiums* ⦿ *Breakfast.*

$

HOTEL

Linderhof Motor Inn. This motel at the west end of Leavenworth is one of the best values in town and, although basic, the rooms are modern and comfortable, with all of the usual amenities and a bit of chintz added for character. **Pros:** across the street from town and shopping; rooms all have microwaves; family-friendly. **Cons:** variety of rates can be confusing. $ *Rooms from: $112* ⊠ *690 U.S. 2* ☎ *509/548–5283, 800/828–5680* ⊕ *www.linderhof.com* ⟳ *34 rooms* ⦿ *Breakfast.*

$

B&B/INN

Mountain Home Lodge. This contemporary mountain inn, built of sturdy cedar and redwood, sits on a 20-acre alpine meadow with breathtaking Cascade Mountains views. **Pros:** pristine luxury; high-quality sports and activities. **Cons:** tough winter transportation; some rooms on the small side. $ *Rooms from: $140* ⊠ *8201 Mountain Home Rd., 3 miles south of Leavenworth* ☎ *509/548–7077, 800/414–2378* 🖨 *509/548–5008* ⊕ *www.mthome.com* ⟳ *10 rooms, 2 cabins* ⦿ *Breakfast.*

$$$

B&B/INN

Pension Anna. Rooms at this family-run Austrian-style pension in the heart of the village are decorated with sturdy imported alpine furniture and fresh flowers, and the beds have cozy comforters. **Pros:** German breakfast is unique; very European feel; nice location. **Cons:** no elevator; some guests have complained about noisy plumbing. ⓢ *Rooms from: $250 ✉ 926 Commercial St. ☎ 509/548–6273, 800/509–2662 ⊕ www. pensionanna.com ↝ 13 rooms, 4 suites* ⎮⃝⎮ *Breakfast.*

$$$

B&B/INN

⌖ **Run of the River.** This intimate, relaxed mountain inn stands on the banks of the Icicle River near Leavenworth, placing the rustic rooms, with timber furnishings, private outside entrances, and decks, close to nature. **Pros:** close to town; abundant healthy breakfasts; lots of outdoor activities. **Cons:** a bit off the beaten path. ⓢ *Rooms from: $230 ✉ 9308 E. Leavenworth Rd. ☎ 509/548–7171, 800/288–6491 ⊕ www. runoftheriver.com ↝ 6 rooms, 1 lodge* ⎮⃝⎮ *Breakfast.*

SPORTS AND THE OUTDOORS

FISHING

Trout are plentiful in many streams and lakes around Lake Wenatchee.

Leavenworth Ranger Station. Get permits here for the Enchantment Lakes and Alpine Lake Wilderness area. ✉ *600 Sherbourne St.* ☎ *509/ 548–6977.*

GOLF

Leavenworth Golf Club. This is an 18-hole, par-71 course. Monday through Thursday, greens fees are $35 for 18 holes or $21 for 9 holes, plus $11 for an optional cart; weekends and holidays, it goes up to $46 and $28, plus $15 for the cart, but pricing drops after 1 pm. ✉ *9101 Icicle Rd., Lakewood* ☎ *509/548–7267* ⊕ *www.leavenworthgolf.com.*

HIKING

The Leavenworth Ranger District has more than 320 miles of scenic trails, among them Hatchery Creek, Icicle Ridge, the Enchantments, Tumwater Canyon, Fourth of July Creek, Snow Lake, Stuart Lake, and Chatter Creek. Both of the following sell the Northwest Forest Pass ($5 day pass; $30 annual pass), which is required year-round for parking at trailheads and for camping in the upper Chiwawa Valley.

Lake Wenatchee Ranger Station. Updates on trails and fire closures are available here. ✉ *22976 Hwy. 207* ☎ *509/763–3103.*

Leavenworth Ranger District. Contact this district office for information on area hikes. ✉ *600 Sherburne St.* ☎ *509/548–6977.*

HORSEBACK RIDING

Eagle Creek Ranch. Rent horses by the hour, or take daylong rides (including lunch) or overnight pack trips ($26–$65) at this ranch. Seasonal sleigh rides are also available ($14–$32). ✉ *7951 Eagle Creek Rd., 8 miles northwest of Leavenworth* ☎ *509/548–7798* ⊕ *www. eaglecreek.ws.*

Icicle Outfitters & Guides. You can enjoy 2- to 4-mile trail rides ($28– $55.50 per person) here, or day-long rides with lunch ($172). ✉ *7373 Icicle Rd.* ☎ *800/497–3912, 509/669–1518* ⊕ *www.icicleoutfitters.com.*

Mountain Springs Lodge. Horseback rides from 50 minutes to all day ($25–$125) long are offered here, as well as daytime sleigh rides ($20), moonlight dinner sleigh rides ($69), breakfast sleigh rides ($36), and snowmobile tours lasting one to five hours ($82.50–$249). ✉ *19115*

15

Chiwawa Loop Rd. ☎ *509/763–2713, 800/858–2276* ⊕ *www. mtsprings.com.*

SKIING

More than 20 miles of cross-country ski trails lace the Leavenworth area.

Leavenworth Ski Hill. In winter enjoy a Nordic ski jump, snowboarding, tubing, and really great downhill and cross-country skiing here. In summer, come for the wildflowers or to catch the Leavenworth Summer Theatre's production of *The Sound of Music*. The ski hill is 1 mile north of downtown Leavenworth. The Play All Day Pass is $25; there's also a Nordic Day Pass ($15), an Alpine Day Pass ($15), and a Tubing Pass ($17). ⊠ *Ski Hill Dr.* ☎ *509/548–5477* ⊕ *www.skileavenworth.com.*

Stevens Pass. There's snowboarding and cross-country skiing here as well as 37 major downhill runs and slopes for skiers of every level. Lift tickets cost $65. ⊠ *U.S. 2, Summit Stevens Pass, 51 miles west of Leavenworth, Skykomish* ☎ *206/812–4510* ⊕ *www.stevenspass.com.*

WHITE-WATER RAFTING

Rafting is popular from March to July; the prime high-country runoff occurs in May and June. The Wenatchee River, which runs through Leavenworth, is considered one of the best white-water rivers in the state—a Class III on the International Canoeing Association scale.

Alpine Adventures. Challenging white-water and relaxing river floats through spectacular scenery are the options here. A Wenatchee River white-water trip with lunch costs $84; a scenic Wenatchee River float (lunch included) is $74. The Methow River drift is $89. An Icicle River run (no lunch) is $49; it fills up fast. ☎ *800/723–8386, 509/470–7762* ⊕ *www.alpineadventures.com.*

Blue Sky Outfitters. Half- and full-day rafting trips on the Methow and Wenatchee rivers are offered by this outfitter. ☎ *206/938–4030, 800/228–7238* ⊕ *www.blueskyoutfitters.com.*

Osprey Rafting Co. This outfitter offers 4½-hour trips on the Wenatchee River for $78.56, which includes wet suits and booties, transportation, and a barbecue lunch; there's a $69.31, 2½-hour trip for travelers short on time. ⊠ *9342 Icicle Rd.* ☎ *509/548–6800, 888/548–6850* ⊕ *www. ospreyrafting.com.*

MOUNT RAINIER
NATIONAL PARK

WELCOME TO MOUNT RAINIER NATIONAL PARK

TOP REASONS TO GO

★ **The mountain:** Some say Mt. Rainier is the most magical mountain in America. At 14,411 feet, it is a popular peak for climbing, with more than 10,000 attempts per year—half of which are successful.

★ **The glaciers:** About 35 square miles of glaciers and snowfields encircle Mt. Rainier, including Carbon Glacier and Emmons Glacier, the largest glaciers by volume and area, respectively, in the continental United States.

★ **The wildflowers:** More than 100 species of wildflowers bloom in the high meadows of the national park; the display dazzles from midsummer until the snow flies.

★ **Fabulous hiking:** More than 240 miles of maintained trails provide access to old-growth forest, river valleys, lakes, and subalpine meadows.

★ **Unencumbered wilderness:** Under the provisions of the 1964 Wilderness Act and the National Wilderness Preservation System, 97% of the park is preserved as wilderness.

1 Longmire. Inside the Nisqually Gate explore Longmire historic district's museum and visitor center, ruins of the park's first hotel, or the nature loop. Nearby, delicate footbridges span the thundering Christine and Narada falls.

2 Paradise. The park's most popular destination is famous for wildflowers in summer and skiing in winter. Skyline Trail is one of many hiking routes that crisscross the base of the mountain; the larger of the two park lodges is also here.

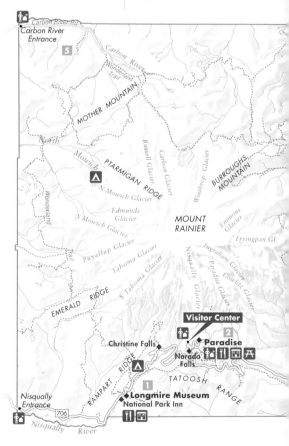

3 **Ohanapecosh.** Closest to the southeast entrance and the town of Packwood, the old-growth trees of the Grove of Patriarchs are a must-see. Another short trail around nearby Tipsoo Lake has great views.

4 **Sunrise and White River.** This side of the park is easy to visit in summer if you enter from the east side, but it's a long drive from the southwest entrance. Sunrise is the highest stretch of road in the park and a great place to take in the alpenglow—reddish light on the peak of the mountain near sunrise and sunset. Mount Rainier's premier mountain-biking area, White River, is also the gateway to more than a dozen hiking trails.

5 **Carbon River and Mowich Lake.** Before entering the isolated northwest corner of the park, visit the Wilderness Information Center in downtown Wilkeson. Near the Carbon River Entrance Station is a swath of temperate forest, but to really get away from it all, follow the winding gravel roads to remote Mowich Lake.

GETTING ORIENTED

The jagged white crown of Mt. Rainier is the showpiece of the Cascades and the focal point of this 337-square-mile national park. The most popular destination in the park, Paradise, is in the southern region; Ohanapecosh, the Grove of Patriarchs, and Tipsoo Lake are in the southeastern corner. Mount Rainier National Park's eastern and northern areas are dominated by wilderness. The snowy folds of the Cascade mountain range stretch out from this Washington park; Seattle is roughly 50 miles north and the volcanic ruins of Mt. St. Helens 100 miles south.

16

Map labels:

Huckleberry Creek

SOURDOUGH MOUNTAINS

SUNRISE RIDGE

410

White River

Mather Memorial Parkway

GOVERNORS RIDGE

Pacific Crest Trail

Sunrise
Visitor Center

4 White River Entrance

White River

GOAT ISLAND MOUNTAIN

410

410

Tipsoo Lake

123

Wonderland Trail

COWLITZ DIVIDE

3

0   2 mi
0   2 km

Grove of the Patriarchs
Stevens Canyon Entrance

Visitor Center

123

Updated by
Shelley Arenas

Like a mysterious, white-clad chanteuse, veiled in clouds even when the surrounding forests and fields are bathed in sunlight, Mt. Rainier is the centerpiece of its namesake park. The impressive volcanic peak stands at an elevation of 14,411 feet, making it the fifth-highest peak in the Lower 48 states. More than 2 million visitors a year enjoy spectacular views of the mountain and return home with a lifelong memory of its image.

The mountain holds the largest glacial system in the contiguous United States, with more than two-dozen major glaciers. On the lower slopes you find silent forests made up of cathedral-like groves of Douglas fir, western hemlock, and western red cedar, some more than 1,000 years old. Water and lush greenery are everywhere in the park, and dozens of thundering waterfalls, accessible from the road or by a short hike, fill the air with mist.

MOUNT RAINIER NATIONAL PARK PLANNER

WHEN TO GO

Rainier is the Puget Sound's weather vane: if you can see it, skies will be clear. Visitors are most likely to see the summit July through September. **Crowds are heaviest in summer,** too, meaning the parking lots at Paradise and Sunrise often fill before noon, campsites are reserved months in advance, and other lodgings are reserved as much as a year ahead.

True to its name, Paradise is often sunny during periods when the lowlands are under a cloud layer. The rest of the year, Rainier's summit gathers lenticular clouds whenever a Pacific storm approaches; once the peak vanishes from view, it's time to haul out rain gear. The rare periods of clear winter weather bring residents up to Paradise for cross-country skiing.

AVG. HIGH/LOW TEMPS.

JAN.	FEB.	MAR.	APR.	MAY	JUNE
36/24	40/26	44/28	53/32	62/37	66/43

JULY	AUG.	SEPT.	OCT.	NOV.	DEC.
75/47	74/47	68/43	57/38	45/31	39/28

PLANNING YOUR TIME

MOUNT RAINIER IN ONE DAY

The best way to get a complete overview of Mount Rainier in a day is to enter via Nisqually and begin your tour by browsing in **Longmire Museum.** When you're done, get to know the environment in and around Longmire Meadow and the overgrown ruins of Longmire Springs Hotel on the ½-mile **Trail of the Shadows** nature loop.

From Longmire, Highway 706 East climbs northeast into the mountains toward Paradise. Take a moment to explore gorgeous **Christine Falls,** just north of the road 1½ miles past Cougar Rock Campground, and **Narada Falls,** 3 miles farther on; both are spanned by graceful stone footbridges. Fantastic mountain views, alpine meadows crosshatched with nature trails, a welcoming lodge and restaurant, and the excellent **Jackson Memorial Visitor Center** combine to make lofty Paradise the primary goal of most park visitors. One outstanding (but challenging) way to explore the high country is to hike the 5-mile round-trip **Skyline Trail** to Panorama Point, which rewards you with stunning 360-degree views.

Continue eastward on Highway 706 East for 21 miles and leave your car to explore the incomparable, thousand-year-old **Grove of the Patriarchs.** Afterward, turn your car north toward White River and **Sunrise Visitor Center,** where you can watch the alpenglow fade from Mt. Rainier's domed summit.

GETTING HERE AND AROUND

CAR TRAVEL

The Nisqually entrance is on Highway 706, 14 miles east of Route 7; the Ohanapecosh entrance is on Route 123, 5 miles north of U.S. 12; and the White River entrance is on Route 410, 3 miles north of the Chinook and Cayuse passes. These highways become mountain roads as they reach Rainier, winding up and down many steep slopes, so cautious driving is essential: use a lower gear, especially on downhill sections, and take care not to overheat brakes by constant use. These roads are subject to storms any time of year and are repaired in the summer from winter damage and washouts.

Side roads into the park's western slope are narrower, unpaved, and subject to flooding and washouts. All are closed by snow in winter except Highway 706 to Paradise and Carbon River Road, though the latter tends to flood near the park boundary. (Route 410 is open to the Crystal Mountain access road entrance.)

Park roads have a maximum speed of 35 mph in most places, and you have to watch for pedestrians, cyclists, and wildlife. Parking can be difficult during peak summer season, especially at Paradise, Sunrise, the Grove of Patriarchs, and at the trailheads between Longmire and

16

Paradise; arrive early if you plan to visit these sites. All off-road-vehicle use—4X4 vehicles, ATVs, motorcycles, snowmobiles—is prohibited in Mount Rainier National Park.

PARK ESSENTIALS

PARK FEES AND PERMITS

The entrance fee of $15 per vehicle and $5 for those on foot, motorcycle, or bicycle, is good for seven days. Annual passes are $30. Climbing permits are $43 per person per climb or glacier trek. Wilderness camping permits must be obtained for all backcountry trips, and advance reservations are highly recommended.

PARK HOURS

Mount Rainier National Park is open 24/7 year-round, but with limited access in winter. Gates at Nisqually (Longmire) are staffed year-round during the day; facilities at Paradise and Ohanapecosh are open daily from late May to mid-October; and Sunrise is open daily July to early September. During off-hours you can buy passes at the gates from machines that accept credit and debit cards. Winter access to the park is limited to the Nisqually entrance, and the Jackson Memorial Visitor Center at Paradise is open on weekends and holidays in winter. In winter, the road from Longmire to Paradise is closed Tuesdays and Wednesdays; the Paradise snow-play area is open Thursdays through Mondays when there is sufficient snow.

CELL PHONE RECEPTION

Cell phone reception is unreliable throughout much of the park, although access is clear at Paradise, Sunrise, and Crystal Mountain. Public telephones are at all park visitor centers, at the National Park Inn at Longmire, and at Paradise Inn at Paradise.

RESTAURANTS

A limited number of restaurants are inside the park, and a few worth checking out lie beyond its borders. Mount Rainier's picnic areas are justly famous, especially in summer, when wildflowers fill the meadows. Resist the urge to feed the yellow pine chipmunks darting about. *Prices in the reviews are the average cost of a main course at dinner or, if dinner is not served, at lunch.*

HOTELS

The Mount Rainier area is remarkably bereft of quality lodging. Rainier's two national park lodges, at Longmire and Paradise, are attractive and well maintained. They exude considerable history and charm, especially Paradise Inn, but unless you've made summer reservations a year in advance, getting a room can be a challenge. Dozens of motels, cabin complexes, and private vacation home rentals are near the park entrances; while they can be pricey, the latter are convenient for longer stays. *Prices in the reviews are the lowest cost of a standard double room in high season.*

TOURS

Fodor's Choice ★ **Gray Line Bus Tours.** Join a 9-hour sightseeing tour from Seattle to Mount Rainier, including a ride on the Mt. Rainier Gondola on Crystal Mountain. ⊠ *4500 Marginal Way SW, Seattle* ☎ *800/426–7532* ⊕ *www. graylineofseattle.com.*

VISITOR INFORMATION
PARK CONTACT INFORMATION
Mount Rainier National Park ✉ *55210 238th Avenue East, Ashford* ☎ *360/569–2211, 360/569-6575* ⊕ *www.nps.gov/mora.*

VISITOR CENTERS
Jackson Memorial Visitor Center. High on the mountain's southern flank, this center houses exhibits on geology, mountaineering, glaciology, and alpine ecology. Multimedia programs are staged in the theater; there's also a snack bar and gift shop. This is the park's most popular visitor destination, and it can be quite crowded in summer. ✉ *Hwy. 706 E, 19 miles east of the Nisqually park entrance* ☎ *360/569–6571* ⊕ *www.nps.gov/mora/planyourvisit/paradise.htm* ☉ *May–mid-Oct., daily 10–6; mid-Oct.–Apr., weekends and holidays 10–5.*

Longmire Museum and Visitor Center. Glass cases inside this museum preserve the park's plants and animals, including a stuffed cougar. Historical photographs and geographical displays provide a worthwhile overview of the park's history. The adjacent visitor center has some perfunctory exhibits on the surrounding forest and its inhabitants, as well as pamphlets and information about park activities. ✉ *Hwy. 706, 10 miles east of Ashford, Longmire* ☎ *360/569–6575* ⊕ *www.nps.gov/mora/planyourvisit/longmire.htm* ☜ *Free* ☉ *July–mid-Oct., daily 9–5; mid-Oct.–June, daily 9–4:30.*

Ohanapecosh Visitor Center. Learn about the region's dense old-growth forests through interpretive displays and videos at this visitor center, near the Grove of the Patriarchs. ✉ *Rte. 123, 11 miles north of Packwood* ☎ *360/569–6581* ⊕ *www.nps.gov/mora/planyourvisit/ohanapecosh. htm* ☉ *June–early Oct., daily 9–6.*

Sunrise Visitor Center. Exhibits at this center explain the region's sparser alpine and subalpine ecology. A network of nearby loop trails leads you through alpine meadows and forest to overlooks that have broad views of the Cascades and Rainier. The Visitor Center has a snack bar and gift shop. ✉ *Sunrise Rd., 15 miles from the White River park entrance* ☎ *360/663–2425* ⊕ *www.nps.gov/mora/planyourvisit/sunrise. htm* ☉ *Early July–early Sept, daily 9–6.*

16

EXPLORING

SCENIC DRIVES

Chinook Pass Road. Route 410, the highway to Yakima, follows the eastern edge of the park to Chinook Pass, where it climbs the steep, 5,432-foot pass via a series of switchbacks. At its top, take in broad views of Rainier and the east slope of the Cascades. The Pass usually closes for the winter in November. ⊕ *www.wsdot.wa.gov/traffic/passes/chinook.*

Mowich Lake Road. In the northwest corner of the park, this 24-mile mountain road begins in Wilkeson and heads up the Rainier foothills to Mowich Lake, traversing beautiful mountain meadows along the way. Mowich Lake is a pleasant spot for a picnic.

Paradise Road. This 9-mile stretch of Highway 706 winds its way up the mountain's southwest flank from Longmire to Paradise, taking you from lowland forest to the ever-expanding vistas of the mountain above. Visit on a weekday if possible, especially in peak summer months, when the road is packed with cars. The route is open year-round though there may be some weekday closures in winter. From November through April, all vehicles must carry chains.

Sunrise Road. This popular (and often crowded) scenic road carves its way 11 miles up Sunrise Ridge from the White River Valley on the northeast side of the park. As you top the ridge there are sweeping views of the surrounding lowlands. The road is open late June to October.

> ### PLANTS AND WILDLIFE IN MOUNT RAINIER
>
> Wildflower season in the meadows at and above timberline is mid-July through August. Large mammals like deer, elk, black bears, and cougars tend to occupy the less accessible wilderness areas of the park and thus elude the average visitor; smaller animals like squirrels and marmots are easier to spot. The best times to see wildlife are at dawn and dusk at the forest's edge. Fawns are born in May, and the bugling of bull elk on the high ridges can be heard in late September and October, especially on the park's eastern side.

HISTORIC SITES

National Park Inn. Even if you don't plan to stay overnight, you can stop by year-round to observe the architecture of this inn, built in 1917 and on the National Register of Historic Places. While you're here, relax in front of the fireplace in the lounge, stop at the gift shop, or dine at the restaurant. ⊠ *Longmire Visitor Complex, Hwy. 706, 10 miles east of Nisqually entrance, Longmire* ☎ *360/569–2411* ⊕ *www. mtrainierguestservices.com/accommodations/national-park-inn.*

SCENIC STOPS

Christine Falls. These two-tiered falls were named in honor of Christine Louise Van Trump, who climbed to the 10,000-foot level on Mt. Rainier in 1889 at the age of 9, despite having a crippling nervous-system disorder. ⊠ *Next to Hwy. 706, about 2½ miles east of Cougar Rock Campground.*

Fodor'sChoice **Grove of the Patriarchs.** Protected from the periodic fires that swept
★ through the surrounding areas, this small island of 1,000-year-old trees is one of Mount Rainier National Park's most memorable features. A 1½-mile loop trail heads through the old-growth forest of Douglas fir, cedar, and hemlock. ⊠ *Rte. 123, west of the Stevens Canyon entrance* ⊕ *www.nps.gov/mora/planyourvisit/ohanapecosh.htm.*

Narada Falls. A steep but short trail leads to the viewing area for these spectacular 168-foot falls, which expand to a width of 75 feet during peak flow times. In winter the frozen falls are popular with ice climbers. ⊠ *Along Hwy. 706, 1 mile west of the turnoff for Paradise, 6 miles east of Cougar Rock Campground* ⊕ *www.nps.gov/mora/planyourvisit/narada-falls.htm.*

FAMILY **Tipsoo Lake.** The short, pleasant trail that circles the lake—ideal for families—provides breathtaking views. Enjoy the subalpine wildflower meadows during the summer months; in early fall there is an abundant supply of huckleberries. ⊠ *Off Cayuse Pass east on Hwy. 410* ⊕ *www.nps.gov/mora/planyourvisit/sunrise.htm.*

> **FLOOD DAMAGE**
>
> Harsh winter weather and heavy spring rains cause road damage and closings every year. Those with the most snow and storm debris usually include Carbon River Road, Stevens Canyon Road, Westside Road to Dry Creek, and Highway 706 from Longmire to Paradise. ∎TIP➜ Before your trip, confirm site and road openings with one of the park's visitor centers.

EDUCATIONAL OFFERINGS

RANGER PROGRAMS

FAMILY **Junior Ranger Program.** Youngsters can pick up an activity booklet at a visitor center and fill it out as they explore the park. When they complete it, they can show it to a ranger and receive a Mount Rainier Junior Ranger badge. ⊠ *Visitor Centers* ☎ *360/569–2211* ⊕ *www.nps.gov/mora/forkids/index.htm* ▢ *Free.*

Ranger programs. Park ranger-led activities include **guided snowshoe walks** in the winter (most suitable for those older than 8) as well as **evening programs** during the summer at Cougar Rock, Ohanapecosh, and White River campgrounds, and at the Paradise Inn. Evening talks may cover subjects such as park history, its flora and fauna, or interesting facts on climbing Mt. Rainier. There are also daily guided programs that start at the Jackson Visitor Center, including meadow and vista walks, tours of the Paradise Inn, and a morning ranger chat. ⊠ *Visitor Centers* ☎ *360/569–2211* ⊕ *www.nps.gov/mora/planyourvisit/rangerprograms.htm* ▢ *Free.*

SPORTS AND THE OUTDOORS

MULTISPORT OUTFITTERS

RMI Expeditions. Reserve a private hiking guide through this highly regarded outfitter, or take part in its one-day mountaineering classes (mid-May through late September), where participants are evaluated on their fitness for the climb and must be able to withstand a 16-mile round-trip hike with a 9,000-foot gain in elevation. The company also arranges private cross-country skiing and snowshoeing guides. ⊠ *30027 Hwy. 706 E, Ashford* ☎ *888/892–5462, 360/569–2227* ⊕ *www.rmiguides.com* ▢ *$991 for four-day package.*

Whittaker Mountaineering. You can rent hiking and climbing gear, skis, snowshoes, snowboards and other outdoor equipment at this all-purpose Rainier Base Camp outfitter, which also arranges for private

16

cross-country skiing and hiking guides. ✉ *30027 Hwy. 706 E, Ashford* ☎ *800/238–5756* ⊕ *www.whittakermountaineering.com.*

BIRD-WATCHING

★ Be alert for kestrels, red-tailed hawks, and, occasionally, golden eagles on snags in the lowland forests. Also present at Rainier, but rarely seen, are great horned owls, spotted owls, and screech owls. Iridescent rufous hummingbirds flit from blossom to blossom in the drowsy summer lowlands, and sprightly water ouzels flutter in the many forest creeks. Raucous Steller's jays and gray jays scold passersby from trees, often darting boldly down to steal morsels from unguarded picnic tables. At higher elevations, look for the pure white plumage of the white-tailed ptarmigan as it hunts for seeds and insects in winter. Waxwings, vireos, nuthatches, sapsuckers, warblers, flycatchers, larks, thrushes, siskins, tanagers, and finches are common throughout the park.

HIKING

Although the mountain can seem remarkably benign on calm summer days, hiking Rainier is not a city-park stroll. Dozens of hikers and trekkers annually lose their way and must be rescued—and lives are lost on the mountain each year. Weather that approaches cyclonic levels can appear quite suddenly, any month of the year. With the possible exception of the short loop hikes listed here, all visitors venturing far from vehicle access points should carry day packs with warm clothing, food, and other emergency supplies.

EASY

Nisqually Vista Trail. Equally popular in summer and winter, this trail is a 1¼-mile round-trip through subalpine meadows to an overlook point for Nisqually Glacier. The gradually sloping path is a favorite venue for cross-country skiers in winter; in summer, listen for the shrill alarm calls of the area's marmots. *Easy.* ✉ *Trailhead at Jackson Memorial Visitor Center, Rte. 123, 1 mile north of Ohanapecosh, at the high point of Hwy. 706* ⊕ *www.nps.gov/mora/planyourvisit/nisqually-vista.htm.*

Sourdough Ridge Trail. The mile-long loop of this self-guided trail takes you through the delicate subalpine meadows near the Sunrise Visitor Center. A gradual climb to the ridgetop yields magnificent views of Mt. Rainier and the more distant volcanic cones of Mt. Baker, Mt. Adams, and Glacier Peak. *Easy.* ✉ *Access trail at Sunrise Visitor Center, Sunrise Rd., 15 miles from the White River park entrance* ⊕ *www.nps.gov/mora/planyourvisit/day-hiking-at-mount-rainier.htm.*

Trail of the Shadows. This ¾-mile loop walk is notable for its glimpses of meadowland ecology, its colorful soda springs (don't drink the water), James Longmire's old homestead cabin, and the foundation of the old Longmire Springs Hotel, which was destroyed by fire around 1900. *Easy.* ✉ *Trailhead at Hwy. 706, 10 miles east of Nisqually entrance* ⊕ *www.nps.gov/mora/planyourvisit/day-hiking-at-mount-rainier.htm.*

MODERATE

Fodor's Choice ★ **Skyline Trail.** This 5-mile loop, one of the highest trails in the park, beckons day-trippers with a vista of alpine ridges and, in summer, meadows filled with brilliant flowers and birds. At 6,800 feet, Panorama Point, the spine of the Cascade Range, spreads away to the east, and Nisqually Glacier tumbles downslope. *Moderate.* ⊠ *Jackson Memorial Visitor Center, Rte. 123, 1 mile north of Ohanapecosh at the high point of Hwy. 706* ⊕ *www.nps.gov/mora/planyourvisit/skyline-trail.htm.*

Van Trump Park Trail. You gain an exhilarating 2,200 feet on this route while hiking through a vast expanse of meadow with views of the southern Puget Sound. The 5.8-mile track provides good footing, and the average hiker can make it up in three to four hours. *Moderate.* ⊠ *Hwy. 706 at Christine Falls, 4.4 miles east of Longmire* ⊕ *www.nps. gov/mora/planyourvisit/van-trump-trail.htm.*

DIFFICULT

Fodor's Choice ★ **Wonderland Trail.** All other Mt. Rainier hikes pale in comparison to this stunning 93-mile trek, which completely encircles the mountain. The trail passes through all the major life zones of the park, from the old-growth forests of the lowlands to the alpine meadows and goat-haunted glaciers of the highlands—pick up a mountain-goat sighting card from a ranger station or visitor center if you want to help in the park's effort to learn more about these elusive animals. Wonderland is a rugged trail; elevation gains and losses totaling 3,500 feet are common in a day's hike, which averages 8 miles. Most hikers start out from Longmire or Sunrise and take 10 to 14 days to cover the 93-mile route. Snow lingers on the high passes well into June (sometimes July); count on rain any time of the year. Campsites are wilderness areas with pit toilets and water that must be purified before drinking. Only hardy, well-equipped, and experienced wilderness trekkers should attempt this trip, but those who do will be amply rewarded. Wilderness permits are required, and reservations are strongly recommended. *Difficult.* ⊠ *Longmire Visitor Center, Hwy. 706, 17 miles east of Ashford; Sunrise Visitor Center, Sunrise Rd., 15 miles west of the White River park entrance* ⊕ *www. nps.gov/mora/planyourvisit/the-wonderland-trail.htm.*

16

MOUNTAIN CLIMBING

Climbing Mt. Rainier is not for amateurs; each year, adventurers die on the mountain, and many become lost and must be rescued. Near-catastrophic weather can appear quite suddenly, any month of the year. If you're experienced in technical, high-elevation snow, rock, and ice-field adventuring, Mt. Rainier can be a memorable adventure. Climbers can fill out a climbing card at the Paradise, White River, or Carbon River ranger stations and lead their own groups of two or more. Climbers must register with a ranger before leaving and check out upon return. A $43 annual climbing fee applies to anyone heading above 10,000 feet or onto one of Rainier's glaciers. During peak season it is recommended that you make a climbing reservation ($20 per group) in advance; reservations are taken by fax beginning in April on a first-come, first-served

basis (find the reservation form at ⊕ *www.nps.gov/mora/planyourvisit/climbing.htm*).

SKIING AND SNOWSHOEING

Mount Rainier is a major Nordic ski center for cross-country and telemark skiing. Although trails are not groomed, those around Paradise are extremely popular. If you want to ski with fewer people, try the trails in and around the Ohanapecosh–Stevens Canyon area, which are just as beautiful and, because of their more easterly exposure, slightly less subject to the rains that can douse the Longmire side, even in the dead of winter. Never ski on plowed main roads, especially around Paradise—the snowplow operator can't see you. Rentals aren't available on the eastern side of the park.

> **GOOD READS**
>
> ■ An excellent general guide to the park, *Mount Rainier: A Visitor's Companion* by Wuerthner and Moore, is now out of print but often available through used booksellers.
>
> ■ For a concise and useful map and guide to Rainier's trail system, buy *50 Hikes in Mount Rainier National Park* by Ira Spring and Harvey Manning, published by Seattle's famed Mountaineers.

★ Deep snows make Mount Rainier a snowshoeing pleasure. The Paradise area, with its network of trails, is the best choice. The park's east side roads, Routes 123 and 410, are unplowed and provide other good snowshoeing venues, although you must share the main routes with snowmobilers.

Paradise Snowplay Area and Nordic Ski Route. Sledding on flexible sleds (no toboggans or runners), inner tubes, and plastic saucers is allowed only in the Paradise snowplay area adjacent to the Jackson Visitor Center. The area is open when there is sufficient snow, usually Thursday through Monday from late December through mid-March. The easy, 3½-mile Paradise Valley Road Nordic ski route begins at the Paradise parking lot, and follows Paradise Valley/Stevens Canyon Road to Reflection Lakes. Equipment rentals are available at Whittaker Mountaineering in Ashford, or at the National Park Inn's General Store in Longmire. ⊠ *Adjacent to the Jackson Visitor Center at Paradise* ☎ *360/569–2211* ⊕ *www.nps.gov/mora/planyourvisit/winter-recreation.htm.*

TOURS AND OUTFITTERS

General Store at the National Park Inn. The store at the National Park Inn in Longmire rents cross-country ski equipment and snowshoes. It's open daily in winter, depending on snow conditions. ⊠ *National Park Inn, Longmire* ☎ *360/569–2411* ⊕ *www.mtrainierguestservices.com/activities-and-events/winter-activities/cross-country-skiing.*

CLOSE UP

Best Campgrounds in Mount Rainier

Four drive-in campgrounds are in the park—Cougar Rock, Ipsut Creek, Ohanapecosh, and White River—with almost 700 sites for tents and RVs. None have hot water or RV hookups; showers are available at Jackson Memorial Visitor Center. For backcountry camping, get a free wilderness permit at a visitor center. Primitive sites are spaced at 7- to 8-mile intervals along the Wonderland Trail.

Cougar Rock Campground. A secluded, heavily wooded campground with an amphitheater, Cougar Rock is one of the first to fill up. Reservations are accepted for summer only. ⊠ *2½ miles north of Longmire* ☏ 877/444-6777.

Mowich Lake Campground. This is Rainier's only lakeside campground.

At 4,959 feet, it's also peaceful and secluded. ⊠ *Mowich Lake Rd., 6 miles east of the park boundary* ☏ 360/569–2211.

Ohanapecosh Campground. This lush, green campground in the park's southeast corner has a visitor center, amphitheater, and self-guided trail. It's one of the first campgrounds to open for the season. ⊠ *Ohanapecosh Visitor Center, Hwy. 123, 1½ miles north of park boundary* ☏ 877/444-6777.

White River Campground. At an elevation of 4,400 feet, White River is one of the park's highest and least wooded campgrounds. Here you can enjoy campfire programs, self-guided trails, and partial views of Mt. Rainier's summit. ⊠ *5 miles west of White River entrance* ☏ 360/569–2211.

WHERE TO EAT

$$$
ECLECTIC
⨯ **National Park Inn Dining Room.** Photos of Mt. Rainier taken by top photographers adorn the walls of this inn's large dining room, a bonus on the many days the mountain refuses to show itself. Meals are simple but tasty: hazelnut chicken, buffalo meat loaf, pot roast with caramelized carrots, beef and buffalo stew, and sautéed brook trout. For a hearty start to the day, try the country breakfast or oatmeal brûlée. $ *Average main: $21* ⊠ *Hwy. 706, Longmire* ☏ 360/569–2411 ⊕ *www.mtrainierguestservices.com* ⌂ *Reservations not accepted.*

$
AMERICAN
FAMILY
⨯ **Paradise Camp Deli.** Grilled meats, sandwiches, salads and soft drinks are served daily from May through early October and on weekends and holidays during the rest of the year. $ *Average main: $8* ⊠ *Jackson Visitor Center, Paradise Rd. E., Paradise* ☏ 360/569–2400 ⊕ *www.mtrainierguestservices.com* ▭ *No credit cards* ☉ *Closed weekdays early Oct.–Apr.*

$$
AMERICAN
⨯ **Paradise Inn.** Where else can you enjoy Sunday brunch in a historic heavy-timbered lodge halfway up a mountain? Tall windows provide terrific views of Rainier, and the warm glow of native wood permeates the large dining room. The lunch menu is simple and healthy—five kinds of burgers (salmon, black bean, chicken, bison, and beef), salads, and the like. For dinner, there's nothing like a hearty plate of the inn's signature bourbon buffalo meat loaf. $ *Average main: $19* ⊠ *E. Paradise Rd., near Jackson Visitor Center, Paradise* ☏ 360/569–2275 ⊕ *www.*

16

mtrainierguestservices.com ✍ *Reservations not accepted* ⏲ *Closed Oct.–late May.*

$ AMERICAN FAMILY 🍴 **Sunrise Day Lodge Food Service.** A cafeteria and grill serve inexpensive hamburgers, chili and hot dogs from early July to early September. [$] *Average main: $8* ✉ *Sunrise Rd., 15 miles from the White River park entrance* ☎ *360/663–2425* 🌐 *www.mtrainierguestservices.com* 💳 *No credit cards* ⏲ *Closed early Sept.–early July.*

PICNIC AREAS

Park picnic areas are open July through September only.

Paradise Picnic Area. This site has great views on clear days. After picnicking at Paradise, you can take an easy hike to one of the many waterfalls in the area—Sluiskin, Myrtle, or Narada, to name a few. ✉ *Hwy. 706, 11 miles east of Longmire* 🌐 *www.nps.gov/mora.*

Sunrise Picnic Area. Set in an alpine meadow that's filled with wildflowers in July and August, this picnic area provides expansive views of the mountain and surrounding ranges in good weather. ✉ *Sunrise Rd., 11 miles west of the White River entrance* 🌐 *www.nps.gov/mora.*

WHERE TO STAY

For expanded hotel reviews, visit Fodors.com.

$$$ 🏨 **National Park Inn.** A large stone fireplace warms the common room of this country inn, the only one of the park's two inns that's open year-round. **Pros:** classic ambience; open all year. **Cons:** jam-packed in summer; must book far in advance; some rooms have shared bath. [$] *Rooms from: $166* ✉ *Longmire Visitor Complex, Hwy. 706, 10 miles east of Nisqually entrance, Longmire* ☎ *360/569–2275* 🌐 *www.mtrainierguestservices.com* 🛏 *25 rooms, 18 with bath* 🍽 *No meals.*

$$$ Fodor's Choice ★ 🏨 **Paradise Inn.** With its hand-carved Alaskan cedar logs, burnished parquet floors, stone fireplaces, Indian rugs, and glorious mountain views, this 1917 inn is a classic example of a national park lodge. **Pros:** central to trails; pristine vistas; nature-inspired details. **Cons:** noisy in high season. [$] *Rooms from: $170* ✉ *E. Paradise Rd., near Jackson Visitor Center, Paradise* ☎ *360/569–2275* 🌐 *www.mtrainierguestservices.com* 🛏 *121 rooms* ⏲ *Closed Oct.–mid-May.*

WASHINGTON WINE COUNTRY

Yakima River Valley

WELCOME TO WASHINGTON WINE COUNTRY

TOP REASONS TO GO

★ **Stay at a spectacular mountain lodge:** The Lodge at Suncadia is one of Washington's premier resorts. Golfers, cross-country skiers, hikers, and families will enjoy this terrific lodge in the beautiful Cascade Mountains.

★ **Washington history:** Yakima Valley Museum is one of the finest museums in the state, with plenty of history of the real West.

★ **Wine tasting:** There are more than 70 wineries in this region, and nearly all of them are excellent. Washington wines' reputation extends globally, and Yakima Valley may be the state's finest wine region.

★ **Eat at a classic diner:** Diners in wine country? There are two terrific ones here. The Red Horse Diner in Ellensburg is more than a hamburger joint, it's a restaurant and museum all in one, built around a mid-1900s Mobil gas station. And Miner's Drive-In, a Yakima icon, serves great old-fashioned hamburgers, fries, and shakes in a truly vintage setting.

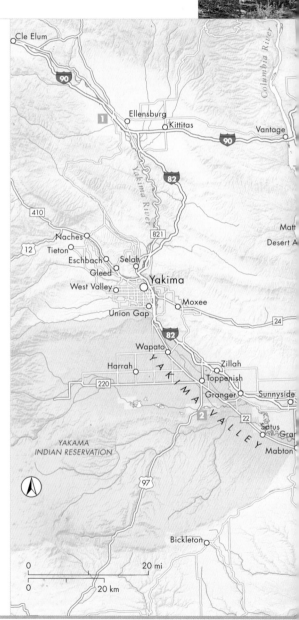

1 Northern Yakima River Valley. Just 80 miles from Seattle over the Cascade Mountains, the historic mining towns of Roslyn and Cle Elum offer quaint shops and one very plush resort. Golf, fishing, hiking, biking, cross-country skiing, and more are readily available in this region. As you follow the Yakima River down past Ellensburg to Yakima, you'll see how irrigation turns a virtual desert into one of the most agriculturally rich regions in the nation. Yakima is the shopping and entertainment hub of the region.

2 Southern Yakima River Valley. From Yakima, which touts itself as the gateway to wine country, visitors can choose from more than 70 wineries, as well as fresh fruits and vegetables of all kinds. The area is one of the most agriculturally diverse in the country, with some outstanding restaurants. History is rich here as well. The Yakama Indian Reservation occupies much of the land, and the history of its people can be seen in several museums around the region, including the museum at the Yakama Nation Cultural Center in Toppenish.

GETTING ORIENTED

The Yakima River Valley encompasses a region of south central Washington that starts just east of Snoqualmie Pass in the Kittitas Valley. It includes the forested eastern slopes and the foothills of the Central Cascades, from Chinook and White Pass all the way down through the Yakima Valley near Benton City. Two interstates meet in Ellensburg. I–90 links Seattle to Cle Elum and Ellensburg before heading east toward Spokane. I–82 branches south off I–90 just east of Ellensburg, and runs through the Yakima Valley to the so-called Tri-Cities (Richland, Pasco, and Kennewick). U.S. 97 is the primary link from Ellensburg north (Wenatchee, Canada's Okanagan Valley) and from Yakima south toward central Oregon.

17

YAKIMA RIVER VALLEY WINERIES

As part of a maturing and successful wine industry in the region, this area now produces a third of the state's wines and has more than 12,000 acres of wine vineyards.

(Above and opposite page top) Hyatt Vineyards (Opposite page bottom) Rows of grapevines are a common sight in the Yakima River Valley.

Horse-drawn plows first started breaking ground in the Yakima Valley more than 150 years ago. While there are still native sagebrush and grasses on the driest and rockiest slopes in the region, much of the Valley and the foothills are now covered with corn and wheat fields, hop yards, orchards, and vineyards. Support for local wineries took a long time to build when the apple growers reigned supreme, but after a quarter-century of serious wine-making, the valley has embraced the wine industry as a tourism attraction and an economic generator.

The Yakima Valley produces excellent reds, among them Cabernet Sauvignon, Cabernet Franc, Merlot, Nebbiolo, Sangiovese, and Syrah. Whites also do well here: Chardonnay, Muscat, Sauvignon Blanc, Sémillon, Viognier, and, in cooler vineyards, Gewürztraminer, Chenin Blanc, and Riesling.

APPLES AND GRAPES

Yakima Valley is at an agricultural crossroads. Apples are still the main crop of the region, but wine vineyards continue to multiply. Among the mistakes of the pioneering grape growers of the 1960s and '70s was overplanting Riesling and Chenin Blanc, which proved hard to market. They compensated by grafting over their vines to more desirable varieties or by replanting. Today Yakima Valley Chardonnay, Cabernet Sauvignon, Merlot, Sangiovese, and Syrah are ranked among the world's best.

YAKIMA'S BEST WINERIES

Stop at the Yakima Valley Visitor Information Center (Exit 34 off I-82) to pick up a wine-tour brochure and map of more than 30 wineries. Most are within a few miles of the freeway and directional signs will help get you to them. Nearly all of Yakima's wineries are worth a visit, but here are three of our favorites.

ZILLAH

Hyatt Vineyards. Big in a physical as well as an enological sense, Hyatt comprises 97 acres of estate vineyards. Established in 1985, the winery, owned by Leland and Linda Hyatt, has always been well respected locally for its Merlot and Cabernet Sauvignon, but lately those wines have been attracting national attention. The late-harvest Riesling here is also worth tasting. The tasting room is well appointed and the staff has wide knowledge of local viniculture. The winery also has spacious well-manicured grounds for picnicking. On clear days there are spectacular views of the Yakima Valley, Mt. Adams, and the Cascade Mountains. ⊠ *2020 Gilbert Rd., off I-82 Exit 52, Zillah* ☎ *509/829–6333* ⊕ *www. hyattvineyards.com* ☙ *Daily 11–5 (closes 4:30 in winter).*

SUNNYSIDE

Tucker Cellars. The Tucker family came to the Yakima Valley as sharecroppers

during the Great Depression. They became successful farmers and were among the first to grow vinifera grapes on a commercial scale. Dean and Rose Tucker founded the winery in 1981; both it and the estate vineyards are family operations involving their four children. Tucker plantings include Riesling, Pinot Noir, Gewürztraminer, Chenin Blanc, Chardonnay, and Muscat Canelli. Attached to the Tucker Cellars tasting room is the family's produce stand, which sells, in season, some of the Yakima Valley's best fruits and vegetables. There's a picnic area. ⊠ *70 Ray Rd., Sunnyside* ☎ *509/837–8701* ⊕ *www.tuckercellars.net* ☙ *Daily 10–5.*

PROSSER

Kestrel Vintners. This is established as one of the Yakima Valley's premium wineries. Although visiting the winery, in the Port of Benton's Prosser Wine and Food Park, doesn't necessarily rank as a great sensory pleasure, tasting the wines does. Kestrel makes mainly reds (Cabernet Sauvignon, Merlot, Syrah), as well as some white (Chardonnay, Viognier), from grapes—some of them estate-grown—that are deliberately stressed to increase the intensity of their flavors. The tasting room sells cheeses and deli items to go with the wines. ⊠ *2890 Lee Rd., in Prosser Wine and Food Park, Prosser* ☎ *509/786–2675* ⊕ *www.kestrelwines. com* ☙ *Daily noon–5.*

17

Updated by
Rob Phillips

The Yakima River binds a region of great contrasts. Snow-capped volcanic peaks and evergreen-covered hills overlook a natural shrub steppe turned green by irrigation. Famed throughout the world for its apples and cherries, its wine and hops, this fertile landscape is also the ancestral home of the Yakama people from whom it takes its name.

The river flows southeasterly from its source in the Cascade Mountains near Snoqualmie Pass. Between the college town of Ellensburg, at the heart of the Kittitas Valley, and Yakima, the region's largest city, the river cuts steep canyons through serried, sagebrush-covered ridges before merging with the Naches River. Then it breaks through Union Gap to enter its fecund namesake, the broad Yakima Valley. Some 200 miles from its birthplace, the river makes one final bend around vineyard-rich Red Mountain before joining the mighty Columbia River at the Tri-Cities.

Mt. Rainier stands west of the Cascade crest but is often more readily seen east of the mountains, where the air is clear and clouds are few. South of Rainier is the broad-shouldered Mt. Adams, the sacred mountain of the Yakama people. The 12,276-foot-tall mountain marks the western boundary of their reservation, second-largest in the Pacific Northwest. Here, today, as they have for centuries, wild horses run free through the Yakama Nation and can be seen feeding along Highway 97 south of Toppenish. Deer and elk roam the evergreen forests, eagles and ospreys soar overhead.

Orchards and vineyards dominate Yakima Valley's agricultural landscape. Cattle and sheep ranching initially drove the economy; apples and other produce came with the engineering of irrigation canals and outlets in the 1890s. The annual asparagus harvest begins in April, followed by cherries in June; apricots and peaches ripen in early to midsummer. Exported throughout the world for the brewing of beer, hops are ready by late August; travelers may see the bushy vines spiraling up fields of twine. The apple harvest runs from late summer through October.

The valley's real fame, however, rests on its wine grapes, which have a growing reputation as among the best in the world. Concord grapes were first planted here in the 1960s, and they still take up large tracts of land. But vinifera grapes, the noble grapes of Europe, now dominate the local wine industry. Merlot and white Burgundies boosted the region, and Syrah is often regarded as the grape of the future. There are fine Cabernets, Grenaches, Rieslings, Chardonnays, Gewürztraminers, Sémillons, Sauvignon Blancs, Chenin Blancs, and Muscats, as well as such lesser-known varietals as Sangioveses, Nebbiolos, and Lembergers.

WASHINGTON WINE COUNTRY PLANNER

WHEN TO GO

Much of the area is considered high desert, with annual rainfall of just 7 inches a year. But in winter, in the higher elevations, it is quite common to have snow on the ground from November until March. This is a decidedly four-season region, with wet, cool, windy springs, beautiful warm summer days, and gorgeous falls with colors to match those of any Northeastern state. Best time to visit is April through October, unless, of course, you're looking to ski, snowboard, or snowmobile.

The main wine-tasting season begins in late April and runs to the end of the fall harvest in November. Winery hours vary in winter, when you should call ahead before visiting. The Yakima Valley Winery Association (⊕ *www.wineyakimavalley.org*) publishes a map-brochure that lists wineries with tasting-room hours. Most are owned and managed by unpretentious enthusiasts, and their cellar masters are often on hand to answer questions.

GETTING HERE AND AROUND

AIR TRAVEL

Although major airlines serve the region's two airports, most people fly into Seattle or Portland, Oregon, and drive to the area.

Horizon Air. There are two nonstops daily between Sea-Tac and Yakima, a 45-minute flight. ☎ *800/547–9308* ⊕ *www.horizonair.com.*

Tri-Cities Airport has a similar schedule from Seattle, a 60-minute trip, with additional nonstop connections to Denver, Portland, and Salt Lake City. Both Yakima and the Tri-Cities are served by Horizon. The Tri-Cities are also served by Delta and United.

Airline Contacts Delta ☎ *800/221–1212* ⊕ *www.delta.com.* **United** ☎ *800/241–6522* ⊕ *www.ual.com.*

Airports Yakima International Airport ✉ *2300 W. Washington Ave., 4 miles southeast of downtown, Yakima* ☎ *509/575–6149.* **Tri-Cities Regional Airport.** This airport is more convenient to Grandview, Prosser, and Benton City. ✉ *3601 N. 20th Ave., Pasco* ☎ *509/547–6352.*

Transfers Taxis and public transit are available at both airports. **Airporter Shuttle.** There are services from Sea-Tac airport (between Seattle and Tacoma) to the Yakima airport ($42.50 in either direction), or downtown Yakima ($40) with stops in downtown Seattle, Cle Elum ($30), and Ellensburg ($35). Trips from the Seattle Amtrak terminal are five dollars more each way. ☎ *866/235–5247* ⊕ *www.*

17

airporter.com. **Yakima City Transit.** In Yakima, this service can provide transportation to hotels. ☎ *509/575–6175* ⊕ *www.yakimawa.gov/services/transit.*

Airport Transportation Diamond Cab. From Yakima Airport, this company will take you pretty much anyplace in Washington State. ☎ *509/453–3113.*

CAR TRAVEL

The Yakima Valley Highway, which turns into Wine Country Road just south of Sunnyside, is a reliable, off-the-beaten-track alternative to I–82 for wine-country visits; but it can be slow, especially through towns, or if farm machinery is on the road. Because of unmarked turns and other potential hazards, it's wise to stick to the freeway after dark. Gas stations in towns, and at major freeway intersections, are typically open well after dark.

Major car rental companies in the area include **Avis** (☎ *509/469–4543 Yakima*), **Budget** (☎ *509/248–6767 Yakima*), **Enterprise** (☎ *509/494– 7111 Yakima, 509/925–5040 Ellensburg*), and **Hertz** (☎ *509/452–9965 Yakima*). Hertz and Budget are available at Yakima International Airport.

RESTAURANTS

South central Washington has a fair share of Mexican food, from taco wagons to fine Mexican restaurants. National fast-food chains, local eateries, and Chicago-style steak houses can be found scattered throughout the region, or sometimes right alongside one another. As a huge agricultural area, the Yakima Valley supplies many of its local restaurants with fresh fruits and vegetables in season. Yakima Valley wines are a staple at virtually all of the fine-dining establishments. Pacific Northwest seafood (particularly salmon) is another staple of the region. *Prices in the reviews are the average cost of a main course at dinner or, if dinner is not served, at lunch.*

HOTELS

Two major freeways, I–90 and I–82, pass through the cities of Ellensburg and Yakima where you'll find the highest concentration of lodgings. A few independent motels are available, but the majority are independently operated under familiar chain names. At the far northeastern end of the region sits Suncadia Resort, offering possibly the finest accommodations in the area. Several bed-and-breakfasts are also available, particularly in the lower Yakima Valley, near the plethora of wineries in the area. It is always prudent to call ahead for reservations, but the busiest tourist times include the third week in April, for Spring Barrel Tasting, and from Memorial Day through Labor Day. *Prices in the reviews are the lowest cost of a standard double room in high season.*

TOURS

Lifelong residents run Yakima Valley Tours' custom agricultural, historical, wine-tasting, and adventure-sports tours. Accent! Tours has informative trips to area wineries. Bus companies such as A & A Motorcoach, and limo services, including Moonlit Ride, conduct charter tours of the Yakima area.

Tour Contacts A & A Motorcoach ✉ *2410 S. 26th Ave., Yakima* ☎ *509/575–3676* ⊕ *www.aamotorcoach.com.* **Accent! Tours** ✉ *1017 S 48th Ave., Suite C, Yakima* ☎ *509/575–3949, 800/735–0428* ⊕ *www.accenttours.com.* **Moonlit Ride Limousine** ✉ *3908 River Rd., Yakima* ☎ *509/575–6846* ⊕ *www.moonlitride.com.* **Yakima Valley Tours** ✉ *551 N. Holt Rd.* ☎ *509/985–8628, 509/840–4777* ⊕ *www.yakimavalleytours.com.*

VISITOR INFORMATION

Yakima Valley Visitor Information Center ✉ *101 Fair Ave., Exit 34 off I-82, Yakima* ☎ *509/573–3388, 800/221–0751* ⊕ *www.visityakima.com.* **Wine Yakima Valley Association** ☎ *800/258–7270, 509/965–5201* ⊕ *www.wineyakimavalley.org.*

NORTHERN YAKIMA RIVER VALLEY

In the upper Kittitas Valley, tucked between the Cascade Mountains to the west and the rugged, snowcapped Sawtooth Mountains to the east, visitors will find the newest in championship golf courses, resort amenities, and fine dining. Plentiful shops, restaurants, museums, and outdoor activities make this one of the most diverse regions of the state. The old-time coal mining towns of Roslyn and Cle Elum are being discovered by more and more travelers seeking good food, fun, and relaxation. The college town of Ellensburg, home of the annual Ellensburg Rodeo on Labor Day, offers a variety of entertainment, restaurants, and hotels. Through it all runs the Yakima River, the lifeblood of this agricultural region, and one of Washington's best trout-fishing rivers.

The city of Yakima is the region's hub, offering all kinds of shopping, including a new Cabela's Outdoor Store and, thanks to a newly refurbished downtown core district, many new restaurants, wineries, and nightlife options. Thousands of acres of orchards, producing cherries, apricots, peaches, pears, plums, nectarines and apples, surround the city. In spring and summer, outdoor enthusiasts flock here to hike, bike, canoe, raft, swim, and fish. Winter sports enthusiasts delight in the multitude of cross-country skiing, snowshoeing, and snowmobiling options, along with downhill skiing at White Pass.

CLE ELUM

86 miles southeast of Seattle.

A former railroad, coal, and logging town, Cle Elum (pronounced "klee *ell*-um") now caters to travelers stopping for a breath of air before or after tackling Snoqualmie Pass. It's also home to the ever-growing Suncadia Resort, possibly Washington's finest destination resort.

GETTING HERE AND AROUND

Cle-Elum is hard to miss; it's just off I–90. Exit 80 will get you to SunCadia Resort. Exit 84 will put you at the west end of Cle Elum, placing you in the business district if you're approaching from Seattle and points west. Exit 85 will deliver you into the eastern boundaries of Cle Elum, but will also put you directly in the business district. Most of the amenities are found within the city limits of Cle Elum and Roslyn.

ESSENTIALS

Visitor Information **Cle Elum/Roslyn Chamber of Commerce** ✉ *401 W. 1st St.* ☎ *509/674–5958* 🌐 *www.cleelumroslyn.org.*

EXPLORING

The Cle Elum Bakery. A local institution, this establishment has been doing business from the very same spot since 1906. Delectable treats from fresh-baked doughnuts and pastries to a fabulous sticky bun–cinnamon roll are available daily. ✉ *501 E. 1st St.* ☎ *509/674–2233* 🕒 *Mon.–Sat. 7–5:30, Sun. 7–3.*

Owens Meats. Across from the Cle Elum bakery is this marvelous smokehouse; established in 1887, it's been run by the Owens family since then. No processed jerky and meats here—just the freshest smoked and cured meats around, including beef jerky that is addictive. ✉ *502 E. 1st St.* ☎ *509/674–2530* 🌐 *owensmeats.com.*

Roslyn. A former coal-mining town just 3 miles northwest of Cle Elum, Roslyn gained notoriety as the stand-in for the fictional Alaskan village of Cicely on the 1990s TV show *Northern Exposure*. A map locating sites associated with filming is available from the city offices at First Street and Pennsylvania Avenue. Roslyn is also notable for its 28 ethnic cemeteries. Established by communities of miners in the late 19th and early 20th centuries, they are clustered on a hillside west of town.

WHERE TO EAT

$ STEAKHOUSE 🍴 **MaMa Vallone's Steak House and Inn.** Set in a building constructed in 1906, the upscale but rustic Western look makes the perfect style for this cozy and informal restaurant that once was a boarding house for unmarried miners. Guests dine at antique tables, and the works of several local artists hang on the walls. Pasta dishes such as the tomato-based *fagioli* (soup with vegetables and beans) and *bagna calda* (a bath of olive oil, garlic, anchovies, and butter for dredging vegetables and meat) attract diners from as far away as Seattle. [$] *Average main: $13* ✉ *302 W. 1st St.* ☎ *509/674–5174* 🌐 *www.mamavallones.com* 🕒 *No lunch.*

$ AMERICAN 🍴 **Sunset Café and Loose Wolf Lounge.** Since 1936 this Western-themed restaurant has been serving breakfast delectables like Texas-sized cinnamon rolls made on-site and comfort food, including homemade ravioli. Italian dishes share the lengthy menu with traditional American favorites such as hamburgers and fried chicken. [$] *Average main: $12* ✉ *318 E. 1st St., Cle Elum* ☎ *509/674–2241.*

WHERE TO STAY

For expanded hotel reviews, visit Fodors.com.

$ HOTEL 🏨 **Econo Lodge—Cle Elum Mountain Inn.** Interiors are simple at this well-kept two-story motel east of downtown, but the large rooms provide home-away-from-home comfort with many amenities. **Pros:** clean, affordable rooms; kitchenettes are an added convenience. **Cons:** no-frills; no pool. [$] *Rooms from: $95* ✉ *906 E. 1st St., Cle Elum* ☎ *509/674–2380, 888/674–3975* 🌐 *www.econolodge.com/hotel-cle_elum-washington-WA242* 🛏 *43 rooms* 🍽 *Breakfast.*

$ B&B/INN 🏨 **Iron Horse Inn Bed and Breakfast.** What was once a boardinghouse for rail workers (1909–74) is now a comfortable country inn owned by

Lodge at Suncadia

the daughter and son-in-law of a one-time lodger. **Pros:** unique lodging experience; on the National Registry of Historic Places. **Cons:** some rooms share bathrooms. [$] *Rooms from: $100* ✉ *526 Marie Ave., South Cle Elum* ☎ *509/674–5939, 800/228–9246* 🌐 *www.ironhorseinnbb.com* 🛏 *11 rooms, 8 with bath* 🍴 *Breakfast.*

$$$$ RESORT FAMILY Fodor's Choice ★ 🏨 **The Lodge at Suncadia.** In the middle of one of the region's premier golf courses (Prospector), this great stone-and-wood lodge blends beautifully with its mountain and forest surroundings. **Pros:** intimate mountain-retreat environment; golfing, fly-fishing, cross-country skiing, and hiking just minutes away. **Cons:** costs can quickly add up for a family visit. [$] *Rooms from: $309* ✉ *3320 Suncadia Trail* ☎ *509/649–6400, 866/904–6300* 🌐 *www.suncadia.com* 🛏 *254 rooms* 🍴 *No meals.*

ELLENSBURG

24 miles southeast of Cle Elum.

This university town is one of the state's friendliest and most easygoing places. "Modern" Ellensburg had its origin in a July 4 fire that engulfed the original city in 1889. Almost overnight, Victorian brick buildings rose from the ashes; many still stand, though their functions have changed. Stroll downtown to discover art galleries, comfortable cafés, secondhand-book and -record stores, an old-fashioned hardware store, and one antiques shop after another.

Central Washington's single biggest event is the Ellensburg Rodeo, held Labor Day weekend. On the national circuit since the 1920s, the rodeo has a year-round headquarters on Main Street where you can buy tickets and souvenirs. You can also get a bird's-eye view of the rodeo grounds from Reed Park, in the 500 block of North Alder Street.

GETTING HERE AND AROUND

Ellensburg is adjacent to I-90, with two exits that will take you right to gas, fast food, and lodging. Follow Main Street north and it will put you into the heart of downtown and Central Washington University.

ESSENTIALS

Visitor Information **Kittitas County Chamber of Commerce** ⊠ *609 N. Main St.* ☎ *509/925-2002, 888/925-2204* ⊕ *www.kittitascountychamber.com.*

EXPLORING

Central Washington University. The nearly 11,000 students here enjoy a pleasant, tree-shaded campus marked by tasteful redbrick architecture. Its 8th Avenue side has several handsome buildings dating from its founding in 1891 as the State Normal School. Near the center of campus is a serene Japanese garden. The Sarah Spurgeon Gallery, in Randall Hall, features the work of regional and national artists as well as students and faculty. ⊠ *400 E. 8th Ave.* ☎ *509/963-1111* ⊕ *www.cwu. edu* ☞ *Free* ☉ *Tours weekdays 10-2.*

Clymer Museum of Art. Half the museum houses the largest collection of works by painter John Clymer (1907-89). The Ellensburg native was one of the most widely published illustrators of the American West, focusing his oils and watercolors on wildlife and traditional lifestyles. The other half features other well-known and aspiring Western and wildlife artists. ⊠ *416 N. Pearl St.* ☎ *509/962-6416* ⊕ *www. clymermuseum.org* ☞ *Free* ☉ *Weekdays 10-5, Sat. 10-4.*

FAMILY **Dick and Jane's Spot.** Nestled in suburbia is the area's most peculiar attraction. The home of artists Dick Elliott and Jane Orleman is a continuously growing whimsical sculpture: a collage of 20,000 bottle caps, 1,500 bicycle reflectors, and other bits. Their masterpiece stands on private property near downtown, but it's still possible to see the recycled creation from several angles; sign the guestbook mounted on the surrounding fence. ⊠ *101 N. Pearl St.* ☎ *509/925-3224* ⊕ *www. reflectorart.com.*

Gallery One. In the 1889 Stewart Building you'll find a community art center with rotating shows by regional artists, a fine gift shop, and art classes. ⊠ *408 N. Pearl St.* ☎ *509/925-2670* ⊕ *www.gallery-one.org* ☞ *Free* ☉ *Mon.-Sat. 11-5, Sun. noon-4.*

Ginkgo and Wanapum State Parks. Separated by I-90, 28 miles east of Ellensburg on the Columbia River, are two state parks. Ginkgo Petrified Forest State Park preserves a fossil forest of ginkgos and other trees. A 3-mile-long trail leads from the interpretive center. Wanapum State Park, 3 miles south, has camping and river access for boaters. ⊠ *I-90 east to Exit 136, Vantage* ☎ *509/856-2700* ⊕ *www.parks. wa.gov* ☞ *Free; parking $10, camping $23* ☉ *Apr.-Oct., daily 6:30-dusk; Nov.-Mar., weekends and holidays 8 am-dusk.*

Olmstead Place State Park. This park and 217-acre working farm encompasses the grounds of an original pioneer farm built in 1875. A 1-mile interpretive trail links eight buildings, including a barn and schoolhouse. During harvest time, the park holds threshing bees, demonstrating historic farming practices. ⊠ *N. Ferguson Rd., ½ mile south of Kittitas Hwy., 4 miles east of Ellensburg* ☎ *509/925–1943* ⊕ *www. parks.wa.gov* ⊠ *Free; parking $10* ⊙ *Apr.–Oct., 6:30 am–dusk; Nov.– Mar., 8 am–dusk.*

Wanapum Dam Visitor Center. Native American and pioneer artifacts are exhibited here as well as displays on modern hydroelectric power. ⊠ *Hwy. 243 S.* ☎ *509/932–3571* ⊕ *www.grantpud.org* ⊠ *Free* ⊙ *Weekdays 8:30–4:30, weekends 9–5.*

WHERE TO EAT

$
AMERICAN

×**The Palace Cafe.** This café has been serving good food to hungry travelers and locals since 1892. They offer a solid menu with standard varieties of steaks, burgers, chicken, and pasta in a Western setting. Their specialty is a prawn strawberry salad, and they have a chicken linguine that is excellent. $ *Average main: $14* ⊠ *323 Main St.* ☎ *509/925–2327* ⊕ *www.thepalacecafe.net.*

$
AMERICAN
Fodor's Choice
★

×**Red Horse Diner.** Step back in time to a 1930s-era service station. Now, however, the service at this refurbished Mobil station includes specialty sandwiches, shakes, and more. While you wait for your burger and fries, check out the hundreds of old metal signs and advertisements that enhance the vintage appeal of this classic burger joint. $ *Average main: $10* ⊠ *1518 W. University Way* ☎ *509/925–1956* ⊕ *www. redhorsediner.com.*

$$
CONTEMPORARY

×**Valley Cafe.** Meals at this vintage art deco eatery consist of Mediterranean bistro-style salads, pastas, and other plates. Featured dinner entrées include pork tenderloin, seared ahi tuna, and chicken marsala. An impressive wine list offers dozens of Yakima Valley options. Owner Greg Beach also owns the wine shop next door. $ *Average main: $22* ⊠ *105 W. 3rd Ave.* ☎ *509/925–3050.*

$$
AMERICAN

×**Yellow Church Café.** Built in 1923 as a Lutheran church, this house of culinary worship now offers seating in the nave or choir loft. Soups, salads, sandwiches, pastas, and home-baked goods are served, as well as dinner specials. Breakfast is popular on weekends. $ *Average main: $18* ⊠ *111 S. Pearl St.* ☎ *509/933–2233* ⊕ *www.yellowchurchcafe.com.*

WHERE TO STAY

For expanded hotel reviews, visit Fodors.com.

$
HOTEL

Best Western Lincoln Inn and Suites. A spacious hostelry one block off Ellensburg's main north–south arterial, the Lincoln Inn offers travelers plenty of elbow room, minimal noise, and lots of amenities and services. **Pros:** very nice motel close to the freeway; caters to business travelers. **Cons:** if you are looking for a less expensive place for a one night's stay, this may be a bit much. $ *Rooms from: $130* ⊠ *211 W. Umptanum Rd.* ☎ *509/925–4244, 866/925–4288* 🖷 *509/925–4211* ⊕ *www. bestwestern.com* ⊅ *55 rooms* ⊙ *Breakfast.*

17

YAKIMA

38 miles south of Ellensburg.

The gateway to Washington wine country is sunny Yakima (pronounced *yak*-imah), home to about 80,000 people within the city limits and another 25,000 in the surrounding area. Spread along the west bank of the Yakima River just south of its confluence with the Naches River, Yakima is a bustling community with lovely parklands and a downtown in the midst of revitalization. Downtown street improvements with period lighting, trees, and planters have created a fresh new "old" feel that is inviting to residents and visitors alike.

Yakima was settled in the late 1850s as a ranching center where Ahtanum Creek joins the Yakima River, on the site of earlier Yakama tribal villages at present-day Union Gap. When the Northern Pacific Railroad established its terminal 4 miles north in 1884, most of the town picked up and moved to what was then called "North Yakima."

Yakima's Mission-style Northern Pacific Depot (1912) is the highlight of its historic North Front Street. Other old buildings face the depot; behind it, colorful Track 29 Mall is in old rail cars. Four blocks east is the ornate Capitol Theatre, built in 1920. The former vaudeville and silent-movie hall is now a performing arts center. Opposite is Millennium Plaza, a public art installation that celebrates the importance of water to the Yakima Valley. Residents and visitors alike enjoy year-round natural beauty in the heart of Yakima, thanks to the city's ongoing restoration and preservation of the Yakima Greenway. The nature area and trails stretch from Selah Gap to Union Gap, and west along the Naches River. The greenway includes more than 10 miles of paved pathway that connects parks, trails, and adjacent protected natural areas.

Yakima is also home to the Central Washington State Fair, the original State Fair of Washington. Drawing over 300,000 people from all over the Northwest, the annual Fair, held in late September, is the showcase for the agricultural bounty of the area and provides big-name entertainment and all the unique and delicious "Fair" fare.

GETTING HERE AND AROUND

Yakima can be reached via air and road. The Yakima International Airport offers commercial flights to and from Seattle daily, and also welcomes private flights from all over. Interstate 82 from Ellensburg to the Tri-Cities and beyond, runs right through the city limits. Highways 12 and 410, known as White and Chinook Pass, pass on either side of Mt. Rainier and connect with I–82 at Yakima, as does Highway 97, which brings travelers from Oregon and points south.

Yakima is the only city in the region with a public transportation system.

Yakima City Transit. Buses operate weekdays 6:15 am to 6:45 pm and Saturday from 8:45 to 6:45 at half-hour intervals on nine routes. The one-way fare is 75 cents. ☎ *509/575–6175* ⊕ *www.ci.yakima.wa.us/services/transit.*

Yakima Valley Museum

ESSENTIALS

Visitor Information Yakima Valley Visitors and Convention Bureau ✉ *10 N. 8th St.* ☏ *509/576–6385* ⊕ *www.visityakima.com.*

EXPLORING

Gilbert Cellars. In downtown Yakima's historic district, this tasting room serves up selections from their family vineyards, specializing in blends of Rhône varietals and an unoaked Chardonnay. In addition to being a tasting room, there are local craft beers available, as well as small plates to accompany your favorite vintage. The downtown location makes the tasting room an ideal place to meet before a night on the town, or to enjoy a glass of wine after dinner. ✉ *5 N. Front St., Yakima* ☏ *509/249–9049* ⊕ *www.gilbertcellars.com.*

FAMILY **McAllister Museum of Aviation.** The history of aviation in central Washington unfolds at the site of this pioneering flight school at Yakima International Airport. The museum includes Charlie McAllister's original pilot's license, signed by Orville Wright. ✉ *2008 S. 16th Ave.* ☏ *509/457–4933* ⊕ *www.mcallistermuseum.org* ✉ *Donations accepted* ⊙ *Thurs. and Fri. 10–4, Sat. 9–4.*

Naches Heights Vineyard. Just a few miles west of Yakima, this winery is located in Washington's newest wine-growing area. Set among organic and biodynamic vineyards, the tasting room has ample seating inside, where you can enjoy the fireplace while contemplating their wines. Outside the tasting room is where you can get away from it all, with a large grassy picnic area laced with paths and four waterfalls. The winery features blends in both red and white. ✉ *2410 Naches Heights Rd., south of Hwy 12, Yakima* ☏ *855/648–9463* ⊕ *www.nhwines.com*

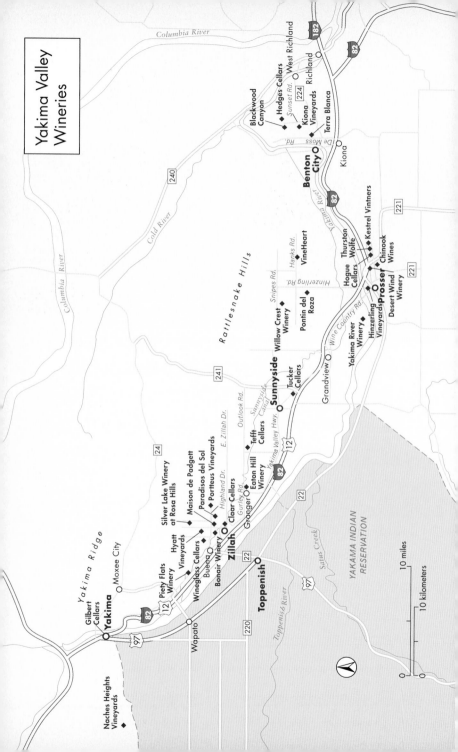

Yakima Valley
Wineries

🕓 *Winter: Sun., Mon., and Thurs. 2–7, weekends 2–9; summer: Mon. and Thurs., 2–7 Fri. and Sat. noon–9, Sun. noon–7; Tues. and Wed. by appointment only.*

Yakima Area Arboretum. Just off I–82, the Yakima Arboretum features hundreds of different plants, flowers, and trees. The park-like Arboretum also sits alongside the Yakima River and the 10-mile-long Yakima Greenway, a paved path that links a series of riverfront parks. A Japanese garden and a wetland trail are the arboretum's highlights. ✉ *1401 Arboretum Dr., off Nob Hill Blvd.* ☎ *509/248–7337* 🌐 *www.ahtrees.org* 🎟 *Free* 🕓 *Daily dawn–dusk.*

FAMILY **Yakima Valley Museum.** Constant exhibits here focus on Yakama native, pioneer, and 20th-century history, ranging from horse-drawn vehicles to a "neon garden" of street signs. Highlights include a fully operating 1930s soda fountain and a model of Yakima native and Supreme Court Justice William O. Douglas's Washington, D.C., office. Other visiting and rotation exhibits are also scheduled throughout the year. ✉ *2105 Tieton Dr.* ☎ *509/248–0747* 🌐 *www.yakimavalleymuseum.org* 🎟 *$5* 🕓 *Tues.–Sat. 10–5.*

WHERE TO EAT

$$ ITALIAN 🍴 **Gasperetti's.** John Gasperetti's restaurant keeps an elegant low profile in a high-traffic area north of downtown. Moderately priced pasta dishes share the menu with a short list of special weekly dinners—meat or seafood entrées with organically grown local produce. The cellar has an excellent selection of wines, including Italian varietals. [$] *Average main: $20* ✉ *1013 N. 1st St.* ☎ *509/248–0628* 🌐 *www.gasperettisrestaurant.com* 🕓 *Closed Sun. No lunch Sat.*

$ AMERICAN FAMILY 🍴 **Miner's Drive-In.** This Yakima icon (actually located in Union Gap) is a must-visit for many travelers coming to or through Yakima. It's an authentic 1940s hamburger joint that has expanded from a traditional drive-in to a family sit-down diner. There are plenty of great-tasting items on the menu, from salads to fish-and-chips, but the real crowd pleaser is the giant "Big Miner"—an old-fashioned burger that knocks any chain burger out of the park. Add a huge basket of fries and a shake, and chances are you'll be full for most of your day. [$] *Average main: $10* ✉ *2415 S. 1st St., Union Gap* ☎ *509/457–8194.*

$ AMERICAN 🍴 **Museum Soda Fountain.** Soda jerks at the Yakima Valley Museum's café make shakes and sundaes plus soups, hot dogs, and sandwiches while a period Wurlitzer spins 1930s big-band records. [$] *Average main: $8* ✉ *Yakima Valley Museum, 2105 Tieton Dr.* ☎ *509/248–0747* ✍ *Reservations not accepted* 🕓 *Closed Sun. and Nov.–Mar.*

$ MEXICAN 🍴 **Santiago's.** Elegant and charming, Jar and Deb Arcand's skylit establishment puts a new spin on Mexican dishes. For chili verde, chunks of pork loin are slow-cooked in jalapeño sauce; the Yakima apple-pork mole is prepared with chocolate and cinnamon. [$] *Average main: $15* ✉ *111 E. Yakima Ave.* ☎ *509/453–1644* 🌐 *www.santiagos.org* 🕓 *Closed Sun. No lunch Sat.*

$$ AMERICAN 🍴 **Second Street Grill.** A hub for Yakima's rejuvenated nightlife, Second Street Grill is located in the heart of downtown. Century-old bare brick walls hung with huge black-and-white photographs and hi-def TVs

provide the setting, and the menu has a similar mix of old and new, featuring a wide array of salads, pastas, and steaks, with a bit of Asian flair thrown in. The restaurant's bar is a happy-hour destination (3 to 6 pm) and a late night hot spot on the weekends, with live music on Saturday. During the warmer months, sidewalk seating is available and recommended as long the weather isn't too warm. $ *Average main: $19* ⊠ *28 N. 2nd St., Yakima* ☎ *509/469–1486* ⊕ *www.secondstreetgrill.com.*

$$$
STEAKHOUSE
✕ **Tony's Steakhouse & Lounge.** The upscale steak house features Kobe rib-eye steaks and other cuts. The specialty menu changes every three months, but standard-cut steaks including filet mignon, New York, and smoked American Kobe prime rib are the specialty here and are available at all times. Unique appetizers and recipes featuring Northwest salmon and other seafood are also featured. Beautiful stonework outside and more stone and hardwood accents inside create elegant dining areas. Tony's is also one of the most popular nightspots in the area for dining or just meeting friends for a glass of Yakima Valley wine. $ *Average main: $30* ⊠ *221 W. Yakima Ave.* ☎ *509/853–1010* ⊕ *www.tonysteakhouse.com* ⊗ *Closed Sun. No lunch Sat.*

WHERE TO STAY

For expanded hotel reviews, visit Fodors.com.

$$
B&B/INN
⛨ **Birchfield Manor.** The valley's most luxurious accommodations are on a plateau just east of Yakima, surrounded by hop yards (fields where most of the brewery hops in the United States are grown), corn, and cattle. **Pros:** a unique experience for this region; good restaurant on-site. **Cons:** a little difficult to find; restaurant only open three nights a week. $ *Rooms from: $170* ⊠ *2018 Birchfield Rd., just south of Hwy. 24* ☎ *509/452–1960, 800/375–3420* ⊕ *www.birchfieldmanor.com* ⇆ *11 rooms* ⦿ *Breakfast.*

$
HOTEL
⛨ **Hilton Garden Inn.** Modern, spacious, and comfortable rooms make this hotel in the heart of downtown Yakima one of the city's finest upscale lodgings. **Pros:** one block from the convention center and within walking distance of dozens of shops; restaurant on-site. **Cons:** in the midst of the concrete jungle. $ *Rooms from: $125* ⊠ *402 E. Yakima Ave.* ☎ *509/454–1111* ⊕ *www.yakima.stayhgi.com* ⇆ *111 rooms, 3 suites* ⦿ *Breakfast.*

$
HOTEL
⛨ **North Park Lodge.** This 2009 addition to the region offers 53 rooms, with grand suites also available. **Pros:** quiet and affordable, with plenty of room for the family; indoor pool. **Cons:** eight miles from Yakima. $ *Rooms from: $100* ⊠ *659 N. Wenas Rd., Selah* ☎ *509/698–6000* ⊕ *www.northparklodge.com* ⇆ *53 rooms* ⦿ *Breakfast.*

SPORTS AND THE OUTDOORS

Apple Tree Golf Course. This beautiful course cut through the apple orchards of West Yakima and is rated as one of the state's top 10. The signature hole on the 18-hole, par-72 course is Number 17, shaped like a giant apple surrounded by a lake. Greens fees run $45–$60. ⊠ *8804 Occidental Rd.* ☎ *509/966–5877* ⊕ *www.appletreeresort.com.*

White Pass Ski Area. A full-service ski area 50 miles west of Yakima toward Mt. Rainier, White Pass is the home mountain of former Olympic medalists Phil and Steve Mahre. Eight lifts serve 47 trails on a vertical drop of 1,500 feet from the 6,000-foot summit. Here you'll find condominiums, a gas station, grocery store, and snack bar. Open woods are popular with cross-country skiers and summer hikers. ⊠ *48935 U.S. 12* ☎ *509/672–3101* ⊕ *www.skiwhitepass.com.*

SHOPPING

Johnson Orchards. This company has been growing and selling fruit—including cherries, peaches, apples, and pears—to the public since 1904. ⊠ *4906 Summitview Ave.* ☎ *509/966–7479.*

Valley Mall. Central Washington's largest shopping center, Valley Mall has all kinds of specialty shops and three major department stores: Sears, Kohl's and Macy's. The area surrounding the mall is the main retail area for the region, featuring several national retailers within a mile radius. Sportsmen and women flock to the Cabela's outdoor store. ⊠ *2529 Main St., off I-82, exit 36, Union Gap* ☎ *509/453–8233.*

Yakima Farmers' Market. Produce vendors gather in downtown Yakima every Sunday, June through October, for the Yakima Farmers' Market. At other times, roadside stands and farms welcome visitors. ⊠ *Yakima Ave. and 3rd St., Downtown.*

SOUTHERN YAKIMA RIVER VALLEY

The lower Yakima Valley encompasses hundreds of thousands of acres both on and off the Yakama Indian Reservation and includes several small towns. Agriculture is the name of the game in this part of the lower valley where everything from apples to zucchinis are grown. Throughout the summer visitors buy or pick all kinds of fresh vegetables and fruits in season. In early May the asparagus grows to cutting height, and soon after that it's time for the cherries to be harvested. Basically, it's one harvest after the next, culminating with apples in late October. Growing conditions also make this area the hot spot for wine-grape growing, and where there are grapes, there are wineries. Some 70 wineries now call the Yakima Valley home, with many of the best wines in the country coming from these vintners. The history of this region stretches back hundreds of years from the time of the Native American Yakama people and early white settlers. Much of this history can be seen in several museums around the region, including the museum at the Yakama Nation Cultural Center in Toppenish.

17

ZILLAH

15 miles southeast of Yakima.

The south-facing slopes above Zillah, a tiny town named after the daughter of a railroad manager, are covered with orchards and vineyards. Several wineries are in or near the community; more are near Granger, 6 miles southeast.

GETTING HERE AND AROUND

The outskirts of Zillah, which is growing to include many new businesses, sits right on I–82 southeast out of Yakima. Downtown Zillah is just up the hill a half-mile or so.

EXPLORING

Bonair Winery. After years of amateur wine-making in California, the Puryear family began commercial wine production in their native Yakima Valley in 1985 under the Bonair Winery name. One of the older Yakima Valley wineries, Bonair offers a large tasting room reminiscent of a European chalet that sits among the vineyards, and a duck pond, which was voted one of Washington's best places for a kiss. Visit the tasting room and you will likely meet the winemaker, Gail Puryear or his wife, the "wine goddess" Shirley. Bonair makes Cabernets, Cabernet Francs, Chardonnays, Gewürztraminer Port, Merlots, Rieslings, and more. Visitors are welcome to picnic here, and vineyard/production tours are available by appointment. ⊠ *500 S. Bonair Rd.* ☎ *509/829–6027* ⊕ *www.bonairwine.com* ☉ *Mar.–Oct., daily 10–6; Nov.–Dec., daily 10–5; Jan.–Feb., weekends noon–5.*

Claar Cellars. Right off of I–82 at Exit 52, Claar Cellars has one of the highest visitor numbers of any Yakima Valley winery. The family-owned estate produces a variety of wines, including some ice wines, Sangiovese, and rare varieties such as Corneauxcopia (a blended variety) and Fouled Anchor Port, which includes cherries, raisins, honey, and maple syrup. They also produce traditional Merlots, Cabernets, Chardonnays, Sauvignon Blanc, and Rieslings. Their grapes come from vineyards in the White Bluffs region, so while the tasting room is easily accessible, it is separated from the vineyards. ⊠ *1001 Vintage Valley Pkwy.* ☎ *509/829–6810* ⊕ *www.claarcellars.com* ☉ *Apr.–Nov., daily 10–6; Dec.–Mar., daily 11–5, or by appointment. May close occasionally for owners' vacations.*

Eaton Hill Winery. Inside the restored Rinehold Cannery building, the rustic Eaton Hill Winery produces Cabernet, Merlot, Chardonnay, Riesling, Sémillon, and various sweeter and fortified wines. ⊠ *530 Gurley Rd., off Yakima Valley Hwy., Granger* ☎ *509/854–2220* ☉ *Mid-Feb.–Nov., daily noon–5.*

Horizon's Edge Winery. With a spectacular view of the Yakima Valley, Mt. Adams, and Mt. Rainier, it is easy to see where Horizon's Edge got its name. The winery makes sparkling wine, Chardonnay, Pinot Noir, Merlot, Cabernet Sauvignon, and Muscat Canelli. ⊠ *4530 E. Zillah Dr., east of Yakima Valley Hwy.* ☎ *509/829–6401* ⊕ *www.horizonsedgewinery. com* ☉ *Mar.–Nov., Thurs.–Mon. noon–5.*

Hyatt Vineyards. This 97-acre estate vineyard and winery sits in the middle of the Rattlesnake appellation and specializes in Chardonnay, Merlot, Syrah, and Cabernet Sauvignon. ⊠ *2020 Gilbert Rd., off Bonair Rd.* ☎ *509/829–6333* ⊕ *www.hyattvineyards.com* ☉ *Apr.–Nov., daily 11–5; Dec.–Mar., daily 11–4:30.*

Maison de Padgett Winery. Owned and operated by a small family, Maison de Padgett produces specialized handcrafted wines in a beautiful winery highlighted by adjoining European-style gardens. Groups of 10 or more should call ahead. ⊠ *2231 Roza Dr., at Highland Dr.* ☎ *509/829–6412* ⊕ *www.maisondepadgettwinery.com* ☉ *Mar.–Nov., Thurs.–Mon. 11–5; Dec.–Feb., by appointment.*

Desert Wind Winery, Prosser

Paradisos del Sol. This is another family-owned winery, operated by veteran wine-grower Paul Vandenberg. The tasting room is a part of the family farmhouse, surrounded by orchards, vineyards, and chickens. Unlike many wineries, the Vandenbergs focus as much on growing the grapes as turning them into wine. Various blends, both white and red, highlight the wine selections. ⊠ *3230 Highland Dr.* ☎ *509/829–9000* ⊕ *www.paradisosdelsol.com* ☉ *Daily 11–6.*

Piety Flats Winery. Just off 1–82 (Exit 44), this former mercantile (circa 1911) and fruit stand is now a winery and tasting room. Offering Syrah, Merlot, Mercantile Red, Carmenere, Junkyard Red, Back Muscat, and more, the winery also offers a number of other Yakima Valley specialty foods and goods, which makes it still a mercantile of sorts. ⊠ *2560 Donald–Wapato Rd.* ☎ *509/877–3115* ⊕ *www.pietyflatswinery.com* ☉ *May–Sept. Mon.–Sat. 10–6, Sun. 10–5; Oct.–Dec. daily 10–5; Jan.– Feb. weekends 11–4; March–Apr. daily 10–5.*

Portteus Vineyards. One of the early Yakima Valley wineries, established in 1981, Portteus is beloved by red-wine drinkers. Production includes Cabernet Sauvignon and Franc, Merlot, Malbec, Syrah, Zinfandel, and port—as well as a robust Chardonnay. Family run, the tasting room is staffed by the second generation of the Portteus family. Grapes are grown at 1,440-foot elevation on 47 acres above Zillah. ⊠ *5201 Highland Dr.* ☎ *509/829–6970* ⊕ *www.portteus.com* ☉ *Daily 10–5.*

Silver Lake at Roza Hills. Bands serenade picnickers on summer weekends on what Silver Lake calls the "viniferanda," above their historic winery, high in the Rattlesnake Hills. With both a large deck and well-manicured lawn with a soothing fountain, visitors are afforded views of the Cabernets, Merlots, Chardonnays, Rieslings, and other vintages in production in the valley below. Sundays in August bring live music and salmon dinners, and the tasting room offers wide views as well. ✉ *1500 Vintage Rd., off Highland Dr.* ☎ *509/829–6235* 🌐 *www.silverlakewinery.com* 🕒 *Apr.–Nov., daily 10–5; Dec.–Mar., Thurs.–Mon. 11–4.*

Wineglass Cellars. This small winery got its name from an unusual collection of antique wine glasses. In the interest of quality and priority, the winery produces limited lots of Merlot, Cabernet Sauvignon, Zinfandel, Sangiovese, Chardonnay, and port. ✉ *206 N. Bonair Rd.* ☎ *509/829–3011* 🌐 *www.wineglasscellars.com* 🕒 *Mid-Feb.–Nov., Thurs.–Sun. 10:30–5.*

WHERE TO EAT AND STAY

For expanded hotel reviews, visit Fodors.com.

$ MEXICAN 🍴 **El Porton.** Authentic, yet inexpensive Mexican fare is what you get here. Savory seafood dishes such as *mariscos al mojo de ajo* (sautéed prawns with mushrooms and garlic) are favorites. Traditional offerings such as beef or chicken burritos and enchiladas, served up in a variety of Mexican styles, round out the menu. [$] *Average main: $14* ✉ *905 Vintage Valley Pkwy., Exit 52 off I–82* ☎ *509/829–9100* ✍ *Reservations not accepted.*

$ HOTEL 🏨 **Comfort Inn–Zillah.** Just a few steps from Claar Cellars off I–82, this clean and modern hotel is a favorite of winery visitors. **Pros:** right on the freeway and the only motel within miles. **Cons:** potential freeway traffic noise. [$] *Rooms from: $100* ✉ *911 Vintage Valley Pkwy.* ☎ *509/829–3399, 800/501–5433* 📠 *509/829–3428* 🌐 *www.comfortinnzillah.com* 🛏 *40 rooms* 🍽 *Breakfast.*

TOPPENISH

17 miles southeast of Yakima.

An intriguing small town with a rustic Old West sensibility, Toppenish—which lies within the Yakama Reservation—blends history and culture, art and agriculture. You can't miss the 70 colorful murals that adorn the facades and exterior walls of businesses and homes. Commissioned since 1989 by the Toppenish Mural Association and done in a variety of styles by regional artists, they commemorate the town's history and Western spirit. Tours in a horse-drawn covered wagon leave from the association's office on Toppenish Avenue.

GETTING HERE AND AROUND

Take Highway 97 out of Yakima, and the four-lane road will take you through Wapato and right to Toppenish. Or follow the signs from I–82 at Zillah. From Oregon and points south Highway 97 also brings you right to Toppenish over Satus Pass.

ESSENTIALS

Visitor Information Toppenish Chamber of Commerce ✉ *504 S Elm St., Toppenish* ☎ *509/865–3262, 800/863–6375* 🌐 *www.toppenish.net.*

EXPLORING

FAMILY **American Hop Museum.** The Yakima Valley grows 75% of the nation's hops and 25% of the world's, and the industry's story is well told at this museum. Exhibits describe the history, growing process, and unique biology of the plant, a primary ingredient in beer. ⌂ *22 S. B St.* ☎ *509/865–4677* ⊕ *www.americanhopmuseum.com* ⊠ *$3* ☉ *Early May–late Sept., Wed.–Sat. 10–4, Sun. 11–4.*

Ft. Simcoe Historical State Park. The residential quarters of an 1856 army fort, 30 miles west of Toppenish, look like a Victorian summer retreat. Exhibits focus on relations between the Yakama people—in the heart of whose reservation the fort stands—and American settlers. ⌂ *5150 Ft. Simcoe Rd.* ☎ *509/874–2372* ⊕ *www.parks.wa.gov* ⊠ *Free* ☉ *Apr.– Oct., daily 6:30 am–dusk.*

Yakama Nation Cultural Center. This six-building complex has a fascinating museum of tribal history and culture, including costumes, basketry, beadwork, and reconstructions of traditional lodges. Tribal dances and other cultural events are often staged in the Heritage Theater; the complex also includes a gift shop, library, and restaurant. ⌂ *Buster Dr. at U.S. 97* ☎ *509/865–2800* ⊕ *www.yakamamuseum.com* ⊠ *$6* ☉ *Weekdays 8–5, weekends 9–5.*

SUNNYSIDE

17

14 miles southeast of Zillah.

The largest community in the lower Yakima Valley and the hometown of astronaut Bonnie Dunbar, Sunnyside runs along the sunny southern slopes of the Rattlesnake Hills.

GETTING HERE AND AROUND

I–82 runs right past Sunnyside as it threads its way down through the Lower Yakima Valley. Three exits put you at either end, and in the middle of Sunnyside.

ESSENTIALS

Visitor Information Sunnyside Chamber of Commerce ⌂ *451 S. 6th St.* ☎ *509/837–5939, 800/457–8089* ⊕ *www.sunnysidechamber.com.*

EXPLORING

Tucker Cellars. Established in 1981 by renowned Washington grape growers Dean and Rose Tucker, Tucker Cellars produces Gewürztraminer, Chenin Blanc, Riesling, Chardonnay, and Pinot Noir. It's next to a fruit and produce market just off the Yakima Valley Highway, about 4 miles east of Sunnyside. ⌂ *70 Ray Rd.* ☎ *509/837–8701* ⊕ *www. tuckercellars.net* ☉ *Daily 10–5.*

WHERE TO EAT

$ ✕ **Dykstra House.** In a wine valley with few upscale restaurants, this AMERICAN 1914 Craftsman house in quiet Grandview has held its own for nearly two decades. Breads are made from hand-ground wheat that's grown locally. Lunch, which is quite a bit less expensive than dinner, features salads, sandwiches, and daily specials. Casual Friday night dinners are Italian; grand Saturday night dinners revolve around chicken, beef, or fish. Local beers and wines are served. [$] *Average main: $15* ✉ *114 Birch Ave., 7 miles southeast of Sunnyside via I–82, Grandview* ☎ *509/882–2082* ✍ *Reservations essential* ⏲ *Closed Sun. and Mon. No dinner Tues.–Thurs.*

$ MEXICAN 🍴 **El Conquistador.** The bright, lively colors and clean, modern-Mexican interior belie the aging facade of this quaint eatery. The menu ranges from burritos, fajitas, and enchiladas mole to shrimp sautéed with green peppers and onions and served with a tangy salsa. Egg dishes are also on the menu, as are some unique Mexican salads and soups. Handcrafted clay masks on the walls add a festive flair. [$] *Average main: $10* ✉ *612 E. Edison Ave.* ☎ *509/839–2880.*

$ AMERICAN 🍴 **Snipes Mountain Microbrewery & Restaurant.** In an imposing log structure that resembles a hunting or ski lodge, the lower valley's oldest and largest brewpub is a grand restaurant with fare ranging from burgers and wood-fired pizzas to pasta dishes, fresh king salmon cooked on an alder plank, prime rib, and rack of lamb. Head brewer Chad Roberts makes handcrafted beers, using locally grown hops, of course. [$] *Average main: $15* ✉ *905 Yakima Valley Hwy.* ☎ *509/837–2739* 🌐 *www.snipesmountain.com.*

WHERE TO STAY

For expanded hotel reviews, visit Fodors.com.

$ B&B/INN 🏨 **Sunnyside Inn Bed & Breakfast.** Built in 1919 as a doctor's residence and office, this two-house inn, remodeled in 2007, is larger than the usual B&B. **Pros:** in the heart of wine country; offering a short drive to several different wineries; free Wi-Fi in rooms. **Cons:** immediate surroundings are not the most appealing. [$] *Rooms from: $100* ✉ *800–804 E. Edison Ave.* ☎ *509/839–5557, 800/221–4195* 🌐 *www.sunnysideinn.com* 🛏 *12 rooms* 🍽 *Breakfast.*

PROSSER

13 miles southeast of Sunnyside.

On the south bank of the Yakima River, Prosser feels like small-town America of the 1950s. The seat of Benton County since 1905, it has a 1926 courthouse and a charming museum in City Park. In 2005, Prosser's Horse Heaven Hills, on the Columbia River's north slope, became Washington's seventh federally recognized wine region.

GETTING HERE AND AROUND

On the lower end of the Yakima Valley, Prosser sits alongside I–82 as it works its way to Benton City and then on to the Tri-Cities (Richland/Kennewick/Pasco). Two exits put you at either end of town.

ESSENTIALS

Visitor Information Prosser Chamber of Commerce ✉ *1230 Bennett Ave.* ☎ *509/786–3177, 800/408–1517* 🌐 *www.prosserchamber.org.*

EXPLORING

Chinook Wines. This small house winery is run by Kay Simon and Clay Mackey, vintners known for their dry wines, including Merlot, Chardonnay, Sémillon and Sauvignon Blanc. The tasting room is within the original farm buildings, and there's a shady picnic area outside.

Hogue Cellars, Prosser

✉ *Wittkopf Loop at Wine Country Rd.* ☎ *509/786–2725* ⊕ *www. chinookwines.com* ⊗ *May–Oct., weekends noon–5, or by appointment.*

Desert Wind Winery. With an expansive tasting room housed in an elegant Southwestern-style building featuring a vast patio overlooking the Yakima River, Desert Wind is one of the highlights of any wine tour in the Valley. Tasters will delight in Sémillon, Barbera, Ruah, Viognier, and various other unique wine selections. Just off I–82, the winery also includes Mojave by Picazo, a small restaurant (open Wednesday–Saturday), and a gift shop with Yakima Valley food products and gift items. Also available on the second floor are four luxury guest suites, $225–$300 per night depending on season and room size. ✉ *2258 Wine Country Rd.* ☎ *509/786–7277* ⊕ *www.desertwindwinery.com* ⊗ *Daily 11–5.*

Hinzerling Vineyards. Billed as the valley's first winery, Hinzerling specializes in dessert and appetizer wines including port, sherry, and Muscat. Vintner Mike Wallace is one of the state's wine pioneers: he planted his first Prosser-area vines in 1972, and established the small winery in 1976. ✉ *1520 Sheridan Rd. at Wine Country Rd.* ☎ *509/786–2163* ⊕ *www.hinzerling.com* ⊗ *Daily 11–4.*

Hogue Cellars. Founded in 1982, Hogue has grown to be one of the largest wineries in the state and has earned multiple awards for its wines. The gift shop carries the winery's famous pickled beans and asparagus as well as Cabernet Sauvignon, Merlot, Chenin Blanc, Rieslings, and Fumé Blanc, among other wines. ✉ *Prosser Wine and Food Park, 2800 Lee Rd.* ☎ *509/786–6108* ⊕ *www.hoguecellars.com* ⊗ *Mar.–Nov., daily 10–5, Dec.–Feb., daily 11–4.*

Kestrel Vintners. Featuring one the oldest vineyards in the Valley, planted in 1973, Kestrel vintners focus on dark red wines including rich Cabernets, Merlots, and Syrahs, among others. ✉ *Prosser Wine and Food Park, 2890 Lee Rd.* ☎ *509/786–2675* 🌐 *www.kestrelwines.com* 🕒 *Daily noon–5.*

Pontin del Roza. Named for its owners, the Pontin family, and the grape-friendly slopes irrigated by the Roza Canal, Pontin del Roza produces Italian-style Sangioveses and Pinot Grigios, as well as Rieslings, Chenin Blancs, Chardonnays, Sauvignon Blancs, and Cabernet Sauvignons. ✉ *35502 N. Hinzerling Rd., 3½ miles north of Prosser* ☎ *509/786–4449* 🌐 *www.pontindelroza.com* 🕒 *Daily 10–5.*

Thurston Wolfe. Established in 1987, Thurston Wolfe features Wade Wolfe's unusual blends of specialty wines, including a white Pinot Gris–Viognier, for instance, and a red mix of Zinfandel, Syrah, Lemberger, and Turiga. One of their popular varieties is Sweet Rebecca, an orange muscat. ✉ *Prosser Wine and Food Park, 588 Cabernet Ct.* ☎ *509/786–3313* 🌐 *www.thurstonwolfe.com* 🕒 *Apr.–early Dec., Thurs.–Sun. 11–5.*

VineHeart. This pleasant boutique winery offers a buttery Riesling, a raspberry-toned Sémillon, a Lemberger, and a Sangiovese, as well as Zinfandel, Cabernet Sauvignon, and Syrah. ✉ *44209 N. McDonald Rd., 7 miles northeast of Prosser* ☎ *509/973–2993* 🌐 *www.vineheart.com* 🕒 *Mon. and Thurs.–Sat. 9–5, Sun. 11–5.*

Willow Crest Winery. Founded by David Minick in 1995, Willow Crest is a small winery with a Tuscan-themed tasting room that pours its own award-winning Syrah as well as Cabernet Franc and Pinot Gris. There's also a café on-site, open May through October. ✉ *Vintners Village, 590 Merlot Dr.* ☎ *509/786–7999* 🌐 *www.willowcrestwinery.com* 🕒 *Daily 10–5.*

Yakima River Winery. Another of the pioneer wineries in the Valley, established by John and Louise Rauner in 1977, Yakima River specializes in barrel-aged reds and a memorable port, along with a new variety, Petit Verdot. ✉ *143302 N. River Rd., 1½ miles south of Wine Country Rd.* ☎ *509/786–2805* 🌐 *www.yakimariverwinery.com* 🕒 *Daily 10–5.*

WHERE TO STAY

For expanded hotel reviews, visit Fodors.com.

$ B&B/INN 🏨 **Vintners Inn.** You'll think you have time-warped back to the turn of the 20th century when you arrive at this 1905 Queen Anne that has been remodeled into a farmhouse-style B&B. **Pros:** winery right next door; central location. **Cons:** bathrooms only have tubs, no showers; three blocks from railroad track, so occasional train noise at night; no TV. [$] *Rooms from: $90* ✉ *1520 Sheridan Ave.* ☎ *509/786–2163, 800/727–6702* 🌐 *www.hinzerling.com* 🛏 *2 rooms* 🍴 *Breakfast.*

akima Valley vineyard

BENTON CITY

16 miles east of Prosser.

The Yakima River zigzags north, making a giant bend around Red Mountain and the West Richland district before pouring into the Columbia River. Benton City—which, with a mere 3,000 residents, is hardly a city—is on a bluff west of the river facing vineyard-cloaked Red Mountain. High-carbonate soil, a location in a unique high-pressure pocket, and geographical anomalies have led to this district's being given its own appellation. You can access the wineries from Highway 224.

GETTING HERE AND AROUND

You'll find Benton City just off of I–82 about halfway between Prosser and Richland. One exit takes off from the Interstate and funnels traffic into the little town and to Highway 224.

EXPLORING

Blackwood Canyon Vintners. Winemaker Michael Taylor Moore freely admits he's pushing the edge, meticulously crafting wines by hand, in the traditional European style of yesteryear. He shuns modern filters, pumps, and even sulfites, and carefully avoids pesticides. Chardonnays, Sémillons, Merlots, Cabernets, and late-harvest wines age *sur lies* (on their sediment) for as long as eight years before release. ✉ *53258 N. Sunset Rd.* ☎ *509/588–7124* ⊕ *www.blackwoodwine. com* ☉ *Daily 10–6.*

Hedges Cellars. This spectacular hillside château winery dominates upper Red Mountain and produces robust red wines. The estate blends Cabernet Sauvignon, Cabernet Franc, Merlot, Syrah, and reserve blends are superb. ⊠ *53511 N. Sunset Rd.* ☎ *509/588–3155* ⊕ *www.hedgesfamilyestate.com* ⊘ *Apr.–Nov., weekends 11–5 or by appointment.*

Kiona Vineyards Winery. John Williams planted the first grapes on Red Mountain in 1975, made his first wines in 1980, and produced the first commercial Kiona Lemberger, a light German red, in the United States. Today Williams's recently constructed 10,000-square-foot tasting room features a 180-degree view of Red Mountain and the Rattlesnake Hills. Kiona also produces premium Riesling, Chenin Blanc, Chardonnay, Cabernet Sauvignon, Merlot, Syrah, Sangiovese, and dessert wines. You can picnic on the patio and, in addition to the wines, a range of meats and cheeses can be purchased. ⊠ *44612 Sunset Rd.* ☎ *509/588–6716* ⊕ *www.kionawine.com* ⊘ *Daily noon–5.*

Terra Blanca. It's named for the calcium carbonate in its soil—Terra Blanca is Latin for "white earth"—and from this unique soil grow wine grapes that produce such specialties as Syrah, Merlot, Cabernet Sauvignon, and Chardonnay. ⊠ *34715 N. Demoss Rd.* ☎ *509/588–6082* ⊕ *www.terrablanca.com* ⊘ *Daily 11–6 (from 10 am Apr.–Oct.).*

SPOKANE AND EASTERN WASHINGTON

WELCOME TO SPOKANE AND EASTERN WASHINGTON

TOP REASONS TO GO

★ **Historic Lodgings:**
Take a step back in time.
Visit the historic hotels and
inns in Spokane, Walla
Walla, and Dayton, which
have been updated with
modern amenities and
high-tech touches, yet retain
the flavor of yesteryear.

★ **Natural Wonders:**
Get off the beaten path
to experience the unique
waters of Soap Lake, see
the cliffs and canyons
along the Columbia River,
and hike in national forests.

★ **Wineries:** Explore
the many wineries in
Walla Walla, Tri-Cities,
and Spokane.

★ **Family Attractions:**
Slip in a little education on
your family vacation by
visiting pioneer museums,
then play at water parks
and Spokane's sprawl-
ing Riverfront Park.

1 **Southeastern Washington.** In the wide-open areas of the Walla Walla and Columbia Valleys, hillsides are covered with rows of grapevines and wind turbines. Lodging, restaurants, museums, and wine-tasting opportunities can be found in Walla Walla and the Tri-Cities. Farther east are historic Dayton and the college town of Pullman.

2 **Spokane.** The second-largest city in Washington is home to one of the state's best hotels, the restored Davenport, and several other historic lodgings. There are numerous restaurants, from fine-dining to family-friendly; a fun kids' museum, new science museum, and interesting history museum; and two especially notable parks (Manito, with its duck pond and Japanese Garden, and Riverfront, with lots of activities for the whole family).

3 **Along Route 90.** The highway through central Washington's desert lands can seem long and boring, but the farmers of Grant County's irrigated lands perk things up a bit with crop signs in the fences and lighted holiday displays. Venture off the main route to discover the stunning Cave B Inn at Sagecliffe by the Columbia River, see pioneer history displays in Ephrata, and experience the healing waters of Soap Lake, before heading back on I-90 through Moses Lake.

GETTING ORIENTED

The main route through eastern Washington is I-90. Coming from the west, as you leave the Cascade Mountains and its foothills behind, the terrain turns to desert and sagebrush, before crossing over the Columbia River and reaching the irrigated areas where fields of crops grow. In this area's barren, dry lands a new type of farming has emerged— wind farms with giant turbines that transform the landscape and provide electricity. The southeast part of the state offers a more verdant setting—rolling hills and fields where rain helps produce abundant crops of grains and wine grapes. The northeast part of the state is flanked by three mountain ranges (Selkirk, Okanogan, and Kettle River), which are considered foothills of the Rocky Mountains; this area is rich with lakes, rivers, cliffs, and meadows, and home to diverse wildlife.

18

Updated by
Shelley Arenas

The Columbia Plateau was created by a series of lava flows that were later deeply cut by glacial floods. Because its soil is mostly made up of alluvial deposits and windblown silt (known to geologists as loess), it's very fertile. But little annual rainfall means that its vast central section—more than 30,000 square miles from the foothills of the Cascades and the northeastern mountains east to Idaho and south to Oregon—has no forests. In fact, except for a few scattered pine trees in the north, oaks in the southwest, and willows and cottonwoods along creeks and rivers, it has no trees.

This treeless expanse is part of an even larger steppe and desert region that runs north into Canada and south to California and the Sea of Cortez. There is water, however, carried from the mountains by the great Columbia and Snake rivers and their tributaries. Irrigation provides the region's cities with shrubs, trees, and flowers, and its fields bear a great variety of crops: asparagus, potatoes, apples, peaches, alfalfa, sweet corn, wheat, lentils, and much more. This bounty of agriculture makes the region prosperous, and provides funds for symphony halls and opera houses, theaters, art museums, and universities.

Southeast of the Columbia Plateau lies a region of rolling hills and fields. Farmers of the Palouse region and of the foothills of the Blue Mountains don't need to irrigate their fields, as rain here produces record crops of wheat, lentils, and peas. It's a blessed landscape, flowing green and golden under the sun in waves of loam. In the Walla Walla Valley the traditional crops of wheat and sweet onions remain, but more than 1,800 acres of grapes now supply more than 100 wineries that have opened in the past few decades. The region is not only fertile, it is historically significant as well. The Lewis and Clark expedition passed through the Palouse in 1805, and Walla Walla was one of the earliest settlements in the inland Northwest.

The northeastern mountains, from the Okanogan to the Pend Oreille Valley, consist of granite peaks, glaciated cliffs, grassy uplands, and sunlit forests. Few Washingtonians seem to know about this region's attractions, however. Even at the height of the summer its roads and trails are rarely crowded.

The hidden jewel of these mountains is the Sanpoil River valley, which is a miniature Yosemite Valley, with vertical rock walls rising 2,000–3,000 feet straight from the river, their height accentuated by the narrowness of the canyon. The valley has no amenities, and is still in the possession of its original owners, the Native Americans of the Colville Reservation, who have preserved its beauty. These wild highlands have few visitor facilities. Towns in the Okanogan Valley and the regional metropolis of Spokane, on the fringes of the region, offer more services.

SPOKANE AND EASTERN WASHINGTON PLANNER

WHEN TO GO

Eastern Washington has four distinct seasons, with generally very hot summers and sometimes very snowy winters. Recreational activities are geared to the specific season, with several downhill ski resorts open for skiing and snowboarding, and Nordic skiing available in the national forests, too. In summer, water activities on the lakes and rivers are popular, and there are many places to pursue hiking, backpacking, cycling, fishing, and hunting. Eastern Washington rarely feels crowded, though popular campgrounds may fill in summer. Lodging rates tend to be higher between Memorial Day and Labor Day, so visiting off-season can reduce costs. Spring and fall are both beautiful seasons to explore the region. In smaller towns certain attractions are open only from May through September, so call ahead to plan visits to sights. Also call well in advance to make reservations during college special-event weekends in Pullman and Walla Walla.

FESTIVALS AND EVENTS

May Spring Release Weekend, Walla Walla wineries

June Celebrate Walla Walla Valley Wine, Walla Walla wineries

July Grant County Food and Wine Festival, Moses Lake

August Peach Festival, Green Bluff (near Spokane)

September Balloon & Wine Festival, Quincy

Farmer Consumer Awareness Day, Quincy

Pig Out in the Park, Spokane

Apple & Harvest Festival, Green Bluff (near Spokane)

Sustainable September Festival, Spokane

Harvest Festival, West Richland

October Apple & Harvest Festival, Green Bluff (near Spokane)

November Tri-Cities Wine Festival, Kennewick

Fall Release Weekend, Walla Walla wineries

Spokane Cork & Keg Festival

December Holiday Barrel Tasting, Walla Walla wineries

Wine Country Holiday Open House, Red Mountain wineries, Tri-Cities

GETTING HERE AND AROUND

AIR TRAVEL

Spokane International Airport is the main hub for air travel in eastern Washington. Smaller airports include Pullman, Tri-Cities, Walla Walla, and Lewiston, Idaho (across the border from Clarkston). Spokane International Airport is served by the airlines listed here; the Tri-Cities Airport is served by Allegiant, Delta, Horizon, and United. Horizon serves the smaller regional airports.

Contacts Alaska Airlines ☎ 800/252–7522 ⊕ www.alaskair.com. **Allegiant Air** ☎ 702/505–8888 ⊕ www.allegiantair.com. **Delta** ☎ 800/221–1212 ⊕ www.delta.com. **Frontier Airlines** ☎ 800/432–1359 ⊕ www.flyfrontier.com. **Horizon Air** ☎ 800/252–7522 ⊕ www.alaskaair.com. **Lewiston-Nez Perce County Airport** ✉ 406 Burrell Ave., Lewiston, Idaho ☎ 208/746–4471 ⊕ www.golws.com. **Southwest** ☎ 800/435–9792 ⊕ www.southwest.com. **Tri-Cities Airport** ✉ 3601 N. 20th Ave., Pasco ☎ 509/547–6352 ⊕ www.portofpasco.org. **United Airlines** ☎ 800/864–8331 ⊕ www.united.com. **US Airways** ☎ 800/428–4322 ⊕ www.usairways.com.

CAR TRAVEL

I–90 is the most direct route from Seattle to Spokane, over the Cascade Mountains (Snoqualmie Pass). U.S. 2 (Stevens Pass), an alternate route, begins north of Seattle near Everett, and passes through Wenatchee and Coulee City. South of I–90, U.S. 395 leads to the Tri-Cities from the east; the Tri-Cities can also be accessed via I–82 from the west. Past the Tri-Cities, continue on I–82 then U.S. 12 to reach Walla Walla. U.S. 195 traverses southeastern Washington to Pullman. Leave U.S. 195 at Colfax, heading southwest on Highway 26 and then 127, and finally U.S. 12 to Dayton and Walla Walla. Gas stations along the main highways cater to truckers, and some are open 24 hours.

RESTAURANTS

Nearly every small town in eastern Washington has at least one fast-food drive-through for a quick meal on the go, but choosing a slower pace will reward visitors with an authentic dining experience that often doesn't cost much more. Local diners and cafés are great spots for getting a hearty breakfast of traditional favorites like farm-fresh eggs or biscuits and gravy. Somewhat surprisingly, several of the small towns have outstanding dining options too; check out our restaurant reviews for Omak, Colville, and Dayton. At many restaurants there's an emphasis on locally grown, organic foods. With the region's many farms, it's easy to source produce, grains, poultry, meat, and dairy items, and some restaurants have their own gardens on-site for the freshest produce of all. Spokane has a good diversity of cuisines and some highly acclaimed restaurants, but up-and-coming Walla Walla is becoming a mecca for foodies and wine lovers too. *Prices in the reviews are the average cost of a main course at dinner or, if dinner is not served, at lunch.*

HOTELS

Family-owned motels and budget chains are prevalent in small towns like Colville, Omak, Grand Coulee, Moses Lake, and Pullman. More of these properties are updating their amenities to include modern touches such as flat-screen TVs; others can feel dated, but at least the prices are reasonable, except during special events when demand spikes create rate hikes. Several pleasant bed-and-breakfasts with friendly innkeepers are found in Spokane, Walla Walla, Dayton, and Uniontown (near Pullman), but with no more than six suites at each it's usually necessary to call ahead for a reservation. There are several historic hotels built in the early 1900s and restored in recent years that are definitely worth visiting in Spokane, Walla Walla, and Dayton. A stay at the Cave B Inn by the Columbia River—in one of its cliff houses, cavern rooms, or luxury yurts—is a recommended destination experience too. *Prices in the reviews are the lowest cost of a standard double room in high season.*

SOUTHEASTERN WASHINGTON

The most populated area in this region is the Tri-Cities—Pasco, Kennewick, and Richland. Each town has its own character, but their proximity makes it easy to access an array of services and attractions like local wineries and pleasant riverfront parks. The town of Walla Walla has a historic downtown shopping district with innovative restaurant choices, wine-tasting rooms, elegant B&Bs, and the impressive Marcus Whitman Hotel. Just outside of town, wineries in bucolic country settings are as enjoyable for picnickers as for serious wine connoisseurs. If you continue east and north on quiet two-lane highways you'll discover Dayton, another historic small town, and Pullman, home of Washington State University.

18

RICHLAND

202 miles southeast of Seattle, 145 miles southwest of Spokane.

Richland is the northernmost of the three municipalities along the bank of the Columbia River known as the Tri-Cities (the others are Pasco and Kennewick). Founded in the 1880s, Richland was a pleasant farming village until 1942, when the federal government built a nuclear reactor on the nearby Hanford Nuclear Reservation. The Hanford site was instrumental in the building of the Tri-Cities, and still plays a major role in the area's economy. In recent years this has also become a major wine producing area. You can find more than 100 wineries within a 50-mile radius, many with tasting rooms.

GETTING HERE AND AROUND

The Tri-Cities Airport in Pasco is served by Allegiant, Delta, Horizon, and United. Taxis and rental cars are available there. Some hotels also offer an airport shuttle. Greyhound Bus Lines and Amtrak's *Empire Builder* both stop in Pasco. Ben Franklin Transit serves all three cities. By car, I–82 is the main east–west highway; from Ritzville or Spokane,

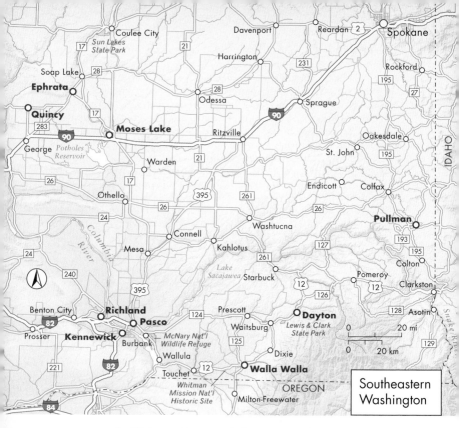

Southeastern
Washington

take Highway 395 to reach the Tri-Cities; from Ellensburg and Yakima, take Highway 82 south and east.

Contact Ben Franklin Transit ☎ *509/735–5100* ⊕ *www.bft.org.*

ESSENTIALS

Visitor Information City of Richland ✉ *505 Swift Blvd.* ☎ *509/942–7390* ⊕ *www.ci.richland.wa.us.* **Tri-Cities Visitor and Convention Bureau.** For winery information and maps, contact Tri-Cities Visitor and Convention Bureau. ✉ *7130 W. Grandridge Blvd., Ste. B, Kennewick* ☎ *800/254–5824, 509/735–8486* ⊕ *www.visittri-cities.com.*

EXPLORING

Barnard Griffin Winery and Tasting Room. Owners Rob Griffin and Deborah Barnard offer a variety of fine wines, including excellent Merlot and Cabernet. The art gallery adds class to the wine-tasting experience. ✉ *878 Tulip La.* ☎ *509/627–0266* ⊕ *www.barnardgriffin.com* ⊗ *Daily 10–5; wine bar Wed.–Sat. 4–9.*

Bookwalter Winery. Next door to Barnard Griffin Winery, Bookwalter produces red wines aged in French oak barrels and whites that are 100% stainless-steel fermented. The classic Merlot is celebrated. Blends are prevalent in both reds and whites. Live music plays Wednesday through Saturday evenings year-round. JBistro restaurant features a changing variety of artisan cheeses, heartier fare such as steaks, burgers, and salmon, and rich desserts. ✉ *894 Tulip La.* ☎ *509/627–5000, 877/667–8300* 🌐 *www.bookwalterwines.com* 🎟 *$10 tasting fee; applied toward wine purchase $35 or more* 🕒 *Sun.–Tues. 11–8, Wed.–Sat. 11–11.*

FAMILY **CREHST Museum** (*Columbia River Exhibition of History, Science, and Technology*). Displays show the area's development from prehistoric times to the nuclear age and there are educational exhibits, some of which are hands-on. The outdoor Boomers on Wheels exhibit depicts local trailer life in the 1940s, when the Hanford Construction Camp was the largest trailer camp in the world. A Lewis and Clark exhibit tells the story of the famous explorers and their expedition through the area more than 200 years ago. Another exhibit highlights fish species of the Columbia River. The area's geology is depicted in a mural and hands-on rock display. ✉ *95 Lee Blvd.* ☎ *509/943–9000, 877/789–9935* 🌐 *www.crehst.org* 🎟 *$5* 🕒 *Mon.–Sat. 10–5, Sun. noon–5.*

WHERE TO EAT AND STAY

For expanded hotel reviews, visit Fodors.com.

$$$ SEAFOOD 🍴 **Anthony's at Columbia Point.** For years the Anthony's chain has been known for fine waterfront dining in western Washington; since 2004 the Tri-Cities has had its own Anthony's on the Columbia River waterfront. Seafood is the specialty—even the appetizers are fish-focused, including pan-fried Willapa Bay oysters and fresh Puget Sound mussels. Dungeness crab (whole, in fettuccine, or in crab cakes), Idaho rainbow trout, char-grilled Alaskan halibut, Northwest cioppino, and several steaks are among the many entrée offerings. Anthony's weekday sunset four-course dinners are also popular. [$] *Average main: $25* ✉ *550 Columbia Point Dr.* ☎ *509/946–3474* 🌐 *www.anthonys.com.*

$ AMERICAN 🍴 **Atomic Ale Brewpub and Eatery.** The staff is friendly at this small, casual brewpub, which serves mainly house-brewed beers. The delicious pizzas are cooked in a wood-fired oven; sandwiches, salads, and soups (including potato, made with the in-house brew) are also fine. Local memorabilia is displayed throughout the restaurant, and the history of the Hanford nuclear plant is depicted in photos on the walls. [$] *Average main: $16* ✉ *1015 Lee Blvd.* ☎ *509/946–5465* 🌐 *www.atomicalebrewpub.com.*

$ HOTEL 🏨 **Red Lion Hotel Richland Hanford House.** Overlooking the Columbia River and convenient for many major Hanford contractors and government facilities, this hotel borders a greenbelt riverfront park and has easy access to trails along the levee; ask for a room with a river view. **Pros:** nice location; free airport shuttle; some rooms have views of river. **Cons:** older hotel, though some rooms have been updated; can get noisy with larger groups/teams. [$] *Rooms from: $139* ✉ *802 George Washington Way* ☎ *509/946–7611* 🌐 *www.redlion.com* 🛏 *142 rooms, 7 suites* 🍽 *Breakfast.*

$ HOTEL FAMILY 🏨 **Shilo Inn Suites Hotel.** Bordering the Columbia River above the mouth of the Yakima, the Shilo Inn has easy access to riverside trails and parks. **Pros:** excellent value; convenient riverfront location walking distance to town and park. **Cons:** rooms by outdoor pool can be noisy; property needs updating; no elevators. [$] *Rooms from: $109* ✉ *50 Comstock St.*

18

☎ *509/946–4661, 800/222–2244* ⊕ *www.shiloinns.com* ⌿ *151 rooms, 13 suites* ⏣ *Breakfast.*

PASCO

10 miles east of Richland.

Tree-shaded Pasco, a college town and the Franklin County seat, is an oasis of green on the Columbia River near a site where the Lewis and Clark expedition made camp in 1805. The city began as a railroad switchyard and now has a busy container port. The neoclassical Franklin County Courthouse (1907) is worth a visit for its fine marble interior.

The Pasco Basin has first-rate vineyards and wineries and some of the state's most fertile land. You can purchase the regional bounty at the farmers' market, held downtown every Wednesday and Saturday morning during the growing season.

GETTING HERE AND AROUND

The Tri-Cities Airport is in Pasco; Allegiant, Delta, Horizon and United operate there. Taxis and rental cars are both available and some hotels offer an airport shuttle. Ben Franklin Transit serves all three cities. By car, I–82 is the main east–west highway; from Ritzville or Spokane, take Highway 395 to reach the Tri-Cities; from Ellensburg and Yakima, take I–82 south and east.

Contact **Ben Franklin Transit** ☎ *509/735–5100* ⊕ *www.bft.org.*

ESSENTIALS

Visitor Information **City of Pasco** ✉ *525 N. Third Ave.* ☎ *509/544–3080* ⊕ *www.pasco-wa.gov.*

EXPLORING

Franklin County Historical Museum. Here you'll find numerous items illustrating local history, including Native American artifacts. Revolving exhibits have featured the Lewis and Clark expedition, the railroad, and World War II. ✉ *305 N. 4th Ave.* ☎ *509/547–3714* ⊕ *www.franklincountyhistoricalsociety.org* ✆ *Donations accepted* ☉ *Tues.–Fri. noon–4.*

Preston Premium Wines. This is one of the Pasco Basin's oldest wineries. The tasting room has great views of surrounding fields, and visitors are welcome to picnic in the winery's park setting. ✉ *502 E. Vineyard Dr.* ☎ *509/545–1990* ⊕ *www.prestonwines.com* ✆ *Free* ☉ *Daily 10–5:30.*

Sacajawea State Park. At the confluence of the Snake and Columbia rivers, this park occupies the site of Ainsworth, a railroad town that flourished from 1879 to 1884. It's named for the Shoshoni woman who guided the Lewis and Clark expedition over the Rocky Mountains and down the Snake River. The 284-acre day-use park has an interpretive center and a large display of Native American tools. A beach, boat launch, picnic area, and children's playground round out the facilities; sand dunes, marshes, and ponds are great for watching wildlife. ✉ *2503 Sacajawea Park Road, Off U.S. 12, 5 miles southeast of Pasco* ☎ *509/545–2361* ⊕ *www.parks.wa.gov* ✆ *Discover*

Pass $10/day or $30/year (valid at all state parks) 🕒 *Apr.–Oct., 6:30 am–dusk.*

WHERE TO EAT AND STAY

For expanded hotel reviews, visit Fodors.com.

$$$ AMERICAN 🍴 **Bin No. 20 Wine Bar and Restaurant.** Opened as a wine bar, Bin No. 20 still carries over 140 kinds of wine, many from Washington state. It expanded beyond the wine focus to become a full-fledged steak and seafood restaurant. Signature dishes include the Bin 20 chop salad and 28-day wet-aged beef fillet and rib-eye steak. On Friday and Saturday nights live smooth jazz accompanies the dinner hours. Happy hour runs 4 to 7 Monday through Thursday. [$] *Average main: $30* ✉ *2525 N. 20th St.* ☎ *509/544–3939* 🌐 *www.bin20.com* 🕒 *No lunch.*

$ HOTEL 🏨 **Red Lion Hotel Pasco.** This full-service hotel is the largest in the Tri-Cities and popular for conventions. **Pros:** as at all other Red Lions, the Roaring Start breakfast buffet is available for $4.95; two restaurants on-site. **Cons:** very large hotel, so some rooms can be a long walk from the lobby. [$] *Rooms from: $129* ✉ *2525 N. 20th St.* ☎ *509/547–0701* 🌐 *www.redlion.com* 🛏 *279 rooms, 10 suites* 🍽 *No meals.*

KENNEWICK

3 miles southwest of Pasco, directly across the Columbia River.

In its 100-year history, Kennewick (*ken*-uh-wick) evolved from a railroad town to a farm-supply center and then to a bedroom community for Hanford workers and a food-processing capital for the Columbia Basin. The name Kennewick translates as "grassy place," and Native Americans had winter villages here long before Lewis and Clark passed through. Arrowheads and other artifacts aside, the 9,000-year-old skeleton of Kennewick Man has been studied by scientists at the University of Washington to determine whether its features are Native American or, as some claim, Caucasian.

GETTING HERE AND AROUND

The Tri-Cities Airport is in nearby Pasco, served by Allegiant, Delta, Horizon, and United. Taxis and rental cars are available and some hotels offer an airport shuttle. Ben Franklin Transit serves all three cities. By car, I–82 is the main east–west highway; from Ritzville or Spokane, take Highway 395 to reach the Tri-Cities; from Ellensburg and Yakima, take I–82 south and east.

Contact **Ben Franklin Transit** ☎ *509/735–5100* 🌐 *www.bft.org.*

ESSENTIALS

Visitor Information **City of Kennewick** ✉ *210 W. 6th Ave.* ☎ *509/585–4200* 🌐 *www.go2kennewick.com.*

EXPLORING

Columbia Park. Adjacent to the Columbia River, this is one of Washington's great parks. Its 4½-mile-long riverfront has boat ramps, a golf course, picnic areas, playgrounds (including an aquatic one), train ride, ropes course, and family fishing pond. In summer, hydroplane races are

18

held here. ✉ *Columbia Trail Dr., between U.S. 240 and the Columbia River* ☎ *509/585–4293* 🌐 *www.go2kennewick.com.*

Badger Mountain Vineyard. A beautiful view of the valley and wine made without pesticides or preservatives is what you'll find here. Badger Mountain was the first wine-grape vineyard in Washington State to be certified organic. ✉ *1106 N. Jurupa St.* ☎ *800/643–9463* 🌐 *www.badgermtnvineyard.com* 🎟 *$5 tasting fee; applied to purchases of bottles* 🕒 *Daily 10–5.*

East Benton County Historical Museum. The entire entryway to the museum is made of petrified wood. Photographs, agricultural displays, petroglyphs, and a large collection of arrowheads interpret area history. Kennewick's oldest park, Keewaydin, is across the street. ✉ *205 Keewaydin Dr.* ☎ *509/582–7704* 🌐 *www.ebchs.org* 🎟 *$4* 🕒 *Tues.–Sat. noon–4.*

Ice Harbor Brewing Company. If you prefer a fine-crafted brew, this 7,000-square-foot brewery has a tasting room, gift shop, and a pub with an antique bar. ✉ *206 N. Benton St.* ☎ *509/582–5340, 888/701–2350* 🌐 *www.iceharbor.com* 🎟 *Free* 🕒 *Mon.–Wed. 11–9, Thurs.–Sat. 11–10, Sun. noon–6.*

Ice Harbor Lock and Dam. At 103 feet, the single-lift locks here are among the world's highest. ✉ *2763 Monument Dr., about 12 miles southeast of Kennewick, Burbank* ☎ *509/547–7781* 🌐 *www.nww.usace.army.mil/Locations/DistrictLocksandDams/IceHarborLockandDam.aspx* 🎟 *Free* 🕒 *Visitor center Apr.–Sept., daily 9–5.*

McNary National Wildlife Refuge. More than 200 species of birds have been identified here, and many waterfowl make it their winter home. But its 15,000 acres of water and marsh, croplands, grasslands, trees, and shrubs are most enjoyable in spring and summer, when there is no hunting. The Environmental Education Center features hands-on exhibits. A self-guided 2-mile trail winds through the marshes, and a cabinlike blind hidden in the reeds allows you to watch wildlife up close. Other recreation includes boating, fishing, hiking, and horseback-riding. ✉ *64 Maple Rd., ¼ mile east of U.S. 12, south of Snake River Bridge, Burbank* ☎ *509/546–8300* 🌐 *www.fws.gov/mcnary* 🎟 *Free, $10 hunting fee* 🕒 *Daily during daylight hrs. Headquarters Mon.–Thurs. 8–4:30, Fri. 8–3:30.*

WHERE TO EAT AND STAY

For expanded hotel reviews, visit Fodors.com.

$$$ AMERICAN

🍴 **The Cedars.** Right on the edge of the Columbia River, Cedars has beautiful views and a 200-foot dock for boaters coming to dine. A deck is open seasonally, and it's popular as an after-work gathering place. The menu includes top-quality steaks, pasta, and poultry. Shellfish are also on the menu, as well as several kinds of fresh fish, including salmon, halibut, swordfish, and ahi tuna. The fish are available with a choice of sauces and the option to be prepared blackened in Cajun spices in a cast iron skillet. An extensive wine list features many local labels. Save room for the house-made mud pie. [$] *Aver-*

age main: $28 ⊠ *355 Clover Island Dr.* ☎ *509/582–2143* ⊕ *www. cedarsrest.com* ⊗ *No lunch.*

$ ☂ **Red Lion Columbia Center.** Talk about convenience: it's next to a regional
HOTEL   shopping mall and a few blocks from the convention center. **Pros:** handy location; good value; seasonal pool. **Cons:** no full-service restaurant (many at the nearby mall); best for business guests. $ *Rooms from: $139* ⊠ *1101 N. Columbia Center Blvd.* ☎ *509/783–0611, 800/733–5466* ⊕ *www.redlion.com* ⤴ *153 rooms, 9 suites* ◎ *No meals.*

WALLA WALLA

52 miles southeast of Kennewick.

Walla Walla, founded in the 1850s on the site of a Nez Perce village, was Washington's first metropolis. As late as the 1880s its population was larger than that of Seattle. Walla Walla occupies a lush green valley below the rugged Blue Mountains. Its beautiful downtown boasts old residences, green parks, and the campus of Whitman College, Washington's oldest institution of higher learning.

A successful downtown restoration has earned Walla Walla high praise. The heart of downtown, at 2nd and Main streets, looks as pretty as it did 60 years ago, with beautifully maintained old buildings and newer structures designed to fit in. Walla Walla's Main Street is the winner of the "Great American Main Street Award" from the National Trust for Historic Preservation. Residents and visitors come here to visit shops, wineries, cafés, and restaurants.

West of town, the green Walla Walla Valley—famous for asparagus, sweet onions, cherries, and wheat—has emerged as Washington's premier viticultural region. Tall grain elevators mark Lowden, a few miles west of Walla Walla, a wheat hamlet that now has several wineries.

18

GETTING HERE AND AROUND

Coming from points west, Walla Walla is reached via I–82 east of the Tri-Cities, then Highway 12, which is still a two-lane highway in places but has recently been expanded west of Walla Walla and into the town. From Spokane and the northeast, travel is all by two-lane highway, going south on Highway 195 to Colfax, then southwest via highways 26 and 127 to Highway 12, then continuing south through Dayton and Waitsburg. Horizon Air runs two daily flights (one on Saturday) each way between Walla Walla and Seattle.

Contacts Horizon Air ☎ *800/252–7522* ⊕ *www.alaskaair.com.* **Walla Walla Regional Airport** ⊠ *45 Terminal Loop Rd., Walla Walla* ☎ *509/525–3100* ⊕ *www.wallawallaairport.com.*

ESSENTIALS

Visitor Information Walla Walla Valley Chamber of Commerce ⊠ *29 E. Sumach St.* ☎ *509/525–0850, 877/998–4748* ⊕ *www.wwvchamber.com.*

EXPLORING

Canoe Ridge Vineyards. Owned by Precept Wine, this vineyard produces Merlot, Cabernet Sauvignon, and Chardonnay. The tasting room is in Walla Walla's historic Engine House. ⊠ *1102 W. Cherry*

St. ☎ *509/525–1843* ⊕ *www.canoeridgevineyard.com* ⊙ *Thurs.–Mon. 11–5.*

FAMILY **Fort Walla Walla Museum.** A few miles west of Walla Walla, the museum occupies 15 acres at Fort Walla Walla Park. A 17-building pioneer village depicts the region's life in the 1800s, and four halls house military, agricultural, and penitentiary exhibits. In 2011, the museum expanded with a new entrance hall and galleries. ⊠ *755 Myra Rd.* ☎ *509/525–7703* ⊕ *www.fortwallawallamuseum.org* 🎫 *$7* ⊙ *Apr.–Oct., daily 10–5; Nov.–Dec., daily 10–4; Jan.–Mar., weekdays 10–4.*

L'Ecole No. 41. Housed in the lower floors of a circa-1915 schoolhouse, this winery produces outstanding Sémillon and Merlot, among other wines. The tasting room is in one of the old classrooms, and details like chalkboards and books add to the restored school's character. ⊠ *41 Lowden School Rd., Lowden* ☎ *509/525–0940* ⊕ *www.lecole.com* 🎫 *$5 tasting fee, refunded with wine purchase* ⊙ *Daily 10–5.*

Pioneer Park. Planted with native and exotic flowers and trees, Pioneer Park is a shady, turn-of-the-20th-century park with a fine aviary. It was originally landscaped by sons of Frederick Law Olmsted, who designed New York City's Central Park. ⊠ *E. Alder St. and Division St.* ⊕ *www.ci.walla-walla.wa.us.*

Seven Hills Winery. Here, owner Casey McClellan makes well-balanced Cabernet Sauvignon, Malbec, and several white wines too. The winery is in Walla Walla's historic Whitehouse-Crawford building. ⊠ *212 N. 3rd Ave.* ☎ *509/529–7198, 877/777–7870* ⊕ *www.sevenhillswinery.com* ⊙ *Weekdays 10–5, Sat. 10–2.*

Sinclair Estate Vineyards. This downtown tasting room for one of Walla Walla's newest wineries opened in 2010, and wines available here include Syrah, Chardonnay, and two blends. Owners Tim and Kathy Sinclair also own Vine and Roses Bed and Breakfast, and their love for French antiques and fine art is evident in the elegant tasting room. There's even a grand piano and live music on Friday evening, with no cover charge. ⊠ *109-B E. Main St.* ☎ *509/876–4300* ⊕ *www.sinclairestatevineyards.com* ⊙ *Sat.–Thurs. 10–5, Fri. 10–5 and 7–10.*

Three Rivers Winery. About a mile east of L'Ecole No. 41, this winery is just off U.S. 12 and is surrounded by vineyards. It produces premium Cabernet Sauvignon, Merlot, Malbec, Petit Verdot, Chardonnay, and Riesling. It also has a nice tasting room, a gift shop, summer concerts, and a 3-hole golf course. ⊠ *5641 Old Hwy. 12* ☎ *509/526–9463* ⊕ *www.threeriverswinery.com* ⊙ *Daily 10–5.*

Waterbrook Winery. The tasting room, part of a facility on 75 acres, has an indoor-outdoor feel, with a spacious patio and outdoor fireplace, hillside views, and natural landscaping and ponds. Waterbrook is best known for Merlot, Chardonnay, and Cabernet. ⊠ *10518 W. U.S. Hwy. 12* ☎ *509/522–1262* ⊕ *www.waterbrook.com* ⊙ *Sun.–Thurs. 10–6, Fri.–Sat. 10–7.*

Whitman College. Large, tree-lined lawns surround the many beautiful 19th-century stone and brick structures of the Whitman College cam-

L'Ecole No. 41 winery

pus. The school began as a seminary in 1859 and became a college in 1883. ⊠ *345 Boyer Ave.* ☎ *509/527–5111* ⊕ *www.whitman.edu.*

FAMILY **Whitman Mission National Historic Site.** This is a reconstruction of Waiilatpu Mission, a Presbyterian outpost established on Cayuse lands in 1836. The park preserves the foundations of the mission buildings, a short segment of the Oregon Trail, and, on a nearby hill, the graveyard where the Native American victims of an 1847 measles epidemic and subsequent uprising are buried. ⊠ *328 Whitman Mission Rd., 7 miles west of downtown* ☎ *509/522–6360, 509/529–2761* ⊕ *www.nps.gov/whmi* ☞ *Free* ☉ *Daily dawn–dusk; visitor center open 9–4.*

Woodward Canyon Winery. Lovers of fine wines make pilgrimages to Woodward Canyon Winery, 12 miles west of Walla Walla, for the superb Cabernet Sauvignon, Chardonnay, and Merlot. The winery occasionally produces other varietals and also has a second label, Nelms Road, that focuses on younger and more affordable red wines. ⊠ *11920 W. U.S. 12, Lowden* ☎ *509/525–4129* ⊕ *www.woodwardcanyon.com* ☞ *$5 or $15 tasting fee* ☉ *Daily 10–5.*

WHERE TO EAT

$ ✕ **Olive Marketplace & Cafe.** Kick back and enjoy good food in a casual CAFÉ environment in this two-level downtown café. Between pouring its first cup of coffee at 8 am and the last glass of wine from the wine bar before closing at 9 pm, the café serves reasonably-priced and varied items. The breakfast menu ranges from classics like eggs Benedict to contemporary dishes like roasted squash hash and poached eggs with polenta cakes. The all-day menu features such standards as vegetarian lasagna and pot pie, along with sandwiches, salads, and seasonal soups. Flatbread pizzas are popular too, including the unique prosciutto and grape, smoked salmon, or spicy adobo braised beef with jalapeños varieties. There's free live music every Thursday night. [$] *Average main: $14* ✉ *21 E. Main St.* ☎ *509/526–0200* 🌐 *www.olivemarketplaceandcafe.com.*

$$$ ITALIAN Fodor's Choice ★ 🍴 **T. Maccarones.** Italian food with a very contemporary flare is the draw at "T-Mac's," along with the neighborly feel of the small, two-level restaurant. It's the kind of place that quickly becomes a favorite for locals. Customers are often greeted personally by friendly owner Tom Maccarone, a native of Walla Walla who returned in 2005 after years in the Seattle area. Chef Preston Crowe's menu focuses on sustainable practices and fresh, local, and organic ingredients for dishes like sweet potato gnocchi and honey cinnamon brined free-range chicken. The T-Mac and Cheese is rich and delicious; desserts are baked in-house. [$] *Average main: $25* ✉ *4 N. Colville St.* ☎ *509/522–4776* 🌐 *www.tmaccarones.com.*

$$$ AMERICAN Fodor's Choice ★ 🍴 **Whitehouse-Crawford Restaurant.** In a former wood mill, this restaurant has gained a reputation for quality and excellence over its decade of existence, thanks to chef Jamie Guerin. Local is the watchword here, where hamburgers are made with grass-fed beef from Blue Valley Meats, and more than a dozen nearby purveyors supply produce, cheese, meat, eggs, and coffee. Try the smoked trout and warm spinach salad, Painted Hills beef tenderloin steak, or roasted rockfish, and save room for the homemade ice cream, which you can take home by the pint. The extensive wine list features many Walla Walla Valley winemakers. [$] *Average main: $28* ✉ *55 W. Cherry St.* ☎ *509/525–2222* 🌐 *www.whitehousecrawford.com* ⏲ *Closed Tues. No lunch.*

WHERE TO STAY

For expanded hotel reviews, visit Fodors.com.

$$$ B&B/INN Fodor's Choice ★ 🏨 **Inn at Abeja.** Twenty-five acres of gardens and vineyards surround a turn-of-the-20th-century farm with guest cottages and suites. **Pros:** beautiful grounds; high-end; very spacious accommodations with kitchens; private tours of the on-site winery. **Cons:** closed from mid-December to February. [$] *Rooms from: $245* ✉ *2014 Mill Creek Rd.* ☎ *509/522–1234* 🌐 *www.abeja.net/inn* 🛏 *4 cottages, 3 suites* ⏲ *Closed mid-Dec.–Feb.* 🍽 *Breakfast.*

$$ B&B/INN 🏨 **Green Gables Inn.** One block from the Whitman Campus, this 1909 Arts and Crafts-style mansion sits among flowering plants and shrubs on a quaint, tree-lined street. **Pros:** mini-fridges in rooms are a nice touch; pretty setting; good room amenities for a B&B. **Cons:** two-night minimum stay on weekends. [$] *Rooms from: $165* ✉ *922 Bonsella St.* ☎ *509/876–4373* 🌐 *www.greengablesinn.com* 🛏 *4 rooms, 1 suite* 🍽 *Breakfast.*

$$ HOTEL Fodor's Choice ★ 🏨 **Marcus Whitman Hotel.** This 1928 hotel is *the* landmark in downtown Walla Walla, and guest quarters include spacious two-room parlor suites and spa suites in the historic tower building. **Pros:** range of accommodations available; downtown location; full breakfast buffet and parking included. **Cons:** no pool; no bathtubs in historic rooms. [$] *Rooms from: $155* ✉ *6 W. Rose St.* ☎ *509/525–2200, 866/826–9422* 🌐 *www.marcuswhitmanhotel.com* 🛏 *127 rooms, 16 suites* 🍽 *Breakfast.*

$$$ B&B/INN Fodor's Choice ★ **Vine and Roses Bed & Breakfast.** Just a block from Pioneer Park (⇨ *Exploring, above*), Walla Walla's finest bed-and-breakfast occupies an 1893 Victorian, extravagantly renovated to create an in-town oasis of luxury and grace. **Pros:** free tastings at the Sinclairs' other business, Sinclair Estate Vineyards; exclusive visits to other wineries can be arranged. **Cons:** as with many B&Bs, this isn't a place to bring kids. [$] *Rooms from: $229* ✉ *516 S. Division St.* ☎ *509/876–2113* 🌐 *www.vineandroses.com* 🛏 *5 suites* 🍴 *Breakfast.*

DAYTON

31 miles northeast of Walla Walla.

The tree-shaded county seat of Columbia County is the kind of Currier & Ives place many people conjure up when they imagine the best qualities of rural America. This tidy town has 117 buildings listed on the National Register of Historic Places, including the state's oldest railroad depot and courthouse.

GETTING HERE AND AROUND

Dayton is northeast of Walla Walla via Highway 12. From the Spokane area, take Highway 195 to Colfax, then veer southwest via Highways 26 and 127 before reaching Highway 12 and continuing into the town.

EXPLORING

Dayton Historical Depot Society. At Washington's oldest standing depot, the Dayton Historical Depot Society houses exhibits illustrating the history of Dayton and surrounding communities. ✉ *222 E. Commercial Ave.* ☎ *509/382–2026* 🌐 *www.daytonhistoricdepot.org* 🎟 *$5* ⏲ *May–Oct., Wed.–Sat. 10–5 (closed noon–1); Nov.–Apr., Wed.–Sat. 11–4.*

OFF THE BEATEN PATH

Palouse Falls State Park. Just north of its confluence with the Snake River, the Palouse River gushes over a basalt cliff higher than Niagara Falls and drops 198 feet into a steep-walled basin. Those who are surefooted can hike to an overlook above the falls, which are at their fastest during spring runoff in March. Just downstream from the falls at the Marmes Rock Shelter, remains of the earliest-known inhabitants of North America, dating back 10,000 years, were discovered by archaeologists. The park has 10 primitive campsites, open year-round, but with no water September through April. ✉ *Palouse Falls Rd. and State Route 261, 38 miles north of Dayton* ☎ *360/902–8844, 888/226–7688* 🌐 *www.parks.wa.gov* 🎟 *Discover Pass (valid at all state parks) $10/day or $30/annually; campsites $12* ⏲ *Summer, daily 6:30 am–dusk; winter, daily 8 am–dusk.*

WHERE TO EAT AND STAY

For expanded hotel reviews, visit Fodors.com.

$$$ FRENCH **Patit Creek Restaurant.** The chef turns out inspired beef, duck, and lamb dishes at this small café, which has been a favorite southeastern Washington eatery for more than 30 years. Portobello mushroom saltimbocca is a popular vegetarian option. Not only can the food be truly sublime, but the service is also excellent. The wine list is short, but has some rare Walla Walla Valley vintages. [$] *Average main: $27* ✉ *725 E. Dayton Ave.* ☎ *509/382–2625* ⏲ *Closed Sun.–Tues. No lunch Sat.*

18

Vine and Roses Bed & Breakfast

$$ AMERICAN

🍴 **Weinhard Café.** The past seems to echo through this restaurant, which is near the Weinhard Hotel and in what was once a pharmacy. Try a panini sandwich for lunch; for dinner, the rib-eye steak with a Cabernet-dried cherry reduction and brussels sprouts or the lamb kebabs with wild rice are good bets. Raspberry-rhubarb pie and coconut-lemon pie are dessert favorites. The menu changes frequently to highlight seasonal specialties. [$] *Average main: $18* ✉ *258 E. Main St.* ☎ *509/382–1681* 🌐 *www.weinhardcafe.com* 🕒 *Closed Mon., brunch only Sun.*

$ HOTEL

🏨 **Weinhard Hotel.** Echoes of the Old West ring through this hotel, built as a saloon and lodge in the late 1800s by the nephew of beer baron Henry Weinhard. **Pros:** friendly, attentive service; rooms reflect the history of the era but have modern features. **Cons:** rooms that face highway and can be noisy; some guests have complained about the continental breakfast. [$] *Rooms from: $125* ✉ *235 E. Main St.* ☎ *509/382–4032* 🌐 *www.weinhard.com* 🛏 *15 rooms* 🍽 *Breakfast.*

SPORTS AND THE OUTDOORS

Bluewood. The Bluewood ski area is 22 miles south of Dayton in the Umatilla National Forest. Though small, with just three triple chairlifts and about two-dozen runs, Bluewood is popular with both skiers and snowboarders because of its especially dry snow and high elevation. The resort also has 5 miles of cross-country trails as well as a restaurant, a pub, a ski shop, and a gift shop. Lift tickets cost $42. ✉ *2000 N. Touchet Rd.* ☎ *509/382–4725* 🌐 *www.bluewood.com* 🕒 *Mid-Nov.–Apr., Thurs.–Sun. 9–4.*

PULLMAN

75 miles south of Spokane.

This funky, liberal town—home of Washington State University—is in the heart of the rather conservative Palouse agricultural district. The town's freewheeling style can perhaps be explained by the fact that most of the students come from elsewhere in Washington.

The Palouse River, the upper course of which flows though the town, is an exception among Washington rivers: because of the high erosion rate of the light Palouse loess soils it usually runs muddy, almost like a gruel during floods (most Washington Rivers run clear, even after major storms). The 198-foot-high Palouse Falls farther downstream, near Washtucna, dramatically drop as a thin sheet of water into a steep box canyon.

GETTING HERE AND AROUND

Horizon Air flies into the local airport, where taxis and rental cars are available to get you to your destination. Most of the hotels have free airport shuttles, too. Pullman is reached via Highway 195, about 75 miles from Spokane.

Pullman-Moscow Regional Airport ⊠ *3200 Airport Complex N.* ☎ *509/338–3223* ⊕ *www.pullman-wa.gov/airport.*

ESSENTIALS

Visitor Information Pullman Chamber of Commerce ⊠ *415 N. Grand Ave.* ☎ *509/334–3565, 800/365–6948* ⊕ *www.pullmanchamber.com.*

EXPLORING

Kamiak Butte County Park. The 3,360-foot-tall butte is part of a mountain chain that was here long before the lava flows of the Columbia basin erupted millions of years ago. The park has great views of the Palouse hills and Idaho's snow-capped peaks to the east, as well as seven primitive campsites, a picnic area, and a 1-mile trail to the top of the butte. ⊠ *902 Kamiak Butte Park Rd., 12 miles north of Pullman, Palouse* ☎ *509/397–6238* ⊕ *www.whitmancounty.org* ⊠ *Free; campsite $15* ☉ *Daily 7–dusk.*

FAMILY

Fodor'sChoice

★

Washington State University. Opened in 1892 as the state's agriculture school, Washington State University today sprawls almost all the way to the Idaho state line. To park on campus, pick up a parking pass in the Security Building on Wilson Road. ⊠ *1 S.E. Stadium Way* ☎ *509/335–3564* ⊕ *www.wsu.edu* ⊠ *Free* ☉ *Daily.*

Ferdinand's. On weekdays between 9:30 and 4:30, you can pop into Ferdinand's, a soda fountain-cheese shop in the food-science building, to buy Aged Cougar Gold, a cheddar-type cheese in a can. ⊠ *2035 N.E. Ferdinand's La.* ☎ *509/335–2141* ⊕ *public.wsu.edu/creamery.*

Museum of Art. The small Museum of Art has lectures, as well as exhibitions that might include turned-wood art, Native American art, or landscaping displays. ⊠ *WSU Fine Arts Center, Wilson Rd. and Stadium Way* ☎ *509/335–1910* ⊕ *museum.wsu.edu* ⊠ *Free* ☉ *School year, Mon.–Wed., Fri. and Sat. 10–4, Thurs. 10–7; call for summer hrs.*

18

Charles R. Conner Museum of Zoology. This museum has the finest collection of stuffed birds and mammals and preserved invertebrates in the Pacific Northwest. ✉ *Abelson Hall, Library Rd. and College Ave.* ☎ *509/335–3515* 🌐 *sbs.wsu.edu/connermuseum* 🎟 *Free* 🕒 *Daily 8–5.*

WHERE TO EAT AND STAY

For expanded hotel reviews, visit Fodors.com.

$ ITALIAN 🍴 **Basilio's Italian Café.** In the heart of downtown, Basilio's serves up such classics as pasta, lasagna, and chicken parmigiana in addition to an assortment of sandwiches and pizzas. Gaze at scenic downtown from the sidewalk seating area. [$] *Average main: $8* ✉ *337 E. Main St.* ☎ *509/334–7663* 🌐 *www.basiliospullman.com.*

$ PIZZA 🍴 **Sella's Calzone and Pastas.** Made daily from scratch, the calzones are always fresh at this cozy storefront. The most popular is the Coug (pepperoni, mushrooms, and black olives), followed by Gourmet (artichoke hearts, sundried tomatoes, and pesto sauce). Pizzas, sandwiches, pastas, and salads are also served. A daily lunch special includes a small calzone with salad or soup. [$] *Average main: $10* ✉ *1115 E. Main St.* ☎ *509/334–1895.*

$ B&B/INN 🏨 **Churchyard Inn.** Registered as a national and state historic site, this 1905 Flemish-style inn, 15 miles southeast of Pullman in Uniontown, was once a parish house for the adjacent church, and then a convent, before becoming a B&B in 1995. **Pros:** welcoming and helpful innkeeper; interesting history; quiet and scenic. **Cons:** no a/c or TVs in rooms. [$] *Rooms from: $95* ✉ *206 St. Boniface St., Uniontown* ☎ *509/229–3200, 800/227–2804* 🌐 *www.churchyardinn.com* 🛏 *5 rooms, 1 suite* 🍽 *Breakfast.*

SPOKANE

75 miles north of Pullman, 282 miles east of Seattle.

Washington's second-largest city, Spokane (spo-*can,* not spo-*cane*) takes its name from the Spokan tribe of Salish Native Americans. It translates as "Children of the Sun," a fitting name for this sunny city. It's also a city of flowers and trees, public gardens, parks, and museums. Known as the "Capital of the Inland Empire," Spokane is the cultural and financial center of the inland Northwest.

Spokane began as a Native American village at a roaring waterfall where each autumn salmon ascended in great numbers. American settlers built a sawmill at the falls in 1873. Several railroads arrived after 1881, and Spokane soon became the transportation hub of eastern Washington. In 1885 Spokane built the first hydroelectric plant west of the Mississippi. Downtown boomed after the fire of 1889, as the city grew rich from mining ventures in Washington, Idaho, and Montana, and from shipping the wheat grown on the Palouse hills.

Until they were cleared away for the 1974 World's Fair, bridges and railroad trestles hid Spokane's magnificent falls from view. Today they form the heart of downtown's Riverfront Park, and the city rises from the falls in a series of broad terraces to the valley's rim. Urban parks are among Spokane's assets. The dry, hot summers here make it easy to plan

Washington State University

golf, fishing, and hiking excursions; long, snowy winters provide nearly five months to enjoy skiing, snowboarding, and sledding.

GETTING HERE AND AROUND

AIRPORT TRANSFERS Many hotels offer a free airport shuttle service. Spokane Transit runs between the airport and downtown, every half-hour 6 am–11 pm weekdays, and hourly on weekends: 6 am–9 pm Saturday and 9–7 Sunday; the 20-minute bus ride costs $1.50. Wheatland Express has shuttle service between the Spokane Airport and Pullman and Moscow, Idaho. Reservations are recommended; the cost is $45 one-way. City Cab serves the Spokane area. Metered fares run about $2.50 a mile. A taxi ride from the Spokane airport to downtown costs about $20.

Contacts Spokane International Airport ⊠ *9000 W. Airport Dr.* ☎ *509/455–6455* ⊕ *www.spokaneairports.net.* **Spokane Transit Authority** ☎ *509/456–7277* ⊕ *www.spokanetransit.com.* **Wheatland Express** ☎ *509/334–2200, 800/334–2207* ⊕ *www.wheatlandexpress.com.* **City Cab** ☎ *509/455–3333* ⊕ *www.spokanecitycab.com.*

BUS TRAVEL Spokane has an extensive local bus system. The fare is $1.50; exact change or a token is required. Pick up schedules, maps, and tokens at the bus depot or the Plaza, the major downtown transfer point.

Contact The Plaza ⊠ *Bus Shop at the Plaza, 701 W. Riverside Ave.* ☎ *509/456–7277* ⊕ *www.spokanetransit.com.*

CAR TRAVEL Spokane can be reached by I–90 from the east or west. U.S. 395 runs north from Spokane to Colville and the Canadian border. Downtown Spokane is laid out along a true grid: streets run north–south, avenues east–west; many are one-way. Spokane's heaviest traffic is on I–90

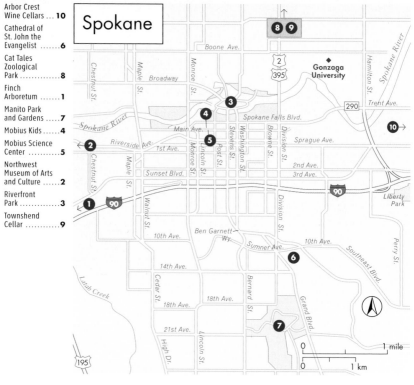

between Spokane and Spokane Valley on weekday evenings. Metered parking is available on city streets; there are also several downtown lots.

TRAIN TRAVEL   Amtrak's *Empire Builder* runs daily between Spokane and Seattle and between Spokane and Portland, stopping at points in between (including Ephrata and Pasco). Reservations are recommended. Round-trip fares vary depending on season; $110 is an average fare between Seattle and Spokane.

Contact Amtrak ☏ *800/872–7245* ⊕ *www.amtrak.com.*

ESSENTIALS

Visitor Information Spokane Area Visitors Information ✉ *201 W. Main St.* ☏ *509/747–3230, 888/776–5263* ⊕ *www.visitspokane.com.*

EXPLORING

TOP ATTRACTIONS

Cathedral of St. John the Evangelist. An architectural masterpiece, the church was constructed with sandstone from Tacoma and Boise and limestone from Indiana. It's considered one of America's most important and beautiful Gothic cathedrals. The cathedral's renowned 49-bell carillon has attracted international guest musicians. ✉ *127 E. 12th Ave.*

A GOOD TOUR

Begin your tour of Spokane west of downtown at the **Finch Arboretum** on Woodland Boulevard off Sunset Boulevard. From the arboretum, head east on Sunset Boulevard, left on Chestnut Street, and left on First Avenue to get to the **Northwest Museum of Arts and Culture.** Riverside Avenue, a block north of First Avenue, leads east to **Riverfront Park.** From here you can see Spokane Falls. If you have kids in tow, make a stop before or after the park at **Mobius Kids,** the children's museum in River Park Square shopping center. Across the street, check out the new **Mobius Science Center.** About 1 mile south of downtown off Grand Boulevard is the **Cathedral of St. John the Evangelist,** and the pleasant **Manito Park and Gardens** are about six blocks south of here.

If you have time to venture out of the city, head north on Division Street, which becomes U.S. 2 (Newport Highway) to **Cat Tales Zoological Park,** about 13 miles from downtown. From here a 2-mile drive east will take you to **Townshend Cellar,** where you can sample Columbia Valley and huckleberry wines (open Fri.–Sun., noon–6). Drive through the countryside another 10 miles south to reach **Arbor Crest Wine Cellars** and its pleasant views of the Spokane River. From here, head north to I–90 for the 6-mile drive back to downtown.

TIMING

You could easily drive the in-city route in an hour. Plan to spend a half-day at Riverfront Park and two hours at the Northwest Museum of Arts and Culture, with at least a half hour to an hour for stops at the other sights. For the destinations outside of the city, figure on driving about 1½ hours round-trip from downtown and making half-hour stops at each site.

18

☎ 509/838–4277 ⊕ www.stjohns-cathedral.org ⊠ Free ⊙ Tours Wed., Fri., Sat. 11–2.

FAMILY
Fodor'sChoice
★
Manito Park and Gardens. A pleasant place to stroll in summer, this 90-acre park has a formal Renaissance-style garden, conservatory, Japanese garden, duck pond, and rose and perennial gardens. Snowy winters find its hills full of sledders and its frozen pond packed with skaters. ⊠ 1702 S. Grand Blvd. ☎ 509/625–6200 ⊕ spokaneparks.org ⊠ Free ⊙ Daily: summer 4 am–11 pm, winter 5 am–10 pm; Japanese garden Apr.–Oct., daily 8 am to ½ hr before dusk.

FAMILY
Mobius Kids Children's Museum. Spokane's museum for children is in the lower level of River Park Square and has six interactive galleries for hands-on learning. Exhibits include a miniature city with safety education features, an art studio, a science exhibit called Geotopica, and a stage with theater equipment and costumes. A partner facility, Mobius Science Center, is across the street. ⊠ 808 W. Main Ave. ☎ 509/624–5437 ⊕ www.mobiusspokane.org ⊠ $6; $15 combined same-day admission with Mobius Science Center ⊙ Tues.–Sat. 10–5, Sun. 11–5.

FAMILY **Mobius Science Center.** Years of effort to create a science education center in Spokane culminated in the opening of Mobius Science Center in the summer of 2012. Across the street from Mobius Kids Children's Museum, the 26,000-square-foot center has 65 interactive science and technology exhibits and also presents special events, camps, and educational programs. ⊠ *811 W. Main Ave., Spokane* ☎ *509/443–5669* ⊕ *www.mobiusspokane.org* ⊑ *$10; $15 combined same-day admission with Mobius Kids Children's Museum* ☉ *Tues.–Sat. 10–6; Sun. 11–5.*

FAMILY **Northwest Museum of Arts and Culture.** Affectionately referred to as the MAC, the museum is in an impressive six-level glass-and-wood structure. It has an audiovisual display and artifacts that trace Spokane's history as well as a fine Native American collection that includes baskets and beadwork of the Plateau nation. The MAC also hosts several traveling exhibits each year. Wander the adjacent Victorian, the Campbell House, to admire the interior or view mining-era exhibits; guided tours are offered four times a day (register in advance when you arrive at the museum). ⊠ *2316 W. 1st Ave.* ☎ *509/456–3931* ⊕ *www. northwestmuseum.org* ⊑ *$7* ☉ *Wed.–Sun. 10–5 (until 8 pm on 1st Fri. of month).*

FAMILY
Fodor's Choice
★

Riverfront Park. The 100-acre park is what remains of Spokane's Expo '74. Sprawling across several islands in the Spokane River, near the falls, the park was developed from old railroad yards. One of the modernist buildings houses an IMAX theater. The opera house occupies the former Washington State pavilion. The outdoor Ice Palace is open mid-October through March. The stone clock tower of the former Great Northern Railroad Station, built in 1902, stands in sharp architectural contrast to the Expo '74 building. A children's train chugs around the park in summer, and a 1909 carousel, hand-carved by master builder Charles I.D. Looff, is a local landmark. Another icon here is the giant red slide shaped like a Radio Flyer wagon. Other attractions include a sky ride over Spokane falls, mini-golf, and amusement rides. ⊠ *507 N. Howard St.* ☎ *509/625–6601* ⊕ *www.spokaneriverfrontpark.com* ⊑ *Park: free. Fees for some attractions; summer day passes: $20* ☉ *Park, daily 4 am–midnight; attraction hrs vary.*

WORTH NOTING

Arbor Crest Wine Cellars. The eclectic mansion of Royal Riblet, the inventor of a square-wheel tractor and the poles that hold up ski lifts, was built in 1924. Sample Arbor Crest wines, enjoy the striking view of the Spokane River below, or meander through the impeccably kept grounds (the house isn't open to tours). Enjoy Sunday evening concerts (5:30 pm–sunset) for $5 from June through September. Local musicians perform Thursday evenings in summer too; no cover charge. ⊠ *4705 N. Fruithill Rd.* ☎ *509/927–9463* ⊕ *www.arborcrest.com* ⊑ *$5 wine tasting fee* ☉ *Daily noon–5; extended hrs in summer.*

FAMILY **Cat Tales Zoological Park.** Among the large cats living at this zoo are lions, tigers, ligers (a combination of lion and tiger), leopards, pumas, and lynxes. Guided tours give background information on the animals. There's also a petting zoo. ⊠ *N. 17020 Newport Hwy., 12 miles north* *of I–90, Mead ☎ 509/238–4126 🌐 www.cattales.org 🎟 $8 ⏲ May–Sept., Tues.–Sun. 10–6; Oct.–Apr., Tues.–Sun. 10–4.*

Finch Arboretum. This mile-long green patch along Garden Springs Creek has an extensive botanical garden with more than 2,000 labeled trees, shrubs, and flowers. Follow the walking tour on well-manicured paths along the creek, or follow your whim—depending on the season—through flowering rhododendrons, hibiscus, magnolias, dogwoods, hydrangeas, and more. ✉ *3404 W. Woodland Blvd.* ☎ *509/624–4832* 🌐 *spokaneparks.org* 🎟 *Free* ⏲ *Daily dawn–dusk.*

Townshend Cellar. A drive to the Green Bluff countryside leads wine lovers to this small winery and its tasting room. Open since 1998, it's won awards for its Cabernet Sauvignon, and also makes Merlot, Chardonnay, and Syrah. Berries from nearby Idaho are used in huckleberry port, blush, and sparkling wine. ✉ *16112 N. Greenbluff Rd., 13 miles northeast of Spokane, Colbert* ☎ *509/238–1400* 🌐 *www.townshendcellar.com* 🎟 *Free* ⏲ *Fri.–Sun. noon–6.*

EN ROUTE

Eastern Washington University. The tree-shaded Cheney campus has six original buildings that are on the National Register of Historic Places, but most of the 300-acre campus consists of post–World War II concrete-and-glass structures. ✉ *526 5th St., about 20 miles west of Spokane, Cheney* ☎ *509/359–6200* 🌐 *www.ewu.edu.*

Gallery of Art. Changing exhibits of works by local and nationally known artists are on show here throughout the school year, and year-end exhibitions showcase student works. ✉ *140 Art Bldg., Cheney* ☎ *509/359–2494* 🌐 *www.ewu.edu/cale/programs/art/gallery.xml* 🎟 *Free* ⏲ *Weekdays, 9–5.*

18

WHERE TO EAT

$ EUROPEAN

🍴 **Catacombs.** Accolades have been won by this underground eatery, both for its unique setting and its menu. It occupies the former boiler room of the Montvale Hotel and, modeling his creation on pubs and underground restaurants he's visited on his travels, owner Rob Brewster has incorporated stone walls, iron chandeliers, lots of brick, and wall tapestries. Try a thin-crust pizza or one of the European specialties, such as Hungarian meatballs. For dessert, pretend you're camping and toast s'mores at your table or try a dessert calzone. Daily happy hour specials include small pizzas and calzones for $5. [$] *Average main: $16* ✉ *10 S. Monroe St.* ☎ *509/838–4610* 🌐 *www.catacombspub.com* ⏲ *Closed Mon. No lunch.*

$$$ SEAFOOD

🍴 **Clinkerdagger.** In a former flour mill with great views of the Spokane River, Clink's has been a Spokane institution since 1974. The seafood, steaks, and prime rib are excellent; the Maytag blue cheese salad and beer-battered fish and chips are both popular at lunch. Some favorite dessert choices include a waffle sundae with two toppings, seasonal fruit crisp, and key lime pie. Happy hour runs daily 3 to 6 and also 9 to close on Friday and Saturday. [$] *Average main: $25* ✉ *621 W. Mallon Ave.* ☎ *509/328–5965* 🌐 *www.clinkerdagger.com* ⏲ *No lunch Sun.*

$ AMERICAN

🍴 **Elk Public House.** This eatery in the relaxed Browne's Addition neighborhood, west of downtown, serves pub food such as lamb sandwiches,

Riverfront Park

burgers, soft tacos, salads, and a spicy gumbo, together with a good selection of microbrews, most from the Northwest. A copper bar stands along one wall, backed by a mirror, giving the interior a saloonlike appearance. Grab an outdoor table in summer if you can. $ *Average main: $10* ✉ *1931 W. Pacific Ave.* ☎ *509/363–1973* ⊕ *www. wedonthaveone.com.*

$ ✕ **Frank's Diner.** Right off the Maple Street Bridge, this is the state's old-
DINER est railroad-car restaurant. Built as an observation car in 1906, it has original light fixtures, stained-glass windows, and mahogany details. Breakfast is the specialty here, and portions are large; for dinner there's such comfort food as turkey with mashed potatoes. Everything is made from scratch. The North Spokane branch is housed in a luxury Pullman car built in 1913. $ *Average main: $9* ✉ *1516 W. 2nd Ave.* ☎ *509/747–8798* ⊕ *www.franksdiners.com* $ *Average main: $9* ✉ *10929 N. Newport Hwy.* ☎ *509/465–2464* ⊕ *www.franksdiners.com.*

$$ ✕ **Latah Bistro.** Tucked into a strip mall in south Spokane near Qual-
ECLECTIC chan Golf Course, Dave and Heather DuPree's neighborhood restau-
Fodor'sChoice rant serves a diverse menu that changes frequently and may include
★ pasta, duck, pork, beef, shrimp, sea bass, ahi tuna, trout, black cod, and scallops. Try the semolina-dusted Idaho rainbow trout with white bean and fennel ragout or long-cooked short ribs with fresh mafaldi pasta. Pizzas, including the eclectic salami and goat cheese pizza, are baked in a wood-burning oven. Save room for dessert. You'll want to try the pumpkin-bread pudding or the "bucket of love" (flourless mini-chocolate cakes dusted with spices). Sunday brunch features varied choices, from pumpkin oatmeal to trout and eggs; a daily frittata is also offered. On Monday, bottles of wine are half off; Thursday

martinis are $5. Enjoy live music on Wednesday. $ *Average main: $24* ✉ *4241 S. Cheney–Spokane Rd.* ☎ *509/838–8338* ⊕ *www.latahbistro. com* ✆ *Brunch on Sun. only; closed Sun. 2–5.*

$$
ECLECTIC
Fodor'sChoice
★
✕ **Luna.** You'll find inventive approaches to classics here, including beef, pork, chicken, salmon, halibut, and lamb. The menu highlights fresh ingredients grown in the restaurant's garden and changes seasonally. Weekend brunch has such treats as Creole cheddar polenta with andouille sausage, duck crepes, and cinnamon walnut bread French toast with bananas. The luscious desserts are worth a visit on their own—especially the six-layer coconut cake (featured in *Bon Appetit* magazine) and shortbread-topped fruit crisp baked in the woodfire oven. Luna is especially known for its extensive wine list, with more than 900 vintages, and has a wine bar as well. The rose terrace and courtyard are open in summer. $ *Average main: $24* ✉ *5620 S. Perry St.* ☎ *509/448–2383* ⊕ *www.lunaspokane.com.*

$$$
SEAFOOD
✕ **Milford's Fish House.** This brick and terra-cotta tile structure was built in 1925, and the terrazzo floor and tin ceiling are relics of that era. The interior's exposed brick walls and wood details, lit by candles, create a romantic environment in which to enjoy the wide array of seafood dishes and steaks. Everything is fresh here, and it is hard to predict what the menu will include, but you might find such offerings as tuna, cod, salmon, snapper, mahimahi, clams, and prawns. Pan-fried oysters are a house specialty. $ *Average main: $27* ✉ *719 N. Monroe St.* ☎ *509/326–7251* ⊕ *www.milfordsfishhouse.com* ✆ *No lunch.*

$$$
ECLECTIC
✕ **Mizuna Restaurant.** Fresh flowers and redbrick walls lend both color and charm to this downtown eatery. Grilled Idaho ruby red trout is served with braised kale and root vegetable hash; New York strip steak comes with sautéed seasonal vegetables and rich blue cheese-crimini mushroom mac and cheese. Local produce is the inspiration for such scrumptious vegetarian fare as white cheddar-and-apple salad and stuffed acorn squash with wild rice. Mizuna's cheese plate gets rave reviews and goes well with the Northwest wines highlighted in the wine bar. Dessert specialties include vegan carrot cake. The patio is open for outdoor dining May through September. $ *Average main: $28* ✉ *214 N. Howard St.* ☎ *509/747–2004* ⊕ *www.mizuna. com* ✆ *No lunch Sun.*

18

$
AMERICAN
✕ **Post Street Ale House.** Adjacent to Hotel Lusso, the Post Street Ale House is a casual eatery with an affordable menu. There's standard pub fare like fish-and-chips, burgers, and sausage dogs, and several kinds of pasta and salads, too. Halibut tacos with corn salsa, served with a cup of black-bean soup, are a great value. More than 25 beers are on tap, and Guinness-braised short ribs also pay homage to the ale. $ *Average main: $11* ✉ *1 N. Post St.* ☎ *509/789–6900* ⊕ *www.hotellusso.com/ dining/alehouse.*

$
ITALIAN
FAMILY
✕ **Rock City Grill.** This upbeat restaurant, which is close to Riverfront Park, has excellent pastas and gourmet wood-fired pizzas, including their most popular, the Thai, with marinated chicken and prawns. Other specialties include bison meat loaf and Jack Daniels whiskey steak. The extensive gluten-free menu features pizza and pasta. Expect some kidding around from the outgoing staff, who will make sure your soft

drinks and lemonades never go empty. Save room for such desserts as tiramisu and the Italian favorite, spumoni ice cream. If you love Thai peanut sauce, take some home; it's available by the bottle. There are late-night pizza specials after 9, and on Sunday there's an all-day happy hour in the bar. $ *Average main: $17* ✉ *808 W. Main St.* ☎ *509/455–4400* ⊕ *www.rockcitygrill.com.*

$$$ ✗ **Santé Restaurant and Charcuterie.** Spectacular French cuisine that isn't
FRENCH   too rich and saucy is the focus here. Local and organic ingredients are creatively presented beginning with the brunch menu, in items like the tasso and leek omelet. The cold fromage plate brings to mind an outdoor picnic, with three cheeses, salami (from the on-site charcuterie), and a baguette. For a heartier meal, try the wild halibut, grass fed beef, heritage chicken, or tofu with pumpkin risotto. The restaurant is small, and service can sometimes be slow; ask for a window seat to people-watch, and remember that the European approach to eating is all about savoring. If there's a wait to be seated, consider browsing in Auntie's Bookstore right next door. $ *Average main: $25* ✉ *404 W. Main St.* ☎ *509/315–4693* ⊕ *www.santespokane.com* ☺ *No dinner Sun.–Tues.*

$ ✗ **Steelhead Bar & Grille.** This casual pub-style eatery is popular for its
AMERICAN   convenient downtown location and affordable prices. Housed in one
FAMILY   of Spokane's many older brick buildings, the interior design has an urban contemporary vibe, with lots of burnished-metal artwork by local artists. About a dozen beers are on tap, but this is a place the whole family can enjoy; there's a decent kids' menu with the usual favorites. Sandwiches and burgers make this a handy place for lunch; kebabs, steak, and halibut-and-chips are heartier fare for dinner, and steelhead is definitely on the menu too. Reservations are not accepted on Friday and Saturday nights. $ *Average main: $15* ✉ *218 N. Howard St.* ☎ *509/747–1303* ⊕ *www.steelheadbarandgrille.com.*

WHERE TO STAY

For expanded hotel reviews, visit Fodors.com.

$$ 🛏 **The Davenport Hotel & Tower.** Two buildings on opposite sides of the
HOTEL   street—one historic, the other a 21-floor modern tower—make up
FAMILY   Washington state's fourth largest hotel and one of its best, with ele-
Fodor's Choice gant accommodations and a plethora of amenities, including good-
★   size TVs. **Pros:** main hotel's historical restoration is a marvel to see; abundant resort-like amenities; experienced service. **Cons:** no coffeemakers or minibars in rooms; no bathtubs in Tower rooms. $ *Rooms from: $190* ✉ *10 S. Post St.* ☎ *509/455–8888, 800/899–1482* ⊕ *www.davenporthotelcollection.com* ⬂ *563 rooms, 48 suites* ⦿❘ *No meals.*

$$ 🛏 **Hotel Lusso.** This classy boutique hotel features guest rooms appointed
HOTEL   with European furnishings and many modern amenities, including flat-screen TVs. **Pros:** small and intimate; luxurious rooms. **Cons:** no pool or similar amenities, though a day pass to the Davenport across the street can be purchased; no coffeemaker or minibar. $ *Rooms from: $159* ✉ *808 W. Sprague Ave.* ☎ *509/747–9750, 800/899–1482* ⊕ *www.davenporthotelcollection.com* ⬂ *36 rooms, 12 suites* ⦿❘ *No meals.*

$ 🏠 **Marianna Stolz House.** Across
B&B/INN from Gonzaga University on a tree-
lined street, this B&B is an American foursquare home built in 1908.
Pros: convenient location; rich history. **Cons:** shared bathroom for
some rooms. [$] *Rooms from: $89*
✉ *427 E. Indiana Ave.* ☎ *509/*
483–4316, 800/978–6587 ⊕ *www.*
mariannastoltzhouse.com ➹ *4*
rooms, 2 with bath ⧆ *Breakfast.*

$ 🏠 **Montvale Hotel.** Housed in one
HOTEL of Spokane's recently restored historic buildings, this intimate boutique hotel has spacious rooms with
comfortable beds, classy retro style,
and flat-screen TVs. **Pros:** helpful
and pleasant service; good value.
Cons: noise from trucks, trains, and
nearby nightlife can be distracting;
very small hotel, so no recreational
amenities. [$] *Rooms from: $110* ✉ *105 First Ave.* ☎ *509/747–1919,*
866/668–8253 ⊕ *www.montvalehotel.com* ➹ *34 rooms, 2 suites*
⧆ *Breakfast.*

$ 🏠 **Red Lion Hotel at the Park.** This hotel is adjacent to Riverfront Park and
HOTEL just a two-block walk from the downtown shopping district. **Pros:** pool
FAMILY area is popular with families; location is great; good service. **Cons:** very
large hotel so gets crowded; rooms that face lobby are noisy. [$] *Rooms*
from: $149 ✉ *303 W. North River Dr.* ☎ *509/326–8000, 800/733–5466*
🖷 *509/325–7329* ⊕ *www.redlion.com* ➹ *400 rooms, 25 suites* ⧆ *No*
meals.

$ 🏠 **Stratford Suites.** Ten minutes from downtown, this newer hotel offers
HOTEL spacious apartment-style suites with full kitchens, one or two bedrooms,
and modern style and amenities, including granite counters and 50-inch
flat-screen TVs. **Pros:** friendly staff; free fresh-baked cookies in the
evening; pet-friendly. **Cons:** no pool; no restaurant on-site; front desk
isn't staffed 24 hours. [$] *Rooms from: $119* ✉ *11808 W. Center La.,*
9 miles west of Spokane, Airway Heights ☎ *509/321–1600, 888/705–*
8877 ⊕ *www.stratfordsuites.com* ➹ *60 suites* ⧆ *No meals.*

NIGHTLIFE AND THE ARTS

NIGHTLIFE

Blue Spark. At the Blue Spark the '80s are still trendy, as evidenced by
the music and interior. It's known for great service, great drinks, and a
party atmosphere. Check out Monday open-mike night, Tuesday trivia,
and live music the rest of the week too. ✉ *15 S. Howard St.* ☎ *509/838–*
5787 ⊕ *www.bluesparkspokane.com.*

Gibliano Brothers. A local magazine named this Spokane's best new nightspot in 2010, when Gibliano Brothers brought dueling pianos to town.

Every Thursday through Saturday four pianists duke it out on the ivories, playing both popular and offbeat tunes—and, of course, they take requests. There's karaoke Sunday through Wednesday nights. ⊠ *718 W. Riverside Ave.* ☎ *509/315–8765* ⊕ *giblianobrothers.com.*

MarQuee Lounge. This is Spokane's most happening dance club, where the young and stylish go to see and be seen. Calling itself a "London style bar," it features a two-story wall of liquor and VIP sections encased in glass. ⊠ *522 W. Riverside Ave.* ☎ *509/838–3332* ⊕ *www.marqueelounge.com.*

THE ARTS

Interplayers Theatre. This professional theater company presents seven main stage productions during September through May; they also offer occasional concerts and participate in downtown Spokane's "First Friday" monthly events. ⊠ *174 S. Howard St.* ☎ *509/455–7529* ⊕ *www.interplayerstheatre.org.*

Spokane Civic Theatre. The long-running community theater presents musicals and dramas on two stages October through June. ⊠ *1020 N. Howard St.* ☎ *509/325–2507* ⊕ *www.spokanecivictheatre.com.*

The Knitting Factory Concert House. National acts, ranging from the Reverend Horton Heat to Josh Ritter and the Royal City Band, are hosted in this 1,500-seat venue. ⊠ *919 W. Sprague Ave.* ☎ *509/244–3279* ⊕ *sp.knittingfactory.com.*

Spokane Symphony. Classical and pops concerts are presented from September to May in the newly restored historic Martin Woldson Theater at The Fox, plus special events such as the *Nutcracker* at the INB Performing Arts Center, free outdoor concerts at city parks in summer, and chamber music in the elegant Davenport Hotel. ⊠ *818 W. Riverside Ave.* ☎ *509/624–1200* ⊕ *www.spokanesymphony.org.*

SHOPPING

Flour Mill. When it was built in 1895, the mill was a huge technical innovation. Today it's home to shops, restaurants, and offices. The mill sits virtually atop the falls, north of the river. ⊠ *621 W. Mallon Ave.* ⊕ *www.flourmillspokane.com.*

River Park Square. Upscale shopping here includes Nordstrom, Apple, Williams-Sonoma, Pottery Barn, The North Face, and other national retailers—more than 30 stores in all. Several restaurants are here or nearby, and there's a 20-screen movie theater. ⊠ *808 W. Main St.* ⊕ *www.riverparksquare.com.*

SPORTS AND THE OUTDOORS

GOLF

Hangman Valley. This 18-hole, par-72 course, has greens fees of $27 weekdays, $29 weekends. ⊠ *2210 E. Hangman Valley Rd.* ☎ *509/448–1212* ⊕ *www.spokanecounty.org/parks.*

Indian Canyon. On the slope of a basalt canyon, this 18-hole course has great views of North Spokane and Mt. Spokane. The greens fees are

$29 weekdays, $31 weekends. ✉ *4304 W. West Dr.* ☎ *509/747–5353* ⊕ *www.spokanegolf.org.*

Liberty Lake. A $6-million course renovation was completed here in 2010, giving it a whole new look. It's near MeadowWood, so avid golfers can visit both and play 36 holes. The greens fees are $27 weekdays, $29 weekends. ✉ *24403 E. Sprague Ave., Liberty Lake* ☎ *509/255–6233* ⊕ *www.spokanecounty.org/parks.*

MeadowWood. This is a Scottish-style course that has been ranked in Washington's top 10 municipal courses. Greens fees are $27 weekdays, $29 weekends. ✉ *24501 E. Valleyway Ave., Liberty Lake* ☎ *509/255–9539* ⊕ *www.spokanecounty.org/parks.*

HIKING

The hills around Spokane are laced with trails, almost all of which connect with 37-mile-long **Centennial Trail,** which winds along the Spokane River. Beginning in Nine Mile Falls, northwest of Spokane, the well-marked trail ends in Idaho. Maps are available at the visitor center at 201 West Main Street. Northwest of downtown at **Riverside State Park,** a paved trail leads through a 17-million-year-old fossil forest in Deep Creek Canyon. From there it's easy to get to the western end of the Centennial Trail by crossing the suspension bridge at the day-use parking lot; trails heading both left and right will lead to the Centennial.

SKIING

49° North. An hour north of Spokane in the Colville National Forest, this is a 2,325-acre family-oriented resort. Lift tickets cost $52 to $57; snowboards and ski package rentals are about $35. ✉ *U.S. 395, 3311 Flowery Trail Rd., Chewelah* ☎ *509/935–6649, 866/376–4949* ⊕ *www.ski49n.com.*

Mt. Spokane. A modest downhill resort, 28 miles northeast of downtown Spokane, Mt. Spokane has a 2,000-foot drop and 10 miles of groomed cross-country ski trails. Snowshoeing and tubing are also options. There's night skiing Wednesday through Saturday. Lift tickets cost $36 to $49. A Discover Pass is required on all vehicles ($10 for one day or $30 annually) and is valid at all Washington state parks. A Sno-Park permit is also required for parking at Nordic skiing trailheads. ✉ *29500 N. Mt. Spokane Park Dr., Mead* ☎ *509/238–2220* ⊕ *www.mtspokane.com.*

18

ALONG ROUTE 90

If you travel along the Interstate at 70+ mph, it might seem that this area is mainly a lot of crop fields and a single town with a big lake. But slow the pace a bit and get off the beaten path to discover family-friendly activities in Moses Lake, including a lively water park and lakefront park for swimming on hot summer days. North in the town of Ephrata, local history is depicted in a pioneer village. Soap Lake is a body of water like no other, with bubbly, mineral-rich water that has been purported to have healing effects for more than a century. Closer to the Columbia River just west of Quincy, the award-winning

Gorge Amphitheatre hosts concerts through the summer. Adjacent to the Gorge is the not-to-be-missed Cave B Inn and Spa, which has luxurious accommodations, fabulous river and canyon views, an estate winery, pool, spa, fine dining, and upscale yurts.

MOSES LAKE

105 miles west of Spokane.

The natural lake from which this sprawling town takes its name seems to be an anomaly in the dry landscape of east-central Washington. But ever since the Columbia Basin Project took shape, there's been water everywhere. Approaching Moses Lake from the west on I–90, you'll pass lushly green irrigated fields; to the east lie vast stretches of wheat. The lakes of this region have more shorebirds than Washington's ocean beaches. Potholes Reservoir is an artificial lake that supports as much wildlife as does the Columbia Wildlife Refuge. The Winchester Wasteway, west of Moses Lake, is a great place to paddle a kayak or canoe and watch birds as you glide along the reedy banks. The airfield north of town was once a major Air Force base, and now serves as a training facility for airline pilots.

GETTING HERE AND AROUND

Moses Lake straddles I–90; it's about 100 miles from Spokane and 175 miles from Seattle. To the north, Highway 17 connects Moses Lake to Ephrata and points north, including Soap Lake and Coulee City.

ESSENTIALS

Visitor Information Moses Lake Area Chamber of Commerce ✉ *324 S. Pioneer Way* ☎ *509/765–7888, 800/992–6234* ⊕ *www.moseslake.com.*

EXPLORING

Columbia National Wildlife Refuge. A great number of birds are attracted to this reserve: hawks, falcons, golden eagles, ducks, sandhill cranes, herons, American avocets, black-necked stilts, and yellow-headed and red-winged blackbirds. The refuge is also home to beavers, muskrats, badgers, and coyotes. ✉ *7 miles northwest of Othello via McMahon Rd. to Morgan Lake Rd.; about 20 miles southeast of Moses Lake, Othello* ☎ *509/546–8300* ⊕ *www.fws.gov/columbia* 🎟 *Free* ☉ *Daily 5–dusk.*

Moses Lake. Claw-shaped, 38-foot-deep, 18-mile-long Moses Lake is filled by Crab Creek—which originates in the hills west of Spokane—with three side branches known as Parker Horn, Lewis Horn, and Pelican Horn. The city sprawls over the peninsulas formed by these "horns," and can therefore be a bit difficult to get around. This is the state's second-largest lake. ✉ *Hwy. 17, off I–90.*

Moses Lake Museum and Art Center. Fossils collected all over North America, including prehistoric land and marine animals, are exhibited here. One gallery also has visual-arts displays. ✉ *Moses Lake Civic Center, 401 S. Balsam St.* ☎ *509/764–3830* ⊕ *www.cityofml.com* 🎟 *Free* ☉ *Mon.–Sat. 11–5.*

Potholes State Park. This park is 25 miles southwest of Moses Lake on the west side of O'Sullivan Dam. Camping and boating, as well as fishing for trout, perch, and walleye, are popular diversions. ✉ *6762 Hwy. 262 E, Othello* ☎ *360/902–8844, 888/226–7688* ⊕ *www.parks.wa.gov* ✉ *Discover Pass (valid at all state parks) $10 per day or $30 for a year; campsite $23–$32* ☉ *Daily: summer, 6:30–dusk; winter, 8–dusk.*

FAMILY **Surf 'n Slide Water Park.** This is a great place to cool off from the hot central Washington sunshine, with an Olympic-sized pool, two 200-foot waterslides, a tube slide, a "baby octopus" slide, and diving boards. ✉ *McCosh Park, 401 W. 4th Ave.* ☎ *509/764–3842* ⊕ *www.cityofml. com* ✉ *$10* ☉ *Early June–Aug., Mon.–Thurs. 11–6:30, Fri.–Sun. 11–7; Memorial Day and Labor Day weekends, 11–7.*

WHERE TO EAT AND STAY

For expanded hotel reviews, visit Fodors.com.

$$ ✕ **Michael's on the Lake.** In the late afternoon golden rays of sunset wash
AMERICAN over the dining room and deck at this lakeside restaurant. Indulge in prime rib or Parmesan-crusted halibut over linguine, or go for the lighter soups and sandwiches. Chocolate lovers will appreciate the dessert menu with choices like mile-high mud pie, half-baked chocolate chip cookies, and chocolate banana bread pudding. Unique appetizers, including prime rib quesadillas and California sushi served in wonton tacos, are half-price during happy hour, daily 4 to 6 and 9 to close. $ *Average main: $22* ✉ *910 W. Broadway Ave.* ☎ *509/765–1611* ⊕ *www.michaelsonthelake.com.*

$$ ✕ **Porter House Steakhouse.** The current owners of one of Moses Lake's
STEAKHOUSE oldest restaurants set out with the goal, ably achieved, of making it a
FAMILY favorite family and group gathering place. As the name implies, steaks are the main event here, ranging from an 8-ounce sirloin to 24-ounce porterhouse. There's even a 4-ounce steak on the kids' menu. Complementing the beef entrées is a variety of chicken, seafood, and pasta dishes. Check out the house-made desserts, including Texas sheet cake and bread pudding with vanilla ice cream. $ *Average main: $22* ✉ *217 N. Elder St.* ☎ *509/766–0308* ⊕ *www.porterhousesteakhouse.net.*

$$ ⌂ **Comfort Suites.** This newer hotel shines with modern style and con-
HOTEL veniences, including granite counters in the bathroom, and flat-screen TVs. **Pros:** clean and modern; nice pool; friendly service. **Cons:** no restaurant; prices steep during some events. $ *Rooms from: $165* ✉ *1700 E. Kittleson Rd.* ☎ *509/765–3731, 877/424–6423* ⊕ *www. comfortsuites.com* ⚲ *60 suites* ❧ *Breakfast.*

SHOPPING

Moses Lake Farmers Market. Vendors come here each Wednesday and Saturday from May to October to sell fresh produce and handmade arts and crafts. ✉ *McCosh Park (next to aquatic center), 401 W. 4th Ave.* ☎ *509/750–7831* ⊕ *www.moseslakefarmersmarket.com* ☉ *Mid-June–mid-Oct., Wed. 2–6, Sat. 7:30–2; May–mid-June and mid- to end Oct., Sat. 7:30–2.*

18

QUINCY

34 miles northwest of Moses Lake.

On the fences along I–90 to George and north on Highway 281 to Quincy, crop identification signs highlight what the Quincy Valley is known for: agriculture. From Thanksgiving to New Year's Eve, these same fields are filled with Christmas motion-light displays, powered by electricity from farmers' irrigation lines—a delightful sight for highway travelers in the dark winter nights. Agriculture hasn't always been king in this area. Though the rich soils attracted many settlers after the railroad made the region accessible in the early 1900s, several serious droughts proved that Mother Nature could not be relied on to water the crops consistently. In the mid-1930s the federal government began to assist with irrigation plans, and by the early 1950s the first systems were in place.

Today the area has 200,000 irrigable acres growing corn, alfalfa, wheat, potatoes, seed, apples, and more. An annual Farmer Consumer Awareness Day is held the second Saturday of September, with farm tours, entertainment, food, arts and crafts, and plenty of fresh produce. Tourism is also growing here, with visitors from across the state and beyond coming to summer concerts at the Gorge Amphitheatre, touring wineries between Quincy and Wenatchee, and hiking and climbing near the Columbia River.

GETTING HERE AND AROUND

Quincy is 11 miles north of I-90's Exit 149, via Highway 281. It's about 2 hours, 45 minutes from Seattle and 2 hours, 30 minutes from Spokane.

EXPLORING

Gorge Amphitheatre. This 20,000-seat amphitheater has won accolades as best outdoor concert venue due to its fine acoustics and stunning vistas of the Columbia River—a setting compared to the Grand Canyon's. Set in one of the sunniest parts of the state, the concert season runs from May to September. Concertgoers often overnight at the adjacent campground or at motels and hotels in Quincy, Moses Lake, and Ellensburg. ⊠ *754 Silica Rd. NW, George* ☎ *509/785–6262.*

WHERE TO EAT AND STAY

For expanded hotel reviews, visit Fodors.com.

$ ✕ **The Grainery.** Quincy farmers David and Harriet Weber opened their
CAFÉ   café to feature their own farm products, including the grains used for
FAMILY   breads and the scrumptious pastries baked in-house. Locals stop in for espresso and giant cinnamon rolls to start their day. Menu items change to reflect what's in season, such as the strawberry summer salad and hearty vegetable soups. Some Friday nights live music plays in the spacious, brightly decorated, country-cozy setting. $ *Average main: $9* ⊠ *101 E St. SE* ☎ *509/797–7240* ⊘ *Closed Sun. No dinner.*

$$$ ⬚ **Cave B Inn and Spa.** Washington's first destination winery resort is
RESORT   built on (and into) ancient basalt cliffs 900 feet above the Columbia
Fodor'sChoice   River; its 15 cliffhouses, cavern (with 12 rooms), and inn all designed
★   to blend into the natural environment, with exterior walls of precast

Cave B Inn & Spa

concrete embedded with rocks. **Pros:** fantastic place to stargaze; quiet and secluded; gorgeous accommodations. **Cons:** very expensive during Gorge Amphitheatre events; no local meal options besides on-site restaurant. $ *Rooms from: $229* ✉ *344 Silica Rd. NW* ☎ *509/785–2283, 888/785–2283* ⊕ *www.sagecliffe.com* ⤴ *12 rooms, 18 suites, 25 yurts* ⊗ *Closed Sun.–Wed. Dec.–Feb.; yurts closed Nov.–Mar.* ⊙| *Breakfast.*

EPHRATA

18 miles northeast of Quincy.

Ephrata (e-*fray*-tuh), a pleasant small farm town and the Grant County seat, is in the exact center of Washington. It was settled quite early because its abundant natural springs made it an oasis in the dry steppe country of the Columbia Basin. Native Americans visited the springs, as did cattle drovers after American ranchers stocked the open range. Ephrata began to grow after the Great Northern Railroad established a terminal here in 1892. Cattlemen took advantage of the railroad to round up and ship out thousands of wild horses that roamed the range. The last great roundup was held in 1906, when the remaining 2,400 horses of a herd that once numbered some 25,000 were corralled and shipped off.

GETTING HERE AND AROUND

Ephrata is about 20 miles north of Moses Lake via Highway 17. Continuing north on the highway leads to the town of Soap Lake, then past state parks, up to Coulee City.

EXPLORING

Grant County Courthouse. Built in the 1920s, the redbrick courthouse has a facade framed by white columns and a majestic set of stairs. Although it may seem antique from the exterior, the building has a unique and progressive feature: it's heated by thermal springs. ✉ *35 C St. NW* ☎ *509/754–2011* 🌐 *www.co.grant.wa.us* 🕑 *Weekdays 8–5.*

FAMILY **Grant County Historical Museum and Village.** More than 30 pioneer-era buildings have been brought here from other parts of Grant County. They include a blacksmith forge, saloon, barber shop, and printing office. ✉ *742 Basin St. N* ☎ *509/754–3334* 🎟 *$3.50* 🕑 *May–Sept., Mon., Tues. and Thurs.–Sat. 10–5, Sun. 1–4.*

Soap Lake. The water is high in dissolved carbonates, sulfates, and chlorides, but even though the lake has long been famous for its mineral waters and therapeutic mud baths, the eponymous small town has never quite succeeded as a resort—perhaps because the miraculous waters have been heavily diluted by irrigation waters. But agriculture is much more profitable anyway, and many other beautiful recreation areas are nearby. ✉ *6 miles north of Ephrata, Soap Lake* 🌐 *www.soaplakecity.org.*

WHERE TO STAY

For expanded hotel reviews, visit Fodors.com.

$ B&B/INN 🏨 **Inn at Soap Lake.** Built in 1905 as a stable and blacksmith shop, this beachside structure was converted to an inn in 1915 during Soap Lake's heyday as a destination for health treatments—most rooms have a soaking tub with the natural mineral-rich water on tap. **Pros:** beautifully landscaped gardens; private beach has lounge chairs; cozy lobby. **Cons:** no pool; registration desk is not staffed, but management is on-site. [$] *Rooms from: $59* ✉ *226 Main Ave. E, Soap Lake* ☎ *509/246–1132, 800/557–8514* 🌐 *www.innsoaplake.com* 🛏 *20 rooms, 8 cottages* 🍴 *No meals.*

$ HOTEL FAMILY 🏨 **Notaras Lodge.** The spacious rooms at this four-building lodge on the shore of Soap Lake are individually decorated; all have a rustic log-style construction. **Pros:** room style is very unusual and fun; helpful staff; interesting grounds. **Cons:** not all rooms have lake views. [$] *Rooms from: $85* ✉ *13 Canna St., Soap Lake* ☎ *509/246–0462* 🌐 *www.notaraslodge.com* 🛏 *8 rooms, 7 suites* 🍴 *No meals.*

NORTHEASTERN WASHINGTON

A technological marvel, the Grand Coulee Dam took nearly a decade to build in the 1930s. Its fascinating history is on display at the year-round visitors center, where tours are also available. The dam created a 150-mile long lake; several campgrounds surround it and recreational activities abound. Farther north, the Colville and Okanogan national forests are comprised of three mountain ranges that are foothills of the Rockies. These wild areas teem with wildlife and natural beauty, yet remain pristine and uncrowded. The small towns of Omak and Colville provide basic services for travelers and a couple of outstanding restaurants.

Northeastern Washington

COULEE DAM NATIONAL RECREATION AREA

60 miles northeast of Ephrata, 239 miles northeast of Seattle, 87 miles northwest of Spokane.

Grand Coulee Dam is the one of the world's largest concrete structures. At almost a mile long, it justly deserves the moniker "Eighth Technological Wonder of the World." Beginning in 1932, 9,000 men excavated 45 million cubic yards of rock and soil and dammed the Grand Coulee, a gorge created by the Columbia River, with 12 million cubic yards of concrete—enough to build a sidewalk the length of the equator. By the time the dam was completed in 1941, 77 men had perished and 11 towns were submerged under the newly formed Roosevelt Lake. The waters backed up behind the dam turned eastern Washington's arid soil into fertile farming land, but not without consequence: salmon-fishing stations that were a source of food and spiritual identity for Native Americans were destroyed. Half the dam was built on the Colville Indian Reservation on the north shore of the Columbia; the Colville tribes later received restitution in excess of $75 million from the U.S. government.

In 1946 most of Roosevelt Lake and the grassy and pine woodland hills surrounding it were designated the Coulee Dam National Recreation Area. Crown Point Vista, about 5 miles west of Grand Coulee on Highway 174, may have the best vantage for photographs of the dam, Roosevelt Lake, Rufus Woods Lake (below the dam), and the town of Coulee Dam.

After nightfall from Memorial Day through September the dam is transformed into an unlikely entertainment complex by an extravagant, free laser-light show. With 300-foot eagles flying across the white water that flows over the dam, the show is spectacular, if hokey. The audio portion is broadcast on 90.1 FM. Show up early to get a good seat. The show starts at 10 pm Memorial Day through July, 9:30 pm in August, and 8:30 pm in September.

GETTING HERE AND AROUND
From Ephrata, take Highway 17 north to reach Grand Coulee. From the Spokane area, U.S. 2 and Highway 174 is the most direct route.

ESSENTIALS
Visitor Information **Grand Coulee Dam Area Chamber of Commerce** ✉ *306 Midway Ave.* ☎ *800/268–5332, 509/633–3074* ⊕ *www.grandcouleedam.org.*

EXPLORING
Colville Indian Reservation. Highway 155 passes through the Colville Indian Reservation, one of the largest reservations in Washington, with about 7,700 enrolled members of the Colville Confederated Tribes. This was the final home for Chief Joseph and the Nez Perce, who fought a series of fierce battles with the U.S. Army in the 1870s after the U.S. government enforced a treaty that many present-day historians agree was fraudulent. Chief Joseph lived on the Colville reservation until his death in 1904. There's a memorial to him off Highway 155 east of the town of Nespelem, 17 miles north of the dam; four blocks away (two east and two north) is his grave. You can drive through the reservation's undeveloped landscape, and except for a few highway signs you'll feel like you've time-traveled to pioneer days. The **Colville Tribal Museum** (✉ *512 Mead Way, Coulee Dam* ☎ *509/633–0751* ☉ *open daily 8:30–5*) is worth a visit. ✉ *Coulee Dam* ⊕ *www.colvilletribes.com/tourism.*

FAMILY   **Grand Coulee Dam Visitor Center.** Colorful displays about the dam, a 13-minute film on the site's geology and the dam's construction, and information about the laser-light show are on offer here. The U.S. Bureau of Reclamation, which oversees operation and maintenance of the dam, conducts tours year-round, weather and maintenance schedules permitting. You can also pick up a self-guided historical walking tour that will take you from the visitor center through the old part of town, across the bridge, and into the old engineers' town. ✉ *Hwy. 155, south of Coulee Dam, Coulee Dam* ☎ *509/633–9265* ⊕ *www.usbr.gov/ pn/grandcoulee* ⌦ *Free* ☉ *Late May–July, daily 8:30 am–11 pm; Aug., daily 8:30 am–10:30 pm; Sept., daily 8:30 am–9:30 pm; Oct., Nov. and Feb.–late May, daily 9–5.*

Lake Roosevelt National Recreation Area. The 150-mile-long lake was created by the Columbia River when it was backed up by Grand Coulee Dam. Several Native American villages, historic sites, and towns lie beneath the waters. ✉ *1008 Crest Dr. (HQ), Coulee Dam* ☎ *509/633– 9441* ⊕ *www.nps.gov/laro* ⌦ *Free; camping $10 May–Sept., $5 Oct.– Apr.* ☉ *Daily 24 hrs.; office weekdays 8–4.*

Steamboat Rock State Park. Here, a 2,200-foot-high flat-topped lava butte rises 1,000 feet above Banks Lake, the 31-mile-long irrigation reservoir filled with water from Lake Roosevelt by giant pumps and siphons. Water is distributed from the south end of the lake throughout the Columbia Basin. The state park has campsites, a swimming area, and boat ramps. In summer it's popular with boaters and anglers, and in winter there's Nordic skiing, snowshoeing, and ice fishing. ✉ *51052 Hwy. 155, 16 miles north of Coulee City, Electric City* ☎ *360/902–8844, 888/226–7688* 🌐 *www.parks.wa.gov* 🎟 *Discover Pass (valid at all state parks) $10 per day or $30 for a year; campsites $23–$32* ⏲ *Daily 6:30–dusk.*

Sun Lakes–Dry Falls State Park. A high point in the coulee, this park has campgrounds, picnic areas, and a state-run golf course that attracts visitors year-round; in summer the lakes bristle with boaters. From the bluffs on U.S. 2, west of the dam, you can get a great view over this enormous canyon. To the north, the banks of the lake are hemmed in by cliffs. At Dry Falls, the upstream erosion of the canyon caused by the floods stops. Below Dry Falls, steep, barren cliffs—some 1,000 feet high—rise from green meadows, marshes, and blue lakes bordered by trees. Most of the water is irrigation water seeping through the porous rock, but the effect is no less spectacular. Eagles and ravens soar along the cliffs, while songbirds, ducks, and geese hang out in the bottomlands.

South of the Sun Lakes, the landscape turns even wilder. The coulee narrows and the cliffs often look like they are on fire, an illusion created by the bold patterns of orange and yellow lichens. The waters of the lakes change, too. The deep blue waters of the small lakes below Dry Falls are replaced by lapis lazuli in the Sun Lakes and turn milky farther south. Presentations at the park's interpretive center at Dry Falls survey the area's geology, and an excellent film describes the great floods. ✉ *34875 Park Lake Road NE, Coulee City* ☎ *360/902–8844, 888/226–7688* 🌐 *www.parks.wa.gov* 🎟 *Discover Pass (valid at all state parks) $10 per day or $30 for a year; camping $23–$35* ⏲ *Daily: summer 6:30–dusk; winter 8–dusk; visitor center May–Sept. daily 9–6, hrs vary offseason.*

WHERE TO EAT AND STAY

For expanded hotel reviews, visit Fodors.com.

$ DINER 🍴 **Flo's Cafe.** One mile south of the dam, this diner dishes up heaps of local color along with loggers' food: biscuits and gravy, corned-beef hash, hamburgers, chicken-fried steak, and chef's salads. Flo's is open for breakfast but closes at 1, so look elsewhere if you want a late lunch. [$] *Average main: $8* ✉ *316 Spokane Way* ☎ *509/633–3216* ⏲ *No dinner.*

$ HOTEL 🏨 **Columbia River Inn.** The well-appointed rooms all have private decks at this inn across the street from Grand Coulee Dam, with easy access to hiking trails and fishing. **Pros:** rooms have microwaves and refrigerators; pretty location. **Cons:** basic rooms on the small side; some visitors have complained about noise. [$] *Rooms from: $105* ✉ *10 Lincoln St., Coulee Dam* ☎ *509/633–2100, 800/633–6421* 🌐 *www.columbiariverinn.com* 🛏 *34 rooms, 1 suite* 🍽 *No meals.*

OMAK

52 miles northwest of Grand Coulee Dam.

Omak is a small mill and orchard town in the beautifully rustic Okanogan Valley of north-central Washington. Lake Omak to the southeast, on the Colville Reservation, is part of an ancient channel of the Columbia River, which ran north prior to the last Ice Age before turning south at Omak in what is now the lower Okanogan Valley.

For years Omak has been criticized by animal lovers for its mid-August Omak Stampede and Suicide Race. During the annual event, wild horses race down a steep bluff and across the Okanogan River. Some horses have been killed and riders seriously injured. Many of the riders are from the Colville Reservation, and elders defend the race as part of Native American culture. Despite the detractors, more spectators attend the event each year.

GETTING HERE AND AROUND

Omak can be reached from the west via Highway 20 from the Methow Valley area. From Ephrata, head north via Highway 17, then Highway 97. From Grand Coulee Dam, take WA 155N.

EXPLORING

FAMILY **Okanogan County Historical Museum.** Okanogan pioneer life is portrayed in the displays here, and there's a replica of an Old West town. Outside are Okanogan's oldest building, a 19th-century log cabin, and antique farm equipment. ⊠ *1410 2nd Ave. N, Okanogan* ☎ *509/422–4272* ⊕ *okanoganhistory.org* 🖾 *$2* ☉ *Memorial Day weekend–Labor Day, daily 10–4; otherwise by appointment.*

Okanogan–Wenatchee National Forest. This is a region of open woods, meadows, and pastoral river valleys in the Okanogan highlands. There's lots of wildlife: deer, black bears, coyotes, badgers, bobcats, cougars, grouse, hawks, and golden eagles. Campgrounds are scattered throughout the region. There are 11 Sno-Parks with groomed trails for snowmobilers, and open areas for cross-country skiing. Ski areas are at Loup Loup Pass (Nordic and alpine) and Sitzmark (alpine only). ⊠ *1240 S. 2nd Ave. (office), Okanogan* ☎ *509/826–3275* ⊕ *www.fs.usda.gov/okawen* 🖾 *Free; permits required at Sno-Parks* ☉ *Office: weekdays 7:45–4:30.*

WHERE TO EAT AND STAY

For expanded hotel reviews, visit Fodors.com.

$ ╳ **Breadline Cafe.** For more than 30 years, Breadline has been a top
ECLECTIC destination for dinner and live music in the Okanogan Valley. A varied
Fodor'sChoice menu highlights local organic produce, locally raised natural Angus
★ beef, crepes, and seafood. You'll find Cajun dishes such as jambalaya, as well as an around-the-world assortment of cuisines, including Italian and Greek. Enjoy the breakfast buffet on Saturday. The bakery features a daily cupcake and other pastries and breads for take-out; or indulge in a decadent dessert with your meal, including brandied bread pudding and soda fountain treats like banana splits and sundaes. There's even ice cream sodas with lemoncello and other liqueurs. $ *Average main: $15*

✉ *102 S. Ash St.* ☎ *509/826–5836* ⊕ *www.breadlinecafe.com* ⊗ *Closed Sun. and Mon. No breakfast Sun.–Fri.*

$
HOTEL
🛏 **Omak Inn.** Just off U.S. 97, this motel is close to restaurants and shopping and has a small patio and expansive lawn for relaxing in the summer heat or walking the dog. **Pros:** most rooms have microwaves and refrigerators; reasonable rates. **Cons:** room style is basic; no elevator. 💲 *Rooms from: $75* ✉ *912 Koala Dr.* ☎ *509/826–3822, 800/204–4800* ⊕ *www.omakinnwa.com* ↰ *66 rooms* ⧉ *Breakfast.*

COLVILLE

115 miles east of Omak.

This small town, the seat of Stevens County, sits in a valley surrounded by lakes, forests, and mountains. The town has many well-maintained old houses and a pleasant, well-to-do atmosphere. Colville became regionally famous in 1983 when Mike Hale opened Hale's Microbrewery—which later moved to the Seattle area.

GETTING HERE AND AROUND

Colville is a direct drive north of Spokane via Highway 395.

ESSENTIALS

Visitor Information Colville Chamber of Commerce ✉ *986 S. Main St., Ste. B* ☎ *509/684–5973* ⊕ *www.colville.com.*

EXPLORING

Colville National Forest. This vast region encompasses mountains, forests, and meadows in the state's northeast corner. Here the desert area ends, and three mountain ranges (Selkirks, Kettle River, and Okanogan)—considered foothills of the Rocky Mountains—traverse the region from north to south. It's a beautiful, wild area, where only the river bottoms are dotted with widely spaced settlements and where the mountains (with an average height of about 4,500 feet) are largely pristine. The streams abound with trout, and the forests with deer and black bears. This is perfect backpacking country, with many trails to remote mountain lakes. ✉ *765 S. Main St. (Forest Service office)* ☎ *509/684–7000* ⊕ *www.fs.usda.gov/colville* ⌷ *Free* ⊗ *Daily dawn–dusk.*

FAMILY
Fort Colville Museum. Visitors here can see a farmstead, lookout tower, trappers' cabins, blacksmith shop, sawmill, and museum. ✉ *700 N. Wynne St.* ☎ *509/684–5968* ⊕ *www.stevenscountyhistoricalsociety.org* ⌷ *$5* ⊗ *May–Sept., Mon.–Thurs. 10–4, Fri.–Sun. 1–4; Oct.–Apr., by appointment.*

WHERE TO EAT AND STAY

For expanded hotel reviews, visit Fodors.com.

$$
PACIFIC
NORTHWEST
Fodor's Choice
★
✕ **Lovitt Restaurant.** Occupying a 1908 farmhouse, it's no surprise that the emphasis here is on farm-fresh ingredients, and owners Norman and Kristen Six are sincerely committed to localized sourcing. Their original Lovitt Restaurant in Chicago won numerous accolades, and their talents have been well received here since their move back to where Norman grew up. The menu is driven by what's in season, but expect to find at least one vegetarian dish, as well as steak and burgers

18

made from grass-fed beef. Flatbread starters come with toppings like Cougar Gold cheese and Dry Fly Gin-cured salmon. Chocolate bon-bons with homemade honey vanilla ice cream and cherry sauce are a favorite dessert item. In summer, enjoy outside dining with views of the bucolic Colville Valley. Reservations, while not required, are recommended due to the distance from Spokane. ⓢ *Average main: $20* ⊠ *149 Hwy. 395 S* ☏ *509/684–5444* ⊕ *www.lovittrestaurant.com* ⊘ *Closed Mon. and Tues. Closed Sun. Oct.–Apr. No lunch.*

$ ⬚ **Benny's Colville Inn.** This is a comfortable family motel nestled in a pris-
HOTEL   tine valley between the Kettle River and Selkirk mountain ranges. **Pros:** family-owned; friendly staff; very affordable. **Cons:** some have com-plained that beds are hard and the older, budget-priced rooms are small. ⓢ *Rooms from: $57* ⊠ *915 S. Main St.* ☏ *509/684–2517, 800/680–2517* ⊕ *www.colvilleinn.com* ⇗ *100 rooms, 5 suites* ⦿ *Breakfast.*

VANCOUVER
AND VICTORIA

WELCOME TO VANCOUVER AND VICTORIA

TOP REASONS TO GO

★ **Stanley Park:** The views, the activities, and the natural wilderness beauty here are quintessential Vancouver.

★ **Granville Island:** Ride the mini-ferry across False Creek to the Granville Island Public Market, where you can shop for delicious lunch fixings; eat outside when the weather's fine.

★ **Museum of Anthropology:** The phenomenal collection of First Nations art and cultural artifacts, and the incredible backdrop, make this a must-see.

★ **The Journey here:** Yup, getting here is one of the best things about Victoria. Whether by ferry meandering past the Gulf or San Juan islands, by floatplane (try to travel at least one leg this way), or on a whale-watching boat, just getting to Victoria from the mainland is a memorable experience.

★ **Butchart Gardens:** A million and a half visitors can't be wrong—these lavish gardens north of town truly live up to the hype.

1 Vancouver. Many people say that Vancouver is the most gorgeous city in North America, and situated as it is, between mountains and water, it's hard to disagree. The Vancouver area actually covers a lot of ground, but the central core—Downtown, Gastown, Yaletown, Chinatown, Stanley Park, and Granville Island—is fairly compact. An excellent public transportation system makes getting around a snap. When in doubt, remember that the mountains are north.

2 Victoria. British Columbia's capital city, Victoria, is a lovely, walkable city with waterfront paths, lovely gardens, fascinating museums, and splendid 19th-century architecture. In some senses remote, it's roughly midway between Vancouver and Seattle and about three hours by car and ferry from either city.

GETTING ORIENTED

The city of Victoria is on Vancouver Island (not Victoria Island). The city of Vancouver is on the British Columbia mainland, not on Vancouver Island, or on Victoria Island (which isn't in British Columbia but rather way up north, spanning parts of Nunavut and the Northwest Territories). For the most part, Vancouver central sits on a peninsula, which makes it compact and easy to explore on foot, especially since most streets are laid out on a grid system. To get your bearings, use the mountains as your "true north" and you can't go too far wrong. All the avenues, which are numbered, have east and west designations; the higher the number, the farther away from the inlet you are. At the southern tip of Vancouver Island, forming the western point of a triangle with Seattle and Vancouver, Victoria dips slightly below the 49th parallel. That puts it farther south than most of Canada, giving it the mildest climate in the country, with virtually no snow and less than half the rain of Vancouver.

19

Updated by
Carolyn B.
Heller, Paige
Donner, and
Chris McBeath

Consistently ranked as one of the world's most livable cities, Vancouver lures visitors with its abundance of natural beauty, multicultural vitality, and cosmopolitan flair. Victoria, the capital of a province whose license plates brazenly label it "The Best Place on Earth," is a walkable, livable seaside town of fragrant gardens, waterfront paths, engaging museums, and beautifully restored 19th-century architecture.

The mountains and seascape make Vancouver an outdoor playground for hiking, skiing, kayaking, cycling, and sailing—and so much more—while the cuisine and arts scenes are equally diverse, reflecting the makeup of Vancouver's ethnic (predominantly Asian) mosaic. Yet despite all this vibrancy, the city still exudes an easy West Coast style that can make New York or London feel, in comparison, edgy and claustrophobic to some.

Victoria was the first European settlement on Vancouver Island, and in 1868 it became the capital of British Columbia. In summer the Inner Harbour—Victoria's social and cultural center—buzzes with visiting yachts, horse-and-carriage rides, street entertainers, and excursion boats heading out to visit pods of friendly local whales. Yes, it might be a bit touristy, but Victoria's good looks, gracious pace, and manageable size are instantly beguiling, especially if you stand back to admire the mountains and ocean beyond.

VANCOUVER

More than 8 million visitors each year come to Canada's third-largest metropolitan area. Because of its peninsula location, traffic flow is a contentious issue. Thankfully, Vancouver is wonderfully walkable, especially in the downtown core. The North Shore is a scoot across the harbor, and the rapid-transit system to Richmond and the airport means that staying in the more affordable 'burbs doesn't have to be synonymous with sacrificing convenience. The mild climate, exquisite natural scenery, and relaxed outdoor lifestyle keep attracting residents, and the number of visitors is increasing for the same reasons. People often get their first glimpse of Vancouver when catching an Alaskan cruise, and many return at some point to spend more time here.

VANCOUVER PLANNER

WHEN TO GO

From June to September, it seems like the entire populace of Vancouver migrates to the beaches, parks, and hiking trails. Daffodils and cherry blossoms transform city streets from March to May. Despite the risk of rain, October's cool, crisp mornings almost invariably give way to marvelous sunshine sparkling through multicolored leaves. Come winter, expect lots of hotel and restaurant bargains.

PLANNING YOUR TIME

If you don't have much time in Vancouver, you'll probably still want to spend at least a half day in Stanley Park: start out early for a walk, bike, or shuttle ride through the park to see the Vancouver Aquarium Marine Science Centre, enjoy the views from Prospect Point, and stroll the seawall. If you leave the park at English Bay, you can have lunch on Denman or Robson Street, and meander past the trendy shops between Jervis and Burrard streets. Or, exit the park at Coal Harbour and follow the Seawall Walk to Canada Place, stopping for lunch at a harbor-front restaurant. A couple of hours at the Granville Island Public Market are also a must.

Walking the downtown core is a great way to get to know the city. Start at Canada Place and head east to Gastown and Chinatown; that's a good half day. Then head north to Yaletown and travel back via Robson Street, by which time you'll have earned yourself a glass of British Columbia wine at one of Vancouver's excellent restaurants.

If you're traveling with children, make sure to check out Science World, Grouse Mountain, and the Capilano Suspension Bridge or Lynn Canyon.

GETTING HERE AND AROUND

AIR TRAVEL

There are direct flights from most major U.S. and international cities to Vancouver International Airport (YVR), with connecting services to Victoria.

CAR TRAVEL

Interstate highway I–5 heads straight up the U.S. coast into Vancouver. However you travel, carry a passport. Without one, even U.S. citizens might not be allowed home. That includes minors. Check out full details in the Travel Smart chapter.

FERRY TRAVEL

Twelve-passenger ferry boats bypass busy bridges and are a key reason why you don't need a car in Vancouver. Aquabus Ferries and False Creek Ferries are private commercial enterprises that provide passenger services between key locales on either side of False Creek. Single-ride tickets range from C$3.25 to C$6.50, depending on the route; day passes are C$15. Aquabus Ferries connections include The Village

19

(Science World and the Olympic Village), Plaza of Nations, Granville Island, Stamp's Landing, Spyglass Place, Yaletown, David Lam Park, and the Hornby Street dock. False Creek Ferries provides service between the Aquatic Centre on Beach Avenue, Granville Island, Science World, Stamp's Landing, and Vanier Park. False Creek and Aquabus ferries are not part of the TransLink system.

Ferry Contacts Aquabus Ferries ☎ *604/689–5858* ⊕ *www.theaquabus.com.* **False Creek Ferries** ☎ *604/684–7781* ⊕ *www.granvilleislandferries.bc.ca.* **Sea-Bus** ☎ *604/953–3333* ⊕ *www.translink.ca.*

TAXI TRAVEL

It can be hard to hail a cab in Vancouver. Unless you're near a hotel or find a taxi rank (designated curbside parking areas), you'll have better luck calling a taxi service. Try Black Top & Checker Cabs or Yellow Cab.

Taxi Companies Black Top & Checker Cabs ☎ *604/731–1111* ⊕ *www.btccabs. ca.* **Yellow Cab** ☎ *604/681–1111* ⊕ *www.yellowcabonline.com.*

PUBLIC TRANSIT TRAVEL

Central Vancouver is extremely walkable, and TransLink, Metro Vancouver's public transport system—a mix of bus, ferry, and the SkyTrain (a fully automated rail system)—is easy and efficient to use. Transfer tickets enable you to travel from one system to the other. The hop-on-hop-off Vancouver Trolley buses circle the city in a continuous loop, and are a great way to see the sights.

Contacts SkyTrain ☎ *604/953–3333* ⊕ *www.translink.ca.* **TransLink** ☎ *604/953–3333* ⊕ *www.translink.ca.* **Vancouver Trolley** ☎ *888/451–5581* ⊕ *www.vancouvertrolley.com.*

TOURS

Edible Canada. Culinary tour company Edible Canada provides guided tours of Granville Island, including a food-focused exploration of the Public Market and a combination market/shopping tour. They also run guided culinary walks around Vancouver's Chinatown, with an optional dim sum lunch. ☎ *604/558–0040, 866/272–8777* ⊕ *www. ediblecanada.com.*

EXPLORING

The city's downtown core includes the main business district between Robson Street and the Burrard Inlet harbor front; the West End that edges up against English Bay; Stanley Park; trendy Yaletown; and Gastown and Chinatown, which are the oldest parts of the city. Main Street, which runs north-south, is roughly the dividing line between the east and west sides. The entire downtown district sits on a peninsula bordered by English Bay and the Pacific Ocean to the west; by False Creek to the south; and by Burrard Inlet, the city's working port, to the north, where the North Shore Mountains loom.

Elsewhere in the city you'll find other places of interest: the North Shore is across Burrard Inlet (Whistler is a two-hour drive from here); Granville Island is south of downtown across False Creek; the West

Side comprises several neighborhoods across from English Bay in the West End. Richmond, where the airport is, is to the south; the suburbs of Burnaby and the Fraser Valley are to the east.

DOWNTOWN AND THE WEST END

Vancouver's compact downtown juxtaposes historic architecture with gleaming brand-new buildings. Sightseeing venues include museums, galleries, and top-notch shopping, most notably along Robson Street, and in and around couture-savvy Sinclair Centre. The harbor front, with the gleaming convention center, has a fabulous water's-edge path all the way to Stanley Park, epitomizing what Vancouver is all about.

Fodor's Choice
★

Bill Reid Gallery. Vancouver's newest aboriginal art gallery, named after one of B.C.'s pre-eminent artists, Bill Reid (1920–98), is as much a legacy of his works as it is a showcase of current artists. Displays include wood carvings, jewelry, print, and sculpture. The gallery may be small but its expansive offerings often include artist talks and other public programs. Bill Reid is best known for his bronze statue, "The Spirit of Haida Gwaii, The Jade Canoe"—measuring 12 ft x 20 ft; the original is an iconic meeting place at the Vancouver International Airport and its image is on the back of the Canadian $20 bill. ⊠ *639 Hornby St., Downtown* ☎ *604/682–3455* ⊕ *www.billreidgallery.ca* ⊠ *C$10* ☉ *Open Wed.–Sun. 11–5.*

Canada Place. Extending four city blocks (about a mile and a half) north into Burrard Inlet, this complex (once a cargo pier) mimics the style and size of a luxury ocean liner, with exterior esplanades. The Teflon-coated fiberglass roof, shaped like five sails (the material was invented by NASA and once used in astronaut space suits), has become a Vancouver skyline landmark. Home to Vancouver's main cruise-ship terminal, Canada Place can accommodate up to four luxury liners at once. Follow the **Canadian Trail** on the west side of the building with displays about the country's provinces and territories; with your smart phone or other device, you can access multimedia content along the trail (there's free Wi-Fi). Also check out the **War of 1812 Experience**, commemorating the bicentennial of this conflict. Canada Place is also home to the luxurious **Pan Pacific Hotel** and the East Building of the **Vancouver Convention Centre** (☎ *604/689–8232*); you can follow the outdoor walkways across the plazas to the Convention Centre's even-more-impressive window-lined West Building. The waterfront promenades, which wind all the way to Stanley Park, present spectacular vantage points to view Burrard Inlet and the North Shore Mountains; plaques posted at intervals offer historical information about the city and its waterfront. ⊠ *999 Canada Place Way, Downtown* ☎ *604/775–7200* ⊕ *www.canadaplace.ca.*

Robson Street. Robson, Vancouver's busiest shopping street, is lined with see-and-be-seen sidewalk cafés, chain stores, and high-end boutiques. The street, which links downtown to the West End, is particularly lively between Jervis and Burrard streets and stays that way into the evening with buskers and entertainers. ⊕ *www.robsonstreet.ca.*

Roedde House Museum. Two blocks south of Robson Street is the Roedde (pronounced *roh*-dee) House Museum, an 1893 house in the Queen Anne Revival style, set among Victorian-style gardens. Tours of the

19

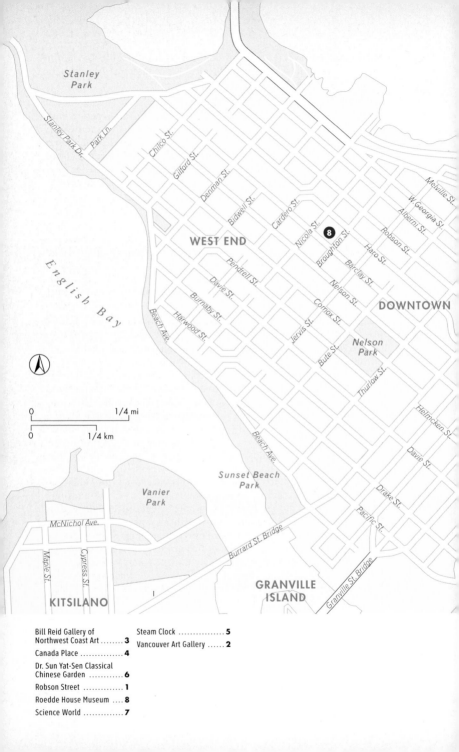

Stanley Park

Stanley Park Dr.

Park Ln.

Chilco St.

Gilford St.

Denman St.

Bidwell St.

Cardero St.

Nicola St.

Broughton St.

Melville St.

W. Georgia St.

Alberni St.

Robson St.

Haro St.

WEST END

Barclay St.

Nelson St.

DOWNTOWN

Pendrell St.

Davie St.

Burnaby St.

Harwood St.

Beach Ave.

Comox St.

Jervis St.

Bute St.

English Bay

8

Nelson Park

Thurlow St.

Helmcken St.

Davie St.

Beach Ave.

Sunset Beach Park

Vanier Park

McNichol Ave.

Burrard St. Bridge

Drake St.

Pacific St.

Granville St. Bridge

Maple St.

Cypress St.

KITSILANO

GRANVILLE ISLAND

0   1/4 mi

0   1/4 km

Vancouver Downtown, Gastown, Chinatown and Yaletown

Burrard Inlet

Coal Harbor Rd.

W.Hastings St.

W.Pender St.

Canada Place Way

4

Vancouver Club

WATERFRONT

Royal Centre

Royal Bank

Sinclair Centre

W.Cordova St.

W.Pender St.

W.Hastings St.

5

GASTOWN

Portside Park

Coal Harbour Rd.

Alexander St.

BURRARD

3

Dunsmuir St.

W.Georgia St.

Christ Church Cathedral

2

GRANVILLE

SKYTRAIN

Cambie St.

Water St.

Cordova St.

Hastings St.

E. Powell St.

Columbia St.

Main St.

Hornby St.

Howe St.

1

Granville St.

Seymour St.

Richards St.

Homer St.

Hamilton St.

Smithe St.

Cambie St.

Beatty St.

Pender St.

Carrall St.

CHINATOWN

Chinatown Memorial Monument

6

Keefer St.

West Han Dynasty Bell

Chinese Cultural Centre Museum and Archives

Burrard St.

Nelson St.

YALETOWN

STADIUM

Expo Blvd.

Pacific Blvd. South

Union St.

Georgia St.

Columbia St.

Main St.

Hamilton St.

Marinaside Ct.

Cambie St. Bridge

False Creek

Creek

7

MAIN STREET

KEY

🚢 SeaBus

restored, antiques-furnished interior take about an hour. On Sunday, tours are followed by tea and cookies. The gardens (free) can be visited anytime. ⊠ *1415 Barclay St., between Broughton and Nicola Sts., West End* ☎ *604/684–7040* ⊕ *www.roeddehouse.org* ⊠ *C$5; Sun. C$6, including tea* ☉ *Open Tues.–Sun. 1–4.*

Vancouver Art Gallery. Painter Emily Carr's haunting evocations of the British Columbian hinterland are among the attractions at western Canada's largest art gallery. Carr (1871–1945), a grocer's daughter from Victoria, fell in love with the wilderness around her and shocked middle-class Victorian society by running off to paint it. Her work accentuates the mysticism and the danger of B.C.'s wilderness, and records the diminishing presence of native cultures during that era (there's something of a renaissance now). The gallery, which also hosts touring historical and contemporary exhibitions, is housed in a 1911 courthouse that Canadian architect Arthur Erickson redesigned in the early 1980s as part of the Robson Square redevelopment. Stone lions guard the steps to the parklike Georgia Street side; the main entrance is accessed from Robson Square or Hornby Street. ⊠ *750 Hornby St., Downtown* ☎ *604/662–4719* ⊕ *www.vanartgallery.bc.ca* ⊠ *C$19.50; higher for some exhibits; by donation Tues. 5–9* ☉ *Open Wed.–Mon. 10–5:30, Tues. 10–9.*

GASTOWN AND CHINATOWN

Gastown and Chinatown are favorite destinations for visitors and residents alike. Gastown is fast becoming überhip as boutiques, ad agencies, and restaurants take over refurbished brick warehouses. Chinatown's array of produce stalls and curious alleyways make it look as if they're resisting gentrification, but inside many of the historic buildings are getting a new lease on life.

Dr. Sun Yat-Sen Chinese Garden. The first authentic Ming Dynasty–style garden outside China, this small garden was built in 1986 by 52 Chinese artisans from Suzhou. It incorporates design elements and traditional materials from several of Suzhou's centuries-old private gardens. No power tools, screws, or nails were used in the construction. Guided tours (45 minutes long), included in the ticket price, are conducted on the hour between mid-June and the end of August (call ahead or check the website for off-season tour times); tours are valuable for understanding the philosophy and symbolism that are central to the garden's design. A concert series, including classical, Asian, world, jazz, and sacred music, plays on Friday evenings in July, August, and early September. The free public park next door is also designed as a traditional Chinese garden. ■ TIP→ Covered walkways make this a good rainy-day choice. ⊠ *578 Carrall St., Chinatown* ☎ *604/662–3207* ⊕ *www.vancouverchinesegarden.com* ⊠ *C$12* ☉ *May–mid-June and Sept., daily 10–6; mid-June–Aug., daily 9:30–7; Oct., daily 10–4:30; Nov.–Apr., Tues.–Sun. 10–4:30.*

Steam Clock. An underground steam system, which also heats many local buildings, supplies the world's first steam clock—possibly Vancouver's most-photographed attraction. On the quarter hour a steam whistle rings out the Westminster chimes, and on the hour a huge cloud of steam spews from the apparatus. The ingenious design, based on an 1875 mechanism, was built in 1977 by Ray Saunders of Landmark Clocks (at 123 Cambie Street) to commemorate the community effort that saved Gastown from demolition. ⊠ *Water St., at Cambie St., Gastown.*

YALETOWN AND FALSE CREEK

In 1985–86 the provincial government cleaned up a derelict industrial site on the north shore of False Creek, built a world's fair, and invited everyone; 20 million people showed up at Expo '86. Now the site of the fair has become one of the largest and most densely populated urban-redevelopment projects in North America.

Tucked into the forest of green-glass condo towers is the old warehouse district of Yaletown. It's one of the city's most fashionable neighborhoods, and the Victorian-brick loading docks have become terraces for cappuccino bars.

FAMILY **Science World.** In a gigantic shiny dome built over the Omnimax theater, this hands-on science center encourages children to participate in interactive exhibits and demonstrations about the natural world, the human body, and other science topics. Exhibits change throughout the year, so there's always something new to see. Adjacent to the museum, the Ken Spencer Science Park is an outdoor exhibit area focusing on environmental issues. It's an easy walk (and mini-ferry ride) from Yaletown; the Main Street/Science World SkyTrain station is on its doorstep, and there's plenty of parking. ⊠ *1455 Quebec St., False Creek* ☎ *604/443–7440* ⊕ *www.scienceworld.bc.ca* ☞ *C$23.50 Science World, C$29 Science World and Omnimax theater* ☉ *July–Labor Day, daily 10–6; Sept.–June, weekdays 10–5, weekends 10–6.*

STANLEY PARK

Fodor'sChoice ★ A 1,000-acre wilderness park, only blocks from the downtown section of a major city, is a rare treasure. Stanley Park is, perhaps, the single most prized possession of Vancouverites, who make use of it fervently to cycle, walk, jog, Rollerblade, play cricket and tennis, and enjoy outdoor art shows and theater performances alongside attractions such as the renowned aquarium.

Lost Lagoon Nature House. For information about guided nature walks in the park, contact the Lost Lagoon Nature House on the south shore of Lost Lagoon, at the foot of Alberni Street. In July and August, the Nature House is open 10 am to 5 pm Tuesday through Sunday; from September through June, they're open Saturday and Sunday only, 10 am to 4 pm. ☎ *604/257–8544* ⊕ *www.stanleyparkecology.ca.*

Prospect Point. At 211 feet, Prospect Point is the highest point in the park and provides striking views of the Lions Gate Bridge (watch for cruise ships passing below), the North Shore, and Burrard Inlet. There's also a year-round souvenir shop, a snack bar with terrific ice cream, and a restaurant. From the seawall, you can see where cormorants build their seaweed nests along the cliff ledges.

Fodor'sChoice ★ **Seawall.** The seawall path, a 9-km (5½-mile) paved shoreline route popular with walkers, cyclists, and in-line skaters, is one of several

19

car-free zones within the park. If you have the time (about a half day) and the energy, strolling the entire seawall is an exhilarating experience. It extends an additional mile east past the marinas, cafés, and waterfront condominiums of Coal Harbour to Canada Place downtown, so you could start your walk or ride from there. From the south side of the park, the seawall continues for another 28 km (17 miles) along Vancouver's waterfront, to the University of British Columbia, allowing for a pleasant, if ambitious, day's bike ride. Along the seawall, cyclists must wear helmets and stay on their side of the path. Within Stanley Park, cyclists must ride in a counterclockwise direction.

The seawall can get crowded on summer weekends, but inside the park is a 28-km (17-miles) network of peaceful walking and cycling paths through old- and second-growth forest. The wheelchair-accessible Beaver Lake Interpretive Trail is a good choice if you're interested in park ecology. Take a map—they're available at the park-information booth and many of the concession stands—and don't go into the woods alone or after dusk.

FAMILY **Vancouver Aquarium Marine Science Centre.** Massive pools with windows below water level let you come face to face with beluga whales, sea otters, sea lions, dolphins, and harbor seals at this research and educational facility. In the Amazon rain-forest gallery you can walk through a jungle populated with piranhas, caimans, and tropical birds, and in summer, you'll be surrounded by hundreds of free-flying butterflies. Other displays, many with hands-on features for kids, show the underwater life of coastal British Columbia and the Canadian Arctic. A Tropic Zone is home to exotic freshwater and saltwater life, including clown fish, moray eels, and black-tip reef sharks. Beluga whale, sea lion, and dolphin shows, as well as dive shows (where divers swim with aquatic life, including sharks) are held daily. Make sure to check out the "4-D" film experience; it's a multisensory show that puts mist, smell, and wind into the 3-D equation. For an extra fee, you can help the trainers feed and train otters, belugas, and sea lions. There's also a café and a gift shop. Be prepared for lines on weekends and school holidays. ■ TIP➔ In summer, the quietest time to visit is before 11 am or after 4 pm; in other seasons, there are fewer crowds before noon or after 2 pm. ✉ *845 Avison Way, Stanley Park* ☎ *604/659–3474* ⊕ *www.vanaqua.org* ✉ *C$27* ⏲ *July–Labor Day, daily 9:30–7; Labor Day– June, daily 9:30–5:30.*

GRANVILLE ISLAND

The creative redevelopment of this former industrial wasteland vies with Stanley Park as the city's top attraction. An active cement works remains at its heart, and is oddly complemented with a thriving diversity of artists' studios, performing arts spaces, an indoor food market, specialty shops, and a jammed-to-the-gunnels marina.

If your schedule is tight, you can tour Granville Island in two to three hours. If you like to shop, you could spend a full day.

Fodor's Choice **Granville Island Public Market.** Dozens of stalls in this 50,000-square-foot
★ building sell locally grown fruits and vegetables direct from the farm and other produce from farther afield; others stock crafts, chocolates,

cheese, fish, meat, flowers, and exotic foods. On Thursdays in summer, farmers sell fruit and vegetables from trucks outside. At the north end of the market, you can pick up a snack, lunch, or coffee from one of the many prepared-food vendors. The Market Courtyard, on the waterside, is a good place to catch street entertainers—be prepared to get roped into the action, if only to check the padlocks of an escape artist's gear. Weekends can get madly busy. ⊠ *1689 Johnston St., Granville Island* ☎ *604/666–5784* ⊕ *www.granvilleisland.com* ⊗ *Open daily 9–7.*

FAMILY **Kids Market.** A converted factory warehouse sets the stage for a slice of kids' heaven on Granville Island. The Kids Market has an indoor play area and two floors of small shops that sell all kinds of toys, magic gear, books, and other fun stuff. ⊠ *1496 Cartwright St., Granville Island* ☎ *604/689–8447* ⊕ *www.kidsmarket.ca* ⊗ *Open daily 10–6.*

Net Loft. A former loft where fishermen used to dry their nets, this blue-and-red building includes a bookstore, a café, and a collection of high-quality boutiques selling imported and locally made crafts, exotic fabrics, handmade paper, and First Nations art. ⊠ *1666 Johnston St., Granville Island* ⊗ *Open daily 10–7.*

THE WEST SIDE AND KITSILANO

Once a hippie haven, Kitsilano has gone upmarket. Distinctive homes and specialty shopping now make up some of the country's most expensive few square miles of real estate. The West Side has the city's best gardens and natural sights; "Kits," however, is really where all the action is.

Fodor's Choice ★ **Museum of Anthropology.** Part of the University of British Columbia, the MOA has one of the world's leading collections of Northwest Coast First Nations art. The Great Hall displays dramatic cedar poles, bentwood boxes, and canoes adorned with traditional Northwest Coast–painted designs. On clear days, the gallery's 50-foot-tall windows reveal a striking backdrop of mountains and sea. Another highlight is the work of the late Bill Reid, one of Canada's most respected Haida artists. In *The Raven and the First Men* (1980), carved in yellow cedar, he tells a Haida story of creation. Reid's gold-and-silver jewelry work is also on display, as are exquisite carvings of gold, silver, and argillite (a black shale found on Haida Gwaii, also known as the Queen Charlotte Islands) by other First Nations artists. The museum's visible storage section displays, in drawers and cases, contain thousands of examples of tools, textiles, masks, and other artifacts from around the world. The Koerner Ceramics Gallery contains 600 pieces from 15th- to 19th-century Europe. Behind the museum are two Haida houses, set on the cliff over the water. Free guided tours—given several times daily (call for confirm times)—are immensely informative. For an extra C$5 you can rent a VUEguide, an electronic device which senses where you are in the museum and shows relevant artist interviews, archival footage, and photographs of the artifacts in their original contexts, on a handheld screen. Arthur Erickson designed the cliff-top structure that houses the MOA, which also has an excellent book and fine-art shop and a café. To reach the museum by transit, take any UBC-bound bus from Granville Street downtown to the university bus loop, a 10-minute walk from the museum. ▥ TIP→ Pay parking is available in the Rose Garden

19

Part of the attraction of the Museum of Anthropology are the exhibits outside the museum, on the cliffs overlooking the water.

parking lot, across Marine Drive from the museum. ⊠ *University of British Columbia, 6393 N.W. Marine Dr., Point Grey* ☎ *604/822–5087* ⊕ *www.moa.ubc.ca* ✉ *C$16.75, Tues. 5–9 C$9* ☉ *Late May–mid-Oct., Tues. 10–9, Wed.–Mon. 10–5; mid-Oct.–late May, Tues. 10–9, Wed.–Sun. 10–5.*

FAMILY **Queen Elizabeth Park.** At the highest point in the city, showcasing 360-degree views of downtown, this 52-hectare (130-acre) park has lavish sunken gardens (in a former stone quarry), a rose garden, and an abundance of grassy picnicking spots. Other park facilities include 18 tennis courts, pitch and putt (an 18-hole putting green), and a restaurant. On summer evenings there's free outdoor dancing on the Plaza—everything from Scottish country dance to salsa, for all ages and levels. In the **Bloedel Conservatory** you can see tropical and desert plants and 100 species of free-flying tropical birds in a glass geodesic dome—the perfect place to be on a rainy day. To reach the park by public transportation, take the Canada Line to King Edward station; from there, it's a six-block walk to the edge of the park (and a hike up the hill to appreciate the views). Cambie Bus 15, which runs south along Cambie Street from the Olympic Village SkyTrain station, will drop you a little closer, at the corner of 33rd and Cambie. ■ TIP➔ **Park activities make for a great family excursion, and unlike Stanley Park with its acres of rain forest, Queen Elizabeth Park is all about the flowers.** ⊠ *Cambie St. and 33rd Ave., Cambie Corridor* ☎ *604/257–8584* ⊕ *www.vancouver.ca/parks* ✉ *Conservatory C$5* ☉ *Park daily year-round; Conservatory May–mid-Sept., weekdays 9–8, weekends 10–9; mid-Sept.–Apr., daily 10–5.*

NORTH SHORE

The North Shore and its star attractions—the Capilano Suspension Bridge, Grouse Mountain, Lonsdale Quay, and, farther east, the lovely hamlet of Deep Cove—are just a short trip from downtown Vancouver.

FAMILY

Fodor's Choice

★

Capilano Suspension Bridge. At Vancouver's oldest tourist attraction (the original bridge was built in 1889), you can get a taste of rain-forest scenery and test your mettle on the swaying, 450-foot cedar-plank suspension bridge that hangs 230 feet above the rushing Capilano River. Across the bridge is the Treetops Adventure, where you can walk along 650 feet of cable bridges suspended among the trees. If you're even braver, you can follow the **Cliffwalk,** a series of narrow cantilevered bridges and walkways hanging out over the edge of the canyon. Without crossing the bridge, you can enjoy the site's viewing decks, nature trails, totem park, and carving center (where you can watch First Nations carvers at work), as well as history and forestry exhibits, a massive gift shop in the original 1911 teahouse, and a restaurant. May through October, guides in 19th-century costumes conduct free tours on themes related to history, nature, or ecology, while fiddle bands, First Nations dancers, and other entertainers keep things lively. In December, more than 250,000 lights illuminate the canyon during the Canyon Lights winter celebration. ■TIP➜ Catch the attraction's free shuttle service from Canada Place; it also stops along Burrard and Robson streets. ✉ *3735 Capilano Rd., North Vancouver* ☎ *604/985–7474* ⊕ *www. capbridge.com* ▦ *C$34.95* ⊗ *Daily.*

FAMILY

Grouse Mountain. North America's largest aerial tramway, the **Skyride** is a great way to take in the city, sea, and mountain vistas (be sure to pick a clear day or evening). The Skyride makes the 2-km (1-mile) climb to the peak of Grouse Mountain every 15 minutes. Once at the top you can watch a half-hour video presentation at the Theatre in the Sky (it's included with your Skyride ticket). Other mountaintop activities include, in summer, lumberjack shows, chairlift rides, walking tours, hiking, falconry demonstrations, and a chance to visit the grizzly bears and gray wolves in the mountain's wildlife refuge. For an extra fee you can also try zip-lining and tandem paragliding, tour the wind turbine that tops the mountain, or take a helicopter flight. In winter you can ski, snowshoe, snowboard, ice-skate on a mountaintop pond, or take Sno-Cat-drawn sleigh rides. A stone-and-cedar lodge is home to snack shops, a pub-style bistro, and a high-end restaurant, with expansive city views. ■TIP➜ The Grouse Grind—a hiking trail up the face of the mountain—is one of the best workouts on the North Shore. Depending on your fitness level, allow between 40 minutes and two hours to complete it (90 minutes is an average time). Then you can take the Skyride down. The BCMC Trail is a less crowded, slightly longer alternative. *(⇨ See the Vancouver Outdoors chapter for more info.)* ✉ *6400 Nancy Greene Way, North Vancouver* ☎ *604/980–9311* ⊕ *www.grousemountain.com* ▦ *Skyride and many activities C$39.95* ⊗ *Daily 9 am–10 pm.*

19

WHERE TO EAT

From inventive downtown bistros to waterfront seafood palaces, to Asian restaurants that rival those in Asia, Vancouver has a diverse array of gastronomical options. Many cutting-edge establishments are defining and perfecting Modern Canadian fare, which incorporates Pacific Northwest seafood—notably salmon and halibut—and locally grown produce, often accompanied by British Columbia wines.

British Columbia's wine industry is enjoying great popularity, and many restaurants feature wines from the province's 100-plus wineries. Most B.C. wines come from the Okanagan Valley in the province's interior, but Vancouver Island is another main wine-producing area. Merlot, Pinot Noir, Pinot Gris, and Chardonnay are among the major varieties; also look for ice wine, a dessert wine made from grapes that are picked while they are frozen on the vines.

Dining is informal. Neat casual dress is appropriate everywhere; nice jeans are fine, though you might want something dressier than sneakers in the evening. A 15% tip is expected. A 5% Goods and Services Tax (GST) is levied on restaurant bills, and an additional 10% liquor tax is charged on wine, beer, and spirits. *Prices in the reviews are the average cost of a main course at dinner or, if dinner is not served, at lunch.*

CENTRAL VANCOUVER

Use the coordinate (✛ B2) at the end of each listing to locate a site on the corresponding map.

DOWNTOWN

$$$$
SEAFOOD
Fodor's Choice
★

✕ **C Restaurant.** Save your pennies, fish fans—dishes such as seared scallops paired with pork belly, apple beignets, and foie gras in a burnt apple sauce; trout served with crispy squid and a chorizo-lemon risotto; or lingcod with poached clams, sidestripe prawns, and bok choy have established this spot as Vancouver's most innovative seafood restaurant. Start with shucked oysters from the raw bar or perhaps the seared scallops with rabbit terrine and carrot panna cotta, and finish with an assortment of handmade chocolate truffles and petits fours. The elaborate tasting menus with optional wine pairings highlight regional seafood. Both the ultramodern interior and the waterside patio overlook False Creek, but dine before dark to enjoy the view. $ *Average main: C$33* ✉ *2–1600 Howe St., Downtown* ☎ *604/681–1164* ⊕ *www.crestaurant.com* ✛ *C5.*

$$$$
MODERN
CANADIAN
Fodor's Choice
★

✕ **Hawksworth Restaurant.** With sleek white tables and sparkling chandeliers, chef David Hawksworth's hotly anticipated restaurant is the kind of place where you can toast a new client or celebrate a romance. The food (and the crowd) is suave and swanky, too. A stellar starter is the yellowfin tuna ceviche tossed with avocado and served over toasted amaranth, but don't overlook the charred octopus salad with smoked potato or the quail paired with glazed sweetbreads and preserved lemon. Although the menu changes frequently, mains might include grilled sturgeon with wild rice and bacon, handmade tagliatelle with walnut pesto and ricotta salata, or the popular crispy chicken paired with bitter greens and a sweet-and-sour vinaigrette. Look out, yoga-pants-wearing Vancouver—fine dining is back. $ *Average main:*

C$33 ✉ *Rosewood Hotel Georgia, 801 W. Georgia St., Downtown* ☎ *604/673–7000* 🌐 *www.hawksworthrestaurant.com* ✥ *E3.*

$$$$ FRENCH 🍴 **Le Crocodile.** Chefs prepare classic Alsatian-inspired food (such as the signature onion tart) at this long-established downtown restaurant. Despite the white-tablecloth sophistication, the breezy curtains, golden yellow walls, and burgundy banquettes keep things cozy. Favorite dishes include lobster with beurre blanc, veal medallions with morel sauce, and sautéed Dover sole. Many lunch options, including a black truffle omelet and a mixed grill of halibut, prawns, and wild salmon, are moderately priced. [$] *Average main: C$34* ✉ *100–909 Burrard St., Downtown* ☎ *604/669–4298* 🌐 *www.lecrocodilerestaurant.com* 🕒 *Closed Sun. No lunch Sat.* ✥ *D3.*

WEST END

$$ JAPANESE 🍴 **Hapa Izakaya.** Serving small plates designed for sharing, this sleek Japanese tapas bar is known for its mackerel, cooked table-side with a blowtorch. Also worth trying are the *ebi mayo* (tempura shrimp with spicy mayonnaise) and the *ishi-yaki* (a Korean-style stone bowl filled with rice, pork, and vegetables). Sake and Japanese beer are the drinks of choice. If you're looking for Japanese fare elsewhere around town, Hapa has branches at 1193 Hamilton Street in Yaletown and at 1516 Yew Street in Kitsilano, one block from Kits Beach. [$] *Average main: C$14* ✉ *1479 Robson St., West End* ☎ *604/689–4272* 🌐 *www.hapaizakaya.com* 🕒 *No lunch* ✥ *C2.*

$$$ MODERN CANADIAN 🍴 **Raincity Grill.** One of the best places to try British Columbian food and wine is this lovely candlelit bistro overlooking English Bay. The menu changes regularly and relies almost completely on local and regional products, from salmon and shellfish to game and fresh organic vegetables. Vegetarian selections are always available, and the exclusively Pacific Northwest and Californian wine list has at least 40 choices by the glass. Popular alternatives include the 100 Mile Tasting Menu (all ingredients are sourced from within 100 miles of the restaurant) and the vegetarian regional tasting menu. The prix-fixe early dinner, served from 5 to 6 pm, is a steal at C$30. Reservations are required for these prix-fixe dinners. [$] *Average main: C$27* ✉ *1193 Denman St., West End* ☎ *604/685–7337* 🌐 *www.raincitygrill.com* ✥ *B2.*

19

GASTOWN AND CHINATOWN

$$$ MODERN CANADIAN Fodor's Choice ★ 🍴 **Boneta.** Some of the city's most innovative dishes—and drinks—grace the tables of this Gastown restaurant, named after co-owner Mark Brand's mother. The tucked-away location in Gaoler's Mews makes the room feel like a secluded speakeasy, as do the almost-too-cool-for-school cocktails, including the Trade Routes (tequila, Benedictine, smoked tea syrup, and lemon oil) and the Roman Holiday (Campari, Cointreau, and citrus). The deep-fried octopus chips, halibut paired with baby artichokes and fava beans, and lamb sirloin with ramps are creations that would make any foodie mother proud. Nobody could say no to the chocolate mascarpone cheesecake with raspberry sorbet and thyme sable cookies. [$] *Average main: C$25* ✉ *12 Water St., Gastown* ☎ *604/684–1844* 🌐 *www.boneta.ca* 🕒 *No lunch* ✥ *G3.*

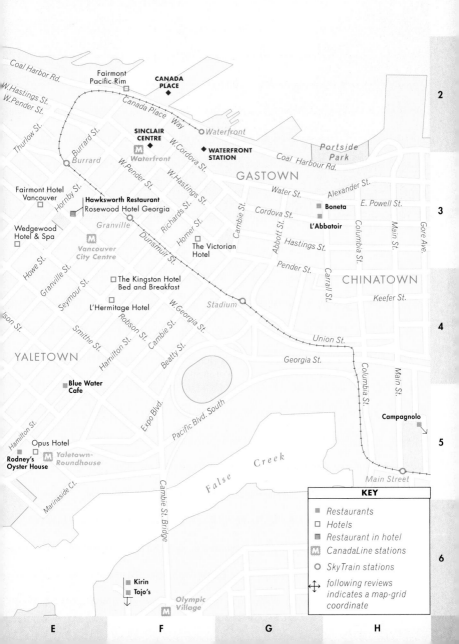

Where to Eat and Stay in Downtown Vancouver

Burrard Inlet

Coal Harbor Rd.

W.Hastings St.
W.Pender St.

Thurlow St.

Fairmont
Pacific Rim

CANADA PLACE

Canada Place Way

○ *Waterfront*

Burrard St.

SINCLAIR CENTRE

Ⓜ *Waterfront*

W. Pender St.

W.Cordova St.

◆ **WATERFRONT STATION**

Coal Harbour Rd.

Portside Park

GASTOWN

Water St.

Alexander St.

E. Powell St.

Fairmont Hotel
Vancouver

Hornby St.

Hawksworth Restaurant
Rosewood Hotel Georgia

Granville

Cordova St.

■ **Boneta**

Wedgewood
Hotel & Spa

Ⓜ *Vancouver City Centre*

Dunsmuir St.

Richards St.

Homer St.

Cambie St.

Abbott St.

L'Abbatoir

Hastings St.

Columbia St.

Main St.

Gore Ave.

Howe St.

Granville St.

Seymour St.

The Victorian
Hotel

Pender St.

Carrall St.

CHINATOWN

Keefer St.

The Kingston Hotel
Bed and Breakfast

W.Georgia St.

○ *Stadium*

L'Hermitage Hotel

Robson St.

Cambie St.

Beatty St.

Smithe St.

Hamilton St.

Union St.

Georgia St.

YALETOWN

Columbia St.

Main St.

■ **Blue Water Cafe**

Expo Blvd.

Pacific Blvd. South

■ **Campagnolo**

Hamilton St.

Opus Hotel

Ⓜ *Yaletown-Roundhouse*

Rodney's Oyster House

Marinaside Ct.

Creek

Cambie St. Bridge

False Creek

Main Street ○

■ **Kirin**
■ **Tojo's**

Olympic Village
Ⓜ

KEY

■ *Restaurants*
□ *Hotels*
■ *Restaurant in hotel*
Ⓜ *CanadaLine stations*
○ *SkyTrain stations*
✛ *following reviews indicates a map-grid coordinate*

Izakaya are Japanese small plates, similar to Spanish tapas.

$$$ MODERN CANADIAN Fodor's Choice ★

🍴 **L'Abbatoir.** Located on the site of Vancouver's first jail, this two-level restaurant with exposed brick walls and classic black-and-white floor tiles has a bold collection of cocktails and an adventurous modern menu. In the glass, choices range from classics like the Hanky Panky (gin, sweet vermouth, and Fernet Branca) to more contemporary concoctions like the Meat Hook (Sazerac rye, Italian vermouth, and 10-year-old whiskey). From the restaurant's name—French for "slaughterhouse" (the surrounding neighborhood was once a meat-packing district)—you'd expect a meat-focused menu, and although you'll find veal sweetbreads on toast or milk-poached pork with salsa verde, seafood shines in dishes like potato gnocchi with scallops and chestnuts or panfried cod paired with an endive tart. Before plotting your escape into the night, share a dark-chocolate pudding for two. [$] *Average main: C$27* ✉ *217 Carrall St., Gastown* ☎ *604/568–1701* 🌐 *www.labattoir.ca* 🕒 *No lunch* ✥ *G3.*

YALETOWN

$$$$ SEAFOOD Fodor's Choice ★

🍴 **Blue Water Cafe.** Executive chef Frank Pabst features both popular and lesser-known local seafood (including frequently overlooked varieties like mackerel or herring) at this fashionable fish restaurant. You might start with Gulf Island scallops baked with tomatoes, olives, and capers; Dungeness crab and white asparagus panna cotta; or a selection of raw oysters. Main dishes are seafood-centric, too—perhaps white sturgeon with beets, or arctic char with trout caviar and pearl couscous. Ask the staff to recommend wine pairings from the B.C.–focused list. You can dine in the warmly lit interior or outside on the former loading dock that's now a lovely terrace. **TIP→ The sushi chef turns out both classic and new creations—they're pricey but rank among the city's best.**

[$] *Average main: C$34* ✉ *1095 Hamilton St., Yaletown* ☎ *604/688–8078* 🌐 *www.bluewatercafe.net* 🕑 *No lunch* ✥ *E4.*

$$ SEAFOOD 🍴 **Rodney's Oyster House.** This faux fishing shack in Yaletown has one of the city's widest selections of oysters (up to 18 varieties), from locally harvested bivalves to exotic Japanese kumamotos. You can pick your oysters individually—they're laid out on ice behind the bar—or try the clams, scallops, mussels, and other mollusks from the steamer kettles. If you're fishing for an afternoon snack, swim in between 3 and 6 (except Sunday) when a light menu of raw oysters, steamed clams, garlic prawns, and a few additional seafood nibbles is served. [$] *Average main: C$18* ✉ *1228 Hamilton St., Yaletown* ☎ *604/609–0080* 🌐 *www.rodneysoysterhouse.com* 🕑 *No lunch Sun.* ✥ *E5.*

STANLEY PARK

$$$$ SEAFOOD FAMILY 🍴 **The Fish House in Stanley Park.** Surrounded by gardens, this 1930s former sports pavilion with a fireplace and two verandas is tucked between Stanley Park's tennis courts and putting green. Chef Karen Barnaby's food, including fresh oysters, grilled ahi tuna with a green-peppercorn sauce, and cornflake-crusted salmon with bacon mashed potatoes, is flavorful and unpretentious. Check the board for the current day's catch. Traditional English afternoon tea is served daily between 2 and 4. [$] *Average main: C$31* ✉ *8901 Stanley Park Dr., Stanley Park* ☎ *604/681–7275, 877/681–7275* 🌐 *www.fishhousestanleypark.com* ✥ *A1.*

GREATER VANCOUVER

Use the coordinate (✥ B2) at the end of each listing to locate a site on the corresponding map.

KITSILANO

$$$$ MODERN CANADIAN 🍴 **Bishop's.** Before "local" and "seasonal" were all the rage, this highly regarded room was serving West Coast cuisine with an emphasis on organic regional produce. The menu changes regularly, but highlights include such starters as elk carpaccio with mountain huckleberries and horseradish crème fraîche. Wild pacific salmon with herb parsnip latkes and locally raised beef tenderloin are among the tasty main dishes. All are expertly presented and impeccably served with suggestions from Bishop's extensive local wine list. The split-level room displays elaborate flower arrangements and selections from owner John Bishop's art collection. [$] *Average main: C$38* ✉ *2183 W. 4th Ave., Kitsilano* ☎ *604/738–2025* 🌐 *www.bishopsonline.com* 🕑 *Closed Mon. No lunch* ✥ *A6.*

$$ THAI Fodor's Choice ★ 🍴 **Maenam.** This moderately priced Thai menu brings this Asian cuisine to a new level. Although some of chef Angus An's dishes may sound familiar—green papaya salad, pad thai, curries—they're amped up with local ingredients, fresh herbs, and vibrant seasonings. Look for delicious innovations, too: perhaps crispy B.C. oysters, a banana blossom salad with a tamarind and palm sugar dressing, or "eight-spice fish" that balances sweet, salty, and sour flavors. The bar sends out equally exotic cocktails, such as the Siam Sun Ray (vodka, lime, chili, ginger, coconut water, and soda). The sleek Kitsilano dining room is stylish enough that you could dress up a bit, but you wouldn't be out of place in jeans. [$] *Average main: C$16* ✉ *1938 W. 4th Ave., Kitsilano* ☎ *604/730–5579* 🌐 *www.maenam.ca* 🕑 *No lunch Sun. and Mon.* ✥ *A6.*

SOUTH GRANVILLE

$$$ INDIAN Fodor's Choice ★ 🍴 **Vij's.** At Vancouver's most innovative Indian restaurant, genial proprietor Vikram Vij and his wife Meeru Dhalwala use local ingredients to create exciting takes on South Asian cuisine. Dishes such as lamb "popsicles" in a creamy curry, spot prawns served with a wheat berry pilaf, or roasted eggplant and butternut squash with black chickpeas are far from traditional but are beautifully executed. Mr. Vij circulates through the room, which is decorated with Indian antiques and whimsical elephant-pattern lanterns, greeting guests and suggesting dishes or cocktail pairings. Expect to cool your heels at the bar sipping a cold beer while you wait up to an hour for a table, but if you like creative Indian fare, it's worth it. [$] *Average main: C$27* ✉ *1480 W. 11th Ave., South Granville* ☎ *604/736–6664* 🌐 *www.vijs.ca* ✍ *Reservations not accepted* ⏲ *No lunch* ✣ *B6.*

$$$$ MODERN CANADIAN Fodor's Choice ★ 🍴 **West.** Contemporary regional cuisine is the theme at this chic restaurant, one of the city's most innovative dining rooms. Among executive chef Quang Dang's creations are grilled quail with chanterelle mushroom tortellini, milk-poached sablefish with spätzle, and herb-crusted lamb served with crispy sweetbreads, beets, and pickled ramps. The decadent desserts might include pears sautéed in maple syrup and paired with a blue cheese biscuit, or a surprisingly delectable tofu "cheesecake" wrapped in a crepe and served with roasted pineapple. If you can't decide, order from the tapas-style "Elements" menu (C$8–C$15) or opt for one of the elaborate multicourse tasting menus (C$58–C$78), which include vegetarian, seafood, and meat options. Marble floors, high ceilings, and a wall of wine make the space feel simultaneously energetic and cozy. [$] *Average main: C$40* ✉ *2881 Granville St., South Granville* ☎ *604/738–8938* 🌐 *www.westrestaurant.com* ✣ *B6.*

FAIRVIEW

$$$ CHINESE 🍴 **Kirin Restaurant.** You can take in the city skyline and the surrounding mountains at this spacious dining room, where the focus is on Cantonese-style seafood, including fish, crab, and lobster fresh from the tanks. The kitchen does an excellent job with vegetables, too; ask for whatever's fresh that day. Dim sum is served daily. It's an easy ride on the Canada Line from downtown to the Broadway/City Hall station, two blocks from the restaurant. [$] *Average main: C$21* ✉ *City Square Shopping Centre, 555 W. 12th Ave., 2nd fl., Fairview* ☎ *604/879–8038* 🌐 *www.kirinrestaurants.com* ✣ *F6.*

$$$$ JAPANESE 🍴 **Tojo's.** Hidekazu Tojo is a sushi-making legend in Vancouver, with thousands of special preparations stored in his creative mind. In this strikingly modern, high-ceilinged space, complete with a separate sake lounge, the prime perch is at the sushi bar, a convivial ringside seat for watching the creation of edible art. The best way to experience Tojo's creativity is to order *omakase* (chef's choice); the chef will keep offering you wildly adventurous fare, both raw and cooked, until you cry uncle. Budget a minimum of C$80 per person (before drinks); tabs topping C$120 per person are routine. [$] *Average main: C$32* ✉ *1133 W. Broadway, Fairview* ☎ *604/872–8050* 🌐 *www.tojos.com* ✍ *Reservations essential* ⏲ *Closed Sun. No lunch* ✣ *F6.*

Chefs prepare regional Canadian cuisine at the popular restaurant West.

MAIN STREET/MT. PLEASANT

$$ ITALIAN 🍴 **Campagnolo.** On a dark block near the Main St./Science World Sky-Train station, this relaxed trattoria lights up the neighborhood with its welcoming vibe and casually contemporary Italian fare. The kitchen cures its own *salumi*, including soppressata, capicola, and various sausages—these make good starters, as do the addictive *ceci* (chick peas). House-made pastas and a small selection of mains take their inspiration from the Emiglia-Romagna and Piemonte regions, updated with B.C. ingredients. Reservations are accepted only for groups of eight or more, but you can unwind with a glass of wine in the lounge if you have to wait. [$] *Average main: C$18* ✉ *1020 Main St., Main St./Mt. Pleasant* ☎ *604/484–6018* 🌐 *www.campagnolorestaurant.ca* ✥ *H5.*

WHERE TO STAY

For expanded hotel reviews, visit Fodors.com.

Accommodations in Vancouver range from luxurious waterfront hotels to neighborhood B&Bs, chain hotels (both luxury and budget), basic European-style pensions, and backpackers' hostels. Although the city is quite compact, each area has its distinct character and accommodation options. All our recommendations are within easy reach of transit that will take you to the major attractions.

The trend toward self-catered apartment suites really struck gold in Vancouver with the 2010 Winter Olympics. The site 🌐 *www.makeyourselfathome.com* (☎ *604/874–7817*) provides a terrific range of private homes and suites available for short-term rentals; this site is especially good for last-minute bookings. *Prices in the reviews are the lowest cost of a standard double room in high season excluding 10% room tax and 5% GST.*

CENTRAL VANCOUVER

DOWNTOWN

Use the coordinate (✢ B2) at the end of each listing to locate a site on the corresponding map.

$$$$ HOTEL **Fairmont Hotel Vancouver.** The copper roof of this 1939 château-style hotel dominates Vancouver's skyline, and the elegantly restored hotel is considered the city's gracious grande dame. **Pros:** full-service spa; great location for shopping; stunning architecture. **Cons:** "standard" room sizes vary greatly. [$] *Rooms from: C$359* ✉ *900 W. Georgia St., Downtown* ☎ *604/684–3131* 🌐 *www.fairmont.com/hotelvancouver* 🛏 *556 rooms, 37 suites* 🍴 *No meals* ✢ *E3.*

$$$$ HOTEL **Fairmont Pacific Rim.** Overlooking the downtown waterfront, this 47-story tower represents the chain's first foray into the condominium-hotel format. **Pros:** prime location; the usual high quality of Fairmont properties. **Cons:** pricey. [$] *Rooms from: C$559* ✉ *1038 Canada Pl., Downtown* ☎ *877/900–5350* 🌐 *www.fairmont.com/pacificrim* 🛏 *37 suites, 340 rooms* 🍴 *No meals* ✢ *F2.*

$$ B&B/INN **Kingston Hotel.** Convenient to shopping and nightlife, the family-run Kingston occupies a four-story elevator building dating back to 1910—exactly the type of establishment you'd expect to find in Europe. **Pros:** great location; breakfast included. **Cons:** some shared bathrooms; limited amenities; early checkout. [$] *Rooms from: C$155* ✉ *757 Richards St., Downtown* ☎ *604/684–9024, 604/684–9024* 🌐 *www.kingstonhotelvancouver.com* 🛏 *52 rooms, 13 with bath* 🍴 *Breakfast* ✢ *F4.*

$$$ HOTEL Fodor's Choice ★ **L'Hermitage Hotel.** Get beyond the marble floors, silk and velvet walls, and gold-cushion benches in the lobby and you'll discover a warm residential character to this boutique hotel. **Pros:** uptown hotel has refreshingly residential vibe; excellent concierge; valet car parking. **Cons:** in the middle of downtown. [$] *Rooms from: C$240* ✉ *788 Richards St., Downtown* ☎ *778/327–4100, 888/855–1050* 🌐 *www.lhermitagevancouver.com* 🛏 *40 rooms, 20 suites* 🍴 *No meals* ✢ *F4.*

$$$$ HOTEL **Loden Hotel.** This gadget-centric boutique hotel has all manner of plug-and-play amenities, including in-room iPod docks and TVs with oversize LCD screens. **Pros:** intimate lounge inspires conversation; central location. **Cons:** limited spa services; dark lobby; service is hit-or-miss. [$] *Rooms from: C$415* ✉ *1177 Melville St., Downtown* ☎ *604/669–5060, 877/225–6336* 🌐 *www.theloden.com* 🛏 *70 rooms, 7 suites* 🍴 *No meals* ✢ *D2.*

$$$$ HOTEL Fodor's Choice ★ **Rosewood Hotel Georgia.** One of Vancouver's newest hotels, the Rosewood Hotel Georgia is also one of its most historic.This 1927 Georgian Revival building once welcomed such prestigious guests as Elvis Presley and Katharine Hepburn. **Pros:** at the center of the city's action; soothing spa; great restaurant. **Cons:** expensive valet parking. [$] *Rooms from: C$379* ✉ *801 W. Georgia St., Downtown* ☎ *604/682–5566* 🌐 *www.rosewoodhotels.com/en/hotelgeorgia* 🛏 *156 rooms* 🍴 *No meals* ✢ *E3.*

$$$$ HOTEL **Shangri-La Hotel.** On the first 15 floors of the tallest building in Vancouver—a 61-story tower of angled glass studded with gold squares that

glint in the sunshine—is this upscale Asian chain's first hotel in North America. **Pros:** first-rate concierge service; stellar spa. **Cons:** public areas could be more inviting; on the city's busiest thoroughfare. [$] *Rooms from: C$375* ✉ *1128 W. Georgia St., Downtown* ☎ *604/689–1120* 🌐 *www.shangri-la.com* 🛏 *81 rooms, 38 suites* 🍴 *No meals* ✣ *D2.*

$$ B&B/INN **Victorian Hotel.** Budget hotels can be handsome, as in the gleaming hardwood floors, high ceilings, and chandeliers at this prettily restored 1898 European-style pension. **Pros:** Gastown location; complimentary breakfast; Wi-Fi access. **Cons:** the neighborhood is relatively safe, but you'll probably want to take a cab after midnight. [$] *Rooms from: C$159* ✉ *514 Homer St., Downtown* ☎ *604/681–6369, 877/681–6369* 🌐 *www.victorianhotel.ca* 🛏 *39 rooms, 18 with bath* 🍴 *Breakfast* ✣ *F3.*

$$$$ HOTEL Fodor's Choice ★ **Wedgewood Hotel & Spa.** A member of the exclusive Relais & Châteaux Group, the lavish Wedgewood is owned by a woman who cares fervently about her guests. **Pros:** personalized service; great location close to shops. **Cons:** small size means it books up quickly. [$] *Rooms from: C$402* ✉ *845 Hornby St., Downtown* ☎ *604/689–7777, 800/663–0666* 🌐 *www.wedgewoodhotel.com* 🛏 *41 rooms, 43 suites* ✣ *E3.*

WEST END

$$ HOTEL Fodor's Choice ★ **Sylvia Hotel.** This Virginia-creeper-covered 1912 building is popular because of its affordable rates and its near-perfect location a stone's throw from the beach on scenic English Bay. **Pros:** beachfront location; close to restaurants; a good place to mingle with the locals. **Cons:** older building; parking can be difficult; walk to downtown is slightly uphill. [$] *Rooms from: C$179* ✉ *1154 Gilford St., West End* ☎ *604/681–9321* 🌐 *www.sylviahotel.com* 🛏 *97 rooms, 22 suites* 🍴 *No meals* ✣ *B2.*

YALETOWN

$$$ HOTEL Fodor's Choice ★ **Opus Vancouver Hotel.** The design team had a ball with this boutique hotel, creating fictitious characters and decorating rooms for each. **Pros:** great Yaletown location, right by rapid transit; funky and hip vibe; the lobby bar is a fashionable meeting spot. **Cons:** surrounding neighborhood is mostly high-rises; trendy nightspots nearby can be noisy at night. [$] *Rooms from: C$259* ✉ *322 Davie St., Yaletown* ☎ *604/642–6787, 866/642–6787* 🌐 *www.opushotel.com* 🛏 *85 rooms, 11 suites* 🍴 *No meals* ✣ *E5.*

19

NIGHTLIFE

Updated by Paige Donner

There's plenty to choose from in just about every neighborhood: hipster Gastown has caught up with Yaletown for clusters of late-night establishments and is now the place to go for racy clubs and trendy wine bars, with venues in the newly cool Chinatown giving them some good competition. The gay-friendly West End is all about bumpin' and grindin' in retro bars and clubs, while a posh crowd of glitterati flocks downtown to Coal Harbour's chic bars and stylish lounges. Meanwhile, Kitsilano (the Venice Beach of Vancouver) attracts a laid-back bunch who like to sip beer and frilly cocktails on cool bar patios with killer views, especially in the summer. And with its fair share of galleries, film festivals, cutting-edge theater, comedy, opera, and ballet, Vancouver (also known as Hollywood North) also has all manner of cultural stimuli that you might be looking for.

L'Hermitage Hotel

Opus Vancouver Hotel

Sylvia Hotel

Wedgewood Hotel & Spa

WHERE TO GET INFORMATION

For event information, pick up a copy of the free *Georgia Straight* (available at cafés and bookstores and street boxes around town) or look in the entertainment section of the *Vancouver Sun*: Thursday's paper has listings in the "Queue" section. Web-surf over to ⊕ *www. gayvan.com* and ⊕ *www.gayvancouver.net* for an insider's look at the gay-friendly scene.

WHERE TO GET TICKETS

Coastal Jazz and Blues Society. Coastal Jazz and Blues Society has a hotline that details upcoming concerts and clubs. The society also runs the Vancouver International Jazz Festival, which lights up 40 venues around town the last week in June. ☎ *888/438–5200* ⊕ *www.coastaljazz.ca.*

Ticketmaster. You can buy half-price day-of-the-event tickets and full-price advance tickets to theater, concerts, festivals, and other performing-arts events in Vancouver from Ticketmaster at **Tickets Tonight**, a kiosk located at the Tourism Vancouver Visitor Centre. Tickets for many events around Vancouver can be booked online. ⊠ *Tourism Vancouver Visitor Centre, 200 Burrard St.* ☎ *855/985–4357* ⊕ *www. ticketmaster.ca.*

DOWNTOWN, COAL HARBOUR, AND THE WEST END

BARS: HOTEL BARS

Hawksworth Bar and Lounge. Vancouver's reigning hotspot, you'll find quality cocktails here blended with house-made bitters, fresh herbs, and other local ingredients. For being so leather-paneled and clubby, it's surprisingly unstuffy. Head barman Brad Stanton has invented (or revived) a few cocktails worth stopping by for, including the Crimson Punch: vodka, honey, and flavors of black cherry, lime, and allspice. The dark mahogany floors and stark white walls of the Prohibition Lounge, also in the Rosewood Georgia Hotel, offer a completely different vibe. ⊠ *Rosewood Hotel Georgia, 801 W. Georgia St., Downtown* ☎ *604/673–7000* ⊕ *www.hawksworthrestaurant.com.*

19

Xi Shi Lounge. In the Shangri-La Hotel, the Xi Shi Lounge has Asian-inspired cocktails served by waitresses in dresses reminiscent of 1920s Shanghai. Weekends are a good time to enjoy the live music and sip on the bar's original cocktail, the Casablanca (sparkling wine, gin, and hints of lemon and peach). The signature Iron Lotus is also blended with sparkling wine, adding vodka, elderflower, and ginger. ⊠ *Shangri-La Hotel, 1128 W. Georgia St., Downtown* ☎ *604/695–1115.*

Yew. The tree-level bar at the Four Seasons provides a diverse environment of glass, natural wood, and sleek granite to reflect B.C.'s stunning natural environment. Happy hour attracts business executives, and at other times you'll see Canucks fans before or after the game. There are more than 150 wines by the glass and a perpetually changing cocktail list. Stop by on Sunday for half-price bottles of wine. ⊠ *Four Seasons Vancouver, 791 W. Georgia St., Downtown* ☎ *604/692–4939* ⊕ *www. yewrestaurant.com.*

BARS: WINE BARS

Wine Room. A new concept in Vancouver, the Wine Room is devoted to nurturing the inner oenophile in all of us by offering wines that you usually can't get by the glass. In other words, at long last there's a place in Vancouver that's taking wine seriously. It's part of Joey Bentall One, but has its own dedicated entrance. Cocktails at the Long Bar aren't too bad, either. Signature martinis include the Hawaiian Hi Five (rum sloshed with fruit juice) and the Thai Lover (lychee-flavored liqueur, pineapple, and passion fruit). ⊠ *507 Burrard St., Coal Harbour* 🕾 *604/915–5639* ⊕ *www.joeyrestaurants.com/bentall-one.*

GAY NIGHTLIFE

1181. This place is all about stylish interior design—plush sofas, glass coffee tables, wood-paneled ceiling—and standard cocktails (think caipirinhas and mojitos). It gets particularly crowded on Saturdays, when a DJ spins behind the bar. ⊠ *1181 Davie St., West End* 🕾 *604/787–7130* ⊕ *www.1181.ca.*

MUSIC

Railway Club. In the early evening, this spot attracts film and media types to its pub-style rooms; after 8 it becomes a venue for local bands. Technically it's a private social club, but everyone of age is welcome. A dartboard offers distraction while you enjoy a cold lager. ⊠ *579 Dunsmuir St., Downtown* 🕾 *604/681–1625* ⊕ *www.therailwayclub.com.*

GASTOWN AND CHINATOWN

BARS AND LOUNGES

Fodor's Choice
★

The Diamond. At the top of a narrow staircase above Maple Tree Square, the Diamond occupies one of the city's oldest buildings. A bartending school by day, cocktail lounge by night, the venue's official name is the Diamond Preparatory School For All Things Drinks. Standing at the bar, co-owner Josh Pape is like a conductor at the symphony. You can choose among "boozy," "proper," or "delicate" options on the drinks menu. The Buck Buck Mule is a refreshing mix of gin, sherry, cucumber juice, cilantro, lime juice, and ginger beer; the Tequila Martinez features tequila, vermouth, Lillet, peach bitters, and an orange twist. ⊠ *6 Powell St., at Carrall St., Gastown* 🕾 *604/568–8272.*

The Keefer Bar. The creative director of cocktails at the Keefer Bar has fully capitalized on the Chinatown connection, using ingredients sourced from local herbalists. Try one of their prescriptions: Lost in Chinatown, a blend of Yellow Chartreuse, Pernod, bourbon, and the exotic-sounding yun xhi syrup. Small plates of Asian dishes make good nibbling. The decor is dark and red, with hanging cylindrical neon lights. There's usually a weekly (and well-attended) burlesque night. ⊠ *135 Keefer St., Chinatown* 🕾 *604/688–1961* ⊕ *www.thekeeferbar.com.*

Fodor's Choice
★

Pourhouse Vancouver. Familiar with the 1862 bartending bible *How To Mix Drinks* by Jerry Thomas? It includes the golden-era-of-cocktails classics from which the Pourhouse draws its inspiration. Before this very first bartending manual was published, there was only an oral tradition of how to blend a mint julep or a sloe gin fizz. Test the bartender's skill and dedication to the bar's theme by asking for a Pick-Me-Up, a Chain-Lightning, or a Corpse Reviver when you drop by this

Yaletown has hip restaurants and bars (many with patios) for lounging in the evening.

Gastown hotspot. ⊠ *162 Water St., Gastown* ☎ *604/568–7022* ⊕ *www.pourhousevancouver.com.*

BARS: WINE BARS

Salt Tasting Room. This place has communal tables, concrete floors, and a selection of local and international wines, beers, and sherries. They're perfect for pairing with the mix-and-match cured meats and artisanal cheese selections that constantly change. By the way, Blood Alley was once the city's meatpacking district. Legend has it that the ghoulish name came from the buckets of blood butchers threw down the cobblestone street. ⊠ *45 Blood Alley, Gastown* ☎ *604/633–1912* ⊕ *www.salttastingroom.com.*

YALETOWN

BARS: BREWPUBS

Yaletown Brewing Company. In a renovated warehouse with a glassed-in brewery turning out several tasty beers, this always-crowded pub and patio has a lively singles' scene. Despite its popularity it still feels like a neighborhood place. ⊠ *1111 Mainland St., Yaletown* ☎ *604/681–2739* ⊕ *www.markjamesgroup.com/yaletown.html.*

BARS: HOTEL BARS

Opus Bar. Local hipsters, executives in suits, and film industry types sip martinis (or perhaps a cocktail made with vodka, passion fruit, and blood oranges) while scoping out the room. The voyeuristic bathrooms have video cameras and one-way glass walls. ⊠ *Opus Hotel, 350 Davie St., Yaletown* ☎ *604/642–0557* ⊕ *www.opusbar.ca.*

19

GREATER VANCOUVER
BARS: BREWPUBS

Dockside Restaurant. A 50-foot aquarium, modern fireplaces, and floor-to-ceiling windows lend atmosphere to a casual seating area where you can take in picturesque Yaletown and North Shore mountain views. Listen to the soft sounds of boats navigating False Creek from the seaside patio as you enjoy a house-brewed German-style beer. ⊠ *Granville Island Hotel, 1253 Johnston St., Granville Island* ☎ *604/685–7070* ⊕ *www.docksidevancouver.com.*

MUSIC

Cellar. This is the city's top venue for jazz, and the calendar features a who's who of the Canadian music scene. Think New York's Village Vanguard, B.C. style. ⊠ *3611 W. Broadway, Kitsilano* ☎ *604/738–1959* ⊕ *www.cellarjazz.com.*

THE ARTS

From performing arts to theater, classical music, dance, and a thriving gallery scene, there's much for an art lover to choose from in Vancouver.

CLASSICAL MUSIC

Vancouver Opera. From October through May, the city's opera company stages four productions a year at the Queen Elizabeth Theatre in downtown Vancouver. ⊠ *Queen Elizabeth Theatre, 630 Hamilton St., Downtown* ☎ *604/683–0222* ⊕ *www.vancouveropera.ca.*

Vancouver Symphony Orchestra. The resident company at the Orpheum Theatre presents classical and popular music. It also has performances at the Chan Centre. ⊠ *Smith St. and Seymour St., Downtown* ☎ *604/ 876–3434* ⊕ *www.vancouversymphony.ca.*

DANCE

Ballet British Columbia. Innovative dances and timeless classics by internationally acclaimed choreographers are presented by the Ballet British Columbia. Most performances are at the Queen Elizabeth Theatre. ⊠ *677 Davie St., Downtown* ☎ *604/732–5003* ⊕ *www.balletbc.com.*

The Dance Center. The hub of dance in British Columbia, this striking building with an art-deco facade hosts full-scale performances, informal showcases, and other events by national and international artists. ▇TIP➔ It often present informal noon performances as part of the Discover Dance! series. ⊠ *677 Davie St., Scotia Bank Dance Centre, Downtown* ☎ *604/606–6400* ⊕ *www.thedancecentre.ca.*

THEATER

Arts Club Theatre Company. This well-regarded company stages productions, a few even by local playwrights, on three principal stages: the Stanley Industrial Alliance Stage, the Revue Stage, and the Granville Island Stage. ⊠ *Stanley Industrial Alliance Stage, 2750 Granville St., at 12th Ave., Shaughnessy* ☎ *604/687–1644* ⊕ *www.artsclub.com.*

Queen Elizabeth Theatre. This is a major venue for ballet, opera, and similar large-scale events. Seating 2,781 people, the Queen Elizabeth is one of the largest theaters in Canada. ⊠ *630 Hamilton St., Downtown* ☎ *604/665–3050.*

Beaches might not be the first thing you think of in Vancouver, but in summer, Kits Beach is quite a hot spot.

SPORTS AND THE OUTDOORS

Updated by
Paige Donner

Exceptional for North American cities, the downtown peninsula is almost entirely encircled by a seawall along which you can walk, in-line skate, cycle, or otherwise propel yourself. It's so popular that it qualifies as an, albeit unofficial, national treasure. There are places along the route where you can rent a bike, skate, canoe, or kayak, or simply go for a swim. Top-rated skiing, snowboarding, mountain biking, fishing, diving, and golf are just minutes away.

BEACHES

Greater Vancouver is well endowed with beaches—from the pebbly coves of West Vancouver to a vast tableau of sand at Spanish Banks—but the waters are decidedly cool, even in summer, and, aside from the kids and the intrepid, the preferred activity is sunbathing. That said, the city provides several exceptional outdoor pools—right smack on the ocean. The most spectacular is Kitsilano Pool, where you can gander up at the North Shore Mountains while swimming lengths or splashing in its shallows. At the city's historic beach and round-the-clock social venue, English Bay, you can swim, rent a kayak—or simply stroll and people-watch. Cosmopolitan Vancouver is also known for its clothing-optional beaches.

All city beaches have lifeguards, bathrooms, and concession stands, and most have paid parking. Liquor and smoking are prohibited in parks and on beaches. With a few exceptions, dogs are not permitted on beaches. For more information, check out the Vancouver Parks website (⊕ *vancouver.ca/parks-recreation-culture/beaches.aspx*).

English Bay Beach. The city's best-known beach, English Bay, lies just to the east of Stanley Park's southern entrance. A long stretch of sable sand, a waterslide, volleyball courts, kayak rentals, and street performers keep things interesting all summer. Known locally for being gay friendly, it draws a diverse crowd. **Amenities:** lifeguards; water sports; food and drink; toilets; parking (fee). **Best for:** swimming; walking; sunset; partiers. ✉ *1791 Beach Ave., between Gilford and Bidwell Sts., English Bay* ☎ *604/665–3424* ⊕ *www.vancouver.ca/parks/rec/beaches.*

Fodor's Choice ★ **Kitsilano Beach.** West of the southern end of the Burrard Bridge, Kits Beach is the city's busiest beach—in-line skaters, volleyball players, and sleek young people are ever present. Facilities include a playground, restaurant, concession stand, and tennis courts. It's also good for windsurfing. **Kitsilano Pool** is here: at 137 meters (445 feet), it's the longest pool in Canada and one of the few heated saltwater pools in the world. **Amenities:** food and drink; lifeguards; parking (fee); toilets. **Best for:** sunrise; sunset; swimming; walking. ✉ *2305 Cornwall Ave., Kitsilano* ☎ *604/731–0011* ⊕ *www.vancouver.ca/parks/rec/beaches.*

Stanley Park. There are two fine beaches accessed from Stanley Park. The most popular with families is **Second Beach,** which has a small sandy area, a playground, and a large heated pool with a slide. **Third Beach** is a little quieter than the other central beaches. It has a larger stretch of sand, fairly warm water, and great sunset views. It's a popular evening picnic spot. **Amenities:** lifeguards; toilets; food and drink; parking (fee). **Best for:** sunset; swimming; walking. ✉ *8001 Stanley Park Dr.* ⊕ *www. vancouver.ca/parks/rec/beaches.*

CYCLING

Although Vancouver has always sported a bike-friendly culture, the city's Downtown Separated Bike Lanes program has made biking even easier. This system of bike lanes protects cyclists by placing a barrier between them and traffic. Look for the lanes downtown, especially along Hornby and Dunsmuir streets. These lanes are in addition to the 16 interconnected bikeways, identified by green bicycle signs, that the city introduced before the 2010 Winter Olympics.

Many TransLink buses have bike racks, and bikes are welcome on the SeaBus and on the SkyTrain at off-peak times. Aquabus Ferries transport bikes and riders across False Creek. If cycling is a key component of your visit, check online with the Vancouver Area Cycling Coalition (⊕ *www.bikehub.ca*).

Lower Seymour Conservation Reserve. Nestled into the precipitous North Shore Mountains, this reserve has 25 km (15.5 miles) of challenging rain-forest trails through alpine meadows, forested slopes, and river flood plains. The meandering **Seymour Valley Trailway** is a 10-km (6-mile) paved pathway, suitable for cyclists, in-line skaters, baby strollers, and wheelchairs. Other trails, like Corkscrew and Salvation, are classified as advanced or even extreme. ✉ *End of Lillooet Rd., North Vancouver* ☎ *604/432–6286* ⊕ *www.metrovancouver.org.*

Seaside Trek. Mostly on paved bike paths, the 9-mile Seaside Trek starts in English Bay and ends at the University of British Columbia, passing through False Creek along the way. ⊠ *Beach Ave. at Gilford St., English Bay.*

Fodor's Choice ★ **Stanley Park Seaside Route.** Vancouver's most popular bike path is the 6½-mile Stanley Park Seaside Route, which follows the perimeter of Stanley Park, hugging the harbor along the way. From here, the views of Lion's Gate Bridge and the mountains to the north are breathtaking. This path converges with the Seaside Trek if you feel like making a day of it. ■ TIP➔ Rent your bike near the entrance to Stanley Park, as there are no rentals once you're inside. ⊠ *W. Georgia St. and Stanley Park Dr., Stanley Park* ☎ *604/873–7526* ⊕ *www.vancouver.ca.*

For detailed route descriptions and a downloadable map, check out ⊕ *www.cyclevancouver.ubc.ca.* Vancouver cycling routes connect with routes on the North Shore, in Richmond and Delta to the south, and in municipalities to the east. For sub-area and region-wide maps, go to the regional transportation authority, TransLink (⊕ *www.translink. bc.ca*). Cycling maps are also available from most bike shops and bike-rental outlets. Helmets are required by law and a sturdy lock is essential.

BIKE RENTALS

Most bike-rental outlets also rent Rollerblades and jogging strollers. Cycling helmets come with the rentals. Locks and maps are also normally supplied.

Bayshore Bike Rentals. If you're starting your ride near Stanley Park, try this friendly store. It has a wide range of bikes as well as baby joggers and bike trailers. ⊠ *745 Denman St., West End* ☎ *604/688–2453* ⊕ *www.bayshorebikerentals.ca.*

Spokes Bicycle Rentals. Located near Stanley Park, Spokes has a wide selection of mountain bikes, tandem bikes, and children's bikes. Everything from hourly to weekly rentals is available. Helmets, locks, and route maps are complimentary. ⊠ *1798 W. Georgia St., West End* ☎ *604/688–5141.*

ECOTOURS AND WILDLIFE-VIEWING

Given a temperate climate and forest, mountain, and marine environments teeming with life, it's no surprise that wildlife-watching is an important pastime and growing business in and around Vancouver. Many people walk the ocean foreshores or park and mountain trails, binoculars or scopes in hand, looking for exceptional or rare birds. Others venture onto the water to see seals, sea lions, and whales—as well as the birds that inhabit the maritime world.

Brackendale Eagles Provincial Park. Between mid-November and mid-February, the world's largest concentration of bald eagles gathers to feed on salmon at Brackendale Eagles Provincial Park, about an hour north of Vancouver on the scenic Sea-to-Sky Highway. ■ TIP➔ The Brackendale Art Gallery has a teahouse that's a good place to stop along the way. ⊠ *Government Rd., off Hwy. 99, Brackendale.*

Sewell's Marina. This marina near the protected waters of Howe Sound runs year-round, two-hour ecotours of the surrounding marine and coastal mountain habitat. Sightings range from swimming seals to soaring eagles. High-speed rigid inflatable hulls are used. ⊠ *6409*

19

Bay St., Horseshoe Bay, West Vancouver ☎ *604/921–3474* ⊕ *www. sewellsmarina.com.*

WHALE-WATCHING

Between April and October pods of orca whales travel through the Strait of Georgia, near Vancouver. The area is also home to harbor seals, elephant seals, bald eagles, minke whales, porpoises, and a wealth of birdlife.

Lotus Land Tours. High-speed covered boats take you out to watch for whales and other wildlife in the Strait of Georgia. The five-hour cruise costs C$175 per adult and includes lunch and a pickup anywhere in Vancouver. The company also offers kayaking tours in Indian Arm and the Gulf Islands, as well as white-water rafting trips on the Elaho and Squamish rivers. ⊠ *1251 Cardero St., West End* ☎ *604/684–4922, 800/528–3531* ⊕ *www.lotuslandtours.com.*

Prince of Whales. This established Victoria operator runs four-hour trips from Vancouver's downtown waterfront (near Waterfront Station) across the Georgia Strait in season. ⊠ *812 Wharf St., Victoria* ☎ *888/383–4884* ⊕ *www.princeofwhales.com.*

Wild Whales Vancouver. Boats leave Granville Island in search of orca pods in the Georgia Strait, often traveling as far as Victoria. Rates are C$125 for a three- to seven-hour trip in either an open or glass-domed boat. Each boat leaves once daily, April through October, conditions permitting. ⊠ *1806 Mast Tower Rd., Granville Island* ☎ *604/699–2011* ⊕ *www.whalesvancouver.ca.*

FISHING

You can fish for salmon all year in coastal British Columbia, weather and marine conditions permitting. Halibut, at 50 pounds and heavier, is the area's other trophy fish. Charters ply waters between the Capilano River mouth in Burrard Inlet and the outer Georgia Strait and Gulf Islands. Your fishing license can be purchased from the boat-rental or tour operator.

Bonnie Lee Fishing Charters. From moorings in the Granville Island Maritime Market, this company runs five-hour fishing trips into Burrard Inlet and the Georgia Strait year-round. Guided outings start at C$395 per person. ⊠ *104-1676 Duranleau St., Granville Island* ☎ *604/290–7447* ⊕ *www.bonnielee.com.*

GOLF

Vancouver-area golf courses offer challenging golf with great scenery. Most are open year-round.

Fodor's Choice ★   **Fraserview Golf Course.** The most celebrated of Vancouver's public courses, the 18-hole Fraserview Golf Course sits on 225 heavily wooded acres overlooking the Fraser River. It has a tree-lined fairway, a driving range, and a lovely clubhouse. There's a golf institute staffed with instructors who teach players of all levels. Golf carts are available on a first-come, first-served basis. ⊠ *7800 Vivian Dr., South Vancouver* ☎ *604/257–6923, 604/280–1818 advance bookings* ⊕ *www.vancouver. ca/parks/golf* ⚑ *18 holes. 6700 yds. Par 72. Green Fee: C$35* ⚲ *Driv-*

ing range, putting green, pitching area, golf carts, rental clubs, pro shop, golf academy/lessons.

Last Minute Golf. For advance tee-time bookings at about 20 Vancouver area courses, or for a spur-of-the-moment game, call Last Minute Golf. The company matches golfers and courses, sometimes at substantial greens-fee discounts. ☎ *604/878–1833, 800/684–6344* ⊕ *www. lastminutegolfbc.com.*

HIKING

If you're heading into the mountains, hike with a companion, pack warm clothes (even in summer) and extra food and water, and leave word of your route and the time you expect to return. Remember that weather can change quickly in the mountains.

Fodor'sChoice **Capilano River Regional Park.** This small but spectacular park is where
★ you'll find old-growth fir trees approaching 61 meters (200 feet). In addition to 26 km (16 miles) of hiking trails in and around Capilano Canyon, there are a dramatic suspension bridge and a salmon hatchery that's open to the public. The park is at the end of Capilano Park Road in North Vancouver. ⊠ *4063–4077 Capilano Park Rd., North Vancouver* ☎ *604/224–5739* ⊕ *www.metrovancouver.org.*

Environment Canada. It's always a good idea to check the weather forecast with Environment Canada. ⊕ *www.weatheroffice.gc.ca.*

Grouse Mountain. Vancouver's most famous, or infamous, hiking route, the Grind, is a 2.9-km (1.8-mile) climb straight up 2,500 vertical feet to the top of Grouse Mountain. Thousands do it annually, but climbers are advised to be very experienced and in excellent physical condition. The route is open daily, 6:30 am to 7:30 pm, from spring through autumn (conditions permitting). Or you can take the Grouse Mountain Skyride to the top 365 days a year; a round-trip ticket is C$39.95. There are additional hiking trails accessible from the gondola, including the Goat Mountain Trail, which can take you even farther up. At the ski resort, drop-in ski and snowboard lessons are C$125, including lift and equipment rental. ⊠ *6400 Nancy Greene Way, North Vancouver* ☎ *604/980–9311* ⊕ *www.grousemountain.com.*

Fodor'sChoice **Stanley Park.** With its moderate walking and easy hiking paths, it's no
★ wonder that Stanley Park attracts 8 million visitors annually. The most picturesque route is the 8.8-km (5½-mile) seawall around its perimeter, but the 1,000-acre park also offers 27 km (167 miles) of well-maintained trails through the coniferous forest, including patches of old growth forest. Here you'll experience a true rain forest and spot birds and small mammals. An easy interior trail runs around Lost Lagoon, and Beaver Lake is a popular destination. Vancouver Aquarium's beluga whales are not to be missed. ⊠ *Northern end of Georgia St.* ☎ *604/602–3088* ⊕ *www.vancouver.ca/parks/parks/stanley.*

HOCKEY

The Canucks have sold out every game since 2004, though tickets can be purchased at legal resale outlets. Watching NHL hockey in a Canadian city is one of sport's greatest spectacles, so try and catch a game if

19

possible. If you can't attend in person, head into any bar on game night, especially on Saturday, which is "Hockey Night" in Canada.

Vancouver Canucks. The city's most beloved sports team, the Vancouver Canucks, plays at Rogers Arena. ⊠ *800 Griffiths Way, Downtown* ☎ *604/899–7676* ⊕ *canucks.nhl.com.*

JOGGING

Vancouverites jog at any time of day, in almost any weather, and dozens of well-trodden routes go through the leafy streets of the city's West Side. The seawall around the downtown peninsula remains the most popular route, though the hilly byways of the North Shore are also popular with serious runners. Visiting runners staying downtown will be drawn to the 8.8-km (5.5-mile) route around Stanley Park, or the 4 km (2.5 miles) around Lost Lagoon.

SKIING AND SNOWBOARDING

While Whistler Resort, a two-hour drive from Vancouver, is the top-ranked ski destination in the region, the North Shore Mountains hold three excellent ski and snowboard areas. All have rentals, lessons, night skiing, eateries, and a variety of runs suitable for all skill levels. The ski season generally runs from early December through early spring. While ski areas and trails are generally well marked, once you ski outside the boundaries you're entering rugged wilderness that can be distinctly unfriendly to humans. Pay close attention to maps and signposts.

Grouse Mountain can be reached by TransLink buses. Cypress and Seymour each run shuttle buses from Lonsdale Quay and other North Shore stops.

Blackcomb and Whistler Mountains. When Whistler and Blackcomb Ski Resorts merged in 1997, they created a snow behemoth not seen in these parts since the last sighting of a yeti—the alpine version of the northwest's infamous Sasquatch. Whistler had already garnered top-notch status, but the addition of Blackcomb left the competition buried in the powder. The numbers are staggering: 410 inches of annual snowfall, over 8,000 skiable acres, 200 named runs, 12 alpine bowls, three glaciers, and the world's most advanced lift system. Point yourself downward on Blackcomb and you can ski or snowboard for a mile from top to bottom. And there are lots of ways to get to the top, either via the Whistler Village, Creekside, or Blackcomb Excalibur gondolas or by taking one of several chairs from the base up the mountain.

According to the locals, many of whom are world-class competitors, picking the day's mountain depends on conditions, time of day, and time of year. While most residents swear by Whistler's bowls and steeps, some prefer the long glade runs and top terrain park of Blackcomb. You can do both in the same day, thanks to the Peak 2 Peak Gondola, which whisks riders along the 2.7-mile journey in just 11 minutes. ⊠ *4545 Blackcomb Way, Whistler Village* ☎ *604/932–3434, 800/766–0449* ⊕ *www.whistlerblackcomb.com.*

Cypress Mountain. The newest of three North Shore commercial ski resorts, Cypress Mountain is nonetheless well equipped, and was made even more so with the completion of freestyle skiing and snowboarding

The hike up Grouse Mountain is no easy feat, but the views from the top, and from Goat Mountain, slightly farther up, are breathtaking.

venues built for the 2010 Winter Olympics. Facilities include five quad or double chairs, 38 downhill runs, and a vertical drop of 1,750 feet. The resort has a snow-tubing area and snowshoe tours. This is also a major cross-country skiing area. ⊠ *Cypress Bowl Rd., West Vancouver* ☎ *604/419–7669* ⊕ *www.cypressmountain.com.*

Grouse Mountain. Reached by gondola from the upper reaches of North Vancouver, much of the Grouse Mountain ski resort inhabits a slope overlooking the city. Although the views are fine on a clear day, at night (the area is known for its night skiing) they're spectacular. Facilities include two quad chairs, 26 skiing and snowboarding runs, and several all-level freestyle-terrain parks. The vertical drop is 1,210 feet. There's a choice of upscale and casual dining in a handsome stone-and-timber lodge. ⊠ *6400 Nancy Greene Way, North Vancouver* ☎ *604/980–9311, 604/986–6262 snow report* ⊕ *www.grousemountain.com.*

FAMILY **Mount Seymour.** A full-service winter activity area, the Mount Seymour ski resort sprawls over 200 acres accessed from eastern North Vancouver. With three chairs for varying abilities; a beginner's rope tow, equipment rentals, and lessons; and toboggan and tubing runs, it's a popular destination for families. Snowboarding is particularly popular. The eateries aren't fancy. ⊠ *1700 Mt. Seymour Rd., North Vancouver* ⊕ *www.mountseymour.com.*

WATER SPORTS

BOATING AND SAILING

With an almost limitless number and variety of waterways, southwestern British Columbia is a boater's paradise. And much of this territory has easy access to marine and public services. One caution: this ocean territory is vast and complex; maritime maps are required. Always consult the Environment Canada marine forecasts (⊕ *www.weatheroffice. gc.ca*).

Blue Pacific Yacht Charters. This company rents speedboats and sailboats for cruising between Vancouver Island and Seattle, including the San Juan Islands, Southern Gulf Islands, and the Sunshine Coast. ✉ *1519 Foreshore Walk, Granville Island* ☎ *604/682–2161, 800/237–2392* ⊕ *www.bluepacificcharters.ca.*

Cooper Boating. Charters sailboats and cabin cruisers, with or without skippers, are available at Cooper Boating. ✉ *1815 Mast Tower Rd., Granville Island* ☎ *604/687–4110, 888/999–6419* ⊕ *www. cooperboating.com.*

CANOEING AND KAYAKING

Kayaking—seagoing and river kayaking—has become something of a lifestyle in Vancouver. While many sea kayakers start out (or remain) in False Creek, others venture into the open ocean and up and down the Pacific Coast. You can white-water kayak or canoe down the Capilano River and several other North Vancouver rivers. And paddling in a traditional, seagoing aboriginal-built canoe is an increasingly popular way to experience the maritime landscape.

FAMILY **Deep Cove Canoe and Kayak Centre.** Ocean-kayak rentals, guided excursions, and lessons for everyone in the family are available between June and September at this company's base in North Vancouver. Winter paddling tours are also available. ✉ *2156 Banbury Rd., North Vancouver* ☎ *604/929–2268* ⊕ *www.deepcovekayak.com.*

Ecomarine Ocean Kayak Centre. Lessons and rentals are offered yearround from this well-regarded company's main branch on Granville Island. There are also locations at Jericho Beach and English Bay. ✉ *1668 Duranleau St., Granville Island* ☎ *604/689–7575, 888/425–2925* ⊕ *www.ecomarine.com.*

SHOPPING

Updated by
Carolyn B.
Heller

Unlike many cities where suburban malls have taken over, Vancouver is full of individual boutiques and specialty shops. Ethnic markets, art galleries, gourmet-food shops, and high-fashion outlets abound, and both Asian and First Nations influences in crafts, home furnishings, and foods are quite prevalent.

Robson Street, particularly the blocks between Burrard and Bute streets, is the city's main fashion-shopping and people-watching artery. The Gap and Banana Republic have their flagship stores here, as do Canadian fashion outlets Club Monaco and Roots. Souvenir shops and cafés fill the gaps. One block north of Robson, **Alberni Street** at Burrard is geared to the higher-income visitor, with names such as Tiffany & Co., Louis Vuitton, Gucci, Coach, Hermés, and Betsey Johnson. In **Gastown,** cool boutiques sell locally designed and one-of-a-kind clothing and accessories, First Nations art, as well as souvenirs—both kitschy and expensive. Bustling **Chinatown**—centered on Pender and Main streets—is full of Chinese bakeries, restaurants, herbalists, tea merchants, and import shops. Frequently described as Vancouver's SoHo, **Yaletown** on the north bank of False Creek is home to boutiques and restaurants—many in converted warehouses—that cater to a trendy, moneyed crowd. On the south side of False Creek, **Granville Island** has a lively food market and a wealth of galleries, crafts shops, and artisans' studios.

DOWNTOWN AND THE WEST END

CLOTHING

Fodor's Choice ★ **Holt Renfrew.** High on the city's ritzy scale, Holt Renfrew is a swanky showcase for international high fashion and accessories for men and women. Think Prada, Dolce & Gabbana, and other designer labels. ⊠ *Pacific Centre, 737 Dunsmuir St., Downtown* ☎ *604/681–3121* ⊕ *www.holtrenfrew.com.*

Lululemon Athletica. Everyone from power-yoga devotees to soccer moms covets the fashionable, well-constructed workout wear with the stylized "A" insignia from this Vancouver-based company. The stores also provide free drop-in yoga classes. There are several branches around town, including 2113 West 4th Avenue in Kitsilano. ⊠ *1148 Robson St., West End* ☎ *604/681–3118* ⊕ *www.lululemon.com.*

Roots. For outdoorsy clothes that double as souvenirs (many sport maple-leaf logos), check out these Canadian-made sweatshirts, leather jackets, and other comfy casuals. In addition to this downtown flagship store, there are branches on South Granville Street in Granville and on West 4th Avenue in Kitsilano. ⊠ *1001 Robson St., West End* ☎ *604/ 683–4305* ⊕ *canada.roots.com.*

DEPARTMENT STORES AND SHOPPING CENTERS

The Bay. A Canadian institution (even though it's now owned by Americans), The Bay was founded as part of the fur trade in the 17th century. A whole department sells the signature tri-color blankets and other Canadiana. ⊠ *674 Granville St., at Georgia St., Downtown* ☎ *604/681– 6211* ⊕ *www.thebay.com.*

GASTOWN AND CHINATOWN

ART AND CRAFTS GALLERIES

Fodor's Choice ★ **Hill's Native Art.** This highly respected store has Vancouver's largest selection of First Nations art. If you think the main level is impressive, go upstairs to where the collector-quality stuff is found. ⊠ *165 Water St., Gastown* ☎ *604/685–4249* ⊕ *www.hills.ca.*

CLOTHING

Dream Apparel & Articles for People. Come here to find a variety of wares by up-and-coming local designers. The creative selections target the hip twentysomething crowd. ⊠ *311 W. Cordova St., Gastown* ☎ *604/683– 7326* ⊕ *www.dreamvancouver.com.*

SHOES

John Fluevog. You might have seen these shops in New York and Los Angeles, but did you know that these funky shoes were created by a Vancouverite? The Gastown location is worth a look for the store itself, with its striking glass facade and soaring ceilings. There's another branch downtown at 837 Granville Street. ⊠ *65 Water St., Gastown* ☎ *604/688–6228* ⊕ *www.fluevog.com.*

19

YALETOWN
FOOD
Swirl. To learn more about British Columbia wines, or to pick up a bottle (or a few), visit the knowledgeable staff at this Yaletown store that stocks more than 650 varieties produced within the province. Complimentary tastings let you try before you buy. ✉ *1185 Mainland St., Yaletown* ☎ *604/408–9463* ⊕ *www.swirlwinestore.ca.*

GRANVILLE ISLAND
Granville Island is a must-do destination for crafts aficionados. Stroll Railspur Alley (off Old Bridge Street), which is lined with working artists' studios; the Net Loft building opposite the Public Market also has several galleries. The "Artists & Artisans of Granville Island" brochure (available at shops around the island or online at ⊕ *www. granvilleisland.com*) has a complete listing of galleries and studios.

FOOD
Edible Canada. Opposite the Granville Island Public Market, this shop sells jams, sauces, chocolates, and hundreds of other edible items from around the province. It's a great place to find gifts for foodie friends. ✉ *1596 Johnston St., Granville Island* ☎ *604/682–6675* ⊕ *www. ediblecanada.com*

KITSILANO
FOOD
Les Amis du Fromage. If you love cheese, don't miss the mind-boggling array of selections from B.C., the rest of Canada, and elsewhere at this shop of delicacies. The extremely knowledgeable mother-and-daughter owners, Alice and Allison Spurrell, and their staff encourage you to taste before you buy. Yum. The shop is located between Granville Island and Kitsilano Beach—useful to know if you're assembling a seaside picnic. ✉ *1752 W. 2nd Ave., Kitsilano* ☎ *604/732–4218* ⊕ *www.buycheese.com.*

SOUTH GRANVILLE
Gallery Row along Granville Street is home to about a dozen high-end contemporary-art galleries. Most are clustered between 5th Avenue and Broadway, but the gallery district extends up to 15th Avenue.

Douglas Reynolds Gallery. In this collection of Northwest Coast First Nations art, particularly strong in woodwork and jewelry, some pieces date back to the 1800s, while others are strikingly contemporary. ✉ *2335 Granville St., South Granville* ☎ *604/731–9292* ⊕ *www. douglasreynoldsgallery.com.*

Robert Held Art Glass. At Canada's largest "hot glass" studio, two blocks west of Granville Street, you can watch glassblowers in action, then browse the one-of-a-kind vases, paperweights, bowls, ornaments, and perfume bottles. Held's glass pieces have been exhibited at the Canadian Museum of Civilization in Ottawa and in galleries across North America. ✉ *2130 Pine St., between 5th and 6th Aves., South Granville* ☎ *604/737–0020* ⊕ *www.robertheld.com.*

A selection of goodies from Les Amis du Fromage

FAIRVIEW
OUTDOOR EQUIPMENT
Mountain Equipment Co-op. This warehouse-style outlet stocks a good selection of high-performance clothing and equipment for hiking, cycling, climbing, and kayaking, as well as just hanging around outdoors. You can rent sports gear here, too. A onetime C$5 membership is required for purchases or rentals. ⊠ *130 W. Broadway, Fairview* ☎ *604/872–7858* ⊕ *www.mec.ca.*

MAIN STREET/MT. PLEASANT
CLOTHING
Barefoot Contessa. This cute shop has a creative take on '40s-style glamour. Look for frilly feminine clothing (dresses, dresses, and more dresses), jewelry, and bags—some by local designers—as well as vintage linens and decorative accessories. ⊠ *3715 Main St., Main St./Mt. Pleasant* ☎ *604/879–1137* ⊕ *www.thebarefootcontessa.com.*

EAST SIDE
SHOPPING CENTERS
Metropolis at Metrotown. With 450 stores—mostly North American chains—this mall is the province's largest shopping destination, easily reached via a 20-minute SkyTrain ride from downtown. Teens and serious shoppers alike flock here. ⊠ *4700 Kingsway, Burnaby* ☎ *604/438–4715* ⊕ *www.metropolisatmetrotown.com.*

RICHMOND
SHOPPING CENTERS

Aberdeen Centre. First-rate Asian restaurants, vendors hawking everything from kimchi to cream puffs, clothing stores stocking the latest Hong Kong styles, and Daiso—a Japanese bargain-hunters' paradise where most items sell for $2—make this swank mall a good introduction to Vancouver's Asian shopping experience. Take the Canada Line south to Aberdeen station, about 20 minutes from downtown. ✉ *4151 Hazelbridge Way, Richmond* ☎ *604/270–1234* ⊕ *www. aberdeencentre.com.*

SPAS

Vancouver's spa scene is as diverse as its population and includes everything from exotic steam experiences to over-the-top indulgences. While many services give the nod to ancient wisdoms such as Ayurveda, you'll also find holistic spa and wellness destinations that incorporate elements of traditional Chinese medicine, Japanese Reiki, and New Age energy therapies, alongside medical aesthetics like Botox, microdermabrasion, and teeth whitening. For authentic spa experiences, here are our top choices:

Absolute Spa at the Century. This expansive spa has an A-list of celebrity clients—Jennifer Lopez, Ethan Hawke, Gwyneth Paltrow, and Ben Affleck, to name a few. What makes this 15,000-square-foot spa really stand out, though, are all the extras that turn even a simple manicure into an experience: every treatment comes with a complimentary eucalyptus steam, a swim in the ozonated pool, and a healthful snack (champagne and chocolate-coated strawberries are optional extras). Jet-lagged? The spa's several branches at Vancouver International Airport give antifatigue treatments and quick chair massages. Prefer to stay put? Absolute Mobile will come to you. ✉ *Century Plaza Hotel, 1015 Burrard St., Downtown* ☎ *604/684–2772* ⊕ *www.absolutespa. com/century-plaza-hotel.*

Absolute Spa at the Fairmont Hotel Vancouver. Although women enjoy the aura and services, this spa is really geared to men—with black-leather pedicure thrones, wide-screen TVs, video games, and computers to check on sports scores and stock prices. Robes and slippers are a bit larger, and many treatments emphasize their manliness, such as the "Gentlemen's Facial" or the "Professional Sports" foot care regimen. ✉ *Fairmont Hotel Vancouver, 900 W. Georgia St., Downtown* ☎ *604/684–2772* ⊕ *www.absolutespa.com/fairmont-hotel-vancouver.*

Miraj. This is just about the most luxuriously authentic steam bath you'll get outside of Turkey. The entire experience feels at the periphery of the *Arabian Nights*, with Middle Eastern–inspired architecture and Jerusalem marble that stays cool to the touch as the temperature rises. A steam includes a light body scrub with black Moroccan soap and the option of a full body massage—highly recommended. Afterward, you get to curl up among the plethora of silk cushions, where you're served Moroccan mint tea and a sweet cake. Snoozing is encouraged. ✉ *1495 W. 6th Ave., South Granville* ☎ *604/733–5151* ⊕ *www.mirajhammam.com.*

Spa Utopia. If you're looking for the ultimate in pampering, it's hard to beat this lavish spa at the Pan Pacific Hotel. Freestanding fountains, floor-to-ceiling windows, and waterfront views add a luxurious touch. There's a wide range of services, but the massages are especially enjoyable; practitioners are trained by the man who wrote the training manual on therapeutic spa massage. For the ultimate treat, book one of the hotel's spa suites and let the treatments come to you. ⊠ *Pan Pacific Hotel, 999 Canada Pl., Downtown* ☎ *604/641–1351* ⊕ *www. spautopia.ca.*

Spruce Body Lab. Urban and hip, Spruce could almost be described as a medical spa since treatments such as Botox and acupuncture are on the menu in addition to regular spa services. Geo-Thermal Stone Therapy, one of the lab's signature treatments, involves the placement of warm and cool stones on the body's different energy centers. It also includes a full body massage, making it a much more dynamic experience than the usual stone massage. ⊠ *1128 Richards St., Yaletown* ☎ *604/683–3220* ⊕ *www.sprucebodylab.com.*

Wedgewood Hotel Spa. What it lacks in size, the Wedgewood Hotel Spa makes up for in intimacy. With only two treatment rooms (each large enough for couples), this second-story spa has understated elegance and graceful attention to detail. Many services include extras like a foot, hand, or scalp massages, and the complimentary steam room gets hot enough to soak the tension out of you. The spa carries Epicuren, a live-enzyme skin-care line favored by many dermatologists. The hotel also has an in-room spa program for guests. ⊠ *Wedgewood Hotel, 845 Hornby St., Downtown* ☎ *604/608–5340* ⊕ *www.wedgewoodhotel. com.*

VICTORIA

19

Updated by
Carolyn B.
Heller

Despite its role as the provincial capital, Victoria was largely bypassed, economically, by Vancouver throughout the 20th century. This, as it turns out, was all to the good, helping to preserve Victoria's historic downtown and keeping the city free of freeways. For much of the 20th century Victoria was marketed to tourists as "The Most British City in Canada," and it still has more than its share of Anglo-themed pubs, tea shops, and double-decker buses. These days, however, Victorians prefer to celebrate their combined indigenous, Asian, and European heritage, and the city's stunning wilderness backdrop. Locals do often venture out for afternoon tea, but they're just as likely to nosh on dim sum or tapas. Decades-old shops sell imported linens and tweeds, but newer upstarts offer local designs in hemp and organic cotton. And let's not forget that fabric favored by locals: Gore-Tex. The outdoors is ever present here. You can hike, bike, kayak, sail, or whale-watch straight from the city center, and forests, beaches, offshore islands, and wilderness parklands lie just minutes away.

VICTORIA PLANNER

WHEN TO GO

Victoria has the warmest, mildest climate in Canada: snow is rare and flowers bloom in February. Summers are mild, too, rarely topping 75°F. If you're here for dining, shopping, and museums, winter is a perfectly nice time for a visit: it's gray and wet, and some minor attractions are closed, but hotel deals abound. If your focus is the outdoors—biking, hiking, gardens, and whale-watching—you need to come with everyone else, between May and October. That's when the streets come to life with crafts stalls, street entertainers, blooming gardens, and the inevitable tour buses. It's fun and busy, but Victoria never gets unbearably crowded.

FESTIVALS

Victoria's top festivals take place in summer, when you're apt to encounter the best weather. For 10 nights in late June, international musicians perform during JazzFest International. Victoria's Inner Harbour becomes an outdoor concert venue in early August for Symphony Splash, when the Victoria Symphony plays a free concert from a barge moored in the middle of the harbor. August and September is the time for the Victoria Fringe Theatre Festival, during which you can feast from a vast menu of offbeat, original, and intriguing performances around town.

PLANNING YOUR TIME

You can see most of the sights in downtown Victoria's compact core in a day, although there's enough to see at the main museums to easily fill two days. Many key sights, including the Royal BC Museum and the Parliament Buildings, are open on some summer evenings as well. You can save time by prebooking tea at the Empress Hotel and buying tickets online for the Royal British Columbia Museum.

You should also save at least half a day or a full evening to visit the Butchart Gardens. The busiest but most entertaining time is during the Saturday-evening fireworks shows. If you have a car, you can make a day of it visiting the nearby town of Sidney and some of the Saanich Peninsula wineries.

An extra day allows for some time on the water, either on a whale-watching trip—it's fairly easy to spot orcas in the area during summer—or on a Harbour Ferries tour, with a stop for fish-and-chips at Fisherman's Wharf. You can also explore the shoreline on foot, following all, or part, of the 7-mile (11-km) waterfront walkway.

GETTING HERE AND AROUND

It's easy to visit Victoria without a car. Most sights, restaurants, and hotels are in the compact walkable core, with bikes, ferries, horse-drawn carriages, double-decker buses, step-on tour buses, taxis, and pedicabs on hand to fill the gaps. Bike paths lace downtown and run along much of Victoria's waterfront, and long-haul car-free paths run to the ferry terminals and as far west as Sooke. Most buses and ferries carry bikes.

AIR TRAVEL

Victoria International Airport (YYJ) is 25 km (15 miles) north of downtown Victoria. The flight from Vancouver to Victoria takes about 25 minutes. The Airporter bus service drops off passengers at most major hotels. There is floatplane service to Victoria's Inner Harbour with West Coast Air and Harbour Air. Kenmore Air has daily floatplane service from May to September from Seattle to Victoria's Inner Harbour.

Contacts and Local Airlines Airporter ☎ 250/386–2525, 877/386–2525 ⊕ www.victoriaairporter.com. **Harbour Air Seaplanes** ☎ 604/274–1277, 800/665–0212 ⊕ www.harbour-air.com. **Kenmore Air** ☎ 425/486–1257, 866/435–9524 ⊕ www.kenmoreair.com. **West Coast Air** ☎ 604/274–1277, 800/665–0212 ⊕ www.westcoastair.com.

FERRY TRAVEL

BC Ferries has daily service between Tsawwassen, about an hour south of Vancouver, and Swartz Bay, at the end of Highway 17, about 30 minutes north of Victoria. Sailing time is 1½ hours. Fares are C$14.85 per adult passenger and C$49.25 per vehicle each way. Vehicle reservations on Vancouver–Victoria routes are optional and cost an additional C$15 to C$17.50. If you're traveling without a car, it's easiest to take a Pacific Coach Lines bus between downtown Vancouver and downtown Victoria; the bus travels on the ferry.

There are several options for getting to Vancouver Island from Washington State: Black Ball Transport operates the MV *Coho*, a car ferry, daily year-round between Port Angeles, Washington, and Victoria's Inner Harbour. The car and passenger fare is US$57; bikes are US$6.50. The *Victoria Clipper* runs daily, year-round passenger-only service between downtown Seattle and downtown Victoria. Trips take about three hours, and the one-way fare from mid-May to late September is US$92; bicycles are an extra US$10, and reservations are recommended. Washington State Ferries runs a car ferry daily from April through December from Anacortes, Washington, to Sidney (some runs make stops at different San Juan Islands), about 30 km (18 miles) north of Victoria. Trips take about three hours. One-way high-season fares are US$59.85 for a vehicle and driver, and bikes are US$6.

Within Victoria, the Victoria Harbour Ferries serve the Inner Harbour; stops include the Fairmont Empress, Chinatown, Point Ellice House, the Delta Victoria Ocean Pointe Resort, and Fisherman's Wharf. Fares start at C$5; multiple-trip and two-day passes are available. Boats make the rounds every 15 to 20 minutes, daily, March through October. The 45-minute harbor tours cost $22, and Gorge cruises cost $26. At 10:45 am on summer Sundays the little ferries perform a water ballet set to classical music in the Inner Harbour.

Ferry Contacts BC Ferries ☎ 250/386–3431, 888/223–3779 ⊕ www.bcferries.com. **Pacific Coach Lines** ☎ 604/662–7575, 800/661–1725 ⊕ www.pacificcoach.com. **Black Ball Ferry Line** ☎ 250/386–2202, 360/457–4491 ⊕ www.ferrytovictoria.com. **Clipper Vacations** ☎ 250/382–8100 ⊕ www.clippervacations.com. **Washington State Ferries** ☎ 206/464–6400, 888/808–7977 ⊕ www.wsdot.wa.gov/ferries. **Victoria Harbour Ferry** ☎ 250/708–0201 ⊕ www.victoriaharbourferry.com.

19

TAXI TRAVEL

In Victoria, call Bluebird, Victoria Taxi, or Yellow Cabs.

Contacts **Bluebird Cabs** ☎ *250/382–2222* ⊕ *www.taxicab.com.* **Victoria Taxi** ☎ *250/383–7111* ⊕ *www.victoriataxi.com.* **Yellow Cab** ☎ *250/381–2222* ⊕ *www.yellowcabofvictoria.com.*

EXPLORING

Exploring Victoria is easy. A walk around downtown, starting with the museums and architectural sights of the Inner Harbour, followed by a stroll up Government Street to the historic areas of Chinatown and Old Town, covers most of the key attractions, though seeing every little interesting thing along the way could easily take two days.

DOWNTOWN VICTORIA

FAMILY **Chinatown.** Chinese immigrants built much of the Canadian Pacific Railway in the 19th century, and their influence still marks the region. Victoria's Chinatown, founded in 1858, is the oldest such district in Canada. If you enter from Government Street, you'll pass under the elaborate **Gate of Harmonious Interest,** made of Taiwanese ceramic tiles and decorative panels. Along Fisgard Street, merchants display paper lanterns and exotic produce. Mah-jongg, fan-tan, and dominoes were games of chance played on **Fan Tan Alley,** said to be the narrowest street in Canada. Once the gambling and opium center of Chinatown, it's now lined with offbeat shops, few of which sell authentic Chinese goods. Look for the alley on the south side of Fisgard Street between Nos. 545½ and 549½. At just two square blocks, Victoria's Chinatown is much smaller than Vancouver's. It's still pleasant to stroll through, particularly as hip boutiques and eateries have moved into the district. ⊠ *Fisgard St., between Government and Store Sts., Chinatown.*

Emily Carr House. One of Canada's most celebrated artists and a respected writer, Emily Carr (1871–1945) lived in this extremely proper, wooden Victorian house before she abandoned her middle-class life to live in the wilds of British Columbia. Carr's own descriptions, from her autobiography *Book of Small,* were used to restore the house. Art on display includes reproductions of Carr's work—visit the Art Gallery of Greater Victoria or the Vancouver Art Gallery to see the originals. ⊠ *207 Government St., James Bay* ☎ *250/383–5843* ⊕ *www.emilycarr.com* ☎ *C$6.75* ☼ *May–Sept., Tues.–Sat. 11–4.*

Fairmont Empress. Opened in 1908 by the Canadian Pacific Railway, the Empress is one of the grand château-style railroad hotels that grace many Canadian cities. Designed by Francis Rattenbury, who also designed the Parliament Buildings across the way, the solid Edwardian grandeur of the Empress has made it a symbol of the city. The elements that made the hotel an attraction for travelers in the past—old-world architecture, ornate decor, and a commanding view of the Inner Harbour—are still here. Nonguests can reserve ahead for afternoon tea (the dress code is smart casual), meet for a curry under the tiger skin in the Bengal Room, enjoy a treatment at the hotel's Willow Stream spa, or sample the superb Pacific Northwest cuisine in the Empress

Room. In summer, lunch, snacks, and cocktails are served on the Terrace Verandah overlooking the Inner Harbour. ⊠ *721 Government St., Downtown* ☎ *250/384–8111, 250/389–2727 tea reservations* ⊕ *www. fairmont.com/empress.*

Parliament Buildings. Officially the British Columbia Provincial Legislative Assembly Buildings, these massive stone structures are more popularly referred to as the Parliament Buildings. Designed by Francis Rattenbury (who also designed the Fairmont Empress Hotel) when he was just 25 years old, and completed in 1897, they dominate the Inner Harbour. Atop the central dome is a gilded statue of Captain George Vancouver (1757–98), the first European to sail around Vancouver Island. A statue of Queen Victoria (1819–1901) reigns over the front of the complex. More than 3,300 lights outline the buildings at night. The interior is lavishly done with stained-glass windows, gilt moldings, and historic photographs, and in summer actors play historic figures from B.C.'s past. When the legislature is in session, you can sit in the public gallery and watch British Columbia's democracy at work (custom has the opposing parties sitting 2½ sword lengths apart). Free, informative, 30- to 45-minute tours run every 20 to 30 minutes in summer and several times a day in the off-season (less frequently if school groups or private tours are coming through). Tours are obligatory on summer weekends (mid-May until Labor Day) and optional the rest of the time. ⊠ *501 Belleville St., Downtown* ☎ *250/387–3046* ⊕ *www. leg.bc.ca* ⊠ *Free* ☉ *Mid-May–early Sept., daily 9–5; early Sept.–mid-May, weekdays 9–5.*

FAMILY
Fodor'sChoice
★
Royal British Columbia Museum. This excellent museum, one of Victoria's leading attractions, traces several thousand years of British Columbian history. Especially strong is its First Peoples Gallery, home to a genuine Kwakwaka'wakw big house and a dramatically displayed collection of masks and other artifacts. The Environmental History Gallery traces B.C.'s natural heritage, from prehistory to modern-day climate change, in realistic dioramas. An Ocean Station exhibit gets kids involved in running a Jules Verne–style submarine. In the Modern History Gallery, a replica of Captain Vancouver's HMS *Discovery* creaks convincingly, and a re-created frontier town comes to life with cobbled streets, silent movies, and the rumble of an arriving train. An IMAX theater presents films on a six-story-tall screen.

19

Optional one-hour tours, included in the admission price, run roughly twice a day in summer and less frequently in winter. Most focus on a particular gallery, though the 90-minute Highlights Tour touches on all galleries. Special exhibits, usually held between April and October, attract crowds despite the higher admission prices. Skip ticket lines by booking online.

The museum complex has several more interesting sights, beyond the expected gift shop and café. In front of the museum, at Government and Belleville streets, is the **Netherlands Centennial Carillon.** With 62 bells, it's the largest bell tower in Canada; the Westminster chimes ring out every hour, and free recitals are occasionally held on Sunday afternoons. Behind the main building, bordering Douglas Street, are the grassy

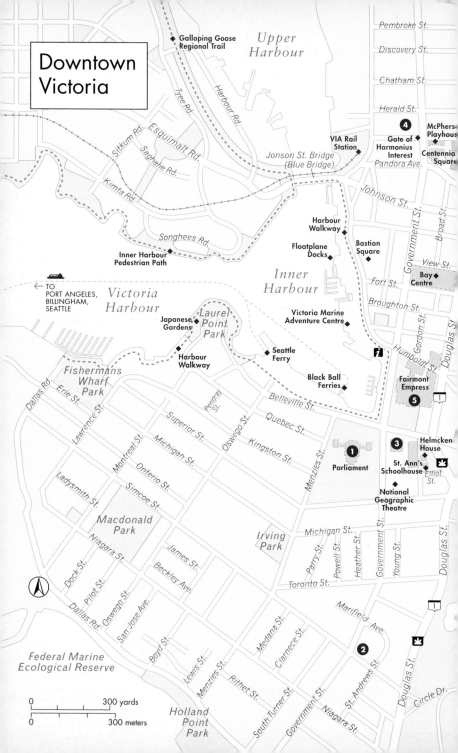

Downtown Victoria

Galloping Goose Regional Trail

Upper Harbour

Pembroke St.

Discovery St.

Chatham St.

Herald St.

VIA Rail Station

Jonson St. Bridge (Blue Bridge)

4

Gate of Harmonius Interest

McPhersn Playhous

Centennia Square

Pandora Ave.

Tyee Rd.

Harbour Rd.

Esquimalt Rd.

Sitkum Rd.

Saghalie Rd.

Kimta Rd.

Songhees Rd.

Inner Harbour Pedestrian Path

Johnson St.

Harbour Walkway

Floatplane Docks

Bastion Square

View St.

Bay Centre

Inner Harbour

Fort St.

Government St.

Broad St.

← TO
PORT ANGELES,
BILLINGHAM,
SEATTLE

Victoria Harbour

Japanese Gardens

Laurel Point Park

Harbour Walkway

Seattle Ferry

Victoria Marine Adventure Centre

Broughton St.

Gordon St.

Humboldt St.

Douglas St.

Black Ball Ferries

Fishermans Wharf Park

Belleville St.

Quebec St.

Fairmont Empress

5

1

Dallas Rd.

Erie St.

Lawrence St.

Montreal St.

Michigan St.

Superior St.

Pendray St.

Oswego St.

Kingston St.

Menzies St.

Ontario St.

Ladysmith St.

Simcoe St.

Parliament

1

3

Helmcken House

St. Ann's Schoolhouse

Elliot St.

Macdonald Park

Niagara St.

James St.

Beckley Ave.

National Geographic Theatre

Government St.

Young St.

Douglas St.

Irving Park

Michigan St.

Toronto St.

Dock St.

Pilot St.

Oswego St.

Dallas Rd.

San Jose Ave.

Boyd St.

Lewis St.

Menzies St.

Rithet St.

Medana St.

Clarnece St.

Parry St.

Powell St.

Heather St.

Marifield Ave.

2

Douglas St.

St. Andrews St.

South Turner St.

Government St.

Niagara St.

Circle Dr.

Federal Marine Ecological Reserve

Holland Point Park

| 0 | | | 300 yards |
| 0 | | | 300 meters |

Central Park

Pembroke St.

Green St.

Royal Athletic Park

Caledonia Ave.

Caledonia Ave.

Herald St.

North St.

Park St.

Fisgard St.

Balmoral St.

Cormorant St.

City Hall

Mason St.

Pandora Ave.

Rudlin St.

Johnson St.

Blanshard St.

Quadra St.

Yates St.

View St.

Cook St.

Fort St.

Broughton St.

Meares St.

Pioneer Square

Courtney St.

Rockland Ave.

Burdett Ave.

Rockland Ave.

Burdett Ave.

Cridge Park

Fairfield Rd.

Humbold St.

McClure St.

Vancouver St.

Theatre Inconnu

Collinson

Richardson St.

Academy St.

Fairfield Rd.

Quadra St.

Southgate St.

Fairfield Rd.

Arbutus Way

Pakington St.

Southgate St.

Heywood Ave.

Vancouver St.

Pendergast St.

Cook St.

Beacon Hill

Sutlej St.

Linden Ave.

Oliphant St.

Park Blvd.

Children's Farm

Leonard St.

KEY	
🛈	Tourist information
⛴	Ferry
- - - -	Pedestrian trail

More than 3,300 lights outline Victoria's Parliament Buildings; like the Fairmont Empress hotel, the buildings have a prominent position in the Inner Harbor, and were designed by the same architect: Francis Rattenbury.

lawns of **Thunderbird Park,** home to 10 totem poles (carved replicas of originals that are preserved in the museum). One of the oldest houses in B.C., **Helmcken House** (☎ *250/356–7226* ⊕ *www.royalbcmuseum. bc.ca* ⊙ *Late May–early Sept., daily noon–4*) was built in 1852 for pioneer doctor and statesman John Sebastian Helmcken. Inside are displays of the family's belongings, including the doctor's medical tools. Behind it is **St. Ann's School House,** built in 1858. One of British Columbia's oldest schools, it is thought to be Victoria's oldest building still standing. Both buildings are part of the Royal British Columbia Museum. ✉ *675 Belleville St., Downtown* ☎ *250/356–7226, 888/447–7977, 877/480– 4887 theater show times* ⊕ *www.royalbcmuseum.bc.ca* 🎟 *C$15, IMAX theater C$11, combination ticket C$23* ⊙ *Oct.–May daily 9–5; Jun.– Sept., Sun.–Wed. 9–5, Thurs.–Sat. 10–10.*

OAK BAY, ROCKLAND, AND FAIRFIELD

The winding shady streets of Victoria's older residential areas—roughly bordered by Cook Street, Fort Street, and the seaside—are lined with beautifully preserved Victorian and Edwardian homes. These include many stunning old mansions now operating as bed-and-breakfasts, and Victoria's most elaborate folly: Craigdarroch Castle. With mansions come gardens, and several of the city's best are found here. Clusters of high-end shops include the extraordinarily British Oak Bay Village, described as a place "behind the Tweed Curtain" for its adherence to Tudor facades and tea shops. Among the lavish waterfront homes are plenty of public parks and beaches offering views across Juan de Fuca Strait to the Olympic Mountains of Washington State.

GETTING HERE AND AROUND

A car or a bike is handy, but not essential, for exploring this area. No wheels? Big Bus, Gray Line, and other tour companies offer Oak Bay and Marine Drive tours.

By public transit, take bus No. 11 or 14 from the corner of Fort and Douglas streets to Moss Street (for the Art Gallery of Greater Victoria), or to Joan Crescent (for Craigdarroch Castle). The walk, about a mile past the antiques shops of Fort Street, is also interesting. Another useful route is bus No. 7: from Johnson and Douglas streets, it travels to Abkhazi Garden and Oak Bay Village.

Abkhazi Garden. Called "the garden that love built," this once-private garden is as fascinating for its history as for its innovative design. The seeds were planted, figuratively, in Paris in the 1920s, when English-woman Peggy Pemberton-Carter met exiled Georgian Prince Nicholas Abkhazi. World War II internment camps (his in Germany, hers near Shanghai) interrupted their romance, but they reunited and married in Victoria in 1946. They spent the next 40 years together cultivating their garden. Rescued from developers and now operated by the Land Conservancy of British Columbia, the one-acre site is recognized as a leading example of West Coast horticultural design, resplendent with native Garry Oak trees, Japanese maples, and mature rhododendrons. The tearoom, in the sitting parlor of the modest, modernist home, serves lunch and afternoon desserts, as well as breakfast on weekends. Watch for evening concerts in the garden. ⊠ *1964 Fairfield Rd., Fairfield* ☎ *250/598–8096* ⊕ *www.conservancy.bc.ca* ☑ *Mar.–Oct. C$10; Nov.–Feb. by donation* ☉ *Daily 11–5.*

Craigdarroch Castle. This resplendent mansion complete with turrets and Gothic rooflines was built as the home of one of British Columbia's wealthiest men, coal baron Robert Dunsmuir, who died in 1889, just a few months before the castle's completion. Now a museum depicting life in the late 1800s, the castle's 39 rooms have ornate Victorian furnishings, stained-glass windows, carved woodwork, and a beautifully restored painted ceiling in the drawing room. A winding staircase climbs four floors to a tower overlooking Victoria. Castles run in the family: son James went on to build the more lavish Hatley Castle west of Victoria. The castle is not wheelchair accessible and has no elevators. ⊠ *1050 Joan Crescent, Rockland* ☎ *250/592–5323* ⊕ *www.thecastle.ca* ☑ *C$13.75* ☉ *Mid-June–early Sept., daily 9–7; early Sept.–mid-June, daily 10–4:30.*

SIDNEY AND THE SAANICH PENINSULA
30 km (18 miles) north of Victoria on Hwy. 17.

Home to the B.C. and Washington State ferry terminals as well as the Victoria International Airport, the Saanich Peninsula, with its rolling green hills and small family farms, is the first part of Vancouver Island that most visitors see. Although it's tempting to head straight for downtown Victoria, 25 minutes to the south, there are many reasons to linger here, including the Butchart Gardens, one of the province's leading attractions. Sidney's parklike waterfront is home to an aquarium and marine ecology center, as well as cafés, restaurants,

19

and a wheelchair-accessible waterfront path.

GETTING HERE AND AROUND

To reach the area by car from downtown Victoria, follow the signs for the ferries straight up Highway 17, or take the Scenic Marine Drive starting at Dallas Road and following the coast north. It joins Highway 17 at Elk Lake (but take a map—even locals get lost). Victoria transit buses serve the area, though not frequently. Bus tours to the Butchart Gardens run several times a day, and many tours take in other sights in the area; several companies also offer winery tours. Gray Line and CVS Cruise Victoria also run shuttles to Butchart Gardens. Cyclists can take the Lochside Trail, which runs from Victoria to Sidney, detouring, perhaps, to some wineries along the way.

WORD OF MOUTH

"Butchart Gardens—beautiful place!! We took the Evening Illuminations tour with Gray Line and got to see the Gardens right before sunset and on into the late night. . . . Seeing the Gardens lit up at night was unique."

—globetrotterxyz

FAMILY
Fodor's Choice
★

Butchart Gardens. This stunning 55-acre garden and National Historic Site has been drawing visitors since it was planted in a limestone quarry in 1904. Seven hundred varieties of flowers grow in the site's Japanese, Italian, rose, and sunken gardens. Highlights include the view over the ivy-draped and flower-filled former quarry, the dramatic 70-foot-high Ross Fountain, and the formal and intricate Italian garden, complete with a gelato stand.

From mid-June to mid-September the gardens are illuminated at night with hundreds of hidden lights. In July and August, kids' entertainers perform Sunday through Friday afternoons; jazz, blues, and classical musicians play at an outdoor stage each evening; and fireworks draw crowds every Saturday night. The wheelchair- and stroller-accessible site is also home to a seed-and-gift shop, a plant identification center, two restaurants (one offering traditional afternoon tea), and a coffee shop; you can even call ahead for a picnic basket on fireworks nights. To avoid crowds, try to come at opening time, in the late afternoon or evening (except Saturday evenings, which also draw many visitors), or between September and June, when the gardens are still stunning. The grounds are especially magical at Christmas, with themed lighting and an ice rink.

The gardens are a 20-minute drive north of downtown; parking is free but fills up on fireworks Saturdays. You can get here by city bus 75 from Douglas Street in downtown Victoria, but service is slow and infrequent. Both Gray Line and CVS Cruise Victoria run shuttles from downtown Victoria, and CVS Cruise Victoria also operates a shuttle from the Swartz Bay ferry terminal. ⊠ *800 Benvenuto Ave., Brentwood Bay* ☎ *250/652–5256, 866/652–4422* ⊕ *www.butchartgardens.com* ☎ *C$29.60* ☉ *Mid-June–Aug., daily 9 am–10 pm; Sept.–mid-June, daily 9 am–dusk.*

FAMILY
Shaw Ocean Discovery Centre. A simulated ride underwater in a deep-sea elevator is just the beginning of a visit to this fun and educational marine interpretive center. Devoted entirely to the aquatic life and

conservation needs of the Salish Sea—the waters south and east of Vancouver Island—the small but modern center displays local sea life, including luminous jellyfish, bright purple starfish, wolf eels, rockfish, and octopi. Hands-on activities and touch tanks delight kids, who also love the high-tech effects, including a floor projection that ripples when stepped on and a pop-up tank you can poke your head into. ⊠ *9811 Seaport Pl., Sidney* ☎ *250/665–7511* ⊕ *www.oceandiscovery.ca* ⊠ *$14* ☉ *July–Aug., daily 10–5; Sept.–June daily 10–4.*

WHERE TO EAT

Wild salmon, locally made cheeses, Pacific oysters, organic vegetables, local microbrews, and even wines from the island's farm-gate wineries (the B.C. government allows really small wineries to sell their wines "at the farm gate") are tastes to watch for. Vegetarians and vegans are well catered to in this health-conscious town, and seafood choices go well beyond traditional fish-and-chips. You may notice an Ocean Wise symbol on a growing number of menus: this indicates that the restaurant is committed to serving only sustainably harvested fish and seafood.

Victoria has a tremendous number of restaurants for such a small city, and the glorious pantry that is Vancouver Island keeps standards up. Restaurants in the region are generally casual. Smoking is banned in all public places, including restaurant patios, in Greater Victoria. Victorians tend to dine early—restaurants get busy at 6, and many kitchens close by 9. Pubs, lounges, and the few open-late places mentioned here are your best options for an after-hours nosh.

Some of the city's best casual (and not-so-casual) fare is served in pubs—particularly in brewpubs; most have an all-ages restaurant as well as an adults-only bar area.

Afternoon tea is a Victoria tradition, as is good coffee in any number of funky local caffeine purveyors around town. *Prices in the reviews are the average cost of a main course at dinner or, if dinner is not served, at lunch, not including 5% GST and 10% liquor tax.*

DOWNTOWN

Use the coordinate (✛ B2) at the end of each listing to locate a site on the corresponding map.

$$$ ✕ **Aura.** Creative Pacific Rim cuisine and the city's best waterfront patio make this chic eatery on the Inner Harbour's south shore a winner. Always using local ingredients, the seasonally changing fare reveals Asian leanings: think poached B.C. salmon paired with barbecued eel and a Japanese rice-cabbage roll; buffalo short ribs braised with fennel and star anise and served with wild mushroom bread pudding; or free-range chicken with a wasabi pea crust. The wine cellar is full of hard-to-find Vancouver Island wines and Okanagan labels. Sleek lines, warm colors, and water-view windows create a room that's both stylish and cozy. $ *Average main: C$25* ⊠ *Inn at Laurel Point, 680 Montreal St., James Bay* ☎ *250/414–6739* ⊕ *www.aurarestaurant.ca* ✛ *C4.*

MODERN
CANADIAN
Fodor's Choice
★

$$ ✕ **Barb's Fish & Chips.** Funky Barb's, a tin-roofed take-out shack, floats on the quay at Fisherman's Wharf, west of the Inner Harbour off St.

SEAFOOD

19

Butchart Gardens

Lawrence Street. Halibut, salmon, oysters, mussels, crab, burgers, and chowder are all prepared fresh. The picnic tables on the wharf provide a front-row view of the brightly colored houseboats moored here, or you can carry your food to the grassy park nearby. Ferries sail to Fisherman's Wharf from the Inner Harbour, or you can work up an appetite with a leisurely stroll along the waterfront. $ *Average main: C$13* ✉ *Fisherman's Wharf, St. Lawrence St., Downtown* ☎ *250/384–6515* ⊕ *www.barbsplace.ca* ☉ *Closed Nov.–early Mar.* ✛ *B5.*

$$$
FRENCH
Fodor's Choice
★

✕ **Brasserie L'ecole.** French-country cooking shines at this informal Chinatown bistro, and the historic room—once a schoolhouse for the Chinese community—evokes a timeless brasserie, from the white linens and patina-rich fir floors to the chalkboards above the slate bar listing the day's oyster, mussel, and steak options. Sean Brennan, one of the city's better-known chefs, works with local farmers and fishers to source the best seasonal, local, and organic ingredients. The menu changes daily but lists such contemporary spins on classic bistro fare as duck breast with chickpea fries and asparagus, or tuna with chervil aioli. Be prepared for lines, as this petite spot does not take reservations. $ *Average main: C$24* ✉ *1715 Government St., Downtown* ☎ *250/475–6260* ⊕ *www.lecole.ca* ⌧ *Reservations not accepted* ☉ *Closed Sun. and Mon. No lunch* ✛ *F2.*

$$$
MODERN
CANADIAN
Fodor's Choice
★

✕ **Cafe Brio.** In this bustling Italian villa–style room, long one of Victoria's favorites, the frequently changing menu adds Mediterranean influences to the regional, mostly organic fare. You might find local rockfish pan-roasted and paired with chickpea polenta, grilled albacore tuna with an olive vinaigrette, red wine-braised duck legs, rigatoni with spicy sausage, or house-made charcuterie. Most dishes come in full- or half-sizes, the better to sample more items or cater to smaller appetites. Virtually everything, including the bread, pasta, and desserts, is made in-house. The 400-label wine list has a top selection of B.C. choices. ⓈAverage main: C$27 ⊠944 Fort St., Downtown ☎250/383–0009, 866/270–5461 ⊕ www.cafe-brio.com ⊘ No lunch ✛ H4.

$$$
MODERN
CANADIAN
✕**Camille's.** Working closely with independent farmers, the chef at this long-established favorite concentrates on such locally sourced products as lamb, duck, and seafood; quail and venison often make an appearance, too. The menu is based on what's fresh, but might include spot-prawn bisque with lemon and ginger; wild salmon with beet papardelle; or organic beef tenderloin. The wine cellar–like backdrop, on the lower floor of a historic building on Bastion Square, is candlelit and romantic, with exposed brick, soft jazz and blues, and lots of intimate nooks and crannies hung with local art. The wine list is well selected. ⓈAverage main: C$28 ⊠45 Bastion Sq., Downtown ☎250/381–3433 ⊕ www. camillesrestaurant.com ⊘ Closed Sun. and Mon. No lunch ✛ E3.

$$
CANADIAN
✕**Mo:Lé.** A good choice for vegans, this brick-lined Chinatown café has plenty of wholesome, organic, local fare for meat eaters, too. At breakfast, large helpings of free-range eggs, locally made sausages, and organic spelt griddle cakes fuel a post-party, pre-yoga crowd. At lunch, locals might pop in for an avocado, seaweed, and sprout sandwich, a yam wrap, or an organic beef burger. The place is tiny, so expect to wait. ⓈAverage main: C$13 ⊠554 Pandora St., Downtown ☎250/385–6653 ⊕ www.molerestaurant.ca ⊜ Reservations not accepted ⊘ No dinner ✛ F2.

$
SEAFOOD
✕**Red Fish Blue Fish.** If you like your fish both yummy *and* ecologically friendly, look no further than this former shipping container on the pier at the foot of Broughton Street. From the soil-topped roof and biodegradable packaging to the sustainably harvested local seafood, this waterfront take-out shop minimizes its ecological footprint. The chef offers a choice of local wild salmon, tuna, oysters, and scallops from the barbecue. Portuguese buns are baked daily for the seafood sandwiches, fish tacos come in grilled tortilla cones, and even plain old fish-and-chips are taken up a notch with a choice of wild salmon, halibut, or cod in tempura batter with hand-cut fries. Be prepared for queues on sunny days. ⓈAverage main: C$12 ⊠1006 Wharf St., Downtown ☎250/298–6877 ⊕ www.redfish-bluefish.com ⊜ Reservations not accepted ⊘ No dinner ✛ E4.

$$$
MODERN
CANADIAN
✕**Ulla Restaurant.** Victoria's foodies are buzzing about this Chinatown restaurant that's serving up some of the city's most innovative fare. From the frequently changing, locally sourced menu, you could choose starters like garlic and celery root ravioli in a basil emulsion or the albacore tuna carpaccio, then continue your meal with chicken (a poached breast and crispy leg paired with tortellini and a trio of carrots and peas), short-rib steak (with Swiss-style potatoes, spring onions, and oyster mushrooms), or halibut (with a lemon and black olive dressing). Vegetarians might opt for a plate of kale shoots, fiddlehead ferns, asparagus, and other delectable plant matter. The high arched windows, solid fir tables, and art-filled walls make the room feel both airy and relaxed.

19

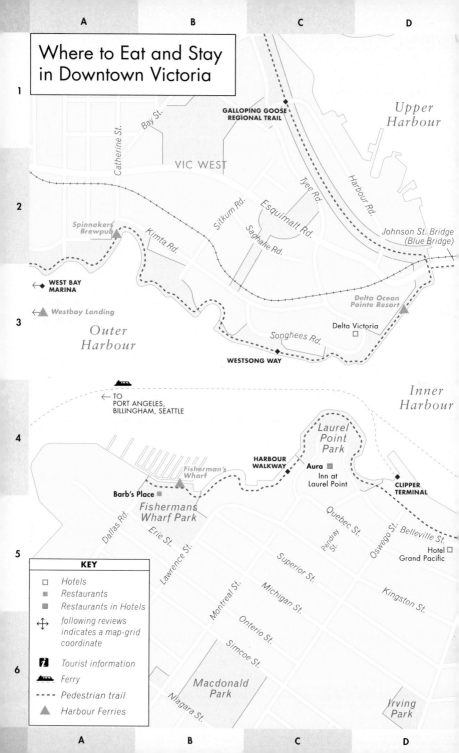

Where to Eat and Stay in Downtown Victoria

A **B** **C** **D**

1

Upper Harbour

GALLOPING GOOSE REGIONAL TRAIL

VIC WEST

Bay St.

Catherine St.

Tyee Rd.

Harbour Rd.

2

Sitkum Rd.

Esquimalt Rd.

Saghalie Rd.

Johnson St. Bridge (Blue Bridge)

Spinnakers Brewpub

Kimta Rd.

West Bay Marina

Westbay Landing

Delta Ocean Pointe Resort

Delta Victoria

3

Outer Harbour

Songhees Rd.

WESTSONG WAY

Inner Harbour

← TO PORT ANGELES, BILLINGHAM, SEATTLE

Laurel Point Park

4

Fisherman's Wharf

HARBOUR WALKWAY

Aura

Inn at Laurel Point

CLIPPER TERMINAL

Barb's Place

Fishermans Wharf Park

Dallas Rd.

Erie St.

Lawrence St.

Quebec St.

Pendray St.

Oswego St.

Belleville St.

Hotel Grand Pacific

5

Superior St.

Kingston St.

Montreal St.

Michigan St.

Onterio St.

Simcoe St.

Niagara St.

6

Macdonald Park

Irving Park

KEY

□	Hotels
■	Restaurants
■	Restaurants in Hotels
⊕	following reviews indicates a map-grid coordinate
🛈	Tourist information
🚢	Ferry
- - -	Pedestrian trail
▲	Harbour Ferries

A **B** **C** **D**

$ *Average main: C$27* ⊠ *509 Fisgard St., Downtown* ☎ *250/590–8795* ⊕ *www.ulla.ca* ⊘ *Closed Sun.–Mon. No lunch* ✛ *E2.*

$$$ ✕ **Zambri's.** This lively trattoria, in a glam space with floor-to-ceiling
ITALIAN   windows and eclectic chandeliers, has a setting to match the top-notch
Italian food. The kitchen uses local and organic ingredients to turn out
contemporary versions of traditional dishes. During the always-busy
lunch service, choose from pizzas, pastas, and hot sandwiches, while
in the evening you might opt for tagliatelle with duck and olive ragù,
grilled tuna with a balsamic vinegar sauce, or crispy pork shoulder
served of a bed of greens, potatoes, and grapes. The mostly Italian
wine list includes lesser-known labels, with many available by the glass.
$ *Average main: C$22* ⊠ *820 Yates St., Downtown* ☎ *250/360–1171* ⊕ *www.zambris.ca* ✛ *G3.*

WHERE TO STAY

For expanded hotel reviews, visit Fodors.com.

Victoria has a vast range of accommodation, with what seems like
whole neighborhoods dedicated to hotels. Options range from city
resorts and full-service business hotels to mid-priced tour-group haunts
and family-friendly motels, but the city is especially known for its lav-
ish B&Bs in beautifully restored Victorian and Edwardian mansions.
*Prices in the reviews are the lowest cost of a standard double room
in high season excluding 10% provincial accommodation tax, service
charge, and 5% GST.*

DOWNTOWN

*Use the coordinate (✛ B2) at the end of each listing to locate a site on
the corresponding map.*

$$$ 🖼 **Beaconsfield Inn.** This 1905 building four blocks from the Inner Har-
B&B/INN   bour is one of Victoria's most faithfully restored, antique-filled man-
sions. **Pros:** luxurious; opportunities to mingle over breakfast or sherry.
Cons: romantic ambience is not suited for kids; several blocks from
shopping and dining. $ *Rooms from: C$199* ⊠ *998 Humboldt St.,
Downtown* ☎ *250/384–4044, 888/884–4044* ⊕ *www.beaconsfieldinn.
com* ⇆ *5 rooms, 4 suites* ❙⊙❙ *Breakfast* ✛ *H6.*

$$$ 🖼 **Delta Victoria Ocean Pointe Resort and Spa.** Across the Johnson Street
HOTEL   Bridge from downtown Victoria, this waterfront resort has all sorts of
amenities, from tennis and squash courts to a popular spa, an around-
the-clock gym, and a waterfront walking path. **Pros:** water views; free
Internet; downtown shuttle and harbor ferry service. **Cons:** not right
downtown; gets busy with conferences. $ *Rooms from: C$229* ⊠ *45
Songhees Rd., Vic West* ☎ *250/360–2999, 800/667–4677* ⊕ *www.
deltavictoria.com* ⇆ *233 rooms, 6 suites* ✛ *D3.*

$$$$ 🖼 **Fairmont Empress.** Opened in 1908, this ivy-draped harborside châ-
HOTEL   teau and city landmark has aged gracefully, with top-notch service and
sympathetically restored Edwardian furnishings. **Pros:** central location;
professional service; great spa and restaurant. **Cons:** small to average-size
rooms and bathrooms; tourists in the public areas; pricey. $ *Rooms from:
C$349* ⊠ *721 Government St., Downtown* ☎ *250/384–8111, 866/540–
4429* ⊕ *www.fairmont.com/empress* ⇆ *436 rooms, 41 suites* ✛ *E5.*

$$$ **Hotel Grand Pacific.** The city's best health club (with yoga classes,
HOTEL squash courts, and state-of-the-art equipment) and a prime Inner
Harbour location appeal to savvy regulars, including Seattleites step-
ping off the ferry across the street. $ *Rooms from: C$199* ⊠ *463
Belleville St., Downtown* ☎ *250/386–0450, 800/663–7550* ⊕ *www.
hotelgrandpacific.com* ⟿ *258 rooms, 46 suites* ⦿*No meals* ✛ *E5.*

$$$$ **Inn at Laurel Point.** A seaside Japanese garden, a museum-quality
HOTEL art collection, and harbor views from every room make this Asian-
Fodor'sChoice inspired independent hotel on the Inner Harbour's quiet south shore a
★ favorite among Victoria regulars. **Pros:** views; quiet, parklike setting.
Cons: 10-minute walk from downtown. $ *Rooms from: C$254* ⊠ *680
Montreal St., Downtown* ☎ *250/386–8721, 800/663–7667* ⊕ *www.
laurelpoint.com* ⟿ *135 rooms, 65 suites* ⦿*No meals* ✛ *C4.*

$$$ **Magnolia Hotel & Spa.** From the on-site spa to the soaker tubs, sauna,
HOTEL and herb tea, the Magnolia, without actually saying so, caters beauti-
fully to the female traveler—though the attention to detail, hop-to-it
staff, and central location won't be lost on men either. **Pros:** great location; friendly and helpful service; welcoming lobby with fireplace, tea,
and coffee. **Cons:** no room service at breakfast; small fitness room; no
on-site pool or hot tub. $ *Rooms from: C$219* ⊠ *623 Courtney St.,
Downtown* ☎ *250/381–0999, 877/624–6654* ⊕ *www.magnoliahotel.
com* ⟿ *64 rooms* ⦿*Breakfast* ✛ *F4.*

OAK BAY AND ROCKLAND

$$$ **Abbeymoore Manor.** This 1912 mansion has the wide verandas, dark
B&B/INN wainscoting, and high ceilings of its era, but the attitude is informal and
welcoming, from the super-helpful hosts to the free snacks to the coffee
on tap all day. **Pros:** good value; friendly hosts; excellent service. **Cons:** a
mile from the Inner Harbour; often booked in advance. $ *Rooms from:
C$199* ⊠ *1470 Rockland Ave., Rockland* ☎ *250/370–1470, 888/801–
1811* ⊕ *www.abbeymoore.com* ⟿ *5 rooms, 2 suites* ⦿*Breakfast* ✛ *H5.*

$$$ **Villa Marco Polo Inn.** A classical European garden with a stone terrace,
B&B/INN reflecting pool, and fountains is all part of the Tuscan-hideaway feel
at this 1923 Italian Renaissance–style manor. **Pros:** lots of comfy common areas; gracious hosts; full concierge services. **Cons:** a mile from
downtown; no elevator. $ *Rooms from: C$215* ⊠ *1524 Shasta Place,
Rockland* ☎ *250/370–1524, 877/601–1524* ⊕ *www.villamarcopolo.
com* ⟿ *4 rooms* ⦿*Breakfast* ✛ *H4.*

SIDNEY AND THE SAANICH PENINSULA

$$$$ **Brentwood Bay Resort & Spa.** Every room has a private ocean-view
RESORT patio or balcony at this adult-oriented boutique resort in a tiny seaside
Fodor'sChoice village. **Pros:** magnificent setting; great food; free Wi-Fi. **Cons:** pricey
★ rates; 30-minute drive from downtown. $ *Rooms from: C$369* ⊠ *849
Verdier Ave., Brentwood Bay* ☎ *250/544–2079, 888/544–2079* ⊕ *www.
brentwoodbayresort.com* ⟿ *30 rooms, 3 suites* ⦿*No meals* ✛ *F1.*

$$$ **Sidney Pier Hotel & Spa.** Stylish and ecologically friendly, this glass-
HOTEL and-stone boutique hotel on the parklike waterfront has helped intro-
duce Sidney to more travelers. **Pros:** lovely views; eco-friendly vibe;
close to ferries and airport. **Cons:** 30 minutes from downtown; no pool.
$ *Rooms from: C$179* ⊠ *9805 Seaport Pl., Sidney* ☎ *250/655–9445,*

19

Inn at Laurel Point

Brentwood Bay Lodge & Spa

866/659–9445 ⊕ *www.sidneypier.com* ⊷ *46 rooms, 9 suites* ⏣ *No meals* ⊕ *H1.*

NIGHTLIFE AND THE ARTS

Monday Magazine. For entertainment listings, pick up a free copy of this artsy magazine every Thursday. You can also check out listings online. ⊕ *www.mondaymag.com.*

Victoria Visitor Information Centre. Tourism Victoria has event listings, and you can buy tickets for many events at the Victoria Visitor Information Centre. ⊠ *812 Wharf St.* ☎ *250/953–2033, 800/663–3883* ⊕ *www. tourismvictoria.com.*

NIGHTLIFE

Victoria's nightlife is low-key and casual, with many wonderful pubs, but a limited choice of nightclubs. Pubs offer a casual vibe for lunch, dinner, or an afternoon pint, often with a view and an excellent selection of beer. The pubs listed here all serve food, and many brew their own beer. Patrons must be 19 or older to enter a bar or pub in British Columbia, but many pubs have a separate restaurant section open to all ages. The city is enjoying a resurgence of cocktail culture, with several of Victoria's trendier restaurants doubling as lounges, offering cocktails and small plates well into the night. Dance clubs attract a young crowd, and most close by 2 am. A dress code (no jeans or sneakers) may be enforced, but otherwise, attire is casual. Smoking is not allowed in Victoria's pubs, bars, and nightclubs—this applies both indoors and on the patio.

BARS AND LOUNGES

Bengal Lounge. Deep leather sofas and a tiger skin help to re-create the days of the British Raj at this iconic lounge in the Fairmont Empress Hotel. Martinis and a curry buffet are the draws through the week. On Friday and Saturday nights a jazz combo takes the stage. ⊠ *Fairmont Empress Hotel, 721 Government St., Downtown* ☎ *250/384–8111* ⊕ *www.fairmont.com/empress.*

Canoe Brewpub. One of Victoria's biggest and best pub patios overlooks the Gorge, the waterway just north of the Inner Harbour. The interior of the former power station has been stylishly redone with high ceilings, exposed bricks, and wood beams. There's a wide range of in-house brews, top-notch bar snacks, and an all-ages restaurant. ⊠ *450 Swift St., Downtown* ☎ *250/361–1940* ⊕ *www.canoebrewpub.com.*

The Superior. Live acoustic blues and jazz and a small-plates menu of local organic fare attract a hip grown-up crowd to this café and nightspot near Fisherman's Wharf. ⊠ *106 Superior St., James Bay* ☎ *250/380–9515* ⊕ *www.thesuperior.ca.*

Swans Brewpub. A stunning array of First Nations masks and other artworks hangs from the open rafters in this popular downtown brewpub, where jazz, blues, and swing bands play nightly. ⊠ *506 Pandora Ave., Downtown* ☎ *250/361–3310* ⊕ *www.swanshotel.com.*

19

DANCE CLUBS

Hermann's Jazz Club. Dinner, dancing, and live jazz are on the menu at this venerable downtown restaurant and jazz club. ✉ *753 View St., Downtown* ☎ *250/388–9166* ⊕ *www.hermannsjazz.com.*

Paparazzi. Victoria's longest-running gay club draws a mixed crowd with fun drag, karaoke, and club nights. ✉ *642 Johnson St., Downtown* ☎ *250/388–0505* ⊕ *www.paparazzinightclub.com.*

THE ARTS
MUSIC

Summer in the Square. Free jazz, classical, and folk concerts; cultural events; and more run all summer at Centennial Square, next to City Hall. Events start daily at noon. ✉ *Centennial Square, Pandora Ave. and Douglas St.* ☎ *250/361–0388* ⊕ *www.victoria.ca.*

Victoria Jazz Society. Watch for music events hosted by this group, which also organizes the annual JazzFest International in late June. ☎ *250/388–4423* ⊕ *www.jazzvictoria.ca.*

Victoria Symphony. With everything from solo performances to chamber music concerts to full-scale orchestral works, the Victoria Symphony has something for everyone. Watch for Symphony Splash on the first Sunday in August, when the orchestra plays a free concert from a barge in the Inner Harbour. ☎ *250/385–6515* ⊕ *www.victoriasymphony.ca.*

THEATER

Belfry Theatre. Housed in a former church, the Belfry Theatre has a resident company that specializes in contemporary Canadian dramas. ✉ *1291 Gladstone Ave., Fernwood* ☎ *250/385–6815* ⊕ *www.belfry.bc.ca.*

SPORTS AND THE OUTDOORS

BIKING

Victoria is a bike-friendly town, with more bicycle commuters than any other city in Canada. Bike racks on city buses, bike lanes on downtown streets, and tolerant drivers all help, as do the city's three long-distance cycling routes, which mix car-free paths and low-traffic scenic routes.

BC Ferries will transport bikes for a nominal fee (just C$2 from Vancouver). You can also rent bikes, bike trailers, and tandem bikes at several Victoria outlets for a few hours, a day, or a week. Helmets are required by law and are supplied with bike rentals.

BIKE ROUTES

Galloping Goose Regional Trail. Following an old rail bed, this 33-mile route officially starts at the Johnson Street Bridge in Victoria. The multi-use trail runs across old rail trestles and through forests west to the town of Sooke, finishing at the abandoned gold-mining town of Leechtown. Just north of downtown it links with the Lochside Regional Trail to Sidney, creating a nearly continuous 62-mile car-free route. ☎ *250/478–3344* ⊕ *www.crd.bc.ca/parks.*

Lochside Regional Trail. This fairly level, mostly car-free route follows an old rail bed for 18 miles past farmland, wineries, and beaches from the ferry terminals at Swartz Bay and Sidney to downtown Victoria. It joins the Seaside Touring Route at Cordova Bay and meets the Galloping

Goose Trail just north of downtown Victoria. ☎ *250/478–3344* ⊕ *www. crd.bc.ca/parks*.

Seaside Touring Route. Starting at the corner of Government and Belleville streets on the Inner Harbour, this 18-mile route, marked with bright yellow signs, leads past Fisherman's Wharf and along the Dallas Road waterfront to Beacon Hill Park. It then follows the seashore to Cordova Bay, where it connects with Victoria's other two long-distance routes: the Lochside and Galloping Goose regional trails.

BIKE RENTALS AND TOURS
Cycle BC Rentals. This centrally located shop rents bikes for adults and children, as well as bike trailers, motorcycles, and scooters. ✉ *685 Humboldt St., Downtown* ☎ *250/380–2453* ⊕ *www.cyclebc.ca*.

CycleTreks. Besides renting bikes, this company also runs bike tours of Victoria, the Gulf Islands, and various parts of Vancouver Island, as well as a vineyard tour of the Cowichan Valley. The staff can give you a ride to the start of Galloping Goose Trail or to Butchart Gardens so that you can pedal back. ✉ *1000 Wharf St., Downtown* ☎ *250/386–2277, 877/733–6722* ⊕ *www.cycletreks.com*.

GOLF
You can golf year-round in Victoria and southern Vancouver Island, and you almost have to, just to try all the courses. Victoria alone has several public golf courses, ranging from rolling sea-view fairways to challenging mountaintop sites. Southern Vancouver Island is home to the Vancouver Island Golf Trail, where you'll find 10 championship courses along a 250-km (150-mile) corridor. Golf Vancouver Island (☎ *888/465–3239* ⊕ *www.golfvancouverisland.ca*) has details.

Bear Mountain Golf & Country Club. Built near the top of a 1,100-foot mountain about 20 minutes north of Victoria, this is widely regarded as the island's most exciting course. Designed by Jack Nicklaus and his son Steve, the Mountain Course has an extra 19th hole built on a cliff ledge with striking views across the city. A second Nicklaus-designed layout, called the Valley Course, is at a slightly lower elevation. ✉ *1999 Country Club Way, off Millstream Rd. and Bear Mountain Pkwy., West Shore* ☎ *250/744–2327, 888/533–2327* ⊕ *www.bearmountain.ca* ⛳ *Mountain Course: 18 holes. 7212 yds. Par 72. Greens Fee: C$129. Valley Course: 18 holes. 7000 yds. Par 71. Greens Fee: C$129.*

HIKING AND WALKING
Victoria is one of the most pedestrian-friendly cities in North America. Waterfront pathways make it possible to stroll virtually all around Victoria's waterfront. For some interesting self-guided walks around the city's historic areas, check out ⊕ *www.victoria.ca/tours* or pick up a free walking-tour map at the city's visitor information center. Though popular with cyclists, the area's long-distance paths are also great for long walks. For views and elevation, check out the trail networks in the area's many provincial and regional parks.

Juan de Fuca Provincial Park. Extending from the Jordan River to near Port Renfrew, Juan de Fuca Provincial Park takes in several beaches, including China Beach, with soft, sandy beaches dotted with driftwood;

19

Sombrio Beach, a popular surfing spot; and Botanical Beach, with its amazing tidal pools. The **Juan de Fuca Marine Trail** is a tough 30-mile hike running along the shore from China Beach, west of the Jordan River, to Port Renfrew. Several trailheads along the way—at Sombrio Beach, Parkinson Creek, and Botanical Beach—allow day hikers to walk small stretches of it. ⊠ *Hwy. 14, between Jordan River and Port Renfrew, Sooke* ☎ *250/474–1336* ⊕ *www.env.gov.bc.ca/bcparks.*

Mount Douglas Regional Park. Trails through the forest to the 758-foot summit of Mt. Douglas reward hikers with a 360-degree view of Victoria, the Saanich Peninsula, and the mountains of Washington State. ⊠ *Off Cedar Hill Rd., Saanich* ☎ *250/475–5522* ⊕ *www.saanich.ca.*

SCUBA DIVING

The waters off Vancouver Island have some of the best scuba diving in the world, with clear waters and rich marine life; visibility is best in winter. The Ogden Point Breakwater and Race Rocks Underwater Marine Park are popular spots close to town. In Brentwood Bay on the Saanich Peninsula are the Glass Sponge Gardens, a sea mountain covered with sponges that were thought to be extinct. Off Thetis Island, near Chemainus, in the Cowichan Valley, divers can explore a sunken 737 jetliner. Dive BC (⊕ *www.divebc.ca*) has details.

Ogden Point Dive Centre. Guided dives, weekend charters, and a water-view café are all available at this PADI-certified dive center at the Ogden Point Breakwater near downtown Victoria. ⊠ *199 Dallas Rd., Downtown* ☎ *250/380–9119, 888/701–1177* ⊕ *www.divevictoria.com.*

Rockfish Divers. Based on the Saanich Peninsula, this internationally accredited PADI dive outfitter offers charters, courses, and equipment rentals. ⊠ *Brentwood Bay Resort & Spa, 849 Verdier Ave., Brentwood Bay* ☎ *250/889–7282, 888/544–2079* ⊕ *www.rockfishdivers.com.*

SHOPPING

Shopping in Victoria is easy: virtually everything is in the downtown area on or near Government Street stretching north from the Fairmont Empress hotel.

SHOPPING DISTRICTS AND MALLS

Chinatown. Exotic fruits and vegetables, children's toys, wicker fans, fabric slippers, and other Chinese imports fill the shops along Fisgard Street. Fan Tan Alley, a narrow lane off Fisgard Street, has more nouveau-hippie goods, with an art gallery and yoga studio tucked in among its tiny storefronts.

Design District. The area where Wharf Street runs into Store Street contains a cluster of Victoria's home decor shops. ⊕ *www.victoriadesigndistrict.com.*

Fodor's Choice ★ **Lower Johnson Street.** This row of candy-color Victorian shopfronts is Victoria's hub for independent fashion boutiques. Storefronts—some closet size—are filled with local designers' wares, funky boutiques, and no fewer than three shops selling ecologically friendly clothes of hemp and organic cotton. ⊠ *Johnson St., between Government and Store Sts., Downtown.*

Fan Tan Alley, in Victoria's Chinatown, is said to be the narrowest street in Canada.

SPECIALTY STORES

Artina's. Canadian-made jewelry—all handmade, one-of-a-kind pieces—fills the display cases at this unique jewelry shop. ⌧ *1002 Government St., Downtown* ☏ *250/386–7000* ⊕ *www.artinas-jewellery.com.*

Munro's Books. This beautifully restored 1909 building houses one of Canada's best-stocked independent bookstores. ⌧ *1108 Government St., Downtown* ☏ *250/382–2464* ⊕ *www.munrobooks.com.*

Fodor's Choice ★ **Silk Road.** For exotic teas (which you can sample at the tasting bar), aromatherapy remedies, and spa treatments (think green-tea facials), stop at this chic tea shop. ⌧ *1624 Government St., Downtown* ☏ *250/704–2688* ⊕ *www.silkroadtea.com.*

SPAS

Since health, nature, and relaxing seem to be the major preoccupations in Victoria, it's not surprising that the city has enjoyed a boom in spas. Aesthetics are important, but natural healing, ancient practices, and the use of such local products as wine and seaweed are more the focus here. Local specialties include vinotherapy (applying the antioxidant properties of wine grapes externally, rather than internally). Here are some local favorites.

Aveda Institute. Vancouver Island's booming spa industry has to be staffed somehow, and this is where the technicians train. Supervised by pros, they offer budget-savvy clients everything from makeup touch-ups to hot-stone massages. Supervised student services top out at around C$65, or you can choose to have your treatment done by a professional. ✉ *1402 Douglas St., Downtown* ☎ *250/386–7993* ⊕ *www.avedainstitutevictoria.ca.*

Le Spa Sereine. A custom-built pedicure room with fully reclining chairs and sunken basins is a draw at this independent downtown spa. Set in an atmospheric old building, it's also known for salt glows, hydrotherapy, reflexology, and Indian head massages. ✉ *1411 Government St., Downtown* ☎ *250/388–4419, 866/388–4419* ⊕ *www.lespasereine.ca.*

Spa at Delta Victoria Ocean Pointe Resort. Organic skin-care products and harbor-view treatment rooms are among the draws at this popular hotel spa. Patrons have access to the hotel's gym and pool. ✉ *Delta Victoria Ocean Pointe Resort, 45 Songhees Rd., Downtown* ☎ *250/360–5938, 800/575–8882* ⊕ *www.thespadeltavictoria.com.*

Spa at the Grand. Traditional Thai, Swedish, and deep-tissue massage, as well as facials and beauty treatments, are among the offerings at this intimate Asian-inspired spa. ✉ *Hotel Grand Pacific, 463 Belleville St., Downtown* ☎ *250/380–7862* ⊕ *www.hotelgrandpacific.com.*

Willow Stream Spa at the Fairmont Empress Hotel. Victoria's most luxurious spa is actually a pretty good value, especially if you arrive, as suggested, an hour before your appointment to soak in the Hungarian mineral bath, sauna, and steam room. ✉ *Fairmont Empress Hotel, 633 Humboldt St., Downtown* ☎ *250/995–4650, 866/854–7444* ⊕ *www. willowstream.com.*

TRAVEL SMART
PACIFIC
NORTHWEST

GETTING HERE AND AROUND

▌AIR TRAVEL

It takes about 5 hours to fly nonstop to Seattle or Portland from New York, 4 hours from Chicago, and 2½ hours from Los Angeles. Flights from New York to Vancouver take about 6 hours nonstop; from Chicago, 4½ hours nonstop; and from Los Angeles, 3 hours nonstop. Flying from Seattle to Portland takes just under an hour; flying from Portland to Vancouver takes an hour and 15 minutes.

Airlines and Airports Airline and Airport Links.com. Airline and Airport Links.com has links to many of the world's airlines and airports. ⊕ *www.airlineandairportlinks.com.*

Airline Security Issues Transportation Security Administration. Transportation Security Administration has answers for almost every question that might come up. It is the most direct resource for confirming what can and cannot be carried on to a plane. ⊕ *www. tsa.gov.*

AIRPORTS

The main gateways to the Pacific Northwest are Portland International Airport (PDX), Sea-Tac International Airport (SEA), and Vancouver International Airport (YVR).

Airport Information Portland International Airport (PDX) ☎ 503/460–4234, 877/739–4636 ⊕ *www.flypdx.com.* **Sea-Tac International Airport (SEA)** ☎ 206/787–5388, 800/544–1965 ⊕ *www.portseattle.org/seatac.* **Vancouver International Airport (YVR)** ☎ 604/207–7077 ⊕ *www.yvr.ca.*

▌TIP➜ Long layovers don't have to be only about sitting around or shopping. These days they can be about burning off vacation calories. Check out ⊕ www. airportgyms.com for lists of health clubs that are in or near many U.S. and Canadian airports.

AIRLINE TICKETS

The least expensive airfares to the Pacific Northwest are often priced for round-trip travel and usually must be purchased in advance. Airlines generally allow you to change your flights for a fee; most low-fare tickets, however, are nonrefundable.

You can often save money on your car rental (a must for most Pacific Northwest itineraries) by booking a fly/drive package through your airline. Many airlines offer deals on rental cars if you book through them.

FLIGHTS

Many international carriers serve the Pacific Northwest with direct flights. These include Air France, All Nippon Airways, British Airways, Cathay Pacific, Emirates, Japan Airlines, and Lufthansa. Vancouver has the most connections with international cities, but Seattle's a close second. U.S. carriers serving the area include Alaska Airlines, American, Delta, and United. JetBlue has daily direct flights from New York's JFK airport, Logan International in Boston, and Los Angeles' Long Beach airport to both Seattle and Portland. Virgin America has daily direct flights to Seattle from San Francisco and Los Angeles (LAX). USAirways flies from Portland and Seattle to Phoenix, Charlotte, and Philadelphia, and from Vancouver to Phoenix. Frontier Airlines, Horizon Air, and United Express provide frequent service between cities in Washington, Oregon, Idaho, Montana, and California. Southwest Airlines has frequent service to Seattle and Portland from cities in California, Nevada, Idaho, and Utah, as well as some other parts of the country. The major regional carrier in western Canada is Air Canada (and its subsidiary, Air Canada Express), which has flights from Seattle and Portland to Vancouver and Victoria, along with many direct flights between Vancouver and major U.S. cities outside the Northwest.

Airline Contacts **Air Canada/Air Canada Express** ☎ 888/247–2262 ⊕ www.aircanada.com. **Alaska Airlines/Horizon Air** ☎ 800/252–7522 ⊕ www.alaskaair.com. **American Airlines** ☎ 800/433–7300 ⊕ www.aa.com. **Delta Airlines** ☎ 800/221–1212 ⊕ www.delta.com. **Frontier Airlines** ☎ 800/432–1359 ⊕ www.frontierairlines.com. **Japan Airlines** ☎ 800/525–3663 ⊕ www.jal.com. **jetBlue** ☎ 800/538–2583 ⊕ www.jetblue.com. **Southwest Airlines** ☎ 800/435–9792 ⊕ www.southwest.com. **United Airlines** ☎ 800/864–8331 for U.S. reservations, 800/538–2929 for international reservations ⊕ www.united.com. **USAirways** ☎ 800/428–4322, 800/622–1015 ⊕ www.usairways.com. **Virgin America** ☎ 877/359–8474 ⊕ www.virginamerica.com.

▮ BOAT AND FERRY TRAVEL

Ferries play an important part in the transportation network of the Pacific Northwest. Some are the sole connection to islands in Puget Sound and to small towns and islands along the west coast of British Columbia. Each day ferries transport thousands of commuters to and from work in the coastal cities. Always comfortable, convenient, and providing spectacular views, ferries are also one of the best ways for you to get a feel for the region and its ties to the sea.

Generally, the best times for travel are 9–3 and after 7 pm on weekdays. In July and August you may have to wait hours to take a car aboard one of the popular ferries, such as those to the San Juan Islands. Walk-on space is almost always available; if possible, leave your car behind. Reservations aren't taken for most domestic routes in Washington.

WASHINGTON AND OREGON

Washington State Ferries carries millions of passengers and vehicles each year on 10 routes between 20 points on Puget Sound, the San Juan Islands, and Sidney, British Columbia. Onboard services vary depending on the size of the ferry, but many ships have a cafeteria, vending machines, newspaper and tourist-information kiosks, arcade games, and restrooms with family facilities. There are discounted fares in off-peak months.

Black Ball Transport's MV *Coho* makes daily crossings year-round from Port Angeles, WA, to Victoria. The *Coho* can carry 800 passengers and 100 cars across the Strait of Juan de Fuca in 1½ hours. Clipper Vacations operates the passenger-only *Victoria Clipper* jet catamaran service between Seattle and Victoria year-round and between Seattle and the San Juan Islands May through September. ▥ TIP→ Victoria Clipper fares are less expensive if booked at least one day in advance, tickets for children under 12 are discounted, and some great package deals are often available online (be sure to ask about any other promotions or deals, too).

Black Ball Transport ☎ 250/386–2202 in Victoria, 360/457–4491 in Port Angeles ⊕ www.cohoferry.com. **Clipper Vacations** ☎ 800/888–2535 in the U.S., 250/382–8100 in Victoria, 206/448–5000 in Seattle ⊕ www.clippervacations.com. **King County Water Taxi** ☎ 206/684–1551 ⊕ kingcounty.gov/transportation/kcdot/WaterTaxi. **Washington State Ferries** ☎ 800/843–3779 automated line in WA and BC, 888/808–7977, 206/464–6400 ⊕ www.wsdot.wa.gov/ferries.

BRITISH COLUMBIA

British Columbia Ferries operates passenger and vehicle service between the mainland and Victoria and elsewhere. Most ferries take reservations.

Information **British Columbia Ferries** ☎ 250/386–3431 in Victoria, 888/223–3779 ⊕ www.bcferries.com.

SIGHTSEEING

Argosy cruising vessels make sightseeing, dinner, weekend brunch, and special-event cruises around Elliott Bay, Lake Union, Lake Washington, the Ballard Locks, and other Seattle waterways.

From Portland, the *Portland Spirit, Willamette Star,* and *Crystal Dolphin* make sightseeing and dinner cruises on the Willamette and Columbia Rivers. Departing from Cascade Locks, Oregon (45 minutes east of Portland), the sternwheeler *Columbia Gorge* cruises the Columbia Gorge and the Willamette River (December only).

Information Argosy Cruises ☎ *206/622-8687, 888/623-1445* ⊕ *www.argosycruises.com.* **Portland Spirit River Cruises** ☎ *503/224-3900* ⊕ *www.portlandspirit.com.*

∎ BUS TRAVEL

Greyhound services the Washington-Oregon region. Its new BoltBus service runs between Vancouver, Bellingham, Seattle, and Portland and features sleek new buses with Wi-Fi, extra legroom, reserved seating, and power outlets. Experience Oregon in Eugene operates charter bus services and scheduled sightseeing tours that last from a few hours to several days. People Mover travels on Highway 26 in Oregon between Bend and John Day. Greyhound serves most towns in British Columbia, and provides frequent service on popular runs. Quick Shuttle runs buses from Sea-Tac airport, downtown Seattle, and Bellingham to various Vancouver spots and hotels.

Pacific Coach Lines runs multiple daily buses between Vancouver and Victoria, including a ferry ride across the Strait of Georgia, and between Vancouver and Whistler Village. The company also has connections from Vancouver International Airport, downtown Vancouver, and the cruise ship terminal, and operates numerous package tours around British Columbia.

Bus Information BoltBus ☎ *877/265-8287* ⊕ *www.boltbus.com.* **Experience Oregon** ☎ *541/342-2662, 888/342-2662* ⊕ *www.experienceoregon.com.* **Greyhound Lines** ☎ *800/231-2222* ⊕ *www.greyhound.com.* **Pacific Coach Lines** ☎ *800/661-1725, 604/662-7575 in Vancouver* ⊕ *www.pacificcoach.com.* **People Mover** ☎ *541/575-2370* ⊕ *www.grantcountypeoplemover.com.*

Quick Shuttle ☎ *800/665-2122, 604/940-4428 in Vancouver* ⊕ *www.quickcoach.com.*

SIGHTSEEING

Gray Line operates a few day trips from Portland, Seattle, and Vancouver, including tours to Mt. Rainier, the San Juan Islands, Multnomah Falls and the Columbia River Gorge, Vancouver, and Victoria, and schedules a variety of popular bus tours and overnight packages around the Pacific Northwest.

∎ CAR TRAVEL

Driver's licenses from other countries are valid in the United States and Canada. International driving permits (IDPs)—available from the American and Canadian automobile associations and Canada's National Auto Club, and, in the United Kingdom, from the Automobile Association and Royal Automobile Club—are a good idea. Valid only in conjunction with your regular driver's license, these permits are universally recognized; having one may spare you having difficulties with local authorities.

Bookstores, gas stations, convenience stores, and rest stops sell maps (about $5) and multiregion road atlases (about $14). Along larger highways, roadside stops with restrooms, fast-food restaurants, and sundries stores are well spaced. Police and tow trucks patrol major highways and lend assistance.

TRAVEL TIMES FROM PORTLAND BY CAR	
Bend	3½–4 hours
Crater Lake National Park	4½–5 hours
Columbia River Gorge/ Mt. Hood	1½ hours
Willamette Valley	1½–2 hours

TRAVEL TIMES FROM SEATTLE BY CAR	
Portland	3–3½ hours
Vancouver	2½–3 hours
Victoria	2½–3 hour drive to Vancouver; 1½ hour ferry ride from Vancouver
Mt. Rainier National Park (Paradise or Longmire entrances)	2½ hours
North Cascades National Park	3–3½ hours
Olympic National Park	2½ hours to Port Angeles; 1 hour from Port Angeles to Hurricane Ridge
Mt. St. Helens	3–3½ hours
Spokane	4½–5 hours
Yakima Valley	2–2½ hours

BORDER CROSSING

⇨ *See also Passports in Essentials below.*

You will need a valid passport to cross the border; passport cards and enhanced driver's licenses are also accepted for land and sea crossings only. In addition, drivers must carry owner registration and proof of insurance coverage, which is compulsory in Canada. The Canadian Non-Resident Inter-Provincial Motor Vehicle Liability Insurance Card, available from any U.S. insurance company, is accepted as evidence of financial responsibility in Canada. If you are driving a car that is not registered in your name, carry a letter from the owner that authorizes your use of the vehicle.

The main entry point into British Columbia from the United States by car is on I–5 at Blaine, Washington, 48 km (30 miles) south of Vancouver. Three highways enter British Columbia from the east: Highway 1, or the Trans-Canada Highway; Highway 3, or the Crowsnest Highway, which crosses southern British Columbia; and Highway 16, the Yellowhead Highway, which runs through northern British Columbia from the Rocky Mountains to Prince Rupert. From Alaska and the Yukon, take the Alaska Highway (from Fairbanks) or the Klondike Highway (from Skagway or Dawson City).

Border-crossing procedures are usually quick and simple. Every British Columbia border crossing is open 24 hours (except the one at Aldergrove, which is open from 8 am to midnight). The I–5 border crossing at Blaine, Washington (also known as the Douglas, or Peace Arch, border crossing), is one of the busiest border crossings between the United States and Canada. An alternate route, the Pacific Highway border crossing (also known as the "truck crossing"), is just east of the Peace Arch crossing and serves all vehicles, not just trucks. Listen to local radio traffic reports for information about border wait times.

CARS RENTAL

■ TIP→ Make sure that a confirmed reservation guarantees you a car. Agencies sometimes overbook, particularly for busy weekends and holiday periods.

Unless you only visit Seattle, Portland, and Vancouver, you will need to rent a car for at least part of your trip. It's possible to get around the big cities by public transportation and taxis, but once you go outside city limits, your options are limited. National lines like Greyhound do provide service between major towns, and Amtrak has limited service between points in Washington, Oregon and British Columbia (allowing you to get from, say, Seattle to Portland, by train), but it is nearly impossible to get to and around the major recreation areas and national parks of each state without your own wheels. For example, there is no public transportation from Seattle to Mt. Rainier National Park.

Rates in Seattle begin at $26 a day ($159 per week) for an economy car. This does not include the 17.2% tax. The tax on rentals at Sea-Tac Airport, which includes an airport concession fee, is more than 30%, so try to rent from a downtown branch. Rates in Portland begin at $26 a day and $167 a week, not including the 17% tax. Rates in Vancouver begin at about C$34 a day or C$155 a week, usually including unlimited mileage. Note that summer rates in all cities can be absurd (up to $65 per day for a compact); book as far in advance as possible, and if you find a good deal, grab it. Car rentals in British Columbia also incur a 12% sales tax. An additional 17% Concession Recovery Fee, charged by the airport authority for retail space in the terminal, is levied at airport locations.

All the major agencies are represented in the region. If you're planning to cross the U.S.–Canadian border with your rental car, discuss it with the agency to see what's involved.

In the Pacific Northwest you must be 21 to rent a car. Car seats are compulsory for children under four years *and* 40 pounds; older children are required to sit in booster seats until they are eight years old *and* 80 pounds. (In British Columbia, children up to 40 pounds or 18 kilos in weight must use a child seat.) In the United States nonresidents need a reservation voucher, passport, driver's license, and insurance for each driver.

ROAD CONDITIONS

Winter driving can present challenges. In coastal areas the mild, damp climate contributes to frequently wet roadways. Snowfalls generally occur in low-lying Portland, Seattle, and Vancouver only once or twice a year, but when snow does fall, traffic grinds to a halt and roadways become treacherous and stay that way until the snow melts.

Tire chains, studs, or snow tires are essential equipment for winter travel in mountain areas. If you're planning to drive into high elevations, be sure to check the weather forecast beforehand. Even the main-highway mountain passes can close because of snow conditions. In winter

state and provincial highway departments operate snow advisory telephone lines that give pass conditions.

ROADSIDE EMERGENCIES

Contacts For police, ambulance, or other emergencies dial 911.

Oregon State Police ☎ 503/378–3720, 800/452–7888.

▎ TRAIN TRAVEL

Amtrak, the U.S. passenger rail system, has daily service to the Pacific Northwest from the Midwest and California. The *Empire Builder* takes a northern route through Minnesota and Montana from Chicago to Spokane, from which separate legs continue to Seattle and Portland. The *Coast Starlight* begins in Los Angeles; makes stops throughout California, western Oregon, and Washington; and terminates in Seattle.

Amtrak's *Cascades* trains travel between Seattle and Vancouver and between Seattle, Portland, and Eugene. The trip from Seattle to Portland takes roughly 3½ hours and costs $24–$59 for a coach seat; this is a pleasant alternative to a mind-numbing drive down I–5. The trip from Seattle to Vancouver takes roughly 4 hours and costs $29–$51. The *Empire Builder* travels between Portland and Spokane (7.5 hours, $53–$90), with part of the route running through the Columbia River gorge. From Portland to Eugene, the trip is just under 3 hours; the cost is $26–$35.

▎TIP→ Book Amtrak tickets at least a few days in advance, especially if you're traveling between Seattle and Portland on summer weekends.

Information Amtrak ☎ 800/872–7245 ⊕ www.amtrak.com.

ESSENTIALS

▌ACCOMMODATIONS

The lodgings we list are the cream of the crop in each price category. Prices are for a standard double room in high season, based on the European Plan (EP) and excluding tax and service charges. Seattle room tax: 15.6%. Elsewhere in Washington: ranges from 10% to 16%. Portland room tax: 11.5% (13.5% at hotels with 50 or more rooms). Elsewhere in Oregon: ranges from 7 to 10%. Vancouver room tax: 14%. Elsewhere in British Columbia: ranges from 12 to 14%. Most hotels and other lodgings require you to give your credit-card details before they will confirm your reservation. Though secure online payment is commonly used for hotel reservations, if you don't feel comfortable providing information this way, ask if you can fax it or provide by phone. However you book, get confirmation in writing and have a copy of it handy when you check in.

▌TIP→ Assume that hotels operate on the European Plan (no meals) unless we specify that they serve breakfast or, in rare cases, other meals are included as well.

BED-AND-BREAKFASTS

The Pacific Northwest is known for its vast range of bed-and-breakfasts, which are found everywhere from busy urban areas to casual country farms and coastal retreats. Many B&Bs here provide full gourmet breakfasts, and some have kitchens that guests can use. Other popular amenities to ask about are fireplaces, jetted bathtubs, outdoor hot tubs, and area activities.

The regional B&B organizations listed here can provide information on reputable establishments.

Reservation Services American Bed & Breakfast Association ⊕ www.abba. com. BBCanada.com ⊕ www.bbcanada. com. British Columbia Bed and Breakfasts ⊕ www.bcbbonly.com. British Columbia Bed and Breakfast Innkeepers Guild ⊕ www. bcsbestbnbs.com. The Canadian Bed and Breakfast Guide ☏ 905/641–8484 ⊕ www. canadianbandbguide.ca. Oregon Bed and Breakfast Guild ☏ 800/944–6196 ⊕ www. obbg.org. Washington Bed and Breakfast Guild ☏ 253/987–6619 ⊕ www.wbbg.com.

CAMPING

Oregon, Washington, and British Columbia have excellent government-run campgrounds. Some accept advance camping reservations. National park campsites—even backcountry sites—fill up quickly and should be reserved in advance. Note that federal forests allow free camping almost anywhere along trails—a good failsafe if you're unable to secure last-minute arrangements at designated sites, and don't mind hauling your gear.

Privately operated campgrounds sometimes have extra amenities such as laundry rooms and swimming pools. For more information, contact the state or provincial tourism department.

Campground Reservations British Columbia Lodgings and Campground Association ☏ 604/945–7676 ⊕ www.travel-british-columbia.com. Discover Camping (British Columbia) ☏ 800/689–9025 ⊕ www. discovercamping.ca. Oregon Parks and Recreation Department. ☏ 800/452–5687 reservations ⊕ www.oregon.gov/oprd/parks. Washington State Parks and Recreation Commission ☏ 888/226–7688 reservations ⊕ www.parks.wa.gov.

HOTELS

When booking a room, always call the hotel's local toll-free number (if one is available) rather than the central reservations number—you'll often get a better price. Deals can often be found at hotel websites. Always ask about special packages or corporate rates. Many properties offer special weekend rates, sometimes up to 50% off regular prices. However, these deals are usually not extended during peak summer months, when hotels are normally full. All hotels listed have private bath unless otherwise noted.

CUSTOMS AND DUTIES

You're always allowed to bring goods of a certain value back home without having to pay any duty or import tax. But there's a limit on the amount of tobacco and liquor you can bring back duty-free, and some countries have separate limits for perfumes; for exact figures, check with your customs department. The values of so-called "duty-free" goods are included in these amounts. When you shop abroad, save all your receipts, as customs inspectors may ask to see them as well as the items you purchased. If the total value of your goods is more than the duty-free limit, you'll have to pay a tax (most often a flat percentage) on the value of everything beyond that limit.

U.S. Information U.S. Customs and Border Protection ⊕ www.cbp.gov.

Information in Canada Canada Border Services Agency ☎ 204/983–3500, 800/461–9999 toll-free within Canada ⊕ www.cbsa-asfc.gc.ca.

EATING OUT

Pacific Northwest cuisine highlights regional seafood and locally grown, organic produce, often prepared in styles that reflect an Asian influence (Seattle, Victoria, and Vancouver have large Asian populations) or incorporate European (often French or Italian) influences. *See our Flavors of the Pacific Northwest feature at the beginning of this book.*

The restaurants we list are the cream of the crop in each price category. Please note that restaurant prices listed as "Average Cost" include a meal consisting of first course, second course, and dessert.

WORD OF MOUTH

Did the resort look as good in real life as it did in the photos? Did you sleep like a baby, or were the walls paper thin? Did you get your money's worth? Rate hotels and write your own reviews or start a discussion about your favorite places in the Forums on www.fodors.com.

MEALS AND MEALTIMES

Unless otherwise noted, the restaurants listed here are open daily for lunch and dinner.

PAYING

Credit cards—Visa and MasterCard, in particular—are widely accepted in most restaurants, especially in Seattle, Portland, and Vancouver. Debit cards are widely accepted in coffeehouses, delis, and grocery stores.

WINES, BEER, AND SPIRITS

Oregon, Washington, and British Columbia all have thriving wineries—many restaurants in major cities and many small towns, and even in wilderness areas, take their wine lists very seriously. Most of Washington's wineries are east of the Cascades in the south-central part of the state, but you'll find a few close to Seattle as well. Oregon's wineries mostly lie in the valleys between the southern Cascades and the coast. British Columbia winemaking has become increasingly prominent, with many wineries opening in the Okanagan Valley. The Washington State Wine Commission (⊕ *www.washingtonwine. org*) and the Oregon Wine Board (⊕ *www. oregonwine.org*) both maintain websites with facts, history, and information on local wineries. The British Columbia Wine Institute's website (⊕ *www.winebc. com*) has facts and information on individual wineries.

Oregon has more than 100 microbreweries, and Washington has no shortage of excellent local microbrews. Both states have festivals and events celebrating their brews—Seattle's Fremont neighborhood has its own Oktoberfest. The website for the Washington Brewers Guild (⊕ *www. washingtonbeer.com*) has info on breweries in the state and events throughout the Pacific Northwest. The Oregon Brewers Guild (⊕ *www.oregonbeer.org*) also has links to breweries and information on events.

You must be 21 to buy alcohol in Washington and Oregon. The legal drinking age in British Columbia is 19.

▌ MONEY

Prices listed for sights and attractions are for adults. Substantially reduced fees are almost always available for children, students, and senior citizens.

CURRENCY AND EXCHANGE
The units of currency in Canada are the Canadian dollar (C$) and the cent, in almost the same denominations as U.S. currency ($5, $10, $20, 1¢, 5¢, 10¢, 25¢, etc.). C$1 and C$2 coins (known as a "loonie," because of the loon that appears on the coin, and a "toonie," respectively) are used in lieu of bills. Canada stopped distributing pennies in 2013. Check with a bank or other financial institution for the current exchange rate. A good way to be sure you're getting the best exchange rate is by using your credit card or ATM/debit card. The issuing bank will convert your bill at the current rate, though foreign transaction fees may still be added.

▌TIP➔ Even if a currency-exchange booth has a sign promising no commission, rest assured that there's some kind of huge, hidden fee. (Oh . . . that's right. The sign didn't say no fee.) And as for rates, you're almost always better off getting foreign currency at an ATM or exchanging money at a bank.

▌ PASSPORTS

All people traveling by air between the United States and Canada are required to present a passport to enter or reenter the United States. To enter Canada (or more precisely, to reenter the U.S. from Canada) by land or sea you need to present either a valid passport or a U.S. Passport Card—sort of a "passport lite" that is only valid for land or sea crossings from Canada, Mexico, the Caribbean, or Bermuda. Enhanced drivers licenses, issued by Washington and other border states, can also be used for land or sea crossings.

For more information on border crossings see Car Travel above.

U.S. passports are valid for 10 years. You must apply in person if you're getting a passport for the first time; if your previous passport was lost, stolen, or damaged; or if your previous passport has expired and was issued more than 15 years ago or when you were under 16. All children under 18 must appear in person to apply for or renew a passport. Both parents must accompany any child under 14 (or send a notarized statement with their permission) and provide proof of their relationship to the child.

The cost to apply for a new passport is $135 for adults, $105 for children under 16; renewals are $110. Allow at least six weeks, sometimes longer for processing, both for first-time passports and renewals. For an expediting fee of $60 you can reduce this time to about two weeks. If your trip is less than two weeks away, you can get a passport even more rapidly by going to a passport office with the necessary documentation. Private expediters can get things done in as little as 48 hours, but charge hefty fees for their services.

U.S. Passport Information U.S. Department of State ☎ 877/487–2778 ⊕ *www.travel.state. gov/passport.*

Canadian Passports Passport Canada ✉ *Foreign Affairs and International Trade Canada, Gatineau, Québec, Canada* ☎ *819/997–8338, 800/567–6868 toll-free Canada and U.S.* ⊕ *www.ppt.gc.ca.*

U.S. Passport & Visa Expediters American Passport Express ☎ *800/455–5166* ⊕ *www. americanpassport.com.* **Passport Express**

☎ *800/362–8196* ⊕ *www.passportexpress.com.* **Travel Document Systems** ☎ *202/638–3800, 800/874–5100* ⊕ *www.traveldocs.com.* **Travel the World Visas** ☎ *202/223–8822, 866/886–8472* ⊕ *www.world-visa.com.*

▍ SAFETY

The most dangerous element of the Northwest is the great outdoors. Don't hike alone, and make sure you bring enough water plus basic first-aid items. If you're not an experienced hiker, stick to tourist-friendly spots like the more accessible parts of the national parks; if you have to drive 30 miles down a Forest Service road to reach a trail, it's possible you might be the only one hiking on it.

▍ TAXES

Oregon has no sales tax, although many cities and counties levy a tax on lodging and services. Room taxes, for example, vary from 7% to 13.5%. The state retail sales tax in Washington is 6.5%, but there are also local taxes that can raise the total tax to almost 10%, depending on the goods or service and the municipality; Seattle's retail sales tax is 9.5%. A Goods and Services Tax (GST) of 5% applies on virtually every transaction in Canada except for the purchase of basic groceries.

In British Columbia an additional Provincial Sales Tax (PST) of 7% applies to most goods and services.

▍ VISITOR INFORMATION

British Columbia Tourism Vancouver Island ⊠ *65 Front St., Suite 501, Nanaimo, British Columbia, Canada* ☎ *250/754–3500* ⊕ *www.seevancouverisland.com.* **Tourism Vancouver Visitor Centre** ⊠ *Vancouver Convention Centre East, 999 Canada Place, Vancouver, British Columbia, Canada* ☎ *604/683–2000* ⊕ *www.tourismvancouver.com.* **Tourism Victoria** ⊠ *Visitors Centre, 812 Wharf St., Victoria,*

WORD OF MOUTH

"We did the train south from Vancouver, and it is much more scenic than I-5. You'll go along the shore in places, where you can see eagles vying with seagulls for fish. Really cool. It leaves Seattle in the morning just once a day, so do plan for that if it interests you."

—sludick

British Columbia, Canada ☎ *250/953–2033, 800/663–3883* ⊕ *www.tourismvictoria.com.*

Oregon Travel Oregon ☎ *800/547–7842* ⊕ *www.traveloregon.com.* **Travel Portland** ⊠ *1000 S.W. Broadway, Suite 2300, Portland, Oregon* ☎ *503/275–9750, 800/962–3700* ⊕ *www.travelportland.com.*

Washington Seattle Convention and Visitors Bureau ☎ *866/732–2695 visitor information, 206/461–5800 main office* ⊕ *www.visitseattle.org.* **Washington State Tourism** ☎ *866/964–8913* ⊕ *www.experiencewa.com.*

INDEX

PHOTO CREDITS

Front cover (Looking Glass Lake, Oregon): Janis Miglavs/age fotostock.1, Konrad Wothe /age fotostock. 2-3, Jeanne Hatch/iStockphoto. 5, Liem Bahneman/Shutterstock. Chapter 1: Experience the Pacific Northwest. 8-9, Martin Bydalek Photography. 10, Rebecca Kennison/wikipedia.org. 11 (left), Lijuan Guo/iStockphoto. 11 (right), Ashok Rodrigues/iStockphoto. 12, Steve Whiston/Burke Museum. 13 (left), Stacey Lynn Payne/iStockphoto. 13 (right), Washington Wine Commission. 16 (left), Christopher Boswell/Shutterstock, 16 (top right), moohaha/Flickr. 16 (bottom center), Elena Korenbaum/ iStockphoto. 16 (bottom right), Brian Holsclaw/Flickr. 17 (top left), The High Desert Museum. 17 (top center), James Hornung/Shutterstock. 17 (bottom left), Neta Delgany/iStockphoto. 17 (bottom center), Chuck Pefley/Almany. 17 (right), Norman Eder/iStockphoto. 18 (left), neelsky/Shutterstock. 18 (top right), moohaha/Flicker. 18 (bottom center), Rimasz/Dreamstime.co. 18 (bottom right), thinair/iStockphoto. 19 (top left), (c) Jdanne I Dreamstime.com. 19 (bottom left), Pike Place Market. 19 (bottom center), Tim Thompson. 19 (right), Lara Swimmer Photography. 20 (left), Kenji Nogai21. 20 (top right), Lissandra Melo/Shutterstock. 20 (bottom center), Natalia Bratslavsky/Shutterstock. 20 (bottom right), WordRidden/Flickr. 21 (top left), Steve Rossett/Shutterstock. 21 (top center) Natalia Braslavsky/ Shutterstock. 21 (right), fotofriends/Shutterstock. 21 (bottom left), Michel Teiten/Wikipedia.com. 21 (bottom center) Royal BC Museum. 22, Kirk Hirota. 23, (left), Victoria Coffee/Kent Colony. 23 (right), ABC pics/Shutterstock. 25 (left), Rachel Coe/Shutterstock. 25 (right), Geoffrey Smith. 26, Matt McGee/ Flickr. 27 Pacific Science Center. 36, Martin Bydalek Photography. 37 (right), Ben Tobin. 37 (left), Campbell Gordon. 39, Stuart Westmorland/age fotostock. 41, Thomas Kitchin & Vict/age fotostock. 42, San Juan Safaris. 43, Sylvain Grandadam/age fotostock. 44, Andy Simonds. Chapter 2: Portland: 45, Brian A. Ridder/Flickr. 46, -b-/Flickr. 47 (left), David Owen/Flikr. 47 (right), Michael Hashizume/ Flickr. 48, Karen Massier/Stockphoto. 57, Greg Vaughan. 60, Greg Vaughan. 69, Rigucci/Shutterstock. 74, Jeff Hobson. 88, Laurelhurst Market. 96 (top), McMenamins Kennedy School. 96 (bottom left), Hotel deluxe. 96 (bottom right), Heathman Hotel.108, EvanLovely/Flickr. 113, Jason Vandewhey/ Shutterstock. 119, LWY/Flickr Chapter 3: The Oregon Coast. 125, Greg Vaughn. 126 (bottom), Jeramey Jannene/Flickr. 126 (center), Aimin Tang/iStockphoto. 126 (top), scaredy_kat/Flickr. 127 (top), Oksana Perkins/iStockphoto.127 (bottom), CVA/Flickr. 128, Tom Wald/iStockphoto. 129 (bottom), John Norris/Flickr. 129 (top), Scott Catron/wikipedia.org. 130, Pacific Northwest USCG/Flickr. 140, Greg Vaughan. 143, OCVA/Flickr. 151, Greg Vaughn. 154, Oregon Coast Aquarium. 163, Greg Vaughn. Chapter 4: Willamette Valley and Wine Country: 177, Greg Vaughn. 178 (bottom), Gathering Together Farms. 178 (top), Don Hankins/Flickr. 179, Doreen L. Wynja. 180, Craig Sherod. 188, Greg Vaughn. 192, Greg Vaughn. 194, Randy Kashka/Flickr. 196, Jason Tomczak. 196-97, Greg Vaughn. 198, Fox Hill Vineyards. 200 (left), Jason Tomczak. 200 (right), REX HILL, Newberg, OR. 201, Doreen L. Wynja. 202 (top), Ponzi Vineyards. 202 (bottom), Vercingetorix Vineyards. 203 (left), Adelsheim Vineyard. 203 (center), Box Hill. 203 (right), Norman Eder/iStockphoto. 205 (left), Pennar-Ash Wine Cellars. 205 (center), Polara Studio. 205 (right), Dundee Bistro. 211, Greg Vaughn. 216, Greg Vaughn. 224, Greg Vaughn. Chapter 5: The Columbia River Gorge and Mt. Hood: 229, Laura Cebulski/iStockphoto. 230, Timberline Lodge. 231 (top), Robert Crum/iStockphoto. 231 (bottom), Christian Sawicki/iStockphoto. 232, Rigucci/Shutterstock. 240, zschnepf/Shutterstock. 242 and 245, GregVaughn. 251, Melissa & Bryan Ripka/Flickr. 252, William Blacke/iStockphoto. Chapter 6: Central Oregon. 257, Mike Houska. 258 (bottom), Black Butte Ranch. 258 (top), Robert O. Brown Photography/iStockphoto. 259, JonDissed/fl ickr. 260, Sunriver Resort. 267, USGS photo by Lyn Topinka/wikimedia. 271, Sunriver Resort. 275, mccun934/flickr. 280, mariachily/fl ickr. Chapter 7: Crater Lake National Park: 285, William A. McConnell. 286 (bottom), Aimin Tang/iStockphoto. 286 (center), Steve Terrill. 286 (top), Ashok Rodrigues/iStockphoto. 287, Michael Rubin/iStockphoto. 288, Vivian Fung/Shutterstock. Chapter 8: Southern Oregon. 297, Greg Vaughn. 298, Michael Dunn-I/Flickr. 299 (top), Michael (a.k.a maik) McCullough/Wikimedia. 299 (bottom), Ellen C. Campbell/Chanticleer Inn. 300, Paula C. Caudill. 305, Larry Turner. 307, nwrafting/fl ickr. 317 and 323, Greg Vaughn. Chapter 9: Seattle. 327 José Fuste Raga / age fotostock. 329, Stephen Finn/Shutterstock. 330, Gregory Olsen/iStockphoto. 331, Mariusz S. Jurgielewicz/Shutterstock. 339, jeffwilcox/Flickr. 340 (top), Mark B. Bauschke/Shutterstock. 340 (bottom), Charles Amundson/Shutterstock. 342 (top), The Tasting Room. 342 (bottom left), piroshky bakery. 342 (bottom right), Beecher's Handmade Cheese. 343 (left), Phillie Casablanca/Flickr. 343 (center), Nick Jurich of fl ashpd.com. 343 (right), eng1ne/Flickr. 344 (top left), Liem Bahneman/Shutterstock. 344 (bottom left), Pike Place Market PDA. 344 (right), World Pictures/Phot / age fotostock. 345 (left), Stephen Power / Alamy. 345 (right), Rootology/wikipedia.org. 347, Mark B. Bauschke/Shutterstock. 350, Laura Komada. 361, Nick Jurich of flashpd.com. 367, Geoffrey Smith. 378 (top), Fairmont Hotels & Resorts. 378 (bottom), Benjamin Benschneider. 380 (top), Mark Bauschke. 380 (bottom left), Pan Pacific Hotel Seattle. 380 (bottom right), Hotel 1000. 385, HeyRocker/Flickr. 387, Elysian

Brewing Company. 389, ebis50/Flickr. 391, Agua Verde Paddle Club. 400, Chris Howes/Wild Places Photography/ Alamy. 406, LegalAdmin/Flickr. 411, Richard Cummins / age fotostock. 415, Joe Becker / age fotostock. Chapter 10: Washington Cascade Mountains and Valleys: 417, Michael Sedam / age fotostock. 418 (bottom), Adrian Baras/Shutterstock. 418 (top), Northwest Trek Wildlife Park. 419, Rodefeld/Flickr. 420, Mrs. Flinger/Flickr. 426, John Carlson. 430, Rodefield/Flickr. 435, Carlos Arguelles/Shutterstock. 443, Richard Cummins / age fotostock. 451, amanderson2/Flickr. 464, tusharkoley/Shutterstock. 466, neelsky/Shutterstock. 467 (bottom), Bill Perry/Shutterstock. 467 (top), Donald A. Swanson/USGS. Chapter 11: San Juan Islands: 469, Edmund Lowe Photograph/Shutterstock. 470 (left), Maria Sats/Shutterstock. 470 (right), funflow/Shutterstock. 471(left), Edmund Lowe Photography/Shutterstock. 471 (right), Monica Wieland/Shutterstock. 472, yel02/Flickr. 481, Hauke Dressler age / fotostock. 487, Bill Stevenson age/fotostock. Chapter 12: Olympic National Park: 491, Rita Bellanca. 492-493, Washington State Tourism. 494, Andrey Lukashenkov/Shutterstock. 501, Lindsay Douglas/Shutterstock. 507, Superstock/age fotostock. Chapter 13: Olympic Peninsula and Washington Coast: 511, Sylvia Grandadam/age fotostock. 514, cdrin/Shutterstock. 521, Ligonograph Dreamstime. com. 530, UnGePhoto/Shutterstock. 533, Keith Lazelle Nature Photography. 538, Konrad Wothe / age fotostock. 542, Seabrook Cottage Rentals. 549, Alan Majchrowicz / age fotostock. Chapter 14: North Cascades National Park: 553, Alan Kearney/age fotostock. 554, WashingtonState Tourism. 555, Iwona Erskine-Kellie/Flickr. 556, Alan Kearney/age fotostock. 562, brewbooks/Flickr. Chapter 15: North Central Washington: 567 and 568 (top), Bill Perry/Shutterstock. 568 (bottom), Galyna Andrushko/Shutterstock. 569(top), Travis Manley/Shutterstock. 569 (bottom), Pierdelune/Shutterstock. 570, Bill Perry/ Shutterstock. 579, Sun Mountain Lodge. 580, brewbooks/Flickr. 587, Natalia Bratslavsky/Shutterstock. Chapter 16: Mount Rainier National Park: 591, chinana, Fodors.com member. 593 (top and bottom), Washington State Tourism. 594, Pat Leahy/Flickr. 602-603, zschnep/Shutterstock. Chapter 17: Washington Wine Country/Yakima River Valley: 607, Bruce Block/iStockphoto. 608, Jackie Johnston. 609 (top), L'Ecole N 41. 609 (bottom), Desert Wind Winery. 610 and 611 (top), Lincoln Potter. 611 (bottom), Karen Massier/iStockphoto. 612, Hogue Cellars. 617, Lodge at Suncadia. 621, David Lynx. 627, Lynn Hawlett. 631, Hogue Cellars. 633,waterfordyork/Stockphoto.Chapter 18: Spokane and Eastern Washington: 635, Michael Sedam / age fotostock. 636 (bottom), fotofriends/Shutterstock.636 (top), Mark Wagner/wikipedia.org. 638, James Hawley/Flickr. 649, Kirk Hirota. 652, Ted Wolfe Photography. 655, Andre Jenny/Alamy. 660, Jame Hawley/Flickr. 669, Cave B Inn at Sangcliffe. Chapter 19: Vancouver and Victoria. 677, Barrett & MacKay / age fotostock. 678, Natalia Bratslavsky/ Shutterstock. 679, Xuanlu Wang/Shutterstock. 680, ABC Pics/Shutterstock. 690, SuperStock / age fotostock.696, Geoff604/Flickr. 699, West Restaurant. 702 (top left), L'Hermitage Hotel. 702 (bottom left), SqueakyMarmot/Flickr. 702 (top right), Opus Hotel. 702 (bottom right), Relais & Chateaux. 705, David Leadbitter/Alamay. 707, Chris Cheadle / age fotostock. 713, Rich Wheater / age fotostock. 717, sashafatcat/Flickr. 726, North Light Images / age fotostock. 730, Xuanlu Wang/Shutterstock. 736, (top) Inn at Laurel Point. 736, (bottom) Brentwood Bay Lodge & Spa. 741, Chuck Pefley / Alamy. Back cover (from left to right): Natalia Bratslavsky/Shutterstock; Rachell Coe/Shutterstock; San Juan Safaris. Spine: Jo Ann Snover/Shutterstock.

ABOUT OUR WRITERS

Shelley Arenas grew up in Spokane and has lived in the Seattle area all of her adult life. She has contributed to Fodor's books for more than a decade, coauthored a guidebook to Seattle for families, and written for regional publications, including *Seattle Woman* magazine. She updated Olympic National Park, North Cascades National Park, Mount Rainier National Park, and Eastern Washington this edition.

Kimberly Bowker grew up hiking and kayaking in the high desert landscape of Central Oregon. She wrote for Bend's daily newspaper before pursuing a freelance writing career, focusing on the topics of travel, craft beer, and love. For more information, visit ⊕ *www.kimberlybowker.com*. She updated the Central Oregon chapter.

Cedar Burnett is a Seattle writer and the mother of an intrepid little traveler. She updated Seattle's Experience, Where to Stay, and Planning sections. Find out more at ⊕ *cedarburnett.com*.

Andrew Collins, a former Fodor's editor, updated Experience the Pacific Northwest, Southern Oregon, Washington Cascade Mountains and Valleys, The San Juan Islands, and the whale-watching feature this edition. A resident of Oregon who travels frequently throughout the region, he has authored more than a dozen guidebooks, is editor in chief of *OutCity* (a GLBT travel and lifestyle magazine on Oregon, Washington, and British Columbia), and produces the website ⊕ *GayTravel.About.com*. He also writes a syndicated monthly travel column, writes about restaurants for *Four Seasons Magazine* and travel for *New Mexico Magazine*; teaches food writing and travel writing for Gotham Writers' Workshop; and has contributed to *Travel & Leisure*, *Sunset*, and dozens of other periodicals.

Portland resident **Christina Cooke** writes about people, places, culture and outdoor adventure for magazines and newspapers across the nation and world. Find out more about her at ⊕ *christinacooke.com*. For this edition, she updated the Portland Where to Eat, Where to Stay, and Nightlife and the Arts sections.

Seattle-based journalist **Rebekah Denn** is a two-time winner of the James Beard award for food writing. She writes about food regularly for *The Seattle Times* and *Sunset* magazine, and was the restaurant critic and food writer for the *Seattle Post-Intelligencer* newspaper. She updated the Seattle Where to Eat section this edition.

A film set first lured **Paige Donner** to Vancouver in the 2000s when she was an entertainment reporter. When she began doing more eco-consulting for film productions was when green-friendly Vancouver became her regular go-to work and outdoor hub. Of course, then she discovered the B.C. local food and wines and was hooked. Paige's articles about the environment, as well as travel and entertainment, have appeared in the *International Herald Tribune*, *Variety*, *New York Times*, *Huffington Post* and *Los Angeles Times*. She worked on Vancouver Sports and the Outdoors, Where to Stay, and Nightlife sections.

While Seattle-based lifestyle and travel writer **Allison Ellis** has traveled to many far-flung destinations, she considers her native Northwest region as the crème de la crème. In addition to updating this edition's Seattle Exploring and Puget Sound Side Trips sections, Allison's travel writing has appeared in a variety of regional publications, including *Seattle Weekly*, *The Seattle Times*, *The Bellevue Visitors Guide*, *ParentMap*, and *Red Tricycle*.

Carolyn B. Heller is the author of two books, *Living Abroad in Canada* and *Moon Handbooks: Ontario*, and has contributed to more than 25 Fodor's guides. Her travel and food articles have appeared in publications ranging from the *Boston Globe* and *Los Angeles Times* to *FamilyFun*, *Real Weddings*, and *Per-*

ceptive Travel. She worked on Vancouver Exploring, Where to Eat, and Shopping.

Adriana Janovich worked as a newspaper reporter for 15 years in Washington state, including the Olympic Peninsula, which she was thrilled to revisit for this edition. She teaches journalism at Central Washington University. She updated the Olympic Peninsula and Washington Coast and North Central Washington chapters.

Brian Kevin explored Mt. Hood and the Columbia River Gorge from a former home base in the Wallowa Mountains. He now lives in a fishing village in coastal Maine, from which he occasionally contributes to publications like *Outside* and *Sierra.* He tweets sardonically at @BrianMT. He updated the Columbia River Gorge and Mt. Hood chapter.

Freelance writer **Rob Phillips** has lived in Central Washington for nearly 50 years. He has written for dozens of publications, mostly on outdoor subjects. His award-winning "Northwest Outdoors" column appears every Tuesday in the *Yakima Herald-Republic.* He updated the Yakima River Valley chapter this edition.

Dave Sandage is a software engineer living in the heart of Willamette Valley wine country. In his spare time he enjoys cooking, wine tasting, and making his own beer and wine. Dave wrote the Willamette Valley wine feature and updated the Willamette Valley and Wine Country chapter.

After three decades in Southern California, **AnnaMaria Stephens** packed it all up and moved to Seattle. Though she misses steady sunshine, the Pacific Northwest makes up for the clouds and drizzle with its stunning views, caffeine-fueled culture, and year-round outdoor play. For this edition, she updated Seattle's Shopping, Nightlife, and Sports and the Outdoors sections.

Lee van der Voo explored the Oregon Coast on forays from her Portland home. She reports on fishing for regional and national publications, and is presently an Alicia Patterson Foundation Fellow. Lee updated the Oregon Coast chapter.

Christine Vovakes, who updated the Crater Lake National Park chapter for this edition, has also contributed to *Fodor's California, Fodor's National Parks of the West,* and *Fodor's Essential USA.* Her travel articles and photographs have appeared in many publications, including *The Washington Post, The Christian Science Monitor, The Sacramento Bee,* and the *San Francisco Chronicle.*

After more than thirteen years living in Oregon, **Crystal Wood** still loves playing tour guide to friends and family. Crystal's vast knowledge of Portland made her the perfect person to update Portland's Exploring, Sports and the Outdoors, and Shopping sections.